COST AND MANAGEMENT ACCOUNTING

Dr. PRASHANTA ATHMA
Professor, Department of Commerce,
Osmania University. Hyderabad,
Andhra Pradesh.

Himalaya Publishing House
ISO 9001:2015 CERTIFIED

First Edition : 2011
Reprint : 2015
Reprint : 2021
Reprint : 2024

Published by : Mrs. Meena Pandey
for **HIMALAYA PUBLISHING HOUSE PVT. LTD.,**
"Ramdoot", Dr. Bhalerao Marg, Girgaon, Mumbai - 400 004.
Phone: 022-23860170, 23863863; **Fax:** 022-23877178
E-mail: himpub@bharatmail.co.in; **Website:** www.himpub.com

Branch Offices :

New Delhi : "Pooja Apartments", 4-B, Murari Lal Street, Ansari Road, Darya Ganj, New Delhi - 110 002. Phone: 011-23270392, 23278631; Fax: 011-23256286

Nagpur : Kundanlal Chandak Industrial Estate, Ghat Road, Nagpur - 440 018. Phone: 0712-2721215, 2721216

Bengaluru : Plot No. 91-33, 2nd Main Road, Seshadripuram, Behind Nataraja Theatre, Bengaluru - 560 020. Phone: 080-41138821; Mobile: 09379847017, 09379847005

Hyderabad : No. 3-4-184, Lingampally, Besides Raghavendra Swamy Matham, Kachiguda, Hyderabad - 500 027. Phone: 040-27560041, 27550139

Chennai : No. 34/44, Motilal Street, T. Nagar, Chennai - 600 017. Mobile: 09380460419

Pune : "Laksha" Apartment, First Floor, No. 527, Mehunpura, Shaniwarpeth (Near Prabhat Theatre), Pune - 411 030. Phone: 020-24496323, 24496333; Mobile: 09370579333

Cuttack : Plot No 5F-755/4, Sector-9, CDA Markat Nagar, Cuttack - 753 014, Odisha. Mobile: 09338746007

Kolkata : 3, S.M. Bose Road, Near Gate No. 5, Agarpara Railway Station, North 24 Parganas, West Bengal - 700 109. Mobile: 09674536325

DTP by : Prerana Enterprises, Mumbai.

Printed at : Geetanjali Press Pvt. Ltd., Nagpur. On behalf of HPH (P).

Dedicated to my Dad

Preface

The book on "Cost and Management Accounting" lays particular emphasis on the Fundamentals of Cost Accounting and Management Accounting; ascertainment of costs; decision making under various situations; analysis of the Financial Statements for a better understanding of the information contained in the Financial Statements; Cost Control and Cost Reduction.

A sincere and an earnest attempt is made to present the information in a non-technical, simple and lucid manner so as to enable the reader to understand the subject matter without difficulty.

The book is designed focussing its attention not only on the Syllabus at the Under Graduate and Post Graduate Level of various Universities but also on general understanding about the Cost and Management Accounting subject. The book contains sufficiently a large number of illustrations for a better grasp in the subject matter. Wherever necessary, working notes and explanations have been provided. Question paper problems of different Universities of different courses including Professional Courses like ICWAI, ICAI and ICS are incorporated in this book and by practicing them, the students will gain confidence to face the exam paper.

Suggestions for improvement of the work are solicited.

I am indebted to good authors on the subject for giving me the requisite knowledge of the subject. I thank my colleagues Dr. Sai Rani, Dr. J. Ravi Kumar, Dr. K. Srinivias, Dr. D. Sridevi, Dr. Sandhya Rani, Dr. M. Ravikanth, Mrs. Nalini, Mrs. Nagamani, Mrs. Uma Devi, Mrs. Shanti, Ms. Santoshi and my students Mrs. Suchitra, Ms. Naganika, Mrs. O. Bhavani, Mrs. Sirisha and Ms. Soujanya for their assistance in the work. My special thanks are to Mrs. Soujanya for her willful cooperation in taking up the typing work.

I also thank the publishers for the timely publication and my special thanks are to Mr. Krishna Poojari, Br. Manager, Hyderbad Branch and Mr. J. Raj Kumar Yadav for the keen interest taken by them in brining out this book.

Dr. PRASHANTA ATHMA

CONTENTS

List of Charts / Graphs

List of Illustrations and Problems

No.	Chapters	Illustrations	Problems
1.	Nature and Scope of Cost Accounting and Management Accounting	—	—
2.	Cost Classification and Importance of Cost Accounting	—	—
3.	Books of Accounts	8	7
4.	Reconciliation of Cost and Financial Accounts	7	10
5.	Materials Cost	14	17
6.	Pricing of Material Issues	10	10
7.	Labor Cost	7	6
8.	Methods of Remunerating Labor	13	8
9.	Overheads	5	5
10.	Re-apportionment and Absorption of Overheads	11	12
11.	Output Costing	9	9
12.	Job Costing	7	8
13.	Contract Costing	10	11
14.	Process Costing	25	22
15.	Operating Costing	12	7
16.	Marginal Costing and Absorption Costing	32	22
17.	Differential Costing	9	8
18.	Budgetary Control	14	16
19.	Standard Costing	—	—
20.	Uniform Costing	—	—
21.	Material Variances	9	7
22.	Labor Variances	9	6
23.	Overhead Variances	9	8
24.	Sales Variances and Control Ratios	7	6
25.	Introduction to Financial Statements Analysis	—	—
26.	Comparative Financial Statements Analysis	6	8
27.	Comparative Common Size Financial Statements	6	6
28.	Trend Analysis	5	5
29.	Ratio Analysis	25	30
30.	Funds Flow Analysis	15	10
31.	Cash Flow Analysis	7	6
32.	Activity Based Costing System	5	3
33.	Cost Audit	—	—
34.	Cost Control and Cost Reduction	—	—
35.	Cost Reporting	—	—
36.	Responsibility Accounting	7	3
	Total	**303**	**276**

Part – I

Introduction

1

NATURE AND SCOPE OF COST ACCOUNTING AND MANAGEMENT ACCOUNTING

Objectives

The objectives of the study are to:

- Learn the cost concepts
- Understand the need for Cost Accounting
- Understand the need for Management Accounting
- Differentiate Cost Accounting from Financial Accounting and Management Accounting
- Know the steps for installation of Cost Accounting
- Get an insight into the various Cost Accounting Standards

INTRODUCTION

Accounting is the language of business. A business enterprise communicates its information through the language of accounting. The enterprise presents such information to those who come into contact with the business in the course of trade.

According to Kohler, "accounting is the recording and reporting of transactions.'' This functional definition emphasizes recording and reporting as the basic functions of accounting.

According to the terminology of American Institute of Certified Public Accountants, Accounting is "the art of recording, classifying and summarizing in a significant manner and in terms of money, transactions and events which are, in part at least, of a financial character, and interpreting the results there-of." An expanded version of this definition shows that accounting is the collection, compilation and systematic recording of business transactions in terms of money, the preparation of financial statements and interpretation of these statements for the benefit of the users of accounting information.

Cost accounting is one of the branches of accounting, the other branches being the Stewardship Accounting, Financial Accounting, Management Accounting, Decision Accounting, Responsibility Accounting, Social Accounting, etc. Each of these branches is for a particular purpose and the prefix used differentiates one from the other, in the context in which it is used.

NATURE AND SCOPE OF COST ACCOUNTING

Cost Accounting is a branch of accounting and has been developed due to the limitations of Financial Accounting. The Financial Accounting system is mainly concerned with the collection, recording, classifying, summarizing and interpreting the results and it is directed towards the preparation of Profit and Loss Account (to ascertain the profit made or loss incurred in the organization for a particular period) and a Balance Sheet (to know the financial position of the organization as on a particular date). Such information is definitely useful to various parties like Shareholders, Creditors, Prospective Investors, Government, Banks etc. But, to the management, the information supplied is not sufficient, as only the overall view of financial position of the business enterprise is provided. In fact, information regarding various functions such as finance, administration, production and distribution is required for the functioning of the enterprise. Financial Accounting is unable to provide the information on costs product-wise, process-wise and activity-wise. Such limitations of Financial Accounting system have led to the emergence of Cost Accounting System.

By the term 'scope', we mean domain or field of activity. The scope of Cost Accounting covers the ascertainment of cost and the control of the same. Cost Accounting provides the management with information relating to the various aspects of performance of an enterprise.

In the earlier stages of its evolution, Cost Accounting confined itself to the accumulation of historical costs and presentation of the same for the sole purpose of cost finding or product costing. However, with the passage of time, its scope was broadened and provision of information for cost control and cost reduction assumed importance than products costing.

In the beginning, Cost Accounting has confined itself to only manufacturing organizations. Now, the techniques of Cost Accounting have gained application in a number of diverse organizations like Hospitals, Educational Institutions, Transport, Local Authorities, Banks and Insurance Companies. Thus, besides the enlargement of its scope, the extent of its application has also become wider.

NEED FOR COST ACCOUNTING

The following limitations of Financial Accounting have resulted in the development of Cost Accounting.

(1) Provides only historical information: Financial Accounting is mainly historical in nature and tells about the cost, which has already been incurred. It does not provide day to day cost information to the management for making effective plans for the future.

(2) **No classification of expenses and accounts:** In Financial Accounting, there is no such-system by means of which accounts are classified so as to give the data regarding costs, departments, processes, products and activities in the manufacturing division. Further, expenses are not classified as to direct and indirect items, the classification of which is very much essential for the control of the costs.

(3) **No data for decision making and comparison:** Financial Accounting does not supply required data for comparison purpose and for taking various financial decisions relating to the expansion and contraction of activities, replacement of labor by machines, introduction of new products, fixation of prices under normal or special conditions, make or buy a component required for the product, etc.

(4) **Price fixation difficult:** As the product wise cost is not supplied by the Financial Accounting System, it is very difficult for the management to fix the price of the product.

(5) **Trading results in total:** Financial Accounting discloses the net trading result of the business as a whole. It does not show profit or loss of different products, departments, processes, jobs etc.

(6) **No control over labor cost:** In Financial Accounting, there is no means of comparing the time clocked with the time booked, which is essential since the payment to the workers is based on the number of hours worked. Further, there is no means of judging the efficient utilization of the labor and as such incentive schemes based on the results cannot be introduced properly.

(7) **No safeguard against the material losses:** Financial Accounting does not provide any safeguard against material losses due to wastage, pilferage, deterioration, obsolescence, etc.

(8) **No controlling techniques:** In the light of the information provided by the Financial Accounting, the techniques of Budgetary Control and Standard Costing, which are very important for planning, control and cost reduction cannot be introduced.

(9) **Lack of scope for performance appraisal:** There is no scope for judging the profitability or otherwise of each line of activity as the profit and loss account discloses the trading result of the organization as a whole.

Product-wise, process-wise and department-wise cost information is required for effective control over cost and overall improvement in efficiency. For the purpose of various managerial decision-making, classification of cost into fixed and variable; direct and indirect cost; controllable and non-controllable cost is a must which is provided under Cost Accounting.

Thus, the above limitations of Financial Accounting have necessitated the need for the development of Cost Accounting system.

Objectives of Cost Accounting

The main objectives of Cost Accounting are cost ascertainment, cost control and ascertainment of profitability.

Cost ascertainment: For the purpose of ascertaining the cost of a product, process or operation, it is necessary to record the expenses incidental thereto. Hence, there is a need for minute sub division of expenses falling under the primary classification of nominal accounts as per the financial records and reclassifying them according to the purpose for which they are incurred.

Basis for estimating: In case of jobbing type of industries and contract business, firms have to submit quotations or estimates for the supply of specific goods or services. In such cases, Cost Accounting records and supplies reliable and useful information about the cost of previous job of a similar nature, which facilitates in making an estimation of cost.

Determination of selling price: Based on the information supplied by the costing records, the price of the product manufactured or services rendered can be determined.

Basis for operating policy: The objective of Cost Accounting is to help the management in the formulation of operating policies. Cost Accounting provides useful information for making various managerial decisions like increase in production, introduction, of a new product, make or buy a component, shut down a plant, selection of a most suitable method of production, etc.

Cost control: For the purpose of cost control, it is a pre-requisite to set standards of performance against which the actual costs can be measured. Budgetary Control and Standard Costing are the two important Cost Accounting techniques, which are used to control the costs. These techniques involve the comparison of the actual costs with the pre-determined costs and ascertain the variances, which are reported to the management for the remedial action.

Cost Concepts

A beginning to the study of Cost Accounting system covers certain familiar cost concepts. which constitutes its basis.

(1) **Cost:** It is the sacrifice made for securing the benefit under consideration. It may be defined as the benefit given up to acquire goods and services. The benefits given up in terms of money may be called as 'cost'. The official terminology of Management Accounting published by Chartered Institute of Management Accountants (CIMA), London 1991 defines the term 'cost' as "the amount of expenditure (actual or notional) incurred on or attributable to a specified thing or activity." This definition refers to the past costs, whether actual or notional, which every

business concern, whether engaged in the production of goods or the provision of services has to incur. The cost is considered as actual if an outlay is involved otherwise it is notional. It may be defined as the value of economic resources consumed for producing a product or rendering a service.

(2) **Costing:** It is the technique and process of ascertaining the cost of activities, products, processes or services. This technique consists of a body of principles and rules, which govern the process of ascertaining the costs. Cost finding is Costing. It is concerned with ascertainment of costs.

(3) **Cost Accounting:** The CIMA official terminology defines Cost Accounting as "the establishment of budgets, standard costs and actual costs of operations, processes, activities or products and the analysis of variance, profitability or the social use of funds." Cost Accounting is classifying, recording and appropriate allocation of expenditure for the determination of the costs of products or services and for the presentation of the information suitably arranged for control and guidance of the management. Accounting for costs is Cost Accounting.

(4) **Cost Accountancy:** As an organized body of knowledge, the term Cost Accountancy may be defined as "the application of costing and cost accounting principles, methods and techniques to the science, art and practice of cost control and ascertainment of profitability. It includes presentation of information for the purpose of managerial decision making" (CIMA official terminology). Thus, Cost Accountancy is a very wide and a comprehensive term.

(5) **Cost Unit:** The ascertainment of cost necessitates the determination of a unit in terms of which costs can be ascertained and expressed. The terminology defines a cost unit as "a unit of product, service or time in relation to which costs are ascertained."

According to the above definition, the choice of a cost unit depends on what is being produced, whether goods or services and what is relevant for the purpose of cost ascertainment. It is the basis for the measurement of costs and making comparison between one period and another, or between actual cost and some pre-determined cost.

Examples of Cost Unit:

Product Industry	*Cost Unit*
Bakery	kilogram
Engineering	job or batch
Steel	tonne
Pencil	gross, dozen, piece
Hospital	patient or bed

(6) Cost Centre: For the purpose of administrative convenience, every large-scale business is divided into a number of departments such as production, administration, marketing and finance, which represent the basic functions of any business organization. These departments are further divided into smaller sections known as cost centres for the purpose of accumulating costs and charging the same to cost units. Cost Centre may be defined as a person, place or item of equipment for which costs are ascertained.

For example, the production activities of an oil industry may be divided into distinct parts such as crushing, refining and finishing. Each of these production lines forms one cost center.

Cost Accounting Organisation

In the case of small concerns, the Cost Accountant is the head of the Cost Accounting Department assisted by cost clerks and in the position of the line manager, he is the subordinate to the Chief Accountant. In the case of large concerns, the organization will be headed by the Chief Accountant or the Finance Manager or the Director of Finance, who is also a Cost Accountant reporting to the Managing Director. Thus, the functions are performed by a large number of persons with division of labor, specialization, decentralization of authority and responsibility.

The Cost Accounting Organization varies from concern to concern depending upon the size of the concern. However, the outlook of Cost Accounting Organization will be more or less similar in case of all the concerns.

The Cost Accounting Organization consists of those persons whose main function is Cost Accounting and Cost Reporting. They are responsible for recording incomes and expenses, preparing statistical data and presenting the same to the management. There should be a perfect understanding and cooperation between the Cost Accounting Department and the other Departments in the concern, as the Cost Accounting Department has to depend upon the other departments, which originate the basic documents.

Cost Accountant: In any manufacturing organization, Cost Accountant is the head of the Cost Accounting Department. In the case of a newly formed undertaking, his role is very important as it is he who comes into the picture for the very purpose of establishing the Cost Accounting Department, designing a suitable system of Cost Accounting, installing it and working the system successfully for achieving the objectives for which it was installed. The Cost Accountant performs certain other functions also like cost ascertainment, cost comparison, cost control, cost reduction and reporting of cost information for managerial decision-making. Thus, as the head of the Cost Accounting Department, he performs a wide variety of functions.

COST ACCOUNTING VS. FINANCIAL ACCOUNTING

The main focus of accounting being provision of business or accounting information, the relationship between Financial Accounting and Cost Accounting appears to be very close. These two branches of accounting are inter disciplinary, though there are various points of distinction, the main point being difference in the reporting aspect.

(1) Financial Accounting provides information about the business in a general way and is both for internal and external purpose. Whereas, Cost Accounting provides information to the management for proper planning, operation, control and decision-making. The information provided is mainly for internal purpose.

(2) Financial Accounting is compulsory and the books are maintained in such a way so as to meet the requirements of Companies Act and Income Tax Act. Cost Accounting records are maintained voluntarily.

(3) Financial Accounts are prepared at the end of the year, whereas, Cost Accounts are prepared as and when required by the management.

(4) Financial Accounting classifies, records and analyses the transactions in a subjective manner according to the value of the expenses. Cost Accounting records expenditure in an objective manner according to the purpose for which the costs are incurred.

(5) Only monetary information is taken in Financial Accounting, whereas, Cost Accounting deals with both monetary and non-monetary information.

(6) In Financial Accounting, emphasis is only on recording aspect without attaching any importance to the control aspect. Cost Accounting has a detailed system of control over all the elements of cost *viz.*, materials, labor and other expenses.

(7) In Financial Accounting, costs are reported in aggregates whereas in Cost Accounting, the costs are broken down on a unit basis.

(8) Actual facts and figures are dealt with in Financial Accounting. Cost Accounting deals partly with facts and figures and partly with estimates.

(9) Valuable information on the relative efficiencies of various workers, plant and machinery is not provided in Financial Accounting system. The same is made available to the management in the case of Cost Accounting System.

(10) There are well-defined rules and regulations, principles and codes in the preparation of Financial Accounts whereas no such thing exists in Cost Accounting System.

INSTALLATION OF COSTING SYSTEM

Cost Accounting System adopted by any company reflects the same principles and purposes, although, their application may vary with circumstances out of necessity. The system adopted should be simple and should suit the nature of the business and the cost involved should not be too high.

The preliminary considerations governing the installation of a Cost Accounting System are:

(1) Simplicity: The system should be simple, easy to operate and the personnel should be capable of understanding the system.

(2) Nature of business: The nature of the business like whether engaged in the production of goods, whether a single product or multi product concern, jobbing type of business or a process type or an assembly unit, etc., also influences the method of Cost Accounting System to be adopted.

(3) Accuracy of data: Before installing the Cost Accounting System, it is also necessary to find out the degree of accuracy required.

(4) Nature of organisation: The existing types of authority relationship, the number of layers and the extent of authority and responsibility in the organization should also be studied as the Cost Accounting System adopted should suit the organization.

(5) Technical aspects: A Cost Accountant should be acquainted with the technical aspects like the nature of products, methods and stages of production.

(6) Flexibility: Any system without flexibility will be outmoded because of fast changes in business and industry. Therefore. the Cost Accounting System to be adopted should be able to take up any changes in the system.

(7) Reconciliation of Cost and Financial Accounts: When Cost and Financial Accounts are maintained independently, there may arise a situation of difference in profits reported by these Accounts. In such a case, there should be a reconciliation of Cost and Financial Accounts. If possible, the Cost and Financial Accounts should be interlocked into one Integral Accounting System in order to avoid the reconciliation work.

Steps to be taken in installing a Cost Accounting System

The following are the steps to be taken into consideration before installation of Cost Accounting System.

(1) Introducing the system: The implications of the system should be explained to all, indicating the benefits that will accrue to each and to the business as a whole, before the system is put into effect. To avoid confusion and overlapping, the system should be introduced in stages.

(2) Study of organisation: To adopt a suitable Cost Accounting System, certain aspects like, the nature of the business and the operations carried on, extent of responsibility and authority attached to the various functionaries, the layout of the factory, etc., are to be studied thoroughly.

(3) Clear-cut objectives: The Cost Accounting System should be simple, but it will have to be elaborative if the objective is to have information which will help the management in exercising control and taking decisions.

(4) Structure of cost accounts: The designing of the system should be such that there is a gradual build up of the cost at each significant stage of production. It should follow the natural production line and the sequence can be simple, analytical or synthetic.

(5) Organising the cost office: To the extent possible, the cost office should be close to the factory, so that, delay in routing out documents or in clearing up discrepancies and doubts is avoided.

(6) Cost office and other departments: The Cost Accounting System should be so designed, that, it serves the requirements of the management, at all levels.

Practical difficulties in the installation of a Cost Accounting System

There are certain practical difficulties in the installation of a Cost Accounting System, which are listed below.

(1) Lack of support: The Cost Accounting System creates a sort of fear in the minds of the people as they treat this system as a device to check their activities and without the consultation and support of departmental heads, the system adopted cannot be a fruitful one.

(2) Non cooperation: Like any other system, Cost Accounting System newly adopted involves additional paper work which is resented by the foremen, supervisors and other staff and without their cooperation the system cannot work smoothly and efficiently.

(3) Shortage of trained staff: The team of Costing Department should consist of well-trained Cost Accountants and when this system is newly introduced, there may arise shortage of Cost Accountants to handle the work of cost analysis, cost control and cost reduction.

(4) Heavy operating cost: The cost involved in the installation of the system will be very high if the system is not designed on the basis of the requirements of the concern.

MANAGEMENT ACCOUNTING

The advancements of Science and Technology have changed the accounting from a mere device of recording to a powerful tool of forecasting, budgeting and budgetary control. Thus, Financial Accounting, besides reporting on business performance, has been supplemented with financial and cost control, budgeting and budgetary control. Precisely, it has led to the emergence of Management Accounting.

The term Management Accounting was first coined and used by the British Team of Accountants that visited the United States in 1950, under the auspices of Anglo American Productivity Council. Since then, it has grown into a full pledged subject and in the recent years, it is looked upon as a subject distinct from Accounting. It is considered as an effective tool in the hands of the management as against the traditional package of accounts.

According to the Institute of Chartered Accountants of England and Wales (ICMA), Management Accounting is "any form of accounting which enables a business to be conducted more efficiently."

Shillinglaw has stated that "accounting which serves management by providing information as to the cost or profit associated with some portion of firm's total operations, is called Management Accounting".

The Management Accounting Team of Anglo American Council on Productivity in its report stated as "Management Accounting is the presentation of accounting information in such a way as to assist management in the creation of policy and the day to day operation of an undertaking. The technique of accounting is of extreme importance as it works in the most nearly universal medium available for the expression of facts so that facts of great diversity can be presented in the same picture. It is not the presentation of these pictures that is the function of management but the use of them."

According to J. Batty, "Management Accounting is the term used to describe the accounting methods, systems and techniques which, coupled with special knowledge and ability, assist the management in its task of maximizing profit or minimizing losses."

From the above definitions, we can draw the following salient features of Management Accounting:

- Management Accounting is concerned with the accounting information which is useful to the management in maximizing profits or minimizing losses.
- It is concerned with the improvement of the efficiency of the various phases of management.

NEED FOR MANAGEMENT ACCOUNTING

A question arises as to what is the need for Management Accounting when Financial Accounting is serving the needs of external users and Cost Accounting is servicing the needs of internal users. Here, what is needed is an integration of both financial and costing information and presentation of the relevant and required information, both quantitative and qualitative, in a suitable manner to the management for the purpose of assisting it to take a number of appropriate managerial decisions.

Management Accounting helps the managerial personnel to perform all the important managerial functions effectively *viz.*, planning, organizing, directing, controlling, co-ordinating, motivating and communicating by providing relevant information timely.

Management Accounting helps in planning by providing various reports which estimate the effects of alternative actions on an enterprise's ability to achieve the desired goals. It provides the necessary information which helps the management to regulate and adjust operations and activities in the light of the changing conditions. By providing performance and control reports highlighting the variances, Management Accounting enables the management to follow the principle of 'management by exception'.

NATURE OF MANAGEMENT ACCOUNTING

Management Accounting is both a science as well as an art. It is concerned with the collection, analysis and communication of accounting information. It is concerned with facts and figures and depends on objectivity and quantification of problems. Science is a systematized body of knowledge where well defined principles are followed. It is a science as, a well defined set of principles are followed. It emphasizes on cause and effect relationship. It is an art as human skills and experience are utilized in taking various managerial decisions.

Management Accounting, with an emphasis on future, deals with data based on projections and estimations for evaluation of various alternative courses of actions. It emphasizes on the classification of costs into fixed and variable and uses the techniques of Break Even Analysis and Marginal Costing for decision-making.

OBJECTIVES AND FUNCTIONS OF MANAGEMENT ACCOUNTING

The main objective or the basic function of Management Accounting is to assist the management in taking various decisions by providing relevant and complete information as and when required. The major functions (objectives) of Management Accounting may be discussed as under.

(1) Provides Relevant Data: Management Accounting collects the most pertinent facts and figures from different sources and presents the same, as and when required, to the internal users in a suitable form and assists them in decision-making.

(2) Validation of Data: The effectiveness of managerial functions depends upon the accuracy and adequacy of various financial data. But some times, apart from the past and present facts, the management may also be interested in prospective events or future data. Therefore, the data contained in the Financial and Cost Accounts are modified in case of Management Accounting and then presented to the management as and when required.

(3) Analysis and Interpretation: Management Accounting, with the help of tools of financial analysis, analyses the data contained in the financial reports to get a better insight into the solvency, liquidity and profitability of the organization and presents to the management, the analyzed results with necessary interpretation.

(4) Facilitates Overall Control: With the help of techniques of cost control like standard costing, budgetary control and responsibility accounting, Management Accounting identifies the areas where the control is required by the management. The actual performance is compared with the standards or budgets set and remedial measures are taken by the management wherever there are adverse variances. Responsibilities are fixed to the personnel concerned for the poor performance.

(5) Provides Qualitative Information: Both, Financial and Cost Accounting, provide only quantitative data and no qualitative data are provided. But, for decision making, management requires qualitative information also. Management Accounting provides a comprehensive report consisting of quantitative data and qualitative data.

(6) Assists in Planning: Management has to formulate various policies, both short term and long term. For future planning, necessary reports, facts and figures are furnished by the Management Accounting. It helps in quantifying the various alternatives in terms of cost, price, income or profit and facilitates comparison to select the best alternative.

Scope of Management Accounting

To serve the various needs of the management, techniques of various disciplines are made used by the Management Accounting. All the tools and techniques which help the Management Accountant in the discharge of his duties fall under the scope of Management Accounting.

Management Accounting gathers maximum data from Financial Accounting. With the help of the financial analysis tools like ratio analysis, comparative financial statements, common size statements, trend analysis, statement of changes in financial analysis, the financial data are analyzed and presented to the management reflecting the financial results and financial position in a suitable manner for decision making. Therefore, Financial Accounting falls within the scope of Management Accounting.

Cost Accounting is another major field from where cost data are collected and with the help of tools like standard costing, budgetary control, marginal costing, absorption costing, inter firm comparison, data are presented to the management for decision-making. Hence, Cost Accounting also falls within the scope of Management Accounting.

Management Accountants present the reports more accurately and usefully by using various statistical and quantitative tools like probability, sampling techniques, linear programming and help the management to take decisions in the midst of numerous and complex problems. Hence, statistical and quantitative techniques also are included in Management Accounting.

Facts and figures are collected, analyzed and presented in the form of various reports to the management which form the basis for decision-making. These reports reflect, both the positive and negative aspects relating to the organization. These internal reports also form the subject matter of Management Accounting.

Role of Management Accountant

Management Accounting represents the blending of the two professions - 'Management' and 'Accounting'. Accounting control and management efficiency - the two important elements for the success of a business concern are completely merged in Management Accounting.

By making a clear shift in the emphasis from mere recording of transactions to their analysis and interpretation, Management Accounting assists the management in achieving better results. It is concerned with the tools and techniques of formulation of budgets and pre-setting of standards as well as evaluation of deviation in actual performance from the standard and also implementation of prompt remedial measures.

Management Accountant helps the managers by providing assistance in the design of an accounting information system; collection of data; maintenance of accounting records; preparation of financial statements, budgets, performance reports and control reports; interpretation of accounting data and reporting of variances.

The role and responsibility of a Management Accountant is one of support. He should ensure that the information system meets the varying needs of the different levels of management.

Management Accounting vs. Financial Accounting

There are certain points of difference between the Management Accounting and Financial Accounting, despite the close inter relationship that exists between the two. The differences are discussed below:

(1) **Focus:** The focus of Financial Accounting is on the enterprise as a whole covering all the aspects of the business operation while the focus of Management Accounting is on the internal details of any particular aspect of business operation.

(2) **Nature:** The nature of Financial Accounting being historical, it serves a limited purpose of throwing light on the events and results of the past. Whereas, Management Accounting is mainly concerned with the future plans and policies and relies on the past records for the formulation of future plans.

(3) **Compulsion:** It is obligatory on the part of every business organization to adopt the Financial Accounting whereas the adoption of the system of Management Accounting is optional.

(4) **Characteristics:** Financial Accounting lays emphasis on the objectivity, validity, absoluteness while Management Accounting lays emphasis on those characteristics like, flexibility, approximation, comparability, etc., which increase the value of information used for a variety of purposes.

(5) **Legal Formalities:** The Companies Act provisions govern the preparation and presentation of annual final accounts of the companies. There is no statutory regulation fixing the norms and standards for preparation of accounting statements in case of Management Accounting as a business concern is free to install the system of Management Accounting.

Cost Accounting vs. Management Accounting

Cost Accounting and Management Accounting, though, both are internal to the organization and have the same objective of assisting the management in the performance of managerial functions, still differ in certain aspects as given below:

(1) Data derivation: While Cost Accounting data are derived from only Financial Accounts, Management Accounting data are derived from both cost accounts as well as financial accounts. Thus, the scope of Cost Accounting is narrow while that of Management Accounting is broad.

(2) Information provided: Cost Accounting provides only cost information for managerial uses whereas Management Accounting provides both cost and financial information.

(3) Emphasis: The main emphasis in Cost Accounting is cost ascertainment and cost control while in Management Accounting, the emphasis is on decision-making.

(4) Installation of the system: Cost Accounting is independent and can be installed without Management Accounting System whereas Management Accounting presupposes the existence of a proper Cost Accounting System.

(5) Purpose: The main purpose of Cost Accounting is to assist the management by reporting current and prospective costs of products, jobs, services, processes, departments etc. It does not provide information for the evaluation of management performance. In case of Management Accounting, the purpose is to provide all accounting information that would assist the management in functioning effectively. It also provides information for the evaluation of management performance.

(6) Techniques employed: In Cost Accounting, techniques like Marginal Costing, Budgetary Control, Standard Costing, etc., are employed. In Management Accounting, in addition to the techniques of Cost Accounting, other techniques like Ratio Analysis, Financial Statement Analysis, Funds Flow and Cash Flow Analysis etc., are used.

(7) Planning: Cost Accounting is concerned mainly with short term planning whereas Management Accounting is equally concerned with short term as well as long term planning.

COST ACCOUNTING STANDARDS

Due to open competition for globalization, the cost management has gained special importance in the business activities. Cost Accounting Standard Board (CASB) set up by the Council of the Institute of Cost and Works Accountants of India will frame the standards on important issues/topics relating to Cost and Management Accounting. It will have a Chairman and other members appointed and nominated by the Council of the Institute.

The CASB will prepare a report of its work each year and sends it to the Council. The work of CASB is to develop Cost Accounting Standard with the following objectives:

- To equip the profession with better guidelines on standard cost accounting practices
- To assist the Cost Accountants in the preparation of uniform cost statements
- To provide guidelines to Cost Accountants to make standard approach towards maintenance of cost.

According to Accounding Record Rules and undertaking Cost Audit under section 209 (1) (d) and section 233B of Companies Law respectively and various other Acts like Income Tax Act, Central Excise Act, Customs Act, Sales Tax Act, etc.

- To assist the management to follow the standard cost accounting practices in the matter of compliance of statutory obligations.
- To help Indian industry and the Government towards a better cost management.

The 'standards' issued by CASB will be recommendatory in nature and every member of the institute is expected to honor the same. Cost Auditors will adopt and encourage the adoption of the standards, wherever applicable, in maintenance of Cost Accounting Record Rules under section 209(1) (d) and report the deviations, if any, in the Cost Audit Reports under section 233B. The Institute will take up thc standards with National Accounting Standard Board to enforce them and to include in Companies Act, 1956. As long as the standards are not enforced by National Accounting Standard Board or by Companies Act, the CASB does not possess the legal authority to impose its views as statutory regulations but it is only by persuasion, the standard can be followed as normal practice by the members of the profession.

Cost Accounting Standards at a glance are given below.

Cost Accounting Standards

CAS No	*Title*	*Objective*	*Useful for*
CAS 1(Final)	Classification of Cost	For preparation of Cost Statements	Assessment of excise duty and other taxes, anti-dumping measures, transfer pricing, etc.
CAS 2 (Final)	Capacity Determination	For determination of capacity	Proper allocation, apportionment and absorption of cost.

CAS No	*Title*	*Objective*	*Useful for*
CAS 3 (Final)	Overheads	For Collection, Allocation, Apportionment and Absorption of overheads	Determining Cost of products, services or activities
CAS 4 (Final)	Cost of Production for Captive Consumption	To determine the assessable value of excisable goods used for captive consumption	Determining Cost of products, services or activities
CAS 5 (Final)	Average (equalized) Cost of Transportation	To determine averaged/equalized transportation cost	Calculating the amount of deduction from assessable value of excisable goods, freight subsidy, Insurance claim valuation, etc.
CAS 6 (Draft)	Arm's Length Price	For computation of Arm's Length Price	Determining Arms Length Price, for transactions between related parties
CAS 7 (Draft)	Costing of Joint Products and By-Products	For Apportionment of Joint costs to individual products	Inventory valuation, Cost of Goods Sold computations,Cost reimbursements under Cost Plus contracts, Transfer Pricing and Insurance settlement computations for Joint products and by-products

Source: *http://myicwai.com/docs/icwaicas1.doc*

Cost Accounting Standard (CAS 1) (Final)**:** ***Classification of Cost*** will be dealt in Lesson 3.

Cost Accounting Standard (CAS 2)**:** ***Capacity Determination***

(http://myicwai.com/docs/icwaicas2.doc)

Cost Accounting Standard issued by the Council of the Institute of Cost and Works Accountants of India on "Capacity Determination" deals with the determination of capacity of a unit.

A better utilization of capacity means better utilization of resources. Utilization of capacity is an important consideration for cost determination and cost reduction. Cost Accounting Records Rules under section 209(1) (d) of Companies Act, 1956 and Cost Audit Report Rules, 2001 under section 233B of the said Act specify that comparative statement of installed capacity and actual capacity utilization is to be recorded and furnished in order to assess the operating level.

The standard prescribes the method of determination of capacity that has to be applied uniformly and consistently. It helps the management to identify the bottlenecks, imbalances and idle capacity for effective use of various resources. It helps in proper allocation, apportionment and absorption of cost.

The standard is applicable for an undertaking, whether existing or new, where there is expansion of more than 5% of the existing capacity due to the introduction of new machines or productive resources. Similarly, the standard is also applicable where there is more than 5% reduction of the existing capacity due to the disposal or withdrawal or impairment of old machines or productive resources.

Certain Important Definitions

'Licensed Capacity' is the production capacity of the plant for which license has been issued by an appropriate authority.

'Installed Capacity' is the maximum productive capacity according to the manufacturers' specification of machines / equipment. Installed capacity of the unit/plant is determined after taking into account imbalances in different machines/ equipment in the various departments/production cost centres in the unit/plant and number of working shifts.

It is determined based on the Manufacturers' Technical specifications; Capacities of individual or interrelated production centres; Operational constraints/capacity of critical machines; Number of shifts and any other factor.

In case, manufacturers' technical specifications are not available, the estimates by technical experts on capacity under ideal conditions may be considered for determination of installed capacity.

In case, a product passes through different production processes and each process is having a different capacity, then, the process which brings effective or ultimate production shall be considered for deciding installed capacity.

'Practical or Achievable Capacity' is the maximum productive capacity of a plant as reduced by the predictable and unavoidable factors of interruption pertaining to internal causes.

Thus, practical capacity is the installed capacity minus the inevitable interruptions due to time lost for preventive maintenance, repairs, set ups, normal delays, weekly off-days and holidays etc. Practical capacity does not consider the external factors causing reduction in production e.g., lack of orders.

Practical capacity or achievable capacity should be determined after adjustment of the following with the installed capacity.

- Available production hours taking into consideration holidays, normal shut down days and normal idle time
- Normal time loss in batch change over, break downs of machines, repairs, etc.
- Loss in efficiency due to ageing of the machines/equipment
- Number of shifts and any other factor

'Normal Capacity' is the production achieved or achievable on an average over a period or season under normal circumstances taking into account the loss of capacity resulting from planned maintenance.

Normal capacity is the practical capacity minus the loss of productive capacity due to external factors. Normal capacity is determined based on the productive capacity achieved over a period of time, say average of three normal years out of preceding five years or expected to be achieved over a period of time, say next three to five years.

This capacity is determined after adjustment of external factors with practical capacity.

Normal capacity of a production process involved in the production of a product or the productive capacity of the plant as a whole should be taken into account to arrive at normal capacity for a product or plant, as the case may be.

The periods influenced by abnormalities should be excluded for this purpose.

In case, the same products with different specifications and of different ranges in terms of size, type, variety etc. are manufactured, then there is a need to determine equivalence among them in order to determine the capacity. In case, some intermediate products/components etc are also produced, they should be taken into consideration for determining equivalent capacity. In case, some machines are leased out/let out or some machines are taken on lease, resulting in decrease/increase in capacity should also be considered.

'Actual Capacity Utilization' is the volume of production achieved in relation to installed capacity.

'Idle Capacity' is the difference between installed capacity and the actual capacity utilization when actual capacity utilization is less than installed capacity.

'Excess Capacity Utilization' is the difference between installed capacity and the actual capacity utilization when actual capacity utilization is more than installed capacity.

'Abnormal idle capacity' is the difference between practical capacity and normal capacity or actual capacity utilization whichever is higher.

Disclosure

The details of basis for arriving at the capacity, variables used and assumptions made should be disclosed. Any change in the installed capacity due to modifications in the machines/equipment or addition of balancing equipment or disposal or impairment of some machines/equipment should be disclosed.

The licensed capacity and installed capacity should be disclosed in absolute term of production whereas practical capacity, normal capacity and actual capacity utilization should be disclosed in absolute term as well as in percentage of installed capacity.

In case some machines are taken on lease or some machines are leased out, their impact in terms of increase/ decrease in capacity should be disclosed separately.

In case of low capacity utilization as compared to the installed capacity, reasons for the same should be disclosed. Comments on the shortfall in production should also specify the factors which are controllable and uncontrollable in short term or in long term.

In case of excess capacity utilization, the same should be disclosed separately in absolute terms and in terms of percentage with reasons.

Exhibit 1

Illustration

Manufacturers' Specifications – capacity per hour	= 500 units
No of shifts (each shift 8 hours)	= 3 shifts
Holidays in a year:	
Sundays	= 52 days
Other holidays	= 13 days

Annual maintenance is done within these 13 hoildays	
Preventive Weekly Maintenance for the machine is on Sunday.	
Normal idle capacity for batch change over, Lunch, personal need, etc	= 1 hr per shift
Production based on sales expectancy in past 5 years	= 30.1, 26.9, 29.7, 24.4 and 30.2 lakh units
Actual Production for the year	= 30.1
Calculation of different Capacities	
Installed Capacity for the machine = 365 * 8 *3 * 500 = 43.8 lakh units	
Practical Capacity = (365 – 52 – 13) * (8 – 1) * 3 * 500 = 31.5 lakh units	
Out of the past five years, normal capacity is average of 3 normal years.	
Normal Capacity = (30.1 + 29.7 + 30.2) /3 = 30.0 lakh units	
Actual Capacity Utilization = 30.1 lakh units = 68.7%	
Idle Capacity = 43.8 – 30.1 = 13.7 lakh unit = 31.3%	
Abnormal idle capacity = 31.5 – 30.1 = 1.4 lakh units	

Source: *http://myicwai.com/docs/icwaicas2.doc*

Cost Accounting Standard (CAS 3) (Final)**:** ***Overheads*** will be dealt in Lesson 10.

Cost Accounting Standard 4 (CAS 4)**:** ***Cost Of Production for Captive Consumption***

(http://myicwai.com/docs/icwaicas4.doc)

The standard deals with determination of cost of production for captive consumption. The Cost Accounting principle for determination of cost of production is well established. Similarly, rules for levy of excise duty on goods used for captive consumption are also well defined. Captive Consumption means the consumption of goods manufactured by one division and consumed by another division(s) of the same organization or related undertaking for manufacturing another product(s). Liability of excise duty arises as soon as the goods covered under excise duty are manufactured but excise duty is collected at the time of removal or clearance from the place of manufacture even if such removal does not amount to sale. Assessable value of goods used for captive consumption is based on cost of production. According to the Central Excise Valuation (Determination of Price of Excisable Goods) Rules 2000, the assessable value of goods used for captive consumption is 110 per cent of cost of production of such goods, and as may be prescribed by the Government from time to time.

The purpose of this standard is to bring uniformity in the principles and methods used for determining the cost of production of excisable goods used for captive consumption. The cost statement prepared based on standard will be used for determination of assessable value of excisable goods used for captive consumption. The standard and its disclosure requirement will provide better transparency in the valuation of excisable goods used for captive consumption.

Cost of Production: It shall consist of Material Consumed, Direct Wages and Salaries, Direct Expenses, Works Overheads, Quality Control cost, Research and Development Cost, Packing cost, Administrative Overheads relating to production. To arrive at cost of production of goods dispatched for captive consumption, adjustment for Stock of work-in-Process, finished goods, recoveries for sales of scrap, wastage, etc. shall be made.

Captive Consumption: It means the consumption of goods manufactured by one division or unit and consumed by another division or unit of the same organization or related undertaking for manufacturing another product(s).

Material Consumed: It shall include materials directly identified for production of goods such as indigenous materials; imported material; bought out items; self manufactured items; process materials and other items.

Cost of material consumed shall consist of cost of material, duties and taxes, freight inwards, insurance, and other expenditure directly attributable to procurement. Trade discount, rebates and other similar items will be deducted for determining the cost of materials. Cenvat credit, credit for countervailing customs duty, Sales Tax set off, VAT, duty drawback and other similar duties subsequently recovered/recoverable by the enterprise shall also be deducted.

Direct wages and salaries shall include house rent allowance, overtime and incentive payments made to employees directly engaged in the manufacturing activities. Direct wages and salaries include fringe benefits such as Contribution to provident fund and ESIS; Bonus/ex-gratia payment to employees; Provision for retirement benefits such as gratuity and superannuation; Medical benefits; Subsidised food; Leave with pay and holiday payment; Leave encashment; Other allowances such as children's education allowance, conveyance allowance which are payable to employees in the normal course of business, etc.

Direct expenses are the expenses other than direct material cost and direct employees' costs which can be identified with the product. Direct expenses include Cost of utilities such as fuel, power, water, steam etc; Royalty based on production; Technical Assistance/know–how fees; Amortized cost of moulds, patterns, patents, etc, Job. charges; Hire charges for tools and equipment; Charges for a particular product designing, etc.

Works overheads are the indirect costs incurred in the production process. Works overheads include Consumable stores and spares; Depreciation of plant and machinery, factory building, etc; Lease rent of production assets; Repair and maintenance of plant and machinery, factory building, etc; Indirect employees cost connected with production activities; Drawing and Designing department cost; Insurance of plant and machinery, factory building, stock of raw material and WIP, etc; Amortized cost of jigs, fixtures, tooling, etc; Service department cost such as Tool Room, Engineering and Maintenance, Pollution Control, etc.

Quality Control Cost: It is the expenses incurred relating to quality control activities for adhering to quality standard. These expenses shall include salaries and wages relating to employees engaged in quality control activity and other related expenses.

Research and Development Cost: The cost incurred for the development and improvement of the process or the existing product shall be included in the cost of production.

Administrative Overheads: It needs to be analyzed in relation to production activities and other activities. Administrative overheads in relation to production activities shall be included in the cost of production. Administrative overheads in relation to activities other than manufacturing activities, e.g., marketing, projects management, corporate office expenses, etc., shall be excluded from the cost of production.

Packing Cost: If product is transferred/dispatched duly packed for captive consumption, cost of such packing shall be included. Packing cost includes both cost of primary and secondary packing required for transfer/dispatch of the goods used for captivc consumption.

Absorption of Overheads: Overheads shall be analysed into variable overheads and fixed overheads. Variable Overheads are the items which change with the change in the volume of production, such as cost of utilities etc. Fixed Overheads are the items whose value does not change with the change in volume of production such as salaries, rent, etc. The variable production overheads shall be absorbed in production cost based on actual capacity utilisation. The fixed production overheads and other similar item of fixed costs such as quality control cost, research and development costs, and administrative overheads relating to manufacturing shall be absorbed in the production cost on the basis of the normal capacity or actual capacity utilization of the plant, whichever is higher.

Valuation of Stock of Work-in-progress and Finished Goods: Stock of work-in-progress shall be valued at cost on the basis of stages of completion as per the cost accounting principles. Similarly, stock of finished goods shall be valued at cost. Opening and closing stock of work-in-progress shall be adjusted for calculation of cost of goods produced and similarly opening and closing stock of finished goods shall be adjusted for calculation of goods despatched. In case the cost of a shorter period is to be determined, where the figures of opening and closing stock are not readily available, the adjustment of figures of opening and closing stock may be ignored.

Treatment of Joint Products and By-Products: A production process may result in more than one product being produced simultaneously. In case, joint products are produced, joint costs are allocated between the products on a rational and consistent basis. In case, by-products are produced, the net realisable value of by-products is credited to the cost of production of the main product.

For allocation of joint cost to joint products, the sales values of products at the split off point i.e. when the products become separately identifiable may become the basis. Some other basis may also be adopted. For example, in the case of petroleum products, each product is assigned certain value based on its certain properties, may be calorific value and these values become the basis of apportionment of joint cost among petroleum products.

Treatment of Scrap and Waste: The production process may generate scrap or waste. Realized or realizable value of scrap or waste shall be credited to the cost of production. In case, scrap or waste does not have ready market and it is used for reprocessing, the scrap or waste value is taken at a rate of input cost depending upon the stage at which such scrap or waste is recycled. The expenses incurred for making the scrap suitable for reprocessing shall be deducted from value of scrap or waste.

Illustration

A production process has three stages.

Stage	*Input material cost (Rs/MT)*	*Processing cost (Rs/MT)*	*Total (Rs/MT)*
1	2000	500	2500
2	2500	1000	3500
3	3500	1000	4500

If during the production process at stage 3, the scrap is produced and the same is recycled at stage 2 after making an expenditure of Rs. 200 per MT to make it suitable for re-processing at stage 2, then scrap will be valued @ Rs. (2500 – 200) i.e. Rs. 2300. If no expenditure is involved to make scrap re-usable, the scrap value will be @ Rs. 2500. The scrap value for the scrap produced during a period calculated at the rate as explained above may be deducted to find out the cost of production for the period.

Miscellaneous Income: Miscellaneous income relating to production shall be adjusted in the calculation of cost of production, for example, income from sale of empty containers used for despatch of the captively consumed goods produced under reference is the miscellaneous income.

Inputs received free of cost: In case, any input material, whether of direct or indirect nature, including packing material is supplied free of cost by the user of the captive product, the landed cost of such material shall be included in the cost of production.

Moulds, Tools, Dies and Patterns, etc., received free of cost: The amortization cost of such items shall be included in the cost of production.

Interest and financial charges: Interest and financial charges being a financial charge shall not be considered to be a part of cost of production.

Abnormal and non-recurring cost: Abnormal and non-recurring cost arise due to unusual or unexpected occurrence of events, such as heavy break down of plants, accident, market condition restricting sales below normal level, abnormal idle capacity, abnormal process loss, abnormal scrap and wastage, payments like VRS, retrenchment compensation, lay-off wages, etc. The abnormal cost shall not form the part of cost of production.

Cost Sheet: The cost sheet should be prepared in the format as par Appendix – 1 or as near thereto as possible. The manufacturer will be required to maintain cost records and other books of account in a manner, which would facilitate preparation and verification of the cost of production. For manufacturers covered under the ambit of Section 209(1) (d) of the Companies Act, 1956, i.e., where Cost Accounting Records are statutorily required to be maintained, the Cost Accountant certifying the cost of production for captive consumption shall verify the correctness of the cost from these records. However, for manufacturers not covered under Section 209(1) (d) of the Companies Act, 1956, it is desirable that they also maintain cost accounting records in line with the records so prescribed as to facilitate determination and certification of cost of production.

Disclosure: If there is any change in cost accounting principles and practices during the concerned period which may materially affect the cost of production in terms of comparability with previous periods, the same should be disclosed.

If opening stock and closing stock of work -in-progress and finished goods are not readily available for certification purpose, the same should be disclosed.

Appendix – 1

Name of the Manufacturer :

Address of the Manufacturer :

Registration No. of the Manufacturer :

Description of product captively consumed :

Excise Tariff Heading :

Statement of Cost of production of ________ manufactured / to be manufactured during the period ________

		Quantity	
Q1	Quantity produced (Unit of Measure)		
Q2	Quantity Dispatched (Units of Measure)		
	Particulars	*Total Cost (Rs.)*	*Cost/Unit (Rs.)*
1.	Material consumed		
2.	Direct Wages and Salaries		
3.	Direct Expenses		
4.	Works Overheads		
5.	Quantity Control Cost		
6.	Research and Development Cost		
7.	Administrative Overheads (relating to production activity)		
8.	Total (1 to 7)		
9.	*Add:* Opening stock of work-in-progress		
10.	*Less:* Closing stock of work-in-progress		
11.	Total (8 + 9 – 10)		

	Particulars	*Total Cost (Rs.)*	*Cost/Unit (Rs.)*
12.	*Less:* Credit for Recoveries/Scrap/By-Products/miscellaneous income		
13.	Packing cost		
14.	Cost of production (11 – 12 + 13)		
15.	*Add:* Inputs received free of cost		
16.	*Add:* Amortized cost of Moulds, Tools, Dies & Patterns etc, received free of cost		
17.	Cost of production for goods produced for captive consumption (14 + 15 + 16)		
18.	*Add:* Opening stock of finished goods		
19.	*Less:* Closing stock of finished goods		
20.	Cost of production for goods dispatched (17 + 18 – 19)		

Seal and Signature of Company's Authorized Representative

I/We have verified above data on test check basis with reference to the books of account, cost accounting records and other records. Based on the information and explanations given to me/us and on the basis of generally accepted cost accounting principles and practices followed by the industry, I/we certify that the above cost data reflect true and fair view of the cost of production.

Date: Seal & Signature of Cost Accountant

Place: Membership No.

Cost Accounting Standard 5 (CAS 5): ***Determination of Average (Equalized) Cost of Transportation*** (http://myicwai.com/docs/icwaicas2.doc)

This standard deals with the determination of average transportation cost of a product.

The cost accounting principles for tracing/identifying an element of cost, its allocation/apportionment to a product or service are well established. Transportation cost is an important element of cost for procurement of materials for production and for distribution of product for sale. Therefore, Cost Accounting Records should present transportation cost separately from the other cost of inward materials or cost of sales of finished goods. The Finance Act 2003 also specifies the certification requirement of transportation cost for claiming deduction while arriving at the assessable value of excisable goods cleared for home consumption/export. There is a need to standardize the record keeping of expenses relating to transportation and computation of transportation cost.

The objectives of the standard are to bring uniformity in the application of principles and methods used in the determination of averaged/equalized transportation cost; to prescribe the system to be followed for maintenance of records for collection of cost of transportation, its allocation/apportionment to cost centres, locations or products and to provide transparency in the determination of cost of transportation.

This standard should be applied for calculation of cost of transportation required under any statute or regulations or for any other purpose. For example, this standard can be used for determination of average transportation cost for claiming the deduction for arriving at the assessable value of excisable goods; Insurance claim valuation; Working out claim for freight subsidy under Fertilizer Industry Coordination Committee; Administered price mechanism of freight cost element; Determination of inward freight costs included or to be included in the cost of purchases attributable to the acquisition; Computation of freight included in the value of inventory for accounting on inventory or valuation of stock hypothecated with Banks/Financial Institution, etc.

Definitions

The following terms are used in this standard with the meaning specified:

Cost of Transportation comprises of the cost of freight, cartage, transit insurance and cost of operating fleet and other incidental charges whether incurred internally or paid to an outside agency for transportation of goods but does not include detention and demurrage charges.

Cost of transportation is classified as inward transportation cost and outward transportation Cost. Inward Transportation cost is the transportation expenses incurred in connection with materials /goods received at factory or place of use or sale/ removal. Outward Transportation cost is the transportation expenses incurred in connection with the sale or delivery of materials or goods from factory or depot or any other place from where goods are sold/removed.

Freight is the charges paid or payable to an outside agency for transporting materials/ goods from one place to another place.

Cartage is the expenses incurred for movement of goods covering short distance for further transportation for delivery to customer or storage.

Transit insurance cost is the amount of premium to be paid to cover the risk of loss/damage to the goods in transit.

Depot is the bounded premises/place managed internally or by an agent, including consignment agent and C&F agent, franchisee for storing of materials/goods for further dispatch including the premises of Consignment Agent and C&F Agent for the purpose. Depot includes warehouses, go-downs, storage yards, stockyards, etc.

Equalized transportation cost means average transportation cost incurred during a specified period.

Equalized freight means average freight.

Maintenance of Records for Ascertaining Transportation Cost

Proper records shall be maintained for recording the actual cost of transportation showing each element of cost such as freight, cartage, transit insurance and others after adjustment for recovery of transportation cost. Abnormal costs relating to transportation, if any, are to be identified and recorded for exclusion of computation of average transportation cost.

In case of a manufacturer having his own transport fleet, proper records shall be maintained to determine the actual operating cost of vehicles showing details of various elements of cost, such as salaries and wages of driver, cleaners and others, cost of fuel, lubricant grease, amortized cost of tyres and battery, repairs and maintenance, depreciation of the vehicles, distance covered and trips made, goods hauled and transported to the depot.

In case of hired transport charges incurred for dispatch of goods, complete details shall be recorded as to date of dispatch, type of transport used, description of the goods, destination of buyer, name of consignee, challan number, quantity of goods in terms of weight or volume, distance involved, amount paid, etc.

Records shall be maintained separately for inward and outward transportation cost specifying the details, particulars of goods dispatched, name of supplier/recipient, amount of freight, etc.

Separate records shall be maintained for identification of transportation cost towards inward movement of material (procurement) and transportation cost of outward movement of goods removed/sold for both home consumption and export.

Records for transportation cost from factory to depot and thereafter shall be maintained separately.

Records for transportation cost for carrying any material/product to job-workers place and back should be maintained separately so as to include the same in the transaction value of the product.

Records for transportation cost for goods involved exclusively for trading activities shall be maintained separately and the same will not be included for claiming any deduction for calculating assessable value of excisable goods cleared for home consumption.

Records of transportation cost directly allocable to a particular category of products should be maintained separately so that allocation in appendix – 3 can be made.

For common transportation cost, both, for own fleet or hired ones, proper records for basis of apportionment should be maintained.

Records for transportation cost for exempted goods, excisable goods cleared for export shall be maintained separately.

Separate records of cost for mode of transportation other than road like ship, air, etc., are to be maintained in appendix – 2 which will be included in the total cost of transportation.

Treatment of Cost

Inward transportation costs shall form the part of the cost of procurement of materials which are to be identified for proper allocation/apportionment to the materials/products. Outward transportation cost shall form the part of the cost of sale and shall be allocated/apportioned to the materials and goods on a suitable basis. Outward transportation cost of a product from factory to depot or any location of sale shall be included in the cost of sale of the goods available for sale.

The following basis may be used, in order of priority, for apportionment of outward transportation cost depending upon the nature of the products, unit of measurement followed and type of transport used:

- Weight
- Volume of goods
- Tonne-Km
- Unit/Equivalent unit
- Value of goods
- Percentage of usage of space

Once a basis of apportionment is adopted, the same should be followed consistently.

For determining the transportation cost per unit, distance shall be factored in, to arrive at weighted average cost. Abnormal and non recurring cost shall not be a part of transportation cost. Penalty, detention charges, demurrage and cost related to abnormal break down will not be included in transportation cost.

Cost Sheet

The cost sheets shall be prepared and presented in a form as per Appendices 1, 2 and 3 or as near thereto. Appendix 1 and Appendix 2 show the details of information to be maintained for compilation of transport cost for own fleet and hired transportation charges respectively. Appendix 1 is applicable where the organization is having its own fleet.

The directly allocable cost of own fleet (outward) shall be identified against different categories of products as per Appendix 3 and same shall be indicated there. Similarly, total common cost of own fleet (outward) shall be apportioned to different categories of products as per Appendix 3 and the basis should be specified. The basis of apportionment may be adopted depending on the nature of product. Similar approach shall also be applied for hired outward transport charges.

More columns may be required to be shown in Appendix 3 specifying different types of transactions. For example: Sale on specific rate basis, sale of waste, scrap, return from customer, goods sent for job work, goods received after job work, etc.

Unit of Measurement (UM) may vary depending upon the nature of the product. For example, Number, MT, Meter, Litre, etc.

Proper records shall be maintained to show separately the Transportation Cost relating to sending of jobs to job contractors/ convertors and receipt back of processed jobs/converted materials.

An enterprise shall be required to maintain cost records and other books of account in a manner which would facilitate preparation and verification of cost of transportation and other related charges and it's apportioning to various products.

Summary

Cost Accounting is one of the branches of accounting, the other branches being the Stewardship Accounting, Financial Accounting, Management Accounting, Decision Accounting, Responsibility Accounting, Social Accounting, etc. The limitations of Financial Accounting, has necessitated the need for the development of Cost Accounting System. The main objectives of Cost Accounting are cost ascertainment, cost control and ascertainment of profitability.

Cost Accountancy is the application of costing and cost accounting principles, methods and techniques to the science, art and practice of cost control and ascertainment of profitability. It includes the presentation of information to the management for the purpose of managerial decision making. Thus, Cost Accountancy is a very wide and a comprehensive term.

The main focus of accounting being provision of business or accounting information, the relationship between Financial Accounting and Cost Accounting appears to be very close. These two branches of accounting are inter disciplinary, though there are various points of distinction, the main point being difference in the reporting aspect.

Management Accounting is concerned with the accounting information which is useful to the management in maximizing profits or minimizing losses. It is concerned with the improvement of the efficiency of the various phases of management. Management Accounting helps the managerial personnel to perform all the important managerial functions effectively *viz.*, planning, organizing, directing, controlling, coordinating, motivating and communicating by providing relevant information timely.

The main objective or the basic function of Management Accounting is to assist the management in taking various decisions by providing relevant and complete information as and when required. All the tools and techniques which help the Management Accountant in the discharge of his duties fall under the scope of Management Accounting.

The CASB develops Cost Accounting Standard to equip the profession with better guidelines on standard cost accounting practices; to assist the Cost Accountants in preparation of uniform cost statements and to provide guidelines to Cost Accountants to make standard approach towards maintenance of Cost. So far, five standards have been issued and two are drafts.

Glossary

- **Management Accounting:** According to the Institute of Chartered Accountants of England and Wales (ICMA) Management Accounting is "any form of accounting which enables a business to be conducted more efficiently".
- **Cost:** is the sacrifice made for securing the benefit under consideration. It may be defined as the benefit given up to acquire goods and services. The amount of expenditure (actual or notional) incurred on or attributable to a specified thing or activity is cost.
- **Costing:** is the technique and process of ascertaining the cost of activities, products, processes or services. This technique consists of a body of principles and rules, which govern the process of ascertaining the costs. Cost finding is Costing.
- **Cost Accounting:** Cost Accounting is classifying, recording and appropriate allocation of expenditure for the determination of the costs of products or services and for the presentation of the information suitably arranged for control and guidance of the management. Accounting for costs is Cost Accounting.
- **Cost Accountancy:** As an organized body of knowledge, the term Cost Accountancy may be defined as "the application of costing and cost accounting principles, methods and techniques to the science, art and practice of

cost control and ascertainment of profitability. It includes presentation of information for the purpose of managerial decision making" (CIMA official terminology).

- **Cost Unit:** The terminology defines a cost unit as "a unit of product, service or time in relation to which costs are ascertained."
- **Cost Centre:** Cost Centre may be defined as a person, place or item of equipment for which costs are ascertained.

Questions

(1) Give any four limitations of Financial Accounting.
(2) What are the objectives of Cost Accounting?
(3) Define Cost Accountancy.
(4) Mention any three points of dissimilarities between Financial Accounting and Cost Accounting.
(5) What is a Cost Centre and Cost Unit?
(6) What are the steps to be taken to install a Cost Accounting System?
(7) Define Management Accounting. Explain the need for Management Accounting.
(8) Discuss the scope of Management Accounting.
(9) Bring out any three differences between Management Accounting and Financial Accounting.
(10) Explain the terms 'Cost Accounting' and 'Management Accounting'. How do they both differ?

❑ ❑ ❑

2

Cost Classification and Importance of Cost Accounting

Objectives of the Study

The objectives of the study are to:

- Understand the basic rules for classification of costs
- Understand the importance of Cost Accounting System
- Critically evaluate the objections against Cost Accounting System
- Learn the relationship of Cost Accounting Department with the other Departments
- Visualize the future of Cost Accounting System

INTRODUCTION

To achieve the managerial objectives, there should be a proper ascertainment, classification and grouping of the costs. Different cost objectives result in different approaches to cost classification and cost accumulation. The process of grouping costs according to their common characteristics may be termed as Cost Classification.

Some of the cost objectives considered very useful and significant in classifying costs are determining product cost for stock valuation and profit measurement; decision-making; planning and control.

COST ACCOUNTING STANDARD 1 (CAS 1): *CLASSIFICATION OF COST*

(http://myicwai.com/docs/icwaicas1.doc)

The standard deals with the principle of classifying costs in the cost statements. The standard on classification of costs deals with the basis of classification of costs and the practice to be adopted for classification of cost elements in regard to its nature and management objective. The statement aims at providing better understanding on classification of cost for preparation of various cost statements required for statutory obligations or cost control measures.

The objective of this Standard is to prescribe the classification of costs for ascertainment of cost of a product or service and preparation of cost statements on a consistent and uniform basis with a view to effect the comparability of the same of an enterprise with that of previous periods and of other enterprises. The classification and its disclosure are aimed at providing better transparency in the cost statement. The standard is also for better adoption of Uniform Costing and Inter-firm Comparison.

BASIC RULES FOR CLASSIFICATION OF COSTS

Classification of cost is the arrangement of items of costs in logical groups having regard to their nature (subjective classification) or purpose (objective classification). Items should be classified by one characteristic for a specific purpose without ambiguity. Scheme of classification should be such that every item of cost can be classified.

Basis of Classification

- Relation to object – traceability
- Functions/activities
- Behavior
- Management decision-making
- Production Process
- Time period

Classification of cost is the process of grouping the components of cost under a common designation on the basis of similarities of nature, attributes or relations. It is the process of identification of each item and the systematic placement of like items together according to their common features. Items grouped together under common heads may be further classified according to their fundamental differences. The same costs may appear in several different classifications depending on the purpose of classification.

PRESENTATION AND DISCLOSURE

The classification of cost item should be done on the 'basis of classification' chosen with pre-determined objective. The classification of cost item should be followed consistently from period to period and preparation of cost statements should be made with reference to a period of time. A change in classification should be made only if it is required by law or for compliance with a Cost Accounting Standard or the change would reset in a more appropriate preparation or presentation of cost statements of an enterprise. Any change in classification of cost which has a material effect on the cost of the product should be disclosed in the cost statements. Where the effect of such change is not ascertainable wholly or partly, the fact should be indicated in the cost statement.

CLASSIFICATION OF COST

Costs are generally classified into the following categories:

(I) Traditional Classification of Cost

Costs should be gathered together in their natural groupings such as material, labor and other expenses. Items of costs differ on the basis of their nature. The elements of cost can be classified into the following three categories *viz.*, Material, Labor and Expenses.

Material Cost is the cost of material of any nature used for the purpose of production of a product or a service. Material cost includes cost of procurement, freight inwards, taxes and duties, insurance, etc. directly attributable to the acquisition. Trade discounts, rebates, duty drawbacks, refunds on account of modvat, cenvat, sales tax and other similar items are deducted in determining the costs of material.

Labor Cost means the payment made to the employees, permanent or temporary, for their services. Labor cost includes salaries and wages paid to permanent employees, temporary employees and also to employees of the contractor. Here, salaries and wages include all fringe benefits like Provident Fund contribution, gratuity, ESI, overtime, incentives, bonus, ex-gratia, leave encashment, wages for holidays and idle time, etc.

Expenses are other than material cost or labor cost which are involved in an activity. Expenditure on account of utilities, payment for bought out services, job processing charges, etc., can be termed as expenses.

These three elements of Cost are further classified into direct and indirect. Direct cost has three components – direct material cost, direct labor cost and direct expenses and indirect cost has three components- indirect material, indirect labor cost and indirect expenses. Sum of all direct costs is called Prime Cost and sum of all indirect costs is called as Overheads.

(1) Direct Material: Raw materials consumed for production of a product or service which are identifiable in the product or service form the direct material cost. Direct Material cost includes cost of procurement, freight inwards, taxes and duties, insurance, etc., directly attributable to the acquisition. Trade discounts, rebates, duty drawbacks, refunds on account of modvat, cenvat, sales tax and other similar items are deducted in determining the costs of direct material. It refers to the cost of material, which forms a major part of the finished product. The other names for this direct material are 'process material', 'prime cost material' '-production material', 'stores material', etc. It comprises all materials specially purchased for a particular job, order, process or product; all material (including primary material) acquired and subsequently requisitioned from the store; components or parts purchased or produced; material passing from one process to another and primary packing materials like wrappings, boxes, etc.

(2) Direct Labor: It is the labor of those workers who are engaged in the production process. It is expended directly upon the materials. The other names for the direct labor are process labor, production labor, operating labor etc. Direct Labor Cost is the cost of wages of those workers who are readily identified or linked with a Cost Centre or Cost Object. Here, the wages of the workers include all fringe benefits like Provident Fund Contribution, Gratuity, ESI, Overtime, Incentives, Bonus , Ex-Gratia, Leave Encashment, Wages for Holidays and Idle Time, etc. Examples of direct labor are machine operators and assemblers.

(3) Direct Expense: This item includes any expenditure other than direct material and direct-labor, which is incurred on a specific cost unit and which can be identified or linked with the Cost Centre or Cost Object. It is incurred for a product or job. This item is also known as chargeable expense. Examples of direct expenses are expenses for special moulds required in a particular Cost Centre; hiring charges for tools and equipments for a Cost Centre; royalties in connection to a product; job processing charges; fee paid to architects, surveyors and other consultants; cost of special moulds, designs and patterns; cost of patents and royalties; license fees etc.

(4) Indirect Material: It is the cost of material which cannot be directly allocable to a particular Cost Centre or Cost Object. Materials which are of small value and cannot be identified in or allocated to a product/service are classified as indirect materials. Examples: Consumable spares and parts; lubricants; nuts; bolts; cotton waste etc.

(5) Indirect Labor: It is that labor which cannot be easily identified with the product or service. Indirect labor cost is the wages of the employees which are not directly allocable to a particular Cost Centre. Examples of indirect labor are salaries of staff in the Administration and Accounts Department and salaries of security staff, foreman, shop clerks, cleaners, supervisors, material handlers, etc.

(6) Indirect Expenses: ICMA defines indirect expenses as "expenses which cannot be allocated but which can be apportioned to or absorbed by Cost Centres or Cost Units. It covers all the expenditure incurred by the manufacturing enterprise from the time production has started to its completion and transfer to finished goods store". Indirect expenses are the expenses other than of the nature of material or labor and cannot be directly allocable to a particular Cost Centre. Examples – insurance, taxes and duties.

(II) Behavioral Classification of Cost

Costs are classified based on behavior as fixed cost, variable cost and semi-variable cost depending upon the response to the changes in the activity levels.

(1) Fixed Cost: ICMA (U.K.) defines fixed cost as "a cost which tends to be unaffected by the variations in the volume of output. Fixed cost depends mainly on the effluxion of time and do not vary directly with volume or rate of output". It is a cost which do not change in total, for a given time period, in spite of change in the level of output. These are also known as standby cost, capacity cost or period cost. While the total fixed cost remains the same, per unit fixed cost decreases with the increase in the output and increases with the decrease in the output.

Examples: rent, salaries to the clerks, depreciation on office facilities, advertising, etc. These costs can also be further classified into :

(i) ***Committed cost*** which are primarily incurred to maintain the company's facilities and physical existence and over which management has little or no discretion. Examples: plant and equipment depreciation, taxes, insurance premium, etc.

(ii) ***Managed costs*** relate to current operations, which must continue to be paid to ensure the continued operating existence of the company. Example: management salaries.

(iii) ***Discretionary costs*** which are not related to current operations or activities and are subject to management decisions and control. Examples: research and development cost, marketing programmes, new system development cost, etc.

(iv) ***Step cost*** which is constant for a given level of output and then increases in a fixed amount at a higher output level. Example: supervisor salary. If the number of workers who are to be supervised is increased, another supervisor will be appointed thereby increasing the cost of supervision.

(2) **Variable Costs:** These costs are those that vary in total amount directly and proportionately with the output. It changes in direct proportion to the level of activity. The ratio between the change in the cost and the change in the level of output is always constant. Direct costs are the costs, which are generally variable costs. Example: cost of raw material. Variable cost has two parts – (a) Variable Direct Cost; and (B) Variable Indirect Costs. Variable indirect costs are termed as variable overhead. Examples of variable cost are materials consumed, direct labor, sales commission, utilities, freight, packing, etc.

(3) **Mixed Costs:** These costs are made up of fixed and variable elements. These costs can be called as semi variable costs or semi fixed costs. They remain constant up to a particular level of output because of the presence of fixed component and thereafter, vary with the volume of output because of the presence of variable component. They are partly affected by fluctuation in the level of activity. Examples of semi-variable cost are Factory supervision, maintenance, power, electricity bill, telephone bill, water bill, salesmen salary and commission, etc.

Note:

The characteristics of fixed costs are: (1) fixed amount within an output range (2) fixed cost per unit decreases with increased output.

The characteristics of variable cost are: (1) The variable cost varies directly with volume of activities or production (2) variable cost remains constant per unit within a range of activity.

(III) Degree of Traceability to the Product

On the basis of traceability or identifiability of the costs with the product manufactured, costs can be classified into direct cost and indirect cost.

(1) **Direct Cost:** These costs are easily traceable or identifiable with a product. Examples: direct materials, direct labor and direct expenses.

(2) **Indirect Cost:** These costs cannot be identified with or traced to a single product because they are common to several products. Indirect expenses are considered as overheads. Examples: indirect material, indirect labor and indirect expenses.

(IV) Degree of Association with the Product

As per the degree of association of costs with the product produced, costs are classified into product cost and period cost.

(1) **Product Cost:** These costs are included in the cost of manufacturing a product and are identifiable with the product. It comprises direct material, direct labor, direct expenses and manufacturing overhead. It is considered as a full Factory Cost.

(2) **Period Cost:** These costs are not included in the stock valuation and are treated as expenses during the period in which they are incurred.

(V) Functional Classification of Costs

Costs should be classified according to the major functions for which the elements are used into the following four major functions

- Production
- Administration
- Selling and Distribution and
- Research and Development Expenditure

Here, the costs are associated with the functions in the business.

(1) Manufacturing/Production/Works/Factory Overhead: Production Cost is the cost of all items involved in the production of a product or service. It includes all direct costs and indirect costs related to the production. Production overhead is the indirect costs involved in the production process. Production overhead is also termed as factory overhead or manufacturing overhead. It is the indirect expense of operating the manufacturing divisions of a concern and includes all expenditure incurred by the undertaking from the receipt of the order till the completion of the product and packed in primary packing. Examples: depreciation and insurance on fixed assets; repairs and maintenance of fixed assets; electricity charges; salaries for staff for production planning, technical supervision, factory administration, etc; normal idle time cost; expenses for stores management; security expenses in the factory; labor welfare expenses; dispensary and canteen expenses; depreciation of plant and machineries; repair and maintenance of factory building and plant and machineries; insurance; quality control, etc.

(2) Administration Overhead: All the indirect expenses incurred in formulating the policy, directing the organization, controlling and managing the operations of an undertaking are considered as administration overhead. Administration costs are expenses incurred for general management of an organization. These are in the nature of indirect costs and are also termed as administrative overhead. Examples of items to be included in administrative overhead are salaries of administrative and accounts staff; general office expenses like rent, lighting, rates and taxes, telephone, stationery, postage etc; bank charges; audit fees; legal expenses; depreciation and repairs and maintenance of office building, etc.

(3) Selling Overhead: The costs of seeking to create and stimulate demand for the products manufactured and of securing orders are considered as selling overheads. Selling costs are indirect costs related to selling of products or services and include all indirect cost in sales management for the organization. Selling Costs include all costs relating to regular sales and sales promotion activities. Examples of expenses which are included in selling cost are salaries, commission and travelling expenses for sales personnel; advertisement cost; legal expenses for debt realization; market research cost; royalty on sales show room expenses; samples and free gifts; bad debts; after sales service cost, etc.

(4) Distribution Overhead: The cost incurred from the time of making the packed product available for dispatch, till the time of making the reconditioned return empty package, if any, available for reuse. Distribution Costs are the cost incurred in handling a product from the time it is completed in the works until it reaches the ultimate consumer. Distribution costs are the costs incurred for distribution of product to customers. Examples of distribution costs are cost of warehousing saleable products; cost of delivering the products to customers; expenses on special packing for bulk transport etc.

(5) Research and Development Costs: These are the costs which are incurred for undertaking research to improve quality of a present product or improve process of manufacture, develop a new product, market research, etc., and commercialization thereof. Research Cost comprises the cost of development of new product and manufacturing process; improvement of existing products, process and equipment; finding new uses for known products; solving technical problem arising in manufacture and application of products, etc. Development cost includes the cost incurred for commercialization/implementation of research findings.

Note

- Primary packaging cost is included in production cost whereas secondary packaging cost is distribution cost.
- In exceptional cases, for example, in case of heavy industries equipment supply, installation cost at delivery site for heavy equipments which involves assembling of parts, testing etc. is included in production cost but not distribution cost. For example: installation cost of a gas turbine at plant site is included in the cost of production of gas turbine.

(VI) Classification by Time

A cost item is related to a specific period of time and costs can be classified according to the system of assessment and specific purpose.

(1) Historical Costs are the actual costs of acquiring assets or producing goods or services. They are 'postmortem' costs which are ascertained after they have been incurred and they represent the cost of actual operational performance. Historical Costing system follows a system of accounting to which all values (in revenue and capital accounts) are based on costs actually incurred or as relevant from time to time.

(2) Pre-determined Costs for a product are computed in advance of production, on the basis of a specification of all the factors affecting cost and cost data. Pre-determined costs may be either standard or estimated.

(3) Standard Costs: A predetermined norm is applied as a scale of reference for assessing actual cost, whether these are more or less. The standard cost serves as a basis of cost control and as a measure of productive efficiency when ultimately posed with an actual cost. It provides management with a medium by which the effectiveness of current results is measured and responsibility of deviation placed. Standard costs are used to compare the actual costs with the standard cost with a view to determine the variances, if any, and analyze the causes for variances and take proper measure to control them.

(4) Estimated Costs of a product are prepared in advance prior to the performance of operations or even before the acceptance of sale orders. Estimated cost is found with specific reference to product in question and activity level of the plant. It has no link with actual and hence it is assumed to be less accurate than the standard cost.

(VII) Relationship with Accounting Period

(1) Capital Cost: This cost is classified as an asset. It is a cost, which provides benefit to the future period. When the asset is used up or written off, this expenditure will flow into the cost stream as an expense.

(2) Revenue Cost: This cost is assumed to benefit only the current period and is classified as an expense.

(VIII) Costs for Decision-Making and Planning

(1) Opportunity Cost: It is the cost of the best alternative foregone for taking up the present alternative under consideration. These costs are measured by the profit that would have been earned had the resources been used for other purpose. These costs are useful for evaluating the alternatives and the usage of scarce resources. Opportunity Cost is always measured in terms of revenue lost. Opportunity Cost is the value of the alternatives foregone by adopting a particular strategy or employing resources in specific manner. It is the return expected from an investment other than the present one. The Opportunity Cost is considered for selection of a project or justification of investment or studying viability of an investment option.

(2) Sunk Cost: It is the cost, which has already been incurred. It is a past cost or commuted cost. Once they have been incurred, they cannot be changed or avoided by any decision that is made in the future. It has nothing to do with decision-making and is also known as Historical Cost. Sunk Costs are those that have been incurred for a project and which will not be recovered if the project is terminated. While considering the replacement of a plant, the depreciated book value of the old asset is irrelevant as the amount is a sunk cost which is to be written off at the time of replacement.

(3) Relevant Cost: It is the cost, which differs between alternatives. It is a future cost, which is affected and changed by a decision. If a cost increases, decreases, appears or disappears as different alternatives are compared, it is a Relevant Cost. These costs are relevant for a specific purpose or situation. In the context of decision making relating to a specific issue, only those costs which are relevant are considered. A particular cost item may be relevant in a decision making and may be irrelevant in some other decision making situation. For example, present depreciated cost of machine is relevant in case of decision of its sale but it is irrelevant in case of decision of its replacement.

(4) Differential Cost: It is the difference in the total cost between any two alternatives. It is equal to the additional variable cost incurred in respect of the additional output plus increase in the fixed cost, if any.

Differential Cost is the change in cost due to a change in the activity from one level to another. Differential Cost is found by using the principle which highlights the points of differences in costs by adoption of different alternatives. This technique is used in export pricing, new products and pricing goods sought to be promoted in new markets, either within the country or outside. The algebraic difference between the relevant costs at two levels of activities is the differential cost. When the level of activity is increased, the increase in cost is known as **Incremental Cost** and when the level of activity is decreased, the decrease in cost is known as **Decremental Cost**.

(5) Replacement Cost is the cost of an asset in the current market for the purpose of replacement. This cost is generally used for determining the optimum time for replacement of an equipment or machine in consideration of maintenance cost of the existing one and its productive capacity.

(6) Marginal Cost is the aggregate of variable costs, i.e. prime cost plus variable overhead. Marginal cost per unit is the change in the amount at any given volume of output by which the aggregate cost changes if the volume of output is increased or decreased by one unit.

Marginal Cost is used in Marginal Costing System. For determining marginal cost, semi-variable costs, if any, are segregated into fixed and variable cost. Then, variable costs plus the variable part of semi-variable costs is the total marginal cost for the volume of production in consideration.

(7) Normal Cost is a cost that is normally incurred at a given level of output in the conditions in which that level of output is achieved. Normal Cost includes those items of cost which occur in the normal situation of production process or in the normal environment of the business. The normal idle time is to be included in the ascertainment of normal cost.

(8) Abnormal Cost is an unusual or a typical cost whose occurrence is usually irregular and unexpected and which is due to some abnormal situation of the production. Abnormal cost arises due to idle time for some heavy break down or abnormal process loss. These are not considered in the cost of production for decision making and charged to profit and loss account.

(9) Avoidable Costs are those costs which under given conditions of performance efficiency should not have been incurred. Avoidable Costs are logically associated with some activity or situation and are ascertained by the difference of actual cost with the happening of the situation and the normal cost. When spoilage occurs in the manufacture in excess of normal limit, the resulting cost of spoilage is avoidable cost. Cost variances which are controllable may be termed as avoidable cost.

(10) Unavoidable Costs are inescapable costs which are essentially to be incurred, within the limits or norms provided for. It is the cost that must be incurred under programmes of business restriction. It is fixed in nature and inescapable.

(11) Imputed Cost: It refers to those costs, which would have been incurred in the absence of a self-owned factor of production. These costs though not incurred in a transaction, but are relevant to the decision, as they pertain to a particular situation. Imputed Cost does not involve any cash outlay. Examples: interest on the internally generated funds, rental value of a company owned property, salaries of the owners of a proprietorship firm, etc.

(12) Out-of-pocket Cost: It signifies the cash associated with an activity. Non-cash cost like depreciation are not included in this type of cost. Example: purchase of raw materials, payment of salaries.

(13) Shut-down Costs: These costs have to be incurred under all situations in the case of temporary cessation of activities of a product or closing down of a department or a division. These costs are always fixed costs.

(IX) Costs for Control

(1) Controllable Cost: The ICMA (U.K.) defines it as "a cost which can be influenced by the action of a specified member of an undertaking". It is the cost over which a manager has a direct and complete decision authority. It can be controlled by a manager at a given organizational level.

(2) Uncontrollable Cost: The ICMA (U.K.) defines it as "a cost which cannot be influenced by the action of a specified member of an undertaking".

(X) Other Costs

(1) Joint Cost: In processing of single raw material or production resources, a situation may arise, where more than one type of finished product may emerge. In such a case, the costs incurred for the production of all these products is considered as Joint Costs. These costs relate to two or more products produced from a common production process. These products are not identifiable as individual types of products, until a certain stage of production known as the split off point. These costs are apportioned to different products only by means of some suitable bases of apportionment.

(2) Common Costs: The costs which are incurred for more than one product, job, territory or any other specific costing object and are not easily identifiable with individual products are called as Common Costs and are generally apportioned. They are common to the costing units like products, processes, functions, responsibilities, customers, sales territories, period of time, etc.

METHODS OF COSTING

Methods of Costing are those which are used to ascertain the cost of a product, service, process or any activity. Techniques are the tools, which are used to exercise control over the costs and also for the decision-making purposes.

There are mainly two methods of costing. They are Job Costing and Process Costing. Other methods of costing are only the variations of these two methods. The variations of Job Costing are Batch Costing and Contract Costing. The variations of Process Costing are Operations Costing, Operating Costing and Unit or Output Costing.

(1) Job Costing: Here, the costs are collected and accumulated for each job, work order of project separately. For the purpose of cost accumulation, a job card is prepared for each job. This method is applicable in industries like machine tool manufacturing, foundries and engineering.

(a) ***Contract Costing:*** This method of ascertaining cost is employed in case of jobs which are big and are spread over long periods of time. A separate account is maintained for each individual contract. Examples: civil and mechanical engineering firms; construction works like dams, bridges, buildings, etc.

(b) ***Batch Costing:*** A batch represents a number of small orders passed through the factory in a lot. Each batch is treated as a cost unit and the costs are ascertained for each batch. Examples: Biscuit manufacturing; drugs and pharmaceutical industries; spare parts and components manufacture.

(2) Process Costing: It is a method of ascertaining costs for each process of manufacture. It is applicable where production is continuous, manufacturing is carried on by different and well defined processes; the finished product of one process become the raw material for the next process; different products with or without by products are produced simultaneously at the same process and where standardized products are manufactured. Examples: Textile industries, Jute manufacturing, etc.

(a) ***Operation Costing:*** Here, each process is sub divided into smaller operations and costs are ascertained for each operation.

(b) ***Output or Unit Costing:*** This method is suitable for industries where manufacture is continuous and units are identical. Cost sheets are prepared to ascertain the cost of the output. Examples: Mines, quarries, oil drilling, breweries, cement work, etc.

(c) ***Operating/Service Costing:*** This method is used to ascertain the costs of services rendered by the industries. *Examples:* transport undertakings, power supply industries, hospitals, hotels, etc.

(3) Multiple Costing: The application of more than one method in respect of the same product is known as Multiple Costing. It is suitable for the industries where a number of component parts are separately produced and subsequently assembled into a final product. Examples: cycle industries, watch making, automobile, engine, radio, typewriter, and aero plane manufacturing companies.

TECHNIQUES OF COSTING

The various techniques of Costing for the control of costs are Historical Costing, Marginal Costing, Absorption Costing, Budgetary Control, Standard Costing and Uniform Costing.

(1) Historical Costing: It is a technique, which aims at recording and ascertaining the cost after they have been incurred. Though it is used for comparison of costs over different periods, it has a limited utility.

(2) Marginal Costing: The term marginal cost refers to the additional cost incurred for every additional unit of output. The Marginal Cost technique aims at segregating the cost into variable and fixed and only variable cost is analyzed for the purpose of decision-making.

(3) Absorption Costing: Here, both the variable and fixed costs are charged to operations, processes or products. Total cost is taken into consideration for decision-making.

(4) Budgetary Control: The official CIMA Terminology defines the term "Budgetary Control" as the establishment of budgets relating the responsibilities of executives to the requirements of a policy and the continuous comparison of actual with budgeted results, either to secure by individual action the objectives of that policy or to provide a basis for its revision.

It involves the following steps:

(i) Establishment of budget.
(ii) Measurement of actual performance.
(iii) Comparison of actual with budgeted results.
(iv) Taking corrective action to prevent recurrence of variations between the actual and budgeted results.
(v) Providing a basis for revision of budgets.

(5) Standard Costing: Under this technique, standards are fixed and a comparison is made between actual costs and predetermined costs and the variances are analyzed for taking remedial action.

(6) Uniform Costing: It is not a separate method of costing. It is a situation where all the firms intending to share the information, follow uniform procedures, methods and practices so that comparison is meaningful.

Cost Sheet or Statement of Cost

Cost sheet is a statement prepared to show the various components of the total cost. It is a memorandum statement. Therefore, it does not form a part of double entry cost accounting records.

In a cost sheet, certain items, which are purely of financial nature, are not included like financial incomes, appropriation of profits, financial charges and abnormal expenses or losses, income tax, provisions, etc.

(1) Financial incomes: interest on investments; interest on bank deposits; transfer fees received; rent receivable; capital profit; dividend received; brokerage, commission or discount received.

(2) Appropriation of profits: transfer to sinking fund, general or specific reserve; dividend paid; tax on income; charitable donations; goodwill or fictitious assets written off.

(3) Purely financial charges: capital losses; damages payable; penalties and fines; expenses on transfer of company's office; interest on bank loan, debentures and mortgage; discount on bonds and debentures; losses on investment; cash discount.

(4) Abnormal expenses or losses: cost of abnormal wastage of material, loss by theft, loss by fire, costs of abnormal idle time.

Cost Sheet for the period ending....

Particulars	*Amount*	*Amount*
Opening stock of Raw materials	xxxx	
Add: Purchase of raw materials	xxxx	
Carriage inward	xxxx	
Freight on purchases	xxxx	
Duty on purchases	xxxx	
Less: Closing stock of raw materials	xxxx	
Defective materials returned	xxxx	
Abnormal wastage of material	xxxx	
***(a)* Cost of Raw Material Consumed**		xxxx
Add: Direct Labour		xxxx
Direct expenses		xxxx
***(b)* Prime Cost**		xxxx
Add: Factory/Works/Production/Manufacturing Overheads:		
Indirect wages	xxxx	
Depreciation on plant and machinery	xxxx	

Particulars		*Amount*	*Amount*
	Insurance on plant and machinery	xxxx	
	Electric power (Factory)	xxxx	
	Motive power	xxxx	
	Oil and waste	xxxx	
	Lighting (Factory)	xxxx	
	Consumable stores	xxxx	
	Store keeping wages	xxxx	
	Factory rent	xxxx	
	Fuel and wastage	xxxx	
Less:	Scrap	xxxx	
Add:	Opening work in progress	xxxx	
Less:	Closing work in progress	xxxx	xxxx
(c)	**Factory / Works / Manufacturing Cost**		xxxx
Add:	Administration Overhead:	xxxx	
	Office salaries	xxxx	
	Depreciation on furniture and fittings	xxxx	
	General expenses	xxxx	
	Directors fees	xxxx	
	Office lighting	xxxx	
	Postage and telegraph	xxxx	
	Telephone charges	xxxx	
	Managers salary	xxxx	
	Managing director's remuneration	xxxx	
	Office stationery	xxxx	xxxx
(d)	**Office Cost or Cost of Production**		xxxx
Add:	Opening stock of finished goods		xxxx
Less:	Closing stock of finished goods		xxxx
(e)	**Cost of Goods Sold**		xxxx
Add:	Selling and distribution :	xxxx	
	Advertisement expenses	xxxx	
	Salary of salesman	xxxx	
	Bad debts written off	xxxx	
	Travelling expenses	xxxx	
	Carriage outwards	xxxx	xxxx
(f)	**Cost of Sales/Total Cost**		xxxx
	Profit / Loss		xxxx
(g)	**Sales**		xxxx

Advantages of Cost Accounting

Cost Accounting is immensely useful in all economic activities. Every economic activity makes a value analysis, wherein, the costs involved in it is compared with the benefits obtained out of it. Here comes the importance of the Cost Accounting System which involves a study of those concepts, tools and techniques which help in the ascertainment and analysis of costs. Cost Accounting aids management in taking various managerial decisions, which are summarized below.

(1) Facilitates cost comparison: Cost Accounting enables the management to make cost comparison of jobs, products, departments, sales territories, etc. both within the firm (intra firm) and with the outside firm (inter firm).

(2) Helps Financial Accounting: In ascertaining the correct value of the closing inventory, the principle of matching cost and revenue under a modern Cost Accounting system is of a great assistance to the management. A good system of Cost Accounting provides a reliable check on the accuracy of Financial Accounting through the reconciliation of cost and financial profits.

(3) **Facilitates planning:** Cost Accounting enables management to know future costs for appropriate plans and decision making besides recording and analyzing past costs and activities for product costing. It also serves as a reliable base for making estimates and submitting tenders.

(4) **Gives detailed cost information:** Cost Accounting classifies cost and revenue by every possible division of the business and supplies the detailed and regular cost information to the management for ascertaining the cost of a product, process, department, division and unit of service.

(5) **Reveals profitable and unprofitable activities:** As costs are ascertained by products, jobs, processes or departments, the management can distinguish between profitable and unprofitable activities and take steps to improve the operating efficiency of unprofitable lines or consider the modification or elimination of such activities.

(6) **Preparation of income statement:** Since cost records show the correct values of closing inventories, preparation of interim profit and loss account on a realistic basis is made possible. Cost Accounting provides various techniques like Perpetual Inventory System, Always Better Control Analysis, etc. to help the management in inventory control.

(7) **Assists management in control of costs:** To ensure that the operations, processes and costs are under control, a concern will have a number of control systems all of which depend upon the detailed and timely cost information. Budgetary Control and Standard Costing are the two important cost accounting techniques which are used to control the costs.

(8) **Reveals idle capacity:** Cost Accounting helps the management to ascertain the cost of idle capacity which may arise due to shortage of demand, breakdown of machinery or other bottlenecks of production and take steps to improve capacity utilization.

(9) **Benefits employees:** The management is in a position to appraise the performance of personnel and introduce incentive wage system based on the operational efficiency of every line of activity disclosed by the Cost Accounting System. A good cost accounting system secures business stability which means continuous and secured employment to employees.

(10) **Benefits creditors:** Cost reports provide not just the present trends of the business but also future prospects of the organization. On the basis of these reports, creditors, debenture holders, banks and other financial agencies are able to form an idea of the financial soundness of the organization.

(11) **Benefits society:** New and improved methods of production, lower production and distribution costs and lower prices, better quality products, etc., which are the results of Cost Accounting System, are of immense benefit to the society as a whole.

(12) **Benefits Government Agencies and Others:** Cost Accounting provides ready figures to the Government, Trade Unions, Wage Tribunals and other bodies, for dealing with a variety of problems regarding price fixation, price control, tariff protection, wage level fixation, etc.

(13) **Assists Management in decision making:** Various managerial decisions like fixation of selling price, add or drop a product, make or buy a component, expansion or contraction of activities can be taken better only with the help of detailed cost information provided by the cost accountant. Cost Accounting assists management in fixing up selling price not only during normal business conditions but also during depression period, when prices may have to be fixed below cost.

Installation of a Cost Accounting System

There is no hard and fast rule for the installation of a Cost Accounting System. Each organization has to design its own system to suit its requirements. While installing a system, management has to evaluate the installation in terms of the cost of installation and the benefits that would derive from the system and install the system when the benefits outweigh the costs.

The general aspects which should be considered before installation of the system are as follows:

(1) **Nature of the business:** The selection of a proper method of costing depends upon the nature of the business, its products, technical aspects, methods and stages of production. Therefore, a proper study of the same is necessary.

(2) **Structure of the organization:** The scope of responsibilities of the managers can be determined only when the structure of the organization, its size and layout is known. This is very much essential for the introduction of the costing system as it will be enable a proper flow of communication, i.e., upward and downward. The existing structure may be disturbed as little as possible while introducing the costing system so as to make the structure suitable.

(3) **Objectives and expectations:** Objectives of the system to be introduced and the expectations of the management from the system should be known. A simple costing system would be introduced if the objective is to ascertain only the cost of each product whereas an elaborate system would be introduced if the objective is to provide cost information which would help the management in controlling the cost and making various decisions.

(4) **Co-operation and support of the staff:** For any system to be successful, the co-operation and support of the staff are essential. Therefore, the system should be designed in consultation with the staff. A sense of cost consciousness

should be instilled in the minds of the managers. The accounting staff may resist the introduction of the costing system for the fear of losing importance and increase and interference in their work. The staff should be clearly explained that the costing system does not replace the existing system but only supplement the financial accounting system. The employees should be educated properly about the benefits of the costing system. Requisite training should be provided to the existing staff.

(5) Standardization of forms: In order to reduce the clerical work to the minimum and save time, it is necessary to standardize the forms to be used in the organization.

(6) Prompt reporting: Information delayed is information denied. Therefore, the cost data must be updated from time to time and accurate data must be made available to the management regularly and promptly as the management has to take several decisions timely.

(7) Flexibility: Any system should be flexible and capable of being adapted to the changing requirements of the business.

(8) Reconciliation of Cost and Financial Accounts: There should be a regular reconciliation of cost and financial accounts when they are maintained separately under non integral system of book keeping.

(9) Current practices: The existing methods and procedures relating to purchase, storage and issue of materials, remunerating labor, apportionment of overheads, etc. should be carefully studied and modified as per the requirements.

(10) Simplicity: The system of costing to be installed should be as simple and easy as possible to understand and operate.

Cost Accounting System should be tailor-made, simple and capable of meeting the requirements of the organization.

LIMITATIONS OF COST ACCOUNTING

In modern times, Cost Accounting has become an indispensable organ of accounting process. In spite of numerous advantages, there are some objections raised against it. They are as follows.

(1) It is unnecessary: It is argued that Cost Accounting is unnecessary and it is just a duplication of accounting work. This argument is based on the premise that in olden times, a good number of firms have proved themselves efficient even without costing techniques.

(2) It is expensive: As Cost Accounting necessitates the maintenance of double set of account books etc., it is very expensive to introduce cost system in a firm. Therefore, a small business concern do not find it economical.

(3) It is monotonous: It is often argued that, it stresses unnecessarily on paper work and routine checking and therefore it is monotonous.

(4) It is a failure: It is argued that in spite of the introduction of Cost Accounting System, the organization could not get the desired results and therefore, the system is a failure.

(5) Unreliable: It is argued that, the results of Cost Accounting are not reliable as the system is based on estimates and estimates cannot be reliable.

(6) Lack of uniformity: This is the greatest limitation of Cost Accounting system and therefore, all Cost Accounting results should be accepted as a reasonable approach to accuracy and not as a precise measurement as Cost Accounting is not an exact science but an art.

(7) Other limitations: The other limitations are arbitrary allocation of joint costs, arbitrary division of costs into direct and indirect, arbitrary apportionment of service departments expenses to other production departments, etc.

In spite of the above limitations of Cost Accounting, if properly used, the benefits of Cost Accounting definitely outweigh its limitations and can be a useful tool for solving many crucial managerial problems.

CRITICAL EVALUATION OF LIMITATIONS

When the so called limitations of Cost Accounting are critically evaluated, one can find that these are not actually the limitations and the benefits of the Cost Accounting system definitely outweigh the drawbacks.

(1) The objection regarding that the Cost Accounting System is unnecessary was true in olden times. But, today, modern industries are running under highly competitive conditions, which require them to control the costs and reduce the selling prices as far as possible. To control the costs, management needs to know detailed cost information for decision-making. This need of cost ascertainment, cost control and decision-making can be served only by Cost Accounting System.

(2) The most powerful argument against the introduction of Cost Accounting System that it involves considerable amount of expenditure is true but, the expenditure incurred on introducing and operating the system will be a profitable investment if due care is taken to devise the Cost Accounting System to suit the size and the need of the organization. The expenditure incurred in the introduction of the system can be treated as an investment and the benefits will surely exceed the costs, if due care is taken.

(3) Though, the introduction of Costing System introduces some additional work and it is true that the forms and the rulings are an integral part of the system, yet, it is not the fault of the system but only the way in which the system is maintained. The forms and the rulings must be revised and updated in the light of altered conditions. Only then, the system will work successfully.

(4) The failure of a system may be due to several causes like lack of support from the top management and employees, lack of adequate facilities etc. If desired results could not be produced, it is not the fault of the system as such but it is the implementation part which is to be looked into. To make the system successful, its utility should be understood clearly by the management and the employees and they should work for the results.

(5) The argument that the Cost Accounting System is not reliable is untenable as estimation of cost is based on scientific techniques and reasoning and past actual figures are taken as the base. Therefore, the estimation is quite near to reality. In certain cases, estimation is the only way as in case of tenders, fixation of standard costs etc. Historical Costing and Standard Costing are the important techniques of costing which are widely used in modern times.

Relationship of Cost Accounting Department with other Departments

The **Design and Development Department,** under the direction of design and development manager, designs and develops products. In this department, cost estimates are needed for each type of material, each item of labor and each machine process before a decision can be made regarding accepting or rejecting a design.

The **Production or Manufacturing Department** includes activities involved in converting raw materials into saleable products. This department needs active and direct support from a number of manufacturing services such as production planning and control, industrial engineering, repairs and maintenance and stores department. The scheduling, manufacturing and inspection of products by the manufacturing departments are measured for efficiency in terms of cost incurred.

The **Personnel Department**, which interviews, screens and selects employees for various job classifications and maintains workers performance records, is interested along with the production department in retaining efficient and satisfied employees. The wage rates and the methods of remuneration agreed upon with the employee, form the basis for the computation of the payroll.

The **Finance Department**, which is responsible for financial administration, relies upon accounting, budgeting and related reports in scheduling cash requirements and expectations.

The **Marketing Department** is concerned with the anticipation and identification of customer needs, creation and stimulation of demand, securing orders and timely distribution. It needs a good product at a competitive price in its dealing with customers. As prices of the product are fixed by adding a predetermined percentage to cost, information regarding cost cannot be ignored. Accurate cost data gives sufficient information to the marketing managers' as to which products are most profitable and assist them greatly in determining sales policies.

The **Customer Service Department** provides a number of services to customers industries which are engaged in the manufacture of equipments such as computers, office machines and capital equipment, small and domestic appliances must provide product support services to buyers. This includes pre-sale and post-sale services. This department is measured for efficiency in terms of costs incurred.

The **Administration Department** provides support to the core functions of the business. This includes formulation of objectives, preparation of corporate plans and issue of directions in order to make sure that the business achieves its objectives and controls total business performance. This department is measured for efficiency in terms of costs incurred.

Thus, the personnel of Cost Accounting Department are posted in different departments to collect the information from various departments on the basis of which the efficiency of each department is judged.

Future of Cost Accounting

With the advent of the factory system, necessity for accurate cost information was felt in order to bring efficiency in production. The growth of heavy industry and mass production methods brought about the development of Cost Accounting.

The scientific management of F.W. Taylor served as an initiative to the development of Cost Accounting. The development of the system of Cost Accounting is of recent origin in India and it started gaining importance when Government of India laid emphasis on industrial development. Further, provision of cost audit under section 233 (B) of the Companies Act has given way to the development of Cost Accounting in India. The various malpractices prevalent in the manufacturing establishment were brought to light by the Vivian Bose Enquiry and it was thought that the audit of financial accounts at the end of the year was insufficient to judge the real efficiency of working of manufacturing organizations. As a result, the concept of cost audit emerged to obtain the best utilization of the resources used in the manufacturing organizations. The Government of India was given the power for ordering cost audit under Section 233 (B) of the Companies Act, 1956. The Government may appoint a cost auditor to conduct cost audit in the following cases

- wherever it is felt necessary to conduct cost audit in the opinion of the Government under Section 233 B of the Companies Act, 1956
- to fix reasonable prices of certain items of production so as to prevent undue profiteering
- to ascertain correct cost of certain units, when Government is approached for probation or for financial help and
- to ascertain correct cost of contract given to private firms under 'cost plus' basis.

SUMMARY

To achieve the managerial objectives, there should be a proper ascertainment, classification and grouping of the costs. The process of grouping costs according to their common characteristics may be termed as Cost Classification. The standard on classification of costs deals with the basis of classification of costs and the practice to be adopted for classification of cost elements in regard to its nature and management objective. The statement aims at providing better understanding on classification of cost for preparation of various cost statements required for statutory obligations or cost control measures.

Classification of cost is the arrangement of items of costs in logical groups having regard to their nature (subjective classification) or purpose (objective classification). Items should be classified by one characteristic for a specific purpose without ambiguity. Any change in classification of cost which has a material effect on the cost of the product should be disclosed in the cost statements. Where the effect of such change is not ascertainable wholly or partly, the fact should be indicated in the cost statement.

The elements of cost are classified into Material, Labor and Expenses. Costs are classified based on behavior as fixed cost, variable cost and semi-variable cost depending upon the response to the changes in the activity levels. According to the degree of traceability to the product, classification is into direct cost and indirect cost. As per the degree of association with the product, they can be classified into product cost and period cost.

Costs are classified according to the major functions, for which the elements are used, into production, administration, selling and distribution and research and development expenditure. A cost item is related to a specific period of time and cost can be classified according to the system of assessment and specific purpose into historical costs, pre-determined costs, standard costs and estimated costs. As per the relationship with accounting period, they may be classified into Capital Cost and Revenue Cost.

There are certain special costs for decision making and planning like opportunity cost, sunk cost, relevant cost, differential cost, replacement cost, marginal cost, normal cost, abnormal cost, avoidable costs, unavoidable costs, imputed cost, out-of-pocket cost and shut down costs. As per the cost which can be controlled or not, the classification is into controllable cost and uncontrollable cost. The other costs are joint costs and common costs.

Methods of costing are those which are used to ascertain the cost of a product, service, process or any activity. Techniques are the tools, which are used to exercise control over the costs and also for the decision-making purposes.

There are mainly two methods of costing. They are Job Costing and Process Costing. Other methods of costing are only the variations of these two methods. The variations of Job Costing are Batch Costing and Contract Costing. The variations of Process Costing are Operations Costing, Operating Costing and Unit or Output Costing. The various techniques of Costing for the control of costs are Historical Costing, Marginal Costing, Absorption Costing, Budgetary Control, Standard Costing and Uniform Costing.

Cost sheet is a statement prepared to show the various components of the total cost. It is a memorandum statement. Therefore, it does not form a part of double entry cost accounting records. In cost sheet, certain items, which are purely of financial nature, are not included like financial incomes, appropriation of profits, financial charges and abnormal expenses or losses, income tax, provisions, etc.

With the advent of the factory system, necessity for accurate cost information was felt in order to bring efficiency in production. The growth of heavy industry and mass production methods brought about the development of Cost Accounting. The importance of Cost Accounting Department is felt in every Department. The personnel of Cost Accounting Department are posted to every department to ascertain the cost of each department to evaluate the efficiency of the departments.

The scientific management of F.W. Taylor served as an initiative to the development of Cost Accounting. The development of the system of Cost Accounting is of recent origin in India and it started gaining importance when Government of India laid emphasis on industrial development. Further, provision of cost audit under section 233 (B) of the Companies Act has given way to the development of Cost Accounting in India.

Glossary

- **Fixed Cost:** a cost which tends to be unaffected by the variations in the volume of output. Fixed cost depends mainly on the effluxion of time and do not vary directly with volume or rate of output.
- **Variable Costs:** are those that vary in total amount directly and proportionately with the output. It changes in direct proportion to the level of activity. The ratio between the change in the cost and the change in the level of output is always constant.

- **Direct Cost:** are easily traceable or identifiable with a product. Examples: direct materials, direct labor and direct expenses.
- **Indirect Cost:** cannot be identified with or traced to a single product because they are common to several products
- **Selling Overhead:** are the costs of seeking to create and stimulate demand for the products manufactured and of securing orders.
- **Distribution Overhead:** are the cost incurred in handling a product from the time it is completed in the works until it reaches the ultimate consumer.
- **Research & Development Costs:** are the costs for undertaking research to improve quality of a present product or improve process of manufacture, develop a new product, market research, etc., and commercialization thereof.
- **Historical Costs:** are the actual costs of acquiring assets or producing goods or services. They are 'post-mortem' costs ascertained after they have been incurred and they represent the cost of actual operational performance.
- **Pre-determined Costs:** for a product are computed in advance of production, on the basis of a specification of all the factors affecting cost and cost data. Pre-determined costs may be either standard or estimated.
- **Opportunity Cost:** is the cost of the best alternative foregone for taking up the present alternative under consideration
- **Sunk Cost:** are those that have been incurred for a project and which will not be recovered if the project is terminated.
- **Relevant Cost:** are the costs relevant for a specific purpose or situation. For example, present depreciated cost of machine is relevant in case of decision of its sale but it is irrelevant in case of decision of its replacement.
- **Differential Cost:** is the difference in the total cost between any two alternatives. It is equal to the additional variable cost incurred in respect of the additional output plus increase in the fixed cost, if any.
- **Replacement Cost:** is the cost of an asset in the current market for the purpose of replacement. It is generally used for determining the optimum time of replacement of an equipment or machine in consideration of maintenance cost of the existing one and its productive capacity.
- **Marginal Cost:** is the aggregate of variable costs, i.e. prime cost plus variable overhead. Marginal cost per unit is the change in the amount at any given volume of output by which the aggregate cost changes if the volume of output is increased or decreased by one unit.
- **Normal Cost:** is a cost that is normally incurred at a given level of output in the conditions in which that level of output is achieved.
- **Abnormal Cost:** is an unusual or a typical cost whose occurrence is usually irregular and unexpected and due to some abnormal situation of the production. Abnormal cost arises due to idle time for some heavy break down or abnormal process loss. They are not considered in the cost of production for decision making and charged to profit and loss account.
- **Avoidable Costs:** are the costs which under given conditions of performance efficiency should not have been incurred. Avoidable costs are logically associated with some activity or situation and are ascertained by the difference of actual cost with the happening of the situation and the normal cost.
- **Unavoidable Costs:** are inescapable costs which are essentially to be incurred, within the limits or norms provided for. It is the cost that must be incurred under programmes of business restriction. It is fixed in nature and inescapable.
- **Imputed Cost:** refers to those costs, which would have been incurred in the absence of a self-owned factor of production. These costs though not incurred in a transaction, but are relevant to the decision, as they pertain to a particular situation. Imputed cost does not involve any cash outlay.
- **Shut down Costs:** have to be incurred under all situations in the case of temporary cessation of activities of a product or closing down of a department or a division. These costs are always fixed costs.
- **Controllable Cost:** is a cost which can be influenced by the action of a specified member of an undertaking. It is the cost over which a manager has a direct and complete decision authority. It can be controlled by a manager at a given organizational level.
- **Uncontrollable Cost:** is a cost which cannot be influenced by the action of a specified member of an undertaking.
- **Joint Cost:** relate to two or more products produced from a common production process. These products are not identifiable as individual types of products, until a certain stage of production known as the split off point. These costs are apportioned to different products only by means of some suitable bases of apportionment.

- **Common Costs:** are incurred for more than one product, job, territory or any other specific costing object and are not easily identifiable with individual products are called as common costs and are generally apportioned.
- **Job Costing:** Here, the costs are collected and accumulated for each job, work order of~ project separately. For the purpose of cost accumulation, a job card is prepared for each job. This method is applicable in industries like machine tool manufacturing, foundries and engineering.
- **Contract Costing:** This method of ascertaining cost is employed in case of jobs which are big and are spread over long periods of time. A separate account is maintained for each individual contract.
- **Batch Costing:** A batch represents a number of small orders passed through the factory in a lot. Each batch is treated as a cost unit and the costs are ascertained for each batch.
- **Process Costing:** is a method of ascertaining costs for each process of manufacture. It is applicable where production is continuous, manufacturing is carried on by different and well defined processes, the finished product of one process become the raw material for the next process, different products with or without by products are produced simultaneously at the same process and where standardized products are manufactured.
- **Operation Costing:** Here, each process is sub divided into smaller operations and costs are ascertained for each operation.
- **Output or Unit Costing:** This method is suitable for industries where manufacture is continuous and units are identical. Cost sheets are prepared to ascertain the cost of the output.
- **Operating/Service Costing:** This method is used to ascertain the costs of services rendered by the industries.
- **Multiple Costing:** The application of more than one method in respect of the same product is known as multiple costing. It is suitable for the industries where a number of component parts are separately produced and subsequently assembled into a final product.
- **Historical Costing:** is a technique, which aims at recording and ascertaining the cost after they have been incurred.
- **Marginal Costing:** The term marginal cost refers to the additional cost incurred for every additional unit of output. The Marginal Cost technique aims at segregating the cost into variable and fixed and only variable cost is analyzed for the purpose of decision-making.
- **Absorption Costing:** Here, both the variable and fixed costs are charged to operations, processes or products. Total cost is taken into consideration for decision-making.
- **Budgetary Control:** involves the establishment of budgets relating the responsibilities of executives to the requirements of a policy and the continuous comparison of actual with budgeted results, either to secure by individual action the objectives of that policy or to provide a basis for its revision.
- **Standard Costing:** Under this technique, standards are fixed and a comparison is made between actual costs and predetermined cost and the variances are analyzed for taking remedial action.
- **Uniform Costing:** is not a separate method of costing. It is a situation where all the firms intending to share the information, follow uniform procedures, methods and practices so that comparison is meaningful.
- **Cost Sheet:** is a statement prepared to show the various components of the total cost.

Questions

(1) How does Costing Methods differ from Costing Techniques?
(2) What are Behavioral Costs and list them out.
(3) What do you understand by the term Opportunity Cost?
(4) How do you classify the costs?
(5) Explain the various methods of classification of costs.
(6) Explain the following terms:
   (a) Sunk cost
   (b) Shut down cost
   (c) Incremental costs
   (d) Out of pocket cost
   (e) Imputed cost
(7) Bring out the significance of Cost Accounting.
(8) Cost Accounting is an aid to Management. Discuss its importance.
(9) What are the steps to be taken to install the Cost Accounting System?
(10) Critically evaluate the limitations of Cost Accounting.
(11) Explain the relationship of Cost Accounting Department with other departments.

❑ ❑ ❑

3

Books of Accounts

Objectives

The main objectives of the study are to

- Learn the basic systems of maintaining Cost Accounts
- Understand the Non-Integral System of Accounting
- Appreciate the need for Integral System of Accounting

Introduction

The importance of Cost Accounting System has led to the establishment of Cost Accounting Departments in most of the industrial enterprises. Cost Accounting records form an important part of a Cost Accounting System. Cost Accounts are essentially maintained on principles of Double Entry Bookkeeping. There are two basic systems of maintaining Cost Accounts. They are:

(1) Independent Cost Accounts or Non-Integrated Accounting (inter-locking) and
(2) Integral or Integrated Accounting

Non-Integrated Accounting

Non-Integrated Accounting is also known as Cost Ledger Accounting System or Independent Cost Accounting System. Under this system, separate sets of books for Cost Accounts and Financial Accounts are maintained. The Cost Ledger is quite independent of the Financial Ledger. While Cost Accountant is responsible for the maintenance of cost accounts, cost reports and statements; Financial Accountant is responsible for financial ledgers.

Principal Ledgers to be maintained in Costing Department

The following important ledgers are kept in Costing Department.

(1) **Cost Ledger:** This is the principal ledger of Costing Department. It contains all impersonal accounts i.e. Nominal Accounts and to some extent Real Accounts. It is similar to General Ledger of Financial Accounting. It is made self-balancing by maintaining control accounts for each of the subsidiary ledgers.

(2) **Stores Ledger:** It is a subsidiary ledger containing all stores accounts. A separate account is opened for each item of stores (i.e., Raw material, components, consumable stores, etc.). Account of each item of stores shows receipt, issue and balance, both in quantity and amount.

(3) **Work in progress Ledger:** It is a subsidiary ledger in which accounts of all jobs undertaken and cost incurred therefore are recorded. Expenditure relating to material, labour and other overheads charged to the jobs will be debited to the respective job and will be credited with the values of goods completed and transferred.

(4) **Finished Goods Ledger:** It is also a subsidiary ledger. This ledger contains an account of completely finished job or product. A separate account is maintained for each type of finished product.

Thus, the above are the principal ledgers to be maintained in Costing Department and it is also necessary to have a separate control account in each of these ledgers.

Principal Accounts to be maintained

When a separate cost ledger is kept, the following accounts are generally maintained.

(1) **General Ledger Adjustment Account (GLA A/C):** This is also known as Financial Ledger Control Account. This ledger is maintained to make cost ledger self-balancing. Expenditure relating to material, labor and other expenses etc. are credited to this account and the sales revenue is debited to this account. Net profit or loss is also transferred to this account. All items of expenses and income, which originate in financial accounts, are routed through this account before an eventual transfer to the relevant control accounts.

If a transaction of internal nature affecting only cost accounts and having no financial implications, i.e., transfer of material from one job to another, transfer from stores ledger control account to work – in-progress control account, then no entry is required in General Ledger Adjustment Account, as double entry is possible without recourse to this balancing account. The balance in this account will always be equal to the sum of all the balances of the impersonal accounts.

(2) **Stores Ledger Control Account:** This ledger is debited with all receipts of materials as per goods received note and credited with all issues of materials as per material requisition note. The balance of this account indicates the total value of materials in stores, which should agree with the aggregate of balance of individual accounts in stores ledger. Abnormal gains or losses in this account, if any, are transferred to the Costing Profit and Loss Account.

(3) **Work-in-progress Ledger Control Account:** This Account indicates the total amount of work-in-progress at any time. This account is debited with cost of production i.e., Direct Material, Direct Labor, Direct Expenses and Production Overhead recovered. The value of finished goods completed in a period and transferred to Finished Goods Control Account is credited to this account. The balance of this account should agree with the sum of balances in individual job order accounts in subsidiary ledger.

(4) **Finished Goods Ledger Control Account:** This account is debited with the value of finished goods transferred from Work-in-progress Control Account and the amount of administration overheads absorbed. This account is credited with the Cost of Sales Account and cost of units sold. The balance of this account indicates the value of finished goods lying at hand.

(5) **Wages Control Account:** Gross Wages (Direct and Indirect) are debited to this account. Direct wages are transferred to Work-in-progress Control Account and indirect wages are transferred to respective Overhead Control Account in production, administration or selling and distribution. Wages paid for abnormal idle time are transferred to Costing Profit and Loss Account directly or through Abnormal Loss Account.

(6) **Production Overhead Account:** This Account is also known as Manufacturing Overhead Account or Works Overhead Account. This account is debited with indirect manufacturing expenses like indirect material, indirect labor and indirect expenses and credited with the account of Manufacturing Overhead Recovered. This absorbed overhead will be debited to Work-in-progress Ledger Control Account. Any balance of this account represents balance of under/over absorbed overhead, which is transferred to Costing Profit and Loss Account.

(7) **Administration Overhead Account:** Administration overhead incurred is debited and administration overhead recovered is credited to this account. The absorbed Administration Overhead will be debited to Finished Goods Ledger Control Account. Any balance in this account represents over or under absorbed administration overhead, which is transferred to Costing Profit and Loss Account.

(8) **Selling and Distribution Overhead Account:** This account is debited with selling and distribution overhead incurred. For selling and distribution overhead recovered, this account is credited and Cost of Sales Account is debited.

(9) Cost of Sales Account: Cost of goods sold and selling and distribution overhead incurred will be debited. The aggregate of cost of goods sold and selling and distribution absorbed is transferred to Costing Profit and Loss Account.

(10) Costing Profit and Loss Account: This account is debited with cost of goods sold, under-absorbed and abnormal losses. Sales value, over-absorbed overhead and abnormal gains are credited to this account. The balance shows profit or loss as per cost books (which is reconciled with financial profit and loss account) and it will be transferred to General Ledger Adjustment Account. In case of profit, Costing Profit and Loss account is debited and General Ledger Adjustment Account is credited where as, in case of loss, Costing Profit and Loss Account is credited and General Ledger Adjustment Account is debited.

Journal Entries

The following are the journal entries to be passed in the Cost Books of Accounts.

Accounting Entries Relating to Material

Journal entry for purchase of Raw-Materials (both direct and indirect; both cash and credit purchases):

Stores Ledger Control Account (SLC A/c) .... Dr.

To General Ledger Adjustment Account (GLA A/c)

Purchase for special Job (both direct and indirect; both cash and credit purchases):

Work-in-progress Ledger Control Account (WIPLC A/c) ..... Dr.

To General Ledger Adjustment Account (GLA A/c)

For Return of materials to the suppliers:

General Ledger Adjustment Account (GLA A/c)...... Dr.

To Stores Ledger Control Account (SLCA/c) (in case of general purchase)

To Work-in-progress Ledger Control Account (WIPLC A/c)

(in case of purchase for special job)

For direct material issued to jobs:

Work-in-progress Ledger Control Account (WIPLC A/c) ..... Dr.

To Stores Ledger Control Account (SLC A/c)

For indirect materials issued to jobs

Production Overheads A/c (POH A/c) .... Dr.

To Stores Ledger Control Account (SLC A/c)

For materials returned from jobs to stores:

Stores Ledger Control Account (SLC A/c)

To Work-in-progress Ledger Control Account (WIPLC A/c)

For materials transferred from one job to another job (eg., Job No. 10 to Job No. 15)

Job No. 15 A/c ....Dr.

To Job No. 10 A/c

Accounting Entries relating to Labor

For total wages and salaries (whether paid or not; whether it is direct or indirect; whether it is relating to production or administrative or selling and distribution activities)

Wages Control A/C (WC A/c).......Dr.

To General Ledger Adjustment Account (GLA A/c)

Wages Absorbed

For Direct Wages

Work-in-progress Ledger Control Account (WIPLC A/c) ..... Dr.

To Wages Control A/C (WC A/c)

For Indirect wages

Production Overheads A/c (POH A/c) .... Dr.

To Wages Control A/C (WC A/c)

For salary to administration staff

Administration Overhead A/c....Dr.

To Wages Control A/C (WC A/c)

For salary to selling and distribution staff

Selling and Distribution Overhead Account ....Dr.

To Wages Control A/C (WC A/c)

Accounting entries for Overhead

For Actual Overhead incurred:

Production Overheads A/c (POH A/c) .... Dr.

Administration Overhead A/c ....Dr.

Selling and Distribution Overhead Account ....Dr.

To General Ledger Adjustment Account (GLA A/c)

For the recovery of overhead expense:

(a) Production overhead expenses

Work-in-progress Ledger Control Account (WIPLC A/c) ..... Dr.

To Production Overheads A/c (POH A/c)

(b) Administration overhead expenses

Finished Goods Ledger Control A/c (FGLC A/c) ...... Dr.

To Administration Overhead A/c

(c) Selling and distribution overhead expenses

Cost of Sales A/c ..... Dr.

To Selling and Distribution Overhead Account

For under/over absorbed overhead: If the actual overhead incurred is equal to the overhead recovered, then there will not be any balance in production overhead account, administration overhead account and selling and distribution overhead account. Any balance in these accounts represents under/over absorbed overhead.

If the actual overhead is more than the overhead recovered, then, it results in under absorbed overhead. If the actual overhead is less than the overhead recovered, then, it results in over absorbed overhead.

There are two approaches for dealing with under/over absorbed overhead. They are as follows.

(a) Transfer all balances under different Overhead Accounts to Costing Profit and Loss Account.

For under absorbed production overhead

Costing Profit and Loss Account A/c ....Dr.

To Production Overheads A/c (POH A/c)

For over-absorbed production overhead

Production Overheads A/c (POH A/c) .... Dr.

To Costing Profit and Loss Account A/c

For under absorbed administration overhead

Costing Profit and Loss Account A/c........Dr.

To Administration Overhead A/c

For over absorbed administration overhead

Administration Overhead A/c ..... Dr.

To Costing Profit and Loss Account A/c

For under absorbed selling and distribution overhead

Costing Profit and Loss Account A/c........Dr.

To Selling and Distribution Overhead Account

For over-absorbed selling and distribution overhead

Selling and Distribution Overhead Account ....Dr.

To Costing Profit and Loss Account A/c

(b) The second approach is to transfer the balances of different overhead accounts to Overhead Adjustment Account, which is eventually transferred to Costing Profit and Loss Account.

For production, administration and selling and distribution overhead under absorbed

Overhead Adjustment A/c ...... Dr.

To Production Overheads A/c

To Administration Overhead A/c

To Selling and Distribution Overhead Account

For production, administration and selling and distribution overhead over-absorbed

Production Overheads A/c ...... Dr.

Administration Overhead A/c ...... Dr.

Selling and Distribution Overhead Account ...... Dr.

To Overhead Adjustment A/c

For transfer of debit balance in overhead adjustment account to Costing Profit and Loss Account

Costing Profit and Loss Account A/c ....Dr.

To Overhead Adjustment A/c

For transfer of credit balance in overhead adjustment account to Costing Profit and Loss Account

Overhead Adjustment A/c ...... Dr.

To Costing Profit and Loss Account A/c

For transfer of goods completed

Finished Goods Ledger Account ...... Dr.

To Work-in-progress Ledger Control Account (WIPLC A/c)

For transfer of units sold

Cost of Sales Account .... Dr.

To Finished Goods Ledger Account

For transfer of cost of sales to Costing Profit and Loss Account

Costing Profit and Loss Account .... Dr.

To Cost of Sales Account

For sales

General Ledger Adjustment Account (GLA A/c)...... Dr.

To Costing Profit and Loss Account

For transferring profit

Costing Profit and Loss Account....... Dr.

To General Ledger Adjustment Account (GLA A/c)

For transferring loss

General Ledger Adjustment Account (GLA A/c) .... Dr.

To Costing Profit and Loss Account

Disadvantages of Non-Integral System

Under Non-Integral System, as two separate sets of books are maintained, one based on the principles of Financial Accounting and another based on the principles of Cost Accounting, there is bound to be a difference in the profits reported by them. Hence, there will be a need to prepare a Reconciliation Statement reconciling the two results shown by the two sets of books.

As two sets of books are maintained, the clerical work would be increased and expenses would also increase.

Illustration 1

In the course of physical verification of stores as on 31st March 1991, the following differences are revealed in case of AB ltd.

Balance

Material	*Units*	*Rate per unit (Rs)*	*Physical*	*Ledger*	*Remark*
A	Nos.	7	600	680	Wrong counting
B	Litres	12	1,100	1,155	Normal evaporation
C	Nos.	6	350	400	Material issued not accounted for
D	Kgs	22	900	930	Shortage due to pilferage and theft
E	Nos.	15	1,475	1,325	150 Nos. received but not entered in the ledger
F	Metres	10	291	291	Obsolete Materials. Realized sale value Rs. 1,650, awaiting dispatch

Prepare Journal entries in the cost ledger to give effects to the above adjustments as called for.

[ICWA, inter]

Solution

Material A: No Journal entry is required. The stock sheet should be altered to 680 Nos. to match with the book balance.

	Particulars		*Dr.*	*Cr.*
Material B	Works Overhead A/c To Stores Ledger Control A/c (Being adjustment made for normal evaporation loss i.e. 55 litres × Rs. 12)	Dr.	660	660
Material C	Work in progress Ledger Control A/c To Store Ledger Control A/c (Being adjustment of issue of material) (50 Nos. × Rs. 6)	Dr.	300	300
Material D	Costing P&L A/c To SLC A/c (Being abnormal loss due to pilferage and theft charged to costing P&L i.e. 30 kgs. × Rs. 22)	Dr.	660	660
Material E	Stores Ledger Control A/c To GLA A/c (Being material received but not taken into stock i.e. 150 × Rs. 15)	Dr.	2,250	2,250
Material F	GLA A/c Costing P&L A/c To SLC A/c (Being obsolete stores sold, the loss being abnormal charged to Costing P&L A/c i.e. 291 meters × Rs. 10)	Dr. Dr.	1,650 1,250	2,910

Illustration 2

The Cost Ledger of Motors Ltd. showed the following balances as on July1st 2007:

	Debit Rs.	*Credit Rs.*
Stores Ledger Control Account	5,250	
WIP Control Account	3,920	
Finished Goods Control Account	2,790	
Works Overhead Account		50
Administration Overhead Account	30	
General Ledger Adjustment Account		11,940
	11,990	11,990

Further balances resulting from the operation for the year ended 30th June 2008 were:

	Rs.
Stores purchases	18,000
Stores issued to production	19,650

Stores issued to repair orders	750
Wages	30,750
Productive labor	29,500
Unproductive labor	1,250
Works overheads allocated to production orders	8,950
Carriage inwards	300
Works expenses	7,000
Administration expenses	900
Administration overhead allocated to production orders	920
Goods finished during the year	58,600
Finished goods sold	60,000
Sales expenses	670

Record the entries in Cost Ledger Accounts for the year ended 30th June 2008

Solution

Dr. **Stores Ledger Control A/c** **Cr.**

Particulars	*Rs.*	*Particulars*	*Rs.*
To balance b/d	5,250	By WIPLC A/c	19,650
To GLA A/c (purchases)	18,000	By Works OH A/c	750
To GLA A/c (carriage inwards)	300	By Balance c/d	3,150
	23,550		23,550
To Balance b/d	3,150		

Note: Carriage inwards can also be presumed to be a part of works overheads.

Dr. **Wages Control A/c** **Cr.**

Particulars	*Rs.*	*Particulars*	*Rs.*
To GLA A/c	30,750	By WIPLC A/c	29,500
		By Works OH A/c	1,250
	30,750		30,750

Dr. **Works OH A/c** **Cr.**

Particulars	*Rs.*	*Particulars*	*Rs.*
To SLC A/c	750	By Balance b/d	50
To Wages Control A/c	1,250	By WIPLC A/c	8,950
To GLA A/c	7,000		
	9,000		9,000

Dr. **Administration OH A/c** **Cr.**

Particulars	*Rs.*	*Particulars*	*Rs.*
To Balance b/d	30	By FGLC A/c	920
To GLA A/c	900	By Balance c/d	10
	930		930
To Balance b/d	10		

Dr. **Sales OH A/c** **Cr.**

Particulars	*Rs.*	*Particulars*	*Rs.*
To GLA A/c	670	By Cost of Sales A/c	670
	670		670

Dr. **WIPLC A/c** **Cr.**

Particulars	*Rs.*	*Particulars*	*Rs.*
To Balance b/d	3920	By FGLC A/c	58,600
To SLC A/c	19,650	By Balance c/d	3,420
To Wages Control A/c	29,500		
To Works OH A/c	8,950		
	62,020		62,020
To Balance b/d	3,420		

Dr. **FGLC A/c** **Cr.**

Particulars	*Rs.*	*Particulars*	*Rs.*
To Balance b/d	2,790	By Cost of Sales A/c	60,000
To Administration OH A/c	920	By Balance c/d	2,310
To WIPLC A/c	58,600		
	62,310		62,310
To Balance b/d	2,310		

Dr. **Cost of Sales A/c** **Cr.**

Particulars	*Rs.*	*Particulars*	*Rs.*
To FGLC A/c	60,000	By GLA A/c (transfer)	60,670
To Sales OH A/c	670		
	60,670		60,670

Dr. **GLA A/c** **Cr.**

Particulars	*Rs.*	*Particulars*	*Rs.*
To Cost of Sales	60,670	By Balance b/d	11,940
To Balance c/d	8,890	By SLC A/c	18,000
		By Wages Control A/c	30,750
		By SLC A/C	300
		By Works OH A/c	7,000
		By Administration OH A/c	900
		By Sales OH A/c	670
	69,560		69,560
		By Balance b/d	8,890

Illustration 3

Journalize the following transactions in a system where Cost Accounts are maintained independently:

	Rs
Purchase of Raw materials	50,000
Direct Materials consumed	25,000
Indirect material consumed	7,500
Material retuned from shop floor	2,500
Material transferred from job No. 20 to Job No.25	500
Total wages and Salaries paid	37,500
Wages booked to production directly	30,000
Indirect wages	7,500
Indirect factory expenses incurred	50,000

Factory overhead absorbed	65,000
Selling and distribution overhead incurred	5,000
Cost of finished goods	85,000
Goods sold (including profit)	90,000

Solution

Particulars		*Dr.* *Rs.*	*Cr.* *Rs.*
Stores Ledger Control A/c To General Ledger Adjustment A/c (Being the stores purchased)	Dr.	50,000	 50,000
WIPLC A/c Factory OH A/c To SLC A/c (Being indirect material consumed)	Dr. Dr.	25,000 7,500	 32,500
SLC A/c To WIPLC A/c (Being material returned from shop floor)	Dr.	2,500	 2,500
Job No.25 A/c To Job No.20 A/c (Being transfer of material from Job No.20 to Job No.25)	Dr.	500	 500
Wages and Salaries Control A/c To GLA A/c (Being total wages and salary paid)	Dr.	37,500	 37,500
WIPLC A/c Factory OH A/c To Wages Control A/c (Being the allocation of wages)	Dr. Dr.	30,000 7,500	 37,500
FOH Control A/c To GLA A/c (Being Indirect expenses incurred)	Dr.	50,000	 50,000
WIPC A/c Dr. To FOH Control A/c (Being factory overhead charged to production)	65,000		 65,000
S&D OH Control A/c Dr. To GLA A/c (Being S&D expenses incurred)	5,000		 5,000
FGLC A/c Dr. To WIPLC A/c (Being cost of completed job from WIP)	85,000		 85,000
Cost Ledger Control A/c To Costing P&L A/c (Being the sales including profit)	Dr.	90,000	 90,000

Illustration 4

The following balances appeared in the books of M/s Ravi Co. Ltd. on 1st Jan 2008:

Particulars	*Rs.*	*Rs.*
General Ledger Adjustment A/c		15,200
Stores Ledger Control A/c	8,750	
Work-in-progress Ledger Control A/c	4,280	
Finished Goods Ledger Control A/c	2,170	
	15,200	**15,200**

On 31st December 2008, the following information was supplied:

	Rs.	*Rs.*
Purchase of goods		60,640
Purchase for special job		1,950
Direct wages	38,627	
Indirect factory wages	9,543	
Administrative salaries	6,731	
Selling and Distribution salaries	4,252	59,153
Production expenses		10,432
Selling and Distribution expenses		6,430
Administrative expenses		9,546
Stores issued to production		56,501
Stores issued to maintenance account		2,586
Return to suppliers		312
Production overhead absorbed by production		23,410
Administrative overhead absorbed by finished goods		15,150
Selling overhead recovered on sales		9,515
Products finished during the year		1,18,517
Finished goods sold at cost		1,33,382
Sales		1,55,000

You are required to record the entries in the Cost Ledger for the year 2008 and prepare a trial balance.

Solution

Accounts in the books of M/s Ravi Co. Ltd.

Dr. **General Ledger Adjustment A/c** **Cr.**

Particulars	*Rs.*	*Particulars*	*Rs.*
To SLC A/c (purchase return)	312	By Balance b/d	15,200
To Costing P&L (sales)	1,55,000	By SLC A/c	60,640
To balance c/d	18,697	By WIPLC A/c	1,950
		By WC A/c	59,153
		By POH A/c	10,432
		By AOH A/c	9,546
		By S&D OH A/c	6,430
		By Costing P&L (profit)	10,658
	1,74,009		1,74,009
		By Balance b/d.	18,697

Dr. **Stores Ledger Adjustment A/c** **Cr.**

Particulars	Rs.	Particulars	Rs.
To Balance b/d	8,750	By WIPLC A/c	56,501
To GLA A/c	60,640	By POH A/c	2,586
		By GLA A/c (purchase return)	312
		By balance c/d	9,991
	69,390		69,390
To Balance b/d	9,991		

Dr. **Wages Control A/c** **Cr.**

Particulars	Rs.	Particulars	Rs.
To GLA A/c	59,153	By WIPLC A/c	38,627
		By POH A/c	9,543
		By AOH A/c	6,731
		By S&D OH A/c	4,252
	59,153		59,153

Dr. **Production Overhead A/c** **Cr.**

Particulars	Rs.	Particulars	Rs.
To WC A/c	9,543	By WIPL A/c	23,410
To GLA A/c	10,432		
To SLC A/c	2,586		
To Overhead Adjustment A/c (over absorption)	849		
	23,410		23,410

Dr. **Work-in-progress Ledger Control A/c** **Cr.**

Particulars	Rs.	Particulars	Rs.
To Balance b/d	4,280	By FGLC A/c	1,18,517
To GLA A/c	1,950	By balance c/d	6,251
To WC A/c	38,627		
To SLC A/c	56,501		
To POH A/c	23,410		
	1,24,768		1,24,768
To Balance b/d	6,251		

Dr. **Administration OH A/c** **Cr.**

Particulars	Rs.	Particulars	Rs.
To WC A/c	6,731	By FGLC A/c	15,150
To GLA A/c	9,546	By Overhead Adjustment A/c (under absorption)	1,127
	16,277		16,277

Dr. **Finished Goods Ledger Control A/c** **Cr.**

Particulars	*Rs.*	*Particulars*	*Rs.*
To Balance b/d	2,170	By COS A/c	1,33,382
To AOH A/c	15,150	By Balance c/d	2,455
To WIPLC A/c	1,18,517		
	1,35,837		1,35,837
To Balance b/d	2,455		

Dr. **Selling and Distribution Overhead A/c** **Cr.**

Particulars	*Rs.*	*Particulars*	*Rs.*
To WC A/c	4,252	By COS A/c	9,515
To GLA A/c	6,430	By Overhead Adjustment A/c (Under absorption)	1,167
	10,682		10,682

Dr. **Cost of Sales A/c** **Cr.**

Particulars	*Rs.*	*Particulars*	*Rs.*
To S&D OH A/c	9,515	By Costing P&L A/c	1,42,897
To FGLC A/c	1,33,382		
	1,42,897		1,42,897

Dr. **Overhead Adjustment A/c** **Cr.**

Particulars	*Rs.*	*Particulars*	*Rs.*
To AOH A/c	1,127	By POH A/c	849
To S&D OH A/c	1,167	By Costing P&L A/c (under absorbed OH transferred to Costing P&L A/c)	1,445
	2,294		2,295

Dr. **Costing P&L of M/s Ravi Co. Ltd. for the year ended Dec. 31, 2008** **Cr.**

Particulars	*Rs.*	*Particulars*	*Rs.*
To Cost of Sales A/c	1,42,897	By GLA A/c (sales)	1,55,000
To OH Adjustment A/c	1,445		
To GLA A/c (profit transferred)	10,658		
	1,55,000		1,55,000

Trial Balance as on December 31, 2008

Particulars	*Dr. (Rs)*	*Cr. (Rs)*
Stores Ledger Control A/c	9,991	
WIPLC A/c	6,251	
FGLC A/c	2,455	
GLA A/c		18,697
	18,697	18,697

INTEGRAL ACCOUNTING

Integral Accounting is a system of accounting in which, both, cost and financial accounts are maintained in same set of books. Under Integral Accounting, finance and costing transactions are recorded in one self-contained ledger which is referred to as Integrated Ledger.

The terminology of CIMA defines Integrated Accounting System as "the interlocking of the financial and cost accounting systems to ensure that all relevant expenditure is absorbed into cost accounts. Under this accounting system, transactions are classified both according to their functions and nature".

The accounts under this system are so designed that full information required both for costing purpose as well as for financial accounting is available from the same set of books.

Features of Integral Accounting

The essential features of Integral Accounting System are as follows.

- The subsidiary ledgers like Stores, Work-in-progress and Finished Goods are maintained in the similar manner as done in case of Non-Integral System.
- Overhead ledger is maintained to contain separate accounts for factory, administration and selling and distribution overhead.
- As all the ledger accounts required (Personal, Real and Nominal) are maintained, General Ledger Control Account is dispensed with.

Pre-requisites for Successful Integration of Accounts

(1) Firstly, the top management of the firm must be convinced about the benefits and extend support for its implementation.

(2) The management has to decide the extent of integration of the two sets of books.

(3) Proper training to Accounts Department personnel should be given because this system involves a complete change from the traditional system of maintaining financial and cost books.

(4) There should be a complete analysis of cost and sales.

(5) A suitable income and expenditure classification and coding system should be devised

(6) There should exist a perfect co-ordination between the Accounts Department and other concerned departments.

Advantages of Integrated System

The adoption of Integral System results in the following benefits to the organization.

(1) This system is simple and economical, because it avoids duplication of accounting and analysis.

(2) As only one set of accounts is maintained, this system eliminates the need for reconciliation of financial and cost accounts.

(3) It reduces the administrative effort and expenditure involved by maintaining only one set of books.

(4) The system facilitates the introduction of Mechanized Accounting.

(5) The necessary data in respect of both the Sets of Accounts, i.e., costing and financial are easily available in a single ledger.

(6) It ensures better coordination in the activities of Cost Accounting and Financial Accounting staff.

(7) The knowledge of Cost and Financial Accounting may be combined together to achieve better results.

Journal Entries

The following are the journals entries to be passed for various transactions under Integral System.

(1) For Materials purchased on cash

Stores Control A/c	Dr.
To Cash A/c	

(2) For Material purchased on credit

Stores Control A/c	Dr.
To Sundry Creditors A/c	

(3) Direct Material issued

WIP A/c	Dr.
To Stores Control A/c	

(4) Indirect Material issued
Relevant Overhead A/c Dr.
To Stores Control A/c

(5) Material returned from shop floor
Stores Control A/c Dr.
To WIP A/c

(6) Material returned to supplier
Creditor A/c Dr.
To Stores Control A/c

(7) Material transferred from Job No.101 to Job No.111
Job No.111 A/c Dr.
To Job No.101

(8) Salary and Wages paid (Direct and indirect)
Wages Control A/c Dr.
To Cash A/c

(9) Direct expenses incurred
WIP A/c Dr.
To Cash A/c

(10) Overhead incurred
Relevant Overhead A/c Dr.
To Cash A/c

(11) Overhead recovered
WIP A/c (For production overhead recovered) Dr.
Finished Stock A/c Dr.
(For administration overhead recovered)
Cost of Sales A/c Dr.
(For Selling and Distribution overhead recovered)
To Relevant Overhead A/c

(12) Overhead on work in progress
WIP A/c Dr.
To Production OH A/c

(13) Finished goods produced
Finished Goods A/c Dr.
To WIP A/c

(14) Goods sold at cost
Cost of Sales A/c Dr.
To Finished Goods A/c

(15) For Sales
Cash or Debtor A/c Dr.
To Sales A/c

(16) Sales Returned
Sales A/c Dr.
To Debtors A/c

(17) Capital work
Sundry Assets A/c Dr.
To WIP A/c

(18) Repair work
Production OH A/c Dr.
To WIP A/c

(19) Under absorbed overhead
P&L A/c Dr.
To relevant Overhead A/c

(20) Over absorbed overhead
Relevant Overhead A/c Dr.
To P&L A/c

Illustration 5

Journalize the following transactions assuming cost and financial accounts are Integrated:

	Rs.
Wages paid (30% indirect)	12,000
Raw material purchases	20,000
Direct material issued to production	15,000
Wages charged to production	9,500

Solution

Journal Entries under Integral System

Particulars		*Dr. (Rs.)*	*Cr. (Rs.)*
Wages Control A/c	Dr.	8,400	
Overhead Control A/c Dr.		3,600	
To Bank A/c			12,000
(Being wages paid)			
Stores Ledger Control A/c	Dr.	20,000	
To Bank A/c			
(Being raw material purchased)			20,000
WIPLC A/c	Dr.	15,000	
To Stores Ledger Control A/c			15,000
(Being direct materials issued to production)			
WIPLC A/c	Dr.	9,500	
To Wages Control A/c			8,400
To Overhead Control A/c			1,100
(Being wages and overhead charged to production)			

Illustration 6

Journalize the following transactions in Financial and Cost Books

		Rs.
(1)	Materials purchased	
	(a) Cash purchases	20,000
	(b) Credit purchases	10,000
	(c) Material purchased for a special job	6,000
(2)	Returns to suppliers	500
(3)	Direct Material issued to Jobs	8,000
(4)	Indirect Material issued to Jobs	1,000
(5)	Material returned from shop floor	300
(6)	Material transferred from Job No.20 to Job No.25	800

Solution

Journal Entries in Financial Books

Particulars		*Dr. (Rs.)*	*Cr. (Rs.)*
(1) *(a)* Purchases A/c	Dr.	20,000	
To Cash A/c			20,000
(Being the amount of cash purchase)			
(b) Purchases A/c	Dr.	10,000	
To Creditor Account			10,000
(Being the amount of credit purchase)			
(c) Purchases A/c	Dr.	6,000	
To Creditor Account			6,000
(Being credit purchase for special job)			
(2) Creditor A/c	Dr.	500	
To Purchases A/c			500
(Being the returns to suppliers)			

No entries will be passed for transaction numbers 3,4,5 and 6 as they affect Cost Ledger only.

Journal Entries in Cost Books

Particulars		*Dr. (Rs.)*	*Cr. (Rs.)*
(1) *(a)* Stores Ledger Control A/c	Dr.	20,000	
To General Ledger Adjustment A/c			20,000
(Being the amount of cash purchases)			
(b) Stores Ledger Control A/c	Dr.	10,000	
To General Ledger Adjustment A/c			10,000
(Being the amount of credit purchases)			
(c) Work In Progress Ledger Control A/c	Dr.	6,000	
To General Ledger Adjustment A/c			6,000
(Being purchases for special job)			
(2) General Ledger Adjustment A/c	Dr.	500	
To Stores Ledger Control A/c			500
(Being the returns to suppliers)			
(3) Work in Progress Ledger Control A/c	Dr.	8,000	
To Stores Ledger Control A/c			8,000
(Being the direct material issued to jobs)			
(4) Production Overhead A/c	Dr.	1,000	
To Stores Ledger Control A/c			1,000
(Being indirect material issued to the jobs)			
(5) Stores Ledger Control A/c	Dr.	300	
To Work in Progress Ledger Control A/c			300
(Being material returned from shop floor)			
(6) Job No.25 A/c	Dr.	800	
To Job No. 20 A/c			800
(Being material transferred from Job No.20 to Job No.25)			

Illustration 7

Dutta Enterprises operates an Integral System of Accounting. You are required to pass the journal entries for the following transactions that took place for the year ended 30-6-1990. (Narration are not required).

Particulars	*Rs.*
Raw material purchased (50% on credit)	6,00,000
Material issued to production	4,00,000
Wages paid (50% direct)	2,00,000
Wages charged to production	1,00,000
Factory overhead incurred	80,000
Factory overhead charged to production	1,00,000
Selling and distribution overhead to production	40,000
Finished goods at cost	5,00,000
Sales (50% credit)	7,50,000
Closing stock	NIL
Receipts from debtors	2,00,000
Payment to creditors	2,00,000

Solution

Journal Entries in the books of Dutta Enterprises

(Integrated Accounting System)

Date	*Particulars*		*LF*	*Dr. (Rs.)*	*Cr. (Rs.)*
(1)	Stores Ledger Control A/c	Dr.		6,00,000	
	To Sundry Creditors A/c				3,00,000
	To Bank or Cash A/c				3,00,000
(2)	Work-in-progress Ledger Control A/c	Dr.		4,00,000	
	To Stores Ledger Control A/c				4,00,000
(3)	Wages Control A/c	Dr.		2,00,000	
	To Cash A/c				2,00,000
(4)	Work-in-progress Ledger Control A/c	Dr.		1,00,000	
	Production Overhead A/c	Dr.		1,00,000	
	To Wages Control A/c				2,00,000
(5)	Production Overhead A/c	Dr.		80,000	
	To Bank or Cash A/c				80,000
(6)	Work-in-progress Ledger Control A/c	Dr.		1,00,000	
	To Production Overhead A/c				1,00,000
(7)	S&D Overhead A/c	Dr.		40,000	
	To Bank or Cash A/c				40,000
(8)	Finished Goods Ledger Control A/c	Dr.		5,00,000	
	To Work-in-progress Ledger Control A/c				5,00,000
(9)	Cost of Sales A/c	Dr.		5,40,000	
	To Finished goods Ledger Control account				5,00,000
	To S&D Overhead A/c				40,000
(10)	Sundry Debtors A/c	Dr.		3,75,000	
	Bank or Cash A/c	Dr.		3,75,000	
	To Sales A/c				7,50,000
(11)	Bank or Cash A/c	Dr.		2,00,000	
	To Sundry Debtors A/c				2,00,000
(12)	Sundry Creditors A/c	Dr.		2,00,000	
	To Bank or Cash A/c				2,00,000

Illustration 8

Messrs Essbee Ltd. maintains Integrated Account of cost and financial accounts. From the following details, write up Control Accounts in general ledger of the factory and prepare a trial balance.

Particulars	*Rs.*
Opening Balances	
Share capital	3,00,000
Reserve	2,00,000
Sundry Creditors	5,00,000
Plant and Machinery	5,75,000
Sundry Debtors	2,00,000
Stores Ledger	1,50,000
Bank and Cash balance	75,000
Transaction during the year were as follows:	
Stores purchased	10,00,000
Stores issued to production	10,50,000
Stores in hand	95,000
Direct wages incurred	6,50,000
Direct wages charged to production	6,00,000
Manufacturing expenses incurred	3,00,000
Manufacturing expenses charged to production	2,75,000
Selling and distribution expenses	1,00,000
Finished stock production (at cost)	18,00,000
Sales at selling pricc	22,00,000
Closing stock of Finished Goods	95,000
Payment to Creditors	11,00,000
Receipts from Debtors	21,00,000

(ICWA Inter, June 1985)

Solution

Dr. **Stores Ledger Control A/c** **Cr.**

Particulars	*Amount (Rs.)*	*Particulars*	*Amount (Rs.)*
To Balance b/d	1,50,000	By WIPLC A/c	10,50,000
To Creditors Control A/c	10,00,000	By POH A/c (bal)	5,000
		By Balance c/d	95,000
	11,50,000		11,50,000
To balance b/d	95,000		

Dr. **Wages Control A/c** **Cr.**

Particulars	*Amount (Rs.)*	*Particulars*	*Amount (Rs.)*
To Bank A/c	6,50,000	By WIPLC A/c	6,00,000
		By POH A/c (difference)	50,000
	6,50,000		6,50,000

Dr. **Production OH A/c** **Cr.**

Particulars	*Amount (Rs.)*	*Particulars*	*Amount (Rs.)*
To SLC A/c	5,000	By WIPLC A/c	2,75,000
To WC A/c	50,000	By P&L A/c (difference)	80,000
To Bank A/c	3,00,000		
	3,55,000		3,55,000

Dr. S&D OH A/c Cr.

Particulars	*Amount (Rs.)*	*Particulars*	*Amount (Rs.)*
To Bank A/c	1,00,000	By COS A/c (transfer)	1,00,000
	1,00,000		1,00,000

Dr. WIP Ledger Control A/c Cr.

Particulars	*Amount (Rs.)*	*Particulars*	*Amount (Rs.)*
To SLC A/c	10,50,000	By FGLC A/c	18,00,000
To WC A/c	6,00,000	By Balance c/d	1,25,000
To POHC A/c	2,75,000		
	19,25,000		19,25,000
To balance b/d	1,25,000		

Dr. FGLC A/c Cr.

Particulars	*Amount (Rs.)*	*Particulars*	*Amount (Rs.)*
To WIPLC A/c	18,00,000	By COS A/c (bal)	17,05,000
		By Balance c/d	95,000
	18,00,000		18,00,000
To balance b/d	95,000		

Dr. Cost of Sales A/c Cr.

Particulars	*Amount (Rs.)*	*Particulars*	*Amount (Rs.)*
To FGLC A/c	17,05,000	By Sales A/c (transfer)	18,05,000
To S&D OH A/c	1,00,000		
	18,05,000		18,05,000

Dr. Sales A/c Cr.

Particulars	*Amount (Rs.)*	*Particulars*	*Amount (Rs.)*
To COS A/c	18,05,000	By Debtor Control A/c	22,00,000
To P&L A/c (profit)	3,95,000		
	22,00,000		22,00,000

Dr. Debtors A/c Cr.

Particulars	*Amount (Rs.)*	*Particulars*	*Amount (Rs.)*
To balance b/d	2,00,000	By Bank A/c	21,00,000
To Sales A/c	22,00,000	By Balance c/d	3,00,000
	24,00,000		24,00,000
To balance b/d	3,00,000		

Dr. **Creditors Control A/c** **Cr.**

Particulars	*Amount (Rs.)*	*Particulars*	*Amount (Rs.)*
To Bank A/c	11,00,000	By Balance b/d	5,00,000
To Balance c/d	4,00,000	By SLC A/c	10,00,000
	15,00,000		15,00,000
		By balance b/d	4,00,000

Dr. **Share Capital A/c** **Cr.**

Particulars	*Amount (Rs.)*	*Particulars*	*Amount (Rs.)*
To balance c/d	3,00,000	By Balance b/d	3,00,000
	3,00,000		3,00,000
		By balance b/d	3,00,000

Dr. **Reserve A/c** **Cr.**

Particulars	*Amount (Rs.)*	*Particulars*	*Amount (Rs.)*
To balance c/d	2,00,000	By Balance b/d	2,00,000
	2,00,000		2,00,000
		By balance b/d	2,00,000

Dr. **Plant & Machinery A/c** **Cr.**

Particulars	*Amount (Rs.)*	*Particulars*	*Amount (Rs.)*
To Balance b/d	5,75,000	By balance c/d	5,75,000
	5,75,000		5,75,000
To balance b/d	5,75,000		

Dr. **Bank A/c** **Cr.**

Particulars	*Amount (Rs.)*	*Particulars*	*Amount (Rs.)*
To Balance b/d	75,000	By WC A/c	6,50,000
To Debtors Control A/c	21,00,000	By POH A/c	3,00,000
		By S&D OH A/c	1,00,000
		By Creditors Control A/c	11,00,000
		By balance c/d	25,000
	21,75,000		21,75,000
To balance b/d	25,000		

Dr. **P&L A/c** **Cr.**

Particulars	*Amount (Rs.)*	*Particulars*	*Amount (Rs.)*
To POH	80,000	By Sales A/c	3,95,000
To balance c/d (profit)	3,15,000		
	3,95,000		3,95,000

TRIAL BALANCE

	Debit (Rs.)	*Credit (Rs.)*
Stores Ledger Control Account	95,000	—
Work-in-progress Ledger Control Account	1,25,000	—
Finished Goods Ledger Control Account	95,000	—
Profit and Loss Account (Profit)	—	3,15,000
Debtors Control account	3,00,000	—
Creditors Control account	—	4,00,000
Share Capital Account	—	3,00,000
Reserve Account	—	2,00,000
Plant and Machinery Account	5,75,000	—
Bank Account	25,000	—
	12,15,000	12,15,000

SUMMARY

The importance of Cost Accounting System has led to the establishment of Cost Accounting Departments in most of the industrial enterprises. Cost accounting records form an important part of a Cost Accounting System. Cost Accounts are essentially maintained on principles of Double Entry Book keeping. There are two basic systems of maintaining cost accounts *viz.*, Independent Cost Accounts or Non- Integrated Accounting (inter-locking) and Integral or Integrated Accounting.

Non-Integrated Accounting is also known as Cost Ledger Accounting System or Independent Cost Accounting System. Under this system, separate sets of books for Cost Accounts and Financial Accounts are maintained.

The Principal ledgers to be maintained in Costing Department are Cost Ledger, Stores Ledger, Work in progress Ledger and Finished Goods Ledger.

The Principal Accounts to be maintained are General Ledger Adjustment Account, Stores Ledger Control Account, Work-in-progress Ledger Control Account, Finished Goods Ledger Control Account, Wages Control Account, Production Overhead Account, Administration Overhead Account, Selling and Distribution Overhead Account, Cost of Sales Account and Costing Profit and Loss Account.

Integral Accounting is a system of accounting in which, both, cost and financial accounts are maintained in same set of books. Under Integral Accounting, finance and costing transactions are recorded in one self-contained ledger which is referred to as Integrated Ledger.

The accounts under this system are so designed that full information required both for costing purpose as well as for financial accounting is available from the same set of books.

Glossary

- **Non-Integrated Accounting:** It is also known as Cost Ledger Accounting System or Independent Cost Accounting System. Under this system, separate sets of books for Cost Accounts and Financial Accounts are maintained.
- **Integral Accounting:** It is a system of accounting in which, both, cost and financial accounts are maintained in same set of books. Under Integral Accounting, finance and costing transactions are recorded in one self-contained ledger which is referred to as Integrated Ledger.
- **Cost Ledger:** This is the principal ledger of Costing Department. It contains all impersonal accounts i.e. Nominal Accounts and to some extent Real Accounts
- **Stores Ledger:** It is a subsidiary ledger containing all stores accounts.

- **Work-in-progress Ledger:** It is a subsidiary ledger in which accounts of all jobs undertaken and cost incurred thereof are recorded.
- **Finished Goods Ledger:** It is also a subsidiary ledger containing an account of completely finished job or product.
- **General Ledger Adjustment Account:** This is also known as Financial Ledger Control Account. This ledger is maintained to make cost ledger self-balancing.
- **Stores Ledger Control Account:** This ledger is debited with all receipts of materials as per goods received note and credited with all issues of materials as per material requisition note.
- **Work-in-progress Ledger Control Account:** This Account indicates the total amount of work-in-progress at any time. This account is debited with cost of production.
- **Finished Goods Ledger Control Account:** This account is debited with the value of finished goods transferred from Work-in-progress Control Account and the amount of administration overheads absorbed. This account is credited with the Cost of Sales Account and cost of units sold. The balance of this account indicates the value of finished goods lying at hand.
- **Wages Control Account:** Gross Wages (Direct and Indirect) are debited to this account. Direct wages are transferred to Work-in-progress Control Account and indirect wages are transferred to respective Overhead Control Account in production, administration or selling and distribution.
- **Production Overhead Account:** This Account is also known as Manufacturing Overhead Account or Works Overhead Account. This account is debited with indirect manufacturing expenses like indirect material, indirect labor and indirect expenses and credited with the account of Manufacturing Overhead recovered.
- **Administration Overhead Account:** Administration overhead incurred is debited and Administration Overhead Recovered is credited to this account.
- **Selling and Distribution Overhead Account:** This account is debited with selling and distribution overhead incurred.
- **Cost of Sales Account:** Cost of goods sold and selling and distribution overhead incurred will be debited.
- **Costing Profit and Loss Account:** This account is debited with cost of goods sold, under-absorbed and abnormal losses. Sales value, over-absorbed overhead and abnormal gains are credited to this account. The balance shows profit or loss as per Cost Books (which is reconciled with financial profit and loss account) and it will be transferred to General Ledger Adjustment Account.

Questions

(1) What do you mean by Non-Integral Accounting System? How does it differ from Integral Accounting System?
(2) What do you understand by Cost Control Accounts?
(3) Briefly explain the principal ledgers to be maintained in the Costing Department.
(4) Define Non-Integral Accounting and explain the principal accounts to be maintained in the Cost Books of Accounts.
(5) Write short notes on *(a)* Cost Ledger *(b)* Stores Ledger *(c)* WIP Ledger *(d)* Finished Goods Ledger.
(6) Define Integral Accounting System and briefly explain the procedure for integration.
(7) Write an explanatory note on integration of cost and financial accounts.
(8) Explain Integrated Accounting System highlighting the advantages of the system.
(9) Explain the basic requirements of an Integral Accounting System.
(10) What is meant by Interlocking System and Integrated System of maintaining Cost and Financial Accounts? Which one would you advise to adopt and why?

PROBLEMS

(1) How will you transact the following in the Material Account and the Stores Ledger?
  (a) Material ledger shows 120 units at an average cost of Rs.10 while the physical count is 110 units, difference due to non-recording of a material requisition note.
  (b) Physical units show 200 while the ledger balance shows a shortage due to non-receipts of an invoice for 20 units for a total cost of Rs. 100.
  (c) Ledger balance indicates an excess of 50 units over the physical balance affected by atmospheric changes, which are normal. The issue rate is Rs. 3 Per unit.
  (d) Physical balance shows a shortage compared to the ledger of 10 units traced to have been an effect of excess issues of material to a production job. The issue price is Rs. 2.50 per unit.

(2) Acme Manufacturing Co. Ltd. opens the costing records, with the balances on 1st July 1991 as follows.

	Rs.	*Rs.*
Material Control A/c	1,24,000	
Work-in-progress A/c	62,500	
Finished Goods A/c	1,24,000	
Production Overhead A/c	8,400	

	Rs.	*Rs.*
Administration Overhead A/c		12,000
Selling and Distribution Overhead A/c	6,250	
General Ledger Control A/c		3,13,150
	3,25,150	3,25,150

The following are the transactions for the quarter ended 30th September 1991:

	Rs.
Materials Purchased	4,80,100
Material issued to jobs	4,77,400
Materials to works maintenance	41,200
Material to administration office	3,400
Material to selling department	7,200
Wages-direct	1,49,300
Wages-indirect	65,000
Transportation for incoming materials	8,400
Production overheads	2,42,250
Absorbed overheads production	3,59,100
Administration Overheads	74,000
Administration allocation to production	52,900
Administration allocation to sales	14,800
Sales overheads	64,200
Sales overheads absorbed	82,000
Finished goods produced	9,58,400
Finished goods sold	9,77,300
Sales realization	14,43,000

Make up the various accounts as you envisage in the Cost Ledger and prepare a Trial Balance as at30th September 1991.

[CA (Fin) May 1992]

(3) In the absence of the Chief Accountant, you have been asked to prepare a month's Cost Accounts for a company, which operates a batch costing system fully integrated with the financial accounts. The following information is provided to you.

Particulars	*Amount (Rs.)*	*Amount (Rs.)*
Balances at the beginning of the month:		
Stores ledger Control Account		25,000
Work in progress Control Account		20,000
Finished Goods Control Account		35,000
Prepaid production overheads brought forward from previous month		3,000
Transactions during the month:		
Materials purchased		75,000
Material issued:		
To Production	30,000	
To Factory Maintenance	4,000	34,000
Materials transferred between batches		5,000
Total wages paid:		
To Direct workers	25,000	
To indirect workers	5,000	30,000
Direct wages charged to batches		20,000
Recorded non-productive time of direct workers		5,000
Selling and distribution overheads incurred		6,000
Other production overheads incurred		12,000
Sales		1,00,000
Cost of finished goods sold		80,000
Cost of goods completed and transferred into finished goods during the month		65,000
Physical value of Work in progress at the end of the month		40,000

The production overhead absorption rate is 150% of direct wages charged to work in progress.

Required: prepare the following accounts for the month:

(a) Stores Ledger Control Account
(b) Work in progress control account
(c) Finished goods Control Account
(d) Production Overhead Control Account
(e) Profit and Loss account

(CA, Inter, May 1981)

(4) Pass the journal entries for the following transaction in a double entry Cost Accounting System:

(a) Issue of materials: Direct – Rs. 5,50,000 Indirect – Rs.1,50,000
(b) Allocation of wages and salaries: Direct – Rs. 2,00,000 Indirect – Rs. 40,000
(c) Overhead absorbed in jobs: Factory – Rs. 1,50,000, Administration – Rs. 50,000 Selling Rs. 30,000
(d) Under/Over absorbed Overheads: Factory (over) – Rs. 20,000, Administration (under) – Rs.10,000.

(ICWA, Inter, June 1979)

(5) Cost Ledger of a company shows the following balances as on Jan 1,1989:

Particulars	*Dr.* *(Rs.)*	*Cr.* *(Rs.)*
Work-In-Progress Control Account	7,840	
Finished Stock Ledger Control Account	5,860	
Works Overhead Suspense Account	400	
Office And Administration Overhead Suspense A/c	200	
Stock Ledger Control Account	10,500	
General Ledger Adjustment A/c		24,800
Transactions for the Year 1989 were:		
Wages-Direct Labor		61,200
Wages-Indirect Labor		2,800
Works overhead allocated to production		18,700
Office and administration overhead allocated		6,200
Stores issued to production		39,300
Goods finished during the year		1,20,000
Finished goods sold(no stock were left at the year end)		1,32,000
Stores purchased		36,000
Stores issued to factory repair orders		1,500
Carriage inward on stores issued for production		600
Work expenses		14,000
Office and administration expenses		6,000

You are required:

(1) Write Cost Ledger accounts recording the above transactions and make necessary transfer to control accounts and
(2) Prepare the Trial Balance as on 31st Dec., 1989.

(CA, Final, OS, May, 1980 adapted)

(**Ans.:** Balances in Stores Ledger Control A/c Rs. 5,700; Work-in- Progress Control A/c Rs.7,040; Works Overhead Suspense A/c Rs. 600 (Dr.) and General Ledger Adjustment A/c Rs.13,340)

(6) The following balances are shown in the cost ledger of Vinayak Ltd. as on 1st Oct., 1990.

Particulars	*Dr.* *(Rs.)*	*Cr.* *(Rs.)*
Work-in-progress Account	7,056	
Factory Overhead Suspense A/c	360	
Finished Stock Account	5,274	
Stock Ledger Control Account	9,450	
Administration Overhead Suspense A/c	180	
General Ledger adjustment A/c		22,320
Transactions for the year 1991 were:		
Stores issued to Production		45,370
Stores purchased		52,400
Material purchased for direct issue to production		1,135
Wages paid (including indirect labor Rs. 2,520)		57,600
Finished goods sold		1,18,800

Particulars	*Dr. (Rs.)*	*Cr. (Rs.)*
Administration expenses		5,400
Selling Expenses		6,000
Factory overhead		15,600
Stores issued to capital work-in-progress		1,500
Finished goods transferred to warehouse		1,08,000
Stores issued to factory repairs		2,000
Factory overhead applied to production		16,830
Administration overhead charged to production		4,580
Factory overhead applied to unfinished work		3,080
Selling overhead allocated to sales		5,500
Stores lost due to fire in stores (not insured)		150
Administration overhead on unfinished work		850
Finished goods stock on 30.9.1991		14,274

You are required to record the entries in the cost ledger for the year ended 30th Sep., 1991 and prepare a trial balance as on that date.

(CA, Inter, Nov., 1982)

(**Ans.:** Balances in Stores Ledger Control A/c Rs. 12,830; Work-in-Progress Control A/c Rs. 22,051; Finished Goods Ledger Control A/c Rs. 14,274; Factory Overhead Suspense A/c Rs. 3,080 (Dr.); Administration Overhead Suspense A/c Rs. 850 (Dr.); Capital Work-in-Progress A/c Rs. 1,500 and General Ledger Adjustment A/c Rs. 54,585)

(7) On 31st March 1989, the following balances were extracted from the books of the Supreme Manufacturing Co.

Particulars	*Dr. (Rs.)*	*Cr. (Rs.)*
Stock Ledger Control Account	35,000	
Work-in-progress Control Account	38,000	
Finished goods Control Account	25,000	
Cost Ledger Control Account		98,000
	98,000	98,000

The following transactions took place in April 1989:

Raw materials:
Purchased Rs.95,000
Returned to suppliers Rs. 3,000
Issued to production Rs. 98,000
Returned to stores Rs. 3,000
Productive wages Rs. 40,000

Indirect labor Rs.25,000
Factory overhead expenses incurred Rs. 50,000
Selling and Administration expenses Rs. 40,000
Finished goods transferred to warehouse Rs. 2,13,000
Cost of goods sold Rs. 2,10,000
Sales Rs. 3,00,000

Factory overheads are applied to production at 150% of direct wages , any under/over absorbed overhead being carried forward for adjustment in the subsequent months. All administration and selling expenses are treated as period costs and charged off to Profit and Loss account of the month in which they are incurred.

Show the following Accounts :

(A) Cost Ledger Control Account, (B) Stock Ledger Control Account, (C) Work-in-Progress Control Account, (D) Finished Goods Control Account, (E) Factory Overhead Control Account, (F) Costing Profit and Loss Account, (G) Trial Balance as at 30th April 1989.

(**Ans.:** (A) Cost Ledger Control Account Rs. 95,000 (B) Stock Ledger Control Account Rs. 32,000 (C) Work-in-Progress Control Account Rs. 20,000 (D) Finished Goods Control Account Rs. 28,000 (E) Factory Overhead Control Account Rs. 15,000 (Dr.) (F) Costing Profit And Loss Account: Profit Rs. 50,000)

❑ ❑ ❑

4

Reconciliation of Cost and Financial Accounts

Objectives

The objectives of the study are to:

- Understand the need for Reconciliation of Cost and Financial Profits
- Analyze the reasons for differences in profits shown by Cost and Financial Accounts
- Reconcile the differences in profits shown by Cost and Financial Accounts

Introduction

A separate set of Books will be required for Costing and Financial purposes, independent of each other, when a large number of Jobs is undertaken or a large number of products are produced. In such a system, when two sets of Books are maintained, two profit and loss accounts will be prepared – one for Costing and other for Financial Books. Profits disclosed by one accounting system tend to differ from that of other accounting system, though both sets of Books are concerned with same basic transactions. This creates problems and a need arises for Reconciliation of Profit shown by two sets of Books. The question of reconciliation of cost and financial accounts arises only under Non-Integral System where cost and financial accounts are separated in contrast with Integrated System where only one set of Books with common Profit and Loss Account is prepared.

Need for Reconciliation

The basic objectives of Reconciliation are:

- To ascertain the reasons for the differences in profit and loss in Cost and Financial Accounts and to indicate the position clearly with an assurance that no mistakes pertaining to accounts have been committed.
- To ensure the mathematical accuracy and reliability of Cost Accounts for the purpose of cost control, and to have check on Financial Accounts.
- To contribute to standardization of policies regarding stock valuation, depreciation and overheads.
- To facilitate better cooperation between financial and cost accounting activities.
- To acquaint management with the reasons for the variations in profits paving way for effective internal control.

REASONS FOR DIFFERENCES IN PROFITS

The disagreement between costing and financial profit is caused by the following:

(1) Items shown only in Financial Accounts: There are a number of items which are included in Financial Accounts but not found in Cost Accounts. These items may be expenditure or appropriation of profit or items of incomes. Expenditure or appropriation of profit items reduces profit while income increases profits shown by Financial Accounts.

***(a)* Purely Financial Charges/Expenses**

Items which are purely of financial nature are charged only in Financial Accounts as a result of which the financial profits would be less as compared to Cost Accounts. These items are:

(i) Loss arising from sale of Fixed Assets
(ii) Loss on Investments
(iii) Discount on Debentures
(iv) Interest on Bank loan, Mortgages and Debentures
(v) Expenses of company's share transfer office
(vi) Interest on proprietors capital
(vii) Damages payable
(viii) Penalties and fines
(ix) Loss due to scrapping of Machinery
(x) Remuneration paid to proprietor

***(b)* Appropriation of Profit**

The distribution/appropriation of profits find place only in Financial Accounts. As a result, if profits after distribution are taken, Financial Accounts Profits would be less than that of the Cost Accounts Profits. The following are the appropriations from financial profits.

(i) Donation and Charities
(ii) Taxes, Income and profits
(iii) Dividend paid on share capital
(iv) Transfer to Reserves, Sinking funds or any other funds e.g.: Dividend Equalization Fund
(v) Provision for Depreciation on fixed assets and for Bad Debts
(vi) Capital expenditure specially charged to Revenue

***(c)* Writing-off of Intangible Assets**

The Intangible Assets written off reduces the profits of Financial Accounts. They are Good will, Patents and Copy Rights, Advertisement, Preliminary Expenses, Organization Expenses, Underwriting Expenses, Underwriting Commission, Discount on issue of Shares/Debentures.

***(d)* Purely Financial Incomes**

The incomes which are purely of financial nature, taken in Financial Accounts, increase the profits of Financial Accounts. The financial incomes are:

(a) Rent receivable
(b) Profit on sale of Investment and Fixed Assets
(c) Transfer fees received
(d) Interest received on Bank Deposits
(e) Dividend received
(f) Brokerage received
(g) Discount or commission received
(h) Bad debts recovered

(2) Item shown only in Cost Accounting

(a) A few items (nominal), which are included in Cost Accounts and not in Financial Accounts, reduce the Cost Accounts Profits. These items are Remuneration paid on owned factors of production employed like

- A Notional charge of interest on owned capital employed in production to show nominal cost.
- Nominal rent for premises owned charged to production for comparison.

(b) Depreciation on Assets is charged even on Negligible Book Value of Assets.

(3) Over and Under Absorption of Overheads: In Cost Accounts, overheads absorbed on the basis of estimation can be more or less than the actual amount incurred. In this way, overheads may not agree with the actual overhead incurred. Profit in Cost Books compared to the Financial Books will be higher or lower depending on the absorption of overheads as to whether the overheads are under absorbed or over-absorbed leading to a difference in profits in two books. Sometimes, selling and distribution expenses are ignored in Cost Accounts and as such costing profit will be higher and thus requires reconciliation.

(4) Difference in Stock Valuation: Valuation of stock in Financial Accounts is based on conservative principle of cost or realizable value which ever is less. In Cost Accounting, different methods of stock valuations are in practice like FIFO, LIFO, Simple or Weighted Average Method. Besides, Work-in-progress in inventory may be valued at Works Cost or Cost of Production basis; Finished Products are valued at Total Cost of Production basis. Since value of stock (Raw Material, Work-in-progress, finished goods) differs in two books, the profits also differ.

(5) Different Methods of charging Depreciation: In Financial Accounting, Depreciation is charged on the basis of different methods like Straight Line Method, Diminishing Balance Method etc., where as in Cost Accounting, Machine Hour Rate or Production Hour Rate or Unit Method may be adopted. These different methods in charging Depreciation cause differences in profit disclosed by two books.

(6) Abnormal Losses and Abnormal Gains: Abnormal items such as abnormal wastage of material by theft, wages of abnormal idle time, cost of abnormal idle facilities, exceptional bad debts, and abnormal gains on manufacturing may be shown in Financial Accounts but are excluded from the Cost Accounts. When these are excluded from Costing Books, Profit of two books will differ.

All the above reasons resulting in differences in profits in the two books necessitate the need for reconciliation of profits.

METHODS OF RECONCILIATION

The reconciliation of costing and financial profits can be attempted either by

(1) preparing Reconciliation Statement or by

(2) preparing Memorandum Reconciliation Account

This reconciliation is similar to Bank Reconciliation Statement.

Reconciliation Statement

Under this method, profit as per Financial Books or Cost Books is taken as the basc profit (starting point) and items causing differences in profits are either added or deducted from it to arrive at profit figure shown by the other set of books. The effect of a particular cause of difference on profit shown by other set of books should be determined. If the cause has increased the profit shown by the other set of books, the amount of such increase should be added to profit as per former set of books which was taken as starting point. In case, the cause (of difference in profit) has decreased the profit shown by the other set of books, the amount of such decrease should be deducted form profit as per former set of books which was taken as starting point. On addition and subtraction of items (causing difference in profit) to the base profit taken as the starting point, the profit as per the other set of books may be arrived at.

Procedure for preparing a Reconciliation Statement

The following steps are adopted to prepare a Reconciliation Statement.

(1) Ascertain the various reasons of disagreement between profits disclosed by the two sets of books of accounts.

(2) If the profit as per Cost Accounts or loss as per Financial Accounts is taken as the base:

Add:

(1) Items of income included in Financial Accounts but not in Cost Accounts.

(2) Items of expenses (as interest on capital, rent on premises etc.,) included in Cost Accounts but not in Financial Accounts.

(3) Amounts of expenses overcharged in Cost Accounts compared to entries in Financial Accounts.

(4) Amounts of incomes shown in excess in Financial Accounts as compared to corresponding entries in Cost Accounts.

(5) Over absorption of overheads in Cost Accounts.

(6) Amount by which closing stock of inventory is undervalued in Cost Accounts (overvalued in Financial Accounts).

(7) Amount by which opening stock is overvalued in Cost Accounts (undervalued in Financial Accounts).

(8) Over charge of Depreciation in Cost Accounts.

Deduct:

(1) Items of income included in Cost Accounts but not in Financial Accounts.

(2) Items of expenses included in Financial Accounts but not in Cost Accounts.

(3) Amounts of incomes shown in excess in Cost Accounts over the corresponding entries in Financial Accounts.

(4) Amounts of expenses shown in excess in Financial Accounts over the corresponding entries in Cost Accounts.

(5) Under absorption of overheads in Cost Accounts (over absorption of overheads in Financial Accounts).

(6) Amount of closing stock overvalued in Cost Accounts (undervalued in Financial Accounts).

(7) Amount of opening stock under valued in Cost Accounts (overvalued in Financial Accounts).

(8) Under charge of Depreciation in Cost Accounts.

(3) After making the above additions and deductions, the resulting figure will be profit/loss as per Financial Accounts/ Cost Accounts.

If the profit as per Financial Accounts (or loss as per Cost Accounts) is taken as the base, them items added above shall be deducted and items to be deducted shall be added. The above procedure should be reversed to find profit/loss as per Cost Accounts Financial Accounts depending upon the starting point.

Memorandum Reconciliation Account

The reconciliation can also be done through preparation of Memorandum Reconciliation Account. This account is a Memorandum Account only and does not form part of Double Entry System. When reconciliation is attempted, profit (as per Cost or Financial Accounting) is shown like opening balance of this Account. All the items of differences required to be deducted are shown on debit side of this account. Items that are to be added are credited to this account. The balancing figure of this account is the profit/loss shown by the other set of accounts.

SPECIMEN OF MEMORANDUM RECONCILIATION ACCOUNT

To Financial Expenses	By profit as per Cost Accounts
– Discount	By financial income
– Fines and Patents	– Rent
– Bank Interest	– Interest
– Underwriters Commission	– Dividend
– Donations	– Profit on sale of goods
– Goodwill written off	By items charged only in Cost Accounts
To under absorption of overheads	– Interest on own capital
To under valuation of opening stock in Cost Accounts	– Rent on own building
To over-valuation of closing stock in Cost Accounts	By over absorption of overheads
To under charge of Depreciation in Cost Accounts	By over-valuation of opening stock in Cost Accounts
To profit as per Financial Accounts	By under valuation of closing stock in Cost Accounts
	By over charge of Depreciation in Cost Accounts

Illustration 1 (when Cost Accounts Profit is given)

The profit as per Cost Accounts is Rs.1,90,000. The following details are ascertained on comparison of Cost and Financial Accounts

	Cost Accounts Rs.	*Financial Accounts* Rs.
(a) Opening Stock		
Materials	30,000	33,000
Work-in-progress	15,000	21,000
(b) Closing Stock		
Materials	40,000	34,000
Work-in-progress	16,200	15,200
Finished Goods	8,000	10,000

(c) Directors fee paid Rs. 2,000; interest paid Rs. 600; reserve for bad and doubtful debts Rs. 400; transfer fees collected Rs. 800 and Dividends received Rs. 500 are exclusively taken in Financial Accounts, but ignored in Cost Accounts.

(d) Rent charged in Cost Accounts but not in Financial Accounts Rs. 4,000.

(e) Preliminary expenses written off Rs. 800 but not charged in Cost Accounts.

(f) Overheads charged in financial books Rs. 1,20,200 but recovered in Costing Rs. 1,26,200.

Find out profit as per Financial Accounts by drawing up a Reconciliation Statement.

Solution

Reconciliation Statement

Particulars	*Amount (Rs.)*	*Amount (Rs.)*
Profit as per Cost Accounts		1,90,000
Add:		
Closing stock of finished goods under valued in Cost Accounts	2,000	
Dividend received taken in Financial Accounts only	500	
Transfer fees ignored in Cost Accounts	800	
Rent charged in Cost Accounts but not in Financial Accounts	4,000	
Over heads over-absorbed in Cost Accounts	6,000	13,300
		2,03,300
Less:		
Opening stock of materials undervalued in Cost Accounts	3,000	
Under valued opening work-in-progress in Cost Accounts	6,000	
Closing stock of materials overvalued in Cost Accounts	6,000	
Closing stock of work-in-progress overvalued in Cost Accounts	1,000	
Director's fee Rs.2,000, interest paid Rs.600 and reserve for bad debts Rs.400 taken in Financial Accounts only	3,000	
Preliminary expenses written off in Financial Accounts	800	**19,800**
Profit as per Financial Accounts		**1,83,500**

Illustration 2 (When profit as per Financial Accounts is given)

The following is a summary of the Trading and Profit and Loss Account of Messrs. Alpha Manufacturing Co. Ltd. for the year ended 31st March 2001.

	Rs.			*Rs.*
To Material consumed	27,40,000	By Sales (1,20,000 units)		60,00,000
To Wages	15,10,000	By Finished Stock (4,000 units)		1,60,000
To Factory Expenses	8,30,000	By Work in Progress:		1,20,000
To Administration Expenses	3,82,400	Materials	64,000	
To Selling and Distribution Expenses	4,50,000	Wages	36,000	
To Preliminary Expenses (written off)	40,000	Factory Expenses	20,000	
To Goodwill (written off)	20,000	By Dividend Received		18,000
To Net Profit	3,25,600			
	62,98,000			62,98,000

The company manufactures a standard unit. In the Cost Accounts:

- Factory expenses have been recovered from production at 20 per cent on Prime Cost;
- Administration expenses are at Rs. 3 per unit on units produced;
- Selling and distribution expenses are at Rs. 4 per unit on units sold.

You are required to prepare a statement of cost and profit in cost books of the company and to reconcile the profit disclosed with that shown in the Financial Accounts.

(CA, Inter)

Solution

Statement of Cost and Profit

Particulars	*Rs.*	*Rs.*
Materials	27,40,000	
Labour	15,10,000	
Prime Cost	42,50,000	
Factory Expenses applied (20% of Prime Cost)	8,50,000	
		51,00,000
Less: Closing Work in Progress		1,20,000

Particulars	*Rs.*	*Rs.*
Works Cost		49,80,000
Add: Administration Expenses (1,20,000 + 4,000) × Rs. 3		3,72,000
Cost of Production		53,52,000
Less: Cost of Closing Finished Stock (4000 units i.e. 4,000/1,24,000 of Rs. 53,52,000)		1,72,645
Cost of Goods Sold		51,79,355
Add: Selling and Distribution Expenses (1,20,000 × Rs. 4)		4,80,000
Total Cost		56,59,355
Profit as per Cost Accounts		3,40,645
Sales (1,20,000 × Rs. 50)		60,00,000

Reconciliation Statement

Particulars	*Amount (Rs.)*	*Amount (Rs.)*
Profit as per Cost Accounts		3,40,645
Add:		
Over-recovery of selling expenses (Rs. 4,80,000 – Rs. 4,50,000)	30,000	
Over-recovery of factory expenses (Rs. 8,50,000 – Rs. 8,30,000)	20,000	
Dividend received	18,000	68,000
		4,08,645
Less:		
Under-recovery of administration expenses (Rs. 3,82,400 – Rs. 3,72,000)	10,400	
Preliminary expenses written off in Financial Accounts	40,000	
Goodwill written off	20,000	
Difference in valuation of finished stock (Rs.1,72,645 – Rs. 1,60,000)	12,645	**83,045**
Profit as per Financial Accounts		**3,25,600**

Illustration 3 (when both the profits as per Financial and Cost Accounts are given)

Managing Director of 'X' Ltd tells you, 'my financial accountant tells me that we have made a profit of Rs. 12,000 this month,' but my cost accountant insists that the figure should be Rs. 13,000. Which one is right? The following information is supplied.

			Financial Accounts Rs.	*Cost Accounts Rs.*
(a)	Stock Valuation			
	Raw Materials :	Opening Stock	22,000	16,000
		Closing Stock	22,000	18,000
	Finished goods :	Opening Stock	50,000	53,000
		Closing Stock	58,000	61,500

(b)	The following items do not appear in the Cost Accounts:	*Rs.*
	Donations to charities	1,500
	Profit on sale of car	1,500
	Exchange rate loss	2,500
	Bad debts written off	500
	Discount allowed	500
	Discount received	400
	Rent Receivable	1,600
(c)	Notional rent is shown in Cost Accounts only	3,000

You are required to prepare a Statement reconciling the two profit figures, starting with financial profit.

Solution

Reconciliation Statement

Particulars	*Amount (Rs.)*	*Amount (Rs.)*
Profit as per Financial Accounts		12,000
Add:		
Difference in stock valuation :		
– over valued opening stock of raw material in Financial Accounts	6,000	
– under valued closing finished stock	3,500	
Donation found in Financial Accounts	1,500	
Exchange rate loss recorded only in Financial Accounts	2,500	
Bad debts written off	500	
Discount allowed	500	14,500
		26,500
Less:		
Under valuation of opening stock of finished goods	3,000	
Over valuation of closing stock of raw material	4,000	
Profit on sale of car ignored in Cost Books	1,500	
Discount received	400	
Rent receivable	1,600	
Notional rent shown only in Cost Books	3,000	**13,500**
Profit as per Cost Accounts		**13,000**

Illustration 4 (when both the profits as per Financial and Cost Accounts are not given)

The following figures were available in respect of Ashok Engineering Company for the year ended 31st March, 2001.

		Financial Accounts Rs.	*Cost Account Rs.*
(a)	Opening Stock		
	Raw Materials	6,000	4,000
	Work-in-progress	7,000	8,500
	Finished stock	5,000	4,500
	Total	**18,000**	**17,000**
(b)	Closing Stock		
	Raw Materials	4,000	5,300
	Work-in-progress	3,000	3,700
	Finished goods	5,900	6,200
	Total	**12,900**	**15,200**
	Purchases	40,000	
	Direct wages	20,000	
	Factory expenses	20,000	21,000 absorbed
	Sales	1,10,000	
	Administration expenses	3,000	2,300 absorbed
	Selling expenses	4,000	4,500 absorbed
	Financial expenses	1,500	
	Interest and Dividend received	2,400	
	Bad debts	500	

Compute profit in Financial Accounts as well as in Cost Accounts and prepare a Reconciliation Statement.

Solution

Statement of Cost and Profit (Cost Books)

Particulars	*Amount (Rs)*
Opening stock of Raw Materials	4,000
Add: Purchase of Raw Materials	40,000
	44,000
Less: Closing Stock of Raw Materials	5,300
Material Consumed	**38,700**
Direct wages	20,000
Prime cost	**58,700**
Factory Overheads	21,000
Add: Beginning work-in-progress	8,500
	88,200
Less: closing work-in-progress	3,700
Works cost	**84,500**
Administration expenses	2,300
Cost of production	**86,800**
Add: Finished Goods (Beginning)	4,500
	91,300
Less: Finished Goods (Closing)	6,200
Cost of Goods Sold	**85,100**
Selling expenses	4,500
Cost of Sales	**89,600**
Profit as per cost accounts	**20,400**
Sales	1,10,000

Profit and Loss Account (Financial Books)

Particulars	*Amount (Rs.)*	*Particulars*	*Amount (Rs.)*
To Opening Stock:		By Sales	1,10,000
Raw Materials	6,000	By Closing Stock:	
Work-in-progress	7,000	Raw Materials	4,000
Finished goods	5,000	Work-in- progress	3,000
To Purchases	40,000	Finished goods	5,900
To Direct wages	20,000	By Interest and Dividend received	2,400
To Factory Expenses	20,000		
To Administration Expenses	3,000		
To Selling Expenses	4,000		
To Financial Expenses	1,500		
To Bad debts	500		
To Net profit as per Financial Accounts	18,300		
Total	**1,25,300**	**Total**	**1,25,300**

Reconciliation Statement

Particulars	*Amount (Rs.)*	*Amount (Rs.)*
Profit as per Cost Accounts		20,400
Add:		
Over absorption of Factory overheads (21,000 – 20,000)	1,000	
Over absorption of Selling expenses (4,500 – 4,000)	500	
Interest and Dividend Received	2,400	3,900
		24,300

Particulars	*Amount (Rs.)*	*Amount (Rs.)*
Less:		
Over valuation of opening stock in Financial Accounts (18,000 – 17,000)	1,000	
Under valuation of closing stock in Financial Accounts (15,200 – 12,900)	2,300	
Financial expenses charged in Financial Accounts	1,500	
Bad debts	500	
Under absorption of Administration Overheads	700	**6,000**
Profit as per Financial Accounts		**18,300**

Illustration 5 (When loss as per Cost/Financial Accounts is given)

	Rs.
From the following figures prepare a Reconciliation Statement:	
Net loss as per financial records	2,08,045
Net loss as per costing records	1,72,400
Works over heads under recovered in costing records	3,120
Administrative overheads recovered in excess	1,700
Depreciation charged in financial records	11,200
Depreciation recovered in costing records	12,500
Interest received not included in costing records	8,000
Obsolescence (Loss) charged in financial records	5,700
Income tax provided in financial books	40,300
Bank interest credited in financial books	750
Stores adjustment (credit in financial books)	475
Value of opening stock in Cost Accounts	52,600
Value of opening stock in Financial Accounts	54,000
Value of Closing stock in Cost Accounts	52,000
Value of Closing stock in Financial Accounts	49,600
Interest charged in Cost Accounts but not in Financial Accounts	6,000
Preliminary expenses written off in Financial Accounts	800
Provision for doubtful debts in Financial Accounts	150

Solution

Reconciliation Statement

Particulars	*Amount (Rs.)*	*Amount (Rs.)*
Loss as per Costing Records		**1,72,400**
Add:		
Works Overheads under absorbed	3,120	
Obsolescence (loss) in Financial Records	5,700	
Income tax	40,300	
Difference in value of opening stock (under valuation in Cost Books)	1,400	
Over valued closing stock in Cost Accounts	2,400	
Preliminary expenses written off	800	
Provision for doubtful debts	150	53,870
		2,26,270
Less:		
Administration Overheads over absorbed	1,700	
Depreciation over absorbed in Cost Accounts	1,300	
Interest received	8,000	
Bank interest	750	
Stores adjustment	475	
Interest charged only in Cost Accounts	6,000	18,225
Loss as per Financial Records		**2,08,045**

Illustration 6 (Where production is below normal production)

The following information is available from the financial books of a company having a normal production capacity of 60,000 units for the year ended 31st March 2004.

(i) Sales Rs. 10,00,000 (50,000 units)
(ii) There was no opening and closing stock of finished units.
(iii) Direct material and direct wages cost were Rs. 5,00,000 and Rs. 2,50,000 respectively.
(iv) Actual factory expenses were Rs. 1,50,000 of which 60% are fixed.
(v) Actual administrative expenses were Rs. 45,000 which are completely fixed.
(vi) Actual selling and distribution expenses were Rs. 30,000 of which 40% are fixed.
(vii) Interest and dividends received Rs. 15,000.

You are required to:

(a) Find out profit as per Financial Books for the year ended 31st March 2004;
(b) Prepare a statement of cost and profit to ascertain the profit as per Cost Accounts for the year ended 31st March 2004 assuming that the indirect expenses are absorbed on the basis of normal production capacity; and
(c) Prepare a statement reconciling profits shown by Financial and Cost Books.

(CA, Inter)

Solution

Profit and Loss Account for the year ended 31.3.2004

Particulars	*Rs.*	*Particulars*	*Rs.*
To Direct Materials	5,00,000	By Sales	10,00,000
To Direct Wages	2,50,000	By Interest and Dividends	15,000
To Factory Expenses	1,50,000		
To Administrative Expenses	45,000		
To Selling and Distribution Expenses	30,000		
To Net Profit	40,000		
	10,15,000		10,15,000

Statement of Cost and Profit (Normal output 60,000 units)

	Rs.	*Rs.*
Direct Materials	5,00,000	
Direct Labor	2,50,000	
Prime Cost		7,50,000
Factory Expenses: Variable (40% of Rs. 1,50,000)	60,000	
Fixed (Rs. 90,000 × 5/6)	75,000	1,35,000
Works Cost	8,85,000	
Add: Administration Expenses (Rs. 45,000 × 5/6)		37,500
Cost of Production		9,22,500
Add: Selling and Distribution Expenses: Variable (60 × Rs. 30,000)	18,000	
Fixed (Rs. 12,000 × 5/6)	10,000	28,000
Cost of Sales	9,50,500	
Profit as per Cost Accounts		49,500
Sales (1,20,000 × Rs. 50)		10,00,000

Reconciliation Statement

Particulars	*Amount (Rs.)*	*Amount (Rs.)*
Profit as per Cost Accounts		49,500
Add:		
Interest and Dividend not recorded in Cost Accounts		15,000
		64,500
Less:		
Expenses under absorbed in Cost Accounts:		
Factory Expenses	15,000	
Administration Expenses	7,500	
Selling and Distribution Expenses	2,000	**24,500**
Profit as per Financial Accounts		**40,000**

Illustration 7 (when Memorandum Account is to be prepared)

The financial Profit and Loss Account of manufacturing company for the year ended 31st March 1998, is given below.

Dr. **Profit and Loss Account** **Cr.**

Particulars	*Amount (Rs.)*	*Particulars*	*Amount (Rs.)*
Opening Stock:		By Sales	4,60,000
Raw Materials	25,000	By Closing Stock:	
Finished Goods	40,000	Raw Materials	30,000
Work-in-progress	12,500	Finished Goods	15,000
	77,500	Work-in-progress	20,700
To Purchases	1,20,000		
To Wages (factory)	30,000		
To Electric Power (factory)	65,000		
To Factory Overheads	45,000		
To Gross Profit c/d	1,88,200		
Total	**5,25,700**	**Total**	**5,25,700**
To Administration Expenses	20,500	By Gross Profit b/d	1,88,200
To Selling and Distribution Expenses	46,500	By Miscellaneous Revenue	26,800
To Bad Debts	15,600		
To Net Profit	1,32,400		
Total	**2,15,000**	**Total**	**2,15,000**

The Cost Accounts of concern showed a net profit of Rs. 1,32,200. It is seen that Costing Profit and Loss Account is arrived at on the basis of figures furnished below:

Opening stock of Raw Material, Finished Stock and Work-in-progress Rs. 90,800

Closing stock of Raw Material, Finished Stock and Work-in-progress Rs. 69,500

Administration expenses are not considered in Cost Accounts.

You are required to prepare a Memorandum Reconciliation Account and reconcile the difference in Profit and Loss Account taking Financial Profit as the base.

Solution

Dr. **Memorandum Reconciliation Account** **Cr.**

Particulars	*Amount (Rs.)*	*Particulars*	*Amount (Rs.)*
To over valuation of opening stock in Cost Accounts	13,300	By net profit as per Financial Accounts	1,32,400
To Miscellaneous Revenue not considered in Cost Accounts	26,800	By over valuation of closing stock in Cost Accounts	3,800
		By Administration expenses not considered in Cost Accounts	20,500
		By bad debts not considered in Cost Accounts	15,600
To profit as per Cost Accounts	1,32,200		
Total	**1,72,300**	**Total**	**1,72,300**

SUMMARY

A need for Reconciliation of Cost and Financial Accounts arises only under Non-Integral System where Cost and Financial Accounts are separated in contrast with Integrated System where only one set of Books with common Profit and Loss Account is prepared.

The main objective of Reconciliation of Cost and Financial Accounts is to ascertain the reasons for the difference in Profits in Cost and Financial Accounts and to reconcile them.

The disagreement between costing and financial profit is caused by the items shown only in Financial Accounts, Purely Financial Charges/Expenses, Appropriation of Profit, Writing off Intangible Assets, Purely Financial Incomes, Items shown only in Cost Accounting, Over and Under Absorption of Overheads, Difference in Stock Valuation, Different methods of charging

Depreciation, Abnormal Losses and Abnormal Gains. All these reasons result in differences in profits in the two books necessitating the need for reconciliation of profits.

The reconciliation of costing and financial profits can be attempted either by preparing Reconciliation Statement or by preparing Memorandum Reconciliation Account.

When Reconciliation is attempted, profit (as per Cost or Financial Accounting) is taken and all the items which increase the profit of the other book are added to the profit taken as per the base set of books and all the items which decrease the profit of the other book are deducted from the profit taken as per the base set of books. The resulting profit would be the profit as per the other set of books.

In case of the Memorandum Reconciliation Account, balance of profit as per Cost or Financial Account is shown like opening balance of this account. All the items of differences required to be deducted are shown on debit side of this account. Items that are to be added are credited to this account. The balancing figure of this account is the profit/loss shown by the other set of accounts.

Glossary

- **Reconciliation Statement:** It is a Statement reconciling the differences in profits shown by Cost and Financial Accounts.
- **Memorandum Reconciliation Account:** It is an Account reconciling the differences in profits shown by Cost and Financial Accounts.

Questions

(1) Indicate the reasons as to why it is necessary for the Cost and Financial Accounts of organization to be reconciled and explain the main reasons of difference which would enter into such accounts.

(2) List out 10 items, either debit or credit, which appear in Financial Accounts but do not appear in Cost Accounts.

(3) Examine the reasons for the difference between Cost and Financial Accounts maintained by the organization.

PROBLEMS

(1) From the following figures, prepare a Reconciliation Statement:

	Rs.
Net profit as per Financial Books	63,780
Net profit as per Costing Books	66,760
Factory on-cost under-recovered in Costing Books	5,700
Administration on-cost recovered in excess	4,250
Depreciation charged in Financial Books	3,660
Depreciation recovered in Costing Books	3,950
Interest received but not Included in Costing Books	450
Income tax provided in Financial Books	600
Bank interest credited in Financial Books	230
Stores adjustment (credited in Financial Books)	420
Depreciation of stock charged in Financial Accounts	860
Dividends appropriated in Financial Accounts	1,200
Loss due to theft and pilferage provided only in Financial Books	260

(2) From the information given below prepare *(i)* a statement showing Costing Profit or Loss and *(ii)* another statement reconciling the costing profits with those shown by Financial Accounts.

Trading and Profit and Loss Account for the year ended 31st December 2008.

Particulars	*Amount (Rs.)*	*Particulars*	*Amount (Rs.)*
To Material consumed	1,00,000	By Sales (1,00,000 units)	2,00,000
To Direct Wages	50,000		
To Indirect Factory Expenses	30,000		
To Office Expenses	9,000		
To Selling and Distribution Expenses	6,000		
To Net profit	5,000		
Total	**2,00,000**	**Total**	**2,00,000**

The normal output of the factory is 1,50,000 units. Factory expenses of a fixed nature are Rs. 18,000. Office expenses are constant for all practical purpose. Selling and Distribution expenses are constant to the extent of Rs. 3,000 and the balance varies with sales.

(Ans: Rs. 15,000)

(3) Ashoka Engineering Co., manufactures two sizes of machine components, size A and B. The following data refer to the year-ended 31.12.1989.

	Size A	*Size B*
Production	125 Units	400 units
Sales	120 units	360 units
Wages cost per unit	Rs. 40	Rs. 30
Material cost per unit	Rs. 15	Rs. 12
Sale price per unit	Rs. 125	Rs. 90

All expenses other than wages and materials are analyzed under 'works overheads' which during the year amounted to Rs. 9,000 and 'office overheads', which amounted to Rs. 10,000. In fixing the selling price, it was estimated that works overheads be taken at 50% on wages and office overhead expenses at $33\frac{1}{3}$ % on works cost.

You are required to compute: *(a)* The total cost of each unit on the basis of the above overhead percentage; *(b)* The net profit for the year shown by the Financial Accounts, valuing unsold stocks at actual material and wages cost plus work overheads at 50% on wages; and *(c)* The reconciliation of net profit in the above with estimated total net profit based on the cost figures.
(Ans: *(a)* Size A – Rs. 100, Size B – Rs. 76, *(b)* Rs. 7,380, *(c)* Rs. 8,040)

(4) The Financial Accounts of a company show a profit of Rs. 6,70,000 for the year ending 31.121991. On further examination of Cost and Financial Accounts the following facts were discovered:

	Rs.
Works on cost under recovered in Cost Books	16,240
Office on cost over-recovered in Cost Books	4,000
Interest on investments not included in Cost Books	16,000
Prepare a statement showing profit as per Cost Accounts.	

(Ans : Rs. 6,66,240)

(5) Find out the profit as per Costing records and Financial Accounts from the following information and reconcile the results:

	Product A	*Product B*
Number of units produced and sold	600	400
Total Direct Materials	Rs. 3,600	Rs. 2,800
Total Direct Wages	Rs. 3,000	Rs. 2,400
Selling price per unit	Rs. 25	Rs. 30

Works on cost is charged at 80% of direct wages and office on cost at 25% of works costs. Actual works expenses amounted to Rs. 4,500 and office expenses to Rs. 3,900. There were no opening and closing stocks.
(Ans: Cost Profit: Rs. 6,850 Financial profit: Rs.6,800)

(6) From the following data, calculate profit or loss in Cost Accounts as well as Financial Accounts and reconcile them.

		Rs.
Sales		2,00,000
Purchases of materials		30,000
Closing stock		5,000
Direct wages		1,00,000
Indirect wages		5,000
Bad debts		1,000
Indirect expenses		20,000
Interest on overdraft		500
Profit on sale of assets		1,000
Selling expenses		20,000
Distribution expenses		10,000
In **Cost Accounts**		
Manufacturing overheads recovered at 30% on direct wages		
Selling overheads recovered	Rs. 15,000	
Distribution overheads recovered	Rs. 7,500	

[Ans: (a) Rs. 22,500, (b) Rs. 19,500]

(7) From the following particulars, prepare a Profit and Loss Account, a statement showing the cost of manufacture and the percentage of each item of cost to total cost. Calculate factory overheads on cost at 25% on prime cost and office overheads on cost at 75% on factory on cost. Prepare statement reconciliation the profit shown by Cost Accounts with that shown by the Profit and Loss Account. The selling price is fixed at cost plus 25%.

	Rs.
Stock of materials (1-7-06)	4,000
Stock of finished goods (1-7-06)	8,000
Stock of materials (31-12-06)	6,000
Stock of finished goods (31-12-06)	2,000
Works expenses	7,750
Purchase or Raw material	24,000
Wages	10,000
Sales	65,000
Office expenses	6,100

[Ans: (a) Rs. 13,150, (b) Rs. 13,000]

(8) The following figures were available about Ashok Engineering Company for the year-ended 31.03.2009:

	Financial Accounts Rs.	*Costs Accounts* Rs.
Opening Stock:		
Raw material	6,000	5,000
Work-in-progress	7,000	6,500
Finished stock	5,000	4,500
Closing Stock :		
Raw material	4,000	4,300
Work-in-progress	3,000	3,700
Finished stock	5,900	6,200
Purchases		40,000
Direct wages		20,000
Indirect wages		3,000
Factory expenses	17,000	21,000 (Absorbed)
Sales	1,10,000	
Administration expenses	3,000	2,300 (Absorbed)
Selling expenses	4,000	4,500 (Absorbed)
Financial expenses	1,000	
Interest and dividend received	1,600	

Compute the profit in Financial Accounts as well as in Cost Accounts and prepare a Reconciliation Statement, showing clearly the reasons for the variance of two profit figures.

[Ans: (a) Rs. 20,450, (b) Rs. 18,500]

(9) From the accounts books of Shankar & Company Ltd., Manufacturing, Trading and Profit and Loss Accounts are reproduced below:

Particulars	*Amount (Rs.)*	*Particulars*	*Amount (Rs.)*
To Raw materials:		By Work-in-progress:	
– Opening stock	29,500	– Material	4,000
– Purchase	1,86,500	– Wages	5,500
		– Works expenses	3,300
To wages	2,98,000	By cost of goods manufactured	6,59,950
To works expenses	1,90,750	By closing stock of raw material	32,000
Total	**7,04,750**	**Total**	**7,04,750**
To cost of goods manufactured	6,59,950	By sales (7,600 units)	9,12,000
To administrative expenses	1,22,500	By finished stock (1,400 units)	1,17,600
To bad debts written off	17,500	By interest on investment	6,800
To net profit transferred to Appropriation Account	2,36,450		
Total	**10,36,400**	**Total**	**10,36,400**

The following information is also available:

(i) Accrued wages, Rs. 17,000 included in wages.

(ii) Works expenses are allocated to production at 60% of direct labour cost.

(iii) Administrative expenses are allocated so as to work out 20% of selling price.

Prepare a Costing Profit and Loss A/c and Statement of Reconciliation between the two accounts (Cost and Financial)

[Ans : (a) Rs. 91,200]

(10) Prepare the following statements from the particulars given below:

(a) Statement of cost of manufacturing and percentage of each item of cost of total cost, calculate factory overheads at 25% of prime cost and office overheads at 75% of factory overheads.

(b) Statement of profit as per Cost Accounts.

(c) Profit and Loss A/c

(d) A Reconciliation Statement

	Rs.
Stock at the beginning:	
Raw material	8,000
Finished articles	16,000
Purchase of raw material	48,000
Wages	20,000
Office expenses	12,200
Works expenses	15,500
Sales.	1,30,000
Stock at the end:	
Raw material	12,000
Finished Articles	4,000
Profit is fixed at 20% on selling price.	

[Ans : *(a)* Rs. 26,000 *(b)* Rs. 26,300]

❑ ❑ ❑

Part – II

Elements of Cost

5

MATERIALS COST

Objectives

The objectives of the study are to:

- Understand the importance of Material Control and
- Learn the various techniques for control of inventory

- **Introduction**
- **Objectives of Material Control**
- **Inventory Control Techniques**
  - **Stock Levels**
    - **Maximum Level**
    - **Minimum Level**
    - **Re-Order Level**
    - **Average Stock Level**
    - **Danger Level**
  - **Economic Order Quantity**
  - **Always Better Control**
  - **Perpetual Inventory Control**
    - **Bin Card**
    - **Stores Ledger**
  - **Stock Turnover Ratios**
  - **Purchase Control**
  - **Just in Time**
- **Bill of Materials**
- **Return of Materials**
- **Transfer of Materials**
- **Summary**
- **Glossary**
- **Questions**

INTRODUCTION

It is the cost of material, which constitutes more than 50 per cent of the total cost of the product or job in several industries. Therefore, there should be a proper control over the material cost. There are two types of material. They are direct material and indirect material.

Direct Materials are those that which can be directly identified with each unit of the finished product. Example: raw cotton in the textile industry, leather for shoemaking industry, sugarcane in sugar industry, etc. The cost of direct material includes:

- All raw materials issued from the store for production
- Material specifically purchased for the specific job
- Material transferred from one cost centre to another centre
- Parts or components purchased or produced for the specific product and
- Primary packing material like wrappings, cartons, bottles, cardboards, etc.

Indirect Materials are those materials, which do not normally form a part of the finished product. They cannot be allocated but can be apportioned or absorbed by cost centres or cost units. The indirect materials include:

- Opening stores used in maintenance of Machinery, Buildings, etc., like lubricants, cotton waste.
- Stores used by the service departments like Power House, Canteen etc. and
- Material, which due to their cost being small, are not considered worth-while to be treated as direct material.

In order to minimize the production costs, it is essential to constitute effective inventory management. For this purpose, it is necessary to design a proper system of purchasing, receiving, storing, issuing and recording of materials.

OBJECTIVES OF MATERIAL CONTROL

The broad objectives of Material Control are:

- To avoid under stocking as it leads to shortage of material and production interruption;
- To avoid overstocking as it results in lock up of capital and high storage cost;
- To purchase material at the most favorable prices resulting in economy of purchasing;
- To give due consideration to the quality of material purchased;
- To minimize the loss of material due to evaporation, obsolescence, pilferage, theft, deterioration, etc., by providing proper storage conditions; and
- To develop a system whereby complete and up-to-date accounting information about the material is available.

INVENTORY CONTROL TECHNIQUES

Inventory includes the stores of raw material, stock of finished goods, work-in-progress and other accessories. It constitutes the principal item in the working capital of the majority of trading and industrial concerns. The various techniques to control inventory are discussed below.

Deciding the various Stock Levels of Inventory

Most of the large companies fix up various stock levels to guard against under stocking and over stocking. The various levels are:

Maximum Level: It indicates the maximum quantity of the inventory items, which can be stored at any given point of time. The basic objective of setting up this level is to ensure that capital is not unnecessarily blocked in stores and also to avoid loss due to obsolescence and deterioration. It is computed by the formula given below.

Maximum Level = (Re-Order level + Re-Order Quantity) – (Minimum Consumption × Minimum Re-Order Period)

Minimum Level: It is that level below which stock should not be allowed to fall. It indicates the minimum stock to be maintained so that there is no risk of stoppage of production.

Minimum Level = Re-Order Level – (Normal Consumption × Normal Re-Order Period)

Re-Order Level: It is the level at which fresh order should be placed for replenishment of stock. It is fixed somewhere between the minimum and maximum level. It is fixed in such a way that before the material ordered is received; there is sufficient material on hand (minimum level) to cover both normal and abnormal circumstances. The factors generally considered for fixing this level are the rate of consumption of material, minimum level and delivery time.

Re-Order Level = Maximum Consumption × Maximum Re-Order Period or
Minimum Level + Consumption during the time required for fresh delivery

Average Stock Level: It is the average of minimum and maximum level.

Average Stock Level = (Minimum Level + Maximum Level) / 2

It is also calculated by taking

(Minimum Level + ½ of Re-Order Quantity)

Danger Level: It is generally below the minimum level. It indicates the urgent action needed for the replacement of stock so that production stoppage can be avoided. It is calculated by taking **Average Consumption × Maximum lead time for emergency purchases.**

Illustration 1

Calculate the Re-Ordering level from the following information:
Maximum consumption = 300 units per day
Minimum consumption = 200 units per day
Re-Order period = 8 to 12 days

Solution

Re-ordering level = Maximum consumption × Maximum Re-Order period
$300 \times 12 = 3600$ units

Illustration 2

Calculate the ordering level of material A from the following particulars.

(i) Minimum limit 500 units
(ii) Maximum limit 2500 units
(iii) Daily requirements of material 200 units
(iv) Time required for fresh delivery 10 days

Solution

Ordering level = Minimum level + Consumption during the time required for fresh delivery
= 500 units + (200 × 10)
= 2500 units

Order for the purchase of the material should be placed when the material in stock reaches 2500 units

Illustration 3

Calculate the Minimum Stock Level, Maximum Stock Level and Re-ordering Level from the following information:
Minimum consumption = 120 units per day
Maximum consumption = 150 units per day
Normal consumption = 120 units per day
Re-Order period = 10 to15 days
Re-Order quantity = 1500 units
Normal Re-Order period = 12 days

Solution

Re-Order level = Maximum consumption × Maximum Re-Order period
= 150 units × 15 days
= 2250 units

Minimum Stock level = Re-Order level – (Normal consumption × Normal Re-Order period)
= 2250 – (120 × 12)
= 810 units

Maximum Stock level = Re-Order level + Re-Order quantity – (Minimum consumption × Minimum Re-Order period)
= 2250 + 1500 – (120 × 10)
= 2550 units

Illustration 4

In manufacturing its product 'A', a company uses three raw materials A, B and C in respect of which the following will apply:

	Raw Materials Usage per Unit	*Re-Order Quantity*	*Price per lb. (Ps.)*	*Delivery Order*		*Minimum Level*
				Period	*Level*	
Product	*(lb.)*	*(lb.)*		*(week)*	*(lb.)*	*(lb.)*
A	10	10,000	10	1-3	7,000	—
B	4	5,000	30	3-5	4,000	—
C	6	10,000	15	2-4	—	2,000

Weekly Production varies from 175 to 225 units averaging 200 units. What would you expect the quantities of the following to be?

(*a*) Minimum Stock of A
(*b*) Maximum Stock of B
(*c*) Re-Order Level of C
(*d*) Average Stock of A

Solution

(*a*) Minimum Stock of A:

Re-Order Level – (Normal Consumption × Normal Re-Order Period)
7,000 – (2,000 × 2 weeks) = 3,000 lbs.

Normal Production per week = $\frac{(175 + 225)}{2}$ = 200 units

Normal Usage of material per unit = 10 lbs.

Normal Consumption of material per week = 200 × 10 = 2,000 lbs.

$$\text{Normal Re-Order Period} = \frac{(\text{Minimum Delivery Period} + \text{Maximum Delivery Period})}{2}$$

= (1 week + 3 weeks) / 2 = 2 weeks

(*b*) Maximum Stock of B:

Re-Order Level + Re-Order Quantity – (Minimum consumption × Minimum Re-Order Period)
= 4,000 + 5,000 – (700 × 3) = 6,900 lbs.

Minimum Production per week = 175 units
Usage per unit of product = 4 lbs.
Minimum Consumption of raw material per week = 175 × 4 = 700 lbs.

(*c*) Re-Order Level of C:

Maximum Consumption × Maximum Re-Order Period
= 1350 × 4 = 5,400 lbs.

Maximum Production per week = 225 units
Usage per unit = 6 lbs.
Maximum consumption of C material = 225 × 6 = 1,350 lbs.

(*d*) Average Stock Level of A:

Minimum Stock Level of A + ½ of Re-Order Quantity of A
= 3,000 + ½ of 10,000 = 8,000 lbs.

Illustration 5

You have been asked to calculate the following level for Part No. 999 from the following information given here under.

(*a*) Re-Ordering Level
(*b*) Maximum Level
(*c*) Minimum Level
(*d*) Danger Level
(*e*) Average Stock Level

The Re-Ordering quantity is to be calculated from the following data.
Total Cost of purchasing relating to the order Rs. 20
Number of units to be purchased during the year 5,000
Purchase price per unit including transportation cost Rs. 50
Annual Cost of storage of 1 unit Rs. 5 (10 % of purchase price)
Lead Time: Average 10 days; Maximum 15 days; Minimum 6 days; Maximum for emergency purchases 4 days.
Rate of consumption: average 15 units; maximum 20 units and minimum 10 units.

Solution

(*a*) Re-Order Level: Maximum consumption × Maximum lead-time
= 20 units × 15
= 300 units

(*b*) Maximum Level = Re-Order Level + Re-Order Quantity – (Minimum consumption × Minimum Lead Time)
300 + 200 – (10 × 6) = 440 units

(*c*) Minimum Level = Re-Order level – (Average consumption × Average Lead time)
300 – (15 × 10) = 150 units

(d) Danger Level = Average consumption × Maximum Lead Time for emergency purchase
$15 \times 4 = 60$ units

(e) Average Stock Level = Minimum Level + ½ of Re-Order Quantity
$150 + \frac{1}{2}$ of $200 = 250$ units

Re-Order Quantity = $\sqrt{2AO/\text{(carrying cost per unit per year or cost per unit} \times \text{rate of carrying cost)}}$

Where,

A = Annual Consumption in units = 5000

O = Ordering Cost per order = Rs. 20

C = Carrying Cost per unit = 10% of 50

Re-Order Quantity = $\sqrt{(2 \times 5000 \times 20) / 10\% \text{ of } 50} = 200$ units

Illustration 6

In ABC Ltd., material consumption was as follows:

Average daily requirements	=	12 units
Usual time required for obtaining supply	=	2 weeks
Maximum requirement in a month of 4 weeks	=	400 units
Minimum requirement in a month of 4 weeks	=	200 units
Economic order size	=	240 units

Time sufficient for emergency supply 2 days

Find out:

(a) Maximum Level
(b) Minimum Level
(c) Ordering Level
(d) Danger Level
(e) Average Stock Level

Solution

(a) Ordering Level = Maximum consumption × Maximum lead time
= $(400/4) \times 2 = 200$ units

(b) Minimum Level = Re-Order level – (Normal consumption × Normal Lead time)
$200 - (72 \times 2) = 56$ units

(c) Maximum Level = Re-Order level + Re-Order Quantity – (Minimum Consumption × Minimum Lead-time)
$200 + 240 - (200/4 \times 2) = 340$ units

(d) Danger Level = Average Consumption × Maximum Lead Time for emergency purpose
$12 \times 2 = 24$ units

(e) Average Stock Level = Minimum Stock Level + ½ of Re-Order Quantity
$56 + \frac{1}{2}$ of $240 = 176$ units

Note: In the absence of information, usual time required 2 weeks is treated as maximum, minimum and average lead-time.

Maximum and Minimum usage are converted per week.

Normal usage per week = $12 \times 6 = 72$ units (taking 6 days in a week).

Illustration 7

Calculate Re-Order Level, Maximum-Level and Minimum-Level of stock from the information given below.

Re-Order quantity- 4000 units

Min-stock level to allow for emergencies-5 weeks.

Average delivery time for suppliers-4 weeks.

Max-stock level allowed by mgmt-20 weeks.

Average rate of consumption-250 units.

Min.consumption in 4 weeks-800 units.

Solution

Re-Order Level = Max.Consumption × Max Re-Order Period
$2{,}250 \times 20 = 45{,}000$ units

where, Max-Consumption = (Avg. Lead Time × Average.Usage) + Safety Stock
= (4 × 250) + (5 × 250)
= 1000 + 1250
= 2250 units

Min-Level = Re-Order Level – (Normal Usage × Normal Lead Time)
= 45,000 – (250 × 4)
= 45,000 – 1000
= 44,000 units

Max-Level = Re-Order Level + Re–Order Quantity – (Min Usage × Min Lead Time)
= 45,000 + 4000 – (200 × 4)
= 49,000 – 800
= 48,200 units

Determination of Re-Order Quantity or Economic Order Quantity

Re-Order Quantity refers to that number of units, which should be ordered at one time so as to minimize the total cost of placing orders and cost of storing the goods as well as interest on the capital invested. It is the quantity, which is most economical to order.

In determining the Economic Order Quantity (EOQ), the problem is to set a balance between the two opposing costs *viz.*, the ordering cost and carrying costs. Ordering cost is the cost of placing an order with the supplier. It includes the cost of stationery, salaries of those engaged in receiving and inspection, salaries of those engaged in placing orders etc. Carrying cost is the cost of holding the stock in storage. Examples: cost of operating the stores (salaries, rent, etc.), insurance, warehousing and storage, material handling and clerical charges, deterioration, spoilage and wastage of material, etc.

The management is tempted on one hand to order huge quantity to reduce the ordering cost by reducing the number of orders but on the other hand, the carrying cost will go up as the stock will remain longer in stores. Hence, the management tries to reconcile them and this reconciliation point is EOQ.

As the number of units per order increase, the ordering cost comes down, while the carrying cost increases. The EOQ, which is the ideal order size, is at a point where the total cost is minimum. The same is represented in the figure below.

Graph: Economic Order Quantity

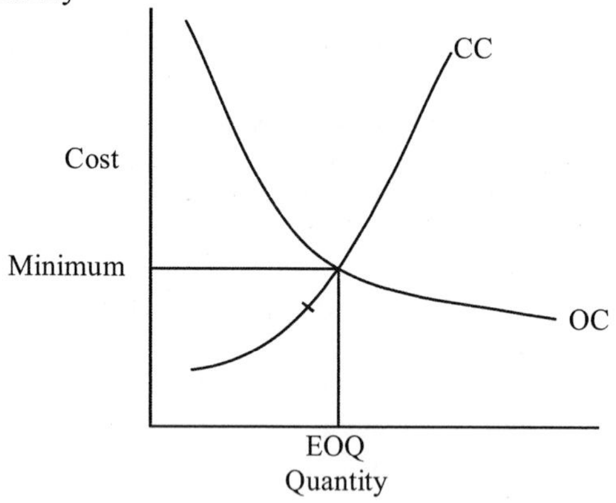

The above graphic method may not provide the accurate EOQ. The same can be determined with the help of a formula.

$EOQ = \sqrt{2AO/C}$

Where,

A = Annual Consumption in units
O = Ordering Cost per order
C = Carrying Cost per unit per annum
Where, Carrying cost is given in percent,

Illustration 8

Find out the Economic Order Quantity from the following particulars.
Annual usage = 6000 units
Cost of material per unit = Rs. 20
Cost of placing and receiving an order = Rs. 60
Annual carrying cost of one unit = 10 % of inventory value.

Solution

$$EOQ = \sqrt{2AO / (\text{cost per unit} \times \text{rate of carrying cost per unit})}$$

$$\sqrt{2 \times 6{,}000 \times 60 / (10\ \% \text{ of } 20)}$$

$$\sqrt{3{,}60{,}000} = 600 \text{ units}$$

Illustration 9

The Shyam bore wells company uses about 75,000 valves per annum and the usage is fairly constant at 6,250 per month. The valves cost Rs. 1.50 per unit when bought in large quantities and the carrying cost is estimated to be 20 % of an average inventory investment on an annual basis. The cost to place an order and process the delivery is Rs. 18. Determine EOQ and the frequency of orders.

Solution

$$EOQ = \sqrt{2AO / (\text{Cost per unit} \times \text{rate of carrying cost per unit})}$$

$$\sqrt{2 \times 75{,}000 \times 18 / (20\ \% \text{ of } 1.50)}$$

$$\sqrt{90{,}00{,}000} = 3{,}000 \text{ units}$$

Frequency of orders = Annual Usage / EOQ

75,000 / 3,000 = 25 orders per day

Illustration 10

A Ltd. Company is committed to supply 24,000 bearings p.a. to B Ltd. Company on a steady daily basis. It is estimated that it costs Re. 0.10 as inventory holding cost per bearing p.m. and that the set up cost per run of bearing manufacture is Rs. 324. Calculate the *(a)* Optimum run size of bearing manufacture and *(b)* Average inventory holding cost per batch.

Solution

(a) $$EOQ = \sqrt{2AO / (\text{Cost per unit} \times \text{rate of carrying cost per unit})}$$

$$\sqrt{2 \times 24{,}000 \times 324 / (.10 \times 12)}$$

$$\sqrt{1{,}29{,}60{,}000} = 3{,}600 \text{ units}$$

(b) Average inventory holding cost per batch:

0.10 × 12 × 1800 = Rs. 2,160

Where, Average inventory = 3,600 / 2 = 1,800 units

Illustration 11

Your factory buys and uses a component for production at Rs 10 per piece. Annual requirement is 2000 units. Carrying cost of inventory is 10 % p.a. and ordering cost is Rs.40 per order. The purchase manager argues that as the ordering cost is very high, it is advantageous to place a single order for the entire annual requirement. He also says that if we order 2000 units at a time, we can get a 2% discount from the supplier. Evaluate this proposal and make your recommendations.

Solution

(a) $$EOQ = \sqrt{2AO / (\text{cost per unit} \times \text{rate of carrying cost per unit})}$$

$$\sqrt{2 \times 2{,}000 \times 40 / (10 \times 10\ \%)}$$

$$\sqrt{1{,}60{,}000} = 400 \text{ units}$$

(b) Frequency of orders: 2,000/400 = 5 orders

	EOQ (400 units) Rs.	*Single Order (2,000 units) Rs.*
Cost of Material (2000 × 10)	20,000	20,000
(–) 2 % discount	—	400
	20,000	**19,600**
Ordering cost (Rs. 40 per order)	200	40
	20,200	**19,640**
Add Carrying Cost (10 % of inv)	200	980
Total Cost	**20,400**	**20,620**

Note: Carrying cost is calculated on average inventory, which is minimum stock plus 50% of ordered quantity.
Carrying Cost: 200 × 10% × 10 = Rs. 200
1000 × 10% × 10 = Rs. 1,000
1,000 – 2% of 1,000 for discount = Rs. 980

As the cost is high under single order, it is advisable to purchase EOQ.

Illustration 12

A firm obtains quantity discounts on its orders of materials as follows:

Price per ton	*Tons*
Rs. 6.00	Less than 250
Rs. 5.90	250 to less than 800
Rs. 5.80	800 to less than 2,000
Rs. 5.70	2,000 to less than 4,000
Rs. 5.60	4,000 and over

The annual demand for the materials is 4,000 tons. Stock holding costs are 20% of material cost p.a. The delivery cost per order is Rs. 6.00. You are required to calculate the best quantity to order.

Solution

	Quantity (units)			
	250 *Rs.*	*800* *Rs.*	*2,000* *Rs.*	*4,000* *Rs.*
Cost of Material	23,600	23,200	22,800	22,400
Order Cost @ Rs. 6 per order	96	30	12	6
Carrying Cost	147.50	464	1,140	2,240
Total Cost	23,843.50	23,694	23,952	24,646
Number of orders:	4,000/250 16	4,000/800 5	4,000/2,000 2	4,000/4,000 1

Material Cost: 250 × 5.90 × 16 = Rs. 23,600
800 × 5.80 × 5 = Rs. 23,200
2,000 × 5.70 × 2 = Rs. 22,800
4,000 × 5.60 × 1 = Rs. 22,400

Carrying cost is calculated on average inventory: Minimum Stock (0) + 50% of quantity ordered.

(0 + 125) = 125 × 5.9 × 20% = Rs. 147.50
(0 + 400) = 400 × 5.8 × 20% = Rs. 464
(0 + 1000) = 1,000 × 5.7 × 20% = Rs. 1,140
(0 + 2000) = 2,000 × 5.6 × 20% = Rs. 2,240

From the above, we can say that the best one is, 800 units as the cost for acquiring is low when compared to other quantities.

Always Better Control

It is a simple but effective technique of inventory control. The main purpose of this tool is to concentrate on the high value items rather than on all the items indiscriminately. All items of material are classified into three categories – high, medium and low value items and named as A, B and C items respectively. The 'A' items should be under the tightest control and it is the responsibility of the most experienced personnel. The 'B' items should be under the normal control procedures and the 'C' items should be under the simple and economical methods of control. This technique is based on the principle of 'management by exception'. It is also known as the Selective Method of Inventory Control. It aims at concentrating efforts on those items where attention is needed the most.

Under this method, the items are listed and ranked in the order of their descending importance (based on cost / value) showing quantity and value of each item.

Uses: The main uses of this technique are:

- This technique ensures closer and stricter control on those items, which represent larger amounts of capital invested.

- It helps in maintaining enough stock for 'C' category items.
- It assists in the maintenance of high stock turnover rate.
- It minimizes the ordering costs and carrying costs with proper economic order quantities.
- It regulates investment in inventory and thus releasing working capital, which can be utilized in the best possible way.

Illustration 13

The following is the information regarding the consumption and price per unit of different items of inventory. Classify the items as per ABC analysis.

Item No.	*Consumption units*	*Rate per unit Rs.*	*Total Value Rs.*
1	12,000	100	12,00,000
2	20,000	65	13,00,000
3	10,000	50	5,00,000
4	50,000	2	1,00,000
5	8,000	25	2,00,000
6	30,000	10	3,00,000
7	50,000	6	3,00,000
8	20,000	5	1,00,000
	2,00,000		**40,00,000**

Solution

ABC analysis requires the annual value of different items to be placed in the order of decreasing total value. First, rank the items in the order of the total value and then group them into A, B and C categories.

Rank	*Item No.*	*Annual Value Rs.*	*Annual Value Percentage*	*Units*	*Units Percentage*
(I)	2	13,00,000	32.5	20,000	10
(II)	1	12,00,000	30.0	12,000	6
(III)	3	5,00,000	12.5	10,000	5
			75		21 'A'
(IV)	7	3,00,000	7.5	50,000	25
(V)	6	3,00,000	7.5	30,000	15
(VI)	5	2,00,000	5.0	8,000	4
			20		44 'B'
(VII)	4	1,00,000	2.5	50,000	25
(VIII)	8	1,00,000	2.5	20,000	10
			5		35 'C'
		40,00,000		**2,00,000**	

Perpetual Inventory Control

According to ICMA, London, it is "a system of records maintained by the controlling department which reflects the physical movements of stock and their current balance".

According to Wheldon, it is "a method of recording stores balances after every receipt and issue, to facilitate regular checking and to obviate closing down for stocktaking".

Thus, the Perpetual Inventory System means, maintenance of stores records such as Bin Card and Stores Ledger. The objective the of Perpetual Inventory Control is to facilitate stocktaking. It includes continuous stocktaking.

A **Bin Card** is a card attached to the bin in which material is stored. The storekeeper records the quantity of material received and issued and strikes the balance after each receipt or issue. All those entries are supported by the documents such as goods received note, material returned note, stores requisition note etc.

BIN CARD

Description — — — — — — — —	Bin No. — — — — — — — —
Minimum Level — — — — — — — —	Code No. — — — — — — — —
Ordering Level — — — — — — — —	Unit — — — — — — — —
Order Quantity — — — — — — — —	Stores Ledger Folio — — — — — — — —

Receipts		*Issues*		*Balance*		*Stock Verification*	
Date	*Ref. No.*	*Quantity*	*Ref.No.*	*Quantity*	*Quantity*	*Date*	*Initials*

Stores Ledger is the chief accounting record for material. The Cost Accounting Department maintains it. It is like Bin Card in form except that it contains column for money values also. The entries in the receipts and issue columns are made from the same documents, which are used for posting in Bin Card. This ledger constitutes a check on the quantity shown in Bin Card.

STORES LEDGER

Name — — — —	Bin No. — — — —	Max. Level — — — —
Code No. — — — —	Location Code — — — —	Min. Level — — — —
Description — — — —	Unit of Quantity — — — —	Re-Order Quantity — — — —
Re-Order Level — — — —		

	Receipts				*Issues*				*Balance*		
Date	*GR No.*	*Qty.*	*Rate*	*Amt.*	*GR No.*	*Qty.*	*Rate*	*Amt.*	*Qty.*	*Rate*	*Amt.*

Under **Perpetual Inventory Control**, the balance of an item of store as shown in Bin Card should agree with that shown in Stores Ledger. Any difference between these two figures may be due to wrong posting or non-posting in either of the perpetual records or due to some arithmetic error in working out the balance. The book balance as shown by the records should agree with actual physical balances in store. This is ensured by continuous stocktaking where, physical verification of every item of stores is done by counting, weighing or measuring. Under this system, a few items of stores are counted daily or at frequent intervals and compared with the perpetual records by the stores auditors. If any difference, an enquiry is made and the difference is adjusted in the records to make them correspond with the physical count.

The main advantages of this technique are:

- Stock records are kept up to date, thus, enabling the preparation of interim financial statements.
- Internal check is done automatically as Stores Ledger is maintained in addition to Bin Card.
- Accurate and reliable inventory balance enables to make proper claim for insurance in case of accident.
- It avoids dislocation in production, which arises in the case of Periodic Stocktaking done at the end of each year.

Stock Turnover Ratios

Another tool for exercising control over inventory is the application of Ratio Analysis to inventory. Stock Turnover is the ratio of the value of material consumed during a period to the average stock of raw material during the period.

Stock Turnover Ratio = Cost of Raw Material Consumed/Average Stock of Raw Material

It is the indicator of the rate of consumption. A high ratio indicates fast moving material and the low ratio indicates slow moving stock. The turnover of different material may be compared to detect those items, which do not move regularly and avoid keeping capital locked up in such undesirable items of material.

Stock Turnover Ratio (STR) can also be calculated in terms of days.

STR in days = Days of the period / STR

If the length of the Stock Turnover Period is short, the material is said to be fast moving. STR is a good measure of the efficiency of the material utilization to detect and control slow and non-moving items. A standard material turnover rate should be computed for each item of material and the actual rate should be compared with the standard rate. If the actual rate is less than the standard, it implies that the actual rate of consumption of the item is less than the standard and the item is thus slow moving. Periodic reports on such material should be prepared and presented to the management for the control purpose.

Illustration 14

Calculate the Material Turnover Ratio for the year 2005 from the following details.

	Material X *Rs.*	*Material Y* *Rs.*
Opening Stock	12,500	43,750
Closing Stock	7,500	31,250
Purchases	95,000	62,500

Determine the fast moving stock.

Solution

$$\text{Material Turnover: } \frac{\text{Cost of raw material consumed}}{\text{Average stock of material}}$$

$$\text{Average Stock of material: } \frac{(\text{Opening stock of material} + \text{Closing stock of material})}{2}$$

$$\text{Material X: } \frac{(12{,}500 + 7{,}500)}{2} = \text{Rs. } 10{,}000$$

$$\text{Material Y: } \frac{(43{,}750 + 31{,}250)}{2} = \text{Rs. } 37{,}500$$

Cost of Raw Material Consumed: Opening Stock + Purchases – Closing Stock
Material X: 12,500 + 95,000 – 7,500 = Rs. 1,00,000
Material Y: 43,750 + 62,500 – 31,250 = Rs. 75,000
Material Turnover
Material X = 1,00,000 / 10,000 = 10 times
Material Y = 75,000 / 37,500 = 2 times
Material X is fast moving material.

Purchase Control

It is an element of Material Control. An efficient purchasing ensures the procurement of materials of the right quality, in the right quantity, at the right time, from the right source and at the right price. There should be a proper organization of the Purchase Department, which in turn depends upon the size of the concern and the management policy. Usually, the large size concerns have a separate Purchase Department headed by a specialist known as Purchase Manager. This Purchase Department takes the task of making all purchases of all types of materials required by the concern. This system is known as Centralized Purchasing. This system has the advantage of having a specialized and expert purchasing staff, better bargaining capacity and better control over purchasing since all records of purchasing transactions are at one place. But, this system leads to higher administration costs and delay in receiving and settling discrepancies.

As opposed to Centralized Purchasing, in case of Decentralized Purchasing, each branch or department makes its own purchases and thus enjoy the benefits of local purchases. Centralized Purchasing System is best suited if the concern is a multi plant concern having plants located far away from one another producing different products from different basic raw materials.

Purchase Procedure: Purchasing starts with the initiation of purchase requisition and ends with the receipt of materials and payment of bills for purchases. The following are the steps usually followed in purchasing and receiving of materials.

- **Purchase Requisition**: Though the purchase of material is the responsibility of the purchase manager, he acts on behalf of the others in the organization who require material. Purchase requisition may be received from the storekeeper when materials reach ordering level or from the production planner for special materials required for the manufacture of a new product or from the plant engineer for repairs and maintenance or from departmental heads for any material required for their departments. It is an internal document representing a formal instruction to the Purchase Manager for the purchase of the material requisitioned in the document. Generally, two copies of requisition are prepared. The original is sent to the Purchase Department and a copy is retained and filed by the requisitionist for future reference.

Purchase Requisition

Department	———————	Date of Requisition	———————
Requisition No.	———————	Date Required	———————

Item No.	*Code No.*	*Description*	*Quantity*	*Purpose*

For use of Purchase Department only			
Purchase Order No.	———————	Requisitioned by	———————
Supplier	———————	Approved by	———————
Date of Delivery	———————		

- **Purchase Order:** After receiving the requisition, the Purchase Manager should find out *(a)* convenient and economical sources of supply; *(b)* invite tenders; *(c)* prepare a comparative statement of tenders and *(d)* select the supplier.

After selecting the supplier, he has to prepare a purchase order. It is a formal document authorizing the supplier to supply the specified material at the price and terms stated there in. It is an important document both from the legal and accounting point of view. Large concerns generally prepare five copies. One copy is sent to the supplier, second one is sent to the Accounting Department and the last one to the Department requisitioning the material as an intimation of the order and expected date of receipt of material.

PURCHASE ORDER

Purchase Requisition No. — — — — — Supplier — — — — —	Quotation No. — — — — — Date — — — — —	Order No. — — — — —

Please supply the following items subject to the terms and conditions printed on the reverse.

Sl. No.	*Code No.*	*Description*	*Quantity*	*Rate*	*Value*

Date of delivery — — — — —
Place of delivery — — — — —
Terms of delivery — — — — —
Terms of payment — — — — —

Signature of the Purchase Manager

↳ **Receipt of Materials:** It is the responsibility of the Receiving Department to receive all the incoming materials after physically verifying the quantity and condition of the materials received.

In small concerns, the storekeeper does the function of both receiving and inspection. Whereas, in large concerns, there are two separate departments, one for Receiving and the other for Inspection.

The particulars of the goods received are entered in a Goods Received Note (GRN). A copy of this GRN is sent to the Purchase Department, to the Department originating the purchase requisition, Stores Department, Accounts Department and the last copy is retained by the Receiving Department for its own file.

Goods received are inspected for the quality to ensure that they comply with the specifications stated in the Purchase Order and the report is to be forwarded to the Purchase Department. In case of discrepancy, the goods are usually returned to the supplier along with a Debit Note informing him that his account is debited with the value of the material concerned. This note may be prepared by the Purchase Department on the basis of inspection report and a copy is sent to the supplier, second one is sent to the Accounts Department for adjustment and the third one is retained by the Purchase Department.

XYZ COMPANY LTD.
GOODS RECEIVED NOTE

Supplier — — — — Date of Delivery — — — —	Purchase Order No. — — — — Delivery Note No. — — — —	GRN No. — — — — Date — — — —

Item No.	*Code*	*Description*	*Quantity Ordered*	*Quantity Received*	*Quantity Rejected*	*Remarks*

Received by ________ Inspected by ________ Approved by ________

↳ **PAYMENT:** Invoice is a document on the basis of which payment is made. When the invoice is received by the Purchase Department, Purchase Manager has to compare it with the purchase order, GRN, inspection report if it is not incorporated in the GRN and debit note. If the invoice is found to be in order, then, he sends it to the Accounts Department for the payment after duly signing it. The Accounts Department checks up the calculations before a voucher authorizing payment is prepared. Then, all the connected documents like Purchase Order, GRN are marked with the invoice number to avoid the possibility of duplicate invoice.

XYZ COMPANY LTD.
DEBIT NOTE

To
The Supplier

No. — — — — — —
Date — — — — — —

We are debiting your account with the value of under mentioned material for the discrepancy.
We wait for your instructions.

Item No.	*Code*	*Description*	*Quantity*	*Rate*	*Amount*

Reasons: Date Received

Purchase Order No. — — — — — —
Suppliers Invoice No. — — — — — —

GRN No. — — — — — —
Signature:

Just in Time

Organisations, in the modern world, are functioning in the highly competitive environment. Therefore, they need to give increased attention to minimizing the costs. Hence, various methods and techniques are used by the cost accountants/entrepreneurs to minimize the costs.

Just-in-time (JIT) is a purchasing and inventory control method in which materials are obtained just in time for production to provide finished goods just in time for sale. Keeping in view the enormous carrying cost of inventory in stores and go down/ warehouses, manufacturers and merchandisers are switching on for more frequent deliveries with shorter purchase order lead times from their suppliers. They are giving increasing attention to reducing stock levels to a minimum through creating closer relationships with suppliers and arranging more frequent deliveries of smaller quantities. With JIT purchasing, the company and the supplier work together cooperatively. Suppliers are expected to guarantee the quality of the material they deliver and inspect it at source.

The official Terminology defines 'Just-in-Time' as a "system whose objective is to produce or to procure products or components as they are required by a customer or for use, rather than for stock. A Just–in–Time system is a 'pull' system, which responds to demand, in contrast to a 'push' system, in which stocks act as buffers between the different elements of the system, such as purchasing, production and sales".

The success achieved by the Japanese firms in international markets by implementing the JIT approach generated interest amongst many western companies in the system. The JIT approach involves a continuous commitment to the pursuit of excellence in all phases of manufacturing systems design and operations. The aim of the JIT is to produce the required items, at the required quality and in required quantities, at the precise time they are required. In particular, the goals of the JIT are to eliminate non – value added activities, to maintain zero inventory, zero break downs and zero defects, have a batch sizes of one and a 100 percent on-time delivery service.

(a) ***Elimination of non – value added activities:*** JIT manufacturing is best described as a philosophy of management dedicated to the elimination of waste, the lead or cycle time, inspection time, move time, queue time and storage time. Of these five steps, only process time actually adds value to the product. Within the JIT philosophy, all the other activities add cost but no value to the product and are thus deemed non-value-added processes. By adopting a JIT philosophy and focusing on reducing lead-time, it is claimed that total costs can be significantly reduced. The ultimate goal of JIT is to convert raw materials to finished products with lead times equal to processing time, thus eliminating all non-value-added activities.

(b) ***Zero Inventory:*** The JIT philosophy extends to adopting JIT purchasing techniques, whereby the delivery of material immediately precedes their use. By arranging with suppliers for more frequent deliveries, the cost of stocks will be minimum. Requiring suppliers to inspect materials before their delivery and guaranteeing their quality, a considerable savings in material handling expenses can be obtained. Giving more business to fewer

suppliers and placing long term purchasing orders can result in this improved service. Therefore, the supplier has an assurance of long-term sales and can plan to meet the demand.

(c) ***Zero break downs:*** A 100 per cent on-time delivery service is possible if and only if there are zero breakdowns, with a pull system problems arising in any part of the system will immediately halt the production line because work centres at the earlier stages will not receive the pull signal and later stages will not have their pull signal answered. Thus, attention is drawn immediately to production problems so that appropriate remedial action can be taken. This is deemed to be preferable to the approach adopted in a traditional manufacturing system where large stock levels provide a cushion for production to continue. This can lead to a situation where major problems can remain hidden or deferred indefinitely, rather than triggering a search for immediate long term solutions.

(d) ***Zero defects:*** The traditional manufacturing approach has been to maintain buffer stocks to avoid workers becoming idle when the preceding production process breakdown or the next item to be processed is defective. Larger quantities of stocks are therefore maintained to protect against shortages caused by poor quality production and machine breakdowns.

In a JIT environment, the emphasis is on preventive maintenance and 'doing the job right the first time', because a defective part or machine breakdown disrupts the flow of production when all processes are operating with a minimal level of inventory. A company operating in a JIT environment becomes very aware of the fact that quality reduces costs because of defects stopping the production line, thus creating re-work and possibly resulting in a failure to meet delivery dates. By adopting new quality awareness programs and implementing statistical process controls, many JIT firms have decreased defect rates, substantially reduced inventories and enhanced the attributes of their products.

(e) ***Batch sizes of one:*** Set-up time is the amount of time required to adjust equipment and to retool for a different product. Long set-up and change over times make the production of batches with a small number of units uneconomical. However, the production of large batches leads to substantial throughput delays and the creation of high inventory levels. Throughput delays arises because, several lengthy production runs are required to process larger batches through the factory. The JIT philosophy is to reduce and eventually eliminate set-up times. By investing in advanced manufacturing technologies, some machine settings can be adjusted automatically instead of manually. Alternatively, some set-up times can be eliminated entirely by redesigning products so that machines do not have to be reset each time a different product has to be made.

If set up times are approaching zero, this implies that there are no advantages in producing in batches. Therefore, the optimal batch size can be one, with a batch size of one; the work can flow smoothly to the next stage without the need for storage and to schedule the next machine to accept this item. Small batch sizes, combined with short throughput times, also enable a firm to adapt more readily to short term fluctuations in market demand, since production is not dependent on long term planning lead times.

(f) ***100 per cent on-time delivery service:*** JIT manufacturing aims to produce the right parts at the right time, only when they are needed and only in the quantity needed. This philosophy has resulted in a 'pull' manufacturing system, which means that parts move through the production system based on end unit demand, focussing on maintaining a constant flow of components than batches of WIP. With the pull system, work on components does not commence until specifically requested by the next process. JIT technique aims to keep the materials moving in a continuous flow with no stoppages and no storage. Thus, JIT philosophy believes in 100 per cent on-time delivery service.

Advantages of JIT

The following are the advantages of JIT system.

- Investment in inventory is reduced because more frequent purchase orders of small quantities are made.
- Carrying cost is reduced as a result of low investment in inventory.
- A reduction in the number of suppliers to be dealt with will result in the reduction of negotiated time and the long run contracts with suppliers will result in minimal paper work.
- Quality costs such as inspection cost of incoming materials or goods, scraps and rework costs are reduced because JIT purchasing assures quick and frequent deliveries of small size orders which results in a low level of inventories causing minimum possible wastage. Therefore, JIT purchasing is frequently applied by organizations dealing in perishable goods.
- JIT helps in reducing waste of time of the work force and the entire production process is concentrated on the time spent in actually producing the products.

Limitations of the JIT

It is considered that JIT is unsuitable in a non-repetitive manufacturing environment such as jobbing shop and small batch production where a wide range of products is produced and the manufacturing system is discontinuous.

The goals of the JIT represent perfection and are unlikely to be achieved in practice.

However, the JIT philosophy relating to the pursuit of excellence and the elimination of waste is applicable to all types of discrete parts manufacturing. Also, the goals offer targets and create a climate for continual improvement and excellence.

Just in Time Manufacturing and Management Accounting

Management Accountants in many organizations have been strongly criticized because of their failure to alter the management accounting system to reflect the move from a traditional manufacturing to a JIT manufacturing system. Conventional management accounting systems can encourage behavior that is inconsistent with a JIT manufacturing philosophy. Management Accounting must support JIT manufacturing by monitoring, identifying and communicating to the decision-makers regarding any delay, error and waste in the system. Modern Management Accounting Systems are now placing greater emphasis on providing information on supplier reliability, set-up times, through put cycle times, percentage of deliveries that are on time and defect rates. All these measures are critical for supporting a JIT manufacturing philosophy.

Material Issues: All materials received by the Stores Department are ultimately meant for the issue to the Production and Service Departments. Since the storekeeper is responsible for receiving and issuing of the material, he should issue only on proper authorization. Material control necessitates Issue Control.

Stores Requisition Note/Material Requisition Note

It is the chief document authorizing the issue of material. It is prepared in triplicate by the Head of the Department requiring the material and two copies are sent to the Stores Department, while the third one is retained by the Requisitioning Department. The store keeper issues the material based on this requisition note after taking the signature of the person receiving them and records in the Bin Card. He sends a copy to the Accounts Department for pricing the issues and making necessary entries in the Stores Ledger.

XYZ COMPANY LTD.

STORES REQUISITION NOTE

Dept. .... Requisition No. .... Date ....

Item No.	*Code*	*Description*	*Quantity*	*Cost Office*	
				Rate	*Amount*

Requisitioned by	....	Bin No.	....	Stores Ledger Folio	....
Issued by	....	Bin Card No.	....		
Received by	....				
Priced by	....				

Bill of Materials

It is a master requisition showing all the material needed for the completion of a job or a batch of production. It is prepared generally by the Engineering or Planning Department soon after an order for production is received. It is, generally used by the Departments having standard material requirements.

The main advantages of this document are:

- It saves time by eliminating the need for preparing separate Material Requisition Notes for various types of material required for the completion of a particular job.
- It is an advance intimation to the storekeeper of the material required.
- Costing of jobs becomes easier when it is sent to the Accounts Department.
- It is an authority to the Production Departments to issue material requisition to the Stores Department, thus reducing the clerical work.

BILL OF MATERIALS

Job No. .... Date ....

Dept. ....

Item No.	*Code*	*Description*	*Quantity*	*Cost Office*	
				Rate	*Amount*

Prepared by .... Date of Issue ....

Checked by .... Issued by ....

Store Keeper ....

RETURN OF MATERIALS

The material may be returned to the Stores Department when it is found to be in excess or defective. The material is returned along with two copies of Material Returned Note. This document is similar to that of Material Requisition Note but printed in a different color for easy identification. The Stores Department retains a copy of it to make necessary entries in the Bin Card and the materials are placed in the appropriate Bins. Second copy is sent to the Cost Office to give a credit to the Department or Job concerned.

XYZ COMPANY LTD.
STORES RETURNED NOTE

Dept. / Job .... No. ....

Dept. Returning .... Date ....

Item No.	*Code*	*Description*	*Quantity*	*Cost Office*	
				Rate	*Amount*

Bin No. .... Received by ....

Stores Ledger Folio .... Priced by ....

Authorized by ....

TRANSFER OF MATERIALS

When material is found to be in excess in a particular department, instead of returning to the Stores Department, it may be transferred to a job requiring such material. This should be done, by intimating the same to the storekeeper by means of a Material Transfer Note. If it is not intimated to the storekeeper, it will result in incorrect costs of the jobs concerned.

XYZ COMPANY LTD.
MATERIAL TRANSFER NOTE

Issuing Dept. .... No. ....
Receiving Dept. .... Date ....

Item No.	*Code*	*Description*	*Quantity*	*Cost Office*	
				Rate	*Amount*

Authorized by .... Received by ....
From Job No. .... To Job No. .... Costed by ....

Summary

It is the cost of material, which constitutes more than 50 per cent of the total cost of the product or job in several industries. Therefore, there should be a proper control over the material cost. In order to minimize the production costs, it is essential to constitute effective inventory management. For this purpose, it is necessary to design a proper system of purchasing, receiving, storing, issuing and recording of materials.

Inventory includes the stores of raw material, stock of finished goods, work-in-progress and other accessories. It constitutes the principal item in the working capital of the majority of trading and industrial concern. The various techniques to control inventory are Stock Levels, Economic Order Quantity, Always Better Control, Perpetual Inventory Control and Stock Turnover Ratios.

Most of the large companies fix up various stock levels to guard against under stocking and over stocking. The various levels are Maximum Level, Minimum Level, Re-Order Level, Average Stock Level and Danger Level.

Economic Order Quantity refers to that number of units, which should be ordered at one time so as to minimize the total cost of placing orders and cost of storing the goods as well as interest on the capital invested. It is the quantity, which is most economical to order.

Always Better Control is a simple but effective technique of inventory control. The main purpose of this tool is to concentrate on the high value items rather than on all the items indiscriminately for the purpose of control. All items of material are classified into three categories – high, medium and low value items and named as A, B and C items respectively.

Perpetual Inventory System means, maintenance of stores records such as Bin Card and Stores Ledger. The objective of Perpetual Inventory Control is to facilitate stocktaking. It includes continuous stocktaking. Under Perpetual Inventory Control, the balance of an item of store as shown in Bin Card should agree with that shown in Stores Ledger.

Stock Turnover Ratio is the indicator of the rate of consumption. A high ratio indicates fast moving material and a low ratio indicates slow moving stock. The turnover of different material may be compared to detect those items, which do not move regularly and avoid keeping capital locked up in such undesirable items of material.

An efficient purchasing ensures the procurement of materials of the right quality, in the right quantity, at the right time, from the right source and at the right price. There should be a proper organization of the Purchase Department, which in turn depends upon the size of the concern and the management policy.

Purchasing starts with the initiation of purchase requisition and ends with the receipt of materials and payment of bills for purchases. All materials received by the Stores Department are ultimately meant for the issue to the Production and Service Departments. Since the storekeeper is responsible for receiving and issuing of the material, he should issue only on proper authorization. Material Control necessitates Issue Control.

The material may be returned to the Stores Department when it is found to be in excess or defective. When material is found to be in excess in a particular department, instead of returning to the Stores Department, it may be transferred to a job requiring such material.

Glossary

- **Direct Materials** are those that which can be directly identified with each unit of the finished product.
- **Indirect Materials** are those materials, which do not normally form a part of the finished product.

- **Inventory** includes the stores of raw material, stock of finished goods, work-in-progress and other accessories.
- **Maximum Level** indicates the maximum quantity of the inventory items, which can be stored at any given point of time.
- **Minimum Level** is that level below which stock should not be allowed to fall. It indicates the minimum stock to be maintained so that there is no risk of stoppage of production.
- **Re-Order Level** is the level at which fresh order should be placed for replenishment of stock.
- **Average Stock Level** is the average of minimum and maximum level.
- **Danger Level** is generally below the minimum level. It indicates the urgent action needed for the replacement of stock so that production stoppage can be avoided.
- **Always Better Control** is a technique of inventory control under which, the items are listed and ranked in the order of their descending importance (based on cost/value) showing quantity and value of each item.
- **Perpetual Inventory Control** is a method of recording stores balances after every receipt and issue, to facilitate regular checking and to obviate closing down for stocktaking.
- **Bin Card** is a card attached to the bin in which material is stored.
- **Stock turnover** is the ratio of the value of material consumed during a period to the average stock of raw material during the period.
- **Purchase Requisition** is an internal document representing a formal instruction to the Purchase Manager for the purchase of the material requisitioned in the document.
- **Stores Requisition Note/Material Requisition Note** is the chief document authorizing the issue of material.
- **Just-in-Time** is a "system whose objective is to produce or to procure products or components as they are required by a customer or for use, rather than for stock. A Just–in–Time system is a `pull' system, which responds to demand, in contrast to a 'push' system, in which stocks act as buffers between the different elements of the system, such as purchasing, production and sales".
- **Bill of Materials** is a master requisition showing all the material needed for the completion of a job or a batch of production.

Questions

(1) What do you understand by Material Control? State its objectives.
(2) Explain and state the factors to be taken into consideration in deciding the following.
  (a) Minimum Level
  (b) Maximum level
  (c) Re-Order Level
(3) What do you understand by ABC Analysis? What are its advantages?
(4) What do you mean by EOQ? How it is calculated?
(5) Describe the procedure for purchasing the material.
(6) Distinguish between Bin Card and Stores Ledger.
(7) Explain briefly the various Inventory Control Techniques.
(8) Write short note on Just-in-Time inventory.
(9) Explain the objectives/goals of JIT.
(10) What is JIT Inventory System? Explain how it eliminates wastage of resources.
(11) Bring out the advantages and limitations of JIT.

PROBLEMS

(1) Calculate Re-Order Level and Re-Order Quantity from the following information.

Maximum Stock Level	8,000 units
Budgeted Consumption:	Maximum 1,200 units per month
	Minimum 80 units per month
Estimated delivery time	Maximum 4 months
	Minimum 3 months

[Ans: Re-Order Level: 4,800 units and Re-Order Quantity: 3,440 units]

Hint: first calculate Minimum Level (2,560 units) and obtain Re-Order Quantity by substituting the values in Maximum Level formula.

(2) A company uses raw material 'A' for a particular product for which the following information is available. Re-Order quantity is 10,000 kgs. and usage per unit of product is 10 kgs.

Delivery period in weeks:	Minimum 1
	Average 2
	Maximum 3

Weekly production varies from 175 to 225 units, averaging 200 units. You are required to calculate:

(a) Minimum Stock Level

(b) Maximum Stock Level

(c) Average Stock Level and

(d) Re-Ordering Level

[Ans: Re-Ordering Level: 6,750 kgs; Minimum Stock Level: 2,750 kgs.; Maximum Stock Level: 15,000 kgs. and Average Stock Level: 7,750 kgs.]

(3) Two materials X and Y are used as follows:

Minimum usage	100 units per each week
Maximum usage	300 units per each week
Normal usage	200 units per each week
Order quantity	X: 1200 units
	Y: 2000 units
Re-Order period	X: 4 to 6 weeks
	Y: 2 to 4 weeks

Calculate: (a) Minimum Level and *(b)* Maximum Level

[Ans.: X: *(a)* Minimum Level 800 units and *(b)* Maximum Level 2600 units
Y: *(a)* Minimum Level 600 units and *(b)* Maximum Level 3000 units]

Note: Re-Order Level X: 1,800 units and Y: 1,200 units.

(4) The particulars of material A are as follows.

Normal usage	10 units per week
Minimum usage	5 units per week
Maximum usage	15 units per week
Re-Order Quantity	60 units per week
Re-Order period	3 to 5 weeks

Calculate:

(a) Re-Order Level

(b) Maximum Stock Level

(c) Minimum Stock Level

(d) Average Stock Level

[Ans.: *(a)* Re-Order Level: 75 units *(b)*Maximum Stock Level: 120 units *(c)* Minimum Stock Level: 35 units and *(d)* Average Stock Level: 65 units]

(5) Compute Minimum and Maximum stock levels from:

Minimum consumption	200 units/day
Maximum consumption	300 units/day
Normal consumption	240 units/day
Re-Order period	10-15 days
Re-Order quantity	1,500 units
Normal Re-Order	12 days

[Ans. Minimum Stock Level: 1,620 units; Maximum Stock Level: 4,000 units]

(6) Two components X and Y are used as follows:

Normal usage	500 per week each
Minimum usage	250 units per week each
Maximum usage	750 units per week each
Re-Order quantity	X: 3000 units
	Y: 5,000 units
Re-Order period	X: 4 to 6 weeks
	Y: 2 to 4 weeks

Calculate for each component:

(a) Re-Order Level

(b) Maximum Stock Level

(c) Minimum Stock Level

(d) Average Stock Level

[Ans.: Re-Order Level: X 4,500 units Y: 3,000 units
Maximum Stock Level: X: 6,500 units Y: 7,500 units

Minimum Stock Level: X: 2,000 units Y: 1,500 units
Average Stock Level: X: 4,250 or 3,500 units Y: 4,500 or 4,000 units]

(7) Two components A and B are used as follows:

Re-Ordering quantity	A: 3,000 units
	B: 4,000 units
Re-Ordering Period	A: 4 to 6 weeks
	B: 2 to 4 weeks
Minimum usage	1,500 units per week each
Normal usage	3,000 units per week each
Maximum usage	4,500 units per week each

You are required to calculate for each of the components:

(a) Re-Order Level
(b) Maximum Stock Level
(c) Minimum Stock Level
(d) Average Stock Level

[Ans.: Re-Order Level: A: 27,000 units B: 18,000 units
Maximum Stock Level: A: 24,000 units B: 19,000 units
Minimum Stock Level: A: 12,000 units B: 9,000 units
Average Stock Level: A: 13,500 or 18,000 units B: 11,000 or 18,000 units]

(8) A company is purchasing 2,000 units of an item per annum at a cost of Rs. 20 per unit. Given ordering cost Rs. 50 and carrying cost 25 %, find out the EOQ.
[Ans.: EOQ: 200 units]

(9) From the following figures, calculate the EOQ.

Annual consumption	4000 kgs.
Cost of placing one order	Rs. 5
Cost per unit	Rs.2 per kg.
Storage and carrying cost	8 % of average inventory

[Ans.: EOQ: 500 kgs.]

(10) A manufacturer buys certain essential spares from outside suppliers at Rs. 40 per set. Total annual requirements are 45,000 sets. The annual cost of investment in inventory is 10% and costs like rent, stationery, insurance, taxes etc. per unit per year work to Re. 1. Cost of placing an order is Rs. 5. Calculate the Economic Order Quantity.
[Ans. EOQ: 2121.32units]

(11) After inviting tenders, two quotations are received as follows:

Supplier A – Rs. 2.20 per unit

Supplier B – Rs. 2.10 per unit plus Rs.2.10 per unit plus Rs. 2,000 fixed charges irrespective of units ordered.

Calculate the order quantity for which the purchase price per unit will be the same. Considering all factors regarding production requirements and availability of finance, the purchase officer wants to place an order for 15,000 units, which supplier should be selected?

[Ans.: Indifference point: 20,000 units; supplier 'A' should be selected]

(12) From the following details, draw a plan of ABC Selective Control.

Item	*Units*	*Unit Cost Rs.*
1	14,000	5.00
2	48,000	3.00
3	3,000	10.00
4	1,200	12.00
5	76,000	2.00
6	40,000	5.00
7	60,000	4.00
8	3,000	6.00
9	1,000	8.00
10	29,999	0.40
11	12,000	7.10
12	4,100	6.20

(13) A firm has 5 different items in its inventory. The relative details are given below. Suggest a breakdown of the items into A, B and C classification.

Item	*Units*	*Unit Cost Rs.*
1	20,000	60.00
2	10,000	100.00
3	32,000	11.00
4	28,000	10.00
5	60,000	3.40

[Ans.: Items 1 and 2 in 'A' Category; items 3 and 4 in 'B' Category; item 5 in 'C' Category]

(14) Draw a plan to classify the items into A, B and C categories.

Item	*Units*	*Unit Cost Rs.*
1	4	40
2	400	5
3	60	1000
4	40	20
5	8	20
6	32	2000
7	48	50
8	10	40
9	200	8
10	500	4
11	240	8
12	280	7
13	20	10
14	40	10
15	400	5

[Ans.: Items 6 and 3 in 'A' Category; items 7,2,10,15,11,12 and 9 in 'B' Category; items 1,4,5,8,13 and 14 in 'C' Category]

(15) From the following data, calculate inventory turnover ratio.
Stock on 1st January Rs. 36,000
Stock on 31st December Rs. 20,000
Purchases during the year Rs. 1,52,000
[Ans.: Inventory turnover ratio: 6 times]

(16) Calculate inventory turnover from the following information.
Maximum stock level 10,000 kgs.
Minimum stock level 4,000 kgs.
Issues during the year 24,000 kgs.
[Ans.: Stock turnover ratio: 3.4 times]

Hint: Average Stock = (Maximum Level + Minimum Level)/2

(17) Minimum stock level 4,000 units
Re-Order quantity 6,000 units
Maximum stock level 12,000 units
Issues 24,000 units
Calculate inventory turnover.
[Ans.: Inventory Turnover: 3.43 times]

Hint: Average stock= Minimum Level + ½ of Re-Order Quantity

❑❑❑

6

PRICING OF MATERIAL ISSUES

Objectives

The objectives of the study are to:

- Learn the methods for pricing the material issues
- Know the conditions to be satisfied before selecting a method of material issues
- Understand the situations under which a particular method is more suitable

INTRODUCTION

The purchase of materials is in anticipation of their use and issue to production. If the material is purchased for a specific job, then, there is no problem as the purchase cost can be debited to the job. In such a case, there will not be any difference between the rate at which the materials are purchased and issued.

Quite often, the materials are purchased from the market and they are put into stock with the existing quantity of material thereby losing their identity. The stock of any item of material may consist of consignments procured at different timings and at different rates. As and when material requisitions are received, these materials are issued from the stores to the different jobs or work orders. Now, the question arises as to at which price, jobs or work orders should be charged for the raw material issued. In preparing cost statements, several methods of pricing the material issued may be used, the choice largely depending on the nature of the material and the particular conditions in the business. The principal methods of issuing materials may be classified into the following.

METHODS OF PRICING ISSUES

Methods of Pricing Issues

ACTUAL COST METHODS

(1) First In, First Out (FIFO)
(2) Last In, Last Out (LIFO)
(3) Highest In, First Out (HIFO)
(4) Next In, First Out (NIFO)
(5) Specific Price Method
(6) Base Stock Method

AVERAGE COST METHODS

(1) Simple Average Method Method
(2) Weighted Average Method Method

NOTIONAL PRICE METHODS

(1) Standard Price Method
(2) Market Price Method
(3) Inflated Price Method

CONDITIONS FOR SELECTING A METHOD

While selecting a method, the following conditions should be satisfied.

- The method should be simple, effective and realistic
- The issue price should fully recover the cost price of the materials
- The issue price must be close to the market price
- It is necessary to consider the effect of the method on the production cost and inventory valuation.

ACTUAL COST METHODS

FIFO Method

Here, it is assumed that the material received first in the stores are issued first and as such the material in stock are the material purchased in the last. However, it does not mean that the physical issue of the stock is actually in the order of FIFO. This method uses the price of the first batch of material purchased for all issues until that batch of materials are fully issued. Later, the materials are issued at the next purchase price and so on. Thus, the materials are issued at the oldest price listed in the Stores Ledger.

Suitability: This method is most suitable in times of falling prices as the material issues to the jobs will be at high price (material issued from the earliest consignments which were purchased at a higher rate) and the material in hand are valued at the price of the latest purchases. This method produces lower profits and results in lower taxes as the cost of goods sold will be higher. In case of inflation, this method is not suitable as the issue price of materials in production will be low while the cost of replacement of materials will be high.

Advantages: The main advantages of this method are:

- Materials are issued in the order of their receipt.
- Valuation of closing stock is at the current market price.
- The method recovers the cost price of the material as the materials are issued at the purchase price and there is no unrealized profit or loss.
- The method is simple to understand and easy to operate.

Disadvantages: The main disadvantages are:

- The cost of production does not reflect the current economic value.
- In case of rising prices, the issue price does not reflect the market price.
- The cost of two jobs of a company will be different, as similar jobs may be charged with material at different prices.

Illustration 1

The "Received" side of the stores ledger accounts shows the following particulars:

Jan 1 Opening Balance: 500 units @ Rs. 4
Jan 5 Received from vendor: 200 units @ Rs. 4.25
Jan 12 Received from vendor: 150 units @ Rs. 4.10
Jan 20 Received from vendor: 300 units @ Rs. 4.50
Jan 25 Received from vendor: 400 units @ Rs. 4

Issues of materials were as follows:

Jan 4 – 200 units; Jan10 – 400 units;
Jan 15 – 100 units; Jan19 – 100 units;
Jan 26 – 200 units; Jan30 – 200 units.

Issues are to be priced on the principle of "First in first out".

Write out the stores ledger account in respect of the materials for the month of January.

Solution

Stores Ledger Account

Date	*Receipts*			*Issues*			*Balance*		
	Quantity	*Unit cost Rs.*	*Total cost Rs.*	*Quantity*	*Unit cost Rs.*	*Total cost Rs.*	*Quantity*	*Unit cost Rs.*	*Total cost Rs.*
Jan 1	—	—	—	—	—	—	500	4	2,000
Jan 4	—	—	—	200	4	800	300	4	1,200
Jan 5	200	4.25	850	—	—	—	300 200	4 4.25	1,200 850
Jan 10	—	—	—	300 100	4 4.25	1,200 425	100	4.25	425
Jan 12	150	4.10	615	—	—	—	100 150	4.25 4.10	425 615
Jan 15	—	—	—	100	4.25	425	150	4.10	615
Jan 19	—	—	—	100	4.10	410	50	4.10	205
Jan 20	300	4.50	1,350	—	—	—	50 300	4.10 4.50	205 1,350
Jan 25	400	4.00	1,600	—	—	—	50 300 400	4.10 4.50 4.00	205 1,350 1,600
Jan 26	—	—	—	50 150	4.10 4.50	205 675	150 400	4.50 4.00	675 1,600
Jan 30	—	—	—	150 50	4.50 4.00	675 200	350	4.00	1,400

Illustration 2

The following is an extract of the record of receipts and issues of sulphur in a chemical factory during Feb 1999.

Feb 1. Opening Balance 500 tonnes @ Rs.200
Feb 3. Issue: 70 tonnes
Feb 4. Issue: 100 tonnes
Feb 8. Issue: 80 tonnes
Feb 13. Received from supplier 200 tonnes @ Rs.190.
Feb 14. Returned from department 15 tonnes
Feb 16. Issue: 180 tonnes

Feb 20. Received from supplier 240 tonnes @ Rs.190
Feb 24. Issue:300 tonnes
Feb 25. Received from supplier 320 tonnes @ Rs 190
Feb 26. Issue: 115 tonnes
Feb 27. Returned from department 35 tonnes
Feb 28. Received from supplier 200 tonnes @ Rs.190

Issues are to be priced on the principle of "First in first out". The stock verifier of the factory had found shortage of 10 tonnes on the 22nd and left a note accordingly.. Draw up priced Stores Ledger Card for material showing the above transactions.

Solution

Stores Ledger Card

Date	*Receipts*			*Issues*			*Balance*		
	Quantity	*Unit cost Rs.*	*Total cost Rs.*	*Quantity*	*Unit cost Rs.*	*Total cost Rs.*	*Quantity*	*Unit cost Rs.*	*Total cost Rs.*
Feb 1	—	—	—	—	—	—	500	200	1,00,000
Feb 3				70	200	14,000	430	200	86,000
Feb 4				100	200	20,000	330	200	66,000
Feb 8				80	200	16,000	250	200	50,000
Feb 13	200	190	38,000				250 200	200 190	50,000 38,000
Feb 14	15 (Material returned)	200	3,000				250 200 15	200 190 200	50,000 38,000 3,000
Feb 16				180	200	36,000	70 200 15	200 190 200	14,000 38,000 3,000
Feb 20	240	190	45,600				70 200 15 240	200 190 200 190	14,000 38,000 3,000 45,600
Feb 22				10	200	2.000	60 200 15 240	200 190 200 190	12,000 38,000 3,000 45,600
Feb 24				60 200 15 25	200 190 200 190	12,000 38,000 3,000 4,750	215	190	40,850
Feb 25	320	190	60,800				535	190	1,01,650
Feb 26				115	190	21,850	420	190	79,800
Feb 27	35 (returns)	190	6,650				455	190	86,450
Feb 28	200	190	38,000				655 (455 + 200)	190	1,24,450

Illustration 3

C Ltd. maintains stores ledger on the basis of FIFO. The following are the transaction relating to purchase of raw slate pieces from a state query and issues to the Production Department.

Jan 7, '96 Purchased 20,000 pieces @ Rs. 100 per 100 pieces
Feb 9 Issued 18,000 pieces
Apr 11 Purchased 40,000 pieces @ Rs. 110 per 100 pieces
May 13 Issued 40,683 pieces
Jul 15 Purchased 50,000 pieces @ Rs. 120 per 100 pieces

Aug 17 Issued 36,141 pieces
Oct 19 Purchased 60,000 pieces @ 130 per 100 pieces
Nov 21 Issued 50,000 pieces

On 1st Jan., 1996, the Firm had stock of 5,000 pieces @ Rs. 95 per 100 pieces. It has been decided by the firm to credit provision for normal damage at 1% on the balance of each quarter . There has been actual damage of 300 pieces at the end of December 1996. Draw up a Stores Ledger Account.

Solution

Stores Ledger A/c

Date	*Receipts*			*Issues*			*Balance*		
	Quantity	*Unit cost Rs.*	*Total cost Rs.*	*Quantity*	*Unit cost Rs.*	*Total cost Rs.*	*Quantity*	*Unit cost Rs.*	*Total cost Rs.*
Jan 1	—	—	—	—	—	—	5,000	0.95	4,750
Jan 7	20,000	1	20,000				5,000 20,000	0.95 1	4,750 20,000
Feb 9				5,000 13,000	0.95 1	4,750 13,000	7,000	1	7,000
Mar 31				70	1	70	6,930	1	6,930
Apr 11	40,000	1.1	44,000				6,930 40,000	1 1.1	6,930 44,000
May 13				6,930 33,753	1 1.1	6,930 37,128.3	6,247	1.1	6,871.7
Jun 30				62	1.1	68.2	6,185	1.1	6,803.5
Jul 15	50,000	1.2	60,000				6,185 50,000	1.1 1.2	6,803.5 60,000
Aug 17				6,185 29,956	1.1 1.2	6,803.5 35,947.2	20,044	1.2	24,052.8
Sep 30				200	1.2	240	19,844	1.2	23,812.8
Oct 19	60,000	1.3	78,000				19,844 60,000	1.2 1.3	23,812.8 78,000
Nov 21				19,844 30,156	1.2 1.3	23,812.8 39,202.8	29,844	1.3	38,797.2
Dec 31				298	1.3	387.4	29,546	1.3	38,409.8

LIFO Method

Here, the material issues are priced under the assumption that the last item materials purchased up to the date of issue is the first to be issued. As such, the inventory valuation is done at the oldest prices of the material purchased and is completely out of the line with current prices.

Suitability: This method is suitable in case of rising prices as the material will be issued for production form the latest consignment, which is closely related to current price levels.

Advantages: The main advantages are:

- Material issues are based on the actual cost; therefore, no artificial profit or loss will result by following this method.
- As the material issues are from the latest consignment, production is charged at the recent prices as far as possible.
- It is simple to operate particularly during periods of steady prices.
- In case of rising prices, this method is suitable as the materials are issued at current market prices which are high, thereby, showing a lower profit compared to FIFO Method, reducing the burden of income tax.

Disadvantages: The main disadvantages are:

- The valuation of closing stock does not reflect the current market prices as such the stock will be understated or overstated in the Balance Sheet.
- When the prices are subject to frequent fluctuations, lots of calculations are involved.
- Like in FIFO method, cost comparison of jobs will be difficult as the material cost of the similar jobs may differ because of issues being made at different prices.

Illustration 4

From illustration 1, prepare a Stores Ledger under LIFO method.

Stores Ledger

Date	*Receipts*			*Issues*			*Balance*		
	Quantity	*Unit cost Rs.*	*Total cost Rs.*	*Quantity*	*Unit cost Rs.*	*Total cost Rs.*	*Quantity*	*Unit cost Rs.*	*Total cost Rs.*
Jan 1	—	—	—	—	—	—	500	4.00	2,000
Jan 4				200	4.00	800	300	4.00	1,200
Jan 5	200	4.25	850				300 200	4.00 4.25	1,200 850
Jan 10				200 200	4.25 4.00	850 800	100	4.00	400
Jan 12	150	4.10	615				100 150	4.00 4.10	400 615
Jan 15				100	4.10	410	100 50	4.00 4.10	400 205
Jan 19				50 50	4.10 4.00	205 200	50	4.00	200
Jan 20	300	4.50	1,350				50 300	4.00 4.50	200 1,350
Jan 25	400	4.00	1,600				50 300 400	4.00 4.50 4.00	200 1,350 1,600
Jan 26				200	4.00	800	50 300 200	4.00 4.50 4.00	200 1,350 800
Jan 30				200	4.00	800	50 300	4.00 4.50	200 1,350

Illustration 5

The following information is provided by Sunrise Co. for fortnight of April 1988 for Material EXE:

Stock on 1-4-88 *Purchased:*	*100 units @Rs. 5 per unit*	*Issued:*	
5.4.88 8.4.88 12.4.88	300 units @ Rs 6 500 units @ Rs 7 600 units @ Rs 8	6.4.88 10.4.88 14.4.88	250 units 400 units 500 units

Calculate: using LIFO and FIFO method:

(a) *(i)* the value of materials consumed during the period
(ii) the value of stock of materials on 15-4-88

(*b*) Explain why the figures in (*i*) and (*ii*) in part (*a*) of this question are different under the two methods of pricing of material issue used. You need not draw up the stores ledger.

(CA, Inter, May, 1989)

Solution

Value of Material EXE consumed
During 1.4.1988 to 15.4.1988 (FIFO Method)

Date	*Description*	*Qty.units*	*Rate (Rs.)*	*Amount (Rs.)*
1.4.88	Opening Balance	100	5	500
5.4.88	Purchased	300	6	1,800
6.4.88	Issued	100	5	500
		150	6	900
8.4.88	Purchased	500	7	3,500
10.4.88	Issued	150	6	900
		250	7	1,750
12.4.88	Purchased	600	8	4,800
12.4.88	Issued	250	7	1,750
		250	8	2,000
15.4.88	Balance	350	8	2,800

Total value of Material EXE consumed during the period under FIFO method comes to Rs.7800 (i.e. Rs.1400+ Rs.2650+ Rs.3750) and the balance of stock on 15-4-88 is of Rs 2800.

Value of Material Exe Consumed (LIFO Method)

Date	*Description*	*Qty.units*	*Rate(Rs.)*	*Amount (Rs.)*
1.4.88	Opening Balance	100	5	500
5.4.88	Purchased	300	6	1,800
6.4.88	Issued	250	6	1,500
8.4.88	Purchased	500	7	3,500
10.4.88	Issued	400	7	2,800
12.4.88	Purchased	600	8	4,800
12.4.88	Issued	500	8	4,000
15.4.88	Balance	350		2,300

Total value of Material EXE consumed during the period under LIFO method comes to Rs. 8,300 (i.e. Rs. 1,500 + Rs. 2,800 + Rs. 4,000) and the balance of stock on 15-4-88 is of Rs 2,300. (100 @ Rs. 5; 50 @ Rs 6; 100 @ Rs. 7 and 100 @ Rs. 8)

The reasons for the difference of Rs. 500 (8,300 – 7,800) is due to different purchase prices paid by the organization on different days of purchase.

HIFO Method

This method is based on the assumption that stock of material should be always priced at the lowest possible price. Therefore, the materials are charged to the jobs at the highest price paid for the materials irrespective of the date of purchase.

Suitability: Under the fluctuating prices, this method is very much suitable as the cost of heavily priced material is recovered from the production at the earliest. This method is rarely found in actual use.

NIFO Method

Here, an attempt is made to value material issues at an actual price, which is as near as possible to the market price. The issues are priced at the price of material, which has been ordered but not yet received. It is a forward-looking method in the sense that issues price reflects current market conditions. This method has also not achieved popularity so far.

Specific Price Method

This method is used where Job Costing Method is in operation and the actual material issued can be identified. Here, materials are purchased and set aside for a particular job or work order. In such a case, the job is charged with the specific price paid for the material.

Base Stock Method

This method is based on the assumption that each concern will always maintain a minimum quantity of material in stock known as 'Safety or Base Stock' and will be used only under an emergency situation. Base Stock is created from the first lot of material purchased and as such it is always valued at the cost price of the first lot. Therefore, the value of inventory is unrealistic because, it does not reflect the current market price. The quantity in excess of the base stock is valued according to one of the other methods such as FIFO, LIFO or Average Price Method.

Illustration 6

The stock of material A as on 1st June, 1998 is 500 units @ Re. 1 per unit. Following purchases and issues of this item were made subsequently:

	Receipts Units	*Rate p.u. Rs.*	*Issues Units*
June 6			200
June 10	400	1.10	
June 15	300	1.20	
June 20			500
June 21			200
June 24	500	1.30	
June 25			300
June 28			300

Prepare a Store Ledger Account showing how the value of the above issues should be arrived at under the Base Stock Method when it operates in conjunction with LIFO. Base stock is 200 units.

Solution:

'A' Stores A/C
(when Base Stock Method operates in conjunction with LIFO)

Date	*Receipts*			*Issues*			*Balance*		
	Quantity	*Unit cost Rs.*	*Total cost Rs.*	*Quantity*	*Unit cost Rs.*	*Total cost Rs.*	*Quantity*	*Unit cost Rs.*	*Total cost Rs.*
June 1	—	—	—	—	—	—	500	1.00	500
June 6				200	1.00	200	300	1.00	300
June 10	400	1.10	440				300 400	1.00 1.10	300 440
June 15	300	1.20	360				300 400 300	1.00 1.10 1.20	300 440 360
June 20				300 200	1.20 1.10	360 220	300 200	1.00 1.10	300 220
June 21				200	1.10	220	300	1.00	300
June 24	500	1.30	650				300 500	1.00 1.30	300 650
June 25				300	1.30	390	300 200	1.00 1.30	300 260
June 28				200 100	1.30 1.00	260 100	200	1.00	200

Average Cost Methods

The Average Method is based on the principle that all of the material in store is so mixed up that an issue cannot be made from any particular lot of purchases. Therefore, it is proper to issue material at the average cost. Here, the material loses its specific identity. Basically, the average prices are of two types, which are discussed below.

Simple Average Method

Here, the material are issued at a price which is calculated by dividing the total of the prices of the material in stock, from which the material to be priced could be drawn, by the number of prices used in that total on the date of the issue. Here, the quantity of different lots is ignored.

Suitability: This method is suitable when the prices of purchases do not show wide fluctuations. It is simple to operate as it takes into account only the prices of the materials.

The disadvantage of this method is that the issue does not reflect the actual cost price and clerical work is more as the average price will have to be calculated each time an issue is made.

Weighted Average Price Method

Here, the issues are made at a price, which is calculated by dividing the total cost of the material in the stock by the number of units in hand. Thus, both the price and quantity of material in store are taken into account. In periods of heavy fluctuations in the prices of material, this method gives better results as it tends to smooth out fluctuations in prices, by averaging the prices of various lots in stock.

This method involves a lot of clerical work as it requires computation of an issue price each time a consignment of material is received and the material cost also does not represent the actual cost price.

Illustration 7

A Company started on 1st Jan 2004, purchased raw materials during 2004 as stated below:

Jan 2	800 kg @ Rs. 62/kg
Feb 26	1200 kg @ Rs. 57/kg
Apr 13	2500 kg @ Rs. 59/kg
Jul 10	3000 kg @ Rs. 56/kg
Sept 18	1500 kg @ Rs. 60/kg
Nov 29	1000 kg @ Rs. 65/kg

While preparing its final account on 31st Dec. 2004, the company had 1200 kg of raw materials in its go down . Calculate the value of closing stock of raw materials according to

(a) First in first out basis

(b) Last in first out basis and

(c) Weighted average basis.

Solution

Valuation of Closing Stock

***(a)* First in first out basis**:

Raw material in hand is 1200 kg. It should be valued @ of last two consignments. The value of closing stock will be :

		Rs.
200 kg	@ 60 /kg	12,000
1000kg	@ 65 /kg	65,000
1200kg		77,000

***(b)* Last in first out basis :**

Raw material in hand is 1200 kg. It should be valued @ of first two consignments. So the value of closing stock will be :

		Rs.
800 kg	@ 62 /kg	49,600
400 kg	@ 57 /kg	22,800
1200 kg		72,400

(c) Weighted Average basis:

Date (2004)	*Price Rs.*	*Qty.*	*Value Rs.*
Jan 2	62	800	49,600
Feb 26	57	1200	68,400
Apr 13	59	2500	1,47,500
Jul 10	56	3000	1,68,000
Sept 18	60	1500	90,000
Nov 29	65	1000	65,000
		10000	5,88,500

Weighted Avg. price = 5,88,500/10,000 = Rs. 58.85
Value of Closing stock = 1,200 × 58.85 = Rs. 70,620

Illustration 8

April 2004
1. Opening Balance 50 tonnes @ Rs 10 a tonne
3. Issued 30 tonnes
4. Received 60 tonnes @ Rs.10.125
5. Issued 25 tonnes (Stock verification reveals a normal loss of one tonne)
6. Received back from complete work order 10 tonnes (Previously issued @ Rs. 10.00 a tonne)
7. Issued 20 tonnes

Assume that the issues of materials are priced on the 'Weighted Average method'.

Calculate the price of 3, 5 and 7th Apr. 2004.

Note: First record loss and then issue if both are on the same day. The cost of normal loss will be borne by good units produced. Therefore, only quantity is reduced.

Solution

Weighted Avg. basis
Stores Ledger

Date	*Receipts*			*Issues*			*Balance*		
2004	*Quantity*	*Unit cost Rs.*	*Total cost Rs.*	*Quantity*	*Unit cost Rs.*	*Total cost Rs.*	*Quantity*	*Unit cost Rs.*	*Total cost Rs.*
Apr 1	—	—	—	—	—	—	50	10	500
Apr 3				30	10	300	20	10	200
Apr 4	60	10.125	607.5				79 (80-1)	10.22	807.5
Apr 5				25	10.22	255.5	54	10.22	552
Apr 6	10	10	100				64	10.19	652
Apr 7				20	10.19	203.8	44	10.19	448.2

Illustration 9

From the following information, prepare a Stores Ledger under (a) Simple Average Method and (b) Weighted Average Method.

Date	*Units*	*Price (Rs.)*
Receipts :		
2.3.99	200	2.00
10.3.99	300	2.40
18.3.99	250	2.60
Issues :		
15.3.99	250	
20.3.99	300	

Solution

***(a)* Simple Average Method :**

Date	*Receipts*			*Issues*			*Balance*		
1999	*Quantity*	*Unit cost Rs.*	*Total cost Rs.*	*Quantity*	*Unit cost Rs.*	*Total cost Rs.*	*Quantity*	*Unit cost Rs.*	*Total cost Rs.*
Mar 2	200	2.00	400	—	—	—	200		400
Mar 10	300	2.40	720				500		1,120
Mar 15				250	2.20	550	250		570
Mar 18	250	2.60	650				500		1,220
Mar 20				300	2.50	750	200		470

March 15th :Issue price: (2 + 2.40)/2 = Rs. 2.20

March 20 th Issue price: (2.40 + 2.60)/2 = Rs. 2.50

***(b)* Weighted Average Method:**

Date	*Receipts*			*Issues*			*Balance*		
1999	*Quantity*	*Unit cost Rs.*	*Total cost Rs.*	*Quantity*	*Unit cost Rs.*	*Total cost Rs.*	*Quantity*	*Unit cost Rs.*	*Total cost Rs.*
Mar 2	200	2.00	400	—	—	—	200	2.00	400
Mar 10	300	2.40	720				500	2.24	1,120
Mar 15				250	2.24	560	250	2.24	560
Mar 18	250	2.60	650				500	2.42	1,210
Mar 20				300	2.42	726	200	2.42	484

Illustration 10

The Stock ledger account for Material X in a manufacturing concern reveals the following data for the quarter ended september 30, 1989:

	Receipts		*Issue*	
	Quantity	*Price (Rs.)*	*Quantity*	*Price (Rs.)*
July 1 Opening Balance	1,600	2.0		
July 9	3,000	2.2		
July 13			1,200	2,556
August 5			900	1,917
August 17	3,600	2.4		
August 24			1,800	4,122
September 11	2,500	2.5		
September 27			2,100	4,971
September 29			700	1,656

Physical verification on September 30, 1989 revealed an actual stock of 3800 units. You are required to:

(a) Indicate the method of pricing employed in the above.

(b) Complete the above account by making entries you would consider necessary including adjustments, if any, and giving explanations for such adjustments.

Solution

(a) The verification of the value of issues applied in the problem shows that Weighted Average method of pricing has been followed.

(b) The complete Stores Ledger Account giving the transactions as stated in the problem together with the necessary adjustments is given below:

Stores Ledger Account (Weighted Avg. Method)

Date	*Receipts*			*Issues*			*Balance*		
	Quantity	*Rate (Rs.)*	*Amount (Rs.)*	*Quantity*	*Rate (Rs.)*	*Amount (Rs.)*	*Quantity*	*Rate (Rs.)*	*Amount (Rs.)*
1-July							1,600	2.00	3,200
9-July	3,000	2.2	6,600				4,600	2.13	9,800
13-July				1200	2.13	2,556	3,400	2.13	7,244
5-Aug.				900	2.13	1,917	2,500	2.13	5,327
17-Aug.	3,600	2.4	8,640				6,100	2.29	13,967
24-Aug.				1800	2.29	4,122	4,300	2.29	9,845
11-Sep.	2,500	2.5	6,250				6,800	2.37	16,095
27-Sep				2100	2.37	4,977	4,700	2.37	11,118
29-Sep.				700	2.37	1,659	4,000	2.37	9,459
30-Sep.				*200	2.37	474	3,800	2.37	8,985

Closing stock 3,800 units @ Rs 2.37 = Rs 8,985 (Rs. 2.365 approximated to Rs. 2.37)

*Shortage of 200 units has been charged at the weighted average price of Rs 2.37 per unit.

NOTIONAL PRICE METHODS

Here, instead of issuing the material at actual prices incurred while purchasing the material, notional, i.e., estimated prices are used for pricing issues.

Standard Price Method

It is a pre determined price and both receipts and issues would be valued at this price. It represents neither cost price nor the market price. The difference between the cost price of the material purchased and the standard price is charged to 'Purchase Price Variance Account'. The standard price is determined for a definite period based on the probable trend of prices, market conditions and discounts, etc.

Advantages: The main advantages of this method are:

- The method is easy to operate, as this method does not involve the fixation of the prices for issues frequently.
- It facilitates cost comparison among different jobs.
- The efficiency in purchasing is reflected by comparison of actual prices with standard prices.

Disadvantages: The main disadvantages are:

- It is difficult to fix the standard price when there are large fluctuations in the market prices of materials.
- Standard price does not reflect the actual cost thus giving rise to unrealized profit or loss.

Market Price Method/Replacement Price Method

Under this method, materials are issued at a price at which they can be replaced without any consideration to the cost of materials purchased. This method is best suited where quotations have to be sent reflecting the latest competitive conditions so far as material are concerned.

Disadvantages: The main points of disadvantages are :

- this method gives rise to unrealized profit or loss as the material issues are not based on costs.
- it is difficult to obtain market price.
- product costs vary according to the variations in the market prices.

Inflated Price Method: It is not a method of valuing issues, but only an accounting procedure to adjust the loss of material due to evaporation, depletion, normal wastage, etc. The issue price is slightly inflated in order to cover such losses and to recover the full cost.

PRICING OF MATERIAL RETURNED TO STORES

Sometimes the material issued for production, may be returned to stores, when the material is found to be in excess. In such a case, the material returned may be valued at the same price at which they were issued and recorded in the stores accordingly. Again, these returned material can be issued first, at the same price. Alternatively, the returned material may be valued at the price at which they were issued and at the time of reissue, these can be charged according to the method used for pricing of material issues.

SUMMARY

The purchase of materials is in anticipation of their use and issue to production. Quite often, the materials are purchased from the market and they are put into stock with the existing quantity of material thereby losing their identity. Now, the question arises as to at which price, jobs or work orders should be charged for the raw material issued. In preparing cost statements, several methods of pricing the material issued may be used, the choice largely depending on the nature of the material and the particular conditions in the business. The principal methods of issuing materials may be classified into Actual Cost Methods, Average Cost Methods and Notional Price Methods.

While selecting a method, the following conditions should be satisfied

- The method should be simple, effective and realistic
- The issue price should fully recover the cost price of the materials
- The issue price must be close to the market price
- It is necessary to consider the effect of the method on the production cost and inventory valuation

Under **FIFO Method,** it is assumed that the material received first in the stores are issued first and as such the material in stock are the material purchased in the last. This method uses the price of the first batch of material purchased for all issues until that batch of materials are fully issued. Later, the materials are issued at the next purchase price and so on. Thus, the materials are issued at the oldest price listed in the Stores Ledger. This method is most suitable in times of falling prices as the material issues to the jobs will be at high price (material issued from the earliest consignments which were purchased at a higher rate) and the material in hand are valued at the price of the latest purchases.

Under **LIFO Method,** the material issues are priced under the assumption that the last item materials purchased up to the date of issue is the first to be issued. As such, the inventory valuation is done at the oldest prices of the material purchased and is completely out of the line with current prices. This method is suitable in case of rising prices as the material will be issued for production from the latest consignment, which is closely related to current price levels.

The other methods of actual costs are HIFO, NIFO, and Specific Price Methods.

The **Average Method** is based on the principle that all of the material in store is so mixed up that an issue cannot be made from any particular lot of purchases. Therefore, it is proper to issue material at the average cost. Here, the material loses its specific identity. Basically, the average prices are of two types.

Under **Simple Average Method,** the material are issued at a price which is calculated by dividing the total of the prices of the material in stock, from which the material to be priced could be drawn, by the number of prices used in that total on the date of the issue. Here, the quantity of different lots is ignored. This method is suitable when the prices of purchases do not show wide fluctuations. It is simple to operate as it takes into account only the prices of the materials.

Under **Weighted Average Price Method,** the issues are made at a price, which is calculated by dividing the total cost of the material in the stock by the number of units in hand. Thus, both the price and quantity of material in store are taken into account. In periods of heavy fluctuations in the prices of material, this method gives better results, as it tends to smooth out fluctuations in prices by averaging the prices of various lots in stock.

Base Stock Method is based on the assumption that each concern will always maintain a minimum quantity of material in stock known as 'Safety or Base Stock' and will be used only under an emergency situation. Base Stock is created from the first lot of material purchased and as such it is always valued at the cost price of the first lot. The quantity in excess of the base stock is valued according to one of the other methods such as FIFO, LIFO or Average Price Method

Sometimes, **Notional Price Methods** are used for pricing material issues. Here, instead of issuing the material at actual prices incurred while purchasing the material, notional i.e. estimated prices are used for pricing issues. Some of such methods are **Standard Price Method**, **Market Price Method/Replacement Price Method** and **Inflated Price Method.**

Sometimes the material issued for production, may be returned to stores, when the material is found to be in excess. In such a case, the material returned may be valued at the same price at which they were issued and recorded in the stores accordingly. Again, these returned materials can be issued first, at the same price. Alternatively, the returned material may be valued at the price at which they were issued and at the time of reissue, these can be charged according to the method used for pricing of material issues.

Glossary

- **FIFO Method:** This method uses the price of the first batch of material purchased for all issues until that batch of materials are fully issued.
- **LIFO Method:** Here, the material issues are priced under the assumption that the last item materials purchased up to the date of issue is the first to be issued.
- **HIFO Method:** The materials are charged to the jobs at the highest price paid for the materials irrespective of the date of purchase.
- **NIFO Method:** The issues are priced at the price of material, which has been ordered but not yet received.
- **Specific Price Method:** Here, materials are purchased and set aside for a particular job or work order. In such a case, the job is charged with the specific price paid for the material.
- **Base Stock Method:** This method is based on the assumption that each concern will always maintain a minimum quantity of material in stock known as 'Safety or Base Stock' and will be used only under an emergency situation.
- **Simple Average Method:** Here, the material are issued at a price which is calculated by dividing the total of the prices of the material in stock, from which the material to be priced could be drawn, by the number of prices used in that total on the date of the issue.
- **Weighted Average Price Method:** Here, the issues are made at a price, which is calculated by dividing the total cost of the material in the stock by the number of units in hand.
- **Notional Price Methods:** Here, instead of issuing the material at actual prices incurred while purchasing the material, notional i.e. estimated prices are used for pricing issues.
- **Standard Price Method:** It is a pre determined price and both receipts and issues will be valued at this price.
- **Market Price Method/Replacement Price Method:** Under this method, materials are issued at a price at which they can be replaced without any consideration to the cost of materials purchased.

Questions

(1) What are the various methods of pricing material issues? Give their advantages and Limitations.
(2) Explain the suitability of each method of valuation of material issue.
(3) What are the features of LIFO method of pricing material issue?
(4) Distinguish between FIFO and LIFO methods of pricing material issue.
(5) Under conditions of rising prices, between FIFO and LIFO methods, which one you recommend and why?
(6) What are the main features which should be considered in selecting a method of pricing Material issues?

PROBLEMS

(1) Show the Stores Ledger entries as they would appear when using:
(a) Last in first out Method
(b) First in first out Method
(c) Simple Average Method and
(d) Weighted Average Method

April 1	Balance in hand b/f 300 units @ Rs. 2.00
April 2	Purchased 200 units @ Rs. 2.20
April 4	Issued 150 units
April 6	Purchased 200 units @ Rs. 2.30
April 11	Issued 150 units
April 19	Issued 200 units
April 22	Purchased 200 units @ Rs. 2.40
April 27	Issued 150 units

[Ans. ***(a)*** **Closing Stock 250 units at Rs. 520** ***(b)*** **250 units at Rs. 595** ***(c)*** **250 units at Rs. 537** ***(d)*** **250 units at Rs. 570]**

(2) The following is an extract of the record of receipts and issues of a material in a factory for the month of June 2004. Prepare the Stores Ledger Account pricing the material under FIFO. The stock verifier of the factory found a shortage of 10 units on 22nd June 2004 and left a note accordingly.

June	1	Opening Balance: 500 units @ Rs. 2 per unit
June	3	Issue of 70 units
June	7	Issue of 150 units
June	12	Received from supplier 200 units @ Rs. 2.10 per unit
June	14	Issue of 180 units
June	20	Received from supplier 250 units @ Rs. 2.20 per unit

June 23 Returns from Production Department of materials issued on 14th June, 20 units
June 24 Issue of 250 units
June 25 Received from supplier 300 units @ Rs. 2.30 per unit
June 28 Issue of 150 units
June 30 Received from supplier 200 units @ Rs. 2.20 per unit
Note: Shortage of 10 units to be treated as an issue

[Ans.: Closing Balance: 140 units @ Rs. 2.20; 20 units @ Rs. 2; 300 units @ Rs. 2.30 and 200 units @ Rs. 2.20 *i.e.*, Rs. 1,482]

(3) Prepare Stores Ledger Account for the following transactions using LIFO.

Jan. 1 Opening Stock 12,000 kgs. at Rs. 7.50 per kg.
1 Purchased 22,000 kgs. at Rs. 7.60 per kg.
2 Issued 5,000 kgs.
5 Issued 7,000 kgs.
12 Issued 8,000 kgs.
13 Surplus from Production Department returned 2,000 kgs. which was issued on 2nd Jan.
18 Issued 12,000 kgs.
22 Purchased 25,000 kgs. at Rs. 7.40 per kg.
28 Issued 7,000 kgs.
31 On Stock verification 500 kgs. was found to be in excess.

[Ans.: *(a)* Surplus material is to be treated as receipt at Rs. 7.6 per unit; *(b)* 500 kgs. of excess material found during physical verification of stock is to be taken as the receipt at the latest purchase price of Rs. 7.4 per unit. *(c)* Closing balance 4,000 units @ Rs. 7.5 + 18,000 units @ Rs. 7.4 plus 500 units @ Rs. 7.4, *i.e.*, total Rs. 1,66,900]

(4) The following transactions took place in respect of an item of material:

Date	*Receipts Qty.*	*Rate Rs.*	*Issues Qty.*
2.3.04	200	2.00	
10.3.04	300	2.40	
15.3.04			250
18.03.04	250	2.60	
20.3.04			200

Record the above transactions in the Stores Ledger, pricing the issues at:
(a) Simple Average Rate
(b) Weighted Average Rate

[Ans.: *(a)* 300 units at Rs. 720 and *(b)* 300 units @ Rs. 2.42]

(5) Bharat Manufacturing Company uses copper wire, which is purchased from the market as and when necessary. The following purchases and issues were made during the month of January 2005.

Jan. 1 Opening Balance 300 kgs. at Rs. 25 per kg (purchase order No. 101)
3 Purchased 500 kgs. @ Rs. 26.60 per kg.
4 Issued 220 kgs. (Material Requisition No. 201)
10 Issued 440 kgs. (Material Requisition No. 202)
20 Purchased 490 kgs. @ Rs. 23 per kg. (Purchase Order No. 102)
25 Issued 300 kgs. (Material Requisition No. 203)
26 Surplus 20 kgs. returned to stock out of quantity issued on Jan. 4th (Material Requisition No. 201)

Prepare the Stores Ledger according to *(a)* FIFO *(b)* LIFO *(c)* Weighted Average Cost Method and *(d)* Simple Average Method.

[Ans. *(a)* 350 units at Rs. 8,090 *(b)* 350 units at Rs. 8,402 *(c)* 350 units at Rs. 8,330 *(d)* 350 units at Rs. 8,649]

(6) Adarsh Company Ltd. purchased and issued the material in the following order.

Jan. 1 Purchased 300 units @ Rs. 3
Jan. 5 Purchased 600 units @ Rs. 4
Jan. 10 Issued 500 units
Jan. 12 Purchased 700 units @ Rs. 4
Jan. 15 Issued 800 units

Jan. 20 Purchased 300 units @ Rs. 5
Jan. 30 Issued 100 units

Ascertain the quantity of closing stocks as on 31st January and state the value under each of the following methods of pricing the issue.

(a) Weighted Average Method
(b) Simple Average Method
(c) LIFO
(d) FIFO

[Ans. *(a)* 500 units at Rs. 2,220 *(b)* 500 units at Rs. 2,188 *(c)* 500 units at Rs. 1,900 *(d)* 500 units at Rs. 2,300]

(7) Satish Ltd. has purchased and issued the material 'M' in the following order.

2004 December

1 Purchased 300 units @ Rs. 3
5 Purchased 600 units @ Rs. 4
6 Issued 400 units
10 Purchased 600 units @ Rs. 4
15 Issued 1,000 units
20 Purchased 400 units @ Rs. 5
23 Issued 200 units

Prepare Stores Ledger under FIFO, Simple Average and Weighted Average Methods.

[Ans.: *(a)* 300 units at Rs. 1,500 *(b)* 300 units at Rs. 1,313 *(c)* 300 units at Rs. 1,431]

(8) The following are the receipts and issues of material during January 2004.

1 Opening Balance 1000 units at Rs. 50 per unit
3 Issue 140 units
4 Issue 200 units
8 Issue 160 units
13 Received from vendor 400 units at Rs. 48 per unit
14 Refund of surplus from a work order 34 units at Rs. 48 per unit
16 Issue 360 units
20 Received from vendor 480 units at Rs. 52 per unit
24 Issue 608 units
25 Received from vendor 640 units at Rs. 50 per unit
26 Issue 524 units
27 Refund of surplus from a work order 24 units (issued on 3rd)
31 Received from vendor 200 units at Rs. 54 per unit

From the above, prepare the Stores Ledger using FIFO and Simple Average Method of pricing.

[Ans.: *(a)* 786 units at Rs. 40,100 *(b)* 786 units at Rs. 40,881]

(9) The following transactions are taken in respect of a material used in a factory.

Date	*Quantity Received*	*Rate per unit Rs.*	*Quantity Issued*
3.1.05	400	2.10	
15.1.05	500	2.20	
19.1.05	—		500
23.1.05	600	2.50	
27.1.05	—		900

Prepare a Stock Ledger Sheet pricing the issues at average rate. Use proper rulings.

[Ans.: Weighted Average Method: Closing Balance 100 units at Rs. 236]

(10) Show the Stores Ledger entries as they would appear using (a) Weighted Average Method and (b) LIFO Method of pricing issues in connection with the following transactions.

April		*Units*	*Value (Rs.)*
1	Balance in hand b/f	300	600
2	Purchased	200	440
4	Issued	150	
6	Purchased	200	460
11	Issued	150	
19	Issued	200	
22	Purchased	200	480
27	Issued	250	

[Ans.: *(a)* 150 units at Rs. 342 *(b)* 150 units at Rs. 300]

❑ ❑ ❑

7

LABOR COST

Objectives

The objectives of this lesson are to:

- Understand the need for control over labor turnover
- Know the difference between Job Evaluation and Merit Rating
- Learn the methods of Time Keeping and Time Booking
- Distinguish Idle Time from Abnormal Idle Time
- Compute Labor Cost

INTRODUCTION

Labor is another element of cost. The accounting and control of labour cost is a major problem for the management, in dealing with which, the Cost Accountant has an important role to play. The responsibility of the Cost Accountants does not lie only with compilation and controlling of labour cost but also lies with the presentation of information on such matters like the costs of recruitment, training of laborers, labor turnover, idle time, overtime, shift work, labor efficiency, wastage, spoilage due to labor faults and various other analyses relating to labor.

DIRECT AND INDIRECT LABOR

Direct labor consists of the wages paid to labor directly involved in the manufacturing process. Direct wages/labor cost refer to the wages which can be identified with and allocated to cost units. For example, wages paid to machine operators, assembly line workers, moulders, etc., are direct wages.

The indirect labor cost is the wages which cannot be allocated, but which can be apportioned to or absorbed by Cost Centres or Cost Units. These costs cannot be conveniently identified with a particular job, product or process. For example, wages paid to foreman, inspectors. watchmen, supervisors, storekeepers, timekeepers, etc., are indirect wages.

ORGANIZATION FOR LABOR CONTROL

There is a need for effective control over labor and labor related costs as labor generally constitute 20 to 25 per cent of the total cost of a product. There are five departments in an organisation which deal with the labor and these are:

(1) Personnel Department
(2) Engineering Department
(3) Time Keeping Department
(4) Payroll Department
(5) Cost Accounting Department

Personnel Department

This department is concerned with the proper relation and training of workers and placing them on jobs for which they are best suited. In consultation with the different departmental heads, the Personnel Department plans the expansion requirements and agrees upon promotions, transfers, number of persons to be hired etc. This Department carries out other functions like the work relating to recruitment, interviewing, testing, physical examination, assignment to jobs, etc.

The Personnel Department prepares an employee's record card whenever a new worker is hired. This card shows the full personal details of the employee, particulars of the previous employment, wages rate, transfers, promotion, details of leave, attendance, emergency address, sickness, wage rate revision, the date of and reasons for leaving, etc. The purpose of this card is to record all the essential information about the workers during his employment in the concern.

EMPLOYEE'S RECORD CARD

Name	:	No.
Address:	Present	
	Permanent	
Date of Birth :	Married/Single	

EMPLOYMENT RECORD

Date	:	
Department	:	
Grade	:	
Designation	:	

WAGE RATE RECORD

Date :	
Rate :	
Particulars :	

PREVIOUS EMPLOYMENT RECORD

Name of previous employment :	
Address :	
Experience :	
Reference :	

EDUCATION AND TRAINING

Qualification :	
School / College :	
Training :	

TIME KEEPING

Year	*Sick Leave*	*Overtime*	*Time lost*

Date Left :
Reasons for leaving :
Remarks :

Labor Turnover

Labor turnover is the percentage change in the labor force of an organization. The number of workers working in an organization keeps changing due to the following reasons.

- Recruitment of new workers
- Deaths
- Retirements
- Promotions
- Removal
- Retrenchment
- Workers leaving the jobs prompted by social and economic factors etc.

The occurrence of some labor turnover is a natural phenomenon as the workers change their jobs due to social and economic factors. A very high labor turnover denotes instability in the labor force.

For the purpose of comparisons between different periods and different undertakings, labor turnover may be expressed as a rate. This rate is computed by following any of the three methods given below.

(i) Separation Method :

$$\text{Labor Turnover Rate : } \frac{\text{Number of employees left during a period} \times 100}{\text{Average number of employees during a period}}$$

This definition does not take into consideration the fact of surplus labor, because, all workers who have left are taken into consideration. This method will not give correct result when the surplus workers are discharged because labor turnover calculated under this method will be high.

(ii) Replacement Method :

$$\text{Labor Turnover Rate} : \frac{\text{Number of employees replaced during a period} \times 100}{\text{Average number of employees during a period}}$$

This definition takes into account the surplus labor and gives correct labor turnover when the factory is expanding because all additions are not taken, only those new workers who have joined in the place of those who have left are taken.

(iii) Flux Method :

$$\text{Labor Turnover Rate} : \frac{(\text{Number of replacements} + \text{number of separations during a period})}{\text{Average number of employees during a period}} \times 100$$

This method shows the total change in the composition of labor force due to separations and additions of workers.

Illustration 1

From the following information, calculate labor turnover rate under *(a)* Replacement Method and *(b)* Flux Method.

Number of workers at the end of the year	5,000
Number of workers at the beginning of the year	4,200

During the year, while 150 got discharged, 50 workers left. 650 workers are recruited, of them 180 workers are recruited in place of those who left and the rest are engaged in accordance with revamping scheme.

Solution

Average number of workers during the year = (4,200 + 5,000) / 2 = 4,600

(a) Replacement Method:

$$\text{Labor Turnover Rate} : \frac{\text{Number of employees replaced during a period} \times 100}{\text{Average number of employees during a period}}$$

$$\frac{180 \times 100}{4600} = 3.91\%$$

(b) Flux Method:

$$\text{Labor Turnover Rate} : \frac{\text{Number of replacements} + \text{number of separations during a period} \times 100}{\text{Average number of employees during a period.}}$$

$$\frac{(180 + 200)\ 100}{4{,}600} = 8.26\%$$

Illustration 2

The extracts from the payroll of ABC Ltd. are as follows.

Number of workers at the end of the year	250
Number of workers at the beginning of the year	200
Number of workers resigned	35
Number of workers discharged	10
Number of workers replaced due to resignations and discharges	25

Calculate labor turnover rate by different methods.

Solution

(a) Separation Method :

Average number of workers = (250 + 200) / 2 = 225

$$\text{Labor Turnover Rate} : \frac{\text{Number of employees left during a period} \times 100}{\text{Average number of employees during a period.}}$$

$$\frac{45 \times 100}{225} = 20\%$$

(b) Replacement Method :

$$\text{Labor Turnover Rate} : \frac{\text{Number of employees replaced during a period} \times 100}{\text{Average number of employees during a period.}}$$

$$\frac{25 \times 100}{225} = 11.11\%$$

(c) Flux Method :

Labor Turnover Rate :

$$\frac{\text{Number of replacements + number of separations during a period} \times 100}{\text{Average number of employees during a period}}$$

$$\frac{(25 + 45)\ 100}{} = 31.11\%$$

Effects of Labor Turnover

A certain amount of labor turnover is desirable because, it helps the firms in adjusting its labor force according to the workload. But, a high labor turnover is always detrimental to the company, as it results in low labor productivity and increased cost of production. This is because :

- Workers who are newly employed take time to learn the work i.e. learning stage.
- Changes in the labor force give rise to interruption in the continuous flow of production.
- Being inexperienced, the new workers cause more depreciation of tools and machinery.
- Selection and training costs of new workers recruited to replace the workers who have left increase the cost of production.

Causes for Labor Turnover

The various causes for labor turnover can be classified under the following three heads :

(a) ***Personal Causes:*** Workers may leave the organization purely on personal grounds like retirement due to old age; domestic troubles and family responsibilities; death; the workers dislike for the job or place; women workers leaving the job after their marriage; accident making the persons incapable and leaving the job for personal betterment.

(b) ***Avoidable Causes:*** Labor turnover may also be due to reasons which could have been avoided like unsatisfactory working conditions; lack of accommodation, medical and transportation facilities; job dissatisfaction on account of working place; low wages and allowances; lack of promotion opportunities; long hours of work; lack of motivation in the company and lack of training for advancement.

(c) ***Unavoidable Causes:*** Labor turnover may be due to compulsory factors like termination of workers due to long absence without intimation; discharge of workers by the management due to their inefficiency; retrenchment due to shortage of work and termination due to criminal prosecution.

As a result, the costs that would be incurred due to labor turnover can be classified into **preventive costs** and **replacement costs**.

Preventive costs are those cost which are incurred to keep the work force satisfied and prevent them from leaving the organization. Examples are cost of welfare activities, medical services, pension schemes, extra bonus and perquisites.

Replacement costs are those costs, which are incurred when the existing labor force is replaced by the new one. The associated costs are cost of recruitment, selection and training of new workers, loss of output due to inexperience or inefficiency of the new workers, cost of defective work of new workers, etc.

As labor turnover has an impact on the cost, care should be taken by the management to keep it as low as possible by concentrating on avoidable causes and incurring preventive costs, after making a cost benefit analysis.

ENGINEERING DEPARTMENT

This Department maintains control over working condition and production methods of each job, department or process. The functions of this department are :

(1) Providing for safe and efficient working conditions
(2) Making job analysis
(3) Preparation of plans and specifications for each job or process
(4) Supervision of production facilities
(5) Conducting time and motion studies for each job
(6) Inspection of job at each stage of production
(7) Setting piece rates

Time Study

It involves determination of standard time for an operation by direct time measurement. It is the art of observing and recording the time required for the completion of a work by 10 to 12 observations with the help of a watch. After determining the standard time, the number of workers required and the cost of completing a job are determined. While fixing the standard time, adequate allowance is made for fatigue, idleness, resetting of machines, tools, etc..

Motion Study

This is the study of movements of workers and machines in performing a particular operation. It is concerned with finding out the standardized methods for performing different operations, identifying and eliminating unnecessary and wasteful operations of workers. Time and motion studies help in determining the best method of doing a job and the standard time allowed for it.

Work Study

Work study serves as an important analytical tool used as a basis for improvement of productivity. The main objective of work study is to bring about an overall improvement by saving time, reducing wastage of materials and developing new methods of work. It is the combination of Method Study and Work Measurement.

Method Study

It is a technique used by engineers for making detailed analysis of the way in which production process is carried on. It involves the examination of the various tasks undertaken, the methods used in their performance, the sequence of operations, plant and equipment available and the factory layout and designing. The study helps in making the best use of the resources available.

Work Measurement

It involves the establishment of the work content of an operation. It consists of conducting both time and motion studies. It determines the effective time required for doing a specified standard task by a worker after separating and eliminating the ineffective or wasteful time.

Job Evaluation

It is a technique, which attempts to show the relative worth of the jobs. This is also a process of review, analysis and systematic classification of a job in accordance with its characteristics. Every job has its own requirements in terms of qualifications, skills, experience, etc. Job evaluation provides the basis on which the management determines the basic wage and salary structure of the various job positions. The objectives of job evaluation are :

(1) to remove discrimination in the wage structure
(2) to evolve an equitable and systematic salary and wage structure
(3) to ensure consistency between the organizations wage structure and that of other organizations
(4) to evolve a proper system of salary and wage structure consistent with the skill required for the job

Merit Rating

Merit rating is a systematic evaluation of an employee's performance on the job in terms of the requirements of the job. The difference between merit rating and job evaluation is that job evaluation is concerned with evaluating a job, whereas merit rating is the comparative appraisal of the individual merits of an employee. Factors like qualification, skill, experience, intelligence, responsibility, leadership qualities, etc., of an individual are considered while rating the workers performance on the job.

The advantages of merit rating are :

(i) it provides a basis for incentive payment
(ii) it improves the productivity of labor
(iii) it highlights the workers skill
(iv) it links the rewards to merit, serving as a motivator

Time Keeping Department

Time Keeping is an important part of the firm's system of accounting and control of labor cost. To show the effective utilisation of labor time, there should be a proper maintenance of records.

In case of small concerns, the Production Department carries out this function. In case of large concerns, there is a separate Time Keeping Department headed by a Timekeeper. Information about the time of arrival, departure, idle time, overtime, etc., is supplied to the Payroll Department to enable the Payroll Department to pay wages to the workers.

Methods of Time Keeping

There are three methods of recording the attendance of the workers. They are :

(i) ***Attendance Registers :*** This is the simplest of all. A manual register will be maintained in which each employee signs on arrival and departure, noting his time 'in' and 'out'. The names of the workers will be entered in the register to record the attendance of each worker everyday. However, this method is simple, inexpensive but outdated. This method is suited for small concerns. In large concerns, there is a scope for mistakes regarding marking of late attendance, short leave, overtime, etc.

(ii) ***Disc or Token System :*** In this system, each worker is allotted an identification number, which is painted or engraved on a metal token (disc) with a hole in it. On entering the gate of the factory, every worker picks up the token bearing his number and drops into a box kept at the factory gate. To allow the latecomers, after the expiry of the time allowed, the first box is removed and replaced by another one into which the latecomers drop their token.

Th attendance of the workers is recorded on the basis of token or disc in the box and missing tokens indicates the absentees. The same procedure is adopted at the departure time in the evening.

The main limitation of this method is, there is every likelihood of a worker dropping the token of an absentee also along with his own token.

(iii) ***Time Recording Clocks :*** Under this system, a card time recording clock is installed in the organisation to record the time of arrival and departure of the workers. At the factory gate, the cards are placed in racks along side the clock. Two racks are kept, one on either side of the time recording clock denoting the 'out' and 'in' racks in order to enable the workers to punch these cards on arrival. On arrival, the worker picks up his clock card from the 'out' rack and inserts it into the slot of the clock on which the date and the time of arrival is printed by the clock in the correct position. After punching, the worker places the same in the 'in' rack.

CLOCK CARD

Name	:		No.	:
Department	:			
Grade	:		Week ending	:
Date	:		Total Hours	:
		Ordinary :	Overtime :	
Total Wages	:			
Less Deduction	:			
Net Pay	:	Signature :		

Time Booking

Time keeping is the recording of the attendance time of the workers, whereas, time booking is the time spent by a worker on each job, process or operation. Every worker who is engaged on a job must specify as to how he has spent the time during which he was present in the factory.

Methods of Time Booking : The recording of work time can be done by any of the following methods :

(i) **Daily Time Sheet**

Time sheet will be filled by the worker himself or by the foreman and it is a record of the nature of work done by and the actual time spent by the worker on each job or operation. This is a simple method, but involves a lot of paper work, because, it has to be compiled daily for the purpose of ascertaining labor cost.

This method of recording time is suitable where workers have to carry out a number of different jobs in a day.

DAILY TIME SHEET

Name : Worker No :
Department : Date :

Job Order No.	*Details of work done*	*Time From To*	*Hours*		*Rate Rs.*	*Amount Rs.*
			Ordinary	*Overtime*		

Signature :
Workman : Foreman : Costing Dept.:

(ii) Weekly Time Sheet

The Weekly Time Sheet records almost the same information as the daily time sheet but the information is for a week. The entries in the weekly time sheet may be inaccurate because the workers may tend to fill up the same for 2/3 days together at one sitting and may forget the actual time spent on certain jobs.

WEEKLY TIME SHEET

Worker's Name : Week ending :
Worker No : Day :
Department : Date :

Job Order No.	*Details of work done*	*Time From To*	*Hours*		*Rate Rs.*	*Amount Rs.*
			Ordinary	*Overtime*		

Signature :
Workman : Foreman : Costing Dept.:

(iii) Job Card

A Job Card is prepared for each job and the workers enter the time of starting as well as completing the job. After completion of the job, the job card is submitted to the foreman along with the work done. The job card also serves as an authorisation to the worker to carry out the job specified therein.

JOB TICKET/CARD

Worker's Name :	Job No. :
Worker's No. :	Dated :
Department :	Starting Time :
Completing Time :	
Signature :	

Workman : Foreman : Costing Dept.:

(iv) Time and Job Card

This card records both the attendance time and the work time of a worker on a job. The difference between the attendance time and the work time is the idle time, which is automatically revealed.

TIME AND JOB CARD

Worker's Name :
Worker No :
Department :

Week ending :
Day :
Date :

Job No.	*Clock In*	*Time Out*	*Job Hours From To*	*Ordinary Time (Hrs)*	*Overtime Time (Hrs)*	*Idle Time Hrs.*

Total :

Signature :
Workman : Foreman : Costing Dept.:

***(v)* Piece Work Card**

This card is allotted to the workers who perform the work on the basis of piece rate. These workers though paid wages not on the basis of time spent but on the basis of output, recording of piecework time is useful for determining the slab rates for piecework.

PIECE CARD WORK

Worker's Name :
Worker No :
Department :

Week ending :
Day :
Date :

Job No.	*Description of Job*	*Time taken*	*Production in units*	*Rejection in units*	*Passed for payment (units)*	*Rate Rs.*	*Amount Rs.*

Total Wages Rs. : ....
Foreman : ....

Payroll Department

This Department is responsible for the computation and disbursement of wages payable to the workers. To ascertain the net wages payable, wage sheet or payroll will be prepared and certain deductions are required to be made from gross wages to ascertain net wages. This Department is responsible for the computation of employee's wages, maintaining a record of job classification and wage rate, receiving time cards piecework cards, etc., verifying and summarising time of each worker and making wage payments.

Pay Slip

At the time of making wage payments, a pay slip will be given to all the workers. This pay slip shows the components of the total salary, deduction made therefrom and the net amount payable.

PAY SLIP

Name of the worker	:		Designation	:
Department	:		Wage period	:
Basic Wage		Rs.		
House Rent Allowance		Rs.		
City Compensatory Allowance		Rs.		
Dearness Allowance		Rs.		
Other Allowances Rs.				
Gross Wages		Rs.		
Less Deduction:				
Provident Fund Contribution		Rs.		
Employees State Insurance Contribution		Rs.		
Income Tax		Rs.		
Total Deductions		Rs.		
Net Amount Payable		Rs.		

Idle Time

Idle time is the difference between the attendance time and job time. This represents the time during which worker has been present in the organisation, but has not spent the same on the job. In spite of it, workers are paid for idle time as they are generally paid on the basis of attendance time. The idle time payment increases the labour cost component of a job as no production is obtained for such payment. Hence, it is necessary to know the causes of such idle time to have control over them.

Causes for Idle Time

The various causes for the idle time are given below.

(1) Time taken from the factory gate to the Department.
(2) Time lost before starting the work.
(3) Waiting for raw material/instructions from superiors.
(4) Time taken in moving from one job to another.
(5) Strikes, lockouts and accidents, etc.
(6) Power failure.
(7) Break down of machinery.
(8) Attending to calls of nature.

Classification of Idle Time

Idle time can be classified into two categories *viz.*, Normal Idle Time and the Abnormal Idle Time.

Normal Idle Time: It is that idle time which is unavoidable, normal and inherent in production. It is the wastage of labor time to be borne by the employer.

Example : the time spent by the workers from the factory gate to the department, time for personal needs, changing over from one job to another, etc.

The cost of normal idle time may be *(a)* charged to the factory overhead or *(b)* wage rate may be increased so as to make allowance for the normal loss of labour hours.

Abnormal Idle Time: It is that time which is not caused or connected with the usual routine of production. For instance, breakdown of machinery, power failure, strikes and lockouts, waiting for tools/raw material/instruction, etc., are certainly within the control of the management and hence abnormal. The cost of abnormal idle time is transferred to Costing Profit and Loss Account.

The idle time can be controlled by proper planning of production, timely provision of tools required, timely instructions and material provided and by careful supervision.

A SPECIMEN OF IDLE TIME CARD

Worker's Name :   Date :
Worker No. :
Department :

Reasons for Idle Time	*Order No.*	*Time (Hours)*			*Cost*	
		From	*To*	*Total*	*Rate Rs.*	*Amount Rs.*
Power Failure Break down of Machinery Waiting for tools/materials Waiting for instructions Strikes Others						

Overtime

Overtime is the extra time put in by the workers beyond their normal hours of work. The overtime work rate is normally double the normal rate per hour. Therefore, overtime is a costly affair and should be avoided as far as possible.

However, inspite of certain negative factors like excess labor cost, extra strain on plant and machinery, effect on the health of the workers, slowing down of normal work, etc., the overtime work is particularly useful in pulling up backlog in production due to shutdown, breakdown of machines, power failures, strikes, etc.

Treatment of Overtime

An overtime premium is an extra payment of wages for additional work done by the workers and it is also a part of the direct labor cost. There are three different ways in which overtime premium may be treated.

(1) Overtime, if it is at the customer's request to expedite delivery, overtime premium should be treated as direct wages and charged to the job concerned.

(2) If the overtime paid is due to general pressure of work, the premium paid should be treated as a part of general overhead.

(3) When overtime is due to abnormal circumstances such as floods, strike etc., should be charged to the Costing Profit and Loss Account.

COST ACCOUNTING DEPARTMENT

This Department is responsible for collecting and analyzing all costs relating to labor. It is the labor time records, which form the basis on which Cost Accounting Department relies.

This Department prepares a document known as Wages Abstract and also presents reports on normal and abnormal idle time, overtime, department labor costs, etc. These reports are then submitted to the management for initiating remedial action.

WAGES ABSTRACT SHEET

Sl. No. :   Week ending :

Worker No.	*Job No.* 1 2 3 4	*Total Direct Hours*	*Rate*	*Indirect Wages*
Total				

The Cost Accounting Department is responsible for the accumulation and classification of all labor costs. The Department along with time cards and job cards, prepares payrolls for the calculation of the labor cost of various job orders, processes, etc.

Wage Rates Calculation

Labor costs represent not only basic wages but also a number of other expenses such as dearness allowance, other allowances, employee's and employer's contribution to provident fund, pension fund, state insurance etc. The labor cost will be arrived at by adding all the expenses relating to labor and dividing it by the number of effective working hours. Once again, the labor cost per hour will be multiplied with the working hours of various jobs to get the labor cost of the jobs respectively.

Illustration 3

From the following particulars, prepare a statement of labor cost showing the cost per day.

(a)	Monthly salary	Rs. 225
(b)	Leave salary	5 % of (a)
(c)	Employer's contribution to provident fund	8 % of (a) and (b)
(d)	Employer's contribution to ESI	3 % of (a) and (b)
(e)	Pro rata expenditure on amenities to labor	Rs. 28 per head per month
(f)	Number of working hours in a month of 25 days :	8 hours per day

Solution

Statement of Labor Cost per day of 8 hours

		Rs.
Basic Salary		225.00
Leave Salary (5% of 225)		11.25
Employer's contribution to Provident fund (8% of 236.25)		18.90
Employer's contribution to ESI	(3% of 236.25)	7.09
Pro rate amenities		28.00
Total for 25 days		290.24
At 8 hours per day for 25 days	= 25 × 8 = 200 hours	
Labor cost per day of 8 hours	= 290.24 × 8 / 200 = Rs. 11.61	
OR		
Labor cost per day of 8 hours	= 290.24 / 25 = Rs. 11.61	

Illustration 4

Calculate the carnings of workers X and Y from the following particulars for a month and allocate the earnings to each Job A, B and C.

		X	*Y*
(a)	Basic Wages (Rs.)	80	80
(b)	D.A.	50%	60%
(c)	Provident Fund on basic wages	8%	8%
(d)	Employer's State Insurance	3%	3%
(e)	Overtime (hours)	12	—
(f)	Idle time and leave (hours)	—	15

The normal working hours for the month is 200hours. Overtime is paid at double the normal wages plus D.A.

Employer's contribution to State Insurance and Provident Fund are at equal rate with the employee contribution. The month contains 25 working days and one paid holiday. The workers were employed on job A, B and C in the following proportions.

	A	*B*	*C*
Workers :			
X (hours)	90	50	60
Y (hours)	90	50	60
Overtime was done on Job B.			

Solution

	Worker X ***Rs.***	***Worker Y*** ***Rs.***
Basic Wages	80.00	80.00
D.A. (50% and 60%)	40.00	48.00
Overtime (12hours @ Re. 1.20)	14.40	
	134.40	**128.00**
Employer's contribution to P.F. (8% of basic wages)	6.40	6.40
Employer's contribution to ESI (3% of basic wages)	2.40	2.40
Total	**8.80**	**8.80**
Gross Wages	143.20	136.80
Allocation of labor cost to jobs :		
Wages (excluding overtime wages)	120.00	128.00
Contribution to P.F. and ESI	8.80	8.80
Total	**128.80**	**136.80**
Normal working hours per month	200	200
Labor cost per hour	128.80/200	136.80/200
=	0.644	0.684

		Total *Rs.*	*Job A* *Rs.*	*Job B* *Rs.*	*Job C* *Rs.*
Worker X :	Ordinary Wages	128.80	57.96	32.20	38.64
	Overtime Wages	14.40	—	14.40	—
Worker Y :	Ordinary Wages	136.80	61.56	34.20	41.04
	Total	280.00	119.52	80.80	79.68

Ordinary Wages = Hours x Rate per hour
Calculation of overtime wages for X :

Basic wager per month	Rs. 80
D.A. per month	Rs. 40
Total	Rs. 120

Normal working hours per month 200
Normal rate per hour 120 / 200 = Re. 0.60
Overtime wages : (Double the normal rate) 2 × 0.60 = Re. 1.20

Illustration 5

A factory department has 180 workers who are paid an average of Rs. 17.50 per week (48 hours), dearness allowance per month (208 hours) of Rs. 130, provident fund deduction is at 8% on gross, of which 1 ⅙% is for family pension fund of half the number of workers and Employees State Insurance deduction is at Rs. 1.25 per month for each. The company gives only a minimum bonus of 8 ⅓% and allows statutory leave of two weeks per year with pay. Show the weekly wage summary for the financial books and the departmental labor hour costs for job costing.

Solution

Weekly Wage Summary

	Rs.
Wages (180 workers @ Rs. 17.50)	3,150.00
Dearness Allowance (130 × 180 × 48/208)	5,400.00
	8,550.00
Bonus (8,550 × 8 ⅓%)	712.50
Total	9,262.50

	Rs.
Less Deductions :	
Provident Fund Contribution ($8\% - 1\frac{1}{6}\%$)	
i.e. ($8,550 \times 6\frac{5}{6}\%$)	584.250
Family Pension ($8550 \times 1\frac{1}{6}\% \times \frac{1}{2}$)	49.875
ESI contribution (180 workers @ Rs. 1.25)	225.000
Total deductions	859.125
Net Wages	8,403.38

Computation of Department Labor Cost

	Rs.
Wages	3,150.00
Dearness Allowance	5,400.00
Bonus	712.50
Providend Fund Contribution	584.25
Family Pension	49.875
ESI Contribution	225.00
Leave Pay (8,550 × 2/52)	328.85
Total Labor Cost	10,450.475

Weekly Labor Hours = 48 hours x 180 workers = 8,640

Labor Cost per hour = 10,450 / 8640 = Rs. 1.21

Illustration 6

A direct worker is paid Rs. 1,600 p.m. as basic wages and Rs. 400 as D.A. per month. His contribution to P.F. is 10% of his basic pay and D.A. His ESI contribution is 5% on basic. Cost of non-monetary benefits to him is estimated as Rs. 200. Actual number of working days (of 8 hours working per day) after adjustment for weekly off, holidays and leaves entitlement are estimated at 250 per year. Normal idle time is 10%.

Calculate wage rate per hour for costing purposes.

Solution

Calculation of Wages

	Rs. (p.m.)
Basic Wages	1600
Dearness Allowance	400
Contribution to Provident Fund (10% of 2000)	200
Contribution to ESI (5% of 1600)	80
Cost of non-monetary benefits	200
Total	2480

Actual number of working days p.m.	250
Less: Normal idle time (10% of 250)	25
Number of working days in a month	225

Total number of working hours = 225 days × 8 hours per day = 1800

Wages per hour = 2,480 / 1800 = Rs. 1.38

Illustration 7

There are 25 direct workers in a factory. During one month, they were paid for 4800 normal working hours at an average rate of Re. 1.50 per hour. In addition, they also worked for 400 over time hours at double pay. (Overtime is due to abnormal reasons). For the purpose of treating labor cost, 40% for fringe benefits is to be added to gross wages. Calculate the total labor cost and show its allocation to different cost elements from the following particulars.

Hours booked on jobs : 4200

Idle time allowed 12 1/2 %

No abnormal idle time was recorded. Actual idle time was in accordance with the standard set for the purpose.

Solution

Statement showing Labor Cost

		Rs.
Normal wages (4,800 hours @ Re. 1.50)		7,200
Overtime wages (400 hours @ Rs. 3)		1,200
Fringe benefits (40% of 8,400)		3,360
Gross Wages		11,760
Total hours : Normal 4800 + 400 Overtime = 5,200		
Labor Cost per hour : 11,760 / 5,200 = Rs. 2.26		
Hours booked on job	4,200	
Add : 12.5 % idle time (4,200 × 12.5%)	525	
Total hours	4,725	

Labor Cost = 4,725 x 2.26 = Rs. 10,678.50

Summary

Labor is the second element of Cost. The Cost Accountant has an important role to play in the Accounting and Control of Labor Cost, a major problem of the Management. The Labor cost consists of Direct and Indirect Wages. Labor constitutes 20 to 25 per cent of the total cost of a product.

Personnel Department, Engineering Department, Time Keeping Department, Payroll Department and Cost Accounting Department are the five departments in an organization, which deal with the labor.

Personnel Department is concerned with the proper relation and training of workers and placing them to job for which they are best suited. Labor turnover is a common phenomenon in every organization. The magnitude of labor turnover differs. Labor turnover is the percentage change in the labor force of an organization. A very high labor turnover denotes instability in the labor force.

A certain amount of labor turnover is desirable because, it helps the firms in adjusting its labor force according to the workload. But, a high labor turnover is always detrimental to the company, as it results in low labor productivity and increased cost of production. In this regard, there are two costs, which are incurred in the organization. They are Preventive Costs and Replacement Costs.

Preventive costs are those costs, which are incurred to keep the work force satisfied and prevent them from leaving the organization. Examples are cost of welfare activities, medical services, pension schemes, extra bonus and perquisites.

Replacement costs are those costs, which are incurred when the existing labor force is replaced by the new one.

As labor turnover has an impact on the cost, care should be taken by the management to keep it as low as possible by concentrating on avoidable causes and incurring preventive costs.

The functions of **Engineering Department** are providing for safe and efficient working conditions, making job analysis, preparation of plans and specifications for each job or process, supervision of production facilities, conducting time and motion studies for each job, inspection of job at each stage of production and setting piece rates.

The **Time Keeping** is an important part of the firm's system of accounting and control of labor cost. To show the effective utilization of labor time, there should be a proper maintenance of records.

In case of small concerns, the Production Department carries out this function. In case of large concerns, there is a separate Time Keeping Department headed by a Timekeeper. Information about the time of arrival, departure, idle time, overtime, etc., is supplied to the Payroll Department to enable the Payroll Department to pay wages to the workers.

Payroll Department is responsible for the computation and disbursement of wages payable to the workers. To ascertain the net wages payable, wage sheet or pay roll will be prepared and certain deductions are required to be made from gross wages to ascertain net wages. This Department is responsible for the computation of employee's wages, maintaining a record of job classification and wage rate, receiving time cards, piece-work cards, etc., verifying and summarizing time of each worker and making wage payments.

The **Cost Accounting Department** is responsible for the accumulation and classification of all labor costs. The Department along with time cards and job cards, prepares payrolls for the calculation of the labor cost of various job orders, processes, etc. This Department prepares a document known as Wages Abstract and also presents reports on normal and abnormal idle time, overtime, department labor costs, etc. These reports are then submitted to the management for initiating remedial action.

Glossary

- **Direct wages:** refers to the wages which can be identified with and allocated to cost units
- **Indirect Wages:** refers to the wages which cannot be allocated, but which can be apportioned to or absorbed by Cost Centres or Cost Units. These costs cannot be conveniently identified with a particular job, product or process
- **Time Study:** involves determination of standard time for an operation by direct time measurement. It is the art of observing and recording the time required for the completion of a work by 10 to 12 observations with the help of a watch
- **Motion Study:** is the study of movements of workers and machines in performing a particular operation. It is concerned with finding out the standardized methods for performing different operations, identifying and eliminating unnecessary and wasteful operations of workers
- **Work Study:** serves as an important analytical tool used as a basis for improvement of productivity. The main objective of work study is to bring about an overall improvement by saving time, reducing wastage of materials and developing new methods of work
- **Method Study:** is a technique used by engineers for making detailed analysis of the way in which production process is carried on. It involves the examination of the various tasks undertaken, the methods used in their performance, the sequence of operations, plant and equipment available and the factory layout and designing
- **Work Measurement:** involves the establishment of the work content of an operation. It determines the effective time required for doing a specified standard task by a worker after separating and eliminating the ineffective or wasteful time
- **Job Evaluation:** is a technique, which attempts to show the relative worth of the jobs. This is also a process of review, analysis and systematic classification of a job in accordance with its characteristics
- **Merit rating:** is a systematic evaluation of an employee's performance on the job in terms of the requirements of the job. To show the effective utilization of labor time, there should be a proper maintenance of records
- **Time Booking:** is the time spent by a worker on each job, process or operation
- **Job Card:** is prepared for each job and the workers enter the time of starting as well as completing the job
- **Piece Work Card:** is allotted to the workers who perform the work on the basis of piece rate to enter the number of units produced
- **Idle Time:** is the difference between the attendance time and job time. This represents the time during which worker has been present in the organization, but has not spent the same on the job
- **Normal Idle Time:** is that idle time which is unavoidable, normal and inherent in production. It is the wastage of labor time to be borne by the employer
- **Abnormal Idle Time:** is that time which is not caused or connected with the usual routine of production.
- **Overtime:** is the extra time put in by the workers beyond their normal hours of work.

Questions

(1) Explain briefly the various departments in an organization, which deal with labor cost.
(2) What is labor turnover? How is it measured? What are its causes and effects on labor costs?
(3) Distinguish 'Time Keeping' from 'Time Booking'.
(4) Distinguish 'Job Evaluation' from 'Merit Rating'.
(5) What is idle time? How is it treated in Cost Accounting?
(6) What is overtime? Explain its treatment in Cost Accounting.
(7) Explain the following terms:
  (a) Time and Motion Study
  (b) Work Study
  (c) Work Measurement
  (d) Method Study

PROBLEMS

(1) From the following data provided to you, find out the Labor Turnover Rate by applying *(a)* Flux Method *(b)* Replacement Method and *(c)* Separation Method.

Number of workers on the payroll:

At the beginning of the month – 500
At the end of the month – 600

During the month, 5 workers left, 20 persons were discharged and 75 workers were recruited. Of these, 10 workers were recruited in the vacancies of those leaving while the rest were engaged for an expansion scheme.

[Ans.: (a) 6.36%; (b) 1.82% and (c) 4.545%]

(2) From the following particulars, you are required to calculate under 'Average Wages Rate', the labor cost chargeable to Job No., 'A' which was completed in 2004.

Basic Wage Rate Rs. 2 per hour and overtime rates are as follows:

Before or after working hours: 150 % of basic wage rate.

Sundays and holidays: 200 % of basic wage rate.

During the year 2004, the following hours were worked:	
Normal Time	2,00,000 hours
Overtime before or after working hours	30,000 hours
Overtime on Sundays and holidays	20,000 hours
Total	2,50,000 hours
For Job 'A' 3500 hours were spent as follows:	
Normal Time	3,000 hours
Overtime before or after working hours	300 hours
Overtime on Sundays and holidays	200 hours
Total	3,500 hours

[Ans.: Average Wage Rate Rs. 2.28 per hour and Labor Cost chargeable to Job 'A' Rs. 7,980]

(3) Calculate normal, overtime and total wages payable to a worker from the particulars given below.

Days	*Hours worked*
Monday	10
Tuesday	9
Wednesday	8
Thursday	12
Friday	9
Saturday	4

Normal working hours = 8 per day; Saturdays: 4 per day.
Normal Rate = Rs. 5 per day
Overtime Rate: up to 9 hours per day – single rate and beyond 9 hours a day – double rate.
[Ans.: Normal Wages Rs. 220 and Overtime Wages Rs. 60]

(4) From the particulars given below, prepare the labor cost per man-day of 8 hours.

(a) Basic salary Rs. 2 per day
(b) Dearness allowance 25 paise per point over 100 cost of living index of working class – current cost of living index 700 points.
(c) Leave salary 10% of *(a)* and *(b)*
(d) Employer's contribution to Provident Fund 8% of *(a)*, *(b)* and *(c)*
(e) Employer's contribution to State Insurance 2.5% of *(a)*, *(b)* and *(c)*
(f) Expenditure on amenities to labor Rs. 20 per head per month.
(g) Number of working days in a month 25 days of 8 hours each.
[Ans.: Rs. 10.524]

(5) From the following information available, you are required to:
Calculate the Net Wages Bill as well as Total Wages Cost; and show necessary journal entries in Financial and Cost Accounts. As per the time cards, the gross earnings of the workmen are Rs. 30,000.The various deductions from the gross earnings are as under:

	Rs.
Employees' Contribution to Provident Fund	2,500
ESI – Employees' Contribution	400
Advances against wages	800
Co-operative dues	600
Income Tax	500
Canteen Charges	100

Company's contributions to Provident Fund and ESI are Rs. 2,500 and Rs. 800 respectively.
Analysis of time cards reveals that 85% of time utilized is on manufacturing operations and the balance is to be treated as indirect.

(I.C.W.A. Inter)

[Ans.: *(a)* Rs. 25,100; Rs. 33,300]

(6) The time taken for a particular operation by operator X in the process division of a manufacturing concern on three different counts was 24, 22 and 27 minutes while that of operator Y was 20, 23 and 26 minutes. It has been ascertained that the rating of X is 70/60 and that of Y is 55/60. Allowance for fatigue, personal needs is assumed at 15%. Calculate, using the above information as a base, for that particular operation:
(a) The standard time, and *(b)* the time allowed under an incentive allowance of 30% of the standard time.

(I.C.W.A. Inter)

[Ans.: *(i)* 28.446 minutes; *(ii)* 36.980 minutes]

❑ ❑ ❑

8

METHODS OF REMUNERATING LABOR

Objectives

The objectives of the study are to:

- Know the essential features of a satisfactory wage system
- Understand the situations where different methods of remunerating labor are applicable
- Learn the pros and cons of different methods of remuneration
- Understand the importance of incentive plans to individuals and group of workers

INTRODUCTION

There are many well-known systems of remunerating labor, each of which specifies a distinct method of calculating the wages payable to workers. In practice, these basic systems have been modified and adopted in numerous ways to suit the needs of individual concerns. This accounts for a very large number of methods of wage payments in use.

The installation of a suitable system of wage payment in a business is of particular interest to the Cost Accountant, because, wage system which allow high wages have the effect of increasing labor costs but this may not always result in high total cost. High wages may have the advantage of increased production as well as productivity and thus result in reducing the impact of fixed overheads and wages on unit cost.

On the other hand, low wages sometimes lead to high unit costs, due to reduced efficiency and increased labor turnover. Therefore, it is the responsibility of the Cost Accountant to suggest the management in achieving efficiency and ensuring economy.

FEATURES OF WAGE SYSTEM

A satisfactory wage system should reflect the following features:

(a) It should guarantee a minimum living wage to all the workers.
(b) It should be flexible and capable of being adapted to the changed circumstances.
(c) It should be consistent with the wage rates prevalent in the industry.
(d) It should reduce labor absenteeism and labor turnover.
(e) It should be based upon scientific time and motion studies.
(f) It should not be in violation of any Government policy.
(g) The system should finally promote healthy industrial relations.

METHODS OF REMUNERATION

Remuneration may be based on time or on piece-work. The following is the classification of methods of remuneration.

Methods of Remuneration

Time Rate System	Payment by Result
Time Rate	Piece-Work
Differential Rate	Combination of Time & Piece Rate
High Wage Plan	Premium Bonus Method
Measured Day Work	Group System

Piece Work Method may be Straight Piece Rate or Differential Piece Rate Methods. Again Differential Piece Rate Method can be Taylor's Differential Piece Rate Method or Merrick Differential Piece Rate Method.

A combination of time and piecework methods consists of Gantt Task Bonus System, Emerson's Efficiency system and Bedaux Points Scheme.

Premium Bonus Methods may be Halsey Plan and Rowan Plan.

I. Time Based System

This system of remunerating labor is the oldest of all the other systems. Under this system, workers are paid according to the time for which they actually work. The wage rate for a day worker may be fixed on hourly, daily, weekly, fortnightly or monthly basis depending upon the nature of his work. This system does not consider the quantity of work done.

Advantages: The advantages of this system are as follows:

(a) Calculation of wages is simple involving less clerical work and is easily understood by the workers.
(b) There is no distinction between efficient and inefficient workers and hence trade unions prefer this system.
(c) The workers are assured of steady and regular income.
(d) Quality of work is better under this system compared to piece rate system.

Disadvantages: The disadvantages of this system are as follows:

(a) This system offers same benefits to all and it does not serve as an incentive to workers to improve their skills.
(b) Equality in wages results in lower production.
(c) Standards for labor are difficult to be set.

Time rate system is suitable where the quality of work is of utmost importance, where the output is beyond the control of the worker and also difficult to measure in quantitative terms.

The various methods of time-based systems are Flat Time Rate, Differential Time Rate, High Wage Plan and Measured Day Work or Graduated Time Rate.

(1) Flat Time Rate or Time Rate

This is the oldest method of remunerating labor. It seeks to pay workers at a particular rate on the number of hours worked or the time actually put in by them as per the attendance record. The amount of wages due to a worker under this method would be arrived at, by multiplying the time clocked by the time rate. This rate is usually fixed taking into consideration the rate prevailing.

Advantages: The advantages of this system are as follows:

(a) It is simple to operate and easy to understand.
(b) This is the ideal method where the nature of work demands skills and craftsmanship.
(c) Suitable to certain types of work, which cannot be quantitatively measured.
(d) This is the only method adopted in case where workers cannot increase their output on account of the restricted speed of the machines on which they work.

Disadvantages: The disadvantages of this system are as follows:

(a) No distinction between efficient worker and an average or slow worker.
(b) It seeks to pay all the employees in a particular grade at the same rate regardless of their performance.
(c) Increases labor turnover as it leads to frustration among the efficient workers.
(d) Workers are inclined to produce as little as possible so that they can increase their wages by working overtime thus leading to low productivity.
(e) It involves high cost of supervision to see whether the workers are spending the time on the job or not.
(f) Standards cannot be set.
(g) Estimates and quotations may give a wrong idea if wages are based on time.

(2) Differential Time Rate

In this case, workers are divided into different grades depending on their relative skills classifying them as A, B and C grades etc. and are paid at different time rates.

This system encourages the workers to improve their performance and efficiency.

(3) High Wage Plan

This is a method of time - based system in which calculation of wages is same as that of other methods. However, it prescribes wages well above the normal basic time rates to those workers who are above the standard of efficiency thus encouraging the efficient workers.

The purpose behind this method is to attract efficient workers who can easily be motivated to achieve predetermined standards of efficiency and output. This method is suitable to the organizations where high quality of work coupled with increased productivity is recognized.

(4) Measured Day Work or Graduated Time Rate

Under this method, the hourly rate of wages is made to comprise both the fixed and variable elements. While the fixed element is dependent upon the nature of the job, the variable element varies for each worker and the same depends upon his merit rating and cost of living index. The aggregate of the fixed and variable part of wages for a day is known as measured day work of a worker.

II. Payment by Results/Piece Rate System

Under this system, payment is made based on the result obtained. The amount of wages depends upon the output turned out by the worker and not upon the time spent by him. Piece rate system is suited where production is standardized and the job is of repetitive nature.

The various methods of result-based systems mentioned above earlier are discussed below.

The different piece - work methods are given below.

(1) Straight Piece Rate Method

Under this method, a rate of wage known as the piece rate is fixed for each operation, job, piece or unit of production by time and motion study.

Considerable care and attention becomes necessary for the fixation of piece rates. It is necessary to determine scientifically, by time and motion study, the time required to complete a unit of production. The time thus arrived at becomes the time allowed or standard time. The total amount of wages depends upon the total output and the piece rate fixed for each unit of the output.

Advantages: The advantages of this system are as follows:

(a) This method is very simple and easy to understand.
(b) It requires less supervision.
(c) Wastage of time gets considerably reduced.
(d) It facilitates production control.
(e) It increases labor efficiency and skill since workers try to adopt improved methods of work.
(f) Workmen get the benefit of increased production and the employer is also, benefited by a saving in overheads.

Disadvantages: The disadvantages of this system are as follows:

(a) This method is not suitable to beginners as, at the initial stage, the output would be low.
(b) The quality of work may be affected when the workers try to increase the production to reap the benefits under this system.
(c) In fixing the piece rate, considerable work and time is involved.
(d) This method cannot be adopted in cases where work is not measurable and where quality is important.

(2) Differential Piece Rate Methods

Under the straight piece rate system, a flat rate per unit is paid for the entire output produced. The flat rate does not serve as an incentive to the increased output. The differential piece rate system seeks to overcome this disadvantage by paying at different rates for different levels of efficiency reflected in the output. The specific level of output is expressed as the standard and different piece rates are fixed for different levels of output at standard, below and above the standard prescribed. The different methods of differential piece rate system are discussed now.

(a) Taylor's Differential Piece Rate method

This method suggests a suitable remuneration to the efficient workers, by an increased piece rate beyond a certain level of output. Under this method, two different rates are fixed, i.e., one, a low rate for output below the standard and the other, a high piece rate for output at or above the standard.

A high task or a standard output and the standard time for the task are determined by time and motion study and this represents 100% efficiency. The worker is paid at a higher piece rate, if he completes the high task within the standard time.

For example, piece rate may be fixed at Re. 0.70 per piece up to a standard of 15 pieces per hour and Rs. 1.10 per piece if the daily production is 15 pieces or more per hour. Thus, if a worker produces 120 pieces in a day of 8 hours, then the wages would be 120 pieces @ Rs. 1.10 i.e. Rs. 132. If he produces 119 pieces, his wages would be 119 pieces @ Re. 0.70 i.e. Rs. 83.3 as his production is less than the standard where the standard production per day is 120 pieces, i.e., 15 pieces × 8 hours.

Illustration 1

With the help of the following information, ascertain the wages paid to workers Sonu & Raju under Taylor's Differential Piece Rate System.

Standard time allowed	50 units per hour
Standard time rate wage	Rs. 10 per hour

Differential piece rates to be applied:
75% of piece rate when below standard
125% of piece rate, when at and above standard
The workers have produced in a day of 8 hours as follows:

Sonu	250 units
Raju	420 units

Solution

Standard time allowed	50 units per hour
Time rate	Rs. 10 per hour

Accordingly, for 50 units per hour, time rate is Rs. 10 per hour
For 1 unit, time rate will be 10/50 = Re. 0.20 per unit
Low piece rate = 75% of piece rate = 75% × 0.20 = Rs. 0.15
High piece rate = 125% of piece rate = 125% × 0.20 = Rs. 0.25
At 50 units per hour, standard output for 8 hours = 400 units
Sonu produces 250 units i.e. less than the standard. Hence, he is entitled to be paid at the lower piece rate i.e. 250 units

× 0.15 = Rs. 37.50

Raju produces 420 units i.e. more than the standard. Hence, he is entitled to be paid at the higher piece rate i.e. 420 units × 0.25 = Rs. 105

Illustration 2

A factory employs two fitters, a welder and a helper on piece rate of Rs. 1,350. The time spent by each of them is 220 ordinary working hours. The rates of pay on time rate basis are Rs. 1.50 per hour for each of the two fitters and Re. 1.00 per hour for the welder and Re. 0.50 per hour for the helper.

Calculate the amount of piecework premium and the share of each worker, when the piece-work premium is divided proportionately on the basis of wages paid on time basis.

Solution

Statement of Labor Cost

Category	*Time taken*	*Rate of Pay* *Rs.*	*Time wages* *Rs.*	*Piece-work premium* *Rs.*
Fitter	220	1.50	330	120
Fitter	220	1.50	330	120
Welder	220	1.00	220	80
Helper	220	0.50	110	40
Total			990	360

Piece Work Premium: 1,350 – 990 = Rs. 360

Ratio for sharing Piece Work Premium = 330: 330: 220: 110

(b) Merrick Differential Piece Rate System

By using three graded piece rates instead of two as advocated by Taylor, this plan is endeavored to overcome the defects of Taylor's Plan. One-piece rate is established for the beginners, one for average workers and one for efficient workers. 83% efficiency is prescribed as the cut off point for the first piece rate. The different piece rates at different levels of efficiency are given below.

Efficiency	*Piece Rates applicable*
Up to 83%	Normal Rate
83% - 100%	10% above normal rate
Above 100%	20% above normal rate

Illustration 3

How much will a worker get under Merrick Differential Piece Rate system?

Standard production per hour = 6 units

Normal Rate per hour Rs. 1.20

In an 8 hour day, units produced by a worker = 32

Solution

Standard production: 6 units per hour

Rate per hour Rs. 1.20

Piece rate = 1.20/6 = Re. 0.20

Worker's efficiency:

If standard output is 48 units (6 units × 8 hours), actual output is 32

(32 × 100) / 48 = 66.6%

Efficiency being less than 83%, the worker is paid at the ordinary piece rate i.e.

32 × 0.20 = Rs. 6.40

Illustration 4

Find out the earnings of the workers on the basis of Merrick's Differential Piece Rate system from the following particulars.

Piece rate 10 paise per unit

Production of workers:

X 90 units

Y 100 units

Z 130 units
Standard production : 120 units
Basic piece rate is guaranteed up to 83% of standard production.

Workers get premium above 83% as follows:
Over 83% to 100% : 110% of the ordinary piece rate
Over 100% : 120% of the ordinary piece rate

Solution

Workers get wages and bonus if standard is achieved i.e.
Below 83% – normal production – Rs. 0.10 per unit
Between 83% to 100% – 110% of normal piece rate: (0.10 × 110)/100 = Re. 0.11 per unit
Over 100% – 120% of normal piece rate: (0.10 × 120)/100 = Re. 0.12 per unit
Standard production: 120 units

X Production: 90 units
Efficiency: (100 × 90) /120 = 75%, which is below 83%
Wages: 90 × 0.10 = Rs. 9

Y Production: 100 units
Efficiency: (100 × 100) /120 = 83.33%, which is above 83% but below 100%
Wages = 100 × .11 = Rs. 11

Z Production: 130 units
Efficiency: (100 × 130) /120 = 108%, which is above 100%
Wages = 130 × .12 = Rs. 15.60

III. Combination of Time and Piece Rate

Under this system, both, time method and piece methods of remunerating labor are combined and various plans are devised as explained below.

(1) Gantt Task Bonus Wages System

This system is a combination of timework and piecework. Under this plan, time rate is paid to a worker whose performance is below standard while others whose performance is above standard are paid at a high piece rate. For those workers whose performance is at standard are paid a bonus of 20 per cent of time rate.

Advantages: The advantages of this system are as follows:

(a) It is simple and easily understandable.
(b) It guarantees time wages.
(c) It offers good incentive to workers to work hard.
(d) It encourages better supervision and planning.
(e) It is a good system for beginners as time rate is guaranteed irrespective of their efficiency levels.

Disadvantages: The disadvantages of this system are as follows:

(a) Standard time and the guaranteed time rate may not be properly mixed.
(b) It categorizes the workers into skilled, semi skilled and unskilled which may not be liked by the workers.
(c) It may not encourage efficiency if workers feel contended with guaranteed time wages.

Illustration 5

The guaranteed time rate is Re. 1 per hour. High piece rate is Re. 0.30 per unit and the standard output is 10 units per hour. In a day of 8 hours, A produces 75 units, B – 80 units and C – 90 units. Calculate the earnings of the workers under Gantt Task Bonus System.

Solution

Standard output at 10 units per hour is 80 units (10 units × 8 hours).

A's output is below the standard, B's output is at the standard and C's output is above the standard. Accordingly, A gets time wages, B gets a bonus of 20% of the time rate and C gets the high piece rate.

Earnings:
A: 8 hours × 1 = Rs. 8
B: 8 hours × 1.2 (i.e. Re. 1 + 20% of Re. 1) = Rs. 9.6
C: 90 × Re. 0.30 = Rs. 27

Illustration 6

Calculate the earnings under Gantt Task Bonus Plan from the following information.

Standard production 80 units in a day of 8 hours, time rate – Rs.2 per hour, Production – A: 75 units; B – 80 units; C – 100 units; D – 64 units.

Solution

Output below standard: payment rate, i.e., Guaranteed day wages
Output at standard – 120% of time rate, i.e., Time rate + 20% of rate as bonus (Rs. 2 + 20%of Rs. 2 i.e. Rs. 2.40)
Output above standard – 120% of piece rate, i.e., High piece rate (120% of Re 0.20 = Re. 0.24)
Piece Rate: Rs. 2 /10 units, i.e. Re. 0.20
Standard output per hour is 80 units/8 hours = 10 units per hour

Worker	*Units*	*Position of Standard*	*Earnings*
A	75	Below Standard	2 × 8 hours = Rs. 16
B	80	At Standard	2.40 × 8 hours = Rs. 19.20
C	100	Above Standard	100 units × 0.24 = Rs. 24
D	64	Below Standard	2 × 8 hours = Rs. 16

(2) Emerson's Efficiency Plan

This scheme is designed to encourage slow workers to improve their performance. It guarantees time wages and encourages efficiency by paying a bonus if the output exceeds 66 2/3% of efficiency. The bonus to be paid at different levels of efficiency, are as follows.

Efficiency	*Emerson's Bonus %*
Below 66 2/3%	No bonus and only time rate wages.
66 2/3%–100%	Bonus is paid on the basis of step bonus rates, i.e., from 1% above wages on 67% efficiency to 20% above wages on 100% efficiency
Over 100%	A bonus of 20% plus a 1% bonus for every 1% increase in efficiency above 100% efficiency.

Note: Emerson used 32 different steps. Step bonus rates are:

Efficiency	*Emerson's Bonus %*
67 to 75%	1%
76 to 85%	4%
87%	7.56%
90 to 95%	10%
96 to 100%	20%

Efficiency percent is calculated as follows:

On time basis: Efficiency % = (Standard time / time taken) × 100

On output basis:

Efficiency % = (Actual output/standard output) × 100

Earnings = Wages + Bonus

This scheme is easy to understand and provides incentive to all types of workers i.e. slow workmen, skilled and efficient workers.

Illustration 7

From the following information, calculate the total earnings under Emerson's Efficiency Bonus Plan.
Standard output in 10 hours = 120 units
Actual output in 10 hours = 132 units
Time rate Rs. 2 per hour

Solution

Earnings = (Time taken × Time rate) + (Emerson Bonus % × Time Taken × Time Rate)
Efficiency % = (Actual production in terms of standard hours × 100) / actual hours worked
(standard hour method)

Actual production in terms of standard hours = (10 × 132 units) / 120 units = 11 hours
Efficiency % = (11 hours × 100) / 10 hours = 110%

OR

Efficiency % (output method) = (Actual output × 100) / standard output
Efficiency % = (132 × 100) / 120 = 110%
For 110% efficiency bonus % = 20% + 10% = 30%
Earnings = (10 × 2) + (30% × 10 × 2)
20 + 6 = Rs. 26

Illustration 8

Standard Output in 10 hours = 100 units i.e., 10 units per hour
Actual Output in 10 hours = 110 units
Rate per hour = Rs. 3
Calculate the earnings under Emerson's Efficiency Bonus system and also calculate the amount of earnings if the actual output is 87 units in 10 hours.

Solution

Efficiency	*Bonus*
Below 66 2/3%	No bonus and only time rate wages
66 2/3 – 100 %	Bonus paid on the basis of Step bonus rates i.e., from 1% above wages on 67% efficiency to 20% above wages on 100% efficiency
Over 100 %	Bonus of 20% + 1% bonus for every 1% increase in efficiency

Earnings = (Time taken × Time rate) + (Time taken × Time rate × Bonus %)
Efficiency % = (110 × 100) / 100 = 110%
For 110 % efficiency, Bonus % = 20% + 10% = 30%
Earnings = (10 × 3) + (10 × 3 × 30%)
= 30 + 9 = Rs. 39
When the actual output is 87 units, efficiency = (87 × 100) / 100 = 87%
At 87% efficiency Bonus will be 7.56%
Earnings = (10 × 3) + (10 × 3 × 7.56%)
= 30 + 2.268 = Rs. 32.268

(3) Bedaux Points Premium System

Under this plan, standard time is divided into standard minutes. Each minute of standard time is called as Bedaux Point or B's, which is indicated on each job ticket. Time wages are paid until 100% efficiency is reached. Above 100% efficiency, bonus is paid on the basis of number of Bedaux Points saved. Bonus at 75% of wages of Bedaux Points saved is paid to the worker and 25% is paid to the foreman.

Earnings = Time Wages + Bonus
Time wages = Hours worked × Rate per hour
Bonus = 75% × Bedaux points saved × rate per minute

The main limitation of this system is, it is not easily understood by workers. Detailed calculation of 'B' units involves heavy clerical expenditure. The main reason for its failure / unpopularity is sharing of bonus by the foreman.

Illustration 9

Standard points for a job = 800 points in 8 hours
Actual points earned = 900 points in 8 hours
Rate Re. 1 per hour
Calculate the earnings under Bedaux Scheme.

Solution

Time rate is guaranteed under Bedaux Scheme
Earnings = (Hours worked × Rate per hour) + (75% of Rate × Bedaux points saved / 60)
Bedaux points saved = Actual points earned – standard points for the job
900 – 800 = 100 points or 100 minutes
Earnings = (8 × 1) + (75% × 1 × 100 / 60)
8 + 1.25 = Rs. 9.25

IV. Premium Bonus Method

This method is a payment by results scheme. Under this system, bonus increases at an increasingly faster rate. Under this system, bonus is paid to each individual worker on the basis of time saved by him in doing a job.

Generally, it is not considered suitable for workers but it is valuable for supervisors and foremen.

Time saved = Time allowed – time taken

Premium bonus methods can be implemented only when the individual worker's performance can be measured. Time wages are guaranteed in most of the cases. The principle of this scheme is to combine the positive features of both, the time rate system and piece rate system as both the employer and the employee share the savings.

(1) Halsey Plan

F.A. Halsey, an American engineer, has introduced this plan in 1891. Under this plan, a standard time is fixed for doing a job by time and motion study. Time rate is guaranteed and 50% of time saved at time rate is paid as bonus and the remaining 50% of the time saved at the time rate goes to the employer. As the benefit is shared by both the employer and the employee equally, this plan is also known as the 'Split Bonus Plan or Fifty-Fifty Plan'.

Advantages: The advantages of this system are as follows :

(a) It guarantees time wages.
(b) It is simple to operate and can be easily understood by the workers.
(c) The benefit of time saved is equally shared, both, by the workers and management.
(d) Efficient workers are encouraged.

Disadvantages: The disadvantages of this system are as follows :

(a) Bonus payment makes workers rush through the work at the expense of quality.
(b) The incentive is not strong enough to induce efficient workers.
(c) Workers may not like to part with half of the share in the benefits to the management.

Note : In case of Halsey Weir Plan, time rate is guaranteed and 1/3rd of time saved multiplied at time rate is paid as bonus to the workers and the remaining 2/3rd of the time saved at the time rate goes to the employer.

Illustration 10

An operator engaged in machining certain components receives an ordinary rate of Rs. 1.60 per day of 8 hours. The standard output for machinery component has been fixed at 80 pieces per hour (time as found for premium bonus). On a certain day, the output of the worker on this machine is 800 pieces. Find the labor cost per 100 pieces and the wages that would have been earned by the workman under the following.

(a) If a bonus of Re. 0.23 is paid per 100 pieces of the extra output.
(b) If paid for on straight piecework basis.
(c) If Halsey Premium bonus system is being adopted.

Solution

(a) Standard Output : 640 units per day (80 pieces × 8 hours)
Bonus Re. 0.23 per 100 pieces of the extra output

		Rs.
	Wages per day (for 640 units)	1.60
	Bonus for extra output of 160 units(800 – 640) 160 × .23/100	0.37
	Total wages per day of 800 pieces	1.97
	Labor cost per 100 pieces = (1.97 × 100) / 800	0.246
(b)	Piece rate for 640 pieces	1.60
	Piece rate for 800 pieces (1.60 × 800 / 640)	2.00
	Labor cost per 100 pieces (2 × 100) / 800	0.25
(c)	Wages per day for 640 pieces	1.60
	Bonus (for half of 160 pieces) (1/2 × 160 × 1.60)/ 640	0.20
	Total wages	1.80
	Labor cost per 100 pieces (1.80 × 100) / 800	0.225

Alternatively, it can be worked out as follows :

Standard given is 80 units in an hour

Standard time for 800 units produced is 800 /80 = 10 hours
Actual time taken is 8 hours
Therefore, time saved is 10 – 8 = 2 hours
Time Rate per hour = 1.60 / 8 = Re. 0.20
Total earnings will be :
Wages for 8 hours = Rs. 1.60
Bonus = 2 hours × .20 × 50% = Re. 0.20
Wages + Bonus = 1.60 + 0.20 = Rs. 1.80

Illustration 11

Calculate the amount of wages and bonus earned by the worker.
Name : Surrender
Job commenced : Monday, 23rd September 2004 at 8 a.m.
Quantity of pieces of work gave out : 638
Quantity of pieces of work passed : 600
Workers rate : 50 paise per hour
Time allowed : 10 pieces per hour
Bonus 40% of time saved
Assume that the employee worked for 9 hours a day up to Friday and up to 1 p.m. on Saturday and no overtime.

Solution

Time allowed is 10 pieces per hour.
Number of pieces passed is 600
Hence, standard time for 600 pieces is 60 hours (600/10)
Time taken on the assumption of 9 hours a day is worked out below.

Monday to Friday (9 hours × 5 days)	45 hours
Saturday (from 8 a.m. to 1 p.m.)	5 hours
Total hours worked :	50
Time allowed :	60

Time saved is (60 – 50) 10 hours

Wages for time taken : 50 hours @ Re. 0.50 per hour	Rs. 25.00
Bonus for time saved : 40% of 10 hours @ Re. 0.50 per hour	Rs. 2.00
Total earnings	Rs. 27.00

(2) Rowan Plan

David Rowan has introduced Rowan Plan in 1901. Here, bonus is that proportion of the wages of time taken, which the time saved bears to the time allowed.

Under this plan, bonus varies according to the extent of time saved. This scheme is also known as Constant Sharing Plan.

The bonus can be calculated by applying the following formula :

Earnings = Time wages + Bonus
Time wages = Time taken × Time rate
Bonus = (Time taken × time rate) × time saved/time allowed

Illustration 12

During the first week of April 1991, the workman Mr. Kalyan manufactured 300 articles. He received wages for a guaranteed 48 hours week @ Rs. 4 per hour. The estimated time to produce one article is 10 minutes and under incentive scheme, the time allowed is increased by 20%. Calculate his gross wages according to :

(a) Piece work with a guaranteed weekly wage
(b) Rowan Premium Bonus and
(c) Halsey Premium bonus 50% to workman.

Solution

Estimated time to produce one article	10 minutes
Standard time to produce one article (increased by 20% i.e. 10 minutes + 20% of 10 minutes)	12 minutes

Standard time to produce 300 articles @ 12 minutes	60 hours or 3600 minutes
Time taken to produce 300 articles	48 hours

(a) Calculation of Gross Wages of Mr. Kalyan if he is paid according to piece method
Wages for 60 hours (time allowed for 300 articles) @ Rs. 4 = Rs. 240

(b) Calculation of Gross Wages if he is paid according to Rowan Premium System
Gross Wages = Actual Wages + Bonus
Wages = Time taken × Time Rate : 48 × 4 = Rs. 192
Bonus = (Time saved × Rate) Time taken / Standard time
Time Saved = Standard Time - Actual Time (60 – 48 hours) = 12 hours
12 × 4 × 48 / 60 = Rs. 38.40
Gross wages = 192 + 38.40 = Rs. 230.40

(c) Calculation of gross wages if he is paid according to Halsey Premium Bonus
Gross Wages = Time Taken × Time Rate + (Time Saved × Time Rate × Bonus %)
48 × 4 + (12 × 4 × 50%)
192 + 24 = Rs. 216

Illustration 13

A worker under the Halsey Method of remuneration has a day rate of Rs. 12 per week of 48 hours, plus a cost of living index of 12 paise per hour worked. He is given 9 hours task to perform, which he accomplishes in 6 hours. He is allowed 30% of the time saved as premium bonus. What would be his total hourly rate of earning and what difference would it make if he was paid under the Rowan method?

Solution

(a)	Under Halsey Plan:	
	Standard time allowed	9 hours
	Actual time taken	6 hours
	Time saved	3 hours
		Rs.
	Standard rate per hour = 12/48 = Re. 0.25	
	Therefore wages for 6 hours = 6 × 0.25 =	1.50
	Cost of Living Index = 6 × .12 =	0.72
	Bonus 30% of time saved = 3 × .25 × 30% =	0.23
	Total earnings for 6 hours =	2.45
(b)	Under Rowan Plan:	
	Wages for 6 hours = 6 × .25 =	1.50
	Cost of living Index = 6 × .12 =	0.72
	Bonus = 0.25 × 3 × 6/9 =	0.50
	Total:	2.72

V. Group System

The individual incentive plans explained so far, are also applicable to the work done by a group of workers. In some cases, individual incentive plans become inappropriate, where production depends upon the collective effort of a group of workers. In such cases, it becomes necessary to introduce bonus schemes for collective efficiency. The bonus calculated for a group should be divided amongst the workers irrespective of the number of workers.

The various types of Group Incentive Plans are :

(1) Priestman's Production Bonus

Under this scheme, a standard in terms of units or points is set for the output to be achieved each week. When the actual output exceeds the standard, workers are paid bonus in proportion to the increase in the production. For example, if the actual output is 1,40,000 units against a standard output of 1,00,000 units, then, workers in addition to their basic wages will receive a bonus equal to 40% of their basic wages. Because, actual output is 140 % of standard output.

***(a)* Rucker Plan or Cost Saving Sharing Plan:** Under this plan, bonus is tied up with value added which is defined as " the increase in realizable value resulting from an allocation in form, location or availability of a product or service, excluding the cost of purchased materials and services"- (CIMA Official Terminology).

Employees receive a constant proportion of value added. For example, if the ratio of direct labor to value added at 70% is taken as standard and if the actual ratio comes to 68%, then, 2% of actual value added is distributed as bonus so that the ratio of direct labor to value added is maintained at 68%.

Under this plan, generally, only 2/3rd of the bonus earned in a given pay period is distributed to the workers and the balance 1/3rd is transferred to the Reserve Fund to be used in a month when performance is below standard. This method is considered superior as it motivates workers to exert extra efforts and also motivates them to be on the look out for the other improvement opportunities like saving in material, improvement in methods, etc.

***(b)* Scanlon Plan:** This is similar to Rucker plan, but with a slight change in the ratio used. Instead of direct labor to value added, the ratio of direct labor to the sales value of production is used. This is vogue in the United States Steel Industry.

***(c)* Cost Premium Method:** Under this plan, the standard cost of production for a particular period is determined. This method is suitable for those industries where, the overhead cost forms a substantial portion of the total cost and an incentive to increased production lowers the cost per unit. The cost thus saved is distributed amongst workers in the form of bonus on an agreed basis.

***(d)* Towne Gain – Sharing Plan:** As under the cost premium method, under this scheme also, the bonus depends upon a saving in the labor cost. This method, named after H.R.Towne, an American who introduced it in 1886, is operated side by side with the time and piece rate systems. On the basis of past results, a standard labor cost per unit is determined and if the actual labor cost per unit is less than the standard, 5% of the saving is distributed among workers, including the foreman, in proportion of their wages.

Summary

There are many well-known systems of remunerating labor, each of which specifies a distinct method of calculating the wages payable to workers.

The installation of a suitable system of wage payment in a business is of particular interest to the Cost Accountant, because, wage system which allow high wages have the effect of increasing labor costs but this may not always result in high total cost. High wages may have the advantage of increased production as well as productivity and thus result in reducing the impact of fixed overheads and wages on unit cost. On the other hand, low wages sometimes lead to high unit costs, due to reduced efficiency and increased labor turnover. Therefore, it is the responsibility of the Cost Accountant to suggest the management in achieving efficiency and ensuring economy.

A satisfactory wage system should reflect the following features:

(a) It should guarantee a minimum living wage to all the workers.
(b) It should be flexible and capable of being adopted to changed circumstances.
(c) It should be consistent with the wage rates prevalent in the industry.
(d) It should reduce labor absenteeism and labor turnover.
(e) It should be based upon scientific time and motion studies.
(f) It should not be in violation of any Government policy.
(g) The system should finally promote healthy industrial relations.

Under Time Based system, workers are paid according to the time for which they actually work. The wage rate for a day worker may be fixed on hourly, daily, weekly, fortnightly or monthly basis depending upon the nature of his work. This system does not consider the quality and quantity of work done.

Time rate system is suitable where the quality of work is of utmost importance, where the output is beyond the control of the worker and also difficult to measure in quantitative terms.

Under Payment by Result system, payment is made based on the result obtained. The amount of wages depends upon the output turned out by the worker and not upon the time spent by him. Piece rate system is suited where production is standardized and the job is of repetitive nature.

The individual incentive plans, are also applicable to the work done by a group of workers. In some cases, individual incentive plans become inappropriate, where production depends upon the collective effort of a group of workers. In such cases, it becomes necessary to introduce bonus schemes for collective efficiency. The bonus calculated for a group should be divided amongst the workers irrespective of the number of workers.

Glossary

- **Time Based System:** Under this system, workers are paid according to the time for which they actually work
- **Differential Time Rate:** In this case, workers are divided into different grades depending on their relative skills classifying them as A, B and C grades, etc., and are paid at different time rates
- **Payment by Results/Piece Rate System:** Under this system, payment is made based on the result obtained

- **Straight Piece Rate Method:** Under this method, a rate of wage known as the piece rate is fixed for each operation, job, piece or unit of production by time and motion study
- **Differential Piece Rate:** The specific level of output is expressed as the standard and different piece rates are fixed for different levels of output at standard, below and above the standard prescribed
- **Taylor's Differential Piece Rate:** Under this method, two different rates are fixed, i.e., one, a low rate for output below the standard and the other, a high piece rate for output at or above the standard
- **Gantt Task Bonus Wages System:** Under this plan, time rate is paid to a worker whose performance is below standard, while others whose performance is above standard are paid at a high piece rate
- **Bedaux Point:** Each minute of standard time is called as Bedaux Point or B's, which is indicated on each job ticket
- **Halsey Plan:** Time rate is guaranteed and 50% of time saved at time rate is paid as bonus and the remaining 50% of the time saved at the time rate goes to the employer

Questions

(1) Explain the features of Wage System.
(2) What are the advantages and disadvantages of time rate and piece rate systems of wage payment? State the situations in which each system is effective and useful.
(3) Explain the various methods of Time-Based System.
(4) Explain Differential Piece Rate Methods.
(5) What measures do you suggest to control key labor costs?
(6) Explain the following:
(a) Gantt Task Bonus Wages System
(b) Emerson's Efficiency Plan
(c) Bedaux Points Premium System
(7) Discuss the merits and demerits of various Premium Bonus Methods
(8) Discuss the various Group Incentive Plans.

PROBLEMS

(1) From the following particulars, calculate the earnings of different workers under Differential Piece Rate Method.

Standard time per unit	6 units
Normal rate	Rs. 5 per hour

Differential piece rates :
80% of piece rate below standard
120% of piece rate at and above standard
In a day of 8 hours, the production for different workers is as under :

Amar	70 units
Badekhan	80 units
Chaplin	90 units
Dharamsingh	100 units

[Ans.: Amar : Rs. 28; Badekhan : Rs. 48; Chaplin : Rs. 54 and Dharamsingh : Rs. 60]

(2) Calculate the earnings of workers A, B and C under Straight Piece Rate System and Merrick's Multiple Piece Rate System from the following particulars.

Normal Rate per hour	Rs. 5.40
Standard time per unit	1 Minute

Output per day is as follows:
Worker A: 390 units
Worker B: 450 units
Worker C: 600 units
Working hours per day are 8
[Ans.: Straight Piece Rate System: A: Rs. 35.10; B: Rs. 40.50 and C: Rs. 54
Merrick Multiple Piece Rate System: A: Rs. 35.10; B: Rs. 44.55 and C: Rs. 64.80]

(3) From the following, calculate the earnings of A under Rowan plan.

Standard time	10 hours
Time rate	Re. 1 per hour
Time taken by A	9 hours

[Ans.: Rs. 9.90]

(4) Calculate the bonus under Halsey Scheme

Standard time	48 hours
Wages per hour	Re. 0.50

Gopal finishes in 36 hours and Ram finishes the job in 25 hours.
[Ans.: Gopal Rs. 21 and Ram Rs. 18.25]

(5) Compute the earnings of a worker from the following data under (a) Halsey and (b) Rowan Premium plan.

Standard time	10 hours
Wage rate per hour	Rs. 6
Time taken	8 hours

[Ans.: Halsey : Rs. 54 and Rowan : Rs. 50.40]

(6) A worker produced 200 units in a week's time. The guaranteed weekly wage payment for 45 hours is Rs. 81. The expected time to produce 1 unit is 15 minutes, which is further raised by 20% under the incentive scheme. What will be the earnings per hour of that worker under *(a)* Halsey and *(b)* Rowan Bonus schemes?

[Ans.: Earnings under *(a)* Halsey : Rs. 420 and *(b)* Rowan : Rs. 390]

(7) From the following particulars, you are required to work out the earnings of a worker for a week under *(a)* Straight Piece Rate; *(b)* Differential Piece Rate; *(c)* Halsey Premium Scheme and *(d)* Rowan Premium Scheme.

Weekly Working hours	48
Hourly wage rate	Rs. 7.50
Piece Rate per unit	Rs. 3.00
Normal time taken per piece	20 minutes
Normal output per week	120 pieces

[Ans. *(a)* Rs. 450; *(b)* Rs. 540; *(c)* Rs. 397.50 and *(d)* Rs. 432]

(8) Sushma produced 1000 units of a product in an 8 hour day. The work standard established by time study is 100 units per hour. If the base hourly rate is Rs. 20, how much income would be received under the following plans?

- Straight Piece Work
- Halsey Plan
- Rowan Plan and
- Gantt Task System

[Ans.: *(a)* Rs. 200; *(b)* Rs. 180; *(c)* Rs. 192; *(d)* Rs. 240]

❑ ❑ ❑

9

OVERHEADS

Objectives

The objectives of the study are to:

- understand the meaning of overheads
- classify the overheads
- know the need for codification of overheads
- learn the procedurc for distribution of overheads

Introduction

Every form of production involves two types of costs - direct costs and indirect costs. The total of all direct costs such as direct material, direct wages and direct expenses is termed as 'Prime cost' and the total of all indirect costs such as indirect material, indirect wages and indirect expenses is known as 'Overheads'. These indirect expenses cannot be charged directly to a specific job, product or service. The indirect portion of the total cost constitutes the overhead cost. Overheads are also known as Loading, Burden, Oncost, Supplementary Costs and Non Production Costs, I.C.M.A. London defined overheads as "an aggregate of indirect material, indirect wages and indirect expenses".

According to Blocker and Welmer "overhead costs are the operating costs of a business enterprise which cannot be traced directly to a particular unit of output. Such costs are invisible or unaccountable".

In the words of Harold J. Wheldon, "overhead may be defined as the cost of indirect material, indirect labour and such other expenses including services as cannot conveniently be charged to specific unit. Alternatively, overheads are all expenses other than direct costs".

Cost Accounting Standard 3 (CAS 3) : *Overheads*

The standard deals with the method of collection, allocation, apportionment and absorption of overheads. In Cost Accounting, the analysis and collection of overheads, their allocation and apportionment to different cost centres and absorption to products or services plays an important role in determination of cost as well as for control purposes. A system of better distribution of overheads can only ensure greater accuracy in determination of cost of products or services. It is, therefore, necessary to follow standard practices for allocation, apportionment and absorption of overheads for preparation of cost statements.

The standard is to prescribe the methods of collection, allocation, apportionment of overheads to different cost centres and absorption thereof to products or services on a consistent and uniform basis in the preparation of cost statements and to facilitate inter-firm and intra-firm comparison. The standardization of collection, allocation, apportionment and absorption of overheads is to provide a scientific basis for determination of cost of different activities, products, services, assets, etc. The standard is to facilitate in taking commercial and strategic management decisions such as resource allocation, product mix optimization, make or buy decisions, price fixation, etc. It aims at ensuring better disclosure requirement and transparency in the cost statement.

The standard should be followed for treatment of overheads by all enterprises including companies covered under Cost Accounting Records Rules issued in pursuant to Sec 209(1)(d) of the Companies Act, 1956 or under the provisions of any other Act, Rules and Regulations.

The standard shall be applied in Cost and Management Accounting practices relating to Cost of products, services or activities; Valuation of stock; Transfer pricing; Segment Performance; Excise/Custom duty, VAT, Income Tax, Service Tax and other levies, duties and abatement fixation and Cost statements for any other purpose.

Classification of Overheads

Overheads may be broadly classified according to functions, elements and behaviour. The following chart gives their classification at a glance.

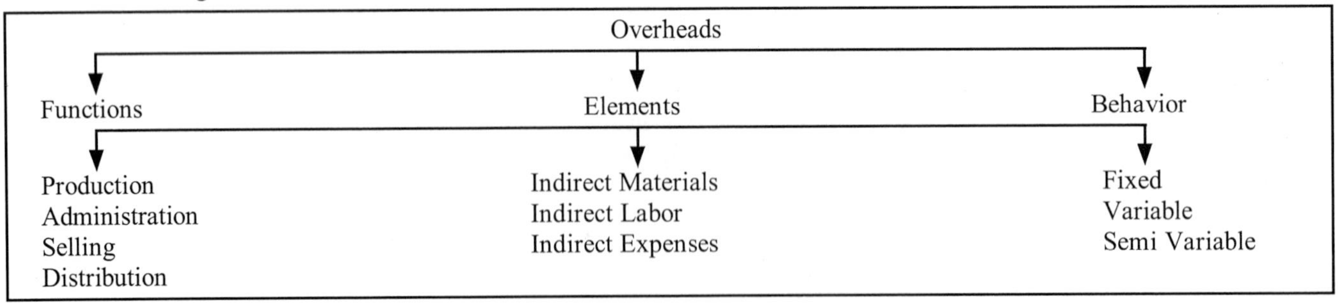

I. According to Functions

This method of classification is based on the major business functions i.e. production, administration, selling and distribution.

(1) Production Overheads: These costs are also known as manufacturing overheads, factory overheads or works overheads. They are the aggregate of the indirect expenses of operating the production division of a concern and include all the indirect expenses incurred to convert the raw material into finished product.

Examples: lubricants; factory power; cotton waste; consumable stores; depreciation and insurance of plant and machinery and factory building; repairs and maintenance; store keeping expenses; indirect wages, etc.

(2) Administration Overheads: The other terms used are general or office overheads. These include all such expenses connected with the direction; control and administration functions of the business excluding those connected with selling and distribution functions.

Examples: office rent and rates; office lighting and heating; office salaries; audit fees; postage and telephone; printing and stationery; legal charges; depreciation of office building and machinery, etc.

(3) Selling Overheads: This type of expenditure is incurred in promoting sales and retaining the customers. It is that portion of the marketing cost, which is incurred in serving orders.

Examples: advertisement; salesmen salaries; brokerage and commission; bad debts; showroom expenses, traveling expenses, etc.

(4) Distribution Overheads: The expenditure incurred from the time product is completed in the factory until it reaches the market or a customer is classified as distribution overheads.

Examples: packing and shipping expenses; carriage outwards; warehousing cost; delivery van costs, etc.

Selling and distribution overheads are incurred after the completion of the production work and hence together are called as "After Production Costs".

II. According to Elements

Under this category, the expenditure is classified into indirect material, indirect labour and indirect expenses.

(1) Indirect Material: It is a cost, which cannot be directly allocated to a particular job or production but is absorbed by cost centres or cost units indirectly.

Examples: nuts and bolts, lubricating oil, gum, sand paper, tools for general use, etc.

(2) Indirect Labor: It is such wages, which cannot be conveniently identified with a particular cost unit.

Examples: gratuity, holiday pay, leave pay, contribution to provident fund, supervisory salary, overtime wages, etc.

(3) Indirect Expenses: All the costs other than indirect material and indirect wages, which cannot be allocated directly to any job, process or work are termed as indirect expenses.

Examples: rent and rates, depreciation, insurance, etc.

III. According to Behavior

This classification is based on the variability of overheads according to the volume of production. On this basis, overheads are classified into fixed overheads, variable overheads and semi fixed or semi variable overheads.

(1) Fixed Overheads: These are period costs, which remain fixed in total amount irrespective of the fluctuations in the volume of output. But, if the change in output is substantial, they also increase in the long run. Though the total cost is constant during a given period, the cost per unit of production varies inversely with the volume of output. These costs are known as period costs because, these are dependent on time rather than on output.

Examples: rent and taxes, salaries of staff, postage, stationery, building depreciation, legal expenses, etc.

(2) Variable Overheads: These costs, in aggregate, change in direct proportion to changes in the volume of output. But, the variable cost per unit of output remains the same.

Examples: indirect material, indirect labor, power, salesmen commission, fuel expenses, etc.

(3) Semi Variable Overheads: These costs are partly fixed and partly variable. They are constant upto a particular level of output and thereafter vary with the change in the level of output.

Examples: depreciation, repairs and maintenance, supervisory salary, etc.

The classification of costs into fixed and variable assumes great importance in planning, decision-making and controlling. The various uses of this classification are given below:

(i) In a flexible budget, we prepare the budget for different levels of activity. In the preparation of flexible budgets, the distinction between fixed and variable cost is necessary as fixed costs remain constant at all the levels of activity, whereas, variable costs vary according to the actual level of output.

(ii) As the main problem of decision making is related to changes in the volume of output, the seggregation of costs into fixed and variable components assumes importance in decisions relating to introduction of new product lines, fixation of selling prices, using alternative methods of production, etc.

(iii) The marginal costing technique is totally dependent on the separation of costs into fixed and variable. In this technique, only variable costs are charged to the product and fixed costs are treated as period costs which can be recovered in the long run from the contribution i.e. sales price in excess of variable cost.

(iv) Classification of costs into fixed and variable facilitates effective cost control by pointing out where the management should concentrate to control the cost. Fixed costs are generally non-controllable in the short run, whereas, variable costs are mostly controllable. For example, material cost which is a variable cost can be controlled by

purchasing in economic lots or purchasing during slack season whereas salaries of the staff, a fixed cost, may not be controllable in the short run.

Any item of overheads arising out of abnormal situation in business activity should not be treated as overheads. They are charged to Costing Profit and Loss Account. Items not related to business activities such as donation, loss / profit on sale of assets etc., are also not to be treated as overheads. Borrowing cost and other financial charges including foreign exchange fluctuations will not form the part of overheads.

Illustration 1

The standard departmental overhead rate is Rs. 15 per hour. Based on the following details provided to you, work out the activity level at which the overhead rate has been fixed.

Activity Level (Hours)	Overheads Allowance (Rs.)
6,000	1,20,000
8,000	1,44,000
10,000	1,68,000

(I.C.W.A. Inter, Dec., 1993)

Solution

Computation of Variable and Fixed Overheads

(1) **Variable Overhead per unit**

$$\frac{\text{Change in Overhead allowance}}{\text{Change in Activity Level}} \quad \frac{\text{Rs.}1,68,000 - \text{Rs.}1,20,000}{10,000\text{ hrs} - 6,000\text{ hrs.}} \quad \frac{\text{Rs.}\,48,000}{4,000\text{ hrs.}}$$

= Rs. 12 per hour

(2) **Fixed Cost** = Rs. 1,20,000 – (6,000 × Rs. 12) = Rs. 1,20,000 – Rs. 72,000
= Rs. 48,000

Fixed Overhead at activity level of 10,000 hours	*(Rs.)*
Total overheads	1,68,000
Less: Variable Overheads (10,000 @ Rs. 12)	1,20,000
Fixed Overheads	48,000

	(Rs.)
Standard Departmental overhead rate	15
Less: Variable overhead rate	12
Fixed overhead rate	3

Calculation of activity level at which the overhead rate has been fixed
= (Fixed Overheads/Fixed Overhead rate) = (Rs. 48,000/Rs. 3 per hour) = 16,000 hrs.
The standard departmental overhead rate is fixed at Rs. 15 based on the activity level of 16,000 hours.

Codification of Overheads

After the classification of overheads as above, each group of overhead is to be given a number or code so that the items of expenses of a similar nature may be grouped together under one head. Such numbers or symbols are called as Standing Order Numbers and are shown on all documents used in Cost Accounting System.

The allocation of code numbers or symbols can be done by following a serial number (1,2,3,4 and so on) or a decimal system (1.1, 1.2, 1.3, 1.4 and so on) or an alphabet (A, B, C, D and so on) or a combination of alphabets and numbers (A1, A2, A3, A4 and so on).

Example: If 'F' denotes Factory Overhead, F1 may indicate Factory Indirect Material, F2 Factory Indirect Labour, F3 Factory Power and so on.

The number of standing order numbers depends on the size of the factory, type of expenses and the extent of control necessary. The codification of overheads should be clear, unambiguous and flexible so that as and when need arises; suitable changes can be made without seriously dislocating the existing system.

DISTRIBUTION OF OVERHEADS

After the classification and codification of overheads, the next step is distribution of overheads. As overhead costs cannot be directly allocated to cost units, the following procedure is followed in the distribution of overhead cost.

(1) Collection of overheads according to standing order numbers.
(2) Allocation and apportionment of overheads to Production and Service Departments on some suitable basis.
(3) Reapportionment of Service Departments costs to Production Departments only
(4) Reapportionment of Service Departments costs to Production Departments and Service Departments and
(5) Absorption of overheads of each of the Production Departments by Cost Units.

Collection of Overheads

Collection of overheads means the pooling of indirect items of expenses from books of account and supportive/ corroborative records into logical groups having regard to their nature and purpose.

Overheads are collected on the basis of pre-planned groupings, called cost pools. Homogeneity of the cost components in respect of their behavior and character is to be considered in developing the cost pool. Variable and fixed overheads should be collected in separate cost pools under a Cost Centre. A great degree of homogeneity in the cost pools are to be maintained to make the apportionment of overheads more rational and scientific. A cost pool for maintenance expenses will help in apportioning them to different Cost Centres which use the maintenance service.

The various items of overheads are collected under separate standing order numbers. The main sources from where overheads collected are invoices, stores requisition slips, wages analysis sheets, cashbook, journal entries and other reports and registers.

Departmentalization of Overheads

In case of multi-product environment, there are common Service Cost Centres which are providing services to the various production cost centres and other Service Cost Centres. The costs of services are required to be apportioned to the relevant cost centres. First step to be followed is to apportion the overheads to different cost centres and then second step is to apportion the costs of Service Cost Centres to Production Cost Centres on an equitable basis. The first step is termed as primary distribution and the second step is termed as secondary distribution of overheads.

The allocation and apportionment of overheads to Production and Service Departments is known as Departmentalisation or Primary Distribution of Overheads. It involves two stages, viz., Allocation and Apportionment of Overheads.

Allocation of Overheads

Allocation of overheads is assigning a whole item of cost directly to a Cost Centre. An item of expense which can be directly related to a Cost Centre is to be allocated to the Cost Centre. For example, depreciation of a particular machine should be allocated to a particular cost centre if the machine is directly attached to the Cost Centre.

It is the process of charging or allotting the full amount of overhead costs to a particular cost centre or cost unit. It is possible only when the expenses can be easily identified with a particular cost centre. It is that part of cost attribution, which charges a specific cost to a Cost Centre/Cost Unit.

Example: salary paid to the foreman of a particular Department, indirect material, indirect wages, overtime, idle time, power (when sub meters are installed in the Department) can be easily identified with a Department and therefore directly charged to that Department.

Apportionment of Overheads

Apportionment of overhead is distribution of overheads to more than one cost centre on some equitable basis. When the indirect costs are common to different cost centres, these are to be apportioned to the cost centres on an equitable basis. For example, the expenditure on general repair and maintenance pertaining to a department can be allocated to that department but has to be apportioned to various machines (Cost Centres) in the department. If the department is involved in the production of a single product, the whole repair and maintenance of the department may be allocated to the product.

When an item of overhead cost cannot be directly identified with a particular Department, such cost is charged to the cost centers on an equitable basis. It refers to the distribution of overheads among Departments or Cost Centres on an equitable basis. It is the allotment of proportions of items of cost to Cost Centres/Cost Units. If an overhead cannot be allocated, it is apportioned. The costs which are common to the cost centres like power of the whole factory, fire insurance, lighting and power, stores and canteen Department expenses, medical and other welfare expenses etc. are to be equitably shared between the various Production and Service Departments.

The main difference between allocation and apportionment of overheads is that allocation deals with the allotment of whole items while apportionment deals with the allotment of proportions of items of overheads.

Apportionment of overheads to Production and Service Departments can be by any of the following methods.

(i) **Service or Use:** Here, the overhead cost borne by each cost centre or cost unit will be in proportion to the service rendered by it. Greater the service rendered by a cost centre/cost unit, larger the amount of overhead cost borne by it. Example: rent is apportioned to the Departments on the basis of floor area occupied by each Department.

(ii) **Survey Method:** When it is difficult to select a suitable base of apportionment, a survey is made of the various factors involved and the overhead cost to be shared by each cost centre/cost unit is determined. Example: Lighting expenses may be apportioned on the basis of a survey of the number of lights and the estimated hours of use.

(iii) **Ability to Pay Method:** Here, the Unit/Department having the largest income is charged with the largest of overhead cost similar to the theory of taxation which holds that those who have the largest income should bear the highest proportion of tax burden. Thus, the most efficient or profitable Department is burdened with the largest share of overhead cost. Therefore, the method is generally considered as an irrational and inequitable method.

Bases of Apportionment:

The most commonly used bases of apportionment of overhead are given below.

	Basis of Apportionment	*Overheads*
(1)	Floor Area	Rent of the building; lighting and heating; rates and taxes; other building expenses like insurance, depreciation and repairs.
(2)	Capital Value	Depreciation, insurance, repairs and maintenance of plant and machinery; insurance of stock.
(3)	Direct Labor hours	General overheads. or machine hours
(4)	Technical Estimates	Lighting; power and steam consumption; managerial salaries; internal transport.
(5)	Number of Workers	Canteen expenses; welfare expenses; time keeping expenses; supervision.
(6)	Weight/Value of Material	Material handling expenses; store keeping expenses.

It should be noted that there is no hard and fast rule regarding the basis of apportionment. The choice of an appropriate method of apportionment is a matter of judgement. Apportionment should be based on the technical opinion of the Department concerned and the expertise of the Cost Accountant.

Illustration 2

Shirisha Company is divided into four Departments A, B, C as Production Departments and D as Service Department. The actual costs for a period are as follows.

	Rs.
Rent	1,000
Repairs to Plant	600
Depreciation of Plant	450
Employer's liability for insurance	150
Supervision	1,500
Fire Insurance in respect of Stock	500
Power	900
Light	120

The following information is available in respect of the four Departments:

	Dept. A	*Dept. B*	*Dept. C*	*Dept. D*
Area (sq. Mts.)	1,500	1,100	900	500
No. of employees	20	15	10	5
Total wages (Rs.)	6,000	4,000	3,000	2,000
Value of Plant (Rs.)	24,000	18,000	12,000	6,000
Value of Stock (Rs.)	15,000	9,000	6,000	—
H.P. of Plant	24	18	12	6

Apportion the cost to the Departments on the most equitable basis.

Solution

Overheads Distribution Statement

Item	*Basis*	*Dept. A* *Rs.*	*Dept. B* *Rs.*	*Dept. C* *Rs.*	*Dept. D* *Rs.*
Rent	Floor Area	375	275	225	125
Repairs	Plant Value	240	180	120	60
Depreciation	Plant Value	180	135	90	45
Light	Floor Area	45	33	27	15
Power	H.P.	360	270	180	90
Supervision	No. of emp.	600	450	300	150
Fire Insurance	Stock Value	250	150	100	—
Insurance	No. of emp.	60	45	30	15
Total		2,110	1,538	1,072	500

Illustration 3

A Company's production for the year ending 30.06.04 is given below.

	Production Department			*Service Department*		
	P1	*P2*	*P3*	*Office*	*Stores*	*Workshop*
Direct Wages (Rs.)	20,000	25,000	30,000			
Direct Material (Rs.)	30,000	35,000	45,000			
Indirect Material (Rs.)	2,000	3,000	3,000	1,000	2,000	2,000
Indirect Wages (Rs.)	3,000	3,000	4,000	10,000	10,000	5,000
Area (sq.mts)	200	250	300	150	100	250
Machinery (Rs.)	30,000	35,000	25,000	—	—	15,000
H.P. of Machinery	15	20	25	—	—	5
Machine hours worked	10,000	20,000	15,000	—	—	—

General expenses : Rent Rs. 12,500; insurance Rs. 1,050; depreciation 15% of the value of machinery; power Rs. 3,800; light Rs. 1,250.

You are required to prepare an Overhead Distribution analysis sheet for the Department showing clearly the basis of apportionment where necessary.

Solution

Statement showing apportionment of Overheads

		Production Department			*Service Department*		
	Basis	*P1* *Rs.*	*P2* *Rs.*	*P3* *Rs.*	*Office* *Rs.*	*Stores* *Rs.*	*Workshop* *Rs.*
Indirect Material		2,000	3,000	3,000	1,000	2,000	2,000
Indirect Wages		3,000	3,000	4,000	10,000	10,000	5,000
Rent Area		2,000	2,500	3,000	1,500	1,000	2,500
Insurance	Machinery	300	350	250	—	—	150
Depreciation	–	4,500	5,250	3,750	—	—	2,250
Power	H.P	877	1,169	1,462	—	—	292
Light	Area	200	250	300	150	100	250
Total		12,877	15,519	15,762	12,650	13,100	12,442

	Basis	Production Department P1 Rs.	P2 Rs.	P3 Rs.	Service Department Office Rs.	Stores Rs.	Workshop Rs.
Secondary Distribution							
Office expenses	D.Wages	3,373	4,217	5,060	-12,650	—	—
Stores expenses	D. Material	3,573	4,168	5,359	—	–13,100	—
Workshop expenses	Machine Hrs.	2,765	5,530	4,147	—	—	-12,442
Total		22,588	29,434	30,328			

Illustration 4

Deccan Manufacturing Ltd. have three departments, which are regarded as Production Departments. Service Departments' costs are distributed to these Production Departments using the 'Step Ladder Method' of distribution. Estimates of factory overhead costs to be incurred by each department in the forthcoming year are as follows. Data required for distribution is also shown against each department:

Department		*Factory Overhead (Rs.)*	*Direct Labor Hours*	*No. of Employees*	*Area in sq.m.*
Production:	X	1,93,000	4,000	100	3,000
	Y	64,000	3,000	125	1,500
	Z	83,000	4,000	85	1,500
Service:	P	45,000	1,000	10	500
	Q	75,000	5,000	50	1,500
	R	1,05,000	6,000	40	1,000
	S	30,000	3,000	50	1,000

The overhead costs of the four service departments are distributed in the same order, viz., P, Q, R and S respectively on the following basis:

Department	*Basis*
P	Number of Employees
Q	Direct Labor Hours
R	Area in square metres
S	Direct Labor Hours

You are required to:

(a) Prepare a schedule showing the distribution of overhead costs of the four Service Departments to the three Production Departments; and

(b) Calculate the overhead recovery rate per direct labor hour for each of the three Production Departments.

(C.A., Inter, May, 1988)

Solution

Statement showing redistribution of Overhead Costs of Service Departments to Production Departments (Step down method)

(Rs.)

Particulars	*Basis of Apportionment*	*Service Depts.* P	Q	R	S	*Production Depts.* X	Y	Z
Factory Overheads	Direct	45,000	75,000	1,05,000	30,000	1,93,000	64,000	83,000
Dept.P	D.L.H	(45,000)	5,000	4,000	5,000	10,000	12,500	8,500
Dept. Q	Area	—	(80,000)	24,000	12,000	16,000	12,000	16,000
Dept. R	D.L.H	—	—	(1,33,000)	19,000	57,000	28,500	28,500
Dept. S		—	—	—	(66,000)	24,000	18,000	24,000
Total (A)						3,00,000	1,35,000	1,60,000
Direct Labor hours (B)						4,000	3,000	4,000
Overhead recovery rate per Direct Labor hour (A) / (B)						Rs. 75	Rs. 45	Rs. 40

Illustration 5

A company manufactures three products PRIMA, DONNA and MEGA. Its market has three zones – North, South and East.

The estimated sales for 1985 are as below:

	North *Rs.*	*South* *Rs.*	*East* *Rs.*
Prima	20,000	8,000	—
Donna	12,000	—	32,000
Mega	—	28,000	16,000

Budgeted advertising outlay is as below:

	North	South	East	Total
Local cost (Rs.)	1,280	1,800	1,680	4,760
General (Rs.)	—	—	—	2,320

Work out a statement to present the advertising cost per cent on sales for each product and for each territory.

(B.Com., Madurai, April, 1986)

Solution

Statement showing allocation and apportionment of Advertising Cost

Advertising Cost	*Basis*	*Sales Territories*			
		Total *Rs.*	*North* *Rs.*	*South* *Rs.*	*East* *Rs.*
Local cost	Direct	4,760	1,280	1,800	1,680
General	% of sales 8:9:12	2,320	640	720	960
Total		7,080	1,920	2,520	2,640
Estimated sales		1,16,000	32,000	36,000	48,000
Advertisement cost as% of sales			6%	7%	5.5%

Apportionment of advertisement cost amongst the products

Territory	*Products*				
	%	*Prima* *Rs.*	*Donna* *Rs.*	*Mega* *Rs.*	*Total* *Rs.*
North	6%	1,200	720	—	1,920
South	7%	560	—	1,960	2,520
East	5.5%	—	1,760	880	2,640
Total advertisement cost		1,760	2,480	2,840	7,080
Estimated sales (given)		28,000	44,000	44,000	1,16,000
Advertisement cost as % of sales		6%	6%	6%	6%

SUMMARY

The total of all direct costs such as direct material, direct wages and direct expenses is termed as 'Prime cost' and the total of all indirect costs such as indirect material, indirect wages and indirect expenses is known as 'Overheads'. These indirect expenses cannot be charged directly to a specific job, product or service. The indirect portion of the total cost constitutes the overhead cost.

Overheads may be broadly classified according to functions, elements and behavior. According to functions, they are classified as Production, Administration, Selling and Distribution Overheads. According to Elements, they are grouped as Indirect Materials, Indirect Labor and Indirect Expenses. According to Behavior, they are classified as Fixed, Variable and Semi Variable Expenses.

After the classification of overheads as above, each group of overhead is to be given a number or code so that the items of expenses of a similar nature may be grouped together under one head. Such numbers or symbols are called as Standing Order Numbers and are shown on all documents used in Cost Accounting System.

After the classification and codification of overheads, the next step is distribution of overheads. The distribution of overhead costs involves

(1) Collection of overheads according to standing order numbers.
(2) Allocation and apportionment of overheads to Production and Service Departments on some suitable basis.
(3) Reapportionment of Service Departments costs to Production Departments only
(4) Reapportionment of Service Departments costs to Production Departments and Service Departments and
(5) Absorption of overheads of each Production Departments by Cost Units.

Glossary

- **Overheads:** include all indirect costs such as indirect material, indirect wages and indirect expenses.
- **Production Overheads:** are the aggregate of the indirect expenses of operating the production division of a concern and include all the indirect expenses incurred to convert the raw material into finished product.
- **Administration Overheads:** include all such expenses connected with the direction, control and administration functions of the business excluding those connected with selling and distribution functions.
- **Selling Overheads:** include expenditure incurred in promoting sales and retaining the customers.
- **Distribution Overheads**: the expenditure incurred from the time product is completed in the factory until it reaches the market or a customer.
- **Indirect Material:** is a cost, which cannot be directly allocated to a particular job or production but is absorbed by cost centres or cost units indirectly.
- **Indirect Labor:** is such wages, which cannot be conveniently identified with a particular cost unit.
- **Indirect Expenses:** are the costs other than indirect material and indirect wages, which cannot be allocated directly to any job, process or work.
- **Fixed Overheads:** are the period costs, which remain fixed in total amount irrespective of the fluctuations in the volume of output.
- **Variable Overheads:** are the costs, in aggregate, change in direct proportion to changes in the volume of output. But, the variable cost per unit of output remains the same.
- **Semi Variable Overheads:** are partly fixed and partly variable costs. They are constant up to a particular level of output and thereafter vary with the change in the level of output.
- **Departmentalization or Primary Distribution of Overheads:** The allocation and apportionment of overheads to Production and Service Departments.
- **Allocation of Overheads:** is the process of charging or allotting the full amount of overhead costs to a particular cost centre or cost unit.
- **Apportionment:** the distribution of overheads among Departments or Cost Centers on an equitable basis. It is the allotment of proportions of items of cost to Cost Centres/Cost Units.

Questions

(1) Define overheads and explain briefly the classification of overheads.
(2) Explain the differences between fixed, variable and semi variable overheads.
(3) Explain the terms allocation, apportionment, reapportionment and absorption of overheads with suitable illustrations.
(4) How do you reapportion the selling and distribution cost?
(5) What are the different methods of apportionment of overheads?
(6) Differentiate Primary Distribution of Overheads from Secondary Distribution of overheads.

PROBLEMS

(1) Swetha Ltd. has four Departments. A, B and C are the Production Departments and D is a Service Department. The actual costs for a period are as follows:

Indirect Materials:		
Department A	Rs.	950
Department B	Rs.	1,200
Department C	Rs.	200
Department D	Rs.	1,500
Indirect Wages:		
Department A	Rs.	900
Department B	Rs.	1,100
Department C	Rs.	300
Department D	Rs.	1,000

Rent Rs. 2,000; repairs Rs. 1,200; depreciation Rs. 900; light Rs. 200; supervision Rs. 3,000; insurance (stock) Rs. 1,000; employees insurance (employer's liability) Rs. 300; power Rs. 1,800
The following data are also available in respect of four Departments.

	Dept. A	*Dept. B*	*Dept. C*	*Dept. D*
Area (sq. Mts.)	150	110	90	50
No. of employees	24	16	12	8
Total wages (Rs.)	8,000	6,000	4,000	2,000
Value of Plant (Rs.)	24,000	18,000	12,000	6,000
Value of Stock (Rs.)	15,000	9,000	6,000	—

Apportion the above costs to various departments on most equitable method.
[Ans.: Dept. A: Rs. 6,055; Dept. B: Rs. 5,265; Dept. C: Rs. 2,635 and Dept. D: Rs. 3,595]

(2) A factory has two Production Departments and two Service Departments. The following figures have been extracted from the books of the respective Departments.

	Production Departments		*Service Departments*	
	Dept. A	*Dept. B*	*Dept. C*	*Dept. D*
Area (sq. Mts.)	1,500	1,100	900	500
No. of employees	40	30	20	10
Total wages (Rs.)	8,000	6,000	3,000	3,000
Value of Plant (Rs.)	16,000	12,000	8,000	4,000
Value of Stock (Rs.)	25,000	15,000	—	—
Lighting units	5,000	3,000	1,500	500

The following figures of actual costs were taken from the financial books :
Supervision Zero; Plant and Machinery repairs Rs. 1,200; light Rs. 1,000; employer's contribution to ESI Rs. 200; rent Rs. 800; depreciation to Plant Rs. 2,000; insurance (stock) Rs. 800; power Rs. 1,000; canteen expenses Rs. 100.
Apportion the above costs to various Departments on most equitable basis.
[Ans.: Dept. A: Rs. 4,300; Dept. B: Rs. 3,070; Dept. C: Rs. 4,830 and Dept. D: Rs. 3,900]

(3) The Overhead expenses of a manufacturing – cum – selling company are recorded in Cost Accounts according to various functions i.e. Production, Administration and Selling and Distribution. From the information given below, show in a statement form the amount of overhead expenses function wise:

	Rs.
Rent of Offices	1,500
Advertising	2,000
Stationery	840
Rates in factory	2,700
Salesmen's commission and expenses	1,400
Insurance of Offices	80
Depreciation of Machinery	6,400
Warehouse rentals	800
Repairs to Plant	1,850
Secretarial wages	3,000
Insurance of factory	1,100
Accounting staff wages	8,200
Delivery charges	450
Factory indirect wages	15,000

[Ans.: Production Department Rs, 27,050; Administration Department Rs. 13,620 and Selling and Distribution Department Rs. 4,650]

(4) A manufacturing concern is divided into four departments. A, B and C are production departments and X is a service department.
The actual expenses for a period are as follows.

	Rs.
Rent	10,000
Depreciation on plant	4,500
Supervisory expenses	15,000
Power	9,000
Repairs to Plant	6,000
Lighting expenses	1,000
Fire insurance on Stock	5,000
Employer's liability for employees insurance	1,500

The following information is available in respect of the four departments:

	Dept A	*Dept B*	*Dept C*	*Dept X*
Area in Sq. ft	1,500	1,100	900	500
Light points	15	11	9	5
Number of employees	200	150	100	50
Total wages (Rs.)	60,000	40,000	30,000	20,000
Value of plant (Rs.)	2,40,000	1,80,000	1,20,000	60,000
Value of stock (Rs.)	1,50,000	90,000	60,000	—

Apportion the costs to the various departments on the most equitable method.

(B.Com., Madras, March 1993)

[Ans.: A - Rs. 21,025; B - Rs. 15,275; C - Rs.10,675 and X - Rs. 5,025; Power is apportioned on the basis of Plant Value]

(5) A company has four departments - L, M and N which are Production Departments and K which is a Service Department. Cost of the department K is apportioned on the basis of wages paid.

The costs for the year 1991 were	*Rs.*
Rent	21,000
Repairs to Plant	1,26,000
Depreciation of Plant	9,450
Light and power	2,100
Supervision	31,500
Repairs to Building	8,400

The following information about departments is available and is used as a basis for distribution.

Departments	*Area.sq.metres*	*No.of employees*	*Wages paid Rs.*	*Value of Plant Rs.*
L	1,500	20	1,26,000	3,15,000
M	1,100	55	84,000	1,89,000
N	900	10	63,000	1,26,000
K	500	5	42,000	—

Apportion these costs to Production Departments.

(B.Com., Bharathidasan, April 1992)

[Ans.: L – Rs. 89,163; M - Rs. 70,297; N – Rs. 38,990]

❑ ❑ ❑

10

RE-APPORTIONMENT AND ABSORPTION OF OVERHEADS

Objectives

The objectives of the study are to:

- learn the methods of re-distributing the Service Department's overheads
- know the methods of absorption of overheads
- understand the treatment for under or over absorption of overheads

INTRODUCTION

The classification, codification and distribution of overheads to production and Service Departments is the first step and the next step is to reapportion the expenses of service Departments to Production Departments as no production takes place in the Service Departments and later the overheads are absorbed by the units produced.

Reapportionment can be in either of the two ways:

- Reapportionment of Service Departments costs to Production Departments only
- Reapportionment of Service Departments costs to Production Departments and Service Departments

After the Service Department's costs are re-apportioned to Production Departments, ultimately they have to be absorbed by Cost Units.

RE-APPORTIONMENT OF SERVICE DEPARTMENT COSTS

It is also called as Secondary Distribution of Overheads. After the overheads are allocated and apportioned to Production and Service Departments and totalled, the next step would be to reapportion the Service Department costs to the Production Departments. This is done because, no cost units pass through Service Departments and the ultimate objective is to charge the overhead cost to Cost Units. Therefore, the costs of Service Departments are reapportioned to Production Departments in order to charge the cost-to Cost Units. The common bases of Secondary Distribution are:

Service Department	*Basis of Apportionment*
(1) Purchase Department	Number of purchase orders/requisitions, number of units/value of material purchased.
(2) Stores Department	Number of material requisitions, quantity/value of material issued.
(3) Time Keeping Department	Number of employees; labor hours, department wages.
(4) Accounts Department	Number of employees.
(5) Repairs and Maintenance Department	Number of hours worked in each department floor area occupied by each department.
(6) Personnel Department Canteen Department Employees Welfare Department Medical Department Recreation Department	Number of employees or wages
(7) Tool Room Department	Direct labor hours, machine hours, wages
(8) Internal Transport Department	Weight/value/goods transported/distance covered
(9) Inspection Department	Inspection hours, value of items inspected
(10) Power House Department	Meter reading; floor space for lighting; heat consumed; % of steam utilization

The manner in which Service Departments costs are reapportioned to Production Departments is given in the chart below.

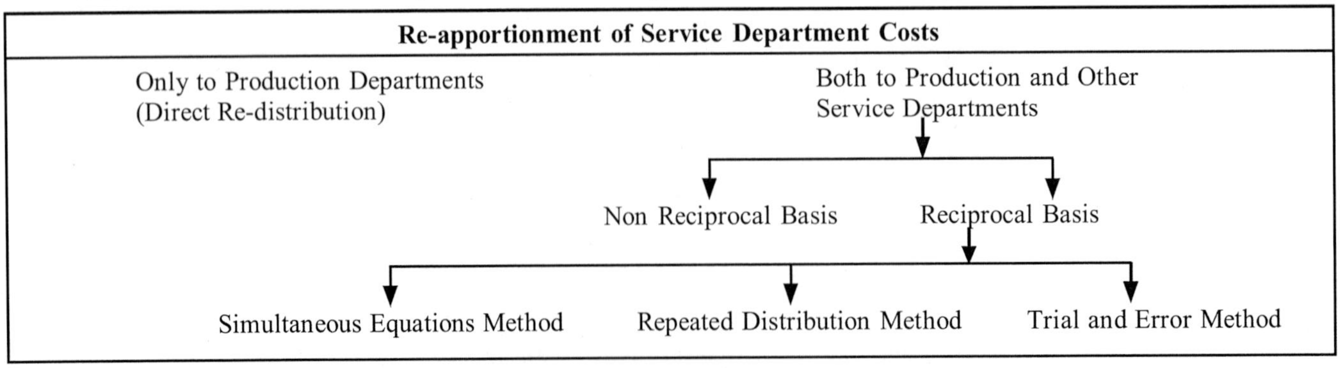

Direct Re-Distribution

Here, the Service Department costs are reapportioned only to Production Departments without considering the service rendered by one Service Department to another or to each other.

Illustration 1

A Company's production for the year ending 30.6.04 is given below.

	Production Department			*Service Department*		
	P1	*P2*	*P3*	*Office*	*Stores*	*Workshop*
Direct Wages (Rs.)	20,000	25,000	30,000			
Direct Material (Rs.)	30,000	35,000	45,000			
Indirect Material (Rs.)	2,000	2,000	3,000	1,000	2,000	2,000
Indirect Wages(Rs.)	3,000	3,000	4,000	10,000	10,000	5,000
Area (sq.mts)	200	250	300	150	100	250
Machinery (Rs.)	30,000	35,000	25,000	—	—	15,000
H.P. of Machinery	15	20	25	—	—	5
Machine hours worked	10,000	20,000	15,000	—	—	—

General expenses: Rent Rs. 12,500; insurance Rs. 1,050; depreciation 15% of the value of machinery; power Rs. 3,800; light Rs. 1,250.

You are required to prepare an Overhead Distribution Analysis Sheet for the Departments Showing clearly the basis of apportionment where necessary.

Solution

Statement showing apportionment of Overheads

		Production Department			*Service Departments*		
	Basis	*P1* *Rs.*	*P2* *Rs.*	*P3* *Rs.*	*Office* *Rs.*	*Stores* *Rs.*	*Workshop* *Rs.*
Indirect Material		2,000	2,000	3,000	1,000	2,000	2,000
Indirect Wages		3,000	3,000	4,000	10,000	10,000	5,000
Rent	Area	2,000	2,500	3,000	1,500	1,000	2,500
Insurance	Machinery	300	350	250	—	—	150
Depreciation	—	4,500	5,250	3,750	—	—	2,250
Power	H.P.	877	1,169	1,462	—	—	292
Light	Area	200	250	300	150	100	250
Total		12,877	14,519	15,762	12,650	13,100	12,442
Secondary Distribution:							
Office expenses	D.Wages	3,373	4,217	5,060	-12,650	—	—
Stores expenses	D. Material	3,573	4,168	5,359	—	-13,100	—
Workshop expenses	Machine Hrs.	2,765	5,530	4,147	—	—	-12,442
Total		22,588	28,434	30,328			

Re-apportionment of Service Department costs to both Production and other Service Departments

Normally, we find a situation where a Service Department renders service not only to Production Departments but also to other Service Departments. For example, Power House Department supplies power not only to Production Departments but also to other Service Departments like Canteen, Maintenance, and Personnel Departments etc. Therefore, the Service Department costs will be distributed not only to Production Departments but also to the other Service Departments either on reciprocal or on non reciprocal basis depending on the inter service rendered.

Non Reciprocal Basis

In non-reciprocal secondary distribution, the costs of service cost centres are apportioned to the production cost centres.

Steps involved:

- The cost of first service cost centre is apportioned on a suitable basis to production cost centres.
- The next step is to apportion the cost of second service centre to the production cost centres as indicated in stage *(i)*.
- The process is to be continued till the costs of all service cost centres are apportioned.

Step Ladder Method

Apportionment of Service Department cost to other Service Departments on non-reciprocal basis is called as Stepladder Method. Here, the cost of that Service Department which renders service to the maximum number of departments is first apportioned amongst the Production Departments and other Service Departments. Thereafter, the next Service Department is taken up for the redistribution of its cost including the apportioned cost of the first Service Department and is apportioned to Production Departments and to other Service Departments and this process goes on until the costs of all the Service Departments are reapportioned.

The limitation of this method is, the reciprocal services rendered by one Service Department to another Service Department are not taken into consideration.

Reciprocal Basis

The services rendered by certain service cost centres are also utilized by other service cost centres. In reciprocal secondary distribution, the cost of service cost centres are apportioned to production cost centres as well as to other service cost centres. This method takes into account the reciprocal services of Service Departments. This method gives cognizance to the fact that when there are two or more Service Departments, they may render service to each other and these inter departmental services are considered while distributing the cost of Service Departments. There are three methods of reapportionment of Service Department costs on a reciprocal basis. They are Simultaneous Equations Method, Repeated Distribution Method and Trial and Error Method.

Repeated Distribution Method: The reapportionment of Service Department costs to other departments is done according to agreed percentages. The process is repeated again and again until the Service Department costs are exhausted or becomes too insignificant.

Steps to be followed under this method are:

- The proportion at which the costs of a service cost centres are to be distributed to production cost centres and other service cost centres are determined.
- Costs of first service cost centres are to be apportioned to production cost centres and service cost centres in the proportion as determined in step (i).
- Similarly, the cost of other service cost centres is to be apportioned.

This process as stated in (ii) and (iii) are to be continued till the figures remaining undistributed in the service cost centres are negligibly small. The negligible small amount left with service centre may be distributed to production cost centres.

Illustration 2

From the following particulars, you are required to calculate the departmental overhead rates for each of the Production Departments assuming that overheads are recovered as a percentage of direct wages.

	Production Overheads			*Service Departments*	
	A	B	C	D	E
Direct wages (Rs.)	8,000	12,000	16,000	4,000	8,000
Direct Material (Rs.)	4,000	8,000	8,000	6,000	6,000
No. of workers	100	150	150	50	50
Electricity (units)	4,000	3,000	2,000	1,000	1,000
Value of assets (Rs.)	1,00,000	70,000	50,000	20,000	1,00,000
No. of light points	10	16	4	6	4
Area (sq. m)	150	250	50	50	50

Expenses:

Power Rs. 2,200; lighting Rs. 400; stores overheads Rs. 1,920; fringe benefits Rs. 6,000; depreciation Rs. 15,000; repairs and maintenance Rs. 10,000; general overheads Rs. 24,000; rent and taxes Rs. 1,100.

You are required to apportion the expenses of Service Department 'E' on the basis of wages and that of 'D' in the ratio of 5 : 2 : 2 : 1 to Departments A, B, C and E respectively using Repetitive Distribution Method.

Solution

Statement of Apportionment of Overheads (Repetitive Distribution Method)

	Production Overheads			*Service Departments*	
	A Rs.	*B* Rs.	*C* Rs.	*D* Rs.	*E* Rs.
Direct Material				6,000	6,000
Direct wages				4,000	8,000
Power (electricity) (4:3:2:1:1)	800	600	400	200	200
Lighting (light points) (5:8:2:3:2)	100	160	40	60	40
Stores overhead (DM) (2:4:4:3:3)	240	480	480	360	360
Fringe benefits (No.of workers) (2:3:3:1:1)	1,200	1,800	1,800	600	600
Depreciation (value of asset) (10:7:5:2:10)	4,411	3,088	2,206	884	4,411
Repairs (asset value)	2,941	2,058	1,470	590	2,941
General (D.Wages) (2:3:4:1:2)	4,000	6,000	8,000	2,000	4,000
Rent (area – 3:5:1:1:1)	300	500	100	100	100
Total	13,992	14,686	14,496	14,794	26,652
Dept. E expenses (D.Wages – 2:3:4:1)	5,330	7,996	10,660	2,666	(-)26,652
	19,322	22,682	25,156	17,460	—
Dept. D expenses (5:2:2:1)	8,730	3,492	3,492	(-)17,460	1,746
	28,052	26,174	28,648	—	1,746
Dept. E expenses	349	524	698	175	(-) 1,746
	28,401	26,698	29,346	175	—
Dept. D expenses	88	35	35	(-) 175	17
	28,489	26,733	29,381	—	17
Dept. E expenses	3	5	9	—	(-) 17
	28,492	26,738	29,390	—	—

Overhead Rate : (Overheads × 100) / Direct Wages

Dept. A : (28,492 × 100) / 8,000 = 356.15%

Dept. B : (26,738 × 100) / 12,000 = 222.81%

Dept. C : (29,390 × 100) / 16,000 = 183.69%

Simultaneous Equation Method

Under this method, simultaneous algebraic equations are used to arrive at the total cost of Service Departments (its own cost plus the proportion of other Service Departments costs). After arriving at the total cost of Service Departments, they are apportioned to the Production Departments as per the service rendered to those departments.

Steps to be followed:

- Proportion of service benefits received by different Cost Centres from a Cost Centre are assessed on the basis of records.
- The same ratios are used as coefficients in the equations framed for apportionment of cost of Service Cost Centres to Production Cost Centres.
- Solution of the equations gives the cost of Service Cost Centres.
- Cost of Service Cost Centres are to be distributed to Production Cost Centres

The simultaneous equation method is to be adopted to take care of secondary distribution of cost of service cost centres to production cost centres with the help of mathematical formulation and solution.

Equation: $X = a + by$

$Y = a + bx$

Where, X = Total cost of Service Department 1

Y = Total cost of Service Department 2

a = its own expenditure

b = % of expenditure in other Service Department costs

Illustration 3

A Company has 3 Production Departments P1, P2 and P3 and 2 Service Departments S1 and S2. During a period, the Departmental Distribution summary has the following towards P1 Rs. 8,000; P2 Rs. 7,000; P3 Rs. 5,000; S1 Rs. 2,340 and S2 Rs. 3,000.

The expenses of S1 and S2 are allocated as follows :

	P1	*P2*	*P3*	*S1*	*S2*
S1	20%	40%	30%	—	10%
S2	40%	20%	20%	20%	—

Apportion the Service Departments expenses to Production Departments by Simultaneous Equation Method.

Solution

Let X be the expenses of Service Department S1

Let Y be the expenses of Service Department S2

Then $X = 2{,}340 + 20\ \%$ of Y (equation 1)

$Y = 3{,}000 + 10\ \%$ of X (equation 2)

$X = 2{,}340 + .2\ Y$ (equation 3)

$Y = 3{,}000 + .1\ X$ (equation 4)

By multiplying the equation 3 with 5 and equation 4 with 1 and rearranging we get,

$5X = 11{,}700 + Y$ (equation 5)

$.1\ X = -3{,}000 + Y$ (equation 6)

By subtracting equation 6 from equation 5, we get

$4.9X = 14{,}700$

Therefore $X = 14{,}700/4.9 = 3{,}000$

By substituting the value of X in equation 3, we get

$3{,}000 = 2{,}340 + .2Y$

$3{,}000 - 2{,}340 = .2Y$

$660 = .2Y$

$Y = 660\ /.2 = 3{,}300$

Total expenses of Department S1 = Rs. 3,000 and Department S2 = Rs. 3,300

Statement of apportionment of Service Department Overheads

	P1 *Rs.*	*P2* *Rs.*	*P3* *Rs.*
As per Primary Distribution	8,000	7,000	5,000
S1 (3000 distributed as per the % given)	600	1,200	900
S2 (3300 distributed as per the % given)	1,320	660	660
Total	9,920	8,860	6,560

Trial and Error Method

Here, the cost of one Service Department is apportioned to the other Service Departments in the given ratio. Then, the cost of second Service Department (along with the share received from the first Service Department) is apportioned to the first and other Service Departments. Like that, the cost of each Service Department is distributed (along with the share received from the other Service Departments) to the other Service Departments. The process is repeated till the amount of Service Departments to be apportioned becomes negligible. Thus, the total cost of the Service Departments to be apportioned to Production Departments is ascertained by trial and error and later they are apportioned to the Production Departments as per the service rendered to those departments.

Steps to be followed:

- The proportion at which the costs of a Service Cost Centre to be distributed to Production Cost Centres and other Service Cost Centres is determined.
- Cost of first Service Cost Centre is distributed to the other Service Centres in the proportion of service they received from the first as assessed in step *(i)*.
- In the next step, total cost of Second Service Cost Centre so arrived has to be distributed to the other Service Centres in the proportion of service they received from the second as assessed in step *(i)*.

Similarly, the cost of other service cost centres are to be apportioned to the service cost centres.This process as described in *(iii)* and *(IV)* is to be continued till the figures remaining undistributed in the Service Cost Centres are negligibly small. At the last, total cost of Service Cost Centres is to be distributed to Production Cost Centres.

Illustration 4

In a factory, there are 3 Production Departments and two Service Departments. Find out their recovery rate with the Trial and Error Method.

	Production Departments			*Service Departments*	
	A *Rs.*	*B* *Rs.*	*C* *Rs.*	*X* *Rs.*	*Y* *Rs.*
Rent	200	350	100	75	50
Electricity	100	150	50	10	10
Insurance	50	75	25	30	20
Depreciation	400	500	300	150	100
Transport	50	25	25	50	75
Total	800	1,100	500	315	255
Estimated working hours	1,000	1,000	1,000		
Apportion the expenses of service departments as follows.					
X	30%	40%	20%	—	10%
Y	10%	20%	50%	20%	—

Solution

Apportionment of Overheads

	Production Departments			*Service Departments*	
	A *Rs.*	*B* *Rs.*	*C* *Rs.*	*X* *Rs.*	*Y* *Rs.*
Total Overheads	800	1,100	500	315	255
(I) Distribution X to Y (10% of 315)					32
(II) Distribution Y to X (20% of 287)				57	
(III) Distribution X to Y (10% of 57)					6
(IV) Distribution Y to X (20% of 6)				1	
	800	1,100	500	373	293

	Production Departments			Service Departments	
	A Rs.	B Rs.	C Rs.	X Rs.	Y Rs.
Overheads of Dept. X charged to Depts. A, B and C as per the % given	112	149	75		
Overheads of Dept. Y charged to Depts. A, B and C as per the % given	29	59	146		
Total Overheads	941	1,308	721		
Working hours Recovery Rate (Total Overheads/working hours)	1,000 0.941	1,000 1.308	1,000 0.721		

Absorption of Overheads

Overhead is absorbed or recovered by the jobs, processess or products by the application of a predetermined rate of absorption. The C.I.M.A. Terminology defines overhead absorption rate as "a means of attributing overhead costs to a product or service base, for example, on direct labor hours, direct labor cost or machine hours".

Absorption of overheads is charging of overheads from cost centres to products or services by means of absorption rates for each cost centre which is calculated as follows:

$$\text{Overhead absorption Rate} = \frac{\text{Total overheads of the Cost Centre}}{\text{Total Quantum of Base}}$$

The base (denominator) is selected on the basis of type of the Cost Centre and its contribution to the products or services, for example, machine hours, labor hours, quantity produced etc.

Overhead absorbed = Overhead absorption rate × units of base in product or service

The various methods used for absorption of factory overheads are given below:

Units or Output Method

This is the simplest method where the rate is obtained by dividing the total overheads of a department by the number of units produced.

$$\text{Overhead Rate} = \frac{\text{Production Overheads}}{\text{Number of units produced}}$$

It is applicable in those organizations where identical cost units are produced. This method is unsuitable if products of different sizes, grades, qualities, etc., are produced according to customer's requirements.

Illustration 5

A company manufactures four products A, B, C and D. For the computation of overhead absorption rate, it has assigned 5, 10, 8 and 4 points to A, B, C and D respectively to compensate the basic differences in the products. The normal capacity is as follows :

	A	B	C	D
Units	2,000	5,000	3,000	4,000

The total overhead cost is estimated at Rs. 6,00,000. Calculate the overhead absorption rates for the products.

Solution

	A	B	C	D
Units produced	2,000	5,000	3,000	4,000
Weights assigned	5	10	8	4
Weighted production (units × weights)	10,000	50,000	24,000	16,000
Ratio	10	50	24	16 = 100

Overheads to be recovered from the products = Total Overheads/Ratio of the Weighted Production.

Dept. A	6,00,000 × 10/100 =	Rs.	60,000
Dept. B	6,00,000 × 50/100 =	Rs.	3,00,000
Dept. C	6,00,000 × 24/100 =	Rs.	1,44,000
Dept. D	6,00,000 × 16/100 =	Rs.	96,000

Direct Material Cost Method

Here, the base is the direct material consumed. The overhead rate is computed by dividing the total overheads by the total cost of direct material consumed and is expressed as a percentage.

$$\text{Overhead Rate} = \frac{\text{Production Overheads}}{\text{Direct Material Cost}} \times 100$$

This method is the only convenient method of absorbing overhead, where the direct material cost represents a substantial proportion of prime cost.

But, this method is quite illogical as in no way the overhead is related to the cost of direct material and it would give misleading results when there is a wide fluctuation in the market prices of direct material cost.

Direct Wages Cost Method

Here, the overhead cost is divided by the direct labor cost to calculate the overhead recovery rate and is expressed as a percentage.

$$\text{Overhead Rate} = \frac{\text{Production Overheads}}{\text{Direct Wages Cost}} \times 100$$

This method is suitable where production is uniform, labor is predominant and all workers earn more or less same hourly wage rate. It gives importance to time factor.

The **limitations** of this method are :

- Where the wage differentials are wide, the overhead rate gets affected by the combination of workers employed on a particular cost unit.
- There may be inaccuracies where workers are paid on the basis of piecework, as the time factor cannot be taken into consideration.
- There is no relationship between direct wages and overheads.
- No distinction is made between work done by skilled and unskilled workers.

Prime Cost Method

This method is a combination of Direct Material and Direct Labor Methods. Here, the assumption is both, material and labor, give rise to factory overhead and therefore the total of the two should be taken as the basis of charging production overhead.

$$\text{Overhead Rate} = \frac{\text{Production Overheads}}{\text{Prime Cost}} \times 100$$

This method is rarely used in practice. It combines the shortcomings of both the Direct Material and Direct Labor Methods.

Illustration 6

The following information relates to the workshop of a factory for a certain period.

Direct Material consumed	Rs.	1,08,000
Direct wages	Rs.	90,000
Overhead charged to the workshop	Rs.	75,000

On one job carried out in the workshop during the period, the following were the relevant data.

Direct Material used	Rs.	18,000
Direct wages	Rs.	14,850

You are required to calculate the overheads to be charged to the job on the basis of (a) Direct Material , (b) Direct Labor and (c) Prime Cost.

Solution

Computation of Overheads charged to the given jobs

(a) Direct Materials Method

$$\text{Overhead Rate} = \frac{\text{Production Overheads}}{\text{Direct Material Cost}} \times 100$$

75,000 × 100 / 1,08,000 = 69.4444%

Overhead Absorption : 18,000 × 69.4444% = Rs. 12,500

(b) Direct Labor Method

$$\text{Overhead Rate} = \frac{\text{Production Overheads}}{\text{Direct Wages Cost}} \times 100$$

75,000 × 100 / 90,000 = 83.3333%

Overhead Absorption : 14,850 × 83.3333% = Rs. 12,375

(c) Prime Cost Method

$$\text{Overhead Rate} = \frac{\text{Production Overheads}}{\text{Prime Cost}} \times 100$$

75,000 × 100 / 1,98,000 = 37.8788%

Prime Cost : 1,08,000 + 90,000 = Rs. 1,98,000

Overhead Absorption : 32,850 × 37.8788% = Rs. 12,443

Prime Cost : 18,000 + 14,850 = Rs. 32,850

Labor Hour Method

As a majority of the items of production overhead fluctuate with the time spent on production of cost unit, it is relevant to charge production overhead on the basis of direct labor hours worked.

$$\text{Overhead Rate} = \frac{\text{Production Overheads}}{\text{Direct Labor Hours}}$$

This method is suitable where production is carried on manually. It gives full consideration to time factor. But, this method does not take into consideration other factors of production.

Illustration 7

A Ltd. Company has three Manufacturing Departments A, B and C and one Service Department Y. The following figures are available for one month of 25 working days of 8 hours each day. All these departments work for all the days and with full attendance.

		Departments			
Expenditure	*Total* *Rs.*	*Y* *Rs.*	*A* *Rs.*	*B* *Rs.*	*C* *Rs.*
Power and lighting	1,100	240	200	300	360
Supervisor's salary	2,000				
Rent	500				
Welfare	600				
Others	1,200	200	200	400	400
Total	5,400				
Supervisor's salary		20%	30%	30%	20%
No. of workers		10	30	40	20
Floor area (sq.ft)		500	600	800	600
Service Department		—	50%	30%	20%

Calculate labor hour rate for each of the Departments – A, B and C.

Solution

Statement showing the distribution of Overheads

	Departments				
Expenditure	*Total Rs.*	*Y Rs.*	*A Rs.*	*B Rs.*	*C Rs.*
Power and lighting	1,100	240	200	300	360
Supervisor's salary (2:3:3:2)	2,000	400	600	600	400
Rent (floor area)	500	100	120	160	120
Welfare (workers)	600	60	180	240	120
Others	1,200	200	200	400	400
Total	5,400	1,000	1,300	1,700	1,400
Service Dept. Y (5:3:2)		-1,000	500	300	200
Total			1,800	2,000	1,600
Labor Hour Rate			1800/6000 0.30	2,000/8,000 0.25	1,600/4,000 0.40

Labor hour rate = Estimated overheads/Direct Labor hours

Labor hours : Dept. A $30 \times 25 \times 8 = 6{,}000$

Dept. B $40 \times 25 \times 8 = 8{,}000$

Dept. C $20 \times 25 \times 8 = 4{,}000$

Machine Hour Rate Method

Machine Hour Rate means the cost of running a machine for one hour. It is calculated by dividing the production overhead by the number of machine hours. This method is suitable where production is predominantly performed by the machines. Machine hour rate is computed for all types of machines used in the manufacturing process as a single machine hour rate to cover the entire factory is unsuitable in view of the variety of machines used.

Steps involved for computation of Machine Hour Rate :

- First, total overheads of the department (both allocated and apportioned) are ascertained for different machines used in the department.
- According to the variability of expenses in relation to the use of machine, the overheads relating to the machine are divided into (a) fixed/standing charges (like supervisor salary, rent, insurance, etc.) and (b) variable/machine charges (like depreciation, repairs and maintenance, power, etc.).
- The effective working hours of the machine are estimated in advance.
- To ascertain the machine hour rate, the overheads pertaining to the machine are divided by the effective machine hours.

Machine Hour Rate = Production Overhead/Effective Machine Hours

If the wages of the machine operator are added to the total overheads allocated to the machine, then, the machine hour rate calculated is called as 'Comprehensive Machine Hour Rate'.

This method is scientific, practical and accurate method of absorption of overheads giving weight age to the time factor. It is an ideal method where machines are predominantly used for production.

But, the method suffers from two drawbacks.

- This method gives inaccurate results where hand labor is equally important.
- It is time consuming and involves a lot of clerical work for maintenance of additional records for the calculation of running hours of each and every machine.

Illustration 8

Calculate the Machine Hour Rate from the following data.

Cost of Machine Rs. 1,16,000

Estimated scrap value Rs. 16,000

Estimated working life 20,000 hours

Estimated maintenance cost during working life of the machine Rs. 24,000

Power used for machine Re. 1 per hour

Rent, rates etc. p.m. (10% to be charged for this machine) Rs. 3,000

Normal machine running hours during a month 200
Standing charges other than rent, rates etc. Rs. 400 p.m.

Solution

Computation of Machine Hour Rate

	Per month	*Per Hour*
Standing Charges :	*Rs.*	*Rs.*
Rent, rates etc. (3,000 × 10%)	300	
Other standing charges	400	
Standing Charges per hour 700/200		3.50
Variable Expenses :		
Depreciation		
(1,16,000 – 16,000 = 1,00,000/20,000)		5.00
Maintenance cost (24,000/20,000)		1.20
Power Consumption		1.00
Machine Hour Rate		10.70

Illustration 9

Calculate the overheads chargeable to the job by the three commonly used methods from the following details relating to the activities of a Production Department during a certain period.

	Rs.
Materials	36,000
Direct Wages	30,000
Labor hours worked	12,000
Hours of machine operator	20,000

Overheads chargeable to the department are Rs. 25,000. On one order carried out in the department during the period, the relevant data were as follows :

	Rs.
Direct wages	4,950
Labor hours	1,650
Machine hours	1,200

Solution

(a) Direct Labor Cost Method : Overheads × 100/Direct wages
25,000 × 100/30,000 = 83.33%
Overheads for the Job would be 83.33% of Direct Wages Rs. 4,950
= 4,950 × 83.33% = Rs. 4,125

(b) Labor Hour Rate : Overheads/Labor hours
25,000/12,000 = Rs. 2.08
Overheads for the Job would be @ Rs. 2.08 for 1,650 labor hours
= 1,650 × 2.08 = Rs. 3,432

(c) Machine Hour Rate : Overheads/Machine hours
25,000/20,000 = Rs. 1.25
Overheads for the Job would be @ Rs. 1.25 for 1,200 machine hours
= 1,200 × 1.25 = Rs. 1,500

Illustration 10

Compute Comprehensive Machine Hour Rate from the following data.

(a) Total cost of machine to be depreciated Rs. 2,30,000
(b) Life of the machine: 10 years
(c) Depreciation is on straight line method
(d) Departmental overheads (annual) : rent, heat and light Rs. 70,000; supervision Rs. 1,04,000
(e) Departmental area is 70,000 square meters
(f) Machine area is 2,500 square meters
(g) 26 machines run in the department

(h) Annual cost of Reserve Equipment for the machine Rs. 1,500
(i) Hours run on production: 1,800
(j) Hours for setting and adjusting: 200
(k) Power cost Re. 0.20 per hour of running time
(l) Labor : when setting and adjusting, full time attention is required and when machine is producing, one worker can look after 3 machines
(m) Labor rate Rs. 6 per hour

Using the machine hour rate as calculated above, work out the amount of factory overhead to be absorbed on the following.

Job No.	*Total hours*	*Production time hours*	*Setting up time hours*
333	100	80	20
444	100	70	30

Solution

Computation of Comprehensive Machine Hour Rate

	Rs.	*Rs.*
Standing Charges:		
Rent, heat and light (70,000 × 2,500/70,000)	2,500	
Supervision (1,04,000/26)	4,000	
Depreciation (2,30,000/10 years)	23,000	
Reserve Equipment cost (1,500/26)	58	
Labor cost during setting and adjusting (200 × 6)	1,200	
Total	30,758	
Hourly standing charges (30,758/1,800)		17.09
Machine Expenses :		
Power		0.20
Labor (6 × 1/3)		2.00
Comprehensive Machine Hour Rate		19.29

Note : It is assumed that there is no power cost, when the machine is being set or adjusted.

Overhead Absorption for the various jobs is :

Job No. 333 : 19.29 × 80 = Rs. 1,543.20
Job No. 444 : 19.29 × 70 = Rs. 1,350.30

Illustration 11

A manufacturing company has supplied the following particulars relating to the activity of its Production Department for the month of March 1988:

Material used (Rs.)	36,000
Direct labor cost (Rs.)	30,000
Direct labor hours worked	24,000
Hours of machine operations	20,000
Factory overhead chargeable to the Department (Rs.)	25,000

On one production order wholly carried out within the Department during this period , the relevant data were:

Material used (Rs.)	2,000
Direct labor (Rs.)	1,650
Direct labor hours	1,650
Machine hours	1,200

Prepare a comparative statement of cost of this order by using the following three methods of recovery of overheads; (1) Direct labor hour rate method (2) Direct labor cost rate method (3) Machine hour rate method.

(B.Com., Hons. Delhi, 1990)

Solution

(1)	Direct Labor Hour Rate Method	=	Factory Overhead/Direct Labor Hours
		=	Rs. 25,000/24,000 = Rs. 1.042 per hour
(2)	Direct Labour Cost Rate	=	Factory Overhead/Direct Labor Cost
		=	Rs. 25,000/30,000 = Re. 0.833 of Direct Labor Cost
(3)	Machine Hour Rate Method	=	Factory Overheads/Machine Hours
		=	Rs. 25,000/20,000 = Rs. 1.25 per hour

Comparative statement of cost of one production order by using different methods of overhead recovery

Elements of Cost	*Labor Hour Rate* *Rs.*	*Labor Cost Rate* *Rs.*	*Machine Hour Rate* *Rs.*
Direct Material	2,000	2,000	2,000
Direct Labor	1,650	1,650	1,650
Factory Overheads			
1,650 hrs × Rs. 1.042	1,719	—	—
Rs. 1,650 × 0.833	—	1,375	—
1,200 hrs × Rs. 1.25	—	—	1,500
Total Factory Cost	5,369	5,025	5,150

Under or Over Absorption of Overheads

Generally, overheads are recovered through products by applying the predetermined rate, as it would not be possible to wait until the production is complete and then ascertain the actual overhead expenses. Therefore, there may be a difference between the overhead recovered and actual overhead incurred resulting in under absorption (if recovered overheads are less than the actual overheads) or over absorption (if recovered overheads are more than the actual overheads). Now, the question arises as to how to treat this under or over absorption of overheads. There are three methods for disposal of the same. They are:

Application of Supplementary Rate

When the difference between applied overhead and actual overhead is significant, it is adjusted by a supplementary rate computed by dividing the amount of under or over absorbed amount by the actual bases. A positive rate set rights the under absorption by adding the under absorbed overhead to the cost of production and a negative rate adjusts the over absorption by deducting the amount of over absorbed overhead from cost of production.

Though this method is suitable only when there is a major change in the method of production resulting in a wide divergence between the anticipated and actual working, it is also used as and when there is a major change in the level of activity.

Write off to Costing Profit and Loss Account

When the difference between recovered and actual overhead is not significant, the under or over absorbed overheads may conveniently be disposed off by writing off to Costing Profit and Loss Account. Even if the difference is significant, it is written off to Costing Profit and Loss Account, if the same is due to abnormal factors like idle facilities, defective planning, etc. This method satisfies the condition that the overhead balance should be closed during the relevant accounting year and not to carry forward to the next year.

Carry over to Next Year's Account

Here, the under or over absorbed overhead is transferred to Overhead Suspense Account and carried forward to the next year, to be absorbed during the subsequent year for computing the recovery rate. This method has a limited application as it is against the cost accounting principles that the costs should be absorbed during the year in which they are incurred.

This method is suitable to those industries, where the demand for their products is fluctuating resulting in fluctuation in production and when the normal business cycle extends over more than a year.

Accounting Treatment of Administration Overheads

There are three ways of accounting for administration overheads.

- Apportioning of administration overheads between Production and Sales Departments recognizing the fact that administration overheads are incurred for the benefit of these two departments. As a result, the administration overheads lose their identity and get merged with production and selling and distribution overheads, thus saving the clerical work involved in apportioning the overheads.

- Charging of administration overheads to the Costing Profit and Loss Account, as they are not directly connected with either production or selling and distribution functions.
- Treating administration overheads as a separate addition to cost of production/sales, they are apportioned by any of the bases such as works cost, sales value or quantity, gross profit on sales, quantity produced, conversion cost, etc.

Accounting Treatment of Selling and Distribution Overheads

The main bases used for absorption of selling and distribution overheads are sales value of goods, cost of goods sold, gross profit on sales and number of orders or units sold, the most logical basis being sale value.

Generally, overheads are recovered through products by applying the predetermined rate as it would not be possible to wait until the production is complete and then ascertain the actual overhead expenses. Therefore, there may be a difference between the overhead recovered and actual overhead incurred resulting in under absorption.

Presentation and Disclosure (CAS – 3)

Once the basis of collection, allocation, apportionment and absorption for different Production Cost Centres are selected, the same shall be followed consistently and uniformly.

Change in the basis for collection, allocation, apportionment and absorption can be adopted only when it is compelled by the change in circumstances like change in technology, refinement and improvement in the basis etc., and the change would provide more scientific approach. In case of such changes, proper disclosure in Cost Records is essential.

Any change in the basis for collection, allocation, apportionment and absorption which has a material effect on the cost of the product should be disclosed in the Cost Statements. Where the effect of such change is not ascertainable wholly or partly, the fact should be indicated in the cost statement.

Treatment of Special Items

(1) Interest on Capital: There is a debate as to whether interest on capital is to be included or not in the Cost Accounts.

(a) Interest on capital is the reward for capital like reward for any other factor of Production. Exclusion of it would distort the cost of the product.
In many management decisions, the cost of capital is a crucial factor especially where such decisions affect the organization's long-term prospects.
The time value of money is recognized only when it is included in Cost Accounts as an element of cost.
The inclusion of cost of capital in Cost Accounts gives a correct picture of profit and loss position of the company.

(b) But, some argue that interest on capital is a finance cost and hence finds no place in Cost Accounts. The amount of interest on capital depends upon the method of capitalization and the financing pattern of the organization.
The calculation of cost of capital is quite a difficult task and it has to be calculated on various sources of capital *viz.*, term loans, debentures, equity capital, preference share capital. The cost of capital depends on various factors like risk, period of maturity, bank rate, etc.
It is also difficult to apportion the cost of capital to different Cost Centres and absorption of it to product cost.

(2) Research and Development Costs: Research and Development (R&D) is a non-recurring expenditure and the benefit of such expenditure is expected to be received in future periods also. It is the expenditure incurred to produce a new product or improve the existing product or to provide a new method of production.
Research costs, are incurred for carrying basic research or applied research. Development cost is incurred to implement the research plan to produce a new product or improve the existing product.
Basic research cost, i.e., costs relating to existing products, methods of operation, technique of production etc. is treated as production overhead for the period during which it has been incurred.
If applied research cost is in relation to improvement of existing product and methods of production, it is treated as manufacturing overhead. If applied research costs are incurred for searching new products / methods of production, such costs are amortized over the period for which benefit from such newly invented or new method of production adopted, is likely to accrue.

If in any year, it is realized that no further benefit is likely to accrue, then the unabsorbed portion of such research cost is written off to Costing Profit and Loss Account of that year.

(3) **Material Handling expenditure:** The expenditure incurred in handling raw materials like unloading, storing, handling the material to work place, handling of work-in-progress and finished goods are apportioned on the basis of physical quantities of different materials and goods handled in the factory.

(4) **Market Research Expenditure:** These are the expenses incurred for market intelligence to ascertain the tastes and habits, market penetration of product, increasing the demand for product, etc., and are treated as selling overhead. If these expenses are for a particular product, it is to be absorbed by that product. Otherwise, they are to be apportioned to different products in the proportion of sales value.

(5) **Subscriptions and donations:** If subscriptions and donations are for the welfare of the workers, or if it is for any technical or research institutions for obtaining data relating to technical, production or scientific nature, then, it is treated as production overhead.
If it is for journals to obtain market data, it is considered as selling overhead. It should be excluded from Cost Accounts if such expenditure is not benefiting the employees.

(6) **After Sales and Service Costs:** If after sales service costs are incurred during the period of guarantee given to customer, they are to be treated as production overhead and absorbed by applying predetermined absorption rates. If these costs are incurred after the guarantee period, they are to be treated as selling overhead.

(7) **Royalties and Patent fees:** These are payable for the use of technology, intellectual property rights, skills brand etc. If the payment of such amount is based on the units sold, they are treated as selling overhead. If it is paid as a fixed rent, it is to be treated as production overhead. If it is paid on the number of units produced, the expenditure is treated as direct expense and forms a part of the cost of the product.

(8) **Training Costs:** If the cost is incurred to train the workers, apprentices and other production staff, it is treated as production overhead. If it is for the training of office and administration staff, it is considered as administration overhead. If the expenditure is for training sales staff, it is treated as selling overhead.

(9) **Taxes:** These are excluded from Cost Accounts as taxes are paid as a per cent of profit earned.

(10) **Major repair:** These are incurred to prolong the useful life of an asset. It has to be added to the asset value and depreciated according to the depreciation policy of the company. If repairs are for upkeep and maintenance of the asset, it should be treated as production overhead.

(11) **Cost of tools:** The cost of large tools is capitalized and depreciation is provided on it. The cost of small tools can be:
(a) Capitalized and depreciation is recovered on production overhead.
(b) Revalued at the end of each accounting year and the difference is charged as production overhead.
(c) Written off to Costing Profit and Loss Account.

(12) **Bad debts:** Bad debts may result due to willful default on the part of the customers or unintentionally. It is treated as selling overhead.

(13) **Notional rent:** It is the rent which is charged for the owned premises so as to represent a benefit enjoyed by the organization though no rent is actually paid. It is treated as administrative overhead.

(14) **Packing expenses:** The primary packing expenses which are included, without which a product cannot be sold is treated as direct cost. Whereas, secondary packing expenses, to facilitate the transportation and distribution of the finished product, is treated as distribution overhead. If packing expenses are incurred to make the product attractive to the customers, then, it is treated as advertising and is included in selling overhead.

SUMMARY

The expenses of Service Departments should be reapportioned to Production Departments and later absorbed by the units produced. This is done because, no cost units pass through Service Departments and the ultimate objective is to charge the overhead cost to Cost Units. Therefore, the costs of Service Departments are reapportioned to Production Departments.

Reapportionment can be in either to (a) Production Departments only or to (b) both the Production Departments and Service Departments.

Under Direct Re-Distribution Method, the Service Department costs are reapportioned only to Production Departments without considering the service rendered by one Service Department to another or to each other.

Under the second method, Service Department costs will be distributed not only to Production Departments but also to the other Service Departments either on reciprocal or on non reciprocal basis depending on the inter service rendered

Reciprocal Method takes into account the reciprocal services of Service Departments. This method gives cognizance to the fact that when there are two or more Service Departments, they may render service to each other and these inter departmental services are considered while distributing the cost of Service Departments

After allocating and apportioning the overhead costs to Production and Service Departments and reapportioning the Service Department costs to Production Departments, the next step is to allocate or allot the costs of Production Cost Centres to the Cost Units passing through them. This process of allotting the overheads to Cost Units is called as 'Absorption of Overheads' or Recovery of Overheads'. By doing this, the Cost Units will receive not only the direct costs but also a share of manufacturing costs.

Overhead is absorbed or recovered by the jobs, processes or products by the application of a predetermined rate of absorption as it would not be possible to wait until the production is complete and then ascertain the actual overhead expenses. Therefore, there may be a difference between the overhead recovered and actual overhead incurred resulting in under absorption (if recovered overheads are less than the actual overheads) or over absorption (if recovered overheads are more than the actual overheads). The same may be disposed off either by application of supplementary rate or writing off to Costing Profit and Loss Account or by carrying over to next year's account.

Glossary

- **Step Ladder Method:** Apportionment of Service Department cost to the other Service Departments on non-reciprocal basis is called as Step Ladder Method.
- **Absorption of Overheads:** allotting the overheads to Cost Units is called as Absorption of Overheads or Recovery of Overheads.
- **Machine Hour Rate:** means the cost of running a machine for one hour.

Questions

(1) What do you understand by absorption of overheads? What are the causes for over or under absorption of overheads?
(2) Explain briefly the various methods of absorption of factory overheads.
(3) How do you dispose of under or over absorbed overheads?
(4) Give the accounting treatment of administration and selling and distribution overheads.
(5) Define machine hour rate and state the steps involved in computation of the same.

PROBLEMS

(1) A company has four Departments A, B and C, which are Production Departments, and D, which is a Service Department. Cost of the Department D is apportioned on the basis of wages paid.
The actual costs for the year 1989 were :

	Rs.
Rent	21,000
Repairs to Plant	1,26,000
Depreciation of Plant	9,450
Light and Power	2,100
Supervision etc.	31,500
Repairs to Building	8,400

The following information about departments is available and is used as a basis for distribution of costs:

Departments	*Area Sq.Metres*	*No. of employees*	*Wages Paid Rs.*	*Value of Plant Rs.*
A	1,500	20	1,26,000	3,15,000
B	1,100	15	84,000	1,98,000
C	900	10	63,000	1,26,000
D	500	5	42,000	

Apportion these costs to Production Departments.
[Ans.: A : Rs. 1,13,954, B : Rs. 75,111, C : Rs. 61,385]

(2) In a factory, there are two Service Departments P and Q and three Production Departments A, B and C. In April 2004, the departmental expenses were:

Departments	Rs.
A	6,50,000
B	6,00,000
C	5,00,000
P	1,20,000
Q	1,00,000

The Service Departments expenses are allocated on a percentage basis as follows :

	Departments				
	A	*B*	*C*	*P*	*Q*
P	30%	40%	15%	—	15%
Q	40%	30%	25%	5%	—

Prepare a statement showing the distribution of the two Service Departments expenses to the three Production Departments under the "Repeated Distribution Method".

[Ans.: Department A- Rs. 7,35,340; B - Rs. 6,86,045 and C – Rs. 5,48,615]

(3) Calculate the overheads chargeable to Production Departments A and B. There are two Service Departments X and Y. X renders service worth Rs. 12,000 to Y and the balance to A and B in the ratio of 3:2. Y renders service to A and B in the ratio of 9:1.

	A	*B*	*X*	*Y*
Floor space (sft)	5,000	4,000	1,000	2,000
Assets (Rs. in lakhs)	10	5	3	1
H.P. of machines	1,000	500	400	100
No. of workers	100	50	50	25
Light and fan points	50	30	20	20

Expenses and charges are :

Depreciation Rs. 1,90,000; rent Rs. 36,000; insurance Rs. 15,200; power Rs. 20,000; canteen expenses Rs. 10,800 and electricity Rs. 4,800

[Ans.: Total expenses of Department A Rs. 1,86,780 and Department B Rs. 90,020]

(4) From the following information, work out the Production Hour Rate of recovery of overheads in Department P1, P2 and P3 under *(a)* Repeated Distribution Method and *(b)* Simultaneous Equation Method.

	Production Departments			*Service Departments*	
	P1 *Rs.*	*P2* *Rs.*	*P3* *Rs.*	*S1* *Rs.*	*S2* *Rs.*
Rent	200	400	150	150	100
Electricity	50	80	30	20	20
Fire Insurance	80	160	60	60	40
Plant depreciation	1,000	1,500	1,000	300	200
Transport	50	50	50	100	150
Estimated working hours	1,000	2,500	1,800		

Expenses of Service Departments S1 and S2 are apportioned as under

	P1	*P2*	*P3*	*S1*	*S2*
S1	30%	40%	20%	—	10%
S2	10%	20%	50%	20%	—

[Ans.: Total Expenses of Department A: Rs. 1,662.76; Dept. B: Rs. 2,605.08 and Dept. C: Rs. 1,731.94
Machine Hour Recovery Rates are Rs. 1.662; Rs. 1.04 and Re. 0.96 respectively]

(5) The New Enterprises Ltd. has Production Departments A, B and C and two Service Departments D and E. The following figures are extracted from the records of the company.

	Rs.
Rent and rates	5,000
General lighting	600
Indirect wages	1,500
Power	1,500
Depreciation of machinery	10,000
Sundries	10,000

The following further details are available :

Items	*Total*	*A*	*B*	*C*	*D*	*E*
Floor Space (sq.ft)	10,000	2,000	2,500	3,000	2,000	500
Light points	60	10	15	20	10	5
Direct wages (Rs.)	10,000	3,000	2,000	3,000	1,500	500
H.P. of Machines	150	60	30	50	10	—
Value of Machinery (Rs.)	2,50,000	60,000	80,000	1,00,000	5,000	5,000
Working hours	—	6,226	4,028	4,056	—	—

The expenses of D and E are allocated as follows :

	A	*B*	*C*	*D*	*E*
D	20%	30%	40%	—	10%
E	40%	20%	30%	10%	—

What is the cost of the article if its Raw Material Cost is Rs. 50, Labour Cost is Rs. 30 and it passes through Departments A, B and C for 4, 5 and 3 hours respectively?

Note : Apportion 'sundries' and 'indirect wages' in proportion of direct wages.

[Ans.: Total Overheads of Service Department D is Rs. 4,625 and E is Rs. 1,575
Overhead Rate : Dept. A – Rs. 1.50; B – Rs. 2.25 and C Rs. 3
Cost of the article : Rs. 106.25]

(6) A manufacturing concern has three production departments P, Q and R and two service departments X and Y. In January 1992, the departmental expenses are:

P - Rs. 20,000; Q - Rs. 17,000; R - Rs. 15,000; X - Rs. 8,000; Y - Rs. 4,000.

The expenses of the service departments are charged on percentage basis as follows:

	P	*Q*	*R*	*X*	*Y*
Dept X	20%	25%	35%	—	20%
Dept Y	40%	25%	25%	10%	—

Prepare overhead distribution summary.

[Ans.: P - Rs. 23,499; Q Rs. 20,571; R Rs. 19,430]

(7). A company has three production departments and two service departments. The following figures are extracted from the books of the company.

	Rs.
Rent	20,000
Indirect wages	6,000
Depreciation	40,000
Lighting	2,400
Power	6,000
Others	40,000

Other particulars:

	A	*B*	*C*	*D*	*E*
Floor space (sq.ft)	4000	5000	6000	4000	1000
Light points	20	30	40	20	10
Direct wages (Rs.)	9000	6000	9000	9000	7000
H.P of machines	75	30	35	10	—
Value of machinery (Rs.)	120000	160000	200000	10000	10000
Working hours	3113	2014	2033	—	—

The expenses of service departments D and E are to be allocated as follows:

	A	*B*	*C*	*D*	*E*
D	20%	30%	40%	—	10%
E	40%	20%	20%	20%	—

You are requested to distribute the service department expenses to the production departments (A, B and C) under simultaneous equation method and calculate hourly rate of each production department.

(B.Com., Bangalore, November 1990)

[Ans.: Department A – Rs. 35,770, Rs.11.49; Department B – Rs. 34,374, Rs. 17.06; Department C – Rs. 44,256, Rs. 21.76]

(8) Machine is purchased for cash @ Rs. 9,200. Its working life is estimated to be 18,000 hours after which its scrap value is estimated at Rs 200. It is assumed from past experience that:

(a) The machine will work for 1,800 hours annually.

(b) The repair charges will be Rs. 1,080 during the whole period of life of the machine.

(c) The power consumption will be 5 units per hour at 6 paise per unit.

(d) Other annual standing charges are estimated to be :

(i) Rent of the Department (machine occupies 1/5th of total space) Rs.780

(ii) Light (12 points in the Department - 2 points engaged in the machine) Rs. 288

(iii) Foreman's salary (1/4th of his time is occupied for the machine) Rs. 6,000

(iv) Insurance premium (fire) for machinery Rs. 36

(v) Cotton waste Rs. 60

Find out the machine hour rate on the basis of the above data for allocation of the works expenses to all jobs for which the machine is used.

[Ans.: Machine Hour Rate: Rs. 1.86]

(9) From the particulars given below, calculate machine hour rate for machine number 333.

Cost of the machine Rs. 45,000; estimated repairs for life of the machine Rs. 9,000; power consumed per hour : 12 units at 10 paise per unit; insurance Rs. 20 per month; lighting (number of points 12 of which 3 are used for the machine) Rs. 60 per month; cotton, waste, oil etc. Rs. 20 per month.

The machine is lodged in a department whose monthly rent is Rs. 500. The machine occupies 1/4 space, one foreman and an attendant are employed on a salary of Rs. 1,000 and Rs. 200 per month respectively and their work is confined not only to this machine but also for one more of a similar type.

[Ans.: Machine Hour Rate Rs. 9.15]

(10) Compute the machine hour rate from the following data.

(a) Cost of machine Rs. 1,00,000; installation charges Rs 10,000; estimated scrap after expiry of its life of 15 years is Rs. 5,000.

(b) Rent and rates of the shop per month Rs. 200

(c) General lighting for the shop Rs. 300 per month

(d) Shop supervisors salary Rs. 600 per month

(e) Insurance Rs. 960 p.a.

(f) Estimated repairs and maintenance Rs. 1,000 p.a.

(g) Estimated working hours of the machine per year (including set up time of 200 hours) 2,200

(h) Power consumption of the machine 10 units per hour at Rs. 30 per 100 units.

The machine occupies 1/4 of the total floor area of the shop.

The supervisor of the shop devotes 1/5th of his time for supervising the machine.

[Ans.: Machine Hour Rate : Rs. 8.95]

(11) The following particulars relate to a new machine purchased :

	Rs.	
Purchase price of the machine	4,00,000	
Installation expenses	1,00,000	
Rent per quarter	15,000	
General lighting for the total area	1,000	per month
Foreman's salary	30,000	per annum
Insurance premium for the machine	3,000	per annum
Estimate repair for the machine	5,000	per annum
Consumable stores	4,000	per annum

Power: 2 units per hour at Rs. 50 per 100 units.

The estimated life of the machine is 10 years and the estimated value at the end of the 10th year is Rs. 1,00,000. The machine is expected to run 20,000 hours in its lifetime. The machine occupied 25% of the total area. The foreman devotes 1/6 of his time for the machine.

Calculate the machine hour rate for the machine.

[Ans.: Machine Hour Rate: Rs. 38.50]

(12) Compute the machine hour rate from the following data:

	Rs.	
Cost of the machine	1,00,000	
Installation charges	10,000	
Scrap value after 15 years life	5,000	
Rent and rates for shop per month	200	
General lighting for shop per month	300	
Insurance for the machine per annum	960	
Repairs and maintenance per annum	1,000	
Power consumption 10 units per hour	—	
Rate of power per 100 units	20	
Estimated working hours per annum:	2,000	hours
Supervisors salary per month	600	

The machine occupies ¼ of the total area of the shop. The supervisor is expected to devote 1/5 of his time on this machine.

(B.Com., Andhra, 1991, B.Com., S.V. University, April, 1992)

[Ans.: Rs. 7.95 per hour]

❑ ❑ ❑

Part – III

Methods of Costing

11

OUTPUT COSTING

Objectives

The objectives of the study are to:

- Know the methods of costing
- Understand the situations where Output Costing can be employed
- Learn the Proforma of a Cost Sheet

METHODS OF COSTING

There are two basic methods of costing, *viz.*, Specific Order Costing and Operation Costing. Specific Order Costing is applicable where the work relates to separate batches, contracts, or jobs. Hence, Batch Costing, Contract Costing and Job Costing come under the category of Specific Order Costing. Operation Costing is applicable in undertakings where:

- there is a single process or operation (Single or Output or Unit Costing)
- the raw materials have to pass through different processes (Process Costing).
- some service is rendered rather than manufacturing the goods (Operating or Service Costing).
- there are different operations to be performed in one process in order to convert the raw materials into finished product (Operation Costing).

Thus, Operation Costing includes Single Costing, Process Costing, Operating Costing, Joint Product Costing and By-Product Costing.

Single Costing is also known as Unit Costing or Output Costing. This method is employed in undertakings and industries, which produce single type of product or more than one product of same kind on a large scale continuously. The units of production are identical and homogeneous and the unit of measurement itself will be the cost unit.

The popular cost units may be one unit as in the case of refrigerators, radios, television sets, coolers, etc., or one litre in case of paints or one tonne in case of coal, iron and steel, 1000 units in case of bricks or one bag of sugar, etc.

From the above cost units, it is clear that, this method will be adopted in sugar mills, iron and steel, brick works, collieries and mining concerns, breweries, cement works, radio, television, refrigerator manufacturing concerns, etc.

ACCUMULATION OF COST

The total cost in a given period is divided by the total number of units produced during that period to arrive at cost per unit. However, the costs are under four headings.

(1) **Materials:** Since single product is manufactured, raw material is directly charged to the production. Analysis of the requisition slips reveals the quantity and values of direct and indirect materials issued. Normal loss of material is adjusted by inflating the issue rate while abnormal loss is charged to Costing Profit and Loss Account.

(2) **Labor:** To control costs effectively, labor cost is prepared separately for each Cost Centre or Production Department through payrolls. Direct labor cost forms a part of prime cost while indirect labor cost is charged to factory overhead.

(3) **Direct Expenses:** As these form a part of prime cost, they are collected separately.

(4) **Overheads:** These are classified as manufacturing, administration, selling and distribution overheads. Generally, these are estimated and charged at pre-determined rates.

Treatment of Scrap and by-products

Scrap consists of spoiled, broken or damaged materials having low value. The value of scrap should be deducted from works cost or works overhead while the realisable value of by-products is deducted from works cost.

Defective products

By incurring some extra cost, defectives can be rectified. If that extra cost is of nominal value, it is treated as works cost; otherwise, it is transferred to "Defectives Account".

Work-in-progress

Generally, work in progress is valued at works cost. However, if it is in the initial stage, it is valued at prime cost. The costs that are collected from various Material Abstracts, Wage Analysis Sheets and Overhead Distribution Summaries are presented in the form of a sheet called as "Cost Sheet" or "Statement of Cost" or in the form of "Production Account".

Cost Sheet is a statement showing the various elements of cost like cost of materials consumed, prime cost, works cost, cost of production and cost of sales. Strictly speaking, it does not include sale proceeds and profits earned. If they are also included, it becomes a "Statement of Profit".

The above information can even be presented in the form of an account known as "Production Account" or "Manufacturing Account". The account is debited with the opening stock and all items of expenses, while sales revenue and closing stock are credited. The difference between the two shows either profit or loss.

Purposes of Cost Sheet

The purposes of Cost Sheet are as follows:

(a) Cost sheet reveals the total cost and unit cost of output.

(b) The break up of total cost, i.e., different elements of cost, are disclosed.

(c) A comparative study of the cost of current period with that of the corresponding previous period are provided.

(d) It acts as a guide to the management in fixation of selling prices and quotation of tenders.

Proforma of a Cost Sheet

Cost Sheet of Chandana Company Ltd. for the year ending

Particulars	*Total Cost*		*Unit Cost*
	Rs.	*Rs.*	*Rs.*
Materials:			
Opening Stock of Materials	xxx		
Add: Raw Materials Purchase	xxx		
Less: Closing Stock of Materials	xxx		
Cost of Raw Material Consumed		xxx	
Add: Direct Wages		xxx	
Add: Direct Expenses		xxx	
Prime Cost		xxx	xxx
Add: **Factory Overhead or Works Overhead**			
Lighting	xxx		
Fuel	xxx		
Water	xxx		

Particulars	*Total Cost*		*Unit Cost*
	Rs.	*Rs.*	*Rs.*
Power	xxx		
Foremen wages	xxx		
Drawing office salary	xxx		
Works office expenses	xxx		
Depreciation on factory land., plant equipment, building, etc.	xxx		
	xxxx		
Less: Scrap value of defective work	xxx		
	xxxx		
Add: Opening Stock of Work in process	xxxx		
Less: Closing Stock of Work in process	xxx	xxxx	xxx
Works cost/Factory cost		xxxx	xxx
Add: **Administration Overhead** :			
Audit Fees	xxx		
Office Rent	xxx		
Insurance, lighting	xxx		
Office salary	xxx		
General Manager salary	xxx		
Director's remuneration	xxx		
Printing and stationery	xxx		
Depreciation on office building	xxx	xxxx	xxx
Cost of Production		xxxx	xxx
Add: Opening Stock of Finished Goods		xxxx	
Less: Closing Stock of Finished Goods		xxxx	
Cost of Goods Sold		xxxx	xxx
Add: Selling and Distribution Overheads:			
Bad debts	xxx		
Travelling expenses of salesmen	xxx		
Delivery expenses	xxx		
Salesmen commission	xxx		
Advertisement	xxx		
Carriage outward	xxx		
Discounts	xxx	xxxx	xxx
Cost of Sales		xxxx	xxx
Profit/Loss		xxxx	xxx
Sales or Selling Price		xxxx	xxx

In case of loss, it has to be deducted from cost of sales to arrive at selling price or sales.

Note: Interest on capital, income tax paid, sales tax paid, provision for discount on debtors and creditors, transfer to sinking fund and general reserve, discounts, dividends, goodwill and preliminary expenses written off will not be taken into consideration while preparing the Cost Sheet.

Quotation or Tenders

Quotation is an invitation or offer. Material and wage costs for tender can be ascertained based on the cost records. Indirect expenses are charged as a percentage to previous year wages. Administration, selling and distribution expenses are allocated as a percentage of previous years work cost. Finally, a percentage of profit is added to the cost so ascertained, to arrive at the estimate for the tender.

Illustration 1

From the following particulars, prepare a cost sheet showing *(a)* cost of materials consumed *(b)* prime cost *(c)* works cost *(d)* cost of production and *(e)* percentage of general overheads to works cost.

	Rs.
Opening Stock of Materials on 01.04.07	20,000
Raw Material Purchased	1,00,000
Finished Goods Stock on 31.03.08	30,000
Sales	6,50,000
Wages	2,50,000
Materials unused	25,000
Finished Goods Stock on 01.04.07	45,000
General expenses	75,000

Solution

Particulars	*Amount (Rs.)*
Materials:	
Opening Stock of Materials	20,000
Add: Raw Materials Purchased	1,00,000
Less: Closing Stock of Materials	25,000
Cost of Raw Material Consumed	95,000
Direct Wages	2,50,000
Prime Cost	3,45,000
Add: Works on cost	—
Works cost/Factory cost	3,45,000
Add: Administration Overhead:	
General expenses	75,000
Cost of Production	4,20,000
Add: Opening Stock of Finished Goods	45,000
Less: Closing Stock of Finished Goods	30,000
Cost of Goods Sold	4,35,000
Profit	2,15,000
Sales or Selling Price	6,50,000

Percentage of General Overhead to Works Cost:

(General Overhead/Works Cost) × 100 = (75,000/3,45,000) × 100 = 21.74%

Illustration 2

In a factory, two types of television sets are manufactured *viz.*, type A and type B models. Find the cost of a television set and profit per television set sold.

	Type A Rs.	*Type B* Rs.
Materials	1,00,000	1,20,000
Labor	50,000	40,000
Other expenses	5,000	4,000

Works on cost is charged at 75% on Labour and Administration Cost is taken at 20% on Works cost. Type A sets sold during the period are 250 @ Rs. 1,500 each and Type B are 300 @ Rs. 1,800 each.

Find the total profit as per Cost Books. Assume that there is no opening or closing stock.

Solution

Cost sheet of Type A and Type B Television Sets.

Particulars	*Type – A (Rs.)*	*Type – B (Rs.)*
Materials	1,00,000	120,000
Direct Labour	50,000	40,000
Other Expenses	5,000	4,000
Prime Cost	1,55,000	1,64,000
Add: Works on cost (75% of Wages)	37,500	30,000
Works cost/Factory cost	1,92,500	1,94,000
Add: Administration Overhead (20% on Works cost)	38,500	38,800
Cost of Production	2,31,000	2,32,800
Profit	1,44,000	3,07,200
Sales	3,75,000	5,40,000

Total Profit: 1,44,000 + 3,07,200 = Rs. 4,51,200

Illustration 3

The accounts of a manufacturing company showed the following details for the year ended 2008.

	Rs.
Materials Used	6,00,000
Production Wages	5,00,000
Works Overhead Expenses	1,00,000
General Expenses	60,000

Prepare a statement showing:

(a) Works cost
(b) Total cost
(c) Percentage of Works Overhead Expenditure to Production Wages and
(d) Percentage of General Expenses to Works Cost

What price should the company quote on the basis of the above information to manufacture a machine which would require materials valued at Rs. 6,000 and wages Rs. 3,000 so that the price will yield a profit of 25% on Selling Price.

Solution

Cost Sheet for the year ending 31.12.2008.

Particulars	*Total Cost Rs.*
Materials used	6,00,000
Direct Wages	5,00,000
Prime Cost	11,00,000
Add: Works on cost	1,00,000
Works cost/Factory cost	12,00,000
Add: Administration Overhead	60,000
Cost of production (Total cost)	12,60,000

Percentage works overhead to wages:

$$\frac{\text{Works Overheads} \times 100}{\text{Wages}} = \frac{1{,}00{,}000 \times 100}{5{,}00{,}000} = 20\%$$

Percentage of/ general overhead to works cost:

$$\frac{\text{General Overheads} \times 100}{\text{Works cost}} = \frac{60{,}000 \times 100}{12{,}00{,}000} = 5\%$$

Statement showing Quotation Price.

Particulars	*Amount (Rs.)*
Materials	6,000
Direct Wages	3,000
Prime Cost	9,000
Add: Works on cost (20% of direct wages)	600
Works cost/Factory cost	9,600
Add: Administration Overhead (5% of works cost)	480
Cost of Production (75)	10,080
Profit (25) $\frac{10,080 \times 25}{75}$	3,360
Quotation price (100)	13,440

Illustration 4

From the following information, prepare a cost sheet.

	Rs.
Opening stock of raw material	10,000
Purchase of raw material	25,000
General expenses	5,000
Administration expenses	1,750
Bad debts	1,200
Income tax paid	5,000
Unused raw material	3,450
Productive wages	2,500
Sales	90,000
Works overhead	2,500
Travelling expenses	1,500

Solution

Cost Sheet showing the various components of cost.

Particulars	*Total Cost Rs.*	*Total Cost Rs.*
Opening stock of raw material	10,000	
Add: purchase of raw material	25,000	
Less: unused material	3,450	
Raw Material Consumed	31,550	
Production wages	2,500	
Prime Cost		34,050
Add: Works on cost		2,500
Works cost/Factory cost		36,550
Add: Administration Overhead:		
Administration expenses	1,750	
General expenses	5,000	6,750
Cost of Production		43,300
Add: Selling and Distribution Overhead:		
Bad debts	1,200	
Travelling expenses	1,500	2,700
Cost of Sales		46,000
Profit		44,000
Sales		90,000

Illustration 5

In a factory, two types of articles are manufactured *viz.*, No.1 and No.2. From the following particulars, prepare a statement of cost showing total cost of each variety and ascertain the total profit. There is no opening or closing stock.

	No.1 *Rs.*	*No.2* *Rs.*
Materials	30,000	50,000
Labor	60,000	70,000

Works on cost is charged at 40% of works cost and office on cost is taken at 20%.

On total cost. No.1 article sold during the period is 180 at Rs. 1,200 each and No. 2 is 200 at Rs. 1,500 each.

(B.Com., Kakatiya, April 1993)

Solution

Determination of Overheads

It is given that works on cost is charged at 40% of works cost. Works Cost Comprises of prime cost plus works overhead. If works cost is assumed to be 100 then prime cost and works on cost will be as follows:

Prime cost	=	60
Works on cost	=	40
Works cost	=	100

Based on relationship of Prime Cost and Works-on Cost, it is possible to find out works on cost for Article No.1 and Article No.2.

	Article No. 1 *Rs.*	*Article No.2* *Rs*
Prime Cost (Given) (Materials + Labor)	90,000	1,20,000
Works on Cost		
(40/60) * 90,000		
(40/60) * 1,20,000	60,000	80,000
Works Cost	1,50,000	2,00,000

It is given that office on cost is 20% of total cost, which comprises of works cost plus office overhead. If total cost is assumed to be Rs. 100, then office overhead and works cost will be as follows:

	Rs.
Works Cost	80
Office Overhead	20
Total Cost	100

Therefore, office overhead is 25% of works cost based on relationship of Works Cost and Office Cost thus determined, it is possible to find the office overhead of Article No. 1 and Article No. 2.

	Article No. 1 *Rs.*	*Article No. 2* *Rs*
Works Cost as above	1,50,000	2,00,000
Office Overhead		
(20/80) * 1,50,000		
(20/80) * 2,00,000	37,500	50,000
Total Cost	1,87,500	2,50,000

Statement showing Cost and Profit

	Article No.1 (*Rs.*)	*Article No.2* (*Rs.*)
Materials Labor	30,000 60,000	50,000 70,000
Prime Cost	90,000	1,20,000
Works Overhead (40% of Works Cost)	60,000	80,000
Works Cost	1,50,000	2,00,000
Office Overheads (20% of Total Cost)	37,500	50,000
Total Cost	1,87,500	2,50,000
Profit	28,500	50,000
Sales	2,16,000	3,00,000

Illustration 6

The standard production for the particular work order is 20 units per day and piece-rate wage is 60 paise per unit if daily production is 20 units or more. The rate is 50 paise per unit if production is less than 20 units. Cost of material is 30 paise per unit. It is proposed to charge factory overheads under one of following methods.

(i) 100% of Labour Cost,

(ii) 80% of Prime Cost.

Tabulate the above data in the form of a suitable statement and indicate the factory cost per unit, under each of the above methods, if the daily production is (a) 15 units (b) 20 units (c) 25 units.

(ICWA, Inter)

Solution

(a) Statement Showing Factory Cost per Unit by Charging Overhead at 100% of Labor Cost

Expenses Item	*Daily Production 15 units (Rs.)*		*Daily Production 20 units (Rs.)*		*Daily Production 25 units (Rs.)*	
	Total per day	*Per unit*	*Total per day*	*Per unit*	*Total per day*	*Per unit*
Material Labour	4.50 7.50	0.30 0.50	6.00 12.00	0.30 0.60	7.50 15.00	0.30 0.60
Prime Cost	12.00	0.80	18.00	0.90	22.50	0.90
Factory Overheads (100% on Labor)	7.50	0.50	12.00	0.60	15.00	0.60
Total Factory Cost	19.50	1.30	30.00	1.50	37.50	1.50

(b) Statement Showing Factory Cost per Unit by Charging Overhead at 80% of Prime Cost

Expenses Item	*Daily Production 15 units (Rs.)*		*Daily Production 20 units (Rs.)*		*Daily Production 25 units (Rs.)*	
	Total per day	*Per unit*	*Total per day*	*Per unit*	*Total per day*	*Per unit*
Material Labor	4.50 7.50	0.30 0.50	6.00 12.00	0.30 0.60	7.50 15.00	0.30 0.60
Prime Cost	12.00	0.80	18.00	0.90	22.50	0.90
Factory Overheads (80% on Prime Cost)	9.60	0.64	14.40	0.72	18.00	0.72
Total Factory Cost	21.60	1.44	32.40	1.62	40.50	1.62

Illustration 7

From the following information, prepare a cost sheet for the month of Dec., 1989:

	Rs.
Stock on Hand – 1st Dec., 1989:	
Raw Materials	25,000
Finished Goods	17,300
Stock on Hand – 31st Dec., 1989:	
Raw Materials	26,200
Finished Goods	15,700
Purchases of Raw Materials	21,900
Carriage on Purchases	1,100
Work in Progress, 1-12-1989 at Works Cost	8,200
Work in Progress, 31-12-1989 at Works Cost	9,100
Sale of Finished Goods	72,300
Direct Wages	17,200
Non-Production Wages	800
Direct Expenses	1,200
Factory Overheads	8,300
Administration Overheads	3,200
Selling and Distribution Overheads	4,200

(M.Com., Madurai Kamaraj, April 1991)

Solution

Cost Sheet for the month ended 31st Dec., 1989

	Rs.	*Rs.*
Stock of Materials on 1-12-1989	25,000	
Add: Purchases	21,900	
Add: Carriage on Purchases	1,100	
	48,000	
Less: Closing Stock on 31-12-1989	26,200	
(a) Material Consumed		21,800
Direct Wages		17,200
Direct Expenses		1,200
(b) Prime Cost		40,200
Factory Overheads		8,300
Non Productive Wages		800
		49,300
Add: Opening Stock of W.I.P		8,200
		57,500
Less: Closing Stock of W.I.P		9,100
(c) Works Cost		48,400
Administration Overhead		3,200
(d) Cost of Production		51,600
Add: Opening Stock of Finished Goods		17,300
		68,900
Less: Closing Stock of Finished Goods		15,700
(e) Cost of Goods Sold		53,200
Selling and Distribution Overheads		4,200
(f) Cost of Sales		57,400
Profit		14,900
(g) Sales		72,300

Illustration 8

The following details are available from the books of Shubhashaya Sea Products Ltd., for the year ending 31st December, 1991:

	Rs.
Direct Wages	6,00,000
Purchase of Materials	7,20,000
Other Materials	36,000
Carriage (factory overhead)	8,640
Wages of Foreman and Storekeepers	48,000
Other Indirect Wages	6,000
Cost of Research and Experiments	30,000
Office Manager's Salary	72,000
Employees' State Insurance	6,000
Power, Fuel and Haulage	54,000
Drawing Office Expenses	36,000
Printing and Stationery	12,000
Counting of Salary	12,000
Sales	18,00,000
Stock 1.1.1991	
Raw Materials	1,20,000
W.I.P	28,800
Finished Products (Units)	6,000
Stock 31.12.1991	
Raw Materials	1,33,440
W.I.P	96,000
Finished Products (Units)	12,000
Income Tax	22,000
Donation	5,000

Selling and Distribution Expenses are to be charged at Re. 1 per unit. During the year 1991, units produced were 96,000. Prepare a Cost Sheet showing the different elements of Cost and the Profit.

(B.Com., Mangalore, May 1992)

Solution

Subhashashya Sea Products Ltd. Cost Sheet for the year ended 31st December 1991

(Production – 96,000 units)

	Units	Rs.	Total (Rs.)	Per Unit (Rs.)
Stock of Raw Materials 1.1.1991		1,20,000		
Add: Purchases		7,20,000		
		8,40,000		
Less: Stock of Materials at close		1,33,440		
Materials-consumed			7,06,560	7.360
Direct Wages			6,00,000	6.250
Prime Cost	96,000		13,06,560	13.6100
Other Materials			36,000	0.3750
Wages of Foreman			48,000	0.5000
Other Indirect Wages			6,000	0.0625
Cost of Research and Experiments			30,000	0.3125
Employees' State Insurance			6,000	0.0625
Power, Fuel and Haulage			54,000	0.5625
Drawing Expenses			36,000	0.3750
			15,22,560	15.860
Add: Opening W.I.P			28,800	0.300
			15,51,360	16.160

	Units	*Rs.*	*Total (Rs.)*	*Per Unit (Rs.)*
Less: Closing W.I.P			96,000	1.000
Works Cost	96,000		14,55,360	15.160
Carriage		8,640		
Office Manager's Salary		72,000		
Printing and Stationery		12,000		
Counting House Salary		12,000	1,04,640	1.090
Cost of Production			15,60,000	16.250
Add: Opening Stock of Finished Goods	6,000		97,500	
	1,02,000		16,57,500	
Less: Closing Stock of Finished Goods	12,000		1,95,000	
Cost of Goods Sold	90,000		14,62,500	
Selling and Distribution Expenses	90,000		90,000	1.000
Cost of Sales	90,000		15,52,500	17.250
Profit			2,47,500	2.750
Sales			18,00,000	20.000

Illustration 9

The Pens manufacturing Company is producing two types of pens 'Deluxe and Popular'. The manufacturing cost for the year ended 31st March 1980 were:

Direct Materials	Rs. 2,00,000
Direct Wages	Rs. 1,12,000
Production Overhead	Rs. 48,000
Total	Rs. 3,60,000

It is ascertained that:

(a) Direct Materials in Deluxe type cost twice as much as that of Popular type.
(b) Direct Wages Popular type were 60% of those for Deluxe type.
(c) Production Overhead was 30 paise per pen for both the types.
(d) Administration Overheads for each type was 200% of Direct Labor.
(e) Selling Cost was 25 paise per pen for both the types.
(f) Production during the year was :
Deluxe type – 40,000 pens of which 36,000 were sold
Popular type – 1,20,000 pens of which 1,00,000 were sold
(g) Selling prices were Rs. 7 per pen of 'Deluxe' type and Rs. 5 per pen of 'Popular' type.

Prepare a statement showing the total cost per pen of each type and the profit made on each type of pen.

(M.Com., Karnataka, 1986)

Solution

Statement Showing the Total Cost and Profit

	Deluxe (40000 Pens)		*Popular (120000 pens)*	
	Total (Rs.)	*Per Pen (Rs.)*	*Total (Rs.)*	*Per Pen (Rs.)*
Direct Materials (Note 1)	80,000	2.00	1,20,000	1.00
Direct Labor (Note 2)	40,000	1.00	72,000	0.60
Prime Cost	1,20,000	3.00	1,92,000	1.60
Production Overhead (Note 3)	12,000	0.30	36,000	0.30
Works Cost	1,32,000	3.30	2,28,000	1.90
Administrative Overheads (200% of Direct Wages)	80,000	2.00	1,44,000	1.20
Cost of Production	2,12,000	5.30	3,72,000	3.10
(–) Closing Stock (Note 4)	21,200	5.30	62,000	3.10
Cost of Goods Sold	1,90,800	5.30	3,10,000	3.10
Selling Expenses (Note 5)	9,000	0.25	25,000	0.25
	1,99,800	5.55	3,35,000	3.35
Profit	52,200	1.45	1,65,000	1.65
Sales (Note 6)	2,52,000	7.00	5,00,000	5.00

Note 1: Consumption of direct material in 'Deluxe' type is twice as much as that of 'Popular' type. Therefore:

Deluxe	Popular
40,000 × 2 = 80,000	1,20,000 × 1 = 1,20,000

Therefore Material Cost is to be divided in the ratio of 80: 120 or 2:3 between Deluxe and Popular.

Deluxe	Popular
(2,00,000/5) × 2 = Rs. 80,000	(2,00,000/5) × 3 = Rs. 1,20,000

Note 2: It is given that direct wages for 'Popular' type were 60% of those for 'Deluxe' type

Suppose wage for Deluxe type = x

	Deluxe	Popular
Therefore Wages	40,000x	1,20,000 × 0.60x

Or 40,000x + [1,20,000 × 0.60x] = Rs. 1,12,000

Or x = Re. 1

Therefore Wage Cost for Deluxe = Rs. 40,000; for Popular = Rs. 72,000

Note 3: Production Overhead

Deluxe 40,000 × Re. 0.30 = Rs. 12,000

Popular 1,20,000 × Re. 0.30 = Rs. 36,000

Note 4: Deluxe = 4,000 in stock @ Rs. 5.30 = Rs. 21,200

Popular = 20,000 in stock @ Rs. 3.10 = Rs. 62,000

Note 5: Deluxe 36,000 × 0.25 = Rs. 9,000

Popular 1,00,000 × Re. 0.25 = Rs. 25,000

Note 6: Deluxe 36,000 × 7 = Rs. 2,52,000

Popular 1,00,000 × 5 = Rs. 5,00,000

SUMMARY

Single Costing is also known as Unit Costing or Output Costing. This method is employed in undertakings and industries, which produce single type of product or more than one product of same kind on a large scale continuously. The units of production are identical and homogeneous and the unit of measurement itself will be the cost unit.

The total cost in a given period is divided by the total number of units produced during that period to arrive at cost per unit.

Cost sheet is a statement showing the various elements of cost like cost of materials consumed, prime cost, works cost, cost of production and cost of sales. Strictly speaking, it does not include sale proceeds and profits earned. If they are also included, it becomes a "Statement of Profit".

Quotation is an invitation or offer. Material and wage costs for tender can be ascertained based on the cost records. Indirect expenses are charged as a percentage to previous year wages. Administration, selling and distribution expenses are allocated as a percentage of previous years work cost. Finally, a percentage of profit is added to the cost so ascertained, to arrive at the estimate for the tender.

Glossary

- **Cost sheet:** a statement showing the various elements of cost like cost of materials consumed, prime cost, works cost, cost of production and cost of sales. Strictly speaking, it does not include sale proceeds and profits earned. If they are also included, it becomes a "Statement of Profit".

Questions

(1) Define Unit Costing and and give examples of industries where it can be used.
(2) What is a Cost Sheet? Explain the purposes served by it.
(3) What are the features of Output Costing? Briefly explain the costing procedure under this method.
(4) What is an Operating Cost? In which industries is this method of costing applicable?
(5) Define Output Costing. Mention the enterprises that use Single or Output Costing.

PROBLEMS

(1) The following information pertains to Alpha Company. Prepare a cost sheet showing *(a)* Cost of materials consumed; *(b)* Prime Cost; *(c)* Works Cost; *(d)* Cost of Production; *(e)* Total Cost; *(f)* Percentage of Works Overheads to Wages and *(g)* Percentage of Office expenses to Works Cost.

	Rs.
Opening Stock of Materials as on 1.4.1999	50,000
Raw Material purchased	15,00,000
Closing Stock of Raw Materials	60,000
Finished Goods Stock on 31.3.2000	1,50,000
Office expenses	1,20,000
Wages	10,30,000
Works overhead	2,60,000
Finished Goods Stock on 1.4.1999	1,20,000
Sale of Finished Goods	31,00,000

The company intends to send a tender for a large plant, which requires materials Rs. 50,000, and incur wages Rs. 35,000. Works overhead are charged at 20% on wages and a profit of 20% on selling price is expected. Show what the amount of tender would be.

[Ans.: *(a)* Rs. 14,90,000; *(b)* Rs. 25,20,000; *(c)* Rs. 27,80,000; *(d)* Rs. 29,00,000; (e) Rs. 28,70,000; *(f)* 25.24%; *(g)* 4.32% Tender amount Rs. 1,19,968]

(2) From the following particulars, prepare a cost statement showing the component of total cost and profit for the year ended 31.12.2008.

	1.1.2008 *Rs.*	*31.12.2008* *Rs.*
Stock of finished goods	16,000	10,000
Stock of raw materials	30,000	40,000
Work-in-progress	12,000	10,000
Transactions during the year:		
Purchase of raw materials	4,00,000	
Carriage inwards	10,500	
Wages	1,50,000	
Work manager's salary	20,000	
Factory employees salaries	40,000	
Factory rent, taxes and insurance	7,500	
Power expenses	10,500	
Other production expenses	40,000	
General expenses	35,000	
Sales	8,00,000	
Income tax	6,000	
Interest on debentures	20,000	
Transfer to sinking fund	40,000	
Goodwill written off	20,500	
Payment of sales tax	36,000	

(B.Com., Andhra University - Adapted)

[**Ans.:** Profit Rs. 94,500]

Hint: Income tax, interest on debentures, transfer to reserves, goodwill, sales tax will not appear in cost sheet.

(3) The following is the Manufacturing and Profit and Loss Account of a company for the year ending 31.03.2008.

Manufacturing and P&L Account

	Rs.		Rs.
Opening stock:			
Materials	2,000	Sales	5,00,000
Finished goods	3,000		
	5,000	Closing Stock:	
Purchase of material	1,50,000	Material 18,500	
Direct wages	1,20,000	Finished goods 3,000	
Power	15,500		
Carriage inwards	2,000		21,500
Royalty	24,000		
Cost of special design	5,000		
Gross profit c/d	2,00,000		
	5,21,500		5,21,500
Rent (office)	5,000	Gross Profit b/d	2,00,000
Rent (factory)	7,000	Interest on loan	4,500
Telephone	3,000	Sale of scrap	750
Advertisement	7,500	Discount received	1,750
Electricity (office)	3,000		
Electricity (factory)	4,500		
Provision for bad debts	10,000		
Income tax	12,000		
Salaries	25,000		
Donation	7,000		
Establishment expenses	10,000		
Depreciation on :			
Office furniture	2,500		
Factory furniture	2,000		
Plant & Machinery	6,000		
Delivery Van	2,000		
Rent on warehouse	6,500		
Net profit	94,000		
	2,07,000		2,07,000

Prepare a Cost Sheet from the particulars given above taking into account the following other details.

(a) 60% of telephone expenses ratio relate to office and 40% to sales department.

(b) 25% of salaries relate to factory, 50% to office and 25% to sales department.

(c) 50% of establishment expenses relate to office and 50% relate to sales department.

[**Ans.:** Profit Rs. 1,16,750]

Hint: Royalty and cost of design form part of cost of raw material consumed. Income tax, provision for bad debts and non-operating incomes are to be excluded.

(4) The following details have been obtained from the cost records of Comet Paints Ltd.

	Rs.
Stock of raw material on 1st September 2008	75,000
Stock of raw material on 30th September 2008	91,500
Direct wages	52,500
Indirect wages	2,750
Sales	2,11,000
Work-in-progress on 1st September 2008	28,000
Work-in-progress on 30th September 2008	35,000
Purchase of raw material	66,000
Factory rent, rates and power	15,000

	Rs.
Depreciation on Plant and Machinery	3,500
Expenses on purchases	1,500
Carriage outwards	2,500
Advertising	3,500
Office rent and taxes	2,500
Travelling expenses	6,500
Stock of finished goods on 1st September 2008	54,000
Stock of finished goods on 30th September 2008	31,000

Prepare a Production Account giving the maximum possible breakup of cost and profit.
[**Ans.:** Profit Rs. 55,250]
Hint: Prime Cost Rs. 1, 03,500, Works Cost Rs. 1,17,750, Total Cost of Production Rs. 1,20,250 and Cost of Sales Rs. 1, 55,750.

(5) The following data have been extracted from the books of Sunshine Industries Ltd for the year 2008.

	Rs.
Opening stock of raw material	25,000
Purchase of raw material	85,000
Closing stock of raw material	40,000
Carriage inwards	5,000
Direct wages	75,000
Indirect wages	10,000
Other direct charges	15,000
Depreciation on Plant and Machinery	1,500
Depreciation on Office Furniture	100
Salary:	
Office	2,500
Salesmen	2,000
Other office expenses	900.
Manager's remuneration	12,000
Rent and rates:	
Factory	5,000
Office	500
Indirect consumption of materials	500
Other factory expenses	5,700
Advance income tax payment	15,000
Bad debts written off	1,000
Advertisement expenses	2,000
Travelling expenses of salesmen	1,100
Carriage outwards	1,000
Sales	2,50,000

The manager has overall charges of the company and his remuneration is to be allocated at Rs. 4,000 to the factory and Rs. 2,000 to the office and Rs. 6,000 to the selling operation.

From the above particulars, prepare a statement showing *(a)* Prime Cost *(b)* Factory Cost *(c)* Cost of Production *(d)* Cost of Sales and *(e)* Net profit.

[**Ans.:** Net profit Rs. 39,200]

(6) The following information pertaining to XYZ Company Ltd. for the year ended 31st March 2008, prepare a Cost Sheet with all detailed information.

	Rs.
Opening stock of raw material	50,000
Material purchased during the year	1,62,500
Counting house salaries	10,000
Carriage and cartage outward	450
Preliminary expenses written off	2,120
Goodwill written off	5,750
Repairs to Plant and Machinery	4,250

	Rs.
Closing stock of raw material	10,350
Drawing office salaries	5,350
Advertisement	3,000
Carriage inwards	1,250
Salesmen travelling expenses	2,500
Bad debts written off	1,680
Rent, rates, taxes and insurance	3,100
Sales	4,50,780
Wages	1,10,000
Director's fees	5,300
Factory gas and water	4,500
Office gas and water	500
Manager's salary (3/5 factory and 2/5 office)	25,000
Salesmen salary and commission	6,500
Depreciation on Furniture written off	1,050
Depreciation on Plant and Machinery	5,500

[**Ans.:** Net profit Rs.58,700]

Hint: Drawing office salaries are treated as factory overhead and counting house salary as general expense.

(7) The following data relating to the working of a factory in 2008 are available:

	Rs.
Material Consumed	2,00,000
Direct wages	1,50,000
Factory expenses	90,000
Administration expenses	88,000
Based on the above data, find out the cost of job to be done in 2009:	
Materials required for the job will be	2,000
Wages for the job will be	2,000

What will be the quotation for the job if a profit at 20% on selling price is required.

[**Ans.:** Rs.7,800]

(8) In respect of a factory, the following figures have been obtained for the year 2008 - Materials Rs.12,00,000, Direct wages Rs.10,00,000, Factory overhead Rs. 6,00,000, Administration overhead Rs. 6,72,000, Selling overhead Rs. 4,48,000, Distribution overhead Rs. 2,80,000 and Profit Rs. 8,40,000. The firm wants to execute a work order in 2009 which requires Rs.16,000 towards materials and Rs. 1 0,000 towards direct wages. Determine the price at which the work order should be accepted so as to enable it to earn the same rate of profit on selling price as in 2008.

[**Ans.:** Rs. 57,602]

(9) In respect of a factory, the following information has been obtained for the year 2007:

Cost of material Rs. 12,00,000; Direct wages Rs. 10,00,000; Factory overhead Rs. 6,00,000; Administration overhead Rs. 6,72,000; Selling overhead Rs. 4,48,000; Distribution overhead Rs. 2,80,000; Sales Rs. 50,40,000.

A work order has been executed in 2008 for which the following expenses have been incurred: Materials Rs. 16,000; Wages Rs. 10,000. Assuming that in 2008, the rate of factory overhead has increased by 10%, distribution overheads have gone down by 10%, selling and administration have each gone up by 25%, at what price should the product be sold so as to earn the same rate of profit on the selling price as in 2007. Factory overhead is based on direct wages and all other overheads are based on factory cost.

[**Ans.:** Tender Rs. 62,200]

❑ ❑ ❑

12

JOB COSTING

Objectives

The objectives of the study are to:

- Understand the meaning of Job Costing
- Know the situations where Job Costing is applicable
- Learn the procedure for adoption of Job Costing

MEANING OF JOB COSTING

Job Costing is also known as Job Order Costing, Production Order Costing or Specific Order Costing. Job Costing means ascertaining the cost of a specific order, or of an individual order or of each job. It is a method applied to determine the cost of specific jobs or lots of production generally manufactured according to customer satisfaction. Every order in Job Costing is separate and it is not essential that the same manufacturing operations be carried out or the same material be utilized in respect of each job. However, a number of identical orders or identical products may be combined to form lots or batches, each such lot or batch constitutes a job order.

C. I. M. A. Terminology defines Job Costing as "a form of specific order costing which applies where work is undertaken to customer's special requirement. As distinct from Contract Costing, each job is of comparatively short duration."

Under this method, production is always against the customer's special requirement. As each job has its own characteristics and requires separate treatment, costs are collected and accumulated according to each job.

For each job, a distinct number is allotted and a separate cost sheet is prepared to ascertain the cost of the job and profit or loss is determined job-wise.

PROCEDURE OF JOB ORDER COST SHEET

There is no continuous process in this system as each job is a separate work. A job cost sheet is prepared for each job and price is quoted separately. A job number or work order number is given to each production order which is made in triplicate – one to the stores department for issue of materials; second one to the costing department and the third to the concerned foreman.

A job cost sheet contains the details pertaining to the cost of direct materials, labor, works overhead, administration, selling and distribution overheads etc. In Job Costing, the requirements of production are determined first and then the expenses are ascertained. The total cost is divided by the number of units produced there under, to determine the cost per unit.

The following procedure is generally followed in case of Job Costing.

- **Job Number** – When an order is accepted, an individual work order number must be assigned to each job so that each job is capable of being identified at all stages of production. Such an assignment of job numbers facilitates reference for costing purposes in the ledger and it is also convenient to use such numbers on various forms and documents.
- **Production Order** – The production control department makes out a production order thereby authorizing to start the work on the job. Several copies of production orders in different colours are prepared to distinguish them easily. These copies are passed on to all the departmental foremen concerned with the job, store keeper for issue of material, tool room as an advance notification of tools required.
- **Job Cost Sheet/Job Card** – It is the unique accounting document showing the cost incurred in doing a job. Receipt of production order is the signal for the cost accountant to prepare a cost sheet in which he will record the cost of material used, labour and machine time consumed. Each concern has to design a sheet to suit its needs. The cost sheet is prepared for each job regardless of time taken for its completion. Material, Labour and Overhead costs are posted periodically to the relevant cost sheet.
  - *(a)* **Material Cost** – On receipt of production order, the shop draws the requisite material from the stores. The material used in manufacturing and/or completing jobs are known as direct material which becomes part of the finished product. Direct materials are directly charged to jobs on which they are used and indirect materials or factory supplies are part of manufacturing overhead and or allocated the various jobs. In a job order cost system, two types of forms may be used. One for an Indirect Material requisition and the second one for a statement of Bill of Material. When the forms are received in the store room, the store keeper will enter the quantity and the cost of material issued in the stores ledger card.
  - *(b)* **Labour Cost** – Direct Labour Cost can be identified with the specific job with the help of job time tickets. When a worker begins to work on an order, the starting time is noted on the ticket and when the job order is finished, the stopping time is written and the time spent on the job is noted. Earnings (Wages) are then computed using the employees hourly rate. The total of direct labour cost is debited to Work-in-Progress Account and the total of Indirect Labour cost is debited to Indirect Manufacturing Cost Control Accounts.
  - *(c)* **Direct Expenses** – These are directly charged to individual jobs for which they are incurred *viz.* Job Ledger Control Account/Work-in-Progress Ledger Control Account. The invoices can be marked with the number of the job, as documentary evidence, to which the cost is to be allocated. It helps the Cost Accounting Department in preparing the summary of direct charges to be posted on individual job cost sheets.
  - *(d)* **Overhead** – Overheads are usually charged to Work-in-Progress by means of a pre-determined absorption rate calculated in advance of production.
- **Completion of Jobs** – As soon as the job is completed, a job completion report is sent by the production shop to the production planning department with a copy to the cost office. The completion report is an indication that the manufacturing operations are over and further expenses on the job should cease so that the cost sheet may now be closed. The expenses booked under each element of cost is totalled up and the grand total of costs is arrived at. The total cost divided by the total number of units produced gives the cost per unit of the job.

  In many cases, a Finished Stock Card which keeps a day to day record of the units completed on a production order is maintained. When the job is completed, the quantity recorded on the Finished Stock Card is totalled up and total number of units completed is posted to the Job Completion Report or to the Production Order, as the case may be.
- **Work-in-Progress** – An incomplete job, i.e., Work-in-Progress is a job on which some manufacturing processes or operations are still due before it can be called as a finished product. The cost of such closing work-in-progress is obtained from work-in-progress account where it appears as a balance entry supported by cost sheets. The closing work-in-progress is carried over to job cost sheet as the opening stock of work-in-progress in the subsequent period.

Suitability of Job Cost Accounting

The following are the situations where Job Cost Accounting can be employed.

(1) **Jobbing Concerns** – Job Costing can be employed in concerns where manufacturing of a variety of products according to customer specifications takes place. These concerns do not generally confine their activities to producing uniformally any specific product for sale in the market. The jobs are all different and non repetitive having different specifications and methods of manufacture and each one requires different types, sizes and quantities of materials and equipment and utilizes different labour hours. Such concerns must use Job Cost Accounting.

(2) Small Concerns – Though manufacturing a number of specific products, small concerns may find process costing difficult to apply due to small sales and no product has a run long enough to establish a product line. A product is manufactured for a few days but when the demand for the product falls, another product is taken up only to be changed over again to a third one after the next few days. On account of frequent changes from one product to another, job costing would be suitable for determining the cost of each lot of products.

(3) Large Concerns – These concerns may manufacture a variety of products. A single department would be manufacturing several products, perhaps all at a time, so that none of the departments is specialized for continuous runs of product lines. As definite process departments cannot be established, job costing is suitable.

Job Costing is applicable to Engineering Concerns, Construction Companies, Ship Building, Furniture Making, Foundries, Machine Manufacturing Industries, Machine tools manufacture, Printers, Hardware, Repair Shops, Automobile Garages, etc.

Advantages of Job Costing System

The main advantages of this system are:

(1) The Cost of Material, Labor and Overhead for every job/product in a department is available daily, weekly or as often as required while the job is still in progress. This enables the management to know the trends of cost and control the efficiency of operations, material and machines by a suitable comparison.

(2) As the cost per job and the profitability of each job undertaken is ascertained, the management can distinguish profitable and unprofitable jobs.

(3) This method of costing becomes the basis for contract costing (cost plus contracts).

(4) It assists in comparing the actual cost with the estimates and enables to take corrective action.

(5) It helps in identifying spoilage and defective work with each job and hence, responsibility can be fixed on persons or departments.

(6) On completion of job, the cost under each element is immediately ascertained. Cost may be compared with the selling price of products in order to determine their profitability and to decide which product lines should be pushed or discontinued. The application of marginal costing may be useful in such situations.

(7) Historical Costs for past periods for each product, compiled by orders, departments or machines provide useful statistics for future production planning and for estimating the costs of similar jobs to be taken up in future. This assists in prompt furnishing of price quotations for specific jobs.

Limitations of Job Costing System

The main limitation of this system are :

(1) It is time consuming and involves, a lot of clerical work, thus making the system expensive.

(2) Job Costing cannot be applied in all types of manufacturing industries specially where there is continuous production and involves many processes.

(3) Since costs are historical in nature, remedial action cannot be taken immediately.

(4) Job Costing does not facilitate control of cost unless it is used with Standard or Estimated Costing.

(5) Each job should be continuously identifiable from the material stage to completion which some times become difficult.

The costing system should be properly developed, periodically evaluated and defined well so that difficulties faced in using the system can be minimized.

Illustration 1

From the following information pertaining to Job No. 101, find the profits.

Material Rs. 5,000, Wages 100 hours at Rs. 3.25 per hour, Rs. 10,500 are towards variable overhead for 3,000 labour hours. The job is quoted for Rs. 7,000.

Solution

Job Cost Sheet No. 101

	Rs.
Material	5,000
Wages for 100 hours @ Rs. 3.25	325
Variable Overhead for 100 hours @ Rs. 3.50 (10,500/3,000 = Rs. 3.50)	350
Total Cost	5,675
Profit	1,325
Quotation price	7,000

Illustration 2

XYZ Ltd. undertook 2 jobs during the last week of March 2008. The details are as follows:

	Job No. 1 (Rs.)	*Job No. 2 (Rs.)*
Material	1,000	800
Direct Expenses	500	400
Wages	800	600
Material Transaferred to Job No. 2	250	250
Material Returned to Stores	75	—
Find the Cost of Each Job.		

Solution

Job Cost Sheet

	Job No.1. Rs.	*Job No.2. Rs.*
Material	1,000	800
Material transfer to Job No. 2	(-) 250	(+) 250
Material returned to stores	(-) 75	—
Material consumed	675	1,050
Wages	800	600
Direct expenses	500	400
Total Cost	1,975	2,050

Illustration 3

Indian Product Ltd. has received an enquiry for the supply of 2,00,000 numbers of a special type of machine screw. Capacity exist for manufacture of the screws in the company's Unit No. 3 but a fixed investment of Rs. 60,000 and a working capital to the extent of 25% of the sale value will be required if the job is undertaken. The costs are estimated as follows:

Raw material 20,000 lbs. at Rs. 2.30 per lb.

Labor hours – direct 18,000 of which 2,000 would be overtime hours payable at double the labor rate.

Labor rate – Re. 1 per hour.

Factory overheads – Re. 1 per direct labour hour.

Selling and distribution cost Rs. 23,000

Materials recovered as scrap at the end of the operations is estimated at Rs. 2,000

The company expects a net return of 25% on the capital employed.

Prepare a cost and price statement indicating the price, which should be quoted to the customer.

(Karnataka – M.Com.)

Solution

Cost and Price Statement for 2,00,000 units of Screws

	Rs.	*Rs.*
Raw Material @ Rs. 2.30 per lb. for 20,000 lbs.	46,000	
Less Scrap value	2,000	44,000
Direct labor:		
16,000 hours @ Re. 1 per hour	16,000	
2,000 hours @ Rs. 2 per hour	4,000	20,000
Prime Cost		64,000
Factory Overhead:		
18,000 hours @ Re. 1		18,000
Works Cost		82,000
Selling & Distribution Overheads		23,000
Total Cost		1,05,000
Profit (25% on capital employed)		23,000
Quotation price		1,28,000

Calculation of profit:

Fixed investment Rs. 60,000

Working capital is 25% of the sales value

Let the sales value be X

Therefore, working capital is 25% of X i.e. (X/4)

Capital Employed = Fixed Assets + Working Capital

Sale Price = Total Cost + 25 % (60,000 + X/4)

X = 1,05,000 + 1/4 (60,000 + X/4)

X = 1,05,000 + 15,000 + X/16

16 X = 16,80,000 + 2,40,000 + X (i.e. Multiplying all the items with 16)

16 X = 19,20,000 + X

16 X – X = 19,20,000

15X = 19,20,000

X = 19,20,000/15 = 1,28,000

Thus, Sales = Rs. 1,28,000

Profit = Sales – Total Cost = 1,28,000 – 1,05,000 = Rs. 23,000

Illustration 4

A factory uses a job costing system. The following data are available from the books at the year ending 31st March 1989:

	Rs.		*Rs.*
Direct material	9,00,000	Selling and distribution overheads	5,25,000
Direct wages	7,50,000	Administrative Overhead	4,20,000
Profit	6,09,000	Factory overhead	4,50,000

Required:

(a) Prepare a Cost Sheet indicating the Prime Cost, Works Cost, Production Cost, Cost of Sales and Sales Value.

(b) In 1989-90, the factory has received an order for a number of jobs. It is estimated that the direct materials would be Rs. 12,00,000 and direct labour would cost Rs. 7,50,000. What would be the price for these jobs if the factory intends to earn the same rate of profit on sales, assuming that the selling and distribution overhead has gone up by 15%? The factory recovers factory overhead as a percentage of direct wages and administrative and selling and distribution overhead as a percentage of works cost, based on the cost rates prevalent in the previous year.

(CA, Inter, November, 1989)

Solution

(a) **Cost Sheet**

For Jobs carried out during March 1988-89

Particulars	*(Rs.)*
Direct materials	9,00,000
Direct wages	7,50,000
Prime Cost	16,50,000
Factory overheads	4,50,000
Works Cost	21,00,000
Administrative overheads	4,20,000
Production Cost	25,20,000
Selling and distribution overhead	5,25,000
Cost of Sales	30,45,000
Profit	6,09,000
Sales Value	36,54,000

Working Notes:

Factory overhead as a % of Direct wages $= \frac{4,50,000}{7,50,000} \times 100 = 60\%$

Administration overhead as a % of Works cost $= \frac{4,20,000}{21,00,000} \times 100 = 20\%$

Selling and distribution overhead as a % of Works cost $= \frac{5,25,000}{21,00,000} \times 100 = 25\%$

Profit on Sales $= \frac{6,09,000}{36,54,000} \times 100 = 16.6667\%$

(b) **Cost Sheet**

For Jobs carried out during 1989-90

Particulars		*(Rs.)*
Direct materials		12,00,000
Direct wages		7,50,000
Prime Cost		19,50,000
Factory overheads (60% of direct wages)		4,50,000
Works Cost		24,00,000
Administrative overheads (20% of works cost)		4,80,000
Production Cost		28,80,000
Selling and distribution overhead (25% of works cost + 15%)		6,90,000
Cost of Sales	(83.3333)	35,70,000
Profit (16.67% of sales)	(16.6667)	7,14,000
Sales Value	**(100.00)**	42,84,000

Selling and distribution overhead = 25% × 24,00,000

= Rs. 6,00,000 + (15% of Rs. 6,00,000)

= Rs. 6,90,000.

Illustration 5

The following information for the year ended March 2008 is obtained from the books and records of a factory.

	Completed Jobs *Rs.*	*Work- in- Progress* *Rs.*
Raw material supplied from stores	90,000	30,000
Wages	1,00,000	40,000
Chargeable Expenses	10,000	4,000
Materials transferred to work-in-progress	2,000	2,000
Materials returned to stores	1,000	—

Factory overhead is 80% of wages and office overhead is 25% of factory cost.

The value of executed contracts during the year was Rs. 4,10,000.

Prepare *(i)* consolidated completed jobs account and *(ii)* consolidated work-in-progress.

Solution

CONSOLIDATED COMPLETED JOBS ACCOUNTS

		Rs.			*Rs.*
To	Raw Material	90,000	By	Materials transferred	2,000
To	Wages	1,00,000	By	Materials returned	1,000
To	Chargeable Expenses	10,000	By	Prime Cost c/d	1,97,000
		2,00,000			**2,00,000**
To	Prime cost b/d	1,97,000			
To	Factory Overhead (80%) of 1,00,000)	80,000	By	Contractee's a/c's	4,10,000
	Factory Cost	**2,77,000**			
To	Office Overhead (25% of factory cost)	69,250			
	Total Cost	**3,46,250**			
To	Profit	63,750			
To		**4,10,000**			**4,10,000**

CONSOLIDATED WORK IN PROGESS

		Rs.			*Rs.*
To	Raw materials	30,000	By	Prime Cost c/d	76,000
To	Transfer from completed jobs	2,000			
To	Wages	40,000			
To	Chargeable Expenses	4,000			
	Prime cost	**76,000**			**76,000**
To	Prime Cost b/d	76,000			
To	Factory Overhead (80% of wages)	32,000			
	Factory Cost	1,08,000	By	Balance c/d	1,35,000
To	Office Overhead (25% of factory cost)	27,000			
		1,35,000			**1,35,000**
To	Balance b/d	1,35,000			

Illustration 6

A shop floor supervisor of a small factory presented the following cost for job no.421 to determine selling price.

	Per unit (Rs.)
Material	70
Direct wages 18hrs@Rs2.5 (Dept. X 8hrs; Dept. Y 6hrs; Dept. Z 4hrs)	45
Chargeable Expenses(special stores items)	5
	120
Add: 33 1/3% for overheads	40
Total cost	160

Analysis of the Profit/Loss Account for 2008 shows the following:

	Rs.	*Rs.*		*Rs.*
Material used		1,50,000	Sales *Less:* Returns	2,50,000
Direct wages :				
Dept. X	10,000			
Dept. Y	12,000			
Dept. Z	8,000	30,000		
Special stores items		4,000		
Overhead :				
Dept. X	5,000			
Dept. Y	9,000			
Dept. Z	2,000	16,000		
Total cost		2,00,000		
Gross profit c/d		50,000		
		2,50,000		**2,50,000**
Selling expenses		20,000	Gross Profit b/d	50,000
Net profit		30,000		
		50,000		**50,000**

It is also noted that average hourly rates for the department X, Y, Z are similar.

Required: (1) Draw up a job cost sheet

(2) Calculate the entire revised cost revised using 2008 actual figures as basics.

(3) Add 20% to total cost to determine selling price.

Solution

In order to prepare the job cost sheet, the overhead rates of different departments will have to be first determined on the basics of previous year's figures. The rates are as follows:

FACTORY OVERHEAD RATES

	Departments	*X* *Rs.*	*Y* *Rs.*	*Z* *Rs.*
(1)	Overheads	5,000	9,000	2,000
(2)	Direct labour hours (Total wages/Hourly Rates)	4,000	4,800	3,200
(3)	Rate per hour (Overheads/Direct labor hours)	1.25	1.875	0.625

COST SHEET OF JOB NO. 421

Particulars		*Rate Rs.*	*Hrs.*	*Amount Rs.*
Material				70.00
Direct Wages:	Dept. X	2.500	8.00	20.00
	Dept. Y	2.500	6.00	15.00
	Dept. Z	2.500	4.00	10.00
Chargeable Expenses				5.00
Prime cost				120.00
Overhead	Dept. X	1.250	8.00	10.00
	Dept. Y	1.875	6.00	11.25
	Dept. Z	0.625	4.00	2.50
Total Cost				**143.75**
Add: Profit 20%of Total Cost				28.75
Selling Price				**172.50**

Illustration 7

Following data refers to the month of December 1991:

	Job 410 *Rs.*	*Job 411* *Rs.*	*Total* *Rs.*
(1) Opening balance of job on 1st December, 1991 :			
Direct Material	80	420	500
Direct Labor	150	450	600
Factory Overheads	200	400	600
	430	1,270	1,700

	Job No	*Rs.*
(2) Direct material requisition during the month of December, 1991:		
	410	120
	411	280
	412	225
	413	300
		925

	Job No.	*Hours*	*Rs.*
(3) Direct labor distribution:			
	410	400	600
	411	200	450
	412	300	675
	413	100	225
		1,000	1,950

(4) Factory overheads are applied to jobs on production according to direct labor hour rate which is Rs. 2
(5) Factory overhead incurred in December, 1991 Rs. 2,100.
(6) Job Nos. 411 and 412 were completed during the month. They were billed to customer at a price which included 15% of the price of the job for selling and distribution expenses and another 10% of price for the profit.

Prepare:
(i) Job Cost Sheet for Job Nos. 411 and 412;
(ii) Determine the price for the job;
(iii) Calculate the value of work in progress; and
(iv) Prepare an income statement showing gross profit for the month of December, 1991.

(B.Com., Madras, September 1991)

Solution

Job Cost Sheet

	Job No. 411 *Rs.*	*Job No. 412* *Rs.*
Opening balance on (01-12-1991)	1,270	Nil
Direct material during month	280	225
Direct labor	450	675
Factory Overhead @ Rs. 2 per hour	400	600
Factory Cost	2,400	1,500
Selling and distribution expenses **(Note 1)**	480	300
Cost of Sales	2,880	1,800
Profit **(Note 1)**	320	200
Billing Price of job	3,200	2,000

		Rs.
Work in progress:		
Opening balance		1,700
Cost incurred during the month:		
Material		925
Labor		1,950
Overhead (1000 × Rs.2)		2,000
		6,575
Less: Jobs completed		
Job No. 411	Rs. 2,400	
Job No.412	Rs. 1,500	3,900
Balance of W.I.P.		2,675

Income Statement	*Rs.*
Selling Price (Rs. 3,200 + Rs. 2,000)	5,200
Less: Factory Cost (2,400 + Rs. 1,500)	3,900
Gross Profit	1,300
Less: Selling and distribution expenses	780
Next Profit	520

Note 1.

Suppose Price		100
Less: Selling expenses	15	
Profit	10	25
Factory Cost		75

For Job No. 411:

(1) If factory cost is 75, selling expenses = Rs. 15
If factory cost is 2,400, selling expenses = (15/75) × 2,400 = Rs. 480

(2) If factory cost is 75, profit = Rs.10
If factory cost is 2,400, profit = (10/75) × 2400 = Rs.320

For Job No. 412:

(1) If factory cost is 75, selling expenses = Rs.15
If factory cost is 1,500, selling expenses = (15/75) × 1,500 = Rs. 300

(2) If factory cost is 75, profit = Rs.10
If factory cost is 1,500, profit = (10/75) × 1500 = Rs.200

SUMMARY

Job Costing is also known as Job Order Costing, Production Order Costing or Specific Order Costing. C.I.M.A. Terminology defines Job Costing as "a form of Specific Order Costing which applies where work is undertaken to customer's special requirement. As distinct from Contract Costing, each job is of comparatively short duration."

A job number or work order number is given to each production order which is made in triplicate - one to the stores department for issue of materials; second one to the costing department and the third to the concerned foreman.

A job cost sheet contains the details pertaining to the cost of direct materials, labor, works overhead, administration, selling and distribution overheads etc. In Job Costing, the requirements of production are determined first and then the expenses are ascertained. The total cost is divided by the number of units produced there-under, to determine the cost per unit.

Job Costing is applicable to Engineering Concerns, Construction Companies, Ship Building, Furniture Making, Foundries, Machine Manufacturing Industries, Machine tools manufacture, Printers, Hardware, Repair Shops, Automobile Garages, etc.

The costing system should be properly developed, periodically evaluated and defined well so that difficulties faced in using the system can be minimized.

Glossary

- Job Costing: means ascertaining the cost of a specific order, or of an individual order or of each job.
- Job Cost Sheet/Job Card: is the unique accounting document showing the cost incurred in doing a job.

Questions

(1) Define Job Costing. In which industries it is used?
(2) Explain the features of Job Costing.
(3) Give an account of merits and limitations of Job Costing.
(4) Describe the procedure for the Job Costing.
(5) Explain the situations where Job Costing is suitable.

PROBLEMS

(1) The following information is extracted from the Job Ledger in respect of Job No. 303:
Materials Rs. 3,400
Wages 80 hours at Rs. 2.50
Variable overheads incurred for all jobs Rs. 5,000 for 4,000 labour hours.
Find the profit if the job is billed for Rs. 4,200.

(B.Com., Osmania)

[**Ans.:** Profit Rs. 500]

(2) What is the cost of a job consuming materials of Rs. 8,000; wages for 200 labour hours at Rs. 5 per hour in Dept. A. and 100 labour hours at Rs. 4 per hour in Dept. B.
The overheads of the factory amounted to Rs. 15,000 for 7,500 total working hours of all departments.

(B.Com., Osmania)

[**Ans.:** Total Cost Rs. 10,000]

(3) Printwell Ltd. took up two jobs during the 1st week of April 1992. The following details are available:

	Job 101 *Rs.*	*Job 102* *Rs.*
Materials supplied	2,000	1,400
Wages paid	900	600
Direct expenses	100	50
Material transfer from 101 to 102	100	100

Find the cost of each job.

(B.Com., Osmania)

[**Ans.:** Cost of Job 101 = Rs. 2,900; Job 102 = Rs. 2,150]

(4) Given: Material Rs. 4,010
Wages : A: 60 hrs. at Rs.3 per hour
B: 40 hrs. at Rs.2 per hour
C: 20 hrs. at Re. 1 per hour
Variable overhead Rs.2 per hour

Fixed overhead Rs. 20,000 for 10,000 hours
Calculate cost of the job

(B.Com., Osmania)

[**Ans.:** Rs. 4,770]

(5) Following information pertains to Bombay Engineering Works, relating to Job No. 120.
Materials Rs. 5,000
Wages:
Department M: 120 hours @ Rs. 5 per our; Department N: 75 hours @ Rs. 3 per hour; Department P: 60 hours @ Rs. 4 per hour
Variable Overhead:
Department M: Rs. 5,000 for 10,000 labour hours
Department N: Rs. 6,000 for 6,000 labor hours
Department P: Rs. 3,000 for 3,000 labor hours
Fixed overheads are estimated to be Rs. 10,000 for 10,000 hours. Calculate the cost of Job No. 120, if 20% profit on cost is charged.
[**Ans.:** Selling Price Rs. 7,818]

(6) The profit and loss account of the previous year is as follows.

		Rs.
Material		47,000
Direct Wages:		
Dept. X		3,000
Dept. Y		2,000
Dept. Z		1,000
Factory Overhead:		
Dept. X		1,500
Dept. Y		4,000
Dept. Z		1,500
Administration Overhead		12,000

Using the previous year's profit and loss account as the basis, calculate the revised cost and the selling price of a product after taking into consideration a profit of 10% on selling price and draw up a Job Cost Sheet.

The selling price of the product has been fixed as follows:	*Rs.*
Material	80
Direct wages: 60 hours @ Re. 1 per hour	60
Dept. 1 - 30 hours	
Dept. 2 - 20 hours	
Dept. 3 - 10 hours	
Prime Cost	140
Profit 25% on cost	35
Selling Price	175

[**Ans.:** Cost: Rs. 252 and Selling Price: Rs. 280]

(7) The Best Corporation takes up two jobs during the last week of January 1999. The following are the details pertaining to Job No. 901 and 902.

	Job No. 901 *Rs.*	*Job No. 902* *Rs.*
Materials Supplied	3,500	2,500
Wages Paid	500	400
Direct Expenses	250	—
Material transferred from 901 to 902	100	100
Material returned to stores	—	75

Find out the cost of each Job.

(B.Com., Osmania adapted)

[**Ans.:** (i) Job No. 901 Rs. 4,150 (ii) Job No. 902 Rs. 2,925]

(8) The expenses of a machine cost centre for a particular month are as follows:

		Rs.
(i)	Power	50,000
(ii)	Maintenance and Repairs	10,000
(iii)	Machine Operator's Wages	2,000
(iv)	Supervision	6,000
(v)	Depreciation	40,000

Other particulars are given below:

Products	*Rate of Production*	*Production in Units*
A	30 Units per hour	1,800
B	10 Units per hour	500
C	6 Units per hour	300
D	4 Units per hour	260

The entire production was to be offered to Government on 'Cost Plus 20% basis'. Materials cost per unit are: A – Rs. 40; B – Rs. 60; C – Rs. 100; D – Rs. 300.

Prepare a statement showing product-wise 'cost' and 'offer price'.

[**Ans.:** Cost of Machine Centre per unit of Product A – Rs. 16; B – Rs. 48; C – Rs. 80
D – Rs. 120. Offer Price per unit of Product A – Rs. 67.20; B – Rs. 129.60;
C – Rs. 216.00; D – Rs. 504.00)

❑ ❑ ❑

13

CONTRACT COSTING

INTRODUCTION

Contract Costing is also known as Terminal Costing. It is a type of Job Costing. In Contract Costing, a contract itself becomes a unit of costing. A contract is an agreement between two parties namely contractor and contractee in which the contractor undertakes to complete the work assigned by the contractee within the specified time for an agreed consideration. The contract is enforceable in a court of law. This method of costing is applicable in construction of buildings, bridges, roads, dams, etc.

According to CIMA, "Contract Costing is a form of specific order costing, attribution of costs to individual contracts".

A Contract Cost is aggregated Costs of a single Contract, usually applies to major long term contracts rather than short term jobs. Contract Costing applies where the work is undertaken to customer's requirements and each order is of long duration as compared to Job Costing.

FEATURES OF CONTRACT COSTING

The following are the features of Contract Costing:

(a) Contracts may be for more than one accounting period.

(b) Contracts are carried out away from Contractor's premises.

(c) Here, the cost unit is a Contract.

(d) In the course of a year, contractor carries out a small number of contracts as the contracts are of large size.

(e) For each contract, a separate account is prepared to ascertain the profit or loss on each contract.

(f) Most of the material is specifically purchased for each contract and if materials are drawn from stores, they are charged to the contract account on the basis of stores requisition note.

(g) Labor and most of the expenses like electricity, telephone, etc., are direct.

(h) Sub contractors may be employed for specialized works like electrical fitting, welding, glass work etc. The cost of such work forms a direct charge to contract.

(i) Plant and equipment may be purchased or hired for the contract.

(j) Payments from the contractee may be made several times based on the work certified by the architect employed by the contractee.

(k) The contract price is normally estimated in advance of the work.

(l) Other clauses may be inserted to allow the contractor to pass on to the customer, the additional costs which are incurred as a result of increase in material, labor and other costs.

(m) As per the agreement, an amount called retention money is withheld by the contractee as a security for any defective work which may be found later on. If the contract is not completed within the stipulated time, the retention money may be adjusted as against penalties.

(n) If extra work of minor nature is done by the contractor, not provided in the contract, the charges made for such work are treated as income and credited to the contract.

Important Costs in Contracts (Recording of Costs)

Under Contract Costing, a contract is basically the Cost Unit and for the purpose of control, it can be regarded as a Cost Centre. Allocation of costs to contract is an important aspect.

A Separate account, the contract account, is opened for each individual contract for the purpose of determining the profit or loss on each contract. The recording procedure of the following costs is mentioned below:

Materials

Materials purchased directly or supplied from the stores or transferred from other contracts will be recorded on the debit side of the contract account. Materials returned to stores/any material transferred to other contracts will be recorded on the credit side of contract account. Amount received from the sale of surplus materials will be recorded on the credit side of the account and any profit or loss arising from the sale will be transferred to Profit and Loss Account. Closing balance of materials will be taken on credit side of the account. Normal wastage should be charged to contracts and abnormal wastage like materials stolen or destroyed by fire are transferred to the Profit and Loss account and are also shown on the credit side of the contract account.

The customer may supply certain materials from own stock to be utilized in construction work. Such materials should not be debited to the contract account, because, such materials do not affect the contract price.

Labor/Wages

Direct wages are charged to the contract concerned. Where workers move from one contract to another contract, separate wage sheets should be prepared and wages may be distributed on the basis of time spent for each contract. The wages of the Head Office and Central Stores are considered as overheads and are charged to contracts on an equitable basis. Wages accrued or outstanding at the end of the period should appear on the debit side of contract account.

Expenses

Expenses are classified into ways, i.e., Direct Expenses and Indirect Expenses. All contract expenses are charged to individual contracts as and when they are incurred.

Indirect expenses like salaries to Engineers, Surveyors, and Supervisors, etc., engaged in various contracts cannot be directly charged to contracts. Such expenses may be distributed to several contracts on some suitable basis as a percentage of material or labor.

Plant and Machinery

There are two ways of treating the charges for the use of Plant and Machinery:

(i) Contract account may be debited with full value of the plant and credited with depreciated value of the plant at the end.

This method is used when the plant has been specifically purchased for a particular contract and will be exhausted at site. The total cost of the plant is debited to the contract account. When the contract is completed or the plant is no longer required, it may be sold at site and contract is credited with the sale proceeds. If it is not sold, the contract account is credited with the Written Down Value (W.D.V.).

(ii) Contract account debited with an hourly rate of depreciation.

This method is used, when the plant is sent to the contract site, only for a short period. It is usual to charge the contract, for use of the plant on a daily or hourly basis. Depreciation is charged at an hourly rate for the hours the plant has worked. If the plant is taken on hire, only the hire charges are debited to the contract account and not depreciation.

SUB CONTRACTS

In general, specialized works passed out to other contractors by the main contractor is called as sub contract. The payment made to sub contractors is charged in total to the debit side of the contract account.

EXTRA WORK

The additional work, being outside the original contract, will be subject to a separate charge. If the additional work is quite substantial, it should be treated as a separate contract and separate account should be opened for it. If it is not very substantial, expenses incurred upon extra work should appear on the debit side of the contract account as "Cost of extra work" and the extra amount which the contractee has agreed to pay should be added to the contract price.

CONTRACT COSTING VS. JOB COSTING

Though the terms Job Costing and Contract Costing are used interchangeably, there exists some minor difference.

(a) A job is a small contract involving production of identical units on order. On the other hand, a contract is a big job.

(b) In Job Costing, the cost unit is relatively small, whereas, in Contract Costing, cost unit is big.

(c) Job Costing is used in connection with machine tools, foundries and general engineering industries. Contract Costing is suitable for printing press, ship building yards, road construction, building and bridge construction and other civil engineering works.

(d) Job work is done in factory premises, whereas, contract work is done at site away from the premises of the business.

Generally, a contract ledger is maintained in which different contract accounts are kept. Each contract is given a number.

The contract account is debited with all expanses incurred and is credited with the contract price (if the contract work is completed) and the closing balances of material, plant, tools, if any. The difference between the two represents either notional profit (if credit total is more than the debit total) or loss which has to be transferred to profit and loss account.

CERTIFICATE OF WORK DONE

As the contract work proceeds, the surveyor appointed by the contractee issues certificate to the extent of the work completed. In normal practice, particularly in case of large contracts, the contractee pays the amount to the contractor against certificate issued by the surveyors. In general, the terms of the contract provide that the whole of the amount shown by the certificate shall not be paid immediately but a percentage thereof shall be retained by the contractee until sometime after the contract is completed. The sum retained is called retention money. If the work has not been certified, the contractee would not make any advance. Such work which has been done but not certified is called work uncertified.

Work certified and work uncertified will appear on the credit side of the contract account under the heading "Work-in-Progress".

When the work certified is not given but cash received from the contractee and retention money are given, the amount of work certified should be calculated first, on the basis of the following formula.

$$\text{Work Certified} = \frac{\text{Cash Received} \times 100}{(100 - \text{\% of Retention money})}$$

PROFIT ON INCOMPLETE CONTRACTS

Many contracts take more than one financial accounting year to complete the project. In this situation, profit on such a contract can be worked out only on its completion but contractor cannot wait for that period to know the profit on such projects. Therefore, profit on partly completed contracts has to be computed and a credit for a part of it is to be taken in the accounts at the year end.

The manner of computation of profit is largely dependent upon the stage of the completion of the work in the contract.

WORK-IN-PROGRESS

Profit should be considered in respect of work certified only; work uncertified should always be valued at cost.

If the contract is incomplete, then, value of work in progress has to be ascertained and credited to contract account, instead of contract price, along with closing stock of tools, plant and materials. If credit total is more than the debit side, the difference is the notional profit otherwise, it is the loss. Part of the notional profit is transferred to reserve and the balance is transferred to profit and loss account as shown below:

(a) If work completed is less than 1/4th of the contract, no estimation of profits should be made.

(b) If work completed is 1/4th or more but less than 1/2 of the contract price, only 1/3rd of the notional profit in proportion to percentage of cash received to work certified should be taken into consideration as profit and the balance should be transferred to Reserve Account.

Transfer of notional profit to profit and loss account:

Notional Profit × 1/3 × % of cash received to work certified

$$\text{\% of cash received to work certified} = \frac{\text{Cash Received}}{\text{Work Certified}}$$

(c) If work certified is 1/2 or more, of the contract price, then, 2/3rd of notional profit in proportion to percentage of cash received to work certified should be transferred to profit and loss account, while the balance is treated as the "Reserve for unrealized Profits".

Transfer of notional profit to profit and loss account:

Notional Profit × 2/3 × % of cash received to work certified

The reserve is deducted from the amount of work in progress in the Balance Sheet.

(d) If the work is nearing to completion, i.e., 90%, then, to the total expenses incurred on account of that contract, estimated costs to complete the work is added to arrive at the estimated cost of the contract. The difference between the contract price and the estimated cost of the contract is the estimated profits. A portion of the estimated profit is credited to Profit and Loss Account, which can be determined by using any of the following formulae.

(i) Estimated Profit × (Work Certified/Contract Price)

(ii) Estimated Profit × (Work Certified/Contract Price) × (Cash Received/Work Certified)

(iii) Estimated Profit × (Cash Received/Work Certified)

(iv) Estimated Profit × (Total Expenditure to date/Estimated Total Cost)

(v) $$\text{Estimated Profit} \times \frac{\text{Total Expenditure to date}}{\text{Estimated Total Cost}} \times \frac{\text{Cash Received}}{\text{Work Certified}}$$

(vi) Notional Profit × (Work Certified/Contract Price)

COST PLUS CONTRACT

A Cost Plus Contract is a contract in which the value of the contract is determined by adding a fixed margin of profit to the total cost of the contract. The contractee agrees to pay this changed value of contract which includes a profit margin as per the agreement. Cost Plus Contract is generally needed where costs of contracts cannot be accurately estimated due to unstable and fluctuating conditions of inputs.

Cost Plus Contracts are useful both to the contractor as well as to the contractee. The contractor is suitably protected against any fluctuations in the prices of materials, labor and overheads which will be used for the completion of the job.

A contractee is protected against an uncertain market which may push up the costs of the contract. The price agreed to be paid by the contractee is based on actual cost.

Sometimes a contract may contain an "escalator clause" which provides for a change in the price of the contract due to change in the prices of raw materials, labor, overheads, etc. The contractor presents evidence of increased costs to the contractee to claim reimbursement.

Illustration 1

Compute a conservative estimate of profit on a contract (which is 80% complete) from the following particulars. Illustrate at least four methods of computing the profit.

	Rs.
Total expenditure to date	2,04,000
Estimated further expenditure to complete the contract	40,800
Contract Price	3,67,200
Work Certified	2,40,000
Work Uncertified	20,400
Cash Received	1,95,840

(B.Com., (Hons.), Delhi, 1997)

Solution

Calculation of estimated profit		
Total Contract Price		3,67,200
Less: Total expenditure to date	2,04,000	
Estimated Expenditure	40,800	2,44,800
Estimated Profit		1,22,400

Profit to be taken to Profit and Loss Account

Method – I: Estimated Profit × (Work Certified/Contract Price)

= 1,22,400 × (2,40,000/3,67,200) = Rs. 80,000

Method – II: $\text{Estimated Profit} \times \dfrac{\text{Work Certified}}{\text{Contract Price}} \times \dfrac{\text{Cash Received}}{\text{Work Certified}}$

= 1,22,400 × (2,40,000/3,67,200) × (1,95,840/2,40,000)

= Rs. 65,280

Method – III: Estimated Profit × (Total Expenditure to date/Estimated Total Cost)

= 1,22,400 × (2,04,000/2,44,800) = Rs. 1,02,000

Method – IV: $\text{Estimated Profit} \times \dfrac{\text{Total Expenditure to date}}{\text{Estimated Total Cost}} \times \dfrac{\text{Cash Received}}{\text{Work Certified}}$

= 1,22,400 × (2,04,000/2,44,800) × (1,95,840/2,40,000) = Rs. 83,232

Alternatively, notional profit can be used to determine amount to be transferred to Profit and Lost account.

Notional Profit = Work certified + Work Uncertified – Total Expenses

= 2,40,000 + 20,400 – 2,04,000 = Rs. 56,400

Since more than half the work is complete, the profit to be taken to Profit and Loss Account may be reduced to 2/3 as shown below:

Rs. 56,400 × 2/3 = Rs. 37,600

Illustration 2

Cost of the contract is Rs. 3,15,000 while the estimated cost is Rs. 35,000. The agreed price of the contract is Rs. 4,50,000. Find out the estimated profit.

Solution

	Rs.
Cost of the contract	3,15,000
Add: estimated cost	35,000
Estimated cost of the contract	3,50,000
Estimated profit	1,00,000
Contract Price	4,50,000

Items that appear on the debit side of the contract account

(a) Direct Material
(b) Direct Labor
(c) Direct Expenses
(d) Establishment Charges
(e) Overheads
(f) Depreciation on plant and machinery, tools, etc.

Items that appear on the credit side of the contract account

(a) Work-in-progress: Certified work and uncertified work
(b) Material returned or lost
(c) Material on hand

(When the contract is for more than one year, the total value of plant and machinery can be taken on the debit side and the closing value on the credit side of contract account instead taking depreciation on the debit side of the contract account.)

Note:

In case of contracts which extend for long periods, generally an escalation clause is included in order to accommodate variation in the cost of materials and labor. This clause provides protection to both the parties on account of changes in the cost of materials and labor.

In case, work-in-progress is not specified but percentage of cash received and the amount of cash received are given, work-in-progress can be ascertained as follows:

$$\text{Work Certified} = \frac{\text{Cash received} \times 100}{\text{\% of cash received}}$$

Illustration 3

Suppose the contractor receives Rs. 60,000 which is only 75% of the work certified, ascertain work certified.

Solution

$$\text{Work Certified} = \frac{\text{Cash received} \times 100}{\text{\% of cash received to work certified}}$$

$$\frac{60{,}000 \times 100}{75} = \text{Rs.}80{,}000$$

Illustration 4

The following was the expenditure on Contract No. 222 for Rs. 60,00,000 which was started in April 2008.

	Rs.
Materials	12,00,000
Wages	15,00,000
Plant	2,00,000
Direct Charges	50,000

Cash received on account up to 31.03.2009 amounted to Rs. 30,00,000 being 75% of the work certified. The value of material on hand as on 31.03.2009 was Rs. 1,00,000. Prepare Contract Account charging 15% depreciation on Plant.

Solution

Contract Account No. 222

		Rs.			*Rs.*
To	Materials	12,00,000	By	WIP	40,00,000
To	Wages	15,00,000	By	Materials	1,00,000
To	Depreciation (15%of 2,00,000)	30,000			
To	Direct Charges	50,000			
To	Notional Profit	13,20,000			
		41,00,000			41,00,000
To	P&L Account	6,60,000			
To	Reserves	6,60,000	By	Notional Profit	13,20,000
		13,20,000			13,20,000

$$\text{WIP} = \frac{30{,}00{,}000 \times 100}{75} = \text{Rs. } 40{,}00{,}000$$

Since the work completed is more than 50% of the contract price, amount to be transferred to Profit and Loss Account is:

Notional profit × 2/3 × % of Cash received

= 13,20,000 × 2/3 × 75% = Rs. 6,60,000

Illustration 5

XYZ contractor has undertaken construction work at a contract price of Rs. 12,00,000 on 1.4.2008. The following are the particulars of the contract up to 31.3.2009.

	Rs.
Materials purchased	2,00,000
Materials issued from stores	8,000
Indirect Expenses	70,000
Labor	2,02,000
Plant	2,81,000
Materials in hand	15,000
Materials lost by fire	5,000
Materials at site on 31.3.2000	8,000
Plant at site	2,40,000

Cash received on account up to 31.3.2009 amounted to Rs. 4,48,000 which represent 80 % of the work certified. Work not certified represent Rs. 80,000.

Prepare the contract account and show the amount to be transferred to Profit and Loss Account. Also prepare Contractee's Account and show how the items would appear in Balance Sheet.

Solution

Contract Account

		Rs.			*Rs.*
To	Materials	2,00,000	By	WIP:	
To	Materials from Stores	8,000		Certified	5,60,000
To	Labor	2,02,000		Uncertified	80,000
To	Indirect Expenses	70,000	By	Materials	15,000
To	Depreciation (2,81,000 – 2,40,000)	41,000	By	Loss of materials	5,000
To	Notional Profit	1,47,000	By	Materials at site	8,000
		6,68,000			6,68,000
To	P&L Account	39,200	By	Notional Profit	1,47,000
To	Reserve	1,07,800			
		1,47,000			1,47,000

$$\text{WIP} = \frac{4,48,000 \times 100}{80} = \text{Rs. } 5,60,000$$

Since the work completed is more than $\frac{1}{4}$th but less than 50% of the contract price, amount to be transferred to Profit and Loss Account is:

Notional Profit × $\frac{1}{3}$ × % of Cash received

= 1,47,000 × $\frac{1}{3}$ × 80% = Rs. 39,200

Contractee's Account

		Rs.			*Rs.*
To	balance c/d	4,48,000	By	Cash	4,48,000
		4,48,000			4,48,000
			By	balance b/d	4,48,000

Balance Sheet

Liabilities		*Rs.*	*Assets*		*Rs.*
Profit & Loss A/c	39,200		Materials in hand		15,000
Less: Loss	5,000	34,200	Materials at site		8,000
			Plant at site		2,40,000
			WIP:		
			Certified	5,60,000	
			Uncertified	80,000	
				6,40,000	
			Less: Reserve	68,600	
				5,71,400	
			Less: Cash Received	4,48,000	1,23,400

Illustration 6

Mr. Satish Kumar undertook a contract for Rs. 15,00,000 on an agreement that 80% of the value of the work done as certified by the architect of the contractee, should be paid immediately and the remaining 20% be retained until the contract was completed.

In 2005-06, the amount expended were:

	Rs.
Materials	1,80,000
Wages	1,70,000
Carriage inward	6,000
Cartage	1,000
Sundry expenses	3,000

The work was certified at Rs. 3,75,000 and 80% of the work was paid as agreed upon. No profit should be taken. In 2006-07, the amount expended were:

	Rs.
Materials	2,20,000
Wages	2,30,000
Carriage inward	23,000
Cartage	2,000
Sundry expenses	4,000

Three fourths of the contract was certified as done, by 31st March 2007 and 80% of this was received accordingly. The cost of uncertified work was ascertained at Rs. 20,000.

From April to 30th September 2007, the amount expended were:

	Rs.
Materials	1,26,000
Wages	1,70,000
Cartage	6,000
Sundry expenses	3,000

On 30th September 2007, the whole contract was completed. Prepare Contract Account and Contractees Account in the books of Contractor.

Solution

Contract Account for the year 2005-06

	Rs.		*Rs.*
To Materials	1,80,000	By Work certified	3,75,000
To Wages	1,70,000		
To Carriage inward	6,000		
To Cartage	1,000		
To Sundry expenses	3,000		
To Notional Profit	15,000		
	3,75,000		3,75,000
To Reserve	15,000	By Notional Profit	15,000
	15,000		15,000

Contract Account for the year 2006-07

	Rs.		Rs.
To WIP b/d	3,75,000	By Reserve	15,000
To Materials	2,20,000	By Work certified	11,25,000
To Wages	2,30,000	Uncertified	20,000
To Carriage inward	23,000		
To Cartage	2,000		
To Sundry expenses	4,000		
To Notional Profit	3,06,000		
	11,60,000		11,60,000
To Profit & Loss a/c	1,63,200	By Notional Profit	3,06,000
To Reserve	1,42,800		
	3,06,000		3,06,000

Profit & Loss Account: 3,06,000 × 2/3 × 80% = Rs.1,63,200

Contract Account up to September 2007

	Rs.		Rs.
To WIP b/d	11,45,000	By Reserves	1,42,800
To Materials	1,26,000	By Contractees a/c	15,00,000
To Wages	1,70,000		
To Cartage	6,000		
To Sundry expenses	3,000		
To Profit	1,92,800		
	16,42,800		16,42,800

Contractee's Account

	Rs.		Rs.
2005-06			
To balance c/d	3,00,000	By Cash	3,00,000
	3,00,000		3,00,000
2006-07			
		By balance b/d	3,00,000
To balance c/d	12,00,000	By Cash	9,00,000
	12,00,000		12,00,000
April 2007-September 2007			
		By balance b/d	12,00,000
To contract a/c	15,00,000	By Cash	3,00,000
	15,00,000		15,00,000

Illustration 7

Utkal construction limited took a contract in 2008 for road construction. The contract price was Rs. 10,00,000 and its estimated cost of completion would be Rs. 9,20,000. At the end of 2008, company has received Rs. 3,60,000 representing 90 percent of work certified. Work not yet certified had cost Rs. 10,000.

Expenditure incurred on the contract during 2008 was as follows Materials Rs. 50,000; Labor Rs. 3,00,000 and Plant Rs. 20,000.

Materials costing Rs. 5,000 were damaged and had to be disposed of for Rs. 1,000. Plant is considered as having depreciated by 25% per cent.

Prepare contract account for 2008 in the books of Utkal Construction Limited. Also show all possible figures that can reasonably credited to profit and loss account in respect of the contract.

Solution

Utkal Construction Limited
Contract Account for 2008

		Rs.			*Rs.*
To	Materials	50,000	By	Materials damaged	5,000
To	Labor	3,00,000	By	Plant at site	15,000
To	Plant	20,000	By	Work-in-progress:	
To	Profit	60,000		Work certified	4,00,000
				Work uncertified	10,000
		4,30,000			**4,30,000**

Amount of Profit that may be taken to Profit and Loss A/c

(i) The contract price is Rs.10,00,000, the work certified is Rs. 4,00,000;

(a) 1/3 of the earned to date may be transferred to Profit And Loss Account 60,000 × 1/3 = Rs. 20,000

(b) Alternatively, the amount calculated under (a) above may be reduced on cash basis: 20,000 × 90/100 = Rs. 18,000

(ii) The estimated profit is Rs. 80,000 (10,00,000 – 9,20,000)

(a) Profit to be transferred to Profit and Loss Account may be calculated on the basis of work certified: 80,000 × 4,00,000/10,00,000 = Rs. 32,000

(b) Profit calculated under (a) above may further be reduced on cash basis*: 32,000 × 90/100 = Rs. 28,800

* is the best alternative under the circumstances.

Illustration 8

SV Construction Ltd. has obtained a contract for construction of a bridge. The value of the contract is Rs. 12 lakhs and the work commenced on 1st October 2007. The following details are shown there in for the year ended 30th September 2008.

	Rs.		*Rs.*
Plant purchases	60,000	Wages accrued as on 30.9.2007	2,800
Wages	3,40,000	Materials at site as on 30.9.2007	4,000
Materials issued to site	3,36,000	Direct expenses accrued as on 30.9.2007	1,200
Direct expenses	8,000	Work not yet certified at cost	14,000
General overheads apportioned	32,000	Cash received being 80% of work certified	6,00,000

Life of plant purchased is 5 years and scrap value is nil.

(1) Prepare the contract account for the year ended 30th September, 2008

(2) Show the a mount of profit which you which consider might be fairly taken on the contract and how you have calculated it.

Solution

S.V. Construction Ltd.
Contract Account

		Rs.	*Rs.*				*Rs.*
To	Materials		3,36,000	By	Work-in-progress:		
To	Wages paid	3,40,000			Work certified (WN 1)	7,50,000	
	Add: Accrued	2,800	3,42,800		Work uncertified	14,000	7,64,000
To	Direct expenses paid	8,000		By	Plant at site		48,000
	Add: Accrued	1,200	9,200	By	Materials at site		4,000
To	Plant purchased		60,000				
To	General overheads		32,000				
To	P&L a/c (WN 2)		19,200				
To	Work-in-progress (Reserver)		16,800				
			8,16,000				8,16,000

Working Notes:

(1) Value of work certified – Cash received is Rs. 6,00,000 representing 80% of work certified, hence the value of the work certified would be Rs. 7,50,000
(i.e. 6,00,000 × 100/80)

(2) The amount of profit taken of profit taken to P & L *A/c* has been calculated as follows:
Total profit made to date – Rs. 36,000. Since the value of work certified is more than one half of the contract price, 2/3rd of profit made to date as reduced on cash basis been taken to the P&L A/c as shown below: Rs. 36,000 × 2/3 × 80/100 = Rs. 19,200.

Illustration 9

The following information related to a building contract for Rs. 10,00,000.

	2007 (Rs.)	*2008 (Rs.)*
Materials issued	3,00,000	84,000
Direct Wages	2,30,000	1,05,000
Direct Expenses	22,000	10,000
Indirect Expenses	6,000	1,400
Work certified	7,50,000	10,00,000
Work uncertified	8,000	—
Materials at site	5,000	7,000
Plant issued	14,000	2,000
Cash received from Contractor	6,00,000	10,00,000

The value of plant at the end of 2007 and 2008 was Rs. 7,000 was Rs. 5,000 respectively.

Prepare *(i)* Contract account and *(ii)* Contractee account for two years 2007 and 2008 taking into consideration such profit for Profit and Loss Account as you think proper.

Solution

Contract Account for 2007

	(Rs.)			*(Rs.)*
To Materials issued	3,00,000	By Materials at site		5,000
To Direct wages	2,30,000	By Plant at site		7,000
To Direct expenses	22,000	By Work-in-progress		
To Indirect expenses	6,000	Work certified	7,50,000	
To Plant issued	14,000	Work uncertified	8,000	7,58,000
To Profit c/d	1,98,000			
	7,70,000			7,70,000
To Profit and Loss A/c	*1,05,600	By Profit b/d		1,98,000
To work-in-progress (Reserve)	92,400			
	1,98,000			1,98,000

Profit taken to profit and loss account:

$$\text{*Total profit} \times 2/3 \times \frac{\text{Cash received}}{\text{Work certified}} = \text{Rs. } 1,98,000 \times 2/3 \times 6,00,000/7,50,000 = 1,05,600$$

Contract Account for 2008

	(Rs.)		*(Rs.)*
To Materials at site b/d	5,000	By Materials at site	7,000
To Plant at site b/d	7,000	By Plant at site	5,000
To Work-in-progress b/d	*6,65,600	By Contractee's A/c	10,00,000
To Materials issued	84,000		
To Direct wages	1,05,000		
To Direct expenses	10,000		
To Indirect expenses	1,400		
To Plant issued	2,000		
To Profit and Loss A/c	1,32,000		
	10,12,000		10,12,000

* Wok-in-progress = 7,58,000 – 92,400 = Rs. 6,65,600

Contractee's Account for 2007 & 2008

2007		*Rs.*	*2007*		*Rs.*
To	Balance c/d	6,00,000	By	Bank	6,00,000
		6,00,000			6,00,000
2008			*2008*		
To	Contract A/c	10,00,000	By By	Balance b/d Bank	6,00,000 4,00,000
		10,00,000			10,00,000

Illustration 10

M/s Manholes and Sewers Ltd. undertook a contract for erecting a sewerage treatment plant for a municipality for a total value of Rs. 24 lakhs. It was expected that the contract would be completed by 31st January 2008.

You are required to prepare a contract account for the year ending 31st January 2007 from the following particulars:

(i) Wages Rs. 6,00,000; *(ii)* Special plant Rs. 2,00,000; *(iii)* Materials Rs. 3,00,000; *(iv)* Overheads Rs. 1,20,000; *(v)* Depreciation @10% to be provided on plant; *(vi)* Materials lying at site on 31-1-2007 Rs. 40,000; *(vii)* Work Certified was to the extent of Rs. 16,00,000 and 80% of the same was received in cash; *(viii)* 5% of the value of materials issued and 6% of wages may be taken to have been incurred for the portion of work completed but not yet certified. *(ix)* Overheads are charged as a percentage of direct wages. *(x)* Ignore depreciation on plant for use on uncertified portion of the work. *(xi)* Ascertain the amount to be transferred to profit and loss account on the basis of realized profit.

(ICWA, Inter, June adapted)

Solution

Contract Account

		Rs.			*Rs.*
To	Materials	3,00,000	By	Materials at site	40,000
To	Wages	6,00,000	By	Plant at site (cost less 10%)	1,80,000
To	Special plant	2,00,000	By	Work-in-progress:	
To	Overheads	1,20,000		Work certified	16,00,000
To	Balance c/d	6,58,200		Work uncertified	58,200
		18,78,200			18,78,200
To	Profit and Loss Account (6,58,200 × 2/3 × 80/100)	3,51,040	By	Balance b/d	6,58,200
To	Work-in-progress A/c (Reserve)	3,07,160			
		6,58,200			6,58,200

Work uncertified is calculated as below:			*Rs.*
(i)	Materials	(5% of Rs.3,00,000)	15,000
(ii)	Wages	(6% of Rs 6,00,000)	36,000
(iii)	Overheads	(20% of Rs 36,000)	7,200
		Work Uncertified	58,200

Overheads as a percent of Direct Wages = (1,20,000/6,00,000) × 100 = 20%

SUMMARY

Contract Costing is also known as Terminal Costing. It is a type of Job Costing. In Contract Costing, a contract itself becomes a unit of costing. A contract is an agreement between two parties namely contractor and contractee in which the contractor undertakes to complete the work assigned by the contractee within the specified time for an agreed consideration. The contract is enforceable in a court of law. This method of costing is applicable in construction of buildings, bridges, roads, dams, etc.

A separate account, the contract account, is opened for each individual contract for the purpose of determining the profit or loss on each contract. In general, specialized works passed out to other contractors by the main contractor is called as sub-contract. The additional work, being outside the original contract, will be subject to a separate charge. If the additional work is quite substantial, it should be treated as a separate contract and a separate account should be opened for it.

A job is a small contract involving production of identical units on order. On the other hand, a contract is a big job. As the contract work proceeds, the surveyor appointed by the contractee issues certificate to the extent of the work completed. In normal practice, particularly in case of large contracts, the contractee pays the amount to the contractor against a certificate issued by the surveyors.

A Cost Plus Contract is a contract in which the value of the contract is determined by adding a fixed margin of profit to the total cost of the contract. The contractee agrees to pay this changed value of contract which includes a profit margin as per the agreement.

Glossary

- **Contract Cost:** is aggregated Costs of a single Contract, usually applies to major long term contracts rather than short term jobs.
- **Sub-Contract:** specialized works passed out to other contractors by the main contractor.
- **Certificate of work done:** As the contract work proceeds, the surveyor appointed by the contractee issues certificate to the extent of the work completed.
- **Cost-Plus Contract:** is a contract in which the value of the contract is determined by adding a fixed margin of profit to the total cost of the contract.

Questions

(1) What is Contract Costing? Give examples of industries where it can be used.

(2) Explain the features of Contract Costing.

(3) Bring out the differences between Contract Costing and Job Costing.

(4) What do you mean by Cost-Plus Contracts?

(5) How do you account for profit on incomplete contracts?

(6) Explain briefly the recording of costs in Contract Account.

PROBLEMS

(1) Prepare Contract Account No. 200 from the following information.

	Rs.
Direct Materials	30,000
Wages	20,000
Plant	15,500
Loose Tools	4,000
Stores issued	6,040
Wages of drivers	3,500
Other charges	2,500
Running Materials	1,500

The contract was completed in 13 weeks. Depreciate plant by 15% while the value of Loose Tools and stores returned amounted to Rs. 2,600 and Rs. 2,040 respectively. The contract price was Rs. 1,00,000. Find Profit.
[**Ans.:** Rs. 36,519]

(2) Constructor Ltd. took a contract in 1999 for road construction for Rs. 10,00,000 and estimated that the cost would be Rs 9,20,000. At the end of 1999, the company received Rs. 3,60,000 being 90% of the work Certified. Certain work not yet certified has a cost of Rs. 10,000. Expenditure incurred was as follows:

	Rs.
Materials	50,000
Labor	3,00,000
Plant	20,000

Materials costing Rs. 5,000 were damaged and disposed of for Rs. 1,000. Plant is considered as having depreciation at 25 %. Prepare contract Account.

(B.Com., Karnataka)

[**Ans.:** Notional Profit Rs. 60,000 and Reserve Rs. 42,000]

(3) Prepare Contract Account from the information given below.

	1998-99 *Rs*	*1999-2000* *Rs.*
Materials	3,00,000	84,000
Wages	2,30,000	1,05,000
Outstanding expenses	35,000	15,400
Materials at end	13,000	7,000
Cash received	6,00,000	10,00,000
Certified completion of work	75%	100%

(B.Com., Osm., Oct-Nov., 1993)

[**Ans.:** 1998-99 : Notional Profit Rs. 1,98,000 1999-2K: Profit Rs. 1,32,000]

(4) How much of profit, if any, would you allow to be considered in the following case?

	Rs.	
Contract Cost	2,80,000	up to date
Contract Value	5,00,000	
Cash received	2,70,000	
Uncertified work	30,000	

Deduction from bills by way of security is 10 per cent.

(B.Com., Osmania, 1995)

[**Ans.:** Profit to be credited to P/L *a/c.* is Rs. 30,000]

(5) Rachana Ltd. furnishes the following information in relation to one of its contracts. The contract commenced on 1-1-89 and was completed on 31-12-90. The contract price was agreed at Rs.13,22,900.

Expenditure during.

	1989 *Rs.*	*1990* *Rs.*
Material issued	3,00,000	3,00,000
Direct expenses	25,000	10,000
Direct wages	3,50,000	3,70,000
Indirect expenses	15,000	16,000
Work done but uncertified	8,000	Nil
Total work certified	7,00,000	Balance of contract price
Plant issued on 1st January	20,000	5,000
Materials at site	5,000	8.000

Depreciation on plant to be charged at 10% p.a. 85% of work certified was received in cash except in the year of completion of contract.

Prepare Contract Account and Contractee's Account for 1989 and 1990 and present the relevant figures in the Balance Sheet for 1989.

(B.Com., Mysore)

[**Ans.:** Profit credited to Profit & Loss *a/c* in 1989 Rs. 1,900; Loss in 1990 Rs. 71,300]

(6) A building contractor have undertaken construction work at contract price of Rs.6,00,000 began the execution of work on 1-1-98. The following are the particulars of contract up to 31-12-98:

	Rs.
Materials issued from stores	4,000
Materials purchased	1,20,000
Labor at site	1,00,000
Indirect expenses	36,000
Plant	1,40,000
Materials returned to store	8,000
Materials lost by fire	2,000
Materials at site on 31st December, 1998	4,000
Plant at site on 31st December, 1998	1,20,000

Cash received on account up to 31st December, amounted to Rs.2,24,000 representing 80 per cent of the work certified. The remaining 20 per cent being retained until completion. The work finished but not certified was Rs. 40,000.

Prepare the Contract Account and state the proportion of profit the contractor would be justified in taking to the credit of the Profit and Loss Account. Also prepare Contractee's Account.

(B.Com., Osmania)

[**Ans.:** Notional Profit Rs. 54,000; Profit transferred to Profit & Loss a/c Rs. 14,400]

(7) The Victory Construction Co. has supplied the following information in respect of a contract for Rs.10,00,000.

	2007 (Rs.)	*2008 (Rs.)*
Materials used	3,00,000	84,000
Direct wages	2,30,000	1,05,000
Direct expenses	22,000	10,000
Indirect expenses	6,000	1,400
Work certified	7,50,000	10,00,000
Work uncertified	8,000	—
Materials at site (31st Dec.)	5,000	7,000
Plant issued (1st Jan.)	14,000	2,000
Value of Plant (31st Dec.)	7,000	5,000
Cash received	6,00,000	10,00,000

From the above details, you are required to prepare
(1) Contract Account for the years 1978 and 1979, and
(2) Contractee's Account.
[**Ans.:** Profit transferred to Costing Profit and Loss Account = Rs. 1,32,000]

(8) The following particulars relate to a contract for Rs.40 lakhs:

Expenses	*2006 Rs.*	*2007 Rs.*	*2008 Rs.*
Materials	4,50,000	7,00,000	6,00,000
Wages	4,30,000	6,00,000	5,00,000
Expenses	20,000	50,000	16,000
Carriage	20,000	60,000	50,000
Work Certified	9,00,000	30,00,000	40,00,000
Work Uncertified	10,000	50,000	—

Plant costing Rs. 1 ,00,000 was brought in the beginning and depreciation was charged at 25% per annum. The contractee was to pay 80% of the work certified every year and settle the account in 2008. Draw contract account for three years and also write contractee's account.
[**Ans.:** Profit transferred to Costing Profit and Loss Account = Rs. 88,000]

(9) The following information relates to a contract for Rs. 75,00,000.

Expenses	*2006 Rs.*	*2007 Rs.*	*2008 Rs.*
Materials	9,00,000	11,00,000	6,28,000
Wages	8,40,000	11,15,000	8,20,000
Expenses	40,000	1,50,000	70,000
Indirect Expenses	15,000	20,000	—
Total work certified	17,50,000	57,50,000	75,00,000
Carriage	5,000	10,000	7,000
Uncertified Work	—	13,500	—
Plant	1,00,000	—	—

The value of plant at the end of 2006 was Rs. 80,000, at the end of 2007 was Rs. 50,000 and at the end of 2008 was Rs. 20,000. The contractee was to pay 90% of the work certified every year and settle the account in 2008. Draw a contract account for three years and show the relevant figures in balance sheet.
[**Ans.:** Profit transferred to Costing Profit and Loss Account in the year 2008 = Rs. 8,16,900]

(10) M/s Excellent Errectors Ltd. took up a contract for construction of a building at a contract price of Rs. 15,00,000. During the first year, the following amounts were spent as against a sum of Rs. 5,62,500, which represented 90% of the work certified and received by the contractor.

Materials	Rs.	2,62,500
Wages paid to workers	Rs.	1,50,000
Overhead expenses	Rs.	37,500
During the second year, the firm spent the following amounts:		
Materials	Rs.	3,75,000
Labor cost	Rs.	3,00,000
Overhead expenses	Rs.	75,000

In the second year, the contract was completed and a sum of Rs. 8,75,000 was received by the contractor. Prepare the contract account and contractee's account for both the years, and calculate the profit.

Note: Consider only 2/5th of the notional profit to be taken to the credit of Profit and Loss A/c in the first year, as the work done is less than 50%.

[Answer:

	I year *Rs.*	*II year* *Rs.*
Notional Profit	1,75,000	2,30,000
Profit to Costing P&L A/C	70,000	2,30,000]

(11) Alcon Construction Company Ltd. commenced its business of construction on 1-1-2008. The trail balance as on 31-12-2008 showed the following balances:

	Dr. (Rs)	*Cr. (Rs)*
Paid-up share capital		1,00,000
Cash received on account of contract (80% of work certified)		1,20,000
Land and buildings		30,000
Machinery at cost (75% at site)		40,000
Bank		4,000
Materials at site		40,000
Direct labor		55,000
Expenses at site		2,000
Lorries and vehicles		30,000
Furniture		1,000
Office equipment		10,000
Postage and telegrams		500
Office expenses		2,000
Rates and Taxes		3,000
Fuel and power		2,500
	2,20,000	**2,20,000**

The contract price is Rs. 3,00,000 and work certified is Rs. 1,50,000. The work completed since certification is estimated at Rs. 1,000 (at cost). Machinery costing Rs. 2,000 was returned to stores at the end of the year. Stock of material at site on 31-12-2008 was of the value of Rs. 5,000. Wages outstanding were Rs. 200. Depreciation on Machinery at 10%. You are required to calculate the profit from the contract and show how the work-in-progress will appear in the balance sheet as on 31-12-2008.

[**Ans.:** Profit Rs. 55,800, Work-in-Progress in Balance Sheet Rs. 4,960]

❑ ❑ ❑

14

PROCESS COSTING

Objectives

The objectives of the study are to:

- Explain the term Process Costing
- Identify the industries where Process Costing is applicable
- Differentiate Process Costing from Job Costing
- Learn the Accounting treatment of Normal Loss, Abnormal Loss and Abnormal Gain
- Ascertain the value of Work-in-Progress with the help of Equivalent Production
- Explain the steps involved in the treatment of inter-process profits
- Apportion the Joint Costs to the Joint and By-Products

INTRODUCTION

There are mainly two methods of ascertaining the cost of products manufactured or services rendered. Process Costing is one such method which is employed in the industries where production moves from one process or department to the next until its final completion and there is a continuous mass production of identical units through a series of processing operations.

MEANING OF PROCESS COSTING

According to CIMA, Process Costing is "the costing method applicable where goods or services result from a sequence of continuous or repetitive operations or processes. Costs are averaged over the units produced during the period".

According to Kohler, process costing is "a method of accounting whereby costs are charged to processes or operations and averaged over units produced, it is employed principally where finished product is the result of a more or less continuous operation as in paper mills, refineries, tanneries and chemical plants, distinguished from job costing, where costs are assigned to specific orders, lots or units".

In Process Costing, costs are accumulated by departments, operations, or processes. The work performed on each unit is standardized or uniform, where a continuous mass production or assembly operation is involved. For example, Process Costing is used by companies that produce appliances, alcoholic beverages, tyres, sugar, breakfast cereals, leather, paint, coal, textiles, lumber, candy, coke, plastics, rubber, cigarettes, shoes, typewriters, cement, gasoline, steel, baby foods, flour, glass, men's suits, pharmaceuticals and automobiles. Process Costing is also used in meat packing and for public utility services such as water, gas and electricity.

FEATURES OF PROCESS COSTING

The following are the features of Process Costing:

(i) The product of one process becomes the input or raw material fo the next process and this transfer from one process to another may be at cost or at cost plus.

(ii) There is a continuous flow of identical units.

(iii) It is difficult to identify a cost unit because each cost unit is part of a process.

(iv) All units produced at a process are identical and cost per unit at a process is determined by averaging.

(v) Cost centers are set up and costs are collected by the centres.

(vi) Processes may involve a normal weight loss which has no sale value or normal scrap which has sale value, abnormal loss or abnormal gain which is valued at cost per unit.

(vii) In Process Costing when manufacturing the main product(s), by-products may emerge. However, these by-products need to be further processed to be marketable.

(viii) It is possible that Joint products may be produced in the processes.

APPLICABILITY OF PROCESS COSTING

Industries using Process Costing in their manufacturing area include chemical processing, oil refining, pharmaceutical, plastics, paints and varnish, soaps, textiles, paper, brick and tile manufacturing, semiconductor chips, beverages and breakfast cereals. It is very useful in bottling companies, canning plants, packing and industries involved in processing milk products.

COMPARISON BETWEEN UNIT COSTING AND PROCESS COSTING

In the case of Unit Costing, per unit cost is determined by averaging the cost incurred. Process Costing is a type of Operation Costing which is used to ascertain the cost of a product at each process or stage of manufacture. Process Costing method is applicable where goods or services result from a sequence of continuous or repetitive operations or processes. Costs are averaged over the units produced during the period.

JOB COSTING VS. PROCESS COSTING

Job Costing	Process Costing
It is used in industries where production is carried on according to specific job order.	It is used in continuous and mass production industries producing like units of standard specification.
Costs are collected to each Job at the end of its completion.	Costs are accumulated and collected for each process at the end of specified accounting period and transferred to next process/department till the last process is completed.
There may or may not be any work in progress at the end of the accounting period.	Normally, there is opening and closing work in progress at the end of the accounting period.
The cost of each Job is ascertained by adding Materials, Labor and Overheads.	The Unit cost is the average cost of the process for a given period.
There is no transfer of work from one Job to another Job.	Costs of one process are transferred to the next process, until goods are completely manufactured.

ADVANTAGES OF PROCESS COSTING

(1) Cost of individual products in each process can be ascertained.

(2) In whichever process excessive cost has been incurred and whereever wastages and scraps are high, cost control is facilitated.

(3) Since output at each process is homogeneous, average cost per unit can be easily calculated.

(4) As the cost incurred in each process is ascertained, employees at the process can be rewarded for cost economies and those not performing can be warned.

(5) Valuation of work in progress, by-products and joint products is facilitated by Process Costing.

DISADVANTAGES OF PROCESS COSTING

(1) Process Costing is historical in nature and suffers from all the limitations of Historical Costing.

(2) Valuation of stock where work is in progress, and ascertainment of cost of by-products and joint products involves lot of estimation.

(3) Under Process Costing, unfinished units (Work-in-Progress) at the end of the period are expressed in terms of completed units by multiplying the same with the degree of completion which is subjective.

ELEMENTS OF PRODUCTION COST

Main elements of Production Cost in Process Costing are:

Material: Direct materials are introduced in the first process and additional material costs if any are introduced in the next processes.

Labor: Remuneration paid to workers is charged to a particular process.

Direct Expenses: Expenses incurred with respect to the production should be charged to the respective processes.

Production Overheads: All indirect material, indirect labor, indirect expenses should be apportioned to each process on the basis of pre-determined rates based on direct materials, direct wages or machine hours.

Illustration 1

Material input in process is 1,000 units valued at Rs. 2,000, direct labor Rs. 1,600, production overheads Rs. 3,000 then, what will be the cost per unit of output?

Solution

Dr. **PROCESS ACCOUNT** **Cr.**

Particulars	*Qty. (units)*	*Amount (Rs.)*	*Particulars*	*Qty. (units)*	*Amount (Rs.)*
To Material	1,000	2,000	By Output transferred to next process	1,000	6,600
To Direct Labor		1,600			
To Production Overheads		3,000			
	1,000	6,600		1,000	6,600

Cost per unit = 6,600/1,000= Rs. 6.60

Illustration 2

A process passes through three distinct processes to completion. These processes are numbered 1, 2 and 3. respectively, During the week ended 15th Jan 2009, 500 units are produced. The following information is obtained:

	Process 1 Rs.	*Process 2* Rs.	*Process 3* Rs.
Direct Materials	1,750	800	500
Direct Labour	1,250	1,000	1,250

The overhead expenses for the period were Rs. 700 apportioned to the processes on the basis of wages.

No work-in-progress or process stocks existed at the beginning or at the end of the week. Prepare Process Accounts.

Solution

Dr. **PROCESS 1 ACCOUNT** **Cr.**

Particulars	*Qty. (units)*	*Amount (Rs.)*	*Particulars*	*Qty. (units)*	*Amount (Rs.)*
To Direct Material	500	1,750	By Process No. 2 a/c	500	3,250
To Direct Labor		1,250	(Output transfer)		
To Overheads		250			
(1,250 × 700)/3,500					
	500	3,250		500	3,250

Cost per unit = 3,250/500 = Rs. 6.50

Dr. **PROCESS 2 ACCOUNT** **Cr.**

Particulars	*Qty. (units)*	*Amount (Rs.)*	*Particulars*	*Qty. (units)*	*Amount (Rs.)*
To Process No.1	500	3,250	By Process 3 a/c	500	5,250
To Direct Material		800	(Output transfer)		
To Direct Labor		1,000			
To Overheads		200			
(1,000 × 700)/3,500					
	500	5,250		500	5,250

Cost per unit = 5,250/500 = Rs.10.50

Dr. **PROCESS 3 ACCOUNT** **Cr.**

Particulars	*Qty. (units)*	*Amount (Rs.)*	*Particulars*	*Qty. (units)*	*Amount (Rs.)*
To Process No.2	500	5,250	By Finished stock	500	7,250
To Direct Material		500	(Output transfer)		
To Direct Labor		1,250			
To Overheads		250			
(1,000 × 700)/3,500					
	500	7,250		500	7,250

Cost per unit = 7,250/500 = Rs. 14.50

Normal Loss and Abnormal Loss

In the process of manufacturing a product, there is bound to be some loss and the number of units introduced may not be equal to the output. This loss can be normal or abnormal. The loss could be waste or scrap or spoilage or defectives.

Waste: That part of basic raw material which is lost in processing without possessing any recovery value is called as waste. It is considered to be normal waste, if it is incidental to manufacturing activities. Examples: Evaporation (Oil & Paints), natural deterioration due to efflux of time, breaking the bulk into desirable shapes, etc. Any waste over and above normal waste is called as abnormal waste and such waste arises on account of pilferage, defective storage, careless handling, defective workmanship, obsolescence, etc. The effect of waste is to reduce the quantity of output. The cost of normal waste is borne by the good production whereas the cost of the abnormal waste is transferred to Costing Profit and Loss Account.

Scrap: It is the incidental residue from certain types of manufacture, usually of small amount and low value, recoverable without further processing. Example: left over pieces of material cuttings and fittings, etc. Scrap value may be credited to Profit and Loss Account or to concerned Process Account or to Factory Overheads Account.

Spoilage: It is that part of production which does not meet the required quality standards. If the spoilage arises under efficient operating conditions and is inherent to the production, it is called as normal spoilage and is uncontrollable in the short run. If the spoilage is over and above the normal spoilage and arises due to inefficient production, it is considered as abnormal spoilage. The examples of abnormal spoilage are – spoilage of work due to machine break-down, accidents, power failure, etc. The cost of normal spoilage is borne by good production and the cost of abnormal spoilage is transferred to Profit and Loss Account. In case, the spoilage has significant market value, it may be sold as seconds.

Defectives: When the production does not meet the quality standards, such products are treated as defectives. These defective products can be rectified and brought upto the standard by incurring additional cost known as rectification cost. The causes for defective products could be due to the use of defective materials, poor workmanship, use of defective machines or tools, etc.,

Normal Loss: During the production process, some loss is unavoidable on account of inherent nature of production and is acceptable to production process. Such loss is called normal loss. The normal loss may or may not have realizable value.

If there is a loss in the form of weight loss, then, such loss has no realizable value. If the loss is scrap which has realizable value then it may be valued at market price. Normal loss is an estimated loss. This estimation is based upon the past experience.

Abnormal Loss: Where the actual output is less than the expected output, the difference is called as abnormal loss. It is over and above the normal loss. The cost of abnormal loss is ascertained as below.

$$\text{Cost of Abnormal Loss} = \frac{\text{Normal Cost of Normal Output}}{\text{Normal Output}} \times \text{Abnormal Loss Units}$$

Normal Cost = Total Cost – Scrap Value

Normal Output = Input units – wastage units – Scrap units i.e. Input units – Normal Loss units

Journal Entries :

(a) Abnormal Loss a/c Dr.
To Process a/c
(Being abnormal loss)

(b) Cash a/c Dr.
To Abnormal loss a/c
(Being scrap value realised)

(c) Costing P&L a/c Dr.
To Abnormal loss a/c
(Being loss transferred to costing P&L)

Actual Output: The output actually achieved in the production process.

Normal/Expected Output: It is the output that should be obtained if the production is carried out under normal circumstances, i.e., Normal Output = Gross Input – Normal Loss.

Illustration 3

In the manufacture of a product, daily input is 500 Kgs of materials @ Rs.10/-. Other expenses are Rs.840/-. Normal wastage is 1% of input and it realizes nothing and 2% scrap realized at Rs.2/-. Actual output is 480 Kgs.

Prepare Process Account and Abnormal Loss Account.

Solution

Dr. **PROCESS ACCOUNT** **Cr.**

Particulars	*Units*	*Amount (Rs.)*	*Particulars*	*Units*	*Amount (Rs.)*
To Material Input	500	5,000	By Wastage @ (1%)	5	—
To Other Expenses		840	By Scrap @ 2% on Input @ Rs.2/-	10	20
			By Abnormal Loss @ Rs.12/-	5	60
			By Actual Output @ Rs.12/-	480	5,760
	500	5,840		500	5,840

Value of abnormal loss:

$$\frac{\text{Normal cost of normal output} \times \text{Abnormal loss account}}{\text{Normal output}}$$

$$= \frac{5000 + 840 - 20}{500 - 5 - 10} \times 5 = \text{Rs. } 60$$

Cost per unit : 5,760/480 = Rs. 12

Dr. **Abnormal Loss Account** **Cr.**

Particulars	*Units*	*Amount (Rs.)*	*Particulars*	*Units*	*Amount (Rs.)*
To Process a/c	5	60	By Cash (Scrap @ Rs.2/- i.e. 5 units * Rs.2/-)	5	10
			By Costing Profit & Loss a/c		50
	5	60		5	60

Abnormal Gain: Accounting Treatment

When the actual output is more than the expected output, the extra units are considered to be abnormal gain units. Abnormal gain is valued at cost i.e. at the normal cost of normal output. To arrive at the actual output, abnormal gain units are added to normal output.

i.e.,	Gross Input Units
Less:	Normal Loss Units
	Normal Output
Add:	Abnormal Gain Units
	Actual Output

Journal Entries:

Process a/c..	Dr.	Xxx	
To Abnormal Gain a/c			xxx
(Being abnormal gain)			
Abnormal Gain a/c..	Dr.	Xxx	
To Normal Loss a/c			xxx
(Being adjustment of normal loss towards abnormal gain)			

Closing Abnormal Account: The balance in the abnormal gain account represents the actual gain made. The gain being abnormal in nature is transferred to Costing Profic and Loss Account.

If there are no losses/gains either normal or abnormal, then input would be equal to quantity output. This output would be transferred to the next process.

Illustration 4

In a factory, 5,000 Kgs material was transferred from Process A to Process B at a cost of Rs. 42,000. The following costs relate to Process B:

Labor Rs. 2,000; Production overheads Rs. 2,000. In Process B, 10% of input is normally lost. Actual output was 4,700 Kgs. Loss realizes Rs. 2 per Kg. Prepare Process B A/c.

Solution

Dr. PROCESS B ACCOUNT Cr.

Particulars	*Units (kgs)*	*Amount (Rs.)*	*Particulars*	*Units (kgs)*	*Amount (Rs.)*
To Process A	5,000	42,000	By Normal Loss	500	1,000
To Labor		2,000	(10% of 5,000 Kgs @ Rs.2/-)		
To Production Overheads		2,000	By Output transfered to		
To Abnormal Gain	200	2,000	Process C a/c @ Rs. 10/-	4,700	47,000
	5,200	48,000		5,200	48,000

Calculation of Cost per unit:

= Normal Cost of Normal Output/Normal Output

= (Total Cost – Scrap)/Gross Input – Normal Loss Units

= (42,000 + 2,000 + 2,000 – 1,000)/5,000 – 500

= Rs. (46,000 – 1,000)/4,500 units

= Rs. 10/- per Kg.

Therefore, **Value of Abnormal Gain** = 200 Kgs × Rs. 10/- = Rs. 2,000

When the output of a process is partly sold and partly transferred to the next process

In certain production processes, the output of the process may be partly sold and partly transferred to the next process for further processing. For example, in Food Processing Industries, part of the output of a Baking Department may be sold and the remaining output is passed on to the finished process for further processing. The part of product sold will contain an element of profit or loss which is debited to Process Account.

Illustration 5

ABC Ltd. Manufactures and sells three chemicals produced by consecutive processes known as A, B and C. The value of normal wastage realized at each processes are as follows: Process A realized Rs. 90 a tonne, Process B realized Rs. 110 a tonne and from C Rs. 200 a tonne. The products of the three processes are dealt with as follows:

	A	*B*	*C*
Sent to warehouse for sale	40%	50%	100%
Passed on the next process	60%	50%	—
The following particulars relate to the month of May:			
Materials used (tonnes)	1,500	163	1,115
Cost per tonne of materials (Rs.)	120	180	80
Manufacturing Expenses (Rs.)	49,950	51,440	40,630
Weight Loss (Wastage)	2%	2%	3%
Normal Loss	5%	10%	15%

Prepare an account for each process, showing the cost per ton of each product.

Solution

Dr. **PROCESS A ACCOUNT** **Cr.**

Particulars	*Tonnes*	*Rs.*	*Particulars*	*Tonnes*	*Rs.*
To Materials (@ Rs.120)	1,500	1,80,000	By Loss in weight		
To Manufacturing Expenses		49,950	(2% of 1,500)	30	
			By Scrap (5% on 1,500		
			@ Rs. 90)	75	6,750
			By Warehouse		
			(40% of 1,395 @ Rs. 160)	558	89,280
			By Process B a/c (transfer		
			60% of 1,395 @ Rs. 160)	837	1,33,920
	1,500	2,29,950		1,500	2,29,950

Cost per unit: 1,33,920/837 = Rs. 160

Working Notes:

(1) Transfer to warehouse = (Rs. 2,29,950 – Rs. 6,750)/(1,500 – 30 – 75) × 558 tonnes = Rs. 89,280

(2) As the question is silent about the nature of loss, it is presumed that both weight loss and scrap are normal.

Dr. **PROCESS B ACCOUNT** **Cr.**

Particulars	*Tonnes*	*Rs.*	*Particulars*	*Tonnes*	*Rs.*
To Process A (transfer)	837	1,33,920	By Loss in weight		
To Materials (@ Rs. 180)	163	29,340	(2% of 1,000)	20	
To Manufacturing Expenses		51,440	By Scrap		
			(10% on 1,000 @ Rs. 110)	100	11,000
			By Warehouse (50% of 880)	440	1,01,850
			By Process C a/c		
			(transfer 50% of 880)	440	1,01,850
	1,000	2,14,700		1,000	2,14,700

Transfer to warehouse = (Rs. 2,14,700 – Rs.11,000)/(1,000 – 120) × 440 tonnes = Rs. 1,01,850

Cost per unit = 1,01,850/440 = Rs. 231.47

Dr. **PROCESS C ACCOUNT** **Cr.**

Particulars	*Tonnes*	*Rs.*	*Particulars*	*Tonnes*	*Rs.*
To Process B (transfer)	440	1,01,850	By Loss in weight		
To Materials (@ Rs. 80)	1,115	89,200	(3% of 1,555)	47	
To Manufacturing Expenses		40,630	By Scrap		
			(15% on 1,555 @ Rs. 200)	233	46,600
			By Warehouse		
			(transfer @ Rs. 145.16)	1,275	1,85,080
	1,555	2,31,680		1,555	2,31,680

Cost per unit: 1,85,080/1,275 = Rs. 145.16

Illustration 6

A product passes through three processes – A, B and C. The details of expenses incurred on the three processes during the year 2007 were as under:

	Process A	*Process B*	*Process C*
Units issued	3,000		
	Rs.	Rs.	Rs.
Cost per unit	50	—	—
Sundry Materials	6,300	1,500	1,500
Labor	13,100	8,000	19,176
Direct expenses	7,100	1,815	8,160
Sales Price of Output (per unit)	80	95	136

Actual output of the three processes was – Process A: 2,550 units: Process B: 1,490 units: Process C: 500 units. Two third of output of Process A and one half of the output of process B was passed on to the next process and the balance was sold. The entire output of process C was sold.

The normal loss of three processes, calculated on the input of every process was:

Process A: 10% Process B: 15% and Process C: 20%.

The loss of process A was sold at Re. 1 per unit, that of Process B at Rs.2 per unit and that of process C at Rs.3 per unit.

Selling and Distribution expenses during the year were Rs. 2,000. These are not allocable to the process but to be considered while drawing the income statement.

Prepare the three Process Accounts and a Statement of Income.

Solution

Dr. **PROCESS A ACCOUNT** **Cr.**

Particulars	*Units*	*Rs.*	*Particulars*	*Units*	*Rs.*
To Units issued	3,000	1,50,000	By Normal Loss a/c (10% of 3,000 @ Re. 1)	300	300
To Sundry Material		6,300	By Abnormal Loss Rs. 65.25	150	9,789
To Labor		13,100	By Process B a/c (2/3 of 2,550) @ Rs. 65.25)	1,700	1,10,925
To Direct Expenses		7,100	By Bank 1/3 of 2,550 @ 80	850	68,000
To P&L a/c (Profit on sale credited to income statement)		12,514			
	3,000	1,89,014		3,000	1,89,014

$$\text{Cost of Abnormal Loss Units} = \frac{\text{Total cost} - \text{value of normal loss}}{\text{Input} - \text{Normal loss in units}} \times \text{Abnormal Loss Units}$$

$$\text{Cost per unit at process A} = \frac{1,76,500 - 300}{3,000 - 300} = \text{Rs. } 65.25$$

Dr. **PROCESS B ACCOUNT** **Cr.**

Particulars	*Units*	*Rs.*	*Particulars*	*Units*	*Rs.*
To Process A a/c	1,700	1,10,925	By Normal Loss a/c 15% of 1,700 @ 2	255	510
To Sundry Material		1,500	By Process C a/c (Output transfer) (Half of 1,490 @ Rs. 8,4.24)	745	62,759
To Labor		8,000	By Bank ½ of 1,490 @95	745	70,775
To Direct Expenses		1,815			
To P&L a/c (Profit on sale credited to income statement)		8,014			
To Abnormal gain (45* 84.24)	45	3,790			
	1,745	1,34,044		1745	1,34,044

Cost per unit at process B = $\frac{\text{Total cost – value of normal loss}}{\text{Input – Normal loss in units}} = \frac{1,22,240 - 510}{1,700 - 255}$ = Rs. 84.24

Cost of Abnormal Gain Units = 45 Units × 84.24 = Rs. 3,790

Dr. **PROCESS C ACCOUNT** **Cr.**

Particulars	*Units*	*Rs.*	*Particulars*	*Units*	*Rs.*
To Process B a/c	745	62,759	By Normal Loss a/c (20% of 745 @ 3)	149	447
To Sundry Material		1,500	By Abnormal Loss	96	14,688
To Labor		19,176	By Bank @ Rs. 136	500	68,000
To Direct Expenses		8,160	By P&L a/c (Loss on Sale)		8,460
	745	91,595		745	91,595

Cost per unit at Process C = $\frac{\text{Total cost – Value of normal loss}}{\text{Input – Normal loss in units}} = \frac{91,595 - 447}{745 - 149}$ = Rs. 153

Cost of Abnormal Loss Units = 96 units × 153 = Rs. 14,688.

Dr. **Abnormal Loss Account** **Cr.**

Particulars	*Units*	*Rs.*	*Particulars*	*Units*	*Rs.*
To Process A a/c	150	9,789	By Cash a/c (@ Re. 1)	150	150
To Process C a/c	96	14,688	By Cash a/c (@ Rs. 3)	96	288
			By P&L a/c		24,039
	246	24,477		246	24,477

Dr. **Abnormal Gain Account** **Cr.**

Particulars	*Units*	*Rs.*	*Particulars*	*Units*	*Rs.*
To Normal Loss a/c (@ Rs. 2) (Loss of income)	45	90	By Process B A/c	45	3,790
To P&L A/c	—	3,700			
	45	3,790		45	3,790

Dr. **Costing P & L a/c** **Cr.**

Particulars	*Rs.*	*Particulars*	*Rs.*
To Selling and Distribution	2,000	By Process A	12,514
To Abnormal loss	24,039	By Process B	8,014
To Process C	8,460	By Abnormal Gain	3,700
		By Net Loss	10,271
	34,499		34,499

PROCESS ACCOUNTS WITH STOCKS

It is quite likely that a process contains stock and the same may be taken in the Process Account or a separate Process Stock Account can be prepared. When a separate Process Stock Account is prepared, the completed output of a process is transferred to its Stock Account and the balance in the Stock Account (after taking opening stock, finished output and closing stock) is transferred to the next process account and the balance in the last Process Stock Account will be transferred to Finished Stock Account.

The following illustrations make the point clear.

Illustration 7

The information given below is extracted from the cost accounts of a factory producing a commodity in the manufacture of which three processes are involved. Prepare Process Cost Account showing the cost of the output and the cost per unit at each stage of manufacture.

(a) The operations in each separate process are completed daily.

	Processes		
	A	*B*	*C*
	Rs.	*Rs.*	*Rs.*
Direct Wages	640	600	1,830
Machine Expenses	360	300	260
Factory Overhead	200	225	315
Raw Materials consume	1,200	—	—
	units	*units*	*units*
Production (Gross)	24,000	—	—
Wastage	1,000	1,000	500
Opening Stock of Raw Materials	—	2,500	10,000
Closing Stock of Raw Materials	—	1,000	5,000

Solution

Dr. **PROCESS 'A' ACCOUNT** **Cr.**

Particulars	*Units*	*Rs.*	*Particulars*	*Units*	*Rs.*
To Raw Material	25,000	1,200	By Normal Wastage	1,000	—
To Direct Wages		640	By Process No. 2 a/c	24,000	2,400
To Machine Expenses		360	(Output transfer @ Re. 0.10)		
To Factory Overheads		200			
	25,000	2,400		25,000	2,400

Cost Per Unit = 2,400/24,000 = Re. 0.10

Dr. **PROCESS 'B' ACCOUNT** **Cr.**

Particulars	*Units*	*Rs.*	*Particulars*	*Units*	*Rs.*
To Opening Stock	2,500	250	By Normal Wastage	1,000	—
(@0.10 paisa 2,400/24,000)			By Closing Stock @ 0.10	1,000	100
To Process A a/c	24,000	2,400	By Process No. C a/c	24,500	3,675
To Direct Wages		600	(Output transfer @0.15)		
To Machine Expenses		300			
To Factory Overheads		225			
	26,500	3,775		26,500	3,775

Cost Per Unit = 3,675/24,500 = Rs. 0.15

Dr. **PROCESS 'C' ACCOUNT** **Cr.**

Particulars	*Units*	*Rs.*	*Particulars*	*Units*	*Rs.*
To Opening Stock @ Re. 0.15	10,000	1,500	By Normal Wastage	500	—
To Process B a/c	24,500	3,675	By Closing Stock @0.15	5,000	750
To Direct Wages		1,830	By Finished Stock a/c	29,000	6,830
To Machine Expenses		260			
To Factory Overhead		315			
	34,500	7,580		34,500	7,580

Cost Per Unit = 6,830/29,000 = Re. 0.24

Note : Opening stock and Clost stock are valued at the cost per unit of previous process as the values are not given in the problem.

Illustration 8

A material used on building is produced in three grades:

Particulars	*Process 1*	*Process 2*	*Process 3*
Raw Materials used (1,000 tonnes) (Rs.)	2,00,000	—	—
Wages (Rs.)	87,500	39,500	10,710
Weight lost (% of input)	5%	10%	20%
Scrap	50 tonnes @ Rs. 50	30 tonnes @ Rs. 500	51 tonnes @ Rs. 50
Sale price per tonne of finished goods (Rs.)	350	500	800

Management expenses were Rs. 17,500 and selling expenses Rs. 10,000. 2/3rd of the output of Process 1 and 50% of the output of Process 2 are passed to the next process and the balance is sold. The entire output of Process 3 is sold. Prepare Process A/cs and a statement of profit.

Solution

Dr. **PROCESS 1 ACCOUNT** **Cr.**

Particulars	*Units*	*Amount (Rs.)*	*Particulars*	*Units*	*Amount (Rs.)*
To Materials	1,000	2,00,000	By N.L. a/c	50	2,500
To Wages		87,500	By Weight Lost (5%)	50	—
			By Process 1 Stock a/c	900	2,85,000
	1,000	2,87,500		1,000	2,87,500

Dr. **PROCESS 1 STOCK ACCOUNT** **Cr.**

Particulars	*Units*	*Amount (Rs.)*	*Particulars*	*Units*	*Amount (Rs.)*
To Process 1 a/c	900	2,85,000	By Process 2 a/c (2/3 × 900)	600	1,90,000
To Profit		10,000	By Sales @ Rs. 350 (1/3 × 900)	300	1,05,000
	900	2,95,000		900	2,95,000

Transfer to Process 2: (2,85,000 / 900) × 600 = Rs. 1,90,000

Dr. **PROCESS 2 ACCOUNT** **Cr.**

Particulars	*Units*	*Amount (Rs.)*	*Particulars*	*Units*	*Amount (Rs.)*
To Process 1 stock a/c	600	1,90,000	By N.L. a/c	30	15,000
To Wages		39,500	By Weight Lost (10%)	60	—
			By Process 2 Stock a/c	510	2,14,500
	600	2,29,500		600	2,29,500

Dr. **PROCESS 2 STOCK ACCOUNT** **Cr.**

Particulars	*Units*	*Amount (Rs.)*	*Particulars*	*Units*	*Amount (Rs.)*
To Process 2 a/c	510	2,14,500	By Process 3 a/c (50% × 510)	255	1,07,250
To Profit		20,250	By Sales @ Rs. 500	255	1,27,500
	510	2,34,750		510	2,34,750

PROCESS 3 ACCOUNT

Dr. Particulars	Units	Amount (Rs.)	Particulars	Units	Amount (Rs.) Cr.
To Process 2 Stock a/c	255	1,07,250	By N.L. a/c	51	2,550
To Wages		10,710	By Weight Lost (20%)	51	—
			By Process 3 Stock a/c	153	1,15,410
	255	1,17,960		255	1,17,960

PROCESS 3 STOCK ACCOUNT

Dr. Particulars	Units	Amount (Rs.)	Particulars	Units	Amount (Rs.) Cr.
To Process 3 a/c	153	1,15,410	By Sales @ Rs. 800	153	1,22,400
To Profit		6,990			
	153	1,22,400		153	1,22,400

STATEMENT OF PROFIT

		Rs.	Rs.
	Profit:		
	Process 1 Stock a/c	10,000	
	Process 2 Stock a/c	20,250	
	Process 3 Stock a/c	6,990	37,240
Less:	Management Expenses	17,500	
	Selling Expenses	10,000	27,500
	Net Profit		9,740

INTER-PROCESS PROFITS

In certain process industries, the output of one process is transferred to the next process not at cost but after adding a percentage of profit. This is done in order to make each process self-dependent and not to depend on the efficiency of the earlier processes.

But, as a result of the transfer of the output of one process to another process at a profit, the stock in each process contains an element of inter-process profits and this has to be eliminated form the stock to ascertain the cost of closing stock for the Balance Sheet purpose.

The question of inter-process profits arises from the second process onwards, as the output of earlier process is transferred at a profit. Therefore, this profit is to be eliminated and the cost of the opening and closing stock has to be ascertained.

The cost of stock is obtained with the help of the following formula:

Cost of Stock = (Cost Column/Total Column) × Stock

The difference between the transfer price and the cost is known as Inter-Process Profit made by the transferror process from transfer of output to the subsequent process.

The procedure involved in inter-process profits is determined in the following illustrations.

Illustration 9

A product passes through three processes before it is completed and transferred to finished stock. From the following data relating to the month of January 2009, prepare process accounts.

Particulars	*Process 1 (Rs.)*	*Process 2 (Rs.)*	*Process 3 (Rs.)*	*Finished Stock (Rs.)*
Opening Stock	500	800	1,000	2,000
Direct Materials	4,000	1,200	1,500	—
Direct Labor	3,500	4,000	3,500	—
Factory Overheads	2,000	2,400	2,000	—
Closing Stock	1,000	400	1,500	3,000

Output of Process 1 to Process 2, of Process 2 to Process 3, of Process 3 to Finished Stock Account is transferred at a profit 25%, 20% and 10% on transfer price, respectively. Finished Stock has been valued at a price at which it was received from Process 3. Sales amounted to Rs. 40,000. Provisions for internal process profits on Jan. 1, 2009 were as follows.

	Rs.
Process 2	140
Process 3	270
Finished Stock	650
	1,060

Solution

Dr. **PROCESS 1 ACCOUNT** **Cr.**

Particulars	*Total Rs.*	*Cost Rs.*	*Profit Rs.*	*Particulars*	*Total Rs.*	*Cost Rs.*	*Profit Rs.*
To Opening Stock	500	500	—	By Process 2 a/c	12,000	9,000	3,000
To Direct Materials	4,000	4,000	—				
To Direct Labor	3,500	3,500	—				
	8,000	8,000	—				
Less: Closing Stock c/d	1,000	1,000	—				
Prime Cost	7,000	7,000	—				
To Factory Overheads	2,000	2,000	—				
Process Cost (75)	9,000	9,000	—				
To Profit (25% on transfer Price) (25)	3,000	—	3,000				
Transfer Price (100)	12,000	9,000	3,000		12,000	9,000	3,000
To Closing Stock b/d	1,000	1,000	—				

Profit = (25/75) × 9,000 = Rs. 3,000

Dr. **PROCESS 2 ACCOUNT** **Cr.**

Particulars	*Total Rs.*	*Cost Rs.*	*Profit Rs.*	*Particulars*	*Total Rs.*	*Cost Rs.*	*Profit Rs.*
To Process 1	12,000	9,000	3,000	By Process 3 a/c	25,000	16,930	8,070
To Opening Stock	800	660	140				
To Direct Materials	1,200	1,200	—				
To Direct Labor	4,000	4,000	—				
	18,000	14,860	3,140				
Less: Closing Stock c/d	400	330	70				
Prime Cost	17,600	14,530	3,070				
To Factory Overheads	2,400	2,400	—				
Process Cost (80)	20,000	16,930	3,070				
To Profit (20% on transfer Price) (20)	5,000	—	5,000				
Transfer Price (100)	25,000	16,930	8,070		25,000	16,930	8,070
To Closing Stock b/d	400	330	70				

Cost of Closing Stock = (Cost column/Total column) × Closing Stock

= (14,860/18,000) × 400 = Rs. 330

Profit = (20/80) × 20000 = Rs. 5,000

Dr. **PROCESS 3 ACCOUNT** Cr.

Particulars	*Total* Rs.	*Cost* Rs.	*Profit* Rs.	*Particulars*	*Total* Rs.	*Cost* Rs.	*Profit* Rs.
To Process 2	25,000	16,930	8,070	By Finished Stock a/c	35,000	23,563	11,437
To Opening Stock	1,000	730	270				
To Direct Materials	1,500	1,500	—				
To Direct Labor	3,500	3,500	—				
	31,000	22,660	8,340				
Less: Closing Stock c/d	1,500	1,097	403				
Prime Cost	29,500	21,563	7,937				
To Factory Overheads	2,000	2,000	—				
Process Cost (90)	31,500	23,563	7,937				
To Profit (10% on transfer Price) (10)	3,500	—	3,500				
Transfer Price (100)	35,000	23,563	11,437		35,000	23,563	11,437
To Closing Stock b/d	1,500	1,097	403				

Cost of Closing Stock = (Cost column/Total column) × Closing Stock
= (22,660/31,000) × 1,500= Rs. 1,097

Profit = (10/90) × 31,500 = Rs. 3,500

Dr. **FINISHED STOCK ACCOUNT** Cr.

Particulars	*Total* Rs.	*Cost* Rs.	*Profit* Rs.	*Particulars*	*Total* Rs.	*Cost* Rs.	*Profit* Rs.
To Process 3	35,000	23,563	11,437	By Sales	40,000	22,893	17,107
To Opening Stock	2,000	1,350	650				
	37,000	24,913	12,087				
Less: Closing Stock c/d	3,000	2,020	980				
	34,000	22,893	11,107				
Add: Profit	6,000	—	6,000				
	40,000	22,893	17,107		40,000	22,893	17,107
To Closing Stock b/d	3,000	2,020	980				

Cost of Closing Stock = (Cost column/Total column) × Closing Stock
= (24,913/37,000) × 3,000 = Rs. 2,020

Profit = (20/80) × 24,000 = Rs. 6,000

Value of Realized Profit

Process Name	*Apparent Profit* Rs.	*Profit in Opening Stock (+)* Rs.	*Unrealized Profit on Closing stock (–)* Rs.	*Actual Profit Realized* Rs.
1	3,000	—	—	3,000
2	5,000	140	70	5,070
3	3,500	270	403	3,367
Finished Stock	6,000	650	980	5,670
Total	17,500	1,060	1,453	17,107

Note: Total of actual profit realized should be equal to the amount in the profit column of finished stock account. Value of Closing Stock for Balance Sheet purpose

	Rs.
Cost of Closing Stock in Process I	1,000
Cost of Closing Stock in Process II	330
Cost of Closing Stock in Process III	1,097
Cost of Closing Stock in Finished Stock Account	2,020
Total	4,447

Illustration 10

A Ltd. produces a product which passes through two processes before it is completed and transferred to finished stock. The following data relate to the month of December:

	Process I Rs.	*Process II* Rs.	*Finished Stock* Rs.
Opening Stock	22,500	27,000	67,500
Direct Materials	45,000	47,250	—
Direct Wages	33,600	33,750	—
Factory Overheads	31,500	13,500	—
Closing Stock	11,100	13,500	33,750
Inter-process profit for opening stock	—	4,500	24,750

Output of process I transferred to process II at 25% profit on the transfer price. Output of Process II is transferred to finished stock at 20% profit on the transfer price. Stock in process is valued at prime cost. Finished stock is valued at the price at which it is received fro process II. The Sales during the period are Rs. 4,20,000.

Prepare process accounts and finished stock account showing the profit element at each.

Solution

Dr. **PROCESS I ACCOUNT** **Cr.**

Particulars	*Total* Rs.	*Cost* Rs.	*Profit* Rs.	*Particulars*	*Total* Rs.	*Cost* Rs.	*Profit* Rs.
To Opening Stock	22,500	22,500	—	By Transfer to Process II a/c	1,62,000	1,21,500	40,500
To Direct Materials	45,000	45,000	—				
To Direct Labor	33,600	33,600	—				
Total	1,01,100	1,01,100	—				
Less: Closing Stock c/d	11,100	11,100	—				
Prime cost	90,000	90,000	—				
To Manufacturing overheads	31,500	31,500	—				
Process cost (75)	1,21,500	1,21,500	—				
Profit (25% on transfer price) (25)	40,500	—	40,500				
Transfer Price (100)	1,62,000	1,21,500	40,500		1,62,000	1,21,500	40,500
To Closing Stock b/d	11,100	11,100	—				

$$\textbf{Profit} = \frac{25}{75} \times 1{,}21{,}500 = \text{Rs. } 40{,}500$$

Dr. **PROCESS II ACCOUNT** **Cr..**

Particulars	*Total* Rs.	*Cost* Rs.	*Profit* Rs.	*Particulars*	*Total* Rs.	*Cost* Rs.	*Profit* Rs.
To Opening Stock	27,000	22,500	4,500	By Transfer to			
To Process I	1,62,000	1,21,500	40,500	Process III a/c	3,37,500	2,27,250	1,10,250
To Direct Materials	47,250	47,250	—				
To Direct Labor	33,750	33,750	—				
Total	2,70,000	2,25,000	45,000				
Less: Closing Stock c/d	13,500	11,250	2,250				
Prime cost	2,56,500	2,13,750	42,750				
To Manufacturing overheads	13,500	13,500	—				
Process cost (80)	2,70,000	2,27,250	42,750				
Profit (20) (20% on transfer price)	67,500	—	67,500				
Transfer Price (100)	3,37,500	2,27,250	1,10,250		3,37,500	2,27,250	1,10,250
To Closing Stock b/d	13,500	11,250	2,250				

$$\text{Cost of Closing Stock} = 13{,}500 \times \frac{2,25,000}{2,70,000} = \text{Rs. } 11{,}250$$

$$\textbf{Profit} = \frac{20}{80} \times 2{,}70{,}000 = \text{Rs. } 67{,}500$$

Dr. **Finished Stock Account** **Cr.**

Particulars	*Total* Rs.	*Cost* Rs.	*Profit* Rs.	*Particulars*	*Total* Rs.	*Cost* Rs.	*Profit* Rs.
To Stock	67,500	42,750	24,750	By Sales	4,20,000	2,47,500	1,72,500
To Process II a/c	3,37,500	2,27,250	1,10,250				
Total	4,05,000	2,70,000	1,35,000				
Less: Closing Stock	33,750	22,500	11,250				
Cost	3,71,250	2,47,500	1,23,750				
Profit	48,750	—	48,750				
	4,20,000	2,47,500	1,72,500		4,20,000	2,47,500	1,72,500
To Closing Stock b/d	33,750	22,500	11,250				

$$\text{Cost of Closing Stock} = \frac{2,70,000}{4,05,000} \times 33{,}750 = \text{Rs.}22{,}500$$

Value of Realized Profit

Process Name	*Apparent Profit* Rs.	*Profit in Opening Stock (+)* Rs.	*Unrealized Profit on Closing Stock (–)* Rs.	*Actual Profit Realized* Rs.
1	40,500	—	—	40,500
2	67,500	4,500	2,250	69,750
Finished Stock	48,750	24,750	11,250	62,250
Total	1,56,750	29,250	13,500	1,72,500

Note: Total of actual profit realized should be equal to the amount in the profit column of finished stock account.

Value of Closing Stock for Balance Sheet purpose

	Rs.
Cost of Closing Stock in Process I	11,100
Cost of Closing Stock in Process II	11,250
Cost of Closing Stock in Finished Stock Account	22,500
Total	44,850

Equivalent Production

Process Costing deals with continuous type of production. In the Process Costing, when the work is not completed such unfinished work is called Work-in-progress (WIP), the accounting for such Work-in-Progress (WIP) is done in terms of Equivalent Production.

An Equivalent Unit is a measure that applies a percentage of completion factor to partially completed units, to calculate the equivalent number of whole units, produced in an accounting period.

In both, opening and closing work-in-progress, equivalent units are calculated for all elements of cost *viz.*, Direct Materials, Direct Labor and Production Overheads.

For the purpose of calculation of Equivalent Production, three statements are prepared:

(a) Statement of Equivalent Production
(b) Statement of Cost per Unit and
(c) Statement of Evaluation.

Statement of Equivalent Production:

Estimating the value of partially completed units as equivalent to fully completed units is called Equivalent Production.

The valuation of equivalent units is done as follows:

Equivalent units = Number of partially completed units × percentage of completion.

If opening WIP is given in the problem with percentage of work completed, then, in the current process, production will be carried forward with rest of the work needed to be completed.

For, e.g., if opening WIP given is 6000 units at Rs. 2000 and % of completion of WIP is given as

Materials – 100%; Labor – 60% and Overheads – 40%, then, the work to be carried forward in material is nil, labor – 40% (100%-60% – completed already), overheads – 60% (100%-40% – completed already).

If both opening and closing work-in-progress are given in the process, then, equivalent units of production for a period can be calculated in any of the three ways.

(1) First-In-First Out
(2) Average Weighted Method
(3) Last-In-First Out Method

However, the first two methods are the most widely used methods.

First-In-First-Out Method (FIFO)

Under this method, it is assumed that the incomplete work on the Opening Work-in-Progress will be first taken up and later, the work on the units introduced in the current period will be taken up. As a result, the valuation of finished stock will include the following costs.

- Cost of Opening Work-in-Progress (Previous period)
- Cost of Opening Work-in-Progress (Current period) and
- Cost of work done on units introduced in the Current period.

While calculating the equivalent units, only work incomplete on Opening Work-in-Progress will be taken. For example, if the degree of completion on Opening Work-in-Progress is 40%, it means that 40% of the work on these units is completed in the previous period and therefore, only 60% of the work will be taken up in the current period.

FIFO method is applicable only when element-wise degree of completion of Opening Work-in-Progress is known.

Illustration 11

Opening work-in-progress (40% completed)	— 2,000 units
Put into the process during the month	— 18,000 units
Transferred to next process	— 16,000 units
Closing Work-in-process (60% completed)	— 4,000 units

Calculate Equivalent Production

Solution

	Equivalent units
Opening work-in-progress (60% unfinished work × 2,000 units)	1,200
Add: No. of units introduced and completed during the month (16,000-2,000): 14,000 × 100%	14,000
Equivalent production: Finished Stock	15,200
Add: Closing stock-work done [4,000 × 60%]	2,400
	17,600

Illustration 12

The following is the information pertaining to process A:

	Units
Opening work-in-progress (30% completed) valued at Rs. 560	— 300
Units introduced during current period	— 800
Finished output during the current period	— 700
Closing work-in-progress (40% completed)	— 100
Cost incurred during the period (Rs.)	— 5,700

Make the necessary calculations and prepare process A Account.

Solution

Statement of Equivalent Production

Items	*Degree of Completion (%)*	*Equivalent Units*
Opening WIP (300)	70%	210
Units introduced and completed (400)	100%	400
Closing stock (100)	40%	40
Total (1,100)		650

Calculation of cost per unit
Cost incurred during the year = Rs. 5,700
Equivalent Production during the period = 650
Cost per unit = 5,700/650 = Rs. 8.7692

Statement of Evaluation

Particulars	*Equivalent units*	*Cost per unit Rs.*	*Total Rs.*
Opening WIP (Previous Period)	—	—	560.000
Opening WIP (Current Period)	210	8.7692	1,841.532
Units introduced and completed during the period	400	8.7692	3,507.680
Cost of Finished Stock			5,909.212
Closing Work-in-progress	40	8.7692	350.768

Dr. **Process A Account** **Cr.**

Particulars	*Costs*	*Rs.*	*Particulars*	*Costs*	*Rs.*
To Opening WIP	300	560	By normal loss	300	—
To Materials	800	5,700	By Finished Stock	700	5,909
			By Work-in-Progress	100	351
	1,100	6,260		1,100	6,260

Illustration 13

During January 1,000 units were introduced into process 1. The normal loss was estimated at 10% on input. At the end of the month 640 units had been produced and transferred to next process, 200 units were uncompleted and 160 units had been scrapped. It was estimated that uncompleted units had reached a stage in production as follows:

Materials	75%
Labor	50%
Overheads	50%

The cost of 1,000 units introduced was Rs. 2,860

Direct materials introduced during the process amounted to Rs. 640

Direct labor cost was Rs. 2,400

Production overheads incurred were Rs. 1,600

Units scrapped realized Re. 1 each. The units scrapped have passed through the process and they were 100% completed as regards material, labor and overheads.

You are required to (a) prepare a statement of Equivalent Production, (b) Evaluate the cost of abnormal loss, finished goods and closing stock and (c) prepare the Process 1 Account and Abnormal Loss Account.

Solution

Statement of Equivalent Production

Output		*Equivalent units*					
Items	*Units*	*Materials*		*Labor*		*Overheads*	
		Qty	*%*	*Qty*	*%*	*Qty*	*%*
Normal loss	100	—	—	—	—	—	—
Abnormal loss	60	60	100	60	100	60	100
Finished production	640	640	100	640	100	640	100
Work-in-Progress	200	150	75	100	50	100	50
Total	1,000	850	—	800	—	800	—

Statement of Cost

Element of Cost	*Cost (Rs.)*	*Equivalent Units*	*Cost per unit (Rs.)*
Materials			
Units introduced	2,860		
Direct Material	640		
	3,500		
Less: scrap value of loss(normal)	100		
Material cost	3,400	850	4
Direct Labor	2,400	800	3
Overheads	1,600	800	2
Total	7,400		9

Statement of Evaluation

Particulars	*Elements of cost*	*Equivalent production*	*Cost per unit (Rs.)*	*Cost (Rs.)*	*Total Cost (Rs.)*
Abnormal loss:	Materials	60	4	240	—
	Labor	60	3	180	—
	Overheads	60	2	120	540
Finished production:	Materials	640	4	2,560	
	Labor	640	3	1,920	
	Overheads	640	2	1,280	5,760
Work-in-progress:	Material	150	4	600	
	Labor	100	3	300	
	Overheads	100	2	200	1,100
					7,400

Dr. **Process I Account** **Cr.**

Particulars	*Units*	*Rs.*	*Particulars*	*Units*	*Rs.*
To units introduced	1,000	2,860	By normal loss (10% of 1,000)	100	100
To Direct Material		640	By abnormal loss	60	540
To Direct Wages		2,400	By Process II		
To Overheads		1,600	(finished production transferred)	640	5,760
			By Work-in-Progress (Balance c/d)	200	1,100
	1,000	7,500		1,000	7,500

Illustration 14

The following data pertain to process 1 for March, 1994 of Beta Ltd :

Opening Work-in-Progress	1,500 units at	Rs. 15,000
Degree of Completion :		
Materials 100%; Labor and overheads 331/3%		
Input Materials :	18,500 units at	Rs. 52,000
Direct Labor		Rs. 14,000
Overheads		Rs. 28,000
Closing work-in-progress	5,000 units	
Degree of Completion :		
Materials 90% : Labor and Overheads	30%	

Normal Process Loss is 10% of total input (opening Work-in-progress units + Units put in)
Scrap value Rs. 2 per unit
Units transferred to the next process – 15,000 units.
You are required to –

(i) Compute equivalent units of production.
(ii) Compute cost per equivalent unit for each cost element i.e., Materials, Labor and Overheads.
(iii) Compute the cost of finished output and closing Work-in-progress.
(iv) Prepare the process and other Accounts.

Assume (a) FIFO method is used by the company, and (b) the cost of opening Work-in-progress is fully transferred to the next process.

Solution

Statement of Equivalent Production

Input		*Output*		*Materials*		*Labor & Overheads*	
Particulars	*Units*	*Particulars*	*Units*	*%*	*Units*	*%*	*Units*
Opening WIP	1,500	Work done	1,500	Nil	Nil	66 2/3	1,000
Introduced	18,500	Completed					
		(15,000-1,500)	13,500	100	13,500	100	13,500
Normal loss			2,000	—	—	—	—
Closing WIP			5,000	90	4,500	30	1,500
Total			22,000		18,000		16,000
		Less: Abnormal Gain	2,000	100	2,000	100	2,000
	20,000		20,000		16,000		14,000

Statement of Cost

Elements of cost	*Cost (Rs)*	*Cost (Rs.)*	*Equivalent Units*	*Cost per Unit (Rs.)*
Materials	52,000			
Less: Scrap Sales	(–)4,000	48,000	16,000	3.00
Labor		14,000	14,000	1.00
Overheads		28,000	14,000	2.00
Total				6.00

Statement of Equivalent Production

Particulars	*Elements of cost*	*Equivalent production*	*Cost per Unit (Rs.)*	*Total Cost (Rs.)*
Opening WIP (Last Year)		—	—	15,000
Additions: (1,500 units):	Materials	—	—	—
	Labor	1,000	1.00	1,000
	Overhead	1,000	2.00	2,000
Opening WIP completed during the year				18,000
Units introduced and completed during the year (15,000 – 1,500)		13,500	6.00	81,000
Cost of units introduced and completed during the year				99,000
Closing WIP (5,000 units):	Materials	4,500	3.00	13,500
	Labor	1,500	1.00	1,500
	Overhead	1,500	2.00	3,000
				18,000
Abnormal Gain		2,000	6.00	12,000

Dr. **Process 1 Account** **Cr.**

Particulars	*Units*	*Rs.*	*Particulars*	*Units*	*Rs.*
Opening WIP	1,500	15,000	Normal Loss	2,000	4,000
Unit Introduced:			Transfer to Next Process	15,000	99,000
Direct Material	18,500	52,000	Closing WIP	5,000	18,000
Direct Labor		14,000			
Overhead		28,000			
Abnormal Gain	2,000	12,000			
	22,000	1,21,000		22,000	1,21,000

Dr. **Abnormal Gain Account** **Cr.**

Particulars	*Units*	*Rs.*	*Particulars*	*Units*	*Rs.*
To Process A/c	2,000	4,000	By Process A/c	2,000	12,000
To Profit & Loss A/c (Abnormal Gain)		8,000			
	2,000	12,000		2,000	12,000

Illustration 15

From the following information about Shreya Co. Ltd. during a period, prepare Process Cost Account for Process 3

Opening Stock in Progress 3 – 1,600 units at Rs. 20,600

Transfer from Progress 2 – 42,400 units at Rs. 3,29,200

Transfer to Progress 4 – 38,400 units

Closing Stock of Progress 3 – 4,000 units

Units scrapped 1,600 units

Direct Material added in Progress 3 – Rs. 1,58,080

Direct Wages – Rs. 78,080

Production Overhead – Rs. 39,040

Degree of Completion

	Opening Stock	*Closing Stock*
Materials	80%	70%
Labor	60%	50%
Overhead	60%	50%

The normal loss in the process was 5% of production and scrap was sold at Rs. 3 per unit.

Solution

Statement of Equivalent Production

Output		*Equivalent Units*					
Items	*Units*	*Material A*		*Material B*		*Labor and Overhead*	
		Qty.	*%*	*Qty.*	*%*	*Qty.*	*%*
Normal Loss	2,000	—	—	—	—	—	—
Finished Production:							
Opening WIP	1,600	—	—	320	20	640	40
Units introduced and Completed (38,400-1,600)	36,800	36,800	100	36,800	100	36,800	100
Closing WIP	4,000	4,000	100	2,800	70	2,000	50
Less: Abnormal Gain	400	400	100	400	100	400	100
Total	44,000	40,400	—	39,520	—	39,040	—

Statement of Cost

Elements of Cost	*Cost (Rs.)*	*Equivalent Units*	*Cost per unit (Rs.)*
Material A			
Transfer from Previous Process	3,29,200		
Less: Value of normal scrap	-6,000		
	3,23,200	40,400	8
Material B added in Process 3	1,58,080	39,520	4
Labor	78,080	39,040	2
Overheads	39,040	39,040	1
Total Cost	5,98,400		

Statement of Evaluation

Particulars	*Elements of Cost*	*Equivalent Production*	*Cost per Unit (Rs.)*	*Cost (Rs.)*	*Total Cost (Rs.)*
Opening WIP	Material A	—	8	—	—
	Material B	320	4	1,280	
	Wages	640	2	1,280	
	Overheads	640	1	640	3,200
Introduced and Completed during the period	Material A	36,800	8	2,94,400	
	Material B	36,800	4	1,47,200	
	Wages	36,800	2	73,600	
	Overheads	36,800	1	36,800	5,52,000
Closing WIP	Material A	4,000	8	32,000	
	Material B	2,800	4	11,200	
	Wages	2,000	2	4,000	
	Overheads	2,000	1	2,000	49,200
Abnormal Gain	Material A	400	8	3,200	
	Material B	400	4	1,600	
	Wages	400	2	800	
	Overheads	400	1	400	6,000
Total Cost (Total Cost – Cost of Abnormal Gain)					5,98,400

Dr. **Process 3 Account** **Cr.**

Particulars	*Units*	*Rs.*	*Particulars*	*Units*	*Rs.*
To balance b/d	1,600	20,600	By normal loss (40,000 × 5%)	2,000	6,000
To Process 2 A/c	42,400	3,29,200	By Process 4 A/c		
To Direct materials		1,58,080	(finished production transferred)	38,400	5,75,800
To Direct wages		78,080	By Work-in-Progress		
To Overheads		39,040	(Balance c/d)	4,000	49,200
To Abnormal Gain	400	6,000			
	44,400	6,31,000		44,400	6,31,000

Dr. **Abnormal Gain Account** **Cr.**

Particulars	*Units*	*Rs.*	*Particulars*	*Units*	*Rs.*
To Process 3 – scrap	400	1,200	By Process 3 A/c	400	6,000
To Profit & Loss A/c		4,800			
	400	6,000		400	6,000

Notes:

(i) Production = Opening Units + Units introduced – Closing Units
1,600 + 42,400 – 4,000 = 40,000 units

(ii) Process 4 accounts transfer: This comprises:

	Rs.
(a) Cost of Opening Stock (Last years)	20,600
(b) Cost of Opening Stock (Current year)	3,200
(c) Charge for units introduced and completed	5,52,000
(d) Cost of Finished Stock	5,75,800

Average Method

Under this method, the cost of Opening Work-in-Progress (Previous period) is added to the cost of Current period, element-wise, to ascertain the total cost. The total cost is then divided by the equivalent units for each element to find out the average cost. This means that the previous prices and the current prices of the input are averaged.

While calculating equivalent units, 100% of finished goods will be taken up without segregating into Opening Work-in-Progress component (Previous period) and the units introduced component(Current period).

The application of Average Cost Method is possible only when the element-wise cost of Opening Work-in-Progress is given in the problem.

Illustration 16

Opening WIP 500 units completed as to Material 60% Rs. 1,500, Labour – 40% Rs. 1,325; Overheads – 40% Rs. 1,200; Units introduced – 6,000 units. Closing WIP – 2,000 units completed as to Material – 80%, Labor – 60%, Overheads – 60%, Material Rs. 7,500, Labor Rs. 5,800 and overheads incurred during the period are Rs. 4,500.

Find out equivalent production using Average Method.

Solution

Statement of Equivalent Production

Output		*Equivalent Units*					
Items	*Units*	*Material A*		*Material B*		*Labor & Overhead*	
		Qty	*%*	*Qty*	*%*	*Qty*	*%*
Finished Stock	4,500	4,500	100	4,500	100	4,500	100
Work-in-Progress	2,000	1,600	80	1,200	60	1,200	60
Total	6,500	6,100	—	5,700	—	5,700	—

Statement of Cost

Element of Cost	*Opening Cost (Rs.)*	*Cost of Input*	*Total Cost*	*Equivalent Units*	*Cost per unit (Rs.)*
Materials	1,500	7,500	9,000	6,100	1.475
Labor	1,325	5,800	7,125	5,700	1.250
Overheads	1,200	4,500	5,700	5,700	1.000

Illustration 17

From the following details, prepare Statement of Equivalent Production, Statement of Cost and find out the value of the units and also prepare Process Account using

(a) Average method *(b)* FIFO method.

Opening Work-in-Progress 3,000 units completed to the extent of Material – 80% Rs. 5,000, Labor 60% Rs. 2,500, Overheads 40% Rs. 2,000. Number of units introduced into process: 6,000. There are 2,000 units in W-I-P and stage of completion is estimated to be Material 80%, Labor 60%, Overheads 40%. 7,000 units are transferred to next process. The process costs for the period are: Material: Rs. 55,200, Labor: Rs. 49,980 and Overheads: Rs. 41,680.

Solution

(a) Average Cost Method

Statement of Equivalent Production

Output		*Equivalent units*					
Items	*Units*	*Material*		*Labour*		*Overhead*	
		Qty	*%*	*Qty*	*%*	*Qty*	*%*
Units introduced Finished and Transferred	7,000	7,000	100	7,000	100	7,000	100
Closing WIP	2,000	1,600	80	1,200	60	800	40
	9,000	8,600	—	8,200	—	7,800	—

Statement of Cost

Element of Cost	*Cost (Rs.)*	*Equivalent Units*	*Cost per unit (Rs.)*
Cost of opening work-in-progress			
Add: cost incurred during process			
Material (5,000 + 55,200)	60,200	8,600	7.0
Labor (2,500 + 49,980)	52,480	8,200	6.4
Overhead (2,000 + 41,680)	43,680	7,800	5.6
			19.0

Statement of Evaluation

Particulars	*Element of cost*	*Equivalent Production*	*Cost per unit (Rs.)*	*Total Cost (Rs.)*
Value of finished goods and value of opening WIP	Material, Labour and Overheads	7,000	19.00	1,33,000
Value of Closing WIP	Material	1,600	7.0	11,200
	Labor	1,200	6.4	7,680
	Overheads	800	5.6	4,480
				23,360

Dr. **Process I Account** **Cr.**

Particulars	*Units*	*Rs.*	*Particulars*	*Units*	*Rs.*
To Opening WIP	3,000	9,500	By Transferred to Next Process	7,000	1,33,000
To Material	6,000	55,200	By Closing W.I.P	2,000	23,360
To Labor		49,980			
To Overheads		41,680			
	9,000	1,56,360		9,000	1,56,360

(b) FIFO Method

Statement of Equivalent Production

Output		*Equivalent units*					
Items	*Units*	*Material*		*Labour*		*Overhead*	
		Qty	*%*	*Qty*	*%*	*Qty*	*%*
Opening WIP	3,000	600	20	1,200	40	1,800	60
Units introduced							
Finished and Transferred (7,000-3,000)	4,000	4,000	100	4,000	100	4,000	100
Closing WIP	2,000	1,600	80	1,200	60	800	40
	9,000	6,200	—	6,400	—	6,600	—

Statement of Cost

	Material	*Labour*	*Overhead*
Cost incurred for the Period (Rs.)	55,200	49,980	41,680
Equivalent Units	6,200	6,400	6,600
Cost per Equivalent Unit (Rs.)	8.90	7.81	6.32

Statement of Evaluation

Element of Cost	*Equivalent Units*	*Cost per Unit Rs.*	*Total Cost Rs.*
Cost of Opening Work-in-Progress:			
Previous period			9,500
Current period:			
Materials	600	8.90	5,340
Labour	1,200	7.81	9,372
Overheads	1,800	6.32	11,376
			35,588
Units introduced in the Current period and completed:	4,000	23.03	92,120
Cost of Finished Stock			1,27,708
Closing Work-in-Progress :			
Material	1,600	8.90	14,240
Labour	1,200	7.81	9,372
Overhead	800	6.32	5,056
Cost of Closing Work-in-Progress			28,668

Cost of Finished Stock = 1,27,708 – 16 for adjustments = Rs. 1,27,692

Note: There is a difference of Rs. 16 which is due to approximations and the same is adjusted in the cost of finished stock.

Dr. **Process Account** **Cr.**

Particulars	*Units*	*Amount Rs.*	*Particulars*	*Units*	*Amount Rs.*
To Opening WIP	3,000	9,500			
Materials	6,000	55,200	By Finished Stock	7,000	1,27,692
Labour		49,980	By Closing WIP	2,000	28,668
Overheads		41,680			
Total	9,000	1,56,360		9,000	1,56,360

Difference between FIFO and Average Costing Method

(1) Under FIFO method, cost of Opening Work-in-Progress in the previous period is treated as previous period cost and not clubbed up with the current period cost. Whereas, under Average Cost Method, previous period cost of Opening Work-in-Progress is added up with the current period cost – element-wise and thus, average cost is ascertained by dividing the total cost with the equivalent units.

(2) While calculating the equivalent units, under FIFO method, Opening Work-in-Progress units are deducted from the completed units and the equivalent units for Opening Work-in-Progress and completed units are calculated separately. Under Average Cost Method there is no such segregation.

(3) FIFO method can be employed for valuation of Opening Work-in-Progress only when the degree of completion of Opening Work-in-Progress is known. Whereas, to adopt the Average Cost Method, it is necessary to know the element-wise cost of Opening Work-in-Progress.

When, both, degree of completion of opening Work-in-Progress and the element-wise costs of opening Work-in-Progress are given, the student may adopt any method *viz.*, FIFO or Average Cost Method.

Joint Products and By-Products

In certain processes, two or more products are produced from the same process and some products may have almost equal value and importance and some products have relatively smaller value. Former products are called Joint Products and later products are called By- Products.

e.g. petrol, diesel, naphtha, kerosene etc produced from the crude oil in oil refining industries and these products are called as Joint Products.

e.g. production of products like bagasse and molasses along with main product sugar in sugar industry are called as By-Products.

The valuation of these joint and by-products can be done under any of the following methods.

(1) Average Unit Cost Method

Under this method, joint costs are apportioned on the basis of average cost of the products. Average cost per unit is arrived at by dividing the total cost with the total output of all the products produced.

Applicability: This method can be used where the cost unit is same for all joint products and the products do not differ much from the other products.

Merits:

(i) Computations are easy and simple.
(ii) Cost of the products is determined in a uniform manner.

Demerits:

(i) If the products are measured in different cost units, then this method cannot be used.
(ii) Products of different grades and quality are assigned the same cost.
(iii) Profit ascertained may not be the real profit as the correct assignable cost may not be charged to different products of different grades and quality.
(iv) Costs determined by this method may not provide an appropriate basis for Price fixation.
(v) Not useful for managerial decision making.

Illustration 18

A producer of toys produces 4 different toys in the following quantities during the month of August:

Toy	*Quantity*
Bunny	2,000
Tom	6,000
Jerry	12,000
Mickey Mouse	10,000

Total cost incurred for all the toys amounted to Rs. 1, 20,000. Calculate cost of the four products using average cost method.

Solution

$$\text{Average cost per unit} = \frac{\text{Total cost incurred}}{\text{Total no. of toys produced}}$$

$$= \frac{1,20{,}000}{30{,}000}$$

= Rs. 4 per toy

Toy	*Quantity Produced*	*Average Cost (Rs.)*	*Cost of Product (Rs.)*
Bunny	2,000	4	8,000
Tom	6,000	4	24,000
Jerry	12,000	4	48,000
Mickey Mouse	10,000	4	40,000
Total	30,000		1,20,000

(2) Physical Measurement Method

Under this method, joint costs are apportioned based on the weight or volume of the products.

Applicability: This method can be used if there is a direct relationship between physical base or weight of the products and the cost incurred on them.

Merits:

(i) This method is appropriate when there is a direct relationship between the weight of the products and the cost incurred on them. The cost is apportioned on the basis of the number of units produced.

(ii) Computations are easy.

Demerits:

(i) This method cannot be used when joint products are expressed in different cost units.

(ii) Cost incurred on joint products may not be in proportion to their physical base.

(iii) The method may assign same cost per unit to a high quality joint product and a low quality joint product.

Illustration 19

In a manufacturing company, 20,000 kilolitres of 'X' is processed to produce 12,000 Kilolitres of 'Y' and 8,000 Kilolitres of 'Z'. The joint cost before separation point came to an amount of Rs. 48,000. From the given particulars, calculate the apportionment of joint cost and the profit of each product under physical measurement method if unit selling price of the products is Rs. 5 and Rs. 3.75

Solution

Total quantity of input of X used is 20,000 kl., to produce 12,000 kl. of Y and 8,000 Kl. of Z.

The ratio for apportionment is 3:2.

Apportionment of Joint cost according to physical measurement

		Y	*Z*	*Total*
(i)	Selling price per unit (Rs.)	5	3.75	
(ii)	No. of units	12,000	8,000	20,000
(iii)	Sales (Rs.)	60,000	30,000	90,000
(iv)	Allocated joint costs (3:2) (Rs.)	28,800	19,200	48,000
(v)	Profit *(iii)* – *(iv)* (Rs.)	31,200	10,800	42,000

(3) Weighted Average Method

In case of heterogeneous products, weighted average method provides a reasonable basis for the allocation of joint costs. Theoretically, this method is superior to the physical quantity method as this method assigns different weights to different products and recognizes the significant characteristics of the output. As the weight factors can reflect the varying amounts of time used and the other significant factors, there would be a positive correlation between these factors and the assigned values of weights. The most widely used weight factor is sale price.

According to this method, the output of each product is multiplied with the respective weight which reflects the collective differences among the products. Weights should be assigned to the products after carefully considering all the relevant characteristics of the product, so as to have reliable results.

Illustration 20

The joint cost incurred by the three products A, B and C is Rs. 22,000. Following are the outputs of the products A, B and C and the assigned weights.

Department	Output	Weight
A	400	1
B	250	2
C	350	4

Allocate the joint costs according to weighted average method.

Solution

Products	*Output*	*Weight*	*Weighted output*	*Ratio*	*Allocated Joint Cost (Rs.)*	*Cost per unit (Rs.)*
A	400	1	400	4/23	3,826	9.565
B	250	2	500	5/23	4,783	19.132
C	350	4	1,400	14/23	13,391	38.260
	1,000		2,300		22,000	

(4) Standard Cost Method

Standard Costs are determined for the products which are taken as the base for apportionment of joint costs to products. Efficiency of this method can be measured by the over recovery or under recovery of costs.

Applicability: This method can be easily adopted by concerns where Standard Costing is in operation.

Merits:

(a) The method does not involve frequent calculations, once standard cost has been determined.

(b) The method indicates the level of efficiency in production.

Demerits:

(a) The use of this method requires setting of standard costs. This involves time and money.

(b) The method may result in over or under recovery of cost.

(c) With change in circumstances, there will be a need to revise standard cost.

(5) Contribution or Gross Margin Method

The joint costs are divided into two types *viz.*, fixed costs and variable costs. Variable joint costs are apportioned to the products based on the output produced or on the basis of the weights of the products. Fixed costs are then apportioned based on the contribution made by each product.

Applicability: This method is applicable only if the joint costs can be separated as variable and fixed costs.

Merits:

(i) Calculations are simple and easy.

(ii) There is a systematic approach in apportionment of costs.

(iii) Apportionment of fixed cost will be subject to the capacity of the products to bear costs.

(iv) The method is suitable where prices of the products are known.

(v) Contribution of the products is taken as the base for apportionment of joint costs which is considered appropriate from managerial decision making point of view.

Demerits:

(i) Costs should be separated into fixed and variable costs.

(ii) It can be used with ease only if marginal costing system is adopted by the concern.

Illustration 21

A manufacturing company is producing three types of soaps Fairy, Snow White and Glamour at a cost of Rs. 149,000 including the fixed cost of Rs. 14,000. The quantities produced and sold are 4,000 soaps, 3,000 soaps and 2,000 soaps respectively and their respective selling prices are Rs. 15, Rs. 20 and Rs. 25 per soap. Apportion the variable cost. Fixed cost is to be approtioned on the basis of contribution margin and ascertain profit from each product.

Solution

Total variable cost = Total cost – Total fixed cost
= Rs. 1,49,000 – Rs. 14,000
= Rs. 1,35,000

Total output = 4,000 + 3,000 + 2,000 = 9,000 soaps

Variable cost per soap = Rs. 1,35,000/9,000
= Rs. 15 per soap

Statement of Apportionment of Joint Cost

Products	*Sales Value Rs.*	*Variable Cost Rs.*	*Contribution Margin (Rs.)*	*Apportioned*	*Profits (Rs.)*
				*Fixed cost**	*(4)-5)=(6)*
1	*2*	*3*	*4*	*5*	*6*
Fairy	4,000 × 15 = 60,000	4,000 × 15 = 60,000	0	0	NIL
S. white	3,000 × 20 = 60,000	3,000 × 15 = 45,000	15,000	6,000	9,000
Glamour	2,000 × 25 = 50,000	2,000 × 15 = 30,000	20,000	8,000	12,000
	1,70,000		35,000	14,000	21,000

* Total fixed cost of Rs. 14,000 is to be distributed to fairy, snow white and glamour in the ratio of their contribution margin, i.e., Nil: 15,000:20,000 or 0:3:4.
Thus fixed cost apportioned to
Fairy = Nil
Snow white = 14,000 × 3/7 = 6,000
Glamour = 14,000 × 4/7 = 8,000

(6) Market Value Method

Apportionment of joint costs on the basis of market value of joint products is the most popular and convenient method. The method is based on the consideration that joint costs should be charged to joint products according to their ability to absorb joint costs. Sales value of products reflects this ability. The cost of each joint product at split off point is obtained by reverse process moving backward from selling price to split off stage. In case one product sells at a higher price, it is believed that more costs have been expended to produce it and therefore larger share of joint costs should be allocated to it than the product with lower selling price. The method has two characteristics:

(i) All joint products enjoy uniform profit margin.

(ii) Changes in selling prices of joint products result in changes in their share in joint costs.

Applicability: The method can be used only where the sale price of joint products is market determined.

Merits:

(i) Computations are simple when market prices are given.
(ii) There is no scope for arbitrariness in apportioning costs.
(iii) All joint products have uniform profit margin.
(iv) Joint products share joint costs in proportion to their ability to bear joint costs.
(v) Method is good for external reporting.

Demerits:

(i) All joint products are not equally profitable. The method neglects this.
(ii) With every change in selling prices of joint products, the cost allocation will also change, though cost structure may remain unchanged.
(iii) It does not consider utilization of productive factors.
(iv) Selling prices of some joint products may be very stable while that of some others may fluctuate markedly. This may make apportionment of joint costs on the basis of market value quite illogical.

There are various variants of market value method.

(7) At the Point of Separation

Under this method the market price of each joint product at separation point is ascertained. Joint costs are apportioned to joint products in the ratio of their sales value at separation point. The method can be applied where such market prices are available .

Merits:

(i) Simple and easy to understand.

Demerits:

(i) It disregards even the logic of 'what the product can bear'.
(ii) Market prices at split off point are generally not available.
(iii) Market prices, even if available, may fluctuate requiring frequent illogical changes in cost allocations.

(8) Market Value after Further Processing

Difficulties in determining market values of joint products at split off point have led to apportionment of joint costs on the basis of market value after further processing. The method is based on the assumption that incurrence of further costs results in corresponding increase in sales value of products. The merit of the method is that market price of saleable products are easily available.

Illustration 22

In a manufacturing company, 20,000 kilolitres of 'X' is processed to produce 12,000 Kilolitres of 'Y' and 8,000 Kilolitres of 'Z'. The joint cost before separation point came to an amount of Rs. 48,000. From the following particulars, calculate the apportionment of joint cost and the profit of each product under *(a)* market value at separation point *(b)* market value after further processing.

	Y *Rs.*	*Z* *Rs.*
Unit selling price of at the separation point	5.00	3.75
Unit selling price after further processing	7.00	7.50
Further processing costs after separation	10,000	15,000

Solution

Computation of share of Joint costs according to Market value at Separation point

		Y	*Z*	*Total*
(i)	Selling price per unit (Rs.)	5	3.75	—
(ii)	No. of units	12,000	8,000	20,000
(iii)	Market value at separation point (Rs.)	60,000	30,000	90,000
(iv)	Allocated joint costs (2:1)* (Rs.)	32,000	16,000	48,000
(v)	Profit *(iii)* – *(iv)* (Rs.)	28,000	14,000	42,000

*Joint costs are allocated on the basis of market value at separation point i.e. 60,000:30,000 or 2:1.

Computation of share of Joint costs according to Market value after further processing

		Y	*Z*	*Total*
(a)	Selling price per unit (Rs.)	7	7.5	
(b)	No. of units	12,000	8,000	20,000
(c)	Market value after further processing (Rs.)	84,000	60,000	144,000
(d)	Allocated joint costs (7:5) (Rs.)	28,000	20,000	48,000
(e)	After separation costs (Rs.)	10,000	15,000	25,000
(f)	Profit *(iii)* – *(iv)* – *(v)* (Rs.)	46,000	25,000	71,000

(c) Market value less further processing cost to complete Individual Joint products

Under this method, further processing cost is deducted from the sales value of joint products for the purpose of calculating the ratio in which the joint costs are apportioned to joint products.

Illustration 23

From the following details of three products A, B and C, apportion joint costs on the basis of sales value less further processing cost method.

Joint Costs:	Rs.
Materials	9,000
Direct Labor	2,000
Overheads	1,000
Total Joint Cost	12,000

The three joint products were further processed and marketed as follows:

Products	*Further processing cost* *Rs.*	*Quantity produced* *Units*	*Selling price per unit* *Rs.*
A	1,000	200	25
B	2,000	50	120
C	2,000	100	90

Solution

Statement of Apportionment of Joint Cost

Product *(1)*	*Final sales value of products* *(2) Rs.*	*Post split off processing cost* *(3) Rs.*	*Sales less further costs* *(2) – (3) Rs.*	*Apportionment of joint costs* *Rs.*
A	5,000	1,000	4,000	(12,000 × 4,000)/15,000 = 3,200
B	6,000	2,000	4,000	(12,000 × 4,000)/15,000 = 3,200
C	9,000	2,000	7,000	(12,000 × 7,000)/15,000 = 5,600
	20,000	5,000	15,000	12,000

(d) Net Value or Net Realizable Value or Reverse Cost Method

Under this method computations are made backward from sales value of joint products to value at split off point. The following costs are deducted from sales value: (a) estimated profit margin (b) selling and distribution expenses (c) costs of processing after split off. The resultant figures after these deductions, represent the net realizable value at split off point. Joint costs are distributed to joint products in the ratio of these values.

Illustration 24

ABC Company is producing three products E, F and G. Joint manufacturing cost for the three products amounted to Rs. 1,20,000. The estimated profit margins on three products are 10%, 20% and 30% sales respectively. Subsequent costs are:

	E (Rs.)	F (Rs.)	G (Rs.)
Direct materials	20,000	50,000	16,000
Direct Labor	34,000	22,000	14,000
Overheads	6,000	8,000	10,000
Total subsequent costs	60,000	80,000	40,000
Sales	1,00,000	1,80,000	80,000

Prepare a statement showing apportionment of joint costs to products E, F and G.

Solution

Statement of apportionment of Joint Costs

Particulars	*Joint products*			*Total (Rs.)*
	E (Rs.)	*F (Rs.)*	*G (Rs.)*	
Sales	1,00,000	1,80,000	80,000	3,60,000
Less estimated profit (10%,20% and 30%)	10,000	36,000	24,000	70,000
	90,000	1,44,000	56,000	2,90,000
Less post split off processing costs	60,000	80,000	40,000	1,80,000
Net realizable value at split off point	30,000	64,000	16,000	1,10,000

Apportionment and Determination of Cost and Profit

Products	*Apportionment of joint cost*		*Post split off Cost (Rs.)*	*Total Cost (Rs.)*	*Sales (Rs.)*	*Profit (Rs.)*
(1)	*(2)*		*(3)*	*(2 + 3) (4)*	*(5)*	*(4 – 5) (6)*
E	1,20,000 × (30,000/1,10,000) =	32,727	60,000	92,727	1,00,000	7,273
F	1,20,000 × (64,000/1,10,000) =	69,818	80,000	1,49,818	1,80,000	30,182
G	1,20,000 × (16,000/1,10,000) =	17,455	40,000	57,455	80,000	22,545
		1,20,000	1,80,000	1,50,000	3,00,000	60,000

Illustration 25

Bright Chemicals Ltd. electrolyses common salt to obtain three joint products – caustic soda, chlorine and hydrogen. During a costing period, the expenditure relating to the inputs for the common process amounted to Rs. 3,50,000. After separation, expenses amounting to Rs. 1,60,000, Rs. 75,000 and Rs. 10,000 were incurred for caustic soda, chlorine and hydrogen respectively. The entire production was sold and Rs. 3,75,000; Rs. 2,50,000 and Rs. 60,000 were realized for caustic soda, chlorine and hydrogen respectively. The selling expenses were estimated at 5% of realizations from sale. The management expected profits @ 15%; 10% and 5% of realizations from sale of caustic soda, chlorine and hydrogen respectively.

Draw a columnar statement showing the apportionment of joint costs and the profitability of each product.

(I.C.W.A. Inter, Dec., 1991)

Solution

Statement showing the Apportionment of Joint Costs and Profitability

Particulars	*Caustic Soda* *Rs.*	*Chlorine* *Rs.*	*Hydrogen* *Rs.*	*Total* *Rs.*
Realisations from sale	3,75,000	2,50,000	60,000	6,85000
Less: Expected Profits				
(15%, 10% and 5% on realization)	56,250	25,000	3,000	84,250
Estimated Total Cost	3,18,750	2,25,000	57,000	6,00,750
Less: Selling Expenses (5% on realization)	18,750	12,500	3,000	34,250
Estimated Cost of Production	3,00,000	2,12,500	54,000	5,66,500
Less: Separation Cost	1,60,000	75,000	10,000	2,45,000
Estimated share of Joint Cost Estimated	1,40,000	1,37,500	44,000	3,21,500
Percentage of Share of Joint Cost in the Total Joint Cost	43.5%	42.8%	13.70%	100%
Actual share of Joint Cost (43.5:42.8:13.75)	1,52,250	1,49,800	47,950	3,50,000
Add: Post Separation Cost	1,60,000	75,000	10,000	2,45,000
Actual Cost of Production	3,12,250	2,24,800	57,950	5,95,000
Add: Selling Expenses (5% on realization)	18,750	12,500	3,000	34,250
Total Cost	3,31000	2,37,500	60,950	6,29,250
Profit (Loss) (Balancing figure)	44,000	12,700	–950	55,750
Sales	3,75,000	2,50,000	60,000	6,85,000

SUMMARY

There are mainly two methods of ascertaining the cost of products manufactured or services rendered. Process Costing is one such method which is employed in the industries where production moves from one process or department to the next until its final completion and there is a continuous mass production of identical units through a series of processing operations.

Industries using Process Costing in their manufacturing area include chemical processing, oil refining, pharmaceutical, plastics, paints and varnish, soaps, textiles, paper, brick and tile manufacturing, semiconductor chips, beverages and breakfast cereals. It is very useful in bottling companies, canning plants, packing and industries involved in processing milk products.

Main elements of Production Cost in Process Costing are Material, Labor and Production Overheads. In the process of manufacturing a product, there is bound to be some loss and the number of units introduced may not be equal to the output. This loss can be normal or abnormal. The loss could be waste or scrap or spoilage or defectives.

Process Costing deals with continuous type of production. In the Process Costing, when the work is not completed, such unfinished work is called work-in-progress, the accounting for such work in progress is done in terms of Equivalent Production.

In both, opening and closing work-in-progress, equivalent units are calculated for all elements of cost viz., Direct Materials, Direct Labor and Production Overheads. For the purpose of calculation of Equivalent Production, three statements are prepared viz., Statement of Equivalent Production; Statement of Cost per Unit and Statement of Evaluation.

If both opening and closing work-in-progress are given in the process, then, equivalent units of production for a period can be calculated in any of the three ways *viz.*, First-In-First Out, Average Weighted Method and Last-In-First Out Method. However, the first two methods are the most widely used methods.

In certain processes, two or more products are produced from the same process and some products may have almost equal value and importance and some products have relatively smaller value. Former products are called Joint Products and later products are called By- Products. The valuation of these joint and by-products can be done under any of the methods *viz.*, Physical Measurement Method, Average Unit Cost Method, Weighted Average Method, Standard Cost Method, Contribution or Gross Margin Method and Market Value Method.

Glossary

- **Process Costing:** is the costing method applicable where goods or services result from a sequence of continuous or repetitive operations or processes. Costs are averaged over the units produced during the period
- **Waste:** that part of basic raw material which is lost in processing without possessing any recovery value
- **Scrap:** is the incidental residue from certain types of manufacture, usually of small amount and low value, recoverable without further processing
- **Spoilage:** is that part of production which does not meet the required quality standards
- **Defectives:** When the production does not meet the quality standards, such products are treated as defectives.

These defective products can be rectified and brought up to the standard by incurring additional cost known as rectification cost

- **Normal Loss:** During the production process some loss is unavoidable on account of inherent nature of production and is acceptable to production process. Such loss is called normal loss
- **Abnormal Loss:** Where the actual output is less than the expected output, the difference is called as abnormal loss. It is over and above the normal loss
- **Inter-Process Profit:** The difference between the transfer price and the cost is known as Inter-Process Profit made by the transferor process from the transfer of output to the subsequent process
- **Equivalent Unit:** is a measure that applies a percentage of completion factors to partially completed units, to calculate the equivalent number of whole units, produced in an accounting period
- **Joint and By- Products:** In certain processes, two or more products are produced from the same process and some products may have almost equal value and importance and some products have relatively small value. Former products are called Joint Products and later products are called By- Products.

Questions

(1) Explain the features of Process Costing and give examples as to where Process Costing is applicable.
(2) Bring out the differences between Process Costing and Job Costing.
(3) Write short notes on Waste, Scrap, Defectives and Spoilage.
(4) Write short notes on Abnormal Loss and Abnormal Gain in Process Costing.
(5) Explain 'Equivalent Production'.
(6) What are Equivalent units of production? Explain the two principal methods of calculating Equivalent Units.
(7) What is By – Product and how is it different from Joint Product? Give a few examples of each.
(8) What are the various methods of accounting for by-products? Briefly explain each of the methods.
(9) Explain what is meant by 'Reverse Cost Method' in By-Product Cost Accounting.
(10) Write short notes on 'Accounting for By-Product'.

PROBLEMS

(1) A product is obtained after passing through three processes. The following information is collected for Jan 2007.

	A	*B*	*C*
Materials (Rs.)	8,690	5,818	5,724
Labor (Rs.)	4,000	8,000	12,000
Output in units	1,350	1,310	1,000
Normal loss	3%	4%	10%
Value of scrap (Rs.)	2	3	6

Additional Information

1,500 units @ Rs. 9 each was introduced in Process A. There was no stock of materials or W.I.P. at the beginning or at the end of month. The production overheads were Rs. 18,000 to be charged on wages.
Prepare Process accounts indicating Normal loss, Abnormal loss and Abnormal gain.
[**Ans.:** Cost per unit: Process A – Rs. 20; Process B – Rs. 36; Process C – Rs. 62]
(**Note:** Production Overheads Rs. 18,000 is distributed in the proportion of wages i.e. 4:8:12)

(2) The product of a company passes through three distinct processes to completion. They are known as A, B, and C. From the past experience it is ascertained that loss is incurred in each process as: Process A-2%, Process B-4%, Process C-5%, In each case, the percentage of loss is computed on the number of units entering the process concerned.
The Loss of each process possesses a scrap value. The loss of process A is sold at Rs. 5 per 100 units, B is sold at Rs.10 per 100 units and that of process C at Rs. 20 per 100 units.
The output of each process passes immediately to the next process and the finished units are passed from process C into stock.

	Processes		
	A *Rs.*	*B* *Rs.*	*C* *Rs.*
Materials consumed	3,000	5,000	7,000
Direct Labor	4,000	4,000	4,720
Manufacturing expenses	2,710	4,425	5,000

10,000 units have been issued to process A at a cost of Rs. 5,000. The output of each process has been as under: Process A 9,700; Process B 9,500; Process C 8,900
There is no work-in-progress in any process.
Prepare Process Accounts. Calculation should be made to the nearest rupee.

[**Ans.:** Cost per unit: Process A – Rs. 1.5; Process B – Rs. 3; Process C – Rs. 5; Abnormal Loss transferred to Costing P&L *a/c* – Rs. 745 and Abnormal Gain transferred to Costing P&L *a/c* – Rs. 545]

(3) In Process B, 50 units of a commodity was transferred from process A at cost of Rs. 910. The additional expenses incurred by the process were Rs. 130. 20% of the units entered are normally lost and sold @ Rs. 4 per unit. The output of the Process was 50 units. Prepare Process B Account and Abnormal Gain Account.

[**Ans.:** Abnormal Gain: 10 Units at Rs. 250; Cost Per Unit – Rs. 25]

(4) A product passes through three processes 1, 2, and 3. The normal wastage of each process is as follows: Process 1-3%, Process 2-4%, Process 3-5%. Wastage of Process 1 was sold @ 0.4 paisa per unit. Process 2 @ 0.60 paisa per unit and that of Process 3 @ 0.8 paisa per unit. 7,500 units were issued to Process1 on 1-4-2007 @ Re.1/-. The other costs were:

	1	*2*	*3*
Sundry Materials (Rs.)	1,750	1,125	2,250
Labor (Rs.)	1,250	2,000	2,750
Direct Expenses (Rs.)	1,230	1,036	727
Actual Output	7,125	6,900	6,275

Prepare Process Accounts assuming that there was no opening or closing stock. Give the Abnormal Wastage and Abnormal Gain Accounts.

[**Ans.:** Cost per unit: Process 1 – Re. 1.60; Process 2 – Rs. 2.25; Process 3 – Rs. 3.20; Abnormal Loss transferred to Costing P&L A/c – Rs. 852 and Abnormal Gain transferred to Costing P&L A/c – Rs. 99]

(5) Textiles industries planned for process. The material produced in three consecutive processes is as follows:

Particulars	*Process 1*	*Process 2*	*Process 3*
Raw materials used	750 tonnes	—	—
Cost per tonne	Rs. 150	—	—
Manufacturing wages and expenses	Rs. 84,750	Rs. 11,730	Rs. 880
Weight lost (% of input of the process)	4%	10%	2%
Scrap (sale price Rs.50 per tonne)	75 tonnes	30 tonnes	5 tonncs
Sale price per tonne	Rs. 310	Rs. 420	Rs. 450

Management expenses were Rs. 3,000 and selling expenses Rs. 5,800. Two third of the output of Process 1 and one third of the output of Process 2 are passed on to the next process and the balances are sold. The entire output of Process 3 is sold. Prepare the three process accounts and a statement of profit. Make approximations, wherever necessary.

[**Ans.:** Cost per unit: Process 1 – Rs. 300; Process 2 – Rs. 390; Profit in Process 1 – Rs. 2,150; Profit in Process 2 – Rs. 7,140; Profit in Process 3 – Rs. 3,360; Net Profit – Rs. 3,850]

(6) In process A, 200 units of raw materials were introduced at a cost of Rs. 2,000. The other expenditure incurred by the process was Rs.1,660. Of the units introduced, 10% are normally lost in the course of manufacture and they possess a scrap value of Rs.3 each. The output of Process A was only 150 units.

Prepare Process A Account and Abnormal Loss Account.

[**Ans.:** Cost of Abnormal Loss: Rs. 600; Abnormal Loss transferred to Costing P&L A/c – Rs. 510]

(7) The information given below is extracted from the cost accounts of a factory producing a commodity in the manufacture of which three processes are involved. Prepare Process Cost Accounts showing the cost of the output and the cost per unit at each stage of manufacture. The value at which units are to be charged to process II and III is the cost per unit of processes one and two respectively.

(a) Wastages are normal and have no realizable value.

(b) Opening and closing stock represent units received from previous process on which no further work has been done in the process concerned.

Process No.	*1(Rs.)*	*2(Rs.)*	*3(Rs.)*
Direct Wages	2,200	3,690	4,200
Machine Expenses	1,200	800	1,000
Factory on Cost	800	1,250	750
Raw Materials consumed	7,000	—	—
	Units	*Units*	*Units*
Input	1,850	—	—
Wastage	120	190	190
Stock on 1-1-2007	—	210	420
Stock on 31-1-2007	—	410	70

[**Ans.:** Finished Output – 1,500 Units at Rs. 25,540]

(8) A product passes through two processes A and B to completion. Output of Process A is transferred to Process B at cost plus 20% and finished goods is similarly transferred to Finished Stock a/c at cost plus a profit of 20% on transfer price. On 31st December 2007, the following information is given to you:

Particulars	*Process A* Rs.	*Process B* Rs.
Materials	10,000	30,000
Labor	15,000	21,000
Closing Stock (valued at prime cost)	5,000	15,000

Out of the finished stock, stock valued at Rs. 30,000 was in hand and the rest was sold for Rs. 60,000. Prepare the Processes and Finished Stock Accounts.

[**Ans.:** Cost of Closing Stock: Process A – Rs. 5,000; Process B – Rs. 14,200 and Finished Stock Account – Rs. 22,720; Actual Profit Realized – Rs. 25,920]

(9) Kalinga manufacturing company manufactures a product that passes through three different processes. Prepare process accounts and finished stock account from the information given below:

	Process A Rs.	*Process B* Rs.	*Process C* Rs.
Direct Materials	30,000	7,500	7,500
Wages	22,500	15,000	15,000
Closing Stock	7,500	8,750	21,300

Finished goods were sold for Rs. 1,30,000 and the value of finished stock at closing was Rs. 5,612. It is the policy of the company to charge 25% on cost price while transferring goods from process A to B and 20% on cost price from B to C to finished stock.

[**Ans.:** Cost of Closing Stock: Process A – Rs. 7,500; Process B – Rs. 7,500; Process C – Rs. 16,500 and Finished Stock Account – Rs. 3,623; Actual Profit Realized – Rs. 67,623]

(10) Product 'A' passes through three processes, before it is transferred to the finished stock. The following information is obtained for the month of July:

	Process I Rs.	*Process II* Rs.	*Process III* Rs.	*Finished Stock* Rs.
Opening Stock	10,000	16,000	20,000	40,000
Direct Materials	80,000	24,000	30,000	—
Direct Wages	70,000	80,000	70,000	—
Manufacturing Overhead	40,000	48,000	40,000	—
Closing Stock	20,000	8,000	30,000	60,000
Profit % on transfer to next process	25%	20%	10%	—
Inter-process profit for opening stock	——	2,790	5,380	13,068

Stock in process is valued at prime cost and finished stock has been valued at the price at which it is received from process III. Sales during the period were Rs. 8,00,000. Prepare Process Cost Account.

[**Ans.:** Cost of Closing Stock: Process I – Rs. 20,000; Process II – Rs. 6,604; Process III – Rs. 21,930 and Finished Stock Account – Rs. 40,396; Actual Profit Realized – Rs. 3,42,168]

(11) In Process X, on 1 March, there was no Opening Work-in-Progress. During the month of March, 1,500 units of material were issued at a cost of Rs. 13,500. Labor and overheads totaled Rs. 6,750 and Rs. 4,950 respectively. On 31st March, 1,125 units were completed and transferred to the next process. On the remaining 375 units, which are incomplete, degree of completion was as follows:

Materials	100%
Labor	60%
Overheads	20%

Prepare: (a) Statement of Equivalent Production
(b) Statement of Cost
(c) Statement of Evaluation
(d) Process Account

[**Ans.:** Equivalent Production: Material – 1,500 units; Labor – 1,350 units and Overheads – 1,200 units; Material Cost per Unit – Rs. 9; Labor Cost per Unit – Rs. 5; Overhead Cost per Unit – Rs. 4.15; Cost of Finished Stock – Rs. 20,391; Cost of Closing Work-in-Progress – Rs. 4,809]

(12) In a manufacturing process opening work-in-progress is valued according to FIFO method. Opening work in progress showed 300 units, 30% completed, valued as follows:

	Rs.
Materials	3,200
Labor	2,500
Overheads	3,300
Total	9,000

In the month of April , materials introduced into the production was Rs. 38,250, labor employed and wages paid were Rs. 29,640 and overheads incurred were Rs. 24,700. Finished production taken into stock in the month was 2,100 units. There was no loss in the process.

At the end of April, the work in progress stock was 400 units, 60% complete as regards to material and 40% as regards to labor and overheads.

You are required to compute equivalent production and prepare process account.

[**Ans.:** Equivalent Production: Material – 2,250 units; Labor – 2,170 units and Overheads – 2,170 units; Material Cost per Unit – Rs. 17; Labor Cost per Unit – Rs. 13.659; Overhead Cost per Unit–Rs. 11.382; Cost of Finished Stock – Rs. 93,503; Cost of Closing Work-in-Progress – Rs. 8,087]

13. Process 2 receives units from Process I and after carrying out work on the units, transfers them to Process 3. For the accounting period, the relevant data were as follows:

Opening WIP 200 units (25% complete) valued at Rs. 5,000

800 units received from Process I valued at Rs. 8,600

840 units were transferred to Process 3

Closing WIP 160 units (50% complete)

The costs of the period were Rs. 33,160 and no units were scrapped.

Required: Prepare the Process Account for Process 2 using the Average Cost method of valuation.

(CA., Inter, Nov., 1995)

[**Ans.:** Equivalent Production: Material – 920 units; Labor – 920 units and Overheads – 920units; Average Cost per Unit – Rs. 50.826; Cost of Finished Stock – Rs. 42,694; Cost of Closing Work-in-Progress – Rs. 4,066].

14. Data relating to work done in Process 'A' of a company during the month of April 2003 is given below:

Opening Work-in-progress (1,000 units)

	Rs.
Materials	40,000
Labour	7,500
Overheads	22,500

	Rs.
Materials introduced in Process 'A' (19,000 units)	7,40,000
Direct Labor	1,79,500
Overheads	5,38,500

Units scrapped	1,500 units
Degree of completion:	
Material	100%
Labor and Overheads	80%
Units finished and transferred to Process 'B'	17,500 units

Normal Loss: 5% of total input including opening WIP.

Scrapped units fetch Rs. 20 per piece.

Required: (a) Statement of Equivalent Production (b) Statement of Cost (c) Statement of distribution of Cost (d) Process 'A' Account and other Accounts.

(ICWA, Inter, Dec., 2000)

[**Ans.:** Equivalent Production: Material – 19,000 units; Labor and Overheads – 18,700 units; Material Cost per Unit – Rs. 40; Labor Cost per Unit – Rs.10; Overhead Cost per Unit–Rs. 30; Cost of Finished Stock – Rs. 14,00,000; Cost of Closing Work-in-Progress – Rs. 72,000; Abnormal Loss Rs. 36,000].

15. The following information is given in respect of Process No. 3 for the month of January 2003. Opening Stock – 2,000 units made-up of:

Direct Materials – I	Rs. 12,350
Direct Materials – II	Rs. 13,200
Direct Labour	Rs. 17,500
Overheads	Rs. 11,000

Transferred from Process No. 2: 20,000 units @ Rs. 6.00 per unit
Transferred to Process No. 4: 17,000 units
Expenditure incurred in Process No. 3:

Direct Materials	Rs. 30,000
Direct Labour	Rs. 60,000
Overheads	Rs. 60,000

Scrap: 1,000 units – Direct Materials 100%, Direct Labour 60%, Overheads 40%
Normal Loss 10% of production.
Scrapped units realized Rs. 4 per unit.
Closing Stock: 4,000 units – Degree of completion: Direct Materials 80%, Direct Labour 60%, Overheads 40%.
Prepare Process No. 3 Account using average price method, along with necessary supporting statements.

(CA., Inter, May 2001)

[**Ans.:** Equivalent Production: Material – I – 20,200 units; Material – II – 19,400 units, Labor 18,600 units and Overheads – 17,800 units; Material – I Cost per Unit – Rs. 6.1955; Material – II Cost per Unit – Rs. 2.2268, Labor Cost per Unit – Rs. 4.1667; Overhead Cost per Unit–Rs. 3.9888; Cost of Finished Stock – Rs. 2,81,822; Cost of Closing Work-in-Progress – Rs. 48,290].

16. In manufacturing the main product A, a company processes, the resulting waste material into two by-products M1 and M2. Using the method of working back from sales value to an estimated cost, you are required to prepare a comparative profit and loss statement of the three products from the following data:
(i) Total cost up to separation point was Rs. 1,36,000.

	A	M_1	M_2
(ii) Sale (all production)	Rs. 3,28,000	Rs. 32,000	Rs. 48,000
(iii) Cost after separation	—	Rs. 9,600	Rs. 14,400
(iv) Estimated Net Profit % to Sale Value	—	20%	30%
(v) Estimated Selling Expenses as % of sale value	20%	20%	20%

(ICWA, Inter, June, 1989)

[**Ans.:** Profit: Product A - Rs. 1,45,600; Product M1 - Rs. 6,400; Product M2 - Rs. 14,400].

17. In a concern engaged in process industry, four products emerge from a particular process of operation. The total cost of input for the period ended 30th September, 2003 is Rs. 2,53,500. The details of output, additional cost after "split-off point" and sales value of the products are appended below:

Product	*Output (kg.)*	*Additional Processing Cost after split-off point (Rs.)*	*Sales value (Rs.)*
A	8,000	60,000	1,68,000
B	5,000	10,000	1,10,000
C	3,000	—	60,000
D	4,000	20,000	90,000

If the products are sold at 'split-off point' without further processing the sales value would have been

Product	*Rs.*
A	1,15,000
B	90,000
C	55,000
D	80,000

You are required to prepare a statement of profitability based on the products being sold:
(g) After further processing, and
(ii) At the split-off point.

(ICWA, Inter, Dec., 1989)

[**Ans.:** (i) Profit: Product – A Rs. 27,000; Product – B Rs. 25,000; Product – C Rs. 15,000; Product – D Rs. 17,500; (ii) Profit: Product – A Rs. 29,527; Product – B Rs. 22,897; Product – C Rs. 13,993; Product – D Rs. 20,353].

18. In a process line of XY Company, three joint products are produced. For the month of May, 2003, the following data were available:

Products	*L*	*M*	*N*
Sales Price per kg.	5	10	20
Post-separation point costs (Rs.)	10,000	5,000	15,000
Output in kg.	2,500	1,000	1,500

Pre-separation point costs amounted to Rs. 20,000.
The joint products are manufactured in one common process, after which they are separated and may undergo further individual processing. The pre-separation point costs are apportioned to joint products according to weight. You are required to prepare a statement showing the estimated profit or loss for each product and in total.

(ICWA, Inter, June, 1990)

[**Ans.:** Profit: Product – L Rs. (7,500); Product – M Rs. 1,000; Product – N Rs. 9,000].

19. In a manufacturing company, 10,000 kilolitres of 'A' is processed to produce 6,000 kilolitres of 'B' and 4,000 kilolitres of 'C'. The joint cost before separation point came to an amount of Rs. 24,000. From the following particulars, calculate the apportionment of joint cost and the profit of each product under *(a)* physical measurement, *(b)* market value at separation point and *(c)* market value after further processing.

	B	*C*
Unit Selling Price at separation point	5.00	3.75
Unit Selling Price after further processing	7.00	7.50
Further Processing Costs after separation	5,000	7,500

(ICWA, Inter, June, 1992)

[**Ans.:** *(a)* B: Rs. 14,400 and Rs. 15,600; C: Rs. 9,600 and 5,400
(b) B: Rs. 16,000 and Rs. 14,000; C: Rs. 8,000 and 7,000
(c) B: Rs. 14,000 and Rs. 23,000; C: Rs. 10,000 and 12,500]

20. In a manufacturing process, in the course of manufacture of the product X, the by-products P and Q also emerge. The pre-separation expenses amount to Rs. 1,19,550. All the three products are processed further and sold in the market (details given below)

	Main Product X	*By-products*	
		P	*Q*
Sales value (Rs.)	90,000	60,000	40,000
Post-separation costs (Rs.)	6,000	5,000	4,000
Profit as a percentage of sales	25	20	15

Total fixed selling and distribution expenses are 10% of the total cost of sales and are apportioned to the three products in the ratio of 20:40:40.

(i) Prepare a statement showing the apportionment of pre-separation costs to the main product and the two by-products.
(ii) If the by-product P is not processed further and can be sold just after separation at Rs. 58,500 without incurring any selling and distribution expenses, would you advise its disposal at that stage?

(I.C.W.A., Inter, June, 1994)

[**Ans.:** X - Rs. 58,510; P – Rs. 37,020; Q – Rs. 24,020. It is advisable to sell By-Product P at split-off stage without further processing]

21. Work out the estimated pre-separation costs per ton of by-products Y and Z from the following data:
Costs of manufacture before separation: Rs. 25,60,000
Main product is X.
There are two by-products Y and Z whose normal selling prices are as under:
Sales price of Y — Rs. 500 per ton
Sales price of Z — Rs. 800 per ton
Selling and distribution expenses have been estimated to be 25% of selling price and the net profit is expected to be 10% of selling price. Costs to manufacture each ton after separation from the main product are: Rs. 95 for by-product Y; Rs. 145 for by-product Z; Assume equal weight for Y and Z.

(I.C.W.A., Inter, Dec., 1994)

[**Ans.:** Y – Rs. 230; Z – Rs. 375]

22. Two products P and Q are obtained in a crude form and require further processing at a cost of Rs. 5 for P and Rs.4 for Q per unit before sale. Assuming a net margin of 25 per cent on cost, their sale prices are fixed at Rs. 13.75 and Rs. 8.75 per unit respectively. During the period, the joint cost was Rs. 88,000 and the outputs were:
P – 8,000 units; Q – 6,000 units
Ascertain the Joint Cost per unit.

(CA., Inter, May, 1998)

[**Ans.:** P – Rs. 8; Q – Rs. 4]

❑ ❑ ❑

15

OPERATING COSTING

Objectives

The objectives of the study are to:

- Adapt the approach according to different services *viz*. Transport Costing, Boiler House Costing, Power House Costing, Canteen Costing, Hospital Costing and Hotel Costing
- Determine the suitable cost unit to be used for cost ascertainment purpose.

INTRODUCTION

Operating Costing is also known as Service Costing. According to Institute of Cost and Management Accountants (UK) Operating Costing is "that form of Costing which applies where standardized services are provided either by an undertaking or by a service cost center within an undertaking". It is a method of costing applied in undertakings which provide service rather than production of commodities.

Examples of service organizations are transport companies (shipping, railways, roadways, airways), catering services (hotels, canteens, cafeteria), public utility services (gas, electricity, steam generation, hospitals, educational institutions), professional services (accounting firms, management consultants, real estate firms).

- The main characteristics of service organizations are:
- Activities are usually labor intensive
- Cost unit is usually difficult to define and
- Major inputs and outputs cannot be stored.

The following cost units are usually applied in different service undertakings

Nature of Business	*Cost Unit*
Electricity supply	per kilowatt hour
Public carriers, trucks, goods trains	per tonne km or per km
Passenger buses and trains	per km
Hospitals	per patient day per bed, per operation
Road maintenance	per km of road
Hotels	per room
Road lighting	per lamp
Canteen	per meal

Collection of Costing Data

Costs are accumulated under various headings suitable for cost control and for decision making. Costs collected are usually grouped under fixed costs and variable costs. The format in which cost data is presented depends upon the nature of the industry and the need of the management.

Classification of Costs in Operating Costing

The following costs are incurred in operating businesses.

(1) Variable or running charges

(2) Maintenance charges

(3) Fixed or standing charges

The cost per unit is calculated as follows:

$$\text{Cost per service unit} = \frac{\text{Total costs for the period}}{\text{Number of service units in the period}}$$

Transport Costing

Transport industries include Air, Water, Road and Railways. Transportation of goods and services happens to be a major economic activity in every country. In a Transport Operating Company, Costing consists of determining the cost of operating a vehicle and the application of cost to a particular unit i.e. per tonne, per mile, per tonne-mile etc. The cost per unit is calculated by taking into account the factors such as type and bulk of goods carried and distance covered etc.

Objectives of Transport Costing

The following are the objectives of Transport Costing

(1) Analyze the Operating Costs: It is useful to analyze operating costs such as cost of petrol, repair expenses, wages etc.

(2) Control the costs: It facilitates control of standing charges and running costs of the vehicle.

(3) Assign cost: It assigns costs to services rendered by each vehicle or group of vehicles.

(4) Compare the costs: It compares the cost of using alternative models of transport with the cost of existing one and compares the cost of running and maintenance of different vehicles.

(5) Fix the service charge for internal transport: Transport costing is used for fixing the charges for using the service of internal transport or the charges for hiring the vehicle.

Examples for costs on Transport Costing

Running Charges:

- Petrol
- Oil
- Grease

Maintenance charges:

- Repairs and maintenance
- Tyres
- Garage charges

Standing Charges:

- Insurance
- Garage costs
- Driver's wage

- Depreciation
- Taxes

The operating cost of the transport company is classified under the following 3 categories:

(A) Operating and Running Charges:- Running costs are the costs of operation, which may vary more or less in direct proportion of distance covered and includes the cost of fuel, lubricants, grease, wear and tear of tyres and wages and salaries of drivers and cleaners. These expenses are variable in nature, because they are dependent on distance covered and trips made.

(B) Maintenance Charges: These are semi-variable in nature and include wear on tyres, repairs and overhauls, painting, hire of spare vehicles when firm's own vehicles are under repairs and garaging etc.

(C) Fixed and Standing Charges: Insurance, tax, depreciation and parts of drivers wages, interest on capital, general supervision, salary of operating managers are items under the category of fixed or standing charges.

The Proforma Cost Sheet for a Transport Company is as under.

XYZ Transport Company Ltd.

COST SHEET

For the month of ——————

Expenses	*Vehicle 1*	*Vehicle 2*	*Vehicle 3*	*Total*
(A) Operating Costs:				
Petrol				
Engine Oil				
Lubricating Oil				
Wages of Drivers				
Depreciation				
Total				
(B) Maintenance Costs:				
Tyres and Tubes				
Repairs Painting Charges				
Overhauling				
Total				
(C) Fixed Costs:				
Garage Rent				
Insurance				
Motor Vehicle Tax				
License Fee				
General Supervision				
Interest on Capital				
Total				
Grand Total (A+B+C)				
Kilometres run				
Load carried (tonnes)				
Days on road				
Capacity utilization				
Cost per tonne km.				
Operating				
Maintenance				
Fixed				

Collection of Cost Data

Each vehicle is given a distinct number. Accumulation and control of costs in Transport Costing are achieved through a daily log sheet and operating cost sheet. An Operating Costing System is a document which contains information regarding each trip.

Daily Log Sheet

Vehicle No. Date:

Driver's Name: Starting Time:

Route No. Returning Time:

Licence No.

Particulars of Journey

Trip No.	*Place From*	*Place To*	*Towns or Packages*		*Kilometres*	*Time*		*Remarks*
			Out	Collected on Route		Out	In	

Supplies
Petrol:
Oil:
Grease:

Time of Workers
Driver:
Mechanic:
Cleaner:
Conductor:

Analysis for Delay
Accident:
Traffic Delay:
Loading/unloading:
Others:

Cost Units

In Transport Costing, tonne per km. or passenger per km. is generally the cost unit. After collecting total cost, the cost per unit is determined. The cost per passenger km. or cost per tonne km. is ascertained as follows:

Cost per passenger or tonne km. = No. of vehicles × Capacity × distance of one trip × No. of days × Passengers travelled/weight carried

Illustration 1

The following statistical data are available regarding the monthly cost of operating 2 trucks by a transport co.:

	Truck No 1 (Rs.)	*Truck No 2 (Rs.)*
Drivers Salaries	6,000	7,500
Cleaners Wages	3,000	3,250
Petrol	750	1,000
Mobile Oil	50	75
Garage Rent	1,250	1,250
Taxes and Insurance	750	750
Depreciation	1,000	1,250
Expenses of Supervision	1,000	1,000
Repairs	420	440
Miscellaneous Overhead	400	400

Both the trucks carried 150 tonnes of goods each during the month of November 2008. The distance covered were 3,500, kms and 5,000 kms respectively.

You are required to prepare an Operating Cost Sheet for November, 2008 from the above data.

Solution

Tonne kms of operation of the 2 trucks are as follows:-

Truck No. 1:

150 tonne × 3,500 kms = 5,25,000 tonne-kms

Truck No. 2:

150 tonne × 5,000 kms = 7,50,000 tonne-kms

Operating Cost Sheet for the month of November, 2008 (Rs. in '000)

Particulars	*Truck No.1* *(Rs.)*	*Truck No.2* *(Rs.)*
Fixed Costs		
Garage Rent	1,250	1,250
Taxes and Insurance	750	750
Supervision	1,000	1,000
Salaries of Drivers	6,000	7,500
Wages of Cleaners	3,000	3,250
Total (a)	12,000	13,750
Variable Costs:		
Petrol	750	1,000
Mobile Oil	50	75
Depreciation	1,000	1,250
Repairs	420	440
Miscellaneous Overheads	400	400
Total (b)	2,620	3,165
Total Cost of Operation (a + b)	14,620	16,915
Cost per tonne-kms (paisa)	2.78	2.25

Note: It is assumed that depreciation charged is based on distance covered, hence taken as Variable Cost.

Illustration 2

You are required to prepare a suggested fare per passenger km. from the following information for a mini bus:

(a) Length of route:30 kms

(b) Purchase price Rs.4,00,000

(c) Part of above cost met by loan, annual interest of which is Rs.10,000 pa.

(d) Other annual charges:

	Rs.
Insurance	15,000
Garage Rent	9,000
Road Tax	3,000
Repairs and Maintenance	15,000
Administration Charges	5,000
Running Expenses:	
Drivers and Conductors salary p.m.	5,000
Repairs/Replacement of Tyres and Tubes p.a.	3,600
Diesel and Oil Cost per km.	5

(e) Effective life of vehicle is estimated at 5 yrs at the end of which it will have a scrap value of Rs.10,000.

(f) Mini bus has 20 seats and is planned to make 6 two way trips for 25 days p.m.

(g) Provide profit @ 20% of total revenue.

Solution

Statement showing the calculation of Suggested Fare

Particulars	*Cost p.a (Rs.)*	*Cost p.m. (Rs.)*
Fixed Expenses		
Interest on Loan	10,000	
Insurance	15,000	
Garage Rent	9,000	
Road Tax	3,000	
Repairs and Maintenance	15,000	
Administration Charges	5,000	
Depreciation (3)	78,000	
	1,35,000	11,250
Running Expenses		
Drivers and Conductors salary		5,000
Repairs/Replacement of Tyres and Tubes	3,600	300
Diesel and Oil cost 9,000 Kms (1) × Rs. 5		45,000
		61,550.00
Add: 20% on Total Revenue (25% of Total Cost)		15,387.50
Total Revenue		76,937.50

Rate per passenger kms. = Total Revenue/Total passenger kms.

Rs. 76,937.50/1, 80,000 passenger kms (W/N 2) = Rs. 0.43 or 43 paisa.

Working Notes:

(1) Total distance traveled by mini bus in 25 days

Length of route (2 Sides) × No. of trips per day × No. of days

60 kms × 6 trips × 25 days = 9,000Kms

(30 Kms × 2 sides i.e. to and fro trip = 60 Kms.)

(2) Total passenger – Kms

Total distance traveled in 25 days × No of seats.

9,000 kms × 20 seats = 1,80,000 passenger Kms.

(3) Depreciation per annum:

(Purchase Price — Scrap Value)/Estimated Life

(Rs. 4,00,000 – Rs. 10,000)/ 5 yrs = Rs. 78,000

Illustration 3

There are two warehouses for storing finished goods in a factory. Warehouse A is at a distance of 10 km and Warehouse B at a distance of 15 km. from the factory. A fleet of 5-tonne Lorries is engaged in transporting the finished goods from the factory. The records show that the Lorries average a speed of 30 km. per hour when running and regularly take 40 minutes to load at the factory. At Warehouse 'A' unloading takes 30 minutes per load while at Warehouse B it takes 20 minutes per load.

Drivers' wages, depreciation, insurance and taxes amount to Rs.18 per hour operated. Fuel, oil, tyres and maintenance cost Rs. 2.40 per kilometer. You are required to draw up a statement showing the cost per tonne kilometre for carrying the finished goods to the two warehouses.

(I.C.W.A.I., Inter, Dec., 1984)

Working Notes:

Calculation of Operating Time

Particulars	*Warehouses*	
	A *Minutes*	*B* *Minutes*
Distance from warehouse to factory		
A – (10 km. @ 30 km. per hour); A – (15 km. @ 30 km. per hour);	20	30
Return Journey	20	30
Loading	40	40
Unloading	30	20
Total Operating Time	110	120
	1 hr. 50 minutes	2 hrs.

Calculation of Operating Charges: per Tonne- Km.

Particulars	*Warehouses*	
	A	*B*
Total tonne-kms. A – (5 tonne × 10 km.); B – (5 tonne × 15 km.):	50.00	75.00
Running charges per Km. (Rs.)	2.40	2.40
Standing charges per hour (Rs.)	18.00	18.00

Calculation of Operating cost per tonne-km.

Particulars	*Warehouse – A*	*Rs.*	*Warehouse – B*	*Rs.*
Running Expenses	(20 km. × Rs. 2.40)	48	(30 km. × Rs. 2.40)	72
Standing Charges	(1 hr. 50 minutes × Rs. 18)	33	(2 hrs. × Rs. 18)	36
Total Operating Cost		81		108
Operating Cost per tonne-km.	(Rs. 81/50)	1.62	(Rs. 108/75)	1.44

Illustration 4

A truck starts with a load of 10 tons of goods from station-P. It unloads 4 tons at station-Q and rest of the goods at station-R. It reaches back directly to station-P after getting reloaded with 8 tons of goods at station-R. The distance between P to Q, Q to R and then from R to P are 40 km., 60 km and 80 km. respectively. Compute 'Absolute tonne-km' and 'commercial tonne-km'.

(CA, Inter)

Solution

			Ton-km
(a)	Absolute tonne-km		
	Station P to station Q	40 km × 10 tonne	400
	Station Q to station R	60 km × 6 tonne	360
	Station R to station P	80 km × 8 tonne	640
			1,400
(b)	Commercial tonne-km		
	Station P to station R	80 km × 10 tonne	800
	Station R to station P	80 km × 8 tonne	640
			1,440

Illustration 5

A manufacturing company runs its boiler on furnace oil obtained from X oil company and Y oil company whose depots are situated at a distance of 24 kms and 16 kms from the factory site.

Transportation of furnace oil is made by company's own tank lorries (two) of 8 ton capacity each. Onward trips are made with full load and the lorries return empty. The filling time take an average of 40 minutes of X oil company and 30 minutes for Y oil company. The empty time in the factory is only 40 minutes for each. The average speed of lorries work out to 24 km per hour.

The varying operating charges average 80 paise per km covered and fixed charges gives an incidence of Rs. 7.50 per hour of operation.

Calculate the transportation cost per tonne-km for each source of furnace oil.

Solution

Calculation of Variable Cost

	Distance X	*Distance Y*
One side distance	24km	16km
Round trip	48km	32km
Variable Cost@0.80 per km	Rs.38.40	Rs.25.60

Calculation of Fixed Cost

	Distance X	*Distance Y*
Actual running time for round trip distance at the speed of 24 km per hour		
X : (48 km/24 km) 60 min		
Y : (32 km/24 km) 60 min	120 min	80 Min
Filling time	40 Min	30 Min
Empty time	40 Min	40 Min
Total time	200 Min	150 Min
Fixed cost @ Rs. 7.50 per hour (200 × 7.50)/60, (150 × 7.50)/60	Rs. 25	Rs. 18.75
Calculation of ton km :		
Capacity (full load)	8 tons	8 tons
Distance with full load	24 km	16km
Tons Km	192	128
Cost per ton km : **X** (38.40 + 25)/192	Re. 0.33	
Y (25.60 + 18.75)/128		Re. 0.347

BOILER HOUSE COSTING

A Boiler House produces steam which is used for power generation, air conditioning and air compression. The main purpose of Boiler House Costing is to ascertain the cost of steam produced. There are many factors such as steam pressure, evaporation, meter reading, distribution to different processes, factory heating, main losses, etc. which should be taken into consideration before ascertaining the cost of 1000 lbs. of steam raised.

Following are the important items of costs relating to Boiler House Costing:

(a) **Supervision:** It includes the wages of foreman and a portion of the salary of works engineer supervision besides other services in the factory.

(b) **Labour:** The labor involved is as (1) Coal handlers (2) Stokers (3) Ash remover

(c) **Maintenance:** The maintenance of Boiler House requires furnace repairs, renewal of fire bars and replacement of fire irons.

(d) **Indirect Material:** This includes the items of small value ranging from service materials to small tools.

(e) **Fuel:** The fuel includes coal or furnace oil.

(f) **Water:** This includes the cost of purification, softening and the cost of supply.

(g) **Fixed overheads:** It includes rates and taxes, depreciation on Plant and Building, insurance and possibly interest on capital.

BOILER HOUSE COST SHEET

Period: ________

Steam produced in 1000 lbs ____
Less boiler house use _______
Mains Losses _______
Total Consumption ______

Particulars	*Current Period*	*Previous Period*	*% increase (or) decrease*	*Remarks*
(1) **Fuel And Labor** Coal and Fuel Oil Electric Power Fuel Handling Ash Removal Disposal Stokers and Coal Wheelers				
(2) **Water** Purchased Softening				
(3) **Indirect Material** Small Tools Service Material				
(4) **Indirect Labor** Supervision Sweeper Cleaner General Laborers, etc.				
(5) **Maintenance** Fixed Plant Meters Boilers Softening Plant Coal Bunkers Furnace Mechanical Stokers Steam Service Pipe Barriers Weighing Machine Other Accessories				
(6) **Fixed Overheads:** Rent Rates, etc. Depreciation on Plant Interest on Capital Steam Mains Allocation of General Factory Overheads				
Total				

Illustration 6

The Boiler House is one of the service departments of a company. Steam is raised and then transferred to production departments and other service departments as required.

The basic monthly budget figures for 2008 are as follows:

Boilers Operating Hours	480
Steam Raised kgs.	80,00,000
Costs:	*Rs.*
Fuel (Variable) (Rs.)	19,200
Chemicals(Variable) (Rs.)	960
Wages (Fixed) (Rs.)	2,400
Sundry Overheads (Rs.)	3,000

The actual figures for February 2008 are as follows:

Steam Raised: kgs	67,50,000
Boiler Operating Hours	432
Costs:	*Rs*
Fuel (Variable) (Rs.)	18,000
Chemical (Variable) (Rs.)	990
Wages (Fixed) (Rs.)	2,200
Sundry Overhead (Fixed) (Rs.)	3,000

It is expected that the price of chemicals for all output will fall by 2% where the boiler operates in excess of 480 hours per month. Sundry fixed costs are expected to fall by Rs. 200 where the boiler is operated for less than 425 hours and to increase from the normal level by Rs. 250 where the boiler is operated for more than 480 hours.

Variable costs vary in proportion to boiler hours.

(a) Prepare a budget summary which shows the cost of the Boiler House in total and per 1,000 kg steam for boiler operating levels of 400,432,480 and 540 hours.

(b) Prepare a Control Statement which compares budget with actual cost of the Boiler House for February where a flexible budgeting system is in operation. Comment on the variance in the statement.

Solution

***(a)* Budget Summary**

Boiler Operating Hours	400.00	432.00	480.000	540.000
Steam Raised (000 Kgs)	6,667.00	7,200.00	8,000.000	9,000.000
Costs:				
Fuel (Variable) (Rs. 40)	16,000.00	17,280.00	19,200.000	21,600.000
Chemicals(Variable) (Rs. 2 per hour)	800.00	864.00	960.000	1,058.400
Wages (Fixed)	2,400.00	2,400.00	2,400.000	2,400.000
Sundry Overheads (Fixed)	2,800.00	3,000.00	3,000.000	3,250.000
Total	22,000.00	23,544.00	25,560.000	28,308.400
Cost ('000 Kg)	3.30	3.27	3.195	3.145

Chemicals price fall by 2% in excess of 480 hours p.m.

Rs. 2 – 2% of Rs. 2 = Rs. 1.96

Cost = 540 × 1.96 = Rs. 1,058.40

***(b)* Control Statement for the month of February**

	Budget	*Actual*	*Variances*
Boiler Operating Hours	432	432	
Steam Raised (000 Kgs)	7,200	6,750	450 (A)
Costs	*Rs.*	*Rs.*	*Rs.*
Fuel (Variable)	17,280	18000	720 (A)
Chemical (Variable)	864	990	126 (A)
Wages (Fixed)	2,400	2,200	200 (F)
Selling Overheads (Fixed)	3,000	3,000	
Total	23,544	24190	646 (A)

Power House Costing

Electricity can be generated by use of either steam or fuel oil. If steam is used for the generation of electricity, a separate Boiler House Cost Sheet is not prepared. Instead, a Power House Cost Sheet is prepared and this facilitates the ascertainment of not only cost of steam but cost of electricity also.

The Cost Department will permanently notice fuel cost, labor cost and the maintenance costs relating to steam raised. Other information of technical nature is watched by engineers.

Power House Operating Cost Sheet

Steam Produced: __________ Steam used for generation of electricity:

Units of electricity generated:

Particulars	*Current Period*	*Previous Period*	*Remarks*
Steam Production Costs:			
Coal			
Water			
Water Softeners			
Wages			
Coal Handling			
Stoking			
Stores			
Repairs and Maintenance			
Depreciation			
Supervision			
Total			
Less: Used In Heating			
Steam Used for Electricity Generation			
Electricity Generation Costs:			
Steam			
Wages			
Stores			
Repairs and Maintenance			
Depreciation			
Supervision			
Interest on Capital			
Total			

Illustration 7

The Iron and steel works which generates its own electricity for the purpose of using the same for running the factory, gives the following information: (per quintal)

(1) Fuel coal consumed during the month: 1,000 quintals @ Rs. 12 per quintal
(2) Oil: 15 quintals @ Rs. 1,000 per quintal p.m.
(3) Water: 2,00,000 litres p.m. @ Re. 1.00 per 1,000 litres.
(4) Cost of steam boiler Rs. 50,000 which has the residual value of Rs. 2,000. The life of steam is 10 years.
(5) Salaries and wages for the boiler house:
    (a) 20 men @ Rs. 150 per month
    (b) 40 men @ Rs. 60 per month
(6) Share of administration charges: Rs. 1,050 per month.
(7) Sale of ash Rs. 300
(8) Generating Plant cost Rs. 1,50,000. Depreciation @ 10%
(9) Repairs and Maintenance of Steam Boiler and Generating Plant Rs. 1,000 p.m.

(10) Salaries and wages for the generating plant:
- *(a)* 10 skilled workers @ Rs. 300 per month.
- *(b)* 15 skilled workers @ Rs. 100 per month.

(11) No of units generated 2,00,000.

(12) 1/10 of units generated were used by generating department itself.

Calculate cost per unit for electricity generated.

(Madurai Kamraj, Nov., 1991)

Solution

Cost Sheet of Iron and Steel works

		P.M. (Rs.)	*Total (Rs.)*
Coal : consumed 1,000 × 12		12,000	
Oil: 15 × Rs. 1,000		15,000	
Water: 2,00,000 litres @ Re. 1 per 1,000 litres		200	
Depreciation of Steam Boiler			
(Cost – Scrap)/Life (50,000-2,000/10)/12 months		400	
			27,600
Less: Sale of ash (for the month)			300
			27,300
Salary and wages of Boiler House			
(a) 20 men @ Rs. 150 per month		3,000	
(b) 40 men @ Rs. 60 per month		2,400	
Salary and Wages of Generating Plant			5,400
Steam Production Cost			**32,700**
(a) 10 skilled workers @ Rs. 300 per month.		3,000	
(b) 15 skilled workers @ Rs. 100 per month.		1,500	4,500
Repairs and Maintenance			1,000
Depreciation of Generating Plant (1,50,000 × 10% × 1/12)			1,250
Share of Administration Charges			1,050
Total	(90%)		40,500
Add: cost of Electricity used in generation	(10%)		4,500
	(100%)		45,000

Total No. of units generated	2, 00,000 units
Less: 10% used by Generating Dept.	20,000 units
Net	1,80,000 units

For 1, 80,000 units, Cost is Rs. 40,500

For 20,000 units, Cost will be (20,000 × 40,500)/1, 80,000 = Rs. 4,500

Cost per unit Rs. 45,000/1,80,000 is Rs. 0.25.

Illustration 8

From the following data pertaining to the year 200-10, prepare a cost sheet showing the cost of electricity generated per unit of KWH by Chambal Thermal Power Station.

Total units generated	20,00,000 kwh
Operating Labor	Rs. 50,000
Repairs and Maintenance	Rs. 50,000
Lubricants, Spares and Stores	Rs. 40,000
Plant Supervision	Rs. 30,000
Administration Overheads	Rs. 20,000

Coal consumed per KWH for the year is 2.5 kg @ Rs. 0.02 per kg. Depreciation charge is 5% on capital cost of Rs. 2,00,000.

Solution

Operating cost sheet for the year 2009-10

	Total Cost *Rs.*	*Cost Per kwh* *Rs.*
Fixed Expenses:		
Plant Supervision	30,000	0.015
Administration Overhead	20,000	0.010
Depreciation @ 5% on Rs. 2,00,000	10,000	0.005
Total (a)	60,000	0.030
Variable Expenses:		
Coal	1,00,000	0.050
Operating Labor	50,000	0.025
Repairs and Maintenance	50,000	0.025
Lubricants and Supplies	40,000	0.020
Total (b)	2,40,000	0.120
Total Cost (a + b)	3,00,000	0.150

Coal consumed is 2.5 kg × 20,00,000 × 0.02 = Rs. 1,00,000

HOSPITAL COSTING

The main purpose of Hospital Costing is to ascertain the cost of providing medical services. There are different departments in a hospital, which are generally formed on the basis of the functions performed by them. The following are the main departments in a hospital:

(1) Out Patient Department
(2) Wards
(3) Medical Services Departments as Diagnostic, X-rays, Radiotherapy and Pathology etc.
(4) General Service Departments, Boiler House, if any, power, heating, lighting, etc: catering, laundry, medical records, workers maintenance, administration, etc.
(5) Miscellaneous Services Departments such as Transport, Dispensary, Cleaning, etc.

Cost of the above (5) departments will have to be apportioned to the other departments on equitable basis. Cost of other department can be determined separately with reference to the units of cost, which are given below:

(1) Out Patient Department	Per out patient attended
(2) Wards	Per new patient attended
(3) Medical Service Departments	
(a) Radiotherapy	Per course of treatment per day
(b) Diagnostic X-Rays	Per 100 units weighted points value
(c) Pathology	Per 100 requests
(4) General Service Departments	
(a) Boiler House	Per 1,000 Lbs steam raised
(b) Heating, Lighting etc.	Per 1,000 cubic feet
(c) Catering	Per person fed per week
(d) Laundry	Per 100 articles laundered
(e) Medical Records	Per weighted unit
(f). Workers Maintenance	Per 1,000 cubic feet
(g) Administration	Suitable % of turnover

The expenses of a hospital can be broadly divided into 2 categories:

(1) Capital expenditure and

(2) Maintenance expenditure: This includes salaries and wages, provision for staff uniforms and clothing, patient clothing, medical and surgical appliances and equipment, fuel, light and power, laundry, water etc.

Services are measured in terms of 'bed-days available' or 'bed-days occupied'. For an operation theatre, cost can be expressed in terms of 'each operation'. Similarly, 'Inpatient-day' might be used as a cost unit for kitchen and laundry; 'outpatient visit' might be used as a cost unit for out-patient departments.

Illustration 9

A Hospital operates a zero bed capacity Special Health Care Department. The said department levies a charge of Rs. 425 per bed day from the patient using its services. The data relating to fees collected and costs for the year 2008 are as under:

	Rs.
Fees collected during the year	34,95,625
Variable Cost based on patient days	13,57,125
Departmental Fixed Cost	6,22,500
Apportioned Cost of the Hospital Administration	10,00,000

Besides the above, nursing staff were employed as per the following scale at Rs. 48,000 p.a. per nurse.

Annual Patient Days	*No. of nurses required*
< 5,000	3
5,000-7,000	4
7,000-9,000	6
>9,000	8

The projections for the year 2009 are as under:

- The cost other than apportioned Overheads will go up by 10%
- The apportioned Overheads will increase by Rs. 2,50,000 p.a.
- The salary of the nursing staff will increase to Rs. 54,000 p.a per nurse.

The occupancy of the bed capacity is not likely to increase in 2009 and consequently the management is actively considering a proposal to close down the department. In that event, the Departmental Fixed Cost can be avoided.

Required:

(i) Present a Statement to show the profitability of the department for the years 2008 and 2009.

(ii) Calculate the:

- Break-even bed capacity for the year 2009.
- Increase in fee per bed required to justify continuance of the department.

Solution

***(a)* Statement of Profitability of Health Care Department for the years 2008 and 2009**

	Year 2008 Rs.	*Year 2009* Rs
Fees Collected (425 per bed day)	34,95,625	34,95,625
Less Variable Cost 2009: (13,57,125 + 10% of 13,57,125)	13,57,125	14,92,837
Total Contribution: (A)		
8,225 bed days × Rs. 260	21,38,500	
8,225 bed days × Rs. 243.5		20,02,788
Fixed Costs:		
Departmental Fixed Cost (4*)	6,22,500	6,84,750
Apportioned Fixed Cost	10,00,000	12,50,000
Nursing staff (6 nurses × Rs. 48,000) (6 nurses × Rs. 54,000)	2,88,000	3,24,000
Total Fixed Cost: (B)	19,10,500	22,58,750
Profit (loss): (A – B)	2,28,000	–2,55,962

Working Notes

(1) Total No. of bed days of occupancy: Total fees collected/Fee per bed day
34,95,625/425 —— 8,225

(2) Variable cost per bed day:

Variable cost per bed day (2008)	Rs. 165.00
Rs. 13,57,125/8,225	
Variable cost per bed day Rs. (2009)	
Rs. 165 + (10% of Rs. 165)	Rs. 181.50

(3) Contribution per bed day

Contribution per bed day (425–165)	260
Contribution per bed day (425–181.50)	243.50

*(4) Departmental Fixed Costs

Departmental Fixed Costs: 2008	Rs. 6,22,500
Departmental Fixed Costs: 2009	Rs. 6,84,750
(6,22,500 + 10% of 6,22,500)	

(5) Nurses Required: Patient days 8,225 are in between 7,000 – 9,000. Hence, six nurses are required.

***(b)* Break even bed capacity for the year 2009**

Total Fixed Costs/Contribution per bed day
22,58,750/243.50 ——— 9,276 bed days (approx).
This is not a valid answer because for 9,276 bed days nurse service required will be as follows.

Nursing staff	8
Remuneration of 8 nursing staff (8 nurses × Rs. 54,000)	Rs. 4,32,000
Departmental Fixed Costs	Rs. 6,84,750
Apportioned Fixed Costs	Rs. 12,50,000
Total Fixed Costs	Rs. 23,66,750

Break-even point Rs. 23,66,750/Rs. 243.50 —— 9,720 bed days

(c) Increase in fee per bed day required to justify continuance of the Special Health Care Department.

Desired Contribution Rs.	22,58,750.00
Bed days of Occupancy	8,225.00
Contribution per bed day Rs. (22,58,750/8,225) *(a)*	274.62
Variable Costs: *(b)* Rs.	181.50
Required fee per bed day: $(a + b)$ Rs.	456.12
Increase in fee per bed day (456.12 – 425 i.e. original fee) Rs.	31.12

CANTEEN COSTING

Now–a– days, many organizations provide the facilities of canteen to workers. Mostly, the intention is to provide subsidized meals with good food stuff. For the purpose of subsidized cost allocation, it may be considered as a service by the Company and the cost accumulation procedure may be oriented accordingly.

Most factory/office canteens are either fully or partly subsidized. Usually, the supervisor who is accountable to the personnel manager or to the works manager runs the canteen, which normally provides main meals, snacks and tea.

Following are the main items of costs relating to Canteen Costing:

(1) *Provision:* It includes items such as meat, fish, poultry, cakes, milk, tea, coffee, flour, soft drinks, etc.

(2) *Labor:* It includes the wages and salaries of canteen staff such as supervisors, cooks, waiters, kitchen assistants and porters.

(3) *Services:* It includes steam, gas, electricity, power, lighting and water.

(4) *Consumable stores:* It will include table linen, cutlery, crockery, glass ware, mops, washing up cloths, drying up cloth, cleaning materials, dustpans and brushes etc.

(5) *Overheads:* These charges include rent, rates, depreciation, insurance, etc.

On the other hand, the receipt from running a canteen may include:

(i) Company Subsidy and

(ii) Sale of Coupons: Usually coupons of different colors are issued to workers, according to the type of meal provided (main meal, snacks, tea, etc.).

Canteen Cost Sheet

Month: Total Cost No. of meals estimated Actual

Items	*Budgeted this month*	*Actual cost to date*	*Remarks*
(1) Wages and salaries:			
Canteen Managers			
Supervisors			
Cooks			
Helpers			
(2) Provision:			
Meat, Fish and Eggs			
Vegetables			
Fruits			
Bread and Cakes			
Biscuits			
Milk			
Soft Drinks, etc.			
(3) Services:			
Steam and Gas			
Electricity			
Power and Light			
(4) Miscellaneous Expenditure:			
Rent and Rates			
Depreciation			
Insurance			
Maintenance			
Total Cost			
Less: Company Subsidy			
Net Cost			
Profit or Loss			
Sales			

Illustration 10

Bright Future Company Ltd. runs a canteen for the welfare of its workers and provides necessary subsidy to the canteens. During the month of August 2008, the following purchases were made:

Commodity	*Quantity (Kgs.)*	*Rate per kg (Rs)*
(1) Tea	4	150
(2) Sugar	50	20
(3) Milk (Litres)	60	24
(4) Atta	210	31
(5) Maida	20	28
(6) Vegetable Ghee	30	210
(7) Besan	12	35
(8) Dal	30	56
(9) Potato	100	10
(10) Green Vegetables	20	12
(11) Spices	2	200

The other expenses for the month were:

Auto Rickshaw Fare	Rs. 100
Salary to Cook (1)	Rs. 2,000 p.m
Salary to Waiters (2)	Rs. 1,000 p.m each
Supervisors Salary	Rs. 4,000 p.m
Fuel, Gas, Coal, etc	Rs. 1,000
Miscellaneous (Crockery and Glassware)	Rs. 1,500
Depreciation on Utensils and Furniture	Rs. 500

Sale of Coupons 7,800 @ Rs. 3.00 per coupon.

Prepare operating cost statement of the canteens for the month of August and find out the amount of subsidy paid by the company.

	Tea	*Sugar*	*Atta*
Opening Balance (kgs)	2	10	30
Closing Balance (kgs)	1	5	20

Solution

Operating Cost Statement of the canteens for the month of August

Opening Stock	*Rs.*	*Rs.*
Tea (2 Kg × Rs. 150)	300	
Sugar (10 Kg × Rs. 20)	200	
Atta (30 Kg × Rs. 31)	930	1,430
Add Purchases:		
Tea (4 Kg × Rs. 150)	600	
Sugar (50 Kg × Rs. 20)	1,000	
Milk (60 litre × Rs. 24)	1,440	
Atta (210 Kg × Rs. 31)	6,510	
Maida (20 Kg × Rs. 28)	560	
Vegetable Ghee (30 Kg × Rs. 210)	6,300	
Besan (12 Kg × Rs. 35)	420	
Dal (30 Kg × Rs. 56)	1,680	
Potato (100 Kg × Rs. 10)	1,000	
Green Vegetables (20 Kg × Rs. 12)	240	
Spices (2 Kg × Rs. 200)	400	20,150
		21,580
Less: Closing Stock		
Tea (1 Kg × Rs. 150)	150	
Sugar (5kg × Rs. 20)	100	
Atta (20 Kg × Rs. 31)	620	870
Cost of Consumption		20,710
Add:		
Auto Rickshaw Fare	100	
Fuel and Gas	1,000	
Salary to Cook (1)	2,000	
Salary to Waiters (2) 1,000 × 2	2,000	
Salary to Supervisor	4,000	
Miscellaneous (Crockery and Glassware)	1,500	
Deprecation	500	11,100
Total Operative Cost for the Month		31,810
Less: Sale of Coupons (7,800 @ Rs. 3.00)		23,400
Subsidy paid by the Company		8,410

HOTEL COSTING

Hotel industry is a service industry and covers various activities like provision of food and accommodations and provides other comforts like recreation, business facilities, and shopping areas for shopping facilities, etc. In order to provide the service, the industry is required to incur various expenses - fixed and variable. Fixed expenses comprise of staff salaries, repairs and renovation, interior decoration, laundry contract, sundries and depreciation on fixed assets. Variable expenses include lighting charges, attendants' salaries, power charges etc.

Illustration 11

A Lodging Home is being run in a small hill station with 50 single rooms. The home offers concessional rates during six off season months in a year. During this period, half of the full room rent is charged. The management's profit margin is targeted at 20% of the room rent. The following are the costs estimated and other details for the year ending 31st March 2008 (assume a month to be of 30 days):

(a) Occupancy during the season is 80% while in the off –season it is 40% only;

(b) Expenses:

	Rs.
Staff Salary (excluding Room Attendant)	2,75,000
Repairs to Building	1,30,500
Laundry and Linen	40,000
Interior and Tapestry	87,500
Sundry Expenses	95,400

(c) Annual depreciation is to be provided for buildings at 5% and on furniture and equipment at 15% on straight line basis.

(d) Room attendants are paid Rs. 5 per room-day on the basis of occupancy of the rooms in a month.

(e) Monthly lighting charges are Rs. 120 per room, except in 4 months of winter when it is Rs. 30 per room and this cost is on the basis of full occupancy for a month.

(f) Total investment in the home is Rs.100 lakhs of which Rs. 80 lakhs relate to building and balance for furniture and equipments.

You are required to work out the room rent chargeable per day both during the season and the off-season months, on the basis of the information provided above.

Solution

Working Notes

		Room Days
(1)	No. of room days in a year	
	Season's occupancy for 6 months @ 80%	
	(50 × 80% × 6 months × 30 days)	7,200
	Off Season's occupancy for 6 months @ 40%	
	(50 × 40% × 6 months × 30 days)	3,600
	Total	10,800 p.a.
(2)	Total full room rent days	
	Season	7,200
	Off-season (in terms of 50% rate on 3,600 days)	1,800
		9,000 p.a.

Statement showing the working of room rent chargeable per day during the season and the off season:

(1) Total estimated cost for the year ending 31-3-2008

	Rs.
Salary	2,75,000
Repairs to Building	1,30,500
Laundry and Linen	40,000
Interior and Tapestry	87,500
Sundry Expenses	95,400
Depreciation 5% of Rs. 80 lakhs (Buildings)	4,00,000
Depreciation 15% of Rs. 20 lakhs (Furniture)	3,00,000
Total Estimated Cost	13,28,400

(2) Attendant's salary for 10,800 room days @ Rs. 5 per day **54,000**

(3) Lighting Charges:

	Rs.
During 6 months season@ Rs. 4 for 7,200 days (Rs. 120/30 days = Rs. 4)	28,800
During 2 months season@ Rs. 4 for 1,200 days (i.e. 2/6 of 3,600)	4,800
During 4 months of winder @ Re. 1 for 2,400 days (i.e. 4/6 of 3,600)	2,400
Total Lighting Charges	**36,000**

Total Estimated Cost (1 + 2 + 3)	**14,18,400**
Total Full Room Rent Days 9,000 p.a. (2)	
Cost per Room Day (14,18,400/9,000)	157.60
Add: Profit Margin at 20% of rent or 25% of Cost	39.40
Room Rent	197.00

During season, room rent of Rs. 197 is to be charged.

During off season, room rent of Rs. 98.50 is to be charged (50% of Full Room Rent)

Illustration 12

PQ Ltd. plans to start a lodging house at a tourist centre with a capacity of 32 single-occupancy rooms. Costs per day per room have been estimated as under.

Costs per day per room	(*Rs.*)
(A) When occupied	
(a) Electricity and utilities	4
(b) Linen, laundry and sanitary supplies	9
(c) Dusting, sweeping and cleaning	2
	15
(B) When unoccupied	2

Over and above these costs, the following expenses represent the estimate of fixed charges per annum (i.e. 365 days):

	(Rs.)
Staff expenses	3,20,000
Other office expenses	64,000
Rates, taxes, insurance, maintenance and depreciation	42,320
	4,26,320

PQ Ltd. defines 100% occupancy to mean all the 32 rooms to fetch revenue for all the 365 days. You are required to answer the following, using planning period of one year:

(i) What should be the tariff per day per room in order to reach break-even at an occupancy level of 50%?
(ii) What would be the profits if the occupancy level reaches: (a) 60%, (b) 70% and (c) 80% respectively?
(iii) What would be the profits, if the tariff per day is reduced by 10% from the answer in (i) above and the occupancy level is 100%?

(I.C.W.A.I., Inter, Dec., 1994)

Solution

(1) Total No. of room days at 100% occupancy per annum
= 32 single rooms × 365 days = 11,680 room days

(2) Total No. of room days at 50% occupancy p.a. = 11,680 × 50/100 = 5,840 room days

(i) Calculation of tariff to reach break-even at 50% occupancy level:

	(Rs.)
Fixed Charges	4,26,320
*Dusting, sweeping and cleaning charges Rs. 2 per day at 100% occupancy level (Rs. 2 × 32 × 365)	23,360
Variable Costs when rooms are occupied (Rs. 13 × 32 × 365) 50/100	75,920
Total cost at 50% occupancy level	5,25,600

*Dusting, sweeping and cleaning charges of Rs. 2 per day are taken at 100% occupancy level as it has to be paid whether rooms are occupied or not occupied.

Tariff to be fixed per room per day to reach the Break-even at 50% occupancy
= Rs. 5, 25,600/5,840 room days = Rs. 90 per day.

(ii) Calculation of Profit at different occupancy levels:

Profit at 60% occupancy level = 11,680 room days × 10/100 × (Rs. 90 – Rs. 13)
= Rs. 89,936

Profit at 70% occupancy level = 11,680 room days × 20/100 × (Rs. 90 – Rs. 13)
= Rs. 1,79,872

Profit at 80% occupancy level = 11,680 room days × 30/100 × (Rs. 90 – Rs. 13)
= Rs. 2,69,808

(iii) Calculation of Profit if tariff per day is reduced by 10%
i.e. (Rs. 90 – Rs. 9 = Rs. 81) and the occupancy level is at 100%
100% occupancy level = 11,680 room days

	(Rs.)
Fixed Charges	4,26,320
Dusting, sweeping and cleaning charges Rs. 2 per day at 100% occupancy level (Rs. 2 × 32 × 365)	23,360
Variable Costs when rooms are occupied (Rs. 13 × 32 × 365)	1,51,840
	6,01,520
Profit (Balancing figure)	3,44,560
Total revenue (11,680 × Rs. 81)	9,46,080

SUMMARY

Operating Costing is also known as Service Costing. It is a method of costing applied in undertakings which provide service rather than production of commodities. Examples of service organizations are transport companies (shipping, railways, roadways, airways), catering services (hotels, canteens, cafeteria), public utility services (gas, electricity, steam generation, hospitals, educational institutions), professional services (accounting firms, management consultants, real estate firms).

In service organizations, activities are usually labor intensive, cost unit is usually difficult to define and major inputs and outputs cannot be stored. Costs are accumulated under various headings suitable for cost control and for decision making. Costs collected are usually grouped under fixed costs and variable costs.

Transport industries include Air, Water, Road and Railways. In a Transport Operating Company, Costing consists of determining the cost of operating a vehicle and the application of cost to a particular unit, i.e., per tonne, per mile, per tonne-mile etc. The operating cost of the transport company is classified into Operating and Running Charges, Maintenance Charges and Fixed or Standing Charges.

A **Boiler House** produces steam which is used for power generation, air conditioning and air compression. The important items of costs relating to Boiler House Costing are Supervision, Labor, Maintenance, Indirect Material, Fuel, Water and Fixed Overhead.

Electricity can be generated by use of either steam or fuel oil. If steam is used for the generation of electricity, a separate Boiler House Cost Sheet is not prepared. Instead, a **Power House** Cost Sheet is prepared and this facilitates the ascertainment of not only cost of steam but electricity also.

The main purpose of **Hospital Costing** is to ascertain the cost of providing medical services. There are different departments in a hospital, which are generally formed on the basis of functions performed by them. The main departments in a hospital are Out Patient Department, Wards, Medical Services Departments, General Service Departments, Boiler House, if any, and Miscellaneous Services Departments.

Now–a–days, many organizations provide the facilities of canteen to workers. Mostly, the intention is to provide subsidized meals with good food stuff. The main items of costs relating to **Canteen Costing** are Provisions, Labor, Services, Consumable Stores and Overheads. On the other hand, the receipt from running a canteen may include Company Subsidy and Sale of Coupons.

Hotel industry is a service industry and covers various activities like provision of food and accommodations and provides other comforts like recreation, business facilities, and shopping areas for shopping facilities, etc.

Glossary

- **Operating Costing:** that form of Costing which applies where standardized services are provided either by an Undertaking or by a Service Cost Centre within an Undertaking.

Questions

(1) What do you mean by Operating Costing? Describe its essential features.
(2) What is Operating Cost? Name the industries where Operating Costing Method is applicable.
(3) Draw a Proforma Cost Sheet of a Transport Company.
(4) Explain briefly various Service Industries where Operating Costing Method is applicable.

PROBLEMS

(1) Mr. Jaidka owns a fleet of taxis and the following information is available from the records maintained by him:

(i)	Number of taxis	10
(ii)	Cost of each taxi	Rs. 20,000
(iii)	Salary of Manager	Rs. 600 p.m.
(iv)	Salary of an Accountant	Rs. 500 p.m.
(v)	Salary of Cleaner	Rs. 200 p.m.
(vi)	Salary of Mechanic	Rs. 400 p.m.
(vii)	Garage rent	Rs. 600 p.m.
(viii)	Insurance premium	5% p.a.
(ix)	Annual tax	Rs. 600 per taxi
(x)	Drivers' salary	Rs. 300 p.m.
(xi)	Annual repairs	Rs. 1,600 per taxi

Total life of taxi is about 2,00,000 kms. A taxi runs in all 3,000 kms. in a month of which 30% it runs empty. Petrol consumption is one litre for 10 kms. @ Rs. 1.80 per litre. Oil and other sundries are Rs. 5 per 100 kms. Calculate the cost of running a taxi per km.

(I.C.W.A., Inter, Dec., 1983)

[**Ans.:** Cost per effective km. run per taxi Rs. 0.85]

(2) The Union Transport Company has been given a twenty kilometre long route to ply a bus. The bus costs the company Rs. 1,00,000. It has been insured at 3% per annum.
The annual road tax amounts to Rs. 2,000. Garage rent is Rs. 400 per month. Annual repair is estimated to cost Rs. 2,360 and the bus is likely to last for five years.

The salary of the driver and the conductor is Rs. 600 and Rs. 200 per month respectively in addition to 10% of takings as commission to be shared equally by them. The manager's salary is Rs. 1,400 per month and stationery will cost Rs. 100 per month. Petrol and oil will cost Rs. 50 per 100 kilometres. The bus will make three round trips per day carrying on an average 40 passengers in each trip. Assuming 15% profit on takings and that the bus will ply on an average 25 days in a month, prepare Operating Cost Statement on a full year basis and also calculate the bus fare to be charged from each passenger kilometre.

(CA., Inter, May, 1992)

[**Ans.:** Bus fare to be charged per passenger km. = Rs. 7.20]

(3) The Holiday Hotel has 40 bedrooms with a maximum occupancy of 490 sleeper nights per week. Average occupancy is 60% throughout the year. Meals provided to guests have been costed and the average food cost per person per day is as follows:

	Rs.
Breakfast	3.60
Lunch	11.00
Dinner	13.40

Direct wages and staff meals per week are as under:

	Rs.
Restaurants and kitchens	3,430
House keeping	1,952
General	1,760

Direct expenses per annum are Rs. 45,760 and housekeeping Rs. 52,000 for the restaurant. Indirect expenses amounted to Rs. 3,41,120, which should be based on floor area occupied by various cost centres. The floor areas are:

	Sq. m.
Bedrooms	3,600
Restaurant	1,200
Service area	600

A net profit of 10% each must be made on the restaurant takings and accommodation takings. You are required to calculate what inclusive terms per person should be charged per day. Show the split between meals and accommodation charges. There is also a proposal to take on hire an adjoining building available and covert it into a pastry shop. The annual cost estimates are:

	Rs.
Rates and taxes	12,000
Wages	54,000
Replacement of utensils	2,400
Depreciation of fixed assets	3,600
Fuel cost	10% of the cost of pastries

Sales are expected to average at Rs. 1, 50,000 per annum. The monthly figures vary according to seasons. Prices shown on the tags are arrived at by marking up the costs by 150%. Calculate the estimated annual profit. Also draw an estimate of cost and profit for the first month when the sales are expected to be Rs. 15,000.

(I.C.W.A.I., Inter)

[**Ans.:** (1) Tariff: Rate per sleeper night:

Meal: Rs. 17,744.81/294	Rs. 60.36
Accommodation: Rs. 8,715.19/294	Rs. 29.74
	Rs. 90.00

(2) Profit Rs. 12,000

(3) Costs: Variable Costs Rs. 12,000;
Fixed Costs Rs. 1,500;
Profit Rs. 1,500]

(4) Elegant Hotel has a capacity of 100 single rooms and 20 double rooms. It has a sport centre with a swimming pool, which is also used by persons other than residents of the hotel. The hotel has a shopping area at the basement and specially restaurant at the roof top. The following information is available.

(i) Average occupancy: 75% for 365 days of the year

(ii) Current costs are:

	Variable cost Rs. per day	Fixed cost Rs. per day
Single room	400	200
Double room	500	250

(iii) Average sales per day of restaurant Rs. 1,00,000; contribution is at 30%. Fixed cost Rs. 10,00,000 per annum.

(iv) The sports centre swimming pool is likely to be used by 50 non-residents daily; average contribution per day per non-resident is estimated at Rs. 50; fixed cost is Rs. 5,00,000 per annum.

(v) Average contribution per month from the shopping arcade is Rs. 50,000; fixed cost is Rs. 6,00,000 per annum.

You are required to find out:

(*a*) Rent chargeable for single and double room per day, so that there is a margin of safety of 20 percent on hire of rooms, and that the rent for a double room should be kept at 120% of a single room.

(*b*) Evaluate the profitability of restaurant, sports centre and shopping area separately.

(CA, Final)

[**Ans.:** Rent per day for single room: Rs. 2,56,64,062/33,945 = Rs. 756 (Appx)
Rent per day for double room: Rs. 756 × 1.20 = Rs. 907 (Appx)
Profitability of restaurant: Rs. 99,50,000
Profitability of sports centre: Rs. 4,12,500
Profitability of shopping area: Rs. Nil]

(5) A hotel has three types of rooms, *viz.*, A, B and C. You are to suggest what rent should be charged for each type of room on the basis of the following information:

(*i*) The rent of B type rooms is to be fixed at 1½ times of the C type rooms and that of A type room as twice of the C type rooms.

(*ii*) There are 20 A type rooms, 30 B type rooms and 100 C type rooms in the hotel.

(*iii*) Normally 60% of A type rooms, 80% of B type rooms and 90% of C type rooms are occupied in summer; and in winter 20% of A type rooms, 20% of B type rooms and 50% of C type rooms are occupied.

(*iv*) Actual expenses are as follows:

(*a*) Staff salary: Rs. 2,20,000 per annum.

(*b*) Room attendants' salary (when occupied):

Room Type	*Summer*	*Winter*
A	Rs. 4.00 per day	Rs. 6.00 per day
B	Rs. 3.00 per day	Rs. 4.50 per day
C	Rs. 2.00 per day	Rs. 3.00 per day

(*c*) Lighting per month if occupied for full month for both summer and winter:
A type room: Rs. 80.00; B type room: Rs. 60.00 and
C type room: Rs. 40.00

(*d*) Power per month if occupied for full month for both summer and winter:
A type room: Rs. 40.00; B type room: Rs. 30.00 and
C type room: Rs. 20.00

(*e*) Repairs and maintenance: Rs. 42,000 per annum

(*f*) Decoration: Rs. 50,000 per annum

(*g*) Sundry expenses: Rs. 76,550 per annum

(*h*) Depreciation on:

— Building @ 5%; cost of building is Rs. 14 lakh.

— Furniture @ 10%; cost of furniture is Rs. 3 lakh.

(*v*) Summer may be assumed for 7 months and winter for 5 months in a year. Normal days in a month may be taken as 30.

(*vi*) Profit on cost is 25%

(C.S., Inter, Dec., 2000)

[**Ans.:** Rent to be recovered per room day = Rs. 8,31,000/41,550 room days = Rs. 20.
Rent to be charged per room day
A type = Rs. 20 × 2 = Rs. 40; B type = Rs. 20 × 1.50 = Rs. 30;
C type = Rs. 20 × 1 = Rs. 20;]

(6) A manufacturing firm facing shortage of electric power supply from the State Electricity Board has set-up its own power generation plant for efficient running of its production units in the factory. The following information has been taken from the records in connection with the generation of power for a month:

(*a*) Number of units generated was 10,00,000 for the month, of which 10% was utilized by the generator department.

(*b*) Consumption data of materials, etc., for the month:

(*i*) Coal consumed – 300 MTs @ Rs. 3,600 per MT

(*ii*) Oil consumed – 4.5 MTs @ Rs. 40,000 per MT

(*iii*) Cost of water extraction and treatment for 6,00,000 litres @ Rs. 1.25 per litre.

(*c*) Steam boiler cost Rs. 20,00,000 with a residual value of Rs. 2,00,000 after a life of 10 years.

(*d*) Salaries and Wages per month:

(*i*) For staff of generating plant – 100 skilled workers @ Rs. 3,000 per month and 150 helpers @ Rs. 1,500 per month.

(*ii*) For staff of boiler house – 60 category A workers @ Rs. 1,500 per month and 100 category 'B' workers @ Rs. 1,000 per month.

(*e*) Cost of generating plant: Rs. 36,00,000 with no residual value. Depreciation at the rate of 10% on straight line basis is to be charged.

(f) Repairs and Maintenance of generation plant and boiler Rs. 50,000 per month.
(g) Share of administrative charges Rs. 40,000 per month.
(h) Sales value of ash disposed Rs. 15,000 per month.
Calculate per unit of electricity generated using a cost sheet format.

(ICWA, Inter, June, 1996)

[**Ans:** Cost per unit generated Rs. 3.512 – Rs. 31,61,000/ 9,00,000 units]

(7) The data given relates to 'Vasanth Talkies', a mini theatre, for the year ending 31st March, 1976:

Salaries:	*Rs.*		*Rs.*
1 Manager	800 p.m	Carbon	7,235
10 Gate Keepers	200 p.m each	Misc. Expenditure	5,425
2 Operators	400 p.m. each	Advertisement	34,710
4 Clerks	250 p.m each	Administration expenses	18,000
Electricity and oil	11,655	Hire of print	1,40,700

The premises are valued at Rs. 6,00,000 and the estimated life is 15 years. Projector and other equipments cost Rs. 3,20,000 on which 10% depreciation is to be charged.

Daily 3 shows are run through out the year. The total capacity is 625 seats which is divided into three classes as follows:

Janata circle	250 seats
Sanman circle	250 seats
Lords circle	125 seats

Ascertain cost per man-show assuming that:

(a) 20% of the seats remain vacant, and
(b) Weightage to be given to the three classes in the ratio 1:2:3.

Determine the rates for each class if the management expects 30% return on gross proceeds. Ignore entertainment taxes.

(B.Com., Madras, April 1983)

[**Ans.:** *(a)* The cost per man show Re. 0.50
(b) Rate for each class: Janata Circle: Re. 0.50; Sanman Circle: Re. 1.00; Lord Circle: Re. 1.50
(c) Man shows per annum Rs. 9,85,500
(d) Number of seats - 1,125]

❑❑❑

Part – IV

Techniques of Costing

16

Marginal Costing and Absorption Costing

Objectives

The objectives of the study are to:

- Distinguish Marginal Cost from Absorption Cost.
- Understand the importance of Breakeven Point.
- Explain the short term decision making with the help of Marginal Costing technique.

Introduction

Decision making involves the choice between various alternatives. In case of long term decision making, management looks beyond the current year and takes into consideration time value of money and return on investment. Whereas, in case of short term decision making, management has to select from among the available alternatives, the best one that can be implemented within a one year period. Such decision making is done with the help of Marginal Costing technique.

Meaning of Marginal Cost

The terminology of CIMA defines Marginal cost as the "cost of one unit of product or service, which would be avoided if that unit were not produced or provided". Marginal cost represents the increase or decrease in total cost which occurs with a small change in outputs say, a unit of output. In Cost Accounting, variable cost represents marginal cost.

Marginal cost is the additional cost of producing an additional output. In other words, it is the amount at any given volume of output by which aggregate variable costs are changed, if the volume of output is changed by one unit.

In this context, a unit may be a single article, a batch of articles, an order, and a stage of production capacity, a process or a department. It relates to the change in output in the particular circumstances under consideration.

Marginal Costing is the principle whereby variable costs are charged to cost units and the fixed costs attributable to the relevant period is written off in full against the contribution for that period. The terminology of CIMA defines Marginal costing as the ascertainment of Marginal cost and the effect on profit of changes in volume or type of output on the company's profit by differentiating between fixed costs and variable costs.

Features of Marginal Costing

The following are the features of Marginal Costing:

(1) Marginal costing differentiates cost into two broad categories, i.e., Fixed Cost and Variable Cost.
(2) It is a technique of ascertaining Marginal cost.
(3) It takes into account only variable cost for Product Costing and Inventory Valuation.
(4) Fixed costs incurred during a particular period are treated as period cost and charged to Profit and Loss Account.
(5) Segregation of expenses as fixed and variable helps the management in taking important decisions.
(6) Contribution is ascertained by deducting variable cost from sales.
(7) Profit is calculated by deducting fixed expenses from contribution.
(8) The profitability of different products is judged by their respective Profit Volume Ratio.

Meaning of Absorption Cost

Absorbed Cost is made up of direct costs plus overhead costs which is allotted to cost units by means of overhead absorption rates. It is the practice of charging all costs, both variable and fixed; and both direct and indirect cost to operations, products or processes.

Absorption Costing is a principle whereby fixed as well as variable costs are allotted to cost units and total overheads are absorbed according to the activity level. Absorption Costing is a technique of cost ascertainment which does not recognise the difference between fixed costs and variable costs. It is a process of determining average total cost by charging all costs both variable and fixed to operational, processes and products. This technique is also known as Product Costing or Full Costing.

Pros and Cons of Absorption Costing

The following are the main advantages of Absorption Costing:

(1) It discloses inefficient or efficient utilisation of production resources by indicating under-absorption or over-absorption of factory overheads.
(2) It will show correct profit calculation, in case, where production is completed and has to be sold in future as compared to variable costing.
(3) It is the basis of cost ascertainment in the absence of the use of Marginal Costing technique.
(4) It helps to conform to accrual and matching concepts which require matching cost with revenue for a particular period.
(5) It avoids separation of costs into fixed and variable elements, which at times is a very difficult task to segregate the total cost into fixed and variable.
(6) It helps to calculate the gross profit and net profit separately in income statement.

The following are the limitations of Absorption Costing:

(1) No distinction is made between the fixed and variable costs in Absorption Costing.
(2) A portion of fixed cost is carried forward to the next period because, closing stock is valued at cost of production which is inclusive of fixed cost.

(3) There is an element of subjectivity as the fixed costs are charged to the products on the basis of overhead absorption rates, which are arbitrary.
(4) Absorption Costing makes comparison and control of cost difficult as increase in the volume of output normally results in reduced unit cost and reduction in output results in an increased cost per unit due to existence of fixed costs.

MARGINAL COSTING VS. ABSORPTION COSTING

Marginal Costing	*Absorption Costing*
Marginal Costing takes into consideration only variable costs	Absorption Costing takes into account total cost i.e., fixed cost and variable cost
Cost per unit will be the same at different levels of output because only variable costs are considered which vary according to the output.	Cost per unit will not be the same at different levels of output as fixed cost remains constant and only variable cost changes.
Inventory is valued at marginal cost	Inventory is valued at cost of production.
There is no scope for over or under absorption of fixed overheads because, only variable costs are considered.	There may be over or under absorption of overheads because of apportionment of fixed costs.
It is an important and helpful technique in taking managerial decisions.	It is not a helpful technique in taking managerial decisions.
Any change in stock carried from one period to another will not affect the profit earned.	Any change in the volume of stock will affect the profit earned.

PREPARATION OF INCOME STATEMENT UNDER MARGINAL COSTING AND ABSORPTION COSTING

In Absorption Costing, the expenses are segregated on functional basis whereas in case of Marginal Costing, it is on the nature of expenses. The following are the proforma for preparing income statement under Absorption Costing and Marginal Costing.

Income Statement (Absorption Costing)

Sales Value		XXXXX
Less: Direct Materials	XXXX	
Direct Labor	XXXX	
Factory Overheads	XXXX	
	XXXX	
Add: Opening Stock	XXXX	
Less: Closing Stock	XXXX	
	XXXX	
Add: Under absorption of Fixed Overheads	XXXX	
Less: Over absorption of Fixed Overheads	XXXX	XXXX
Gross Profit		XXXX
Less: Administration Expenses	XXXX	
Selling & Distribution Expenses	XXXX	XXXX
Net Profit		XXXX

Income Statement (Marginal Costing)

Sales Value		XXXX
Less: Direct Materials	XXXX	
Direct Labor	XXXX	
Variable Factory Overheads	XXXX	
Variable Selling and Distribution expenses	XXXX	XXXX
Net Profit		XXXX

Illustration 1 (When there is production but no Sales)

From the following costing data, prepare the profit statement of ABC Ltd. using:

(a) Absorption Costing *(b)* Marginal Costing

Sales	—	Nil
Normal Capacity	—	60,000 units per month
Actual Production	—	66,000 units
Variable cost	—	Rs. 5 per unit
Fixed overheads	—	Rs. 1,80,000 per month or Rs. 3 per unit at normal capacity
Other Fixed expenses	—	Rs. 10,000

Solution

Income Statement (Absorption Costing)

	Rs.	*Rs.*
Sales		—
Less: Variable cost @ Rs 5 per unit (66,000 units × Rs. 5)	3,30,000	
Fixed Overheads (66,000 units × Rs. 3)	1,98,000	
Cost of goods Manufactured	5,28,000	
Less: Closing Inventory	5,28,000	
Cost of goods sold	—	
Less: Over absorption of Fixed overheads (6000 units × Rs. 3)	18,000	18,000
Gross Profit		18,000
Less: Other Fixed Expenses		10,000
Net profit		8,000

Income Statement (Marginal Costing)

	Rs.	*Rs.*
Sales		
Less: Variable cost(66,000 units × Rs. 5)	3,30,000	
Less: Closing Stock	3,30,000	
Contribution	—	—
Less: Fixed Overheads	1,80,000	
Other fixed expenses	10,000	1,90,000
Net loss		1,90,000

Illustration 2 (When sales are less than production)

From the following costing data prepare the income statement of XYZ Ltd. using

(a) Absorption Costing and *(b)* Marginal Costing

Sales	—	40,000 units
Production	—	80,000 units
Selling price @ Rs. 20 per unit		
Direct Material	—	Rs. 3,00,000
Direct Labor	—	Rs. 5,00,000
Fixed Overheads @ Rs. 3 per unit		
Fixed Overheads	—	Total – Rs. 2,40,000
Selling and Distribution expenses	—	Rs. 80,000

Solution

Income Statement (Absorption Costing)

		Rs.	*Rs.*
Sales (40000 units x Rs.20)			8,00,000
Less:	Direct Material	3,00,000	
	Direct Labor	5,00,000	
	Fixed Overheads	2,40,000	
		10,40,000	
Less:	Closing Stock $\frac{40,000}{80,000}$ 10,40,000	5,20,000	5,20,000
	Gross Profit		2,80,000
Less:	Selling and Distribution Overheads		80,000
	Net Income		2,00,000

Income Statement (Marginal Costing)

		Rs.	*Rs.*
Sales			8,00,000
Less:	Variable cost:		
	Direct Material	3,00,000	
	Direct Labor	5,00,000	
		8,00,000	
Less:	Closing Stock {(40,000/80,000) × 8,00,000}	4,00,000	
		4,00,000	
Add:	Selling and Distribution Costs	80,000	4,80,000
	Contribution		3,20,000
Less:	Fixed Overheads		2,40,000
Net Income			80,000

Note: Stock Valuation will be at total cost under Absorption Costing whereas in case of Marginal Costing, it will be valued at Marginal Cost of Production. As a result, whenever there is only Closing Stock, the profit will be higher under Absorption Costing as compared to under Marginal Costing as cost of Closing Stock will be higher under Absorption Costing.

Illustration 3 (when production is equal to sales)

The following data relates to PQR Ltd. You are required to prepare Income Statement under Absorption Costing and Marginal Costing.

Production	—	1,00,000 units
Sales	—	1,00,000 units
Selling Price @ Rs 10 per unit		
Direct Material @ Rs. 2 per unit		
Direct Labor @ Rs. 4 per unit		
Factory Overheads:		
Fixed	—	Rs. 30,000
Variable @ Re 1 per unit		
Other fixed expenses	—	Rs. 80,000

Solution

Income Statement (Absorption Costing)

		Rs.	Rs.
Sales (1,00,000 units × Rs. 10)			10,00,000
Less:	Direct Material (Rs. 2 × 1,00,000 units)	2,00,000	
	Direct Labor (Rs. 4 × 1,00,000 units)	4,00,000	
	Variable Factory Overheads (Rs. 1 × 1,00,000 units)	1,00,000	
	Fixed Factory overheads	30,000	7,30,000
	Gross Profit		2,70,000
Less:	Other fixed expenses		80,000
	Net Profit		1,90,000

Income Statement (Marginal Costing)

		Rs.	Rs.
Sales			10,00,000
Less:	Variable Cost		
	Direct Material	2,00,000	
	Direct Labor	4,00,000	
	Variable Factory Overheads	1,00,000	7,00,000
Contribution			3,00,000
Less:	Fixed Cost		
	Fixed Factory Overheads	30,000	
	Other Fixed Expenses	80,000	1,10,000
	Net Income		1,90,000

Note: When Production is equal to Sales, there will not be any closing stock. In the absence of stocks, profit will be the same under both the methods.

Illustration 4 (When sales are more than production)

You are required to prepare Profit and Loss Statement under Absorption Costing and Marginal Costing using the following data.

Opening Stock	—	5,000 units (valued at Total Cost Rs. 3,00,000 and Marginal Cost Rs. 2,50,000)
Units produced	—	5,000 units
Sales	—	10,000 units
Selling price per unit	—	Rs. 100
Variable Production cost per unit	—	Rs. 50
Fixed factory Overheads	—	Rs. 1,00,000 or Rs. 10 per unit
Selling and Administration Expenses	—	Rs. 50,000 (Fixed)

Solution

Profit and Loss Statement (Absorption Costing)

	Rs.	*Rs.*
Sales (10,000 × Rs. 100)		10,00,000
Less: Variable Production Cost (5,000 Units × Rs. 50)	2,50,000	
Fixed Factory Overheads (5,000 units × Rs. 10)	50,000	
	3,00,000	
Add: Opening Stock	3,00,000	
	6,00,000	
Add: Under absorption of Factory Overheads (5,000 units × Rs. 10)	50,000	6,50,000
Gross Profit		3,50,000
Less: Selling and Administrative Expenses		50,000
Net Profit		3,00,000

Profit and Loss Statement (Marginal Costing)

	Rs.	*Rs.*
Sales		10,00,000
Less: Variable Cost		
Variable Production Cost	2,50,000	
Opening Stock	2,50,000	5,00,000
Contribution		5,00,000
Less: Fixed Cost		
Fixed Factory Overheads	1,00,000	
Selling and Administration Expenses	50,000	1,50,000
Net Profit		3,50,000

Note: When there is only Opening Stock, profit will be higher under Abnormal Costing as compared to Marginal Costing method of valuation of stock as the cost of Opening Stock will be higher under Absorption Costing.

When both, Opening Stock and Closing Stock are given, profit will be more under Abnormal Costing if Closing Stock is more than Opening Stock and profit will be more under Marginal Costing if Opening Stock is more than Closing Stock.

BREAKEVEN (OR COST VOLUME PROFIT) ANALYSIS

The study of Cost-Volume-Profit Analysis is often referred to as Breakeven Analysis. It is a logical extension of Marginal Costing. It is based on the principle of classifying operating expenses into fixed and variable. It has become a powerful instrument in the hands of policy makers to maximize profits.

There may be a change in the level of production due to many reasons like competition, introduction of a new product, trade depression or boom, increased demand for products, change in selling prices of products, etc. In such cases, Management must study the effect on profit on account of the changing levels of production. Breakeven Analysis is a technique which is an aid to management in this respect.

Breakeven Analysis in its narrower sense, is concerned with finding out Breakeven Point, i.e., level of activity where the total cost equals total sales. In its broader sense, it means that system of analysis which determines the probable profit at any level of production. As Breakeven Analysis establishes relationship between cost, volume and profit, it is also known as 'Cost Volume Profit Analysis' or CVP Analysis.

The study of Breakeven Analysis can be made by *(i)* establishing a mathematical relationship between cost- volume-profits and *(ii)* by preparing Breakeven Charts.

In order to understand the mathematical relationship between cost, volume and profit, it is desirable to understand the following concepts.

(i) Contribution
(ii) Profit Volume (P/V) Ratio or Contribution/Sales
(iii) Breakeven Point
(iv) Margin of Safety

(i) Contribution: It is the difference between the Sales and the Marginal Cost of sales and it contributes towards Fixed Expenses and Profit.

Income Statement

	Sales	xxxx
Less:	Variable Cost	xxxx
	Contribution	xxxx
Less:	Fixed cost	xxxx
	Profit/Loss	xxxx

Contribution = Sales – Marginal cost

(or) Contribution = Fixed Expenses + Profit

(or) Contribution = Fixed Expenses – Loss

***(ii)* Profit Volume (P/V) Ratio:**

P/V Ratio is calculated as under

$$\text{P/V Ratio} = \frac{\text{Contribution}}{\text{Sales}} \times 100$$

$$\text{Or} \quad \frac{\text{Fixed Expenses} + \text{Profit}}{\text{Sales}} \times 100$$

$$\text{Or} \quad \frac{\text{Sales} - \text{Variable Costs}}{\text{Sales}} \times 100$$

$$\text{Or} \quad \frac{\text{Change in Profits or Contributions}}{\text{Change in Sales}}$$

Higher the P/V Ratio, greater will be the profit and lower the P/V Ratio, lesser will be the profit. Hence, it should be the goal of every concern to increase or improve the P/V Ratio.

P/V Ratio is very useful and is used for the calculation of

(i) Breakeven Point (Value) $= \dfrac{\text{Fixed Costs}}{\text{P/V Ratio}}$

(ii) Value of Sales to earn a desired amount of Profit

$$\frac{\text{Fixed Costs} + \text{Desired Profit}}{\text{P/V Ratio}}$$

(iii) Variable Costs = Sales (1 – P/V Ratio)

(iv) Profit = (Sales × P/V Ratio) – Fixed cost

(v) Fixed Cost = (Sales × P/V Ratio) – Profit

(vi) Margin of Safety $= \dfrac{\text{Profit}}{\text{P/V Ratio}}$

(vii) Contribution= Sales X PV Ratio

***(iii)* Breakeven Point:** It is a point of no-profit-no-loss. At this point, contribution is equal to fixed cost. A concern which attains Breakeven point at less number of units will definitely be better than another concern where breakeven point is achieved at more units of production.

$$\text{Breakeven Point (in units)} = \frac{\text{Total Fixed Expenses}}{\text{Selling price per unit} - \text{Marginal cost per unit}}$$

$$\text{(or)} \quad = \frac{\text{Total Fixed Expenses}}{\text{Contribution per unit}}$$

Breakeven Point (in value)

$$\frac{\text{Fixed Cost} \quad \text{Sales}}{\text{Sales} - \text{Variable Cost}} \text{ (or) } \frac{\text{Fixed Cost}}{\text{P/V Ratio}}$$

(iv) **Margin of Safety:** It is the difference between the Actual Sales and Breakeven Sales. Sales or output beyond breakeven point is known as Margin of Safety because, this Margin of Safety Sales generates profit, as fixed expenses are already recovered at breakeven point itself. It can also be expensed in percentage.
It is calculated with the help of the following formula:

$$\text{Margin of Safety} = \frac{\text{Profit}}{\text{P/V Ratio}}$$

Margin of Safety (M/S) = Actual Sales – Breakeven Sales
Efforts should be made by the management to increase the Margin of Safety.

Assumptions Underlying Breakeven Analysis

The Breakeven Analysis is based on the following assumptions:

(1) All costs can be separated into fixed and variable components.
(2) Variable cost per unit remains constant and total variable cost varies in direct proportion to the volume of production.
(3) Total fixed cost remains constant.
(4) Selling price does not change as volume changes.
(5) There is only one product or in the case of multiple products, the sales mix does not change. In other words, when several products are being sold, the sale of various products will always be in some predetermined proportion.
(6) There is no synchronization between production and sales.
(7) Productivity per worker does not change.
(8) There will be no change in general price level.

Breakeven Chart

A Breakeven Chart is a graphical representation of Marginal Costing. This chart shows the inter-relationship between profit, volume and cost. It shows the break-even point and also indicates the estimated profit or loss at varying levels of activity. There are three methods of drawing a Breakeven Chart.

First Method: On the X-axis of the graph, the number of units produced and sold is plotted, and on the Y-axis, costs and sales revenues are shown. The fixed cost line is drawn parallel to X-axis. This line indicates that fixed expenses remain constant irrespective of production. The variable costs for different levels of activity are plotted over the fixed cost line. The variable cost line is joined to fixed cost line at zero volume of production. This line can also be regarded as the total cost line because, it starts from point where fixed cost has been incurred and variable cost is zero. Sales values at various levels of output are plotted, joined and the resultant line is sales line. The sales line will cut the total cost line at a point where total costs equals to total revenues and this point of intersection of two lines is known as Breakeven Point – the point of no profit no loss. Loss and profit as shown in the chart states that if production is less then Breakeven Point, the business shall be running at a loss and if the production is more than Breakeven level, profit shall result.

Output (Units)	*Sales (Rs.)*	*Total Cost (Rs.)*	*Fixed Cost (Rs.)*	*Variable Cost (Rs.)*
0	0	20,000	20,000	0
1,000	30,000	45,000	20,000	25,000
2,000	60,000	70,000	20,000	50,000
3,000	90,000	95,000	20,000	75,000
4,000	1,20,000	1,20,000	20,000	1,00,000
5,000	1,50,000	1,45,000	20,000	1,25,000
6,000	1,80,000	1,70,000	20,000	1,50,000

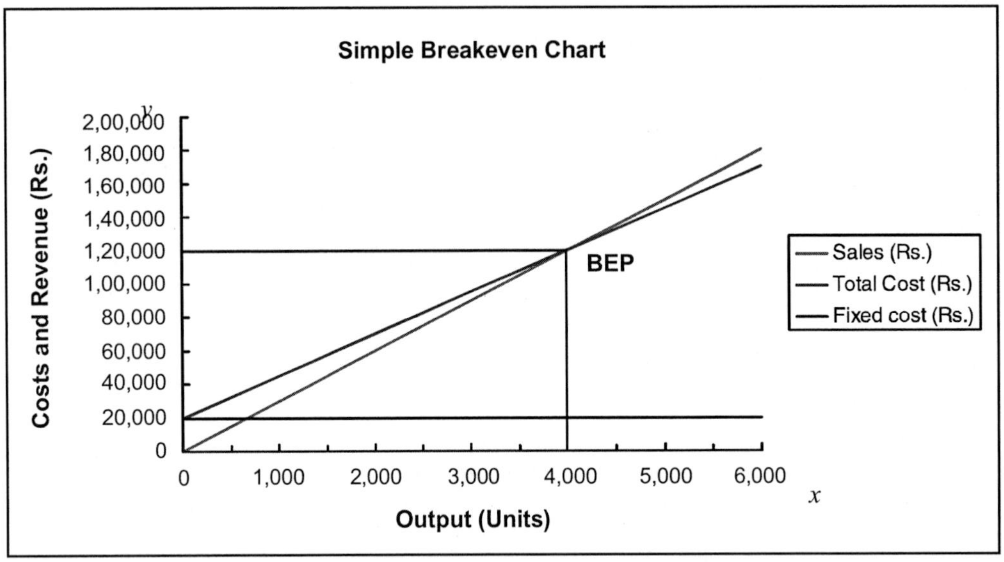

Second Method: A variation of the first method is that, variable cost line is plotted first and then the fixed cost line is plotted over the variable cost line. The latter line is the total cost line because, it is drawn over the variable cost line and represents total cost at various levels of output. The method is more helpful to management for decision making because it shows the recovery of fixed costs at various levels of production before profits are realized and contributions at various levels of production are automatically disclosed in the chart as the variable cost line starts from zero.

Output (Units)	*Sales (Rs.)*	*Total Cost (Rs.)*	*Fixed Cost (Rs.)*	*Variable Cost (Rs.)*
0	0	20,000	20,000	0
1,000	30,000	45,000	20,000	25,000
2,000	60,000	70,000	20,000	50,000
3,000	90,000	95,000	20,000	75,000
4,000	1,20,000	1,20,000	20,000	1,00,000
5,000	1,50,000	1,45,000	20,000	1,25,000
6,000	1,80,000	1,70,000	20,000	1,50,000

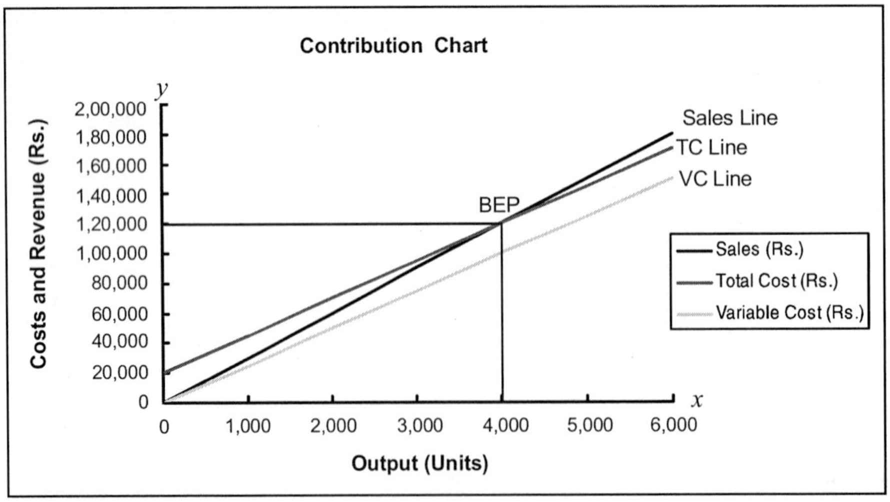

Third Method: Under this method, the fixed cost line is drawn parallel to X-axis. The contribution line is drawn from origin and this line goes up with the increase in output. The sales line is plotted as usual. The question of interaction of sales line with cost line does not arise because the total cost line is not drawn in this method. Here, Breakeven Point is that point where the contribution line cuts the fixed cost line. At this point, contribution is equal to fixed expenses and there is no profit no loss. If contribution is more than fixed expenses, profit shall arise and if the contribution is less than fixed expenses it would result in loss.

Output (Units)	*Sales (Rs.)*	*Total Cost (Rs.)*	*Fixed Cost (Rs.)*	*Variable Cost (Rs.)*	*Contribution (Rs.)*
0	0	20,000	20,000	0	0
1,000	30,000	45,000	20,000	25,000	5,000
2,000	60,000	70,000	20,000	50,000	10,000
3,000	90,000	95,000	20,000	75,000	15,000
4,000	1,20,000	1,20,000	20,000	1,00,000	20,000
5,000	1,50,000	1,45,000	20,000	1,25,000	25,000
6,000	1,80,000	1,70,000	20,000	1,50,000	30,000

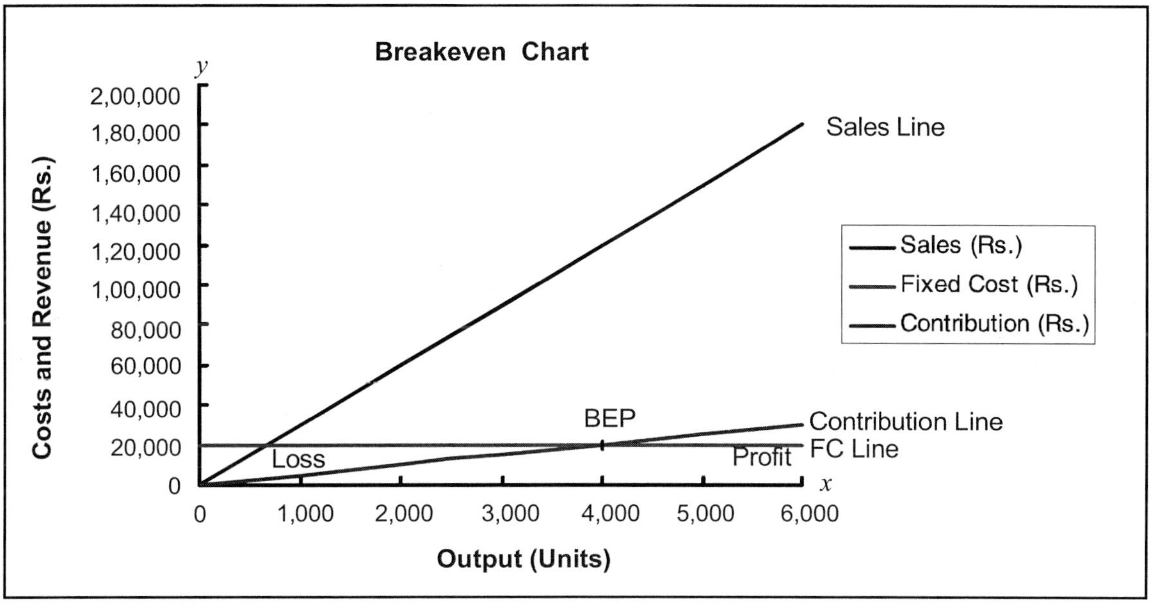

Angle of Incidence: This is the angle formed at the Breakeven Point at which the sales line cuts the total cost line. This angle indicates the rate at which profits are being made. Larger Angle of Incidence is an indication that profits are being made at a high rate. On the other hand, a small angle indicates a low rate of profit and suggests that variable costs form a major part of cost of production. A large Angle of Incidence with a high Margin of Safety indicates the most favorable position of a business and even the existence of monopoly conditions.

Advantages of Breakeven Charts

The following are the benefits of Breakeven Charts.

(1) Information provided by the Breakeven Chart can be understood by the management more easily than contained in profit and loss account and the cost statements because, a Breakeven Chart is a simple presentation of cost, volume and profit structure of the company

(2) The chart is very useful for taking managerial decisions because, it shows the effect on profits of changes in fixed costs, variable costs, selling price and volume of sales.

(3) The chart is very useful for forecasting costs and profits at various volumes of sales.

(4) It is a tool for cost control because it shows the relative importance of fixed costs and the variable cost.

(5) Profitability of various products can be studied with the help of these charts and a most profitable product mix can be adopted.

(6) Profits at different levels of activity can also be ascertained

(7) The profit potentialities can be judged from a study of the position of the Breakeven Point and the Angle of Incidence in the Breakeven Chart.

(8) It is helpful in the determination of sales price, which would give desired profits or a Breakeven Point.

(9) It is helpful in knowing the effect of increase or reduction in selling price.

Limitations of Breakeven Charts

Breakeven Charts suffers from the following limitations.

(1) A Breakeven Chart is based on a number of assumptions which may not hold good. Fixed costs vary beyond a certain level of output. Variable costs do not vary proportionately if the law of diminishing or increasing returns is applicable in the business. Sales revenues do not vary proportionately with changes in volume of sales, due to a reduction in the selling price as a result of competition or increased production.

(2) In Breakeven Chart, we see that total cost line and sales line look straight. But, in practice, the total cost and sales lines are not straight lines because the assumptions do not hold good.

(3) The effect of various product mixes on profits cannot be studied from a single Breakeven Chart.

(4) A Breakeven Chart doesn't take into consideration capital employed which is a very important factor in taking managerial decisions. Therefore, managerial decisions on the basis of Breakeven Chart may not be reliable.

(5) A limited amount of information can be shown in a Breakeven Chart. A number of charts may have to be drawn up to study the effects of changes in fixed costs, variable costs and selling prices.

In-spite of the above Limitations, the Breakeven Chart is a useful management device for analyzing the problems, if it is constructed and used by those who fully understand its limitations.

Illustration 5

Determine the amount of fixed expenses from the following particulars.

Sales: Rs. 2,80,000;

Direct Material: Rs. 80,000;

Direct Labor: Rs. 40,000;

Variable Overheads Rs. 30,000 and

Profit Rs. 60,000.

Solution

Marginal cost equation is

Sales – Variable Cost = Fixed Cost + Profit

Sales = Rs. 2,80,000

Variable Cost = 80,000 + 40,000 + 30,000 (Direct Material + Direct Labor + Variable Overheads) = Rs.1,50,000

Profit = Rs. 60,000

Fixed Cost = ?

Applying the figures in the equation: Sales – Variable Cost = Fixed Cost + Profit, we get

2,80,000 – 1,50,000 = F + 60,000

Fixed Cost = 2,80,000 – 1,50,000 – 60,000

Fixed Cost = Rs.70,000

Illustration 6

Calculate BEP from the following information: (in units and value)

Fixed Expenses – Rs. 1,00,000

Variable Cost (per unit) – Rs.13

Selling Price (per unit) – Rs.15

Solution

(1) Contribution = Selling price per unit – Variable Cost per unit
= 15 – 13 = Rs. 2

(2) $\text{P/V Ratio} = \dfrac{\text{Contribution}}{\text{Sales}}\ 100 = \dfrac{2}{15} \times 100 = 13.33\% \text{ or } 13\tfrac{1}{3}\%$

(3) $\text{Breakeven Point (in Value)} = \dfrac{\text{Fixed Expenses}}{\text{P/V Ratio}}$

$$= \frac{1,00,000}{13\frac{1}{3}\%} = \text{Rs.}7,50,000 \text{ (approximated)}$$

(4) $\text{Breakeven point (in units)} = \dfrac{F}{\text{Contribution per unit}} = \dfrac{1,00,000}{2} = 50,000 \text{ units}$

Illustration 7

From the following information, calculate *(i)* P/V Ratio *(ii)* Breakeven point and *(iii)* Fixed Cost.

Year	*Sales Rs.*	*Profit Rs.*
2007	1,50,000	20,000
2008	1,70,000	25,000

Solution

(1) P/V Ratio $= \dfrac{\text{Change in profit}}{\text{Change in sales}} = \dfrac{5{,}000}{20{,}000} = 25\%$

(2) Breakeven point (in Rs.) $= \dfrac{\text{Fixed Cost}}{\text{P/V Ratio}}$

Contribution $= 1{,}50{,}000 \times \dfrac{25}{100} =$ Rs. 37,500

→ Contribution = Fixed Cost + Profit

→ 37,500 = Fixed Cost + 20,000

→ Fixed Cost = 37,500 – 20,000 = Rs. 17,500

Breakeven point $= \dfrac{17{,}500}{25\%} =$ Rs. 70,000

P/V Ratio = 25%, Breakeven Sales= Rs.70,000, Fixed Cost = Rs.17,500

Illustration 8

A company has fixed expenses of Rs. 90,000 with sales at Rs. 3,00,000 and a profit of Rs. 60,000 during the first half year. If in the second half year, the company suffered a loss of Rs. 30,000, calculate:

(a) The P/V Ratio, Breakeven point and Margin of Safety for the first half year
(b) Expected sales volume for the next second half of the year assuming that selling price and fixed expenses remain unchanged.
(c) The Breakeven point and Margin of Safety for the whole year.

(CS., Inter, June, 1998)

Solution

(a) *(i)* P/V Ratio $= \dfrac{\text{Contribution}}{\text{Sales}} \times 100 = \dfrac{1{,}50{,}000}{3{,}00{,}000} \times 100 = 50\%$

[Contribution = 90,000 (Fixed expenses) + 60,000 Profit = Rs.1,50,000]

(ii) Breakeven point $= \dfrac{\text{Fixed Cost}}{\text{P/V Ratio}} = \dfrac{90{,}000}{50\%} =$ Rs. 1,80,000

(iii) Margin of Safety = Actual sales – BEP sales
= 3,00,000 – 1,80,000 = Rs. 1,20,000

(b) Expected sales volume $= \dfrac{\text{Fixed cost} - \text{Loss}}{\text{P/V Ratio}} = \dfrac{90{,}000 - 30{,}000}{50\%} =$ Rs. 1,20,000

(c) (i) Breakeven point (for the whole year)

$= \dfrac{\text{Fixed cost for the whole year}}{\text{P/V Ratio}} = \dfrac{1{,}80{,}000}{50\%} =$ Rs. 3,60,000

(ii) Margin of Safety = Actual sales – BEP sales
Actual Sales = 3,00,000 (for first half year) + 1,20,000 (for second half of the year) = Rs. 4,20,000
Margin of Safety = 4,20,000 – 3,60,000 = Rs. 60,000 Or
Margin of Safety = Profit (or loss)/PV Ratio 30,000/50% = Rs. 60,000

Illustration 9

MRS Manufacturers Ltd's., budget production is 3,00,000 units at a Variable Cost of Rs. 10 each. The Fixed Costs are Rs. 20,00,000. The selling price is fixed to yield 20% on cost. Find out (a) P/V Ratio (b) Breakeven production in units and in value.

Solution

Sales = Fixed Cost + Variable Cost + Profit
= 20,00,000 + 30,00,000 + 20% of 50,00,000
= Rs. 60,00,000

Contribution = Sales – Variable Cost
= 60,00,000 – 30,00,000 = Rs. 30,00,000

Sale price = 60,00,000/3,00,000 = Rs. 20

Contribution per unit = 20 – 10 = Rs. 10

(a) $$\text{P/V Ratio} = \frac{\text{Contribution}}{\text{Sales}} \times 100 = \frac{30,00,000}{60,00,000} \times 100 = 50\%$$

(b) $$\text{Breakeven Point (in units)} = \frac{\text{Fixed Cost}}{\text{Contribution per unit}} = \frac{20,00,000}{10} = 2,00,000 \text{ units}$$

Breakeven Point (in Value) = BEP units × Sale price
= 2,00,000 × 20
= Rs. 40,00,000

Illustration 10

Calculate *(a)* BEP units and value *(b)* Sales to earn a profit of Rs. 20 per unit *(c)* Profit to reach a sales target of Rs. 2,50,000.

Selling Price: Rs. 200 per unit; Variable Cost Rs.100 per unit; Total Fixed Cost: Rs. 96,000

Solution

Contribution = Sales – Variable Cost
= 200 – 100 = Rs. 100 per unit

$$\text{P/V Ratio} = \frac{100}{200} \times 100 = 50\%$$

(a) $$\text{BEP (in units)} = \frac{\text{Fixed Cost}}{\text{Contribution per unit}} = \frac{96,000}{100} = 960 \text{ units}$$

BEP (in value) = BEP units × Sale price
= 960 × 200 = Rs.1,92,000

$$\text{(or) Fixed Cost / PV Ratio} = \frac{96,000}{50\%} = \text{Rs. } 1,92,000$$

(b) $$\text{Sales required to earn a profit of Rs. 20 per unit} = \frac{\text{Fixed Cost + Profit}}{\text{Contribution per unit}}$$

Suppose N units are sold.

$$\rightarrow N = \frac{96,000 + (\text{Rs. } 20 \times N)}{100}$$ (Desired profit is Rs. 20 per unit)

$\rightarrow$ 100N = 96,000 + 20 N

$\rightarrow$ 100N – 20N = 96,000

$\rightarrow$ 80N = 96,000

$$\rightarrow N = \frac{96,000}{80} = 1,200 \text{ units}$$

(c) Sales $= \dfrac{\text{Fixed Cost + Profit}}{\text{P/V Ratio}}$

$= 2{,}50{,}000 = \dfrac{96{,}000 + P}{50\%}$

$= 2{,}50{,}000 \times 50\% = 96{,}000 + P$

$\rightarrow$ 1,25,000 = 96,000 + P

$\rightarrow$ P = 1,25,000 – 96,000 = Rs. 29,000

Illustration 11

From the following data, find out *(i)* Sales and *(ii)* New Breakeven sales, if selling price is reduced by 10%.

Fixed Cost	Rs. 4,000
Breakeven sales	Rs. 20,000
Profit	Rs. 1,000
Selling Price per unit	Rs. 20

(C.S., Inter, Dec, 1994)

Solution

(i) Fixed Cost = Rs. 4,000

Breakeven Sales = Fixed Cost/PV Ratio

$$\text{P/V Ratio} = \frac{\text{Fixed Cost}}{\text{B.E. Sales}} = \frac{4{,}000}{20{,}000} \times 100 = 20\%$$

$$\text{Sales} = \frac{\text{Fixed Cost + Profit}}{\text{P/V Ratio}} = \frac{4{,}000 + 1{,}000}{20\%} = \text{Rs. } 25{,}000$$

(ii) New selling price = Rs. 20 – 10% = 20 – 2 = Rs. 18

If PV Ratio is 20%, Variable Cost is 80% in 100% Sales

Variable Cost = 80% of Rs. 20 = Rs. 16 per unit

New Contribution = Rs. 18 – 16 = Rs. 2

$$\text{New P/V Ratio} = \frac{\text{Contribution}}{\text{Sales}} \times 100 = \frac{2}{18} \times 100 = \frac{200}{18} = 11\frac{1}{9}\%$$

$$\text{New Breakeven Sales} = \frac{\text{Fixed Cost}}{\text{P/V Ratio}} = \frac{4{,}000}{11\frac{1}{9}} = \text{Rs. } 36{,}000 \text{ (Approximated)}$$

Illustration 12

From the following data, compute Breakeven sales and Margin of Safety.

Sales	Rs. 10,00,000
Fixed Cost	Rs. 3,00,000
Profit	Rs. 2,00,000

(C.S., Inter, Dec., 1994)

Solution

Contribution = Fixed Cost + Profit

= 3,00,000 + 2,00,000 = Rs. 5,00,000

$$\text{P/V Ratio} = \frac{\text{Contribution}}{\text{Sales}} = \frac{5{,}00{,}000}{10{,}00{,}000} \times 100 = 50\%$$

$$\text{Breakeven sales} = \frac{\text{Fixed Cost}}{\text{P/V Ratio}} = \frac{3{,}00{,}000}{50\%} = \text{Rs. } 6{,}00{,}000$$

$$\text{Margin of Safety} = \frac{\text{Profit}}{\text{P/V Ratio}} = \frac{2,00,000}{50\%} = \text{Rs. } 4,00,000 \quad \text{Or}$$

Margin of Safety = Actual Sales – Breakeven Sales

10,00,000 – 6,00,000 = Rs. 4,00,000

Illustration 13

A Company sells its product at Rs. 15 per unit. In a period, if it produces and sells 8,000 units, it incurs a loss of Rs. 5 per unit. If the volume is raised to 20,000 units, it earns a profit of Rs. 4 per unit. Calculate Breakeven point both in terms of value, and in units.

Solution

Average cost at 8,000 units volume

= Selling price per unit + Loss per unit

→ 15 + 5 = Rs.20

Average cost at 20,000 units volume = 15 – 4 = Rs. 11

Total cost at 8,000 units volume = 8,000 × 20 = Rs. 1,60,000

Total cost at 20,000 units volume = 20,000 × 11 = Rs. 2,20,000

$$\text{Variable Cost per unit} = \frac{\text{Change in Total Cost}}{\text{Change in Volume of Production}}$$

$$= \frac{2,20,000 - 1,60,000}{20,000 - 8,000} = \frac{60,000}{12,000} = \text{Rs. } 5$$

Fixed Cost = Total Cost – Variable Cost

= 1,60,000 – (8,000 × 5) = 1,60,000 – 40,000

= Rs. 1,20,000

$$\text{P/V Ratio} = \frac{\text{Contribution}}{\text{Sales}} = \frac{15\text{-}5}{15} \times 100 = 66\frac{2}{3}\%$$

$$\text{Breakeven sales} = \frac{\text{Fixed Cost}}{\text{P/V Ratio}} = \frac{1,20,000}{66\frac{2}{3}\%} = \text{Rs. } 1,80,000$$

$$\text{Breakeven point (in units)} = \frac{\text{Fixed Cost}}{\text{Contribution per unit}} = \frac{1,20,000}{10} = 12,000 \text{ units}$$

Contribution per unit = 15 – 5 = Rs. 10 per unit

Illustration 14

Construct a BEP chart from the following:

Units	*Total Cost (Rs.)*	*Revenue/(Sales) (Rs.)*	*Fixed Cost (Rs.)*
0	30,000	0	30,000
1,000	50,000	28,000	30,000
2,000	70,000	56,000	30,000
3,000	90,000	84,000	30,000
4,000	1,10,000	1,12,000	30,000
5,000	1,30,000	1,40,000	30,000
6,000	1,50,000	1,68,000	30,000
7,000	1,70,000	1,96,000	30,000

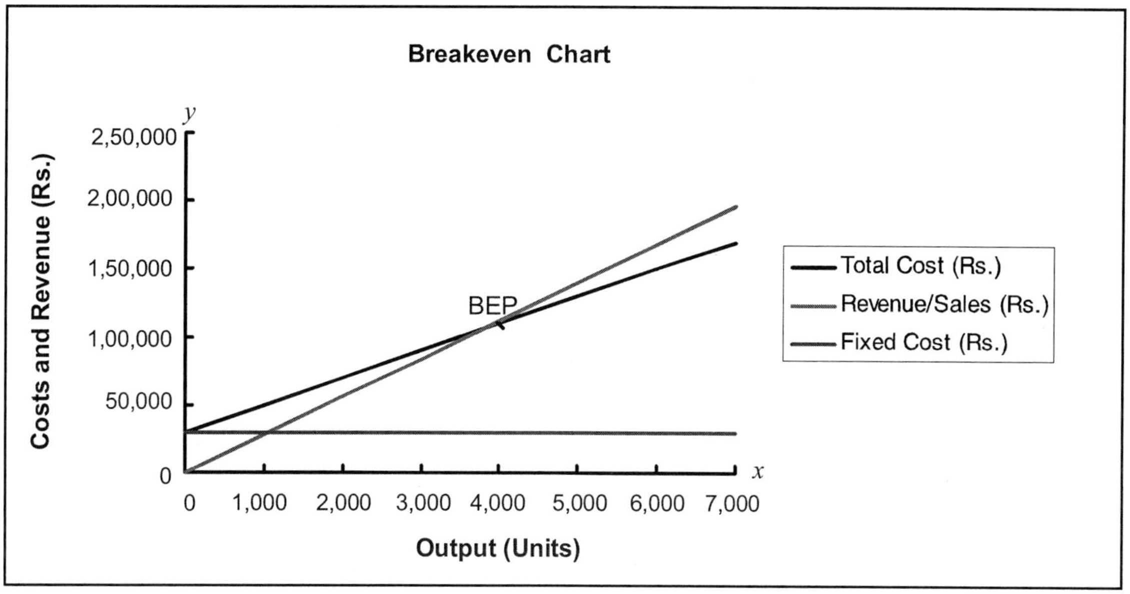

Illustration 15

From the following information of a company which produces three products, calculate *(a)* Composite P/V Ratio *(b)* Composite Breakeven point.

Product	*Sales Revenue* *Rs.*	*Variable cost* *Rs.*
X	20,000	10,000
Y	40,000	14,000
Z	60,000	36,000

Fixed Cost: Rs. 50,000

Solution

Product	*Sales Revenue* *Rs.*	*Variable cost* *Rs.*	*Contribution* *(S - V) Rs.*	*P/V Ratio* *(C/S X100)*
X	20,000	10,000	10,000	50%
Y	40,000	14,000	26,000	65%
Z	60,000	36,000	24,000	40%
	1,20,000	60,000	60,000	50%

(a) Composite P/V Ratio $= \dfrac{\text{Total Contribution}}{\text{Total Sales}} \times 100$

$$= \frac{60{,}000}{1{,}20{,}000} \times 100 = 50\%$$

(b) Composite Breakeven Point (in Value) $= \dfrac{\text{Total Fixed Cost}}{\text{Composite P/V Ratio}}$

$$\rightarrow \frac{50{,}000}{50\%} = \text{Rs. } 1{,}00{,}000$$

DECISION MAKING

Marginal Costing is a very useful and important technique for the management in decision making. The information provided by the Total Cost or Absorption Cost Method is not sufficient in solving the management problems. Marginal Costing differentiates total costs into fixed cost and variable cost and helps in ascertaining marginal cost and the effect on the profit of changes in the volume or type of output on the company's profit.

The following are some of the important decisions where Marginal Costing technique is applied

(i) Pricing Decisions
(ii) Make or Buy Decisions
(iii) Product / Sales Mix Decisions
(iv) Key or Limiting Factor
(v) Shut Down or Continue Decision
(vi) Alternative Methods of Production
(vii) Accept or Reject an Offer

I. Pricing Decisions

The technique of Marginal Costing can be applied to the pricing of products. In normal circumstances, the price of a product would cover the total cost plus a margin of profit. Any product which generates revenue in excess of its variable cost contributes towards the recovery of fixed costs and results in profits. Once the fixed costs are recovered at a particular level of production, the additional units produced would contribute towards profit. But, selling prices are not always determined by the cost of production and they may be determined by market conditions and sometimes the firm may have to sell its products below the total cost. Therefore, the pricing decision is different under different circumstances. Some of the circumstances are as follows:

Pricing during Recession

During recession, the prices fall and the product may be sold below the total cost. In case there is a temporary fall in the demand due to recession, leading to the reduction in the price temporarily, the price so reduced should be at least equal to the marginal cost. If the selling price at which goods can be sold is equal to marginal cost or more than the marginal cost, the product should be continued. In this case, the loss will be to the extent of the fixed cost uncovered. Fixed cost will be incurred even if the product is discontinued. If the product is sold at a price which is little more than the marginal cost, the loss on account of fixed expenses can be reduced.

If the selling price is below the marginal cost, loss will be more than the fixed cost because, the variable costs are not recovered fully. In such a case, the production of that particular product should be discontinued. But there are certain circumstances, where production is continued even if the selling price is below the marginal cost. The following are some of them.

(a) Introduction of new product in the market
(b) Exploring foreign markets
(c) Closure of a business
(d) Clearing the stock of perishable nature
(e) Utilization of surplus resources which otherwise would go waste
(f) Elimination of competitors from the market
(g) To avoid retrenchment of workers
(h) To push the sale of a joint product

Illustration 16

Bell Electronics decides to effect a 10% reduction in the price of its product because; it is felt that such a step may lead to a greater volume of sales. It is anticipated that there are no prospects of a change in fixed costs and variable cost per unit. The directors would like to maintain net profit at the present level.

The following information has been obtained from its books.

	Rs.
Sales 15,000 units	4, 50,000
Variable Costs – Rs 25 per unit	
Fixed Costs	50,000

How would the management proceed to implement this decision?

Solution

Calculation of Present level of profit

Income Statement of Bell Electronics

	Rs.
Sales: 15,000 units	4,50,000
— Variable cost (Rs. 25 × 15,000 units)	3,75,000
Contribution	75,000
— Fixed costs	50,000
Profit	25,000

Calculation of Sales required to earn the present level of profit (Rs. 25,000)

	Rs.
Selling Price per unit	30
Less: 10% reduction in price	3
New Selling Price per unit	27
Less: Variable cost per unit	25
Contribution per unit	2

Required Sales = (Fixed Cost + Desired Profit)/Contribution per unit

= (50,000 + 25,000)/2 = 75,000/2 = 37,500 units

If the company reduces the selling price by Rs. 3 per unit and wishes to earn the present level of profit of Rs. 25,000, then it has to raise the sales by 22,500 units (37,500 – 15,000).

Verification

	Rs.
Sales (Rs. 27 × 37,500 units)	10,12,500
Less: Variable Cost (Rs. 25 × 37,500 units)	9,37,500
Contribution	75,000
Less: Fixed Cost	50,000
Profit	25,000

Illustration 17

A Manufacturer of plastic buckets makes an average profit of Rs. 450 per piece on a selling price of Rs. 14.50 by producing and selling 50,000 pieces at 50% potential capacity. His cost of sales is:

	Rs.
Direct Material	3.00
Direct Wages	1.00
Factory Overheads (50% Fixed)	5.00
Selling Overheads (75% Fixed)	1.00

During the Current year, he intends to produce the same number of units, but anticipates that:

(i) Fixed cost will go up by 10%

(ii) Material and labor costs will go up by 3%

(iii) Selling price will remain unchanged.

Under these circumstances, he obtains an offer for a further 20% of his capacity. What minimum price you would recommend for acceptance to ensure an overall profit of Rs. 2,50,000?

Solution

Statement of contribution for the current year prior to acceptance of 20% excess order

Particulars	*Rs. Per Piece*	*Total Rs.*
Sales	14.50	7,25,000
Direct Material (Rs. 3 + 3% of Rs. 3)	3.09	1,54,500
Direct Labor (Re. 1 + 3% of Re. 1)	1.03	51,500
Variable Factory Overheads (50% of Rs. 5)	2.50	1,25,000
Variable Selling Overheads (25% of Re. 1)	0.25	12,500
Marginal Cost	6.87	3,43,500
Contribution	7.63	3,81,500

	Rs.
Fixed cost: Factory overheads (50,000 × 2.5 = 1,25,000 + 10% of 1,25,000)	1,37,500
Selling overheads (50,000 × 0.75 = 37,500 + 10% of 37,500)	41,250
Total Fixed overheads	1,78,750
Profit = Contribution – Fixed cost	
(3,81,500 – 1,78,750)	2,02,750
Profit Planned	2,50,000
Therefore, Increase in profit or contribution expected = Rs. (2,50,000 – 2,02,750)	47,250
Now, Marginal cost of additional 20,000 pieces i.e. Rs. 20,000 × 6.87	1,37,400
(Order for 20% of 1,00,000 units capacity)	
Add: Additional profit required	47,250
Total Sales expected	1,84,650
Therefore, Selling Price per unit = Rs. (1,84,650/20,000)	9,233

Illustration 18

A firm having a capacity of 65,000 units per year produces 50,000 units which are consumed in domestic market at Rs. 12 per unit. The cost sheet of the product is given as under:

			Rs.
Direct Material			4.00
Direct Labor			3.00
Factory Overheads:	Fixed	0.50	
	Variable	1.50	2.00
Administrative Expenses			1.00
Selling and Distribution Expenses			
	Fixed	0.25	
	Variable	0.50	0.75
			10.75

A foreign customer is interested in the product but he is willing to buy only 15,000 units at a price of Rs. 10 per unit. Advise whether the order should be accepted. What will be your advice if the order were from domestic merchant?

Solution

Income Statement

	Present Position (50,000 units) Rs.	*Export Order (15,000 units) Rs.*	*Position after Export Order Receipt (65,000 units) Rs.*
Sales	6,00,000	1,50,000	7,50,000
Less: Variable Cost:			
Direct Material	2,00,000	60,000	2,60,000
Direct Labor	1,50,000	45,000	1,95,000
Variable Factory Overheads	75,000	22,500	97,500
Variable S&D Expenses	25,000	7,500	32,500
Contribution	1,50,000	15,000	1,65,000
Less: Fixed Cost:			
Fixed Factory Overheads	25,000		25,000
Fixed S & D Expenses	12,500		12,500
Administration Expenses	50,000		50,000
Net Profit	62,500	15,000	77,500

It is advisable to accept the foreign order as it increases the net profit by Rs. 15,000.

*(b)*If the order were from a domestic merchant, it is advisable to reject the order, as the price reduction will affect the normal market conditions.

Illustration 19

A manufacturing company has an installed capacity of 1,50,000 units per annum. Its cost structure is given below.

	(per unit) *Rs.*
Variable costs	10
Labor (minimum Rs.1,00,000 per month)	10
Overheads	4
Fixed Overheads: Rs.1,92,300 per annum	

Semi-variable overheads Rs.60,000 per annum at 75% capacity, which increases by Rs.4,000 per annum for every 5% increase in capacity utilization for the year as a whole. The capacity utilization for the next year is estimated at 75% for three months, 80% for six months and 90% for the remaining part of the year. If the company is planning to have a profit of 20% on the selling price, calculate the selling price per unit.

(CA, Final, November, 2003)

Solution

Working notes:

(1) Average installed capacity (in units) per month:

=(Total annual installed capacity/12 months)

=1,50,000 units/12 months=12,500 units per month

(2) Total Labor Cost at different Capacity Utilization

Capacity Utilization	75%	80%	90%
Expected Production per month(in units)	9,375	10,000	11,250
Labor cost of expected production(Rs.)	93,750	1,00,000	1,12,500
Minimum labor cost per month(Rs.)	1,00,000	1,00,000	1,00,000
Budgeted labor cost per month(Rs.)	1,00,000	1,00,000	1,12,500
Number of months during which the production equals expected production	3	6	3
Total labor cost for production months at different capacity utilization (Rs.)	3,00,000	6,00,000	3,37,500

(3) Computation of Total Semi-Variable Overheads

Capacity utilization	75%	75%-80%	80%-85%	85%-90%
Semi-variable overheads (Rs.)	60,000	64,000	68,000	72,000

(4) Total Annual Production

Months	1-3	4-9	10-12
Total number of units produced	28,125 (9,375 units × 3 months)	60,000 (10,000 units × 6 months)	33,750 (11,250 units × 3 months)
Total annual production=1,21,875 units			

Statement showing computation of selling price per unit

Months	1-3	4-9	10-12	Total
Total number of units produced (Refer to working note 4)	28,125	60,000	33,750	1,21,875
Variable cost (Rs.)	2,81,250	6,00,000	3,37,500	12,18,750
Labor Cost (Rs.) (refer to working note 2)	3,00,000	6,00,000	3,37,500	12,37,500
Overhead (Rs.)	1,12,500 (28,125 units × Rs. 4)	2,40,000 (60,000 units × Rs. 4)	1,35,000 (33,750 units × Rs. 4)	4,87,500 —
Total semi-variable overheads (refer to working note 3)				72,000
Fixed overheads(Rs.)				1,92,300
Total cost (Rs.)				32,08,050
Add: profit (20% on selling price or 25% on cost)				8,02,013
Sales Revenue (Rs.)				40,10,063
Selling price per unit (Rs.40,10,063/1,21,875 units)				32.90

II. Make or Buy Decision

The management very often faces a problem as to whether component parts should be manufactured by itself or they should be purchased from an outside supplier. When a company has surplus capacity to manufacture, then, it should utilize its idle capacity instead of buying them from outside supplier. But, before arriving at such a decision, it should compare the marginal cost of manufacturing that particular part with the price quoted by the outside supplier. In case, the price quoted is lower than the marginal cost of manufacture, then, it is advisable to buy the part and not to manufacture.

Illustration 20

The total costs of manufacturing a component part are as under:

	Rs.
Material	250
Labor	100
Variable Expenses	50
Fixed Expenses	100
	500

The same component part is available in the market at Rs. 450. Should the firm make it or buy it?

Solution

To arrive at the decision as to whether the firm should make the component part or buy, we should compare the marginal cost of manufacturing the component with the price at which it is available in the market.

Calculation of Marginal cost:

	Rs.
Material	250
Labor	100
Variable Expenses	50
	400

Since the marginal cost of manufacturing the part i.e., Rs. 400 is less than the price at which it is available in the market, i.e., Rs 450, the firm should manufacture the component part.

By manufacturing the part, the company gets an additional contribution of Rs.50 per part (Rs.450- Rs. 400).

Illustration 21

Auto parts Ltd. has an annual production of 90,000 units for a major component. The components cost structure is as given below:

	Rs.
Material	270 per unit
Labor (25% fixed)	180 per unit
Expenses:	
Variable	90 per unit
Fixed	135 per unit
Total	675 per unit

(a) The purchase manager has an offer from a supplier who is willing to supply the component at Rs. 540. Should the component be purchased and production stopped?

(b) Assume the resources now used for this components manufacture are to be used to produce another new product for which the selling price is Rs.485.

In the latter case, material price will be Rs. 200 per unit. 90,000 units of this product can be produced, at the same cost basis as above for labor and expenses. Discuss whether it would be advisable to divert the resources to manufacture that new product, on the footing that the component presently being produced would, instead of being produced, be purchased from the market.

(CA., Inter)

Solution

***(a)* Statement showing the Variable Cost and Purchase Cost of Component**

	Per unit *Rs.*	*Total (90,000 units)* *Rs.*
Variable cost:		
Material	270	2,43,00,000
Labor (75% of Rs. 180)	135	1,21,50,000
Expenses	90	81,00,000
Total Variable Cost	495	4,45,50,000
(When component is produced)		
Purchase Price	540	4,86,00,000
Excess of purchase price over Variable cost	45	40,50,000

Since, fixed expenses remain constant; it is evident from the above statement that if the component is purchased from the outside supplier, the company will have to pay Rs 45 per unit more. Therefore, the company should not stop the production.

***(b)* Statement showing the contribution per unit if the existing resources are used for the production of new product**

	Per Unit *Rs.*	*Per Unit* *Rs.*
Selling Price of new product		485
Less: Material	200	
Labor (variable)	135	
Expenses (variable)	90	425
Contribution per unit from the new product		60
Loss per unit if the present component is purchased		45
Net Savings		15

The above details show that if the company diverts its resources for the production of another new product, it will benefit by Rs. 15 per unit. It is, therefore, advisable to use the resources to manufacture the new product and component should be purchased from the market.

Illustration 22

A firm needs a component in an assembly operation. If it wants to do the manufacturing itself, it would need to buy a machine for Rs. 4 lakhs which would last of 4 years with no salvage value. Manufacturing costs in each of the 4 years would be Rs. 6 lakhs, Rs.7 lakhs, Rs.8 lakhs and 10 lakhs respectively. If the firm had to buy the component from a supplier, the component would cost Rs. 9 lakhs, Rs. 10 lakhs, Rs.11 lakhs and Rs.14 lakhs respectively in each of the 4 years. However, the machine would occupy floor space which could have been used for another machine. This latter machine could be hired at no cost to manufacture an item, the sale of which would produce net cash flows in each of the 4 years of Rs.2 lakhs; it is impossible to find room for both the machines and there are no other external effects. The cost of capital is 10% and PV factor for each of the 4 years is 0.909, 0.826, 0.751 and 0.683 respectively. Should the firm make the component or buy from outside?

(CA, Final, May 1999, adapted)

Solution

Evaluation of Make or Buy Proposal

(Rs. in lakhs)

Year	*Present Value Factor at 10%*	*When the Component is Manufactured*		*When the Component is bought*	
		Cash outflow (Capital cost, Manufacturing Cost + Opportunity Cost) *Rs.*	*Present Value of Cash Outflows* *Rs.*	*Cash Outflow (cost of buying)* *Rs.*	*Present value* *Rs.*
0	1.000	4	4.0000	—	—
1	.909	6+2	7.2720	9	8.181
2	.826	7+2	7.4340	10	8.260
3	.751	8+2	7.5100	11	8.261
4	.683	10+2	8.1960	14	9.562
			34.4120		34.264

Saving in buying: Rs. 34.412 lakh – Rs. 34.264 lakh
= Rs. 0.148 lakhs

Thus, it is beneficial to buy the component from outside.

Note: The loss of Rs. 2 lakhs cash inflow for each of the 4 years due to inability of the firm to operate another machine when it manufactures the component is to be treated as an opportunity cost.

III. Product Mix Decision

Another important area where the management faces a problem is, as to whether it should produce one product or more than one product. This decision is arrived on the basis of contribution of each product. Thus, the management should select that product mix which yields maximum contribution. But, if there is a shortage or limited supply of certain other resources like for example, the machine hours, then the contribution is linked with such resource for taking a decision.

Illustration 23

A company has 3 alternative choices of a product mix. It produces two products X and Y. It can produce either

(a) 200 units of X and 400 units of Y or

(b) 300 units of X and 300 units of Y or

(c) 400 units of X and 200 units of Y

	X (Rs)	*Y (Rs)*
Selling Expenses per unit	200	150
Variable Costs per unit	160	120
Fixed expenses: Rs. 8,000		

You have to decide the best product mix.

Solution

Statement showing contribution per unit

	X (Rs)	*Y(Rs)*
Selling Price per unit	200	150
Less: Variable Expenses per unit	160	120
Contribution per unit	40	30

(a) Calculation of contribution if the company produces 200 units of X and 400 units of Y

	Rs.
Contribution from 200 units of X (200 units × Rs. 40)	8,000
Contribution from 400 units of Y (400 units × Rs. 30)	12,000
Total Contribution	20,000

Profit = Contribution – Fixed expenses

= 20,000 – 8,000 = Rs. 12,000

(b) Calculation of contribution if the company produces 300 units of X units and 300 units of Y

	Rs.
Contribution from 300 units of X (300 units × Rs. 40)	12,000
Contribution from 300 units of Y (300 units × Rs. 30)	9,000
Total Contribution	21,000

Profit = Contribution – Fixed expenses

= 21,000 – 8,000 = Rs. 13,000

***(c)* Calculation of contribution if company produces 400 units of X and 200 units of Y**

	Rs.
Contribution from 400 units of X (400 units × Rs. 40)	16,000
Contribution from 200 units of Y (200 units × Rs. 30)	6,000
Total Contribution	22,000

Profit = Contribution – Fixed expenses

= 22,000 – 8,000 = Rs. 14,000

Since contribution from 400 units of X and 200 units of Y is the maximum, the company should select this product mix to increase its profit.

Illustration 24

Allied Manufacturing Company gives you the following information.

	Product A *Rs.*	*Product B* *Rs.*
Fixed Overhead: Rs.15,000 p.a.		
Direct Materials	15	20
Direct Labor @ Re.1 per hour.	5	10
Variable Overhead (100% of Direct Labor)		
Selling Price	50	90

You are required to present a statement showing the marginal cost of each product and recommend which of the following sales mixes should be adopted

(i) 900 units of A and 600units of B

(ii) 1,800 units of A only

(iii) 1,200 units of B only and

(iv) 1,500 units of A and 500 units of B.

Solution

Marginal Cost Statement

	Product A Rs.	Product B Rs.
Direct Material	15	20
Direct Labor	5	10
Variable overhead	5	10
Marginal cost	25	40
Contribution	25	50
Selling Prices	50	90

Statement Showing Contribution and Profits of various Sale Mix alternatives

Sales Mix	*Contribution per unit Rs.*	*Total Contribution Rs.*	*Fixed Cost Rs.*	*Profit Rs.*
900 units of A	25	22,500		
and 600 units of B	50	30,000		
		52,500	15,000	37,500
1,800 units of A only	25	45,000	15,000	30,000
1,200 units of B only and	50	60,000	15,000	45,000
1,500 units of A	25	37,500		
and 500 units of B	50	25,000		
		62,500	15,000	47,500

Hence, the sales mix (iv) is recommended as it yields maximum profit i.e. Rs.47,500.

IV. Key or Limiting Factor

Very often, the company faces the problem of non-availability of input factors in adequate quantities. Such a factor is called as Key or Limiting Factor. CIMA, England defined, Limiting Factor as 'the factor in the activities of an undertaking which at a particular point in time or over a period will limit the volume of output". Key factor may be in the form of shortage of raw material, labor hours, machine hours, finance, etc. In the presence of a limiting factor, selection of the product will be on the basis of contribution per unit of key factor.

Illustration 25

A company manufactures and markets three products A, B and C. All the three products are made from the same set of machines. Production is limited by machine capacity. From the data given below, indicate priorities for products A, B, and C with a view to maximize the profits.

Particulars	*Product A (Rs)*	*Product B (Rs)*	*Product C (Rs)*
Raw Material cost per unit	2.25	3.25	4.25
Direct Labor cost per unit	0.50	0.50	0.50
Other Variable cost per unit	0.30	0.45	0.71
Selling Price per unit	5.00	6.00	7.00
Standard Machine time required per unit	39 mins	20 mins	28 mins

In the following year, the company faces extreme shortage of raw materials. It is noted that 3 kg, 4 kg, and 5 kg of raw materials are required to produce one unit of A, B and C respectively. How would products priorities change?

(CS, Inter, Dec., 1977)

Solution

Particulars	*A* *Rs.*	*B* *Rs.*	*C* *Rs.*
Selling price per unit	5.00	6.00	7.00
Less: Variable cost per unit			
Raw Material	2.25	3.25	4.25
Direct Labor	0.50	0.50	0.50
Other Variable Cost	0.30	0.45	0.71
Total Variable Cost per unit	3.05	4.20	5.46
Contribution per unit	1.95	1.80	1.54
Standard machine time per unit	39 min	20 min	28 min
Contribution per machine minute	5 paisa	9 paisa	5 ½ paisa
Priorities for products	III	I	II
Raw materials required to produce one unit (kgs)	3	4	5
Contribution per kg of Raw	(1.95/3)	(1.80/4)	(1.54/5)
Materials (Rs)	0.65	0.45	0.308
Priorities for products	I	II	III

Illustration 26

The following data are given

	Product A *Per unit* *Rs.*	*Product B* *Per unit* *Rs.*
Direct Material	20	10
Direct Labor @ 3 per hour	6	9
Variable Overhead @ Rs. 4 per hour	8	12
Selling Price	90	100
Standard Time	2 hrs	3hrs

State which product you would recommend to manufacture when

(i) Labor time is the key factor

(ii) Sales is the key factor

Solution

		Product A *Rs.*	*Product B* *Rs.*
Selling Price (1)		90	100
Direct Material		20	10
Direct Labor		6	9
Variable Overhead		8	12
Marginal Cost (2)		34	31
Contribution [(1)-(2)]		56	69
(i) Contribution per Labor hour		(56/2)=28	(69/3)=23
(ii) Contribution per Rupee of Sale Value		(56/90)=0.62	(69/100)=0.69

Remarks:

(1) Product A is recommended when labor hour is the limiting factor as contribution per hour of Product A is greater than that of Product B.

(2) Product B is recommended when sales is the limiting factor as contribution per rupee of sale value of Product B is greater than that of Product A.

(3) When no limiting factor is considered, Product B is more profitable as its contribution per unit is more than that of product A.

Illustration 27

From the following data, which product would you recommend to be manufactured in a factory, time being the key factor?

	Per unit of Product A Rs.	*per unit of Product B Rs.*
Direct material	24	14
Direct Labor (Re 1 per hr)	2	3
Variable Overhead (Rs 2 per hr)	4	6
Selling Price	100	100
Standard time to produce	2 hrs	3 hrs

Solution

Particulars	*Product A (per unit) Rs.*	*Product B (per unit) Rs.*
Selling Price	100	100
Less: Variable expenses		
Direct Materials	24	14
Direct Labor	2	3
Variable overhead	4	6
Contribution per unit	70	77
Standard time to produce	2 hrs	3 hrs
Contribution per hour	70/2 = Rs. 35	77/3 = Rs. 25.67

Thus, it is clear from the above statement that during shortage of labor, Product A is more profitable than product B. If there were to be no shortage, then, Product B would have been preferred.

V. Shut down/Closing or Continue Decision

Very often, it becomes necessary for a firm to temporarily suspend or close the activities of a factory due to trade recession. The decision to close down or suspend its activities should depend on Marginal Cost Analysis. If the products are making a contribution towards fixed expenses, then, it is preferable to continue because, the losses will be minimized.

Sometimes, if the firm is closed down, certain fixed expenses can be avoided and certain other fixed expenses may be incurred for closing down the activities. In such a case, the firm is advised to continue, when the contribution is more than the difference between the fixed expenses incurred in normal operation and the fixed expenses incurred during the shut down.

Illustration 28

A Ltd. is experiencing recessionary difficulties and as a result, its directors are considering whether or not the factory should be closed till the recession has passed.

The annual flexible budget is compiled giving the following details.

	Fixed costs		*Production capacity(FC+VC)*			
	Close down *Rs.*	*Normal* *Rs.*	*40%* *Rs.*	*60%* *Rs.*	*80%* *Rs.*	*100%* *Rs.*
Direct Material	—	—	12,000	18,000	24,000	32,000
Direct Labor	—	—	10,000	15,000	20,000	25,000
Factory Overheads	6,000	8,000	10,000	11,000	12,000	13,000
Administration OHs	4,000	6,000	6,500	7,000	7,500	8,000
S & D Overheads	4,000	6,000	7,000	8,000	9,000	10,000
Miscellaneous	1,000	1,000	1,500	2,000	2,500	3,000
	15,000	21,000	47,000	61,000	75,000	91,000

The following additional information has been supplied

(a) Present sales at 50% capacity are estimated at Rs. 30,000 p.a.
(b) Closing down costs would amount to Rs. 4,500
(c) Maintenance of plant would cost Rs. 800 p.a.
(d) On reopening the factory, the cost of overhauling the plant would be Rs. 2,000 and Rs. 1,400 for training of personnel.
(e) A market research consultant has revealed that sales would take an upward swing to around 70% capacity at prices which would produce revenue of Rs. 1,00,000 in approximately twelve months time.

You are required to advise the directors whether to close down for 12 months or continue operations.

Solution

Statement of Profit and Loss

Particulars	*Production Capacity*		
	0% *Rs.*	*50%* *Rs.*	*70%* *Rs.*
Sales	—	30,000	1,00,000
Less: Variable Costs	—	33,000	47,000
Contribution	—	(3,000)	53,000
Less: Fixed Costs	15,000	21,000	21,000
Other Fixed Costs:			
Closing Down Costs	4,500	—	—
Plant Maintenance	800	—	
Reopening Cost	2,000	—	
Personnel Training	1,400		
Profit/(Loss)	(23,700)	(24,000)	32,000

Working Notes:

(1) Calculation of variable costs at 50% capacity

At 60% capacity, total cost is Rs. 61,000

At 40% capacity, total cost is Rs. 47,000

<u>20%</u> Difference in Capacity, <u>14,000</u> change in costs

Variable costs for 10% capacity level

20% — 14,000

10% — ?

= (14,000/20) × 10 = Rs. 7,000

Therefore, for 10% increase in capacity, the variable costs will be Rs. 7000.

	Rs.
Total costs at 40% capacity	47,000
+ 10% increase in capacity	7,000
Total costs at 50% capacity	54,000
Fixed costs (Normal)	21,000
Variable cost at 50% capacity	33,000

(2) Calculation of variable costs at 70% capacity

	Rs.
Total costs at 60% capacity	61,000
+ 10% increase in capacity	7,000
Total costs at 70% capacity	68,000
– Fixed costs (Normal)	21,000
Variable Cost at 70% capacity	47,000

It is advisable to continue operations at 70 per cent capacity

Illustration 29

Universe Ltd. manufactures 20,000 units of 'X' in a year at its normal production capacity. The unit cost as to variable costs and fixed costs at this level are Rs. 13 and Rs. 4 respectively.

Due to trade depression, it is expected that only 2,000 units of 'X' can be sold during the next year. The management plans to shut-down the plant. The fixed costs for the next year then, is expected to be reduced to Rs. 33,000. Additional costs of plant shut-down are expected at Rs. 12,000. Should the plant be shut-down? What is the shut-down point?

(CA, Final, May, 1996)

Solution

Note: The decisions regarding the plant shut-down and the calculation of shut-down point requires the figure of selling price per unit of the units sold. As the selling price (per unit) is not given, the selling price per unit is assumed to be Rs. 20.

Statement of cost for taking a decision about shut-down of plant

	Plant is operated *Rs.*	*Plant is shut-down* *Rs.*
Variable cost	26,000 (2,000 units × Rs. 13)	—
Fixed cost	80,000 (2,000 units × Rs. 4)	33,000 (un escapable cost)
Additional shut-down cost	—	12,000
Total Cost	1,06,000	45,000
State of Loss: Sales	40,000 (2,000 units × Rs. 20)	—
Less: Total cost (as above)	1,06,000	45,000
Loss	(66,000)	(45,000)
	(if continued)	(if shut-down)

Decision: A comparison of loss figures indicated as above points out, that, loss is reduced if the plant is shut-down. In fact, by doing so, the concern's loss would be reduced by Rs. 21,000.

Calculation of Shut-down point:

$$\text{Shut-down point} = \frac{\text{Total fixed cost} - \text{Shut down costs}}{\text{Contribution per unit}}$$

$$= \frac{\text{Rs.}80{,}000 - \text{Rs.}45{,}000}{\text{Rs. }20 - \text{Rs.}13}$$

= 5,000 units

VI. Alternative Methods of Production

When a company has different alternative methods of production, then it should select that alternative, which gives maximum contribution assuming that fixed expenses remain same for all the alternatives.

Illustration 30

PQ Ltd. can produce its product on Machine X or Machine Y. From the following data, advise on which machine should the product be produced?

	Machine X	*Machine Y*
Machine hours per year	2,500	2,500
Output per hour (Units)	20	30
Selling Price per unit (Rs.)	100	100
Variable Cost per unit (Rs.)	50	60
Fixed Cost per unit (Rs.)	30	30

Solution

Statement of Profit/Loss

	Machine X *Rs.*	*Machine Y* *Rs.*
Selling price per unit	100	100
Less: Variable Cost per unit	50	60
Contribution per unit	50	40
Output per hour (units)	20	30
Contribution per hour (Rs.)	1,000	1,200
Machine hours per year	2,500	2,500
Annual Contribution (Rs.)	25,00,000	30,00,000

Since Annual contribution from Machine Y is highest, the company should produce on machine Y.

VII. Accept or Reject an offer

Sometimes, the management may have to face a situation where it has to decide as to whether to accept a foreign offer or reject. In such cases, the decision would be in favour of acceptance of the offer, if there is contribution from the acceptance of the offer. Normally, tapping the unutilized capacity to produce would not entail any additional fixed costs and as a result, the additional contribution from the acceptance of foreign offer would add to the existing profit in the home market or enable to cover the uncovered portion of the fixed costs.

Illustration 31

A Company manufacturing a specialized motor part is operating at 60 per cent of its capacity of producing 10,000 units per month. Its monthly budget for fixed expenses (inclusive of depreciation) is Rs. 6 lakhs per month. The direct cost of making the part is as under :

Direct Material	–	Rs. 55.00
Direct Labour	–	Rs. 10.00
Expense	–	Rs. 25.00

The company has invested Rs. One crore in the business and is currently earning a return of 7.2 per cent per annum before taxes. The managing director is prepared to accept new business at any price which will raise the return of investment to 20 per cent before taxes.

A car manufacturer has offered to buy 4,000 units of the part every month if it could be supplied at Rs. 120 per unit. Would you advise the company to accept the offer.

(Meerut 1968 R)

Solution

Total capacity is 10,000 units per month.

Utilized Capacity is 60% of 10,000, i.e., 6,000 units per month.

Fixed Costs are Rs. 6,00,000 per month.

Direct Costs are Rs. 55 + Rs. 10 + Rs. 25 = Rs. 90 per unit.

Total Investment = Rs. 1,00,00,000

Earnings Rate = 7.2% p.a., i.e., Rs. 7,20,000 p.a.

So, Earnings per month = Rs. 60,000.

Now, we can calculate the selling price per unit from the facts mentioned above.

Computation of Selling Price
Output 6,000 units per month

Items	*Total Amount Rs.*	*Per unit Rs.*
Direct Costs	5,40,000	90
Fixed Costs	6,00,000	100
Total Cost	11,40,000	190
Profit	60,000	10
Sales	12,00,000	200

The above calculations show that the total cost of the product is Rs. 190 per unit. But the offer which the company has received is at Rs. 120 per unit. Hence it appears that if this offer is accepted, the company will have to suffer a loss of Rs. 70 (190-120) per unit. But this analysis is fallacious because fixed costs are not affected by the utilization of unutilized capacity of the plant and hence they are deemed to be irrelevant. Here, only variable costs are relevant and worth consideration. As such, here the selling price of the product will be compared with its direct or variable costs and if the selling price is sufficiently higher than the variable costs of the product, the offer should be accepted. The following statement clearly shows the profitability of this proposal.

Statement Showing Profit or Loss on Proposed Offer

	Present Output 6,000 units p.m.		*Proposed Output 4,000 units p.m.*		*Total output 10,000 Units p.m.*
	Per unit Rs.	*Total Amount Rs.*	*Per unit Rs.*	*Total Amount Rs.*	*Total Amount Rs.*
Sales	200	12,00,000	120	4,80,000	16,80,000
Less: Direct Costs	90	5,40,000	90	3,60,000	9,00,000
Contribution	110	6,60,000	30	1,20,000	7,80,000
Less: Fixed Costs	100	6,00,000	—	—	6,00,000
Net Profit p.m.	10	60,000	30	1,20,000	1,80,000
Net Profit p.a.		7,20,000	—	14,40,000	21,60,000
Return on Investment of Rs. 1 crore					21.6%
Management's expectations					20%

The above statement shows that the company will earn an additional amount of Rs. 14,40,000 per annum by accepting this offer and the total annual profit of the company will be increased from the present level of Rs. 7,20,000 to Rs. 21,60,000. This increased profit is 21.6% of the company's investment. Hence, the managing director will accept this offer because this return is more than his desired limit of 20%.

Illustration 32

The A B C Co. is currently operating at an annual production volume of 7,50,000 direct labour hours. Its annual operating capacity which can not be exceeded is 10,00,000 direct labour hours. Recently a private brand distributor has offered to buy 1,00,000 units of the company's product at a special price of Rs. 10.50 per unit. The regular selling price is Rs. 12.90 per unit. The standard cost sheet for one unit of the product appears as follows:

Materials 6kg. @ Re. 0.40 per kg.	Rs. 2.40
Direct Labor 2 hours @ Rs. 2.50 per hour	Rs. 5.00
Overhead:	
Variable 2 hours @ Re. 0.75	Rs. 1.50
Fixed 2 Hours @ Rs. 1.20	Rs. 2.40
	Rs. 11.30

(a) Would it be profitable for the company to accept the offer?

(b) Would your answer be different if the offer was called for 2,50,000 units of the product in place of 1,00,000 units? Why?

Solution

(a) To decide whether the offer should be accepted or not, we have to compare the incremental revenue and incremental costs.

Incremental Revenue from the sale of 1,00,000 units @ Rs. 10.50		Rs. 10,50,000
Incremental Costs:		
Material @ Rs. 2.40 per unit	Rs. 2,40,000	
Direct Labor @ Rs. 5 per unit	Rs. 5,00,000	
Variable Overhead @ Rs. 1.50 Per unit	Rs. 1,50,000	Rs. 8,90,000
Incremental Profit		Rs. 1,60,000

Thus, it would be profitable for the company to accept the offer for the purchase of 1,00,000 units at the price of Rs. 10.50 per unit.

(b) If the order is for 2,50,000 units in place of 1,00,000 units, the position will be different. The total capacity is 5,00,000 units (10,00,000 labour hours/2 hours). The present production and sales are 3,75,000 units (7,50,000 labour hours/2 hours). Thus, the unutilized capacity is 1,25,000 units. The order for 2,50,000 units can be accepted only if *(a)* a new plant is purchased or *(b)* the sales at the regular price are curtailed by 1,25,000 units, i.e., from 3,75,000 units to 2,50,000 units.

If the first option is exercised, there will be a substantial increase in company's fixed costs due to installation of the new plant. Besides, the company will have to face many problems related to financing and acquisition of the new plant.

The effect of second option on company's profits will be as follows:

		Rs.
Incremental Revenue from new order of 2,50,000 units @ Rs. 10.50 per unit		26,25,000
Incremental Costs:		
Material @ Rs. 2.40 per unit	Rs. 6,00,000	
Direct Labor @ Rs. 5 per unit	Rs. 12,50,000	
Variable Overhead @ Rs. 1.50 per unit	Rs. 3,75,000	22,25,000
Incremental Profit		4,00,000
Less: Variable Profit* foregone on the sales of 1,25,000 units which could be sold at the regular price of Rs. 12.90 (1,25,000 × Rs. 4)		5,00,000
Net Loss		1,00,000

Variable Profit = Selling Price – Variable Cost.

12.90 – 8.90 = Rs. 4.00

Thus, we can say that it is not profitable to accept the offer for the sale of 2,50,000 units @ Rs. 10.50 per unit.

SUMMARY

Decision making involves the choice between various alternatives. In case of long term decision making, management looks beyond the current year and takes into consideration time value of money and return on investment. Whereas, in case of short term decision making, management has to select from among the available alternatives, the best one that can be implemented within a one year period. Such decision making is done with the help of Marginal Costing technique.

The terminology of CIMA defines Marginal costing as the ascertainment of Marginal cost and the effect on profit of changes in volume or type of output on the company's profit by differentiating between fixed costs and variable costs.

Absorption Costing is a technique of cost ascertainment which does not recognize the difference between fixed costs and variable costs. It is a process of determining average total cost by charging all costs both variable and fixed to operational, processes and products.

The study of Cost-Volume-Profit Analysis is often referred to as Breakeven Analysis. It is a logical extension of Marginal Costing. It is based on principles of classifying operating expenses into fixed and variable. It has become a powerful instrument in the hands of policy makers to maximize profits. A Breakeven Chart is a graphical representation of Marginal Costing. This chart shows the inter-relationship between profit, volume and cost. It shows the break -even point and also indicates the estimated profit or loss at varying levels of activity.

Marginal Costing is a very useful and important technique for the management in decision making. The information provided by the Total Cost or Absorption Cost Method is not sufficient in solving the management problems. Marginal Costing differentiates costs into fixed cost and variable cost and helps in ascertaining marginal cost and the effect on the profit of changes in the volume or type of output on the company's profit. The important decisions where Marginal Costing technique is applied are Pricing Decisions, Make or Buy Decisions, Product / Sales Mix Decisions, Key or Limiting Factor, Shut Down or Continue Decision, Alternative Methods of Production and Accept or Reject an Offer.

Glossary

- **Marginal Cost:** the cost of one unit of product or service, which would be avoided if that unit were not produced or provided.
- **Marginal Costing:** the ascertainment of Marginal cost and the effect on profit of changes in volume or type of output on the company's profit by differentiating between fixed costs and variable costs.
- **Absorbed Cost:** is the cost which is equal to direct costs plus overhead costs and which is allotted to cost units by means of overhead absorption rates.
- **Absorption Costing:** is a principle whereby fixed as well as variable costs are allotted to cost units and total overheads are absorbed according to the activity level.
- **Breakeven Analysis:** means that system of analysis which determines the probable profit at any level of production. As Breakeven Analysis establishes relationship between cost, volume and profit, it is also known as 'Cost Volume Profit Analysis' or CVP Analysis
- **Contribution:** It is the difference between the Sales and the Marginal Cost of sales and it contributes towards Fixed Expenses and Profit.
- **Margin of Safety:** It is the difference between the Actual Sales and Breakeven Sales. It is the sales or output beyond breakeven point.
- **Breakeven Chart:** is a graphical representation of Marginal Costing. This chart shows the inter-relationship between profit, volume and cost. It shows the breakeven point and also indicates the estimated profit or loss at varying levels of activity.
- **Angle of Incidence:** This is the angle formed at the Breakeven Point at which the sales line cuts the total cost line. This angle indicates the rate at which profits are being made.

Questions

(1) Explain the concepts of Marginal Cost and Absorption Cost.
(2) Differentiate Marginal Costing from Absorption Costing.
(3) Discuss the importance of Breakeven Analysis.
(4) What are the limitations of Breakeven Analysis?
(5) Explain the technique of Marginal Costing and state its importance in decision making.
(6) Explain briefly the various decisions that can be taken with the help of Marginal Costing.

PROBLEMS

(1) From the following cost, production and sales data of XY Company, prepare a comparative income statement for the three years under (1) the Absorption Costing (ii) the Direct Costing Method.
Indicate the unit cost for each year under each method. Also evaluate the closing stock. The company produces a single article for sale:

	Situation		
	A	*B*	*C*
Production and sales	*1976*	*1977*	*1978*
Opening stock	—	—	10,000
Units produced	50,000	70,000	60,000
Units sold	50,000	60,000	66,000
Closing stock	—	10,000	4,000
Cost incurred	*1976* *Rs.*	*1977* *Rs.*	*1978* *Rs.*
Direct Materials	1,00,000	1,44,000	1,27,200
Direct Labor	1,50,000	2,16,000	1,74,000
Direct labor hours	1,00,000	1,44,000	1,16,000
Direct expenses	48,000	72,000	56,000
Factory and Administration Overheads	72,000	72,000	70,000
Variable selling costs	2,50,000	3,00,000	3,40,000
Fixed selling costs	50,000	50,000	50,000

Selling price Rs. 20 per unit
Fixed costs are to be recovered on actual activity.

(ICWA, Inter)

[**Ans.:** *(a)* Absorption Costing Method:
Cost per unit of sales: A-Rs. 13.40; B-Rs. 13.03; C-Rs. 13.04
Closing Stock: A-Nil; B- Rs. 72,000; C-Rs. 28,525
(b) Direct Costing Method:
Variable Cost per unit of sales: A-Rs. 10.96; B-Rs. 11.17; C-Rs. 11.14
Closing Stock: A- Nil; B- Rs. 61,714; C- Rs. 23,937]

(2) Your company has a production capacity of 2,00,000 units per year. Capacity utilization is reckoned as 90%. Standard variable production costs are Rs. 11 per unit and factory costs are Rs. 3,60,000 per year. Variable selling costs are Rs. 3 per unit and fixed costs are Rs. 2,70,000 per year. The unit selling price is Rs. 20. In the year just ended on 30th June 2004, the production was 1,60,000 units and sales were 1,50,000 units. The closing inventory for 2004 was 20,000 units. The actual variable production costs for the year were Rs. 35,000 above the standard.
Calculate the profit for the year
(i) By the Absorption Costing Method and
(ii) By the Marginal Costing Method
(iii) Explain the difference in the profits.
[**Ans.:** *(i)* Profit: Rs. 2,59,375 *(ii)* Profit: Rs. 2,39,375 *(iii)* The difference in profits, Rs. 20,000 is due to theelement of fixed factory cost included in the valuation of opening and closing stock under Absorption Costing Method]

(3) PQR Ltd., has following data

Sales	*1997-98*	*1998-99*
P/V Ratio	8,00,000	
Margin of Safety sales	50%	37.5%
as % of Total Sales	40%	21.87%

The company could maintain its level of 1997-98 in 1998 – 99 by reducing selling price. You are required to calculate the following: *(i)* sales for 1998-99 *(ii)* Breakeven sales for 1998-99.

(CA, Inter, Nov,1999)

[**Ans.:** (1) Rs. 6,40,000 (2) Rs. 5,00,000]

(4) *(i)* Ascertain profit when sales Rs. 2,00,000; Fixed Cost Rs. 40,000; BEP Rs. 1,60,000
(ii) Ascertain Sales, when Fixed Cost is Rs. 20,000; Profit Rs.10,000; BEP Rs. 40,000

(CA, Inter, May, 1999)

[**Ans.:** *(i)* Rs. 10,000 *(ii)* Rs. 60,000]

(5) XYZ Ltd. furnishes the following:

	Year-2001	
	First half year (Rs.)	*Second half (Rs.)*
Sales	8,10,000	10,26,000
Profit earned	21,600	64,800

Assuming fixed cost remain same in both the periods, calculate *(i)* P/V Ratio *(ii)* Fixed cost *(iii)* The amount of profit or loss when sales are Rs. 6,48,000 *(iv)* The amount of sales required to earn profit of Rs. 1,08,000.

(B.Com., Hons., Delhi)

[**Ans.:** *(i)* 20% *(ii)* Rs.1,40,000 *(iii) Loss:* Rs.10,800 *(iv)* Rs. 12,42,000]

(6) The following cost and sales of a manufacturing company for the first and second half of 2008-2009 are given.

	I half year Rs.	*II half year Rs.*
Sales	24,00,000	30,00,000
Total costs	21,80,000	26,00,000

Calculate: *(i)* Contribution/Sales Ratio *(ii)* Fixed cost *(iii)* BEP (Sales) *(iv)* MOS as a percentage of sales.
[**Ans.:** *(i)* 30% *(ii)* Rs. 10,00,000 *(iii)* Rs. 33,33,333 *(iv)* 38.3%]

(7) The Rates of variable cost to sales is 70%. The Breakeven point occurs at 60% of the capacity sales. Find the capacity sales when fixed costs are Rs. 90,000. Also, compute profit at 75% of capacity sales.

(C.A., Intermediate, Nov., 1997)

[**Ans.:** *(i)* Rs. 3,00,000 *(ii)* Rs. 5,00,000]

(8) XYZ Ltd has been offered a choice to buy Machine 'A' or Machine 'B'. From the following data, you are required to compute:

(a) Breakeven point for each of the Machine.
(b) The level of sales at which both Machines earn equal profit.

	Machine	
	A	B
Fixed cost (Rs.)	10,000	10,000
Profit at given level of production (Rs.)	30,000	16,000
Production	30,000	24,000

The market price of the product is expected to be Rs.10 per unit.
[**Ans.:** *(a)* Machine A 5,000 units of Rs. 50,000; Machine – 'B' 4000 units of Rs.40,000 *(b)* 7000 units]

(9) You are given the following data:

	Rs.
Fixed cost	2,000
Profit	2,000
Sales	10,000
Variable Cost – 60% of sales	

Find : *(i)* Breakeven sales
(ii) What should be the sales to earn a profit of Rs. 6,000 and
(iii) Margin of safety when sales are Rs. 25,000

[**Ans.:** *(i)* Rs. 5,000 *(ii)* Rs. 20,000 *(iii)* Rs. 20,000]

(10) S.N. furnishes the following information relating to the half year ended 30 June, 2008.

Fixed cost	Rs. 45,000
Sales	Rs. 1,50,000
Profit	Rs. 30,000
During the second half of the year, the company has projected a loss of	Rs. 10,000

Calculate: *(a)* The breakeven point and margin of safety for six months ending 30 June, 2008.
(b) Expected sales volume for the second half of the year, assuming that fixed cost and P/V ratio remain constant in the second half of the year.
(c) The breakeven point and margin of safety for the whole year of 2008.

[**Ans.:** *(a)* Rs. 90,000 and Rs. 60,000 *(b)* Rs. 70,000 *(c)* Rs. 1,80,000 and Rs. 40,000)

(11) If Margin of Safety is Rs. 2,40,000 (40% sales) and P/V Ratio is 30% of ABC Ltd., calculate its *(i)* Breakeven sales *(ii)* Amount of profit on sales of Rs. 9,00,000.

(C.A., Inter, May, 1997)

[**Ans.:** (1) Rs. 3,60,000 (2) Rs. 1,62,000]

(12) The sales turnover and profit during two periods were as follows:

Period	*Sales Rs.*	*Profit Rs.*
1	2,00,000	20,000
2	3,00,000	40,000

(1) What would be Profitable Trading Results with sales of Rs. 1,80,000
(2) What amount of sales will yield a profit of Rs. 50,000?
[**Ans.:** (1) Rs. 16,000 (2) Rs. 3,50,000]

(13) *(a)* Calcutta Company Ltd. manufactures and sells four types of products under the brand names Ace, Utility, Luxury and Supreme. The sales mix in value comprises of:

Brand	*Percentage*
Ace	33 1/3%
Utility	41 2/3%
Luxury	16 2/3%
Supreme	8 1/3%
	100 %

The total budgeted Sales (100%) are Rs.6,00,000 per month
The operating costs are:

Ace	60% of selling price
Utility	68% of selling price
Luxury	80% of selling price
Supreme	40% of selling price

The fixed costs are Rs.1,59,000 per month. Calculate the Breakeven point for the product on an overall basis.
(b) It has been proposed to change the sales mix as follows, the total sales per month remaining Rs.6,00,000:

Brand	*Percentage*
Ace	25 %
Utility	40 %
Luxury	30%
Supreme	5%
	100%

Assuming that this proposal is implemented, calculate the new Breakeven point.

(CA, Final, November, 1986)

[**Ans.:** *(a)* Overall P/V ratio: 35%; Breakeven Point (sales value) Rs. 4,54,286 *(b)* New P/V ratio: 31.8%; New Breakeven point (sales value) Rs. 5,00,000]

(14) ABC Ltd. has developed a new product which is about to be launched into the market. The variable cost of selling the product is Rs.17 per unit. The marketing department has estimated that at a price of Rs.25, annual demand would be 10,000 units. However, if the sale price is set abovc Rs. 25, sales demand would fall by 500 units for each Re.0.50 increase above Rs.25. Similarly, if the price is below Rs.25, demand would increase by 500 units for each Re.0.50 stepped reduction in price below Rs.25.
Required: determine the price which would maximize ABC Ltd.'s profit in the next year.

(CA, Final, May, 1995)

[**Ans.:** Total contribution would be maximum at a sale price of Rs. 26 per unit and sales demand of 9,000 units]

(15) Chum Chum Ltd. Is about to introduce a new product with the following estimates:

Price per unit (Rs.) (Demand)	*Demand (in thousand units)*
30-00	400
31-50	380
33-00	360
34-50	340
36-00	315
37-50	280
39-00	240

Costs:

Direct material	Rs. 12 per unit
Direct labor	Rs. 3 per unit
Variable overhead	Rs. 3 per unit
Selling expenses	10% on sales
Fixed production overheads	Rs. 14,40,000
Administration expenses	Rs. 10,80,000

Judging from the estimates, determine the tentative price of the new product to earn maximum profit.

(CA, Final, Nov., 1991)

[**Ans.:** The tentative price of the new product should be Rs. 36 per unit. At this price, the profit of Chum-Chum Ltd. is maximum at Rs. 20,16,000]

(16) An enthusiastic marketing manager suggests to his managing director that only if he is permitted to reduce the selling price of product by 20%, he would be able to achieve a 30% increase in sales volume. The managing director, finding that the sales volume increase exceeds in percentage the extent of requested reduction in price, gives the clearance. You are given the following information:

Present selling price per unit	Rs. 7.50
Present volume of sales	2,00,000 Nos.
Total variable costs	Rs. 10,50,000
Total fixed costs	Rs. 3,60,000

Assuming no changes in the costs pattern in coming period:

(i) Examine the consequences of the managing director's decision assuming that 30% increase in sales in realized.

(ii) At what volume of sales can the present quantum of profits be maintained?

[**Ans.:** *(a)* Present level of profit: Rs. 90,000

(b) After reduction of 20% selling price: Loss Rs. 1,65,000

(c) Sales required at the present level of profits: Rs. 36,00,000]

(17) A manufacturer with an overall capacity of one lakh machine hours (inter-change-able among the products) has been so far producing a standard mix of 15,000 units of product A; 10,000 units of products B and C each. On experience, the total expenditure (exclusive of the fixed charges) is to be Rs. 2.09 lakh and the unit variable cost ratio among the products approximates 1:1.5:1.75 respectively. The fixed charges come to Rs. 2 per unit. When the unit selling prices are Rs. 6.25 for A; Rs. 7.5 for B and Rs. 10.5 for C; 'C' incurs loss. Hence, he desires to change the product mix as under:

	Mix 1	*Mix 2*	*Mix 3*
A	18,000	15,000	22,000
B	12,000	6,000	8,000
C	7,000	13,000	8,000

As a cost accountant, what mix will you recommend?

(M.Com., UOM, May 1982)

[**Ans.:** Profit: Mix I: Rs.(6,300); Mix II: Rs. (450); Mix III Rs. 300. Hence, proposed Mix III is more profitable among the alternative mixes available]

(18) The Fast Bicycles Ltd. manufactures a number of cycle parts. The cost per unit of part No. 845 is as follows:

	Rs.
Materials	3.00
Labor (25% Fixed)	2.00
Expenses: Variable	1.00
Fixed	1.50
	7.50

The company is informed by an outside firm that the part can be supplied by it at Rs. 6, quality and regular supplies guaranteed. The present consumption and production is 50,000 units per annum. Do you recommend that the production be stopped and the part be purchased?

Will your answer be different, if the men and plant required for making part No. 845 can be used to turn out a defense item for which a price of Rs. 4.25 is offered?

(M.Com., UOM, March, 1989)

[**Ans.:** Manufacture the component as Variable Cost of manufacturing i.e. Rs. 5.50 is less than the supplier's price of Rs. 6.00]

(19) A machine manufactures 10,000 units of a part at a total cost of Rs.21 of which Rs.18 is variable. This part is readily available in the market at Rs.19 per unit. If the part is purchased from the market, then, the machine can either be utilized to manufacture a component in same quantity contributing Rs.2 per component or it can be hired out at Rs.21,000. Recommend which of the alternative is profitable?

(CA, Final, May, 1997)

[**Ans.:** *(a)* Manufactured internally- Cost Rs. 1,80,000; *(b)* purchased from the market and the machine is utilized to manufacture 10,000 units of a component- Cost Rs. 1,70,000; *(c)* hiring out the machine –Cost Rs. 1,69,000. 3rd alternative is the best]

(20) A company produces three products from an imported material. The cost structure per unit of the products is as under:

	Product		
	A *Rs.*	*B* *Rs.*	*C* *Rs.*
Sales Value	200	300	250
Direct Material	50	80	60
Direct Wages Rs.6 per hour	60	120	108
Variable Overheads	30	60	54

Out of Direct Material 80% is of the imported material @ Rs.10 per kg.

Prepare a statement showing comparative profitability of the three products under the following scenarios:

(i) Imported Material is in restricted supply.

(ii) Production Capacity is limiting factor.

(iii) When maximum sales potential of products A and B are 1,000 units each and that of product 'C' is 500 units for specific requirement, availability of imported material is restricted to 10,000 kgs. per month, how the profit could be maximized?

(CA, Final, November, 1997)

[**Ans.:** *(i)* Product 'A' is most profitable *(ii)* Product 'A' is most profitable *(iii)* No. of units- A: 1,000; B: 562; C: 500 and Maximum Profit- A: Rs. 60.000; B: Rs. 22,450; C: Rs. 14,000]

(21) The flexible budget of a company is as follows :

Particulars	*Production Capacity*			
	40% (Rs.)	*60% (Rs.)*	*80% (Rs.)*	*100% (Rs.)*
Costs:				
Direct Labor	1,60,000	2,40,000	3,20,000	4,00,000
Direct Material	1,20,000	1,80,000	2,40,000	3,00,000
Production Overheads	1,14,000	1,26,000	1,38,000	1,50,000
Administrative Overheads	58,000	62,000	66,000	70,000
Sales Overheads	62,000	68,000	74,000	80,000
Total	5,14,000	6,76,000	8,38,000	10,00,000

Due to recession in the economy, the company is operating at 50% capacity. In about twelve months time, sales are expected to be about 75% of normal capacity and the revenue to be produced in the second year will amount to Rs. 9,00,000. The present revenue from sales at 50% capacity amounts to Rs. 4,95,000 for a complete year. If the directors decide to close down the factory for a year, it is estimated that:

(a) The present fixed costs would be reduced to Rs. 1,10,000 per annum;

(b) Closing down costs would amount to Rs. 75,000

(c) Maintenance of plant would cost Rs. 10,000 per annum and

(d) On reopening the factory, the cost of overhauling would require Rs.40,000.

Present the information to the company indicating whether it is desirable to close down the factory

(M.Com., UOM, May 1983)

[**Ans.:** *Loss: (a)* if factory is continued-Rs.1,00,000 and *(b)* if factory is closed-Rs. 2,35,000 *(c)* Profit likely to be earned next year- R.s 1,02,500. Hence, continue to run the plant]

(22) The following information for the year 2008 relates to a mechanical toys factory:

		Rs.
Material Cost		1,20,000
Labor Cost		2,40,000
Fixed Overheads		1,20,000
Variable Overheads		60,000
Units produced 12,000		
Total capacity 20,000 units	Selling price per unit – Rs. 50	

The firm has an offer for the purchase of 5,000 units at a price of Rs. 40 per unit. If the offer is accepted, it would lead to (i) a saving of Re. 1 per unit in material cost on all units manufactured; (ii) an increase in overhead by Rs. 35,000 and (iii) a drop in overall efficiency by 2 per cent on the entire production. Would you advise acceptance of the offer?

[**Ans.:** The increase in the net profit of Rs. 61 is very insignificant. Therefore, it is not advisable to accept the offer at Rs. 40]

❑ ❑ ❑

17

DIFFERENTIAL COSTING

Objectives

The objectives of the study are to:

- Understand the concept of Differential Cost
- Differentiate Differential Cost from Marginal Cost
- Appreciate the significance of Differential Costing technique in decision making

INTRODUCTION

A manager has to take several decisions in the course of time for the maximization of profits of the company. He has to choose the best alternative among the available alternatives. In such a case, he has to compare the additional costs and the additional revenues while switching over from one alternative to another alternative. This is where the technique of Differential Costing helps him in decision making.

MEANING OF DIFFERENTIAL COST

Differential Costs are the increase or decrease in the total costs that result from producing additional or fewer units, or from the adoption of an alternative course of action. The alternative course of action may arise due to a change in sales volume, alternative method of production, change in product/sales mix, make or buy, refuse or accept decisions, addition of a new product, exploring a new market, decision to drop a product line, etc.

Differential Cost may be referred to as either Incremental Cost or Decremental Cost. When there is an increase in the total cost due to an increase in the level of production, it is called Incremental Cost, and when there is a decrease in the total cost due to a decrease in the level of production, it is called as Decremental Cost.

MARGINAL COST VS. DIFFERENTIAL COST

Marginal Cost represents the increase or decrease in the total cost which occurs with a small change in output say, a unit of output. In Cost Accounting, Variable Costs represent Marginal Cost.

Differential Cost is the change (increase or decrease) in the total cost (variable as well as fixed) due to a change in the level of activity, technology or production process or method of production. In other words, it can be defined as the cost of one unit of product or service which would be avoided if that unit was not produced or provided.

The main point which distinguishes Marginal Cost and Differential Cost is that of change in fixed cost when volume of production increases or decreases by a unit of production. In the case of Differential Cost, variable as well as fixed cost, i.e., both the costs change due to a change in the level of activity, whereas under Marginal Costing, only variable cost changes due to a change in the level of activity.

If at any level of output, an increase in the output by one or more units, the increase in costs associated with such an increase in output represents Marginal Cost. Marginal Cost is variable in relation to output. This concept helps us in determining the PV ratio, break-even point and margin of safety. It is an important concept in Cost-Accounting and is useful for managerial decision making as well. Here, costs have a linear relationship with output. Marginal Cost excludes fixed costs, whereas Differential Cost includes certain fixed costs. It helps in pricing and product mix decision to be taken to improve operating results.

Characteristics of Differential Cost

(1) The data used for Differential Cost Analysis are costs, revenues and investments involved in the decision making problem.
(2) Differential Cost does not find a place in the accounting records. It can be determined from the analysis of routine accounting records.
(3) Total Differential Cost is considered in Differential Cost Analysis. Cost per unit is not taken into consideration.
(4) Differential Cost Analysis determines the choice for future course of action and hence it deals with the future costs. Historical Costs or Standard Costs may be used but they should be suitably adjusted to future conditions.
(5) Differential Costing involves the study of difference in costs between two alternatives.
(6) The changes in costs are measured from a common base point which may be a present course of action or present level of production.
(7) The alternative which shows the highest difference (surplus) between the Incremental Revenue and the Differential Cost is the one which is considered to be the best choice.

Managerial Applications of Differential Cost Analysis

The following are the decisions which can be taken with the help of Differential Cost Analysis.

- Determination of the most profitable level of production and price.
- Introduction of new products.
- Acceptance of an offer at a lower selling price.
- Changing the product mix.
- Changing the method of production.
- Discontinuing a product to avoid the losses and increase profits.
- Decision to drop a product line.
- Make or buy decisions.
- Decision regarding the depth of processing.
- Shut-down decisions.
- Determining a suitable price at which raw materials may be purchased.

Illustration 1

A company's flexible budget at various levels of production reveals the following:

Output in 000s Units	*Selling price per Unit Rs.*	*Total Semi-fixed Costs Rs. (000)*	*Total Variable Costs Rs. (000)*	*Total fixed cost Rs. (000)*
30	24	150	418	142
60	22	150	818	142
90	20	170	1,278	142
120	18	170	1,578	142
150	16	200	1,778	142
180	14	200	1,902	142

You are required to:

(1) Prepare a schedule showing the total Differential Cost and Increments in Revenue.
(2) At what level should the company set its level of production?
(3) What selling price is recommended by you in order to maximize the profits?

Solution

Schedule showing the Differential Cost and Incremental Revenue

Output (no 000)	*Selling price per unit Rs.*	*Sales Value Rs. (000)*	*Incremental Revenue Rs. (000)*	*Semi fixed cost Rs. (000)*	*Variable Cost Rs. 000*	*Fixed Cost Rs. 000*	*Total Cost Rs. 000*	*Differential Cost Rs. 000*
30	24	720	—	150	418	142	710	—
60	22	1,320	600	150	818	142	1,110	400
90	20	1,800	480	170	1,278	142	1,590	480
120	18	2,160	360	170	1,578	142	1,890	300
150	16	2,400	240	200	1,778	142	2,120	230
180	14	2,520	120	200	1,902	142	2,244	124

It is profitable for the company to increase the level of production so long as the incremental revenue is more than the differential cost. It is not advisable to increase the level of production to such a level where the Differential Costs are more than the Incremental Revenue. In the given problem, the company should set the level of production at 1,50,000 units because after this level Differential Costs exceed the Incremental Revenue.

The selling price recommended for the company is Rs 16/- per unit at an activity level of 1,50,000 units.

Illustration 2

Somesh of Agra, presently operates its plant at 80% of the normal capacity to manufacture a product only to meet the demand of Government of Tamil Nadu under a rate contract. He supplies the product for Rs.4,00,000 and earns a profit margin of 20% on sales realizations. Direct cost per unit is constant.

The indirect costs as per his budget projections are:

Indirect Costs	*20,000 units (80% capacity) Rs.*	*22,500 units (90% capacity) Rs.*	*25,000 units (100% capacity) Rs.*
Variable Cost	80,000	90,000	1,00,000
Semi-Variable Cost	40,000	42,500	45,000
Fixed Cost	80,000	80,000	80,000

He has received an export order for the product equal to 20% of its present operations. Additional packing charges on this order will be Rs.1,000. Arrive at the price to be quoted for the export order to give him a profit margin of 10% on the export price.

Solution

Working notes:

Direct Cost per unit	*Rs.*
Selling Price per unit (Rs. 4,00,000/20,000 units)	20
Less: Profit Margin (20% × Rs. 20)	4
Total Cost	16
Less: Indirect Costs (Rs. 2,00,000/20,000 units)	10
Direct Cost per unit	6

2. Statement of Differential Cost for 4,000 units (20% of 20,000 units)

	Present Production 20,000 units Rs.	*Proposed Production 24,000 units Rs.*	*Differential Cost for 4,000 units Rs.*
Direct Cost @ Rs.6/- p.u.	1,20,000	1,44,000	24,000
Indirect Cost:			
Variable Cost @ Rs.4/-p.u	80,000	96,000	16,000
Semi-Variable Cost	40,000	44,000	4,000
Fixed Cost	80,000	81,000	1,000
Total Cost	3,20,000	3,65,000	45,000

Computation for the price to be quoted for the export order of 4,000 units

	Rs.
Differential Cost (Refer to working note 2)	45,000
Add: Profit (10% of export price or 1/9th of cost)	5,000
Price to be quoted	50,000

Export price per unit: Rs. 2.50 (Rs.50,000/4000 units)

Illustration 3

A company has a capacity of producing 1,00,000 units of a certain product in a month. The sales department reports that the following schedule of sale price is possible:

Volume of production %	*Selling price per unit* *Paise*
60	90
70	80
80	75
90	67
100	61

The variable cost of manufacture between these levels is 15 paise per unit and fixed cost Rs.40,000.

Prepare a statement showing incremental revenue and differential cost at each stage. If there is an offer at 50 paise per unit for the balance capacity over the maximum profit volume for export price, and price quoted will not affect the internal sale price, will you advise accepting this bid and why?

Solution

Statement showing Incremental Revenue and Differential Cost

Capacity %	*Output* (units)	*Variable Cost (Rs)*	*Fixed Cost (Rs)*	*Total Cost (Rs)*	*Selling Price (Rs)*	*Sales Value (Rs)*	*Differential Cost (Rs)*	*Incremental Revenue (Rs)*
60	60,000	9,000	40,000	49,000	0.90	54,000	—	—
70	70,000	10,500	40,000	50,500	0.80	56,000	1,500	2,000
80	80,000	12,000	40,000	52,000	0.75	60,000	1,500	4,000
90	90,000	13,500	40,000	53,500	0.67	60,300	1,500	300
100	1,00,000	15,000	40,000	55,000	0.61	61,000	1,500	700

At 80% capacity, profit will be the maximum, as, after this level, the Differential Cost is more than the Incremental Revenue.

It is advisable to accept the bulk order of export at a price of 50 paise per unit because, the balance capacity of 20,000 units will add Rs. 10,000 (20,000 × 0.50) to the sales revenue and the cost shall increase by only Rs. 3,000 (20,000 × 0.15). The incremental revenue of Rs. 10,000 is much more than the differential cost of Rs. 3,000, it will increase the profit by Rs. 7,000.

Illustration 4

Sports Specialists Ltd. is famous for specialized manufacture of quality chess boards sets. Presently, the company is working below its normal capacity of 1,000 units per month. The company sells its chess boards' sets in the national market at Rs. 150 per unit. During April 2008, 600 units were sold which is the regular sales volume for each month all through the year.

The unit cost of production is:

	Rs.
Direct Material	60
Direct Labor	30
Factory Overhead	30
Selling and Administration Overhead	15

The company has received an export order on 20-4-08 for supply of 600 units to be dispatched by 30-6-08. However, the order stipulates the price per unit as Rs. 100 only. The cost analysis indicated that the cost of direct material and direct labor that are to be incurred on the export order would be the same amount per unit as the regular line of production. However, an amount of Rs. 2,000 will have to be incurred on special packing, labeling, get up, etc. No additional factory, selling or administrative overhead costs would be incurred in executing the export order since the firm is operating below normal capacity.

Using Differential Cost Analysis Method, prepare the income statement to show whether the acceptance of the export order would be profitable to the company. Assumptions and comments, if any, may be given separately.

Solution

Assumption and comments:

(1) The company has received an export order on 20-4-08 for the supply of 600 units to be dispatched by 30-6-08. Therefore, the production of units for export can be planned for two months i.e. May and June 2008.

The total units of sales for 2 months are:

Regular domestic sales for		
2 months:	May – 600 units	
	June – 600 units	1,200 units
Export sales		600 units
Total sales in 2 months		1,800 units

(2) Since normal capacity is 1,000 units per month, total production capacity available is 2,000 units in 2 months. Therefore, as per the given data, there is no problem of capacity.

(3) Preparation of income statement for May and June, 2008 using Differential Costing Method

Particulars	*Domestic Sales*	*Export Sales*	*Total Sales*
Production and sales (units)	1,200	600	1,800
Selling price p.u (Rs)	150	100	—
Sales (units x S.P. p.u) (A)	1,80,000	60,000	2,40,000
Costs:			
Direct Material @Rs. 60 p.u	72,000	36,000	1,08,000
Direct labor @ Rs. 30.p.u	36,000	18,000	54,000
Factory Overheads@ 30.p.u	36,000	—	36,000
Selling and administration Overheads			
@ Rs.15 p.u	18,000	—	18,000
Special Packing etc.	—	2,000	2,000
Total cost (B)	1,62,000	56,000	2,18,000
Profit: (A) – (B)	18,000	4,000	22,000

Analysis: For the period of 2 months: May and June, 2008, acceptance of the export order results in the increase in company's profit by Rs. 4,000. Hence, the export order should be accepted.

Illustration 5

A manufacturing concern sells one of its products under the brand name 'utility' at Rs. 3.50 each, the cost of which is Rs. 3.00 each. After further processing, which entails additional material and labor cost of Rs. 2.50 and Rs. 2.00 per number respectively, 'utility' is converted into another product 'Ace' which is sold at Rs. 8.00 each. The concern at present procures per day 600 numbers of each of the two products for which 2,500 labor hours are utilized. The factory overheads have been budgeted as under:

Labor hours	2,000	2,500	3,000	3,500
Factory Overheads (Rs)	700	800	900	1,000

The following alternative proposals have been put forth for varying the sales mix:

(a) To process the entire quantity of 'utility' so as to convert it into 600 numbers of 'Ace'. This will need an additional 500 labor hours.

(b) To continue the present level of output of 'utility' but double the production of 'Ace'.

You are required to work out the incremental profit/loss involved in each of the two proposals and to offer suggestions.

Solution

First proposal:	*Rs.*	*Rs.*
Incremental Revenue (600 Ace × Rs. 4.50)		2700
Less: Differential Cost:		
Material 600 × 2.50	1,500	
Labor 600 × 2.00	1,200	
Overheads 900 – 800	100	2,800
Incremental Loss		(100)
Second proposal:		
Incremental Revenue 600 × 8.00		4,800
Less: Differential Cost:		
600 units up to 'utility' stage 600 × 3	1,800	
Conversion cost from 'utility' to ace	2,800	
(Calculated in 1 above)		(4600)
Incremental Profit		200

It is advisable to accept the second proposal, provided, facilities exist for the production of additional numbers of 'utility' and to convert them into 'Ace'. The first proposal results into a loss and hence it, is not acceptable.

Illustration 6

The following extracts from sales budget of a company for the current year:

		(Rs. '000)
Sales: 40,000 units @ Rs. 25 per unit		1,000
Selling costs:		
Advertisement	100	
Salesmen salaries	80	
Travelling expenses	50	
Rent of sales office	10	
Other	10	250

The management is considering a proposal to establish a new market in the Eastern Region in the next year. It is proposed to increase the advertising expenditure by 25% and appoint sales supervisor at a salary of Rs. 30,000 per year to establish a market. This will involve additional traveling, and the traveling expenses shall increase by 10%.

Target annual sales volume at the existing selling price for the new market is 10,000 units. The estimated variable cost of production is Rs. 12 per unit.

Should the company try to establish the new market?

Solution

Statement showing Budgeted, Current and Incremental Cost and Revenue:

(Rs.000)

Particulars		*Budgeted cost and Revenue*	*Proposed cost and Revenue*	*Incremental cost and Revenue*
Sales (units)		40,000	50,000	10,000
		Rs.	*Rs.*	*Rs.*
Sales revenue	(A)	1,000	1,250	250
Selling costs:				
Advertising		100	125	25
Salesmen salaries		80	110	30
Travelling expenses		50	55	5
Rent of sales office		10	10	—
Others		10	10	—
Total selling costs:	(B)	250	310	60

Particulars	Budgeted cost and Revenue	Proposed cost and Revenue	Incremental cost and Revenue
	Rs.	Rs.	Rs.
Variable cost of production @ Rs. 12.p.u (C)	480	600	120
Total cost: (B + C) = D 730	910	180	
Profit: (A –D)	270	340	70
Percentage rate of return on sales value	27%	27.2%	28%

Since the incremental rate of return is higher than the budgeted rate of return, the proposal to establish a new market may be accepted.

Illustration 7

The components of an item are manufactured by another unit under the same management. The unit at present manufactures 1,00,000 units (the present requirements of the main factory) at the following costs:

	Rs.
Materials	5,00,000
Labor	2,50,000
Overheads	2,00,000
	9,50,000

Labor is paid @ Rs. 2 per unit and the fixed D.A and other allowances monthly. The components required by the main factory are to be increased by 20%. The components factory can increase production up to 25% without any additional labor force. Overheads are variable to the extent of 25% of the present amount.

The additional requirement may be purchased from the market at Rs. 8.50 per unit. Suggest which will be better.

Solution

	Rs.
Differential cost of producing 20,000 units:	
Materials 20,000 × 5	1,00,000
Labor (Variable) 20,000 × 2	40,000
Labor (Fixed)	—
Overheads (variable) 20,000 × 0.50	10,000
Overheads (fixed)	—
	1,50,000
If purchased from outside, cost is (20,000 × 8.50)	1,70,000

Since the cost of producing is less than the cost of purchase, it is better to produce than buy.

Illustration 8

A.P. Ltd. has an annual production of 90,000 units of a motor component. The component cost structure is as below:

	Rs. per unit
Materials	270
Labor (25% fixed)	180
Variable Expenses	90
Fixed Expenses	135
	675

The Purchase manager has an offer from a supplier who is willing to supply the component at Rs. 540. Should the component be purchased and production stopped?

(a) Assume the resources now used for this components manufacture are to be used to produce another new product for which the selling price is Rs. 485.

The material price will be Rs. 200 per unit, 90,000 units of this product can be produced at the same cost basis as above for labor and expenses.

Discuss whether it would be advisable to divert the resources to manufacture the new product, assuming that the component presently being produced would, instead of being produced, be purchased from the market.

Solution

Statement of Cost of the Component

Particulars	*Per unit (Rs.)*	*Total for 90,000 units (Rs.)*
Material	270	2,43,00,000
Labor	135	1,21,50,000
Expenses	90	81,00,000
Total variable cost	495	4,45,50,000
Cost of purchase from outside	540	4,86,00,000
Excess of purchase price over variable cost	45	40,50,000

Since the purchase from outside involves payment of Rs. 45 more per unit and for 90,000 units, it amounts to Rs. 40,50,000, the company should not stop the production of the component. It is assumed here that the fixed expenses are not being affected by the decision.

In case, the facilities made available are diverted to produce another (new) product:

		Rs.
Selling price per unit of the new product		485
Material cost	200	
Labor	135	
Variable expenses	90	
Total Valiable Cost		425
Contribution per unit		60

Thus, it is found that the company benefits by Rs. 15 per unit (Rs. 60 – Rs. 45) and on 90,000 units the company will save (90,000 × Rs. 15) Rs. 13,50,000. Therefore, it is advisable to divert the resources to manufacture the new product and the component presently being produced be purchased from outside.

Illustration 9

ABC Ltd. is at present operating at 80% capacity level, the production being 15,000 per annum. It operates a flexible budgetary control system. The following relevant cost data are obtained from the company's budget at different capacity utilization levels:

Particulars	*Capacity Utilisation Level*	
	80% Rs.	*100% Rs.*
Sales	20,00,000	25,00,000
Variable overheads	2,25,000	2,50,000
Semi-variable overheads	1,05,000	1,11,000
Fixed overheads	4,00,000	4,70,000
Output (in units)	15,000	18,750

Material and labor cost per unit is constant under the present conditions. The management expects a profit margin of 10% on sales.

You are required to compute the Differential Cost of production for producing additional 3,750 units by increasing the capacity utilization level to 100%.

Solution

(1) Computation of cost of Material and Labor at 80% capacity:

		Rs.
Sales at 80% capacity		20,00,000
Less: Profit margin (10% on sales)		2,00,000
Cost of sales		18,00,000
Less: Overheads:		
Fixed	Rs. 4,00,000	
Semi-variable	Rs. 1,05,000	
Variable:	Rs. 2,25,000	
		7,30,000
Cost of Materials and Labor (at 80% capacity)		10,70,000

(2) Cost of Materials and Labor at 100% capacity:
10,70,000 × 100/80 = Rs. 13,37,500

Computation of Differential Cost of producing 3,750 additional units:

		Rs.	
Particulars	*80%*	*Capacity Level* *100%*	*20% (Differential Cost of 3,750 units)*
Production and Sales (units)	15,000	18,750	3,750
	Rs.	*Rs.*	*Rs.*
Material and Labor Cost	10,70,000	13,37,500	2,67,500
Variable Overheads	2,25,000	2,50,000	25,000
Semi-variable Overheads	1,05,000	1,11,000	6,000
Fixed Overheads	4,00,000	4,70,000	70,000
Total Cost	18,00,000	21,68,500	3,68,500

SUMMARY

Differential Costs are the increase or decrease in the total costs that result from producing additional or fewer units or from the adoption of an alternative course of action. The alternative course of action may arise due to change in sales volume, alternative method of production, change in product/sales mix, make or buy, refuse or accept decisions, addition of a new product, exploring a new market, decision to drop a product line, etc.

Differential Cost may be referred to as either Incremental Cost or Decremental Cost. When there is an increase in the total cost due to an increase in the level of production, it is called Incremental Cost, and when there is a decrease in the total cost due to a decrease in the level of production, it is called as Decremental Cost.

The main point which distinguishes Marginal Cost and Differential Cost is that of change in fixed cost when the volume of production increases or decreases by a unit of production. In the case of Differential Cost, variable as well as fixed cost, i.e., both the costs, change due to a change in the level of activity, whereas under Marginal Costing, only variable cost changes due to a change in the level of activity.

The decisions which can be taken with the help of Differential Cost Analysis are Determination of the most profitable level of production and price, Introduction of new products, Acceptance of an offer at a lower selling price, Changing the product mix, Changing the method of production, Discontinuing a product to avoid the losses and increase profits, decision to drop a product line, Make or buy decisions, Decision regarding the depth of processing and Shut-down decisions.

Glossary

- **Differential Cost:** is the increase or decrease in the total costs that result from producing additional or fewer units or from the adoption of an alternative course of action.

- **Incremental Cost:** is an increase in the total cost due to an increase in the level of production.
- **Decremental Cost:** is a decrease in the total cost due to a decrease in the level of production.

Questions

(1) What do you understand by the concept "Differential Cost"?
(2) Differentiate Differential Cost from Marginal Cost.
(3) What are the situations under which Differential Costing technique is useful?
(4) What are the characteristics of Differential Costing?
(5) Explain briefly with suitable examples the managerial decisions taken with the help of Differential Costing technique.

PROBLEMS

(1) Modern sewing machines co. manufactures hand operated sewing machines. Prepare a schedule showing the Differential Costs and Incremental Revenues at each stage from the following data. At what volume the company should set its level of production?

Output (in lakhs)	*Selling Price per machine (Rs.)*	*Total Semi Fixed Cost (Rs.in lakhs)*	*Total Variable Cost (Rs. in lakhs)*	*Total Fixed Cost (Rs. in lakhs)*
0.60	240	30	83.6	28.4
1.20	220	30	163.6	28.4
1.80	200	34	255.6	28.4
2.40	180	34	315.6	28.4
3.00	160	40	355.6	28.4
3.60	140	40	380.6	28.4

[**Ans.:** The company should set its level of output at 3.0 lakh units because upto this level, Incremental Revenue exceeds Differential Cost.]

(2) A company has a capacity of producing 1,00,000 units of a certain product in a month. The sales department reports that the following schedule of sale price is possible.

Volume of production %	*Selling price per unit paise*
60	0.90
70	0.80
80	0.75
90	0.76
100	0.68

The Variable cost of manufacture between these levels is 20 paise per unit and fixed cost Rs. 40,000.
Prepare a statement showing Incremental Revenue and Differential Cost at each stage. At which volume of production will the profit be maximum.
If there is an offer at Re.1 per unit for the balance capacity over the maximum profit volume for export price, and price quoted will not affect the internal sale price, will you advise accepting this bid and why?
(**Ans.:** *(a)* At 90% capacity, profit will be the maximum as after this level the Differential Cost is more than Incremental Revenue. *(b)* It is advisable to accept the bulk order of export at a price of Re.1 per unit The incremental revenue is Rs.10,000 and the differential cost is Rs. 2,000)

(3) A manufacturing concern sells one of its product under the brand name 'Rough' at 4.50 each, the cost of which is 4.00 each. After further processing, this entails additional material and labor cost of Rs.2.50 and 2.00 per number respectively. 'Rough' is converted into another product 'Tough' which is sold at Rs.8.00 each. The concern at present procures per day 800 numbers of each of the two products for which 3,500 labor hours are utilized.
The factory overheads have been budgeted as under

Labor hours	3,000	3,500	4,000	4,500
Factory overheads (Rs.)	800	900	1,000	1,100

The following alternative proposals have been put forth for varying sales mix.
(a) To process the entire quantity of 'Rough' so as to convert it into 800 numbers of 'Tough'. This will need an additional 500 labor hours.
(b) To continue the present level of output of 'Rough' but double the production of 'Tough'
You are required to work out the incremental profit/loss involved in each of the two proposals and to offer your suggestions.
[**Ans.:** Proposal I: Incremental Loss Rs. 100 and Proposal II: Incremental Profit Rs. 300]

(4) The components of an item are manufactured by another unit under the same management. The unit at present manufactures 1,00,000 units (the present requirements of the main factory) at the following costs.

	Rs.
Materials	5,00,000
Labor	3,00,000
Overheads	2,00,000
	10,00,000

Labor is paid @ Rs 3 per unit, the fixed D.A and other allowances monthly. The components are required by the main factory are to be increased by 25%. The components factory can increase production upto 30% with out any additional labor force. Overheads are variable to the extent of 20% of the present amount.

The additional requirement may be purchased from the market at Rs. 8.00 per unit. Suggest which will be better.

[**Ans.:** Cost of producing Rs. 2,10,000 and the cost of purchase is Rs. 2,00,000]

(5) Sports specialists Ltd. are famous for specialized manufacture of quality bats. Presently, the company is working below its normal capacity of 1200 units per month. The company sells its bats in the national market at Rs. 145 per unit. During March 2008, 500 units were sold which are the regular sales volume for each month all through the year.

The unit cost of production is:

Direct Material	Rs. 50
Direct Labor	Rs. 25
Factory Overhead	Rs. 30
Selling & Distribution Overhead	Rs. 20

The company has received an export order on 25-03-08 for the supply of 800 units to be dispatched by 30-5-08. However, the order stipulates the price per unit as Rs. 110 only. The cost analysis indicated that the cost of direct material and direct labor that are to be incurred on the export order would be the same amount per unit as the regular line of production. However, an amount of Rs. 1,500 will have to be incurred on special packing, labeling, getup etc. No additional Factory, Selling or Administrative Overhead costs would be incurred in executing the export order since the firm is operating below normal capacity,

Using Differential Cost Analysis Method, prepare the income statement to show whether the acceptance of the export order would be profitable to the company. Assumptions and comments if any may be given separately.

(**Ans.:** Acceptance of the export order results in company's profit by Rs. 6,000.)

(6) The following is the extract from sales budget of a company for the current year.

		(Rs. 000)
Sales: 35,000 units @ Rs. 25 per unit		875
Selling costs:		
Advertisements	90	
Salesmen salaries	60	
Travelling expenses	40	
Rent of sales office	15	
Others	10	
	215	

The management is considering a proposal to establish a new market in the eastern region in the next year. It is proposed to increase the advertising by 20% and appoint an additional sales supervisor at a salary of Rs. 20,000 per year to establish a market. This will involve additional traveling and traveling expenses shall increase by 10%.

Target annual sales volume at the existing selling price for the new market is 5,000 units. The estimated cost of production is Rs. 10 per unit.

Should the company try to establish the new market?

[**Ans.:** Since the incremental rate of return 33% is lower than the budgeted rate of return 35.43%, the proposal to establish new market may not be accepted.]

(7) XYZ Ltd has an annual production of 1,00,000 units of a machine manufacturing component. The component cost structure is as below:

	Rs. Per unit
Material	300
Labor (30% fixed)	150
Variable Expenses	200
Fixed Expenses	130
	780

The purchase manager has an offer from a supplier who is willing to supply the component at Rs.580. Should the component be purchased and production stopped?

(a) Assume the resources now used for this components manufacture are to be used to produce another new product for which the selling price is Rs. 600.

The material price will be Rs. 250 per unit. 1,00,000 units of this product can be produced at the same cost basis as above for labor and expenses. Discuss whether it would be advisable to divert the resources to manufacture the new product, assuming that the component presently being produced would, instead of being produced, be purchased from the market.

[**Ans.:** *(a)* Purchase from outside involves payment of Rs 25 more per unit. The company should not stop the production of the component. *(b)* In case the facilities made available are diverted to produce another (new) product, the company benefits by Rs.20 per unit. Therefore, it is advisable to divert the resources to manufacture the new product and the component presently being produced be purchased from outside.]

(8) XYZ Ltd is at present operating at 80% capacity level the production being 10,000 units per annum. It operates a flexible budgetary control system. The following relevant cost data are obtained from the company's budget at different capacity utilization levels.

Particulars	*Capacity Utilization Levels*	
	80%	*100%*
	Rs.	*Rs.*
Sales	15,00,000	20,00,000
Variable Overheads	2,00,000	2,25,000
Semi-variable Overheads	1,00,000	1,10,000
Fixed Overheads	3,00,000	4,00,000
Output (in units)	10,000	15,000

Material and Labor Cost per unit is constant under the present conditions. The management expects a profit margin of 15% on sales.

You are required to compute the Differential Cost of producing additional 5,000 units by increasing the capacity utilization level to 100%.

[**Ans.:** Differential Cost Rs. 2,93,750]

❑ ❑ ❑

18

BUDGETARY CONTROL

Objectives

The objectives of the study are to:

- Understand the importance of Budgets and Budgetary Control
- Learn the preparation of various Budgets
- Highlight the significance of Zero Based Budgeting

- **Introduction**
- **Budget: Meaning and Definition**
- **Essentials of a Budget**
- **Budgeting**
- **Budgetary Control**
- **Essentials of Budgetary Control**
- **Forecast vs. Budget**
- **Classification of Budgets**
- **Budget Committee**
- **Budget Officer/Budget Controller**
- **Budget Manual**
- **Fixation of the Budget Period**
- **Determination of Key Factor**
- **Functional Budgets**
  - **Sales Budget**
  - **Production Budget**
  - **Production Cost Budget**
  - **Direct Material Budget**
  - **Direct Labor Budget**
  - **Factory Overheads Budget**
  - **Administrative Overheads Budget**
  - **Selling and Distribution Overheads Budget**
  - **Capital Expenditure Budget**
  - **Cash Budget**
    - **Receipts and Payments Method**
    - **Adjusted Profit and Loss (or) Net Income Method.**
    - **Balance Sheet Method**

INTRODUCTION

The future should be planned. The Business budget is a plan for future, which is expressed, in monetary or physical terms. Budgets are nothing but the expressions, largely in financial terms of management's plan for operating and financing the enterprise, during a specific period of time. The act of planning as to how the amount should be spent is known as Budgeting. The act of continuously monitoring and taking timely corrective actions is Budgetary Control. Therefore, Budgetary Control has become an essential tool of management for controlling costs and maximizing profits.

Cost Accountancy is the application of costing and cost Accounting Principles, Methods and Techniques to the science, art and practice of cost control. The chief tools for cost control are Budgetary Control, Standard Costing and Cost Audit.

BUDGET: MEANING AND DEFINITION

A Budget is a detailed plan of operations for some specific future period. It is an estimate prepared in advance of the period to which it applies. It acts as a business barometer, as it is a complete programme of activities of the business for the period covered. It is a quantitative statement of goals and objectives expressed in monetary terms.

The chartered Institute of Management Accountants, London, defines a budget as "a financial and/or quantitative statement, prepared prior to a defined period of time, of the policy to be pursued during that period for the purpose of attaining a given objective."

"A Budget is a written plan covering projected activities of a firm for a definite period." — Dickey.

A budget is a projection or estimate of future output, costs and revenues. It is a formal means of expressing the management intentions of a company for a coming period. A year is the basic time frame, though it can be almost any length of time-quarter, month, and week or in a day. Once the budget is agreed upon and adopted, it becomes a sort of an intruction communicating to each executive, his role in business activity and the level of production, sale or expenditure he has to achieve or the limits with in which he has to operate.

Budget is an annual estimate of revenue and expenditure of a State, Organization, Cooperative Institutions, Local Bodies, State Governments, Union Governments, UGC, Family or an Individual. It indicates as to where the revenue comes from and where it goes. Inadequate provision in the Budget would necessitate additional expenditure to complete the work. Otherwise, the work or project would have to be discontinued or abandoned midway with the resultant economic and social evils of increasing costs and deferred benefits to the society at large. On the other hand, provision in excess of the needed amount would tend to result in squandering the moneys on the works which could have been completed with lesser amount of money. Great care has, therefore, to be exercised in preparing the Budget. It is prudent to avoid deficit or surplus.

Though, generally, a budget is always imagined to be in financial terms, it can also be in terms of machine hours, personnel or any other facility.

A Budget should be:

- based on objectives
- realistic
- flexible

- prepared early and
- easily understood

Essentials of a Budget

The following are the essentials of a Budget.

(a) A Budget is prepared in advance for a defined period of time.

(b) It forms the basis for future plan of actions.

(c) It relates to a future period and is based on objectives to be achieved.

(d) The given objectives must be laid before the budget is prepared.

(e) The budget is a monetary and/or quantitative statement of policy formulated by the management.

Thus, a budget fixes targets in terms of rupee or quantity against which the actual performance is measured. Therefore, a budget can be taken as a document, which is closely related to both the management function as well as the accounting function of an organisation.

The Importance of a budget increases as the size of the organization increases. Budgets are helpful for coordinating the various activities such as production and sales and are used as a means of communication. The ideas of top management are communicated through budgets to lower level, who gives them the practical shape. Budgets are helpful in developing a teamwork which is essential to achieve common objectives of the organization. Thus, a budget is essential to plan for the future, to motivate the staff associated, to co-ordinate the activities of departments and to control the performance of various departments.

Budgeting

According to National Association of Accounting (NAA), Budgeting is the process of planning all flows of the financial resources into within and from an entity during some specified future period. It includes providing for the detailed allocation of expected available future resources to projects, functions, responsibilities and time period.

Budgeting is a process of preparing and using budgets for planning and control of performance. It is an exercise in allocating scarce economic resources and financial resources among alternative uses. The ultimate aim of budgeting is to allocate the limited resources most effectively for achieving the goals of an organization. Budgeting is the actual act of preparing the budget. It is the process of evolving the final statement. Budget is the end product of Budgeting.

Budgetary Control

An understanding of the term 'control' is essential before any attempt is made to gain an idea about 'Budgetary Control'. Control includes some sort of comparison of performance with predetermined plan, in order to take some remedial measures for any deficiencies. Planning and Control are the two related activities of management. Budget is simply a plan of action. Hence, the technique of Budgetary Control is an important tool of management.

Budgetary Control refers to the principles, procedures and practices of achieving given objectives through Budgets. Both, Budgets and Budgetary Control, are the two important tools in the hands of management to achieve the desired results.

The Charted Institute of Management Accountants, London, defines Budgetary Control as "The establishment of budgets relating to the responsibilities of executives to the requirements of a policy and the continuous comparison of actual with budgeted results, either to secure by individual action the objective of that policy or to provide a basis for its revision".

J. Batty defines it as "A System which uses budget as a means of planning and controlling all aspects of producing and/ or of selling commodities and services".

Budgetary Control involves the following:

(a) The objects are set by preparing budgets.

(b) The business is divided into various Responsibility Centres for preparing various budgets.

(c) If the actual performance is less than the budgeted norms; a remedial action is taken immediately.

Essentials of Budgetary Control

The essentials of Budgetary Control are:

(1) Budgeting is the starting point of Budgetary Control.

(2) Budgets are to be classified based on their functions.

(3) Actual data should be computed.

(4) A continuous comparison of actual with budgeted figures is to be made.

(5) Variances, if any, are to be analyzed.

(6) Corrective actions are to be initiated to ensure that actuals are in line with budgeted performance.

(7) Budgets are to be revised, if necessary.

An effective budgeting system is vital to the success of a business firm. The main objectives of Budgetary Control may be summarized as follows:

***(a)* Planning:** Budgeting is a planning device. Almost all the business activities require some planning to ensure efficient and maximum use of scarce resources. The first step in planning is, defining a company's broad aims and objectives. The budget is a detailed schedule of the proposed combination of the various factors of production. Budgets present the plan, objectives and policies of an enterprise and express them in numerical terms.

Since Budgets are prepared for every function or segment of a business, all levels of management are drawn into the planning function, besides keeping every manager sufficiently informed as to the future with respect to the objectives, goals, policies, rules, procedures and programmes. Planning is, thus, a necessary ingredient of budgetary control and budgeting is an important managerial tool of planning.

***(b)* Co-ordination:** Co-ordination means developing and maintaining various activities within the concern in proper relationship with one another. It is the process by which each subdivision of a concern works towards the common goal or objective with due regard to all other sub-divisions. There is a need for co-ordination between the production department and sales department. A production department should ensure adequate production to meet the anticipated demand of the sales department; sufficient material, labor and other facilities should be made available to facilitate higher production. If needed, production capacity must be increased. In turn, finance manager has to ensure adequate cash to meet greater output requirement.

Co-ordination of the various activities of an organization is also achieved by operating the technique of Budgetary Control. Effective co-ordination is also dependent upon adequate communication. Every member of the management should be informed in advance as to *(i)* What is planned? *(ii)* How it is planned and *(iii)* When and by whom it is to be accomplished? The individual responsibility is thus fixed, as a result, it becomes easy to ascertain, whether co-ordination is being achieved or not, by the control techniques.

***(c)* Control:** Control follows planning and co-ordination. The need to keep a strict control on costs is thus impressed upon every manager.

In exercising the control over the activities, the budget aims at the following:

(i) When budget is being formulated, departments analyze their plans for the future and submit estimates as per their requirements, justifying each of their demands by demonstrating a need.

(ii) After budgets of different departments have been revised and approved, they become targets that set desirable limits on spending.

At the end of the budget period, a comparison of actual expenditure with budget expenditure is made as a means of judging performances and fixing responsibility for deviation.

FORECAST VS. BUDGET

A forecast is the statement of facts likely to occur. According to Chartered Institute of Management Accounts London, forecast is a "statement of probable events". At planning stage, it is necessary to prepare forecasts of action for the business in future. Plans or budgets are prepared on the basis of these forecasts in order to achieve the objectives of the organization. The forecast of a function need not necessarily be coordinated. The desired coordination is obtained before finalization of the budget. Thus, a forecast is a perquisite to planning.

Forecasts results in planning and planning results in Budgeting. However, this inter relationship does not mean that a forecast and budget are one and the same. A forecast denotes some degree of looseness while a budget denotes a definite target.

The differences between a forecast and budget are as follows:

(a) According to Terminology, a forecast is an assessment of probable future events. A budget on the other hand is a blue print for a projected plan of action of a definite period of time.

(b) Forecasting precedes thc preparation of budget. It relates to probable events whereas a budget is based on the implications of a forecast and relates to planned events.

(c) A forecast does not lay down any target in the form of commitment which management aims at attaining while budget lays down a target.

(d) A forecast merely takes note of the future events while a budget aims at controlling and shaping them.

(e) A budget may be prepared for the business as a whole, covering all the activities, or for a particular function or segment of the business. A forecast usually covers a specific business function.

(f) A Budget is not merely a planning device but a controlling tool also. However, being a statement of future events, a forecast is not a means of control.

(g) The function of forecasting ends with the assessment of probable future events. However, budgeting starts where forecasting ends.

CLASSIFICATION OF BUDGETS

Budgets can be classified into different categories from different points of view.

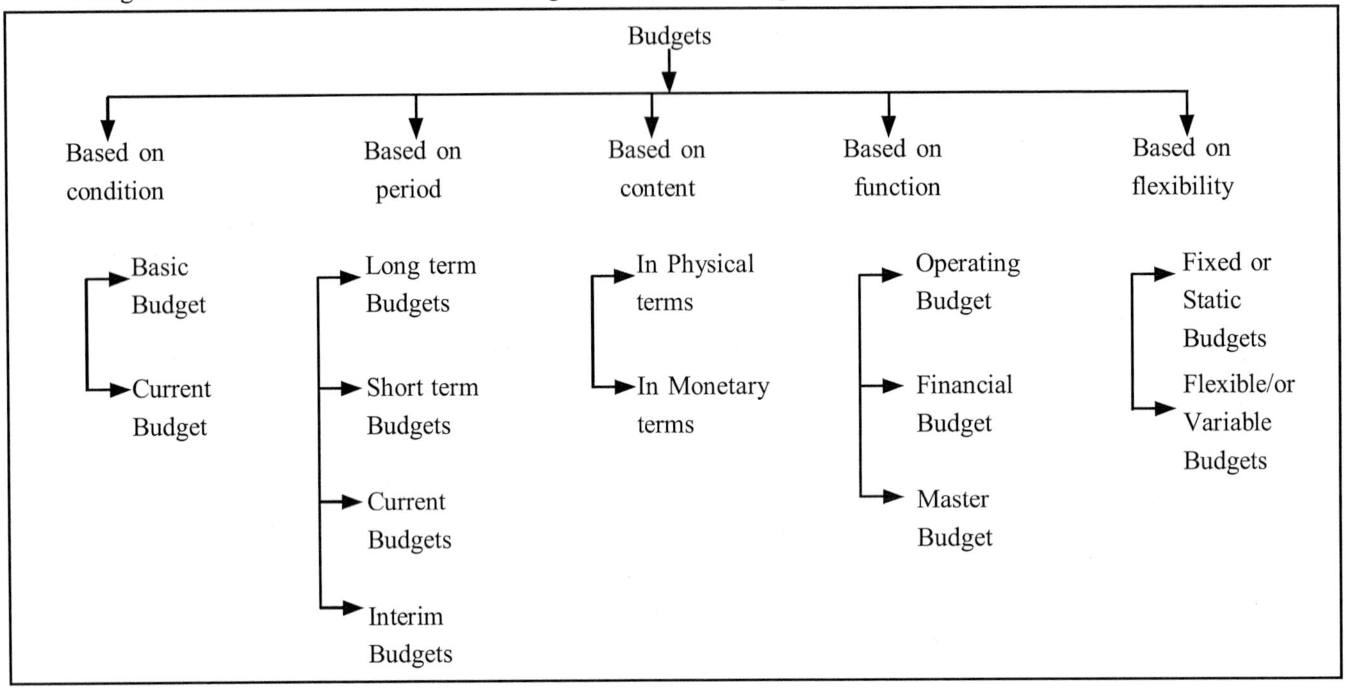

(I) Based on Condition

According to condition, Budgets are classified as Basic and Current Budgets.

***(a)* Basic Budget:** Budgets prepared and used for a long period of time without alteration are called as Basic Budgets.

***(b)* Current Budget:** Budgets which are related to current conditions are called current Budgets. It is more realistic in nature. It is for a short period.

(II) Based on Period

Based on time, Budgets are classified into Long term, Short term, Current and Interim Budgets.

***(a)* Long term Budgets:** They are prepared for a long period. These are generally prepared by a financial controller exclusively for the top-level management. These are useful for organizations having a long gestation period, generally expressed as a percentage or in physical terms, e.g. Capital Expenditure Budgets, R&D Budgets, etc.

***(b)* Short term Budgets:** They are for a short period. They are useful in case of consumer goods industries. These Budgets are used by the lower level management, e.g., Material Budget, Cash Budget.

***(c)* Current Budget:** As per ICWA London, "Current Budget is a Budget which is established for use over a short period of time and is related to current condition". It is for a very short period say a quarter or a month. They are essentially short-term budgets adjusted to current conditions or prevailing circumstances.

***(d)* Interim Budgets:** They are the budgets prepared in between two budget periods. These are then integrated with the budget of the following period.

(III) Based on Content

On the basis of content, budgets are in physical terms and monetary terms.

***(a)* In Physical Terms:** Budgets are expressed in terms of Quantity only. They do not include value, e.g., Production budget, material budget, etc.

***(b)* In Monetary terms:** Budgets are expressed in terms of Quantities as well corresponding values, e.g., Cash Budget, Sales Budget, Purchase Budget, etc.,

(IV) Based on Function

Based on function, budgets are grouped into Operating, Financial and Master Budgets.

***(a)* Operating Budgets:** These Budgets relate to different operations or activities of a firm. The number of budgets depends on the size and nature of the business. The Budget shows planned operations for the coming period, including revenues, expenses and related changes in the inventory. It covers in its ambit the budgets like Sales Budget, Production Budget, Cost of Production Budget, etc. Thus, it is the principal part of Master Budget of the Business.

Operating Budget usually consists of 2 parts:

***(i)* Program Budget:** It consists of estimated revenues and costs of the major programmes that the company plans to undertake during the forth-coming period. Such Budgets can be proposed in respect of each project or product line giving details of revenue, costs and resultant profit in respect of each one of them. Such Budgets are useful in a way that they provide an overall picture of the various projects or products. However, they are not suitable for exercising control over individuals since various persons may be responsible for the total operation. It is also termed as a Project or Product Budget.

***(ii)* Responsibility Budget:** It is a budget which identifies the revenues and costs, with the individual responsibility for their incurrence. Such a budget is an excellent control device since it identifies with the individual only such revenues and costs which are controllable by him. The data regarding actual results are collected from different operations and compared with the budgeted figures to find out whether the individual has achieved what was expected of him.

***(b)* Financial Budget:** Financial Budgets are concerned with cash receipts and disbursements, working capital, capital expenditure, financial position, etc., e.g., Working Capital Budget, Capital Budget, Income Statement Budget, Research and Development Budget, etc.

***(c)* Master Budget:** As per ICWA London, "Master Budget is the Summary Budget incorporating its Functional Budgets". This is prepared by the budget officer for the benefit of the top-level management. It is used as an effective control device. It interprets different Functional Budgets and covers within its range the preparation of projects income statement and projected balance sheet.

(V) Based on flexibility

On the basis of flexibility, budgets are classified into Fixed or Static Budgets and Flexible or Variable Budgets.

***(a)* Fixed or Static Budgets:** According to ICWA London, "A fixed Budget is a budget which is designed to remain unchanged irrespective of the level of activity actually attained". This is generally based on fixed volume of an activity; as such it is not useful for managerial purposes.

***(b)* Flexible or Variable Budgets:** These are also called as Sliding Scale Budgets, Control type Budgets. According to ICWA London, "A Flexible Budget is a budget which is designed to change in accordance with the level of activity actually attained". It provides the budgeted costs at any level of activity. A series of budgets for different levels of activity can be prepared.

BUDGET COMMITTEE

The Budget Committee is a group of representatives of various functions in the organization. As all functions are inter related, it is necessary to discuss the targets so that a mutually agreed program is determined which requires the coordination in budget making. The main functions of the Budget Committee are to:

- Receive and review budget estimates from the respective divisions or departments and make appropriate recommendations for their improvement.
- Recommend decisions on budget matters in case there is a conflict between departments or divisions.
- Recommend changes and approval of the final budget.
- Receive, study and analyze periodic reports comparing the budgets with the actual performance and consider policies with respect to follow up procedures.
- Make recommendations for the revision of the budget when conditions warrant and also for the changes in the budget policies and procedures for greater effectiveness as well as for the Budget Manual.

BUDGET OFFICER/BUDGET CONTROLLER

The functionary who heads the Budget Committee is the Budget Director or the Budget Controller. He is appointed to administer the budget program. His primary responsibility is to coordinate the various phases of the program, assemble the component parts and to identify the problems.

The Budget Director is not expected to prepare budgets. He has to simply direct and supervise budget programs. He reviews the departmental budgets to make certain that they are in harmony and will achieve the common goal. He then assembles the final departmental budgets into a Master Budget. He should have knowledge regarding the technical details of the business and should report directly to the President or the Chief Executive of the organization. Thus, he needs to act as a mediator.

BUDGET MANUAL

ICMA England defines a Budget Manual as "a document, schedule or booklet which sets out, *inter alia*, the responsibilities of the persons engaged in the routine of and the forms and records required for Budgetary Control. Thus, it is a written document which guides the executives in preparing various budgets. It should be clear and there should be no ambiguity in it. The manual is subdivided into different sections for the purpose of easy handling. They are:

- Income Statement Budget
- Statement of Retained Earning Budget
- Budgeted Balance Sheet or Position Statement Budget

FIXATION OF THE BUDGET PERIOD

The period for which budget should be framed depends upon the nature of the industry, peculiar characteristics of the organization and the need for control of performance and cost. It is not possible to suggest a Budget Period which will be uniformly suitable for all purposes. In industries, in which capital expenditure is high and long term planning is necessary, budget periods of up to 20 years may be required. Example: Ship building and electric supply industries. On the other hand, industries where fashion and weather factors (readymade fabrics and food processing industries) exert a great influence on demand, planning may have to be done for shorter period say a season or quarter. However, it is necessary for control purposes to prepare budgets both for long as well as short periods.

DETERMINATION OF KEY FACTOR

Key Factor is also known as the "Limiting Factor" or "Principal Budget Factor". It is defined as "the factor the extent of whose influence must first be assessed in order to ensure the functional budgets are capable of fulfillment." It would be desirable to prepare first the budget relating to Key Factor and then prepare the other budgets. Generally, the Principal Budget Factor is sales but sometimes depending upon circumstances, labor, plant capacity, availability of material and time, financial resources may also serve as Limiting Factors.

The Key Factor should be correctly identified and examined. Keeping in view the Limiting Factors, the volume of sales and volume of production should be coordinated so that targets can be easily reached. The key factors need not be of a permanent nature. In the long run, the management may overcome the key factors by introducing new products, by changing material mix or by working overtime or extra shifts, etc.

FUNCTIONAL BUDGETS

There are various functional budgets which are explained below.

Sales Budget: Sales Budget is an estimate of expected sales during a budget period. It lays down a comprehensive plan and program for sales department. Sales Manager is responsible for preparing Sales Budgets. It expresses the figures in Quantity as well as in value. It is generally prepared Territory Wise (Area wise). The degree of accuracy with which sales are estimated determines the success of budgeting exercises. The following points should be taken into account while preparing Sales Budgets.

(i) Sales figures
(ii) Assessment of Sales
(iii) Availability of key factor
(iv) Seasonal fluctuation
(v) Availability of financers
(vi) General trade prospects
(vii) Order book position
(viii) Market intelligence
(ix) External environment
(x) Policy Implication

Illustration 1

XYZ & Co., manufactures two products X and Y and sells them through two divisions east and west. For the purpose of submission of sales budget to the budget committee, the following information has been made available:

Budgeted Sales for the current year were:

Product	East	West
X	400 units @ Rs. 9	600 units @ Rs. 9
Y	300 units @ Rs.21	500 units @ Rs. 21

Actual sales for the current year were:

Product	East	West
X	500 units @ Rs. 9	700 units @ Rs. 9
Y	200 units @ Rs.21	400 units @ Rs.21

Adequate market studies reveal that product X is popular but under – priced. It is observed that if price of X is increased by Re. 1, it will find a ready market. On the other hand, Y is over priced to customers and market could absorb more if sales price of Y be reduced by Re. 1. The management has agreed to give effect to the above price changes.

From the information based on these price changes and reports from salesmen, the following estimates have been prepared by divisional managers.

Percentage increase in sales over current budget is:

Product	**East**	**West**
X	+10%	+5%
Y	+20%	+10%

With the help of an intensive advertisement campaign, the following additional sales above the estimated sales of divisional managers are possible:

Product	**East**	**West**
X (units)	60	70
Y (units)	40	50

You are required to prepare a Budget for sales incorporating the above estimates and show the budgeted and actual sales of the current year.

Solution

Division	*Product*	*Budget for future period*			*Budget for current period*			*Actual sales for current period*		
		Qty	*Price Rs.*	*Value Rs.*	*Qty*	*Price Rs.*	*Value Rs.*	*Qty*	*Price Rs.*	*Value Rs.*
East	X	500	10	5,000	400	9	3,600	500	9	4,500
	Y	400	20	8,000	300	21	6,300	200	21	4,200
	Total	**900**		**13,000**	**700**		**9,900**	**700**		**8,700**
West	X	700	10	7,000	600	9	5,400	700	9	6,300
	Y	600	20	12,000	500	21	10,500	400	21	8,400
	Total	**1,300**		**19,000**	**1,100**		**15,900**	**1,100**		**14,700**
Total	X	1,200	10	12,000	1000	9	9,000	1200	9	10,800
	Y	1,000	20	20,000	800	21	16,800	600	21	12,600
	Total	**2,200**		**3,2000**	**1,800**		**25,800**	**1,800**		**23,400**

Illustration 2

A Company has four sales territories 1,2,3 and 4 each salesman is expected to sell the following number of units during the first quarter of 1989. Assume the average selling price to be Rs. 30

Territory	*1*	*2*	*3*	*4*
January	1,000	1,500	2,500	3,500
February	2,000	1,800	2,800	4,000
March	2,500	2,000	3,000	4,500

Prepare the sales Budget for the first quarter of the year.

Solution

Sales Budget (First Quarter)

Territory	*January*		*February*		*March*		*Total*	
	Units	*Value (Rs.)*	*Units*	*Value (Rs.)*	*Units*	*Value (Rs.)*	*Units*	*Value (Rs.)*
1	1,000	30,000	2,000	60,000	2,500	75,000	5,500	1,65,000
2	1,500	45,000	1,800	54,000	2,000	60,000	5,300	1,59,000
3	2,500	75,000	2,800	84,000	3,000	90,000	8,300	2,49,000
4	3,500	1,05,000	4,000	1,20,000	4,500	1,35,000	12,000	3,60,000
Total	8,500	2,55,000	10,600	3,18,000	12,000	3,60,000	31,100	9,33,000

Production Budget

It is a forecast of a number of units to be produced during the Budget period. It is prepared in relation to the sales budget. The number of units to be produced is arrived after taking into account opening and closing stock. This is prepared by factory in-charge or production manager. The factors to be considered are:

- Sales budget
- Plant Capacity
- Lag time
- Stock Quantity to be held
- Availability of key factor
- Production planning

The Production Budget is prepared in two parts namely;

- **Production Volume Budget:** It shows the physical units of the product to be manufactured; and
- **Cost of Production or Manufacturing Cost Budget:** It gives details of the budgeted cost under material, labor and factory overheads.

The following steps are involved in the preparation of Production Budget:

(1) Production Planning: Production planning plays a very important part in the preparation of Production Budget. Production planning on sound lines takes into consideration optimum utilization of plant capacity by eliminating or reducing the limiting factors and both, bottle necks in production like shortage of material, labor etc. and proper planning of production. It levels out seasonal fluctuations of sales so that optimum inventory of finished goods, components and work – in – progress is maintained.

(2) Consideration of plant capacity: The total quantities of each of the products or group of products which the firm is capable of producing are determined. This requires co-ordination of Production Budget with Plant Utilization Budget.

(3) Co-ordination with Sales Budget: Proper co-ordination between Production and Sales Budget is necessary to avoid imbalances of sales and production.

(4) Inventory Policy Consideration: The extent to which inventory of finished goods is to be carried depends up on several factors such as future sales potential, availability of storage facilities, the risk and cost of stock out and cost of carrying inventory. The budgeted quantity of production is computed as follows:

Units to be produced = Budgeted sales + desired closing stock of finished goods – opening stock of finished goods.

(5) Policy of Management: Management policy as to whether certain components or parts should be produced or procured from out side should also be taken before finally preparing the budget.

Production Cost Budget

This is the quantity of products to be manufactured expressed in terms of cost. Basically, there are three elements of costs namely Direct Material, Direct Labor and Overheads. Separate budgets for each of these elements have to be prepared.

Direct Material Budget

Standard Costing, greatly facilities the preparation of a Materials Budget. When standard cost records are not available, the details have to be adjusted to the period during which manufacturing takes place. Materials are controlled on the basis of price and usage, after allowing for normal wastage. Technical experts decide on the best and most economical material to use for each purpose. While preparing the Material Budget, the following factors must be taken into account.

(1) The quantities of materials to be required for the Production Budget
(2) The probable dates by which materials required must be available
(3) Storage facilities available
(4) Availability of credit facilities and other financial resources
(5) Price trends in the market
(6) The anticipated cost of the purchase to be made
(7) Nature of materials, i.e., seasonal or otherwise

Direct Labor Budget

A similar procedure to the above applies to direct labor. The labor shown in the production budgets are used with the wage rates which are likely to apply during the period of production. Wages are controlled according to the rates paid and the efficiency of the operator. In order to control the labor costs, the planning department has to establish standard by listing the operations, indicating the tools and equipment needed, stating the grade of employees, and setting the standard operation time in standard direct labor hours.

Overheads Budget

Overheads Budget has to be assembled from a detailed information from past records. It has to be updated to allow for the changes in the future costs and related activity. It is compiled on the basis of Department Overhead Expense Budgets and Cost Centre Budgets. The overheads may relate to factory, general administration, selling and distribution functions. Accordingly, separate budgets are prepared for factory overheads, administrative overheads and selling and distribution overheads.

Illustration 3

The following information has been made available from the records of Atul tools Ltd. for the last 6 months of 2008 (and of only sales of January 2009) in respect of product X.

(1) The units to be sold in different months are:

July 1,100	August 1,100	September 1,700	October 1,900
November 2,500	December 2,300	January 2,000	

(2) There will be no work-in-progress at the end of any month.

(3) Finished units equal to half-of-sales for the next month will be in stock at the end of every month (including June).

(4) Budgeted production and production cost for the year ending 31/12/08 are as follows:

Production(units)	22,000
Direct materials per unit	Rs. 10.00
Direct Wages per unit	Rs. 4.00

Total factory overheads apportioned to product Rs. 88,000

Prepare:

(a) A Production Budget for each of the last 6 months of 2008

(b) A Summarized Production Cost Budget for the same period.

Solution

(a) Production Budget for 6 months

Particulars	*July*	*August*	*September*	*October*	*November*	*December*
Sales (in units)	1,100	1,100	1,700	1,900	2,500	2,300
(+) Closing stock (1/2 of sales for next month)	550	850	950	1,250	1,150	1,000
	1,650	1,950	2,650	3,150	3,650	3,300
(-) Opening stock (last months closing stocks)	550	550	850	950	1,250	1,150
Production in units	1,100	1,400	1,800	2,200	2,400	2,150

(b) Production Cost Budget for 6 months

Production for 6 months (July to December)

(1,100 + 1,400 + 1,800 + 2,200 + 2,400 + 2,150) = 11,050 units

		Rs.
Direct materials @ Rs. 10 per unit (11,050 × 10)	=	1,10,500
Direct Wages @ 4 per unit (11,050 × 4)	=	44,200
Factory overheads (88,000 × 6/12)	=	44,000
Total Production Cost	=	1,98,700

Note : Factory overheads are taken for 6 months.

Illustration 4

A company manufactures product A and B. During the year ending 31/12/08, it is expected to sell 15,000 kg. of product A and 75,000 kg of product B at Rs. 30 and Rs. 16 per kg respectively. The direct materials P, Q and R are mixed in the proportion of 3:5:2 in the manufacture of product A. Material Q and R are mixed in the proportion of 1:2 in the manufacture of product B. The actual and Budgeted inventories for the year are given below:

		Opening Stock Kg.	*Expected closing Stock Kg.*	*Anticipated cost Per Kg. (in Rs.)*
Materials	P	4,500	3,000	12
	Q	3,000	6,000	10
	R	30,000	9,000	8
Product	A	3,000	1,500	—
	B	4,000	4,500	—

Prepare Production and the Material Budget showing the expenditure on purchase of materials for the year ending 31st December 2008.

Solution

Production Budget for the year ending 31/12/08 (Units)

Particulars	*Product A (Kg.)*	*Product B (Kg.)*
Sales	15,000	75,000
(+) Closing Stock	1,500	4,500
	16,500	79,500
(-) Opening Stock	3,000	4,000
Production	13,500	75,500

Material Budget for the year ending 31/12/08

Particulars	*P (Kg)*	*Q (Kg)*	*R (Kg)*
For Product A 13500 Kg in 3:5:2	4,050	6,750	2,700
For product B 75500 Kg in 1:2 (Q&R)	—	25,167	50,333
Material Consumption	4,050	31,917	53,033
(+) Closing Stock	3,000	6,000	9,000
	7,050	37,917	62,033
(-) Opening Stock	4,500	3,000	30,000
Material Purchase Budget	2,550	34,917	32,033
Cost per (Kg)	Rs. 12	Rs. 10	Rs. 8
Expenditure on purchase of Materials for 2008 (Rs.)	30,600	3,49,170	2,56,264

Illustration 5

The direct labor hours requirement of 3 of the products manufactured in a factory, each involving more than one labor operation is estimated as follows:

Direct Labor Hours per unit (in minutes)

		Products		
		1	**2**	**3**
Operation	**1**	18	42	30
	2	—	12	24
	3	9	6	—

The factory works 8 hrs per day, 6 days in a week. The budget quarter is taken as 13 weeks and during a quarter, lost hours due to leave and holidays and other causes are estimated to be 124 hrs.

The budgeted hourly rate for the workers manning the operation 1,2 and 3 are Rs. 2.00, Rs. 2.50 and Rs. 3.00 respectively. The budgeted sales of the products during the quarter are:

Product	1	9000 units
	2	15,000 units
	3	12,000 units

There is a carryover of 5,000 units of product 2 and 4,000 units of product 3 and it is proposed to build up a stock at the end of the budget quarter which are as follows:

Product	1	1,000 units
	3	2,000 units

Prepare a Manpower Budget for the quarter showing for each operation *(i)* direct labor hours *(ii)* direct labor costs and *(iii)* the number of workers.

Solution

Man Power Budget

Operation	*Hourly Rate (Rs.)*	*Product 1*		*Product 2*		*Product 3*		*Total*		*Number of workers*
		D.L.hrs	*Cost Rs.*	*D.L.hrs*	*Cost Rs.*	*D.L.hrs*	*Cost Rs.*	*D.L.hrs*	*Cost Rs.*	
I	2.00	3,000	6,000	7,000	14,000	5,000	10,000	15,000	30,000	30
II	2.50	—	—	2,000	5,000	4,000	10,000	6,000	15,000	12
III	3.00	1,500	4,500	1,000	3,000	—	—	2,500	7,500	5
Total		4,500	10,500	10,000	22,000	9,000	20,000	23,500	52,500	47

Working Notes:

(1) Production Budget (Units)

Particular	*Product – 1*	*Product – 2*	*Product – 3*
Sales	9,000	15,000	12,000
(+) Closing Stock	1,000	—	2,000
	10,000	15,000	14,000
(-) Opening Stock	—	5,000	4,000
Production Budget	10,000	10,000	10,000

(2) Total available hours in a quarter per man :

Total hours = 8*6*13 = 624

(-) Hours lost due to leave etc. = 124

Total available hours per man = 500

(3) Calculation of direct labor hours, direct labor cost and number of men has been made as follows:

Operation I:

Product 1: Direct labor hrs = (18 × 10,000)/60 = 3,000 hrs

Direct labor cost = 3,000 × 2 = Rs. 6,000

Product 2: Direct labor hrs = (42 × 10,000)/60 = 7,000 hrs

Direct labor cost = 7,000 × 2 = Rs. 14,000

Product 3: Direct labor hrs = (30 × 10,000)/60 = 5,000 hrs

Direct labor cost = 5,000 × 2 = Rs. 10,000

Operation II:

Product 1: Direct labor hours = Nil

Direct labor cost = Nil

Product 2: Direct labor hours = (12 × 10,000)/60 = 2,000

Direct labor cost = 2,000 × 2.5 = Rs. 5,000

Product 3: Direct labor hours = (24 × 10,000)/60 = 4,000

Direct labor cost = 4,000 × 2.5 = Rs. 10,000

Operation III:

Product 1: Direct labor hours = (9 × 10,000)/60 = 1,500

Direct labor cost = 1500 × 3 = Rs. 4,500

Product 2: Direct labor hours = (6 × 10,000)/60 = 1,000

Direct labor cost = 1,000 × 3 = Rs. 3,000

Product 3: Direct labor hours = Nil

Operation I: $\text{No. of men required} = \dfrac{\text{Direct labor hrs required}}{\text{Total available hours per man}} = \dfrac{15{,}000}{500} = 30 \text{ Men}$

Operation II: $\text{No. of men required} = \dfrac{\text{Direct labor hrs required}}{\text{Total available hours per man}} = \dfrac{6{,}000}{500} = 12 \text{ Men}$

Operation IIII: $\text{No. of men required} = \dfrac{\text{Direct labor hrs required}}{\text{Total available hours per man}} = \dfrac{2{,}500}{500} = 5 \text{ Men}$

Factory Overheads Budget

Manufacturing or Factory Overheads include the cost of indirect material, indirect labor and indirect expenses. The manufacturing overheads can be classified into three categories *(i)* Fixed, i.e., which tend to remain constant irrespective of any change in the volume of output *(ii)* Variable, i.e., which tends to vary with the output and *(iii)* Semi – variable, i.e., which are partly variable and partly fixed. The Manufacturing Overheads Budget will provide an estimate of these overheads to be incurred in the budget period.

Illustration 6

From the following average figures of previous quarters, prepare a manufacturing overheads budget for the quarter ending 31/3/09. The budgeted output during this quarter is 4,000 units.

Fixed Overheads Rs. 20,000

Variable Overheads Rs. 10,000 (varying @ Rs. 5 per unit)

Semi – Variable Overheads Rs. 10,000 (40% fixed and 60% varying @ Rs. 3 per unit)

Solution

Manufacturing Overhead Budget for the quarter ending 31/3/09

Particulars	*Amount (Rs.)*	*Amount (Rs.)*
Fixed Overheads		20,000
Variable Overheads (4000 × 5)		20,000
Semi-Variable Overheads		
Fixed: (40% of Rs. 10,000)	4,000	16,000
Variable: 4000 units (@ Rs. 3 per unit)	12,000	
Total Overheads Cost		56,000

Administrative Overheads Budget

The Budget covers the expenses of all administrative office and management salaries. A careful analysis of the need of all administrative departments of the enterprise is very necessary. The minimum requirements for the efficient operation of each department can be estimated on the basis of costs for prior years and after a study of the plans and responsibilities of each administrative department for the budget period. The budget for the entire administrative division will be prepared by totaling the separate budgets of all administrative departments.

Selling and Distribution Overheads Budget

The Budget includes all expenses relating to selling, advertising, delivery of goods to customer etc. It is better if such costs are analyzed according to products, types of customer, territories and the sales departments in the organization itself. The responsibility for the preparation of this budget rests with the executives of the sales departments. There must be a co-ordination of selling expenses with the volume of sales expected and an effort should be made to control the costs of distribution. The preparation of the budget would depend on the analysis of the market situations by the Management, advertising policies, research programmes and the fixed and the variable elements.

Illustration 7

You are requested to prepare a Sales Overheads Budget from the estimates given below:

	Rs.
Advertisement	2,500
Salaries of the sales department	5,000
Expenses of the sales department	1,500
Counter Sales men's salaries and Dearness allowance	6,000

Commission to counter salesmen is at 1% on their sales; Traveling salesman commission is at 10% on their sales and expenses at 5% on their sales. The sales during the period were estimated as follows:

	Counter Sales (Rs.)	*Traveling sales men's (Rs.)*
	80,000	10,000
	1,20,000	15,000
	1,40,000	20,000

Solution

Sales Overhead Budget

Estimated Sales

Particulars	*(80,000 + 10,000) 90,000 Sales (Rs.)*	*(1,20,000+15,000) 1,35,000 Sales (Rs.)*	*(1,40,000 + 20,000) 1,60,000 Sales (Rs.)*
Fixed Overheads			
Advertisements	2,500	2,500	2,500
Salaries of sales department	5,000	5,000	5,000
Expenses of sales department	1,500	1,500	1,500
Counter salesmen's salaries and D.A	6,000	6,000	6,000
	15,000	15,000	15,000
Variable Overheads			
Counter salesmen commission @ 1% on their sales	800	1,200	1,400
Traveling salesmen commission @ 10% on their sales	1,000	1,500	2,000
Expenses @ 5% on Traveling Salesmen sales	500	750	1,000
	2,300	3,450	4,400
Total Sales Overheads	17,300	18,450	19,400

Illustration 8

The following is the information regarding the Budgeted and Actual Production Cost for the 6 months ending 31-12-08.

Units produced		*40,000 Budgeted*		*50,000 Actual*	
		Units	*Amount Rs.*	*Units*	*Amount Rs.*
(I)	Material Consumed	45,000	1,35,000	55,000	1,90,000
(II)	Wages at 3 hours per Unit (Rs.1.50 per hr)		1,80,000		2,45,000
(III)	Variable Overheads @ Rs.2 per unit		80,000		1,25,000
(IV)	Fixed Overheads		75,000		1,00,000

During the Budget Period:

(i) Production is expected to increase up to 60,000 units.

(ii) The prices of materials are expected to increase further in the same manner as they had increased over the budget price.

(iii) Labor charges are expected to increase by 50 paise per hour above the actual rates shown above, though efficiency is expected to decline by 20%.

(iv) Fixed Overheads are expected to increase by 20%.

(v) Loss of material is expected to be unaffected.

(vi) Variable Overheads are expected to increase by 10%.

You are required to prepare a Production Cost Budget for the 6 months ending 30th June 2009.

Solution

Elements of Cost	*Budget for 6 months ending 31.12.08 Production: 40,000 units*			*Actual for 6 months ending 31.12.08 Production: 50,000 units*			*Budget for 6 months ending 30th June 2009 Production: 60,000*		
	Units/ hrs	*Rate Rs.*	*Amount Rs.*	*Units/ hrs*	*Rate Rs.*	*Amount Rs.*	*Units/ hrs*	*Rate Rs.*	*Amount Rs.*
Material	45,000	3.00	1,35,000	55,000	3.455	1,90,000	66,000	3.978	2,62,548
Wages	1,20,000	1.50	1,80,000	1,50,000	1.633	2,45,000	2,16,000	2.133	4,60,728
Variable Overheads	40,000	2.00	80,000	50,000	2.500	1,25,000	60,000	2.750	1,65,000
Fixed Overheads			75,000			1,00,000			1,20,000
			4,70,000			6,60,000			10,08,276

Notes:

(1) Actual Material Consumed has been 10% over production in 2008. It continues to be 10% in 2009 also.

(2) The cost of material during 6 months ended 31.12.08 should have been as per budget prices Rs 1,65,000 (55,000 units × Rs. 3. However, actual cost of material is Rs 1,90,000. It means, cost of material has gone up by Rs. 25,000 (Rs. 1,90,000 – Rs. 1,65,000) resulting in 15.15 percent increase in 2008. The same trend is expected to continue in 2009. The price of materials therefore comes to Rs. 3.978 per unit (Rs. 3.455 + 15.15% of Rs. 3.455).

(3) Since the efficiency has gone down by 20% for manufacturing one unit, 3.6 labor hours (i.e. 3 hours +20% of 3 hours) will be taken in 2009. The total number of labor hours for 60,000 units will therefore be 2,16,000.

(4) Labor Hours = Production × 3 hours

(5) Factory Overheads in 2009 = 1,00,000 + 20 % of 1,00,000 = Rs. 1,20,000

Capital Expenditure Budget

The Budget provides guidance as to the amount of the capital that may be needed for procurement of capital assets during the budget period. The budget is prepared after taking into account the available productive capacities, probable reallocation of existing assets and possible improvement in production techniques. If necessary, separate budget may be prepared for each item of assets, such as building budget, a plant and equipment budget, etc.

Cash Budget

A Cash Budget contains detailed estimate of cash receipts (cash inflows) and disbursements (cash outflows) for the budget period or for some other specific period. A Cash Budget is extremely important since business operations require adequate cash to acquire materials and meet various expenses and loan obligations. The preparation of cash budget has the following objectives.

(1) to indicate the effect on the cash position of seasonal requirements, large inventories, unusual receipts and slowness in colleting receivables.

(2) to indicate the cash requirements needed for a plant or Equipment Expansion Programme.

(3) to indicate the availability of cash for taking advantage of discounts.

(4) to assist in planning the financial requirements of bond retirements, income tax installments and payments to pension and retirement funds.

(5) to show the availability of excess funds for short term or long-term investments.

(6) to show the surplus/deficit of cash so as to make arrangement for short term investment of surplus cash or arrange for borrowings to meet the deficiencies.

Preparation of Cash Budgets: A Cash Budget may be prepared by following any of the three generally accepted procedures.

(1) Receipts and Payments Method

(2) Adjusted Profit and Loss (or) Net Income Method

(3) Balance Sheet Method

(1) Receipts and Payment Method

In this method, the cash receipts from various sources and cash payments to different agencies are estimated. The Receipts and Payments may be divided into two specific categories. They are:

(i) Receipts:
(a) Capital and *(b)* Revenue

(ii) Payments:
(a) Capital and *(b)* Revenue

Capital Receipts would be: *(i)* The proceeds of issue of shares or debentures or loans to be raised, and *(ii)* sale proceeds of long-term investments or fixed assets. Revenue Receipts would be from: (i) cash sale of goods or services *(ii)* receipt from customers or clients and *(iii)* other business receipts like commission, income from investment, etc.

Capital payments would be: *(i)* Redemption of redeemable preference shares *(ii)* payment of long-term loans and *(iii)* purchase of fixed assets, etc. Revenue payments may be of the following types: *(i)* payments for materials supplied *(ii)* payments of wages *(iii)* payments of overheads *(iv)* other payments like interest on loans and income tax , etc and *(v)* payment of dividends.

To the opening balance of cash of a period, the estimated cash receipts are added and the estimated cash payments are deducted to find out the closing balance. This closing balance of a particular period will become the opening balance of cash for the next period.

Illustration 9

Prepare a Cash Budget for the months of May, June and July 2009 on the basis of the following information.

(1) Income and Expenditure Forecasts

Month	*Credit Sales* *Rs.*	*Credit Purchases* *Rs.*	*Wages* *Rs.*	*Manufacturing Expenses* *Rs.*	*Office Expenses* *Rs.*	*Selling Expenses* *Rs.*
March	60,000	36,000	9,000	4,000	2,000	4,000
April	62,000	38,000	8,000	3,000	1,500	5,000
May	64,000	33,000	10,000	4,500	2,500	4,500
June	58,000	35,000	8,500	3,500	2,000	3,500
July	56,000	39,000	9,500	4,000	1,000	4,500
August	60,000	34,000	8,000	3,000	1,500	4,500

(2) Cash balance on 1st May 2009 Rs. 8,000.

(3) Plant costing Rs. 16,000 is due for delivery in July, payable 10% on delivery and the balance after 3 months.

(4) Advance tax of Rs. 8,000 each is payable in March and June.

(5) Period of credit allowed *(i)* by suppliers – 2 months, and *(ii)* to customers – 1 month.
(6) Lag in payment of manufacturing expenses – 1/2 month.
(7) Lag in payment of office and selling expenses – one month.

Solution

Cash budget

Particulars	*May* *Rs.*	*June* *Rs.*	*July* *Rs.*
Opening Balance	8,000	13,750	12,250
Estimated Cash Receipts:			
Debtors (Credit Sales)	62,000	64,000	58,000
Total Cash Receipts	70,000	77,750	70,250
Estimated Cash Payments:			
Creditors (Credit Purchases)	36,000	38,000	33,000
Wages	10,000	8,500	9,500
Manufacturing Expenses	3,750	4,000	3,750
Office Expenses	1,500	2,500	2,000
Selling Expenses	5,000	4,500	3,500
Plant-Payment on Delivery	—	—	1,600
Advance Tax	—	8,000	—
Total Cash Payments	56,250	65,500	53,350
Closing Balance	13,750	12,250	16,900

Working notes:

(1) Closing balance of May becomes the opening balance for June and closing balance of June will become the opening balance for July.
(2) The period of credit allowed to customers is one month. The amount of credit sales in April shall be collected in May and so on.
(3) The period of credit allowed by supplies is 2 months, the payment for credit purchases in March shall be made in May and so on .
(4) One half of the manufacturing expenses of April and one half of those of May shall be paid in May, i.e. (1/2 of Rs. 3000, i.e. last month) + (1/2 of Rs. 4,500, i.e. current month), i.e. Rs. 3,750 and so on .
(5) Office and selling expenses of April shall be paid in May and so on .

(2) Adjusted Profit and Loss Account Method

In this method, the Cash Budget is prepared on the basis of opening cash and bank balances, projected Profit and Loss Account and the balances of the various assets and liabilities. Cash from operations is ascertained by adjusting the figure of profit in the light of non-cash items such as depreciation, loss on sale of capital assets, preliminary expenses written off, etc. These items do not affect cash position though they are charged to the Profit and Loss Account; therefore, they are added back to the profit or deducted from loss, as the case may be. Likely issue of new shares, realization from sale of fixed assets or raising longterm loans is taken as other sources of cash. Similarly, likely redemption of preference shares, payment of long term loan, purchase of fixed assets, payments of dividends, etc., are taken as applications of cash. Moreover, increase in current liabilities such as creditors, bills payable, etc., will mean less cash payments or decrease in current assets such as debtors, stock, bill receivables, prepaid expenses etc., will mean less investment in these assets or cash realized and therefore they will be all taken as sources of cash. Decrease in current liabilities or increase in current assets on the same basis will result in a decline in cash resources.

Illustration 10

The following data are available. You are required to prepare a Cash Budget according to adjusted Profit and Loss Account Method.

Balance Sheet

Liabilities	*Amount Rs.*	*Assets*	*Amount Rs.*
Share Capital	1,00,000	Premises	50000
General Reserve	20,000	Machinery	25,000
P&L A/c	10,000	Debtors	40,000
Creditors	50,000	Closing Stock	20,000
Bills payable	10,000	Bills Receivable	5,000
Outstanding Rent	2,000	Prepaid Commission	1,000
		Bank	51,000
	1,92,000		1,92,000

Dr. Projected Trading and Profit and Loss A/C for the year ended 31.12.2009 Cr.

Particulars		*Amount Rs.*	*Particulars*	*Amount Rs.*
To Opening Stock		20,000	By Sales	2,00,000
To Purchases		1,50,000	By Closing Stock	15,000
To Octroi		2,000		
To Gross Profit		43,000		
		2,15,000		2,15,000
To Interest		3,000	By Gross Profit b/d	43,000
To Salaries		6,000	By Sundry Receipts	5,000
To Depreciation		7,500		
(10% on premises and machinery)				
To Rent	6,000			
(+) Outstanding (CY)	1,000			
	7,000			
(–) last year	2,000	5,000		
To Commission	3,000			
(+) last year	1,000	4,000		
To Office Expenses		2,000		
To Advertisement Expenses		1,000		
To Net Profit c/d		19,500		
		48,000		48,000
To Dividends		8,000	By balance of profit from last year	10,000
To Addition to Reserves		4,000	By Net Profit b/d	19,500
To Balance c/d		17,500		
		29,500		29,500

Closing balances of certain items: Share Capital of Rs 1,20,000; 10% Debentures Rs 30000; Creditors Rs. 40,000; Debtors Rs. 60,000; Bills Payable Rs. 12,000; Bills Receivable Rs. 4,000; Furniture Rs. 15,000; Plant Rs. 50,000 (both these assets are to be purchased by the end of the year).

Cash Budget

Particulars	*Amount* Rs.	*Amount* Rs.
Opening balance as on 1st Jan 2009		51,000
Add:		
Net profit for the year	19,500	
Depreciation	7,500	
Decrease in Bills Receivable	1,000	
Increase in Bills Payable	2,000	
Issue of Share Capital (1,20,000 -1,00,000)	20,000	
Issue of Debentures	30,000	
Decrease in Prepaid Commission	1,000	
Decrease in Stock (20,000 – 15,000)	5,000	86,000
		1,37,000
Less:		
Purchase of Plant	50,000	
Purchase of Furniture	15,000	
Increase of Debtors	20,000	
Decrease of Creditors	10,000	
Decrease in outstanding rent	1,000	
Dividends paid	8,000	1,04,000
Closing Balance as on 31.12.2009		33,000

(3) Balance Sheet Method

In this method, at the end of each period, a projected Balance Sheet is drawn up setting out the various assets and liabilities, except cash and bank balances. The balancing figure would be the estimated closing cash/bank balances. Thus, under this method, closing balances other than cash/bank will have to be ascertained first, to draw up a Budgeted Balance Sheet. This can be done by adjusting the anticipated transactions of the year in the opening balances. This method is not recommended.

Illustration 11

From the following Budgeted Balance sheet as at 31/12/07, Budgeted Profit and Loss Account for the year ended 31/12/08 and the estimated figures for 2008, you are required to prepare the Cash Forecast of the Empire Manufacturing co. Ltd. for the year ending 31/12/08.

Budget Balance Sheet As on 31/12/07

Liabilities	*Amount* (Rs.)	*Assets*		*Amount* (Rs.)
Issued share capital	70,00,000	Freehold Building	35,00,000	
Capital Reserve	7,00,000	(–) Depreciation	3,50,000	31,50,000
Profit and Loss A/c	11,20,000	Plant and Machinery	56,00,000	
15% Debentures	7,00,000	(–) Depreciation	11,20,000	44,80,000
Trade Creditors	4,20,000	Motor Vehicles	11,20,000	
Proposed Dividends	2,80,000	(–) Depreciation	2,80,000	8,40,000
Liabilities for Expenses	56,000	Stock		7,00,000
		Debtors		6,30,000
		Bank		4,76,000
	1,02,76,000			1,02,76,000

Budgeted Profit and Loss Account for the year ended 31/12/08

Particulars	*Amount Rs.*	*Particulars*	*Amount Rs.*
To Administrative Expenses	4,82,440	By Gross profit b/d	21,00,000
To Selling Expenses	6,99,160	By Dis. Received	1,01,610
To Financial Expenses	1,33,000	By Int. Received	17,360
To Net profit c/d	9,04,400		
	22,19,000		22,19,000
To Dividends paid	5,60,000	By Bal b/d	11,20,000
To Balance taken to Balance Sheet	14,64,400	By net profit b/d	9,04,400
	20,24,400		20,24,400

Estimated Figures as at 31/12/08

Particulars	*Amount (Rs.)*
Issued Share Capital	77,00,000
Capital Reserve	7,00,000
Profit and Loss Account	14,64,000
15% Debentures	10,50,000
Trade Creditors	4,92,000
Liabilities for Expenses	63,000
Freehold Building (at book value after deducting total Depreciation Rs. 4,20,000)	30,80,000
Plant and Machinery (at book value after deducting total Depreciation Rs. 16,80,000)	53,20,000
Motor Vehicle (at book value after deducting total depreciation Rs. 5,60,000)	8,40,000
Stock	7,56,000
Debtors	5,60,000

Solution

Cash Forecast for the year ending 31/12/08

Particulars	*Amount (Rs.)*	*Amount (Rs.)*
Budgeted Cash Balance as on 1st Jan 08		4,76,000
Receipts: Cash from operations:		
Net Profit	9,04,400	
(+) Non-cash charges:		
Depreciation	9,10,000	
	18,14,400	
(+) Increase in Creditors	70,000	
Increase in liabilities for expenses	7,000	
Reduction in Debtors	70,000	
	19,61,400	
(–) Increase in Stock	56,000	
		19,05,400
Issue of Equity Shares		7,00,000
Issue of 15% Debentures		3,50,000
Total Cash Receipts (i)		34,31,400

Particulars	*Amount (Rs.)*	*Amount (Rs.)*
Payments:		
Purchase of Plant and Machinery		14,00,000
Purchase of motor vehicles		2,80,000
Payments of dividends: 2007	2,80,000	
2008	5,60,000	8,40,000
Total Cash Payments (ii)		25,20,000
Cash Balance at the end of the year (i)-(ii)		9,11,400

Working notes: (1) Depreciation to be written off during 2008.
Balance in depreciation provision as on 31st December.

Particulars	*2007. Rs.*	*2008 Rs.*	*Increase Rs.*
Free holdings	3,50,000	4,20,000	70,000
Plant & Machinery	11,20,000	16,80,000	5,60,000
Motor Vehicles	2,80,000	5,60,000	2,80,000
	17,50,000	26,60,000	9,10,000

Fixed Assets acquired during 2008

Particulars	*Plant & Machinery (Rs.)*	*Motors Vehicles (Rs.)*
Book values as on 31.12.08	53,20,000	8,40,000
(+) Depreciation Provision Cost on 31.12.08	16,80,000	5,60,000
	70,00,000	14,00,000
(–) Cost on 31.12.07	56,00,000	11,20,000
	14,00,000	2,80,000

Master Budget

According to ICMA Terminology, "A Master Budget is the Summary Budget incorporating its component functional budgets and which is finally approved, adopted and employed". Accordingly, it comprises of the Functional Budget summaries in the form of budgeted profit and loss account and approved and accepted by the management.

The Master Budget projects the activities of a business during the budget period, and thus it is a profit plan. It represents the standards to be achieved by the various departments working together.

Illustration 12

A Glass Manufacturing Company requires you to calculate and present the budget for the next year from the following information

Toughened Glass	Rs. 3,00,000
Bent Toughened Glass	Rs. 5,00,000
Direct Material Cost	60% of Sales
Direct Wages	20 workers @ Rs. 150 per month
Factory Overheads:	
Indirect Labor:	
Work Manager	Rs. 500 Per Month
Foreman	Rs. 400 Per Month

Stores and Spares 2½% in Sales

Depreciation on Machinery	Rs. 12,600
Light and Power	Rs. 5,000
Repairs and Maintenance	Rs. 8,000

Other Sundries 10% on Direct Wages

Administration, Selling and Distribution Expenses Rs 14,000 per year

Solution

Master Budget for the period ending on....

Particulars	*Amount (Rs.)*	*Amount (Rs.)*
Sales (as per sales budget):		
Toughened Glass		3,00,000
Bent Toughened Glass		5,00,000
		8,00,000
(–) Cost of production (as per Cost of Production Budget)		
Direct Materials (60% of Rs. 8,00,000)	4,80,000	
Direct Wages (20 × 150 × 12)	36,000	
Factory Overheads Variable:		
Stores and Spares (2½% of sales)	20,000	
Light and Power	5,000	
Repairs & Maintenance	8,000	
Fixed: Works Managers Salary (500 × 12)	6,000	
Foreman's Salary (400 × 12)	4,800	
Depreciation	12,600	
Sundries (10% × 36,000)	3,600	5,76,000
Gross profit		2,24,000
(–) Selling Administration and Distribution OH		14,000
Net Profit		2,10,000

FIXED AND FLEXIBLE BUDGETS

Budgets can be classified into Fixed and Flexible budgets which are explained below.

Fixed Budget

According to the Charted Institute of Management Accountants, London, "A Fixed Budget is a budget which is designed to remain unchanged irrespective of the level of activity actually attained."

It is based on single level of activity. A Fixed Budget Performance Report compares data from actual operations with the single level of activities reflected in the budget. It acts as a target for the forth-coming period. It represents a point fixed in advance with which actual results are compared. Fixed Budgets do not change with production level changes.

In practice, Fixed Budget is rarely used. The main reason is that, the actual output is often significantly different from the budgeted output. A Fixed or Static Budget is satisfactory only when company's activities can be estimated with in close limits.

Flexible Budget

A Flexible Budget is defined in the terminology of Cost Accounting, issued by Institute of Cost and Management Association (UK) as "A budget which by recognizing the difference between fixed, semi-fixed and variable cost is designed to change in relation to the level of activity attained."

A Flexible Budget is a budget that is prepared for a range, i.e., for more than one level of activity. It is a set of alternative budget to different expected levels of activity. The Flexible Budget is also known as Variable Budget, Dynamic Budget, Sliding Scale Budget, Step Budget, Expenses Formula Budget and Expenses Control Budget.

A Flexible Budget provides information to managers for multiple levels of output in case actual output is different from the expected levels. The Performance Reports at the end of the accounting period are compared with a budget based on actual output attained during the period.

Features of the Flexible Budget

A Flexible Budget has the following features:

(1) It covers a range of activities (output).

(2) It is flexible, i.e., easy to change with variation in production levels.

(3) It facilitates performance measurement and evaluation.

Steps in Flexible Budgeting

The following steps are involved in developing a Flexible Budget:

(1) Deciding the range of activities to which budget is to be prepared.

(2) Determining the cost behavior patterns (fixed, variable, semi-variable) for each element of cost to be included in the Budget.

(3) Selecting the activity levels (generally in terms of production) to prepare budgets at those levels.

(4) Preparing the budget at each activity level selected by associating the activity level with corresponding costs. The corresponding costs to be attached with each activity level are determined in terms of their behavior, i.e., fixed, variable and semi-variable.

Advantages of Flexible Budgeting

Flexible Budgeting is budgeting that is automatically tailored to any level of activity. It provides a better evaluation of efficiency by relating inputs to outputs. Although it is most often associated with the control of overheads, a Flexible Budget may also include direct materials and direct labor.

A Flexible Budget is a great planning and coordinating tool. It becomes a frame of reference - a set of expectations against which actual results can be compared.

The main advantages of Flexible Budgeting are listed below.

(1) Highlights all Departures: A Flexible Budget highlights all departures from the efficient performance. As the actual results are compared with the budgeted results for the same levels of activity, efficiency and inefficiency are clearly indicated.

(2) Organised Procedures for Planning: Budgets containing estimated costs are plans for action. But, they are so, only when they are drawn for various possible volumes. Since future is uncertain, planning can be effective only with the help of a set of budgets made for alternative outcomes.

(3) Better Control: In management aspects of Cost Accounting, budgets are used to evaluate the performance of the department managers. A comparison of actual performance with the budgeted performance aids the management in evaluating whether the departmental manager has succeeded in attaining the targets set for him.

(4) Management by Exception: The deviation between the figures of performance budget and the actual results is the variance. The significant variances are investigated for corrective action. This process is called "Management by Exception" (MBE) as the management concentrates only on the deviations/variances.

(5) Localized Decisions: A Flexible Budget framework is most useful for localized Decision Centers. A number of variables could be used to build revenue and cost functions. For a particular budget area, the relevant variable or variables could be selected.

Methods of constructing a Flexible Budget

A Flexible Budget can be constructed according to any one of the following methods:

(1) Multi Activity Method: This method involves computing budget figures for different levels of activity within a range. Preparation of budget according to this method involves the following steps:

(i) Determination of the units in which the different levels of activity are to be expressed. The levels of activity are generally expressed in production units or in terms of sales values. However, the levels of activity may also be expressed in terms of labor or machines hours.

(ii) The fixation of the Budget Cost Allowance for the Budget Centers. According to the Chartered Institute of Management Accountants, London, the Budget Cost Allowance means "the cost which a Budget Centre is expected to incur during a given period of time in relation to the level of activity attained by the Budget Centre."

(iii) Determination of the different levels of activity for which the Flexible Budget is to be prepared. This method is also called as Tabular Method.

(2) Formula Method: This is also known as the Budget Cost Allowance Method. The following steps are taken in this method.

(i) A budget is prepared for the expected normal level of activity.

(ii) Ratios are worked out showing the relationship of each expense or group of expenses per unit level of activity.

Thus, total cost for any level of activity can be computed on basis of the following formula:

Total Costs= Fixed Costs + (Actual units of activity × Variable cost per unit of activity).

(3) Graphic Method: According to this method, the costs are classified according to their variability as fixed, variable and semi variable. Estimates of different costs are made for different levels of activity. The data are then plotted on a graph paper showing the costs at different levels of activity. The budgeted levels of activity are on the horizontal scale and the amount of budgeted costs is on the vertical scale. Budgeted costs can be shown in graph regarding each item of expenditure for each department or for the business as a whole.

Illustration 13

The expenses for budgeted production of 10,000 units in a factory are furnished below:

	Per Unit (Rs.)
Materials	70
Labor	25
Variable Overheads	20
Fixed Overheads (10,000)	10
Variable Expenses (Direct)	5
Selling Expenses (10% Fixed)	13
Distribution Expenses (20% Fixed)	7
Administration Expenses (Rs.50,000)	5
Total Cost per unit	155

Prepare a budget for production of

(a) 8,000 units and 6,000 units *(c)* Also indicate the cost per unit at both the levels.

Assume the administration expenses are fixed for all levels of production.

Solution

Flexible Budget

Particulars	*10,000 units*		*8,000 units*		*6,000 units*	
	Per Unit Rs.	*Amount Rs.*	*Per Unit Rs.*	*Amount Rs.*	*Per Unit Rs.*	*Amount Rs.*
Production Expenses						
Materials	70.0	7,00,000	70.000	5,60,000	70.000	4,20,000
Labor	25.0	2,50,000	25.000	2,00,000	25.000	1,50,000
Overheads	20.0	2,00,000	20.000	1,60,000	20.000	1,20,000
Direct Variable Expenses	5.0	50,000	5.000	40,000	5.000	30,000
Fixed Overheads:						
Fixed Expenses (Rs 1,00,000)	10.0	1,00,000	12.500	1,00,000	16.667	1,00,000
Selling Expenses:						
Fixed	1.30	13,000	1.625	13000	2.167	13,000
Variable	11.70	1,17,000	11.700	93,600	11.700	70,200
Distribution Expenses:						
Fixed	1.40	14,000	1.750	14000	2.333	14,000
Variable	5.60	56,000	5.600	44,800	5.600	33600
Administration Expenses	5.00	50,000	6.250	50,000	8.333	50,000
	155.00	15,50,000	159.425	12,75,400	166.800	10,00,800

LIMITATIONS OF BUDGETARY CONTROL

Although Budgetary Control is immensely useful, Budget cannot be considered to be a managerial tool which is perfect. It is not free from the following limitations, which have been summarized by welsels in his book "Budgeting, Profit Planning and Control" under the following major heads.

(1) **The Budget plan is based on estimates:** The success of Budgetary Control depends upon the accuracy of forecasts on which budgets are prepared. Since forecasts cannot be considered to be an exact science, the accuracy of data on which the estimates are based determines the adequacy or otherwise of a Budgetary Programme. If forecasts are made on the basis of inadequate and inaccurate data, the budgeted figures would be far away from the reality and the target set would also be inaccurate.

(2) **The likelyhood of becoming rigid:** A Budget Programme should be dynamic and flexible, being capable of being adapted to changed circumstances. But, when the budgets are prepared with predetermined targets of program, there is a general tendency to consider them as fixed. In such cases, the Budgetary Program becomes rigid and when it becomes rigid and final, it is not easy for the management to bring changes in the budgeted figures due to change in circumstances.

On the other hand, if it is felt that the budgeted figures are not final and subject to frequent changes, the personnel are bound to loose faith on Budgetary Program.

While it is necessary to introduce the elements of flexibility during the formative period, frequent revisions are not advisable.

(3) **Execution of Budgeted Plan will not occur automatically:** Unless there is an active cooperation between the different levels of management, no budget will automatically become a success. Budgetary Control implies the preparation of budgets and its administration also. But most of the personnel is of the opinion that the preparation of budget is the end, but, they should know that no budget will be successful unless it is properly executed.

(4) **Not a substitute for Management:** It is to be clearly understood that Budgetary Control is not a substitute for Management but is only a tool in the hands of management to perform their functions more effectively.

(5) **It is an expensive tool:** It is commented that implementing a Budgetary Control is a costly affair as it necessitates the employment of specialized staff which small concerns may not afford.

(6) **Suitability:** It is not suitable where frequent changes occur. This system proves to be useless in those firms where policies, processes, techniques are subject to frequent changes.

(7) **Uncontrollable factors:** There are many factors on which success of Budgetary Control depends on which; management has on control.

(8) **Opposition against the very spirit of Budgeting:** Always there will be active and passive resistance to Budgetary Control from various levels of management. No Budgetary Control is successful unless there is full co-operation from all the individuals concerned.

(9) **Time Factor:** It is felt that preparation of a Budget involves a lot of time. Better results from Budget will rise over a longer period of time. Accuracy in budgeting comes through experience. Management must not expect too much during the development period.

(10) **Conflict among different departments:** Budgetary Control may lead to conflict among the functional departments. Every department worries about its own department with out considering the business goal. Every department tries to get maximum allocation of funds, which creates conflict among the departments.

(11) **Support from top management:** The success of Budgetary Control mainly depends upon the full co-operation and support from top management. The top management must be enthusiastic about the success of the system and must give full support. Any lack of support from the top management results in the failure of Budgetary Control.

(12) **Discourages efficiency:** Under Budgetary Control System, the targets are set and given to every individual in the organization. Once the target is given, it is a common tendency in every one to fulfill the target without working hard to achieve more. Even the efficient will be contended, by achieving the targets. Hence, under Budgetary Control System, there is no incentive to improve efficiency.

(13) **Suitable only in static conditions:** Budgetary Control is suitable only when frequent changes are not expected. But, in most of the cases, the future is uncertain.

Thus, Budgetary Control suffers from the above the limitations or disadvantages which it has to overcome.

TRADITIONAL SYSTEM OF BUDGETING

The traditional technique of budgeting is based on prior years' performance. The type of budgeting process assumes that the allocation of financial resources in the prior year are correct and will continue in the future as well. In this method, the preparation of budget mainly comprises simple extrapolation of the last years' level of spending to the current years' level of spending with adjustment for the expected changes in the cost. Here, only incremental change or additions to previous budget levels are made. Therefore, it is also called as 'Incremental Budgeting System'. Here, the budget changes in increments or small movements from the previous year.

The preparation of budgets is a unique task having long-term implications on the pace and growth of the organization. A budget serves as a guide to the spending units to incur expenditure and to achieve the targets as envisaged. The estimates are prepared by "pushing forward the previous year's figures with slight adjustment. As such, budgets in their present form have outlived their utility on all counts. The corrective measures to remedy the situation lie in modernizing the technique of budget preparation.

Limitations of Traditional Budgeting

The following are the limitations of Traditional Budgeting:

- Using the previous years' performance as a base for current years' budget is meaningless because the modern conditions are dynamic. Therefore, they require fresh review of every task in the new dimension.
- The previous years' inefficiencies and wastes are automatically carried forward in the current years budgeting.
- The traditional budgeting results in undesirable allocation of resources. In it, the funds are likely to be allocated to the non-essential programs and priority programs suffer because of lack of funds.
- There is no relationship between the inputs (expenditures made) and the output (results obtained). It does not provide rigorous cost benefit analysis.
- It provides inadequate information to the management for decision-making.

In order to make the effective allocation of limited resources, a budget system should answer the following questions.

(i) Whether the expenditure for the activity is justifiable?

(ii) How much amount should be spent for that activity?

(iii) How that amount can be spent effectively?

ADVANTAGES OF BUDGETARY CONTROL

In modern business world, the Budgetary Control has become an essential tool of management for controlling costs and maximizing profits. It helps the management to perform their functions effectively. It acts as a tool to compare actual performance with planned performance and measure any deviations. It helps to correct the deviations from pre-planned path. It uncovers uneconomic operations, weaknesses in the organization structure and minimizes the wastage of time and finance. It acts as a friend, philosopher and a guide to the management. Its advantages can be summarized as follows.

(1) **Promotes efficiency:** It acts as a yardstick against which the actual performance is compared with and necessary corrections can be made so that it promotes efficiency and thereby help the management in taking future course of action.

(2) **Coordination among the Departments:** Coordination is established among the different departments and individuals through planning policy and control.

(3) **Helps in utilizing limiting factors economically:** Limiting factors can be utilized properly by the application of this system. Otherwise, less important factors can play the most significant role, without however, utilizing the scarce factors which should have been used in view of their importance.

(4) **Provides a valuable aid to control:** It provides a valuable aid to the management by several managerial functions and thus helps the management to adopt the future course of action in a scientific way.

(5) **Helps to control:** The top management can exercise control over the various activities of the business since each and every aspect of the business is reviewed.

(6) **Maximization of profit:** Budgetary Control helps to maximize profits by exercising control over various capital and revenue expenditure. To achieve this aim, a proper planning and coordination of different functions is undertaken.

(7) **Specific aims:** Budgetary Control helps the management to achieve common specific aims of the organization with proper plans, policies and good set up for the organisation. Every Department is given target to be achieved. All efforts of all the individuals and departments are properly coordinated to achieve specific aims of the organisation without much wastage of finance and efforts.

(8) **Brings economy in working:** With proper planning and coordination, it brings efficiency and economy in the working of the business enterprise.

(9) **Management by Exception:** Budgetary Control provides a tool for measuring managerial performance by providing targets for various departments. The performance of each department is measured by comparing the actual performance with the budgeted performance. The system enables the introduction of Management by Exception as, only an exceptional item, where there is a variance is reported to the management.

(10) **Buck passing avoided:** Budgetary Control establishes Divisional and Departmental responsibilities. It prevents "buck-passing" when the budget figures are not met as responsibilities are fixed to the managers.

(11) **Guards against undue optimism:** As targets are fixed by the top executive, after cool and careful thought, it guards against undue optimism of leading to over expansion.

(12) **Acts as Safety Signal:** It acts as a safety signal for the management. It shows when to proceed cautiously and when manufacturing or merchandising expansion can be safely undertaken. It serves as an automatic check on the judgment of the executives as losses are revealed on time which is a caution to the management to stop wastage.

(13) **Adoption of Uniform Policy:** Uniform Policy without the disadvantage of military type of business organisation can be pursued by all the divisions of the business by means of centralization of Budgetary Control.

(14) **Decrease in production costs:** Seasonal variations in production can be reduced by developing new "fill in products". This results in decreasing the cost of production by increasing the volume of output.

(15) **Adoption of Standard Costing Principles:** The use of budget figures as measures of operating performance and financial position makes possible adoption of the Standard Costing Principles in divisions other than the Production Division.

(16) **Corrective action:** Budgetary Control helps to point out deviations regularly so that necessary action is taken at the earliest by the management. In the absence of a Budgetary Control System, the deviations can be determined only at the end of the financial year.

(17) **Consciousness:** It creates budget consciousness among the employees. By fixing targets for the employees, they are made conscious of their responsibilities. Everybody is aware of one's duties.

(18) **More economical use of capital:** Budgetary Control helps the management in obtaining the most profitable combination of different factors of production. This results in more economical use of capital.

(19) **Favor with Credit Agencies:** Managements who have developed a well-ordered budget plan and who operates accordingly, receive greater favor from Credit Agencies.

(20) **Optimum capitalization:** It helps to judge as to what extent financing will be necessary, avoiding the possibility of both, over and under capitalization.

(21) **Introduction of Incentive Schemes:** Budgetary Control helps the management to introduce incentive schemes of remuneration basing on the performance measured in terms of budgeted performance.

(22) It provides a basis for internal audit.

(23) It helps the management in identifying unprofitable or less profitable activities so as to discontinue them.

(24) It ensures availability of sufficient working capital and channelises capital expenditure into most profitable lines.

(25) It guides the management in Research and Development.

ZERO BASED BUDGETING (ZBB)

Zero Based Budgeting is the latest technique of budgeting and it has an increased use as a management tool. The technique was first used in America in 1962. The former President of America, Jimmy Carter, used the technique, when he was the Governor of Georgia, of conducting state expenditure. Later, it has become popular in other countries also.

Zero Based Budgeting (ZBB) is budgeting with the base zero. All existing programs have to be justified in the same way as new proposals. The current activities will have to be compared with alternative uses for available resources. It is the opposite of "Incremental Budgeting Process" where, line-by-line approval is accorded to specific categories of expenditure. An across-the-board percentage increase or decrease is effected there in, which hardly induces the managers to reduce the costs.

The basic concept of ZBB is to start budgeting from Zero Base (scratch or clean slate). Under ZBB, every manager or division head has to justify his claims for financial resources for particular activity under his charge. The expenditure on every activity (current or proposed) is reviewed and justified in terms of the organizations objectives and goals. The main point of difference between the Traditional Budgeting and ZBB is that, while the former concerns predominantly with marginal change in resource allocation, the latter works under the assumption that at the time of preparing budget, the expenditure in every item of budget is zero. A manager has to therefore justify a budget requirement in detail (i.e. purpose of activity, possible alternative for it, consequences of not carrying out such an activity etc.) from the scratch.

Peter A Pyhrr, a former Budget Director with Texas Instruments in USA, widely regarded as the father of ZBB defines it as "a planning budgeting process which requires each manager to justify his entire budget request in detail from scratch (hence Zero Base) and shifts the burden of proof to each manager to justify why he should spend any money at all. The approach requires that all activities, be analyzed in `decision packages' which are evaluated by systematic analysis and ranked in order of importance."

Under the Traditional Budgeting, it is possible that the funds are allocated to the non-essential activities while the essential and high priority programs suffer from lack of funds. But, ZBB calls for a fresh examination of every program or activity from a Zero Base instead of only increases or decreases in spending. Every ongoing activity is also scrutinized in the same manner like a new one proposed to be under taken. Therefore, it provides a rational method and allows reallocation of resources from low to high priority programs.

According to the ICMA Terminology, Zero Based Budgeting also designated as Priority Base Budgeting is a method of budgeting, where by, all activities are revaluated each time a budget is set and each activity is valued and a combination of activities are chosen to match funds available.

Generally, the following points are to be considered before introducing ZBB,

- Is it absolutely necessary?
- What should be the qualitative features of current activities?
- Will production be continued according to the existing system
- What is the cost of production under current conditions?

In this way, cost reduction is possible in the enterprises after a careful analysis. However, it takes a long time to implement this method although, through a minute review of the present system, overheads can be controlled.

Stages in ZBB

ZBB involves the following stages:

(1) Each separate activity of the organization is identified and is called a Decision Package. A Decision Package is a document that identifies and describes a specific activity in such a manner that the management can

(a) Evaluate it and rank it against other activities competing for limited resources and

(b) Decide whether to approve or disapprove it

(2) Each Decision Package must be justified, i.e., it should be enquired into whether a Decision Package promotes the goals of an enterprise.

(3) If justified, then, the cost of minimum efforts needed to sustain each Decision Package is determined.

(4) Alternatives for each Decision Package are considered in order to select better and cheaper option for a package.

(5) Incremental Decision Packages are also justified and costed in the above manner. The incremental packages describe the costs and benefits of additional work that could be done above the required, by the base package, for the minimum amount of work needed to carry out the activity.

(6) Managers rank their Decisions Package in order of priority for resource allocation.

(7) Resources are allocated to the Packages.

Advantages of ZBB

ZBB offers the following advantages to the organization.

(1) It represents a move towards allocation of resources by need and benefit and thus resulting in an efficient allocation of resources.

(2) It identifies and eliminates wastages and obsolete operations.

(3) It ensures that the best possible methods of performing jobs are caused and thus, new ideas emerge.

(4) It creates a questioning attitude rather than the one which accepts the current practices, without any evaluation.

(5) It leads to increased staff involvement which may lead to improved motivation and greater interest in the job.

(6) It increases communication with in the organization.

(7) Managers become more aware of the costs of inputs which help them identify priorities.

(8) The documentation of decisions packages provides management with a deep, coordinated knowledge of all organizations activities.

(9) It is useful especially for service departments where it is difficult to identify output.

Disadvantages of ZBB

The following are the limitations from which ZBB suffers.

(1) The costs involved in preparing a vast number of decision packages in large firms are very high.

(2) It is very time consuming and a large amount of additional paper work is involved.

(3) Managers develop fear and feel threatened by ZBB and therefore may oppose new ideas and changes.

(4) The ranking of decision packages and allocation of resources is subjective, to a certain degree, which can result in departmental conflict.

(5) Administration and communication of ZBB process may become critical problems as more managers become involved in this process than in most budgeting and planning procedures and these problems are further compounded in large organizations.

PROGRAMME BUDGETING

Programme Budgeting is used in non profit or non commercial organizations to enable them to make more informed decisions about resource allocation. Programme Budgeting differs from traditional non profit and non manufacturing budgets in the sense that the latter are prepared as line item budget where as the former are prepared on the basis of programs, i.e., planned activities and have specified objectives. In Programme Budgeting, budgets for line/functional items for the whole departments are not presented.

Programme Budgeting is taken by extending the planning period beyond the one-year budget period. It is the counter part of the long-term planning process which is operated in the profit oriented organizations. It is based on a rational model of decision making and involves the following stages:

(1) Identify and define the objectives of programme.
(2) Select performance or output measures to assess the effectiveness of the programme.
(3) Identify and evaluate alternative methods of achieving the objectives laid down for each specific programme. For this, cost and benefits associated with each alternative course of action should be detailed.
(4) Select the appropriate programmes on the basis of Cost-Benefit Analysis.
(5) Implement the selected alternative and monitor its performance to ensure that the objectives of the programmes are achieved given the resources allocated to those programmes.

Advantages of Programming Budgeting

The following are the benefits of Programming Budgeting.

(1) It leads to more effective allocation of resources by cutting across departmental barriers, providing to managers specific information related to the activities and by coordinating scarce resources and skilled personnel located in different departments on a particular programme or project.
(2) It compels the management to identify and evaluate activities, functions or programmes which are carried out in terms of their objectives, efficiency and effectiveness.
(3) Programme Budgeting provides adequate information which will enable the management to assess the effectiveness of its plans and to focus on the organisation's output (the objectives to be achieved).

PERFORMANCE BUDGETING

Performance Budgeting as a budgeting method was first introduced in USA around 1950. Performance Budgeting aims to formulate budgets in term of activities, programmes and functions. The essence of this budgeting lies in ascertaining activities and related costs and to measure efficiency achieved thereby.

According to the National Institute of Bank Management, Bombay, Performance Budgeting technique is, the process of analyzing, identifying, simplifying and crystallizing specific performance objectives of a job to be achieved over a period, in the framework of the organisational objectives, the purpose and objectives of the job. The technique is characterized by its specific direction towards the business objectives of the organisation. Thus, Performance Budgeting lays immediate stress on the achievement of specific goals over a period of time. It enables the organisation to be sensitive and adaptive, preventing it from developing rigidities which may retard the process of growth.

Performance Budgeting involves three levels of management:

(1) Policy Management – identification of needs, analysis of options, selection of programmes and allocation of resources.
(2) Resource Management – establishment of basic support system consisting of budgeting structures and financial management practices.
(3) Programme Budgeting – implementation of policies and related operations, accounting, reporting and evaluating.

Thus, a Performance Budget is one that presents the purposes and objectives for which, funds are required, the cost of achieving them and the quantitative data measuring the accomplishments and work performed under each programme. Performance Budgeting involves the following steps:

- activity classification in terms of functions, programmes and activities;
- financial and physical measurement of activities;
- reporting the progress of performance at periodic intervals; and
- restructuring of the accounting system.

The main objectives of Performance Budgeting are:

(a) To coordinate the physical and financial aspects;
(b) To improve the budget formulation, review and decision making at all levels of management;
(c) To facilitate better appreciation and review by controlling authorities (Legislatures, Board of Trustees or Governors, etc.) as the presentation is more purposeful and intelligible;
(d) To make more effective performance audit possible; and
(e) To measure progress towards long-term objectives which are envisaged in the development plan.

The responsibility for preparing the Performance Budget of each Department lies on the respective Department Head. Each departmental head will be supplied with a copy of the section of the Master Budget appropriate to his sphere. The report may be daily, weekly or monthly depending upon the size of the business and the budget period. These reports will be in the form of comparison of budgeted and actual figures, both periodic and cumulative. The purpose of submitting these reports is to convey promptly the information about the deviation in actual and budgeted activity to the person who has the necessary authority and responsibility so that he may take necessary action to correct any deviation from the budget.

Illustration 14

Z ltd. had a profit plan approved for selling 5,000 units per month at an average price of Rs 10 per unit. The budgeted variable cost of production was Rs. 4 per unit and fixed costs were budgeted at Rs. 20,000, the planned income being Rs. 10,000 per month. Due to shortage of raw materials, only 4,000 units could be produced and the cost of production increased by 50 paisa per unit. The selling price was raised by Re. 1.00 per unit. In order to improve the production process, an expenditure of Rs. 1,000 was incurred for research and development activities.

You are required to prepare a Performance Budget and Summary Report.

Solution

Z Ltd. Performance Budget

Particulars	*Original Plan (5,000 units) (Rs.)*	*Adjusted Plan (4,000 units) (Rs.)*	*Actual Plan (4,000 units) (Rs.)*
Sales Revenue	50,000	40,000	44,000
(–)Variable Costs	20,000	16,000	18,000
Contribution	30,000	24,000	26,000
(–) Fixed Cost	20,000	20,000	21,000
Net Income	10,000	4,000	5,000

Summary Report

Planned Income	Rs. 10,000
(1) Selling Price Variance (4,000 × (11-10))= Rs. 4,000 (Favorable)	
(2) Variable Cost Variance [4,000 × (4-4.5)] = Rs. 2,000 (Adverse)	
(3) Fixed Cost Variance [21,000 – 20,000] = Rs. 1,000 (Adverse)	
(4) Profit Volume Variance [1,000 × 6] = 6,000 (adverse)	Rs. 5,000 (Adverse)
Actual Income	Rs. 5,000

SUMMARY

Budgets are the blue prints which speak about the probable future course of action. The primary objective of Budgetary Control is to help the management in systematic planning and controlling with proper communication network. A properly prepared and implemented budget reaps many advantages to the organization, ultimately, resulting in achieving the main target of profit maximization. But, it should be cost effective, prepared in a realistic manner and implemented properly. However, a proper organization is essential for the successful preparation, maintenance and administration of budgets.

There must be an organizational chart showing the hierarchy with chief executive at the apex, who appoints a Budget Officer assisted by a Budget Committee consisting of all functional heads. They decide the Budget Period, Budget Centers and also prepare a Budget Manual which spells out the duties and responsibilities of various executives in the organization.

The process of budget setting starts with the Sales Budget. Production Budget follows, which in turn, necessitates budget for Materials, Direct Labor and Overheads. These and other budgets are assembled into a Master Budget which becomes a governing document and virtually a forecasted profit and loss account. Best Budgets are the ones which are prepared on standard costs. To be meaningful, budgets have to be flexible rather than static. A flexible budget is prepared for several levels of activity, but, at minimum, it is for at least three levels viz., most optimistic, the most pessimistic and the most likely levels.

Zero Based Budgeting is the latest technique of budgeting and it has an increased use as a management tool. Zero Based Budgeting (ZBB) is budgeting with the base zero. All existing programs have to be justified in the same way as the new proposals. The current activities will have to be compared with alternative uses for available resources. It is the opposite of "Incremental Budgeting Process" where, line-by-line approval is accorded to specific categories of expenditure. Every on going activity is also scrutinized in the same manner like a new one proposed to be under taken. Therefore, it provides a rational method and allows reallocation of resources from low to high priority programs.

Glossary

- **Budget:** a blueprint enunciating the future and a projection or estimate of future output, costs and revenues.
- **Budgeting:** the task of preparation of budget or the cost of building the budget.
- **Budgetary Control:** a system of management control and accounting in which all the operations are forecasted and the actuals are compared with the forecasted figures.

- **Forecast:** assessment of probable future events and precedes the budget.
- **Budget Manual:** document which clearly defines the responsibilities and duties of various people relating to framing of budgets.
- **Budget Period:** the period for which budget should be framed. It depends upon the nature of industry, the peculiar characteristics of the organization and the need for control of performance and costs.
- **Sales Budget:** the starting point, based on product, territory and customer. This is the budget on which all other operating and financial budgets depend.
- **Production Budget:** an estimate of the production quantity required based on the sales forecast and budgeted inventory levels.
- **Material Budget:** the budget which sets out the quantity and volume of different types of materials to be purchased during the budget period taking into consideration the level of production activity and the inventory levels.
- **Direct Labor Budget:** a budget prepared for estimates of the department's labor hours which will be required to meet the planned production. Where different grades of labor exist, these should be specified separately in the budget.
- **Manufacturing Overheads Budget:** contains the expected cost of all indirect manufacturing elements necessary to meet the production budget.
- **Cash Budget:** expected cash inflows and outflows during the budget period adjusted for opening and closing balances
- **Master Budget:** a summary of all functional budgets in a capsule form.
- **Fixed Budget:** a budget designed to remain unchanged irrespective of the level of activity actual attained.
- **Flexible Budget:** a budget designed to furnish budgeted costs for any level of activity actually attained.
- **Performance Budget:** a budget which specifies output or results to be achieved along with the inputs or expenditure to be incurred during the budget period.
- **Zero Based Budgeting:** an operating, planning and budgeting process which requires each manager to justify his entire budget in detail from scratch.

Questions

(1) Define Budget, Budgeting and Budgetary Control. Explain the important objectives of Budgetary Control.
(2) What are the advantages of Budgetary Control?
(3) Explain the limitations of and objectives of Budgetary Control.
(4) What is Sales Budget? How is it prepared?
(5) Distinguish between a Forecast and Budget.
(6) What is meant by Master Budget?
(7) What is meant by Flexible Budget and explain its advantages.
(8) Write the Classification of Budgets.
(9) What do you understand by Budgetary Control? What are the essentials for the success of the system of Budgetary Control?
(10) Explain briefly the following: (a) Master Budget (b) Labor Budget (c) Overheads Budget
(11) Differentiate between the Fixed Budgeting and Flexible Budgeting.
(12) Explain Performance Budgeting.
(13) What is Programming Budgeting? Explain its advantages.
(14) Write a short note on Budget Period.
(15) What is meant by Key Factor?
(16) What is Zero Based Budgeting?

PROBLEMS

(1) The Golden Company Ltd. manufactures two products A and B and gives you the following particulars. The Sales Department of the company has three departments in different areas of country.
The sales budget for the year ending 31st Dec., 2008 was:

	Units
Product A:	
Department 1	6,00,000
Department 2	11,25,000
Department 3	3,60,000
Product B:	
Department 1	80,000
Department 2	12,00,000
Department 3	40,000

Sales price are Rs. 3,000 and Rs. 4,000 in all departments respectively.
It is estimated that with rigorous sales promotion, the sale of B in department 1 will increase by Rs. 3,50,000. It is also expected by increasing production and arranging extensive advertisement, department 3 will be able to increase the sales of B to Rs. 1,00,000. It is recognized that the estimated sales by department 2 represents an unsatisfactory target. It is agreed to increase both estimates by 20%.
Prepare Sales Budget for the year.
[**Ans.:** A – Rs. 69,30,000 and B – Rs. 1,07,60,000]

(2) From the following information, prepare Production Budget of Arun Sales Corporation for the year ended June 30, 2008.

Product	*Sales (Units)*	*Estimated Stock (Units) July 1, 2007*	*Estimated Stock (Units) June 30, 2008*
A	1,50,000	14,000	15,000
B	1,00,000	5,000	4,500
C	70,000	8,000	8,000

[**Ans.:** A – 1,51,000; B – 99,500; C – 70,000 Units]

(3) From the following data, prepare a Production Budget for the ABC Co..Ltd:
Stocks for the budgeted period as on:

Product	*1st Jan*	*30th June*
A	8,000	10,000
B	9,000	8,000
C	12,000	14,000

Requirements to fulfill sales program :

A	60,000 units
B	50,000 units
C	80,000 units

Normal loss in production:

A	4%
B	2%
C	6%

[**Ans.:** A – 64,583 Units; B – 50,000 Units; C – 87,234 Units]

(4) Gamma Engineering Company Ltd. manufactures two products X and Y. An estimate of the number of units expected to be sold in the first seven months of 2008 is given below:

Months	*Product X*	*Product Y*
January	500	1,400
February	600	1,400
March	800	1,200
April	1,000	1,000
May	1,200	800
June	1,200	800
July	1,000	900

It is anticipated that:
1. There will be no work in progress at the end of any month; and
2. Finished units equal to half the anticipated sales for the next month will be in stock at the end of each month (including December, 2007)

The budgeted production costs for the year ending 31st December, 2008 are as follows:

	Product X	*Product Y*
Production (Units)	11,000	12,000
Direct Material per unit (Rs.)	12	19
Direct Wages per unit (Rs.)	5	7

Other manufacturing charges apportionable to each type of product X: Rs. 33,000 and Y Rs. 48,000
You are required to prepare:
(a) a Production Budget showing the number of units to be manufactured each month.
(b) a summarized Production Cost Budget for the 6-month period January to June, 2008.
Hint: Assume Manufacturing Expenses are variable.
[**Ans.:** X – Rs. 1,11,000; Y – Rs. 1,90,500]

(5) From the following figures prepare the Raw Materials Purchase Budget for January

Material (units)

	A	*B*	*C*	*D*	*E*	*F*
Estimated stock on January 1	16,000	6,000	24,000	2,000	14,000	28,000
Estimated stock on January 31	20,000	8,000	28,000	4,000	1,60,000	32,000
Estimated Consumption	1,20,000	44,000	1,32,000	36,000	88,000	1,72,000
Standard price per unit	25p	5p	15p	10p	20p	30p

[**Ans.:** Total Estimated Purchases Rs. 1,28,300]

(6) The sales director of a manufacturing company reports that next year he expects to sell 54,000 units of a certain product. The Production Manager consults the Store Keeper and caste his figures as follows:
Two kinds of Raw Materials A and B are required for manufacturing the product. Each unit of the product required 2 units of A and 3 units of B. The estimated opening balances at the commencement of the next year are:
Finished product – 10,000 units, A – 12,000 units, B – 15,000 units
The desirable closing balances at the end of the next year are:
Finished product – 14,000 units, A – 13,000 units, B – 16,000 units
Draw up a Quantitative Chart showing the Material Purchases Budget for the next year.
[**Ans.:** A – 1,17,000 units; B – 1,75,000 units]

(7) From the given particulars presented by P. Ltd., you are asked to prepare a Material Budget. Estimated sales 50,000 units (each unit of the production requires 2 units of Material X and 4 units of Material Y).

Estimated Opening Balance:
Finished Goods 10,000 units
Material-X 15,000 units
Material-Y 25,000 units

Material on order (opening):
Material-X 80,00 units
Material-Y 12,000units

Estimated Closing Balance:
Finished Goods 6,000 units
Material-X 16,000 units
Material-Y 30,000 units

Materials in order (closing):
Material -X 6,000 units
Material-Y 8,000 units
(*Hint:* the treatment of materials on order is same as that of stock of materials)
[**Ans.:** X – 91,000 units; Y – 1,85,000 units]

(8) Sangitha Food Products Limited has prepared the following sales budget for the first five months of 2009:

	Sales Budget (in units)
January	10,800
February	15,600
March	12,200
April	10,400
May	9,800

The inventory of finished product at the end of every month is equal to 25% of the sales estimate for the next month. On January 1, 2009, there were 27,000 units of product in hand. There is no work-in progress at the end of any month. Every unit of product requires two types of materials in the following quantities.
Material A 4 units
Material B 5 units
Material equal to 1\2 of the next months production are to be on hand at the end of every month. This requirement was met on 1st January 2009.
Prepare a Materials Budget for the first quarter of 2009 in a logical form showing the quantities of each of material to be purchased.
[**Ans.:** Material requirements for the first quarter of 200: Material A = 1,50,500 units;
Material B = 1,88,125 units)]

(9) From the information given below, prepare Manufacturing Overhead Budget for the quarter ending December 31, 2008.

Budget output during the quarter	5,000 units
Fixed Overheads	Rs. 30,000
Variable Overheads (varying at the rate of Rs. 5 per unit)	Rs. 15,000

Semi Variable Overheads @ Rs. 3 per unit (40% fixed and 60% varying)
[**Ans.:** Total Overheads Cost Rs. 76,000]

(10) Prepare Manufacturing Overheads Budget and ascertain the manufacturing overheads rates at 50% and 70% capacities. The following particulars are given at 60% capacity.

	Rs.
Variable Overheads:	
Indirect Material	6,000
Indirect Labor	18,000
Semi Variable Overheads:	
Electricity (40%fixed)	30,000
Repairs and Maintenance (20%variable)	3,000
Fixed Overhead:	
Depreciation	16,500
Insurance	4,500
Salaries 15000	
Total Overheads	93,000

Estimated Direct Labor Hours 1,86,000 hours
[**Ans.:** Total Overheads: 50% Rs. 85,900; 60% Rs. 93,000; 70% Rs. 1,00,100]

(11) You are required to prepare the Sales Overhead Budget from the forecast given below:

	Rs.
Advertisement	5,000
Salaries of Sales Department	10,000
Expenses of Sales Department	3,000
Counter Salesmen Salary Allowances	12,000

Commission at 10% on the sales and Traveling Expenses are at 5% on the sales. Sales have been budgeted as under:

Period	*Counter Sales* *Rs.*	*Traveling Salesmen's Sales* *Rs.*
A	1,60,000	20,000
B	2,40,000	30,000
C	2,80,000	40,000

[**Ans.:** Period A – Rs. 34,600; Period B – Rs. 36,900; Period C – Rs. 38,800]

(12) Following information is about a Ltd. Concern. You are required to prepare a Selling Overhead Budget.

	Rs.
Advertisement	2,000
Salaries of Sales Department	2,000
Expenses of Sales Department (Fixed)	950
Salesmen Remuneration:	
Salaries	6,000

Commission @1% on sales affected
Carriage Outwards: estimated @5% on sales
Agents Commission 6% on sales:
Sales during the period were estimated as follows:
Rs. 1,00,000 including Agents sales Rs. 10,000
Rs. 1,50,000 including Agents sales Rs. 20,000
Rs. 2,00,000 including Agents sales Rs. 20,000
[**Ans.:** Rs. 17,450; Rs. 20,950; Rs. 23,950]

(13) A firm expects to have Rs. 30,000 in the bank on 1st Jan 2008, and requires you to prepare an estimate of Cash Position during the three months May to July 2008. The following information is supplied to you.

Month	*Sales* *Rs.*	*Purchases* *Rs.*	*Wages* *Rs.*	*Factory Expenses* *Rs.*	*Office* *Rs.*	*Selling* *Rs.*
March	40,000	24,000	6,000	3,000	4,000	3,000
April	46,000	28,000	6,500	3,500	4,000	3,500
May	50,000	32,000	6,500	4,000	4,000	3,500
June	72,000	36,000	7,000	4,400	4,000	4,000
July	84,000	40,000	7,250	4,250	4,000	4,000

Other information:

(1) 25% of the sales is in cash and the remaining amount is collected in the month following that of sales.
(2) Suppliers supply goods at two months credit
(3) Delay in payment of wages and all other expenses - one month
(4) Income tax of Rs. 1,000 is due to be paid in May
[**Ans.:** Cash Balance: May Rs. 25,500; June Rs. 35,000; July Rs. 48,600]

(14) National Products Limited wants to approach for a temporary overdraft facility for the quarter beginning 1st October 2008. During the period of these 3 months, the company will be manufacturing mostly for stock. You are required to prepare Cash Budget for the above period from the following data indicating the overdraft facility required by the company at end of each month.

	Sales *Rs.*	*Purchases* *Rs.*	*Wages* *Rs.*
August	3,60,000	2,49,600	24,000
September	3,84,000	2,88,000	28,000
October	2,16,000	4,86,000	22,000
November	3,48,000	4,92,000	20,000
December	2,52,000	5,36,000	30,000

(a) 50 % of the credit sales are realized in the month following sales and the 50 % in the second month following.
(b) Creditors are paid in the month following the month of purchases
(c) Estimated Cash at Bank as on 1st October, 2008 Rs. 50,000.
[**Ans.:** Balance at the end of October Rs. 1,12,000; Overdraft at the end of November Rs. 94,000 and December Rs. 3,34,000]

(15) Johnson and Company produces an article, the estimated cost per unit are given below.

	Rs.
Material 60	
Labor	48
Expenses	12
Variable Overheads	18

Semi Variable Overheads at 100% activity level (10,000 units) are estimated to be Rs. 2,40,000 and these overheads vary in steps of Rs. 12,000 for each change in output of 1,000 units.
Fixed Overheads are estimated at Rs. 3,00,000. The selling price per unit is also estimated at Rs. 240.
Prepare a Flexible Budget at 50%, 70% and 90% levels of capacity.
[**Ans.:** Budgeted Profit: 50% Rs. 30,000; 70% Rs. 2,10,000; 90% Rs. 3,90,000]

(16) Excellent Engineering Works had prepared its budget for 2008, based on the production of one-lakh units of their only product as follows:

	(Rs. '000)
Raw Material	252
Direct Labor	75
Direct Expenses	10
Work Overheads (60% Fixed)	225
Administrative Overheads	40
Selling Overheads (50%Fixed)	20

For want of demand, the actual production for that period was only 60,000 units. Calculate the budgeted cost per unit under both the original plan under actual performance.
[**Ans.:** Total Cost: Original Plan: Rs. 6,22,000; Revised Plan Rs. 4,47,200]

❑❑❑

19

STANDARD COSTING

Objectives

The objectives of the study are to:

- Learn the need for the technique of Standard Costing
- Understand the basic concepts of Standard Cost and Standard Costing
- Know the types of Standards
- Differentiate Standard Costing from Budgetary Control

INTRODUCTION

In the earlier lessons, you have learnt about certain techniques of Costing like Variable / Marginal Costing, Absorption Costing and Differential Costing. In this lesson, you will learn another technique of Costing *viz.*, Standard Costing, which helps in setting up the standards for different elements of costs and controlling the costs.

NEED FOR STANDARD COSTING

In general, costs may be divided into two broad categories – Historical Costs and Pre-determined Costs. Historical costs are the actual costs that are ascertained after they are incurred. Pre-determined costs, on the other hand, are the future costs which are calculated in advance of production so that the inefficiency and waste may be detected at the source. Pre-determined costs that are ascertained on a scientific basis, result in Standard Costs.

In the initial stages of development of Cost Accounting, Historical Costing was the only system in use for cost ascertainment and presentation of costs. But, such a system has the following limitations.

- Historical Costing is not an effective method of exercising cost control because; it does not provide a yardstick with which actual performance may be compared. It only indicates the actual cost, which is of little value in measuring performance efficiency.
- Historical Costing is not preceded by planned costs, which are a must for effective cost control. Costs are already incurred before the cost figures can become available to management. Thus, inefficiencies and errors in production are not revealed until damage has occurred. Therefore, management will not be able to take necessary corrective action in good time. It is just a post-mortem of expenses incurred.
- Historical cost is valid only for one accounting period for which it has been ascertained and that too obtained too late, therefore, it is not of much use in price quotations and production planning.
- Historical Costing is comparatively an expensive system of costing as it involves the maintenance of a larger volume of records.

Due to the above limitations of Historical Costing, the need for Standard Costing was felt.

CONCEPTS

The main concepts in Standard Costing are Standard Cost and Standard Costing.

Standard Cost

A Standard Cost is a pre-determined cost. It is a determination in advance of production, of what the cost should be. A standard is a norm or a criterion. A standard figure is one which may be used as a yardstick for measuring the efficiency or otherwise of the actual performance.

The ICWA, London has defined it as "a pre-determined cost, which is computed in advance of production on the basis of specifications of all the factors affecting costs and used in standard costing".

In the words of Brown and Howard, "the standard cost is a pre-determined cost which determines what each product or service should cost under given circumstances".

Standard cost is a target cost which must be attained. The main objective of standard costs is to look forward and assess what the cost should be as different from what the cost has been in the past.

Standard Costing

It is the preparation of standard costs and applying them to measure the variations of actual costs from the standard costs and analyzing the causes of variations with a view to maintain maximum efficiency in production.

According to ICMA, London, standard costing is defined as "the preparation and the use of standard costs, their comparison with actual costs and analyzing of variances to their causes and points of incidence".

Standard costing system involves:

- The setting of standard costs for different elements of cost, i.e., material, labor and overheads
- Ascertainment of actual costs
- Comparison of actual costs with standard costs to find out the variances
- Analyzing the variances for ascertaining reasons thereof and
- Reporting the variances and analysis thereof, to the management, for appropriate action wherever necessary.

PRE-REQUISITES TO STANDARD COSTING

The following pre-requisites may be considered to be the steps/principles involved in its application and operation.

- Sound organisation structure with well defined authority relationships
- Methods, operations and processes capable of being standardized
- A sufficient volume of standardized products or components produced

- Determination of standard cost for each product, recording of actual costs incurred, comparison of standard and actual costs, analyzing variances and taking remedial action
- Determination of the type of standard to be used

TYPES OF STANDARDS

As the value of Standard Costing depends upon the standards set, the same should be realistic and capable of attainment rather than being based on mere aspirations. The standards may be classified into two main standards – Basic Standards and Current Standards.

Basic Standard

It is a standard established for use unaltered over a long period of time. It is fixed for long periods so as to help forward planning. They are established and operated without revision for a number of years and are not adjusted to current market conditions. Thus, these standards are of no practical utility from the point of view of cost control and may be suitable for those items of cost which are fixed in nature like rent, manager's salaries, etc.

Current Standards

Current Standards are related to current conditions and are established for use over a short period of time. They are of three types – ideal, expected and normal standards.

- **Ideal Standards:** These are theoretical standards, which can be attained under the most favorable conditions possible. They are based upon a very high degree of efficiency, which are rather impossible to achieve. They presupposes that the performance of men, materials and machines is perfect and thus make no allowance for loss of time, accidents, machine breakdowns, wastage of material and any other type of waste or loss.
  The utility of this standard is that, it sets a target, which though not attainable in practice, is always aimed at. The main limitation is that, they show adverse variances as a permanent feature, which discourages the employees and no serious attention is given to such variances.
- **Expected/Attainable Standards:** These standards are anticipated to be attained during a future period. They are based on expected performance after making a reasonable allowance for unavoidable losses and other inevitable lapses from perfect efficiency like machine breakdown, idle time, etc. Therefore, these standards are more realistic. Hence, they are best suited from control point of view because these standards reveal real variances from the attainable performance.
- **Normal Standard:** This standard is known as past performance standard because it is based on the average performance in the past. The aim is to eliminate the variations in the cost, which arise out of trade cycle. It is difficult to follow normal standards in practice, as it is not possible to forecast performance with a reasonable degree of accuracy for a long period of time. These are attainable under anticipated normal conditions only. Therefore, normal standards may not be a useful device for the purpose of cost control.

STANDARD COSTING AND BUDGETARY CONTROL

Both, Standard Costing and Budgetary Control are effective tools to management in controlling costs. Both the techniques are based on the same principles *viz.*, establishment of pre-determined targets, comparison of actual performance with the pre-determined targets and taking corrective measures wherever necessary. Though, both are effective means of exercising cost control, they differ in the following respects.

Standard Costing	*Budgetary Control*
Standard Costs are based on technical assessments, e.g., standard labor cost is determined on the basis of time and motion study.	Budgets are based on past figures adjusted to future needs.
Standard Costs are developed mainly for the manufacturing function. Standards are compiled for various elements of costs.	Budgets are compiled for different functions of the business, i.e., production, sales, purchases, etc.
Standards set up targets to be attained by actual performance. Standard Costing gives importance to costs approaching the standard costs.	Budgets set up maximum limits of expenditure above which, the actual expenditure should not normally exceed.
Standard Costs are projection of Cost Accounts as they aim at efficiency at every point.	Budgets are projection of Financial Accounts as they aim at overall efficiency.
Variances are usually revealed through accounts such as material price variance and material usage variances.	Variances are not revealed through the accounts but are revealed in total.
Standard Costs do not tell what the costs are expected to be but tell about what the costs should be.	Budgets are anticipated or expected costs meant to be used for forecasting cash.
Standard Costing is intensive in application as it calls for a detailed analysis of variances.	Budgetary Control is extensive in nature and the degree of analysis tends to be much less than in Standard Costing

Both, Standard Costing and Budgetary Control, are complimentary to each other and for maximum efficiency, both should be used simultaneously.

Advantages of Standard Costing

Standard Costing overcomes the weaknesses of Historical Costing system and it is a very important managerial tool for cost control. The chief advantages of Standard Costing are summarized as follows.

- **Effective Cost Control:** By setting the level of costs, the actual costs are compared with the yardsticks to ascertain efficiency or inefficiency of actual performance and taking remedial action on the basis of variances so revealed. Thus, it facilitates the control of costs.
- **Helps in Planning:** Establishing standards is a very useful exercise in planning and budgeting, which instills in the management, a habit of thinking in advance.
- **Provides incentives:** The standards provide incentives to the employees and motivate them to work with a greater effort. Schemes may be formulated to reward the employees who attain the standards. This increases efficiency and productivity.
- **Fixing prices and formulating policies:** Standard Costing provides a valuable guidance to the management in the formulation of price and production policies like preparing price lists, planning production of new products and furnishing cost estimates to higher levels.
- **Facilitates coordination:** While establishing standards, the performance of different departments is taken into account and thus, coordination of various functions is achieved.
- **Eliminates wastes:** By fixing standards, certain wastes such as idle time, material wastage, lost machine hours etc. are reduced. Standard Costing makes all the executives cost conscious which increases efficiency and productivity all round.
- **Valuation of stocks:** Standard Costing simplifies the valuation of stock, as the stock is valued at standard costs.
- **Management by exception:** It is only in the case of above or below standard performance that, management focuses their attention on the exceptional items.
- **Economical and simple:** Standard Costing results in a saving in the cost of costing system as the clerical work associated with costing is reduced and it results in reduction in paper work in accounts and needs lesser number of forms and records.

Disadvantages/Limitations of Standard Costing

The following are some of the limitations of Standard Costing.

- The technique of Standard Costing may not be applicable in small concerns, as the establishment of standards requires high degree of skill. For, e.g., standard time fixation involves a costly process of time and motion study.
- For fixing responsibilities, variances should be segregated into controllable and uncontrollable variances. But, the division is a difficult task. The executive may be made responsible for controllable variances only.
- Inaccurate and unreliable standards cause misleading results and thus, may not enjoy the confidence of the users of the system.
- The technique of standard costing may not be very effective in the case of individuals dealing with non-standard products and the jobs, which changes with the requirement of the customers.
- If the standards set are too high, its non-achievement results in frustration and build up resistance from the employees. If the standards set are too low, it will be easily achieved without putting any extra efforts.

Establishment of Standards

Various factors have to be taken into consideration while setting standards as the success of Standard Costing System depends on the reliability, accuracy and acceptance of standards. A Standard Committee, consisting of representatives from the various departments like production, purchase, personnel, sales etc. should be set up to assist the Cost Accountant in his task of setting standards. Standard should be established for each element of cost.

Direct Material: Here, standards are determined for quantity of material required for the production and the standard price per unit of material.

- **Material Quantity Standard:** While setting quantity standard, quality and size of the material item should be standardized. Based on the standard specification of material planned by the engineering department, the standard quantity of the material is determined. The allowances should be made for the normal wastage such as cutting in cloth or metals etc. The main aim of material quantity standard is to achieve mass economies in material usage.
- **Material Price Standard:** The cost accountant in collaboration with the purchase officer sets the standard price for each item of material. The main objective of material price standard fixation is to increase efficiency in the purchasing so that the price of the material may be kept low. While setting the material price standard, the factors

to be considered are purchase price of recent orders, prices specified in the long-term contracts, forecast of the commodity price trends, provision for the discount, packing and delivering charges, etc.

Direct Labor: The standard for the direct labor cost, are, the standard time and standard price.

- **Labor Time/Efficiency Standard:** Time and motion study carried out in conjunction with a study to determine the most efficient method of working will determine the standard time. Due allowances should be made for fatigue, receiving instructions, idle time, tool setting, etc.
- **Labor Rate:** Standard rates of pay should be established for every category of labor. Establishment of standard rates does not pose any problem in those industries where wage rates are fixed by contract laws, wage tribunals and wage boards. Fixation of standard rates are done having regard to the current rate of pay and any anticipated variations.

Where workers are paid on time basis, it is necessary to establish the labor rate standard for each operation, the wage rate of each grade of labor and the grades of labor to be employed, i.e., male or female, skilled, unskilled or semi skilled, etc.

Where workers are paid on piece basis, a standard rate will be fixed per piece.

Overheads: Overheads are segregated into fixed and variable overheads and standard overhead rate should be determined for both, according to the function wise classification of overheads – manufacturing, administrative, selling and distribution so that the exact place of overhead variances may be located and corrective action may be taken.

Here, developing standard for overheads involve determination of the standard overhead costs and estimation of production, i.e., standard level of activity reduced to a common base such as direct labor hours, units of production, machine hours, etc.

$$\text{Standard Overheads Rate} = \frac{\text{Standard Overhead Cost for the period}}{\text{Standard Production in units/hours}}$$

STANDARD HOUR

Production is generally expressed in physical units such as kilos, tones, litres, dozens, gallons, numbers, etc. When different types of products are manufactured in a concern, it is difficult to express all the products in one common unit. Therefore, production is expressed in standard hours, as the factor is common to all operations. A standard hour is an hour, which measures an amount of work that should be performed in one hour under standard conditions. In the words of ICMA, London, a standard hour is "a hypothetical hour which represents the amount of work which should be performed in one hour under standard conditions".

STANDARD COST CARD

It is a record of standard material, labor and overhead costs maintained for each product or service showing the quantity and the price of each material item to be consumed, the time and the rate of labor required, the overheads to be absorbed and the total cost for the product. It is also known as Standard Cost Sheet.

Specimen of Standard Cost Card

Product: *Date of setting standard:*

Unit: *Date of Revision:*

Elements of Cost	*Quantity/Hour*	*Rate* *Rs.*	*Standard Cost or Sales* *Rs.*
(1) Direct Material:			
Material A	10 units	2	20
Material B	20 units	3	60
	30 units		80
Less: Normal Loss (10%)	3 units		6
Normal Output	27 units		74
(2) Direct Labor	25 hours	2	50
(3) Overheads:			
Variable	10 hours	1	10
Fixed	10 hours	0.50	5
Total Cost			139.00
Profit (10%)			13.90
Selling Price			152.90

VARIANCE ANALYSIS

Cost Variance is the difference between the standard costs and the comparable actual cost incurred during a given period. Analysis of variances helps in controlling the performance in achieving the profit planned.

Variance analysis is the process of analyzing the variances by sub dividing the total variance in such away that the management can assign responsibility for any off standard performance.

When the actual cost is lower than the standard cost, it is a favorable variance and when actual cost is higher that the standard cost, the variance in unfavorable or known as adverse variance. Any variance that has a favorable effect on profit is a favorable variance and variance that has an adverse or unfavorable effect on the profit is termed as an adverse variance. A favorable variance is the reflection of efficiency and an unfavorable variance indicates inefficiency, provided, standard costs have been correctly set.

A variance can be considered as a controllable variance if it can be regarded as the responsibility of a particular person with the result that his degree of efficiency can be reflected in its size. Example, excess usage of material is usually the responsibility of the foreman concerned. If the excessive usage is due to the defective material, then, the responsibility may rest with the inspection department for the non-detection of the defects. If the variance is due to certain factors beyond the control of the management, then, the variance is known as uncontrollable variance. Example, a change in the market price of material, increase in the labor rates, etc.

The management should emphasize more on controllable variances, as they require investigation and a possible corrective action.

Analysis of variance enables the management to follow the technique of 'management by exception' where they exercise control only in case of unfavorable variance, as they cannot devote their limited time to every item.

REVISION OF STANDARDS

Standard Cost may be set for any specified period but normally, an annual period may be considered as reasonable. A large number of factors, both internal and external, influence the determination of standard cost and any change in these factors may result in revision of the standards set.

Standards may be revised when:

- Price level change
- Errors in setting standards are located
- Methods of production undergo change
- Designs or specifications of products change
- Technological advances take place
- Wage rates change substantially
- Variations of actual performance from standard is very large
- Capacity of plant changes

SUMMARY

Standard Costing is a technique, which helps in setting up the costs for different elements of costs and controlling the costs. The limitations of Historical Costing have given rise to the emergence of Standard Costing. The system of Standard Costing involves setting up of standards for each element of costs; measuring the actual costs and comparing them with standard costs to ascertain the variances; analyzing the variances for ascertaining the reasons thereof and reporting the variances to the management for appropriate actions wherever necessary.

The standards may be classified mainly into Basic Standards and Current Standards. Again, Current Standards consist of Ideal Standards, Expected Standards and Normal Standards. Though, both Standard Costing and Budgetary Control are effective tools to management in controlling costs, they differ on various counts. Standards should be established for each element of cost and a Standard Cost Sheet should be prepared.

Analysis of variances, enable the management to follow the technique of 'management by exception'. The success of Standard Costing system depends on the reliability, accuracy and acceptance of the standards.

Glossary

- **Historical Costs:** are the actual costs that are ascertained after they are incurred
- **Pre-determined Costs:** are the future costs which are calculated in advance of production
- **Standard:** is a norm or a criterion used as a yardstick for measuring the efficiency or otherwise of the actual performance.
- **Standard Cost:** is a cost determined in advance of production of what the cost should be

- **Standard Costing:** is the preparation of standard costs and applying them to measure the variations from the standard costs and analyzing the causes of variations with a view to maintain maximum efficiency in production.
- **Basic Standard:** is established for use unaltered over a long period of time
- **Current Standards:** are related to current conditions and are established for use over a short period of time
- **Ideal Standards:** are theoretical standards, which can be attained under the most favorable conditions possible
- **Expected Standard:** is anticipated to be attained during a future period
- **Normal Standard:** is based on the average performance in the past
- **Standard Hour:** is an hour which measures an amount of work that should be performed in one hour under standard conditions
- **Standard Cost Card:** is a record of standard material, labor and overhead costs maintained for each product or service showing the quantity and the price of each item of cost. It is also known as Standard Cost Sheet
- **Variance Analysis:** is the process of analyzing the variances by sub dividing the total variance in such a way that the management can assign responsibility for any off standard performance.

Questions

(1) Define Standard Costing. In what type of industry is Standard Costing employed?

(2) How does Standard Costing differ from Historical Costing? Discuss the advantages and disadvantages of Standard Costing.

(3) Distinguish Budgetary Control from Standard Costing.

(4) Describe briefly the procedure of establishing Standard Costing within the division of material, labor and overhead costs.

(5) Explain the concepts – Standard Hour, Standard Cost Card and Variance Analysis.

(6) Explain the different types of Standards in detail.

(7) Explain in detail the circumstances that necessitate the revision of Standards.

❑ ❑ ❑

20

UNIFORM COSTING

Objectives

The objectives of the study are to:

- Understand the concepts of Uniform Costing and Inter-Firm Comparison
- Identify the areas where uniformity can be achieved
- Assess the importance of Uniform Costing and Inter Firm Comparison

INTRODUCTION

Industrial sector comprises of a large number of industries engaged in the production and sale of a variety of goods and services. Within an industry, there are a large number of firms engaged in the production of a single product, e.g., sugar industry consists of a large number of firms producing sugar. There may be differences due to ownership, capital employed but they possess one common feature, i.e., production of sugar. Therefore, the nature of activities conducted will also be similar. When similarity rules, each firm would be curious to compare its achievements and costs with the other firms. This inter firm comparison can only be possible when there is Uniform Costing System.

Different firms adopt different Methods and Techniques of Costing and as a result of which, the profits of the firms differ to the extent of the effect of these various procedures on profits. In order to make a useful and meaningful comparison of the performance of the firms, Uniform Methods and Procedures are to be adopted necessitating the need for Uniform Costing.

MEANING

Uniform Costing refers to a system of costing under which several undertakings use the same costing principles or practices. The basic idea behind the uniform costing is that the different concerns in an industry should adopt a common method of costing and apply uniformly the same principles and techniques for better cost comparison and common good. It is neither a separate method of Cost Accounting like Specific Order Costing or Operation Costing nor a separate technique of costing like Marginal Costing or Standard Costing, but, is only a particular system of costing which takes the help of both the methods and techniques of costing.

Uniform Costing seeks to introduce certain common principles and practices which help to provide a common denominator in the collection, presentation and interpretation of the costing data in different enterprises.

ICMA defines Uniform Costing as "the use by several undertakings of the same costing principles and/or practices". According to the Chambers of Commerce of the United States "Uniform Cost Accounting comprises a set of principles and in some cases, of accounting methods which when incorporated in the accounting systems of the individual members of the industry will result in obtaining of cost figures by the individual members of the industry which will be on a comparable basis. Uniform Cost Accounting does not mean the preparation of average or standard cost figures for the industry nor the inclusion in costs of predetermined or fixed elements of cost."

In general, Uniform Costing may be considered as a technique as it is used mainly for maintaining uniform procedures in the organization which would like to compare their costs and reduce the costs.

APPLICABILITY OF UNIFORM COSTING

This system can be usefully employed in

(1) A single enterprise having a number of branches, each having separate manufacturing unit.
(2) A number of concerns, each belonging to the same industry and affiliated to the same trade association, cartel, pool, etc.
(3) Industries which are similar, e.g., textiles – Cotton, Jute and Woolen; Mining Iron, Mica, Manganese; Gas and Electricity, etc.

SCOPE OF UNIFORM COSTING

Uniform costing may be applied advantageously in an organization having a number of branches each of which may be a separate manufacturing unit or in a number of units in the same industry bound together through a trade association or otherwise; industries which are similar and having common operations and procedures, e.g., Jute and Woolen textiles, Cotton, Gas, Electricity and Transport.

Uniform Costing is used in case of the following:

- Firms belonging to the same industry having similarity in size, method and technology, type, organisational structure and age of equipment used.
- Individual departments or functions which are similar in different industries (or) sectors of the Economy.
- Uniform costing is done in all the organisations with the objectives like comparison of costs, reduction in costs and improvement in performance, fixing uniform prices, cutting or eliminating unfair trade practices etc.
- In some organisations, the Head Office controls the operation of Uniform Costing but in other organisations, the different units of the same industry may be bound together by a trade association for the purpose of Uniform Costing.

NEED FOR UNIFORM COSTING

The need for Uniform Costing arises because of the fact that different units use different costing procedures due to:

- **Size of the Business:** the size of the business differs because of division of work, responsibility and level of expenditure incurred being different in small and large concerns. In small concerns, a single proprietor manages the whole affairs while departmentation in large scale concerns is applied.
- **Nature of Business:** the nature of business differs because of the different techniques employed i.e. capital intensive techniques vs. labor intensive techniques.
- **Product Differentiation:** Difference may arise in the quality of finished product, raw material, change in the material mix. These factors also lead to different costing methods.

Therefore, the above factors have to be leveled out to adopt Uniform Costing System.

Objectives of Uniform Costing

The objectives of Uniform Costing are as follows:

(1) Fixation of Common Price

It avoids cut-throat competition among the member units as common price is fixed which is acceptable to all and this helps in bringing stability of the processes of products manufactured.

(2) Improving Performance

It will help in improving the performance of inefficient units by standardizing several common practices.

(3) Inter-Unit Comparison of Cost of Production

It enables the member units to use this system as yardstick of their achievements and performances by comparing costs and profitability of such units.

(4) Control of Costs

It helps to control the cost by eliminating the unprofitable ventures and inefficiencies. It also helps in reduction in costs and improvement in the quality of the products through member units.

(5) Measure Efficiency

It measures the efficiency of all the units in the industry by establishing common standards. It also determines the common policy for the participating units.

(6) Controls Production

It controls the production by maintaining and stabilizing demand for the product in the market. It also improves the production capacity level and labor efficiency by comparing production cost of different units with each other.

(7) Create Confidence in the Public

It helps in achieving a common selling price for all the participating units which instills confidence in the public that selling prices are established by producers who have full knowledge of the cost of products offered for sale.

Areas of Uniform Costing

In the development of Uniform Costing System, uniformity is required regarding the following points:

- Method of Costing to be adopted, i.e., whether Job Costing or Process Costing or a variation of either of them to be used
- Determination of Cost Units and Cost Centres
- Definitions of different Elements of Cost
- Basis of segregation of costs into fixed, variable and semi variable categories
- Basis of allocation and apportionment of costs to production and service departments and of service departments to production departments
- Basis of recovery of production overheads
- Method of accounting for administration, selling and distribution overheads
- Treatment of purchases, material handling and upkeep expenses
- System of material control, pricing of issues, valuation of stock
- Methods of remunerating labor
- Methods of accounting for overtime pay, bonus and other miscellaneous allowances paid to labor
- Treatment of research and developments costs
- Rates of depreciation to be used in case of fixed assets
- Method of presenting cost information to the management.
- Method of recording accounting information (whether non-integral or integral system to be used)

Driving forces for applicability of Uniform Costing

The following are the driving forces for the wide application of Uniform Costing.

Rationalization and Scientific Management

Rationalization provides uniformity in the production system and the Scientific Management helps in determining the suitable wage system, providing incentive to produce more and thereby earn more remuneration. Rationalization and Scientific Management which aim at cost reduction and improved production made Uniform Costing to be highly desirable

Growth of Combinations, Syndicate and Other Forms of Association

The Combinations and Syndicates find Uniform Costing highly useful for the purpose of uniformity in the procedures followed for obtaining cost details.

Industries under State Ownership

When several industries of similar nature are run and controlled by the state such as Iron and Steel Industry in India, each unit prefers to adopt the Uniform Costing to compare the reports and information of each unit from time to time.

Statutory Requirements

Due to mushroom growth of industrial units, there was a need to regulate and control industries enacts by legislation to provide basis for cost-determination, sale-price and cost audit. In this situation, the units of the Industry prefer to choose Uniform Costing.

PRE-REQUISITES FOR INSTALLATION OF UNIFORM COSTING SYSTEM

The installation of Uniform Costing requires certain conditions to be fulfilled. They are:

(1) Mutual Relationship among Participating Members

The member units participating in the Uniform Costing plan should have mutual trust, co-operation and confidence. Every participating member should be willing to supply the required information to a central body appointed by themselves.

(2) Spirit of Sharing Experience

The bigger units should be prepared to share their experiences and knowledge with the smaller concerns so that the latter may be able to improve their performances.

(3) Free Exchange of Ideas

The participating members should be free to exchange their ideas and they should not hide information from each other.

(4) Absence of Rivalry

There should not be any rivalry and competition among the participating members.

(5) Leveling the Key Factors

Certain key factors such as methods of production, size of the organization, methods and principles of cost accounting peculiar to individual units should be carefully noted. These key factors affect the cost of different undertakings in the same industry which will make cost comparison difficult. These varying factors should be leveled out by giving a weightage on an equitable basis.

(6) Cost Manual

A Cost Manual which contains the recommended Cost Accounting Plan should be prepared and circulated amongst the members.

(7) Adequate Information for Categorization

Adequate qualitative and quantitative information should be available for categorizing long term and short term differences in order to make comparison useful.

(8) Central Organization

There should be a Central Organization for the collection, co-ordination and the presentation of information.

(9) Proper Explanation of the Scheme

The scheme must be properly explained to all the concerned units and they should be convinced about its utility and they all should work for its success.

UNIFORM COSTING MANUAL

Uniform Costing Manual is a formal document which lays down the recommended cost principles, plans and procedures to be adopted by the participating members. It serves as a formal evidence of the adoption of Uniform Costing System and act as a guide to the participating members. The successful implementation and effective management of Uniform Costing System presupposes the existence of a Uniform Cost Manual.

A typical Costing Manual may contain the following:

(1) Introduction

The introduction part of the manual may include the statement of objectives and the purpose of the system, scope of the system and advantages to be derived, which helps educating the management to appreciate the system and the extent of co-operation necessary.

(2) Organisation

It should also provide the steps necessary for developing and operating the system and the state in which the system is to be introduced.

(3) Accounting System and Plans

These include general principles of accounting to be adopted, nature of coding system, terminology to be used and classification and description of accounts.

(4) Presentation of Information

It must contain detailed instructions regarding the presentation of data. The presentation of contents of the manual may take the form of descriptive method, step by step method (or) the hand book method. The adoption of a particular method depends upon factors such as nature and size of the participating units, extent of uniformity desired etc.

(5) Comprehensive Reference Book

It should serve as a comprehensive reference book on "accounting procedures" useful to the executives and accountants in solving problems of installation of the recommended uniform methods.

Thus, for the successful implementation and effective management, a well written uniform costing manual is an essential prerequisite.

ADVANTAGES OF UNIFORM COSTING

(1) Management Control

It is a useful tool for management control. Standard norms of operation and performance are set for the industry as a whole. The member units can measure their own performances with norms so set for the industry and improve their own working.

(2) Healthy Competition

Cut-throat competition is avoided in the line of trade, and business is carried on healthy lines.

(3) Improvement in Efficiency

Every weaker participating member increases the efficiency by following the standard and efficient methods of production.

(4) Benefits to Weaker Units

Research and Development is carried out by big concerns and the smaller participating members of the industry draws the benefit of research and development carried out under this system, which will lead to economy as a whole in the industry.

(5) Cost Consciousness

It creates cost consciousness among the member units and provides them the best system of cost control and cost presentation in the entire industry.

(6) Availability of Data

It furnishes reliable data which helps the Government in fixing wages easily through Minimum Wages Act (or) Wage Boards. It also helps the Government to fix the selling price and thus have effective price control.

(7) Fixation of Selling Price

The prices fixed with the help of Uniform Costing will be more reliable and representative of the whole industry.

(8) Economy

It leads to economy as individual units need not indulge in expensive experimentation to achieve efficiency. The bigger units assist the smaller units by providing requisite information relating to Cost Accounting Methods.

(9) Comparative Assessment

Uniform Costing facilitates a comparative assessment of the performance of the public and private sector in the same industry.

(10) Helps in Cost Audit and Inter Firm Comparison

Cost audit is facilitated with the help of Uniform Costing System. The system facilitates the comparison of results of one firm with those of the other forms. Thus, Uniform Costing is a must for Inter-Firm Comparison.

(11) Benefits the Trade Association and Industry

Uniform Costing enables the trade associations and the industry to place relevant cost data before the Government and trade unions for negotiations in respect of matters such as tariffs, subsidies, price fixation, wage revisions etc.

LIMITATIONS OF UNIFORM COSTING

The following are the limitations of Uniform Costing System.

(1) Individual Units Differ

It is difficult to apply the Uniform Costing as the individual units differ in respect of key factors such as methods of production, size of the organization, methods of accounting, location, age and condition of plant, nature of labor force, capital investment and degree of mechanization.

(2) Monopolistic Conditions

Uniform Costing may promote monopolistic tendencies in the industry which may turn out to be detrimental to the interest of customers.

(3) High Cost

The smaller units cannot afford to set up Uniform Costing as the cost of installation is very high.

(4) Lack of Trust and Confidence

The system may not prove to be a success as the member units do not have trust and confidence in the other units and do not provide full information relating to technical procedures and cost information.

Further, the utility of Uniform Costing may be reduced because of non-cooperation of the participating members.

Inter-Firm Comparison

Inter-Firm Comparison (IFC) is the technique which studies the performances, efficiencies, costs and profits of various concerns in an industry, with the help of exchange of information in order to have a relative comparison. The Uniform Cost System is the very basis on which Inter-Firm Comparison is made.

IFC involves the process by bringing together the members of identical firms and collecting their business figures and statistics through a neutral organization in which the participating firms repose their full confidence.

The figures under comparison may relate to

(1) The financial results *viz.*, the position assets, liabilities, profit, capital employed, etc.
(2) Cost structure of the products *viz.*, material cost, labor cost, overhead, etc.
(3) Physical and operational performance such as output or operation per man hour, expressed in terms of productivity ratios and percentages.

The main **objectives** of Inter Firm Comparison are:

(1) To know one's weak points in comparison with other firms and to improve the efficiency in future.
(2) To locate the spots of dis-economies so that action may be taken to effect economy by eliminating such sources of in-economies
(3) To know whether the profits of the firm are adequate and further to improve profitability position by comparing its profits with the member firms.

Procedure for Inter Firm Comparison

The following procedure is adopted for Inter Firm Comparison.

- Data are collected from various participating organizations by central agency like Trade Association or Chambers of Commerce.
- The data are analysed and presented in such a manner that data furnished by an individual company are kept secret.
- The management of various participating organizations are provided with information which will enable them to determine the efficiency by comparing the performance of other companies within the industry.
- Weaknesses are highlighted and an attempt is made to show as to why the efficiency of an organization is less than that of the other organizations.
- Financial and cost ratios are used.

An Inter Firm Comparison is not possible unless the 'like' is compared with the 'like'. Thus, a Uniform Costing System is a pre-requisite to an Inter Firm Comparison. Therefore, it is essential that those firms only should compare their performance with the other firms which are employing Uniform Costing System. In fact, Inter Firm Comparison is a natural outcome of Uniform Costing System.

Advantages of Inter-Firm Comparison

Inter-Firm Comparison offers the following benefits to the member firms.

(1) It spots the inefficiencies in the organization and thus brings stability in the cost structure and presentation of information.
(2) It creates cost consciousness among the participating firms.
(3) It helps the member firms to reduce their costs by comparing their costs with the other firms in case their costs are more.
(4) It improves productivity of labor, usage of materials and utilization of capacity.
(5) It helps Government, Regulatory Agencies and Researchers in obtaining useful information to conduct in-depth studies and to formulate suitable policies for regulation and control of industry and business.
(6) Secrecy is maintained as the firms are known by the code numbers and the figures are shown in ratios.
(7) A continuous review of the operations and policies of the business as a whole is made by the management.
(8) IFC improves the efficiency of participating firms as it reveals the relative strengths and weaknesses of each participating firm in relation to the other in the industry.
(9) It facilitates Government to take suitable decisions to control and regulate the industry and business in respect of price fixation, granting of subsidies and loans protection, tariffs, etc.
(10) Expertise and experience of the Central Organization are made available to the member units.
(11) It is also useful in evaluating business results and return on capital invested which in turn, helps in project appraisal and evaluation, conducting feasibility studies, capital budgeting, investment decisions, etc.
(12) It checks the unhealthy competition.

LIMITATIONS OF INTER-FIRM COMPARISON

Inter-Firm Comparison suffers from the following limitations.

(1) The main limitation of IFC springs from the differences in the nature of the participating units. This makes comparability difficult.

(2) In the absence of Central Organization, this scheme cannot be operated to its best advantage.

(3) Most of the members do not disclose the relevant data as they think the information is confidential and should not be revealed to the other member firms.

(4) Unreliable information is supplied for comparison in the absence of a proper Cost Accounting System in a firm.

(5) Time factor is totally ignored and no attention is given to the level of technology and technological developments.

Inspite of the above limitations, the advantages outweigh the limitations and IFC proves to be a very useful technique to be adopted.

SUMMARY

Uniform Costing refers to a system of costing under which several undertakings use the same costing principles or practices. The basic idea behind the uniform costing is that the different concerns in an industry should adopt a common method of costing and apply uniformly the same principles and techniques for better cost comparison and common good.

Uniform Costing can be usefully employed in a single enterprise having a number of branches, each having a separate manufacturing unit; in a number of concerns, each belonging to the same industry and affiliated to the same trade association, cartel, pool etc. and in industries which are similar, e.g., textiles – Cotton, Jute and Woolen; Mining Iron Mica, Manganese; Gas and Electricity, etc.

The objectives of Uniform Costing are Fixation of Common Price, Improving Performance, Inter-Unit Comparison of Cost of Production, Control of Costs, Measure Efficiency, Control Production and create confidence in the Public.

The various driving forces for the wide application of Uniform Costing are Rationalization and Scientific Management; Growth of Combinations, Syndicate and Other Forms of Association; Industries under State Ownership and Statutory Requirements.

The installation of Uniform Costing requires certain conditions to be fulfilled like Mutual Relationship among Participating Members; Spirit of Sharing Experience; Free Exchange of Ideas; Absence of Rivalry; Leveling the Key Factors; Cost Manual; Adequate Information for Categorization; Central Organization and Proper Explanation of the Scheme.

Uniform Cost Manual is a formal document which lays down the recommended cost principles, plans and procedures to be adopted by the participating members. It serves as a formal evidence of the adoption of Uniform Costing System and act as a guide to the participating members.

Inter-Firm Comparison (IFC) is the technique which studies the performances, efficiencies, costs and profits of various concerns in an industry, with the help of exchange of information in order to have a relative comparison. The Uniform Cost System is the very basis on which Inter-Firm Comparison is made.

IFC involves the process by bringing together a member of identical firms and collecting their business figures and statistics through a neutral organization in which the participating firms repose their full confidence.

IFC, though it suffers from certain limitations, the advantages outweigh the limitations and IFC proves to be a very useful technique to be adopted.

Glossary

- **Uniform Costing:** refers to a system of costing under which several undertakings use the same costing principles or practices.
- **Uniform Cost Manual:** is a formal document which lays down the recommended cost principles, plans and procedures to be adopted by the participating members. It serves as a formal evidence of the adoption of Uniform Costing System and act as a guide to the participating members.
- **Inter-Firm Comparison:** is the technique which studies the performances, efficiencies, costs and profits of various concerns in an industry, with the help of exchange of information in order to have a relative comparison.

Questions

(1) What do you understand by Uniform Costing and explain its importance.

(2) What are the objectives of Uniform Costing?

(3) Explain the pre-requisites for installation of Uniform Costing.

(4) What do you understand by IFC Scheme? Bring out its merits.

❑ ❑ ❑

PART – V

VARIANCE ANALYSIS

21

MATERIAL VARIANCES

Objectives

The objectives of the study are to:

- analyse the causes for Material Variances
- identify the persons responsible for the variances
- learn the computation and analysis of Material Variances

INTRODUCTION

In the earlier lesson, you have learnt about setting of standards for each element of cost and the concept of analysis of variance. The total Cost Variance is divided into Direct Material Cost Variance, Direct Labor Cost Variance and Overhead Variance. In this lesson, you will learn the computation of Material Variances. Analysis of Material Variances enables one to ascertain the causes for the Material Variances, identify the persons responsible for variances and help to take remedial measures.

MATERIAL VARIANCES

In case of Material, the various variances to be calculated are:

- Material Cost Variance
- Material Price Variance
- Material Usage Variance
- Material Mix Variance
- Material Yield Variance

The following chart shows the division and sub division of Material Variances.

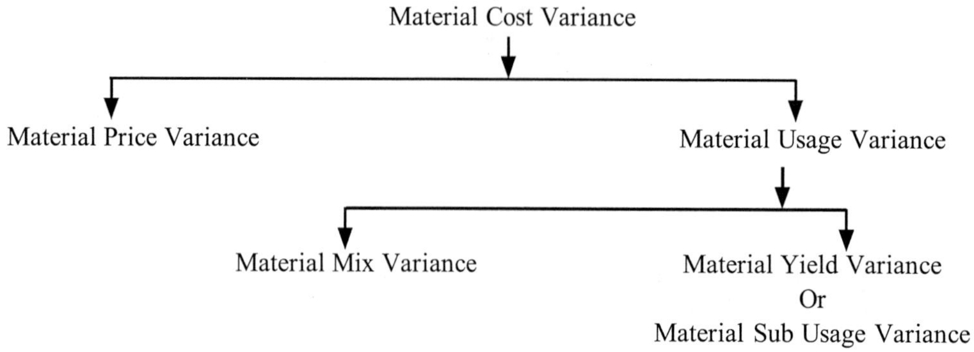

MATERIAL COST VARIANCE

It is the difference between the Actual Cost of materials used and the Standard Cost of material allowed for the actual output achieved. It is computed as:

Material Cost Variance = Standard Cost of material for Actual Output – Actual Cost of material used

Standard Cost of Material = Standard Quantity for Actual Output × Standard Price

Actual Cost of Material = Actual Quantity used × Actual Price

Therefore, Material Cost Variance = (Standard Quantity for Actual Output × Standard Price) – (Actual Quantity × Actual Price)

Here, it is necessary to calculate the standard quantity of material allowed for actual output.

Standard Quantity of Material allowed for actual output is:

Actual Output × Standard Quantity of Material per unit of Standard Output

or

= (Standard Quantity × Actual Output)/Standard Output

Material Cost Variance is a favorable variance if actual cost is less than the standard cost of material allowed, as it will have a favorable impact on profit and vice versa.

MATERIAL PRICE VARIANCE

It is that portion of Material Cost Variance, which is due to the difference between the standard price of material specified and the actual price for the material used.

Material Price Variance = (Standard Price – Actual price) Actual Quantity of Material used

Material Price Variance is a favorable variance if actual price is less than the standard price as it has the effect of reducing the cost and thereby increasing the profit and vice versa.

Analysis of Material Price Variance will help in locating the cause and the person responsible for a particular cause.

Possible Cause	Person Responsible
● Change in material price	Uncontrollable
● Change in quality or specification of material purchased on account of non availability of standard quality	Uncontrollable
● Change in the amount of taxes and duties	Uncontrollable
● Inefficient buying	Purchase Officer
● Rush order to meet shortage of supply	Purchase Officer/ Store Keeper
● Emergency purchases on the request of the Production/Department	Production Manager/ Sales Manager
● Failure to take advantage of off season price	Finance Manager
● Loss of discount	Accounts Officer

MATERIAL USAGE/QUANTITY VARIANCE

It is that portion of Material Cost Variance, which is due to the difference between the standard quantity specified and the actual quantity used.

Material Usage Variance = (Standard Quantity for Actual Output – Actual Quantity) Standard Price

Material Usage Variance is a favorable variance if actual consumption is less than the standard consumption for the same level of output.

Analysis of Material Usage Variance will help in locating the cause and the person responsible for a particular cause.

Possible Cause	Person Responsible
● Excessive wastage of material	Foreman
● Theft/Pilferage of material	Foreman/Storekeeper
● Poor inspection of raw material	Store keeper/ Receiving Department
● Careless handling	Store keeper/ Receiving Department
● More wastage due to poor quality of material	Purchase Officer
● Wrong specification	Planning Engineer
● More wastage due to wrong mixture of material	Production Department
● Incorrect setting of standard usage	Cost Accountant
● Improper maintenance of machines leading to Breakdowns and more use of material	Plant Engineer

Verification: Material Cost Variance = Material Price Variance + Material Usage Variance

Illustration 1

For producing a commodity, the standard quantity of material required was fixed at 10 Kg. and standard price was fixed at Rs. 2 per kg. The actual quantity consumed was 12 kgs. and the actual price paid was Rs. 1.90 per kg. Calculate Material Price Variance, Material Quantity Variance and Material Cost Variance.

Solution

Material Price Variance = (SP – AP) AQ

$(2 - 1.90)\ 12 =$ Rs. 1.20 (f)

Material Quantity Variance = (SQ – AQ) SP

$(10 - 12)\ 2 =$ Rs. 4 (a)

Material Cost Variance = $(SQ \times SP) - (AQ \times AP)$

$(10 \times 2) - (12 \times 1.90) =$ Rs. 2.80 (a)

Verification: Material Cost Variance = Material Price Variance + Material Usage Variance

2.80 (a) = 1.20 (f) + 4 (a)

Illustration 2

A manufacturing concern, which has adopted standard costing, furnishes the following information.

Standard: Materials for 70 kg. finished products = 100 kg.

Price of materials Re. 1 per kg.

Actual :	Output	2,10,000 kgs.
	Materials used	2,80,000 kgs.
	Cost of materials	Rs. 2,52,000

Calculate: *(a)* Material Price Variance

(b) Material Quantity Variance

(c) Material Cost Variance

Solution

As output is given, first calculate the standard quantity required for the actual output.

Standard Quantity for Actual Output: (Standard Quantity × Actual Output) / Standard Output

(100 × 2,10,000)/70 = 3,00,000 units

Actual Price = Actual Cost/Actual Quantity

2,52,000/2,80,000 = Re. 0.90

(a) Material Price Variance = (SP – AP) AQ

(1 – 0.90) 2,80,000 = Rs. 28,000 (f)

(b) Material Usage Variance = (SQ for actual output – AQ) SP

(3,00,000 – 2,80,000) 1 = Rs. 20,000 (f)

(c) Material Cost Variance = (SQ for actual output x SP) – (AQ × AP)

(3,00,000 × 1) – (2,80,000 × 0.90) = Rs. 48,000 (f)

Verification: Material Cost Variance = Material Price Variance + Material Usage Variance

48,000 (f) = 28,000 (f) + 20,000 (f)

Illustration 3

From the following particulars find the

(a) Material Price Variance

(b) Material Quantity Variance

(c) Material Cost Variance

Quantity of material purchased	3,000 units
Value of material purchased	Rs. 9,000

Standard quantity of materials required per ton of finished product is 25 units

Standard rate of material	Rs. 2 per unit
Opening stock of material	nil
Closing stock of material	500 units
Finished production during the period	80 tons

Solution

Actual Price = 9,000 / 3,000 = Rs. 3 per unit

Actual Quantity = Opening Stock + Purchases + Closing Stock

NIL + 3,000 – 500 = 2,500 units

As output is given, first calculate the standard quantity required for the actual output.

Standard Quantity for actual output:

(Actual Output × Standard Quantity per unit of output) / Standard Output

(80 × 25) / 1 = 2,000 units

Material Price Variance = (SP – AP) AQ

(2 – 3) 2,500 = Rs. 2,500 (a)

Material Quantity Variance = (SQ for actual output – AQ) SP

(2,000 – 2,500) 2 = Rs. 1,000 (a)

Material Cost Variance = (SQ for actual output × SP) – (AQ × AP)

(2,000 × 2) – (2,500 × 3) = Rs. 3,500 (a)

Verification: Material Cost Variance = Material Price Variance + Material Usage Variance

3,500 (a) = 2,500 (a) + 1,000 (a)

MATERIAL MIX VARIANCE

One of the reasons for Material Usage Variance is wrong mixture of materials where more than one type of material is used for producing the finished product. It is that portion of the Material Usage Variance, which is due to the difference between the standard and actual composition of materials.

It may arise in industries like chemicals, rubber, textile, construction work etc. due to non- availability of the requisite quantity of one or more of the specified material for the mix or may arise due to non-purchase of a particular material at the proper time. The variance due to the first reason is uncontrollable whereas variance due to the second reason is controllable and it is on account of inefficiency of the Purchase Department.

Increase in the proportion of cheaper material results in favorable Material Mix Variance and *vice versa*. The use of more expensive material in large proportions results in adverse variance.

***(a)* When the weight of actual mix and standard mix do not differ:**

Material Mix Variance = (Standard Quantity – Actual Quantity) Standard Price

A point to be noted here is, Material Mix Variance will be the same as that of the Material Usage Variance if there is no difference between the standard output specified and the actual output achieved.

***(b)* When the weight of actual mix and standard mix differ:**

Material Mix Variance = (Revised Standard Quantity – Actual Quantity) Standard Price

Here, when the weight of actual and standard mix is not the same, the standard quantity is to be revised to adjust the total weight of standard mix to the total weight of actual mix.

$$\text{Revised Standard Quantity} = \frac{\text{Total Weight of Actual Mix}}{\text{Total Weight of Standard Mix}} \times \text{Standard Quantity}$$

Material Yield Variance (MYV)

It is that portion of Material Usage Variance, which is due to the difference between the standard yield specified and the actual yield obtained. It arises in process industries like chemicals, where loss in production is inevitable. The standard yield is the output expected from the standard input of raw material. It measures the abnormal loss or saving (abnormal gain) of materials.

All other Material Variances calculated so far, are the input variances, whereas the Material Yield Variance is the output variance. While other variances represent a gain or loss on the cost of the material input, Material Yield Variance represents a gain or loss in output in terms of finished production.

A low actual yield results in unfavorable yield variance, which shows that the actual output was less for the material consumed or consumption of material was more than the standard quantity specified for that level of output.

Material Yield Variance arises in the following two situations:

***(a)* When the weight of Standard and Actual mix do not differ:**

Material Yield Variance = (Actual Yield – Standard Yield) Standard Rate

Standard Rate = Standard cost of standard mix/standard output

***(b)* When the weight of Standard and Actual mix differ:**

Material Yield Variance = (Actual Yield – Revised Standard Yield) Standard Rate

$$\text{Revised Standard Yield} = \frac{\text{Total Weight of Actual Mix}}{\text{Total Weight of Standard Mix}} \times \text{Standard Yield}$$

When the mix differ, it is necessary to revise the standard yield as per the actual mix weight.

Verification

Material Usage Variance = Material Mix Variance + Material Yield Variance

When the output is not given and the standard mix and actual mix weight differ, in such a case, a Material Sub Usage Variance is calculated.

Material Sub Usage Variance

Material Sub Usage Variance = (Standard Quantity for actual output – Revised Standard Quantity) Standard Price

It is a favorable variance if revised standard quantity is less than the standard quantity. When Material Sub Usage Variance is calculated,

Material Usage Variance = Material Mix Variance + Material Sub Usage Variance

Note: When the standard and actual mix weights do not differ,

Material Usage Variance = Material Mix Variance + Material Yield Variance

When the standard and actual mix weight differ, then,

Material Usage Variance = Material Mix Variance + Material Yield Variance

OR

Material Usage Variance = Material Mix Variance + Material Sub Usage Variance

In this Case, Material Yield Variance = Material Sub Usage Variance

Illustration 4

A company produces a certain chemical, the standard material cost being:

40% of material X at Rs. 20 per ton.

60% of material Y at Rs. 30 per ton.

A standard loss of 10% is expected in production. During one month, 171 tons of chemical was processed from the use of 90 tons of material 'X' at Rs. 18 per ton and 110 tons of material 'Y' at Rs. 34 per ton. Calculate Material Variances.

Solution

	Standard			*Actual*		
	Quantity	*Price Rs.*	*Cost Rs.*	*Quantity*	*Price Rs.*	*Cost Rs.*
X	80	20	1,600	90	18	1,620
Y	120	30	3,600	110	34	3,740
	200		5,200	200		5,360
Loss (10%)	20			29		
Output	180			171		

(a) Material Price Variance = (SP – AP) AQ

X : (20 – 18) 90 = Rs. 180 (f)

Y : (30 – 34) 110 = Rs. 440 (a)

Rs. 260 (a)

(b) Material Usage Variance = (SQ for actual output – AQ) SP

SQ for actual output = (Actual Output × SQ)/Standard Output

X (171 × 80)/180 = 76 units

Y (171 × 120)/180 = 114 units

Material Usage Variance

X: (76 – 90) 20 = Rs. 280 (a)

Y: (114 – 110) 30 = Rs. 120 (f)

Rs. 160 (a)

(c) Material Cost Variance = (SQ for actual output × SP) – (AQ × AP)

X = (76 × 20) – (90 × 18) = Rs. 100 (a)

Y = (114 × 30) – (110 × 34) = Rs. 320 (a)

Rs. 420 (a)

Verification: Material Cost Variance = Material Price Variance + Material Usage Variance

420 (a) = 260 (a) + 160 (a)

Weight of Actual and Standard Mix are same:

(d) Material Mix Variance = (SQ – AQ) SP

X (80 – 90) 20 = Rs. 200 (a)

Y (120 – 110) 30 = Rs. 300 (f)

Rs. 100 (f)

(e) Material Yield Variance = (Standard Yield – Actual Yield) Standard Rate per unit of output

Standard Rate per unit of output = Standard Cost/Standard Yield

5200 / 180 = Rs. 28.8889

(180 – 171) 28.8889 = Rs. 260 (a)

Verification: Material Usage Variance = Material Mix Variance + Material Yield Variance

160 (a) = 100 (f) + 260 (a)

Illustration 5

The standard material cost for an output of 100 kgs of chemical 'D' is made up of:

Chemical A: 30 kg. @ Rs. 4 per kg.

Chemical B: 40 kg. @ Rs. 5 per kg.

Chemical C: 80 kg. @ Rs. 6 per kg.

In a batch, 500 kgs. of chemical 'D' were produced from a mix of:

Chemical A: 150 kgs. at a cost of Rs. 588

Chemical B: 220 kgs. at a cost of Rs.1,056

Chemical C: 380 kgs. at a cost of Rs.2,860

Calculate the Material Variances.

Solution

	Standard		*Actual*	
	Quantity	*Price Rs.*	*Quantity*	*Price Rs.*
A	30	4	150	3.92
B	40	5	220	4.80
C	80	6	380	7.53
	150		750	
Output	100 Kgs.		500 Kgs.	

(a) Material Price Variance = (SP – AP) AQ

A : (4 – 3.92) 150 = Rs. 12 (f)

B : (5 – 4.80) 220 = Rs. 44 (f)

C : (6 – 7.53) 380 = Rs. 580 (a)

Rs. 524 (a)

Material Usage Variance = (SQ for actual output – AQ) SP

SQ for actual output = (Actual Output × SQ)/Standard Output

A (500 × 30)/100 = 150 units

B (500 × 40)/100 = 200 units

C (500 × 80)/100 = 400 units

Material Usage Variance

A: (150 – 150) 4 = Rs. 0

B: (200 – 220) 5 = Rs. 100 (a)

C: (400 – 380) 6 = Rs. 120 (f)

Rs. 20 (f)

Material Cost Variance = (SQ × SP) – (AQ × AP)

A = (150 × 4) – 588 = Rs. 12 (f)

B = (200 × 5) – 1056 = Rs. 56 (a)

C = (400 × 6) – 2860 = Rs. 460 (a)

Rs. 504 (a)

Verification: Material Cost Variance = Material Price Variance + Material Usage Variance

504 (a) = 524 (a) + 20 (f)

Weight of actual and standard mix differ:

(b) Material Mix Variance = (RSQ – AQ) SP

$$\text{Revised Standard Quantity} = \frac{\text{Total Weight of Actual Mix}}{\text{Total Weight of Standard Mix}} \times \text{Standard Quantity}$$

A = (750 × 30)/150 = 150
B = (750 × 40)/150 = 200
C = (750 × 80)/150 = 400

Material Mix Variance

A: (150 – 150) 4 = Rs. 0
B: (200 – 220) 5 = Rs.100 (a)
C: (400 – 380) 6 = Rs.120 (f)
Rs. 20 (f)

Material Sub Usage Variance = (SQ for actual output– RSQ) SP

A: (150 – 150) 4 = Rs. 0
B: (200 – 200) 5 = Rs. 0
C: (400 – 400) 6 = Rs. 0
Rs. 0

Verification: Material Usage Variance = Material Variance + Material Sub Usage Variance
20 (f) = 20 (f) + 0

Illustration 6

Calculate the Material Variances for each of the following:

(a)	Opening Stock	100 kg.
	Purchased during the period	3,000 kg. cost Rs. 6,200
	Standard	2 kg. per unit at Rs. 2 per kg.
	Original Budget	2,000 units
	Production	1,600 units
	Sales	1,400 units
	Closing Stock	200 kg.
(b)	Purchased during the period	6,000 kg. cost Rs. 2,400
	Standard	3 kg. per unit at Re. 0.50 per kg.
	Production	2,000 units
	Closing Stock	400 kg.

Solution

(a) *(i)* Material Price Variance: (Standard Price – Actual Price) Actual Quantity
(2 – 2.0667) 3,000 = Rs. 200 (a)

(ii) Material Usage Variance: (Standard Quantity for Actual Output – Actual Quantity) Standard Price
(3,200 units – 3,000 units) Rs. 2 = Rs. 400 (f)
Standard Quantity for Actual Output = 1,600 units × 2 = 3,200 units

(iii) Material Cost Variance:
(Standard Quantity for Actual Output × Standard Price) – (Actual Quantity × Actual Price)
(3,200 × 2) – (3,000 × 2.0667) = Rs. 200 (f)

Verification: Material Cost Variance = Material Usage Variance + Material Price Variance
Rs. 200 (f) = Rs. 400 (f) + Rs. 200 (a)

(b) *(i)* Material Price Variance: (Standard Price – Actual Price) Actual Quantity
(0.50 – 0.40) 5600 = Rs. 560 (f)

(ii) Material Usage Variance:
(Standard Quantity for Actual Output – Actual Quantity) Standard Price
(6000 – 5600) 0.50 = Rs. 200 (f)
Standard Quantity for Actual Output = 2,000 units × 3 = 6,000 kg.
Actual material used is taken (6000 – 400 closing stock = 5600).

It can be calculated on purchases also.

(iii) Material Cost Variance:

(Standard Quantity for Actual Output × Standard Price) – (Actual Quantity × Actual Price)

(6000 × 0.5) – (5600 × 0.40) = Rs. 760 (f)

Verification: Material Cost Variance = Material Usage Variance + Material Price Variance

Rs. 760 (f) = Rs. 200 (f) + Rs. 560 (f)

Note: Material Price Variance is calculated at the time of purchases only. It can be calculated on Material Used also.

Illustration 7

Eskay Ltd. produces an article by blending two basic raw materials. The following standards have been set up for raw materials:

Materials	Standard Mix	Standard Price per kg.
A	40%	Rs. 4.00
B	60%	Rs. 3.00

The standard loss in processing is 15%. During September 1990, the company produced 1700 kg. of finished output.

	Stock on 1.1.90	Stock on 30.09.90	Purchased during Sep., 1990	
A	35 kg.	5 kg.	800 kg.	Rs. 3,400
B	40 kg.	50 kg.	1,200 kg.	Rs. 3,000

Calculate the following Variances:

(a) Material Price Variance, *(b)* Material Usage Variance, *(c)* Material Yield Variance, *(d)* Material Mix Variance and *(e)* Total Material Cost Variance. Assume first in first out method for issue of material. The opening stock is to be valued at standard price.

(CA, Inter, November, 1991)

Solution

Material Consumed: Opening Stock + Purchases – Closing Stock

Material A: 35 + 800 – 5 = 830

Material B: 40 + 1200 – 50 = 1,190

Material	*Standard*			*Actual*		
	Quantity	*Price (Rs.)*	*Amount (Rs.)*	*Quantity*	*Price (Rs.)*	*Amount (Rs.)*
A	808	4	3,232	830	4.0964	3,400
B	1,212	3	3,636	1,190	2.5210	3,000
Input	2,020		6,868	2,020		6,400
Less 15%	303			–320		
Output	1,717			1,700		

(a) Material Price Variance: (Standard Price – Actual Price) Actual Quantity

Material A: (4-4.0964) 830 = Rs. 80 (a)

Material B: (3-2.5210) 1190 = Rs. 570 (f)

Total Rs. 490 (f)

(b) Material Usage Variance :

(Standard Quantity for Actual Output – Actual Quantity) Standard Price

Material A: (800-830) 4 = Rs. 120 (a)

Material B: (1,200-1,190) 3 = Rs. 30(f)

Total Rs. 90 (a)

Standard Quantity for Actual Output: (Actual Output/Standard Output) Standard Quantity

Material A: (1,700/1,717) 808 = 800

Material B: (1,700/1,717) 1212 = 1,200

(c) Material Yield Variance: (Standard Yield – Actual Yield) Standard Rate

(1,717-1,700) 6,868/1,717 = Rs. 68 (a)

(d) Material Mix Variance: (Standard Quantity – Actual Quantity) Standard Price

Material A: (808-830) 4 = Rs. 88 (a)

Material B: (1,212-1,190) 3 = Rs. 66 (f)

Total Rs. 22 (a)

(e) Material Cost Variance:

(Standard Quantity for Actual Output x Standard Price) – (Actual Quantity × Actual Price)

Material A: (800 × 4) – (830 × 4.0964) = Rs. 200 (a)

Material B: (1,200 × 3) – (1,190 × 2.5210)= Rs. 600 (f)

Total Rs. 400 (f)

Verification: Material Cost Variance = Material Usage Variance + Material Price Variance

Rs. 400 (f) = Rs. 90 (a) + Rs. 490 (f)

Material Usage Variance = Material Mix Variance + Material Yield Variance

Rs. 90 (a) = Rs. 22 (a) + Rs. 68 (a)

Illustration 8

From the data given below, calculate:

(a) Individual Material Price Variances for the two materials X and Y assuming that price variances are calculated at the time of purchase.

(b) Individual Material Usage Variances for materials X and Y assuming that there was no stock in progress either at the commencement or at the end of the period.

	X		*Y*	
	Quantity	*Value*	*Quantity*	*Value*
Raw Material Purchases	2,000 kg.	Rs. 4,000	5,000 kg.	Rs. 6,250
Issues to Works	2,150 kg.		3,950 kg.	
Works Stock of Material:				
Opening	300 kg.		1,000 kg.	
Closing	200 kg.		1,250 kg.	

Standard Price: Material X: Rs. 1.90 per kg.

Material Y: Rs. 1.30 per kg.

Standard Usage:	Material X	Material Y
Product A	1.0kg.	1kg.
Product B	0.5kg.	1kg.

Output during the period: Product A: 1,130 units

Product B: 2,550 units

(ICWA, Inter, June, 1989)

Solution

(a) Material Price Variance: (Standard Price – Actual Price) Actual Quantity

Material X: (1.90-2) 2,000 = Rs. 200 (a)

Material Y: (1.30-1.25) 5,000 = Rs. 250 (f)

Total Rs. 50 (f)

(b) Material Usage Variance: (Standard Quantity for Actual Output – Actual Quantity) Standard Price

Material X: (2,405-2,250) 1.90= Rs. 294.50 (f)

Material Y: (3,680-3,700) 1.30= Rs. 26.00 (a)

Total Rs. 268.50 (f)

Standard Quantity for Actual Output:

Product A: 1,130 units × 1 kg = 1,130 kg.

Product B: 2,550 units × 0.5 kg = 1,275 kg.

Total: Material X 2,405 kg.

Product A: 1,130 units × 1 kg = 1,130 kg.

Product B: 2,550 units × 1 kg = 2,550 kg.

Total: Material Y 3,680 kg.

Actual Quantity used: Opening Stock + Issues – Closing Stock

Material X: 300 + 2,150 – 200 = 2,250 kgs.

Material Y: 1,000 + 3,950 – 1,250 = 3,700 kgs.

Illustration 9

X Ltd. is producing floor covers in roll of standard size measuring 3 meters wide and 30 meters long by feeding raw materials to a continuous process machine. Standard mixture fixed for a batch of 900 sq. meters of floor cover is as follows:

2,000 kg. of Material A at Re. 1.00 per kg.

800 kg. of Material B at Re. 1.50 per kg.

20 gallons of Material C at Rs. 30 per gallon.

During the period, 1,505 standard size rolls were produced from the material issued for 150 batches. The actual usage and the cost of materials were:

3,00,500 kg. of Material A at Rs. 1.10 pe rkg.

1,19,600 kg. of Matrial B at Rs. 1.65 per kg.

3,100 gallon of Material C at Rs. 29.50 per gallon.

Present the figures to management showing the break up of Material Cost Variances arising during the period.

(ICWA, Inter, December, 1984)

Solution

Material	*Standard*			*Actual*	
	Quantity (Kgs)	*Price (Rs.)*	*Amount (Rs.)*	*Quantity (Kgs)*	*Price (Rs.)*
A	2,000	1.00	2,000	3,00,500	1.10
B	800	1.50	1,200	1,19,600	1.65
C	20 gallons	30	600	3,100 gallons	29.50
Output	10 Rolls		3,800	1,505 Rolls	

(a) Material Price Variance: (Standard Price – Actual Price) Actual Quantity

Material A: (1-1.10) 3,00,500 = Rs. 30,050 (a)

Material B: (1.50-1.65) 1,19,600 = Rs. 17,940 (a)

Material C: (30-29.50) 3,100 = Rs. 1,550 (f)

Total Rs. 46,440 (a)

(b) Material Usage Variance:

(Standard Quantity for Actual Output – Actual Quantity) Standard Price

Material A: (3,01,000-3,00,500) 1 = Rs. 500 f)

Material B: (1,20,400-1,19,600) 1.5 = Rs. 1,200 (f)

Material C: (3,010-3,100) 30 = Rs. 2,700 (a)

Total Rs. 1,000 (a)

Standard Quantity for Actual Output: (Actual Output / Standard Output) Standard Quantity

Material A: (1,505/10) 2000 = 3,01,000

Material B: (1,505/10) 800 = 1,20,400

Material C: (1,505/10) 20 = 3,010

Standard size of one roll= 3m × 30m = 90 sq. meters

Output of one batch in sq. meters = 900

Number of rolls produced in one batch: 900/90 = 10

(c) Material Cost Variance:

(Standard Quantity for Actual Output × Standard Price) – (Actual Quantity × Actual Price)

Material A: (3,01,000 × 1) – (3,00,500 × 1.10) = Rs. 29,550 (a)

Material B: (1,20,400 × 1.5) – (1,19,600 × 1.65) = Rs. 16,740 (a)

Material C: (3,010 × 30) – (3,100 × 29.50) = Rs. 1,150 (a)

Total Rs. 47,440 (a)

(d) Material Mix Variance: (Standard Quantity– Actual Quantity) Standard Price

Material A: (3,00,000-3,00,500) 1 = Rs. 500 (a)

Material B: (1,20,000-1,19,600) 1.5 = Rs. 600 (f)

Material C: (3,000 – 3,100) 30 = Rs. 3,000 (a)

Total Rs. 2,900 (a)

Standard Quantity for 150 batches

Material A: 150 × 2,000 = 3,00,000

Material B: 150 × 800 = 1,20,000

Material C: 150 × 20 = 3,000

(e) Material Yield Variance: (Standard Yield for Actual Input – Actual Yield) Standard Rate

(1,500 – 1,505) 380 = Rs. 1,900 (f)

Standard Rate: Standard Cost / Standard Yield: 3,800 / 10 Rolls = Rs. 380 per Roll

Standard Yield = 10 Rolls × 150 batches = 1,500 Rolls

Verification: Material Cost Variance = Material Usage Variance + Material Price Variance

Rs. 47,440 (a) = Rs. 1,000 (a) + Rs. 46,440 (a)

Material Usage Variance = Material Mix Variance + Material Yield Variance

Rs. 1,000 (a) = Rs. 2,900 (a) + Rs. 1,900 (f)

SUMMARY

Material Variances arise due to a change in the actual price and/or quantity of material from the standard prescribed. Analysis of variances helps in locating the causes and the persons responsible for a particular cause.

Material Price Variance arises due to the difference between the standard price of material specified and the actual price for the material used. Material Usage Variance arises due to a difference between the standard and actual composition of materials and also due to the difference between the standard yield specified and the actual yield obtained. It is subdivided into Material Mix Variance and Material Yield Variance or Material Sub Usage Variance.

While the material price, usage and mix variances are the input variances, the material yield variance is the output variance. The first three variances represent a gain or loss in the cost of material input, whereas the yield variance represents a gain or loss in the output in terms of finished production.

Glossary

- **Material Cost Variance:** It is the difference between the Actual Cost of Materials used and the Standard Cost of Material allowed for the actual output achieved.
- **Material Price Variance:** It is that portion of Material Cost Variance, which is due to the difference between the standard price of material specified and the actual price for the material used.

- **Material Usage Variance:** It is that portion of Material Cost Variance, which is due to the difference between the standard quantity specified and the actual quantity used.
- **Material Mix Variance:** It is that portion of the Material Usage Variance, which is due to the difference between the standard and actual composition of materials.
- **Material Yield Variance:** It is that portion of Material Usage Variance, which is due to the difference between the standard yield specified and the actual yield obtained.

Questions

(1) Identify the causes for the Material Price Variance and the persons responsible for the same.
(2) How do you compute the various Material Variances?
(3) How do you control the variances in Material?

PROBLEMS

(1) Suppose the standards fixed for a product are 10 kgs. costing Rs. 100. But, on the completion of the job, the cost accountant reveal that the quantity consumed for that product was 12 kgs. costing Rs. 126. Find out the variances of quantity, price and cost of the material.
[**Ans.:** Material Price Variance Rs. 6 (a); Material Usage Variance Rs. 20 (a); Material Cost Variance Rs. 26(a)]

(2) The standard cost card shows the following details relating to the material required to produce 1 kg. of output.

Quantity of raw material	3 kgs.
Price	Re. 0.76 per kg.
Actual production data:	
Production during one-month	1,000 kgs.
Quantity used	3,500 kgs.
Price	Re. 1 per kg.

Calculate Material Cost Variance, Material Price Variance and Material Usage Variance.
[**Ans.:** Material Cost Variance Rs. 1,220 (a); Material Price Variance Rs. 840 (a) and Material Usage Variance Rs. 380 (a)]

(3) Calculate Material Cost Variance, Material Price Variance and Material Usage Variance.

Material	*Standard Quantity (Kgs)*	*Standard Price. per kg (Rs.)*	*Actual Quantity (Kgs)*	*Actual Price per kg (Rs.)*
L	30	5	28	6.00
M	40	4	42	3.50
	70		70	

[**Ans.:** Material Cost Variance Rs. 5 (a); Material Price Variance Rs. 7 (a) and Material Usage Variance Rs. 2 (f)]

(4) The standard cost of a chemical mixture is as under.
8 tons of material A @ Rs. 20 per ton
12 tons of material B @ Rs. 30 per ton
Standard Yield is 90% of input.
Actual cost for the period is as under:
9 tons of material A @ Rs. 15 per ton
15 tons of material B @ Rs. 34 per ton
Actual yield is 18.2 tons.
Compute all the five material variances.
[**Ans.:** Material Price Variance Rs. 15 (a); Material Usage Variance Rs.104.236(a); Material Cost Variance Rs.119.23 (a); Material Mix Variance Rs.6 (a) and Material Sub Usage Variance Rs.98.232 (a)]

(5) Calculate different Material Variances from the data given below.

	Standard			*Actual*		
	Quantity	*Price Rs.*	*Cost Rs.*	*Quantity*	*Price Rs.*	*Cost Rs.*
A	1000	10	10,000	1090	11	11,990
B	250	20	5,000	400	18	7,200
C	400	15	6,000	380	17	6,460
D	600	10	6,000	610	9	5,490
	2,250		27,000	2,480		31,140

[**Ans.:** Material Price Variance Rs. 440 (a); Material Usage Variance Rs. 3,700 (a); Material Cost Variance Rs. 4,140 (a); Material Mix Variance Rs. 940 (a) and Material Sub Usage Variance Rs. 2,760 (a)]

(6) The standard mix of product A2 is as follows:

Kg.	*Material*	*Price per kg. Rs.*
45	X	6.00
25	Y	4.50
30	Z	9.50

The standard loss in production is 10% of input. There is no scrap value. Actual production for the material was 7425 kg. of A2 from 80 mixes. Actual purchases and consumption of material during the month were:

Kgs	*Material*	*Price per kg Rs.*
4200	X	6.50
1700	Y	4.25
2600	Z	9.75

You are required to calculate the following variances for presentation to the management:
(1) Material cost variance
(2) Material price variance
(3) Material mix variance
(4) Material yield variance

(C.S., Inter, Dec., 1998)

[**Ans.:** (1) Material cost variance = Rs. 4,806.25 (A)
(2) Material price variance = Rs. 2,325 (A)
(3) Material mix variance = Rs. 812.50 (A)
(4) Material yield variance = Rs. 1,668.75 (A)]

(7) Gemini Chemical Industries provide the following information from their records.

Material	*Quantity (kgs)*	*Rate per kg (Rs.)*
A	8	6.00
B	4	4.00

During April 1988, 1000 kgs. of Gemco were produced. The actual consumption of materials is as under:

Material	*Quantity (kgs)*	*Rate per kg (Rs)*
A	750	7.00
B	500	5.00

Calculate: *(a)* Material Cost variance
(b) Material price variance
(c) Material usage Variance

(C.A., Inter, May, 1989)

[**Ans.:** *(a)* Material Cost variance = Rs. 1,350 (A)
(b) Material price variance = Rs. 1,250 (A)
(c) Material usage Variance = Rs. 100 (A)]

❑ ❑ ❑

22

LABOR VARIANCES

Objectives

The objectives of the study are to:

- analyze the causes for Labor Variances
- identify the persons responsible for the variance
- learn the computation and analysis of Labor Variances

INTRODUCTION

In this lesson, you will learn the computation and analysis of Labor Variances; variances relating to the second element of cost. The analysis and computation of Labor Variances is similar to that of Material Variances. Whenever the standards specified for direct labor differ from the actual, Labor Variances arise, necessitating an investigation into and an analysis of Labor Variance.

LABOR VARIANCES

In case of Labor, the various variances to be calculated are:

- Labor Cost Variance
- Labor Rate/Price Variance
- Labor Efficiency/Time/Usage Variance
- Labor Mix Variance
- Labor Idle Time Variance
- Labor Yield Variance or Labor Sub Usage/Labor Revised Efficiency Variance

The following chart shows the division and sub division of Labor Variances.

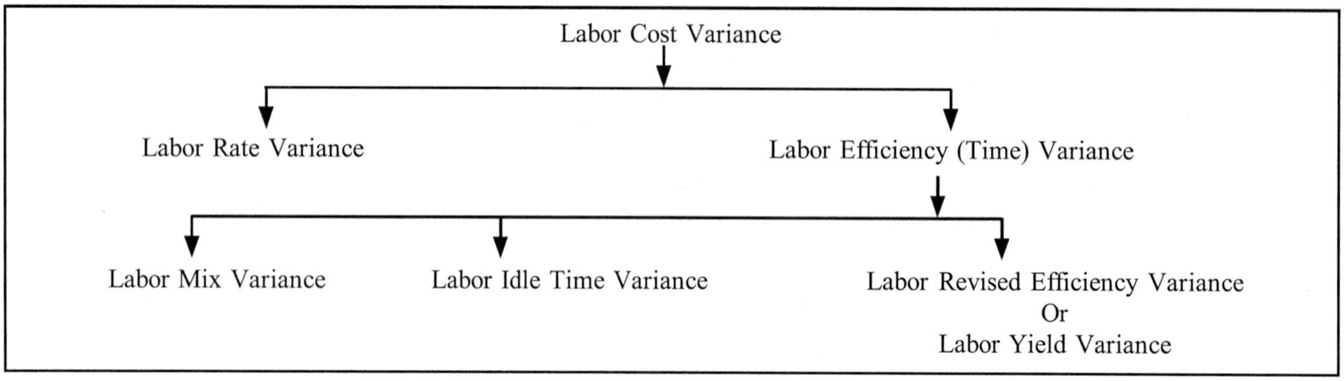

LABOR COST VARIANCE

It is the difference between the standard direct labor cost specified for the activity achieved and the actual direct labor cost incurred. It is also known as Wages Variance.

Labor Cost Variance is equal to

(Standard Time for Actual Output × Standard Rate) – (Actual Time × Actual Rate)

OR

Standard Cost of labor for actual output – Actual Cost of labor

LABOR RATE VARIANCE

It is that portion of the Labor Cost Variance, which is due to the difference between the standard rate specified and the actual rate paid.

Labor Rate Variance = (Standard Rate – Actual Rate) Actual Time

The possible reasons for Labor Rate Variance are change in the basic wage rates, use of a different method of wage payment, employing workers of grades different from the standard grades specified, unscheduled overtime, new workers not being paid at full rates, promotion of employees without proper authorization and paying them rates fixed for higher job classification, etc.

Often, Labor Rate Variance will be uncontrollable, as labor rates are usually determined by demand and supply conditions in the labor market or use of a grade of labor other than that specified due to non availability of the labor grade specified. But, when a foreman carelessly employs a wrong grade of labor on a job, he may be held responsible.

It is considered as a favorable variance if actual rate of pay to the labor is less than the specified standard rate.

LABOR TIME VARIANCE/LABOR EFFICIENCY VARIANCE

It is that portion of Labor Cost Variance, which is due to the difference between labor hours specified and the actual labor hours expended.

Labor Time Variance = (Standard time for actual output – Actual time) Standard Rate

It is a favorable variance, if actual time taken is less than the standard time specified.

This type of variance arises due to the improper working conditions, insufficient training to workers, lack of proper supervision, defective tools/machines, increase in labor turnover, machine breakdown, non employment of right men for the right job etc.

Verification: Labor Cost Variance = Labor Rate Variance + Labor Efficiency Variance

Illustration 1

Compute Labor Rate Variance, Labor Efficiency Variance and Labor Cost Variance.

Standard hours for production	2,21,000
Actual hours worked	2,00,000
Standard labor rate per hour	Re. 0.10
Actual labor rate per hour	Re. 0.12

Solution

Labor Rate Variance:	(Standard Rate – Actual Rate) Actual Time	
	(0.1 - 0.12) 2,00,000	= Rs. 4,000 (a)
Labor Efficiency Variance:	(Standard Time – Actual Time) Standard Rate	
	(2,21,000 – 2,00,000) 0.1	= Rs. 2,100 (f)

Labor Cost Variance: (Standard Time × Standard Rate) – (Actual Time × Actual Rate)

(2,21,000 × 0.1) – (2,00,000 × 0.12) = Rs. 1,900 (a)

Verification: Labor Cost Variance = Labor Rate Variance + Labor Efficiency Variance

1,900 (a) = 4,000 (a) + 2,100 (f)

Illustration 2

A group of workers normally consists of 10 men, 5 women and 5 boys, paid at standard hourly rates of Rs. 4, Rs. 3 and Rs. 2 respectively. In a normal working week of 40 hours, the group is expected to produce 1,000 units of output.

In a certain week, the group consisted of 13 men, 4 women and 3 boys. They worked for 72 hours and actual wages paid amounted to Rs. 2,500. The output of the group was 1,000 units.

Calculate the Labor Cost Variance, Labor Rate Variance and Labor Efficiency Variance.

Solution

(a)

	Standard Time		*Actual Time*	
Men	10 × 40 hours	= 400 hours	13 × 72 hours	= 936 hours
Women	5 × 40 hours	= 200 hours	4 × 72 hours	= 288 hours
Boys	5 × 40 hours	= 200 hours	3 × 72 hours	= 216 hours
		800 hours		1,440 hours

Standard Cost:

Men	400 × 4	= Rs. 1600
Women	200 × 3	= Rs. 600
Boys	200 × 2	= Rs. 400
		Rs. 2,600

Labor Cost Variance = Standard Cost – Actual Cost

Rs. 2,600 – 2,500 = Rs. 100 (f)

Actual Labor Rate: 2,500/1,440 = Rs. 1.736

(b) Labor Rate Variance: (Standard Rate – Actual Rate) Actual Time

Men	(4 – 1.736) 936	= 2,119.104 (f)
Women	(3 – 1.736) 288	= 364.032 (f)
Boys	(2 – 1.736) 216	= 57.024 (f)
		2,540.160 (f)

(c) Labor Efficiency Variance: (Standard Time – Actual Time) Standard Rate

Men	(400 – 936) 4	= 2,144 (a)
Women	(200 - 288) 3	= 264 (a)
Boys	(200 - 216) 2	= 32 (a)
		2,440 (a)

Verification: Labor Cost Variance = Labor Rate Variance + Labor Efficiency Variance

100 (f) = 2,540 (f) + 2,440 (a)

Illustration 3

The standard costs on materials and labor for manufacturing a unit of a certain product are estimated as under:

Materials 100 kgs. at Rs. 2 per kg.

Wages 20 hours at Rs. 1.5 per hour

On completion of the manufacturing of a unit of that product, the actuals are recorded as under.

Materials 80 kgs. at Rs. 3 per kg.

Wages 25 hours at Rs. 2 per hour

Calculate the Material and Labor Variances.

Solution

Material Variances:

(a) Material Usage Variance = (Standard Quantity – Actual Quantity) Standard Price

(100 – 80) 2 = Rs. 40 (f)

(b) Material Price Variance = (Standard Price – Actual Price) Actual Quantity
(2 – 3) 80 = Rs. 80 (a)

(c) Material Cost Variance = (Standard Quantity × Standard Price) – (Actual Quantity × Actual Price)
(100 × 2) – (80 × 3) = Rs. 40 (a)

Verification: Material Cost Variance = Material Usage Variance + Material Price Variance
40 (a) = 40 (f) + 80 (a)

Labor Variances:

Labor Rate Variance: (Standard Rate – Actual Rate) Actual Time
(1.5 – 2.0) 25 = Rs. 12.50 (a)

Labor Efficiency Variance: (Standard Time – Actual Time) Standard Rate
(20 – 25) 1.5 = Rs. 7.50 (a)

Labor Cost Variance: (Standard Time × Standard Rate) – (Actual Time × Actual Rate)
(20 × 1.5) – (25 × 2) = Rs. 20.00 (a)

Verification: Labor Cost Variance = Labor Rate Variance + Labor Efficiency Variance
20(a) = 12.50 (a) + 7.50 (a)

Labor Efficiency Variance is further divided into 3 sub variances – Idle Time Variance, Labor Mix Variance and Labor Revised Efficiency Variance

IDLE TIME VARIANCE

It is that portion of Labor Efficiency Variance, which is due to abnormal idle time such as time lost due to machine breakdown, power failure, strikes etc.

Idle Time Variance = Idle Time × Standard Rate

It is always an adverse variance as idle hours represent a loss.

LABOR MIX/GANG COMPOSITION VARIANCE

It arises only when more than one grade of workers are employed. It shows to the management as to how much of the Labor Cost Variance is due to the change in the composition of labor force.

***(a)* When total standard time and actual time are same**

Labor Mix Variance = (Standard Time – Actual Time) Standard Rate

***(b)* When total standard time and actual time differ**

Labor Mix Variance = (Revised Standard Time – Actual Time) Standard Rate

If the total actual time of labor differs from the total standard time of labor, standard time is revised to adjust the total time of standard mix to the total time of actual mix.

$$\text{Revised Standard Time} = \frac{\text{Total time of actual labor composition}}{\text{Total time of standard labor composition}} \times \text{Standard Time}$$

It is a favorable variance, if actual time consumption is less than the standard time stipulated.

LABOR REVISED EFFICIENCY VARIANCE

This is also a sub variance of Labor Efficiency Variance and arises due to the factors other than those which give rise to Idle Time Variance and Labor Mix Variance.

Labor Revised Efficiency Variance = (Standard Time for actual output – Revised Standard Time) Standard Rate

Verification: Labor Efficiency Variance = Labor Idle Time Variance + Labor Mix Variance
+ Labor Revised Efficiency Variance

Illustration 4

A contract job is scheduled to be completed in 30 weeks with a labor component of 100 skilled operatives, 40 semi skilled operatives and 60 unskilled operatives. The standard weekly wages of each type of operatives are skilled Rs. 60, semi skilled Rs. 36 and unskilled Rs. 24. The work is actually completed in 32 weeks with a labor force of 80 skilled, 50 semi skilled and 70 unskilled operatives and the actual weekly wage rates average Rs. 65 for skilled, Rs. 40 for semi skilled and Rs. 20 for unskilled labor.

Analyze the variances in labor cost.

Solution

	Standard		*Actual*	
Category	*Time (Weeks)* *Rs.*	*Rate* *Rs.*	*Time (Weeks)*	*Rate*
Skilled	100 × 30 = 3,000	60	80 × 32 = 2,560	65
Semi Skilled	40 × 30 = 1,200	36	50 × 32 = 1,600	40
Unskilled	60 × 30 = 1,800	24	70 × 32 = 2,240	20
	6,000		6,400	

					Rs.
Labor Cost Variance:					
Skilled	(3,000 × 60)	—	(2,560 × 65)	=	13,600 (f)
Semi Skilled	(1,200 × 36)	—	(1,600 × 40)	=	20,800 (a)
Unskilled	(1,800 × 24)	—	(2,240 × 20)	=	1,600 (a)
					8,800 (a)
Labor Efficiency Variance:					
Skilled	(3,000 – 2,560) 60			=	26,400 (f)
Semi Skilled	(1,200 – 1,600) 36			=	14,400 (a)
Unskilled	(1,800 – 2,240) 24			=	10,560 (a)
					1,440 (f)
Labor Rate Variance:					
Skilled	(60 – 65) 2,560			=	12,800 (a)
Semi Skilled	(36 – 40) 1,600			=	6,400 (a)
Unskilled	(24 – 20) 2,240			=	8,960 (f)
					10,240 (a)

Verification: Labor Cost Variance = Labor Efficiency Variance + Labor Rate Variance

8,800 (a) = 1,440 (f) + 10,240 (a)

Mix total not same:

Labor Mix Variance = (Revised Standard Time – Actual Time) Standard Rate

$$\text{Revised Standard Time} = \frac{\text{Total Actual Mix}}{\text{Total Standard Mix}} \times \text{Standard Time}$$

Revised Standard Time :

Skilled	(6,400 × 3,000) / 6,000 = 3,200 weeks	
Semi Skilled	(6,400 × 1,200) / 6,000 = 1,280 weeks	
Un Skilled	(6,400 × 1,800) / 6,000 = 1,920 weeks	

Labor Mix Variance :

Skilled	(3,200 – 2,560) 60	=	Rs. 38,400 (f)
Semi Skilled	(1,280 – 1,600) 36	=	Rs. 11,520 (a)
Un Skilled	(1,920 – 2,240) 24	=	Rs. 7,680 (a)
			Rs. 19,200 (f)

Labor Revised Efficiency Variance : (Standard Time – Revised Standard Time) Standard Rate

Skilled	(3,000 – 3,200) 60	=	Rs. 12,000 (a)
Semi Skilled	(1,200 – 1,280) 36	=	Rs. 2,880 (a)
Un Skilled	(1,800 – 1,920) 24	=	Rs. 2,880 (a)
			Rs. 17,760 (a)

Verification: Labor Efficiency Variance = Labor Mix Variance + Labor Revised Efficiency Variance
1,440 (f) = 19,200 (f) + 17,760 (a)

LABOR YIELD VARIANCE

It is that portion of Labor Efficiency Variance, which is due to the difference between actual output of workers and standard output of workers specified.

NOTE: When output is given, we can as well find out the Labor Yield Variance.

- **When total standard time and actual time are same**

  Labor Yield Variance = (Standard yield – Actual yield) Standard rate per hour

  $$\text{Standard Rate per hour} = \frac{\text{Standard Cost}}{\text{Standard yield}}$$

- **When total standard time and actual time are not same**

  Labor Yield Variance = (Revised Standard yield – Actual yield) Standard rate per hour

  $$\text{Revised Standard Yield} = \frac{\text{Total actual time}}{\text{Total standard time}} \times \text{Standard Yield}$$

Verification: Labor Efficiency Variance = Labor Mix Variance + Labor Yield Variance **Or**
Labor Mix Variance + Labor Revised Efficiency Variance

Illustration 5

From the following, calculate labor variances.

	Standard			*Actual*		
	Hours	*Rate*	*Amount*	*Hours*	*Rate*	*Amount*
(a) Skilled	2,400	2	4,800	2,400	2.25	5,400
(b) Unskilled	1,200	1	1,200	1,200	1.25	1,500
	3,600		6,000	3,600		6,900
Output	1,000			2,000		

Solution

(a) Labor Cost Variance: (Standard Time for actual output x Standard Rate) – (Actual Time x Actual Rate)

Standard Time for actual output:

Skilled: 2,000 × (2,400 / 1,000) = 4,800 hours

Unskilled: 2,000 × (1,200 / 1,000) = 2,400 hours

			Rs.
Skilled:	(4,800 × 2) – (2,400 × 2.25)	=	4,200 (f)
Unskilled:	(2,400 × 1) – (1,200 × 1.25)	=	900(f)
			5,100 (f)

(b) Labor Rate Variance: (Standard Rate – Actual Rate) Actual Time

Skilled:	(2 – 2.25) 2,400	=	600 (a)
Unskilled:	(1 – 1.25) 1,200	=	300 (a)
			900 (a)

(c) Labor Efficiency Variance: (Standard Time for actual output – Actual Time) Standard Rate

Skilled:	(4,800 – 2,400) 2	=	4,800(f)
Unskilled:	(2,400 – 1,200) 1	=	1,200 (f)
			6,000 (f)

Verification: Labor Cost Variance = Labor Efficiency Variance + Labor Rate Variance
5,100 (f) = 6,000 (f) + 900 (a)

Mix total same:

(d) Labor Mix Variance: (Standard Time – Actual Time) Standard Rate

Skilled:	(2,400 – 2,400) 2	=	0
Unskilled:	(1,200 – 1,200) 1	=	0
			0

(e) Labor Yield Variance: (Standard Yield – Actual Yield) Standard Rate per unit of output

Standard Rate per unit of output = Standard Cost/Standard Output

= 6,000/1,000 = Rs. 6

(1,000 – 2,000) 6 = Rs. 6,000 (f)

Verification: Labor Efficiency Variance = Labor Mix Variance + Labor Yield Variance

6,000 (f) = 0 + 6,000 (f)

Illustration 6

A gang of workers normally consisted of 30 men, 15 women and 10 boys. They are paid at standard rates as under.

Man	Re. 0.80
Woman	Re. 0.60
Boy	Re. 0.40

In a normal working week of 40 hours, the gang is expected to produce 2,000 units of output.

During the week ended 31st December, the gang consisted of 40 men, 10 women and 5 boys. The actual wages paid were at Re. 0.70; Re. 0.65 and Re. 30 respectively. 4 hours were lost due to abnormal idle time and 1,600 units were produced.

Calculate labor variances.

Solution

	Standard			*Actual*		
Category	*Time (hours)*			*Time (hours)*		
Men	30 × 40	=	1,200	40 × 40	=	1,600
Women	15 × 40	=	600	10 × 40	=	400
Boys	10 × 40	=	400	5 × 40	=	200
			2,200			2,200
Output			2,000 units			1,600 units

Standard Time for actual output:

Men:	1,200 × (1,600/2,000) = 960 hours
Women:	600 × (1,600/2,000) = 480 hours
Boys:	400 × (1,600/2,000) = 320 hours

(a) Labor Cost Variance:

					Rs.
Men	(960 × .80)	—	(1,600 × .70)	=	352 (a)
Women	(480 × .60)	—	(400 × .65)	=	28 (f)
Boys	(320 × .40)	—	(200 × .30)	=	68 (f)
					256 (a)

(b) Labor Rate Variance:

Men	(.80 – 70) 1,600	=	160 (f)
Women	(.60 – .65) 400	=	20 (a)
Boys	(.40 – .30) 200	=	20 (f)
			160 (f)

(c) Labor Efficiency Variance:

Men	(960 – 1,600) .80	=	512 (a)
Women	(480 – 400) .60	=	48 (f)
Boys	(320 – 200) .40	=	48 (f)
			416 (a)

Verification: Labor Cost Variance = Labor Rate Variance + Labor Efficiency Variance

256 (a) = 160 (f) + 416 (a)

Mix total not same:

Idle Time:

Men	40 × 4	=	160 hours
Women	10 × 4	=	40 hours
Boys	5 × 4	=	20 hours

(d) Idle Time Variance: Idle Time × Standard Rate

Men	160 × .80	=	128 (a)
Women	40 × .60	=	24 (a)
Boys	20 × .40	=	8 (a)
			160 (a)

Labor Mix Variance: (Revised Standard Time – Actual Time) Standard Rate

$$\text{Revised Standard Time: } \frac{\text{Total Actual Mix}}{\text{Total Standard Mix}} \times \text{Standard Time}$$

Now, actual time worked is calculated after deducting idle time

Actual Time:

Men	1600 – 160 =	1,440 hours
Women	400 – 40 =	360 hours
Boys	200 – 20 =	180 hours
		1,980 hours

Revised Standard Time:

Men	1,200 × (1,980/2,200) = 1,080
Women	600 × (1,980/2,200) = 540
Boys	400 × (1,980/2,200) = 360

(e) Labor Mix Variance:

Men	(1,080 – 1,440) .80	=	288 (a)
Women	(540 – 360) .60	=	108 (f)
Boys	(360 – 180) .40	=	72 (f)
			108 (a)

(f) Labor Revised Efficiency Variance:

(Standard Time for actual output – Revised Standard Time) Standard Rate

Men	(960 –1,080) .8	=	96 (a)
Women	(480 – 540) .6	=	36 (a)
Boys	(320 – 360) .4	=	16 (a)
			148 (a)

Verification: Labor Efficiency Variance = Idle Time Variance + Labor Mix Variance + Labor Revised Efficiency Variance

416 (a) = 160 (a) + 108 (a) + 148 (a)

Illustration 7

The following details are available from the records of ABC Ltd. engaged in manufacturing article A for the week ended 28th February. The standard labor hours and rates of payment per article A were as follows:

	Hours	*Rate per hour (Rs.)*	*Total (Rs.)*
Skilled labor	10	3.00	30
Semi-skilled labor	8	1.50	12
Unskilled labor	16	1.00	16
			58

The actual production was 1,000 articles A for which the actual hours worked and rates are given below:

	Hours	*Rate per hour (Rs.)*	*Total (Rs.)*
Skilled labor	9,000	4.00	36,000
Semi-skilled labor	8,400	1.50	12,600
Unskilled labor	20,000	0.90	18,000
			66,600

From the above set of data, you are asked to calculate: *(i)* Labor Cost Variance, *(ii)* Labor Rate Variance, *(iii)* Labor Efficiency Variance, and *(iv)* Labor Mix Variance.

(C.S., Inter, Dec., 1994)

Solution

Basic data for Standard and actual labor cost of producing 1,000 articles of 'A' and standard cost of actual labor hours.

Labor	*Standard Cost*			*Actual Cost*			*Std. Cost of actual*
	Hours	*Rate Rs.*	*Amount Rs.*	*Hours*	*Rate Rs.*	*Amount Rs.*	*labor hrs (Actual hrs × Std. Rate) Rs.*
Skilled	10,000	3.00	30,000	9,000	4.00	36,000	27,000
Semi-skilled	8,000	1.50	12,000	8,400	1.50	12,600	12,600
Unskilled	16,000	1.00	16,000	20,000	0.90	18,000	20,000
Total	34,000		58,000	37,400		66,600	59,600

Calculation of Labor Variances:

(i) Labor Cost Variance

= Standard cost – Actual Cost

= Rs. 58,000 – Rs. 66,600 = Rs. 8,600 (A)

(ii) Labor Rate Variance

= Actual hours (Standard rate – Actual rate)

(Or)

= Standard cost of actual hours – Actual cost

= Rs. 59,600 – Rs. 66,600 = Rs. 7,000 (A)

(iii) Labor Efficiency Variance

= Standard rate of standard mix (Total standard hours for actual output – Total actual hours)

= Rs. 58,000/34,000 × (34,000 – 37,400) = Rs. 5,800 (A)

(iv) Labor Mix Variance:

= Total actual hours (Standard rate of standard mix – standard rate of actual mix)

= 37,400 [(58,000/34,000) – (59,600/37,400)] = Rs. 4,200 (F)

Summary of Labor Variance

	Rs.
Rate Variance	7,000 (A)
Efficiency Variance	5,800 (A)
Mix Variance	4,200 (F)
Labor Cost Variance	8,600 (A)

Illustration 8

The standard labor complement and the actual labor complement engaged during the month are given below:

	Skilled	*Semi-skilled*	*Unskilled*
(a) Standard number of workers in group	30	10	10
(b) Standard wage rate (Rupees per hour)	5	3	2
(c) Actual number of workers employed during the month in the group	24	15	12
(d) Actual wage rate per hour (Rs.)	6	2.5	2

During the month of 200 working hours, the group produced 9,600 standard hours of work.

Required: Calculate Wage Rate Variance, Labor Efficiency Variance, Labor Mix Variance and Total Labor Cost Variance.

(I.C.W.A., Inter, June, 1995)

Solution

Basic Data

Category workers	*No. of Workers*	*Hours p.m.*	*Total Hours*	*Std. rate*	*Std. Labor cost Rs.*	*Std. Rate per hour of group Rs.*
(1) Standard Labor hour rate of Standard group						
Skilled	30	200	6,000	5	30,000	
Semi-skilled	10	200	2,000	3	6,000	
Unskilled	10	200	2,000	2	4,000	
Total			10,000		40,000	4.00
(2) Standard Labor hour rate of Actual group						
Skilled	24	200	4,800	5	24,000	
Semi-skilled	15	200	3,000	3	9,000	
Unskilled	12	200	2,400	2	4,800	
Total			10,200		37,800	3.71
(3) Actual Labor hour rate of Actual group						
Skilled	24	200	4,800	6	28,800	
Semi-skilled	15	200	3,000	2.50	7,500	
Unskilled	12	200	2,400	2	4,800	
Total			10,200		41,100	4.03

Particulars	*Hours*	*Rate p.h Rs.*	*Amount Rs.*
(1) Standard Cost of Output	9,600	4.00	38,400
(2) Actual hours at Standard Rates of standard Group	10,200	4.00	40,800
(3) Actual hours at Standard Rate of actual group	10,200	3.71	37,842
(4) Actual Wages paid to the group			41,100

Calculation of Variances

Total labor cost variance	(1) – (4)	2,700 (A)
Wages rate variance	(3) – (4)	3,258 (A)
Labor efficiency variance	(1) – (2)	2,400 (A)
Labor mix variance	(2) – (3)	2,958 (F)

Illustration 9

The following was the composition of a gang of workers in a factory during a particular month, in one of the production departments. The standard composition of workers and wage rate per hour were as below:

Skilled : Two workers at a standard rate of Rs. 20 per hour each.

Semi-skilled : Four workers at a standard rate of Rs. 12 per hour each.

Unskilled : Four workers at a standard rate of Rs. 8 per hour each.

The standard output of the gang was four units per hour, of the product.

During the month in question, however, the actual composition of the gang and hourly rates paid were as under:

Nature of worker	*No. of workers*	*Wage rate paid per worker per hour engaged*
Skilled	2	Rs. 20
Semi-skilled	3	Rs. 14
Unskilled	5	Rs. 10

The gang was engaged for 200 hours during the month, which included 12 hours when no production was possible, due to machine breakdown, 810 units of the product were recorded as output of the gang during the month.

You are required: *(a)* to compute the standard unit labor cost of the product; *(b)* to compute the total variance in labor cost during the month; and *(c)* analyze the variance in (b) above into sub-variances and reconcile.

(I.C.W.A., Inter, Dec., 1996)

Solution

Basic Data

Actual production during the month	810 units
Actual Labor hours engaged	200 hours

Computation of Labor Cost

Type of worker	*No. of workers*	*Actual hours worked*	*Actual Wages for actual hours*		*Std. wages for actual hours*	
			Per hr. (Rs.)	*Total (Rs.)*	*Per hr. (Rs.)*	*Total (Rs.)*
Skilled	2	200	20	8,000	20	8,000
Semi-skilled	3	200	14	8,400	12	7,200
Unskilled	5	200	10	10,000	8	8,000
Total				26,400		23,200

Type of worker	*No. of workers*	*Rate P.H.*	*Std. wages for actual hours in Std. gang*		*Std. wages for actual hours worked (200-12)*	
			Hours	*Amount (Rs.)*	*Hours*	*Amount (Rs.)*
Skilled	2	20	200	8,000	188	7,520
Semi-skilled	4	12	200	9,600	188	9,024
Unskilled	4	8	200	6,400	188	6,016
Total				24,000		22,560

		(Rs.)
Std. wages for actual output	810 × (Rs. 120/4)	24,300
Actual wages for actual output	810 × (Rs. 26,400/810)	26,400
Total Labor Cost Variance		2,100 (A)

Computation of Labor Cost per unit

		(Rs.)
Labor Cost		
Skilled	(2 workers @ Rs. 20)	40
Semi-skilled	(4 workers @ Rs. 12)	48
Unskilled	(4 workers @ Rs. 8)	32
Total Labor Cost per hour		120
Std. output per gang hour		4 units
Std. Labor Cost per unit	(Rs. 120/4)	Rs. 30

Computation of Labor Variances:

(1) Total Labor Cost Variance

Actual wages for actual hours – Std. wages for actual output

= Rs. 26,400 – Rs. 24,300 = Rs. 2,100 (A)

(2) Labor Rate Variance

Actual wages for actual hours – Std. wages for actual hours

= Rs. 26,400 – Rs. 23,200 = Rs. 3,200 (A)

(3) Labor Efficiency Variance

Actual hours at Std. rate – Std. wages for actual output

= Rs. 23,200 – Rs. 24,300 = Rs. 1,100 (F)

(4) Labor Gang Variance

Std. wages for actual hours – Std. wages for actual hours in Std. gang

Rs. 23,200 – Rs. 24,000 = Rs. 800 (F)

(5) Labor Idle Time Variance

Std. wages for actual hours in Std. gang – Std. wages for actual hours

= Rs. 24,000 – Rs. 22,560 = Rs. 1,440 (A)

(6) Labor Yield Variance

Std. wages for actual hours – Std. wages for actual output

= Rs. 22,560 – Rs. 24,300 = Rs. 1,740 (F)

Summary of Labor Variances

Rate Variance		3,200 (A)
Efficiency Variance		
(i) Gang Variance	800 (F)	
(ii) Idle Time Variance	1,440 (A)	
(iii) Yield Variance	1,740 (F)	1,100 (F)
Total Labor Cost Variance		2,100 (A)

Reconciliation Statement

		(Rs.)
Std. Labor Cost or actual output		24,300
Add: Adverse Cost Variances		
Labor Rate Variance	3,200	
Labor Idle Time Variance	1,440	4,640
		28,940
Less: Favorable Cost Variances		
Labor Gang Variance	800	
Labor Yield Variance	1,740	2,540
Actual Labor Cost		26,400

SUMMARY

Labor Variances analyze the variances in labor, labor being the second element of cost. Labor variances can be analyzed as Labor Cost Variance, Labor Rate/Price Variance and Labor Efficiency/Time/Usage Variance. Again, Labor Efficiency Variance can be split into Labor Mix Variance, Labor Idle Time Variance, Labor Yield Variance or Labor Sub Usage/Labor Revised Efficiency Variance. The analysis of variances in labor is similar to that of Material Variances. Labor Variances arise due to the difference in the standards specified and the actual thus, calling for an investigation and analysis of variances.

Glossary

- **Labor Variance:** The difference between the standards specified for direct labor and the actual
- **Labor Cost Variance:** the difference between the standard direct labor cost specified for the activity achieved and the actual direct labor cost incurred
- **Labor Rate Variance:** that portion of the Labor Cost Variance, which is due to the difference between the standard rate specified and the actual rate paid
- **Labor Efficiency Variance:** that portion of Labor Cost Variance, which is due to the difference between labor hours specified and the actual labor hours expended
- **Labor Idle Time Variance:** that portion of Labor Efficiency Variance, which is due to abnormal idle time such as time lost due to machine breakdown, power failure, strikes etc
- **Labor Mix Variance:** shows to the management as to how much of the Labor Cost Variance is due to the change in the composition of labor force
- **Labor Sub Efficiency Variance:** arises due to the factors other than those which give rise to Idle Time Variance and Labor Mix Variance
- **Labor Yield Variance:** that portion of Labor Efficiency Variance, which is due to the difference between actual output of workers and standard output of workers specified

Questions

(1) Discuss briefly the causes for various Labor Variances.

(2) How are the Labor Variances calculated?

PROBLEMS

(1) From the following information, calculate labor cost variances.

Gross direct wages	Rs. 3,000
Standard hours produced	1,600
Standard rate per hour	Rs. 1.50
Actual hours paid	1,500

[**Ans.:** Labor Cost Variance Rs. 600 (a); Labor Price Variance Rs. 750 (a) and Labor Efficiency Variance Rs. 150 (f)]

(2) Calculate Labor Cost Variance, Labor Price Variance and Labor Efficiency Variance

Standard hours	40 @ Rs. 3 per hour
Actual hours	50 @ Rs. 4 per hour

[**Ans.:** Labor Cost Variance Rs. 80 (A); Labor Price Variance Rs. 50 (A) and Labor Efficiency Variance Rs. 30 (A)]

(3) Calculate all labor variances.

	Standard			*Actual*		
	Hours	*Rate Rs.*	*Amount Rs.*	*Hours*	*Rate Rs.*	*Amount Rs.*
(a) Skilled	6,000	2	12,000	5,800	2.5	14,500
(b) Semi	8,000	1	8,000	8,500	1.0	8,500
(c) Unskilled	12,000	0.50	6,000	12,500	0.6	7,500
	26,000		26,000	26,800		30,500

[**Ans.:** Labor Cost Variance Rs. 4,500 (A); Labor Price Variance Rs. 4,150 (A); Labor Efficiency Variance Rs. 350 (A); Labor Mix Variance Rs. 450 (F) and Labor Yield Variance Rs. 800(a)]

(4) Find out different labor variances.

	Standard	*Actual*
Output	1,000 units	1,200 units
Rate of payment	Rs. 6 per unit	wages paid with bonus Rs. 8,000
Time taken	50 hours	40 hours

[**Ans.:** Labor Cost Variance Rs. 800 (A); Labor Price Variance Rs. 3,200 (A) and Labor Efficiency Variance Rs. 2,400 (F)]

(5) A gang of workers usually consists of 10 men, 5 women, and 5 boys in a factory. They are paid a standard hourly rate of Rs.1.25, Re.0.80 and Re. 0.70 respectively. In a normal working week of 40 hours the gang is expected to produce 1000 units of output.

In a certain week, the gang consisted of 13 men, 4 women and 3 boys. Actual wages paid at the rates of Rs.1.20, Re.0.85 and Re. 0.65 respectively. Two hours were lost due to abnormal idle time and 960 units of output were produced. Calculate various labor variances

(C.S., Inter. June 1993)

[**Ans.:**
(1) Labor cost variance = Rs. 70 (A)
(2) Labor rate variance = Rs. 24 (F)
(3) Labor efficiency variance = Rs. 94 (A)
(4) Labor mix variance = Rs. 62 (A)
(5) Labor idle time variance = Rs. 40 (A)
(6) Labor Yield Variance = Rs. 8 (F)]

❑❑❑

23

OVERHEAD VARIANCES

Objectives

The objectives of the study are to:

- Ascertain the causes for Overhead Variances and
- Learn the computation and analysis of Overhead Variances

INTRODUCTION

The last cost variance to be studied in the Variance Analysis is the Overhead Variance. Overhead is the aggregate of indirect material cost, indirect labor cost and indirect expenses incurred. Two way and three way classification of overhead variance computation is the matter of this lesson.

OVERHEAD COST VARIANCE

It is the difference between the Standard Overhead Cost allowed for the actual output achieved and the Actual Overhead Cost incurred. The Overhead Cost Variance can be classified as follows.

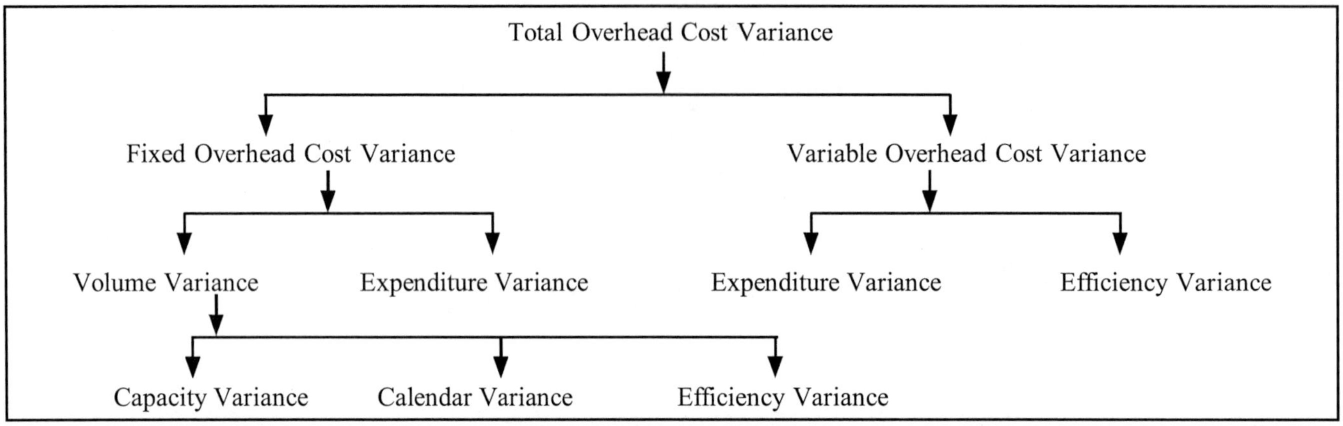

The analysis of Overhead Variance by expenditure and volume is called as Two Way Variance Analysis. When the Volume Variance is further analyzed to know the reasons for the change in output, it is called as Three Way Variance Analysis as it is classified into three variances, i.e., Capacity Variance, Calendar Variance and Efficiency Variance.

Under Standard Costing, overhead rates are pre determined per hour or per unit of output. Standard overheads are calculated by multiplying the actual hours or actual units produced with the standard overhead rates.

Overhead Variance can be classified into Variable Overhead and Fixed Overhead Variance. First, Variable Overhead Variance is dealt with.

Variable Overhead Variance

It is the difference between the Standard Variable Overhead Cost allowed for the actual output achieved and the Actual Variable Overhead Cost. This is also known as Expenses or Spending or Cost Variance.

Variable Overhead Variance:

(Standard Variable Overhead Rate per unit – Actual Variable Overhead Rate per unit) Actual Output

OR

(Standard hours for actual output × Standard Variable Overhead Rate) - Actual Overhead

Variable Overhead Expenditure/Price/Budget Variance

It is that portion of the Overhead Variance, which is due to the difference between the standard price of the service specified and the actual price paid.

(Standard Rate per hour – Actual Rate per hour) Actual hours worked

Variable Overhead Efficiency Variance

It is that portion of the Overhead Variance, which is due to the difference between the budgeted efficiency of production and the actual efficiency attained.

(Standard Time for actual output – Actual Time) Standard Rate per hour

Verification: Variable Overhead Variance = Variable Overhead Expenditure Variance + Variable Overhead Efficiency Variance

Illustration 1

Standard hours allowed per unit	2 hours
Standard cost allowed per direct labor hour	Rs. 4
Actual production (units)	100
Actual direct labor hours	175
Actual Overheads incurred	Rs. 550

Determine Variable Overhead Variances.

Solution

(1) Variable Overhead Variance:

(Standard Variable Overhead Rate per unit – Actual Variable Overhead Rate per unit) Actual Output

OR

(Standard hours for actual output × Standard Variable Overhead Rate) – Actual Overhead

(100 × 8) – 550 = Rs. 250 (f)

Standard Variable Overhead per unit:

Standard time for 1 unit = 2 hours

Standard cost per hour = Rs. 4

Standard Cost per unit = Rs. 4 × 2 hours per unit = Rs. 8

(2) Variable Overhead Efficiency Variance:

(Standard Time for actual output – Actual Time) Standard Rate per hour

(2 × 100) – 175) 4 = Rs. 100 (f)

(3) Variable Overhead Expenditure Variance:

(Standard Rate per hour – Actual Rate per hour) Actual hours worked

(4 – 550/175) 175 = Rs. 150 (f)

Verification: Variable Overhead Variance = Variable Overhead Efficiency Variance + Variable Overhead Expenditure Variance

250 (f) = 100 (f) + 150 (f)

Illustration 2

From the following data, compute variable overhead variances.

	Standard	*Actual*
Number of units	15,000	8,000
Capacity (hours)	30,000	17,000
Variable Overheads (Rs)	30,000	15,000

Solution

Standard Variable Overhead per unit	30,000/15,000 = Rs. 2
Standard Variable Overhead per hour	30,000/30,000 = Re. 1
Actual Variable Overhead per unit	15,000/8,000 = Rs. 1.875
Actual Variable Overhead per hour	15,000/17,000 = Re. 0.882

(1) Variable Overhead Cost Variance:

(2 – 15,000/8,000) 8,000 = Rs. 1,000 (f)

(2) Variable Overhead Expenditure Variance:

(1 – 15,000 /17,000) 17,000 = Rs. 2,000 (f)

(3) Variable Overhead Efficiency Variance:

(16,000 – 17,000) 1 = Rs. 1,000 (a)

Standard time for actual output = 8,000 × 30,000 / 15,000 = 16,000 hours

Verification: Variable Overhead Variance = Variable Overhead Expenditure Variance + Variable Overhead Efficiency Variance

1,000(f) = 2,000 (f) + 1,000 (a)

Fixed Overhead Cost Variance

It is that portion of the total Overhead Cost Variance, which is due to the difference between the Standard Cost of Fixed Overhead allowed for the actual output achieved and the Actual Fixed Overhead incurred.

(Actual Output × Standard Fixed Overhead Rate per unit) – Actual Fixed Overhead

OR

(Standard Hours for actual output × Standard Rate per hour) – Actual Fixed Overhead

Actual Fixed Overhead = Actual hours × Actual fixed overhead rate per hour

Expenditure or Budget or Spending Variance

It is that portion of the Fixed Overhead Variance, which is due to the difference between the Budgeted Fixed Overhead and the Actual Fixed Overhead incurred during a period. It shows efficiency in spending.

The variance may arise due to a rise in general price level, changes in production methods or ineffective control.

Expenditure Variance = Budgeted Fixed Overhead for actual hours – Actual Fixed Overhead

VOLUME VARIANCE

It is due to the difference between the Standard Cost of Fixed Overhead allowed for actual output and the Budgeted Fixed Overhead for the period during which the actual output has been achieved. It shows over or under absorption of overhead.

If the actual output is more than the budgeted output, there is over recovery of fixed overhead and volume variance is favorable and *vice versa*.

The variance may be due to poor efficiency of workers or machinery, lack of orders, shortage of power, ineffective supervision, more or less working days, excess plant capacity, labor problems, defective materials, inefficient planning etc.

Volume Variance:

Standard Rate per unit (Actual Output – Budgeted Output)

OR

Standard Rate per hour (Standard Hours for actual output – Budgeted Hours)

Verification: Fixed Overhead Cost Variance = Expenditure Variance + Volume Variance

CAPACITY VARIANCE

It is that portion of the Volume Variance, which is due to working at higher or lower capacity than the standard capacity. It indicates under or over utilization of plant and equipment and arises due to idle time, strikes and lock- outs, breakdown of the machinery, shortage of material and labor, power failure, absenteeism, overtime, changes in number of shifts etc.

Capacity Variance:

Standard Rate per unit (Revised Budgeted Units – Budgeted Units)

OR

Standard Rate per hour (Revised Budgeted Hours – Budgeted Hours)

CALENDAR VARIANCE

It is that portion of the Volume Variance, which is due to the difference between the actual number of working days and the number of working days in the budget period. The variance is favorable if actual number of working days is more than the budgeted days and *vice versa*.

It is the increase or decrease in production due to more or less working days at the rate of budgeted capacity multiplied with the standard rate per unit.

Calendar Variance:

(Standard hours for actual number of days × Standard Overhead Rate) – Standard Overhead for Standard Period

EFFICIENCY VARIANCE

It is that portion of the Volume Variance, which is due to the difference between the budgeted efficiency of production and the actual efficiency achieved.

Efficiency Variance:

(Actual Production – Standard Production for actual time) Standard Rate per unit

OR

(Standard Hours produced – Actual Hours) Standard Rate per hour

Note: Standard Production /Standard Hours mean budgeted production or hours adjusted to increase or decrease in production due to capacity or calendar variances.

Illustration 3

Following information is available form the records of a factory.

	Budget	*Actual*
Fixed Overhead for June (Rs.)	10,000	12,000
Production in June (units)	2,000	2,100
Standard time per unit (hours)	10	
Actual hours worked in June		22,000

Compute necessary Fixed Overhead Variances.

Solution

Standard Fixed Overhead Rate per unit = Budgeted Overhead/Budgeted Output

10,000 / 2,000 = Rs. 5 per unit

(1) Fixed Overhead Cost Variance

(Actual Output × Standard Fixed Overhead Rate per unit) – Actual Fixed Overhead

OR

(Standard Hours for actual output × Standard Rate per hour) – Actual Fixed Overhead

(2,100 × 5) – 12,000 = Rs. 1,500 (a)

(2) Fixed Overhead Expenditure Variance

Budgeted Fixed Overhead for actual hours – Actual Fixed Overhead

10,000 – 12,000 = Rs. 2,000 (a)

(3) Fixed Overhead Volume Variance

Standard Rate per unit (Actual Output – Budgeted Output)

OR

Standard Rate per hour (Standard Hours for actual output – Budgeted Hours)

5 (2,100 – 2,000) = Rs. 500 (f)

Verification: Fixed Overhead Cost Variance = Expenditure Variance + Volume Variance

1,500 (a) = 2,000 (a) + 500 (f)

(4) Fixed Overhead Capacity Variance

Standard Rate per unit (Revised Budgeted Units – Budgeted Units)

OR

Standard Rate per hour (Revised Budgeted Hours – Budgeted Hours)

5 (2,200 – 2,000) = Rs. 1,000 (f)

Standard Time for Standard Output = 2000 × 10 = 20,000 hours

Standard Rate per unit of output = 10,000/2,000 = Rs. 5

Revised Budgeted Units = Actual Time × Standard Output/Standard Time

22,000 × 2,000 / 20,000 = 2,200 units

(5) Fixed Overhead Efficiency Variance

(Actual Production – Standard Production for actual time) Standard Rate per unit

OR

(Standard Hours produced – Actual Hours) Standard Rate per hour

(2,100 – 2,200) 5 = Rs. 500 (a)

Verification: Fixed Overhead Volume Variance = Fixed Overhead Capacity Variance + Fixed Overhead Efficiency Variance

500 (f) = 1,000 (f) + 500 (a)

Illustration 4

The following information was obtained from the records of a manufacturing unit using Standard Costing System.

	Standard	*Actual*
Production (units)	4,000	3,800
Working days	25	28
Fixed Overheads (Rs)	44,000	40,000

You are required to calculate the necessary Overhead Variances.

Solution

Standard Fixed Overhead Rate per unit = Budgeted Overhead/Budgeted Output

44,000 / 4,000 = Rs. 11 per unit

(1) Fixed Overhead Cost Variance

(Actual Output × Standard Fixed Overhead Rate per unit) – Actual Fixed Overhead

OR

(Standard Hours for actual output × Standard Rate per hour) – Actual Fixed Overhead

(3,800 × 11) – 40,000 = Rs. 1,800 (f)

(2) Fixed Overhead Expenditure Variance

Budgeted Fixed Overhead for actual hours – Actual Fixed Overhead

44,000 – 40,000 = Rs. 4,000 (f)

(3) Fixed Overhead Volume Variance

Standard Rate per unit (Actual Output – Budgeted Output)

OR

Standard Rate per hour (Standard Hours for actual output – Budgeted Hours)

11 (3,800 – 4,000) = Rs. 2,200 (a)

Verification: Fixed Overhead Cost Variance = Expenditure Variance + Volume Variance

1,800 (f) = 4,000 (f) + 2,200 (a)

(4) Calendar Variance

Standard fixed overheads for actual number of days – Budgeted Fixed Overhead

49,280 – 44,000 = Rs. 5,280 (f)

Standard Fixed Overheads for actual number of days = 28 × 44,000/25 = Rs. 49,280

(5) Fixed Overhead Efficiency Variance

(Actual Production – Standard Production for actual time) Standard Rate per unit

OR

(Standard Hours produced – Actual Hours) Standard Rate per hour

(3,800– 4,480) 11 = Rs. 7,480 (a)

Standard Production for actual time = 28 × 4000/25 = 4,480 units

Verification: Fixed Overhead Volume Variance = Fixed Overhead Calendar Variance + Fixed Overhead Efficiency Variance

2,200 (a) = 5,280 (f) + 7,480 (a)

Illustration 5

(a) The Budget for a period indicates:

Works Overhead Fixed	Rs.	50,000
Works Overhead Variable	Rs.	1,50,000
Normal Activity		100%

During the period, the actual activity was only 70% of the normal load for a total expenditure of Rs. 1,50,000. What are the budget and volume variances?

(b) Determine the budget and capacity variances from the following data:

Estimated Factory Overhead	Rs.	25,000
Estimated Direct Labour Hours		5,000
Actual Overhead Expenses	Rs.	26,500
Applied Overhead Expenses	Rs.	22,500

(I.C.W.A., Inter, Dec., 1990)

Solution

(a) **(1) Budgeted Works Overhead for Actual Quantity**

	(Rs.)
Fixed	50,000
Variable (1,50,000 × 70%)	1,05,000
Total	1,55,000

(1) Actual Works Overhead for actual activity = Rs. 1,50,000

(2) Recovered Works Overhead for actual activity

	(Rs.)
Fixed (50,000 × 70%)	35,000
Variable	1,05,000
Total	1,40,000

Overhead Budget Variance

Budgeted Overheads – Actual Overheads

= 1,55,000 – 1,50,000 = Rs. 5,000 (F)

Overhead Volume Variance

Recovered Overheads – Budgeted Overheads

= 1,40,000 – 1,55,000 = Rs. 15,000 (A)

(b) (1) **Overhead Budget Variance**

Budgeted Overheads – Actual Overheads

= 25,000 – 26,500 = Rs. 1,500 (A)

(2) **Overhead Capacity Variance**

Standard Overhead rate per hour (Standard Hours for actual production – Budgeted hours)

= 5 (4,500 – 5,000) = Rs. 2,500 (A)

Standard Overhead rate per hour = 25,000/5,000 = Rs. 5

Standard Hours for actual production = $\frac{22,500}{25,000}$ 5 = 4,500

Illustration 6

In Department A of a plant, the following data are submitted for the week ended 31st March, 2003:

Standard Output for 40 hours per week	1,400 units
Budgeted Fixed Overheads	Rs. 1,400
Actual Output	1,200 units
Actual hours worked	32 hours
Actual fixed Overheads	1,500

You are required to prepare a Statement of Variances

(I.C.W.A., Inter, June, 1993)

Solution

Calculation of Fixed Overhead Variances

(1) **Fixed Overhead Cost Variance**

Recovered Fixed Overheads – Actual Fixed Overheads

= (Re. 1 × 1,200 units) – Rs. 1,500 = Rs. 300 (A)

(2) **Fixed Overhead Expenditure Variance**

Budgeted Fixed Overheads – Actual Fixed Overheads

= Rs. 1,400 – Rs. 1,500 = Rs. 100 (A)

(3) **Fixed Overhead Volume Variance**

Recovered Fixed Overheads – Actual Fixed Overheads

= Rs. 1,200 – Rs. 1,400 = Rs. 200 (A)

Fixed Overhead Volume Variance can be further analyzed into:

(a) Fixed overhead Efficiency Variance

Standard Overhead rate per hour (Std. Hrs. for actual output – Actual hrs.)

= (1,400 / 40) × (40/1,400 × 1,200) – (32)
= 35 × (480/14 –32) = 35 × (480 – 448)/14 = 35 × 32/14 = Rs. 80 (F)

(b) Fixed Overhead Capacity Variance
Standard Overhead rate per hour (Actual hours – Budgeted hours)
= 35(32 – 40) = Rs. 280 (A)

Summary of Fixed Overhead Variances

Expenditure Variance		100 (A)
Volume Variance		
(a) Efficiency Variance	80 (F)	
(b) Capacity Variance	280 (A)	200 (A)
Fixed Overhead Cost Variance		300 (A)

Illustration 7

The following data has been collected from the cost records of a unit for computing the various fixed overhead variances for a period:

Number of budgeted working days	25
Budgeted man-hours per day	6,000
Output (budgeted) per man-hour (in units)	1
Fixed overhead cost as budgeted	1,50,000
Actual number of working days	27
Actual man-hours per day	6,300
Actual output per man-hour (in units)	0.9
Actual fixed overhead incurred	1,56,000

Calculate fixed overhead variances – *(a)* Expenditure Variance, *(b)* Calendar Variance, *(c)* Capacity Variance, *(d)* Efficiency Variance, *(e)* Volume Variance, *(f)* Fixed Cost Variance.

(I.C.W.A., Inter, Dec., 1995)

Solution

Computation of Fixed Overhead Variances

***(a)* Fixed Overhead Expenditure Variance**
Actual Fixed Overhead – Budgeted Fixed Overhead
= Rs. 1,56,000 – Rs. 1,50,000 = Rs. 6,000 (A)

***(b)* Fixed Overhead Calendar Variance**
Budgeted Fixed Overhead – [(Budgeted Fixed Overhead/ Budgeted working days) X Actual working days]
= Rs. 1,50,000 – [(Rs. 1,50,000/25 days) × 27 days]
= Rs. 1,50,000 – Rs. 1,62,000 = Rs. 12,000 (F)

***(c)* Fixed Overhead Capacity Variance**
[{Budgeted Fixed Overhead/Budgeted working days} × Actual Working days]
– Actual Fixed Overhead for actual production
= Rs. 1,62,000 – (6,300 × 27 × Re. 1)
= Rs. 1,62,000 – Rs. 1,70,100 = Rs. 8,100 (F)

***(d)* Fixed Overhead Efficiency Variance**
(Actual hours worked × Standard Fixed Overhead rate per hour) – Standard Fixed Overhead for Actual production
= (6,300 × 27 × .9 × Re.1) – (6,300 × 27 × 1 × Re. 1)
Rs. 1,53,090 – Rs. 1,70,100 = Rs. 17,010 (A)

(e) **Fixed Overhead Volume Variance**

Calendar + Capacity + Efficiency

= Rs. 12,000 (F) + 8,100 (F) + Rs. 17,010 (A) = Rs. 3,090 (F)

(f) **Total Fixed Cost Variance**

Expenditure Variance + Volume Variance

= Rs. 6,000 (A) + Rs. 3,090 (F) = Rs. 2,910 (A)

Working Notes:

Std. Fixed Overhead rate = Rs. 1,50,000/(6,000 × 25 hrs.) = Re. 1

Illustration 8

The following data is given:

	Budget	*Actuals*
Production (in units)	400	360
Man hours to produce above	8,000	7,000
Variable overheads (in rupees)	10,000	9,150

The standard time to produce one unit of the product is 20 hours. Calculate variable overhead variances and give necessary journal entries to record the transactions.

(C.A. Inter, Nov., 1997)

Solution

(1) **Standard variable overhead per unit**

Rs. 10,000/400 units = Rs. 25

(2) **Standard variable overhead per hour**

Rs. 10,000/8,000 hours = Rs. 1.25

(3) **Standard variable overhead (for actual output or variable overhead recovered)**

= Actual output × Standard variable overhead per unit

= 360 units × Rs. 25 = Rs. 9,000

(4) **Budgeted variable overhead (based on actual hours worked)**

= Actual hours worked X Std. Variable overhead per hour

= 7,000 hrs × Rs. 1.25 = Rs. 8,750

(5) **Standard hours for actual output**

= Actual output × Standard hours per unit

= 360 units × 20 hours = 7,200 hours

Variances:

(i) **Variable Overhead Variance**

= Standard variable overhead – Actual variable overhead

= Rs. 9,000 – Rs. 9,150 = Rs. 150 (A)

(ii) **Variable Overhead Budget (expenditure) Variance**

= Budgeted variable overhead – Actual variable overhead

= Rs. 8,750 – Rs. 9,150 = Rs. 400 (A)

(iii) **Variable Overhead Efficiency Variance**

= Standard variable overhead per hour (Standard Hours for actual output – Actual hours)

= Rs. 1.25 (7,200 hours – 7,000 hours) = Rs. 250 (F)

Summary of Variable Overhead Variances

		(Rs.)
Variable Overhead Budget (expenditure) Variance	400 (A)	
Variable Overhead Efficiency Variance		250 (F)
Variable Overhead Variance		150 (A)

Journal Entries:

			Rs.	Rs.
(1)	Variable Overhead A/c	Dr.	8,750	
	Variable Overhead Expenditure Variance A/c	Dr.	400	
	To Creditors for Expenses A/c			9,150
(2)	Work-in-Progress A/c	Dr.	9,000	
	To Variable Overhead A/c			8,750
	To Variable Overhead Efficiency Variance A/c			250

Illustration 9

Premier industries has a small factory where 52 workers are employed on an average for 25 days a month and they work 8 hours per day. The normal down time is 20%. The firm has introduced standard costing for cost control. Its monthly budget for November, 2003 shows that the budgeted variable and fixed overheads for the month are Rs. 99,840 and Rs. 2,08,000 respectively.

The firm reports the following details of actual performance for November, 2003, after the end of the month:

Actual hours worked	:	8,100 hrs
Actual Production expressed in standard hours	:	8,800
Actual variable overheads	:	Rs. 1,02,000
Actual fixed overheads	:	Rs. 2,00,000

You are required to calculate: *(a)* Variable overhead expenditure variance; *(b)* Variable overhead efficiency variance; *(c)* Fixed overhead budget variance; *(d)* Fixed overhead capacity variance; *(e)* Fixed overhead efficiency variance; *(f)* Capacity ratio; *(g)* Efficiency ratio; *(h)* Activity ratio.

(I.C.W.A., Inter, Dec., 1998)

Solution

Budgeted hours for November 2003	= (52 × 25 × 8) × 80%		= 8320
Budgeted Variable Overhead	= Rs. 99,840,	∴ Rate per hour	= Rs. 12
Budgeted Fixed Overhead	= Rs. 2,08,000,	∴ Rate per hour	= Rs. 25

The variances and ratios are worked out as follows:

(1) Variable Overhead Expenditure Variance

= Budgeted Variable O.H. for hours worked – Actual variable overhead

= 8,100 × Rs. 12 – 1,02,000 = Rs. 4,800 (A)

(2) Variable Overhead Efficiency Variable

= (Production in Standard hours – Actual hours) × Standard Rate

= (8,800 – 8,100) × Rs. 12 = Rs. 8,400 (F)

(3) Fixed Overhead Budget Variance

= Budgeted Fixed Overheads – Actual Fixed Overhead

= Rs. 2,08,000 – Rs. 2,00,000 = Rs. 8,000 (F)

(4) Fixed Overhead Capacity Variance

= (Capacity available – Capacity used) × Standard Rate

= (8,320 – 8,100) × Rs. 25 = Rs. 5,500 (A)

(5) Fixed Overhead Efficiency Variance

= (Production in Standard hours – Actual hours) × Standard Rate

= (8,800 – 8,100) × Rs. 25 = Rs. 17,500 (F)

(6) Capacity Ratio

= Actual hours worked / Budgeted hours = 8,100/8,320 = Rs. 97.4%

(7) Efficiency Ratio

= Production Standard hours/Actual hours worked = 8,800/8,100 = Rs. 108.6%

(8) Activity Ratio

= Production in Standard hours/Budgeted Standard hours = 8,800/8,320 = Rs. 105.8%

SUMMARY

The last cost variance to be studied in the Variance Analysis is the Overhead Variance. It is the aggregate of indirect material cost, indirect labor cost and indirect expenses incurred.

Under Standard Costing, overhead rates are pre determined per hour or per unit of output. Standard overheads are calculated by multiplying the actual hours or actual units produced with the standard overhead rates.

Overheads Variance can be classified into Variable Overhead and Fixed Overhead Variance. Variable Overhead Variance is further analyzed into Expenditure Variance and Efficiency Variance. Fixed Overhead Cost Variance is sub divided into Volume Variance and Expenditure Variance. Again, Expenditure Variance is classified into Capacity Variance, Calendar Variance and Efficiency Variance.

The analysis of Overhead Variance by Expenditure and Volume is called as Two Way Variance Analysis. When the Volume Variance is further analyzed to know the reasons for the change in output, it is called as Three Way Variance Analysis as it is classified into three variances i.e. Capacity Variance, Calendar Variance and Efficiency Variance.

The analysis of Variances is done for the purpose of cost control.

Glossary

- **Overhead Cost Variance:** the difference between the Standard Overhead Cost allowed for the actual output achieved and the Actual Overhead Cost incurred.
- **Variable Overhead Variance:** the difference between the Standard Variable Overhead Cost allowed for the actual output achieved and the Actual Variable Overhead Cost. This is also known as Expenses or Spending or Cost Variance.
- **Variable Overhead Expenditure/Price/Budget Variance:** that portion of the Overhead Variance, which is due to the difference between the standard price of the service specified and the actual price paid.
- **Variable Overhead Efficiency Variance:** that portion of the Overhead Variance, which is due to the difference between the budgeted efficiency of production and actual efficiency attained.
- **Fixed Overhead Variance:** that portion of the total Overhead Cost Variance, which is due to the difference between the Standard Cost of Fixed Overhead allowed for the actual output achieved and the Actual Fixed Overhead incurred.
- **Expenditure or Budget or Spending Variance:** that portion of Fixed Overhead Variance, which is due to the difference between the Budgeted Fixed Overhead and the Actual Fixed Overhead incurred during a period. It shows efficiency in spending.
- **Volume Variance:** the difference between the Standard Cost of Fixed Overhead allowed for actual output and the Budgeted Fixed Overhead for the period during which the actual output has been achieved. It shows over or under absorption of overhead.
- **Capacity Variance:** that portion of the Volume Variance, which is due to working at higher or lower capacity than the standard capacity.
- **Calendar Variance:** that portion of the Volume Variance, which is due to the difference between the actual number of working days and the number of working days in the budget period.
- **Efficiency Variance:** that portion of the Volume Variance, which is due to the difference between the budgeted efficiency of production and the actual efficiency achieved.

Questions

(1) Explain with suitable examples *(a)* Volume Variance, *(b)* Efficiency Variance and *(c)* Capacity Variance.

(2) What are the differences between two variance and three variances analysis of indirect manufacturing cost? What are the variances computed in each case and how are they calculated?

PROBLEMS

(1) For the month of March, you are given the following figures for a manufacturing firm.

	Standard	*Actual*
Number of units	20,000	10,000
Capacity (hours)	45,000	30,000
Variable Overheads (Rs)	45,000	25,000

Calculate necessary variances.
[**Ans.:** Overhead Cost Variance: Rs. 2,500 (a); Overhead Expenditure Variance: Rs. 5,000 (f) and Overhead Efficiency Variance: Rs. 7,500 (a)]

(2) From the following, calculate Overhead Variance.

	Standard	*Actual*
Production (units)	4,000	3,800
Working days	20	21
Fixed Overhead (Rs.)	40,000	39,000
Variable Overhead (Rs.)	12,000	12,000

(3) A company forecasts its overhead expenditure for a period as under.
Rs. 30,000 for 10,000 hours
Rs. 27,500 for 9,000 hours
Rs. 25,000 for 8,000 hours
The normal volume of activity is 10,000 hours. During a period, 8,750 hours were utilized for a total overhead expenditure of Rs. 28,750 of which fixed overheads totaled Rs. 5,250.
The standard utilization of labor hours is less by 5 per cent. How will you analyze the Overhead Variance?

(4) Calculate appropriate Cost Variances form the following.

Items	*Budget*	*Actual*
Number of working days	20	2
Man hours per day	8,000	8,400
Output per man hour (units)	1.00	0.90
Overhead Cost (Rs.)	1,60,000	1,68,000

(5) Shreya Ltd. has provided the following information.

	Budget	*Actual*
Number of Working days	25	27
Production (units)	25,000	30,000
Fixed Overheads (Rs)	40,000	42,000

Budgeted fixed overhead rate is Re. 1.00 per hour. The actual hours worked are 38,000
Calculate the necessary variances.
[**Ans.:** Efficiency Variance: Rs. 10,000 (f); Capacity Variance: Rs. 5,200 (a); Calendar Variance: Rs. 3,200 (f); Volume Variance: Rs. 8,000 (f) and Expenditure Variance: Rs. 2,000 (a)]

(6) The following information has been obtained from the records of a manufacturing organization using the Standard Costing System:

	Standard	*Actual*
Production (Units)	4,000	3,800
Working Days	20	21
Fixed Overheads (Rs.)	40,000	39,000
Variable Overheads (Rs.)	12,000	12,000

You are required to calculate the following Overhead Variances:

(i) Variable Overhead Variance;

(ii) Fixed Overhead Variance; *(a)* Expenditure variance; *(b)* Volume Variance; *(c)* Efficiency Variance; *(d)* Calendar Variance.

Also prepare a statement reconciling the Standard Fixed Overhead worked out by using the Standard Overhead Rate and the Actual Fixed Overhead.

(I.C.W.A., Inter, Dec., 1991)

[**Ans.:** *(i)* Variable Overhead Variance: Rs. 600 (A), *(ii)* Fixed Overhead Cost Variance : Rs. 1,000 (A); Fixed Overhead Expenditure variance Rs. 1,000 (F); Fixed Overhead Volume variance Rs. 2,000 (A); Fixed Overhead Efficiency Rs. 4,000 (A); Fixed Overhead Calender Variance Rs. 2,000 (F)]

(7) AB Company Limited is having Standard Costing System in operation for quite sometime. The following data relating to the month of April, 2003 is available from the cost records:

	Budgeted	*Actual*
Output (in units)	30,000	32,500
Operating Hours	30,000	33,000
Fixed Overheads (Rs.)	45,000	50,000
Variable Overheads (Rs.)	60,000	68,000
Working days	25	26

You are required to work out the relevant variances (on the basis of output)

(I.C.W.A., Inter, June, 1994)

[**Ans.:** *(i)* Variable Overhead Variance: Rs. 3,000 (A); Variable Overhead Expenditure Variance Rs. 2,000 (A); Variable Overhead Efficiency Variance Rs. 1,000 (A); *(ii)* Fixed Overhead Cost Variance : Rs. 1,250 (A); Fixed Overhead Expenditure Variance Rs. 5,000 (A); Fixed Overhead Volume Variance Rs. 3,750 (F); Fixed Overhead Efficiency Rs. 750 (A); Fixed Overhead Capacity Variance Rs. 4,500 (F); Fixed Overhead Calendar Variance Rs. 1,800 (F); Revised Fixed Overhead Capacity Variance Rs. 2,700 (F)]

(8) A company has a normal capacity of 120 machines, working 8 hours per day of 25 days in a month. The fixed overheads are budgeted at Rs. 1,44,000 per month. The standard time required to manufacture one unit of product is 4 hours.
In April, 2003, the company worked 24 days of 840 machine hours per day and produced 5,305 units of output. The actual fixed overheads were Rs. 1,42,000.
Compute: *(i)* Efficiency variance, *(ii)* Capacity variance, *(iii)* Calendar variance, (iv) Expense variance, *(v)* Volume variance, *(vi)* Total fixed overheads variance.

(C.A., Inter, May, 1998)

[**Ans.:** *(i)* Efficiency Variance Rs. 6,360 (F), *(ii)* Capacity variance Rs. 17,280 (A), *(iii)* Calendar variance Rs. 5,760 (A), *(iv)* Expense Variance Rs. 2,000 (F), *(v)* Volume Variance Rs. 16,680 (A), *(vi)* Total Fixed Overheads Variance Rs. 14,680 (A)]

❑ ❑ ❑

24

Sales Variances and Control Ratios

Objectives

The objectives of the study are to:

- Learn the various Sales Variances
- Understand the need for and the essentials for an effective reporting of the variances
- Know the disposition of variances
- Identify the ratios used for controlling the costs

Introduction

Cost Variances relating to material, labor and overhead, learnt in the earlier lessons though invaluable, to obtain full advantage of Standard Costing System, it is necessary to compute Sales Variances. In this lesson, you will learn about Sales Variances to have a complete analysis of Profit Variance because, profit is the difference between sales and cost. You will also learn the Control Ratios.

Sales Variance

While cost variances are concerned with unit cost and their effect on budgeted profit due to favourable or adverse variances, the sales variances affect the budgeted profit due to changes in sales revenue, i.e., changes caused by either a variation in selling prices or sales quantities. They may be computed to show the effect on sales values or calculated to show the effect on profit. The first method is Turnover or Value Method and the second one is Profit or Margin Method of calculating Sales Variances.

Turnover/Value Method

The various Main and Sub-variances of sales computed under this method are shown in the chart below:

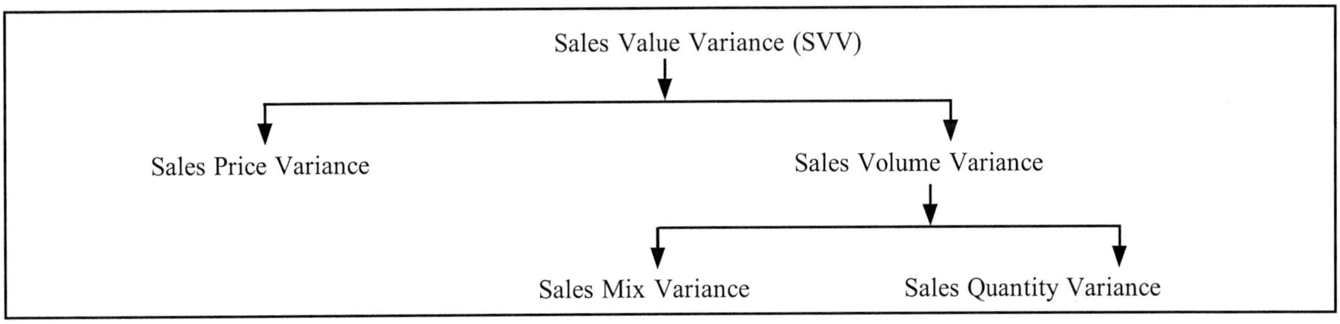

(a) **Sales Value Variance:** It is the difference between the budgeted and the actual value of sales effected during a period.

Sales Value Variance = (Actual Sales – Budgeted Sales)
= (Actual Quantity sold × Actual Sales Price) – (Standard Quantity to be sold × Standard Sales Price)

It is a favourable variance if actual sales are greater than the budgeted sales as this would increase the profit. Sales Value Variance arises due to a difference in the quantity sold or difference in the sales mix.

(b) **Sales Price Variance:** This is the sub-variance of the Sales Value Variance and it is that portion of Sales Value Variance which is due to the difference between the standard price specified and the actual price charged.

Sales Price Variance = (Actual Sales Price – Standard Sales Price) Actual Quantity sold

If actual price is more the standard price, there will be a favourable variance and *vice versa.* This variance may arise due to unforeseen competition, depression, etc.

(c) **Sales Volume Variance:** It is that portion of Sales Value Variance which is due to the difference between the actual quantity of sales and the budgeted quantity of sales.

Sales Volume Variance = (Actual quantity sold – Standard quantity to be sold) Standard Sales Price.

The reasons for the variance may be unforeseen competition, depression, ineffective advertising and sales promotion.

Verification: Sales Value Variance = Sales Price Variance + Sales Volume Variance

(d) **Sales Mix Variance**: It is that portion of Sales Volume Variance, which is due to the difference between the actual composition and standard composition of the sales mix.

Sales Mix Variance = Standard Value of Actual Sales Mix – Standard Value of Revised Mix

OR

(Actual Quantity sold – Revised Standard Quantity) Standard Sales Price

$$\text{Revised Standard Quantity} = \frac{\text{Budgeted Quantity of any one product}}{\text{Total Budgeted Quantity}} \times \text{Total Actual Quantity}$$

This variance arises only when more than one type of product is dealt with. It is a favourable variance if Actual Sales are more than the Revised Sales.

(e) **Sales Quantity Variance:** This is also a sub-variance of Sales Volume Variance, which arises due to the difference between the Revised Standard Quantity and Budgeted Sales Quantity.

Sales Quantity Variance = Revised Standard Sales – Budgeted Sales

OR

(Revised Standard Quantity – Budgeted Quantity) Standard Sales Price

It is a favorable variance if revised standard sales are more than the budgeted sales.

Verification: Sales Volume Variance = Sales Mix Variance + Sales Quantity Variance

Illustration 1

From the following data, calculate Sales Variances.

Product	*Standard*		*Actual*	
	Units	*Unit Price (Rs)*	*Units*	*Unit Price (Rs)*
A	1,500	30	2,000	29
B	1,000	50	700	50
Total:	2,500		2,700	

Solution

(a) Sales Price Variance: (Standard Price-Actual Price) Actual Quantity

A: (30-29) 2,000 = Rs. 2,000 (a)

B: (50-50) 700 = —

Total: Rs. 2,000 (a)

(b) Sales Volume Variance: (Standard Quantity-Actual Quantity) Standard Price

A: (1,500-2,000) 30 = Rs. 1500 (f)

B: (1,000-700) 50 = Rs. 1500 (a)

Total: NIL

(c) Sales Value Variance: (Actual Quantity × Actual Price) – (Standard Quantity × Standard Price)

A: (2,000 × 29) – (1,500 × 30) = Rs. 13,000 (f)

B: (700 × 50) – (1,000 × 50) = Rs. 15,000 (a)

Total Rs. 2,000 (a)

Verification: Sales Value Variance = Sales Price Variance + Sales Volume Variance

2,000 (a) = 2,000 (a) + 0

(d) Sales Mix Variance: Standard Value of Actual Sales Mix – Standard Value of Revised Sales Mix

(Actual Quantity Sold – Revised Standard Quantity) Standard Sales price

$$\text{Revised Standard Quantity} = \frac{\text{Budgeted Quantity of any one product}}{\text{Total Budgeted Quantity}} \times \text{Total Actual Quantity}$$

A: (1,500 × 2,700)/2,500 = 1,620

B: (1,000 × 2,700)/2,500 = 1,080

Sales Mix Variance:

A = (2,000-1,620) 30 = Rs. 11,400 (f)

B = (700 –1,080) 50 = Rs. 19,000 (a)

Total: Rs. 7,600(a)

(e) Sales Quantity Variance = Revised Standard Sales – Budgeted Sales

OR

(Revised Standard Quantity – Budgeted Quantity) Standard Sales Price

A: (1,620 – 1,500) 30 = Rs. 3,600 (f)

B: (1,080 – 1,000) 50 = Rs. 4,000 (f)

Total Rs. 7,600 (f)

Verification: Sales Volume Variance = Sales Mix Variance + Sales Quantity Variance

0 = 7,600 (a) + 7,600 (f)

Illustration 2

From the budgeted and actual sales for May 1999 in respect of three products given below, calculate sales variances.

Product	*Standard*		*Actual*	
	Units	*Unit Price (Rs)*	*Units*	*Unit Price (Rs)*
X	5,000	5	5,000	5.00
Y	4,000	6	6,000	6.25
Z	3,000	7	4,000	6.75
Total:	12,000		15,000	

Solution

(a) Sales Value Variance: (Actual Quantity × Actual Price) – (Standard Quantity × Standard Price)

X: (5,000 × 5.00) – (5,000 × 5) = NIL

Y: (6,000 × 6.25) – (4,000 × 6) = Rs. 13,500 (f)

Z: (4,000 × 6.75) – (3,000 × 7) = Rs. 6,000 (f)

Total: Rs. 19,500 (f)

(b) Sales Price Variance: (Standard Price – Actual Price) Actual Quantity

X: (5 – 5.00) 5,000 = NIL

Y: (6 – 6.25) 6,000 = Rs. 1,500 (f)

Z: (7 – 6.75) 4,000 = Rs. 1,000 (a)

Total: Rs. 500 (f)

(c) Sales Volume Variance: (Standard Quantity – Actual Quantity) Standard Price

X: (5,000 – 5,000) 5 = NIL

Y: (4,000 – 6,000) 6 = Rs. 12,000 (f)

Z: (3,000 – 4,000) 7 = Rs. 7,000 (f)

Total: Rs. 19,000 (f)

Verification: Sales Value Variance = Standard Price Variance + Sales Volume Variance

19,500 (f) = 500 (f) + 19,000 (f)

(d) Sales Mix Variance: Standard Value of Actual Mix Sales – Standard Value of Revised Mix

OR

(Actual Quantity sold – Revised Standard Quantity) Std. Sales price

$$\text{Revised Standard Quantity} = \frac{\text{Budgeted Quantity of any one product}}{\text{Total Budgeted Qty}} \times \text{Total Actual Quantity}$$

X: (5,000 × 15,000)/12,000 = 6,250 Units

Y: (4,000 × 15,000)/12,000 = 5,000 Units

Z: (3,000 × 15,000)/12,000 = 3,750 Units

Sales Mix Variance

X = (5,000 – 6,250) 5 = Rs. 6,250 (a)

Y = (6,000 – 5,000) 6 = Rs. 6,000 (f)

Z = (4,000 – 3,750) 7 = Rs. 1,750 (f)

Total: Rs. 1,500 (f)

(e) Sales Quantity Variance: (Revised Standard Quantity – Standard Quantity) Standard Price

X: (6,250 – 5,000) 5 = Rs. 6,250 (f)

Y; (5,000 – 4,000) 6 = Rs. 6,000 (f)

Z: (3,750 – 3,000) 7 = Rs. 5,250 (f)

Total: Rs. 17,500(f)

Verification: Sales Volume Variance = Sales Mix Variance + Sales Quantity Variance

19,000 (f) = 1,500 (f) + 17,500 (f)

Illustration 3

From the following information about sales, calculate: *(i)* Total Sales Variance, *(ii)* Sales price Variance, *(iii)* Sales Volume Variance, *(iv)* Sales Mix Variance, *(v)* Sales Quantity Variance.

Product	*Standard*		*Actual*	
	Units	*Rate (Rs.)*	*Units*	*Rate (Rs.)*
A	5,000	5	6,000	6
B	4,000	6	5,000	5
C	3,000	7	4,000	8

(a) **Total Sales Variance**

Standard Sales – Actual Sales

= Rs. 70,000 – Rs. 93,000 = Rs. 23,000 (F)

(b) **Sales Price Variance**

Actual Quantity of Sales (Standard Sales Price – Act Sales Price)

A = 6,000 (5 – 6) = 6,000 (F)

B = 5,000 (6 – 5) = 5,000 (A)

C = 4,000 (7 – 8) = 4,000 (F) = Rs. 5,000 (F)

(c) **Sales Volume Variance**

Standard Sales Price (Standard Quantity – Act Quantity)

A = 5 (5,000 – 6,000) = 5,000 (F)

B = 6 (4,000 – 5,000) = 6,000 (F)

C = 7 (3,000 – 4,000) = 7,000 (F) = Rs. 18,000 (F)

(d) **Sales Mix Variance**

Standard Sales Price (Revised Standard Quantity – Act Quantity)

A = 5 (6,250 – 6,000) = 1,250 (A)

B = 6 (5,000 – 5,000) = 0

C = 7 (3,750 – 4,000) = 1,750 (F) = Rs. 500 (F)

(e) **Sales Quantity Variance**

Standard Sales Price (Standard Quantity – Revised Standard Quantity)

A = 5 (5,000 – 6,250) = 6,250 (F)

B = 6 (4,000 – 5,000) = 6,000 (F)

C = 7 (3,000 – 3,750) = 5,250 (F) = Rs. 17,500 (F)

Revised Standard Quantity

A = (5,000/12,000) 15,000 = 6,250

B = (4,000/12,000) 15,000 = 5,000

C = (3,000/12,000) 15,000 = 3,750

MARGIN/PROFIT METHOD

This method of analyzing sales value measures the effect on profit of deviations of actual from the budgeted sales. It assumes all costs are standards.

(a) **Total Sales Margin Variance:** It is the difference between Actual Profit and Budgeted Profit.

Total Sales Margin Variance = Actual Profit – Budgeted Profit

Or

(Actual Quantity sold × Actual Profit per unit) – (Budgeted Quantity × Budgeted Profit)

(b) **Sales Margin Price Variance:** It is that portion of the total Sales Margin Variance which is due to the difference between the Actual Price of quantity of sales effected and the Standard Price of those sales.

Sales Margin Price Variance = (Actual Selling Price per unit – Standard Price per unit) Actual Quantity sold

Or

(Actual Profit per unit –Standard Profit per unit) Actual Quantity Sold

The possible reasons for this type of variance are unexpected competition and a rise in general price level, which are uncontrollable and may be due to poor quality of products for which Production Manager is responsible.

(c) **Sales Margin Volume Variance:** It is that portion of Total Sales Margin Variance which is due to the difference in the Actual Quantity sold and Budgeted Quantity of Sales.

Sales Margin Volume Variance = (Actual Quantity sold – Budgeted Quantity of sales) Standard Profit per unit

Verification: Total Sales Margin Variance = Sales Margin Price Variance + Sales Margin Volume Variance

(d) **Sales Margin Quantity Variance:** It is that portion of Sales Margin Volume Variance due to the difference between the actual and Budgeted Quantity sold of each product.

Sales Margin Quantity Variance = (Standard Proportion for Actual Sales – Budgeted Quantity of Sales)
Standard Profit per unit

Or

Revised Standard Profit –Budgeted Profit

(e) **Sales Margin Mix Variance:** It arises due to the different proportion of Actual Sales Mix.

Sales Margin Mix Variance = (Actual Quantity sold – Standard Proportion for Actual Sales)
Standard Profit per unit

Or

Standard Profit – Revised Standard Profit

Verification: Sales Margin Volume Variance = Sales Margin Quantity Variance + Sales Margin Mix Variance

Illustration 4

Compute the following variances from the data given below: (1) Total Sales Margin Variance; (2) Sales Margin Volume Variance; (3) Sales Margin Price Variance; (4) Sales Margin Quantity (Sub-volume) Variance.

Product	*Budgeted quantity units*	*Actual quantity units*	*Budgeted sale price per unit Rs.*	*Actual sale price per unit Rs.*	*Standard cost per unit Rs.*
X	240	400	50	45	30
Y	160	200	25	20	15

(C.A., Inter, May, 1992)

Solution

Working Notes:

(1) *(a)* **Actual Margin per unit**

(Actual sales price per unit – Standard cost per unit)

Product X	= Rs. 45 – Rs. 30	= Rs. 15
Product Y	= Rs. 20 – Rs. 15	= Rs. 5

(b) **Budged Margin per unit**

Budgeted sales price per unit – Standard cost per unit

Product X	= Rs. 50 – Rs. 30	= Rs. 20
Product Y	= Rs. 25 – Rs. 15	= Rs. 10

(2) *(a)* **Actual Profit**

Actual quantity of product units sold × Actual margin per unit

Product X	= Rs. 400 × Rs. 15	= Rs. 6,000
Product Y	= Rs. 200 × Rs. 5	= Rs. 1,000
		7,000

(b) **Budgeted Profit**

Budgeted quantity of units to be sold × Budgeted margin per unit

Product X	= Rs. 240 × Rs. 20	= Rs. 4,800
Product Y	= Rs. 160 × Rs. 10	= Rs. 1,600
		6,400

(3) ***(a)*** **Budgeted Margin per unit on actual mix**

$$= \frac{(\text{Rs. } 20 \times 400) + (\text{Rs.} 10 \times 200)}{600} = \frac{\text{Rs. } 8,000 + \text{Rs.} 2,000}{600} = \text{Rs. } 16.666$$

(b) **Budgeted Margin per unit on budgeted mix**

$$= \frac{(\text{Rs. } 20 \times 240) + (\text{Rs.} 10 \times 160)}{400} = \frac{\text{Rs. } 4,800 + \text{Rs.} 1,600}{400} = \text{Rs. } 16$$

(1) Total Sales Margin Variance

Actual Profit – Budgeted Profit

= Rs. 7,000 – Rs. 6,400 = Rs. 600 (F)

(2) Sales Margin Volume Variance

Budgeted margin per unit (Actual quantity – Budgeted quantity)

X: Rs. 20 (400 – 240) = Rs. 20 × 160 = Rs. 3,200 (F)

Y: Rs. 10 (200 – 160) = Rs. 10 × 40 = Rs. 400 (F)

= Rs. 3,600 (F)

(3) Sales Margin Price Variance

Actual quantity (Actual margin per unit – Budgeted margin per unit)

X: Rs. 400 (Rs. 15 – Rs. 20) = Rs. 2,000 (A)

Y: Rs. 200 (Rs. 5 – Rs. 10) = Rs. 1,000 (A)

= Rs. 3,000 (A)

(4) Sales Margin Mix Variance

Total actual quantity (Budgeted margin per unit on actual mix – Budgeted margin per unit on budgeted mix)

= 600 (Rs. 16.666 – Rs. 16) = Rs. 400 (F)

(5) Sales Margin Quantity (sub-volume)Variance

Budgeted margin per unit on budgeted mix (Total actual quantity – Total budgeted quantity)

= Rs. 16 (600 – 400) = Rs. 3,200 (F)

Summary of Sales Margin Variances

		Rs.
Price VarianceVolume Variance		3,000 (A)
(i) Mix Variance	400 (F)	
(ii) Quantity Variance	3,200 (F)	3,600 (F)
Sales Margin Variance		600 (F)

Illustration 5

A company uses standard costing system. The sales data for a period are as under:

Product	*Budgeted Sales Units*	*Budgeted Selling Price Per Unit*	*Actual Sales Units*	*Actual Sales Value Rs.*
A	1,280	20	650	12,350
B	3,200	12	3,900	50,700
C	1,920	16	1,950	29,250

The cost data are as under:

	A	*B*	*C*
Standard Cost Per Unit	16	10	13
Actual Cost Per Unit	18	12	13

You are required to calculate the following for the period: *(i)* Gross Margin Total Sales Variance; *(ii)* Gross Margin Sales Volume Variance; *(iii)* Gross Margin Mix Variance; *(iv)* Gross Margin Sales Quantity Variance; *(v)* Sales Price Variance; *(vi)* Total Cost Variance.

(C.A., Inter, May, 1995)

Solution

Working Notes:

Basic data

Particulars	*Products*	*Sales Units*	*Selling price per unit Rs.*	*Cost per unit Rs.*	*Profit per unit Rs.*	*Total Profit Rs.*
(1) Budgeted Data	A	1,280	20	16	4	5,120
	B	3,200	12	10	2	6,400
	C	1,920	16	13	3	5,760
Total		6,400				17,280
(2) Actual Data	A	650	19	16	3	1,950
	B	3,900	13	10	3	11,700
	C	1,950	15	13	2	3,900
Total		6,500				17,550

(1) Budgeted Margin per unit on actual mix

Product	*Units*	*Per unit Rs.*	*Total Rs.*
A	650	4	2,600
B	3,900	2	7,800
C	1,950	3	5,850
Total	6,500		16,250

= Rs. 16,250/6,500 = Rs. 2.50

(2) Budgeted margin per unit on budgeted mix

= Rs. 17,280/6,400 units = Rs. 2.70

Calculation of Variances

(i) **Gross Margin Total Sales Variance**

Actual Profit – Budgeted Profit

= Rs. 17,550 – Rs. 17,280 = Rs. 270 (F)

(ii) **Gross Margin Sales Volume Variance**

= Budgeted margin per unit (Actual Quantity – Budgeted Quantity)

A = Rs. 4 (650 units – 1,280 units) = 2,520 (A)

B = Rs. 2 (3,900 units – 3,200 units) = 1,400 (F)

C = Rs. 3 (1,950 units – 1,920 units) = 90 (F) = Rs. 1,030 (A)

(iii) **Gross Margin Sales Mix Variance**

Total actual quantity (Budgeted margin per unit on actual mix – Budgeted margin per unit on budgeted mix)

= 6,500 units (Rs. 2.50 – Rs. 2.70) = Rs. 1,300 (A)

(iv) **Gross Margin Sales Quantity Variance**

Budgeted Margin per unit on budgeted mix (Total Actual Quantity – Total Budgeted Quantity)

= Rs. 2.70 (6,500 units – 6,400 units) = Rs. 270 (F)

(v) **Sales Price Variance**

Actual sales volume (Actual selling price – Budgeted selling price)

A = 650 units (Rs. 19 – Rs. 20) = 650 (A)

B = 3,900 units (Rs. 13 – Rs. 12) = 3,900 (F)

C = 1,950 units (Rs. 15 – Rs. 16) = 1,950 (A) = Rs.1,300 (F)

(vi) **Total Cost Variance**

Standard Cost for Actual Quantity – Actual Cost

Actual Quantity (Standard Cost Price – Actual Cost Price)

A = 650 units (Rs. 16 – Rs. 18) = 1,300 (A)

B = 3,900 units (Rs. 10 – Rs. 12) = 7,800 (A)

C = 1,950 units (Rs. 13 – Rs. 13) = — = Rs. 9,100 (A)

Summary of Variances

		(Rs.)
Sales Price Variance		1,300 (F)
Sales Volume Variance		
(a) Gross Margin Sales Mix Variance	1,300 (A)	
(b) Gross Margin Sales Quantity Variance	270 (F)	1,030 (A)
Gross Margin Total Sales Variance		270 (F)
Total Cost Variance		9,100 (A)

Illustration 6

The standard cost data of three products X,Y and Z manufactured by a company are given below together with the budgeted sales and unit selling prices for 2002 – 03:

Particulars	*X*	*Y*	*Z*
Budgeted Sales (Units)	25,000	20,000	15,000
Selling price per unit (Rs.)	40	60	80
Cost per unit (Rs.)	28	48	64

In April, 2002 the Cost department of the company gathered the following details for 2002 – 03:

Particulars	*X*	*Y*	*Z*
Budgeted Sales (Units)	20,000	22,000	16,000
Average sales realization per unit (Rs.)	42	56	81
Actual cost per unit (Rs.)	30	50	63

You are required to determine: *(a)* the budgeted and the actual profit for 2002 – 03; *(b)* the variance in profit analyzed into *(i)* Cost variance; *(ii)* Sales price variance; *(iii)* Sales value variance.

(I.C.W.A., Inter, June, 1996)

Solution

Basic Data

Products	*Sales Units*	*Selling price per unit Rs.*	*Cost per unit Rs.*	*Profit per unit Rs.*	*Total Profit Rs.*
Budgeted Data					
X	25,000	40	28	12	3,00,000
Y	20,000	60	48	12	2,40,000
Z	15,000	80	64	16	2,40,000
Total					7,80,000

Products	*Sales Units*	*Selling price per unit Rs.*	*Cost per unit Rs.*	*Profit per unit Rs.*	*Total Profit Rs.*
Actual Data					
X	20,000	42	30	12	2,40,000
Y	22,000	56	50	6	1,32,000
Z	16,000	81	63	18	2,88,000
Total					6,60,000

Profit Variance

= Rs. 7,80,000 – Rs. 6,60,000 = Rs. 1,20,000 (A)

Calculation of Variances

(1) Total Cost Variance

Actual units sold (Standard Cost – Actual Cost)

X = 20,000 (28 – 30) = 40,000 (A)
Y = 22,000 (48 – 50) = 44,000 (A)
Z = 16,000 (64 – 63) = 16,000 (F) = Rs. 68,000 (A)

(2) Selling Price Variance

Actual Units sold (Standard Price – Actual Price)

X = 20,000 (40 – 42) = 40,000 (F)
Y = 22,000 (60 – 56) = 88,000 (A)
Z = 16,000 (80 – 81) = 16,000 (F) = Rs. 32,000 (A)

(3) Sales Volume Variance

Standard Profit (Budgeted Volume – Actual Volume)

X = 12 (25,000 – 20,000) = 60,000 (A)
Y = 12 (20,000 – 22,000) = 24,000 (F)
Z = 16 (15,000 – 16,000) = 16,000 (F) = Rs. 20,000 (A)

Summary of Variances

	(Rs.)
Total Cost Variance	68,000 (A)
Selling Price Variance	32,000 (A)
Sales Volume Variance	20,000 (A)
Profit Variance	1,20,000 (A)

REPORTING OF VARIANCES

Variances are not ends themselves. The variances should be communicated to the top-level management. The management, based on variance, will go for an analysis and investigation. This investigation may culminate in cost reduction.

Reporting of variances can be done in two ways *viz.*, in absolute terms and in relative terms. Due to the difference in size, technology, quantity of sales, etc., variances may not give correct inferences when compared with other Unit or with previous accounting period's variance.

For the purpose of effective cost control, it is essential that, reports exhibiting variances from standards for each element of cost of each department and operation should be quickly and effectively presented to the management for the purpose of corrective action. The management should speedily investigate variances and, where possible, make decisions to prevent recurrence of adverse variances.

For an effective reporting under Standard Costing, it is essential that the following should be fulfilled:

(1) The report should be simple, clear and quick. The variance arising out of each factor should be correctly segregated so that there may be correct reporting to the Management.
(2) Authority and Responsibility of each employee should be clearly laid down so that responsibility may be fixed and corrective action may be taken.

(3) The report should show the results of the period in view and assess the level of efficiency achieved. It should also show a comparison of results achieved with those planned.
(4) Special attention should be focussed on significant variances; there by, following the principle of exception rule. Controllable variances should be separated from uncontrollable variances.
(5) Wherever possible, the use of charts and graphs should be made in variance reports.
(6) Depending upon the level of management, reporting of variances should be made to suit the needs of different levels of management. The reports should be broad based to the top level management and should be a detailed one showing the causes of each variance alongside the persons who may be held responsible for each variance to the lower levels of management.

Disposition of Variances

Cost Variances may be disposed off in any one of the following 3 ways:

(1) Transfer to Current Profit and Loss Account: Here, closing stock of raw material, work in progress and finished goods and cost of goods sold are valued at standard price and all variances are closed by debiting to profit and loss account for unfavourable variances and crediting to profit and loss account for favourable variances. This method is suitable when distribution of variances to various products is difficult on account of a large number of diverse products being manufactured.
(2) Allocation of variances to Cost of Goods Sold and Inventories: The allocation of variances is made to work in progress account, finished account and cost of goods sold account on a percentage basis according to the closing balance of each account. This method gives good results when standards set are too high or too low and do not reflect currently attainable cost levels. Closing stock of work in progress, finished goods and cost of goods sold are shown at their actual costs.
(3) Transfer of Variances to subsequent financial year: In this method, unfavorable variances and favourable variances may be set-off against favourable and unfavourable variances respectively, in the subsequent years. Though not a popular method, it is justified when the normal business cycle is more than one year.

Cost Control Ratios

The management can compute different ratios relating to short-term financial position, profitability, capital structure, leverage, etc. Here, the discussion is limited to only operating cost (control) ratios. These ratios help in comparison of variances of different firms and for different periods, i.e., inter firm and intra firm comparison.

A number of ratios are used for reporting to the management to show whether the deviations of the actual performance from the budgeted performance are favorable or unfavorable to assist the management in their control work. They are as given below:

(1) Efficiency Ratio shows whether the time taken in production is more or less than the standard time allowed. It indicates the efficiency attained in production, over a period.

$$\text{Efficiency Ratio} = \frac{\text{Standard hours for Actual Output}}{\text{Actual hours worked}} \times 100$$

(2) Activity Ratio measure the level of activity attained during the period. It shows the extent to which the production facilities have been utilized as compared with that contemplated in budgets.

$$\text{Activity Ratio} = \frac{\text{Standard hours for Actual Output}}{\text{Budgeted hours}} \times 100$$

(3) Calendar Ratio indicates whether all the budgeted working days in a budgeted period have been available in actual practice.

$$\text{Calendar Ratio} = \frac{\text{Available working days}}{\text{Budgeted working days}} \times 100$$

(4) Standard Capacity Usage Ratio indicates the extent to which, the maximum possible number of working hours are budgeted to be worked.

$$\text{Standard Capacity Usage Ratio} = \frac{\text{Budgeted hours}}{\text{Maximum possible hours in budget period}} \times 100$$

(5) Actual Capacity usage Ratio indicates the extent to which the budgeted hours of working are actually utilized.

$$\text{Actual Capacity Usage Ratio} = \frac{\text{Actual hours worked}}{\text{Maximum possible hours in budget period}} \times 100$$

Illustration 7

Following information is available for S Ltd:

Standard working: 8 hours per day and 5 days per week

Maximum Capacity	50 employees
Actual working	40 employees
Actual hours expected to be worked per 4 weeks	6,400
Standard hours expected to be earned per 4 weeks	8,000
Actual hours worked in the 4-week period	6,000
Standard hours worked in the 4-week period	7,000

In this period there was a Special holiday due to national event.

Calculate: *(a)* Efficiency ratio *(b)* Activity ratio *(c)* Calendar ratio *(d)* Standard Capacity Usage ratio *(e)* Actual Capacity utilization Ratio

Solution

(a) Efficiency Ratio : Standard hours/Actual hours

(7,000 × 100)/6,000 = 117%

(b) Activity Ratio : Standard Hours/Budgeted Hours

(7,000 × 100)/6,400 = 109%

(c) Calendar Ratio : Available working days/Budgeted working days

[(5 × 4) – 1]/(5 × 4) = 95%

(d) Standard Capacity Usage Ratio: Budgeted hours/Maximum possible hours in budgeted period

(6,400 × 100)/8,000 = 80%

(e) Actual capacity utilization ratio: Actual hours / maximum possible hours in the budgeted period

(6000 × 100)/8,000 = 75%

SUMMARY

Cost Variances are concerned with unit cost and their effect on budgeted profit due to favorable or adverse variances. Whereas, the Sales Variances affect the budgeted profit due to changes in sales revenue which is caused by either a variation in selling prices or sales quantities. Sales Variances may be computed either by turnover method or by profit method.

The variances must be reported to the management for the purpose of corrective action. For an effective reporting, the report should be simple, clear and quick. Special attention should be focused on significant variances, thus, following the principle of exception rule. Wherever possible, charts and graphs must be used in variance reports.

Cost Variances may be disposed off either by transfer to current profit and loss account or by allocating variances to cost of goods sold and inventory or by transferring to subsequent financial year.

A number of control ratios are used for reporting to the management to show whether the deviations of the actual performance from the budgeted performance are favorable or unfavorable. The various control ratios are efficiency ratio, activity ratio, calendar ratio, standard capacity usage ratio and actual capacity usage ratio.

Glossary

- **Sales Variance:** affect the budgeted profit due to changes in sales revenue, i.e., changes caused by either a variation in selling price or sales quantitly.
- **Sales Value Variance:** the difference between the budgeted and actual value of sales effected during a period.
- **Sales Price Variance:** is the sub-variance of the sales value variance and it is that portion of sales value variance which is due to the difference between the standard price specified and the actual price charged.
- **Sales Volume Variance:** is that portion of sales value variance, which is due to the difference between the actual quantity of sales and the budgeted quantity of sales.
- **Sales Mix Variance:** is that portion of sales volume variance, which is due to the difference between the actual composition and standard composition of the sales mix.
- **Sales Quantity Variance:** is also a sub-variance of sales volume variance which arises due to the difference between the Revised Standard Quantity and Budgeted Sales Quantity.

- **Cost Control Ratios:** are used for reporting to the management to show whether the deviations of the actual performance from the budgeted performance are favorable or unfavorable to assist the management in their control work.
- **Efficiency Ratio:** shows whether the time taken in production is more or less than the standard time allowed. It indicates the efficiency attained in production, over a period.
- **Activity Ratio:** measures the level of activity attained during the period. It shows the extent to which the production facilities have been utilized as compared with that contemplated in budgets.
- **Calendar Ratio:** indicates whether all the budgeted working days in a budgeted period have been available in actual practice.
- **Standard Capacity Usage Ratio:** indicates the extent to which, the maximum possible number of working hours are budgeted to be worked.
- **Actual Capacity usage Ratio:** indicates the extent to which the budgeted hours of working are actually utilized.

Questions

(1) Explain why sales variances arise and how the different variances are calculated.
(2) Explain the factors to be considered while reporting of variance to the management and how to dispose off the variances.
(3) Explain briefly the different cost control ratios computed to assist the management in their control work.

PROBLEMS

(1) From the following information given below, calculate all sales variances.

Standard:

Product L 5,000 units sold @ Rs. 5

Product M 4,000 units sold @ Rs. 6

Actual:

Product L 6,000 units sold @ Rs. 6

Product M 3,500 units sold @ Rs. 5

[**Ans.:** SVV: Rs. 4,500 (f); SPV: Rs. 2,500 (f); Sales Volume Variance : Rs. 2,000 (f); SMV: Rs. 722 (a); SQV: Rs. 2,722(f)]

(2) From the following information of a company, calculate Sales Variances.

Budgeted Sales:	A:	1,200 units @ Rs. 15
	B:	800 units @ Rs. 20
	C:	2,000 units @ Rs. 40
Actual Sales:	A:	800 units @ Rs. 18
	B:	880 units @ Rs. 20
	C:	2,640 units @ Rs. 38

[**Ans.:** SVV: Rs. 18,320 (a); SPV: Rs. 2,880 (a); Sales Volume Variance: Rs. 21,200 (f); SMV: Rs. 12,080 (f); SQV: Rs. 9,120 (f)]

(3) From the following data, relating to two products A and B, calculate Sales Variances.

	Budget			*Actual*		
Product	*Quantity*	*Price Rs.*	*Value Rs.*	*Quantity*	*Price Rs.*	*Value Rs.*
A	2,000	5	10,000	1,500	6	9,000
B	2,500	10	25,000	3,000	9	27,000
Total			35,000			36,000

[**Ans.:** SVV: Rs. 1,000 (f); SPV: Rs. 1,500 (a); Sales Volume Variance: Rs. 2,500 (f); SMV: 0 SQV: Rs. 2,500 (f)]

(4) From the following information relating to the month of January, calculate Capacity Ratio and Efficiency Ratio.

	Budget	*Actual*
Units Produced	12,000	12,600
Hours worked	24,000	26,400

[**Ans.:** Capacity Ratio: 110% and Efficiency Ratio: 95.45%]

(5) Calculate Efficiency Ratio, Activity Ratio and Capacity Ratio from the following figures.

Budgeted Production	88 units
Standard hours per unit	10
Actual Production	75 units
Actual working hours	600

[**Ans.:** Efficiency Ratio: 125%; Activity Ratio: 23% and Capacity Ratio: 68.18%]

(6) SQC Ltd. provides the following data for the month of October, 2003

Product	*Budget*		
	Budgeted Sales Quantity	*Budgeted Selling Price Per Unit (Rs.)*	*Standard Cost Per Unit (Rs.)*
A	2,160	12	9
B	1,440	5	3

Product	*Actual*		
	Actual Sales Quantity	*Actual Selling Price Per Unit (Rs.)*	*Actual Cost Per Unit (Rs.)*
A	2,240	11	8
B	960	6	5

You are required to compute: *(i)* Sales margin quantity variance *(ii)* Sales margin mix variance *(iii)* Sales margin volume variance *(iv)* Sales margin price variance *(v)* Sales margin total variance.

(C.A., Inter, Nov., 1999)

[**Ans.:** *(i)* Sales margin quantity variance Rs. 1,040 (A); *(ii)* Sales margin mix variance Rs. 320 (F); *(iii)* Sales margin volume variance Rs. 720 (A); *(iv)* Sales margin price variance Rs. 1,280 (A) *(v)* Sales margin total variance Rs. 2,000 (A)]

❑ ❑ ❑

Part – VI

Financial Statements Analysis

25

INTRODUCTION TO FINANCIAL STATEMENTS ANALYSIS

Objectives

The objectives of the study are to:

- understand the meaning of financial statements and their analysis
- highlight the importance of financial analysis
- describe the techniques of financial analysis
- state the limitations of financial analysis
- prepare comparative statements and interpret the data given therein

Meaning of Financial Statements

In order to take right decisions at right time, the management is equipped with sufficient past and present information about the firm and its operations. Much of the information that is used by the management is derived from the financial statements and is known as financial information.

A Financial Statement is a collection of data organized according to logical and consistent accounting procedures. The term Financial Statements, refer to a package of Financial Statements, *viz.*, Balance Sheet, Profit and Loss Account, etc. It also includes Profit and Loss Appropriation Account, Statement of Retained Earnings, Statement of Sources and Uses of Funds, Directors' Report and Auditors' Report and a copy of the Chairman Speech delivered at the Annual General Meeting. Some times, it includes the Schedules and Explanatory Footnotes. These statements are intended to supplement the data contained in Financial Statement and thus, increase the value of such statements to the user.

Nature of Financial Statements

The Financial Statement reflects the financial position of the company as at a point of time (Balance Sheet) and the financial result of the company for a particular period (Profit and Loss Account). The data exhibited in the Financial Statements are the result of the combined effect of recorded facts, accounting conventions adopted and personal judgement.

***(a)* Recorded Facts**

The data used for preparing Financial Statements are drawn from the accounting records. The facts which are not and cannot be recorded in the books are not taken in Financial Statements irrespective of their materiality. For example, as per the accounting records, the fixed assets are shown at the cost price which is a recorded fact. Its market value or the replacement cost is not stated in the Balance Sheet as it is not recorded in the books. Therefore, the Balance Sheet does not show the financial position of the business in terms of current economic conditions. The Balance Sheet shows the historical cost rather than current cost.

Certain facts, which cannot be recorded in the books, are some times shown as footnotes. Examples are Valuation of Stock, Unclaimed Preference Dividend, and Amount of Contingent Liabilities, etc. The information disclosed in the footnotes makes the Financial Statements more meaningful and useful.

***(b)* Accounting Conventions**

The Financial Statements are affected to a great extent by Accounting Principles, Concepts and Conventions like Going Concern Concept, Accounting Period Concept, Matching Concept, Conservatism Convention, Consistency Convention, Monetary Postulate, Realization Postulate etc.

These concepts and conventions provide a guideline to the accountant for arriving at the decision as to the amount to be charged to the Profit and Loss Account of the current year and amount to be carried forward as an expired cost to be shown in the Balance Sheet .

***(c)* Personal Judgement**

Though the concepts and conventions provide guidelines in the preparation of the Financial Statements, the personal judgement has its own role to play in the preparation of Financial Statements. For example, in the application of depreciation, the accountant has scope of exercising his personal judgement in the use of the depreciation method and in deciding the rate of depreciation. Again, in deciding the method of valuing the stock in trade, he can make a choice of the various methods available like FIFO, LIFO, and Average Methods etc. Whether a particular item should be capitalized or charged to Profit and Loss Account again depends to a great extent on the personal judgement of the accountant.

The accounting records are materially affected by the personal judgement. But, the existence of the consistency principle serves as a check on the power of the accountant to use his personal judgement. The area of the application of his personal judgement is reduced as the accountant is guided by the past accounting practices.

Objectives of Financial Statements

A thorough understanding of Financial Statements is the starting point for the development of financial skills. Different statements are prepared for different purposes in mind. The main purpose of Financial Statements is to convey an understanding of some financial aspects of a business firm. They are prepared to present a periodical review or report on the progress by the management and deal with the results achieved during the period under review. They reveal the financial health in terms of progress, position, and prospects of a business on a certain date. It shows the position of the firm at a moment of time as in the case of Balance Sheet or may reveal a series of activities over a given period of time as in the case of Income Statement.

Parties Interested in Financial Statements

The accounting information is needed by a variety of people and their outlook often differs very widely. Owners, Managers, Creditors, Potential Investors, Employees, Customers and Tax Authorities are the persons who are directly interested in the financial information. The indirect users include Financial Analysts, Trade Unions, and Trade Associations etc.

(1) The owners have invested their financial resources in the firm and therefore would like to know periodically the performance of the firm, the prospects of their investments and to elect to sell or continue ownership.
(2) Managers are the custodians of the investment of shareholders and are responsible for the overall performance of the firm. They need accounting information to review the company's progress, position and prospects to decide upon the course of action to be taken in future.
(3) Creditors supply the financial resources to the firm. They are interested in the accounting information to determine the degree of risk to which they are exposed.
(4) Potential investors need accounting information to get an idea about the firm's financial strengths and performance. They are generally interested in earnings, dividends and growth trends of the firm.
(5) Employees can bargain on matters relating to salary determination, bonus, working conditions, fringe benefits, etc., on the basis of the information revealed in the Financial Statements.
(6) Customers get an insight into the prices being charged by the firm by a careful study of the Financial Statements.
(7) The Tax department of the Government has an interest in the accounting information for determining the taxable income of the firm.
(8) Stock Exchange acts as a watchdog of corporate investors and it is interested in the accounting information to protect investor's interest in the listed companies.
(9) Researchers like Economists, Company Law Boards, and Public Accounts Committee, etc., need accounting information for a wide and varied reasons.

LIMITATIONS OF FINANCIAL STATEMENTS

Though the Financial Statements have the appearance of completeness, exactness and finality, they suffer from the following limitations.

(1) The Financial Statements are only interim reports. The exact position of the company can be known only when the business is liquidated or sold.
(2) As the allocation of costs and income to the various accounting period depends on the personal judgement of the accountant, the quality of the team which organises the whole show affects the quality of the statements.
(3) The Financial Statements are affected by various concepts, therefore, Balance Sheet does not show the financial position of the concern as is claimed by it. Balance Sheet is a collection of various unamortized costs rather than market or replacement values.
(4) Financial Statements reflect only the recorded facts. Those facts, which cannot be expressed in terms of money, do not find place in Financial Statements. For example, working conditions of the company, quality of the product introduced by the company, etc., though important, they do not appear in Financial Statements.

Thus, the Financial Statements show the position of financial accounting rather than financial position of the business.

TYPES OF FINANCIAL STATEMENTS

The term Financial Statements refer to atleast two statements, which the accountant prepares at the end of a given period of time for the business enterprise. These statements are Profit and Loss Account and Balance Sheet.

Profit and Loss Account

It is also called as Income Statement. It shows the net result of the business enterprises. This statement matches revenues with the costs incurred in the process of earning revenue. It takes into consideration all expenses and losses and incomes and gains relating to a particular period. It is also called Nominal Account.

Balance Sheet

It is also called as a Sheet of Balances, a Statement of Assets and Liabilities and a Statement of Sources and Uses of Capital. The same are explained below.

(1) As a Sheet of Balances

Balance Sheet is a Sheet, which discloses the names of all such accounts, which show balances. The accounts, which have no balances, do not find a place in the Balance Sheet. For example, certain items like Purchases, Sales, Salaries, Wages, etc., are transferred to Trading and Profit and Loss Account and hence, do not show any balance. Therefore, they do not appear in the Balance Sheet. Whereas, Buildings, Machinery, Furniture, Debtors, Creditors, Capital accounts are not transferred to Profit and Loss Account and show balances. Hence, they are shown in the Balance Sheet.

Some times, the amount shown in advertisement account, discount allowed on shares and debentures, preliminary expenses are not transferred to Profit and Loss Account in full. They are spread over a number of years for which the benefit is likely to accrue from them. In such a case, these accounts show some balances and they appear in the Balance Sheet until they are written off.

(2) As a Statement of Assets and Liabilities

Here, the Sheet of Balances is divided into two equal parts. On the left side of this sheet, such accounts which have credit balances are shown and on the right side, such accounts which have debit balances are shown. The left side is called Liabilities side and the right hand side is called as Assets side. As the Balance Sheet shows Assets and Liabilities, it is defined as a Statement of Assets and Liabilities.

In case of Manufacturing Companies, the arrangement of assets is in the order of permanence, in a Banking Business, in the order of liquidity and in Insurance Enterprises, in the order, which is neither an order of permanency nor liquidity.

(3) As a Statement of Sources and Uses of Capital

Here, capital means total capital of the business. The sources of capital are shown on the liability side and uses of the total capital on the asset side of the Balance Sheet. The total on the two sides of the Balance Sheet must be equal, as uses of capital in the business cannot be more than the sources of capital.

PREPARATION AND PRESENTATION OF FINANCIAL STATEMENTS

According to Modus Operandi of Analysis, a Financial Analysis may be Vertical or Horizontal. Under Horizontal Presentation, the assets and liabilities are shown side by side, assets on the right hand side and liabilities on the left-hand side. The Horizontal Analysis is a Dynamic Analysis measuring change of position or trend of the business over a number of years. Under Vertical Presentation, the assets and liabilities are presented one below the other. The Vertical Presentation is a Static Analysis measuring the position at a point of time or for a period.

Format of Balance Sheet

Horizontal

(Order of liquidity)

XYZ Co, Balance Sheet as on March 31, 2001

Liabilities	*Rs.*	*Assets*	*Rs.*
Current Liabilities:		**Current Assets:**	
Creditors		Cash in Hand	
Bills Payable		Cash at Bank	
Bank Loan		Debtors	
Outstanding Expenses		Bills Receivable	
Income Received in Advance		Stock-in-Trade	
		Outstanding income	
Fixed Liabilities:		**Fixed Assets:**	
Loan		Furniture	
Mortgage Loan		Plant and Machinery	
Capital:		Buildings	
X Capital		Land	
Y Capital		Goodwill	
Z Capital			

Vertical Presentation

XYZ Co, Balance Sheet as on March 31, 2000

Uses of Funds:

Fixed Assets:	*Cost* *Rs.*	*Depreciation* *Rs.*	*Net* *Rs.*
Land			
Buildings			
Plant and Machinery			
Furniture			
Current Assets:			
Stock in Trade			
Sundry Debtors			
Cash at Bank			

Fixed Assets:	*Cost* *Rs.*	*Depreciation* *Rs.*	*Net* *Rs.*
Cash in Hand *Less:* **Current Liabilities:** Sundry Creditors Bills Payable Outstanding Expenses			
Net Working Capital (Current Assets – Current Liabilities)			
Total Net Assets or Total Uses (Fixed Assets + Net Working Capital)			
Sources of Funds: Owners Funds Share Capital Reserves Undistributed Profits			
Outsiders Funds: Debentures Loans Borrowings			
Total Sources			

The Income Statement can be a Single Step or a Multiple Step.

Single Step Income Statement

	Rs.
(1) Income: Sales Dividends Interest on Securities Royalties Miscellaneous	
(2) Deduction from Income: Cost of Goods Sold Selling, General and Administration Expenses Interest on Debentures Amortization of Discount on Debentures Other Interest Loss on Sale of Properties Provision for Taxation	
Net Income for the Year (1-2)	

Multiple Step Income Statement

A Co. Ltd. Profit and Loss Account for the year ending March 31, 2001

	Rs.
Net Sales *Less:* Cost of Goods Sold	
Gross Profit	
General and Administration Expenses Office Salaries Taxes Insurance Depreciation Other Administrative Expenses Selling Expenses: Salesmen Salaries Advertisements Travelling and Entertainment Expenses Freight and Delivery Charges Depreciation on Transport Vehicles	
Total Operating Expenses	
Operating Profits (Gross Profit – Operating Expenses) *Add:* Non-Operating Income: Interest Received Dividend Earned Rent and Other Incomes Received *Less:* Non-Operating Expenses (Interest)	
Profit before Income Tax *Less:* Tax	
Profit after Tax	

Profit and Loss Appropriation shows the utilization of profit earned by the company. The account is debited with dividend declared both on equity share capital and preference share capital and the amount transferred to reserves. The balance in this account is shown on the liability side of Balance Sheet under owners' funds.

Statement of Sources and Uses of Working Capital, summaries, the changes in the working capital, during a stated period of time. The excess of sources over uses indicates increase in working capital and the excess of uses over sources reflect decrease in working capital during the period.

FINANCIAL STATEMENTS ANALYSIS

Financial Statements, *viz.*, Profit and Loss Account and Balance Sheet are the indicators of two significant factors, i.e., profitability and financial soundness. Financial Statements prepared in an absolute manner, do not convey anything to a layman. Therefore, there should be a proper regrouping and analysis of the statements to make them more meaningful for the user. Analysis of Financial Statements means presentation of the information in such a manner so as to afford a full diagnosis of the profitability and financial position of the firm concerned.

The data provided in the Financial Statements should be methodically classified and compared with figures with previous periods (Intra-firm comparison) or other similar firms (Inter firm comparison) in order to have a clear understanding of the profitability and financial position.

An External Analyst usually relies on the published information. It is the Internal Analyst who would really know the full story behind each and every figure of the Financial Statement and he would also get supplementary information to properly assess the significance of the figures. Such analysis is more reliable than done by an outsider.

The process of critical examination of the financial information contained in the financial statements in order to understand and make decisions regarding the operations of the firm is called 'Financial Statements Analysis'. It is basically a study of the relationship among various financial facts and figures as given in a set of financial statements.

Financial Statement Analysis of a firm can be undertaken in different ways. There is no 'the best type' of Financial Statement Analysis which can be applied to all the firms under all the situations. For e.g., Financial Statement Analysis can be done on the basis of number of firms, party who is analysing and interpreting, number of year's figures used, etc.

The term 'financial analysis' include both 'analysis and interpretation'. The term analysis means simplification of financial data, by methodical classification, given in the financial statements. Interpretation means explaining the meaning and significance of the data so simplified. These two are complimentary to each other. Analysis is useless without interpretation and interpretation without analysis is difficult or even impossible.

SIGNIFICANCE OF FINANCIAL ANALYSIS

Financial analysis is the process of identifying the financial strengths and weaknesses of the firm by properly establishing relationships between the items of the Balance Sheet and the Profit and Loss Account. Financial Analysis can be undertaken by management of the firm, or by parties outside the firm, *viz.*, owners, trade creditors, lenders, investors, labour unions, analysts and others. The nature of analysis will differ depending on the purpose of the analyst. A technique frequently used by an analyst need not necessarily serve the purpose of other analyst because of the difference in the interests of the analysts. Financial analysis is useful and significant to different users in the following way.

(i) **Useful to the finance manager:** Financial Analysis focuses on highlighting the facts and relationships related to managerial performance, corporate efficiency, financial strengths and weaknesses and credit worthiness of the company. A finance manager must be well equipped with the different tools of analysis to make rational decisions for the firm. The tools for analysis help in studying accounting data, so as to determine the continuity of the operating policies, investment value of the business, credit ratings and testing the efficiency of operations. The techniques are equally important in the area of financial control, enabling the finance manager to make constant reviews of the actual financial operations of the firm as a whole and in part, to analyse the cause of major deviations, which result in corrective action wherever indicated.

(ii) **To the management:** The importance of Financial Analysis is not limited to the finance manager alone. Its scope of importance is quite broad which include top management. Management of the firm would be interested in every aspect of the Financial Analysis. It is their overall responsibility to see that the resources of the firm are used most efficiently, and that the firm's financial condition is sound.

Financial Analysis helps the management in measuring the success or otherwise of company's operations, appraising the individuals performance and evaluate the system of internal control.

(iii) **To the Trade Creditors:** A creditor, through an analysis of Financial Statements appraises not only the ability of the company, at a particular point of time, to meet its obligations, but also judges the probability of its continued ability to meet all its financial obligations. Trade creditors are particularly interested in the firm's ability to meet their claims over a very short period of time. Their analysis will, therefore, confine to the evaluation of the firms liquidity position.

(iv) **Lenders:** Suppliers of long-term debt, on the other hand, are concerned with the firm's long-term solvency and survival. They analyse the firm's profitability over time, its ability to generate cash to be able to pay interest and repay principal and the relationship between various sources of funds (capital structure relationships). Long-term creditors do analyse the historical Financial Statements. But, they place more emphasis on the firm's projected Financial Statements to make analysis about its future solvency and profitability.

(v) **Investors:** Investors, who have invested their money in the firm's shares, are interested about the firm's earnings. As such, they concentrate on the analysis of the firm's present and future profitability. They are also interested in the firm's financial structure to know the extent it influences the firm's earnings and risk.

The shareholders or investors evaluate the efficiency of the management and determine whether a change is needed or not. However, in some large companies, the shareholders interest is limited to decide whether to buy, sell or hold the shares.

(vi) **Labour Unions:** Labour unions analyse the Financial Statements to assess whether the company is earning a fair rate of return on invested capital, whether it can presently afford a wage increase and whether it can absorb a wage increase through increased productivity or by raising prices.

(vii) **Others:** The economists, researchers analyse the Financial Statements to study the present business and economic conditions. The Government agencies need financial analysis for price regulations, rate settling and other similar purposes.

Purpose of Financial Statements Analysis

Analysis reveals the trends and tendencies, relative importance of each item, relationship and inter relationships between items and the changes that have taken place among them. Therefore, the purpose of Financial Analysis is to know these things so as to identify the financial strengths and weaknesses of the business firm.

Financial Analysis is undertaken by the management of the firm or by parties outside to it, namely owners, creditors, investors, etc. The nature and type of analysis varies according to the specific interest or purpose of the analyst.

Analysis of Financial Statements reveals important facts and relationships concerning the managerial performance and the efficiency of the firm. Broadly, the objectives of the analysis are to understand the information contained in Financial Statements with a view to know the weaknesses and strengths of the firm and to make a forecast about the future prospects of the firm and thereby enabling the Financial Analysts to take different decisions regarding the operation of the firm. Generally, Financial Analysis is undertaken to serve the following purposes (objectives).

- To assess the present profitability and operating efficiency of the firm as a whole as well as for its different departments, thus, to judge the financial health of the firm.
- To find the relative importance of different components of the financial position of the firm.
- To identify the reasons for change in the profitability/financial position of the firm.
- To judge the ability of the firm to pay the principal and interest, arrangements for amortization of debt and security available for the loans and thus to assess the short term as well as the long-term liquidity position of the firm.
- Through an analysis of the Financial Statements of the firms, an economist can gauge the extent of concentration of economic power and pitfalls in the financial policies pursued. The employees and their unions can know how the firm stands in relation to labour and its welfare. Again, Financial Statement Analysis provides the basis for many governmental actions relating to licensing, controls, fixing of prices, ceiling of profits, dividend freeze, tax subsidy and other concessions.

Thus, the analysis of Financial Statements will help the management at self-appraisal and the very statements help the shareholders (owners) and others to judge the performance of the management.

Tools of Financial Analysis

Financial Statement Analysis is done to emphasise the comparative and relative importance of the data presented and at the same time evaluates the position of the firm. This purpose of financial data analysis is satisfied, by using various suitable techniques. The techniques show the relationships and changes. Most widely known techniques of Financial Statements Analysis are:

- Comparative Statements
- Common Size Statements
- Trend Analysis
- Ratio Analysis
- Funds Flow Analysis and
- Cash Flow Analysis

When a number of years are involved in the analysis, the analysis is referred to as "Horizontal or Dynamic Analysis". Such an analysis suggests probabilities, weaknesses or strengths and includes data from year to year. The tem Vertical or Static Analysis is used when data for one accounting period is taken.

(i) Comparative Statements

These are the statements showing the financial position of a firm at different periods of time. The elements of financial position are shown in a comparative form to give an idea about the financial position of two or more periods. For the purpose of financial analysis, generally, the two important Financial Statements, namely, Balance Sheet and Income Statement are prepared in a comparative form. The financial data will be comparative only when same accounting principles are used in preparing these statements. If this is not the case, then, the deviation in the use of accounting principles should be mentioned as a footnote. The analyst can draw useful conclusions when figures are given in a comparative form. Comparative figures indicate the trend and direction of financial position and operating results. This analysis is also known as 'Horizontal Analysis'.

The comparative statements show the absolute data (in rupees), increase or decrease in absolute figures and increase or decrease in terms of percentage. These statements reflect the effects of the conduct of a business. It gives a considerable amount of information, which is of value in forming an opinion regarding the progress of the enterprise.

Recognizing the importance of comparative figures, the Companies Act 1956 made it compulsory to show the figures of the previous years also in the Balance Sheet to facilitate comparison.

(ii) Common Size Statements

Here, the data in Balance Sheet and Profit and Loss Account are shown in analytical percents, i.e., percentages or ratios to total assets, total liabilities and total net sales thus, a common base for comparison is supplied. The relationship of the individual numbers to the totals is stated in simple terms. Here, the total of the assets, the total of the liabilities, the total of the net sales is taken as 100 percent and the ratio of each asset to total asset, the ratio of each liability to the total liabilities and the ratio of each item in income statement to the net sales is computed. Therefore, this statement is also known as 100 percent statement.

These statements indicate the relationship of different items of a Financial Statement with some common item by expressing each item as a percentage to the common item. The percentage, thus, calculated can be easily compared with the corresponding percentages to some other firms, as the numbers are brought to a common base, i.e., per cent. Such statements allow an analyst to compare the operating and financing characteristics of the two companies of different sizes in the same industry. Common Size Statements are useful, both, in intra-firm comparisons over a series of different years and also in making inter firm comparisons for the same year or for several years. This analysis is also known as 'Vertical Analysis'.

(iii) Trend Analysis

Here, a series of Financial Statements may be analysed by studying the trends of various data shown in the statement. Such an analysis of the trend is helpful in budgeting and forecasting. Here, a statement of one period is taken as a base with reference to which all other statements are studied. Every item in the base statement is taken as 100. If the amount of an item in another statement is more than that in the base statement, the trend percentage will be more than 100 and *vice versa*. Thus, the percentages of different items for various periods are calculated and comparison is made. Trend ratios are computed by dividing each amount in the current statement by the corresponding item in the base statement.

Trend analysis emphasizes the changes in the operating and financial data over a period of time and makes possible a horizontal study of the data. It shows the direction of the change, i.e., upward or downward. The main objection to such an analysis is that the selected base year may not be a representative one. In such a case, the entire analysis would be a futile one.

It is a technique of studying several Financial Statements over a series of years. Using the previous year's data of a business enterprise, trend analysis can be done to observe the percentage changes over time in the selected data. The trend percentage is the percentage relationship, which each item of different years bear to the same item in the base year. Trend Analysis is important because, with its long run view, it may point out to the basic changes in the nature of the business. By looking at a trend in a particular ratio, one may find whether the ratio is falling, rising or remaining relatively constant. From this observation, a problem is detected or the sign of good management is found.

(iv) Ratio Analysis

It describes the significant relationship which exists between figures shown in a Balance Sheet, in a Profit and Loss Account, in a Budgetary Control System or in any other part of the accounting organization. As a technique of Financial Analysis, accounting ratios measure the comparative significance of the individual items of the Income and Position Statements. It is possible to assess the profitability, solvency and efficiency of an enterprise through the technique of ratio analysis.

(v) Funds Flow Analysis

It refers to the movement of funds into the business and out of the business during a given accounting period. The flow of funds into the business is called as sources of funds and flow of funds out of the business is called as uses or applications of funds. The difference in the inflow or outflow of funds is the change in the working capital during a given accounting period. When the sources of funds exceed the uses of funds, it results in an increase in the working capital and when the uses exceed the sources of funds, it is a case of decrease in the working capital.

The main sources of funds are funds from operations, issue of share capital, issue of debentures, sale of fixed assets and long term borrowings and the applications of funds are purchase of fixed assets, repayment of borrowings, redemption of debentures, payment of dividends and taxes.

(vi) Cash Flow Analysis

It refers to the analysis of actual movement of cash into and out of an organization. The flow of cash into the business is called as cash inflow or positive cash flow and the flow of cash out of the firm is called as cash outflow or a negative cash flow. The difference between the inflow and outflow of cash is the net cash flow representing surplus or a deficit. Cash Flow Statement is prepared to project the manner in which the cash received has been utilized during an accounting year. It includes only cash transactions. It is a statement, which shows the sources of cash receipts and also the purposes for which payments are made. Thus, it summarises the causes for the changes in cash position of a business enterprise between dates of two Balance Sheets.

LIMITATIONS OF FINANCIAL ANALYSIS

Though Financial Analysis is quite powerful in determining financial strengths and weaknesses of a firm, the analysis is based on the information available in the Financial Statements. As such, the Financial Analysis also suffers from serious limitations of Financial Statements. Hence, the financial analyst must be careful about the impact of price level changes, window dressing of Financial Statements, changes in accounting policies of a firm, accounting concepts and conventions, personal judgement, etc. Some other limitations of financial analysis are:

(i) Financial analysis does not consider price level changes.
(ii) Financial analysis may be misleading on account of changes in accounting procedure followed by a firm.
(iii) Financial analysis is just a study of interim reports.
(iv) Monetary information alone is considered in financial analysis, while non monetary factors are ignored.
(v) The Financial Statements are prepared on the basis of going concern concept; as such it does not give an exact position.

SUMMARY

A Financial Statement is a collection of data organized according to logical and consistent accounting procedures. The term Financial Statements, refer to a package of Financial Statements, *viz.*, Balance Sheet, Profit and Loss Account etc. It also includes Profit and Loss Appropriation Account, Statement of Retained Earnings, Statement of Sources and Uses of Funds, Directors' Report and Auditors' Report and a copy of the Chairman Speech delivered at the Annual General Meeting. Some times, it includes the Schedules and Explanatory Footnotes. These statements are intended to supplement the data contained in Financial Statements and thus, increase the value of such statements to the user.

The Financial Statement reflects the financial position of the company as at a point of time (Balance Sheet) and the financial result of the company for a particular period (Profit and Loss Account). The data exhibited in the Financial Statements are the result of the combined effect of recorded facts, accounting conventions adopted and personal judgements.

The accounting information is needed by a variety of people and their outlook often differs very widely. Owners, Managers, Creditors, Potential Investors, Employees, Customers and Tax Authorities are the persons who are directly interested in the financial information. The indirect users include Financial Analysts, Trade Unions, and Trade Associations, etc.

According to Modus Operandi of Analysis, a Financial Analysis may be Vertical or Horizontal. Under Horizontal Presentation, the assets and liabilities are shown side by side, assets on the right hand side and the liabilities on the left-hand side. The Horizontal Analysis is a Dynamic Analysis measuring the change of position or trend of the business over a number of years. Under Vertical Presentation, the assets and liabilities are presented one below the other. The Vertical Presentation is a Static Analysis measuring the position at a point of time or for a period.

The Income Statement can be a Single Step or a Multiple Step.

Profit and Loss Appropriation shows the utilization of profit earned by the company. The account is debited with dividend declared both on equity share capital and preference share capital and the amount transferred to reserves. The balance in this account is shown on the liability side of Balance Sheet under owners' funds.

Statement of Sources and Uses of Working Capital, summaries, the changes in the working capital, during a stated period of time. The excess of sources over uses indicates increase in the working capital and the excess uses over sources reflect decrease in the working capital during the period.

Financial Statements, *viz.*, Profit and Loss Account and Balance Sheet are the indicators of two significant factors, i.e., profitability and financial soundness. Financial Statements prepared in an absolute manner, do not convey anything to a layman. Therefore, there should be a proper regrouping and analysis of the statements to make them more meaningful for the user. Analysis of Financial Statements means presentation of the information in such a manner so as to afford a full diagnosis of the profitability and financial position of the firm concerned.

The process of critical examination of the financial information contained in the financial statements in order to understand and make decisions regarding the operations of the firm is called 'Financial Statement Analysis'. It is basically a study of the relationship among various financial facts and figures as given in a set of financial statements.

The term 'Financial Analysis' include both 'Analysis and Interpretation'. The term analysis means simplification of financial data, by methodical classification, given in the financial statements. Interpretation means explaining the meaning and significance of the data so simplified. These two are complimentary to each other. Analysis is useless without interpretation and interpretation without analysis is difficult or even impossible.

Financial Analysis can be undertaken by the management of the firm, or by the parties outside the firm, *viz.*, owners, trade creditors, lenders, investors, labour unions, analysts and others. The nature of analysis will differ depending on the purpose of the analyst.

Most widely known techniques of Financial Statements Analysis are Comparative Statements, Common Size Statements, Trend Analysis, Ratio Analysis, Funds Flow Analysis and Cash Flow Analysis.

The financial analyst must be careful about the impact of price level changes, window dressing of Financial Statements, changes in accounting policies of a firm, accounting concepts and conventions, personal judgements, etc.

Glossary

- **Financial Statements:** Financial statements contain summarized information of the firm's financial affairs, organized systematically. They are the means to present the firm's financial situation to users. These statements refer to Balance Sheet and Profit and Loss Account.
- **Interpretation:** Explaining the meaning and significance of the data analysed.
- **Financial Statement Analysis:** It is a process of synthesis and summarization of financial and operative data with a view to getting an insight into the operative activities of a business concern.
- **Vertical Analysis:** Analysis made to review and analyse the financial statements of one particular year only.
- **Horizontal Analysis:** Analysis made to review and analyse the financial statements of a number of years and therefore, are based on the financial data taken from several years.
- **Comparative Statement Analysis:** Statements showing the financial position of a firm at different periods of time.

Questions

(1) What do you mean by a Balance Sheet?
(2) Explain the different ways of presentation of Balance Sheet.
(3) Explain Single Step and Multiple Step Income Statement.
(4) What do you understand by Financial Statements? What is the nature of Financial Statements?
(5) Who are the parties interested in the Financial Statements and why are they interested in them?
(6) Bring out the limitations of the Financial Statements.
(7) Explain the different techniques for the analysis of Financial Statements.

❑❑❑

26

Comparative Financial Statements Analysis

Objectives

The objectives of the study are to:

- Highlight the importance of Financial Statements Analysis and Interpretation
- Present Comparative Balance Sheet
- Explain Comparative Income Statement

Introduction

Financial Statements are the outcome of summarizing process of Accounting. A complete set of Financial Statements consists of Income Statement or Profit and Loss Account, Balance Sheet or Position Statement, Statement of changes in Owner's Accounts, i.e., Profit and Loss Appropriation Account and Statement of Changes in Financial Position.

The importance of Financial Statements lies not in their preparation but in their analysis. The Financial Analysis emphasize on evaluating the financial position and the results of the operations of a business. It involves presentation of information useful to the business managers, investors, creditors and all others interested in the information contained in the Financial Statements.

Financial Statements Analysis consists of both analysis and interpretation. While Analysis is the methodological classification of the data, Interpretation explains the meaning and significance of the data so classified. These two are complementary to each other. Analysis is useless without Interpretation and Interpretation is rather difficult or impossible without Analysis.

The various tools for Analysis are Comparative Financial Statements, Common-Size Statements, Trend Analysis, Ratio Analysis, Funds Flow Analysis and Cash Flow Analysis.

In this lesson, Comparative Financial Statements Analysis is discussed.

Comparative Financial Statements Analysis

The two comparative statements used in the process of analysis are Balance Sheet and Income Statement. Here, both the Profit and Loss Account and Balance Sheet are prepared by providing columns for the figures for both, the current year as well as for the previous year and for the changes during the year, both in absolute and relative terms. As a result, it is possible to find out not only the balances of accounts as on different dates and summaries of different operational activities of different periods, but also the extent of their increase or decrease between these dates. The figures in the comparative statements can be used for identifying the direction of changes and also the trends in different indicators of performance of an organization.

The following steps may be followed to prepare the Comparative Statements.

Step 1: List out the absolute figures in rupees at two points of time (as shown in columns 2 and 3 of Exhibit 1)

Step 2: Find out the change in absolute figures by subtracting the first year figure (Col.2) from the second year figure (Col.3) and indicate the change as increase (+) or decrease (-) and put it in column 4.

Step 3: Calculate the percentage change as

$$\frac{\text{Absolute Increase or Decrease Figure (Col. 4)}}{\text{First year Absolute Figure (Col. 2)}} \quad 100$$

Step 4: Take the percentage change in Column 5.

Exhibit – 1

Particulars	*First Year*	*Second year*	*Absolute Increase (+) or Decrease (-)*	*Percentage Increase (+) or Decrease (-)*
Column 1	*2*	*3*	*4*	*5*
	Rs.	*Rs.*	*Rs.*	*%*

The procedure for computing and interpreting Comparative Statements is the same for both, Balance Sheet and Profit and Loss Account, i.e., Income Statement.

COMPARATIVE STATEMENTS

The Comparative Statements show the absolute data (in rupees), increase or decrease in absolute figures and increase or decrease in terms of percentage. These statements reflect the effects of the conduct of a business. It gives a considerable amount of information, which is of value in forming an opinion regarding the progress of the enterprises.

Recognizing the importance of comparative figures, the Companies Act 1956 made it compulsory to show the figures of the previous years also in the Balance Sheet to facilitate comparison.

Illustration 1

From the following, prepare a Comparative Statement.

Trading and Profit and Loss A/c of Y Ltd

(Rs. In '000)

	2007	*2008*		*2007*	*2008*
To Cost of Goods Sold	100	120	By sales	200	250
To Office and Administration Expenses	20	20			
To Selling and Distribution Expenses	10	20			
To Other Expenses	30				
To Net Profit	40	90			
	200	250		200	250

Solution

Comparative Statement Analysis

	2007 *Rs.*	*2008* *Rs.*	*Change* *Rs.*	*Change in %*
Sales	200	250	+50	+25.00
Cost of Goods Sold	100	120	+20	+20.00
Gross Profit	100	130	+30	+30.00
Office and Administration Expenses	20	20	—	0
Selling and Distribution Expenses	10	20	+10	100.00
Total Operating Expenses	30	40	+10	+33.33
Operating Profit	70	90	+20	+28.57
Other Expenses	30	—	–30	–100.00
Net Profit	40	90	+50	125.00

Illustration 2

From the following information, prepare a Comparative Balance Sheet.

	2007 *Rs.*	*2008* *Rs.*
Capital	10,000	10,000
Reserves	500	600
Debentures	—	100
Land and Building	10,000	6,000
Creditors	200	—
Bills Payables	400	300
Machinery	1,000	3,000
Current Assets	100	2,000

Solution

Comparative Analysis of Balance Sheet

	2007 *Rs.*	*2008* *Rs.*	*Change* *in Rs.*	*Change in %*
Capital and Liabilities:				
Capital	10,000	10,000	—	—
Reserves	500	600	+100	+20.00
Debentures	—	100	+100	α
Bills payables	400	300	–100	–25.00
Creditors	200	—	–200	–100.00
Total Liabilities	11,100	11,000	–100	–00.90
Assets:				
Land and Building	10,000	6,000	–4,000	–40.00
Machinery	1,000	3,000	+2,000	+200.00
Current Assets	100	2,000	+1900	+1900.00
Total Assets	11,100	11,000	–100	–00.90

Illustration 3

Convert the following Income Statement into a Comparative Income Statement of BCR Co. Ltd and interpret the changes in 2008 in the light of the condition in 2007.

Particulars	*2007* *Rs.*	*2008* *Rs.*
Gross Sales	30,600	36,720
Less: Sales Returns	600	700
Net Sales	30,000	36,020
Less: Cost of Goods Sold	18,200	20,250
Gross Profit (A)	**11,800**	**15,770**
Less: Operating Expenses		
Administration Expenses	3,000	3,400
Sales Expenses	6,000	6,600
Total Expenses (B)	**9,000**	**10,000**
Income form Operations (A – B)	2,800	5,770
Add: Non-Operating Income	300	400
Total Income	**3,100**	**6,170**
Less: Non-Operating Expenses	400	600
Net Profit before Tax	2,700	**5,570**
Less: Tax say @ 50%	1,350	2,785
Net Profit After Tax	**1,350**	**2,785**

Solution

Comparative Income Statement for the years 31st March 2007 and 2008

Particulars	*2007*	*2008*	*Absolute Increase (+) or Decrease (-)*	*Percentage Increase (+) or Decrease (-)*
Column 1	*2*	*3*	*4*	*5*
	Rs.	*Rs.*	*Rs.*	*%*
Gross Sales	30,600	36,720	+6,120	+20.00
Less: Sales Returns	600	700	+100	+16.67
Net Sales	30,000	36,020	+6,020	+20.07
Less: Cost of Goods Sold	18,200	20,250	+2,050	+11.26
Gross Profit (A)	**11,800**	**15,770**	**+3,970**	**+33.64**
Less: Operating Expenses				
Administration Expenses	3,000	3,400	+400	+13.33
Sales Expenses	6,000	6,600	+600	+10.00
Total Expenses (B)	**9,000**	**10,000**	**+1,000**	**+11.11**
Operating Profit (A-B)	**2,800**	**5,770**	**+2,970**	**+106.07**
Add: Non-Operating Income	300	400	+100	+33.33
Total Income	**3,100**	**6,170**	**+3,070**	**+99.03**
Less: Non-Operating Expenses	400	600	+200	+50.00
Net Profit before Tax	**2,700**	5,570	+2,870	+106.30
Less: Tax @ 50%	1,350	2,785	+1,435	+106.30
Net Profit after Tax	**1,350**	2,785	+1,435	+106.30

Interpretation

(i) The Gross Profit has increased in 2008 compared to 2007 as the sales have gone up.

(ii) The percentage of operating profit has increased as the increase in Gross Profit is more than the increase in operating expenses.

The overall performance of the company has improved in the year 2008, as the increase in sales is much more than that of costs.

Illustration 4

From the following Income Statement of Madhu Co.Ltd., prepare a Comparative Income Statement for the year 2007 and 2008 and interpret the same.

Particulars	*2007 Rs.*	*2008 Rs.*
Sales	4,00,000	6,50,000
Purchases	2,00,000	2,50,000
Opening Stock	20,600	32,675
Closing Stock	32,675	20,000
Salaries	16,010	18,000
Rent	5,100	6,000
Postage and Stationery	3,200	4,100
Advertising	2,600	4,600
Commission on Sales	3,160	3,500
Postage Paid	200	500
Loss on Sale of Asset	4,000	2,000
Profit on Sale of Investment	3,000	4,500

Solution

Comparative Income Statement of Madhu Co. Ltd for the year ended 2007 and 2008

Particulars	*2007*	*2008*	*Absolute Increase (+) or Decrease (-)*	*Change % Increase (+) or Decrease (-)*
Column 1	*2*	*3*	*4*	*5*
	Rs.	*Rs.*	*Rs.*	*%*
Sales	4,00,000	6,50,000	+2,50,000	+62.50
Less: Cost of Goods Sold:				
Opening Stock	20,600	32,675	+12,075	+58.62
Add: Purchases	2,00,000	2,50,000	+50,000	+25.00
Less: Closing Stock	32,675	20,000	(–)12,675	(–)38.79
Cost of Gods Sold	**1,87,925**	**2,62,675**	**+74,750**	**+39.78**
Gross Profit (A)	**2,12,075**	**3,87,325**	**+1,75,250**	**+82.64**
Less: Operating Expenses:				
Salaries	16,010	18,000	+1,990	+12.43
Rent	5,100	6,000	+ 900	+17.65
Postage and Stationery	3,200	4,100	+ 900	+28.13
Advertising	2,600	4,600	+2,000	+76.92
Commission on Sales	3,160	3,500	+ 340	+10.76
Postage Paid	200	500	+ 300	+150.00
Total Expenses (B)	**30,270**	**36,700**	**+ 6,430**	**+21.24**
Operating Profit (A-B)	**1,81,805**	**3,50,625**	**+1,68,820**	**+92.86**
Add: Non-Operating income:				
Profit on Sale of Investment	3,000	4,500	+1,500	+50.00
Total Income	**1,84,805**	**3,55,125**	**+1,70,320**	**+92.16**
Less: Non-operating Expenses:				
Loss on Sale of Asset	4,000	2,000	(–)2,000	(–)50.00
Net Profit	**1,80,805**	**3,53,125**	**+ 1,72,320**	**+95.31**

Interpretation

(i) The Comparative Balance Sheet of the company reveals that there has been an increase in the sales by Rs. 2,50,000, i.e., 62.5% whereas cost of goods sold has increased only by Rs. 74,750, i.e., 39.78%. This reveals that the company has made efforts to reduce the cost of goods sold, thereby, the gross profit of the company has increased by Rs. 1,75,250, i.e., 82.64%.

(ii) The operating expenses of the company has increased by Rs. 6,430, i.e., 21.24% only and the operating profit has increased by Rs. 1,68,820, i.e., 92.86%.

(iii) The net profit of the company has increased by 95.31%, i.e., Rs. 1,72,320

(iv) The overall financial result of the company is good.

Illustration 5

The following are the balance Sheets of J Ltd., at the end of 2007 and 2008.

Prepare a Comparative Balance Sheet and study the financial position of the concern.

Balance Sheets of J Ltd. at the end of 2007 and 2008 *Rs.('000)*

Liabilities	*2007 Rs.*	*2008 Rs.*	*Assets*	*2007 Rs.*	*2008 Rs.*
Equity Share Capital	600	800	Land and Buildings	370	270
Reserves and Surplus	330	222	Plant and Machinery	400	600
Debentures	200	300	Furniture and Fixtures	20	25
Long-term Loans	150	200	Other Fixed Assets	25	30
Bills Payable	50	45	Cash in hand and at Bank	20	80
Sundry Creditors	100	120	Bills Receivable	150	90
Other Current Liabilities	5	10	Sundry Debtors	200	250
			Stock	250	350
			Prepaid expenses	—	2
	1,435	1,697		1,435	1,697

Solution

For the purpose of the analysis, Horizontal Balance Sheet may be presented vertically with major heads of assets and liabilities.

Comparative Balance Sheets of J Ltd. as on 31st December 2007 and 2008 *(Rs. '000)*

	2007	*2008*	*Absolute Increase/Decrease*	*Change % Increase (+)/ Decrease (-)*
	Rs.	*Rs.*	*Rs.*	
Assets:				
Current Assets:				
Cash and Bank	20	80	+60	+300
Bills Receivable	150	90	(–)60	(–)40
Sundry Debtors	200	250	+50	+25
Stocks	250	350	+100	+40
Prepaid Expenses	—	2	+2	α
Total Current Assets	**620**	**772**	**+152**	**+24.52**
Fixed Assets:				
Land and Buildings	370	270	**(–)100**	(–)27.03
Plant and Machinery	400	600	**+200**	+50
Furniture and Fixtures	20	25	**+5**	+25
Other Fixed Assets	25	30	**+5**	+20
Total Fixed Assets	**815**	**925**	**+110**	**+13.50**
Total Assets	**1,435**	**1,697**	**+262**	**+18.26**

	2007	*2008*	*Absolute Increase/Decrease*	*Change % Increase (+)/ Decrease (-)*
	Rs.	*Rs.*	*Rs.*	
Liabilities and Capital:				
Current Liabilities:				
Bills Payable	50	45	(–)5	**(–)10**
Sundry Creditors	100	120	+20	**+20**
Other Current Liabilities	5	10	+5	**+100**
Total Current Liabilities	**155**	**175**	**+20**	**+12.90**
Debentures	200	300	+100	**+50**
Long Term Loans	150	200	+50	**+33.33**
Total Outsiders Liabilities	**505**	**675**	**+170**	**+33.66**
Equity Share Capital	600	800	+200	**+33.33**
Reserves and Surplus	330	222	(–)108	**(–)32.73**
Total Liabilities and Capital	**1,435**	**1,697**	**+262**	**+18.26**

Interpretation

(i) The Comparative Balance Sheet of the company reveals that during the year 2008, there has been an increase in Fixed Assets by Rs. 1,10,000, i.e., 13.5% while long term liabilities have relatively increased by Rs. 1,50,000 and Equity Share Capital has increased by Rs. 2 Lakhs. This fact depicts that the policy of the company is to purchase Fixed Assets from long-term source of finance thereby not affecting the Working Capital.

(ii) The Current Assets have increased by Rs. 1,52,000, i.e., 24.52%. The current liabilities have increased only by Rs. 20,000, i.e., 12.9%. This further confirms that the company has raised long term finances even for the Current Assets resulting in an improvement in the liquidity position of the Company.

(iii) Reserves and Surplus have decreased from Rs. 3,30,000 to Rs. 2,22,000, i.e., 32.73% indicating that the Company has utilized Reserves and Surplus for the payment of dividend to the shareholders either in cash or by issuing bonus shares.

(iv) The overall financial position of the company is satisfactory.

Illustration 6

From the following Balance Sheet and Income statement of Day Dreaming Co.Ltd. for the year ending 2007and 2008, prepare Comparative Statements.

Income Statement

(Rs. in Lakhs)

Particulars	*2007*	*2008*
Net Sales	900	1,050
Cost of Goods Sold	650	850
Administrative Expenses	40	40
Selling Expenses	20	20
Net Profit	**190**	**140**

BALANCE SHEET

(Rs. in Lakhs)

	2007	*2008*
Equity Share Capital	600	600
6% Preference Share Capital	500	500
Reserves	400	445
Debenture	300	350
Bills Payable	250	275
Creditors	150	200
Tax payable	150	200
Total Liabilities	**2,350**	**2,570**

	2007	*2008*
Land	300	300
Buildings	500	470
Plant	400	470
Furniture	300	340
Stocks	400	500
Cash	450	490
Total Assets	**2,350**	**2,570**

Solution

Comparative Income Statement of Day Dreaming Co. Ltd. for the years ended 2007 and 2008

(Rs. in Lakhs)

Particulars	*2007*	*2008*	*Increase (+) or Decrease (-)*	*Change in %*
	Rs.	*Rs.*	*Rs.*	
Net Sales	900	1,050	150	16.67
Less: Cost of Goods Sold	650	850	200	30.77
Gross Profit (A)	250	200	(–)50	(–)20
Operating Expenses:				
Administration Expenses	40	40	0	0.00
Selling Expenses	20	20	0	0.00
Total Operating Expenses (B)	**60**	**60**	**0**	**0.00**
Operating Profit (A – B)	**190**	**140**	**(–)50**	**(–)26.32**
Other Expenses				
Net Profit	190	140	(–)50	(–)26.32

Comparative Balance Sheet of Day Dreaming Co. Ltd. at the end of the years 2007 and 2008

(Rs. in Lakhs)

Particulars	*2007*	*2008*	*Increase (+) or Decrease (-)*	*Change %*
	Rs.	*Rs.*	*Rs.*	
ASSETS				
Current Assets				
Stocks	400	500	100	25.00
Cash	450	490	40	8.89
Total Current Assets	**850**	**990**	**140**	**16.47**
Fixed Assets				
Land	300	300	0	0.00
Buildings	500	470	–30	–6.00
Plant	400	470	70	17.50
Furniture	300	340	40	13.33
Total Fixed Assets	**1,500**	**1,580**	**80**	**5.33**
Total Assets	**2,350**	**2,570**	**220**	**9.36**
LIABILITIES AND CAPITAL				
Current Liabilities				
Bills Payable	250	275	25	10.00
Creditors	150	200	50	33.33
Tax payable	150	200	50	33.33
Total Current Liabilities	**550**	**675**	**125**	**22.73**

Particulars	*2007*	*2008*	*Increase (+) or Decrease (-)*	*Change %*
	Rs.	*Rs.*	*Rs.*	
Debenture	**300**	**350**	**50**	**16.67**
Equity Share Capital	600	600	0	0.00
6% Preference Share Capital	500	500	0	0.00
Reserves	400	445	45	11.25
Total Shareholders Funds	**1,500**	**1,545**	**45**	**3.00**
Total Liabilities	**2,350**	**2,570**	**220**	**9.36**

Interpretation

(i) The Comparative Income Statement reveals that there has been an increase in sales by 16.67% while the cost of goods sold has increased by 30.77% thereby resulting in a decline in the Gross Profit by 20%. Although the Operating Expenses have remained constant, there has been a decrease in Net Profit by 26.32%, because of decline in Gross Profit.

(ii) The companies current assets have increased by Rs. 140 lakhs, i.e., 16.47% whereas the current liabilities have increased by Rs. 125 lakhs (22.73%).

(iii) Shareholders funds have increased by Rs. 45 lakhs, i.e., 3%.

(iv) The overall financial position of the company is satisfactory.

SUMMARY

Financial Statements are the end products of the financial accounting practices. The two major Financial Statements are the Balance Sheet and the Income Statement. Financial Statement Analysis is a study of the relationship among various financial facts and figures as given in a set of Financial Statements. Financial Analysis focuses on highlighting the facts and relationships related to managerial performance, corporate efficiency, financial strengths and weaknesses and credit worthiness of the company.

Most widely known techniques of Financial Statements Analysis are Comparative Statements Analysis, Common-Size Statements Analysis, Trend Analysis, Ratio Analysis Funds Flow Analysis and Cash Flow Analysis.

Glossary

- **Analysis:** is the methodological classification of the data.
- **Interpretation:** explains the meaning and significance of the data classified.
- **Comparative Statements:** shows the absolute data (in rupees), increase or decrease in absolute figures and increase or decrease in terms of percentage.

Questions

(1) Explain the concept of Financial Statements.

(2) State briefly the techniques of Financial Statement Analysis.

(3) Distinguish between Vertical and Horizontal Analysis of financial data.

(4) Explain the meaning of Analysis and Interpretation.

(5) What are the limitations of Financial Analysis?

(6) Bring out the importance of Financial Analysis.

(7) Explain the procedure for preparing the Comparative Financial Statements.

(8) State the different types of Financial Analysis and discuss the limitations of Financial Analysis.

(9) What is the importance of Comparative Statements? Illustrate your answer with particular reference to Comparative Income Statement and state briefly how they are prepared.

(10) What do you understand by analysis and interpretation of Financial Statements? Discuss their importance.

PROBLEMS

(1) From the following information of Narsimham Company Ltd., prepare a Comparative Income Statement for the years 2004-2005

	2004 *Rs.*	*2005* *Rs.*
Gross Sales	7,25,000	8,15,000
Less: Returns	25,000	15,000
Net Sales	7,00,000	8,00,000
Cost of Goods Sold	5,95,000	6,15,000
Gross Profit	1,05,000	1,85,000
Other Expenses		
Selling and Distribution Expenses	23,000	24,000
Administration Expenses	12,700	12,500
Total Expenses	**35,700**	**36,500**
Operating Income	69,300	1,48,500
Add: Other Income	1,200	8,050
	70,500	**1,56,550**
Less: Non Operating Expenses	1,750	1,940
Net Profit	**68,750**	**1,54,610**

(2) The following are the Balance Sheets of Mohan Ltd., at the end of 2004 and 2005.

Rs.'000

Liabilities	*2004* *Rs.*	*2005* *Rs.*	*Assets*	*2004* *Rs.*	*2005* *Rs.*
Equity Share Capital	400	600	Land and Buildings	270	170
Reserves and Surplus	312	354	Plant and Machinery	310	786
Debentures	50	100	Furniture and Fixtures	9	18
Long-term Loans	150	255	Other Fixed Assets	20	30
Accounts Payable	255	117	Loans and Advances	46	59
Other Current Liabilities	7	10	Cash at Bank	118	10
			Accounts Receivable	209	190
			Inventory	160	130
			Prepaid Expenses	3	3
			Other Current Assets	29	40
	1,174	1,436		1,174	1,436

Prepare a Comparative Balance Sheet and study the financial position of the company.

(3) The following are the Balance Sheets of Devi Co. Ltd at the end of 2002 and 2003. Prepare a Comparative Balance Sheet and study the financial position of the concern.

Liabilities	*2002* *Rs.*	*2003* *Rs.*	*Assets*	*2002* *Rs.*	*2003* *Rs.*
Equity Capital	1,20,000	1,85,000	Fixed Assets	1,40,000	1,95,000
Preference Capital	70,000	95,000	Stock	40,000	45,000
Reserves	30,000	35,000	Debtors	70,000	82,500
P&L A/c	17,500	20,000	Bills Receivables	20,000	50,000
Bank O.D.	35,000	45,000	Prepaid Expenses	6,000	8,000
Creditors	25,000	35,000	Cash at Bank	40,000	48,500
Provision for Taxation	15,000	22,500	Cash in Hand	5,000	29,000
Proposed Dividend	8,500	20,500			
	3,21,000	4,58,000		3,21,000	4,58,000

(4) From the following information, prepare a Comparative Statement and Comment.

(Rs. In Lakhs)

	2008 *Rs.*	*2007* *Rs.*
Share Capital	2,400	2,400
Reserves	400	500
Fixed Assets	2,900	2,800
Investments	—	100
Cash	1,000	800
Current Liabilities	1,200	800
Current Assets	100	—

(5) Prepare Comparative Size Balance Sheets from the following data and comment upon the financial position of the company.

BHARATH LTD.

Balance Sheet on March 31

(Rs. in Crores)

Liabilities	*2007* *Rs.*	*2008* *Rs.*	*Assets*	*2007* *Rs.*	*2008* *Rs.*
Share Capital	70	70	Fixed Assets	120	100
Reserves	120	70	Current Assets		
Secured Loans	20	25	Stocks	80	60
Unsecured Loans	10	15	Debtors	40	30
Current Liabilities	30	20	Cash	10	10
	250	200		250	200

(6) The income statements of a concern are given for the years ending on 31st March 2007 and 2008. Rearrange the figures in a comparative form and study the profitability position of the concern.

Particulars	*2007* *Rs.('000)*	*2008* *Rs. ('000)*
Net sales	785	900
Cost of Goods Sold	450	500
Operating Expenses		
General	70	72
Administrative and Selling Expenses	80	90
Non-operating		
Interest Paid	25	30
Income Tax	70	80

(7) From the following balance sheets of Mohan metal works, prepare a Comparative Balance Sheet and comment upon the significant changes which have taken place during the year 2008.

BALANCE SHEETS (As at 31st March 2007 and 2008)

Liabilities	*2007* *Rs.*	*2008* *Rs.*	*Assets*	*2007* *Rs.*	*2008* *Rs.*
Equity Share Capital	800	1,200	Debtors	418	380
Capital Reserve	120	220	Cash	236	20
General	444	418	Stocks	320	260
Reserve	80	100	Others	64	26
Sinking Fund	400	650	Investment	540	340
Debentures	510	234	Furniture	18	36
Creditors	14	20	Building	620	1572
Others			Land	40	60
			Other Assets	112	148
	2,368	2,842		2,368	2,842

(8) The following are the Balance Sheets of a concern for the years 2007 and 2008. Prepare a Comparative Balance Sheet and study the financial position of the concern.

BALANCE SHEET AS ON 31ST MARCH

Particulars	*2007* *Rs.*	*2008* *Rs.*
Liabilities:		
Equity Share Capital	6,00,000	8,00,000
Reserves and Surplus	3,30,000	2,22,000
Debentures	2,00,000	3,00,000
Long Term Loans	1,50,000	2,00,000
Bills Payable	50,000	45,000
Sundry Creditors	1,00,000	1,20,000
Other Current Assets	5,000	10,000
Total	14,35,000	16,97,000
Assets:		
Land and Building	3,70,000	2,70,000
Plant and Machinery	4,00,000	6,00,000
Furniture and Fixtures	20,000	25,000
Other Fixed Assets	25,000	30,000
Cash and Bank	20,000	80,000
Bills Receivable	1,50,000	90,000
Sundry Debtors	2,00,000	2,50,000
Stocks	2,50,000	3,50,000
Preliminary Expenses	—	2,000
	14,35,000	16,97,000

❑ ❑ ❑

27

Comparative Common Size Financial Statements Analysis

Objectives

The objectives of the study are to:

- Understand the preparation of Common Size Statements and
- Learn the interpretation of the given data

Introduction

In the previous lessons, you have learnt about the Financial Statements Analysis, its importance, advantages and disadvantages, and also of Comparative Statements, its preparation and interpretation of data. In this lesson, you will learn about the preparation of Common Size Statements and the interpretation of the given data.

Common Size Financial Statements Analysis

Common Size Statement is also known as Component Percentage Statement is a financial tool for studying the key changes and trends in the financial position (Balance Sheet) and financial result (Profit and Loss Account) of a company. Here, each item in the statement is stated as a percentage of some total, of which that item is a part. Thus, each percentage exhibits the relation of the individual item to its respective total. For example, assets may be chosen as a measure (base or total) for balance sheet items and sales as a measure (base/total) for Profit and Loss Account.

Common Size Analysis is of immense use for comparing enterprises which differ substantially in size as it provides an insight into the structure of the financial statements. Inter-firm comparison or comparison of the company's position with the related industry as a whole is possible with the help of (Vertical) Common Size Statement Analysis.

Procedure for Common Size Statements

The following procedure may be adopted for preparing Common Size Statements.

(i) List out absolute figures in rupees at two points of time, say year 1, and year 2 (Column 2 and 4 of Exhibit 1)

(ii) Choose a common base (as 100). For example, Sales revenue total may be taken as base (100) in case of Profit and Loss Account and the Total Assets or Total Liabilities as base (100) in case of Balance Sheet.

(iii) Convert all items of Col. 2 and 4 as a percentage of that total. Column 3 and 5 portray these percentages in exhibit 1.

EXHIBIT 1
COMMON SIZE STATEMENT

Particulars	*Year one*	*Percentage*	*Year two*	*Percentage*
Column 1	*2*	*3*	*4*	*5*

The purpose of Common Size Analysis is to know the importance of each item in the total. Hence, this analysis can be done for one year also.

Common Size Statements

Here, the data in Balance Sheet and Profit and Loss Account are shown in analytical percents, i.e., percentages or ratios of total assets, total liabilities and total net sales thus, a common base for comparison is supplied. In simple terms, the relationship of the individual number is stated to the total. Here, the total of the assets, the total of the liabilities, the total of the net sales is taken as 100 percent and the ratio of each asset to total asset, the ratio of each liability to the total liabilities and the ratio of each item in income statement to the net sales is computed. Therefore, this statement is also known as 100 Percent Statement or Component Percentages. The Common Size Statement is reduced to the total of 100 and each individual item is stated as a percentage of the total of 100.

Illustration 1

From the following, construct a Comparative Common Size Statement.

	2007-2008 *Rs.*	*2008-2009* *Rs.*
Sales	5,00,000	6,00,000
Cost of Goods Sold	3,75,000	4,40,000
Selling Expenses	20,000	40,000
Administrative Expenses	30,000	40,000
Financial Expenses	10,000	5,000

Solution

Common Size Statement Analysis

	2007-2008		*2008-2009*	
	Rs.	*%*	*Rs.*	*%*
Sales	5,00,000	100	6,00,000	100.00
Less: Cost of Goods Sold	3,75,000	75	4,40,000	73.33
Gross Profit (a)	1,25,000	25	1,60,000	26.67
Selling Expenses	20,000	4	40,000	6.67
Administrative Expenses	30,000	6	40,000	6.67
Total Operating Expenses (b)	50,000	10	80,000	13.33
Operating Profit (a-b)	75,000	15	80,000	13.33
Less: Financial Expenses	10,000	2	5,000	0.83
Net Profit	65,000	13	75,000	12.50

Illustration 2

From the following income statement of ‘A’ Ltd. for the year ending March 31, 2007 and 2008, prepare Common Size Statement.

	31-03-2007 Rs.	31-03-2008 Rs.
Gross Sales	1,51,500	1,41,540
Less: Returns	1,500	1,540
Net Sales	1,50,000	1,40,000
Less: Cost of Goods Sold	1,05,000	99,400
Gross Profit	45,000	40,600
Expenses		
Selling	7,500	7,500
General	4,500	4,500
Financial	750	620
Total Expenses	12,750	12,620
Net Profit	32,250	27,980

Solution

Common Size Income Statement of A' Ltd. for the year ending March 31, 2007 and 2008.

	2007		2008	
	Rs.	%	Rs.	%
Gross Sales	1,51,500	101.00	1,41,540	101.10
Less: Returns	1,500	1.00	1,540	01.10
Net Sales	1,50,000	100.00	1,40,000	100.00
Less: Cost of Goods Sold	1,05,000	70.00	99,400	71.00
Gross Profit (A)	45,000	30.00	40,600	29.00
Expenses				
Selling	7,500	5.00	7,500	5.40
General	4,500	3.00	4,500	3.20
Financial	750	0.50	620	0.40
Total Expenses (B)	12,750	8.50	12,620	9.00
Net Profit (A-B)	32,250	21.50	27,980	20.00

Illustration 3

Convert the following Balance Sheets into Common size Balance Sheet and interpret the results.

Balance Sheet as on 31-03-2004 and 2005 (Rs. in lakhs)

Liabilities	2004 Rs.	2005 Rs.	*Assets*	2004 Rs.	2005 Rs.
Equity Share Capital	1,000	1,200	Debtors	450	390
Capital Reserves	90	185	Cash	200	15
General Reserves	500	450	Stocks	320	250
Sinking Fund	90	100	Investment	300	250
Debentures	450	650	Building Less Depreciation	800	1,400
Sundry Creditors	200	150	Land	198	345
Others	15	20	Furniture and Fittings	77	105
	2,345	2,755		2,345	2,755

Solution

Common size Balance Sheet at the end 31st March 2004 and 2005 (Rs. in Lakhs)

Particulars	*2004*		*2005*	
	Rs.	*%*	*Rs.*	*%*
Capital and Reserves:				
Equity Share Capital	1,000	42.64	1,200	43.56
Capital Reserves	90	3.84	185	6.72
General Reserves	500	21.32	450	16.33
Sinking Fund	90	3.84	100	3.63
Total Capital and Reserves	**1,680**	**71.64**	**1,935**	**70.24**
Long Term Debts:				
Debentures	450	19.19	650	23.59
Current Liabilities:				
Sundry Creditors	200	8.53	150	5.44
Other Creditors	15	0.64	20	0.73
Total Current Liabilities	215	9.17	170	6.17
Total Liabilities	**2,345**	**100**	**2,755**	**100**
Fixed Assets:				
Buildings	800	34.12	1,400	50.82
Land	198	8.44	345	12.52
Furniture and Fittings	77	3.28	105	3.81
Total Fixed Assets	**1,075**	**45.84**	**1,850**	**67.15**
Current Assets:				
Debtors	450	19.19	390	14.16
Cash	200	8.53	15	0.54
Stocks	320	13.64	250	9.07
Total Current Assets	**970**	**41.36**	**655**	**23.77**
Investments	300	12.8	250	9.07
Total Assets	**2,345**	**100**	**2,755**	**100**

Interpretation

(i) In the year 2005, both, current assets and current liabilities decreased compared to 2004 but the decrease in current assets is more than the decrease in the current liabilities. The decrease in current liabilities was merely 3% where as current assets decreased from 41.36% to 23.78%. The decrease in cash is more than the decrease in any other current asset. As a result, the firm may face difficulties in payment of daily expenses.

(ii) In 2005, both fixed assets and the fixed liabilities increased but the increase in the fixed assets is more than the increase in fixed liabilities. The firm sold investments to acquire fixed assets. Increase in the fixed assets is more than the increase in capital and reserves.

(iii) The firm has undertaken expansion program by purchasing land and buildings. Therefore, the productive efficiency of the firm may increase in coming years.

The overall financial position of the firm is satisfactory. It should improve its cash position.

Illustration 4

From the given Financial Statements, prepare an Analysis Sheet using Common Size method of analysis for the given financial years.

Income Statement for the year

Particulars	*2004* *Rs.*	*2005* *Rs.*
Net Sales	5,00,000	4,95,000
Cost of Goods Sold	3,78,000	3,60,000
Operating Expenses	62,500	60,000
Depreciation	22,000	22,000
Income from Investment	70,000	89,000
Income Tax	32,500	40,000

Balance Sheets as on_____

Particulars	*31.12.2004* *Rs.*	*31.12.2005* *Rs.*
Liabilities		
Share Capital	2,00,000	2,90,000
Reserves	40,220	40,000
P&L A/c	15,555	14,292
Long Term Loan	18,965	19,262
Creditors	5,125	5,125
Bills Payable	2,300	2,195
Accounts Payable	13,000	15,000
Outstanding Expenses	2.220	1,011
	2,97,385	**3,86,385**
Assets		
Land and Buildings	50,000	70,000
Plant and Machinery	1,00,000	1,00,000
Furniture	30,000	62,500
Stocks	7,165	8,192
Debtors	40,000	52,000
Bills Receivable	50,000	49,020
Cash	—	20,000
Prepaid Expenses	20,220	25,173
	2,97,385	**3,86,885**

Solution

Common size Income Statement for the year ended 31 Dec. 2004 and 2005

Particulars	*2004*		*2005*	
	Rs.	*%*	*Rs.*	*%*
Net Sales	5,00,000	100.0	4,95,000	100.00
Less: Cost of Goods Sold	3,78,000	75.6	3,60,000	72.73
Gross Profit	1,22,000	24.4	1,35,000	27.27
Less: Operating Expenses	62,500	12.5	60,000	12.12
Less: Depreciation	22,000	4.4	22,000	4.44
Operating Profit	37,500	7.5	53,000	10.71
Add: Income from Investment	70,000	14.0	89,000	17.98
Profit before Tax	1,07,500	21.5	1,42,000	28.69
Less: Income Tax	32,500	6.5	40,000	8.08
Net Profit after Tax	75,000	15.0	1,02,000	20.61

Common size Balance Sheet as on 31st Dec., 2004 and 31st Dec., 2005

	2004		*2005*	
	Amount *Rs.*	*%*	*Amount* *Rs.*	*%*
Liabilities:				
Share Capital	2,00,000	67.25	2,90,000	74.96
Reserves	40,220	13.52	40,000	10.34
Profit and Loss Account	15,555	5.23	14,292	3.69
Long Term Loan	18,965	6.38	19,262	4.98
Creditors	5,125	1.72	5,125	1.32
Bills Payable	2,300	0.77	2,195	0.57
Accounts Payable	13,000	4.37	15,000	3.88
Outstanding Expenses	2,220	0.75	1,011	0.26
Total Liabilities	**2,97,385**	**100.00**	**3,86,885**	**100.00**

	2004		2005	
	Amount Rs.	*%*	*Amount Rs.*	*%*
Assets:				
Land and Buildings	50,000	16.81	70,000	18.09
Plant and Machinery	1,00,000	33.63	1,00,000	25.85
Furniture	30,000	10.09	62,500	16.15
Stocks	7,165	2.41	8,192	2.12
Debtors	40,000	13.45	52,000	13.44
Bills Receivable	50,000	16.81	49,020	12.67
Cash	—	—	20,000	5.17
Prepaid Expenses	20,220	6.80	25,173	6.51
Total Assets	**2,97,385**	**100.00**	**3,86,885**	**100.00**

Interpretation

(i) On comparison of the cost of goods sold percentage to sales of both the years, it is observed that the company has tried to reduce its cost to improve its profit margin.

(ii) The profitability position of the company has improved compared to the previous year as the profit after tax percentage has gone up by 5.61%.

(iii) The company has gone for issue of share capital and raising long term loans in order to finance the purchase of fixed assets like land and buildings and furniture.

(iv) The company has also improved its liquidity position as it has increased its current assets mainly cash balances by 5.17%.

(v) By observing the increase in the percentage of current assets compared to current liabilities, we can predict that the company is having a very good liquidity position.

Company's operations are good and are improving year by year.

Common Size Analysis can be done not only for one or more years, it can also be done for two enterprises at a time consider the following example.

Illustration 5

The following figures are extracted from the books of Kranthi Ltd. and Hema Ltd. for the year ending 31st March, 2009.

Kranthi Ltd.

Particulars	*Rs.*	*Particulars*	*Rs.*
Sales	3,15,000	Advertising	2,520
Purchases	1,57,500	Commission on Sales	3,150
Opening Stock	29,400	Discount Allowed	840
Closing Stock	33,600	Interest Paid	2,100
Salaries	15,540	Loss on Sale of Asset	4,830
Rent	5,040	Profit on Sale of Investment	3,999
Postage and Stationery	2,100	Provision for Taxation	21,000

Hema Ltd.

Particulars	*Rs.*	*Particulars*	*Rs.*
Sales	4,00,000	Advertising	2,600
Purchases	2,00,000	Commission on Sales	3,160
Opening Stock	20,600	Discount Allowed	—
Closing Stock	32,675	Interest Paid	200
Salaries	16,010	Loss on Sale of Asset	4,000
Rent	5,100	Profit on Sale of Investment	3,000
Postage and Stationery	3,200	Provision for Taxation	20,000

You are required to prepare a Common Size Income Statement.

Solution

Common Size Income Statements of Kranthi and Hema Ltd. for the year ended 31st March, 2009

Particulars	*Kranthi Ltd.*			*Hema Ltd.*		
	R.s	*Rs.*	*%*	*Rs.*	*Rs.*	*%*
Sales		3,15,000	100		4,00,000	100
Less: Cost of Goods Sold						
Opening Stock	29,400			20,600		
Add: Purchases	1,57,500			2,00,000		
	1,86,900			**2,20,600**		
Less: Closing Stock	33,600	1,53,300	48.67	32,675	1,87,925	46.98
Gross Profit (A)		**1,61,700**	**51.33**		**2,12,075**	**53.02**
Operating Expenses:						
Salaries		15,540	4.93		16,010	4.00
Rent		5,040	1.6		5,100	1.28
Postage and Stationery		2,100	0.67		3,200	0.8
Advertising		2,520	0.8		2,600	0.65
Commission on Sales		3,150	1		3,160	0.79
Discount Allowed		840	0.27		—	—
Total Operating Expenses (B)		**29,190**	**9.27**		**30,070**	**7.52**
Operating Profit (A-B)		**1,32,510**	**42.07**		**1,82,005**	**45.50**
Add: Non-Operating Profit:						
Profit on Sale of Investment		3,999	1.27		3,000	0.75
		1,36,509	**43.34**		**1,85,005**	**46.25**
Less: Financial Expenses:						
Interest Paid		2,100	0.67		200	0.05
Less: Non-Operating Expenses:						
Loss on Sale of Asset		4,830	1.53		4,000	1
Profit Before Tax		1,29,579	41.13		1,80,805	45.20
Provision for Taxation		21,000	6.67		20,000	5
Profit After Tax		**1,08,579**	**34.47**		**1,60,805**	**40.20**

Interpretation

(i) Hema Ltd. has earned more profit compared to Kranthi Ltd.
(ii) Hema Ltd. has worked hard to reduce its cost of goods sold in order to get improved profits.
(iii) The interest paid is also less by Hema Ltd., compared to Kranthi Ltd.
(iv) Both the companies profitability is satisfactory but Kranthi Ltd. needs to cut down its cost in order to boost up its profits.

Illustration 6

The following are the Balance Sheets of Harsha Ltd. as on 31st December, 2004 and 2005.

Liabilities	*2004 Rs.*	*2005 Rs.*	*Assets*	*2004 Rs.*	*2005 Rs.*
Equity Capital	1,00,000	1,65,000	Fixed Assets	1,20,000	1,75,000
Preference Capital	50,000	75,000	Stock	20,000	25,000
Reserves	10,000	15,000	Debtors	50,000	62,500
Profit and Loss Account	7,500	10,000	Bills Receivables	10,000	30,000
Bank Overdraft	25,000	25,000	Prepaid Expenses	5,000	6,000
Creditors	20,000	25,000	Cash at Bank	20,000	26,500
Provision for Taxation	10,000	12,500	Cash in Hand	5,000	15,000
Proposed Dividend	7,500	12,500			
	2,30,000	**3,40,000**		**2,30,000**	**3,40,000**

Prepare a Common Size Balance Sheet and interpret the same.

Common Size Balance Sheet of Harsha Ltd. as on 31st Dec., 2005 and 2006

	2005		*2006*	
	Amount Rs.	*%*	*Amount Rs.*	*%*
Equity Capital	1,00,000	43.48	1,65,000	48.53
Preference Capital	50,000	21.74	75,000	22.05
Reserves	10,000	4.34	15,000	4.41
Profit and Loss Account	7,500	3.26	10,000	2.95
Total	**1,67.500**	**72.82**	**2,65,000**	**77.94**
Current Liabilities				
Bank Overdraft	25,000	10.87	25,000	7.35
Creditors	20,000	8.7	25,000	7.35
Provision for Taxation	10,000	4.35	12,500	3.68
Proposed Dividend	7,500	3.26	12,500	3.68
Total	**62,500**	**27.18**	**75,000**	**22.06**
Total Liabilities	**2,30,000**	**100**	**3,40,000**	**100**
Current Assests				
Stock	20,000	8.7	25,000	7.35
Debtors	50,000	21.74	62,500	18.38
Bills Receivables	10,000	4.35	30,000	8.82
Prepaid Expenses	5,000	2.17	6,000	1.78
Cash at Bank	20,000	8.7	26,500	7.79
Cash in Hand	5,000	2.17	15,000	4.41
Total	**1,10,000**	**47.83**	**1,65,000**	**48.53**
Fixed Assets (net)	1,20,000	52.17	1,75,000	51.47
Total Assets	**2,30,000**	**100**	**3,40,000**	**100**

Interpretation

(i) In the year 2006, Current Assets have increased from 47.83% to 48.53%, Cash Balances increased to 4.41% from 2.17%.

(ii) Current Liabilities decreased from 27.18% to 22.06% implying that the company has paid the current liabilities from current assets, even then, the liquidity position is reasonably good.

(iii) Fixed Assets Increased from Rs. 1,20,000 in 2005 to Rs. 1,75,000 in 2006 as a result of purchase of fixed assets by additional issue of share capital.

(iv) The overall financial position of the company is satisfactory.

SUMMARY

Common Size Statements help in knowing the "make up" or structure of the balance sheet and the income statements. The trend revealed by the common size statements is more authentic because it shows qualitative assessment depicted by absolute figures. As each item is expressed as a percentage of the total, the relative size of each component of a subdivision of the balance sheet and the income statements can also be expressed as a percentage of the total of that division.

Glossary

- **Common Size Financial Statements:** Common size statements are those in which figures are converted into percentages to some common base.
- **Inter Firm Comparison:** Comparison between two or more firms to measure the performance is called inter firm comparison.

Questions

(1) What do you mean by Common Size Statements? How do you prepare them?

(2) Distinguish Comparative Statements from Common Size Statements.

PROBLEMS

(1) Convert the following income statement into common size statement and interpret the changes in 2005 in the light of the conditions in 2004.

	2004 *Rs.*	*2005* *Rs.*
Gross Sales	30,600	36,720
Less: Sales Returns	600	700
Net Sales	30,000	36,020
Less: Cost of Goods Sold	18,200	20,250
Gross Profit	11,800	15,770
***Less:* Operating Expenses**		
Administration Expenses	3,000	3,400
Sales Expenses	6,000	6,600
Total Expenses	**9,000**	**10,000**
Income from Operations	2,800	5,770
Add: Non-Operating Income	300	400
Total Income	**3,100**	**6,170**
Less: Non-Operating Expenses	400	600
Net Profit	**2,700**	**5,570**

(2) Following are the Balance Sheets of Reddy Ltd. as on 31 March 2003 and 2004.

Liabilities	*2003* *Rs.*	*2004* *Rs.*	*Assets*	*2003* *Rs.*	*2004* *Rs.*
Share Capital	2,400	3,600	Land and Buildings	1,620	1,040
Reserves and Surplus	1,872	2,124	Plant and Machinery	1,860	4,716
Debentures	300	600	Furniture and Fixtures	54	108
Long-term Debt	900	1,530	Other Fixed Assets	120	180
Bills Payable	1,530	702	Long Terms Loans	276	354
Other Current Liabilities	42	60	Cash and Bank Balances	708	60
			Bills Receivable	1,254	1,120
			Stock	960	780
			Prepaid Expenses	18	18
			Other Current Assets	174	240
	7,044	**8,616**		**7,044**	**8,616**

Analyze the financial position of the company with the help of the Common Size Balance Sheet.

(3) The accompanying balance sheet and profit and loss account related to SUMO Logistics Pvt. Ltd. Convert these into common size statements.

Previous Year = 2005 Current Year = 2006 **(Rs. '000)**

Particulars	*Previous Year*	*Current Year*
Liabilities:		
Equity Share Capital (of Rs. 10 each)	240	240.00
General Reserve	96	182.00
Long Term Loans	182	169.50
Creditors	67	52.00
Outstanding Expenses	6	—
Other Current Liabilities	9	6.50
Total Liabilities	**600**	**650.00**
Assets :		
Fixed Assets net of accumulated depreciation	402	390
Cash	54	78
Debtors	60	65
Inventories	84	117
Total Assets	**600**	**650**

Income Statement for the year ended

Rs.'000

Particulars	*Previous Year*	*Current Year*
Gross Sales	370	480
Less: Returns	20	30
Net Sales	350	450
Less: Cost of Goods Sold	190	215
Gross Profit	160	235
Less: Selling and Administration Expenses	50	72
Operating Profit	110	163
Less: Interest Expenses	20	17
Earnings before Tax	90	146
Less: Taxes	45	73
Earnings After Tax	45	73

(4) You are required to prepare a Comparative Statement of Proprietor's Funds and comment thereon.

	2008 (Rs.)	*2009 (Rs.)*
Preference Share Capital	50,000	50,000
Equity Share Capital	1,50,000	1,75,000
Capital Reserves	25,000	25,000
Revenue Reserves	25,000	50,000
Building	1,25,000	1,30,000
Plant	50,000	50,000
Goodwill	50,000	45,000
Cash	5,000	7,500
Debtors	35,000	45,000
Stocks	30,000	45,000
Creditors	25,000	17,500
Bills Payable	5,000	2,500
Overdraft	15,000	2,500

(5) From the following information, prepare a Common Size Statement and Comment.

Balance Sheets of Nizam Ltd. as at 31st March 2008 and 2009

Liabilities	*2008 Rs.*	*2009 Rs.*	*Assets*	*2008 Rs.*	*2009 Rs.*
Equity Share Capital	17,000	30,000	Land and Building	15,000	20,000
General Reserves	1,000	2,000	Plant and Machinery	5,000	10,000
Preference Capital	5,000	6,000	Stocks	10,000	12,000
Long-Term Loans	3,000	2,000	Debtors	6,000	3,000
Short-Term Loans	7,000	5,000	Cash	2,000	3,000
Bills Payable	3,000	2,000	Bills Receivable	2,000	3,000
Creditors	4,000	4,000			
	40,000	**51,000**		**40,000**	**51,000**

(6) Prepare Common Size Balance Sheets from the following data and comment upon the financial position of the company.

Balance Sheet on March 31st

(Rs. in lakhs)

Liabilities	*2008*	*2009*	*Assets*	*2008*	*2009*
Share Capital	50	90	Fixed Assets	100	120
Reserves	120	70	Current Assets:		
Secured Loans	20	25	Stocks	80	60
Unsecured Loans	10	15	Debtors	40	30
Current Liabilities	30	20	Cash	10	10
	230	**220**		**230**	**220**

❑ ❑ ❑

28

TREND ANALYSIS

Objectives

The objectives of the study are to:

- Understand the meaning of Trend Percentages
- Explain the procedure for calculation of the Trend Percentages
- To learn the interpretation of the given data

INTRODUCTION

In the previous chapter, the procedure for preparing common size statements is explained. Common size statements indicate the relationship of various items with some common item (expressed as a percentage of the common item). In this chapter, another tool for the analysis of data, i.e., Trend Analysis is explained.

TREND ANALYSIS: MEANING

The financial statements may be analysed by computing trends of series of information. Trend Analysis determines the direction upwards or downwards and involves the computation of the percentage relationship that each item in the various years bears to the same item in the base year. The base year could be the earliest year involved in comparison or the latest year or any intervening year. But, it should not be an abnormal year where rare situations have taken place in that year. In case of Comparative Analysis, an item is compared with itself in the previous year to know whether it has increased or decreased or remained constant. In case of Common-Size Analysis, an item (say cost of goods sold) is observed to know whether its proportion is increasing or decreasing in the common base (say sales). But, in case of Trend Analysis, we would like to know the behavior of the same item over the period say during the last 5 years. Take for example, administrative expenses, whether they are exhibiting increasing tendency or decreasing tendency or remaining constant over the period of comparison. Generally, Trend Analysis is done for reasonably long period. The trend percentages disclose the changes in the operating and financial data between the specific periods taken for the study. From the Trend Analysis, one can form an opinion as to whether favorable or adverse tendencies are reflected by the data.

PROCEDURE FOR CALCULATING TREND PERCENTAGES

The following is the procedure for calculating the Trend Percentages.

- One year is taken as the base year. Generally, the first or the last year is taken as the base year.
- The figure of the base year is taken as 100.
- The trend percentages are calculated in relation to the base year. This is done by dividing each year's figure with the base year's figure and multiplied with 100.

If a figure in other years is less than the figure in the base year, the trend percentage will be less than 100 and it will be more than 100 if the figure in other years is more than the base year figure.

$$\text{Trend Percentage} = \frac{\text{Present year value}}{\text{Base year value}} \times 100$$

PRECAUTIONS

Certain precautions should be taken while calculating Trend Percentages as the increase or decrease in Trend Percentages may lead to wrong conclusions, if studied in isolation.

The base period should be carefully selected. The base period should be a normal period. The accounting procedures and conventions used for collecting data and preparation of financial statements should be similar; otherwise the figures will not be comparable.

The interpretation of trend analysis involves a cautious study. The mere increase or decrease in trend percentage may give misleading results. For example, an increase of 20% in current assets may be treated as favorable. If this increase in current assets is accompanied by an equivalent increase in current liabilities, then this increase will be unsatisfactory. The increase in sales may not increase profits if cost of production has gone up.

ANALYSIS OF TREND PERCENTAGES

Here, a series of Financial Statements may be analyzed by studying the trends of various data shown in the statement. Such an analysis of the trend is helpful in budgeting and forecasting. Here, a statement of one period is taken as a base with reference to which all other statements are studied. Every item in the base statement is taken as 100. If the amount of an item in another statement is less than that in the base statement, the trend percentage will be less than 100 and *vice versa*. Thus, the percentages of different items for various periods are calculated and a comparison is made. Trend ratios are computed by dividing each amount in the current statement by the corresponding item in the base statement.

Trend analysis emphasizes the changes in the operating and financial data over a period of time and makes possible a horizontal study of the data. It shows the direction of the change i.e. upward or downward. The main objection to such an analysis is that the selected base year may not be a representative one. In such a case, the entire analysis would be a futile one.

Illustration 1

From the following data relating to the liabilities of the Balance Sheet of Shreya Ltd. for the period 31st March 2001 to 2004, you are required to calculate the Trend Percentages taking 2001 as the base year.

(Rs. in lakhs)

	2001	*2002*	*2003*	*2004*
Share Capital	100	125	130	150
Reserves and Surplus	50	60	65	75
12% Debentures	200	250	300	400
Bank Overdraft	10	20	25	25
Profit and Loss Account	20	22	28	26
Sundry Creditors	40	70	60	70
Outside Creditors	2	3	5	4

Solution

Calculation of trend percentages of Shreya Ltd.

	2001	*2002*	*2003*	*2004*
Share Capital	100	125	130	150
Reserves and Surplus	100	120	130	150
12% Debentures	100	125	150	200
Bank Overdraft	100	200	250	250
Profit and Loss Account	100	110	140	130
Sundry Creditors	100	175	150	175
Outside Creditors	100	150	250	200

Illustration 2

Calculate the trend percentages from the following figures of Sales, Stock and Profit of X Ltd., taking 2001 as the base year and interpret them.

(Rs.in lakhs)

Year	*Sales Rs.*	*Stock Rs.*	*Profit before tax Rs.*
2001	1,881	709	321
2002	2,340	781	435
2003	2,655	816	458
2004	3,021	944	527
2005	3,768	1,154	627

Solution

Trend Percentages (base year 2001 = 100)

(Rs. in Lakhs)

Year	*Sales Rs.*	*Trend %*	*Stock Rs.*	*Trend %*	*Profit Rs.*	*Trend*
2001	1,881	100	709	100	321	100
2002	2,340	124	781	110	435	136
2003	2,655	141	816	115	458	143
2004	3,021	161	944	133	527	164
2005	3,768	200	1,154	163	627	195

Interpretation

(i) The sales have continuously increased in all the years up to 2005. The percentage in 2005 is 200 as compared to 100 in 2001. The increase in sales is quite satisfactory.

(ii) The figures of stock have also increased over a period of 5 years. The increase in stock in 2005 is more as compared to earlier years.

(iii) Profit has substantially increased. The profits have increased more than sales (upto the year 2004) which show that there is a proper control over cost of goods sold.

The comparative increase in profits is much higher in 2004 and 2005 as compared to 2003.

Illustration 3

The following data is available from the Profit and Loss Account of Deepak Ltd.

(Figures in Rs.)

Particulars	*2003*	*2004*	*2005*	*2006*
Sales	3,10,000	3,27,500	3,20,000	3,32,500
Wages	1,07,500	1,07,500	1,15,000	1,20,000
Selling Expenses	27,250	29,000	29,750	27,750
Gross Profit	90,000	95,000	77,500	80,000

You are required to show Trend Percentages of different items.

Solution

Trend ratios of different items (Base year = 2003)

Particulars	*2003*	*2004*	*2005*	*2006*
Sales	100	106	103	107
Wages	100	100	107	112
Selling expenses	100	106	109	102
Gross Profit	100	106	86	89

Interpretation

(i) The sales for the years 2004 and 2006 have increased but the sales for the year 2005 have decreased. It is not a good sign for the business.

(ii) The wages paid to the employees is continuously increasing whereas the selling expenses are also increasing, by and large. However, there is a decline in the year 2006.

(iii) The gross profit for the year 2003 is 100 and for the year 2004, it is 106 but it has gradually decreased for the periods 2005 and 2006.

(iv) The firm should reduce its expenses in order to increase the gross profit.

The overall performance is not satisfactory.

Illustration 4

From the following data relating to the assets side of Balance Sheet of ABC Ltd for the period ended 31st Dec. 2003 to 31st Dec 2006, calculate trend percentages.

(Rs. in Lakhs)

Particulars	*2003*	*2004*	*2005*	*2006*
Cash	100	120	80	140
Debtors	200	250	325	400
Stocks	300	400	350	500
Other Current Assets	50	75	125	150
Land	400	500	500	500
Buildings	800	1,000	1,200	1,500
Plant	1,000	1,000	1,200	1,500

Solution

Trend Percentages

(Rs. in Lakhs)

Assets	*2003*	*Trend %*	*2004*	*Trend %*	*2005*	*Trend %*	*2006*	*Trend %*
Current Assets:								
Cash	100	100	120	120	80	80	140	140
Debtors	200	100	250	125	325	162.50	400	200
Stocks	300	100	400	133.33	350	116.67	500	166.67
Other Current Assets	50	100	75	150	125	250	150	300
Total A	**650**	**100**	**845**	**130**	**880**	**135.38**	**1,190**	**183.08**
Fixed Assets:								
Land	400	100	500	125	500	125	500	125
Buildings	800	100	1,000	125	1,200	150	1,500	187.5
Plant	1,000	100	1,000	100	1,200	120	1,500	150
Total B	**2,200**	**100**	**2,500**	**113.64**	**2,900**	**131.82**	**3,500**	**159.00**
A + B	**2,850**	**100**	**3,345**	**117.36**	**3,780**	**132.63**	**4,690**	**164.56**

Interpretation

(i) The total assets have exhibited a continuous increasing trend over the period.

(ii) The current assets increased much faster than the fixed assets.

(iii) Sundry Debtors and Other Current Assets in Current Assets segment and Buildings and Plant in Fixed Assets segment have shown higher growth.

Illustration 5

From the following data relating to the Liabilities side of Balance Sheet of X Ltd., for the period 31st Dec., 2003 to 31st Dec, 2006 calculate trend percentages taking 2003 as the base year.

(Rs. in Lakhs)

Liabilities	*2003*	*2004*	*2005*	*2006*
Equity Share Capital	1,000	1,000	1,200	1,500
General Reserves	800	1,000	1,200	1,500
12% Debentures	400	500	500	500
Bank Overdraft	300	400	550	500
Bills Payable	100	120	80	140
Sundry Creditors	300	400	500	600
Outstanding Liabilities	50	75	125	150

Solution

Trend Percentages

(Rs. in Lakhs)

Liabilities	*2003*	*Trend %*	*2004*	*Trend %*	*2005*	*Trend %*	*2006*	*Trend %*
Shareholder funds								
Equity Share Capital	1,000	100	1,000	100	1,200	120	1,500	150
General reserves	800	100	1,000	125	1,200	150	1,500	187.5
Total A:	**1,800**	**100**	**2,000**	**111.11**	**2,400**	**133.33**	**3,000**	**166.67**
Long term debts								
12 % Debentures	400	100	500	125	500	125	500	125
Total B:	**400**	**100**	**500**	**125**	**500**	**125**	**500**	**125**
Current Liabilities								
Bank overdraft	300	100	400	133.33	550	183.33	500	166.67
Bills Payable	100	100	120	120	80	80	140	140
Sundry Creditors	300	100	400	133.33	500	166.67	600	200
Outstanding Liabilities	50	100	75	150	125	250	150	300
Total C :	**750**	**100**	**995**	**132.67**	**1,255**	**167.33**	**1,390**	**185.33**
Total (A + B + C)	**2,950**	**100**	**3,495**	**118.47**	**4,155**	**140.85**	**4,890**	**165.76**

Interpretation

(i) Share holders funds have increased over the period, because of retaining the profits in the business in the form of reserves. Share capital also increased may be due to the issue of fresh shares or bonus shares.

(ii) The increase in current liabilities is more than that of Long term liabilities.

(iii) The Sundry creditors have doubled, may be due to the credit policy of the management. Other current liabilities exhibited a 200% increase which needs to be closely watched.

Summary

Trend Analysis is an important tool of Horizontal Financial Analysis. This method is immensely helpful in making a comparative study of the financial statements of several years. The Trend Percentages show the relationship of each item with its preceding year's percentages. These trend ratios may be compared with that of the industry in order to know the strong and weak points of a concern.

Glossary

- **Trend Analysis:** Study of the financial statements in percentages that each item bears to the same item in the base year, over a period of time.
- **Base Year:** The year which is taken as the base to calculate the trend ratio for an item in the profit and loss account or balance sheet.

Questions

(1) How are the Trend Ratios computed?
(2) What are the precautions to be taken into account at the time of computing trend ratios?
(3) What is a base year?
(4) Explain the usefulness of trend percentages in the interpretation of financial performance of a company.
(5) Critically examine the various tools available for financial analysis. What are the limitations of such tools?

PROBLEMS

(1) From the following particulars extracted from P&L A/c of Prashanth Ltd., you are required to calculate the trend percentages.

Year	*Sales (Rs.)*	*Wages (Rs.)*	*Bad debts (Rs.)*	*Profit after tax (Rs.)*
2003	3,50,000	50,000	14,000	16,000
2004	4,15,000	60,000	26,000	24,500
2005	4,25,000	72,200	29,000	45,000
2006	4,60,000	85,000	33,000	60,000

(2) Calculate the trend percentages from the following figures of ABC Ltd., taking 2000 as base and interpret them.

Year	*Sales (Rs.)*	*Stocks (Rs.)*	*Profit before tax (Rs.)*
2000	1,500	700	300
2001	2,140	780	450
2002	2,365	820	480
2003	3,020	930	530
2004	3,500	1,160	660
2005	4,000	1,200	700

(3) From the following data relating to the Liabilities side of Balance Sheet of Madhuri Ltd., as on 31st March 2006, you are required to calculate the trend percentages taking 2002 as the base year.

(Rs. in Lakhs)

Liabilities	*2002*	*2003*	*2004*	*2005*	*2006*
Share capital	100	125	130	150	160
Reserves and Surplus	50	60	65	75	80
12% Debentures	200	250	300	400	400
Bank overdraft	10	20	25	25	20
Profit and Loss A/c	20	22	28	26	30
Sundry Creditors	40	70	60	70	75

(4) From the following data relating to the liabilities of the Balance sheet of Shreya Ltd. for the period 31-03-1996 to 31-03-1999, you are required to calculate the Trend percentages taking 1996 as the base year and comment.

(Rs.in lakhs)

	1996	*1997*	*1998*	*1999*
Share Capital	1,000	1,000	1,200	1,500
Reserves and Surplus	800	1,000	1,200	1,500
12% Debentures	400	500	500	500
Bank Overdraft	300	400	550	500
Bills Payables	100	120	80	140
Sundry Creditors	300	400	500	600
Outstanding Liabilities	50	75	125	150

(5) Calculate the Trend percentages from the following figures of X 'Ltd. taking 1991 as the base.

(Rs.in lakhs)

Year	*1991*	*1992*	*1993*
Sales	2,655	3,021	3,768
Stocks	816	944	1,154
Profit before tax	458	527	672

❑ ❑ ❑

29

Ratio Analysis

Objectives

The objectives of the study are to:

- Gain an insight into the different types of Ratios
- Understand the significance of Ratio Analysis
- Learn the computation Financial Statements from incomplete data

Introduction

One of the important tools of Financial Analysis is Ratio Analysis. A Ratio may be defined as the indicated quotient of two mathematical expressions. It is a statistical yardstick to measure the relationships between two variables or figures which may be expressed as a percent or as a quotient. Ratio analysis involves determining and interpreting numerical relationships based on Financial Statements.

An accounting figure, unless related to some other relevant information, conveys no purposeful meaning. The relationship between the two related accounting figures, expressed mathematically, is known as a 'Financial Ratio'. In Financial Analysis, Ratios are used as yardstick for evaluating the financial position and performance of a firm.

Persons Interested

The persons interested in the analysis of Financial Statements can be grouped as under.

***(a)* Creditors:** They can be classified as Short Term Creditors and Long Term Creditors.

Short-Term Creditors: These persons are concerned with the firm's ability to pay its bills promptly, as they hold obligations that will mature soon. It is the amount of the liquid assets that the firm possesses, determine the ability of the firm to pay off current liabilities. These persons are interested in the liquidity ratios like current ratio and quick ratio, interest coverage ratio and turnover ratios.

Long-Term Creditors: As these persons hold bonds or mortgages against the firm, they are interested in the current payments of interest and eventual repayment of the principal amount. They are interested both in liquidity and profitability of the firm. In the short run, the firm must be sufficiently liquid and in the long run, the firm should have adequate profits. In case, earnings decline, the working capital position would indicate the ability of the firm to pay interest and principal. Interest coverage position of the firm would be of particular interest to such long-term creditors.

***(b)* Investors/Owners/Stockholders:** The owners of the firm are interested in the policies of the firm that affect the market price of the shares. They are also interested in the liquidity and profitability ratios as without liquidity, the firm would not be in a position to pay cash dividends and without profitability, it would not be possible for the firm to declare dividends. Earning per share, dividend per share, market price per share, price earning ratio and dividend yield are of particular interest to the owners.

***(c)* Financial Executives:** In order to make intelligent decisions, the management is interested in evolving analytical tools to measure costs, efficiency, liquidity and profitability. For the financial executives, various ratios like profitability ratios, liquidity ratios, solvency ratios and turnover ratios are helpful for decision making.

Standards for Comparison

For the useful interpretation of the financial statements, there is a need for comparison. A single ratio does not indicate favorable or unfavorable condition. It should be compared with some standard. The various standards for comparison are given below.

(1) Intra Firm Comparison: One way of comparison of ratios is, to compare the present ratios with the ratios calculated from the past financial statements of the same firm. This method is the easiest way to evaluate the performance of a firm over a period of time. It indicates the direction of the change and reflects whether the performance of the firm has improved, deteriorated or remained stable over time. But, the comparison is valid only when the accounting policies of the firm have not changed over a period of time.

(2) Inter Firm Comparison: Another way of comparison is, to compare the ratios of one firm with the calculated ratios of select firms belonging to the same industry. This type of comparison provides relative strengths and weaknesses of the firm. It is easy to compare, as it is not difficult to get the published financial statements of the similar firms.

(3) Projected Ratios Comparison: Here, the future ratios are used as standards for comparison with the past/present ratios of the firm. For calculating the future ratios, the projected or proforma financial statements of the same firm are taken. Such comparison reflects the strengths and weaknesses in the past and the future. Corrective actions can be initiated if the future ratios indicate weak financial position.

(4) Average Ratios Comparison: The ratios of the firm may be compared with the average ratios of the industry of which the firm is a member. This type of comparison is important in view of the fact that each industry has its own characteristics which influence the financial and operating relationships. But, the difficulty is, the firms within the same industry differ widely in their accounting principles and practices. Industry ratios prove to be very useful in evaluating the financial condition and performance of the firm provided the accounting data for the firm in the industry are standardised and extremely weak and strong firms are eliminated.

Types of Ratios

There are various types of ratios which are classified mainly into Structural Ratios, Liquidity Ratios, Profitability Ratios, Turnover Ratios and Miscellaneous Group.

I. Structural Group/Leverage/Capital Structure Ratios

Leverage ratios indicate long term financial strength of the company. The short term creditors like bankers and suppliers of raw materials are satisfied with the firm's current debt paying ability, whereas, the long term creditors like debenture holders, financial institutions are more concerned with the firm's long term financial strength.

Leverage ratios indicate the funds provided by the owners and creditors, thus, identifying the sources of funds. They provide a measure of the degree of risk resulting from debt financing. The manner in which the funds are being provided has a number of implications. Between debt and equity, though debt is a cheaper source of funds, it is more risky from the firm's point of view. Irrespective of profits made, the firm has to pay interest on the debt funds. But, the advantage of debt capital is that the existing shareholders can retain their control over the firm with a limited stake and their earnings would be magnified when the firm invest the funds raised and earns a rate of return higher than the interest rate on the debt funds. This process of magnifying the shareholders earnings through the employment of debt is called as **'trading on equity'.** At the same time, if the cost of debt is higher than the firms overall rate of return, the shareholders earnings would be reduced and there is also a threat of insolvency if the firm is not able to pay the interest charges to the debenture holders. If the firm is actually liquidated, then, the worst sufferers would be the shareholders as they are the residual owners. Thus, the use of debt magnifies the shareholders earnings and at the same time increases the risk. Hence, it is a double-edged sword.

Debt Equity Ratio = Long Term Debt/Shareholders Equity

Or

Total Debt/Shareholders Equity

It is a measure of the relative claims of creditors and owners against the firms' assets. Shareholders equity is equal to the net worth. It includes share capital (both equity and preference capital), reserves and undistributed profits excluding past accumulated losses and deferred expenditures (fictitious assets).

A high ratio shows that the claims of creditors are greater than those of owners and it is unfavorable from the firms' point of view. A highly debt financed company suffers great strains during the periods of low profits as it cannot discharge the obligations of the creditors.

A low debt equity ratio implies a greater claim of owners than creditors. It represents a satisfactory capital structure from the point of view of creditors since a high proportion of equity provides a larger margin of safety for them. But, there is a disadvantage to the shareholders during the periods of good economic conditions if the firm employs a low amount of debt.

Thus, there is a need to strike a proper balance between the use of debt and equity.

II. Liquidity Ratios

It measures the ability of the firm to meet its current obligations. It is necessary for a firm to meet its obligations as they become due. The firm should ensure that it does not suffer from lack of liquidity and at the same time it should not have too much liquidity. The failure of a company to meet its obligations will result in bad credit ratings and lack of creditor confidence. It may also result in lawsuits leading to closure of the company. At the same time, a very high degree of liquidity is also not good, as idle assets earn nothing. Therefore, there is a need for a proper balance between liquidity and lack of liquidity. The extent of liquidity or lack of it, is indicated by current ratio and quick ratio.

(A) Current Ratio: It is a ratio between the current assets and the current liabilities. Current assets include all those assets which are cash or can be quickly converted into cash within a period of one year such as marketable securities, stocks, debtors, prepaid expenses, bills receivable, bank and cash. Current liabilities are those obligations maturing within a period of one year and include creditors, bills payable, accrued expenses, income tax liability and long term debt maturing in the current year. The ratio indicates the availability of current assets in rupees for every one rupee of current liability. It measures the firm's short-term solvency.

Current Ratio = Current Assets/Current Liabilities

A high current ratio indicates that the firm is liquid and has the ability to pay its bills. A relatively low ratio is considered as an indication that the firm will find difficulty in paying its bills. As a conventional rule, a current ratio of 2:1 is considered as satisfactory. The logic here is, in a worst situation, even if the value of current assets becomes half of its value, the firm will be able to meet its obligations. But in reality, the firms with less than 2:1 current ratio may also be doing well, while the firms with 2:1 or more may be finding difficulties in paying the bills. The reason is, current ratio is only a test of quantity and not quality. There may be doubtful and slow paying debtors or slow moving and unsaleable stock of goods, as a result of which, the firm's ability to pay bills is impaired and its short term solvency is threatened. Thus, too much reliance should not be placed on the current ratio. Further investigation about the quality of the current assets should be made. However, this ratio is a quick and crude measure of the firm's liquidity.

(B) Quick Ratio/Acid Test Ratio: It establishes a relationship between quick or liquid assets and current liabilities. Quick assets are those assets which can be converted into cash immediately or reasonably soon without a loss of value and include all current assets except stocks and prepaid expenses. Stocks normally requires some time for realizing into cash and its value has a tendency to fluctuate. Prepaid expenses are excluded, as they cannot be converted into cash.

Quick Ratio = Quick Assets/Current Liabilities or Quick Assets/Quick Liabilities

Generally a quick ratio of 1:1 is considered as satisfactory. It is more penetrating test of liquidity than the current ratio, but this ratio should be used cautiously. A higher ratio need not necessarily imply a sound liquidity position and a low ratio, a bad liquidity position. This is because, all book debts need not be liquid and cash may be immediately needed to pay operating expenses. At the same time, inventories are not absolutely non-liquid. Thus, a company may be facing a problem with a high value of quick ratio and on the other hand a company with a low value of quick ratio may really be prospering and paying its current obligations on time if it has been managing its inventories very efficiently. Therefore, the firm should compare its current ratio and quick ratio with the industry averages to get an idea regarding the firm's relative current financial position. Quick Liabilities are Current Liabilities less Bank Overdraft.

Illustration 1

The working capital of AB Ltd. has deteriorated in the recent year and now stands as under:

Current Liabilities	*Rs.*	*Current Assets:*	*Rs.*
Creditors	2,45,000	Inventory	2,80,000
Bank Loan	1,05,000	Debtors	1,75,000
		Cash	35,000

Calculate Current Ratio

Solution

Current Ratio = Current Assets/Current Liabilities 4,90,000/3,50,000 = 1.4

Illustration 2

Calculate Current Ratio and Quick Ratio from the following information:

Liabilities	*Rs.*	*Assets*	*Rs.*
Sundry Creditors	10,000	Stocks	30,000
Bills Payable	7,500	Sundry Debtors	35,000
Tax Payable	9,000	Cash Balance	10,000
Outstanding Expenses	16,000	Bills Receivable	15,000
Debentures	75,000	Prepaid Expenses	5,000
		Land and Building	1, 00,000
		Goodwill	50,000

Solution

Current Ratio: Current Assets/Current Liabilities

Current Assets = Rs. 30,000 + Rs. 35,000 + Rs. 15,000 + Rs. 10,000 + Rs. 5,000 = Rs. 95,000

Current Liabilities = Rs. 10,000 + Rs. 7,500 + Rs 9,000 + Rs. 16,000 = Rs. 42,500

Current Ratio = 95,000/42,500 = 2.23

Quick Ratio Quick Assets/Current Liabilities

Quick Assets = Current Assets – Stocks – Prepaid Expenses

95,000 – 30,000 – 5,000 = Rs. 60,000

Quick Ratio = 60,000/42,500 = 1.41

Illustration 3

Following is the information given to you.

Current Ratio 2.5

Working Capital Rs. 60,000

Find out *(a)* Current Assets and *(b)* Current Liabilities

Solution

Working Capital = Current Assets – Current Liabilities

Current Ratio = Current Assets:Current Liabilities

Current Ratio of 2.5 means Current Assets are 2.5 and Current Liabilities are 1

Then, Working Capital will be 2.5 – 1 = 1.5

If 1.5 Working Capital = Rs. 60,000

Then, Current Assets 2.5 = 60,000 × 2.5/1.5 = Rs. 1,00,000

1 Current Liabilities = 60,000 × 1/1.5 = Rs. 40,000

Illustration 4

The following information of a company is given. Find out *(a)* Current Assets *(b)* Working Capital

Current Ratio = 2.25

Current Liabilities = Rs. 50,000

Solution

Working Capital = Current Assets – Current Liabilities

Working Capital =2.25-1=1.25

1 = Rs. 50,000

1.25=?

(50,000 × 1.25)/1= Rs. 62,500

Current Assets = 2.25

1 = 50,000, 2.25=?

(50,000 × 2.25)/1= Rs. 1,12,500

Verification : Working Capital = Current Assets – Current Liabilities

Working Capital = 1,12,500 – 50,000

Working Capital = Rs. 62,500

Illustration 5

Calculate Liquid Ratio from the following information.

Current Liabilities	*Rs.*	*Current Assets*	*Rs.*
Trade Creditors	2,50,000	Cash	50,000
Bills payable	1,00,000	Inventory	3,00,000
Outstanding Expenses	50,000	Debtors	2,00,000

Solution

Liquid Ratio = Liquid Assets/Current Liabilities

Liquid Assets = Cash + Debtors (50,000 + 2,00,000) = Rs. 2,50,000

Current liabilities = 2,50,000 + 1,00,000 + 50,000 = Rs. 4,00,000

= 2,50,000/4,00,000 = 0.625

Illustration 6

The following information of a company is given.

Current ratio = 2.5

Liquid ratio = 1.5, Stock = 15,000

Find out *(a)* Liquid assets *(b)* Current assets *(c)* Current liabilities *(d)* Working capital

Solution

(a) Inventory Ratio = Current Ratio – Liquid Ratio

Inventory Ratio = 2.5-1.5

Inventory Ratio = 1

Stock 15,000 = 1

Liquid Assets = 1.5

1 = 15,000

1.5 = ?

(15,000 × 1.5)/1 = Rs. 22,500

(b) Current Assets = 2.5 (15,000 × 2.5)/1

Current Assets = Rs. 37,500

(c) Current Liabilities, Current Ratio = 2.5:1

Current Assets = 2.5 and Current Liabilities = 1

Current Liabilities = (37,500 × 1)/ 2.5 = Rs. 15,000

(d) Working Capital = Current Assets – Current Liabilities

37,500 – 15,000 = Rs. 22,500

Illustration 7

Given

Acid test ratio = 1.5, Current Ratio =2.8

Working capital = Rs. 36,000. Find out *(a)* Current Assets *(b)* Current Liabilities *(c)* Liquid Assets and *(d)* Inventory

Solution

	Current Ratio	= 2.8:1
	Working Capital	= Current Assets - Current Liabilities
	Working Capital	= 2.8 – 1 = 1.8
	Working Capital	= 1.8 = Rs. 36,000
(a)	Current Assets	= 2.8
	Current Assets	= (36,000 × 2.8)/1.8 = Rs. 56,000
(b)	Current Liabilities	= (36,000 × 1)/1.8 = Rs. 20,000
(c)	Liquid Assets	= Liquid Assets/Current Liabilities = 1.5
	Liquid Assets	= (1.5 × 20,000)/1 = Rs. 30,000
(d)	Inventory	= Current Assets – Liquid Assets
		= 56,000 – 30,000 = Rs. 26,000

Illustration 8

Current Ratio 1.75; Quick Ratio 1.25; Inventory Rs. 1,00,000

Find out Current Ratio; Current Liabilities; Liquid Assets and Working Capital.

Solution

	Inventory Ratio	= Current Ratio – Liquid Ratio
		= 1.75 – 1.25 = 0.5
(i)	Current Assets :	
	Inventory 0.5	= Rs. 1,00,000
	Current Assets 1.75	= (1,00,000 × 1.75)/0.5 = Rs. 3,50,000
(ii)	Current Liabilities :	
	Current Ratio	= Current Assets/Current Liabilities
	Current Assets 1.75	= Rs. 3,50,000
	Current Liabilities 1	= (3,50,000 × 1)/1.75 = Rs. 2,00,000
(iii)	Liquid Assets	= Current Assets – Inventory
		= Rs. 3,50,000 – Rs. 1,00,000 = Rs. 2,50,000
(iv)	Working Capital	= Current Assets – Current Liabilities
		= 3,50,000 – 2,00,000 = Rs. 1,50,000

III. Profitability Ratios

For the survival and growth of the firm over a long period of time, profits are a must for the firm. Profit is the difference between the total revenues and the total expenses over a period of time. The firm will have no future if it fails to make sufficient profits and profit is the ultimate output. To measure the operating efficiency of the firm, profitability ratios are calculated. Apart from the management of the company, creditors and owners are also interested in the profitability ratios, as they would like to know the return on their investments. The various profitability ratios are given below.

(A) Operating Ratio: It shows the relationship between the total operating expenses and the net sales. Total operating expenses include cost of goods sold and other operating expenses like administration and selling and distribution expenses. Financial costs like dividends and interest including income tax are excluded.

$$\text{Operating Ratio} = \frac{\text{Cost of goods sold + Other operating expenses}}{\text{Net sales}} \times 100$$

A high operating ratio is considered as unfavorable, since it leaves a very small amount of operating income to meet non-operating expenses. This ratio is a yardstick of operating efficiency. To know the behavior of each individual expense item, the ratio of each individual operating expenditure to sales may be calculated.

(B) Operating Profit Ratio: It is a ratio between the operating profit and the net sales. It can also be calculated by subtracting operating ratio from 100.

$$\text{Operating Profit Ratio} = \frac{\text{Operating profit}}{\text{Net sales}} \times 100$$

A lower operating ratio results in a higher operating profit ratio enabling the firm to meet interest, income tax and dividends and retain profits for expansion. This ratio indicates the ability of the firm to withstand the adverse conditions.

(C) Gross Profit Margin: It reflects the efficiency with which the management produces each unit of product. It shows the relationship between gross profit and net sales. Gross profit is the excess of net sales over cost of goods sold. The ratio is expressed as a percentage.

$$\text{Gross Profit Margin} = \frac{\text{Gross Profit}}{\text{Net Sales}} \times 100$$

A high ratio implies that the firm is able to produce at relatively a lower cost. It is a sign of good management. The ratio can be increased by higher sales price or lower cost of goods sold or a combination of variations in sales prices and costs.

(D) Net Profit Margin: To earn an adequate net profit, a reasonable gross profit margin is necessary. Net Profit is obtained after deducting operating and non-operating expenses from the gross profit. Here, the Net Profit after taxes is expressed as a percentage of Net Sales.

$$\text{Net Profit Margin} = \frac{\text{Net Profit after Taxes}}{\text{Net Sales}} \times 100$$

It indicates the overall efficiency of the firm, to turn each rupee of sales into net profit. It shows the management's efficiency in manufacturing, administering and selling the products. A high net profit margin would enable the firm to survive in the face of falling sales price, rising cost of production or declining demand for the product.

By linking both Gross Profit Margin and Net Profit Margin, the firm's profitability can be interpreted more meaningfully. Inspite of an increase in the gross profit margin over years, if net profit margin as either remained constant or declined or not increased as fast as gross margin, it is an indication that the operating expenses relating to sales have been increasing.

(E) Interest Coverage Ratio: This ratio is used to test the firm's debt servicing capacity. It is also known as Times – Interest – Earned. It shows, how many times the interest charges are covered by the funds that are ordinarily available to pay the interest charges.

$$\text{Interest Coverage Ratio} = \frac{\text{Earnings before Interest and Taxes}}{\text{Interest charges}}$$

Income tax is excluded in the numerator as; taxes are calculated after paying the interest. It shows the margin available to the long-term creditors in paying their interest charges. It also indicates the extent to which the earnings may fall without causing any difficulty to the firm regarding the payment of the interest charges. A high ratio means, the firm is very conservative in using the debt and credit is not utilized to the best advantage of the shareholders. A lower ratio implies excessive use of debt or inefficient operations.

(F) Return on Investment: Here, investment may mean total assets, capital employed or the owner's equity. Accordingly, the following ratios may be calculated.

(i) **Return on Assets** $= \dfrac{\text{Net Profit after Taxes}}{\text{Total Assets}}$

This ratio is a useful measure of the profitability of all financial resources invested in the firm's assets. It evaluates the performance of the divisions in a multi-divisional firm. It evaluates the use of total funds without any regard to the sources of funds.

(ii) **Return on Capital Employed** $= \dfrac{\text{Net Profit after Taxes}}{\text{Capital Employed}}$

Capital Employed is the permanent capital, which includes owner's funds and non-current liabilities.

Owners funds = Equity Share Capital + Preference Share Capital + Reserves + Undistributed Profits - Fictitious Assets. Capital Employed can also be calculated by adding Working Capital (Current Assets – Current Liabilities) to the Non-Current Assets.

The return on capital employed shows, how well the management has utilized the funds supplied by the creditors and owners. A higher ratio is a positive sign. The relative operational efficiency of the firm will be known by comparing it with the ratios of similar business and industry average.

(iii) **Return on Shareholders Equity** $= \dfrac{\text{Net Profit after Taxes}}{\text{Shareholders Equity}}$

Shareholders Equity is known as networth or owners funds. The ratio shows the profitableness of the owner's investments. When compared with ratios of other similar firms or industry average, the relative performance and the relative strength of the company in attracting future investment is revealed.

Illustration 9

From the following information, calculate Operating Ratio and Operating Profit Ratio.

Cost of Goods Sold	Rs. 5,20,000
Operating Expenses	Rs. 1,80,000
Net Sales	Rs. 8,00,000

Solution

Operating Ratio = (Cost of Goods Sold + Other Operating Expenses)/Net Sales

= (5,20,000 + 1,80,000)/8,00,000 = 0.875 or 87.5%

Operating Profit Ratio = 100% – Operating Ratio

= 100% – 87.5% = 12.5%

Illustration 10

A firm has profit before interest and taxes of Rs. 3,20,000; interest charges of Rs. 16,000; taxes of Rs. 60,000; total assets of Rs. 10,00,000 and total liabilities of Rs. 6,00,000. What is its *(a)* Return on Equity and *(b)* Interest Coverage?

Solution

	Rs.
Earnings before Interest and Taxes	3,20,000
Less: Interest	16,000
Earnings before Taxes	3,04,000
Less: Taxes	60,000
Earnings after Taxes	2,44,000

(a) Return on Equity = (Earnings after taxes/Equity) × 100

Equity = Total Assets – Total Liabilities

10,00,000 – 6,00,000 = Rs. 4,00,000

Return on Equity = (2,44,000/4,00,000) × 100 = 61%

(b) Interest Coverage = Earnings before interest and taxes/Interest

3,20,000/16,000 = 20 times

Illustration 11

From the following particulars, calculate interest coverage ratio and offer your comment.

Net income after taxes	Rs. 2,00,000
Fixed interest charges	Rs. 27,000

Income tax paid is 50% on profit.

Solution

Profit after tax is Rs. 2,00,000 after deducting a tax of 50%. The profit after tax is calculated as under.

Profit after tax = Earnings before interest and taxes – interest – taxes

In the problem, profit after tax is given. We have to work back to know EBIT.

If Profit before tax is Rs. 100, Profit after tax is Rs.50 after deducting a tax of Rs. 50.

Therefore, EBT = (2,00,000 × 100)/50 =	Rs. 4,00,000
Add Interest	Rs. 27,000
EBIT	Rs. 4,27,000

Interest Coverage = EBIT/Interest 4,27,000/27,000 = 15.82 times

The financial position of the company to meet the interest charges out of the current earnings is sound.

IV. Turnover Ratios/Activity Ratios: The funds of creditors and owners are invested in various kinds of assets to generate sales and profits. The activity ratios evaluate the efficiency with which the firm manages and utilizes its assets. They indicate the speed with which the assets are being converted or turned over into sales. A relationship between sales and various assets is established. The various turnover ratios are given below.

***(a)* Inventory/Stock Turnover Ratio:** Here, the efficiency of the firm's inventory management is reflected.

$$\text{Inventory Turnover Ratio} = \frac{\text{Cost of goods sold or Net Sales}}{\text{Average Inventory or Closing Stock}}$$

Cost of goods sold = Opening Stock + Purchases + Direct Expenses – Closing Stock

Average Inventory = (Opening Stock + Closing Stock)/2

The formula Cost of Goods Sold/Average Inventory, is more appropriate as both the numerator (cost of goods sold) and the denominator (Average inventory), are valued at cost and are comparable.

***(b)* Debtors Turnover Ratio and Collection Period:** The liquidity position of the firm depends on the quality of debtors to a great extent. Collection period shows the average number of days for which the firm must wait after making a credit sale before collecting cash from the customers.

$$\text{Debtors Turnover Ratio} = \frac{\text{Credit Sales}}{\text{Average Debtors or Closing Debtors}}$$

Debtors include bills receivable. If credit sales information is not given, total sales are assumed to be credit sales. Higher the ratio, greater is the efficiency in the management of debtors.

$$\text{Average Collection Period} = \frac{\text{Days or weeks or months in a year}}{\text{Debtors Turnover Ratio}}$$

The Collection period indicates the rapidity or slowness in the collection of the amount from the debtors. A short collection period implies a prompt payment by debtors. It also indicates a very restrictive credit and collection policy. Though, such a policy avoids bad debts losses, it also curtails sales resulting in low profits. A long collection period implies a too liberal and inefficient credit and collection performance. Here, there are chances of bad debt losses.

To have a more detailed idea of quality of debtors, ageing schedule can be prepared by breaking down debtors according to the length of time for which they have been outstanding. Ageing schedule clearly spots out the slow paying debtors.

***(c)* Fixed Assets Turnover Ratio:** It measures the efficiency with which the firm is utilizing its investment in fixed assets. It is obtained by dividing the sales with the depreciated value of fixed assets.

$$\text{Fixed Assets Turnover} = \frac{\text{Cost of Goods Sold}}{\text{Net Fixed Assets}}$$

Or

$$\text{Fixed Assets Turnover} = \frac{\text{Net Sales}}{\text{Net Fixed Assets}}$$

A high fixed assets turnover indicates efficient utilization of fixes assets in generating sales and a low ratio indicates inefficient management and utilization of fixed assets.

***(d)* Total Assets Turnover:** The firm must manage its total assets efficiently and generate maximum sales through their proper utilization.

$$\text{Total Assets Turnover} = \frac{\text{Cost of Goods Sold or Net Sales}}{\text{Total Assets}}$$

Total Assets include Net Fixed Assets and Current Assets. The ratio shows the firms ability to generate sales from all the financial resources connected to the firm. A higher ratio indicates the firm's ability to produce a large volume of sales with a small total assets base.

***(e)* Capital Employed Turnover:** This ratio examines the effectiveness in utilizing the capital employed. The higher the ratio, the more efficient utilization of owners and long term creditor's funds.

$$\text{Capital Employed Turnover} = \frac{\text{Net Sales}}{\text{Capital Employed}}$$

Illustration 12

Calculate stock turnover ratio from the following information.

Opening Stock Rs. 29,000; Closing Stock Rs. 31,000; Sales Rs. 3,20,000; Gross Profit 25%

Solution

Stock Turnover = Cost of Goods Sold/Average or Closing Stock

If Gross Profit is 25% of Sales, then, Cost of Goods Sold is 75% of sales

Cost of goods sold = 3,20,000 × 75% = Rs. 2,40,000

Average Stock = (Opening Stock + Closing Stock)/2

= (29,000 + 31,000)/2 = Rs. 30,000

Stock Turnover = 2,40,000/30,000 = 8 times

Illustration 13

A firm has a cost of goods sold of Rs. 8,00,000; sales of Rs.10,00,000 and an asset turnover of 4. What is the rate of return on asset?

Solution

Return on assets = (Profit after tax/Total Assets) × 100

Assets turnover = Cost of goods sold/Total assets

Therefore, total assets = Cost of goods sold/Assets turnover

8,00,000/4 = Rs. 2,00,000

Profit = Sales – Cost of goods sold

10,00,000 – 8,00,000 = Rs. 2,00,000

Return on Assets = (2,00,000 × 100)/2,00,000 = 100%

Illustration 14

Kiran Stores Ltd. carries on an average stock valued at a cost price of Rs. 40,000 and turns this over five times per year. If his stocks are marked up by 25% on cost price, what is his gross profit for the year?

Solution

Average Stock = Rs. 40,000

Stock Turnover = Cost of Goods sold/Average stock, i.e., 5 times

Cost of Goods sod = Average Stock × Stock Turnover

40,000 × 5 = Rs. 2,00,000

Gross Profit = 2,00,000 × 25% = Rs. 50,000

Illustration 15

A company has the shareholders equity of Rs. 6,00,000. Fixed assets are 60% of the shareholders equity, while the fixed assets turnover is 4. If the company has an inventory turnover of 6, determine the amount of inventory.

Solution

Fixed assets = 60% of Rs. 6,00,000, i.e., Rs. 3,60,000

Fixed Assets Turnover = Cost of goods sold or sales/Fixed Assets

Sales = Fixed Assets × Fixed Assets Turnover

= 3,60,000 × 4 = Rs. 14,40,000

Stock Turnover = Sales/Closing Stock

Closing Stock = Sales/Stock Turnover

= 14,40,000/6 = Rs. 2,40,000

Illustration 16

A company has an inventory of Rs. 3,60,000; Debtors Rs. 2,00,000 and an inventory turnover of 12. The gross profit margin of the company is 10% and its credit sales are 30% of the total sales. Calculate the average collection period.

Solution

Stock Turnover Ratio = Cost of goods sold/Stock

Cost of goods sold = Stock × Stock Turnover

3,60,000 × 12 = Rs. 43,20,000

Gross profit = 10% of sales

If sales = Rs. 100, Gross Profit = Rs. 10, then, Cost of goods sold will be Rs. 90

Cost of goods sold 90 = Rs. 43,20,000

Sales 100, will be equal to (43,20,000 × 100)/90 = Rs. 48,00,000

Credit Sales = Rs. 48,00,000 × 30% = Rs. 14,40,000

Debtors Turnover = Credit Sales/Debtors

14,40,000/2,00,000 = 7.2 times

Collection Period = No. of days in a year/Debtors Turnover

365/7.2 = 50.69 days or 51 days

Illustration 17

From the following particulars, you are required to calculate :

(a) Debtors Turnover and

(b) Average Collection period

	March 31,2007 *Rs.*	*March 31, 2008* *Rs.*
Net Sales	8,00,000	7,50,000
Debtors at the beginning of the financial year	1,66,000	1,60,000
Debtors at the end of the financial year	2,94,000	1,72,000

Solution

Debtors Turnover = Credit Sales/Average Debtors

Average Debtors = (Opening Debtors + Closing Debtors)/2

(1,66,000 + 2,94,000)/2 = Rs. 2,30,000

(1,60,000 + 1,72,000)/2 = Rs. 1,66,000

Debtors Turnover 2007 = 8,00,000/2,30,000 = 3.48 times

2008 = 7,50,000/1,66,000 = 4.52 times

Average Collection Period = No. of days in a year/Debtors Turnover

2007 : 365/3.48 = 104.89 days or 105 days

2008 : 365/4.52 = 80.75 days or 81 days

Illustration 18

Shirish Stores Ltd. made credit sales of Rs. 36,00,000 during the year 2000. If the collection period is 30 days and the year is assumed to be 360 days, calculate

(a) Debtors Turnover

(b) Average Debtors and

(c) Debtors at the end if the debtors at the end are more than the beginning debtors by Rs. 16,000.

Solution

(a) Collection Period = No. of days in a year/Debtors Turnover

Debtors Turnover = No. of days in a year/Collection Period

360/30 = 12 times

(b) Debtors Turnover = Credit Sales/Average Debtors

Average Debtors = Credit Sales/Debtors Turnover

36,00,000/12 = Rs. 3,00,000

(c) Let Opening Debtors be Rs. x

Closing Debtors = Opening Debtors + Rs. 16,000, i.e., x + 16,000

Average Debtors = (Opening Debtors + Closing Debtors)/2

3,00,000 = (x + x + 16,000)/2

3,00,000	= (2x + 16,000)/2
3,00,000 × 2	= 2x + 16,000
6,00,000	= 2x + 16,000
6,00,000 – 16,000	= 2x
5,84,000	= 2x
x = 5,84,000/2	= 2,92,000

Therefore, Opening Debtors = Rs. 2,92,000

Closing Debtors = 2,92,000 + 16,000 = Rs. 3,08,000

Illustration 19

Net Sales Rs. 5,00,000	Bills Receivables Rs. 40,000
Debtors Rs. 1,20,000	Calculate Debtors Turnover

Solution

Debtors Turnover = Credit Sales/Debtors

= 5,00,000/1,60,000 = 50/16 = 3.125 times

Collection Period = Number of Days in a year/Debtors Turnover

= 365 × 16/50 = 116.8 days or 117 days

Note: Debtors include Bills Receivables

Illustration 20

Following are the ratios of the trading activities of National Traders Ltd.

Debtors Velocity	3 months	Creditors Velocity	2 months
Stock Velocity	8 months	Gross Profit ratio	25%
Gross Profit	Rs. 4,00,000	Closing Stock was Rs. 10,000 above the opening stock	
Bills Receivables	Rs. 25,000	Bills Payable	Rs. 10,000

Find out

- Sales
- Sundry Debtors
- Closing Stock and
- Sundry Creditors

Solution

(i) Sales :

Gross Profit = 25% = Rs. 4,00,000

Sales 100% = 4,00,000 × 100/25 = Rs. 16,00,000

(ii) Sundry Debtors :

Debtors Velocity (Collection Period) = 3 months

Receivables Turnover = 12 months/3 months = 4 times

Receivable Turnover = Credit Sales/Average Receivable

Average Receivables = 16,00,000/4 = Rs. 4,00,000

Debtors = Average Receivables – Bills Receivable

4,00,000 – 25,000 = Rs. 3,75,000

(iii) Closing Stock :

Stock Velocity 8 months

Stock Turnover = 12 months/8 months = 1.5 times

Stock Turnover = Cost of goods sold/Average Stock

Where Cost of Goods sold = Sales 16,00,000 – Gross Profit 4,00,000 = Rs. 12,00,000

Average Stock = 12,00,000/1.5 = Rs. 8,00,000

Average Stock = (Opening Stock + Closing Stock)/2

If Opening Stock is assumed to be x, then, Closing Stock will be x + 10,000

Average Stock × 2 = Opening Stock + Closing Stock

$8,00,000 \times 2 = x + x + 10,000$

$2x + 10,000 = 16,00,000$

$x = (16,00,000 - 10,000)/2$

$x = 15,90,000/2 = \text{Rs. } 7,95,000$

Opening Stock = Rs. 7,95,000 and Closing Stock = 7,95,000 + 10,000 = Rs. 8,05,000

(iv) Sundry Creditors :

Creditors Velocity 2 months

Creditors Turnover = 12 months/2 months = 6 times

Creditors Turnover = Credit Purchases/Average Payables

Cost of goods sold = Opening Stock + Purchases – Closing Stock

Purchases = Cost of goods sold – Opening Stock + Closing Stock

= 12,00,000 – 7,95,000 + 8,05,000 = Rs. 12,10,000

Average Payables = Credit Purchases/Creditors Turnover

= 12,10,000/6 = Rs. 2,01,667

Creditors = Average Payables – Bills Payable

= 2,01,667 – 10,000 = Rs. 1,91,667

V. Miscellaneous Ratios

(a) **Earnings per share** = $\dfrac{\text{Net Profit after Taxes} - \text{Preference Dividends}}{\text{Number of Equity Shares}}$

Earnings per share shows the profitability of the firm on a per share basis. It is a valuable and widely used ratio, though it does not reflect how much is paid as dividend and how much is retained in the business. Earnings per share over years indicate whether the firms earning power on per share basis has changed or not over that period.

(b) **Dividends per share** = $\dfrac{\text{Earnings paid to Equity Shareholders}}{\text{Number of Equity Shares}}$

The net profits after taxes though belong to shareholders, the owners are interested in the amount of earnings which are actually distributed and paid as cash dividends. Therefore, the present and the potential investors are more interested in dividend per share rather than earning per share.

Another ratio, which may be of more interest to the shareholders, is Dividend Payout Ratio. It indicates how much dividend per share is paid out of earning per share.

Dividend Payout Ratio = $\dfrac{\text{Dividend Per Share}}{\text{Earning Per Share}}$

(c) **Dividend and Earning Yields**

Dividend Yield = $\dfrac{\text{Dividend Per Share}}{\text{Market Value of the Share}}$

Earnings Yield = $\dfrac{\text{Earnings Per Share}}{\text{Market Value of the Share}}$

Earnings Yield is also known as Earnings Price Ratio.

The above Yield ratios evaluate the share holders return in relation to the market value of the share. As the information on the market value per share is not generally available from the financial statements, it has to be collected from the stock exchanges.

(d) **Price Earning Ratio** = $\dfrac{\text{Market Value of the Share}}{\text{Earnings per Share}}$

It is the reciprocal of the earnings yield. It indicates the investors expectations about the firms performance. The Security Analysts use this ratio widely to evaluate the firms performance as expected by the investors.

Illustration 21

A company has a net profit after tax Rs. 2,40,000 and pays cash dividends of Rs. 96,000 on its 72,000 shares outstanding at a time when the share is selling for Rs. 20. What is the dividend yield and dividend payout ratio?

Solution

(a)	Dividend Yield	=	Dividend per share/Market price per share
	Dividend per share	=	96,000/72,000 = Rs. 1.33
	Dividend Yield	=	1.33/20 = 0.0665 or 6.65%
(b)	Dividend Pay-out Ratio	=	Dividend per share/Earning per share
	Earning Per Share	=	Earnings after tax/No. of shares
		=	2,40,000/72,000 = Rs. 3.33
	Dividend pay-out Ratio	=	1.33/3.33 = 0.399

Du- Pont Analysis Chart

The return on capital employed indicates the earning power of an enterprise. It is a combination of profit margin and capital employed turnover.

Return on Capital Employed = Profit Margin × Capital Employed Turnover

$$= \frac{\text{Operating Profit}}{\text{Net Sales}} \times \frac{\text{Net Sales}}{\text{Capital Employed}}$$

$$= \frac{\text{Operating Profit}}{\text{Capital Employed}}$$

The above analysis of ratio has been presented by Du-Pont Company of U.S.A. through a chart, which is given below.

Du-Pont Chart

Return on Investment

(Operating Profit/Capital Employed)

Profit Margin × **Investment Turnover**

Profit Margin		Investment Turnover
↓		↓
Operating Profit / Sales		Sales / **Investment**
↓		↓
Sales – **Operating Expenses**		Fixed Assets + **Working Capital**
↓		↓
Cost of Goods Sold + Administration, Selling and Distribution expenses		Current Assets – Current Liabilities

The above chart shows the interpretation of profitability and turnover (activity) ratios. The Profit Margin Ratio shows the margin the firm gets through carrying on its business and the investment turnover ratio shows the speed at which the assets are usefully employed in the business. Thus, the overall performance or efficiency of a firm is a result of its working and operations. The performance can be improved either by increasing the profit margin or accelerating the pace of rotation of funds for business activity.

Increase in the profit margin can be achieved either by controlling the costs or by increasing the sales or both. The investment turnover can be increased either by limiting the investment in fixed assets or working capital without adversely affecting the sales or by increasing the sales for a given level of investment.

The above analysis gives a clear picture of the areas, which need management's attention for a better performance.

Illustration 22

The following are the abridged accounting reports prepared for Shanti Ltd.

Income Statement for the year ending 31.03.2000

			Rs.
Credit Sales			3,00,000
Less: Cost of Goods Sold			
Opening Stock		1,00,000	
Purchases		2,05,000	
		3,05,000	
Less: Closing Stock		80,000	
			2,25,000
Gross Profit			75,000
Less: Operating Expenses			57,000
Net Profit Before Tax			18,000
Less: Provision for Tax			8,000
Net Profit After Tax			10,000

Balance Sheet of Shanti Ltd. as on 31.03.2000

Liabilities		*Rs.*	*Assets*		*Rs.*
Accounts Payable	87,000		Cash	30,000	
Accrued Expenses	8,000		Bill Receivables	60,000	
Provision for Tax	5,000		Inventory	80,000	
		1,00,000			1,70,000
Loan on Mortgage		25,000	Fixed Assets:		
Shareholders Funds			Buildings	65,000	
Capital	80,000		Machinery	40,000	
Reserves	30,000		*Less:* Depreciation	25,000	
Unappropriated Profits	15,000				80,000
		1,25,000			
		2,50,000			2,50,000

Identify and calculate the following ratios.

(*a*) The rapidity with which accounts receivable are collected

(*b*) The ability of the company to meet its current liabilities

(*c*) What 'mark up' has been attained?

(*d*) The efficiency with which funds represented by inventories are being utilized and managed?

(*e*) The ability of the company to meet quickly demands for payment of amounts due.

(*f*) The relative importance of proprietorship and liabilities as sources of funds.

Solution

(*a*) Average Collection Period = (Number of days in a year × Debtors)/Sales

= (365 × 60,000)/3,00,000 = 73 days

(*b*) Current Ratio = Current Assets/Current Liabilities

= 1,70,000/1,00,000 = 1.7

(*c*) Gross Profit Margin = (Gross Profit × 100)/Sales

= (75,000 × 100)/3,00,000 = 25%

(*d*) Inventory Turnover = Cost of Goods Sold/Average Stock

Average Stock = (1,00,000 + 80,000)/2 = 90,000

Inventory Turnover = 2,25,000/90,000 = 2.5 times

(*e*) Quick Ratio = Quick Assets/Current Liabilities

= 90,000/1,00,000 = 0.9

Quick Assets = 30,000 + 60,000 = Rs. 90,000

(*f*) Equity Capital to Liabilities = Shareholders Funds/Total Liabilities
= 1,25,000/2,50,000 = .5 or 50%

COMPUTATIONS OF FINANCIAL STATEMENTS FROM INCOMPLETE DATA

Sometimes, situations may arise wherein the complete data required for the preparation of the financial statements like Trading Account, Profit and Loss Account and Balance Sheet may not be available. Only the various ratios may be given along-with a few figures. In such a case, start with the ratio for which the absolute figures are available and find out the missing figures for the other items. The following illustrations enable you to understand better as to how missing figures are to be ascertained and how the financial statements are prepared.

Illustration 23

Assume that a firm has owners' equity Rs. 5,00,000. The ratios for the firm are :

Current debt to total debt 0.45

Total debt to owners equity 0.65

Fixed assets to owners' equity 0.55

Total assets turnover 3 times

Inventory turnover 6 times

Complete the following Balance Sheet, from the above information.

Liabilities		*Assets*	
Current Debt.	xxxx	Cash	xxxx
Long Term Debt.	xxxx	Inventory	xxxx
Total Debt.	xxxx	Total Current Assets	xxxx
Owners Equity	xxxx	Fixed Assets	xxxx
Total	xxxx	Total	xxxx

Solution

Total Debt 0.65 × owners equity
0.65 × 5,00,000 = Rs. 3,25,000

Fixed Assets 0.55 × owners equity
0.55 × 5,00,000 = Rs. 2,75,000

Total Capital Total Debt + Owners Equity
3,25,000 + 5,00,000 = Rs. 8,25,000

Total assets consisting of current assets and fixed assets must be equal to total capital of Rs. 8,25,000. Out of this total assets, fixed assets are Rs. 2,75,000 therefore current assets are Rs. 5,50,000 (8,25,000 – 2,75,000).

Sales :

Assets turnover = Sales / Assets

Sales = Assets × Assets turnover, i.e., 8,25,000 × 3 = Rs. 24,75,000

Inventory:

Inventory turnover = Sales/Inventory

Inventory = Sales/Inventory turnover, i.e., 24,75,000/6 = Rs. 4,12,500

Cash = Current Assets – Inventory
5,50,000 – 4,12,500 = Rs. 1,37,500

Current Debt = .45 × Total Debt
= .45 × 3,25,000 = Rs. 1,46,250

Long Term Debt = Total Debt – Current Debt
= 3,25,000 – 1,46,250 = Rs. 1,78,750

Now, we can prepare the Balance Sheet:

Liabilities	*Rs.*	*Assets*	*Rs.*
Current Debt.	1,46,250	Cash	1,37,500
Long term Debt.	1,78,750	Inventory	4,12,500
Total Debt.	3,25,000	Total Current Assets	5,50,000
Owners Equity	5,00,000	Fixed Assets	2,75,000
Total	8,25,000	Total	8,25,000

Illustration 24

Using the following information, complete the Balance Sheet given below.

Total debt to net worth : 0.45 to 1

Turnover of total assets based on year end sales figures: 3

Gross profit 40%

Average collection period (based on 360 days year) 30 days

Inventory turnover (based on cost of goods sold and year end inventory) 4 times

Acid test ratio 0.90

Balance Sheet

	Rs.		*Rs.*
Notes and Accounts Payable	??????	Cash	??????
Common Stock	2,30,000	Accounts Receivable	??????
Retained Earnings	3,70,000	Inventory	??????
		Plant and Equipment	??????
	????????		??????

Solution

Debt to Net worth ratio : Total Debt/Net Worth

Net Worth = Common Stock + Retained Earnings, i.e., 2,30,000 + 3,70,000 = Rs. 6,00,000

Total Debt = Net Worth × Debt to Net Worth Ratio

= 6,00,000 × .45 = Rs. 2,70,000

Total Debt (Notes and accounts payable) = Rs. 2,70,000

With total debt of Rs. 2,70,000, the total of liabilities side would be Rs. 8,70,000 which will be the total of assets.

Total Assets Turnover = Sales/Total Assets

Sales would be equal to Total Assets × Total Assets Turnover

i.e., 8,70,000 × 3 = Rs. 26,10,000

Gross Profit Ratio = (Gross Profit × 100)/Sales

Gross Profit = 26,10,000 × 40% = Rs. 10,44,000

Cost of Goods Sold = Sales – Gross Profit

= 26,10,000 – 10,44,000 = Rs. 15,66,000

Assuming all sales are credit sales, the figure of Accounts Receivable would be determined as follows.

Collection Period = 360/Accounts Receivable Turnover

Accounts Receivable Turnover = 360/30 = 12 times

Accounts Receivable Turnover = Credit Sales/Average Debtors

Average Debtors = Credit Sales/Accounts Receivable Turnover

= 26,10,000/12 = Rs. 2,17,500

In the absence of Opening and Closing Receivables, the available receivables of Rs. 2,17,5000 will be taken as Closing Receivables.

Inventory Turnover = Cost of Goods Sold/Closing Inventory

Closing Inventory = 15,66,000/4 = Rs. 3,91,500

Acid Test Ratio = Liquid Assets/Current Liabilities

Liquid Assets = Current Liabilities × Acid Test Ratio, i.e., 2,70,000 × .90 = Rs. 2,43,000

Liquid Assets = Cash + Accounts Receivables

Cash = Liquid Assets – Accounts Receivables, i.e., 2,43,000 – 2,17,500 = Rs. 25,500

Balance Sheet

	Rs.		*Rs.*
Notes and Accounts Payable	2,70,000	Cash	25,500
Common Stock	2,30,000	Accounts Receivable	2,17,500
Retained Earnings	3,70,000	Inventory	3,91,500
		Plant and Equipment	2,35,500
	8,70,000		8,70,000

Illustration 25

From the following particulars, prepare the Balance Sheet of Shreya Ltd. as at March 31, 2000

Current Ratio	2
Working Capital	Rs. 5,00,000
Capital Block to Current Asset	3:2
Fixed Asset to Turnover	2:3
Cash Sales/Credit Sales	2:3
Debentures/Share Capital	1:3
Stock Velocity	3 months
Credit Velocity	3 months
Debtors Velocity	3 months
Gross Profit Ratio	30%
Capital Block:	
Net profit	15% of Turnover
Reserve	5% of Turnover

Solution

Working Capital = Current Assets – Current Liabilities

Current Ratio = Current Assets/Current Liabilities

Current Ratio 2 implies Current Liabilities are 1 and Current Assets are 2

Current Assets 2 – Current Liabilities 1 = Working Capital 1

Working Capital 1= Rs. 5,00,000

Current Liability 1 = Rs. 5,00,000

Current Assets 2 = 5,00,000 × 2 = Rs. 10,00,000

Capital Block (Equity Funds + Debentures) to Current Assets Ratio = 3:2

If Current Assets are 2, the amount = Rs. 10,00,000

Capital Block 3 = 10,00,000 × 3/2 = Rs. 15,00,000

Total Assets = Total Liabilities

Total Liabilities or Total Assets = Long Term Funds (Capital Block) + Current Liabilities

= 15,00,000 + 5,00,000 = Rs. 20,00,000

Fixed Assets = Total Assets – Current Assets
= 20,00,000 – 10,00,000 = Rs. 10,00,000

Fixed Assets to Sales = 2 : 3 which means if Fixed Assets are 2, sales are 3

Fixed Assets 2 = Rs. 10,00,000

Sales 3 = 10,00,000 × 3/2 = Rs. 15,00,000

Proportion of Cash Sales to Credit Sales = 2 : 3

Cash Sales = 15,00,000 × 2/5 = Rs. 6,00,000

Credit Sales = 15,00,000 × 3/5 = Rs. 9,00,000

Gross Profit = Sales × Gross Profit Ratio, i.e., 15,00,000 × 30% = 4,50,000

Cost of Goods Sold = Sales – Gross Profit
15,00,000 – 4,50,000 = Rs. 10,50,000

Debtors Velocity = 3 months

Debtors Turnover = Months in a Year/Velocity
12/3 = 4 times

Debtors Turnover = Credit Sales/Debtors

Debtors = Credit Sales/Debtors Turnover, i.e., 9,00,000/4 = Rs. 2,25,000

Stock Velocity = 3 months

Stock Turnover = Months in a Year/Velocity
12/3 = 4 times

Cost of Goods Sold = 70% of Rs. 15,00,000 sales = Rs. 10,50,000

Stock = Cost of Goods Sold/Stock Turnover
10,50,000/4 = Rs. 2, 62,500

Other Current Assets = Current Assets – Stock – Debtors
10,00,000 – 2,62,500 – 2,25,000 = Rs. 5,12,500

Cost of Goods Sold = Opening Stock + Purchases – Closing Stock

Purchases = Cost of Goods Sold + Closing Stock – Opening Stock
10,50,000 + 2,62,500 – Nil = Rs. 13,12,500

Creditors Velocity = 3 months

Creditors Turnover = Months in a Year/Velocity
12/3 = 4 times

Creditors Turnover = Credit Purchases/Creditors

Creditors = Credit Purchases/Creditors Turnover, i.e., 13,12,500/4 = Rs. 3,28,125

Other Current Liabilities = Current Liabilities – Creditors
5,00,000 – 3,28,125 = Rs. 1,71,875

Debentures to Share Capital Ratio = 1:3 (Share Capital 3 + Debentures 1 = Total 4)

Profit = 15% of Rs. 15,00,000 = Rs. 2,25,000

Reserves= 5% of Rs. 15,00,000 = Rs. 75,000

Capital Block = Share Capital + Debentures + Net Profit + Reserves

15,00,000 = (Share Capital + Debentures) + 2,25,000 + 75,000

SD = 15,00,000 – 2,25,000 – 75,000

SD= 12,00,000

Debentures = 12,00,000 × 1/4 = Rs. 3,00,000

Share Capital = Rs. 12,00,000 × 3/4 = Rs. 9,00,000

Balance Sheet

Liabilities	*Rs.*	*Assets*	*Rs.*
Share Capital	9,00,000	Fixed Assets (Net)	10,00,000
Reserves	75,000	Current Assets :	
Profit and Loss Account	2,25,000	Stocks	2,62,500
Debentures	3,00,000	Debtors	2,25,000
Current Liabilities:		Other Current Assets	5,12,500
Creditors	3,28,125		
Other Current Liabilities	1,71,875		
	20,00,000		20,00,000

Significance of Ratio Analysis

The significance of Ratio Analysis is reflected in the following points.

(i) Ratios reveal useful trends for the assessment of financial health and operational efficiency of an enterprise.

(ii) Ratios reflect the solvency and liquidity position of the firm.

(iii) Ratios facilitate inter-firm comparison by establishing suitable relationships between various relevant factors in a concern which are compared with the same in other units in the industry or average for the industry as a whole.

(iv) It facilitates intra-firm comparison wherein the departmental efficiency can be judged and appropriate decisions taken in several directions.

(v) Ratios also serve as barometers for future. They are helpful in forecasting and planning the business activities for the future period as they have predictory value.

(vi) Ratios are employed to diagnose the financial health and flow of funds of a firm. They are used to locate the symptoms of problems so as to take steps to overcome them.

Limitations of Ratio Analysis

Though, Ratio Analysis is a widely used technique to evaluate the financial position and performance of a business, it suffers from the following limitations.

(i) The proper basis for comparison is difficult to decide.

(ii) Because of differences in situation of two companies or of one company over years, the comparison is rendered difficult.

(iii) The interpretation of ratios calculated from historical financial statements becomes invalid, because of price level changes.

(iv) The differences in the definitions of items in the Balance Sheets and Income Statements make the interpretation of ratios difficult.

(v) The ratios calculated at a point of time are less informative and defective as they suffer from short term changes.

(vi) As the ratios are generally calculated from past financial statements, they do not indicate the future. The Financial Analysts are more interested in what happens in future whereas the ratio indicates what happened in the past.

Inspite of the above problems, ratio analysis is a useful tool. The Analysts should make necessary adjustments before using them. If used intelligently, they can provide useful insights into firms operations.

Summary

One of the important tools of Financial Analysis is Ratio Analysis. A Ratio may be defined as the indicated quotient of two mathematical expressions. It is a statistical yardstick to measure the relationships between two variables or figures which may be expressed as a percent or as a quotient. Ratio analysis involves determining and interpreting numerical relationships based on Financial Statements.

The persons interested in the analysis of Financial Statements can be grouped as Creditors – Short-Term Creditors and Long-Term Creditors; Investors/Owners/Stockholders and Financial Executives. For the useful interpretation of the financial statements, there is a need for comparison. A single ratio does not indicate favourable or unfavourable condition. It should be compared with some standard. The various standards for comparison are Intra Firm Comparison, Inter Firm Comparison, Projected Ratios Comparison, and Average Ratios Comparison. There are various types of ratios which are classified mainly into Structural Ratios, Liquidity Ratios, Profitability Ratios, Turnover Ratios and Miscellaneous Group.

The return on capital employed indicates the earning power of an enterprise. The return is a combination of profit margin and capital employed turnover. This analysis of ratio has been presented by Du-Pont Company of U.S.A. through a chart known as Du-Pont Chart. It shows the interpretation of profitability and turnover (activity) ratios. The Profit Margin Ratio shows the margin the firm gets through carrying on its business and the investment turnover ratio shows the speed at which the assets are usefully employed in the business. Thus, the overall performance or efficiency of a firm is a result of its working and operations. The performance can be improved either by increasing the profit margin or accelerating the pace of rotation of funds for business activity.

In order to make effective use of Ratios, the Analysts should make necessary adjustments before using them. If used intelligently, they can provide useful insights into firms operations.

Glossary

- **Ratio:** is the indicated quotient of two mathematical expressions. It is a statistical yardstick to measure the relationships between two variables or figures which may be expressed as a percent or as a quotient.
- **Ratio Analysis:** involves determining and interpreting numerical relationships based on Financial Statements.
- **Intra Firm Comparison:** is to compare the present ratios with the ratios calculated from the past financial statements of the same firm.
- **Inter Firm Comparison:** is to compare the ratios of one firm with the calculated ratios of select firms belonging to the same industry.
- **Projected Ratios Comparison:** Here, the future ratios are used as standards for comparison with the past/present ratios of the firm. For calculating the future ratios, the projected or proforma financial statements of the same firm are taken.
- **Average Ratios Comparison:** The ratios of the firm are compared with the average ratios of the industry of which the firm is a member.
- **Leverage Ratios:** indicate long term financial strength of the company.
- **Trading on Equity:** The process of magnifying the shareholders earnings through the employment of debt.
- **Liquidity Ratio :** measures the ability of the firm to meet its current obligations.
- **Current Ratio:** is a ratio between current assets and current liabilities.
- **Quick Ratio/Acid Test Ratio:** It establishes a relationship between quick or liquid assets and current liabilities
- **Operating Ratio:** shows the relationship between total operating expenses and net sales.
- **Operating Profit Ratio:** is a ratio between operating profit and net sales.
- **Gross Profit Margin:** reflects the efficiency with which the management produces each unit of product. It shows the relationship between gross profit and net sales
- **Interest Coverage Ratio:** is used to test the firm's debt servicing capacity. It is also known as Times – Interest – Earned. It shows, how many times the interest charges are covered by the funds that are ordinarily available to pay the interest charges.
- **Return on capital employed:** shows how well the management has utilized the funds supplied by the creditors and owners
- **Activity Ratios:** evaluate the efficiency with which the firm manages and utilizes its assets. They indicate the speed with which the assets are being converted or turned over into sales. A relationship between sales and various assets is established.
- **Collection period:** indicates the rapidity or slowness in the collection of the amount from the debtors.
- **Fixed Assets Turnover Ratio:** measures the efficiency with which the firm is utilizing its investment in fixed assets. It is obtained by dividing the sales with the depreciated value of fixed assets.
- **Capital Employed Turnover:** examines the effectiveness in utilizing the capital employed. The higher the ratio, the more efficient utilization of owners and long term creditor's funds.
- **Earnings per share:** shows the profitability of the firm on a per share basis.
- **Dividend Payout Ratio:** indicates how much dividend per share is paid out of earning per share.
- **Price Earning Ratio:** is the reciprocal of the earnings yield. It indicates the investors expectations about the firms performance.

Questions

(1) What is a Ratio? What are the uses of Ratio Analysis?
(2) How would you analyze the financial position of a company from the view point of an investor and a creditor?
(3) Write a brief note on the importance of Ratio Analysis to the different categories of users (C.S. Final, June 1988)
(4) Write a short note on 'Trading on Equity'.
(5) Explain the various accounting ratios which serve as an indication of profitability of the firm.
(6) Give a brief account of ratios to analyze the liquidity position of a business concern.
(7) Explain in detail the 'Du-Pont Chart'.

(8) Explain the role of Ratio Analysis in the interpretation of financial statements. Examine the limitations of Ratio Analysis, if any (M.Com. Madras University, 1997).

(9) What are turnover ratios? How are they calculated? Explain the significance of turnover ratios.

PROBLEMS

Liquidity Ratios

(1) If a company merchandise inventory is Rs. 1,20,000; total current liabilities are Rs. 80,000; Acid Test Ratio is 2:1, what is current ratio?

[**Ans.:** Current ratio = 3.5 times]

(2) If Apple Company Ltd.'s Current Ratio is 5.5:1, Quick Ratio is 4 to 1; Inventory is Rs. 30,000 what are the current liabilities?

[**Ans.:** Current liabilities Rs. 20,000]

(3) You are given the following information about two companies:

	Company A *Rs.*	*Company B* *Rs.*
Cash	180	140
Debtors	1,420	3,200
Inventory	1,800	5,400
Bills Payable	270	1,000
Creditors	500	4,000
Accrued Expenses	150	125
Tax Payable	750	1,000

Calculate liquidity ratios for the two companies and give your interpretation of the liquidity position of the companies, as revealed by the ratios.

[**Ans.:** Current ratio Company A : 2.03:1; Company B : 1.43:1
Quick ratio Company A : 0.95:1; Company B : 0.54:1]

(4) From the following balance sheet and information, calculate ratios for *(a)* testing liquidity and *(b)* solvency.

Balance sheet as on 31.3.2008 *(Rs. in '000)*

Liabilities		*Rs.*	*Assets*	*Rs.*
Equity		20	Goodwill	12
Capital Reserves		4	Fixed Assets	28
8% Loan on Mortgage		16	Stocks	6
Trade Creditors		8	Debtors	6
Bank Overdraft		2	Investments	2
Taxation:			Cash	6
Current		2		
Future		2		
Profit and Loss A/c				
Profit for 2008 after tax and interest on fixed deposits	12,000			
Less: Transfer to Dividend	(–)2,000			
Reserves	(–)4,000	6		
		60		60

[**Ans.:** Current ratio 1.67, Quick ratio 1.17, Long-term debt Equity ratio 1:2, Total debt Equity ratio 7:8]

Profitability Ratios:

(5) If net income of Simco Ltd. is Rs. 1,22,600.(after tax at 50%); its fixed interest charges on Debenture amount to Rs. 4,800. Calculate the Interest Coverage Ratio.

[**Ans.:** Interest coverage ratio 51.08]

(6) Calculate and comment on the rate of return on total assets from the following data of two companies:

	Gama Ltd	*Lama Ltd.*
Sales	x x x	Rs. 2,52,75,000
Total Assets	Rs. 42,50,000	x x x
Net Profit on Sales	6%	4%
Turnover of Assets	6 times	6 times
Gross Margin	Rs. 20,68,000	12%

[**Ans.:** Rate of return on total assets, Gama Ltd. 36%, Lama Ltd. 24%]

(7) From the following information of Nidhi Ltd. for the year 1999, calculate *(i)* Gross Profit Ratio, *(ii)* Net Profit Ratio, *(iii)* Operating Ratio, *(iv)* Operating Profit Ratio, *(v)* Return on assets, *(vi)* Assets Turnover, *(vii)* Return on Equity

Total Assets of the company	Rs. 16,00,000
Borrowed Capital @ 8% interest per annum 50% of the total assets	
Direct Cost for the year	Rs 9,60,000
Operating expenses	Rs, 1,60,000
The goods are sold to customers at 150% of the direct cost	
Assume tax rate	50%

[**Ans.:** *(i)* 33.33% *(ii)* 8.89% *(iii)* 77.78% *(iv)* 22.22% *(v)* 8% *(vi)* 0.6 times *(vii)*16%]

(8) Compute return on capital employed from the following details:

Net Profit after tax	Rs. 43,000
Rate of Income tax	50%
14% Debentures	Rs. 1,00,000
Share Capital	Rs. 2,50,000
Profit and Loss Account	Rs. 1,58,000
Loss on Issue of Debentures	Rs. 8,000

[**Ans.:** 8.6%]

(9) The following are the summarised P&L A/c of Alind Products Ltd. for the year ending 31st March 2008, and the Balance Sheet as on that date.

PROFIT AND LOSS ACCOUNT

	Rs.		*Rs.*
To Opening Stock	99,500	By Sales	8,50,000
To Purchase (credit)	5,45,250	By Closing Stock	1,50,000
To Expenses	14,250		
To Gross Profit	3,41,000		
	10,00,000		10,00,000
To Operating Expenses	1,95,000	By Gross Profit	3,41,000
To Non Operating Expenses	5,000	By Non-operating Income	9,000
To Net Profit	1,50,000		
	3,50,000		3,50,000

BALANCE SHEET

	Rs.		*Rs.*
Equity Share Capital	2,00,000	Land and Building	1,50,000
Reserves	90,000	Plant and Machinery	80,000
P& L A/c	1,50,000	Stocks	1,50,000
Bills Payable	60,000	Sundry Debtors	41,000
		Bills Receivable	30,000
		Cash at Bank	49,000
	5,00,000		5,00,000

From the above statements you are required to calculate the following ratio;

(i) Gross profit ratio

(ii) Net profit ratio

(iii) Operating profit ratio

(iv) Operating ratio

(v) Return on capital employed

[**Ans.:** *(i)* 40.1% *(ii)* 17.64% *(iii)* 17.18% *(iv)* 82.82% *(v)* 34.09%.]

(10) Following is the income statement of Strong Ltd. for the year ending 31st March, 2008.

INCOME STATEMENT

Particulars	*Rs.*	*Particulars*	*Rs.*
To Opening Stock	45,750	By Sales	3,00,000
To Purchases	1,89,150	By Closing Stock	59,100
To Carriage	1,200		
To Wages	3,000		
To Gross Profit	1,20,000		
	3,59,100		3,59,100
To Administrative Expenses	60,600	By Gross Profit	1,20,000
To Finance Expenses		By Non-operating Income:	
Interest	720	Interest	900
Discount	1,440	Dividend	2,250
Bad Debts	2,040	Profit on Sale of Securities	450
S&D Expenses	7,200		
Non-operating Expenses	1,200		
To Net Profit	50,400		
	1,23,600		1,23,600

You are required to calculate:

(a) Gross profit Ratio *(b)* Net profit Ratio *(c)* Operating Ratio *(d)* Operating Profit Ratio *(e)* Stock Turnover Ratio.

[**Ans.:** *(a)* 40% *(b)* 16.8% *(c)* 84% *(d)* 16% *(e)* 3.43 times]

(11) From the following information, you are required to compute the cost of goods sold :

Current liabilities	Rs. 9,00,000
Inventory turnover ratio	8
Current ratio	2.5:1
Acid Test ratio	2.1:1

[**Ans.:** Cost of goods sold = Rs. 28,80,000]

Turnover Ratios:

(12) M/s Hema Raj & Co. sells goods on cash as well as on credit. The following particulars are extracted from their books of accounts for the year 2007-08.

	Rs.
Total Gross Sales	1,00,000
Cash Sales (included in above)	20,000
Sales Returns	7,000
Total Debtors for Sales as on 31.3.2008	9,000
Bills Receivable on 31.3.2008	2,000
Provision for Doubtful Debts on 31.3.2008	1,000
Trade Creditors on 31.3.2008	10,000

Calculate the average collection period.

[**Ans.:** 50 days]

(13) Following are the ratios relating to the activities of National Traders Limited:

Debtors' velocity	3 months
Stock velocity	8 months
Creditors' velocity	2 months
Gross Profit Ratio	25%

Gross Profit for the year ended 31st March, 2008 amounts to Rs. 4,00,000; Closing Stock of the year is Rs. 10,000 above the Opening Stock. Bills Receivable amount to Rs. 25,000 and the Bills Payable to Rs. 10,000. Find out *(i)* Closing Stock *(ii)* Sundry Creditors.

[**Ans.:** *(i)* Rs. 1,55,000 *(ii)* Rs. 1,91,667]

(14) The Balance sheet of Star Ltd., as at 31st March 2008 is given below

Liabilities	*Rs.*	*Assets*	*Rs.*
Equity share capital	6,00,000	Plant and Machinery	4,50,000
Reserves	1,80,000	Furniture	50,000
Creditors	1,20,000	Stocks	1,80,000
		Debtors	1,20,000
		Cash at Bank	1,00,000
	9,00,000		9,00,000

The other details are as follows:

(a) Total Sales during the year have been Rs. 10,00,000 out of which cash sales amounted to Rs. 2,00,000.

(b) The Gross Profit has been earned @ 20%

(c) Amount as on 1.4.07

	Rs.
Debtors	80,000
Stock	1,40,000
Creditors	30,000

(d) Cash paid to creditors during the year Rs. 2,10,000

You are required to calculate the following ratios:

(i) Debtors Turnover Ratio

(ii) Creditors Turnover Ratio

(iii) Stock Turnover Ratio

(iv) Fixed Assets Turnover Ratio

[**Ans.:** *(i)* 8 times *(ii)* 4 times *(iii)* 5 times *(iv)* 2 times]

(15) M/s.Rakesh &Co. supplies you the following information for the year ending 31st March 2008.

Credit sales	Rs. 1,50,000
Cash sales	Rs. 2,50,000
Returns inwards	Rs. 25,000
Opening stock	Rs. 25,000
Closing stock	Rs. 35,000

Find out Inventory turnover when Gross profit ratio is 20%.

[**Ans.:** 10 times]

(16) Following are the ratios relating to the activities of National Traders Limited:

Debtors' velocity	3 months
Stock velocity	8 months
Creditors' velocity	2 months
Gross Profit Ratio	25%

Gross Profit for the year ended 31st March,1992 amounts to Rs. 4,00,000, Closing Stock of the year is Rs. 10,000 above the Opening Stock. Bills Receivable amount to Rs. 25,000 and the Bills Payable to Rs. 10,000. Find out *(i)* Sales *(ii)* Sundry Debtors.

[**Ans.:** *(i)* 16,00,000 *(ii)* 4,00,000]

(17) Rearrange the following statements in a form suitable for analysis and calculation of five ratios which are significant in analysing the financial trend of the business:

Condensed Balanced Sheet

	2007 *Rs.*	2008 *Rs.*
Assets:		
Cash at Bank	15,380	26,020
Trade Debtors	11,260	11,710
Stocks	56,160	49,460
Fixed Assets *Less:* Depreciation	2,17,200	2,19,810
	3,00,000	3,07,000
Liabilities:		
Creditors	20,000	16,000
Bills Payable	12,750	6,500
Debentures	1,00,000	1,00,000
Reserves and Surplus	67,250	84,500
Paid-up Capital	1,00,000	1,00,000
	3,00,000	3,07,000
Sales	1,80,000	1,95,000

[**Ans.:**	2007	2008
Current Ratio	2.5	3.88
Quick Ratio	0.82	1.68
Debt-Equity Ratio	0.59	0.54
Stocks Turnover Ratio	3.21times	3.94 times
Debtors Turnover Ratio	15.98	16.65
Fixed Assets Turnover Ratio	1.21	1.13]

(18) From the following details calculate *(i)* Sales and *(ii)* Sundry Debtors,

Debtors Velocity 3 months		Gross Profit	Rs. 8,00,000
Gross Profit ratio		25% Bills Receivables	Rs. 30,000

(M.Com., O.U., January, 1997)

[**Ans.:** *(i)* Rs. 32,00,000 *(ii)* Rs. 7,70,000]

(19) Summarised data taken from the statement of a company are given below.

	Rs.
Net Sales	2,40,00,000
Net Income from Operations	60,00,000
Net Income after Interest and Tax	30,00,000
Average Total Assets	1,20,00,000
Average Shareholder's Equity	80,00,000

Compute the rate for management and shareholder's purpose.

[**Ans.:** Return on assets — 25%, Return on equity — 37.5%]

Miscellaneous :

(20) From the following Balance Sheet and the sub-joined information of a company, you are required to calculate:

Current Ratio

Quick Ratio

Inventory Turnover

Average collection period presuming 360 days in a year

Owned funds to liabilities ratio.

Balance Sheet

Liabilities	*Rs.*	*Assets*	*Rs.*
Share Capital	2,00,000	Goodwill	1,20,000
Reserves and Surplus	58,000	Plant and Machinery	1,50,000
Debentures	1,00,000	Stocks	80,000
Creditors	40,000	Debtors	45,000
Bills Payable	20,000	Cash	17,000
Other Current Liabilities	2,000	Miscellaneous Current Assets	8,000
	4,20,000		4,20,000

Sales (credit) for the year Rs. 4,00,000
Gross Profit Rs. 1,60,000
[**Ans.:** *(i)* 2.4, *(ii)* 1.13, *(iii)* 3 times, *(iv)* 41.5 days, *(v)* 1.6]

(21) From the following information, calculate the Net worth and Reserves and Surplus
Equity Rs. 20,000; Debentures Rs. 20,000; Long term Loans Rs. 30,000;
Bonds (Short term) – Rs. 20,000; Creditors – Rs. 20,000; Debt Equity Ratio = 2:1
[**Ans.:** Net worth, Rs. 25,000, Reserves Rs. 5,000]

(22) From the following information, calculate interest and dividend.
Interest Coverage Ratio = 15 times
Fixed charges coverage = 10 times
Earning before interest and tax = Rs. 6,00,000
[**Ans.:** Interest = Rs. 40,000, Fixed cost coverage = Rs. 60,000, Dividend Rs. 20,000]

(23) From the ratios and other data set forth below for Maruti Vahan Ltd., indicate your interpretation of the company's financial condition.

	3rd year	2nd year	1st year
Current Ratio	302%	278%	265%
Acid Test Ratio	99%	110%	155%
Working Capital Turnover (times)	3.25	3.00	2.75
Receivables Turnover	7.2	8.41	9.83
Collection Period	50	43	37
Inventory to Working Capital	110%	100%	95%
Inventory Turnover (times)	5.41	6.01	6.11
Income Per Equity Share	Rs. 2.5	Rs. 4.0	Rs.5.10
Net Income to Net Worth	7%	8.5%	11.07%
Operating Expenses to Net Sales	25%	23%	22%
Sales Increase During the Year	23%	16%	10%
Cost of Goods Sold to Net Sales	73%	71%	70%
Dividends Per Share (Rs.)	3	3	3
Fixed Assets to Net Worth	22.7%	18.0%	16.4%
Net Profit to Net Sales	2.0%	5.09%	7.03%

(24) From the following balance sheet of Hindustan Ltd., as on 31st March 2008,calculate *(i)* Current Ratio *(ii)* Quick Ratio *(iii)* Absolute Liquidity Ratio *(iv)* Ratio of Inventory to Working Capital *(v)* Ratio of Current Assets to Fixed Assets *(vi)* Debt to Equity Ratio.

Balance Sheet

Liabilities	*Rs.*	*Assets*	*Rs.*
Equity Share Capital	10,00,000	Goodwill (at cost)	5,00,000
6% Preference Share Capital	5,00,000	Plant and Machinery	6,00,000
General Reserves	1,00,000	Land and Buildings	7,00,000
Profit and Loss Account	4,00,000	Furniture and Fixtures	1,00,000
Provision for Tax	1,76,000	Stock in Trade	6,00,000
Bills Payable	1,24,000	Bills Receivable	30,000
Bank Overdraft	20,000	Debtors	1,50,000
Creditors	80,000	Bank	2,00,000
12% Debentures	5,00,000	Marketable Securities	20,000
	29,00,000		29,00,000

[**Ans.:** *(i)* 2.5 times *(ii)* 1 time *(iii)* 0.55 times *(iv)* 1 time *(v)* 1:1.9 *(vi)* 1:4]

(25) The following information is extracted from the published accounts of Strong Ltd. and Weak Ltd.

(Rupees in lakhs)

	Strong Ltd.	*Weak Ltd.*
Sales	32.00	30.00
Net profit after tax	1.23	1.58
Equity share capital Rs.10 per share		
Fully paid up	10.00	8.00
Reserves	2.32	6.42
Long term debt	8.00	6.60
Creditors	3.82	5.49
Bank credit	0.60	2.00
Fixed assets	15.99	15.90
Inventories	3.31	8.09
Other current assets	5.44	4.52

Calculate profitability and activity ratios for the two companies from the fore-going data and offer a brief comment.

[**Ans.:**	Strong Ltd.	Weak Ltd.
Net Profit Ratio	3.84%	5.27%
Return on Investment	6.05%	7.52%
Earning Per Share (Rs.)	1.23	1.975
Debt-Equity Ratio	0.65:1	0.45:1]

(26) The following are the figures relating to trading activities of Bharath Traders Ltd., for the year ended 31-3-2008.

	Rs.
Sales	2,60,000
Stock (1.4.2007)	33,000
Sales Returns	10,000
Administration Expenses	49,000
Non-operating Income	6,000
Purchases	1,61,000
Stock (31.3.2008)	49,000
Direct Expenses	5,000
Selling and Distribution Expenses	11,000
Non-Operating Expenses	2,000

Arrange the above figures in a form suitable for analysis and compute the following ratios :

(i) Gross Profit Ratio
(ii) Operating Ratio
(iii) Cost of Sales Ratio
(iv) Administrative Expenses Ratio
(v) Selling and Distribution Expenses Ratio
(vi) Net Profit Ratio
(vii) Stock Turnover.

[**Ans.:** *(i)* 40%, *(ii)* 84%, *(iii)* 60%, *(iv)* 19.6%, *(v)* 4.4%, *(vi)* 17.6%, *(vii)* 3.66 times.]

Balance Sheet:

(27) Using the following Ratios, make a Balance Sheet at a sales of Rs. 36 lakhs.

Sales/total Assets	3
Sales/fixed Assets	5
Sales/current Assets	7.5
Sales/inventory	20
Sales/debtors	15
Current Ratio	2
Total Assets/net Worth	2.5
Debt/equity Ratio	1:1

[**Ans.:** Balance Sheet Total Rs. 12,00,000]

(28) From the following information, make out a statement of proprietor's funds with as many details as possible:
Current Ratio 2.5;
Liquid Ratio 1.5
Proprietary Ratio (fixed assets/proprietary funds) 0.75;
Working Capital Rs. 60,000
Reserves and Surplus Rs. 40,000
Bank Overdraft Rs.10,000; and
There is no long-term loan or fictitious assets
[**Ans.:** Proprietor Funds Rs. 2,40,000]

(29) From the following information of Nahar Ltd., complete the Proforma Balance Sheet given below if its sales are Rs. 32,00,000

Sales to Net worth	—	2.3 times
Current Debt to Net worth	—	42%
Total Debt to Net worth	—	75%
Current Ratio	—	2.9 times
Net Sales to Inventory	—	4.7 times
Average Collection Period	—	64 days
Fixed Assets to Net worth	—	53.2%

Proforma Balance Sheet

Net Worth	xx	Fixed Assets	xx
Long Term Debt	xx	Cash	xx
Current Debt	xx	Stocks	xx
		Debtors	xx

[**Ans.:** Balance Sheet Total Rs. 24,34,783]

❑ ❑ ❑

30

FUNDS FLOW ANALYSIS

Objectives

The objectives of the study are to:

- Understand the importance of Working Capital and the causes for the changes in the working capital
- Appreciate the need for Funds Flow Statement
- Learn the technique of preparation of Funds Flow Statement

INTRODUCTION

Every transaction brings about a change in the financial position of the business and thus, alters the composition of net worth (owners' funds), liabilities and assets. This implies a dynamic situation, involving continuous movement of funds in and out of the business. While the Balance Sheet reveals the financial position as at a point of time, it cannot by itself, in its usual form, reveal the changes in the financial position between any two given dates.

The 'Funds Flow Statement', which is also known as the 'Statement of Sources and Uses of Funds', is another analytical tool for analysis of financial statements, financial planning and control. Kholer has defined this statement as "a statement of changes in financial position or statement of sources and applications of funds in which elements of net income and working capital contributing to an understanding of the whole of financial operations during the reporting period replace totals of these items".

Thus, the Funds Flow Statement reveals the volume of financial transactions and explains the flow of funds taking place within a business during a particular period of time, and its effect on the working capital. It is a supplement to the two principal financial statements. It describes the sources from where funds are obtained and the uses of these funds, in a condensed form.

The word 'Funds' has different meanings. In the narrow sense, it is defined as cash resources of the business. But, 'Funds' is a broader term than cash. In the broader sense, it includes all resource of the business whether in the form of men, material, money or machinery, etc. Flows in the cash account are only a part of the wider funds movement and many of these movements do not involve cash such as purchase or sale of goods on credit, i.e., credit transactions.

The third interpretation of 'Funds' is working capital. There is in fact a variety of definitions ranging from liquidity, i.e., cash at one extreme to total resources at the other. The other definitions of Funds refer to Working Capital, gross or net. In the context of preparation of Fund Flow Statement, 'Funds' refers to Net Working Capital.

FLOW OF FUNDS

Flow of Funds means 'change in funds' or 'change in working capital'. Whenever there is a change in the funds, it is presumed that flow in funds has taken place. The flow in funds can be inflow as well as outflow. An inflow of funds will increase the working capital.

There will be no flow of funds, if a transaction involved *(i)* both current accounts only; or *(ii)* both non-current accounts only. A non-current account means either a non-current asset (Fixed Asset) or a non-current liability (long term liabilities).

In other words, a cross transaction (a transaction involving a fixed asset/fixed liability on the one hand and a current asset/current liability on the other) will result in flow of funds.

(1) Transactions involving accounts from current and non-current categories and thus, resulting in flow of funds

(a) Purchased Machinery for Rs. 30,000

This transaction increases machinery and reduces cash. Due to reduction in cash balance without a corresponding change in any other current items, the working capital will decrease. (The reduction in cash reduces current assets without reducing current liabilities as a result, the difference between the two, gets reduced).

(b) Shares issued Rs. 2,00,000

In this case, non-current liability, i.e., share capital is increased and a current asset, i.e., cash is increased. As a current asset is increased without any change in any other current item, working capital gets increased.

(2) Transactions involving accounts from current category only and thus, not resulting in flow of funds

(a) Cash collected from Debtors Rs. 4,000

Cash and Debtors are both current assets. This transaction results in an increase in cash and a decrease in debtors by the same amount, thus, the total of current assets stand at the same level thereby causing no change in the working capital.

(b) Acceptance given to Creditors Rs. 3,000

Both Creditors and Bills Payable are current liabilities. By giving acceptance to creditors, creditors decrease on one hand and bills payable increase on the other, by the same amount. Since this transaction does not affect the total amount of current assets and also the total amount of current liabilities, the difference between the two, i.e., current assets and current liabilities remains unchanged. Thus, there is no flow of funds, i.e., no change in the working capital.

(c) Paid Creditors Rs. 1,000

By paying the creditors; cash, a current asset is reduced on one hand and creditors, a current liability, are reduced on the other hand by the same amount. Since the difference between the current assets and current liabilities will be the same as it was before, there will be no flow of funds, i.e., no change in working capital.

(3) Transactions involving accounts from non-current category only and thus, not resulting in flow of funds

(a) Land exchanged for Machinery Rs. 10,00,000

Both land and machinery are non-current assets. By exchanging land for machinery, land is reduced and machinery is increased but the total of non-current assets, remains unaffected. Further, there is no change in any current asset or current liability. Hence, there will be no change in the funds.

(b) Preference shares are converted into equity shares Rs. 10,00,000

Preference share capital and equity share capital are both non-current liabilities. By conversion, equity share capital stands increased and at the same time, preference share capital gets reduced to the same extent. As no current category item is affected, there will be no change in funds, i.e., Working Capital.

IMPORTANCE OF FUNDS FLOW STATEMENT

Generally, a business concern prepares two financial statements, i.e., Income Statement or Profit and Loss Account which reveals the net result of trading operations over a period of time and a Position Statement or Balance Sheet which reflects the state of assets and liabilities of a company on a particular date.

The above two statements – though fulfil the highly important function of picturising the financial result and the position of the business, they do not throw light on the sources and uses of funds and changes that have taken place, between two balance sheet dates. This information is made available by preparing a statement of Sources and Uses (Applications) of Funds also called as, 'where got where gone statement', or 'Funds Flow Statement'.

The Funds Flow Statement highlights the sources and uses of working capital and reveals the changes in the financial position of the business between two balance sheet dates. Thus, the main purposes of such a statement are:

(1) To understand the flow of funds in a business, *viz.*, Funds taken as *(a)* Cash; *(b)* Net Working Capital; or *(c)* Total Financial Resources.
(2) To appreciate the role of Working Capital.
(3) To understand and interpret the changes that have taken place in working capital and analyze the causes thereof.
(4) To ascertain the sources and uses of working capital.
(5) To point out the financial strengths and weaknesses of the business concern particularly of its financing policies.

USES OF FUNDS FLOW STATEMENT

Funds Flow Statement is of great value to management, owners, creditors, bankers, money lending institutions, etc. The uses of the 'statement' are as follows:

(1) It explains the financial consequences of business operations

This statement answers questions such as:

(a) Where have the profits gone?
(b) Why is there an imbalance between liquidity and profitability position of the enterprise?
   (1) In spite of profits, why is the liquidity position bad or
   (2) In spite of losses, how is the business having a comfortable liquid position?
(c) How was it possible for the concern to distribute dividends, in excess of earnings, or in the presence of net loss, for the period?

The answers to the above questions enable the management to direct the funds to those channels which would be more profitable to the organization and improve the liquidity and profitability position of the business.

(2) Forecasting Value

There should be optimum utilization of available resources for the overall growth of an enterprise. This objective can be achieved by preparing a projected Funds Flow Statement and allocating the resources properly.

(3) Testing Value

The Funds Flow Statement tests the efficiency with which the working capital has been used by the management. The adequacy or inadequacy of working capital will be revealed. The possible steps to be taken by the management to make an effective use of surplus working capital or make arrangements for providing funds in case of inadequacy of working capital will also be revealed.

(4) Decision making value

Funds Flow Statement reveals the credit worthiness of the enterprise, the sources of repayment of loans raised, funds generated through normal business operations and how the management has utilized the funds in the past. Further, it reveals the likely uses of funds in the future. As a result, outsiders like creditors can decide about providing loans.

The shareholders can decide whether the management is effective or not in managing the funds. Further, mismanagement can also be identified and prevented.

The information revealed can be used by the management to shape its future financing policies and capital expenditure programs.

TECHNIQUE OF PREPARATION OF FUNDS FLOW STATEMENT

The technique of preparation of Funds Flow Statement involves essentially three steps.

(i) Schedule of changes in working capital: This schedule is prepared to determine the increase or decrease in working capital, the figure of which is included in Funds Flow Statement.

(ii) Funds from operations: It is ascertained by adjusting the profit (or loss as the case may be) in respect of certain items like depreciation, non operating incomes and non operating expenses. Funds from operations will also appear in the Funds Flow Statement.

(iii) Funds Flow Statement (on working capital basis): This statement is prepared with non-current segment items to collaborate the change in working capital, as revealed by the schedule of changes in working capital.

Schedule of Changes in Working Capital

This statement is prepared from the current items of balance sheet, i.e., current assets and current liabilities in order to calculate the increase or decrease in working capital. Non-current items are ignored as working capital is the difference between current assets and current liabilities. In order to know whether there is an increase or decrease in working capital, the following rules must be followed:

(1) An increase in a current asset between two balance sheet dates results in an increase in the working capital and a decrease in a current asset would result in a decrease in working capital.

(2) An increase in a current liability, between two balance sheet dates, decreases working capital whereas a decrease in a current liability would increase the working capital.

The following illustrations will make the above rules clear.

Illustration 1

Prepare a schedule of changes in working capital from the given consolidated Balance Sheet.

Liabilities	*31.03.08* *Rs.*	*31.03.09* *Rs.*	*Assets* *Rs.*	*31.03.08* *Rs.*	*31.03.09*
Share Capital	80,000	95,000	Fixed Assets	90,000	1,00,000
Reserves	20,000	25,000	Current Assets	30,000	50,000
Current Liabilities	20,000	30,000			
	1,20,000	1,50,000		1,20,000	1,50,000

Schedule of Changes in Working Capital

Particulars	*31.03.08*	*31.03.09*	*Change in Working*	
			Increase (+)	*Decrease (–)*
	Rs.	*Rs.*	*Rs.*	*Rs.*
Current Assets	30,000	50,000	20,000	—
Current Liabilities	20,000	30,000	—	10,000
			20,000	10,000
Increase in Working Capital			—	10,000
			20,000	20,000

Note: Though there is an increase in both current assets and current liabilities, the increase in current assets is more than the increase in current liabilities, thus resulting in an increase in working capital.

Illustration 2

The following are the particulars of A Ltd. for 31.03.08 and 31.03.09.

Particulars	*31.03.08.* *Rs.*	*31.03.09* *Rs.*
Fixed Assets	5,90,000	5,20,000
Current Assets	4,10,000	3,80,000
	10,00,000	9,00,000
Equity Capital	5,00,000	5,00,000
Reserves	2,75,000	2,00,000
Current Liabilities	2,25,000	2,00,000
	10,00,000	9,00,000

Prepare a statement of changes in working capital.

Solution

Schedule of changes in working capital

Particulars	*31.03.08* *Rs.*	*31.03.09* *Rs.*	*Change in Working Capital* *Increase (+)* *Rs.*	*Decrease (–)* *Rs.*
Current Assets	4,10,000	3,80,000	—	30,000
Current Liabilities	2,25,000	2,00,000	25,000	—
			25,000	30,000
Decrease in Working Capital			5,000	—
			30,000	30,000

Illustration 3

The following are the summarized balance sheets of X & Y Co., as on 31.03.08 and 31.03.09.

Balance Sheets

Particulars	31.03.08 Rs.	31.03.09 Rs.	Particulars	31.03.08 Rs.	31.03.09 Rs.
Capital:					
Equity Shares	80,000	80,000	Fixed Assets	60,000	50,000
Preference Shares	—	20,000	Debtors	80,000	48,000
General Reserve	4,000	4,000	Stocks	20,000	70,000
Profit and Loss Account	8,000	10,800	Prepaid expenses	2,600	1,000
Debentures	22,000	25,600	Cash	400	7,000
Creditors	24,000	26,000			
Bank Overdraft	25,000	9,600			
	1,63,000	1,76,000		1,63,000	1,76,000

You are required to prepare a schedule showing changes in working capital.

Solution

Schedule of changes in Working Capital

Particulars	*31.03.08* *Rs.*	*31.03.09* *Rs.*	*Change in Working Capital* *Increase (+)* *Rs.*	*Decrease (–)* *Rs.*
Current Assets				
Debtors	80,000	48,000	—	32,000
Stocks	20,000	70,000	50,000	—
Prepaid Expenses	2,600	1,000	—	1,600
Cash	400	7,000	6,600	—
Current Liabilities				
Creditors	24,000	26,000	—	2,000
Band Overdraft	25,000	9,600	15,400	—
			72,000	35,600
Increase in Working Capital			—	36,400
			72,000	72,000

The preparation of Schedule of changes in Working Capital, to ascertain the increase or decrease in working capital between two balance sheet dates, constitutes the first step in the preparation of Fund Flow Statement on working capital basis. The remaining two steps are *(a)* ascertaining funds from operations and *(b)* preparation of Funds Flow Statement.

Sources and Application of Funds

'Funds' are interpreted, to mean Working Capital (Net Working Capital). As net working capital is excess of current assets over current liabilities, funds represent that portion of current assets which are not financed by current liabilities (i.e., financed from the long-term/Non-current sources).

Sources of Funds

The sources of funds can be classified as external sources and internal sources. External sources of funds are those sources which are raised from outside the business, to augment the funds. The external sources are *(a)* additional capital raised *(b)* increase in long term borrowings.

As opposed to external sources, internal sources consist of resources raised within the organization internally. Every profitable sale brings in funds in excess of the cost of goods sold. Thus, profit generated by the business is an important internal source of funds. In determining profit, revenues during the period are matched against the expenses, whether it involves the use of funds or not, during the current period. Thus, the amount of profit requires adjustment in respect of transactions that do not involve the use of funds – e.g., Depreciation, amortization of expenses etc.

Surplus or worn out assets could be sold and this also constitutes an internal source of funds.

Applications (Uses) of Funds

Funds are usually used for *(i)* financing expansion in fixed assets *(ii)* redeeming/repaying *(a)* long term borrowings (b) redeemable preference shares, if any; and *(iii)* financing increase in Working Capital.

Possibility of alternative treatment of certain items:

It is necessary to identify the non-current and current items from the Balance Sheet as a preparatory step before an attempt is made to prepare the Funds Flow Statement. In respect of majority of the items, clear cut classification into non-current and current items is easy. In respect of certain items like Provision for Taxation and Proposed Dividends, there is a possibility of alternative treatment, i.e., an item can be considered as a non-current item or a current item. It is necessary to take a decision at the outset as to whether these items are going to be classified as non-current or current, because, that would decide the place where these items will be taken up for consideration. If these items are to be classified as current items, then, they would appear in the 'schedule of changes in the working capital' and thus, will not be considered in calculating funds from operations nor would they appear in the Funds Flow Statement. Similarly, if these items are classified as non-current, then, they will not be appearing in the schedule of changes in working capital but would influence the funds from operations and a related item would find a place in Funds Flow Statement.

Funds from Operations

Funds from Operations are an important source. Profit is the result of excess of revenues over expenses and belongs to the owners and thus is a non-current segment item. Profit increases the working capital. It is realized only when operations take place and that is why profit constitutes an important component in the funds provided by operations. However, the profit as shown by Profit and Loss Account requires certain adjustments to calculate the funds provided by operations.

The items of expenses charged and revenues earned do not in certain cases, involve the flow of funds during the current period. Depreciation written off during the current period is merely a method of showing the expired cost of the asset concerned and thus does not involve any outflow of funds during the current period (The outflow of funds take place only at the point of time when that asset was originally purchased). It is only an accounting way of matching the cost of fixed assets with the benefit derived from those assets. As charging depreciation does not involve the use of funds during the current period, it is added back to the net profit to determine funds provided by operations. Adding back depreciation should not be misinterpreted to mean that 'depreciation is a source of funds'. It is to be noted that it is the operations that constitute the source and not charging depreciation. Otherwise, if depreciation were to be really a source of funds, more and more depreciation can be charged and funds provided by operations would be increased accordingly. However, in view of the tax deductibility nature of depreciation, charging depreciation reduces taxable profits (Profit before taxes) and thus influences the tax amount payable, which in turn affects the profit after tax. Thus, depreciation is not to be treated as a source of funds directly, except to the extent of tax shield, depreciation in an indirect sense, provides increased funds from operations.

Similarly, certain expenses/losses, incurred in the past, may be wholly or partially written off during the current period. Such write offs of intangible assets/deferred revenue expenditure do not involve any outflow of funds during the current period and hence, added back to the net profit to derive funds from operations.

There are certain transactions like profit/loss on the sale of fixed assets and non-operating income like dividends from investment, which cannot strictly be called as arising due to regular operations of business. Hence, as the intention is to calculate funds from operations for the purpose of highlighting the amount that was made available through 'operations; it is considered necessary to exclude the effect of such items. Thus, if profit on sale of a fixed asset was included in profit and loss account, this must be subtracted from the net profit to determine funds from operations. Similarly, if there was a loss on sale of fixed asset, the loss charged to profit and loss account must be added back to the net profit to ascertain funds from operations.

When all the details are available, it is relatively easy to calculate the 'Funds from Operations'. However, if the total information is not available, then, it is necessary, based on the clues provided, to find out the hidden information and finally ascertain 'funds from operations'.

Ascertaining the amount of Depreciation

Sometimes, the problem contains either the profit and loss account in full or a relevant extracts thereof. In such a case, the amount charged as depreciation during that period can easily be ascertained. However, when details regarding the income statement are not given, the depreciation amount has to be ascertained from other available information.

When the opening balance and the closing balance of the asset concerned, at their depreciated value (cost less depreciation till date) are available, in such a case, assuming that there were no purchases and sales of the asset concerned during the year, the difference between the opening balance and the closing balance of the asset concerned must be considered, as the depreciation charged. However, sometimes, the method of presenting the information can be different. The fixed assets are allowed to appear at cost (i.e., their cost value) on the assets side of the balance sheet and the depreciation amount charged is credited to Depreciation Fund Account (also called, Accumulated Depreciation Account) and this account can either be shown as a deduction from the asset concerned or allowed to appear on the liabilities side. Whatever be the procedure adopted, the increase in the amount of accumulated depreciation, during the year, (assuming that there are no purchase and sale of fixed assets), must be taken as the amount of depreciation charged during that year.

The following accounts may be prepared to ascertain the missing information.

Dr. **Accumulated Depreciation A/c** *Cr.*

	Amount Rs.		*Amount Rs.*
To Asset (depreciation on asset sold)	....	By Balance b/d	....
To Balance c/d	......	By P&L A/c (depreciation charged during the year)	......

Dr. **Asset A/c** *Cr.*

	Amount Rs.		*Amount Rs.*
To Balance b/d	....	By Accumulated Depreciation A/c	....
To P&L A/c (if Gain on sale)	....	By Cash-sale	....
To Cash (Purchase)	....	By P&L A/c (if Loss on sale)	....
		By Balance c/d	....

Gain/ Loss on Asset sold

Book Value	XXX
Less Depreciation	XX
Written down Value	XXX
Sale Price	XXX
Gain/Loss on sale	XXX

Illustration 4

Extracts of Balance Sheets

	31.03.08 Rs.	*31.03.09 Rs.*		*31.03.08 Rs.*	*31.03.09 Rs.*
Accumulated Depreciation	10,000	19,000	Furniture	30,000	24,000

Net profit for the year is Rs. 80,000.

You are informed that during the year, some old furniture (original cost Rs. 6,000) was sold for Rs. 4,000. Accumulated depreciation on that asset till date was Rs. 2,500. Calculate gain on sale of furniture.

Solution

Dr. **Accumulated Depreciation Account** *Cr.*

	Rs.		*Rs.*
To Furniture A/c (Depreciation on Furniture Sold)	2,500	By Balance b/d	10,000
To Balance c/d	19,000	By P&L A/c	11,500
	21,500		21,500

Dr. **Furniture Account** *Cr.*

	Rs.		*Rs.*
To Balance b/d	30,000	By Cash A/c	4,000
		By Accumulated Depreciation A/c	2,500
To Profit and Loss A/c (gain on sale)	500	By Balance c/d	24,000
	30,500		30,500

	Rs.
Original Cost of Furniture sold	6,000
Accumulate depreciation of furniture sold	2,500
Written down Value	3,500
Sale Value	4,000
Gain on sale of furniture	500

Amortization of Expenses and Writing off Intangible Assets

Sometimes, a firm desires to write off a portion of its intangible assets like goodwill, patents, copy rights etc., by charging some amount to profit and loss account. Similarly, it may desire to write off deferred revenue expenditure like preliminary expenses, discount on issue of shares, etc., by charging some amount to profit and loss account. Thus, these amounts written off, like depreciation, are non-cash costs and reduce the amount of profit but do not affect the funds provided by operations. For this reason, such amounts written off must be added back to the net profit to determine the funds provided by operations.

TREATMENT OF CERTAIN ITEMS

Certain items like provision for taxation, proposed dividends and investments may be treated as either current items or non-current items. Depending upon the decision, the accounting treatment of these items varies.

Provision for Taxation

Provision for tax may be treated as a current liability or as a non-current liability.

***(a)* As a Current Liability**

Provision for taxation represents the amount likely to be paid as tax after the assessment is complete, during the next accounting period. Thus, provision for taxes can be treated as a current liability. As per the provisions of tax laws, generally, advance tax is paid on a quarterly basis. Thus, about three-fourth of the total amount of tax payable would have already been paid as an advance tax. Further, the amount of provision for taxation shown in the previous Balance Sheet can be reasonably assumed as to have been paid during the current year.

When provision for taxation is treated as a current liability this item would appear in schedule of changes in working capital. When provision for taxation is treated as a current item, its actual payment will not reduce the working capital. Because, cash, a current asset, and provision for taxation, a current liability are simultaneously getting reduced (as both are current items this is not a cross transaction and hence working capital is not affected). That is why the actual tax paid during the year will not be shown as a use in the Funds Flow Statement.

***(b)* As a non-current liability**

When provision for taxation is taken as an appropriation of profits, it is to be treated as a non-current liability. When provision is made, there is no change in working capital as it involves two fixed/non-current liabilities, i.e., Profit and Loss Appropriation Account and Provision for Taxation Account. This will not be taken to statement of changes in working capital, as it is being treated as a non-current item. Provision made during the current year will be found out by preparing the provision for taxation account and added back to net profit as reported in profit and loss account, to ascertain funds from operations.

When tax is paid, it will be taken as an appropriation of funds and will be shown as a use in Funds Flow Statement because, it will then involve 'provision for tax' a non-current liability and cash account which is a current asset.

Provision for Taxation Account

	Rs.		Rs.
To Bank (Tax paid)	....	By Balance b/d	....
To Balance c/d	....	By P&L A/c (Balancing Figure) (Provision made during the year)	....

Note:

(1) When provision for taxation appears clearly as a current liability, it must be taken as such.

(2) When provision for taxation appears, above current liabilities, then a choice exists, i.e., it may be treated either as *(a)* a current liability or *(b)* a non-current liability. In such a case, it is advisable to put up clearly a note and spell out how it is treated.

Proposed Dividends

This item is similar to the provision for taxation explained above. It can be treated either as a current liability or as a non-current liability and the treatment will differ based on the decision. However, when proposed dividends are approved in the Annual General Body Meeting of shareholders, it certainly becomes a current liability and must be treated as such.

***(a)* As a current liability**

When it is considered as a current liability, proposed dividends will be taken in the statement of changes in working capital. When dividends are proposed and declared, they will have to be paid within 42 days of their declaration. In case it is treated as current liability, it will appear as one of the items in the schedule of changes in working capital. Dividends paid will not be shown as an application of funds in Funds Flow Statement as the two accounts affected would be current items only, i.e., Cash Account and Proposed Dividends Account.

***(b)* As a non-current liability**

Proposed dividends may be taken as simply the appropriation of profits, i.e., the amount instead of appearing as a part of the Profit and Loss Appropriation Account, now appears to the credit of a separate account. In such a case, when dividends are proposed, the two accounts affected would be of non-current nature only, i.e., Profit and Loss Appropriation Account and Proposed Dividends Account. Hence, this item will not find a place in the statement of changes in working capital. Proposed dividends for the current year will be found out by preparing the account and will be added back to the current year's profits in order to ascertain funds from operations, if such amount of dividends proposed has already been charged to profits. On payment of dividends, there will be an outflow of funds (as cash will be reduced which is a current asset and proposed dividends, a non-current liability will also be reduced), it will be shown as an application/use of funds.

Dr. **Proposed Dividend Account** *Cr.*

	Rs.		Rs.
To Bank (Dividends paid) A/c	....	By Balance b/d	....
To Balance c/d	....	By P&L A/c (Balancing Figure) (Provision made during the year)	....

Interim Dividend

Sometimes, companies pay an interim dividend between two usual annual dividends. Such interim dividend paid reduces the balance of Profit and Loss Appropriation Account. Hence, the amount of the interim dividend paid must be added, to the difference between the opening and closing balances of Profit and Loss Accounts in order to estimate the profit made during the year. The interim dividends paid will be shown as a use in the Funds Flow Statement.

Investments

If a company purchases shares in some other company with the intention of acquiring control, investment would be considered as a non-current item, i.e., as a fixed asset. In such a case, the changes in this item, if any, would appear in the Funds Flow Statement. However, when surplus liquid funds are available for short periods and they are invested outside the business, such investments must be treated as a current segment item only. In such a case, the changes in this item, if any, would appear in the schedule of changes in working capital.

Provision for Doubtful Debts

As the entire amount of outstanding debtors may not be realized, based on past experience, a particular proportion of the sum of debtors is provided as Provision for Doubtful Debts to meet the loss when bad debts actually arise. Usually, Provision for Doubtful Debts, is subtracted from the sundry debtors, on the assets side of Balance sheet and thus the debtors appear at their expected realizable value. Sometimes, Provision for Doubtful Debts Account may also be shown on the liabilities side of the Balance sheet. Irrespective of this difference in presentation, the effect of this item is similar i.e., to the extent of the provision for doubtful debts (created by debiting profit and loss account), the sundry debtors, a current asset, appears at a reduced value. Thus, this item must be treated as a current item only. This item would appear in the schedule of changes in working capital, whether shown on the assets side of Balance Sheet (as a deduction from sundry debtors) or shown separately on the liabilities side of Balance Sheet. When ascertaining funds provided by operations, the amount of provision for doubtful debts made during the year should not be added back to the net profit for the year. (i.e. should be ignored).

METHODS OF ASCERTAINING FUNDS FROM OPERATIONS

Funds from Operations can be ascertained, either in a statement form or in an account form.

***(a)* Statement Form**

Profit earned during a period, provides additional funds, while, the loss suffered by the business would decrease the funds available with the business. The figure of net profit, as shown in Profit and Loss Account, requires certain adjustments for ascertaining funds from operation. The adjustments are necessary because, the income statement is the combined result of both past and current decisions, whereas, movement in the funds is related to current decisions only. The following adjustments are necessary in this connection:

(i) All such expenses which have been charged to the profit and loss account thus, reducing the profit but did not involve the use of working capital during the current period, should be added to the profit. The items to be added are Depreciation; Amortisation of Goodwill, patents, etc., Amortisation of preliminary expenses; Amortisation of deferred revenue expenditure and Amortisation of discount on sale of shares and debentures.

(ii) Loss on sale of fixed assets, if any, is charged to profit and loss account and thus reduces the net profit for the year. However, this item does not use any working capital during the year. It is necessary to add back this item for the purpose of ascertaining funds from operations.

(iii) Gain on sale of fixed assets, if any, is taken on the credit side of profit and loss account, thus increasing the profit. However, this is not a regular operation and hence subtracted from the net profit, to arrive at funds from operations.

(iv) All such incomes which have been added to revenue thus increasing the profit but have not contributed to working capital are to be subtracted. The items to be deducted are Profit on revaluation of non-current assets; Dividends and interest on long term investments.

Thus, starting with the net profit for the year (or net loss), as shown by the Profit and Loss Account, different items as explained above, are to be added/subtracted to ascertain Funds from Operations.

***(b)* Account Form**

An alternative method of ascertaining funds from operations is by recasting the Profit and Loss Account.

(a) Only business revenues arising from regular operations, providing working capital are included on the income side; this implies that the items to be deducted as explained above will not be now shown on the income side.

(b) Only those operating business expenses, which involve the use of working capital will be shown on the debit side of profit and loss account, this implies that the items to be added as explained above will not be now shown on the expenditure side.

The balancing figure of such a re-casted Profit and Loss Account will represent the amount of net working capital provided by the business operations (i.e., funds from operations).

Sometimes, in the problem, the comparative balance sheets only are given, and the income statement is not given. In such a case, the following procedure can be adopted to ascertain funds from operations.

(i) Compare the opening and closing balances of the profit and loss appropriation account and take the difference between the two as profit for the year (after all the adjustments have been done) as the starting figure for converting it into funds from operations.

(ii) Under such circumstances, it would be necessary to compare the opening and closing balances on accounts like general reserves and consider *(a)* increase in general reserves as arising due to transfer from profit and loss account and hence add back this figure to the figure shown in *(i)* above. *(b)* Alternatively, if there is a decrease in general reserves, it has to be verified whether this decrease is because of capitalization of reserves for the purpose of issuing bonus shares, and if it is not so, it can be assumed that the reduction in the general reserves is because of transferring the amount to the credit of current year's profit and loss account and hence deduct this figure from the figure shown in *(i)* above.

(iii) Funds from operations can be ascertained by preparing the Profit and Loss Adjustment Account, on a memorandum basis.

(iv) After opening the account, all the items to be added as explained above will be shown on the debit side of the account and the items to be deducted will be taken on the credit side of the account. Now, the balancing figure in this account will represent funds from (or used for) operations.

FUNDS FLOW STATEMENT

Funds Flow Statement is prepared by taking into consideration only the non-current segment items. A comparison of opening and closing balances of *(a)* Equity Share Capital Account *(b)* Preference Share Capital Account *(c)* Debentures or Long-Term Loans Account will reveal *(i)* additions to these items (issue of shares/debentures) and *(ii)* repayment/redemption of preference shares and or debentures. This information can also bye found out by preparing the accounts concerned. Depending on the information given and clues provided, the missing information can be ascertained, by preparing the concerned accounts.

The following is the usual form of presenting the Funds Flow Statement.

Funds Flow Statement

(A) Sources of funds:

(1) Funds from Operations
(2) Issue of Share Capital
(3) Issue of Debentures
(4) Long Term Loans raised
(5) Sale of Fixed Assets
(6) Other items if any

(B) Application of funds:

(1) Purchase of Fixed Assets
(2) Repayment of Long Term Liabilities
(3) Redemption of Preference Share Capital

Increase/Decrease in Working Capital (A-B)

Illustration 5

Prepare a Funds Flow Statement from the following information.

Comparative Balance Sheet

	31.03.08 *Rs.*	*31.03.09* *Rs.*		*31.03.08* *Rs.*	*31.03.09* *Rs.*
Capital	80,000	1,00,000	**Fixed Assets:**		
Reserves	30,000	45,000	Machinery	60,000	70,000
Accumulated Depreciation			Furniture	40,000	40,000
on Machinery	10,000	15,000			
Current Liabilities:			**Current Assets:**		
Creditors	25,000	30,000	Stocks	20,000	30,000
Bills Payable	10,000	2,000	Debtors	15,000	25,000
Expenses Payable	20,000	8,000	Cash	40,000	35,000
	1,75,000	2,00,000		1,75,000	2,00,000

Net profit for the year Rs.15,000.

Solution

Schedule of Changes in Working Capital

Particulars	*31.03.08* *Rs.*	*31.03.09* *Rs.*	*Change in Working Capital* *Increase (+)* *Rs.*	*Decrease (–)* *Rs.*
Current Assets:				
Stocks	20,000	30,000	10,000	—
Debtors	15,000	25,000	10,000	—
Cash	40,000	35,000	—	5,000
Current liabilities:				
Creditors	25,000	30,000	—	5,000
Bills Payable	10,000	2,000	8,000	—
Expenses Payable	20,000	8,000	12,000	—
			40,000	10,000
Increase in Working Capital			—	30,000
			40,000	40,000

Dr. **Accumulated Depreciation Account** *Cr.*

	Rs.		*Rs.*
To Balance c/d	15,000	By Balance b/d	10,000
		By Depreciation Charged (Balancing Figure)	5,000
	15,000		15,000

Dr. **Machinery Account** *Cr.*

	Rs.		*Rs.*
To Balance b/d	60,000	By Balance c/d	70,000
To Cash Purchase (Balancing Figure)	10,000		
	70,000		70,000

Dr. **Share Capital Account** *Cr.*

	Rs.		*Rs.*
To Balance c/d	1,00,000	By Balance b/d	80,000
		By Cash (Balancing Figure)	20,000
	1,00,000		1,00,000

Dr. **Reserves Account** *Cr.*

	Rs.		*Rs.*
To Balance c/d	45,000	By Balance b/d	30,000
		By Net Profit	15,000
	45,000		45,000

Funds from Operations

	Rs.
Net Profit	15,000
Add: Depreciation Charged	5,000
Funds from Operations	20,000

Funds Flow Statement for the year ended 31-03-2009

		Rs.
(A)	**Sources:**	
	Funds from Operations	20,000
	Issue of Share Capital	20,000
		40,000
(B)	**Applications:**	
	Purchase of Machinery	10,000
	Increase in Working Capital	30,000
		40,000

Illustration 6

From the following Profit and Loss Account and Balance Sheets, you are required to prepare:

(A) A Schedule of Changes in Working Capital and

(B) A Funds Flow Statement.

Dr. **Profit and Loss Account for the year ended 31-03-2009** *Cr.*

	Rs.		Rs.
To Cost of Sales	19,80,000	By Sales	25,20,000
To Expenses	4,08,000	By Equipment A/c (Profit on Sale)	12,000
To Depreciation on Building and Equipment	60,000		
To Administrative Expenses	72,000		
To Net Profit	12,000		
	25,32,000		25,32,000

Comparative Balance Sheet

	31.03.08 Rs.	*31.03.09* Rs.		*31.03.08* Rs.	*31.03.09* Rs.
Capital	3,60,000	4,44,000	**Fixed Assets:**		
Reserves	1,51,800	1,63,800	Land	48,000	96,000
Accumulated Depreciation:			Buildings and Equipment	3,60,000	5,76,000
On building and Equipment	1,20,000	1,32,000			
Current Liabilities:			**Current Assets:**		
Sundry Creditors	2,40,000	2,34,000	Cash	60,000	72,000
Outstanding Expenses	24,000	48,000	Debtors	1,68,000	1,86,000
Bills Payable	12,000	13,200	Stocks	2,64,000	96,000
			Advances	7,800	9,000
	9,07,800	10,35,000		9,07,800	10,35,000

Cost of Equipment sold was Rs. 72,000.

Solution

Schedule of Changes in Working Capital

Particulars	*31.03.08* Rs.	*31.03.09* Rs.	*Change in Working Capital* *Increase* Rs.	*Decrease* Rs.
Current Assets:				
Cash	60,000	72,000	12,000	—
Debtors	1,68,000	1,86,000	18,000	—
Stocks	2,64,000	96,000	—	1,68,000
Advances	7,800	9,000	1,200	—
Current Liabilities:				
Sundry Creditors	2,40,000	2,34,000	6,000	—
Outstanding expenses	24,000	48,000	—	24,000
Bills Payable	12,000	13,200	—	1,200
			37,200	1,93,200
Decrease in Working Capital			1,56,000	—
			1,93,200	1,93,200

Dr. **Building and Equipment Account** *Cr.*

	Rs.		*Rs.*
To Balance b/d	3,60,000	By Bank (sale)	36,000
To Profit and Loss A/c (Gain on Purchase)	12,000	By Accumulated Depreciation (on Equipment sold)	48,000
To Bank (Purchase) (Balancing Figure)	2,88,000	By Balance c/d	5,76,000
	6,60,000		6,60,000

Dr. **Accumulated Depreciation Account** *Cr.*

	Rs.		*Rs.*
To Buildings and Equipment A/c (Depreciation on Building and Equipment sold) (Balancing Figure)	48,000	By Balance b/d	1,20,000
		By Profit and Loss a/c (depreciation charged)	60,000
To Balance c/d	1,32,000		
	1,80,000		1,80,000

Calculation of sale value of Equipment

	Rs.
Cost of Equipment sold	72,000
Depreciation on asset sold	48,000
Book value	24,000
Gain on sale	12,000
Sale proceeds	36,000
Funds from operations	
Net profit	12,000
Add: Depreciation	60,000
	72,000
Less: Gain on Sale of Equipment	12,000
Funds from Operations	60,000

Dr. **Reserves Account** *Cr.*

	Rs.		*Rs.*
To Balance c/d	1,63,800	By Balance b/d	1,51,800
		By Net Profit	12,000
	1,63,800		1,63,800

Funds Flow Statement for the year ended 31-03-2009

			Rs.
(A) Sources:			
Funds from Operations			60,000
Sale of Equipment			36,000
Issue of Share Capital			84,000
			1,80,000
(B) Applications:			
Purchase of Land			48,000
Purchase of Equipment			2,88,000
			3,36,000
Decrease in Working Capital (B-A)			1,56,000

Illustration 7

Prepare funds flow statement from the given below balance sheets and other information:

Comparative Balance Sheets

	31.03.08 Rs.	*31.03.09 Rs.*		*31.03.08 Rs.*	*31.03.09 Rs.*
Share Capital	1,00,000	1,20,000	**Fixed assets:**		
General Reserve	85,000	65,000	Land	85,000	1,15,000
Profit and Loss A/c	40,000	50,000	Furniture	60,000	55,000
Accumulated Depreciation A/c	15,000	20,000			
Current liabilities:			**Current assets:**		
Sundry creditors	20,000	25,000	Debtors	25,000	20,000
Bank overdraft	10,000	15,000	Stocks	45,000	60,000
			Cash	40,000	35,000
			Advertisement Expenses (Deferred Revenue Expenditure)	15,000	10,000
	2,70,000	2,95,000		2,70,000	2,95,000

Old Furniture costing Rs. 12,000 was sold for Rs. 10,000 and Accumulated Depreciation on it was Rs. 6,000. General Reserve was utilized for Issue of Bonus Shares.

Solution

Schedule of Changes in Working Capital

Particulars	*31.03.08*	*31.03.09*	*Change in Working Capital*	
	Rs.	*Rs.*	*Increase Rs.*	*Decrease Rs.*
Current Assets				
Stocks	45,000	60,000	15,000	—
Debtors	25,000	20,000	—	5,000
Cash	40,000	35,000	—	5,000
Current Liabilities				
Creditors	20,000	25,000	—	5,000
Bank Overdraft	10,000	15,000	—	5,000
			15,000	20,000
Increase in Working Capital			5,000	—
			20,000	20,000

Dr. **Land Account** *Cr.*

	Rs.		*Rs.*
To Balance b/d	85,000	By Balance c/d	1,15,000
To Cash (Purchase) (Balancing Figure)	30,000		
	1,15,000		1,15,000

Dr. **Accumulated Depreciation Account** *Cr.*

	Rs.		*Rs.*
To Furniture A/c (Depreciation on Furniture)	6,000	By Balance b/d	15,000
To Balance c/d	20,000	By P&L Account (Depreciation Charged) (Balancing Figure)	11,000
	26,000		26,000

Furniture Account

Dr.	Rs.		Cr. Rs.
To Balance b/d	60,000	By Accumulated Depreciation A/c (Sold Furniture)	6,000
To Profit and Loss A/c (gain)	4,000	By Cash (Sale Value)	10,000
To Cash A/c (New Purchase) (Balancing Figure)	7,000	By Balance c/d	55,000
	71,000		71,000

Gain on Sale of Furniture

	Rs.
Cost of Furniture	12,000
Depreciation on Furniture Sold	6,000
Book Value	6,000
Sale Proceeds	10,000
Gain on Sale	4,000

Advertising Account
(Deferred Revenue Expenditure)

Dr.	Rs.		Cr. Rs.
To Balance b/d	15,000	By Adjusted Profit and Loss A/c (Balancing Figure)	5,000
		By Balance c/d	10,000
	15,000		15,000

General Reserve Account

Dr.	Rs.		Cr. Rs.
To Share Capital A/c (Bonus Shares) (Balancing Figure)	20,000	By Balance b/d	85,000
To Balance c/d	65,000		
	85,000		85,000

Share Capital Account

Dr.	Rs.		Cr. Rs.
To Balance c/d	1,20,000	By Balance b/d	1,00,000
		By General Reserve (on Bonus Shares) (Balancing Figure)	20,000
	1,20,000		1,20,000

Adjusted Profit and Loss Account

Dr.	Rs.		Cr. Rs.
To Advertising A/c (Expenses Written-off Deferred Expenditure)	5,000	By Balance b/d	40,000
To Depreciation charged	11,000	By Furniture A/c (Gain on sale)	4,000
To Balance c/d	50,000	By Funds From Operations (Balancing Figure)	22,000
	66,000		66,000

Funds Flow Statement for the year ended 31-03-2009

	Rs.
(A) Sources	
Funds from operations	22,000
Sale of furniture	10,000
	32,000
(B) Applications	
Purchase of furniture	7,000
Purchase of land	30,000
	37,000
Decrease in Working Capital (B-A)	5,000

Note:

Issue of bonus shares from General Reserve affects two Non-Current Accounts i.e., General Reserve and Share Capital Account. Hence this item does not find place in Fund Flow Statement as there is no flow of funds.

Illustration 8

The following are the summaries of balance sheets of a company as on 31st March 2008 and 2009.

Liabilities	*2008 Rs.*	*2009 Rs.*	*Assets*	*2008 Rs.*	*2009 Rs.*
Share Capital	8,00,000	12,00,000	Land and Buildings (at cost)	6,00,000	8,00,000
General Reserve	5,00,000	7,00,000	Plant and Machinery (at cost)	9,20,000	12,60,000
Depreciation Fund	1,60,000	2,40,000	Inventories	3,60,000	4,00,000
Debentures	3,20,000	1,60,000	Debtors	2,00,000	3,10,000
Proposed Dividend	80,000	1,20,000	Cash	1,00,000	30,000
Provision for Tax	80,000	1,10,000			
Sundry Creditors	2,40,000	2,70,000			
	21,80,000	28,00,000		21,80,000	28,00,000

A machinery which was purchased earlier for Rs. 1,20,000 was sold for Rs. 8,000. The book value of the machine was Rs. 12,000. The company also purchased new equipments during the year.

The company has issued new shares to the extent of Rs.4,00,000 for cash.

Prepare a Funds Flow Statement.

Solution

Schedule of changes in Working capital

Particulars	*31.03.08*	*31.03.09*	*Change in Working Capital*	
			Increase	*Decrease*
	Rs.	*Rs.*	*Rs.*	*Rs.*
Current Assets:				
Inventories	3,60,000	4,00,000	40,000	—
Debtors	2,00,000	3,10,000	1,10,000	—
Cash	1,00,000	30,000	—	70,000
Current Liabilities:				
Sundry Creditors	2,40,000	2,70,000	—	30,000
			1,50,000	1,00,000
Increase in Working Capital			—	50,000
			1,50,000	1,50,000

Note: Cost of machinery purchased earlier = 1,20,000
Book value of machinery = 12,000

Depreciation on machinery sold = Rs. 1,08,000

Written Down value of machine sold	=	Rs. 12,000
Sale value	=	Rs. 8,000
Loss on sale	=	Rs. 4,000

Dr. **Machinery Account** *Cr.*

	Rs.		*Rs.*
To Balance b/d	9,20,000	By Depreciation fund	1,08,000
To Bank (Purchase) (Balancing Figure)	4,60,000	By Cash (sale)	8,000
		By P&L A/c (loss)	4,000
		By Balance c/d	12,60,000
	13,80,000		13,80,000

Dr. **Depreciation Fund Account** *Cr.*

	Rs.		*Rs.*
To Machinery A/c (Depreciation on asset sold)	1,08,000	By Balance b/d	1,60,000
To Balance c/d	2,40,000	By P&L Adjustment A/c (Provision Made) (Balancing Figure)	1,88,000
	3,48,000		3,48,000

Dr. **Reserve Account** *Cr.*

	Rs.		*Rs.*
To Depreciation Fund A/c	1,88,000	By Balance b/d	5,00,000
To Provision for Tax A/c	1,10,000	By Funds From Operations (Balancing Figure)	6,22,000
To Machinery A/c (Loss on Sale)	4,000		
To Proposed Dividend A/c	1,20,000		
To Balance c/d	7,00,000		
	11,22,000		11,22,000

Dr. **Provision for Tax Account** *Cr.*

	Rs.		*Rs.*
To Cash A/c (Tax Paid)	80,000	By Balance b/d	80,000
To Balance c/d	1,10,000	By Profit and Loss Adjustment A/c (Provision Made) (Balancing Figure)	1,10,000
	1,90,000		1,90,000

Dr. **Proposed Dividends Account** *Cr.*

	Rs.		*Rs.*
To Cash A/c (Dividend Paid)	80,000	By Balance b/d	80,000
To Balance c/d	1,20,000	By P&L Adjustment A/c (Provision Made Balancing Figure)	1,20,000
	2,00,000		2,00,000

Funds Flow Statement

	Rs.
(A) Sources	
Funds From Operations	6,22,000
Proceeds from Issue of Share Capital (12,00,000 – 8,00,000)	4,00,000
Proceeds from Sale of Machinery	8,000
	10,30,000

	Rs.
(B) Applications	
Purchase of Machinery	4,60,000
Purchase of Land and Buildings (8,00,000 – 6,00,000)	2,00,000
Payment of Tax	80,000
Redemption of Debentures (3,20,000 – 1,60,000)	1,60,000
Payment of Dividends	80,000
	9,80,000
Increase in Working Capital (A-B)	50,000

Illustration 9

From the following balance sheet of Shreya Ltd., prepare a Funds Flow Statement for the year 2009.

Liabilities	*31.03.08 Rs.*	*31.03.09 Rs.*	*Assets*	*31.03.08 Rs.*	*31.03.09 Rs.*
Share Capital	75,000	1,00,000	Goodwill	25,000	20,000
9% Redeemable			Land and Buildings	50,000	42,500
Preference Shares	37,500	25,000	Plant and Machinery	20,000	50,000
Capital Reserve	—	5,000	Investments	5,000	7,500
General Reserve	10,000	12,500	Sundry Debtors	35,000	42,500
Profit and Loss A/c	7,500	12,000	Stock	19,500	27,500
Proposed Dividend	10,500	12,500	Bills Receivable	5,000	7,500
Provision for Tax	10,000	12,500	Cash at Bank	3,500	2,500
Sundry Creditors	6,500	12,000	Cash in Hand	2,500	2,000
Bills Payable	5,000	4,000	Preliminary Expenses	4,000	2,500
Liability for Expenses	7,500	9,000			
	1,69,500	2,04,500		1,69,500	2,04,500

Additional Information

(1) A part of land was sold out in 2009, and the profit was credited to capital reserve.
(2) A machine has been sold for Rs. 2,500 (written down value of the machine was Rs.3,000). Depreciation of Rs. 2,500 was charged on plant in 2009.
(3) An interim dividend of Rs. 5,000 has been paid in 2009.
(4) An amount of Rs. 500 has been received by way of dividend on investment in 2009.

Solution

(Note: (a) Provision for tax and proposed dividends are treated as non-current items.)

Schedule of changes in working capital

Particulars	*2008*	*2009*	*Change in Working Capital*	
	Rs.	*Rs.*	*Increase Rs.*	*Decrease Rs.*
Current Assets				
Sundry Debtors	35,000	42,500	7,500	—
Stock	19,500	27,500	8,000	—
Bills Receivable	5,000	7,500	2,500	—
Cash at Bank	3,500	2,500	—	1,000
Cash in Hand	2,500	2,000	—	500
Current Liabilities				
Sundry Creditors	6,500	12,000	—	5,500
Bills Payable	5,000	4,000	1,000	—
Liability for Expenses	7,500	9,000	—	1,500
			19,000	8,500
Increase in Working Capital			—	10,500
			19,000	19,000

Dr. **Plant Account** *Cr.*

	Rs.		*Rs.*
To Balance b/d	20,000	By Depreciation	2,500
To Bank A/c (Purchase) (Balancing Figure)	35,500	By Bank A/c (Sale)	2,500
		By Profit and Loss Adjustment Account (Loss)	500
		By Balance c/d	50,000
	55,500		55,500

Dr. **Proposed Dividends Account** *Cr.*

	Rs.		*Rs.*
To Cash A/c (Dividend Paid)	10,500	By Balance b/d	10,500
To Balance c/d	12,500	By P&L Adjustment A/c(Balancing Figure)	12,500
	23,000		23,000

Dr. **Provision for Tax Account** *Cr.*

	Rs.		*Rs.*
To Cash (Tax Paid) A/c	10,000	By Balance b/d	10,000
To Balance c/d	12,500	By Profit and Loss Adjustment A/c (Provision Made) (Balancing Figure)	12,500
	22,500		22,500

Dr. **Investments Account** *Cr.*

	Rs.		*Rs.*
To Balance b/d	5,000	By Balance c/d	7,500
To Bank A/c (Balancing Figure)	2,500		
	7,500		7,500

Dr. **Profit and Loss Adjustment Account** *Cr.*

	Rs.		*Rs.*
To Capital Reserve (Closing Balance)	5,000	By Balance b/d	7,500
To General Reserve (Closing Balance)	12,500	By General Reserve Balance b/d	10,000
To Loss on Sale of Plant	500	By Land A/c (Gain on Sale)	5,000
To Provision for Tax	12,500	By Dividend Received on Investment	500
To Proposed Dividend	12,500	By Funds From Operations (Balancing Figure)	46,000
To Depreciation on Plant	2,500		
To Interim Dividend	5,000		
To Goodwill Written-off	5,000		
To Preliminary Expenses	1,500		
To Balance c/d	12,000		
	69,000		69,000

Profit on Sale of Land is credited to Capital Reserve. The amount credited to Capital Reserve stands at Rs. 5,000 which is considered to be the Profit on Sale of Land.

Dr. **Land and Building Account** *Cr.*

	Rs.		*Rs.*
To Balance b/d	50,000	By Bank A/c (Sale) (Balancing Figure)	12,500
To Profit and Loss Adjustment A/c (Gain on Sale)	5,000	By Balance c/d	42,500
	55,000		55,000

Note :

(1) When accumulated depreciation is not given, depreciation on assets will be transferred to P&L A/c. If accumulated depreciation account appears in Balance sheet, then, depreciation on asset will be taken to accumulated depreciation account and only the provision for depreciation made during the year will be taken to Profit and Loss Account.

(2) Goodwill is an intangible asset and Preliminary Expenses is a fictitious asset. Any reduction in these two assets amount to writing off. Goodwill account is reduced by Rs.5,000 (Rs.25,000-Rs.20,000)and preliminary expenses is reduced by Rs.1,500 (Rs.4,000-Rs.2,500). Hence taken on the debit side of P&L A/c.

Funds Flow Statement
For the year ended 31-03-2009

	Rs.	*Rs.*
(A) Sources		
Funds From Operations	46,000	
Issue of Equity Shares (1,00,000-75,000)	25,000	
Sale of Land and Buildings	12,500	
Dividend Received on Investments	500	
Sale of Plant and Machinery	2,500	86,500
(B) Applications		
Redemption of Preference Shares (37,500-25,000)	12,500	
Purchase of Plant	35,500	
Payment of Tax	10,000	
Payment of Dividends	10,500	
Purchase of Investments	2,500	
Payment of Interim Dividend	5,000	76,000
Increase in Working Capital (A-B)		10,500

(b) **When provision for Tax and Proposed dividends are treated as Current items**

Schedule of Changes in Working Capital

Particulars	*2008*	*2009*	*Change in Working Capital*	
	Rs.	*Rs.*	*Increase Rs.*	*Decrease Rs.*
Current Assets:				
Sundry Debtors	35,000	42,500	7,500	—
Stocks	19,500	27,500	8,000	—
Bills Receivable	5,000	7,500	2,500	—
Cash at Bank	3,500	2,500	—	1,000
Cash in Hand	2,500	2,000	—	500
Current Liabilities:				
Sundry Creditors	6,500	12,000	—	5,500
Bills Payable	5,000	4,000	1,000	—
Liability for Expenses	7,500	9,000	—	1,500
Provision for Tax	10,000	12,500	—	2,500
Proposed Dividend	10,500	12,500	—	2,000
			19,000	13,000
Increase in Working Capital			—	6,000
			19,000	19,000

Note

(1) When provision for tax and proposed dividends are taken as Current Liabilities, tax paid and dividend paid will not appear as application of funds as the two accounts affected will be only current accounts i.e., provision and cash.

(2) There is no need for the preparation of Proposed Dividend Account and Provision For Tax Account

(3) Adjusted Profit and Loss Account will be the same excepting for the two items provision for tax of Rs. 12,500 and proposed dividend of Rs. 12,500. Therefore, funds from operations will be Rs. 21,000 (46,000-12,500-12,500).

(4) Interim dividend of Rs. 5,000 will appear as application of funds. It is not the same as the last year dividend paid which appears in Proposed Dividend Account.

Funds Flow Statement
For the year ended 31-03-2009

		Rs.	*Rs.*
(A) Sources			
Funds From Operations		21,000	
Proceeds from Issue of Equity Share Capital		25,000	
Amount realized from Sale of Land and Buildings		12,500	
Dividend Received on Investments	500		
Amount Realized from Sale of Plant and Machinery	2,500		
Total sources			61,500
(B) Applications			
Redemption of Preference Shares		12,500	
Purchase of Plant		35,500	
Payment of Interim Dividend		5,000	
Purchase of Investment		2,500	
Total Applications			55,500
Increase in Working Capital (A-B)			6,000

Illustration 10

From the following Balance Sheets of A Co. prepare a Statement of Funds Flow:

Liabilities	*2008* *Rs.*	*2009* *Rs.*	*Assets*	*2008* *Rs.*	*2009* *Rs.*
Share Capital	4,00,000	5,00,000	Land and Buildings	4,00,000	3,80,000
General Reserve	1,00,000	1,20,000	Machinery	3,00,000	3,38,000
Profit and Loss A/c	61,000	61,200	Stock	2,00,000	1,48,000
Bank Loan (Long term)	1,40,000	—	Debtors	1,60,000	1,28,400
Sundry Creditors	3,00,000	2,70,400	Cash	1,000	1,200
Provision for Tax	60,000	70,000	Bank	—	16,000
			Goodwill	—	10,000
	10,61,000	10,21,600		10,61,000	10,21,600

Additional Information

During the year *(a)* Dividend of Rs. 46,000 was paid; *(b)* Assets of another company were purchased for a consideration of Rs. 1,00,000 payable in shares. The following assets were purchased: Stock Rs. 40,000; Machinery Rs. 50,000; *(c)* Machinery was further purchased for Rs. 16,000; *(d)* Depreciation written off on Machinery Rs. 24,000; *(e)* Income Tax provided during the year Rs. 66,000; *(f)* Loss on sale of Machinery Rs.400 was written off to General Reserve.

Note: Increase in Goodwill of Rs. 10,000 is purchased by issue of share capital (i.e., balance in capital account).

Statement of Changes in Working Capital

Particulars	*2008*	*2009*	*Change in Working Capital*	
			Increase	*Decrease*
	Rs.	*Rs.*	*Rs.*	*Rs.*
Current Assets				
Stock	2,00,000	1,48,000	—	52,000
Debtors	1,60,000	1,28,400	—	31,600
Cash	1,000	1,200	200	—
Bank	—	16,000	16,000	—
Current Liabilities				
Sundry Creditors	3,00,000	2,70,400	29,600	—
			45,800	83,600
Decrease in Working Capital			37,800	—
			83,600	83,600

Dr. **Land and Building Account** *Cr.*

	Rs.		*Rs.*
To Balance b/d	4,00,000	By Depreciation (Balancing Figure) By Balance c/d	20,000 3,80,000
	4,00,000		4,00,000

Dr. **Machinery Account** *Cr.*

	Rs.		*Rs.*
To Opening Balance b/d To Share Capital A/c (Purchase) To Cash (Purchase)	3,00,000 50,000 16,000	By Depreciation By General Reserve A/c (Loss on Sale) By Cash A/c (Sale) (Balancing Figure) By Closing Balance c/d	24,000 400 3,600 3,38,000
	3,66,000		3,66,000

Dr. **Share Capital Account** *Cr.*

	Rs.		*Rs.*
To Balance c/d	5,00,000	By Balance b/d By Machinery A/c (Purchase) By Stock A/c (Purchase) By Goodwill A/c (Balancing Figure)	4,00,000 50,000 40,000 10,000
	5,00,0000		5,00,000

Dr. **Provision for Tax Account** *Cr.*

	Rs.		*Rs.*
To Cash A/c (Tax Paid) (Balancing Figure) To Balance c/d	56,000 70,000	By Balance b/d By Profit and Loss Adjustment A/c	60,000 66,000
	1,26,000		1,26,000

Dr. **General Reserve Account** *Cr.*

	Rs.		*Rs.*
To Machinery A/c (Loss on Sale) To Closing Balance c/d	400 1,20,000	By Balance b/d By Profit and Loss Adjustment A/c (Balancing Figure)	1,00,000 20,400
	1,20,400		1,20,400

Dr. **Goodwill Account** *Cr.*

	Rs.		*Rs.*
To Share Capital A/c (Balancing Figure)	10,000	By Balance c/d	10,000
	10,000		10,000

Dr. **Profit and Loss Adjustment Account** *Cr.*

	Rs.		*Rs.*
To General Reserve To Income Tax Provision To Depreciation on Land and buildings Machinery To Dividend To Balance c/d	20,400 66,000 20,000 24,000 46,000 61,200	By Balance b/d By Funds From Operations (Balancing Figure)	61,000 1,76,600
	2,37,600		2,37,600

Funds Flow Statement

	Rs.
(A) Sources	
Funds From Operations	1,76,600
Proceeds from Issue of Shares	40,000
Amount realized from Sale of Machinery	3,600
Total (A)	2,20,200
(B) Applications	
Purchase of Machine for Cash	16,000
Payment of Bank Loan	1,40,000
Payment of Tax	56,000
Dividend Paid	46,000
Total (B)	2,58,000
Decrease in Working Capital (B-A)	37,800

Illustration 11

From the following details relating to the accounts of ABC & Co .Ltd., prepare a Statement of Sources and Application of Funds.

	31.12.2001 *Rs.*	*31.12.2000* *Rs.*
Liabilities:		
Share Capital	4,00,000	3,00,000
Reserves	1,00,000	80,000
Profit and Loss A/c	50,000	30,000
Debentures	1,00,000	1,50,000
Income Tax Provision	40,000	50,000
Trade Creditors	70,000	90,000
Proposed Dividend	40,000	30,000
	8,00,000	7,30,000
Assets:		
Goodwill	90,000	1,00,000
Plant and Machinery	4,29,250	2,98,000
Debentures Discount	5,000	8,000
Prepaid Expenses	5,750	4,000
Investment	60,000	1,00,000
Sundry Debtors	1,10,000	1,60,000
Stock	80,000	50,000
Cash at bank	20,000	10,000
	8,00,000	7,30,000

(1) 15% deprecation has been charged in the accounts on Plant and Machinery.
(2) Old machine costing Rs. 50,000 (WDV Rs. 20,000) has been sold for Rs. 35,000.
(3) A machine costing Rs. 10,000 (WDV Rs. 3,000) has been discarded.
(4) Rs. 10,000 profits has been earned by sale of investments.
(5) Debentures have been redeemed at 5% premium.
(6) Rs.45,000 income tax has been paid and adjusted against Income Tax Provision Account.

(CAIIB, Part II – Adapted)

Solution

Statement of Changes in Working Capital

Particulars	*2000* *Rs.*	*2001* *Rs.*	*Change in Working Capital* *Increase* *Rs.*	*Decrease* *Rs.*
Current Assets:				
Stocks	50,000	80,000	30,000	—
Prepaid expenses	4,000	5,750	1,750	—
Debtors	1,60,000	1,10,000	—	50,000
Cash at Bank	10,000	20,000	10,000	—
Current Liabilities:				
Trade Creditors	90,000	70,000	20,000	—
			61,750	50,000
Increase in Working Capital			—	11,750
			61,750	61,750

ABC & Co.

Statement of Source and Application of Funds
(for the year ended 31st December 2001)

		(Rs.)
Sources of Funds:		
Share Capital	1,00,000	
Sale of Machine	35,000	
Sale of Investments	50,000	
Funds from Operations	1,84,250	3,69,250
Application of Funds:		
Purchase of Machinery	2,30,000	
Redemption of Debentures	52,500	
Payments of Dividend	30,000	
Payment of Income Tax	45,000	3,57,500
Increase in Working Capital		11,750

[**Note:** If Provision for taxation is considered as a current liability, then net increase in working capital would be Rs. 21,750 and Funds from Operations Rs. 1,49,250]

Dr. **Share Capital Account A/c** *Cr.*

	Rs.		*Rs.*
To Balance c/d	4,00,000	By Balance b/d	3,00,000
		By Cash – balancing figure (additional issue)	1,00,000
	4,00,000		4,00,000

Dr. **Debentures A/c** *Cr.*

	Rs.		*Rs.*
To Cash (Balancing Figure)	52,500	By Balance b/d	1,50,000
To Balance c/d	1,00,000	By Profit and Loss A/c – premium (50,000 × 0.05)	2,500
	1,52,500		1,52,500

Reserve A/c

Dr.	Rs.		Cr. Rs.
To Balance c/d	1,00,000	By Balance b/d	80,000
		By Profit and Loss A/c – balancing figure (further appropriation)	20,000
	1,00,000		1,00,000

Plant and Machinery A/c

Dr.	Rs.		Cr. Rs.
To Balance b/d	2,98,000	By Machine Discarded	3,000
To P&L A/c (Gain)	15,000	By Cash-sale of old machine	35,000
To Cash (Purchase) (Balancing Figure)	2,30,000	By Depreciation on the balance: (.15 × 2,75,000)	41,250
		By Depreciation on Machinery Purchased (.15 × 2,30,000)	34,500
		By Balance c/d	4,29,250
	5,43,000		5,43,000

[Note if x = purchase of machinery, then 3,13,000 + x = 5,08,500 + .15x, solving, we get, x = Rs. 2,30,000]

Provision for Income Tax A/c

Dr.	Rs.		Cr. Rs.
To Cash – Payment of tax	45,000	By Balance b/d	50,000
To Balance c/d	40,000	By Profit and Loss A/c (further appropriation)	35,000
	85,000		85,000

Investment A/c

Dr.	Rs.		Cr. Rs.
To Balance b/d	1,00,000	By Cash-sale	50,000
To P&L A/c. (Gain on sale)	10,000	By Balance c/d	60,000
	1,10,000		1,10,000

Proposed Dividend A/c

Dr.	Rs.		Cr. Rs.
To Cash A/c (payment of dividend)	30,000	By Balance b/d	30,000
To Balance c/d	40,000	By Profit and Loss A/c (appropriation)	40,000
	70,000		70,000

Profit and Loss A/c

Dr.	Rs.		Cr. Rs.
To Goodwill written off	10,000	By Balance b/d	30,000
To Discount on Debentures written off	3,000	By Profit on sale of Investment	10,000
To Premium on redemption of Debentures	2,500	By Profit on sale of Machine	15,000
To Proposed Dividend	40,000	By Funds from Operations	1,84,250
To Reserves	20,000		
To Loss on Machine discarded	3,000		
To Provision for Income Tax	35,000		
To Depreciation on Plant and Machinery	75,750		
To Balance c/d	50,000		
	2,39,250		2,39,250

Illustration 12

From the following Balance Sheets of AB & Co., prepare a statement of changes in working capital and funds flow statement.

Balance Sheet of AB & Co. (for two years)

Liabilities	*2000 Rs.*	*2001 Rs.*	*Assets*	*2000 Rs.*	*2001 Rs.*
Equity Share Capital	1,30,000	2,00,000	Goodwill	45,000	40,000
8% Redeemable Preference Share capital	60,000	40,000	Land and Buildings	95,000	82,000
Capital Reserve	—	10,000	Plant	30,500	1,00,000
General Reserve	15,000	20,000	Investments	10,000	12,000
Profit and Loss Account	15,000	20,000	Debtors	60,000	84,000
Proposed Dividend	20,000	30,000	Stock	30,000	50,500
Creditors	15,500	25,500	Bills Receivables	9,000	11,000
Bills Payable	10,000	9,000	Cash	6,000	4,000
Provision for Taxation	20,000	22,000	Bank	5,000	3,500
Liabilities for Expenses	12,000	15,000	Preliminary Expenses	7,000	4,500
	2,97,500	3,91,500		2,97,500	3,91,500

(1) A piece of land had been sold in 2001 and the profit on sale has been credited to capital reserve.
(2) A Machine has been sold for 6,000. The WDV of the machine was Rs. 7,000. Depreciation of Rs. 6,000 is charged on plant in 2001.
(3) The investments are all trade investments. Rs. 2,000 by way of divided is received including Rs. 800 from pre-acquisition profit, which has been credited to investment account.
(4) An interim dividend of Rs. 12,000 has been paid in 2001.

(CAIIB, Part II – Adapted)

Solution

Statement of Changes in Working Capital

Particulars	*2000 Rs.*	*2001 Rs.*	*Change in Working Capital* Increase Rs.	Decrease Rs.
Current Assets:				
Stock	30,000	50,500	20,500	—
Debtors	60,000	84,000	24,000	—
Bills Receivable	9,000	11,000	2,000	—
Cash	6,000	4,000	—	2,000
Bank	5,000	3,500	—	1,500
Current Liabilities:				
Creditors	15,500	25,500	—	10,000
Bills Payable	10,000	9,000	1,000	—
Liabilities for Expenses	12,000	15,000	—	3,000
Provision for Taxation	20,000	22,000	—	2,000
			47,500	18,500
Increase in Working Capital			—	29,000
			47,500	47,500

Funds Flow Statement
(For the year ended 31st Dec., 2001)

	Rs.	Rs.
Sources of Funds:		
Funds from Operation	65,300	
Equity Share Capital (2,00,000 – 1,30,000)	70,000	
Sale of Land	23,000	
Dividend Received	2,000	
Sale of Machine	6,000	
Total Sources		1,66,300

	Rs.	Rs.
Application of Funds:		
Redemption of Preference Shares	20,000	
Proposed Dividend	20,000	
Interim Dividend	12,000	
Purchase of Plant	82,500	
Purchase of Investments	2,800	
Total Applications		1,37,300
Net Increase in Working Capital		29,000

Dr. **Plant and Machinery A/c** *Cr.*

	Rs.		Rs.
To Balance b/d	30,500	By Depreciation	6,000
To Cash (Purchase) (Balancing Figure)	82,500	By Loss on sale	1,000
		By Cash	6,000
		By Balance c/d	1,00,000
	1,13,000		1,13,000

Dr. **Investment A/c** *Cr.*

	Rs.		Rs.
To Balance b/d	10,000	By Dividend	800
To Cash – Purchase	2,800	By Balance c/d	12,000
	12,800		12,800

Dr. **Land and Building A/c** *Cr.*

	Rs.		Rs.
To Balance b/d	95,000	By Cash A/c – sale of land	23,000
To Capital Reserve	10,000	By Balance c/d	82,000
	1,05,000		1,05,000

Dr. **Proposed Dividend A/c** *Cr.*

	Rs.		Rs.
To Cash A/c (Last year's paid)	20,000	By Balance b/d	20,000
To Balance c/d	30,000	By Profit and Loss A/c (balancing figure)	30,000
	50,000		50,000

Dr. **Profit and Loss A/c** *Cr.*

	Rs.		Rs.
To General Reserve (20,000 – 15,000)	5,000	By Balance b/d	15,000
To Interim Dividend	12,000	By Dividend Received (2,000 – 800)	1,200
To Proposed Dividend	30,000	By Funds from Operations	65,300
To Goodwill Written off	5,000		
To Loss on Plant	1,000		
To Depreciation on sale of Plant	6,000		
To Preliminary Expenses	2,500		
To Balance c/d	20,000		
	81,500		81,500

Illustration 13

The following Balance Sheets of XYZ & Co. Ltd. for the years 2000 and 2001 are given. You are required to prepare statement of changes in Working Capital and a Funds Flow Statement.

Balance Sheet of XYZ & Co.

(Figures are as at 31st December) (Rs '000)

Liabilities	*2000 Rs.*	*2001 Rs.*	*Assets*	*2000 Rs.*	*2001 Rs.*
Share Capital	150.0	225.0	Land	150.0	150.0
Share Premium	—	7.5	Plant	156.0	150.0
General Reserve	75.0	90.0	Furniture	10.5	13.5
Profit and Loss Account	15.0	25.5	Investment	90.0	120.0
Debentures	105.0	75.0	Debtors	45.0	105.0
Depreciation on Plant	75.0	84.0	Stock	90.0	97.5
Depreciation on Furniture	7.5	9.0	Cash	45.0	67.5
Provision for Tax	30.0	45.0			
Sundry Creditors	129.0	142.5			
	586.5	703.5		586.5	703.5

Additional information:

(1) Plant purchased for Rs. 6,000(depreciation value Rs. 3,000) was sold for cash Rs. 1,200 on 30th September 2001.
(2) On 29th June 2001, Furniture was purchased for Rs. 3,000.
(3) Deprecation on Plant is 8% and Deprecation on Furniture is 12½% on average cost.
(4) Dividend 22½% on original share capital.

(CAIIB, Part II – Adapted)

Solution

Statement of Changes in Working Capital

Particulars	*2000*	*2001*	*Change in Working Capital*	
	Rs.	*Rs.*	*Increase Rs.*	*Decrease Rs.*
Current Assets:				
Stock	90,000	97,500	7,500	—
Debtors	45,000	1,05,000	60,000	—
Cash	45,000	67,500	22,500	—
Current Liabilities:				
Sundry Creditors	1,29,000	1,42,500	—	13,500
			90,000	13,500
Increase in Working Capital			—	76,500
			90,000	90,000

Funds Flow Statement
(For the year ended 31st Dec., 2001)

	Rs.	*Rs.*
Sources of Funds:		
Funds from Operation	89,550	
Share Capital (2,25,000 – 1,50,000)	75,000	
Share Premium	7,500	
Sale of Plant	1,200	
Total Sources		1,73,250
Application of Funds:		
Redemption of Debentures	30,000	
Purchase of Furniture	3,000	
Purchase of Investments	30,000	
Payment of Dividend (1,50,000 × 22.5%)	33,750	
Total Applications		96,750
Net Increase in Working Capital		76,500

Dr. **Plant A/c** *Cr.*

	Rs.		*Rs.*
To Balance b/d	1,56,000	By Provision for Depreciation on Plant A/c	3,360
		By P&L A/c - Loss on sale	1,440
		By Cash	1,200
		By Balance c/d	1,50,000
	1,56,000		1,56,000

Dr. **Provision for Depreciation on Plant A/c** *Cr.*

	Rs.		*Rs.*
To Plant (accumulated depreciation on Plant sold)	3,360	By Balance b/d	75,000
To Balance c/d	84,000	By P&L A/c (depreciation on Plant sold) (6,000 × .08 × 9/12)	360
		By P&L A/c (depreciation)	12,000
	87,360		87,360

Dr. **Investment A/c** *Cr.*

	Rs.		*Rs.*
To Balance b/d	90,000	By Balance c/d	1,20,000
To Cash - Purchase	30,000		
	1,20,000		1,20,000

Dr. **Furniture A/c** *Cr.*

	Rs.		*Rs.*
To Balance b/d	10,500	By Balance c/d	13,500
To Cash - Purchase	3,000		
	13,500		13,500

Dr. **Provision for Depreciation on Furniture A/c** *Cr.*

	Rs.		*Rs.*
To Balance c/d	9,000	By Balance b/d	7,500
		By P&L A/c (depreciation)	1,500
	9,000		9,000

Dr. **General Reserve A/c** *Cr.*

	Rs.		*Rs.*
To Balance c/d	90,000	By Balance b/d	75,000
		By Profit and Loss A/c	15,000
	90,000		90,000

Dr. **Provision for Tax A/c** *Cr.*

	Rs.		*Rs.*
To Balance c/d	45,000	By Balance b/d	30,000
		By Profit and Loss A/c	15,000
	45,000		45,000

Dr. **6% Debenture A/c** *Cr.*

	Rs.		*Rs.*
To Cash A/c - Redemption	30,000	By Balance b/d	1,05,000
To Balance c/d	75,000		
	1,05,000		1,05,000

Dr. **Profit and Loss A/c** *Cr.*

	Rs.		*Rs.*
To Reserves	15,000	By Balance b/d	15,000
To Dividends	33,750	By Funds from Operations	89,550
To Provision for Income Tax	15,000		
To Depreciation on Plant sold	360		
To Depreciation on Balance of Plant	12,000		
To Depreciation on Furniture	1,500		
To Loss on sale of Plant	1,440		
To Balance c/d	25,500		
	1,04,550		1,04,550

Illustration 14

The comparative Balance Sheets of Beta Trading Company are indicated in condensed form as under:

(Rs.)

	31st December, 2002		*31st December, 2001*	
Fixed assets	5,20,000		4,80,000	
Less: Depreciation	1,40,000	3,80,000	1,08,000	3,72,000
Investment at cost		50,000		1,00,000
Stocks		90,500		55,600
Sundry debtors		1,67,800		1,18,300
Cash and bank balance		47,500		49,800
Preliminary expenses		—		7,200
		7,35,800		7,02,900
Share capital				
Ordinary shares of Rs. 100 each issued for cash		4,00,000		3,60,000
General Reserve		60,000		1,10,000
Surplus in P&L A/c		33,450		20,450
Sundry creditors		1,95,350		1,33,650
Proposed Dividend		15,000		28,800
Provision for taxation		32,000		50,000
		7,35,800		7,02,900

The net profit for the year (after providing for depreciation Rs. 40,000, writing off preliminary expenses Rs. 7,200 and making provision for taxation Rs. 32,000) mounted to Rs. 38,000. The company sold during the year old machinery costing Rs. 9,000 for Rs. 3,000. The accumulated depreciation on the said machinery was Rs. 8,000. A portion of the company's investment became worthless and was written off to general reserve. The cost of such investment was Rs. 50,000. During the year, the company paid an interim dividend of Rs. 10,000 and directors have recommended a final dividend of Rs. 15,000 for the year 2002. Prepare – *(a)* statement of sources and applications of funds for the year ended 31st December, 2002 and *(b)* schedule of working capital changes.

(C.S., Inter, June, 1994)

Solution

Calculation of Funds from Operations

		(Rs.)
Net Profit for the Year		38,000
Add: Provision for Depreciation	40,000	
Preliminary expenses written off	7,200	47,200
		85,200
Less: Profit on Sale of Machinery	2,000	2,000
Funds from Operations		83,200

Dr. **Fixed Assets A/c** *Cr.*

	Rs.		*Rs.*
To Balance b/d	4,80,000	By Depreciation fund account	8,000
To Bank (Purchase of assets)	49,000	By Bank (Sale of Machinery)	3,000
To Profit and Loss Account (gain on sale)	2000	By Balance c/d	5,20,000
	5,31,000		5,31,000

Dr. **Depreciation Fund A/c** *Cr.*

	Rs.		*Rs.*
To Fixed Asset A/c	8,000	By balance b/d	1,08,000
To Balance c/d	1,40,000	By Profit and Loss A/c	40,000
	1,48,000		1,48,000

	Rs.
Cost of Fixed Assets	9000
Less Depreciation	8000
Written down value	1000
Sale value	3000
Profit on sale	2000

Dr. **Investment A/c** *Cr.*

	Rs.		*Rs.*
To Balance b/d	50,000	By Balance c/d	1,00,000
To General Reserve	50,000		
	1,00,000		1,00,000

Statement of Sources and Application of Funds for the Year ended 31st December, 2002

	Rs.
Sources of Funds:	
Funds from Operation	83,200
Issue of Capital	40,000
Sale of Machinery	3,000
	1,26,200
Application of Funds:	
Dividend Paid	15,000
Interim Dividend	10,000
Purchase of Fixed Assets	49,000
Increase in Working Capital	52,200
	1,26,200

Schedule of Working Capital Change

(Rs.)

Particulars	*2001*	*2002*	*Increase*	*Decrease*
Current Assets:				
Cash and Bank	49,800	47,500	—	2,300
Sundry Debtors	1,18,300	1,67,800	49,500	—
Stocks	55,600	90,500	34,900	—
Total (A)	2,23,700	3,05,800		
Current Liabilities:				
Sundry Creditors	1,33,650	1,95,350	—	61,700
Provision for Taxation	50,000	32,000	18,000	—
Proposed Dividend	28,800	15,000	13,800	—
Total (B)	2,12,450	2,42,350		
Net Working Capital (A)-(B)	11,250	63,450		
Increase in Working Capital	52,200	—	—	52,200
Total	63,450	63,450	1,16,200	1,16,200

Illustration 15

The following Balance Sheets of Chandan Products Ltd. for the years 2001 and 2002 are available:

Particulars	*2001* *Rs.*	*2002* *Rs.*
Liabilities		
Share Capital	6,00,000	7,00,000
General Reserve	2,00,000	2,50,000
Capital Reserve (Profit on sale of investments)	—	10,000
Profit and Loss Account	1,00,000	2,00,000
7% Debentures	3,00,000	2,00,000
Creditors for Expenses	10,000	12,000
Creditors for Supply of Goods	1,60,000	2,50,000
Proposed Dividend	30,000	35,000
Provision for Taxation	70,000	75,000
	14,70,000	17,32,000
Assets		
Fixed Assets	10,00,000	12,00,000
Less: Accumulated Depreciation	2,00,000	2,50,000
	8,00,000	9,50,000
Investments (at cost)	1,80,000	1,80,000
Stock (at cost)	2,00,000	2,70,000
Sundry Debtors (Less Provision for Rs. 20,000 and Rs. 25,000 respectively)	2,25,000	2,45,000
Bills Receivable	40,000	65,000
Pre-payment of Expenses	10,000	12,000
Miscellaneous Expenditure	15,000	10,000
	14,70,000	17,32,000

Other information: *(i)* During the year 2002, fixed assets (WDV Rs. 10,000, depreciation written off Rs. 30,000) was sold for Rs. 8,000. *(ii)* The proposed dividend of last year was paid in 2002. *(iii)* During the year 2002, investments costing Rs. 80,000 were sold and later in the year, investments of the same cost were purchased. *(iv)* Debentures were redeemed at a premium of 10% in 2002. *(v)* Liability for taxation for 2001 came to Rs. 55,000. *(vi)* During the year 2002, bad debts written off were Rs. 15,000 against the provision account. Prepare a Funds Flow statement

(C.S., Inter, Dec., 1996)

Working Notes

Dr. **Fixed Assets A/c** *Cr.*

	Rs.		*Rs.*
To Balance b/d	10,00,000	By Scrapped Assets A/c	40,000
To Bank-Purchase(Balancing figure)	2,40,000	By Balance c/d	12,00,000
	12,40,000		12,40,000

Dr. **Accumulated Depreciation A/c** *Cr.*

	Rs.		*Rs.*
To Scrapped Assets A/c (depreciation on asset sold)	30,000	By Balance b/d	2,00,000
To Balance c/d	2,50,000	By Profit and Loss A/c –Depreciation for the year (Balancing figure)	80,000
	2,80,000		2,80,000

Dr. **Scrapped Assets A/c** *Cr.*

	Rs.		*Rs.*
To Fixed Assets A/c	40,000	By Accumulated Depreciation A/c	30,000
		By Bank-Sale proceeds	8,000
		By Profit and Loss A/c — Loss on sale of Assets (Balancing figure)	2,000
	40,000		40,000

Dr. **Investment A/c** *Cr.*

	Rs.		*Rs.*
To Balance b/d	1,80,000	By Bank A/c – sale (80,000 + 10,000 gain)	90,000
To Bank-Purchase	80,000	By Balance c/d	1,80,000
To Capital reserve (Profit on sale of Investment)	10,000		
	2,70,000		2,70,000

Dr. **Proposed Dividend A/c** *Cr.*

	Rs.		*Rs.*
To Cash A/c (Dividend Paid)	30,000	By Opening Balance b/d	30,000
To Closing Balance c/d	35,000	By P&L A/c (Balancing figure)	35,000
	65,000		65,000

Dr. **Provision for Taxation A/c** *Cr.*

	Rs.		*Rs.*
To Cash A/c (tax paid)	55,000	By Opening Balance b/d	70,000
To Closing Balance c/d	75,000	By P&L A/c (Balancing figure)	60,000
	1,30,000		1,30,000

Calculation of Funds from operations

		(Rs.)
Profit and Loss A/c balance as on 31-12-2002		2,00,000
Add:		
Depreciation Written off	80,000	
Loss on Sale of Scrapped Assets	2,000	
Miscellaneous Expenditure Written off	5,000	
Appropriation to General Reserve	50,000	
Provision for Premium on Redemption of Debentures	10,000	
Proposed Dividend	35,000	
Provision for Taxation	60,000	2,42,000
		4,42,000
Less: Balance as on 1-1-2002		1,00,000
Funds from Operations		3,42,000

Funds Flow Statement of Chandan Products Ltd. for the Year ended 31st Dec., 2002

	(Rs.)
Sources of Funds	
Issue of Share Capital	1,00,000
Sale of Investments	90,000
Sale of Scrapped Assets	8,000
Funds from Operations	3,42,000
Total	5,40,000

	(Rs.)
Application of Funds	
Purchase of Fixed Assets	2,40,000
Purchase of Investments	80,000
Redemption of Debentures	1,00,000
Premium on Redemption of Debenture	10,000
Payment of Dividend	30,000
Payment of Taxes	55,000
Increase in Working Capital (Balancing figure)	25,000
Total	5,40,000

Schedule of Change in Working Capital

(Rs.)

Particulars	*2001*	*2002*	*Increase*	*Decrease*
Current Assets:				
Sundry Debtors (net)	2,25,000	2,45,000	20,000	—
Stock	2,00,000	2,70,000	70,000	—
Bills Receivables	40,000	65,000	25,000	—
Expenses Prepaid	10,000	12,000	2,000	—
Total (A)	4,75,000	5,92,000	—	—
Current Liabilities:				
Creditors for Expenses	10,000	12,000	—	2,000
Creditors for Supply of Goods	1,60,000	2,50,000	—	90,000
Total (B)	1,70,000	2,62,000	—	—
Working Capital (A)-(B)	3,05,000	3,30,000	—	—
Increase in Working Capital	25,000	—	—	25,000
	3,30,000	3,30,000	1,17,000	1,17,000

SUMMARY

The 'Funds Flow Statement', which is also known as the 'Statement of Sources and Uses of Funds', is one of the analytical tools for analysis of financial statements, financial planning and control. The Funds Flow Statement reveals the volume of financial transactions and explains the flow of funds taking place within a business during a particular period of time, and its effect on the working capital. It is a supplement to the two principal financial statements *viz.*, Profit and Loss Account and Balance Sheet. It describes the sources from where funds are obtained and the uses of these funds, in a condensed form.

In the context of preparation of Fund Flow Statement, 'Funds' refer to Net Working Capital. The technique of preparation of Funds Flow Statement involves essentially three steps. Preparation of Schedule of changes in working capital to determine the increase or decrease in working capital, ascertainment of Funds from Operations and preparation of Funds Flow Statement.

The Sources of funds are Funds from Operations; Proceeds from Issue of Share Capital; Proceeds from Issue of Debentures; Long Term Loans raised; Sale of Fixed Assets etc. The Applications of funds are Purchase of Fixed Assets; Repayment of Long Term Liabilities; Redemption of Preference Share Capital, Payment of Dividends and Tax etc. The difference between the sources and uses of funds is Increase/Decrease in Working Capital.

Glossary

- **Funds Flow Statement:** a statement of changes in financial position or statement of sources and applications of funds in which elements of net income and working capital contributing to an understanding of the whole of financial operations during the reporting period replace totals of these items".
- **Flow of Funds:** means 'change in funds' or 'change in working capital'.

Questions

(1) What are 'Funds from Operations'?
(2) What is a 'Funds Flow Statement'?
(3) How do you treat the following items in the calculation of funds from operations?
Depreciation charged during the year.
Deferred revenue expenditure written off.
Gain on sale of fixed assets.
Loss on sale of Fixed Assets.
(4) Where do the following items appear in Funds Flow Statement?
Dividend paid, when proposed dividends are treated as non-current liabilities.
Tax paid when provision for taxation is treated as a current liability.
(5) What are the sources and uses of funds?
(6) "The True Funds flow from depreciation is the opportunity saving of cash outflow through taxation". Illustrate with a numerical example.
(7) Explain the importance and uses of Funds Flow Statement
(8) Explain why and how 'funds from business'(net profit) are converted to ' Funds from Operations'.
(9) Explain the possibility for alternative treatment of proposed dividends and provision for taxation in the preparation of Funds Flow Statement.

PROBLEMS

(1) Prepare a Funds Flow Statement for X co. from the following Balance Sheets.

	31-3-2008 *Rs.*	*31-3-2009* *Rs.*		*31-3-2008* *Rs.*	*31-3-2009* *Rs.*
Liabilities			**Assets**		
Share Capital	25,00,000	20,00,000	Fixed Assets	15,50,000	15,00,000
Reserves and Surplus	7,50,000	2,50,000	Investments	75,000	—
Proposed Dividend	5,00,000	6,00,000	Stock	37,50,000	39,37,500
Secured Loans	12,50,000	14,00,000	Debtors	20,00,000	17,50,000
Current Liabilities	25,00,000	30,00,000	Cash and Bank	1,25,000	62,500
	75,00,000	72,50,000		75,00,000	72,50,000

Additional Information

(1) Dividend paid Rs. 2,50,000

(2) Depreciation on fixed assets for the year was Rs. 1.5 lakhs (Rs. 1,50,000).

[**Ans.:** Increase in Working Capital Rs. 6,25,000 and Funds From Operations Rs. 8,00,000]

(2) Prepare a Funds Flow Statement from the following Consolidated Balance Sheet.

	31-3-2008 Rs.	*31-3-2009 Rs.*		*31-3-2008 Rs.*	*31-3-2009 Rs.*
Liabilities			**Assets**		
Share capital	6,00,000	7,00,000	Fixed assets	10,20,000	12,40,000
General Reserve	3,00,000	4,00,000	Investments (Long Term)	60,000	1,60,000
P&L A/c	1,20,000	1,40,000			
Debentures	2,00,000	4,00,000	Current Assets	4,80,000	7,50,000
Depreciation Reserve	1,80,000	2,60,000	Discount on Debentures	10,000	—
Current Liabilities	1,50,000	2,20,000			
Provision for Doubtful Debts	20,000	30,000			
	15,70,000	21,50,000		15,70,000	21,50,000

During the year, a dividend of 15% was paid for 2008 and asset costing Rs. 80,000 (Depreciation provided Rs. 34,000) was disposed off for Rs. 50,000.

[**Ans.:** Increase in Working Capital Rs. 1,90,000 and Funds from Operations Rs. 3,30,000]

(3) From the following Consolidated Balance Sheet, prepare a Funds Flow Statement:

	31-3-2008 Rs.	*31-3-2009 Rs.*		*31-3-2008 Rs.*	*31-3-2009 Rs.*
Liabilities			**Assets**		
Share Capital	1,50,000	2,00,000	Goodwill	57,500	45,000
18% Redeemable			Land	1,00,000	85,000
Preference Share Capital	75,000	50,000	Plant	40,000	1,00,000
General Reserve	20,000	35,000	Debtors	80,000	1,00,000
Profit and Loss A/c	15,000	24,000	Stock	38,500	54,500
Proposed Dividend	21,000	25,000	Bills Receivable	10,000	15,000
Sundry Creditors	27,500	41,500	Cash	7,500	5,000
Bills Payable	10,000	8,000	Bank	5,000	4,000
Provision for Tax	20,000	25,000			
	3,38,500	4,08,500		3,38,500	4,08,500

Additional information

Depreciation of Rs. 5,000 and Rs. 10,000 has been charged on Plant and Land respectively in 2009.

An interim dividend of Rs. 10,000 has been paid in 2009

Income tax Rs. 17,500 has been paid during the year 2009.

[**Ans.:** Increase in Working Capital Rs. 25,500 and Funds from Operations Rs. 1,09,000]

(4) From the following figures, prepare a statement showing Application and Sources of Funds for the financial year 2008-2009.

	31-3-2008 Rs.	*31-3-2009 Rs.*		*31-3-2008 Rs.*	*31-3-2009 Rs.*
Liabilities			**Assets**		
Equity Share Capital	6,00,000	7,00,000	Fixed Assets (Net)	10,20,000	12,40,000
8% Preference			Investment	60,000	1,60,000
Share Capital	4,00,000	2,00,000	Current Assets	4,80,000	7,50,000
Debentures	2,00,000	4,00,000	Discount on Debentures	20,000	10,000
Reserves and Surplus	2,20,000	5,40,000			
Current Liabilities	1,60,000	3,20,000			
	15,80,000	21,60,000		15,80,000	21,60,000

You are informed that during the year *(a)* A machine with a book value of Rs. 80,000 was sold for Rs. 50,000 *(b)* Preference share redemption was done at a premium of 15% on 31st March 2009 *(c)* Dividend at 15% was paid on equity shares for 2008 and *(d)* Depreciation charged during the year was Rs. 1,20,000.

[**Ans.:** Increase in Working Capital Rs. 1,10,000 and Funds from Operations Rs. 6,32,000]

(5) Prepare a statement from the figures given below showing applications and sources of funds during the year.

	1-4-2001 Rs.	*31-3-2002* Rs.		*1-4-2001* Rs.	*31-3-2002* Rs.
Share Capital	6,00,000	7,00,000	Fixed Assets	10,20,000	12,40,000
Debentures	2,00,000	4,00,000	Investments	60,000	1,60,000
General Reserve	3,00,000	4,00,000	Current Assets	4,80,000	7,50,000
P&L A/c	1,20,000	1,40,,000	Discount on Debentures	10,000	—
Depreciation Reserve	1,80,000	2,60,000			
Provision for Doubtful Debts	20,000	30,000			
Current Liabilities	1,50,000	2,20,000			
	15,70,000	21,50,000		15,70,000	21,50,000

During the year, a dividend @ 15% was paid for 2000 and asset costing Rs. 80,000 (Deprecation provided Rs. 34,000) was disposed of for Rs. 50, 000.

(CAIIB, Part II – Adapted)

[**Ans.:** Net increase in Working Capital: Rs. 2,00,000; Funds from operations: Rs. 3,40,000; Total of funds statement: Rs. 6,90,000]

(6) From the following Balance Sheets and Information of Everest Ltd. for 2001 and 2002, draw out a Funds Flow statement and statement of changes in working capital for 2002.

Balance Sheets of Everest Ltd.

	2001 Rs.	*2002* Rs.
Liabilities		
Equity share capital	2,00,000	3,00,000
8% Preference share capital (redeemable)	1,00,000	50,000
General reserve	20,000	30,000
Capital reserve	—	25,000
Profit and loss account	18,000	27,000
Proposed dividend	28,000	39,000
Sundry creditors	25,000	47,000
Bills payable	10,000	6,000
Liabilities for expenses	8,000	6,000
Provision for taxation	28,000	32,000
	4,37,000	5,62,000
Assets		
Goodwill	50,000	40,000
Land and building	1,00,000	75,000
Plant	90,000	1,91,000
Trade investment	10,000	35,000
Sundry debtors	60,000	90,000
Stock	85,000	78,000
Bills receivable	15,000	18,000
Cash in Hand	7,000	6,000
Cash at bank	10,000	22,000
Preliminary Expenses	10,000	7,000
	4,37,000	5,62,000

(i) In 2002 Rs. 18,000 depreciation has been written off from plant account and no depreciation has been charged on land and building *(ii)* A piece of land has been sold out and the balance has been revalued, profits on revaluation and sales being transferred to capital reserve. There is no other entry in capital reserve account. *(iii)* A plant was sold for Rs. 12,000 (w.d.v. Rs. 15,000) *(iv)* Rs. 2,100 dividend has been received, but it includes Rs. 600 pre-acquisition dividend. *(v)* An interim dividend of Rs. 10,000 has been paid in 2002.

(C.S., Inter, Dec., 1995)

[**Ans.:** FFO Rs. 1,00,500 Increase in Working Capital Rs. 17,000]

(7) From the figures given below, prepare a statement showing the application and sources of funds during the year 2001-2002.

	31st March, 2001 *Rs.*	*31st March, 2002* *Rs.*
Assets		
Fixed assets (net)	5,10,000	6,20,000
Investments	30,000	80,000
Current assets	2,40,000	3,75,000
Discount on debentures	10,000	5,000
	7,90,000	10,80,000
Liabilities		
Share capital (Equity)	3,00,000	3,50,000
Share capital (Preference)	2,00,000	1,00,000
Debentures	1,00,000	2,00,000
Reserves	1,10,000	2,70,000
Provision for doubtful debts	10,000	15,000
Current liabilities	70,000	1,45,000
	7,90,000	10,80,000

You are informed that during the year: *(i)* A machine costing Rs. 70,000 (book value Rs. 40,000) was disposed of for Rs. 25,000 *(ii)* Preference share redemption was carried out at a premium of 5% *(iii)* Dividend at 15% was paid on equity shares for the year 2001.

Further *(a)* The provision for depreciation stood at Rs. 1,50,000 on 31-3-2001 and at Rs. 1,90,000 on 31-3-2002 *(b)* Stock which ws valued at Rs. 90,000 as on 31-3-2001 was written up to its cost Rs. 1,00,000 for preparing the profit and loss account for 2002.

(C.S., Inter, June, 1996)

[**Ans.:** FFO Rs. 2,90,000 Increase in Working Capital Rs. 45,000]

(8) The summarized Balance Sheets of NVS Shanti Products for the years ended 31-3-2001 and 31-3-2002 are given below:

(Rs. In'000)

Capital and Liabilities	*31-3-2001*	*31-3-2002*	*Assets*	*31-3-2001*	*31-3-2002*
Share capital	500	500	Land and buildings	180	200
General reserve	200	220	Plant and machinery	210	276
Profit and loss account	40	32	Other fixed assets	30	45
Bank loan (long-term)	—	100	Investments	50	50
Creditors	158	172	Stock	200	190
Provision for taxation	45	30	Debtors	170	195
			Cash at bank	103	98
	943	1,054		943	1,054

Prepare a statement of sources and application of funds given the following additional information relating to the year ended 31-3-2002. *(a)* Dividend amounting to Rs. 30,000 was paid during the year. *(b)* Provision for taxation made Rs. 12,000. *(c)* Machinery worth Rs. 15,000 (book value) was sold at a loss of Rs. 3,000. *(d)* Investment costing Rs. 10,000 was sold for Rs. 12,000 *(e)* Depreciation provided on assets:

Land and buildings	Rs. 5,000
Plant and machinery	Rs. 20,000

(I.C.W.A., Inter, June,1997)

[**Ans.:** FFO Rs. 55,000 Decrease in Working Capital Rs. 4,000]

(9) Prepare a Funds Flow Statement and a statement of changes in working capital from the following particulars furnished by X Company Ltd.

(Rs. In lakhs)

	End of 2001	*End of 2002*
Owner's Equity and liabilities		
Share capital	50	50
Reserves and Surplus	60	70
Long-term debt	95	80
Short-term bank borrowings	70	80
Trade creditors	50	60
Provisions	20	15
Total	345	355
Assets		
Fixed assets (net)	180	190
Inventories	70	60
Debtors	60	70
Cash	20	15
Other assets	15	20
Total	345	355

The Income Statement of X Company Ltd. for the year 2002 is given below:

(Rs. Lakhs)

To Cost of goods sold	520	By Sales	800
To Operational expenses	150		
To Non-operational expenses	50		
To Interest	30		
To Tax	20		
To Dividend	20		
To Balance c/d	10		
	800		800

(C.S., Inter, June, 1997)

[**Ans.:** FFO Rs. 80 lakhs Decrease in Working Capital Rs. 15 lakhs]

(10) From the following Balance Sheets of XYZ Co. Ltd., prepare a Funds Flow Statement:

(Rs. '000)

Liabilities	*2001*	*2002*	*Assets*	*2001*	*2002*
Equity share capital	600	800	Goodwill	230	180
Preference capital	300	200	Land and buildings	400	340
General reserve	80	140	Plant and machinery	160	400
Profit and loss a/c	60	96	Debtors	320	400
Proposed dividend	84	100	Stock	154	218
Creditors	110	166	Bills receivable	40	60
Bills payable	40	32	Cash	30	20
Tax provision	80	100	Bank	20	16
	1,354	1,634		1,354	1,634

Additional information: *(i)* Proposed dividend made during 2001 has been paid during 2002. *(ii)* Depreciation: *(a)* Rs. 20,000 on plant and machinery; and *(b)* Rs. 40,000 on land and buildings. *(iii)* Interim dividend has been paid Rs. 40,000 in 2002. *(iv)* Income-tax Rs. 70,000 has been paid during 2002.

(C.S., Inter, Dec., 1997)

[**Ans.:** FFO Rs. 4,36,000 Increase in Working Capital Rs. 1,02,000]

❑ ❑ ❑

31

CASH FLOW ANALYSIS

Objectives

The objectives of the study are to:

- Understand the concept of Cash Flow Statement
- Appreciate the need for Cash Flow Statement
- Learn the technique of preparation of Cash Flow Statement

INTRODUCTION

The Balance Sheet and Income Statement/Profit and Loss Account are the two traditional basic financial statements of a business enterprise. A Balance Sheet reflects the financial position of a firm as at a particular date i.e. the last day of the Financial Year *viz.*, 31st March. An Income Statement focuses on the financial result (Profit/Loss) of a firm during the period. Cash is the most important asset of an organization. It is required to meet various expenses like payments to its suppliers, day to day expenses, salaries, wages, interest and dividend, etc. It is the life blood of a business enterprise. It is very essential for a business to maintain an adequate balance of cash. Many a time, in-spite of earning profits, its cash position may not be good.

This chapter describes the third financial statement that a company is required to prepare, namely the Cash Flow Statement. The objective of the Cash Flow Statement is to provide information about the cash flows associated with operating, investing and financing activities of the firm during the accounting period.

MEANING

Cash Flow Statement is a statement which indicates the sources and uses of cash during an accounting period. The sources of cash reflect the activities/transactions which generate cash inflows and the uses of cash reflect the activities which cause cash out flows. Therefore, it is also called as "Where Got Where Gone Statement".

The purpose of preparing a Cash Flow Statement is to explain increase/decrease in the cash balance between two points of time. A Cash Flow Statement is prepared, in the same pattern as the Funds Flow Statement is prepared. Just as net profit is adjusted to ascertain Funds from Operations, Funds from Operations are now adjusted to ascertain Cash from Operations.

CLASSIFICATION OF CASH FLOWS

According to AS-3 (Revised), the Cash Flow Statement should report cash flows during the period classified by operating, investing and financing activities, thus, cash flows are classified in to three main categories:

(1) Cash Flows from Operating Activities
(2) Cash Flows from Investing Activities
(3) Cash Flows from Financing Activities

(1) Cash Flows from Operating Activities

Operating Activities are the principal revenue generating activities of the enterprise and include activities other than that of investing or financing activities.

The amount of cash flows arising from Operating Activities reflect upon the operating capability of the enterprise in generating sufficient cash flows to pay dividends, repay loans and make new investments without recourse to external sources of financing.

The Examples of cash flows (both, Inflow and Outflow) from Operating Activities are:

(1) Cash receipts from the sale of goods and rendering of services.
(2) Cash receipts from royalties, fees and commissions.
(3) Cash payments to supplies of goods and services.
(4) Cash payments to and on behalf of employees.
(5) Cash receipts and cash payments of an insurance enterprise for premiums and claims, annuities and other policy benefits.
(6) Cash payment or refund of income taxes unless they can be specifically identified with Financing and Investing Activities, and
(7) Cash receipts and payments relating to future contracts, forward contracts, option contracts and swap contracts when the contracts are held for dealing or trading purposes.

(2) Cash Flows from Investing Activities

Investing activities are the acquisition and disposal of long term assets and other investments not included in cash equivalents. The separate disclosure of cash flows arising from Investing Activities is important because the cash flows represent the extent to which expenditures have been made for resources intended to generate future income and cash flows.

Examples of Cash Flows arising from Investing Activities are:

(1) Cash payments to acquire fixed assets. These payments are capitalized research and development cost and self constructed fixed assets.
(2) Cash receipts from disposal of fixed assets.
(3) Cash payments to acquire shares, warrants or debt instruments of other enterprises and interests in joint ventures.
(4) Cash receipt from sale of shares, warrants or debt instruments of other enterprises and interest in joint ventures.
(5) Cash advances and loans made to third parties.
(6) Cash receipts from the repayment of advances and loans made to third parties.
(7) Cash payments for future contracts, forward contracts, option contracts and swap contracts except when the contracts are held for dealing or trading purposes or the payments are classified as financing activities.
(8) Cash receipts from futures contracts, forward contracts, option contracts and swap contracts except when the contracts are held for dealing or trading purposes or the receipts are classified as financing activities.

(3) Cash Flows from Financing Activities

Financing Activities are the activities that result in changes in the size and composition of the owners' capital and borrowings of the enterprise.

Examples of cash flows arising from Financing Activities are

(1) Cash proceeds from issuing shares or other similar instruments.
(2) Cash proceeds from issuing debentures, loans, notes, bonds and other short or long term instruments, and
(3) Cash repayments of amounts borrowed such as redemption of debentures, bonds, preference shares.

TREATMENT OF SOME TYPICAL ITEMS

AS-3 (Revised) has also provided for the treatment of cash flows from some peculiar items as discussed below:

(1) Extraordinary Items: The cash flows associated with extraordinary items should be classified as arising from Operating, Investing or Financing Activities and should be disclosed appropriately as such in the Cash Flow Statement to enable users to understand their nature and effect on the present and future cash flows of the enterprise.

(2) Interest and Dividends: Cash flows from interest and dividends received and paid should be disclosed separately. The treatment of interest and dividends received and paid depends upon the nature of the enterprise for this purpose, the enterprises are classified as *(i)* Financial enterprises and *(ii)* Other enterprises.

(i). Financial Enterprises: In the case of financial enterprises, cash flows arising from interest paid and interest and dividend received should be classified as cash flows arising from operating activities.

(ii) Other Enterprises: In the case of other enterprises, cash flows arising from interest paid should be classified as cash flows from Financing Activities while interest and dividends received should be classified as cash flows from Investing Activities. Dividend paid should be classified as cash flows from financing activities.

(3) Taxes on Income: Cash flows arising from taxes in income should be separately disclosed and should be classified as cash flows from Operating Activities unless they can be specifically identified with financing and Investing Activities.

(4) Acquisitions and Disposal of subsidiaries and other business units: The aggregate cash flows arising from acquisitions and disposals from subsidiaries or other business units should be presented separately and classified as Investing Activities. An enterprise should disclose, in aggregate, in respect of both acquisition and disposal of subsidiaries or other business units during the period each of the following:

(a) The total purchase or disposal consideration, and

(b) The portion of the purchase or disposal consideration discharged by means of cash and cash equivalents.

(5) Foreign currency cash flows: Cash flows arising from transactions in a foreign currency should be recorded in an enterprise's reporting currency by converting the foreign currency into the reporting concern currency at the exchange rate prevailing between the two countries, at the date of the cash flow. The effect of changes in exchange rates on cash and cash equivalents held in a foreign currency should be reported as a separate part of the reconciliation of the changes in cash and cash equivalents during the period.

(6) Non–Cash Transactions: Many investing and Financing Activities do not have a direct impact on current cash flows although they do affect the capital and asset structure of an enterprise.

Examples of non-cash transactions are:

(i) The acquisition of assets by assuming directly related activities.

(ii) The acquisition of an enterprise by means of issue of shares and

(iii) The conversion of debt to equity.

FORMAT OF CASH FLOW STATEMENT

AS-3 (Revised) has not provided any specific format for preparing a Cash Flow Statement. However, an idea of the suggested format can be inferred from the illustrations appearing in the appendices to the accounting standard. The Cash Flow Statement should report cash flows during the period classified by operating, investing and financing activities.

A widely used format of Cash Flow Statement is given below:

Cash Flow Statement

(for the year ended...........)

	Rs.	*Rs.*
Cash Flows from operating activities		
Cash receipts from customers	xxx	
Cash paid to suppliers and employees	xxx	
Cash generated from operations	xxx	
Income-tax paid	xxx	
Cash flow before extraordinary items	xxx	
Extraordinary items	xxx	
Net cash from (used in) Operating activities	xxx	
Or		
Net profit before tax and extraordinary items		
Adjustments for non-cash and non-operating items		
(List of individual items such as depreciation, foreign exchange loss, loss on sale of fixed assets, interest income, dividend income, interest expense etc.)	xxx	

	Rs.	*Rs.*
Operating profit before working capital changes	xxx	
Adjustments for changes in current assets and current liabilities	xxx	
(List of individual items)		
Cash generated from (used in) operations before tax	xxx	
Income tax paid	xxx	
Cash flow before extraordinary items	xxx	
Extraordinary items (such as refund of tax)	xxx	
Net cash from (used in) Operating Activities		xxx
Cash Flows From Investing Activities		
Individual Items of cash inflows from Investing Activities	xxx	
(Sale of fixed assets, sale of investments, interest received, dividend received)		
Individual Items of cash outflows from Investing Activities		
(Purchase of fixed assets, purchase of investments, etc.)	xxx	xxx
Net cash from (used in) Investing Activities		xxx
Cash Flows From Financing Activities		
Individual Items of cash inflows from Financing Activities	xxx	
(Proceeds from issue of shares, long-term borrowings)		
Individual Items of cash outflows from Financing Activities		
(Repayments of long–term borrowings, interest paid, dividend paid etc.)	xxx	xxx
Net cash from (used in) Financing Activities		
Net Increase (Decrease) in cash and cash equivalents		
Cash and cash equivalents at the beginning of the period		xxx
Cash and cash equivalents at the end of the period		xxx

Format of Cash Flow Statement Approved by SEBI

Cash Flow Statement

(for the year ended ....)

XYZ Ltd.	*Rs.*
(A) Cash Flow From Operating Activities	
Net Profit/Loss before tax and extraordinary items	
Adjustments for:	
Depreciation	
Gain/Loss on sale of fixed assets	
Foreign exchange	
Miscellaneous expenditure written off	
Investment income	
Interest	
Dividend	
Operating Profit before working capital changes	
Adjustments for:	
Trade and other receivables	
Inventories	
Trade payables	
Cash generated from operations	
Interest paid	
Direct taxes paid	
Cash flow before items	
Extraordinary items	
Net Cash from Operating Activities	
(B) Cash Flow From Investing Activities	
Purchase of fixed assets	
Sales of fixed assets	
Purchase of investments	
Sale of investments	
Interest received	
Dividend received	
Net cash from/used in Investing Activities	

XYZ Ltd.	*Rs.*
(C) Cash Flow From Financing Activities	
Proceeds from issue of share capital	
Proceeds from long-term borrowings/banks	
Payment of long-term borrowings	
Dividend paid	
Net Increase/Decrease in Cash and Cash Equivalents	
Cash and Cash Equivalents as at........... (Opening Balance)	________
Cash and Cash Equivalents as at .... (Closing Balance)	________

USES AND SIGNIFICANCE OF CASH FLOW STATEMENT

Cash Flow Statement is of vital importance to the Financial Management. It is an essential tool of financial analysis for short-term planning.

The preparation of Cash Flow Statement particularly projected Cash Flow Statement has many uses. The following are some of the more important uses:

(1) Changes in cash balance between two points of time and the contributing factors for such change are clearly revealed. The Cash Flow Statement would explain:
   (a) The presence of a very low cash balance in-spite of huge operating profits; or
   (b) The presence of a high level of cash balance in-spite of a very low level of profits.

(2) When projected Cash Flow Statements are prepared, they help the management in various ways, particularly in the short range planning, when they are prepared on a monthly-basis. The projected Cash Flow Statements help in:
   (a) The determination of cash requirements during a given period and to make timely arrangements.
   (b) Identification of the size of surplus and the time for which such surplus funds are likely to be available.
   (c) Judging the ability of the firm to repay/redeem the debt/preference shares.
   (d) Examining the possibility of maintaining/increasing dividends.
   (e) Assessing the capability to finance replacement of fixed assets.
   (f) Assessing the capability of the firm to finance expansion.
   (g) More efficient and effective management of cash flows.

(3) Since a Cash Flow Statement is based on the cash basis of accounting, it is very useful in the ascertainment of cash position of a firm.

(4) A comparison of the historical and projected Cash Flow Statements can be made so as to find the variations and deficiency or otherwise in the performance so as to enable the firm to take immediately and an effective action.

(5) A series of intra-firm and inter-firm Cash Flow Statements reveals whether the firm's liquidity is improving or deteriorating over a period of time and in comparison to other firms over a given period of time.

(6) Cash Flow Analysis is more useful and appropriate than Funds Flow Analysis for short term financial analysis.

(7) Cash Flow Statement prepared according to AS-3 (Revised) is more suitable for making comparisons than the Funds Flow Statement as there is no standard format used for the same.

(8) Cash Flow Statement provides information of all activities classified under Operating, Investing and Financing Activities.

LIMITATIONS OF CASH FLOW STATEMENT

Cash Flow Statements suffer from the following limitations:

(1) Cash Flow Statement ignores the basic accounting concept of accrual basis, as it is based on cash basis of accounting.

(2) Some people feel that as working capital is a wider concept of funds, a Funds Flow Statement provides a more complete picture than the Cash Flow Statement.

(3) Cash Flow Statement is not suitable for judging the profitability of a firm as non-cash changes are ignored while calculating cash flows from Operating Activities.

(4) The cash position may not represent the real liquidity position of the business as it can be easily influenced by postponing the purchases and other payments.

Inspite of the above limitations, still, Cash Flow Statement can be considered as a useful tool as it discloses the volume as well as the speed at which, the cash, flows in to the different segments of the business.

Cash Flow Analysis and Funds Flow Analysis

Following are certain points of difference between Cash Flow Analysis and Funds Flow Analysis.

(1) Funds Flow Analysis deals with a change in the working capital position between the two balance sheet dates whereas the Cash Flow Analysis is concerned only with the changes in cash positions.

(2) Cash Flow Analysis is more useful as a tool in short range planning whereas Funds Flow Analysis is more useful in long range planning.

(3) An increase in a current liability or a decrease in a current asset (other than cash) will result in an increase in cash. Whereas, such changes will result in decrease in working capital. Similarly, a decrease in a current liability or an increase in a current asset (other than cash) will result in a decrease in cash, whereas such changes would increase the working capital.

Procedure for Preparing a Cash Flow Statement

Cash Flow Statement is not a substitute of Income Statement, i.e., a Profit and Loss Account, and a Balance Sheet. It provides additional information and explains the reasons for changes in cash and cash equivalents, derived from financial statements at two points of time. The procedure for preparing a Cash Flow Statement is different from the procedure followed in respect of Profit and Loss Account and Balance Sheet. It is prepared with the help of financial statements. **The basic information required for the preparation of a Cash Flow Statement is obtained from the following three sources:**

(i) Comparative Balance Sheets at two points of time, i.e. in the beginning and at the end of the accounting period.

(ii) Income Statement of the current accounting period or the Profit and Loss Account.

(iii) Some selected additional data to extract the hidden transactions.

The preparation of a Cash Flow Statement involves the following steps:

Step 1. Compute the net increase or decrease in cash and cash equivalents by making a comparison of these accounts given in the comparative balance sheets.

Step 2. Calculate the net cash flow provided from (used in) Operating Activities by analyzing the Profit and Loss Account, Balance Sheet and Additional Information. There are two methods of converting net income into net cash flows from Operating Activities: the **Direct Method** and the **Indirect Method**.

Step 3. Calculate the net cash flow from Investing Activities (Cash Inflows – Cash Outflows).

Step 4. Calculate the net cash flow from Financing Activities (Cash Inflows – Cash Outflows).

Step 5. Prepare a formal Cash Flow Statement highlighting the net cash flow from (used in) Operating, Investing and Financing Activities separately.

Step 6. Make an aggregate of net cash flows from the above three activities and ensure that the total net cash flow is equal to the net increase or decrease in cash and cash equivalents as calculated in Step 1.

Step 7. Report significant non-cash transactions that did not involve cash or cash equivalents in a separate schedule to the Cash Flow Statement e.g., purchase of machinery against issue of share capital or redemption of debentures in exchange for share capital.

Methods for Calculation of Cash from Operations

Information on cash flows is useful in determining whether or not an enterprise will continue to exist in the long run. The net effect of various transactions in a business during a particular period is either net profit or net loss. Usually, net profit results in inflow of cash and net loss in outflow of cash. But, it is not necessary that the net profit is equal to cash inflow or net loss is equal to cash outflow. This is because of certain non-cash and non-operating items (expenses or incomes) charged to the Income Statement, i.e., Profit and Loss Account, which do not affect cash flows.

Income Statement is prepared on accrual basis of accounting. Whereas, Cash Flow Statement is prepared on cash basis of accounting. Here lies the fundamental difference, which needs an adjustment.

There are two methods of reporting cash flows from Operating Activities: the Direct Method and the Indirect Method.

Direct Method

Under the Direct Method, cash receipts (inflows) from operating revenues and cash payments (outflows) for Operating Expenses are calculated to arrive at cash flows from Operating Activities. The difference between the cash receipts and cash payments is the net cash flow provided by (or used in) Operating Activities. The following are the examples of cash receipts and cash payments (called cash flows) resulting from Operating Activities:

(a) Cash receipts from the sale of goods and rendering of services;

(b) Cash receipts from royalties, fees, commissions and other revenues;

(c) Cash payment to suppliers for goods and services;

(d) Cash payment to and on behalf of employees;

(e) Cash receipts and cash payment of an insurance enterprise for premiums and claims, annuities and other policy benefits;

(f) Cash payments or refund of income taxes unless they can be specifically identified with Financing and Investing Activities; and

(g) Cash receipts and payments relating to future contracts, forward contracts, option contracts and swap contracts when the contracts are held for dealing or trading purposes.

The information about major classes of gross cash receipts and gross cash payments may be obtained either:

(i) From accounting records of the enterprise; or

(ii) By adjusting sales, cost of sales (interest and similar income and interest expense and similar charges for a financial enterprise) and other items in the statement of profit and loss for:

(a) Changes in inventories and operating receivables and payables during the accounting period;

(b) Other non-cash items; and

(c) Other items for which the cash effects are investing or financing cash flows.

Illustration 1

From the following calculate cash from operations:

Profit and Loss Account for the year ended 31st March, 2002

Particulars	*(Rs. '000)*	*Particulars*	*(Rs. '000)*
To Salaries	5,000	By Gross profit	25,000
To Rent	1,000	By Profit on sale of land	5,000
To Depreciation	2,000	By Income-tax refund	3,000
To Loss on sale of plant	1,000		
To Goodwill written off	4,000		
To Proposed dividend	5,000		
To Provision for tax	5,000		
To Net profit	10,000		
	33,000		33,000

(C.S., Inter, Dec., 1997)

Solution

Calculation of Cash from Operations

		(Rs. '000)
Net Profit		10,000
Add: Non-Cash items:		
Depreciation	2,000	
Loss on Sale of Plant	1,000	
Goodwill written off	4,000	
Proposed Dividend	5,000	
Provision for Tax	5,000	17,000
		27,000
Less: Non-Operating income:		
Profit on sale of Land	5,000	
Income Tax refund	3,000	8,000
Funds from Operations		19,000
Add: Decrease in Current Assets	NIL	
Increase in Current Liabilities	NIL	
Less: Increase in Current Assets	NIL	
Decrease in Current Liabilities	NIL	NIL
Cash from Operations		19,000

Illustration 2

From the following information prepare a Cash Flow Statement of XYZ Ltd for the year ended 2007. (Direct Method)

Balance sheet *(Rs. in '000)*

Liabilities	*March 2006 (Rs.)*	*March 2007 (Rs.)*	*Assets*	*March 2006 (Rs.)*	*March 2007 (Rs.)*
Issued and paid up Capital	2,000	2,000	Long-term Assets (Net)	1,500	2,500
Profit and Loss A/c	200	250	Closing stock	400	800
Mortgage Loan	—	1,000	Prepaid Administrative Expenses	100	200
Tax unpaid	50	100	Trade Debtors	200	250
Trade Creditors	500	1,000	Cash	550	600
	2,750	4,350		2,750	4,350

Statement of Profit for the year ended March 31, 2007 *(Rs. in '000)*

Particulars	*Rs.*	*Rs.*
Sales		5,000
Opening Stock	400	
Add: Purchases	3,500	
	3,900	
Less: Closing stock	800	
Cost of Goods Sold	3,100	3,100
Gross profit		1,900
Less: Administration Expenses	1,300	
Depreciation	250	
Provision for tax	150	1,700
Net Profit		200
Less: Payment of Dividends		150
Current Year Profit		50
Add: Profit and Loss A/c (2006)		200
Balance on 31 March 2007		250

You are also informed that a new Building was purchased on 15 June 2007 for Rs. 14,50,000/-

Solution

Cash Flow Statement for the year ended on 31st March 2007 *(Rs. in '000)*

	Rs.	*Rs.*
Cash flows from Operating Activities :		
Cash receipts from customers	4,950	
Cash paid to suppliers and employees	(4,200)	
Cash generated from operations	750	
Income tax paid	(100)	
Net cash generated from operating activities		650
Cash flows from Investing Activities :		
Purchase of new building	(1,450)	
Net cash used in Investing Activities		(1,450)
Cash flows from Financing Activities :		
Raising of mortgage loan	1,000	
Dividend paid	(150)	
Net cash provided by Financing Activities		850
Net increase in cash and cash equivalents		50
Add : Cash and cash equivalents at the beginning of the period		550
Cash and cash equivalents at the end of the year		600

Working Notes

(Rs. in '000)

			Rs.
(1)	Calculation of cash receipts from customers:		
	Sales for the year as per profit statement		5,000
	Add : Trade Debtors as an 31st March 2006		200
			5,200
	Less: Trade Debtors as on 31st March 2007		250
	Cash receipts from customers		4,950
(2)	Calculation of cash paid to supplier and employees:		
	(A)	Purchases for the year as per statement of profit	3,500
		Add: Trade creditors as on 31st March 2006	500
			4,000
		Less: Trade creditors as on 31st March 2007	1,000
		Cash paid to creditors for purchase of goods (A)	3,000
	(B)	Administrative expenses as per statement of profit	1,300
		Add: Prepaid expenses as on 31st March 2006	100
			1,400
		Less: Prepaid expenses as on 31st March 2007	200
		Cash paid to services (B)	1,200
	Cash paid to supplier and employees (A + B)		4,200
(3)	Calculation of tax paid:		
	Opening balance of tax unpaid		50
	Add: Provision made during the year		150
			200
	Less: Closing balance of tax unpaid		100
	Tax paid during the year		100

Indirect Method

Under the Indirect Method, the net cash flow from Operating Activities is determined by adjusting net profit or loss for the effect of:

(a) Non-cash items such as depreciation, provisions, deferred taxes, and unrealized foreign exchange gains and losses, and

(b) Changes in inventories and operating receivables and payables during the period;

(c) All other items for which the cash effects are investing or financing cash flows.

The Indirect Method is also called as Reconciliation Method as it involves a reconciliation of net profit or loss as given in the Profit and Loss Account and the net cash flow from Operating Activities as shown in the Cash Flow Statement. In other words, net profit or loss is adjusted, for non-cash and non-operating items which may have been debited or credited to Profit and Loss Account, as follows:

Calculation of Cash Flow From Operating Activities

	Amount (Rs.)	*Amount (Rs.)*
Net Profit before Tax and extraordinary Items		xxxxxx
Add: Non-cash and non-operating items which have already been debited to P&L A/c:		
(a) Depreciation	xxx	
(b) Transfer to Reserves and provisions	xxx	
(c) Goodwill written off	xxx	
(d) Preliminary expenses written off	xxx	
(e) Other intangible assets written off such as discount or loss on issue of shares/debentures, underwriting commission etc.	xxx	
(f) Loss on sale or disposal of fixed assets	xxx	
(g) Loss on sale of investments	xxx	
(h) Foreign exchange loss	xxx	xxxxxx

		Amount (Rs.)	Amount (Rs.)
Less:	Non-cash and non-operating items which have already been credited to P&L A/c:		
	(a) Gain on sale of fixed assets	xxx	
	(b) Profit on sale of investments	xxx	
	(c) Income from interest or dividends on investments	xxx	
	(d) Appreciation	xxx	
	(e) Reserves written back	xxx	
	(f) Foreign exchange gain	xxx	xxxxxx
	Operating Profit before working capital changes		
	Adjustments for changes in Current Operating Assets and Current Liabilities:		
Add:	Decrease in Accounts of Current Operating Assets (except cash and cash equivalents):		
	Decrease in Trade Debtors	xxx	
	Decrease in Inventories/Stock-in-trade	xxx	
	Decrease in Prepaid Expenses etc.	xxx	
Add:	Increase in Accounts of Current Operating Liabilities (except Bank Overdraft):		
	Increase in Creditors	xxx	
	Increase in Bills Payable	xxx	
	Increase in Outstanding Expenses	xxx	xxxxxx
Less:	Increase in Accounts of Current Operating Assets (As stated above)	xxx	xxxxxx
Less:	Decrease in Accounts of Current Operating Liabilities (except Bank Overdraft)	xxx	
	Cash generated from (used in) operations before tax	xxx	xxxxxx
Less:	Income tax paid		xxx
	Cash flow before extraordinary items		xxx
Add/Less:	Extraordinary items if any		xxx
	Net Cash Flow from (Used in) Operating Activities		xxx

Illustration 3

From the following information, you are required to prepare a Cash Flow Statement of XYZ Co. Ltd. for the year ended 31st March 2008 using the Indirect Method.

Balance sheets

Liabilities	*March 2007 (Rs.)*	*March 2008 (Rs.)*	*Assets*	*March 2007 (Rs.)*	*March 2008 (Rs.)*
Share Capital	1,00,000	1,00,000	Plant and Machinery	80,000	1,21,000
Secured Loans	—	40,000	Inventory	20,000	40,000
Creditors	20,000	40,000	Debtors	10,000	20,000
Tax payable	4,000	8,000	Cash	20,000	13,000
P&L A/c	9,000	10,000	Prepaid Expenses	3,000	4,000
	1,33,000	1,98,000		1,33,000	1,98,000

Profit and Loss Account
(for the year ended 31st March, 2008)

	Rs.		*Rs.*
To Opening Inventory	20,000	By Closing Stock	40,000
To Purchases	1,35,000	By Sales	1,50,000
To Gross Profit c/d	35,000		
	1,90,000		1,90,000

	Rs.		*Rs.*
To General Expenses To Depreciation To Taxes To Net Profit c/d	15,000 10,000 7,000 3,000	By Gross Profit b/d	35,000
	35,000		35,000
To Dividend To Balance c/f	2,000 10,000	By Balance b/f By Net Profit b/d	9,000 3,000
	12,000		12,000

Solution

Cash Flow Statement
(for the year ended 31st March 2008)

	Rs.	*Rs.*
Cash Flows from Operating Activities		
Net Profit before tax and extraordinary items	10,000	
Adjustments for non-cash and non-operating items:		
Add: Non-cash and non-operating items which have already been debited to profit and loss a account :		
Depreciation	10,000	
Less: Non-cash and non-operating items credited to profit and loss account	—	
Operating Profit Before Working Capital Changes		20,000
Adjustments for changes in current operating assets and liabilities :		
Add: Increase in Creditors		20,000
Less: Increase in Inventory	20,000	
Increase in Debtors	10,000	
Increase in Prepaid Expenses	1,000	(31,000)
Cash from Operations before Tax		9,000
Less: Income Tax Paid	3,000	(3,000)
Net Cash from Operating Activities		6,000
Cash Flows From Investing Activities		
Purchase of Plant and Machinery (2)	(51,000)	(51,000)
Net cash from Investing Activities		(45,000)
Cash Flows From Financing Activities		
Proceeds from raising of Secured Loans	40,000	
Dividend paid	(2,000)	
Net cash provided by Financing Activities		38,000
Net Decrease in Cash and Cash Equivalents		(7,000)
Cash and cash equivalents at the beginning of the period		20,000
Cash and cash equivalents at the end of the period		13,000

Working Notes

		Rs.
(1)	Calculation of Income-tax paid :	
	Opening Balance of Tax Payable	4,000
	Add: Tax provided/charged during the year	7,000
		11,000
	Less: Closing Balance of Tax Payable	8,000
	Tax paid during the year	3,000
(2)	Calculation of Purchase of Plant and Machinery	
	Opening Balance of Plant and Machinery	80,000
	Less: Depreciation charged during the year	10,000
		70,000
	Closing Balance of Plant and Machinery	1,21,000
	Plant and machinery purchased during the year	51,000

(1) Tax Payable A/c

	Rs.		Rs.
To Cash - Tax Paid (Diff.)	3,000	By Balance b/d	4,000
To Balance c/d	8,000	By P and L A/c (Current Year Provision)	7,000
	11,000		11,000

(2) Plant and Machinery A/c

	Rs.		Rs.
To Balance b/d	80,000	By Depreciation	10,000
To Cash Purchase (Diff.)	51,000	By Balance c/d	1,21,000
	1,31,000		1,31,000

Illustration 4

Ever Green limited has submitted the following condensed Balance Sheets as on 31 March 2007 and the Statement of Income and Reconciliation of Retained Earnings ended 31st March, 2007.

Balance Sheet

Liabilities	*March 2006 (Rs.)*	*March 2007 (Rs.)*	*Assets*	*March 2006 (Rs.)*	*March 2007 (Rs.)*
Share Capital	30,000	40,000	Fixed Assets	70,000	80,000
General Insurance	8,000	10,000	*Less:* Accumulated depreciation	22,500	26,000
Retained Earnings	6,000	9,000			
6 % Debentures	20,000	12,500		47,500	54,000
Loans on Mortgage	—	4,000	Stock	12,500	20,000
Sundry Creditors	18,500	10,500	Sundry Debtors	18,000	15,000
Outstanding Wages	300	500	Cash in Hand/Bank	9,500	8,900
Provision for Tax	7,500	14,000	Prepaid Expenses	300	600
			Preliminary Expenses	2,500	2,000
	90,300	1,00,500		90,300	1,00,500

Statement of Income and Reconciliation of Retained Earnings
(For the year ended 31st March 2007)

		Rs.
Sales		1,50,000
(–) Cost of goods sold:		
Stock 1-4-06	12,500	
Purchases	1,00,000	
	1,12,500	
(–) Closing Stock (31-03-07)	20,000	(–) 92,500
		57,500
(–) Wages		(–) 4,000
Gross Income		53,500
Sundry Expenses	20,500	
Preliminary Expenses	500	
Depreciation	3,500	(–) 24,500
		29,000
(–) Provision for Income tax		(–) 14,000
Net Income		15,000
General Reserve	2,000	
Dividend paid	10,000	(–) 12,000
Net Income for the year (Retained)		3,000
Add Retained Earnings on 31-03-2006		6,000
Retained Earnings on 31-03-2007		9,000

Additional Information

During the year, the company purchased a Building for Rs. 10,000

You are required to prepare a Cash Flow Statement for the year ended 31st March 2007 using *(i)* the Direct Method and *(ii)* the Indirect Method.

Solution

Direct Method

Cash Flow Statement

(for the year ended 31.03.2007)

	Rs.	*Rs.*
Cash Flows from Operating Activities		
Cash receipts from customers [working note *(i)*]	1,53,000	
Cash paid to suppliers and employees [working note *(ii)*]	(1,32,600)	
Cash generated from operations	20,400	
Income tax paid [Working Note *(iii)*]	(7,500)	
Net cash provided by operating activities		12,900
Cash Flows From Investing Activities		
Purchase of Building	10,000	
Net cash from Investing Activities		(10,000)
Cash Flows From Financing Activities		
Proceeds from issue of share capital	10,000	
Raising of loans on mortgage	4,000	
Redemption of debentures	(7,500)	
Dividend paid	(10,000)	
Net cash from Financing Activities		(3,500)
Net Decrease in Cash and cash equivalents		(600)
Cash and cash equivalents at the beginning of the period		9,500
Cash and cash equivalents at the end of the period		8,900

Working notes

		Rs.
(i)	**Calculation of cash receipts from customers**	
	Sales for the year as per Statement of Income	1,50,000
	Add: Trade Debtors as on 31st March, 2006	18,000
		1,68,000
	Less: Trade Debtors as on 31st March, 2007	15,000
	Cash receipts from customers	1,53,000
(ii)	**Calculation of cash paid to suppliers and employees**	
	Purchase for the year as per statement of income	1,00,000
	Add: Trade creditors as on 31st March, 2006	18,500
		1,18,500
	Less: Trade creditors as on 31st March, 2007	10,500
	Cash paid to suppliers for purchase of goods (a)	1,08,000
	Wages as per Statement of Income	4,000
	Add: Wages outstanding at the beginning	300
		4,300
	Less: Wages outstanding at the end	500
	Wages paid (b)	3,800
	Sundry Expenses as per income statement	20,500
	Less: Prepaid expenses as on 31st March 2006	300
		20,200
	Add: Prepaid expenses as on 31st March 2007	600
	Cash paid to employees and other operating expenses (c)	20,800
	Cash paid to suppliers and employees (a + b + c)	1,32,600
(iii)	**Calculation of income tax paid :**	
	Provision for income tax in the beginning of the year	7,500
	Add: provision made during the year	14,000
		21,500
	Less: Closing balance of provision for tax	14,000
	Income tax paid during the year	7,500

Indirect Method

Cash Flow Statement (for the year ended 31.03.2007)

	Rs.	*Rs.*
Cash Flows from Operating Activities		
Net profit before tax and extraordinary items	29,000	
Adjustments for non-cash and non-operating items:		
Depreciation	3,500	
Preliminary expenses written off	500	
Operating profit before working capital changes	33,000	
Adjustments for changes in current operating assets and liabilities :		
Increase in stock	(7,500)	
Decrease in debtors	3,000	
Increase in prepaid expenses	(300)	
Decrease in creditors	(8,000)	
Increase in wages outstanding	200	
Cash generated from operations before tax	20,400	
Less: Income tax paid	7,500	
Net cash from Operating Activities		12,900
Cash flows from Investing Activities		
Purchase of building	(10,000)	
Net cash from Investing Activities		(10,000)
Cash Flows From Financing Activities		
Proceeds from issue of share capital	10,000	
Redemption of debentures	(7,500)	
Raising of loans on mortgage	4,000	
Dividend Paid	(10,000)	
Net Cash from Financing Activities		(3,500)
Net decrease in cash and cash equivalents		(600)
Cash and cash equivalents at the beginning of the period		9,500
Cash and cash equivalents at the end of the period		8,900

Illustration 5

The following details are available from a company.

Liabilities	*31.03.2006* *Rs.*	*31.03.2007* *Rs.*		*31.03.2006* *Rs.*	*31.03.2007* *Rs.*
Share Capital	35,000	37,000	Cash	4,500	3,900
Debentures	6,000	3,000	Debtors	7,450	8,850
Reserve for Doubtful Debts	350	400	Stocks	24,600	21,350
Trade Creditors	5,180	5,920	Land	10,000	15,000
P&L A/c	5,020	5,280	Goodwill	5,000	2,500
	51,550	51,600		51,550	51,600

In addition, you are given:

(1) Dividend paid total Rs. 1,750

(2) Land was purchased for Rs. 5,000

(3) Amount provided for amortization of goodwill Rs. 2,500

(4) Debentures paid Rs. 3,000

Solution

Direct Method

Cash Flow Statement (for the year ended 31st March, 2007)

	Rs.	Rs.
Cash Flows From Operating Activities		
Increase in the Balance of P&L A/c	260	
Adjustments for non-cash and non-operating items:		
Reserve for Doubtful Debts	50	
Dividend	1,750	
Goodwill written off	2,500	
Operating profit before working capital changes	4,560	
Adjustments for changes in current operating assets and liabilities:		
Increase in Trade Creditors	740	
Increase in Debtors	(1,400)	
Decrease in stock	3,250	
Cash generated from operations	7,150	
Income tax paid	—	
Net cash from operating activities		7,150
Cash Flows From Investing Activities		
Purchase of Land	(5,000)	(5,000)
Net cash used in Investing Activities		
Cash Flows From Financing Activities		
Proceeds from issue of share capital	2,000	
Redemption of debentures	(3,000)	
Dividend paid	(1,750)	(2,750)
Net Decrease in cash and cash equivalents		(600)
Cash and cash equivalents at the beginning of the period		4,500
Cash and cash equivalents at the end of the period		3,900

Illustration 6

The following are the comparative Balance Sheets of XYZ Ltd., as on 31st March 2006 and 2007.

Liabilities	*2006 Rs.*	*2007 Rs.*	*Assets*	*2006 Rs.*	*2007 Rs.*
Share Capital			Land	10,000	15,000
(Share of Rs. 10 each)	35,000	37,000	Stocks	24,600	21,350
Profit and Loss A/c	5,040	5,280	Goodwill	5,000	2,500
9 % Debentures	6,000	3,000	Cash in Bank	4,200	3,500
Creditors	5,160	5,920	Temporary Investments	300	400
			Debtors	7,100	8,450
	51,200	51,200		51,200	51,200

Other particulars provided to you are:

(a) Dividends declared and paid during the year Rs. 1,750.

(b) Land was revalued during the year at Rs. 15,000 and the profit on revaluation was transferred to Profit and Loss Account.

You are required to prepare a Cash Flow Statement for the ended 31-03-2007.

Cash Flow Statement
(for the year ended 31st March, 2007)

	Rs.	*Rs.*
Cash Flows From Operating Activities		
Increase in the balance of P&L A/c	240	
Adjustments for non-cash and non-operating items:		
Profit on revaluation of land	(5,000)	
Goodwill written off	2,500	
Dividend declared	1,750	
Operating profit before working capital changes	(510)	
Adjustments for changes in Current Operating Assets and Liabilities:		
Increase in Creditors	760	
Decrease in stock	3250	
Increase in Debtors	(1,350)	
Increase in temporary Investments	(100)	
Cash generated from operations	2,050	
Income tax paid	—	
Cash flows from extraordinary items	—	
Net cash from Operating Activities		2,050
Cash Flows From Investing Activities	NIL	NIL
Cash Flows From Financing Activities:		
Proceeds from issue of share capital	2,000	
Redemption of debentures	(3,000)	
Dividend paid	(1,750)	
Net cash from Financing Activities		(2,750)
Net Decrease in cash and cash equivalents		(700)
Cash and cash equivalents at the beginning of the period		4,200
Cash and cash equivalents at the end of the period		3,500

Illustration 7

From the following information as contained in the Income Statement and the Balance Sheet of Strong Ltd., you are required to prepare a Cash Flow Statement using *(i)* Direct Method; and *(ii)* Indirect Method;.

Income Statement and Reconciliation of Earnings for the year ended 31st March, 2002

	(Rs.)	*(Rs.)*
Net Sales		40,32,000
Less : Cost of sales	31,68,000	
Depreciation	96,000	
Salaries and wages	3,84,000	
Operating expenses	1,28,000	
Provision for taxation	1,40,800	39,16,800
Net operating profit		1,15,200
Non-recurring income:		
Profit on sale of equipment		19,200
Profit for the year		1,34,400
Retained Earnings (Balance in Profit and Loss Account brought forward)		2,42,880
		3,77,280
Dividend declared and paid during the year		1,15,200
Profit and Loss Account Balance as on 31st March, 2002		2,62,080

Comparative Balance Sheets

	As on 31-3-2001 (Rs.)	*As on 31-3-2002 (Rs.)*
Fixed Assets:		
Land	76,800	1,53,600
Building and Equipments	5,76,000	9,21,600
Current Assets:		
Cash	96,000	1,15,200
Debtors	2,68,800	2,97,600
Stocks	4,22,400	1,53,600
Advances	12,480	14,400
Total	14,52,480	16,56,000
Capital	5,76,000	7,10,400
Surplus in Profit and Loss A/c	2,42,880	2,62,080
Sundry Creditors	3,84,000	3,74,400
Outstanding Expenses	38,400	76,800
Income-tax Payable	19,200	21,120
Accumulated Depreciation on Building and Equipments	1,92,000	2,11,200
Total	14,52,480	16,56,000

Cost of equipment sold was Rs. 1,15,200.

(C.S. Inter, Dec., 1999)

Solution

***(i)* Direct Method**

Strong Ltd.

Cash Flow Statement for the year ended 31-3-2002

	(Rs.)	*(Rs.)*
(A) Cash Flows from Operating Activities		
Cash receipts from customers	40,03,200	
Cash paid to suppliers and employees	(33,84,320)	
Cash generated from operations	6,18,880	
Income-tax paid	(1,38,880)	
Net Cash from Operating Activities (A)		4,80,000
(B) Cash Flows from Investing Activities		
Purchase of land	(76,800)	
Purchase of building and equipment	(4,60,800)	
Sale of equipment	57,600	
Net Cash used in investing Activities (B)		(4,80,000)
(C) Cash Flows from Financing Activities		
Issue of share capital	1,34,400	
Dividend paid	(1,15,200)	
Net Cash from Financing Activities (C)		19,200
Net Increase in Cash and Cash Equivalent (A+B+C)		19,200
Cash and Cash Equivalents at the beginning		96,000
Cash and Cash Equivalents at the end		1,15,200

Working Notes:

(i) **Cash receipts from customers**

	(Rs.)
Sales	40,32,000
Add: Debtors at the beginning	2,68,800
	43,00,800
Less: Debtors at the end	2,97,600
	40,03,200

(ii) **Cash paid to suppliers and employees**	(Rs.)	(Rs.)
Cost of goods sold	31,68,000	
Add: Operating expenses	1,28,000	
Salaries and Wages	3,84,000	
		36,80,000
Add: Creditors at the beginning	3,84,000	
Outstanding expenses at the beginning	38,400	
Stock at the end	1,53,600	
Advance at the end	14,400	5,90,400
		42,70,400
Less: Creditors at the end	3,74,400	
Outstanding expenses at the end	76,800	
Stock at the beginning	4,22,400	
Advances at the beginning	12,480	8,86,080
		33,84,320

(iii) **Income-tax paid**	(Rs.)
Income-tax payable at the beginning	19,200
Add: Provisions for taxation	1,40,800
	1,60,000
Less: Tax payable at the end	21,120
Tax paid during the year	1,38,880

(iv) **Accumulated Depreciation Written off on Equipment Sold**	(Rs.)
Accumulated Depreciation at the beginning	1,92,000
Add: Depreciation for the year	96,000
	2,88,000
Less: Accumulated Depreciation at the end	2,11,200
	76,800

(v) **Sale Price of Equipment**	(Rs.)
Cost price	1,15,200
Less: Accumulated depreciation	76,800
	38,400
Add: Profit on Sale	19,200
Sale price	57,600

(vi) **Purchase of Building and Equipments**	(Rs.)
Balance at the beginning	5,76,000
Less: Cost of equipments sold	1,15,200
	4,60,800
Balance at the end	9,21,600
Purchase	4,60,800

***(ii)* Indirect Method**

Strong Ltd.
Cash Flow Statement for the year ended 31-3-2002

		(Rs.)	*(Rs.)*
(A)	**Cash Flows from Operating Activities**		
	Net Profit before taxation and extraordinary items	2,56,000	
	Adjustment for Depreciation	96,000	
	Operating profit before working capital changes	3,52,000	
	Increase in debtors	(28,800)	
	Decrease in stock	2,68,800	
	Increase in advances	(1,920)	
	Decrease in creditors	(9,600)	
	Increase in outstanding expenses	38,400	
	Cash generated from operations	6,18,880	
	Income-tax paid	(1,38,880)	
	Net Cash from Operating Activities		4,80,000
(B)	**Cash Flows from Investing Activities**		
	Purchase of land	(76,800)	
	Purchase of building and equipment	(4,60,800)	
	Sale of equipment	57,600	
	Net Cash used in investing Activities		4,80,000
(C)	**Cash Flows from Financing Activities**		
	Issue of share capital	1,34,400	
	Dividend paid	(1,15,200)	
	Net Cash from Financing Activities		19,200
Net Increase in Cash and Cash Equivalents (A+B+C)			19,200
	Cash and Cash Equivalents at the beginning		96,000
	Cash and Cash equivalents at the end		1,15,200

SUMMARY

Cash is the most important asset of an organization. It is the life blood of a business enterprise. Cash Flow Statement is a statement which indicates the sources and uses of cash during an accounting period. Cash flows during the period are classified by Operating, Investing and Financing Activities.

The amount of cash flows arising from Operating Activities reflect upon the operating ability of the enterprise in generating sufficient cash flows to pay dividends, repay loans and make new investments without recourse to external sources of financing. Investing activities are the acquisition and disposal of long term assets and other investments not included in cash equivalents. The separate disclosure of cash flows arising from Investing Activities is important because the cash flows represent the extent to which expenditures have been made for resources intended to generate future income and cash flows. Financing Activities are the activities that result in changes in the size and composition of the owners' capital and borrowings of the enterprise.

Cash Flow Statement is of vital importance to the Financial Management. It is an essential tool of financial analysis for short-term planning. Cash Flow Statement can be considered as a useful tool as it discloses the volume as well as the speed at which the cash, flows into the different segments of the business.

The basic information required for the preparation of a Cash Flow Statement is obtained from the three sources *viz.*, Comparative Balance Sheets at two points of time, i.e., at the beginning and at the end of the accounting period; Income Statement of the current accounting period or the Profit and Loss Account; Some selected additional data to extract the hidden transactions.

There are two methods of reporting cash flows from Operating Activities - the Direct Method and the Indirect Method. Under the Direct Method, cash receipts (inflows) from operating revenues and cash payments (outflows) for Operating Expenses are calculated to arrive at cash flows from Operating Activities. The difference between the cash receipts and cash payments is the net cash flow provided by (or used in) Operating Activities.

Under the Indirect Method, the net cash flow from Operating Activities is determined by adjusting the net profit or loss for the effect of Non-cash items such as depreciation, provisions, deferred taxes, and unrealized foreign exchange gains and losses; Changes in inventories and operating receivables and payables during the period and all other items for which the cash effects are investing or financing cash flows.

Glossary

- **Cash Flow Statement** is a statement which indicates the sources and uses of cash during an accounting period.
- **Operating Activities** reflect upon the operating ability of the enterprise in generating sufficient cash flows to pay dividends, repay loans and make new investments without recourse to external sources of financing.
- **Investing activities** are the acquisition and disposal of long term assets and other investments not included in cash equivalents.
- **Financing Activities** are the activities that result in changes in the size and composition of the owners' capital and borrowings of the enterprise

Questions

(1) What do you understand by Cash Flow Statement?
(2) Explain briefly the Classification of Cash Flows.
(3) Give a Format of Cash Flow Statement.
(4) Explain the significance of a Cash Flow Statement.
(5) What are the limitations of Cash Flow Statement?
(6) How does a Cash Flow Statement differ from a Funds Flow Statement?
(7) Explain the methods for calculation of Cash from Operations.
(8) Explain briefly, the procedure for preparing a Cash Flow Statement.

PROBLEMS

(1) From the following information, calculate Cash from Operations.

(Rs.)

Particulars	*2001*	*2002*
Profit and Loss Account (credit)	40,000	50,000
Debtors	20,000	26,000
Bills Receivable	20,000	12,000
Prepaid Rent	2,000	3,000
Prepaid Insurance	1,000	800
Goodwill	20,000	14,000
Depreciation	32,000	40,000
Creditors	20,000	30,000

[**Ans.:** Cash from Operations Rs. 35,200]

(2) From the following financial statements and additional data condensed from reports of Sweet Grapes Limited, prepare a Cash Flow Statement for the year ended 31st March 2007 using *(i)* the Direct Method and *(ii)* the Indirect Method

Profit and Loss Account
for the year ended 31st March

(Rs. in '000)

		2006 Rs.		*2007 Rs.*
Sales		1,000		1,400
Less: Cost of Sales:				
Stock (Opening)	250		120	
Purchase	850		800	
	1,100		920	
Less: Stock (closing)	120		160	
		980		760
Gross Profit		20		640
Less: Operating expenses		280		320
Net Profit		(260)		320
Balance of undistributed profit b/f		180		80
Balance available for distribution		(80)		240
Less: dividend paid		—		200
Balance of undistributed profit c/f		(80)		40

Balance Sheets As at 31st March

(Rs. in '000)

Capital/Liabilities	*2006 Rs.*	*2007 Rs.*	*Assets*	*2006 Rs.*	*2007 Rs.*
Expenses payable	50	40	Cash	80	100
Sundry Creditors	150	260	Prepaid expenses	10	20
Long-term loans	400	200	Sundry Debtors	10	20
Paid-up capital	200	400	Stock	120	160
Profit and Loss			Investments	100	240
Appropriation A/c	—	40	Fixed Assets	400	400
			Profit and Loss A/c	80	—
	800	940		800	940

Additional Information:

(a) Depreciation charges for the year Rs. 40,000

(b) There are no sales of fixed assets during the period.

[**Ans.:** Net cash from Operating Activities Rs. 4,00,000; Net cash used in Investing Activities Rs. 1,80,000; Net cash used in Financing Activities Rs. 2,00,000; Net increase in cash and cash equivalents Rs. 20,000]

(3) The Balance Sheets of Y Ltd. as on 1-4-07 and 31-3-08 are given below

Liabilities	*1.4.07 Rs.*	*31.03.08 Rs.*	*Assets*	*1.4.07 Rs.*	*31.03.08 Rs.*
Share Capital	1,25,000	1,53,000	Cash	10,000	47,000
Bank Loan	40,000	50,000	Debtors	30,000	50,000
Loan from Financial	25,000	—	Stocks	35,000	25,000
Institution			Machinery	80,000	55,000
Creditors	40,000	44,000	Land	40,000	50,000
Profit and Loss A/c	1,00,000	1,20,000	Buildings	35,000	60,000
			Goodwill	1,00,000	80,000
	3,30,000	3,67,000		3,30,000	3,67,000

Other Information:

(a) Dividend paid Rs. 15,000 during the year.

(b) Rs. 20,000 worth of Machinery was sold at book value.

With the help of the above information, prepare a 'Cash Flow Statement'.

[**Ans.:** Net cash from Operating Activities Rs. 54,000; Net cash used in Investing Activities Rs. 15,000; Net cash used in Financing Activities Rs. 2,000; Net increase in cash and cash equivalents Rs. 37,000]

(4) Balance Sheets of A and B on 1st January, 1993 and 31st March, 1993 were as follows:

Liabilities	*1.1.1993 Rs.*	*31.12.1993 Rs.*	*Assets*	*1.1.1993 Rs.*	*31.12.1993 Rs.*
Creditors	40,000	44,000	Cash	10,000	7,000
Loan from Mrs. A	25,000	—	Debtors	30,000	50,000
Loan from Bank	40,000	50,000	Stocks	35,000	25,000
Capital	1,25,000	1,53,000	Machinery	80,000	55,000
			Land	40,000	50,000
			Buildings	35,000	60,000
	2,30,000	2,47,000		2,30,000	2,47,000

During the year, a Machine costing Rs. 10,000 (accumulated depreciation Rs. 3,000) sold for Rs. 5,000. The provision for depreciation against Machinery as on 1st January, 1993 was Rs. 25,000 and on 31st March, 1993 Rs. 40,000. Net Profit for the year 1993 amounted to Rs. 45,000. You are required to prepare a Cash Flow Statement.

(B.Com., Madras, April 1980)

[**Ans.:** Net cash from Operating Activities Rs. 59,000; Net cash used in Investing Activities Rs. 30,000; Net cash used in Financing Activities Rs. 32,000; Net decrease in cash and cash equivalents Rs. 3,000]

(5) Swastik Oils Ltd. has furnished the following information for the year ended 31st March 2003:

Particulars	*Rs. in Lakhs*
Net Profit	37,500.00
Dividend (including interim dividend paid)	12,000.00
Provision for Income-Tax	7,500.00
Income-Tax paid during the year	6,372.00
Loss on Sale of Assets (net)	60.00
Book Value of Assets Sold	277.00
Depreciation Charged to P&L Account	30,000.00
Profit on Sale of Investments	150.00
Interest Income on Investments	41,647.50
Value of Investments sold	3,759.00
Interest Expenses	15,000.00
Interest Paid During the Year	15,780.00
Increase in Working Capital (excluding cash and bank balances)	84,112.50
Purchase of Fixed Assets	21,840.00
Investments on Joint Venture	5,775.00
Expenditure on Construction work-in-progress	69,480.00
Proceeds from Long-Term Borrowings	38,970.00
Proceeds from Short-Term Borrowings	30,862.50
Opening Cash and Bank Balances	11,032.50
Closing Cash and Bank Balances	2,569.00

You are required to prepare the Cash Flow Statement in accordance with AS-3 for the year ended 31st March, 2003. (Make assumptions wherever necessary).

(C.S., Inter, June, 2004)

[**Ans.:** Net cash used for Operating Activities Rs. 4,333.50; Net cash used in Investing Activities Rs. 51,321.00; Net cash from Financing Activities Rs. 42,052.50; Net increase in cash and cash equivalents Rs. 13,602.00]

(6) Following information is available from the books of Standard Company Ltd.

(Rs.)

Particulars	*2001*	*2002*
Profit Made During the year		2,50,000
Income Received in Advance	500	600
Prepaid Expenses	1,600	1,400
Debtors	80,000	95,000
Bills Receivable	25,000	20,000
Creditors	45,000	40,000
Bills Payable	13,000	15,000
Outstanding Expenses	2,500	2,000
Accrued Income	1,500	1,200

Calculate Cash flow from operations.

(C.S., Inter, Dec., 1996)

[**Ans.:** Cash flow from operations Rs. 2,62,900]

❑ ❑ ❑

Part – VII

Cost Control and Cost Reduction

32

ACTIVITY BASED COSTING SYSTEM

Objectives

The objectives of the study are to:

- Understand the concept of Activity Based Costing System
- Learn the tools and techniques of Cost Management
- Know the application of Activity Based Costing System

INTRODUCTION

Cost Accounting is accounting for cost aimed at providing cost data, statements and reports for the purpose of managerial decision making. Cost accounting is the application of costing and cost accounting principles, methods and techniques to the science, art and practice of cost control and ascertainment of profitability. It is the process of accounting from the point at which expenditure is incurred or committed to the establishment of its ultimate relationship with cost centres and cost units.

Management decisions are taken, by many companies, by using product costs derived from information that was required to meet the needs of external financial accounting. Product costs calculated to meet the financial accounting requirements can be inaccurate as a measure of resources consumed by each individual product. But it can still provide information that is sufficiently accurate at the aggregate level for valuing stocks and measuring profits.

Instead of investing in two separate systems – one for stock valuation and the other for decision making – over the years, most companies have invested in a single system designed to meet stock valuation requirements. A system designed to meet stock valuation requirements accurately measures direct labor and material resources consumed by products but overheads are generally spread across all products on some arbitrary basis.

Traditional costing systems use volume-related measures, such as direct labor hours, machine hours, and number of employees, etc., to allocate overheads to products. Volume-related allocation bases accurately measure resources that are consumed in proportion to the number of units produced of the individual products. Such resources include direct labor, materials, energy for activities that are related to physical volume. Non-volume related activities consist of support activities such as material handling, material procurement, performing set-ups, and production scheduling and first-item inspection activities. Traditional product cost systems, which assume that products consume all resources in proportion to their production volumes, thus, report inaccurate/distorted product costs.

Traditional product costing systems were designed decades ago when most companies manufactured a narrow range of products, and direct labor and materials were the dominant factory costs. Overhead costs were relatively small, and the distortions arising from inappropriate overhead allocations were not significant. Information processing costs were high, and it was therefore difficult to justify more sophisticated overhead allocation methods.

Today, companies produce a wide range of products; direct labor represents only a small fraction of total costs, and overhead costs are of considerable importance. Simplistic overhead allocations using a declining direct labor base cannot be justified, particularly when information processing costs are no longer a barrier to introducing more sophisticated cost systems. The modern day intense global competition has made decision errors due to poor cost information, more probable and more costly. The increased opportunity cost of having poor cost information, and the decreased cost of operating more sophisticated cost systems, has increased the demand for more accurate product costs. It is against this background that Activity Based Costing has emerged.

Cooper and Kaplan (1988) have developed a more refined approach for assigning overheads to products and computing product costs. They called this approach as Activity-Based Costing (ABC). It is claimed that ABC provides product cost information that is useful for decision-making purposes

MEANING

Activity Based Costing (ABC) is that costing in which costs are first traced to activities and then to products. The ABC is a costing system which focuses on activities that are performed to produce products. It is the activities which become the focal points for cost accumulation. Here, the assumption is that activities are responsible for the incurrence of costs and it is the products which create demand for activities. Costs are charged to products based on the usage of each activity for the production. Here, costs are, first traced to the activities and then to the products unlike in Traditional Product Costing System where the costs are first traced to an organizational unit, such as Department or Plant. It means, under both ABC and Traditional Costing System, the second and final stage consists of tracing the costs to the product. By emphasizing activities, ABC tries to ascertain the factors that cause each major activity, cost of such activities and the relationship between activities and products produced.

DEFINITION

The CIMA official terminology defines ABC as "cost attribution to cost units on the basis of benefit received from indirect activities, e.g., ordering, setting up, assuring quality". ABC has also been defined as "the collection of financial and operational performance information tracing the significant activities of the firm to product costs".

Activity Based Costing (ABC) is a new term developed for finding out the cost. The basic feature of ABC is its focus on activities as the fundamental cost objects. It uses activities as the basis for calculating the costs of products and services.

Horgren Foster and Datar opine, "ABC is not an alternative costing system to Job Costing or Process Costing. Rather, ABC is an approach to developing the cost numbers used in job costing or process costing systems. The distinctive feature of ABC is its focus on activities as the fundamental cost objects. In contrast, more traditional approaches to developing the cost numbers used in job or process costing systems rely on general purpose (generic) accounting systems not tailored to the activities found in individual organizations. The ABC approach is more expensive than traditional approaches. ABC has the potential, however, to provide managers with information they find more useful for costing purposes".

TOOLS AND TECHNIQUES OF COST MANAGEMENT

Cost Management involves initiating and making decisions that improve the cost leadership of an organization. It involves generation of cost information and its active use to plan and control the costs. This involves a regular flow of reliable and relevant cost information to the managers for decision making. There are various tools and techniques of Cost Management and one such technique is Activity Based Costing. Some of the other tools are explained below:

Total Quality Management

Here, the management develops policies and practices to ensure that the firm's products and services exceed the customers' expectations in terms of reliability, durability, serviceability and product functionality. Kaizen is the key to ongoing improvement as it stands for continuous effort with no end.

Benchmarking

Here, the company continuously evaluates its performance in terms of its competitors who are the models to learn and improve in the critical areas. Improvements are implemented to reach or beat the performance of the competitors. Xerox Corporation of USA was the pioneer in benchmarking.

Target Costing

A target cost is the market determined price minus the desired profit. It is the difference between the sale price required to capture the desired market share and the desired profit per unit. A target cost is established at different stages of a new product and a comparison is made between the actual costs with the target costs in order to control and reduce the costs.

Back Flush Costing

Here, the allocation of cost is delayed till the product is manufactured or sold. Once the production of the product is completed or it is sold, the allocation of materials and conversion costs is triggered. Whereas, in case of conventional system, the allocation of cost arises with the actual use of the resources. This new technique eliminates the work-in-process account as the manufacturing costs are charged directly to the finished goods. It is considered as 'back flush' costing as it is the opposite of allocation procedures which 'flushes' costs through the accounting records as the work progresses.

DESIGN OF ACTIVITY-BASED COST SYSTEMS

Activity Based Costing emphasizes the need to obtain a better understanding of the behavior of overhead costs and thus, ascertains what causes overhead costs and how they relate to products. Kaplan and Cooper of Harvard Business School, who have developed this new approach in costing to calculate product costs, claim that the costs should be classified as long-term variable costs and short-term variable costs, i.e., ABC recognizes that in the long run most costs are not fixed and it seeks to understand the forces that cause overhead costs to change over time. ABC system assumes that cash outflows are incurred to acquire a supply of resources (e.g., labor, materials, and machinery) which are then consumed by activities. In other words, it is assumed that activities cause costs and also that products (or services) create demand for activities. A link is made between activities and products by assigning costs of activities to products based on individual product's consumption or demand for each activity. ABC system simply recognizes that businesses must understand the factors that drive each major activity, the cost of activities and how activities relate to products. The design of ABC systems involves the following stages:

(1) Identifying the major activities that take place in an organization;
(2) Creating a cost pool/cost centre for each activity;
(3) Determining the cost driver for each major activity;
(4) Assigning the cost of activities to product's according to the product's demand for activities.

(1) Identifying Activities

The first stage is to identify the major activities in the organization. Examples of activities include machine-related activities (e.g., machining cost centres), direct labor-related activities (e.g., assembly departments) and various support activities such as ordering, receiving, materials handling, administration, production scheduling, packing and dispatching.

Activities are composed of units of work or tasks. For example, purchasing of materials might be identified as a separate activity. This activity consists of the aggregation of many different tasks, such as receiving a purchase request, identifying suppliers, preparing purchase order, mailing purchase orders and performing follow ups. Activities are identified by carrying out an activity analysis. However, the activities chosen should be at a reasonable level of aggregation based on costs versus benefit analysis.

The final choice of activities must be a matter of judgement but it is likely to be influenced by factors such as the total cost of the activity centre (it must be of significance to justify separate treatment) and the ability of a single driver to provide a satisfactory determinant of the cost of the activity. Where the latter is not possible, further decomposition of the activity will be necessary.

(2) Assigning Costs to Activity Cost Centre

The second stage requires that a cost centre/cost pool be created for each activity. For example, the total cost of all set-ups might constitute one cost centre for all set-up related costs.

After the activities have been identified, the cost of resources consumed over a specified period must be assigned to each activity. Many of the resources/expenses will be directly attributable to specific activity centres but others/overheads may be indirect and jointly shared by several activities. These costs will have to be apportioned on some suitable basis.

(3) Selecting Appropriate Cost Drivers

In order to assign the costs attached to each activity cost centre, to products, a cost driver must be selected for each activity centre. The term 'cost driver' is used to describe the events or forces that are the significant determinants of the cost of the activities. Several factors must be borne in mind when selecting a suitable cost driver. First, it should provide a good explanation of costs in each activity cost pool. A cost driver should be easily measurable, the data should be relatively easy to obtain and be identifiable with products. The costs of measurement should therefore be taken into account. Using cost drivers that capture the number of transactions generated by an activity is an important technique for reducing measurement costs in the design of ABC systems

Cost Drivers

The following are the examples of some of the cost drivers in Activity Based System.

(1) Number of receiving orders for the Receiving Department
(2) Number of purchase orders for the cost of operating the Purchase Department
(3) Number of dispatch orders for the Dispatch Department
(4) Number of units
(5) Number of set-ups
(6) Value of materials in a product
(7) Number of materials handling hours
(8) Number of inspections
(9) Number of schedule changes
(10) Number of parts received per month
(11) Amount of labor cost incurred
(12) Number of direct labor hours
(13) Number of labor transactions
(14) Number of machine hours used on a product
(15) Number of set up hours
(16) Number of sub-assemblies
(17) Number of vendors
(18) Number of units scrapped
(19) Number of purchasing and ordering hours
(20) Number of customer orders processed
(21) Number of employees

However, care should be taken to ensure that cost drivers represent a reasonably homogeneous measure of the output for each activity. If cost drivers are non-homogeneous, there is a danger that they will not provide a satisfactory explanation of activity costs. Where transaction cost drivers are non-homogeneous and it is not feasible to measure duration of an activity, the problem can be resolved by weighing the cost drivers.

In most situations, data may not be available relating to the past costs of activities or potential cost driver volumes. To ascertain potential cost drivers, interviews will be required with the personnel involved with the specific activities. The interviews will seek to ascertain what causes the particular activity to consume resources and incur costs. The final choice of a cost driver is likely to be based on managerial judgement after taking into account the factors outlined above.

(4) Assigning the Cost of the Activities to the Products:

The final stage involves applying the cost driver rates to the products. Therefore, the cost driver must be measurable in a way that enables it to be identified with individual products. Thus, if set-up hours are selected as a cost driver, there must be a mechanism for measuring the set-up hours consumed by each product. Alternatively, if the number of set-ups is selected as the cost driver, measurements by products are not required since all products that require a set-up are charged with a constant set-up cost. The ease of obtaining data on cost driver consumption by products is therefore a factor that must be considered during the third stage when an appropriate cost driver is being selected.

SUITABILITY OF ABC SYSTEM

The use of ABC system is steadily increasing, particularly in case of organizations which are faced with an increased product diversity, product complexity and intense competition. It can be successfully implemented in manufacturing, marketing and administrative organizations as well as in case of service and non-profit organizations.

CLASSIFICATION OF ACTIVITIES

Under ABC system, the activities are classified into three major categories that drive expenses at the product level. They are unit-level activities, batch-level activities and product-sustaining activities.

(a) Unit–Level Activities

Unit Level Activities are the activities whose costs are strongly correlated to the number of units produced. Examples are use of indirect materials; inspection or testing of every item produced or say every 100th item produced and indirect consumables. They are performed each time a unit of the product or service is produced. Expenses in this category include direct labor, direct materials, energy costs and expenses that are consumed in proportion to machine processing times. Unit–level activities consume resources in proportion to the number of units produced.

(b) Batch–Related Activities

Batch-Level Activities are the activities whose costs are driven by the number of batches of units produced. Such activities are Material ordering, Machine set-up costs and inspection of products like first item of every batch. The cost of batch-related activities varies with the number of batches made, but is fixed for all units within the batch. Traditional Costing System treats batch-related expenses as fixed costs. However, the more the batch-related activities are required, the more the organization must eventually spend to supply resources to perform these activities. Thus, ABC system provides a mechanism for assigning some of the costs of complexity such as set-ups, customer ordering and purchasing to the products or services that cause the activity.

(c) Product-Sustaining Activities

These activities are performed to support different products in the product line. They are performed to enable individual products to be produced and sold, but the resources consumed by these activities are independent of the number of units or batches of the product produced. Engineering resources devoted to maintaining coherent specifications for individual products and their routing through the plant can be taken as an example of product-sustaining activities. The expenses of product-sustaining activities will tend to increase as the number of products manufactured is increased. ABC uses product level bases such as number of active part numbers and number of engineering change notices to assign these costs to products. Product-Level Activities are driven by the creation of a new product line and its maintenance, and the example is Advertisement Costs, if advertisement is for individual products, designing the product and producing parts to a certain specification.

(d) Facility-Sustaining Activities

One additional expense category that cannot be directly attributed to individual products is Facility-Sustaining Activities. These are performed to sustain a facility's general manufacturing process. Examples of facility-sustaining activities include administration, plant management, accounting services, lighting and heating of the factory. These activities are necessary to sustain the manufacturing process and are common and joint to all products manufactured in the plant. Therefore, these costs are not assigned to products under ABC system. Instead, they are regarded as common costs to all the products made in the plant and deducted in a lump sum from the total of the operating margins from all product lines. Facility-Level Activities are related to maintaining the building and other facilities required by a concern.

COMPARING ABC WITH CONVENTIONAL COSTING SYSTEM

In Traditional Costing System, overhead costs are assumed to be influenced by only units produced, which implies that costs of batch level, product level and facility level activities are fixed costs, i.e., costs which remain constant irrespective of the production volume. Unit-Based Cost Systems charge variable overheads directly to the products and apportion the fixed overhead to individual products using the base of number of units produced.

In ABC, variable overhead is appropriately traced to individual products. The costs incurred when the units are produced are traditionally treated as variable overhead. But, charging of fixed overheads on the basis of units made, as in Traditional Costing, is likely to be arbitrary and also may not reflect activities and cost actually consumed by the products. ABC system recognizes the fact that many fixed overhead costs vary in proportion to changes in other than production units. This recognition under ABC is an improvement over Product Costing procedure (as compared to Traditional Costing). It means, under ABC system, the other two level activities, *viz.*, batch level and product level, which are non-unit based cost drivers are assumed to influence fixed overhead costs. By establishing the link between these cost drivers and fixed overhead costs, they are finally traced to individual products. The diagrams given below reflect an overview of product cost determination under Traditional Costing and ABC system. Under both the costing systems, a two stage allocation procedure is followed.

In Traditional Costing System, in the first stage, overhead costs are allocated to production departments. They are pooled/ collected department-wise. In the next stage, Departmental Overhead Allocation Rates are used to re-apportion the overhead cost of Service Departments to Production Departments. Therefore, only fewer cost pools exist.

Under ABC system, first, overhead costs are assigned to each major activity and not to departments. Many activity-based cost pools or cost centres are created separately for production as well as service activities. In the next stage, overhead costs of the production and service activities (service departments) are assigned directly to specific products through applying cost driver rates. Thus, in ABC system, there is no need to allocate/re-apportion overheads of Service Departments to Production Departments.

(A) TRADITIONAL PRODUCT COSTING SYSTEM

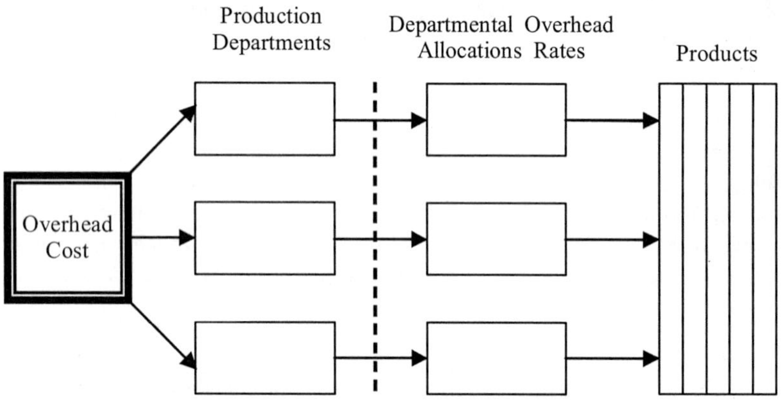

(B) ACTIVITY BASED PRODUCT COSTING SYSTEM

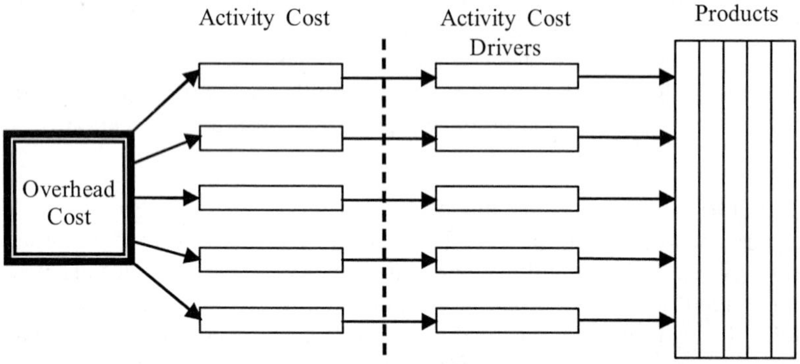

Figure: Comparison of Traditional and Activity Based Costing Systems (Adapted from Innes and Mitchell (1990))

The distortions arising from the use of Traditional Product Costing Systems are most pronounced in organizations that produce a diverse range of products which differ in volume and complexity. Cooper and Kaplan (1991) (the authors of ABC system) use the following example to illustrate the inability of Traditional Costing Systems to report accurate product costs:

Consider two hypothetical plants turning out a simple product: ballpoint pens. The factories are of the same size and have the same capital equipment. Every year, Plant I make ten lakh units of only one product: blue pens. Plant II, a full-line producer, also produces blue pens, but only one lakh per year. Plant II also produces a variety of similar products: eighty thousand black pens, thirty thousand red pens, five thousand green pens, five hundred lavender pens, and so on. In a typical year, Plant II produces up to one thousand product variations, with volumes ranging between one hundred and one lakh units. Its aggregate annual output equals 10 lakh pens of Plant I.

The first Plant has a simple production environment and requires limited manufacturing support facilities. With its higher diversity and complexity of operations, the second plant requires a much larger support structure. For example, one thousand different products must be scheduled through the plant, and this requires more people for scheduling machines, performing set-ups, inspecting items, purchasing, receiving and handling materials, and handling a large number of individual requests. Expenditure on support overheads will therefore be much higher in the second plant, even though the number of units produced is identical, both plants will have approximately the same amount of direct labor hours, machine hours and material purchases. The much higher expenditure on support overheads in the second plant cannot therefore be explained in terms of direct labor, machine hours operated or the amount of materials purchased. Traditional Costing Systems, however, use these volume bases to allocate support overheads to products.

Cooper and Kaplan use the two-plant example to illustrate the distortion in product costs that can arise if traditional volume-related bases such as direct labor hours, machine hours or material costs are used to allocate support department costs to products. For example, in the second plant, the cost system will allocate to blue pens, which represent 10% of the plant's output (1,00,000/10,00,000), approximately 10% of the factory expenses. Similarly, the same method of allocation is employed in case of green pens, which represent 0.5% of the plant's output (5,000/10, 00,000). In fact, if each pen requires approximately the same number of machine hours, direct labor hours or material cost, the reported cost per pen will be identical. Thus, blue and green pens will have identical product costs, even though green pens are ordered, manufactured, packaged and dispatched in much lower volumes.

The small-volume products, such as the green and lavender pens, place a much higher relative demand on the support departments than their low share of volume might suggest. Intuitively, it must cost more to produce a low-volume green pen; than a high-volume blue pen. Traditional volume-based costing systems therefore tend to over cost high-volume products and under cost low-volume products. To remedy this discrepancy, ABC expands the second stage overhead assignment bases used for assigning overheads to products.

In order to illustrate the differences between Traditional Product Costing Systems and ABC systems, Cooper and Kaplan initially focused on the allocation of the costs of non-volume-related activities. Consider, for example, an activity such as setting up a machine to produce a different product. When the machine is changed from one product to another, set-up resources are consumed according to the number of units produced after completing the set-up.

Suppose that the cost of resources consumed by set-up activities is Rs. 1,20,000/- and only two products are produced– product L (a low-volume product) and product H (a high-volume product). Production for the period was 5,000 units of product L and 45,000 units of product H. The low volume product is produced in batches of 500 units whereas the high volume product is produced in batches of 9,000 units, thus, product L requires 10 set-ups and product H, five set-ups.

With the Traditional Product Costing System, the set-up costs would be allocated to the production departments and then charged to products using volume-related bases such as machine hours or direct labor hours. Assuming that both products required the same number of machine or direct labor hours per unit, then, the Traditional System would allocate 10% (5,000/ 50,000) of the set-up costs to product L and 90% (45,000/50,000) to product H. Thus, set-up costs of Rs. 12,000/- (Rs. 1,20,000 × 10%) would be allocated to product L and Rs 1,08,000 (Rs. 1,20,000 × 90%) would be allocated to product H. The overall outcome is that, a set-up cost of Rs. 2.40 would be attributed to each product (Rs. 12,000/5,000 units) for product L and Rs. 2.60 (Rs. 1,08,000/45,000 units) for product H.

With the ABC System, costs are traced to products according to the product's demands for activities. Product L has consumed two-thirds (10 out of 15 set-ups) and product H has consumed one-third (5 out of 15 set-ups) of the set-up resources. Thus, set-up costs of Rs. 80,000 would be traced to product L and Rs.40,000 would be traced to product H. The set-up cost per unit is Rs.16 for Product L (Rs. 80,000/5,000 units) and Rs. 0.89 (Rs. 40,000/45,000 units) for product H. Cooper and Kaplan argue that, Traditional Cost System reports distorted product costs whenever the cost of non-volume-related activities is significant. In particular, low-volume products tend to be under-costed and high-volume products over costed. Assuming that the selling price for product L was marginally higher than product H, the message from Traditional Cost System is to de-emphasize product H and focus on more profitable especially low volume products similar to product L. In reality, this strategy would be disastrous since product H is cheaper to make and replacing the lost output with low volume speciality products will further increase the overheads relating to support activities.

Illustration 1

Company Aditya produces two products A and B. Both are produced on the same equipment and use similar processes. The products differ by volume. Product A is a low-volume product while B is a high -volume product. Details of products input, output and the cost of activities are as follows:

Product	*Machine Hours Per unit*	*Direct Labor Hours per unit*	*Annual Output (units)*	*Total Machine Hours*	*Total Direct Labor Hours*	*No. of Purchase orders*	*No. of Set-ups*
A	10	20	5,000	50,000	1,00,000	400	200
B	10	20	50,000	5,00,000	10,00,000	800	300
Total				5,50,000	11,00,000	1,200	500

The cost centre costs are Rs. 22,00,000 but have been further analyzed as follows:

	Rs.
Volume related	5,50,000
Purchasing-related	6,00,000
Set-up-related	10,50,000

Apportion the cost centre costs to the products A and B under Traditional Cost System and Activity Based Costing System.

Solution

(A) Traditional Costing System

Cost-centre costs to be allocated	Rs. 22,00,000
Overhead rate per machine hour	Rs. 22,00,000/5,50,000 = Rs. 4 per hour
Overhead rate per direct labor hour	Rs. 22,00,000/11,00,000 = Rs. 2 per hour
Cost per unit : A	Rs. 4 × 10 machine hours = Rs. 40 per unit
B	Rs. 4 × 10 machine hours = Rs. 40 per unit
OR	
A	Rs. 2 × 20 labor hours = Rs. 40 per unit
B	Rs. 2 × 20 labor hours = Rs. 40 per unit
Total Cost allocated to products: A	5,000 units × Rs. 40 per unit = Rs. 2,00,000
B	50,000 units × Rs. 40 per unit = Rs. 20,00,000

(B) ABC System

Particulars	Activities		
	Volume related	Purchasing related	Set up related
Cost traced to activities (Rs.)	5,50,000	6,00,000	10,50,000
Cost Driver	5,50,000 machine hours	1,200 purchase orders	500 set-ups
Cost per unit of consumption	Rs.1.00 per hour	Rs. 500 per order	Rs. 2,100 per set up
Costs traced to products:			
Product A	50,000 hours × Re. 1 per hour	400 orders × 500	200 × 2,100
	Rs. 50,000	Rs. 2,00,000	Rs. 4,20,000
Product B	5,00,000 hours × Re. 1 per hour	800 × 500	300 × 2,100
	Rs. 5,00,000	Rs. 4,00,000	Rs. 6,30,000

Cost per unit:

Total Cost for Product A = Rs. 50,000 + 2,00,000 + 4,20,000 = Rs. 6,70,000

Cost per unit = Rs. 6,70,000/5,000 units = Rs. 134 per unit

Total Cost for Product B = Rs. 5,00,000 + 4,00,000 + 6,30,000 = Rs. 15,30,000

Cost per unit = Rs. 15,30,000/50,000 units = Rs. 30.60 per unit.

Illustration 2

X Manufacturing Company has been using a cost system that allocates all factory overhead costs to products based on 350 per cent of direct labor cost. The company has just decided to use Activity Based Cost System that traces indirect costs to products based on consumption of major activities as indicated below.

Activity	*Annual Cost Driver Quantity*	*Cost*	*Product's Cost Driver Consumption*
Labor	Rs. 6,00,000	Rs. 60,000	Rs. 20,000
Machinery	40,000 hours	Rs. 10,00,000	1600 hours
Set-up	20,000 hours	Rs. 2,00,000	200 hours
Production order	4,000 orders	Rs. 4,00,000	24 orders
Material handling	2,000 requisitions	Rs. 40,000	10 requisitions
Parts Administration	24,000 parts	Rs. 9,60,000	36 parts

Required:

Compare the total annual costs of the product using both the traditional volume-based and new ABC system.

Solution

Statement Showing Calculation of Total Cost Under Traditional and ABC System

Cost System	*Pool Rate*	*Cost Driver Consumption*	*Cost Assignment Rs.*
(I) Traditional Cost System	350% of direct labor cost	Rs. 20,000	70,000
(II) ABC System			
(i) Labor	(Rs. 60,000/6,00,000) × 100 =10%	Rs. 20,000	2,000
(ii) Machinery	Rs. 10,00,000/40,000 hours = Rs. 25 per hour	1,600 hours	40,000
(iii) Set-up	Rs. 2,00,000/20,000 hours = Rs. 10 per hour	200 hours	2,000
(iv) Production order	Rs. 4,00,000/4,000 orders = Rs. 100 per order	24 orders	2,400
(v) Material handling	Rs. 40,000/2,000 requisition per requisition = Rs. 20	10 requisitions	200
(vi) Parts administration	Rs. 9,60,000/24,000 parts = Rs. 40 per part	36 parts	1,440
Total			48,040

Conclusion: The total cost of product under ABC is Rs. 48,040/- and under Traditional Cost system, it is Rs. 70,000/-

Illustration 3

XYZ manufacturing company has three accounts clerks responsible for processing purchase invoices. Each clerk is paid a salary of Rs. 1,00,000 p.a. and is capable of processing 5,000 invoices per year. In addition to the salary, the company spends Rs. 30,000 per year for forms, postage, etc. During the year, 12,500 invoices were processed.

Required:

(1) Calculate the activity rate for the purchase order activity. Break the activity into fixed and variable components.
(2) Compute the total activity availability and classify this into used and unused activity.
(3) Calculate the total cost of resources supplied and break this into activity usage and unused activity.

Solution

(1) Activity Rate	= Total cost/No. of invoices = (3 × 1,00,000 + 30,000)/15,000 = Rs. 22 per invoice No. of invoices = 3 clerks × 5,000 invoices = 15,000
(a) Fixed Activity Rate	= 3,00,000/15,000 = Rs. 20 per invoice
(b) Variable Activity Rate	= 30,000/15,000 = Rs. 2 per invoice
(2) Activity Availability	= Activity Usage + Unused Activity = 12,500 invoices + 2,500 invoices = 15,000 invoices
(3) Cost of resources supplied	= Cost of activity used + Cost of unused activity = (2 × 12,500) + (20 × 2,500) = 3,25,000 + 50,000 = Rs. 3,75,000/-

Note: For unused activity, there will be no variable cost.

Illustration 4

XYZ Company produces two types of similar products. Activity data is as follows:

Activity Usage Measures	*Deluxe*	*Product-Costing Data* *Regular*	*Total*
Units produced per year	10,000	60,000	70,000
Prime Costs (Rs.)	50,000	4,00,000	4,50,000
Direct Labor Hours	10,000	50,000	60,000
Machine Hours	20,000	1,00,000	1,20,000
Production Hours (Set-ups)	15	5	20
Number of Moves	100	50	150

Activity Cost Data (Overhead Activities)

Activity	*Activity Cost (Rs.)*
Setting up equipment	1,00,000
Material Handling	50,000
Power	50,000
Testing	60,000
Total	2,60,000

Required:

(1) Calculate the consumption ratios for each activity
(2) Group - Activities Based
(3) Calculate a rate for each pooled group of activities.
(4) Using the pool rates, calculate unit product costs.

Solution

(1) Consumption Ratios

Overhead Activity	*Deluxe*	*Regular*	*Activity Driver*
Set-ups	15/20 = 0.75	5/20 = 0.25	Production Hours
Material handling	100/150= 2/3	50/150 = 1/3	No. of Moves
Power	20,000/1,20,000 = 0.1667	1,00,000/1,20,000 = 0.8333	Machine Hours
Testing	10,000/60,000 = 0.1667	50,000/60,000 = 0.8333	Direct Labor Hours

(2) Group – Activity Based

Batch – level: (a) Set-ups and Material Handling

Unit – level: Unit: Power and Testing

(3) Rate for each Pooled Group of Activities

Batch – level Pool	*Rs.*
Set-ups	1,00,000
Material Handling	50,000
Total	1,50,000
Pool Rate	Pooled Cost/No. of set ups = 1,50,000/20 = Rs. 7,500 per set up
Unit – level Pool	
Power	50,000
Testing	60,000
Total	1,10,000
Pool Rate	= Pool Cost/No. of Machine Hours = 1,10,000/1,20,000 = 0.9166 per machine hour

(4) Unit Costs: Activity Based Costing

Particulars	*Deluxe (Rs.)*	*Regular (Rs.)*
Prime Costs	50,000	4,00,000
Overhead Costs:		
Batch Level Pool (Production Hours, i.e., set-ups)	(Rs. 7,500 × 15) 1,12,500	(Rs. 7,500 × 5) 37,500
Unit Level Pool (Machine Hours)	(Rs. 0.9166 × 20,000) 18,332	(Rs. 0.9166 × 1,00,000) 91,660
Total Manufacturing costs	1,80,832	5,29,160
Unit Cost (Total cost/No. of units)	(1,80,832/10,000) 18.08	(5,29,160/60,000) 8.82

Illustration 5

X Co. has been incurring two types of overhead costs – material handling and quality inspection. The costs expected for these categories for the coming year is as follows:

Material handling	Rs. 5,00,000
Quality inspection	Rs. 15,00,000

The company currently charges overhead using direct labor hours and expected actual capacity. Direct labor hours are 50,000

The factory manager has been asked to submit a bid for the proposed job. The following data has been collected for the purpose.

Direct Materials	Rs. 20,000
Direct Labor (500 hours)	Rs. 50,000
Number of Material moves	10
Number of inspections	5

The manager has been informed that this is a highly competitive bid. Before submitting the bid for the proposed job, he wants to assess the effect of the ABC approach. For this purpose, he estimates that the expected number of material moves for all jobs during the year is 1,000 and he expects 5,000 quality inspections in total, to be performed.

Required:

(a) Compute the total cost of the proposed job using direct labor hours to assign overhead. Assume the bid price is full manufacturing cost plus 25%;

(b) Compute the total cost of the job using the number of inspections to allocate the quality inspections costs. Assume bid price is full manufacturing costs plus 25%. What should be his bid using this approach?

(c) Which approach do you think best reflects the actual cost of the job. Explain.

Solution

(a) Total Overhead = Rs. 5,00,000 + 15,00,000 = Rs. 20,00,000/-

Plant wide absorption rate = Rs. 20,00,000/50,000 hours = Rs. 40 per hour

Statement Showing Cost and Bid Price of the proposed Job
(Based on Direct Labor Hour Basis)

	Rs.
Direct Materials	20,000
Direct Labor	50,000
Prime Cost	70,000
Overhead Costs	(500 hours × Rs. 40) = 20,000
Total Manufacturing Cost	90,000
Add: 25% on cost	(90,000 × 25%) = 22,500
Bid Price	1,12,500

(b) In ABC approach, consumption ratios are different for overhead activities. Therefore, overhead pools are formed for each activity. The overhead rates for each of these pools are as follows.

Material Moves = Rs. 5,00,000/1,000 moves = Rs. 500 per move

Quality inspection = Rs. 15,00,000/5,000 quality = Rs. 300 per inspection.

Statement showing Cost and Bid Price of the proposed job
(Based on Activity Based Costing Approach)

	Rs.
Direct materials	20,000
Direct labor	50,000
Prime Cost	70,000
Add: Overhead Costs	
Material handling (10 moves × Rs. 500 per move)	5,000
Quality inspection (5 inspections × Rs. 300 per inspection)	1,500
Total Manufacturing Cost	76,500
Add: 25% on cost (Rs. 76,500 × 25%)	19,125
Bid price	95,625

(c) The total cost of the proposed job under traditional cost assignment is Rs. 1,12,500 and under ABC approach, it is Rs. 95,625. The traditional approach overestimates the overhead, and therefore, the company using this system would overbid the proposed job. ABC approach best reflects the actual cost of the proposed job.

Importance and Advantages of ABC System

An efficient system of costing is of great value to management and control functions. The following are the advantages of ABC system (over Traditional System).

(1) By focusing on cause-and-effect-relationship in the cost incurrence, ABC brings accuracy and reliability in product cost determination.

(2) By providing more reliable product cost data, ABC improves greatly the manager's decision-making. It also enables managers to control many fixed overhead costs by exercising more control over the activities which cause the incurrence of these fixed costs.

(3) As more accurate cost data of product is readily available, fixation of selling prices of the products is more accurate and reliable.

(4) ABC is particularly well suited to the service sector, since the majority of costs consist of overheads that are not volume-related or easily assigned to products.

(5) Activity Based Systems assigns costs to segments based on a segment's consumption or demand for each activity. Consequently, resource consumption by different segments such as products or consumers is more accurately measured, and thus activity-based profitability analysis is likely to provide more meaningful information than an analysis based on Traditional Cost Systems.

ABC system is clearly superior in terms of accuracy of cost measurement than traditional cost systems. Nevertheless, many firms may choose to retain their Traditional Cost System on cost-benefit criteria. ABC system varies in their degree of sophistication; some systems use a small number of activity pools and cost drivers whereas others use many pools and cost drivers. Clearly, the greater the degree of sophistication, the greater is the cost of operating the system. The benefits derived from implementing ABC are likely to be influenced by the level of competition faced, the number of products sold, and the diversity of the product range and the proportion of overheads of a firm's cost structure. Companies operating in a more competitive environment have a greater need for more accurate cost information, since competitors are more likely to take advantage of any error arising from the use of distorted cost information.

Summary

Traditional Product Costing Systems reports distort product costs whenever an organization produces a diverse range of low-volume and high-volume products. Activity Based Costing emphasizes the need to obtain a better understanding of the behavior of overhead costs, and thus, ascertain what causes overheads and how they relate to products. By emphasizing activities, ABC tries to ascertain the factors that cause each major activity, cost of such activities and the relationship between activities and products produced.

The design of ABC system involves identifying the major activities that take place in an organization; creating a cost pool/cost centre for each activity; determining the cost driver for each major activity and assigning the cost of activities to products according to the product's demand for activities.

ABC system is clearly superior in terms of accuracy of cost measurement than traditional cost systems. The benefits derived from implementing ABC are likely to be influenced by the level of competition faced, the number of products sold, and the diversity of the product range and the proportion of overheads of a firm's cost structure. Companies operating in a more competitive environment have a greater need for more accurate cost information, since competitors are more likely to take advantage of any errors arising from the use of distorted cost information.

Glossary

- **Activity Based Costing:** is that costing in which costs are first traced to activities and then to products. The ABC is a costing system which focuses on activities performed to produce products. Activities become the focal points for cost accumulation
- **Total Quality Management:** Here, the management develops policies and practices to ensure that the firm's products and services exceed the customers' expectations in terms of reliability, durability, serviceability and product benchmarking
- **Target Costing:** A target cost is the market determined price minus the desired profit. It is the difference between the sale price required to capture the desired market share and the desired profit per unit
- **Back Flush Costing:** Here, the allocation of cost is delayed till the product is manufactured or sold. Once the production of the product is completed or it is sold, the allocation of materials and conversion costs is triggered
- **Benchmarking:** Here, the company continuously evaluates its performance in terms of its competitors who are the models to learn and improve in the critical areas
- **Cost Drivers:** are the events or forces that are the significant determinants of the cost of the activities
- **Unit-Level Activities:** are performed each time a unit of the product or service is produced. These activities consume resources in proportion to the number of units produced
- **Batch-Related Activities:** are performed each time a batch of goods is produced. The cost of batch-related activities varies with the number of batches made, but is fixed for all units within the batch
- **Product-Sustaining Activities:** are performed to support different products in the product line to enable individual products to be produced and sold, but the resources consumed by these activities are independent of how many units or batches of the product are produced
- **Facility-Sustaining Activities:** are performed to sustain a facility's general manufacturing process. These activities are necessary to sustain the manufacturing process and are common and joint to all products manufactured in the plant

Questions

(1) What is Activity Based Costing? Why is it needed?
(2) What is a Cost Driver? What is the role of Cost Driver in tracing costs to products?
(3) Explain the steps in applying Activity Based Costing (ABC).
(4) Distinguish between Activity Based Costing and Traditional Costing System.
(5) What are the benefits of Activity Based Costing?
(6) When do you recommend Activity Based cost allocation?
(7) Define unit level activities, batch level activities, product level activities and facility level activities.
(8) Mr. X owns a large department store in Hyderabad. For last several years, the accountant has applied overheads to the various departments – produce, meat, diary, canned foods, bakery, floral etc – based on the employee hours worked. The son of Mr. X, a Commerce student at Osmania University, has suggested his father to consider Activity Based Costing (ABC). In an attempt to implement ABC, Mr. X and his son have identified the following activities. They need your help in determining a Cost Driver for each of the activities.

Cost Pool

(a) Placing orders;
(b) Checking out Customers;
(c) Bagging groceries;
(d) Delivering groceries;
(e) Stocking shelves;
(f) Sanitorial and Maintenance;

(g) Training employees;
(h) Administrative;
(i) Advertising and Marketing;
(j) Accounting and Legal service.
(**Ans.:** Cost drivers are
(a) Number of orders;
(b) Number of customers or Sales volume;
(c) Number of Customers or Sales volume;
(d) Number of delivery orders;
(e) Hours worked for stocking;
(f) Square feet/area occupied;
(g) Number of employees;
(h) Number of departments or Sales volume;
(i) Number of advertisement campaigns;
(j) Number of transactions or sales volume.

PROBLEMS

(1) A manufacturing company gives you the following information relating to its products lines:

	Product A	*Product B*
Number of units produced	100	20
Machine set-up hours per product line	10	10
Direct labor hours per unit	2	2

Total budgeted machine set-up related cost Rs. 10,800

Required:

(a) Allocate machine set-up related cost to the product lines A and B using direct labor hour rate.

(b) Allocate machine set-up related cost to the product lines using ABC.

(c) Show cost per unit of A and B using (a) and (b) above.

(d) Is overhead allocation to product A and B lines evidence of product diversity or volume diversity?

(2) You are given the following information in respect of a manufacturing company producing three products:

(1) Budgeted overhead expenses:	*Rs.*
Machine Depreciation and Maintenance	1,68,000
Receiving	83,720
Engineering	72,000
Machine set-up	7,480
Inspection	38,400
	3, 69,600

(2) Other particulars:

	Products			*Total*
	A	*B*	*C*	
Units produced and sold	28,000	18,000	6,000	
Direct material cost per unit	Rs. 40	Rs. 30	Rs. 26	
Direct labor cost per unit	Rs. 24	Rs.28	Rs.20	
Machine hour per unit	1.5	2	1	84,000
Number per product line:				
Receiving orders	16	40	200	256
Production orders	14	12	19	45
Production runs	4	8	22	34
Inspections	8	4	20	32

Required:

(a) Statement showing total cost per unit for each product using machine hour rate.

(b) Statement showing total cost per unit of each product using relevant activities for recovery of overhead expenses:

(c) Explain the reason for differences, if any, in costs between *(a)* and *(b)*.

(3) A manufacturing company recently introduced product B to complement its regular product A. The company accumulates all overhead in a single cost pool and allocates it using machine hours. The company wants to switch over to ABC. A study reveals that much overhead cost relates to machine set-ups and engineering changes. The number of engineering changes may be taken as the activity drivers for the two new cost pools. Machine hours may be continued to be the base for allocating all remaining overhead.

You are given the following information of the company for the year ended 31.3.2000

	Product A	*Product B*	*Total*
Units produced	9,960	40	10,000
Direct material cost per unit	Rs. 50	Rs. 500	
Direct labour cost	Rs. 9,96,000	Rs. 80,000	Rs. 10,76,000
Machine hours	2,200	192	2,392
Machine set-ups	50	100	150
Engineering changes	80	120	200
Overheads:			*Rs.*
Machine set-up related			48,000
Engineering related			1,67,280
Others			3,82,720
		Total	5,98,000

Required:

(a) Using traditional costing system, determine the total and unit cost for each product line.

(b) Using ABC, determine the total and unit cost for each product line.

(c) What percentage of total overhead did the two costing systems treat differently? By what percentage did the cost of product B change as a result of the change in the system?

❑ ❑ ❑

33

COST AUDIT

Objectives

The objectives of the study are to:

- Understand the importance of Cost Audit
- Learn the provisions of Cost Audit
- Know the techniques of Auditing

MEANING

The term audit in its most popular connotation is understood to mean as an expert examination of financial books and records to ensure that the financial statements represent true and fair view of the state of affairs. Cost audit is of a very recent origin and there are very few countries which have introduced Statutory Cost Audit, i.e., compulsory audit in this field.

Cost Audit was introduced for the first time in India by an Amendment of Companies Act, 1965. This amending Act accommodated the provision for the maintenance of cost accounting records and audit thereof u/s 209(1)(d) and 233(2) of the Companies Act. The object of the cost audit is to ensure that the accounts on which the auditor is reporting, show a true and fair view and are not misleading. It is also a systematic examination of books and records of the business with a view to establish their credibility.

Cost Audit is a part of the work of the internal auditor and is primarily concerned with the audit of cost accounts. Cost Audit must be carried out systematically after the auditor having prepared a programme.

Cost Audit has two major activities, *viz.*, verification of cost accounting records like the accuracy of Cost Accounts, Cost Reports, Cost Statements, Cost Data, Costing Techniques, etc., and examination of these records to ensure that, they adhere to the cost accounting principles, plans, procedures and objectives.

DEFINITION

ICWA London (UK) defines Cost Audit as, "The verification of cost accounts and a check on the adherence to the cost accounting plan".

According to W.M. Harper, "Cost Audit is the verification of the correctness of the cost accounts and of the adherence to proper cost accounting procedures".

Cost Audit is verifying the correctness of cost accounts, cost reports, cost data and costing methods.

The important aspects of Cost Audit are: *(a)* Propriety Audit and *(b)* Efficiency Audit.

(a) Propriety Audit: It is the audit of executive action and plans bearing on finance and expenditure of the company.

(b) Efficiency Audit: It ensures application of the basic economic principle that resources flow into the most remunerative channels.

IMPORTANCE OF COST AUDIT

Cost Audit is becoming important because it has proved to be an effective tool of control in the hands of the management. It also keeps a check and safeguards the interests of the shareholders, consumers and the Government. As a tool of internal management, cost audit points out the weakness of cost accounting systems and also brings efficiency at all levels of the management. It also helps the Government in fixing the prices of various commodities and reliable cost data.

In India, cost audit has already gained popularity and by now it has been made compulsory for 26 companies (Sec. 233B): Cement, Cycles, Caustic Soda, Tyres and Tubes, Room air conditioners, Refrigerators, Automobile batteries, Electric lamps, Electric fans, Electric motors, Motor vehicles, Tractors, Aluminium, Vanaspati, Bulk drugs, Sugar, Cotton textiles, etc.

Cost Audit aims at examining that there is no undue wastage or losses and the costing system brings out the correct and realistic cost of production or processing. It provides the management with such information useful for decision making like price to be fixed for a product, avoidance of wastage, reorganize sales or inventory systems, to make the work more efficient, suggest better utilization of resources and to monitor the working of internal control and internal check systems.

SCOPE OF COST AUDIT

The scope of Cost Audit includes:

(1) Materials: The cost auditor generally verifies the following items relating to materials:

(a) Goods inward procedure
(b) Store-Keeping arrangement
(c) Accounting for scrap, wastage, material transfers
(d) Perpetual inventory system
(e) Materials Pricing methods used
(f) Adequacy of stock checking methods

(2) Wages

- *(a)* Documents used in preparation of payroll
- *(b)* Wage rate changes, authorization for wage payments and overtime payments
- *(c)* Time recording
- *(d)* Internal Check Systems

(3) Overheads

- *(a)* Classification of overheads
- *(b)* Overhead budgets
- *(c)* Apportionment and allocation of overheads
- *(d)* Methods of absorption
- *(e)* Accounting treatment of under and over absorption

(4) General

- *(a)* Methods of establishing standards, revision of standards
- *(b)* Methods of calculating standard cost variances
- *(c)* Accounting codes and instructions

Functions/Objectives

Cost Audit may be undertaken by the Government, Trade Associations, Labor Tribunals and by the Organizations themselves. Objectives of cost audit may be divided into two parts:

- *(a)* General Objectives
- *(b)* Social Objectives

General Objectives

1. To verify that cost accounts have been properly maintained and compiled according to the cost accounting system employed
2. To check their adherence to cost accounting plan
3. To detect errors and to prevent frauds and possible misappropriations
4. To determine the inventory valuation as accurately as possible
5. To verify the cost of each cost unit and cost centre to ensure that these are accurately ascertained
6. To help in fixation of prices of goods and services supplied by the company
7. To ensure that company is making optimum use of resources available in the firm of men, materials and machines
8. To make inter-firm comparisons and advise the management about the areas where performance may be improved

Social Objectives

1. These help in fixation of reasonable prices by the company
2. To guard against evasion of tax by correct valuation of inventory leading to correct profit figures
3. To help identify unproductive product lines so that resources may be diverted from un-economical to economical channels and from unproductive to productive channels
4. To provide reliable cost data, where escalation clauses are in operation in respect of certain contracts
5. To create cost consciousness in society in respect of utilization of national resources available in the form of financial, physical and human resources

Types of Cost Audit

0Cost Audit is divided mainly into two types, *viz.*, on the basis of the person who conduct the audit and on the basis of the persons who direct the audit to be performed.

On the basis of the person who conduct the audit: Cost Audit can be internal cost audit or external cost audit.

- ***(a)*** **Internal Cost Audit:** It is conducted by the persons, who are in the regular employment of the company as the part of the system of internal control and internal check. It is oriented towards the objectives of the management, primarily for system compliance and decision making purposes.
- ***(b)*** **External Cost Audit:** It is conducted by outside parties or organizations and is not a part of the regular organizational procedure. It is oriented towards the objectives of the persons who direct the audit to be performed, example Government, Trade Association, etc.

On the basis of the persons who direct the audit to be performed: According to this, Cost Audit is classified as follows;

- ***(a)*** **Cost Audit on behalf of the Management:** The main objective of this audit is to see that, the cost data placed before the management are verified and reliable and they are prepared in such detail as will serve the purpose of the management in taking appropriate decision.
- ***(b)*** **Cost Audit on behalf of a Customer:** In case of cost plus contracts, often, the buyer of the contract insists on a cost audit to satisfy about the correct ascertainment of cost.

(c) **Cost Audit on behalf of Government:** The Government may order that a cost audit may be conducted when it is approached with request for subsidies, protection, etc., to satisfy itself whether the need is genuine or made up, whether the industry seeking assistance is efficiently run, etc. This audit may be conducted in public interests also to establish the fair price of an essential commodity.

(d) **Cost Audit by Trade Association:** The Trade Association may seek full information on the costing system, level of efficiency, utilization of capacity, etc. It may also require a cost audit when its activities include maintenance of the price of the products manufactured by its member units or where there is a pooling or contributory arrangement by all the members of the Association.

(e) **Statutory Cost Audit:** Section 233B of Companies Act stipulates Cost Audit for certain types of companies or industries. The Government orders the conduct of cost audit from time to time, whenever it feels that such type of audit is necessary for a particular company.

STATUTORY AUDIT

"Audit which is based on legislative enactments", Financial Audit is governed by Section 224-227 under Indian Companies Act 1956. Cost Audit has been made statutory in respect of industries engaged in Manufacturing, Processing, Mining and Production. Till date, 43 products have been recognized under the category of Statutory Audit.

Vivian Bose Enquiry Commission has laid foundation for the emergence of Statutory Cost Audit in India.

Need for Statutory Cost Audit

The need for Statutory Cost Audit is felt in the following situations:

***(a)* Price Fixation:** When and where the Government intends to fix the price of important commodities under rational basis, Cost Audit is made compulsory.

***(b)* Tariff Protection:** Tariff is the sum total of import duties and taxes on products. When the extent and the need for tariff protection to be given to a particular industry are to be decided, the need for Cost Audit is felt.

***(c)* Cost – Plus Contracts:** When contracts are placed on cost plus basis, Cost Audit provides ready data certified through its accuracy for the purpose of payment to the contractor company.

***(d)* Mismanagement:** When there are reasons to doubt that the prices are going up, profiteering is resorted to or production is hampered due to mismanagement or inefficiencies or fraudulent management exists, Cost Audit is of great assistance in revealing the true state of affairs.

Provisions Relevant to Statutory Cost Audit

(a) Sec. 233 – B: Various facets of auditors and their role

(b) Sec. 209 (1) (d): Cost Auditing (Record) Rules , 1968

(c) Cost Audit (Report) Rules 1968: Sec 233 – B(4), Sec. 227 (1), Sec. 642 (1) (6)

ADVANTAGES OF COST AUDIT

The following are the main advantages of cost audit to Management: Cost Accountant, Shareholders, Tax-payers, Government and Consumers.

(1) Cost Audit will establish the accuracy of cost accounts and will assist in prevention of errors and frauds. It will also help to improve cost accounting methods and techniques to facilitate prompt and reliable information to the management. It creates cost consciousness, results in improved cost accounting methods and helps to have better internal control.

(2) It will help the management in taking important decisions because prompt, accurate and reliable information is made available to the management with the help of cost audit.

(3) It will help in reducing cost of production because a close check will be maintained on all wastages relating to materials, labor and overheads. Wastages will be promptly reported to the management, so that there may not be recurrence of those wastages.

(4) It will bring more reliability on the costing data and hence, can be more effective for inter-firm comparison.

(5) Management by exception is possible since cost audit separates efficient from inefficient operations and fixes individual responsibility for inefficient operations.

(6) Analysis of variances is facilitated with cost audit because a comparison of actual with standard production and sales is made. Hence, the systems of standard costing and budgetary control will be gainfully applied with cost audit. It improves the effectiveness of cost control and cost presentation by introducing efficient routines, reducing expenditure and ensuring promptness.

(7) Cost Audit assists the financial auditor because he can safely rely on many important costing data such as cost of closing stock of raw materials, work-in-progress and finished goods. In financial accounts, closing stock is valued at cost or market price, whichever is lower. The actual cost of closing stock can be reliably taken from costing books. In other matters, like payment of commission on gross profit, production, bonus to staff, etc., the

data supplied by cost accounts, audited by cost auditor can be taken as correct by the financial auditor. Thus, the task of the financial auditor is greatly facilitated if cost accounts are audited.

(8) Cost Audit is very useful in public undertakings, because it pinpoints the inefficiency of the employers. Thus, it will help in reducing cost of production of goods produced by such organizations. Making goods available to the masses at cheaper rates is the prime need of the day and cost audit will help in this direction.

(9) Cost Audit will promote better understanding between the persons at the realm of the affairs and the persons at the bottom. The cost data audited by the cost auditor will prove useful in settling trade disputes for wages, bonus, share in profits, etc.

(10) The existence of cost audit has a great moral influence on the employees, as a result of which the efficiency is increased.

(11) The goods and the trade associations may require cost audit for the purpose of fixing ceiling prices to prevent excessive profit making. The Government may also require cost audit to give protection to certain industries in public interest. It contributes to the betterment of the economy by increasing productivity and performance.

(12) Cost Audit Reports raise the status of Cost Accountant. Being external, it helps in improving costing methods and can solve specific problems which ultimately raise the status of Costing Department.

(13) It provides information relating to weak, inefficient or mismanaged units for taking proper corrective action. It also helps to identify the symptoms of sickness in a unit.

Differences between Cost Audit and Financial Audit

	Cost Audit	Financial Audit
(1) Meaning and Aim	It is the verification of cost accounts and a check on the adherence of cost accounting plan. It stresses propriety of expenditure and efficiency of performance through analysis of expenditure incurred.	It is to verify the financial accounts and report whether balance sheet and profit and loss account have been drawn properly and whether they exhibit a true and fair view of the state of affairs of the concern. Its aim is to prevent the errors and frauds and prevention of their recurrence. It is more of a honesty audit.
(2) Coverage	It covers cost accounts like cost transactions, policies, procedures techniques in great detail.	It covers financial accounts like financial transactions and procedures.
(3) Mandatory Nature	Not compulsory. Prescribed only for specified industries from time to time.	Compulsory under law for all the companies.
(4) Major Objective	Expression of opinion on propriety of expenditure, efficiency of performance, etc.,	Expression of opinion on true and fair view presented by financial statements.
(5) Periodicity	As per the Government Order or at regular intervals which may exceed one year.	Usually one year.
(6) Appointing Authority	The Board of Directors' with prior approval of Central Government.	Members in the Annual General Meeting.
(7) Approach	It imparts a forward looking approach besides checking of cost records	It is generally a post mortem check to see that the expenditure recorded has been actually incurred. It is concerned with the past and historical in nature.
(8) Concerned with	It is to verify the accuracy of cost of each job, product process, unit, etc., and is concerned with the analysis of information and its prompt presentation to the management for taking managerial decisions, i.e., price fixing, make or buy, etc. A cost auditor is to find out what the cost should be.	It is concerned with totality of the picture in respect of profit and financial position. A financial auditor is not to arrive at what the cost should have been and is merely concerned with the detection of errors and frauds and improvement in the accounting system.
(9) Reports	Cost auditor reports to the management except in case of statutory audit in which case he reports to the Government.	Financial auditor reports to the shareholders of the company.
(10) Difference in treatment	There is a difference in treatment of certain cost factors as valuation of stock, depreciation, interest on capital, etc., in cost audit as compared to financial audit.	Financial audit treats valuation of stock, depreciation, interest on capital, etc., in a different way as compared to cost audit.

Cost Audit Programme

An audit programme sets out the schedule of work to be done, its distribution among the staff, time sequence, etc. No standard pattern can be laid down for the cost audit programme. Cost audit programme is effective by the nature and size of the business, attitude of the management and its existing system. The cost auditor should have a cost audit programme, which should be specific to the unit concerned. In a cost audit programme, the following actions would be taken by the auditor. They are:

Impact of Cost

The auditor should audit the impact of the different elements of costs on the total cost and the cost which is getting acquainted with the company and the industry as a whole. The auditor should know the methods and processes of production, raw materials used and their sources, degree of automation, liquidity of both the company and the industry. He should also study the Provisions of Companies' Memorandum and Articles of Association.

Comparison

Auditors should compare the actual production and sales with the budget estimates with a view to finding the efficiency of the Budgetary Control System.

Analysis of Variances

An analysis of Cost Variances is made to confirm that they are being correctly interpreted to the management. If most of the cost variance is adverse or unfavorable, it is a proof enough that unattainable standards have been set or the management control is too loose.

Listing of Priorities

It is necessary to draw up a list of priorities, if more than one alternative is to be followed up.

Critical Examination

As the top manager is a busy person, he may not have enough time to go through all the problems and as such he will look after only those problem cases requiring the policy decisions. The auditor has to critically examine all the statements put forward to the management for taking managerial decisions. Auditor should also review frequently every system laid down or action taken by the lower management.

Discussion of Queries

Auditor has to discuss the questions or queries that arise during the course of examination with the concerned officer and he has to follow-up to ensure that agreed action has actually taken place. The benefit of any scheme or technique lies not simply in finding out the problem, but setting it in motion.

Verification of Accounts

For verification of the correctness of Cost Accounts, auditor can follow the same procedure of Financial Audit, i.e., vouching, checking and ticking, test checks, audit notes and questionnaires.

Reconciliation of Priorities

Priorities as per Cost Accounts should be reconciled with that of Financial Accounts.

Cost Audit Procedure

A cost auditor follows more or less the same procedure as the financial auditor and it was recommended by W.M. Harper. The cost procedure can be stated as follows:

(a) An audit programme is laid down and followed.
(b) Only a proportion of day-to-day transactions is checked, i.e., exact analysis is of considerable importance.
(c) Audit note sheets are compiled.
(d) Unusual items are examined and queries follow-up until the auditor is certain that he has the full explanation.

Auditing Techniques

The auditor while checking the costing system, uses a variety of techniques. Some important techniques are:

Vouching

Vouching is the examination of the evidence offered in substantiation of the entries in the books and it is also a proof that no entries have been omitted from the books. To substantiate an entry in the books of accounts, the auditor has to examine the supporting documentary evidences such as vouchers, receipts, invoices, minutes, contracts, correspondence, etc.

Check Marks and Ticking

In order to indicate that the work has been completed, some check marks and ticks with pencil or ink will be adopted by the auditor.

Test Checks

This technique may be employed by the auditor where transactions are numerous and the audit checks are a few. In such cases, statistical techniques like sampling may be employed and there is no need to undertake a cent per cent check.

Audit Notes and Questionnaires

A careful and precise note must be taken of all the material facts uncovered in the course of audit such as errors discovered, defects in the system of accounting or internal control and working details supporting the annual statement of accounts. The auditor may issue questionnaires to the different departmental managers so as to find an answer for each question.

A questionnaire on material (Stores Department) is given below:

(1) Are Goods Received Note obtained for all incoming goods?
(2) Are Bin Cards entered daily from Goods Received Notes?
(3) Are Store Requisitions checked as to authorization?
(4) Are goods taken from the stores recorded daily on Bin Cards?
(5) Have Stores Debit Note been received for all materials returned to store?
(6) Have they been recorded at once on Bin Card?
(7) Have the work rules been observed at all times before admission to the stores?
(8) Have all known losses, with their causes been reported at once?
(9) Have fire appliances been checked regularly?
(10) Have weighing machines been regularly maintained?
(11) Has the inspector's attention been called to all cases of damages to goods?
(12) Have you any suggestions to put forward to the management regarding the work of your Department?

Audit Report

After the completion of audit, the auditor should report the correctness or otherwise of the system and his recommendations. The report should be concise and rendered speedily so as to be of effective use to the management. Earlier, no standard form of an audit report was laid down but after the Cost Audit (Report) Rules, were formed in 1967 as amended in 1969 and 1971, the cost auditor is required to make a report in the form and in accordance with the procedure laid down.

Section 233-B

Appointment of Cost Auditor u/s 233-B (2)

The cost auditor has to be appointed by the Board of Directors under section 233-B of the Companies Act subject to the prior approval of the Company Law Board. This will be done on receipt of specific order from the Company Law Board for getting audited the cost accounting records of a particular year for specified products. Application in prescribed form (23-C) is submitted to the Central Government with the prescribed fee along with a copy of the Board's Resolution.

Eligibility for appointment u/s 233-B (1)

The following persons are eligible to be appointed as cost auditor u/s 233 (B)

(a) Cost Accountant within the meaning of the Cost and Works Accountants Act, 1959, or
(b) Any such Chartered Accountant within the meaning of Chartered Accountant Act, 1949 and has passed Part I of the Management Accountancy Examinations of ICAI or
(c) Any other person as may possess prescribed qualification.

Disqualification for appointment as Cost Auditor u/s 233-B(5)

U/s 233 – B (5), the following persons are disqualified for appointment as Cost Auditor:

(a) An officer or employee of the company
(b) A person who is the partner of the company
(c) A Body Corporate
(d) A person who is indebted to the company for more than Rs. 1,000 or may have given any guarantee
(e) A person who is a financial auditor of a company

Rights of Auditor u/s 233 B and 227 (1)

The rights of the Adutior are:

(1) Right to access the Books of Accounts and Vouchers.
(2) Right to get information relevant to audit.
(3) Right to get all the facilities and assistance from the company.
(4) Right to get remuneration for the services rendered.

Duties and Responsibilities of Cost Auditor u/s 233 B

The following are the duties and respossibilites of a Cost Auditor:

(1) Liable to the company if he does not perform his duties properly
(2) Owes legal responsibility to the third party if the party has been misled by his audit certificate.
(3) Should maintain his working papers as an evidence of his having carried out his duties.
(4) Should not disclose confidential information.
(5) Responsible to answer queries raised by the Central Government.
(6) Criminally liable for falsification of books.

Cost Accounting (Record) Rules 1968 u/s 209 (1) (d)*

Cost Audit Branch under the Ministry of Corporate Affairs is manned by the professionals drawn from the Indian Cost Accounts Service (ICAS) and primarily deals with sections 209 (1) (d) and 233B of the Companies Act, 1956.

The Branch, under section 209 (1) (d) formulates and notifies Cost Accounting Records Rules (CARRs) for various industries. Such rules prescribe the manner in which cost records are to be maintained by a specified class of companies. The Branch also undertakes rationalization of existing CARRs to reflect the changes in technology, manufacturing processes and accounting standards.

Books of Account to be kept by Company u/s 209

The following are the books to be maintained by a company u/s 209:

(1) Every company shall keep, at its registered office, proper Books of Account with respect to:
(a) All sums of money received and expended by the company and the matters in respect of which the receipt and expenditure take place;
(b) All sales and purchases of goods by the company;
(c) The assets and liabilities of the company;
(d) In the case of a company pertaining to any class of companies engaged in production, processing, manufacturing or mining activities, such particulars relating to utilization of material or labor or other items of cost as may be prescribed, if such class of companies is required by the Central Government to include such particular in the books of account.

Provided that all or any of the books of account aforesaid may be kept at such other place in India as the Board of Directors may decide and when the Board of Directors so decides, the company shall, within seven days of decision, file with the Registrar, a notice in writing giving the full address of that other place.

(2) Where a company has a branch office, whether in or outside India, the company shall be deemed to have complied with the provisions of sub-section (1), if proper books of account relating to the transactions effected at the branch office are kept at that office and proper summarized returns, made up to date at intervals of not more than three months, are sent by the branch office to the company at its registered office or the other place referred to in sub-section (1).

(3) For the purposes of sub-sections (1) and (2), proper books of account shall not be deemed to be kept with respect to the matters specified therein,–
(a) If such books as are necessary to give a true and fair view of the state of the affairs of the company or branch office, as the case may be, and to explain its transactions are not kept properly; and
(b) If such books are not kept on accrual basis and according to the double entry system of accounting.

(4) The books of account and other books and papers shall be open to inspection by any director during business hours.

(4A) The books of account of every company relating to a period of not less than eight years immediately preceeding the current year together with the vouchers relevant to any entry in such books of account shall be preserved in good order :

Provided that in the case of a company incorporated less than eight years before the current year, the books of account for the entire period preceeding the current year together with vouchers relevant to entry in such books of account shall be so preserved.

(5) If any of the persons referred to sub-section (6) fails to take all reasonable steps to secure compliance by the company with the requirements of this section, or has by his own wilful act been the cause of any default by the company thereunder, he shall, in respect of each offence, be punishable with imprisonment for a term which may extend to six months, or with fine which may extend to one thousand rupees, or with both:
(a) provided that in any proceedings against a person in respect of an offence under this section consisting of a failure to take reasonable steps to secure compliance by the company with the requirements of this section, it shall be a

Source: *www.mca.gov.in/MinistryWebsite/dca/mcaoffices/cab.html*

defence to prove that a competent and reliable person was charged with the duty of seeing that those requirements were complied with and was in a position to discharge that duty:

(b) provided further that no person shall be sentenced to imprisonment for any such offence unless it was committed wilfully.

(6) The persons referred to in sub-section (5) are the following, namely:–

(a) where the company has a managing director or manager, such managing director or manager and all officers and other employees and agents as defined in sub-section (6) of section 240 but excluding bankers, auditors and legal advisor;

(b) where the company has neither a managing director nor manager, every director of the company;

(c) every officer and other employee and agent (defined as aforesaid) of the company.

(7) If any person, not being a person referred to in sub-section (6), having been charged by the Managing director, manager or Board of Directors, as the case may be, with the duty of seeing that the requirements of this section are complied with, makes default in doing so, he shall, in respect of each offence, be punishable with imprisonment for a term which may extend to six months, or with a fine which may extend to one thousand rupees, or with both.

AUDIT OF COST ACCOUNTS IN CERTAIN CASES U/S 233B

Under section 233B, orders are issued to individual companies for conducting cost audit of cost records in accordance to Cost Audit Report Rules by a Cost Auditor appointed by the Board of Directors with the prior approval of the Ministry.

(1) Wherein the opinion of the Central Government, it is necessary to do so in relation to any company required under clause (d) of sub-section (1) of section 209 to include in its books of account the particulars referred to therein, the Central Government may, by order, direct that an audit of cost accounts of the company shall be conducted in such manner as may be specified in the order by an auditor who shall be a cost accountant within the meaning of the Cost and Works Accounts Act, 1959 (23 of 1959) :

Provided that, if Central Government is of the opinion that sufficient number of cost accountants within the meaning of the Cost and Works Accountants Act, 1959 (23 of 1959), are not available for conducting the audit of the cost accounts of companies generally, that Government may, by notification in the Official Gazette, direct that, for such period as may be specified in the said notification, such chartered accountant within the meaning of the Chartered Accountants Act, 1949 (38 of 1949), as possesses the prescribed qualifications, may also conduct the audit of the cost accounts of companies, and thereupon a chartered accountant possessing the prescribed qualifications may be appointed to audit the cost accounts of the company.

(2) The auditor under this section shall be appointed by the Board of Directors of the company in accordance with the provisions of sub-section (1B) of section 224 and with the previous approval of the Central Government; provided that before the appointment of any auditor is made by the Board, a written certificate shall be obtained by the Board from the auditor proposed to be so appointed to the effect that the appointment, if made, will be in accordance with the provisions of sub-section (1B) of section 224.

(3) An audit conducted by an auditor under this section shall be in addition to an audit conducted by an auditor appointed under section 224.

(4) An auditor shall have the same powers and duties in relation to an audit conducted by him under this section as an auditor of a company has under sub-section (1) of section 227 and such auditor shall make his report to the Central Government in such form and within such time as may be prescribed and shall also at the same time forward a copy of the report to the company.

(5)(a) A person referred to in sub-section (3) or sub-section (4) of section 226 shall not be appointed or re-appointed for conducting the audit of the cost accounts of a company. (b) A person appointed, under section 224, as an auditor of a company, shall not be appointed or re-appointed for conducting the audit of the cost accounts of that company. (c) If a person, appointed for conducting the audit of cost accounts of a company, becomes subject, after his appointment, to any of the disqualifications specified in clause (a) or clause (b) of this sub-section, he shall, on and from the date on which he becomes so subject, cease to conduct the audit of the cost accounts of the company.

(6) Upon receipt of an order under sub-section (1), it shall be the duty of the company to give all facilities and assistance to the person appointed for conducting the audit of the cost accounts of the company.

(7) The company shall, within thirty days from the date of receipt of a copy of the report referred to in sub-section (4), furnish the Central Government with full information and explanations on every reservation or qualification contained in such report.

(8) If, after considering the report referred to in sub-section (4) and the information and explanations furnished by the company under sub-section (7), the Central Government is of the opinion that any further information or explanation is necessary, that Government may call for such further information and explanation and thereupon the company shall furnish the same within such time as may be specified by the Government.

(9) On receipt of the report referred to in sub-section (4) and the information and explanations furnished by the company under sub-section (7) and sub-section (8), the Central Government may take such action on the report, in accordance with the provisions of this Act or any other law for the time being in force, as it may consider necessary.

(10) The Central Government may direct the company whose cost accounts have been audited under this section to circulate to its members, along with the notice of the annual general meeting to be held for the first time after the submission of such report, the whole or such portion of the said report as it may specify in this behalf.

(11) If default is made in complying with the provisions of this section, the company shall be liable to be punished with a fine which may extend to five thousand rupees, and every officer of the company who is in default, shall be liable to be punished with imprisonment for a term which may extend to three years, or with the fine which may extend to five thousand rupees, or with both.

SCOPE OF FUNCTIONS

Cost Audit Branch (CAB) under the Ministry of Corporate Affairs performs the following functions:

(1) Matters falling under section 209 (1) (d) of the Companies Act, 1956:

- Prescription of Cost Accounting Records Rules in respect of various industries/products.
- Rationalization of existing Cost Accounting Record Rules to reflect the changes in technology, manufacturing processes and accounting standards.
- Holding of meeting of the Informal Advisory Committee, which includes all the three professional Institutes (ICAI, ICSI, and ICWAI), Tariff Commission and Ministry of Finance, Industry Associations, etc., for finalization of the new Rules and Amendments in the existing Rules.
- Laying the notified rules in both Houses of Parliament after legal vetting and publication in the Gazette.

(2) Matters falling under section 233B of the Companies Act, 1956:

- Prescription of Cost Audit Report Rules, including review and rationalization of the existing ones.
- Issue of Cost Audit Orders on eligible companies.
- Processing of applications (Form 23C) for approval of appointment of Cost Auditors.
- Processing of requests for exemption/withdrawal of Cost Audit Orders.
- Receipt and review of Cost Audit Reports.
- Providing Cost Audit Reports and other information/analytical data to other Government departments/organizations/ agencies, as and when required.
- Monitoring of compliance with the provisions of Section 209 (1) (d) and Section 233B of the Companies Act, 1956 and issue of show cause notices to the defaulting companies.
- Initiating prosecution proceedings against the errant companies for defaults/violations by referring the matter to the concerned Registrar of Companies.
- Initiating action against the errant Cost Auditors under Section 224 and Section 233B of the Companies Act, 1956.

(3) To carry-out data mining and industry-wise economic analysis of all industries/sectors.

(4) Inspection of companies under Section 209A (1) of the Companies Act.

(5) Providing expert opinion on various matters as referred to Cost Audit Branch.

(6) Attending to all Court and Parliament matters relating to Cost Audit Branch.

COST ACCOUNTING RECORD RULES (CARRs)

In exercise of the powers conferred by sub-section (1) of section 642, read with clause (d) of sub-section (1) of section 209 of the Companies Act, 1956, Central Government has prescribed Cost Accounting Record Rules for various industries and products. All companies engaged in production, processing, manufacturing or mining activities, in respect of industries or products specified in the Cost Accounting Record Rules, as applicable, are required to keep at its registered office proper books of account relating to utilisation of material or labour or to other items of cost as prescribed under the said Rules.

These rules do not apply to a company, –

(1) wherein, the aggregate value of Machinery and Plant installed as on the last date of the preceeding financial year, does not exceed the limit as specified for a small scale industrial undertaking under the provisions of Industries (Development and Regulation) Act, 1951 (65 of 1951); and

(2) the aggregate value of the turnover made by the company from sale or supply of all its products or activities during the preceeding financial year does not exceed ten crores of rupees.

To view/download full list of industries and products covered under section 209 (1) (d) of the Companies Act, 1956 and to view/download full text of each Cost Accounting Record, Rules.

COST AUDIT REPORT RULES

In exercise of the powers conferred by sub-section (4) of section 233B, read with sub-section (1) of section 227 and clause (b) of sub-section (1) of section 642 of the Companies Act, 1956, Central Government has notified Cost Audit Report Rules from time to time. In supersession of the Cost Audit (Report) Rules, 1996, Cost Audit Report Rules, 2001 were notified vide G.S.R. 924(E) dated 27th December 2001. These rules were further amended in the year 2006 vide The Cost Audit Report (Amendment) Rules, 2006.

Cost Audit Reports are required to be e-filed for every financial year within 180 days from the date of close of its financial year.

Cost Audit (Report) Rules 1968

In exercise of power conferred by Section 233 B (4) read with Section 227 (1) and Section 642 (1) (6) of the Companies Act 1956, the Central Government of India u/s 209 (1) (d) of Companies Act 1956 issued the following rules.

Application

These rules shall apply to every company in respect of which an Audit of the Cost Accounting Records has been ordered by the Central Government. u/s 233 (1) of the Indian Companies Act 1956.

Form of Report

Every Auditor who conducts an audit of the Cost Accounting Records of the company shall make the report in triplicate to the Company Law Board laid down in Schedule annexed to these rules and at the same time forward a copy of the report to the company.

He shall also reply to any clarification sought by the Company Law Board within the specified time on the audit report submitted by him.

Time limit for Report

The cost auditor shall send his report to the Company Law Board and to the company within sixty days before the Annual General Meeting of the company.

Cost Auditor is to be furnished with Cost Accounting Records, etc.

The Company and every officer thereof shall make available cost accounting records to the cost auditor within 90 days from the end of the financial year of the company.

Penalties

Default by cost auditor in complying with the provisions of Rule 3 or Rule 4, he shall be punishable with a fine which may extend to Rs 500.

Default by the company in complying with the provisions of Rule 5, the company and every officer of the company, who is in default shall be punishable with fine which may extend to Rs. 500.

Schedule

COST AUDIT REPORT

A certified letter alongwith 16 appendices is to be furnished by the Cost Auditor.

(1) General

- *(a)* Name and address of the company
- *(b)* Name and address of the cost auditor
- *(c)* Government order
- *(d)* The financial year for which cost audit is prepared
- *(e)* Any foreign collaborations can be mentioned

(2) Cost Accounting System

- *(a)* Cost Accounting plan laid down in the organization by the cost auditor is mentioned

(3) Financial Position

- (a) Capital employed = Fixed Assets + Current Assets – Current Liabilities
- *(b)* Net Worth = Share Capital + Reserves and Surpluses – Accumulated Losses – Intangible Assets
- *(c)* Ratios = Profit/Capital Employed or Net Sales; Current Assets/Current Liabilities; Net worth/Long-term Liabilities
- *(d)* Income on Investments outside India
- *(e)* Capital Gains
- *(f)* Non recurring incomes

(4) Production

- *(a)* Licensed capacity, installed capacity
- *(b)* Actual Production

- *(c)* Percentage of actual production to installed capacity
- *(d)* Installed capacity on a single shift or multiple shift

(5) Process of manufacture

- *(a)* The stages in manufacture and the expenses incurred in each stage

(6) Raw Material

- *(a)* Major raw material
- *(b)* Significant transport cost
- *(c)* Freight, free on board, ocean freight
- *(d)* Insurance
- *(e)* Customs duty
- *(f)* Inland freight charges
- *(g)* Standard and actual quantities

(7) Power and Fuel

- *(a)* Quantity rate per unit
- *(b)* Total cost separately for each major product
- *(c)* Major form of fuel, coal, furnace, oil and electricity

(8) Wages and Salary

- *(a)* Direct labor, Indirect labor for separate department
- *(b)* Total man hours available
- *(c)* Average number of workers, incentives

(9) Stores and Spares

- *(a)* Per unit information
- *(b)* Slow moving spares, i.e., which do not move for more than 24 months

(10) Depreciation

- *(a)* Method adopted
- *(b)* Compared with depreciation u/s 205 (2)
- *(c)* Product on which depreciation is charged at 100 per cent should be spread over economic life of the product
- *(d)* Basis of allocation of depreciation on common assets in various departments has to be mentioned

(11) Overheads

- *(a)* Factory overheads
- *(b)* Administration overheads
- *(c)* Selling and distribution overheads
- *(d)* Annual bonus
- *(e)* Interest on borrowings
- *(f)* Bad debts, donation, retrenchment, large variances have to be recorded

(12) Royalty or technical aid

- *(a)* Total amount of royalty
- *(b)* Royalty Per unit of product

(13) Sales

- *(a)* Total sales, net sales, average sales per unit
- *(b)* Export sales, differential sales

(14) Abnormal non recurring losses

- *(a)* Strikes, lockouts, their impact on production and sales

(15) Other items

(16) Auditors conclusions and observations

- *(a)* Point of transactions, wrong in principles or apparently unjustifiable
- *(b)* Inefficient utilization of resources
- *(c)* Increase in cost of production due to controlled factors
- *(d)* Adequacy of budgetary control systems
- *(e)* Scope and performance of internal audit
- *(f)* Suggestions
- *(g)* Rectification of imbalances
- *(h)* Fuller utilization of installed capacity
- *(i)* Concentration on areas offering scope for cost reduction, increased productivity, limiting factors causing bottlenecks and improved inventory policies

Points to be considered

(*a*) Separate reports for each factory in case of the organization having more factories.
(*b*) Separate reports for each factory in case of organization having variety of products.
(*c*) The cost audit report, should be authenticated by the cost auditor
(*d*) The cost audit report has to be neatly stitched, bound in a fine cloth and send by registered post with acknowledgement due or courier.

MANAGEMENT AUDIT

Management Audit is the appraisal of management performance of an organization and ensures that at every stage of planning and operation, the accounting records, procedure of information are not only in accordance with correct principles, but also indicate that the facts and trends are correct and trust worthy. Management covers the fields of efficiency audit and propriety audit.

Efficiency Audit is one in which facts are collected, actual performance is measured and compared with standards of the organization, any negative deviations are noted down thereby initiating steps to minimize these deviations. The results so obtained by comparing, are compared with the results of the other companies engaged in same industry.

Propriety Audit ensures that every rupee invested in the business enters into highly remunerative channels, i.e., the best of the available courses is taken up while making a decision.

Areas of Management Audit

Management Audit includes

(*a*) Transactional Audit: Ensures cross checking;
(*b*) Systems Audit: Going through the accounts associated;
(*c*) Policy Audit: Evaluating Management Policies

Areas: Stores; Production; Sales; Finance

(1) Stores

Transactional Audit

(*a*) Stores ledger posting is checked with goods receivable note and material requisition
(*b*) Check stores ledger, bin card and physical balances and reconcile the differences
(*c*) For selected items, the rates adopted for pricing of receipts as well as issues are to be checked
(*d*) The rate at which closing stocks are valued for selected items is to be checked

Systems Audit

(*a*) Check from purchasing routine starting from preparation of stores indent to passing of bill for payment
(*b*) Inspection notes, rejection reports and actions taken up by the company
(*c*) Routine check for disposal and used/damaged stores
(*d*) Routine check for ensuring that stocks are not issued in excess of standard fixed

Policy Audit

(a) Maximum level of stock fixed are correct is to be verified
(*b*) Ensure that ordering quantity is based on EOQ
(*c*) Setting standards for stores consumption

(2) Production

Transaction Analysis

(*a*) Check all production records, so as to ensure that quantities of Work in Progress and quantities of finished goods have been correctly arrived at
(*b*) Ensure that defectives, scrap, wastage, etc., were properly collected, accounted and disposed off
(*c*) Link up production with cost records
(*d*) Check up sales at normal rates and concessional rate
(*e*) In case of sub-contracting, check all dispatches to and receipts from the sub-contractor and reconcile the amounts paid with quantities received

Systems Audit

(*a*) Check how production is measured
(*b*) Ensure production is correctly recorded
(*c*) Test check finished goods ready for dispatch
(*d*) Calculate yield variances and ensure that it is within the norm

Policy Audit

(*a*) Investigate into all charges made in the production programme and ascertain profitability
(*b*) Investigate into lapses of production and their causes

(3) Sales

Transaction Audit

(a) Check all dispatches from finished goods godown with invoices
(b) Check the stocks of selected items in the finished stores godown and compare with the book balance
(c) Check the postings in Debtor's Ledger and ensure that credit policy has been followed
(d) Check invoices

Systems Audit

(a) Ensure selling and distribution charges are properly allocated to each territory
(b) Examine whether the incidence of selling and distribution costs are correctly ascertained
(c) Examine whether the variances are correctly calculated, computed, investigated and acted upon
(d) Check on the incentive scheme

Policy Audit

(a) Investigate into changes in sales policies and comment upon the profitability
(b) Work out the total turnover and sales participation ratio and comment on the trend
(c) Ascertain whether the selling and distribution costs are beneficial
(d) Confirm, whether present policy is prudent, safe and beneficial

(4) Finance

Transaction Audit

(a) Check ledger and cash book with primary document
(b) Check whether all vouchers and primary documents have been properly certified
(c) Verify actual cash balances and book balances and reconcile the differences
(d) Check Petty Cash Book, Income and Expenditure books and ensure that all expenses are properly accounted for

Systems Audit

(a) Levels of authority for sanctioning expenses have been correctly observed
(b) Systems of financing the cash requirements are checked
(c) Check the existing system for preparing and creating the cash budget report thereon
(d) Check the present system of debt collection and payment to debtors and report on working

Policy Audit

(a) Check the extent of capitalization and report on under or over capitalization
(b) Review long and short term cash position
(c) Calculate the return on investment and report on reasonableness

SUMMARY

The term Audit in its most popular connotation is understood to mean as an expert examination of financial books and records to ensure that the financial statements represents true and fair view of the state of affairs. Cost Audit is the verification of Cost Accounts and a check on the adherence to the cost accounting plan.

Cost Audit has two major activities *viz.*, *verification* of cost accounting records like the accuracy of Cost Accounts, Cost Reports, Cost Statements, Cost Data, Costing Techniques, etc., and *examination* of these records to ensure that, they adhere to the cost accounting principles, plans, procedures and objectives.

The important aspects of Cost Audit are Propriety Audit and Efficiency Audit. Propriety Audit is the audit of executive action and plans bearing on finance and expenditure of the company. Efficiency Audit ensures application of the basic economic principle that 'resources flow into the most remunerative channels'.

Cost Audit may be undertaken by the Government, Trade Associations, Labor Tribunals and by the Organizations themselves. Cost Audit is divided mainly into two types *viz.*, on the basis of the persons who conduct the audit and on the basis of the persons who direct the audit to be performed.

Cost Audit may be Internal or External. Internal Cost Audit is conducted by the persons, who are in the regular employment of the company as a part of the system of internal control and internal check. It is oriented towards the objectives of the management, parimarily for system compliance and decision making purposes. External Cost Audit is conducted by the outside parties or organizations and is not a part of the regular organizational procedure. It is oriented towards the objectives of the persons who direct the audit to be performed, example Government, Trade Association, etc.

Cost Audit Programme sets out the schedule of work to be done, its distribution among the staff, time sequence, etc., Vouching is the most important technique used by the Cost Auditor. It is the examination of the evidence offered in substantiation of the entries in the books and it is also a proof that no entries have been omitted from the books. To substantiate an entry in the books of accounts, the auditor has to examine the supporting documentary evidences such as vouchers, receipts, invoices, minutes, contracts, correspondence, etc. In order to indicate that the work has been completed, some check marks and ticks with pencil or ink will be adopted by the auditor. Test Checks may be employed by the auditor where transactions are numerous and the audit checks are few. A careful and precise note must be taken of all the material facts uncovered in the course of audit such as errors detected, defects in the system of accounting or internal control and working details supporting the annual statement of accounts. The auditor may issue questionnaires to different departmental managers so as to find an answer to each question. After the completion of audit, the auditor should report the correctness or otherwise of the system and his recommendations.

All companies engaged in production, processing, manufacturing or mining activities, in respect of industries or products specified in the Cost Accounting Record Rules, as applicable, are required to keep at its registered office proper books of account relating to utilization of material or labor or to other items of cost as prescribed. Cost Audit Reports are required to be e-filed for every financial year within 180 days from the date of close of its financial year.

Management Audit is the appraisal of management performance of an organization and ensures that at every stage of planning and operation, the accounting records, procedure of information are not only in accordance with correct principles, but also indicate that the facts and trends are correct and trustworthy. Management covers the fields of efficiency audit and propriety audit.

Glossary

- **Cost Audit:** The verification of cost accounts and a check on the adherence to the cost accounting plan.
- **Propriety Audit:** It is the audit of executive action and plans bearing on finance and expenditure of the company. It ensures that every rupee invested on the business enters into highly remunerative channels i.e., the best of the available courses is taken up while making a decision.
- **Efficiency Audit:** It ensures application of the basic economic principle that resources flow into the most remunerative channels. It is one in which facts are collected, actual performance is measured and compared with standards of the organization, any negative deviations are noted down thereby initiating steps in minimizing these deviations.
- **Internal Cost Audit:** It is conducted by the persons, who are in the regular employment of the company as a part of the system of internal control and internal check. It is oriented towards the objectives of the management, primarily for system compliance and decision making purposes.
- **External Cost Audit:** It is conducted by the outside parties or organizations and is not a part of the regular organizational procedure. It is oriented towards the objectives of the persons who direct the audit to be performed, example Government, Trade Association, etc.,
- **Statutory Audit:** It is based on legislative enactments. Cost Audit has been made statutory in respect of industries engaged in Manufacturing, Processing, Mining and Production.
- **Vouching:** It is the examination of the evidence offered in substantiation of the entries in the books and it is also a proof that no entries have been omitted from the books.
- **Management Audit:** It is the appraisal of management performance of an organization and ensures that at every stage of planning and operation, the accounting records, procedure of information are not only in accordance with correct principles, but also indicates that the facts and trends are correct and trust worthy.

Questions

(1) What do you understand by Cost Audit?
(2) Explain the importance of Cost Audit.
(3) Discuss the scope of Cost Audit.
(4) What are the various objectives of Cost Audit?
(5) Explain the different types of Cost Audit.
(6) Discuss the need for Statutory Cost Audit.
(7) Discuss the merits of Cost Audit.
(8) Bring out the differences between Cost Audit and Financial Audit.
(9) How Cost Audit Program is a conducted?
(10) Discuss the various techniques adopted by an auditor for checking the costing system.

❑ ❑ ❑

34

Cost Control and Cost Reduction

Objectives

The objectives of the study are to:

- **Explain the concept of Cost Control and Cost Reduction**
- **Differentiate Cost Control from Cost Reduction**
- **Learn the techniques of Cost Control and Cost Reduction**
- **Analyze the areas of Cost Reduction**

INTRODUCTION

The basic objective of Cost Accounting is controlling the cost and reducing the cost. Controlling is that part of the management activity wherein managers compare the actual performance against the planned performance, find out the deviations and take remedial steps to correct the deviations, thus, control helps the correction.

MEANING OF COST CONTROL

Cost Control is defined as "The Regulation by executive action of the costs of operating an undertaking particularly where such action is guided by Cost Accounting". According to this definition, Cost Control needs regulatory action. Cost Control is exercised through setting standards or targets and comparing the actual performance with the pre-determined one. Corrective action is taken to ensure that future performance confirms to the set standards, in case any deviation is observed.

COST CONTROL TECHNIQUES

The following are considered as the important techniques for Cost Control:

(1) Material/Inventory Control
(2) Labor Control
(3) Work and Methods Study
(4) Time Study
(5) Coding and Classification
(6) Budgetary Control
(7) Standard Costing
(8) Control of Capital Expenditure
(9) Responsibility Accounting
(10) Productivity and Accounting Ratios

Material/Inventory Control is the system devised and adopted for controlling investment in inventory. It involves inventory planning and decision- making with regard to the quantity and time of purchase, fixation of stock levels, maintenance of stores and continuous stock-taking. Inventory Control includes control of not only the physical stock but also of the funds invested in it. Accordingly, the twin objectives of Inventory Control are *(a)* to maintain a balanced inventory and *(b)* to keep the amount invested in inventories as low as possible without hampering either the flow of production or deliveries of finished goods.

Labor Control: Labor cost constitutes quite a significant proportion of the total cost. Labor Cost Control includes control over recruitment, giving increment and promotions; formulation of wage policy and incentive schemes and allocation of cost. For effective control of labor cost, management compares the actual labor cost of products or services with the standard labor cost of product or services and this comparison helps the management in planning for improvement in labor costs in future periods. Time Keeping and Time Booking helps in the calculation of wages to be paid to the workers. Devising a good wage policy is essential for the smooth running of the organization.

Work Study: It is a systematic recording of the existing methods of work; analyzing and examination of existing and proposed methods of performing a work; developing and applying new and improved methods of work for simplification of existing methods and better utilization of available resources. It aims at most effective use of existing or proposed plant and human effort. It comprises two main techniques *viz.*, Methods Study and Time Study.

Method Study involves the use of Motion Study which aims at finding out the most scientific and simple way of performing an operation or doing a job by eliminating all wasteful movements and reducing fatigue to the minimum.

Time Study measures the requirements for the task and fixes the standard time required to perform an operation or job. It helps to eliminate waste, minimize damage and wear and tear.

Coding and Classification: The arrangement of items in a logical sequence having regard to their nature or the purpose to be fulfilled is called as classification. It is the process of arranging items into groups according to their likeness. After classifying all the items of stores, it becomes necessary to allot code numbers to the classified items. If the stores items are allotted scientific classification code numbers, it is possible to have a complete catalogue of coding system and all those who deal with materials become conversant with it. Classification of expenses of similar nature into a group helps in an effective analysis and control of the expenses. Classification and Coding helps to reduce cost by making it possible to find wanted items easily and faster to simplify record keeping.

Budgetary Control: It is defined as the establishment of budgets relating the responsibilities of the executives to the requirements of a policy and a continuous comparison of actual with the budgeted results, either to secure by individual action the objectives of that policy or to provide a basis for revision. An important characteristic of the Budgetary Control is comparing actual performance with prior estimates or targets laid down in the budget to make sure that actual performance is steering in the right direction. The Budgetary Control coordinates the various activities of the firm and secures cooperation of all concerned so that the common objective of the firm may be successfully achieved. It forces executives to think and think as a group. It makes control possible by a continuous comparison of the actual performance with that of the budget.

Standard Costing is the name given to the technique whereby standard costs are pre-determined and subsequently compared with the recorded actual costs. It is thus, a technique of cost ascertainment and cost control. The technique of Standard Costing can be used in conjunction with any method of costing. Standard Costing simplifies the work of valuing inventory and serves as the basis of inventory valuation. If inventories are valued at standard cost, stores ledger can be maintained in terms of quantities only. Being pre-determined costs, standard costs are very useful in planning, budgeting and decision making. Standard costing facilitates timely presentation of cost reports to the management pinpointing the significant variances.

Control of Capital Expenditure: The capital expenditure on fixed assets can be controlled by preparing a Capital Expenditure Budget. It relates to projects involving huge capital outlay and long-term commitment. The Capital Expenditure Decisions affect operations of business over a series of years. Therefore, Capital Expenditure Budget should be prepared carefully to ensure that capital outlays are used only in most profitable alternatives and do not endanger the financial position of the company.

Responsibility Accounting: It means an accounting process, which reports as to how well managers of Responsibility Centres have fulfilled their responsibility. It is closely related to the goal of controllability. Those elements in a certain area of activity which are controllable are identified and a person is given the responsibility for managing such elements. Thus, individuals in an organization are made responsible for only those elements which can be controlled by them. Responsibility Accounting focuses on Responsibility Centres. The managers of different Activity Centres are responsible for controlling the costs of their Centres. The performance is constantly compared to the standards set and this process is very useful in exercising cost controls.

Productivity and Accounting Ratios: It refers to the effective use of expenditure on resources required for the production of goods or rendering of services. It refers to the rate of production in terms of materials, labor hours, machine hours or any other effective basis. It is the ratio of Output to Input or Return to Input or Gross Income to Gross Expense. A high ratio reduces costs and increases output and thus, increases profitability.

Essentials for Success of Cost Control

Essentials for success of Cost Control are given as under:

- Targets or standards should be laid for each area of responsibility and cost for each area of responsibility should be collected.
- Actual performance should be measured against the standards.
- Reporting of efficiency or inefficiency displayed by each person should be prompt. Information delayed is information denied.
- Taking corrective action to eliminate the variances so that cost may be controlled and maximum efficiency is achieved.
- Reviewing periodically, the standards or targets in the light of changed circumstances.
- There should be effective Budgetary Control and proper setting up of standards for effective system of cost control.

Meaning of Cost Reduction

According to the Chartered Institute of Management Accountants, London, "Cost Reduction is the achievement of real and permanent reduction in unit cost of goods manufactured or services rendered without impairing their suitability for the use intended".

Cost Reduction requires co-operation at all levels. It requires motivating the staff, training and educating them, offering incentives and promotions for better performance, etc. All this will result in Cost Reduction.

Characteristics of Cost Reduction

- Cost Reduction should be real one which comes through greater productivity.
- Reduction must be a permanent one.
- The reduction should not result from reduction in price of inputs or labor, etc., which is short lived, rather it should be through improvements in methods of production.
- Reduction should not result in loss of quality of the products or services rendered.
- Cost Reduction should aim at elimination of wasteful elements.

Cost Reduction Program

Cost Reduction aims to bring about real and permanent reduction in costs. Therefore, it should not be a loose-end haphazard program. It should be a well coordinated program which is formulated at the initiative of the management.

The organization for formulating a Cost Reduction program differs from concern to concern based on the nature of the business, size of the concern and individual requirements.

A special Cost Reduction program is brought into action to meet the required needs. Short-term Cost Reduction plans are set to tide over current difficulties. Long-term Cost Reduction plans improve major reductions in cost and involve capital expenditure.

Cost Reduction program consists of the following steps

- Firstly, Centres where costs are incurred are identified and grouped on the basis of departmental responsibilities.
- Value Analysis scheme is submitted for each such group to see whether optimum efficiency is achieved or not in its performance.
- Lastly, appropriate techniques are applied to reduce costs.

Cost Control vs. Cost Reduction

Cost Control	Cost Reduction
Cost Control aims at controlling the cost.	Cost Reduction aims at achieving the real and permanent reduction in the cost of goods or services.
Cost Control is static in nature.	Cost Reduction is dynamic in function.
Cost Control is achieved by setting standards, ascertaining actual performance and then comparing it with the target.	Cost Reduction is not concerned with the maintenance of performance according to the target set.
Cost Control is only a means to an end.	Cost Reduction is the end in itself. Cost Reduction begins where Cost Control ends.
Cost Control is a preventive function as it aims to see that the actual cost do not exceed the pre-determined cost.	Cost Reduction is a corrective function. It aims at bringing forth the savings by challenging the standards and improving them.

Tools and Techniques of Cost Reduction

The tools for Cost Reduction are mostly the same as followed for Cost Control. They are Budgetary Control, Standard Costing, Work-Study and Method-Study, Coding and Classification, Improvement in Design and Substitute Material Utilization.

Automation: In large organizations, cost data is so heavy that manual operations cannot process it satisfactorily and with speed. With the help of mechanical devices, summaries and reports can be prepared promptly without errors and at a low cost and a large number of routine organizations functions can be carried out well. If reducing costs is a step-by-step process, adding new technology is really the final step. The deployment of automated systems lets companies cut their workforce costs while maintaining quality. Automation, with its integrated logistics, material handling, and warehousing systems, work force management can both proactively and reactively address the critical issues of cost cutting and reduction.

Operations Research: It is a scientific quantitative method to solve complex management problems subject to many variables and constraints. It is a mixed term approach to problem solving where number of researchers drawn from different disciplines and professions work under a common roof. Each researcher sees problem from specialized eyes and then join hands with the other. Operations Research can help organization in achieving billion dollars saving with improved market shares through the development, implementation of its strategic investment, procurement, inventory, production, marketing decision simulations out of its existing management information data base, integrating supply chain into Total Quality Management on its existing IT architecture.

Product Planning and Control: Cost Control refers to management's effort to influence the actions of individuals who are responsible for performing tasks, incurring costs, and generating revenues. First, managers plan the way they want people to perform, then they implement procedures to determine whether actual performance complies with these plans. Cost Control is a continuous process that begins with the annual budget. As the fiscal year progresses, management compares actual results to those projected in the budget and incorporates into the new plan the lessons learned from its evaluation of current operations. Through the budget process and accounting controls, management establishes overall company objectives, defines the centres of responsibility, and determines specific objectives for each responsibility centre, and designs procedures and standards for reporting and evaluation. The planning process, then, provides for two types of control mechanisms: feed forward, which provides a basis for control at the point of action (the decision point); and feedback, which provides a basis for measuring the effectiveness of control after implementation. Management's role is to feed forward a futuristic vision of where the company is going and how it is to get there, and to make clear decisions coordinating and directing employee activities. Management also oversees the development of procedures to collect, record, and evaluate feedback.

Inventory Control: Inventory includes raw materials, work–in–progress, finished goods and consumables and maintenance supplies. Inventory control is the system which ensures the provision of required quantity of inventories of the required quality at the required time with a minimum investment. A proper system of Inventory Control lowers the costs and helps in an uninterrupted production and supply of finished goods to the customer without losing them. The various techniques of Inventory Control are:

(i) **Always Better Control Analysis (ABC):** It is a technique wherein the items of stores are classified into Category 'A' consisting of items of store that have high value and low quantity; Category 'B' consisting of those items that require substantial investment but not as much as the items of Category 'A' and Category 'C' consisting of those items that do not require much investment and which are least costly items and where the quantity is usually large. Category 'A' is given utmost attention and care as they are very costly and not much control is exercised over the items of Category 'C'. In case of Category 'B' items, ordinary stores routine control is exercised. By doing so, the investment in inventory can be regulated and funds can be utilized in the best possible way.

(ii) **Inventory Turnover:** It is a ratio which measures the number of times a firm's average inventory is sold during a year. It reflects upon the usage of stock. A high ratio indicates fast moving stock which has to be replaced fast, while a low ratio indicates slow moving stock and therefore, attempt should be made to keep these stocks at the lowest level. Such a step prevents unnecessary investment in inventories.

(iii) **Just-in-Time Inventory System:** Here, the supply of items fully coincides with their demand and stocks are eliminated to the extent possible. This system ensures maximum economy in material handling costs, ordering costs and stock holding cost and the chances of loss due to pilferage, leakage and spoilage are reduced to the minimum.

(iv) **Vital – Essential – Desirable Analysis:** Here, the classification of materials is done on the basis of their criticality for production. The items are classified into **vital** which are very critical for production, **essential** which are very important for production and **desirable** which are required for production but the Production Department can manage without them for some period. Such an analysis ensures that there is uninterrupted supply of vital material.

(v) **Economic Order Quantity (EOQ):** It is that level of material to be ordered where the aggregate of two costs *viz.*, Ordering Cost and Holding Costs of inventory is the minimum. Ordering Costs increase for a fewer quantities whereas Carrying Costs will be lower. Thus, while determining EOQ, a balance has to be struck between these two opposing costs.

(vi) Fixation of Stock Levels: The main objective of Inventory Control is to maintain the raw materials as low as possible and at the same time, material must be made available as and when required by the Production Department. Thus, there should be neither under stocking nor over stocking. Hence, various stock levels like Maximum Level, Minimum Level, Re-order Level, Danger Level, Safety Level and Average Stock Level are fixed to have a proper balance between under stocking and over stocking.

Training Schemes: Training programs can help in identifying areas for cost prevention and reduction, understanding the factors driving costs in areas such as distribution, inventory management, space management, corporate purchasing, fleet planning, airport and flight operations, etc., applying cost reduction strategies using worksheets to organize and manipulate data, developing and implementing effective cost-containment programs, sustaining the impact of cost-reduction program, and finally assuring participation at all levels. Training can help managers at all levels and also workers to improve their understanding of key drivers of profitability and shareholder value, develop a Cost Re-Balancing Program that will ensure the long-term financial viability, identify crucial areas where costs can be prevented or reduced and thereby creating and implementing a formal cost review process.

Simplification and Variety Reduction: Diversification means entry into new product line, processes, services or market. It may be horizontal or vertical. Though, it is necessary for growth, stability, flexibility and to earn more profit; reduction in variety results in low costs, due to reduction in tool setting costs and higher productivity leading to reduced costs and reduced sales. It also results in reduction of inventory of raw material and finished goods and improved service for the customer. On the reducing complexity front, the latest panacea is to build up an application integration framework based on services and open standards, in addition-to consolidation, elimination of redundant systems, and settling for less feature-laden applications. Overall, a reduction in complexity, and an increase in consolidation and data centre automation, should reduce the human labor needed to keep systems running, potentially freeing up resources to work on innovating rather than maintaining.

Business Forecasts: It enables one to achieve a permanent transformation in ones cost structure, embedding the appropriate scrutiny and controls that will prevent slippage. Business forecast helps in choosing the right approach to an overhead review through *(a)* Radical cost reduction *(b)* Continuous improvement *(c)* A mid way – rebalancing of resources *(d)* Timescales and *(e)* Staff involvement. It also helps in avoiding cuts to strategically important capabilities, understanding the business imperatives, identifying where greatest value will be added and creating cost reduction plans that support the strategic imperative. Forecasting helps in knowing the high costs of forecasting errors and best practice in approaches to forecasting

Standardization – Cost Reduction Opportunities: Standard part lists can be 50 times less than proliferated lists and Standardization Results for Standard parts are easier to get and fewer types need to be purchased. The results will be in terms of economies of scale and this results from larger purchases and material overhead of the standard parts can be one-tenth that of proliferated lists. Implementing Standardization with a practical procedure developed to standardize part and materials for new designs can reduce costs. Products can be rationalized to eliminate or outsource the most unusual products that have the most unusual parts and materials. Total cost measurements should be implemented to justify standardization efforts and encourage picking standard parts. Standardization leads to reduction in capital investment say elimination of unnecessary stock and reduction in prices due to larger batch quantities and improvement in quality.

Market Research: is generally either primary or secondary. In Secondary Research, the company uses information compiled from other sources that appears applicable to a new or existing product. Primary Market Research involves testing such as focus groups, surveys, field tests, interviews or observation, conducted or tailored specifically to that product.

A list of questions that can be answered through Market Research are:

- What is happening in the market? What are the trends? Who are the competitors?
- How do consumers talk about the products in the market?
- Which needs are important? Are the needs being met by current products?

Marketing Research, or Market Research, is a form of business research and is generally divided into two categories: consumer market research and business-to-business (B2B) market research, which was previously known as industrial marketing research. Consumer marketing research studies the buying habits of individual people while business-to-business marketing research investigates the markets for products sold by one business to another.

Consumer market research is a form of applied sociology that concentrates on understanding the behaviors, whims and preferences of consumers in a market-based economy, and aims to understand the effects and comparative success of marketing campaigns.

Thus, **Marketing Research** is the systematic and objective identification, collection, analysis, and dissemination of information for the purpose of assisting the management in decision making related to the identification and solution to problems and opportunities in marketing. It reveals several issues related to why organizations undertake cost reduction exercises. It details which cost reduction activities are most popular in the focus areas and explains the success of organizations in reducing costs in each focus area, while minimizing negative impact to morale, IT operations and the business. Market research presents specific issues and challenges in each focus area, along with mitigating steps and best practices.

Quality Control: It ensures through a system of testing and inspection that the performance comes up to the required standards and specifications as regards quality. The objective is to place quality products in the hands of the customers according to their preferences to provide control over the performance of the manufacturer. Detection of sub-standard work in the earlier stages of manufacturing saves further costs on subsequent operations. Quality Control ensures stable, reliable, and continuous measurement, reduces costs and time for analysis, eliminates manual measurement errors and reduces workload.

Value Analysis: It is the scientific approach to cost reduction. It aims at cost reduction by increasing the value in a product. It is a creative approach to identify unnecessary costs, which do not improve the products quality or efficiency and do not provide any additional satisfaction to the customers. It aims at eliminating such costs. It is considered as the effective tool for cost reduction. Cost Reduction is effected in two ways.

(a) By economizing expenditure and increasing productivity

(b) By improving the use value and esteem value of product.

Use Value refers to those qualities and characteristics which make a product useful and esteem value refers to those properties which make it attractive and create in it an aesthetic value.

Value Analysis attempts to achieve the maximum possible value for a given cost by following various techniques for reducing the costs. Keeping in view the wide applicability of this technique, Value Analysis is used instead of Value Engineering.

Value Analysis is a scientific aid which lays emphasis on reaching new ideas, exploring new ways of improving performance which ultimately leads to addition in the quality and reduction in the cost of the product.

Procedure of Value Analysis

The following is the procedure:

(1) Defining the problem, i.e., ascertaining whether the product has full use value and esteem value, if not in what respect it is lacking and to that extent, action may be planned on those lines.
(2) Obtaining all relevant data regarding the use of the product, cost of product, selling and distribution, competitive products, etc.
(3) Studying and assessing the alternatives which reduce cost.
(4) Examining the feasibility of the alternatives. Best alternative proposed is reviewed by the management and authority is granted for its development
(5) Implementation
(6) Follow up, i.e., to ascertain whether the proposals have achieved the reduction in costs that were planned.

For the success of Value Analysis, active participation of various departments, team and personnel heading the Value Analysis team is required. The team generally includes a design engineer, a production engineer, cost accountant, system expert, market analyst, etc.

Value Engineering

The concept evolved from the work of Lawrence Miler who, in 1970's was a purchase engineer with G.E. Miler was assigned the task of purchasing the materials to permit this. Often he was unable to obtain the specific material or component specified by the designer, so Miler thought, "if he cannot obtain the product, he must obtain an alternative". Miler observed that many of the substitutes were providing equal or better performance at a lower cost and from this evolved the first definition of Value Engineering.

It is an organized approach to providing the necessary function at the lowest cost. The concept of Value Engineering is cost validation exercise, which did not affect the quality of the product. It is an organized approach to the identification and elimination of unnecessary costs.

The following steps are involved in Value Engineering practice:

- Preparing and administering maintenance programs
- Forecasting expenditure flows
- Advising on cost limits and preparing budgets
- Advising on cash flow forecasting
- Cost analysis
- Cost benefit analysis
- Undertaking feasibility studies
- Investment appraisal

Value Engineering is a practice where goal is always, to achieve value for money. Value Engineering found its first applications in US manufacturing at the end of World War II. The introduction to construction in the early 1960's was founded by the US military and expanded throughout the US government. Subsequently, its use has spread globally.

Today, Value Engineering is not only recognized but also acclaimed as one of the best value improving practices that management can employ. The successful application to strategic planning, quality improvement, management studies, manufacturing and construction has demonstrated both its versatility and its durability as a management practice.

The following are the features of Value Engineering:

- Value Engineering is function based
- Value Engineering is multi-disciplinary
- Value Engineering follows a specific methodology

In industry, Value Engineering enables to

- reduce time to market
- reduce product and operating tools
- use resources more effectively
- compute successfully internationally
- increase employee involvement/contribution

Areas Covered by Cost Reduction

The areas covered under Cost Reductiopn are described below:

(1) **Product Design:** At the time of introducing a new design and at the time of seeking new improvements in existing design, the scope of Cost Reduction should be investigated. All comparative costs should be studied. The impact of design modification on the following costs should be examined.

(i) Materials: Using cheaper substitutes, superior chemical properties, etc.

(ii) Labor: Reducing labor time, fatigue and monotony.

(iii) Tools and equipment: Use of efficient tools and equipment.

(iv) Standardization and Simplification: Promoting, Modification and Product design.

(v) Packing and Transport: Contributing to safety and economy in packing and transport.

(vi) After Sales Service: Cost of after sale services should come down due to modification.

(2) **Organization Structure:** It should be planned in such a way that it should be smooth, efficient and cost effective.

(i) Functions and responsibilities should be defined.

(ii) Tasks should be assigned with targets.

(iii) Authority should match responsibility.

(iv) Overlapping of functions should be avoided.

(v) Two way channel of communication is to be established.

(3) **Production Methods:** The type of plant and machinery, tools and equipment, labor and material mix and the technique of using all these should result in cost economy. Degree of capital intensity should lead to maximum cost saving.

(4) **Plant Layout:** Plant layout should avoid problems in movement of labor, material and equipment and facilitate smooth movement of raw material, work-in-progress and finished products.

(5) **Production Schedules:**

The following points should be kept in mind for proper production scheduling.

(i) There should be an optimum batch size.

(ii) Underloading and overloading of machines should be avoided.

(iii) There should be proper synchronization between output and input.

(iv) Excess stocking or understocking of finished products should be avoided.

(v) It should lead to optimum utilization of facilities already created.

(6) **Material Purchase and Handling Procedures:**

(i) There should be a clear layout of procedures in purchases, receipts and issue of materials.

(ii) Periodical review and thorough study should be done on Economic Order Quantity, Safety Stock and Re-order Level.

(iii) Proper measures should be taken to control spoilage, wastage and shortage.

(7) **Personnel:**

Prospects of cost saving in personnel function should be explored in the following ways:

(i) Methods should be adopted to reduce per unit labor cost.

(ii) Implement voluntary retirement schemes to get rid of excess unwanted work-force.

(iii) Research should be conducted for simplification of work to reduce labor content and labor time and fatigue.

(iv) Create better working conditions and improve labor relations.

(8) **Financial Management:** The scope for reducing cost is more through managing the financial resources in a better way. The following steps can be followed.

(i) Determination of optimum capital required.
(ii) Raising funds from cheaper source of finance.
(iii) Optimum mix of capital.
(iv) Avoiding both over capitalization and under capitalization.
(v) Avoid shortage of working capital as well as excess working capital.
(vi) There should be strict control on the use of financial resources.

Advantages of Cost Reduction

The following are the benefits that would result from Cost Reduction Program.

(1) Cost Reduction leads to higher profits.
(2) It increases the competitive strength of the organization.
(3) Cost Reduction may lead to productive use of society's resources at macro level, which leads to a higher rate of economic growth.
(4) Cost Reduction increases the resistance of the undertaking to face ups and downs in business.
(5) Firms which are successful in reducing the costs also force their competitors to earn efficient ways of doing things.
(6) Cost efficient firms grow at a faster rate and diversify at a faster rate.

Summary

The basic objective of Cost Accounting is controlling the cost and reducing the cost. Controlling is that part of the management activity wherein the managers compare the actual performance against the planned performance, find out the deviations and take remedial steps to correct the deviations. Thus, control helps the correction.

Cost Control is the Regulation by executive action of the costs of operating an undertaking particularly, where such action is guided by Cost Accounting. The important techniques for Cost Control are Material/Inventory Control, Overhead Control, Budgetary Control, Standard Costing, Control of Capital Expenditure, Responsibility Accounting and Productivity and Accounting Ratios.

Cost Reduction is the achievement of real and permanent reduction in the unit cost of goods manufactured or services rendered without impairing their suitability for the use intended. As Cost Reduction aims to bring about real and permanent reduction in costs, it should not be a loose-end haphazard program. It should be a well coordinated program which is formulated at the initiative of the management.

The important techniques for Cost Control are Automation, Operations Research, Product Planning and Control, Inventory Control, Training Schemes, Simplification and Variety Reduction, Business Forecasts, Standardization, Market Research and Quality Control.

The various areas covered by Cost Reduction are Product Design, Organization Structure, Production Methods, Plant Layout, Production Schedules, Material Purchase and Handling Procedure, Personnel, Financial Management and Value Analysis.

Cost Reduction Program leads to higher profits; increases the competitive strength of the organization; results in productive use of society's resources at macro level, which leads to a higher rate of economic growth; increases the resistance of the undertaking to face ups and downs in business; successful firms force their competitors to earn efficient ways of doing things and cost efficient firms grow at a faster rate and diversify at a faster rate.

Glossary

- **Cost Control:** The Regulation by executive action of the costs of operating an undertaking particularly where such action is guided by Cost Accounting.
- **Inventory Control:** is the system devised and adopted for controlling investment in inventory. It involves inventory planning and decision-making with regard to the quantity and time of purchase, fixation of stock levels, maintenance of stores and continuous stock-taking.
- **Work Study:** is a systematic recording of the existing methods of work; analyzing and examination of existing and proposed methods of performing a work; developing and applying new and improved methods of work for simplification of existing methods and better utilization of available resources.
- **Method Study:** involves the use of Motion Study which aims at finding out the most scientific and simple way of performing an operation or doing a job by eliminating all wasteful movements and reducing fatigue to the minimum.
- **Time Study:** measures the requirements for the task and fixes the standard time required to perform an operation or job. It helps to eliminate waste, minimize damage and wear and tear.
- **Classification:** The arrangement of items in a logical sequence having regard to their nature or the purpose to be fulfilled. It is the process of arranging items into groups according to their likeness.

- **Budgetary Control:** the establishment of budgets relating the responsibilities of executives to the requirements of a policy and a continuous comparison of the actual with the budgeted results, either to secure by individual action the objectives of that policy or to provide a basis for revision.
- **Standard Costing:** is the technique whereby standard costs are pre-determined and subsequently compared with the recorded actual costs. It is thus a technique of cost ascertainment and cost control.
- **Responsibility Accounting:** an accounting process, which reports as to how well managers of Responsibility Centres have fulfilled their responsibility. It is closely related to the goal of controllability.
- **Productivity:** refers to the effective use of expenditure on resources required for the production of goods or rendering of services. It refers to the rate of production in terms of materials, labor hours, machine hours or any other effective basis.
- **Operations Research:** is a scientific quantitative method to solve complex management problems subject to many variables and constraints.
- **Inventory Control:** is the system which ensures the provision of required quantity of inventories of the required quality at the required time with a minimum investment.
- **Always Better Control Analysis (ABC):** a technique wherein the items of stores are classified into Category 'A' consisting of items of store that have high value and low quantity; Category 'B' consisting of those items that require substantial investment but not as much as the items of Category 'A' and Category 'C' consisting of those items that do not require much investment and which are least costly items and where the quantity is usually large.
- **Inventory Turnover:** It is a ratio which measures the number of times a firm's average inventory is sold during a year. It reflects upon the usage of stock.
- **Just-in-Time Inventory System:** a system where the supply of items fully coincides with their demand and stocks are eliminated to the extent possible.
- **Vital – Essential – Desirable Analysis:** a system where the classification of materials is done on the basis of their criticality for production. The items are classified into **vital** which are very critical for production, **essential** which are very important for production and **desirable** which are required for production but the Production Department can manage without them for some period.
- **Economic Order Quantity (EOQ):** is that level of material to be ordered where the aggregate of two costs viz., Ordering Cost and Holding Costs of inventory is the minimum.
- **Marketing Research:** is the systematic and objective identification, collection, analysis, and dissemination of information for the purpose of assisting the management in decision making related to the identification and solution of problems and opportunities in marketing.
- **Quality Control:** ensures through a system of testing and inspection that the performance comes up to the required standards and specifications as regards quality.
- **Value Analysis**: is the scientific approach to cost reduction. It aims at cost reduction by increasing the value in a product. It is a creative approach to identify unnecessary costs, which do not improve the products quality or efficiency and do not provide any additional satisfaction to the customers.

Questions

(1) What do you understand by the terms 'Cost Control' and 'Cost Reduction'?

(2) Bring out the differences between 'Cost Control' and 'Cost Reduction'.

(3) Explain briefly the techniques of Cost Control.

(4) Explain briefly the techniques of Cost Reduction.

(5) Analyse the various areas where Cost Reduction is possible.

❑❑❑

35

COST REPORTING

Objectives

The objectives of the study are to:

- Understand the General Principles of Reporting
- Highlight the needs of different levels of management
- Learn the different types of reporting

INTRODUCTION

The ultimate objective of any Costing System is the maximization of profit through cost control techniques. Cost presentation plays a very important role in achieving this objective. It helps the management in taking proper action. Cost information may be presented and communicated to the management through Reports, Charts and Graphs. Presenting and Reporting of information to the management closes the Control Cycle. Reporting is considered as the last function of Accounting. Characteristically, the accountant has considered himself as successful in the following shapes:

First, as a Recorder,

Second, as a Classifier,

Third, as a Summarizer, and

Fourth, as a Reporter

Reporting is a communication process that facilitates detection and correction of mistakes. The Cost Accountant should evolve an efficient and suitable system of reporting and presentation of cost and other financial information to the management. The reporting system should be designed to meet the needs of individual concerns and should be frequently reviewed and adjusted in accordance with the requirements.

In a small business, the management keeps in close contact with the various activities of the business and the need for presenting and reporting of information may not be keenly felt. But, with the growth in the size of a business, the top management gets fewer opportunities to come in contact with the activities of the business and its control becomes more and more remote. Control is such a situation which is achieved mainly through reports. In fact, no planning and control procedure is complete without an effective system of reporting of operating results.

General Principles of Reporting [Basic Rules]

The basic rules of report presentation are listed below:

(i) **Good form and content:** A report should be in a suitable form, having a suggestive title, sub headings and paragraph division. It should be addressed to those for whom it has been prepared, it should state by whom it is submitted, be dated and duly signed. The language used in the report should be clear and unambiguous and vital information should be in eye-catching position. Contents of a Report depend upon a very large number of factors and no rules can be laid in this regard. However, the contents should be in a logical sequence like the following:

(a) Summary of the present position

(b) Courses of action, which might be taken with the expected results

(c) Recommendations and the reasons for their submission

(ii) **Promptness:** The importance of promptness in reporting cannot be over emphasized. A report must be prepared and presented before it becomes a matter of the past. In many cases, promptness in reporting is more important than any other of the general principles of reporting. Information delayed is information denied. If, for, e.g., reporting is delayed, an opportunity for action may be lost or some wrong decision may be taken in the absence of information. In order to achieve promptness in reporting, the method of collecting the data should be improved, thereby increasing the speed with which the final information becomes available. Use of mechanical devices in accounting not only helps in prompt reporting but also avoids clerical errors.

(iii) **Accuracy:** Data presented in the reports should be accurate but not extremely accurate at the cost of promptness. It is better to have approximate but timely reports than to have very accurate but late reports. The margin of error allowed depends upon the purpose for which the report is being prepared. Use of mechanical aids in accounting can prove extremely useful for ensuring the accuracy of the reports.

(iv) **Simplicity:** Reports should also possess the quality of simplicity. It should avoid technical jargon to avoid confusion. The reports should not attempt to portray very much. A series of simple statements is usually preferred to a single comprehensive one overloaded with details that little information can be gathered from it and that too with difficulty.

(v) **Comparative Figures:** When presenting information, it is often useful if additional figures are included to show a comparison either with past performance or with a predetermined target. This facilitates a better assessment of the current performance. For instance, a statement of monthly costs may have columns for "this month", "last month", "same month last year" and "average monthly costs for the year to date" with actual and budgeted figures. As an alternative to absolute comparison, reports may highlight the significant deviations from standards or past performance. Such reports take the minimum time of the recipient of the report and also enable their attention focused on significant exceptions and this is called "reporting by exception".

(vi) **Cost of Reporting:** Reporting costs money and is an expensive activity where considerable time is spent in analyzing data and preparing reports. The cost of reporting should be compared with the value of advantage gained from the report or the loss sustained by not reporting. In other words, the cost of maintaining a system of reporting should be commensurate with the benefits derived therefrom.

(vii) **Needs of different levels of Management:** Reports are prepared to meet the needs of the different levels of management. The details to be shown in the report should be designed to suit those levels for, e.g., while reporting to the top management, broad trends and significant exceptions may be summarized on plant wise basis. Reports to departmental managers should be more detailed covering the department concerned and reports to the lower management level like section supervisors should be still more detailed.

(viii) **Use of visual aids:** Visual aids like Charts, Graphs and Diagrams should be used in the reports, wherever possible. These facilitate quick grasp of the significant trends and leave a lasting impression in the mind.

Reporting to different Levels of Management

One of the general principles of reporting is that the system of reporting should be designed in such a way so as to meet the informational needs of the different levels of management. In any organization, there are three distinct levels of management - the Top Management, Middle Management and Junior or Lower or Operational Management. The contents of the reports depend upon the level to which reporting is done. For, e.g., reports for top management have to be comprehensive and concise and as we move to the lower level of management, reports have to be more detailed and specific.

The various levels of management and their reporting needs are discussed as follows:

Top Management Level: The top level management comprises of Board of Directors (B.O.D.), Managing Director or General Manager, Assistant General Manager or any other Chief Executive by whatever name called. These managers at the top level are concerned more with the formulation of business policies and working plans than in the day-to-day functioning of the business. They are, therefore, interested in the overall efficiency or inefficiency of the business as reflected in Profit and Loss Account and Balance Sheet so much so that a monthly Profit and Loss Account and Balance Sheet may be prepared and presented to them. Reports for Top Management should be summarized by totals only and the areas of shortfall and variations should be indicated to enable the top management to take action. Such reports should show the efficiency of plans, soundness of organization, etc.

Reports for the top management include the following:

(1) Periodical Profit and Loss Account and Balance Sheet
(2) Master Budget
    (A combination of all the budgets put together, i.e., comprehensive of all the budgets)
(3) Capital Budget
(4) Reports on Research and Development Activities
(5) Management Ratios – showing overall financial position
    e.g., Return on Capital Employed, Gross Profit Ratio, Liquidity Ratios, etc.
(6) Summaries of Cost of Production in various departments, showing element wise classification
(7) Plant Utilization Reports
(8) Variance Analysis Reports
(9) Report on Spoiled and Defective Work
(10) Overheads and Labor Efficiency Reports
(11) Inventory Position and Inventory Turn over
(12) Productivity Reports

Middle Level Management

This comprises of the heads of various departments such as Sales Manager, Production Manager, and Purchase Manager, etc. The main difference between the Top Management and Departmental Management is that the latter has to operate within the framework of policy laid down by the former. Thus, the Departmental Managers are primarily concerned with the execution of plans, administration of policies, directing operating supervisors and appraising their performance. The reports for this level should show the efficiency and cost data relating to their respective areas or departments.

Reports for Middle or Coordinating Level include the following:

(1) Reports on Material Price and Usage Variances
(2) Reports on Labor Rate and Efficiency Variance
(3) Overheads Variance Report
(4) Department Efficiency Reports
(5) Reports on Costs (element-wise)
(6) Idle Time Report
(7) Report on Wastage of Materials
(8) Report on Production
(9) Plant Utilization Report
(10) Report on Sales, etc.

Junior or Operating or Lower Level Management

This Level comprises Supervisors, Foreman, and Section Chiefs, etc. They are concerned with the day-to-day operations of the various sections of the business and have no say in decision making activities. The difference between the reports to this level and the reports to the top level and middle level of management is that, in the case of former, reports are likely to be in physical units only (though these may also be both in physical and monetary terms) while reports to the latter are in physical as well as monetary terms. Moreover, reports to the Junior Level are prepared by the supervisors themselves without any expert advice and therefore these may not be in a proper form.

Reports to Operating Management are detailed and specific, restricted only to the activity with which they are concerned. Examples of such Reports are:

(i) Cost of Product Report
(ii) Material consumed and Material Variance Report
(iii) Report on Scrap, Shortage and Defective Output
(iv) Labor Utilization, Labor Turnover, Idle Time, Overtime, Absenteeism and Labor Efficiency Reports
(v) Analysis of Sales by the products, lines and regions
(vi) Sales Operating Statement, etc.

FORMS OF REPORTING

Reports may be presented in the following forms:

Verbal (or Oral) – This type of reporting takes place in Group Meetings, Conferences, Seminars etc.

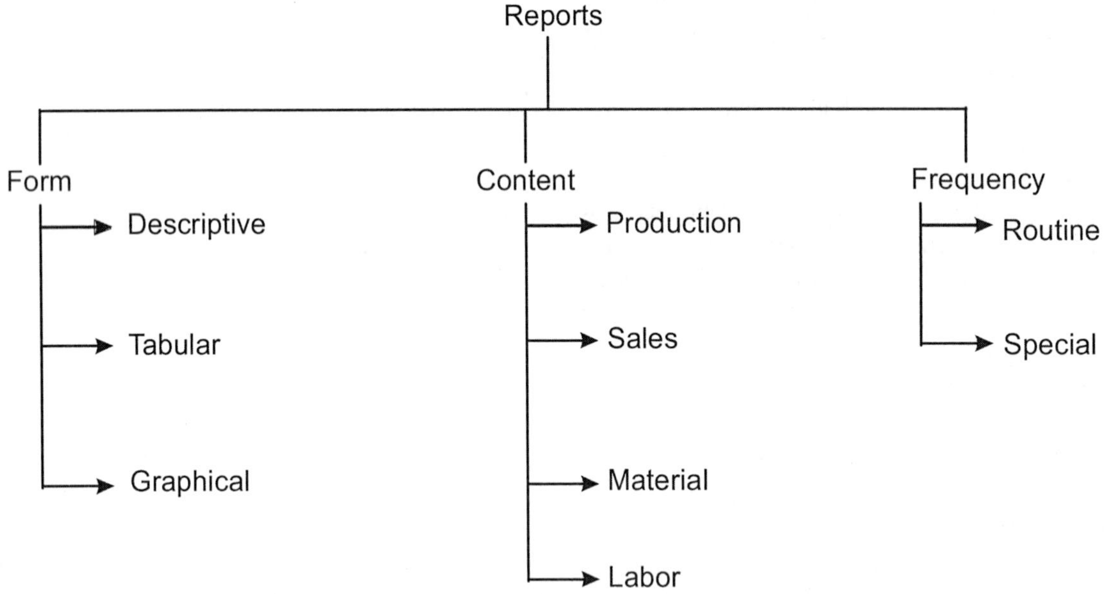

Written: This is the most common form of reporting to the management. There are various types of written reports as discussed below:

CLASSIFICATION OF REPORTS

Reports may be classified by their Form, Content and Frequency. This is shown below:

A report, to be described fully, must show its class under frequency, form and contents, e.g., a Special Tabular Sales Report, Routine Descriptive Product Report, etc.

The various types of reports shown in the above chart are described below:

According to Form

A report can be classified into Descriptive, Tabular and Graphical.

Descriptive Form: These are written in narrative or descriptive style. These should be in a proper format with suitable headings, sub headings and paragraphs. The language used is the report should be simple and clear. As these types of reports do not make use of tables and diagrams, they are less effective as compared to the reports using graphs, diagrams, etc.

Tabular Form: In this type of reports, data is presented in the form of tables. Such tables may be designed to show comparison with budgeted or past performance. This form of reporting is usefully employed in presenting cost data, profit or loss, comparative profitability, etc. Such reports are definitely more effective than descriptive reports because important figures may be written in bold type or may be underlined so as to attract the eye of the recipient.

Graphical Form: Factual information is often clearer and easier to understand if presented in graphical or pictorial form. This itself justifies the use of graphs in reports to the management. Graphic Presentation makes an otherwise dull and confusing data interesting and attractive and is considered to be the most appealing form of reporting. However, graphical form suffers from a limitation that graphs cannot be read to the degree of exactness to which they are drawn. In brief, graphical form is extremely useful because of the following reasons:

(1) Graphs and diagrams are attractive to the eyes

(2) They give a bird's eye view of the entire data and are comparatively easily understood

(3) They have a greater memorizing effect

(4) They facilitate comparison of data, e.g., actual with the standard cost, etc.

The several types of graphs and diagrams used in management reporting are given below:

***(i)* Bar Chart:** This is a very common type of chart in which bars of thick lines (vertical or horizontal) represent the magnitude of values. The longer the line, the higher is its magnitude. Vertical bars are generally preferred because they give a better look. It should be noted that it is the length of the bars that matters and not the width and therefore they have a standard width. Bar charts may be of the following types:

***(a)* Simple Bar Chart:** These charts are used to depict only one variable, e.g., comparative figures of sales, production, etc., for various periods may be shown as given below:

Year	*Production (in tons)*
2005	10,000
2006	25,000
2007	20,000
2008	22,500

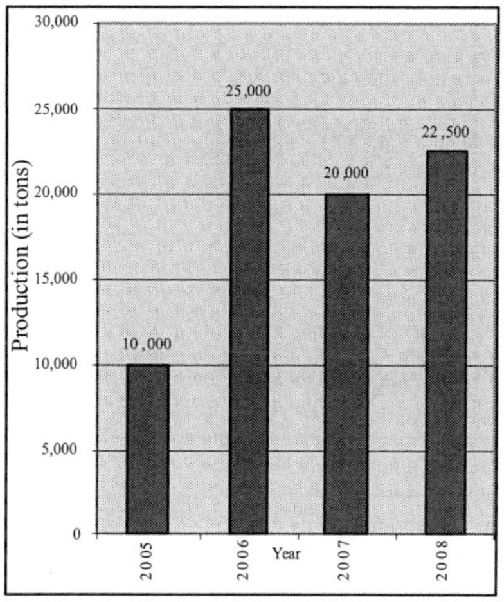

***(b)* Multiple Bar Chart:** These charts are represented by two or more sets of connected data. These are used whenever a comparison between two or more related variables is to be made over a period of time preferably each bar in a particular set should be represented by distinctive colors or designs.

Year	*Production (Rs. in Lakhs)*	*Sales (Rs. in Lakhs)*
2005	9.72	22.45
2006	15.20	26.12
2007	9.45	16.34
2008	10.80	34.20

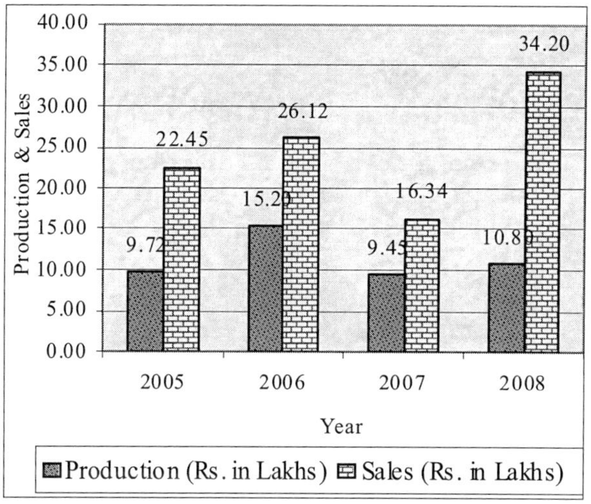

***(c)* Sub-divided Bar Charts:** These charts are used to present such data which are shown in parts or which are the totals of various subdivisions. The bars are subdivided in the ratio of components, the portion of each component being colored or shaded differently for the purpose of distinguishing between the different components. Such charts may be used in reports to show analysis of cost or sales by their constituent elements.

Year	*Product A (Rs.)*	*Product B (Rs.)*
Sales	6,00,000	6,50,000
Materials	3,50,000	3,00,000
Wages	2,00,000	2,00,000
Overheads	1,00,000	1,00,000
Profit	-50,000	50,000

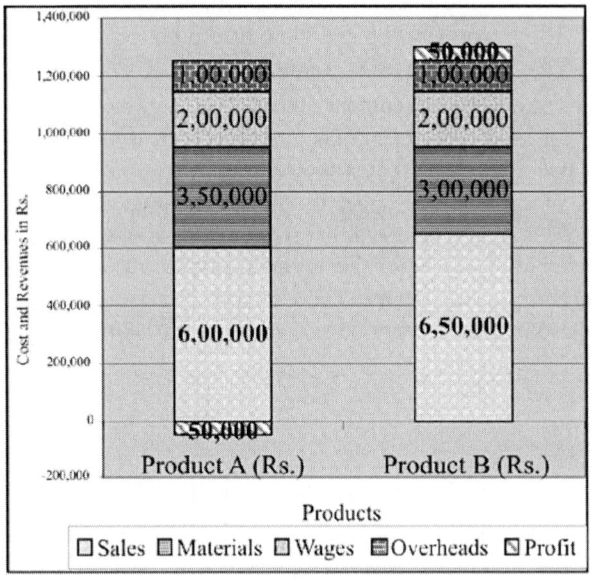

***(d)* Percentage Bar Chart:** These are common size bars where length of the bar is kept equal to 100% and segments are cut in these bars to represent the components (in percentages) of an aggregate. Such bars have an added advantage of comparison on a relative basis. [The length of the bar is always equal to 100% and it is subdivided]

Expenses & Profits	*2007*		*2008*	
	Per Unit (Rs.)	*Percentage*	*Per Unit (Rs.)*	*Percentage*
Materials	20.00	50	24.00	48
Labor	10.00	25	11.00	22
Overheads	6.00	15	9.00	18
Profit	4.00	10	6.00	12
Total	**40.00**	**100**	**50.00**	**100**

Pie or [Circular] Charts: These are like percentage charts but these are presented as segments of a circle instead of components of a bar. Such charts show the relationship of parts to the whole. The angles at the centre of a circle equal 360^0 and various segments of a circle are reduced in proportion to 360^0. Then, these segments are measured on the circle with the help of a protractor. For identification, different colors or designs may be used for different components.

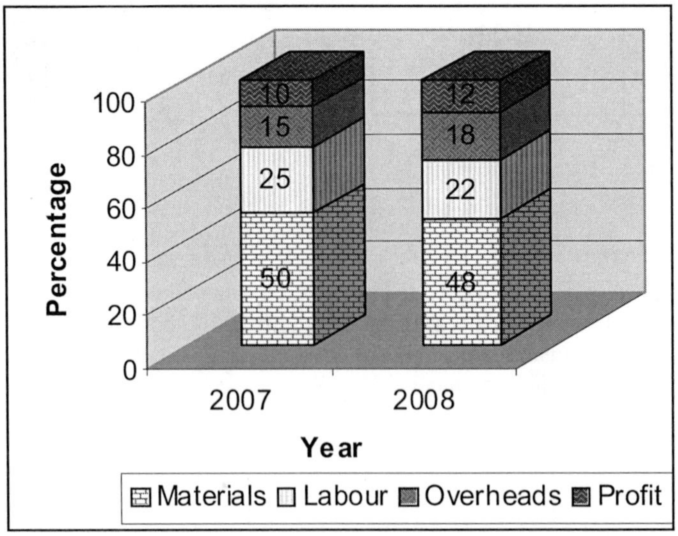

	Rs.	*Sectors*
Materials	20,000	200°
Labor	5,000	50°
Factory Overheads	5,000	50°
Office Overheads	5,000	50°
Selling and Distribution Overheads	1,000	10°
Total	36,000	360°

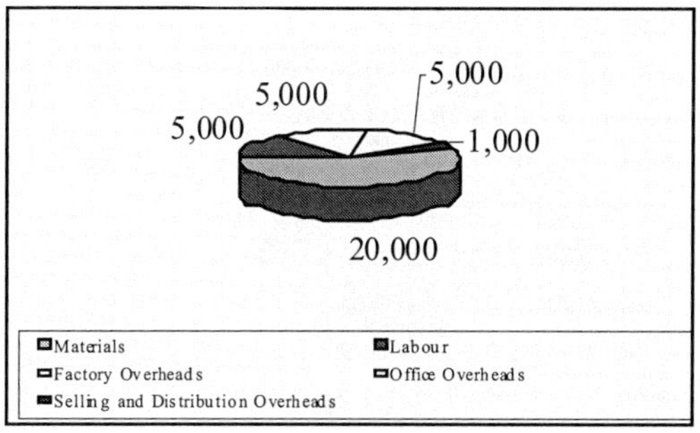

The limitation of a pie chart is that, it is less effective than the bar diagrams for accurate reading and interpretation particularly, when the difference between the components is very small.

Gnatt Chart (Progress Chart): This is a variant of the bar chart in which bars are drawn horizontally. The Gnatt charts are widely used in the industry for facilitating a comparison of the actual performance with that of the budgeted. This can be differentiated in the chart through thick and thin lines or *vice-versa*. It is used mostly for comparing the accomplished targets as against the planned targets.

'Z' Chart or Zee Chart: This chart depicts three curves on a single graph and on completion; these 3 curves take the shape similar to that of the letter 'Z'. This is the reason why it is called a 'Z' chart. The 3 curves display:

(a) The current figures for the period concerned

(b) Cumulative amounts to the latest date

(c) The moving annual total or 'trends'.

Silhouette Charts: In these charts, a particular year or period is taken as the base period. The value of the item concerning the base period is taken to be zero and through this a line parallel to the 'X' axis is drawn. It is called the base line or reference line. Any value more than the base value is plotted above the base line and any value less than this base value is plotted below the base line. Then, these plotted points are joined together. The area between the base line and the joint line is shaded with dark color. This makes the presentation of information very attractive.

Control Charts: This chart was originated by Dr. W.A. Shewhart. It is a device used for the control of progresses. It helps in revealing the variations from the established standard. It consists of the following horizontal lines.

(1) Reference Line (Central Line): It indicates the designed standard

(2) Upper Control Limit Line (UCL)

(3) Lower Control Limit Line (LCL)

The control is done through two charts *viz.*, the mean chart and the range chart. As the process proceeds, mean and a small range of sample data are plotted on the graph. If the point plotted falls within the control limits, there is nothing to worry. If this point falls outside the control limits, it is considered to be dangerous. In case, plotted points are moving towards a particular limit, machine may be stopped and re-set to avoid the out of control situation.

Break Even Charts: These charts show the cost-volume profit relationship indicating the BEP, i.e., a point at which sales revenue is equal to the total cost where there is no profit or no loss.

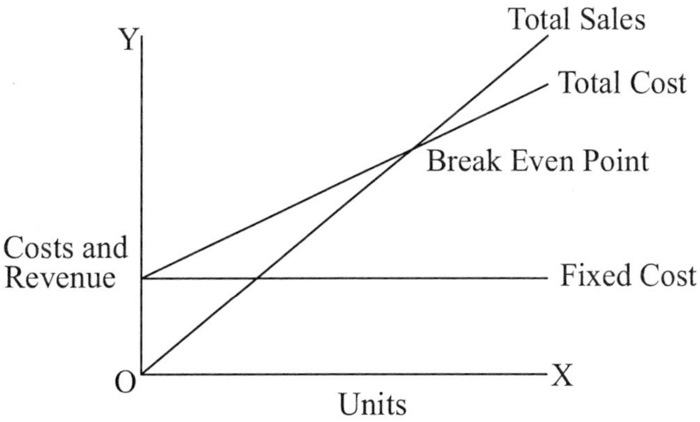

According to Contents

According to the contents, Reports are divided into reports on Material, Labor, Overheads, Reports to Production Departments and Sales Departments.

Reports on Materials

(i) Material Productivity Report
(ii) Purchase Department Costs
(iii) Material Price Trends
(iv) Normal and Abnormal Loss of Material
(v) Inventory Position Report
(vi) Supply Position Report
(vii) Ratio of Material Consumed to Cost of Product
*(viii)*Material Cost Variances, etc.,

Reports on Labor

(i) Idle Time Report
(ii) Labor Absenteeism Report
(iii) Labor Productivity Report
(iv) Labor Turnover Report
(v) Report on Accidents
(vi) Labor Cost Variances
(vii) Overtime and Shift Working Report
*(viii)*Ratio of Direct Wages to Cost of Production
(ix) Recruitment and Training Cost Reports, etc.

Reports on Overheads

(i) Report on Overhead Absorption Ratio
(ii) Overhead Variances Report
(iii) Administrative Overheads Report
(iv) Selling and Distribution Cost Reports
(v) Research and Development Cost Reports
(vi) Ratio of Overheads to Cost of Production
(vii) Fixed and Equitable Overhead Reports
*(viii)*Repairs and Maintenance Cost Reports
(ix) Power Cost Report, etc.

Reports to Production Department

(i) Report on Material Consumption
(ii) Report on Labor Cost
(iii) Report on Overhead Absorption
(iv) Cost of Production of Jobs
(v) Cost Variances – Material, Labor and Overheads
(vi) Labor Utilization, Idle Time, Overtime with Causes
(vii) Machine Utilization and Idle Capacity
*(viii)*Reports on Labor Turnover and Absenteeism
(ix) Spoilage, Defective Work, Scrap and Waste
(x) Material and Labor Cost/unit
(xi) Control Ratios – ratio of Various Elements of Cost to Total Product Cost.

Reports to Sales Department

(i) Sales Analysis – Productwise, Areawise, Salesman Wise, etc.
(ii) Sales Variances
(iii) Selling and Distribution Costs
(iv) Market Research Activities
(v) Reports on Bad Debts and Credit Control

(vi) Cash Collection Reports
(vii) Warehousing and Showroom Expenses Report
(viii) Advertisement Cost Reports
(ix) Analysis of Orders needed, Executed and in Hand
(x) Ratios like Selling Overheads its Cost of Sales, etc.

According to Frequency of Reporting

Reports may be grouped into Routine Reports and Special Reports. Routine reports are submitted to the management at predetermined time schedules. It is a usual practice to keep a time schedule for release of such reports. In many cases, routine reports are printed or cyclostyled, leaving blank columns to be filled in. The executive in-charge of the reporting should keep a programme control chart and enter therein the reports released from time to time. Examples of routine reports are variance reports, inventory position reports, idle time and overtime reports, etc.

Special Reports

Certain problems may very often come up in businesses which requires investigation. Results of investigation and measures suggested are presented through Special Reports. The form of these reports depends upon the nature of the problem in question. The interval at which Routine or Periodic Report should be submitted should be specifically laid down but, Special Reports can be submitted only after proper investigation has been made. No specific matters can be laid down for such investigations.

Special Reports might be required for the following matters:

(1) Problems of capital investment
(2) Effect of surplus capacity on cost of product
(3) Delays in production and its effect on cost of product
(4) Problems of make or buy decisions
(5) Problems of price fixation
(6) Effect of change in the product methods, systems and designs
(7) Effect of market research
(8) Starting new department or installing new plants
(9) Closing down a particular department
(10) The most suitable method of raising long-term capital
(11) Improving the profitability of the different products
(12) Study of the economic changes
(13) Study of the change in the Government policy and its effect on cost and profit
(14) Schemes regarding the cost reduction
(15) Financial position of the organization
(16) Selling the product below the cost during temporary crisis
(17) Cost of keeping excessive stocks of raw material, finished goods and losses due to shortages
(18) Problem of labor turnover and its effects
(19) Effect of sales promotion schemes
(20) Welfare schemes
(21) Material price changes
(22) Stocks turn over
(23) Cost of training
(24) Under and/or over absorption of overheads
(25) Depreciation of assets
(26) Occurrence of accidents, etc.

Summary of reporting practices observed in 30 leading companies and the trends as given by NAA Research Series No. 28. (NAA Bulletin, Vol. 36)

(1) To reduce the figure presented to the management (particularly the top management) to a minimum consistent with the needs of the individual recipient. The principal techniques to accomplish this are:
(a) Begin each report with a summary
(b) Concentrate attention on the items requiring action
(c) Reduce the number of figures/digits to be remembered or compared

(d) Use a variety of devices to emphasize significant points

(2) To produce reports in a clear, attractive and easily readable form. A variety of techniques are used to achieve this including avoidance of closely packed masses of figures, use of color in the reports and standardizing terminology, arrangement of report content and format of reports.

(3) To stress timeliness of information particularly where the figures measure current performance or indicate a need for current action.

(4) To utilize as far as possible terminology and language which is familiar to the recipients of reports and to avoid technical accounting terms where non-technical terms can be used to convey the same meaning.

(5) To use a variety of communication media to the effectiveness of presentation and to improve management's overall understanding of the information presented.

(6) To accept responsibility for the analysis and interpretation of accounting figure by including in accounting reports the comments designed to bring out significance of the figure of the recipients of the reports. The analysis is frequently in the form of a letter or written comments on or accompanying the report.

Another classification of Reports is according to the users', i.e., the person to whom reporting is done. Accordingly, Reports may be classified into External Reports and Internal Reports.

On the basis of users → Reports for external use
→ Reports for internal use

External Reports

Strictly speaking, the enterprise is not answerable to anyone other than to, its proprietors – shareholders in a company, but in reality, it is the management that asks for accounts. However, in an organized society, reporting to shareholders has assumed a wider dimension. The annual reports to shareholders are public documents. Copies of such reports are to be filed with the Registrar of companies as well as with stock exchanges. In the interest of general understanding, the final statements of accounts are expected to conform to certain minimum standards of disclosure and to disclose certain basic details. In India, this is laid down by schedule VI in the Companies Act. It is thus the Government which tries to protect the investing public from mischievous management. In the U.S.A., the quality of the final reporting practices of manufacturing concern has stemmed from four principal sources.

(i) Gradual recognition by some managers of their public recognition

(ii) Increasing criticism of management accounting and reporting practices by a number of influential groups and individuals outside the management class.

(iii) Direct Federal Government Legislation such as the Securities Act 1933-34

(iv) Recognition by the American accounting profession and acceptance by the business community of some accounting and reporting standards.

Regarding development of external reporting in U.K., the Jenkins Committee on Company Law says "the recommendations on accounting principles periodically issued by the Institute of Chartered Accountants in England and Wales to their members have already done much to ensure that the standards of accounting are reasonably uniform and constantly rising. These recommendations are based on close and constant study of the relevant problems which are ever changing and primarily it is to the initiative of the professional association that we must look if the general principles of the Act are to effectively apply to practice."

In India however, no specific individual or body can claim for the rise in the standards and content of external reporting. Company Legislations followed the pattern of corresponding English legislation. English practices came to be adopted in India too. Pact in respect of final accounts and information contained therein, the Indian Law has for long been ahead of the law in the U.K. For this, the Government in pre-independence days deserves the credit.

External reports are those which are prepared for external parties. These reports are:

(a) **Annual Accounts for shareholders:** It is obligatory to send to the shareholders of a company the annual accounts (Income Statement, Balance Sheet and Directors' Report). Adequate efforts have been made in western countries to improve the quantity and quality of information to be included in such reports.

(b) **Reports to Government Authorities:** In our country, it has been made obligatory to send a copy of annual accounts to the Registrar of companies. In addition, Sales Tax Returns, IT Returns, Excise Duty Returns are to be prepared and submitted to several authorities.

(c) **Reports to Stock Exchange:** If the shares of the company are listed on Stock Exchange, a report in the prescribed form has to be submitted to the Stock Exchange authorities and a copy of the annual accounts has also to be sent to them.

(d) **Report to Credit Institutions:** A report has to be sent to the Credit Institutions from whom credit facilities are to be availed.

INTERNAL REPORTS

As opposed to External Reporting (published annual reports of companies); Internal Reports refer to the reports to the various levels of management. These are not public documents. They generally do not have to conform to any statutory standards. They are basically vehicles for carrying information to the various levels of management. Such reports are prepared keeping in view the recipient of the reports – his accomplishments, his time for scanning the reports, the purpose to be served by the reports, etc.

Internal Reports are those which are prepared for the use of the internal parties like different levels of management, employees, etc. These are not public documents and do not conform to any statutory standards.

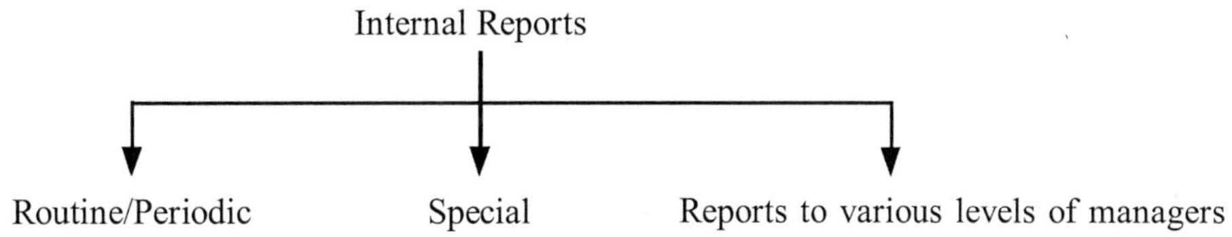

Internal Reports can be divided into Routine and Special Reports. Routine Reports are sent when a system of control exists. To activate the control function, periodically, reports are sent to the various levels of management. It is the feedback because; the basic data for this information had gone from the recipient. It is sent back to him in a different shape. The periodicity and information and details of the reports depend upon the various levels of management. The report should be so framed as to bring out significant information more prominently by special colors on special type of print as there is a tendency to neglect the routine reports by the recipient because of their routine nature.

Special Reports are required for special purposes. Matters which require treatment in Special Reports are political and economical development at home and abroad; Results of market analysis and sales research including methods of design, attitudes and possible moves by competitors; Material Reports by the purchase department on purchasing problems and by the cost accountant on the implications of price movements; Technological developments in the industries which may offer competition; Patent rights and changes in patent laws; Information about competitive products; Comparative performance and cost of existing product plant and more up to date equipment; Wages and other costs connected with labor, Industrial relations, taxation, trade association matters; Important matters revealed by costing system and the results in terms of costs of contemplated alternative lines of action; Reports by the secretary on company matters and legal obligation; Reports by consultants and outside advisers on financial, commercial and management problems including recommendations by the auditor.

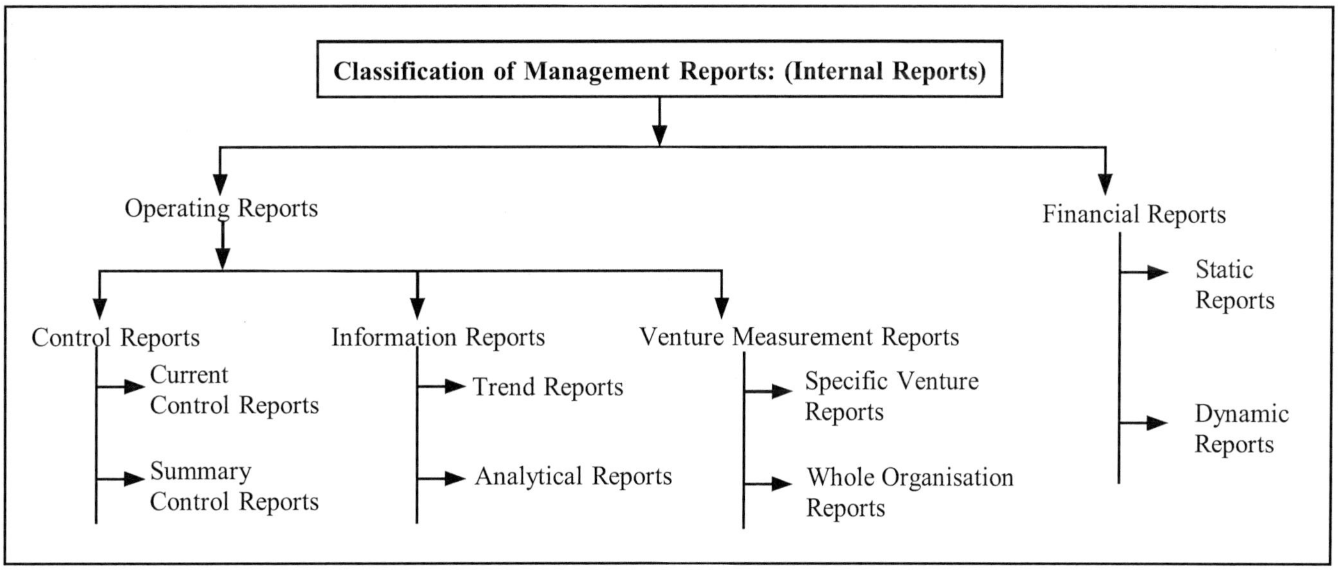

Operating Reports

These reports provide information about the operations of the company at different functional levels. These reports are classified into Control, Information and Venture Measurement Reports.

Control Reports

On the basis of Control, the reports can be classified into Current Control and Summary Control Reports. **Current Control Reports** are intended to spot deviations from the budgeted performance without loss of time, so that prompt control action can be taken. They relate to a small fragment of a whole period. **Summary Control Reports** are intended to summarize the deviations from objectives over a certain period so that control can be initiated at higher levels. Current control reports relate to deviations in a short period of time and require actions at lower levels only.

Information Reports

These Reports provide useful information which will enable programme and policy formulation for the future. **Trend reports** provide information in a comparative fashion over a period of time. It will clearly depict the direction of events over a period of time. Graphical representations can be effectively used in trend reports. **Analytical Reports** provide information in a classified manner about composition of certain results so that one can identify specific factors in the overall total. For example, the composition of various elements of cost in the total cost of a product can be depicted. This can be done by a histogram with markings for each element.

Venture Measurement Reports

These reports are intended to communicate in a summarized form the results of operations. These may be located in respect of any specific venture or of the organization as a whole. The reports in either case will cover a specific period.

Financial Reports

These reports provide information about the financial position as on specific dates or the movement of finance during a specified period. Balance sheet is a Static Report whereas funds flow statement is Dynamic Report. Cash flow statement and statement showing the financial positions are example of dynamic reports as compared to the budget.

Review of Reports

It is necessary to constantly review the utility of reports so that no executive is starved of information and no one is fed with unwanted data. A report should not be a burden to the sender and a nuisance to the receiver. It is necessary to constantly review the utility of the organization reports through the processes of self-examination. Each executive should ask certain questions about the reports that he receives. The following are the questions:

(1) Do I want this data?
(2) Are they relevant to my position?
(3) Do they come in time?
(4) Do they come at the right frequency?
(5) Are they accurate enough?
(6) Is their presentation in the best form for me?

Management Accounting and Information Reporting System is information for management which should be relevant, comprehensive and accurate. The system to deal with data-input should be flexible to ensure a realistic response to the needs of the management and changing business environment. It is the duty of the Management Accountant to evolve a suitable system of reporting cost, financial and non-financial information relating to the various activities in a quick, correct and efficient manner.

A sound MIS ensures:

(a) Right information at the right time, to the right person and in the right manner
(b) Regularity in the periodicity of information flow
(c) Information geared towards aiding management decision for planning and control by highlighting control areas and suggesting control actions as well.
(d) Screening all information at the point of transmission in order to select the relevant details and reject all irrelevant details, keeping an eye on the diverse needs of the different levels of management.
(e) A built in system of link-up and follow-up.

Thus, there should be a proper reporting system in any organization for its success.

SUMMARY

Cost presentation plays a very important role in achieving maximization of profit through cost control techniques. Cost information may be presented and communicated to the management through Reports, Charts and Graphs. Reporting is considered as the last function of Accounting.

Reporting is a communication process that facilitates detection and correction of mistakes. The Cost Accountant should evolve an efficient and suitable system of reporting and presentation of cost and other financial information to the management. The reporting system should be designed to meet the needs of the individual concerns and should be frequently reviewed and adjusted in accordance with the requirements.

One of the general principles of reporting is that the system of reporting should be designed in such a way so as to meet the informational needs of the different levels of management. In any organization, there are three distinct levels of management - the Top Management, Middle Management and Junior or Lower or Operational Management. The contents of the reports depend upon the level to which reporting is done.

Reports may be presented in Verbal (or Oral) form or in written form. Reports may be classified by their Form, Content and Frequency. Reports may be grouped into Routine Reports and Special Reports.

It is necessary to constantly review the utility of reports so that no executive is starved of information and no one is fed with unwanted data. A report should not be a burden to the sender and a nuisance to the receiver. It is necessary to constantly review the utility of organization reports through the processes of self-examination.

Management Accounting and Information Reporting System is information for management which should be relevant, comprehensive and accurate. Thus, there should be a proper reporting system in any organization for its success.

Glossary

- **Reporting:** is a communication process that facilitates detection and correction of mistakes.
- **Bar Chart:** is a very common type of chart in which bars of thick lines (vertical or horizontal) represent the magnitude of values. The longer the line, the higher is its magnitude.
- **Sub-divided Bar Charts:** are used to present such data which are shown in parts or which are the totals of various subdivisions.
- **Pie or [Circular] Charts:** are like percentage charts but these are presented as segments of a circle instead of components of a bar.
- **Z' Chart or Zee Chart:** depicts three curves on a single graph and on completion, these 3 curves take the shape similar to that of the letter 'Z'.
- **Control Chart:** was originated by Dr. W.A. Shewhart. It is a device used for the control of progresses. It helps in revealing the variations from the established standard.
- **Break Even and Profit Volume Charts:** show the cost-volume profit relation ship indicating the BEP, i.e., a point at which sales revenue is equal to the total cost where there is no profit or no loss.
- **Venture Measurement Reports:** are intended to communicate in a summarized form the results of operations.
- **Financial Reports:** provide information about the financial position as on specific dates or the movement of finance during a specified period.
- **Management Accounting and Information Reporting System:** is information for management which should be relevant, comprehensive and accurate.

Questions

(1) What do you mean by Reporting?

(2) What are the basic rules of Reporting?

(3) Explain the various informational needs of different levels of Management.

(4) Give a brief description of various types of Reports.

(5) How do you classify the Reports according to Contents?

(6) Explain the classification of Reports according to the users of Reports.

(7) Classify the Internal Reports.

(8) What is the need for Review of Reports?

❑❑❑

36

Responsibility Accounting

Objectives

The objectives of the study are to:

- Understand the meaning of Responsibility Accounting
- Know the steps/process of implementation of Responsibility Accounting
- Learn the importance of different Centres and the reports
- Evaluate the Divisional Performance

Introduction

An organization is a group of persons who work together for one or more goals or objectives. It consists of human beings. An organisation has one or more leaders, called managers. They decide the goals of the organisation and communicate the same to the members of the organization. A manager can supervise only a limited number of subordinates. A manager should take responsibility on behalf of subordinates. The following organisation chart can disclose the responsibilities of each manager of the organisation.

Organisation Chart

Board of Directors of the company is responsible to the shareholders for the overall conduct of the company's affairs. General Manager reports to the Board of Directors regarding the functioning of all the departments. Functional managers are responsible for the activities going on in their departments. Production manager is responsible for producing budgeted quantities within the specified budgeted cost. Marketing manager is responsible for increasing the revenue by securing orders from the customers. Personnel Manager is responsible to recruit right people in the organisation. Finance manager is responsible to raise funds for the organisation from the cheapest sources and invest in better alternatives.

These functional managers are responsible in the sense that they are held accountable for the work done by their organisation units.

Financial Performance of the organisation can be measured by the whole organisation taken as one unit or by every division taken as one unit. For measuring the performance of the organisation as a whole, Financial Accounting will suffice. Standard Costing, Budgetary Control, Marginal Costing and Responsibility Accounting are useful to the management for controlling the costs.

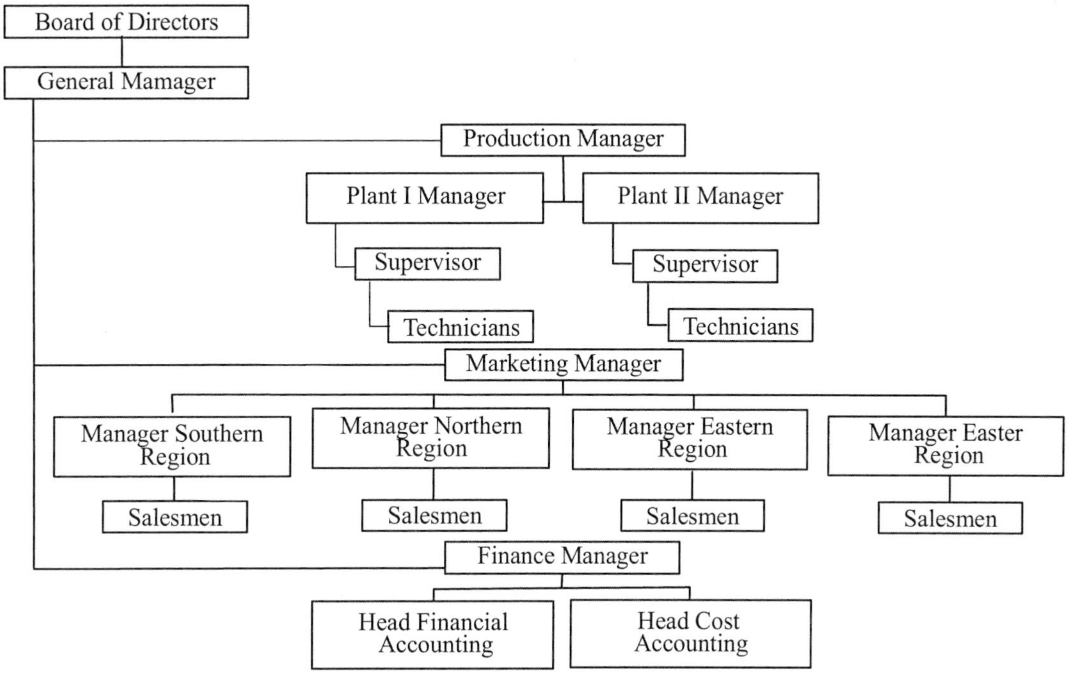

In case of Standard Costing, Budgetary Control, and Marginal Costing, emphasis is on the devices of control and not on those who use such devices whereas, in case of Responsibility Accounting, the emphasis is on men rather than on machines. Responsibility Accounting is a system of control, where, responsibility is assigned for the control of costs. The persons are made responsible for the control of costs. The responsibility of the persons at the Responsibility Centres is to find out the reasons for variance between the budgeted and the actual performance.

MEANING

The term 'Responsibility Accounting' means an accounting process which reports as to how well managers of responsibility centres have fulfilled their responsibility. It is closely related to the goal of controllability. Those elements in a certain area of activity which are controllable are identified and a person is given the responsibility for managing such elements. Thus, individuals in an organization are made responsible for only those elements which can be controlled by them.

In Responsibility Accounting, the areas of responsibility are defined for which managers are held responsible. They are charged with only those items over which they can exercise direct control and are held responsible only for those items. Here, the managers should actively participate in establishing the goals or budgets which are attainable with efficient and effective performance, against which their performance is measured. Responsibility Centre managers should try to accomplish the budgets established for their areas of responsibility and control reports should contain significant information related to each area of responsibility.

DEFINITIONS

The following definitions are given by various authors.

According to **Institute of Cost and Works Accountants of India**, Responsibility Accounting is "a system of Management Accounting under which accountability is established according to the responsibility delegated to various levels of management and a management information and reporting system instituted to give adequate feedback in terms of the delegated responsibility.

Under this system, divisions or units of an organisation under a specified authority in a person are developed as Responsibility Centres and evaluated individually for their performance."

Charles, T. Horngreen says "Responsibility Accounting is a system of accounting that recognizes various Responsibility Centres throughout the organisation and reflects the plans and actions of each of these centres by assigning particular revenues and costs to the one having the pertinent responsibility. It is also called Profitability Accounting and Activity Accounting."

According to **Anthony and Reece**, "Responsibility Accounting is that type of Management Accounting that collects and reports both planned and actual accounting information in terms of Responsibility Centres."

According to **David Fanning**, Responsibility Accounting "is a system or mechanism for controlling the wider freedom of action that executive's decision Centre managers in other words are given by senior management and for holding those executives responsible for the consequences of their decisions."

From the above definitions, the following characteristics of the Responsibility Accounting emerge:

(1) The organization is divided into various Responsibility Centres

(2) The objectives of responsibilities for each Centre are set

(3) The Cost Centres are put under certain persons and adequate authority is delegated to them

(4) The actual performance is recorded

(5) The variance between Budgeted and Actual figures is ascertained and the concerned executives are held responsible

Responsibility Accounting focuses on Responsibility Centres. The managers of different Activity Centres are responsible for controlling the costs of their centres. The performance is constantly compared to the standards set and this process is very useful in exercising cost controls.

Process of Implementation of Responsibility Accounting

Responsibility Accounting is used as a control device. Responsibility Accounting helps the management in achieving organizational objectives. The following steps are involved in Responsibility accounting.

(1) Responsibility Centres

The organization is divided into various Responsibility Centres. Each Responsibility Centre is put under the charge of a responsibility manager. These managers are responsible for the performance of their divisions.

(2) Setting the Objectives

The objectives are set in consultation with the managers of the Responsibility Centres. This helps to get the full information from the managers about their departments. The goals of the organization must be properly communicated to their subordinates, so that they will help in achieving the goals.

(3) Recording Actual Performance

The actual performance of each Responsibility Centre is measured and recorded. It helps in future for comparison with the standards.

(4) Comparison

The actual performance is compared with the objectives set for Responsibility Centres. It helps in assessing the work of these centres.

(5) Variance

The variance is ascertained by comparing the actual perfomance with the standards set. Variance means the difference between standard objectives and actual performance. This variance may be favorable or unfavorable. If actual performance is less than the standard objectives, it is unfavorable performance. In case, actual performance is more than the standard objectives, it is a favorable performance.

(6) Action

Timely action is taken and necessary corrective measures are initiated on the basis of the variance so that the work does not suffer in future.

Responsibility Centres

A small firm may possibly be managed by a small group of people. But the activities of a large firm are difficult to be supervised by an individual or by a small group of people. For effective control of its activities, a large firm is divided into some segments like divisions, departments and so on. Each segment has certain activities to perform; its manager is assigned specific authority and responsibility to carryout those activities and is held responsible for his actions and decisions affecting those activities.

Process

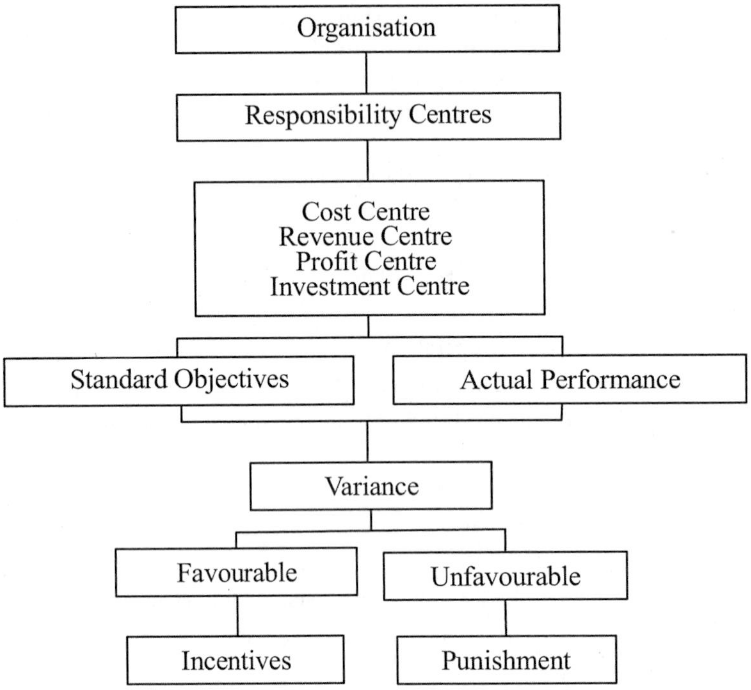

The units of an organisation for the purpose of control are called Responsibility Centres. A Responsibility Centre is a unit of an organisation under the supervision of a manager, who has the responsibility for the activities of that unit.

According to Anthony and Reece, "A Responsibility Centre is like an engine in that it has inputs, which are physical quantities of material, hours of various types of labour and a variety of services; it works with these resources usually; working capital and fixed assets are also required. As a result of this work, it produces outputs, which are classified either as goods, if they are tangible or as services, if they are intangible. These goods or services go either to other Responsibility Centres within the company or to customers in the outside world."

According to the above definition, Responsibility Centres have the following characteristics.

(a) Each Responsibility Centre has inputs like material, labour and services

(b) Responsibility Centre produces outputs – goods or services

(c) Responsibility Centres require working capital and fixed assets

(d) Goods produced in one Responsibility Centre are transferred to another Responsibility Centre within the company or to the outside customers.

Responsibility Accounting is used to measure both inputs and outputs. Inputs of Responsibility Centre are measured as costs. Any input of the Centre can be expressed in monetary terms. Outputs i.e. goods and services are measured as revenues by Responsibility Centres. It is easy to measure the value of revenue when goods or services are sold to the outsiders. But it is difficult to measure when outputs are used within the organisation. A number of approaches can be followed for this purpose. Usually, the methods suggested are: *(a)* Market Price *(b)* Cost Based Price *(c)* Full Cost Price.

Responsibility Centres, for planning and control purposes, are classified into the following classes:

(1) Cost Centre

(2) Revenue Centre

(3) Profit Centre

(4) Investment Centre

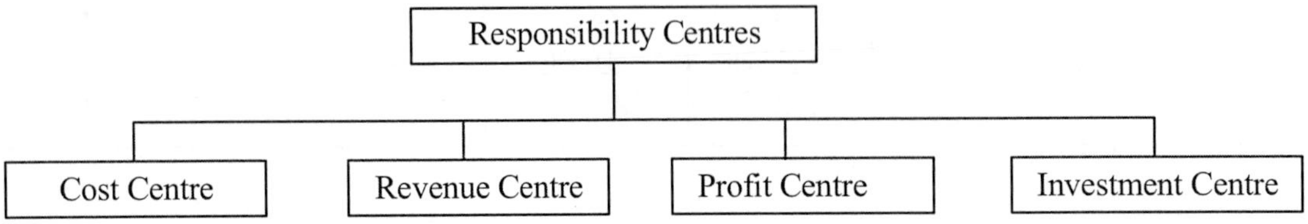

(1) Cost Centre

A Cost Centre is the Centre where inputs are measured in monetary terms. In Cost Centre of responsibility, the accounting system records only the cost incurred in the centre. Performance of Cost Centre is measured by the monetary terms of input only, where, cost of operating the division is directly traceable to it.

Performance of the Cost Centre manager will be judged on the basis of the cost incurred in his centre. Compare actual inputs to some predetermined level that represents efficient utilization. The variance between the actual and the budget would be indicative of the efficiency of the division.

Examples of Cost Centres are Production Department, Service Department, Marketing Department, Sales Region and Single Sales Representative.

Benefits of Cost Centre

Through the Cost Centre, the following benefits are available:

- Each Cost Centre can control the cost
- Cost Centre increases the efficiency of the operation
- The cost per unit of the product would be indicative of the efficiency of the department
- A comparison of the actual number of units produced with the units produced in previous period leads to improvement in the performance.

Limitations of Cost Centre

The following are the limitations of the Cost Centre

- It ignores output measured in financial terms
- Cost Centre manager is not responsible for common costs, which is common in the organisation.
- The efficiency and effectiveness of the Responsibility Centre cannot be measured, if elements in Cost Centre are not measured in monetary terms.

Illustration 1

The following information is available relating to the cost of production of X Limited:

Cost Item		*Amount (Rs.)*
Direct Material		80,000
Direct Labor		52,000
Overheads		
Supervision	15,200	
Indirect labor	26,400	
Supplies	4,800	
Other Overheads	9,600	56,000
		1,88,000

It may be assumed that X Ltd. has four departments – two production (A and B) and two service (C and D). Assume that the overheads are absorbed by 2:3:4:3 ratio. The company's estimated cost for these departments are Rs. 1,20,000, 40,000, 18,000, and 15,000 respectively. Production Departments share the material and labor in the ratio of 8:2.

Measure the performance of departments of X Limited.

Solution

Responsibility Centre

		Production Departments		*Service Departments*	
Particulars	*Total* Rs.	*A* Rs.	*B* Rs.	*C* Rs.	*D* Rs.
Direct Material (8:2)	80,000	64,000	16,000	—	—
Direct Labor (8:2)	52,000	41,600	10,400	—	—
Prime Cost (A)	1,32,000	1,05,600	26,400		

Particulars	Total Rs.	Production Departments A Rs.	Production Departments B Rs.	Service Departments C Rs.	Service Departments D Rs.
Factory Overheads					
Supervision (2:3:4:3)	15,200	2,533	3,800	5,067	3,800
Indirect Labor (2:3:4:3)	26,400	4,400	6,600	8,800	6,600
Supplies (2:3:4:3)	4,800	800	1,200	1,600	1,200
Other Overheads (2:3:4:3)	9,600	1,600	2,400	3,200	2,400
Total Overheads (B)	56,000	9,333	14,000	18,667	14,000
Total Cost (A + B)	**1,88,000**	**1,14,933**	**40,400**	**18,667**	**14,000**
Estimated Cost	**1,93,000**	**1,20,000**	**40,000**	**18,000**	**15,000**
Variance	**5,000 F**	**5,067 F**	**400 A**	**667 A**	**1,000 F**

(2) Revenue Centre

It is a segment of the organization which is primarily responsible for generating sales revenue. A Revenue Centre manager does not have control over the cost or the investment in assets, but generally has control over some of the expenses of the marketing department. This centre's performance is measured by comparing the actual revenue with the budgeted revenue and the actual marketing expenses with that of the budgeted marketing expenses. Examples of Revenue Centre are Marketing Manager of a product line or an individual sales representative.

(3) Profit Centre

Responsibility Centres may have both inputs and outputs. The inputs are taken as costs and outputs are taken as revenues. Managers of profit centres have control over both the costs and the revenues because profit is the difference between the revenues and the costs. The main purpose of a Profit Centre is to earn profit. Management decides to make a Responsibility Centre as a Profit Centre when it thinks that the outputs are capable of being measured in monetary terms and that it would be beneficial to do so.

A division of the company which produces and markets the products may be called a Profit Centre.

Benefits of Profit Centre

- A Profit Centre provides more effective assessment of the manager's performance
- A Profit Centre manager is motivated to make decisions about inputs and outputs
- There is accountability for the transfer of goods to another department or selling to the outsiders.

Illustration 2

Raymonds Limited employs a Budgetary Control System and measures its performance on segmented basis of its product line Divisions A and B. The budgeted and actual sales figures for the month of March are as follows:

Division	*Budgeted*		*Actual*	
	Units	*Amount Rs.*	*Units*	*Amount Rs.*
A	25,000	2,50,000	27,000	2,70,000
B	60,000	3,00,000	60,000	3,60,000

The standard unit controllable variable costs are Rs. 3 and 2 for the products A and B respectively. But actual variable manufacturing costs during March were Rs. 90,000 and Rs. 1,25,000 for the products A and B respectively. The firm's budgeted controllable fixed costs for the month are Rs. 25,000 each for the products A and B, whereas, the actual amounted to Rs. 24,000 for product A and Rs. 28,000 for product B.

The attributable budgeted segment costs are: Rs. 45,000 and Rs. 70,000 for the products A and B respectively but actual costs incurred were Rs. 50,000 and Rs. 75,000 for A and B respectively. The common costs are assumed to be Rs. 55,000 to be apportioned on the basis of segment sales revenue.

From the above information, prepare a Performance Evaluation Report, if the Raymonds Ltd. employs Profit Centre basis of Divisional Performance Measurement.

Solution

Performance Evaluation Report

(Rs. in thousands)

Particulars	*Product A*			*Product B*			*Total*		
	Budget Rs.	*Actual Rs.*	*Variance Rs.*	*Budget Rs.*	*Actual Rs.*	*Variance Rs.*	*Budget Rs.*	*Actual Rs.*	*Variance Rs.*
Sales Revenue	250	270	20F	300	360	60F	550	630	80F
Less: Controllable Variable Cost	75	90	15A	120	125	5A	195	215	20A
Controllable Contribution Margin	**175**	**180**	**5F**	**180**	**235**	**55F**	**355**	**415**	**60F**
Less: Controllable Fixed Cost	25	24	1F	25	28	3A	50	52	2A
Controllable Segment Margin	**150**	**156**	**6F**	**155**	**207**	**52F**	**305**	**363**	**58F**
Less: Attributable Segment Cost	45	50	5A	70	75	5A	115	125	10A
Segment Profit Contribution	**105**	**106**	**1F**	**85**	**132**	**47F**	**190**	**238**	**48F**
Less: Common Costs (250:300 – Sales Ratio)	25	25		30	30		55	55	
Net Income	**80**	**81**	**1F**	**55**	**102**	**47F**	**135**	**183**	**48F**

(4) Investment Centre

It is a division of an organization wherein its performance is assessed by considering not only its costs and revenues but also by establishing a relationship between the profit (difference between revenues and costs), capital invested or employed and revenue. It is responsible for both profits and investments. When only top management takes the decision regarding the capital expenditure decision, i.e., capital budgeting decision, there will be only one Investment Centre covering the entire organization. Whereas, when such decision making is delegated to the divisional heads, there will be more number of Investment Centres. Thus, the number of Investment Centres will be fewer compared to Profit or Cost Centres. Therefore, all the Investments Centres are normally Profit Centres and Cost Centres but not all Profit Centres are Investment Centres.

The performance of a division is measured by establishing a relationship between its net income and total capital employed in that division.

Illustration 3

Division A and B are both considering an outlay on new investment projects.

Particular	*Division A*	*Division B*
Investment Accodingly (Rs.)	2,00,000	2,00,000
Net return on the new investment (Rs.)	32,000	32,000
Current ROI	18%	11%

The company's cost of capital is 13%. Should the project be accepted or rejected?

Solution

$$\text{ROI on New Investment} = \frac{\text{Net Return}}{\text{New Investment}} \times 100$$

$$\text{Division A} = \frac{32,000}{2,00,000} \times 100 = 16\%$$

$$\text{Division B} = \frac{32,000}{2,00,000} \times 100 = 16\%$$

Division A should reject the new investment as its ROI is 16%, though more than the cost of capital, it is less than the current ROI of 18%.

Division B can accept the new investment as its ROI of is 16%, which is more than the current ROI of 11%.

OBJECTIVES OF RESPONSIBILITY PERFORMANCE REPORTING

Responsibility Performance Reporting is the reporting phase of Responsibility Accounting. The main objectives of Responsibility Reporting are

- To determine the degree of performance in the area of responsibility for which the concerned Responsibility Centre's manager is directly responsible and
- To formulate measures to improve the performance of the Responsibility Centre's manager after ascertaining the deviation of the actual performance from the budgeted performance.

REPORTS

The reports can be Responsibility Reporting for Cost Centres and Profit Centres. Responsibility Report contains items and information which are required by the concerned Responsibility Centre Manager and which are within his responsibility area. Responsibility Reporting goes on aggregating information as the reports are prepared for higher level managers in the organizational hierarchy. The amount of detail decreases as reports reach higher and higher levels of management. If the information is too detailed and voluminous, the managers cannot make effective use of information as the time at their disposal is very limited. In case, detailed information is required, they can get it and might seek it, if they are concerned about some particular elements of cost.

Responsibility Accounting Reports for Profit Centres are normally in the form of income statements. Here, the principle of controllability is applied. The managers at the lower level are responsible for the product lines and they are subordinate to the managers of the geographical areas, who in turn are responsible to the Managing Director of the organization.

The main point in reporting is to convey the best information.

Illustration 4

Sony Dresses Limited manufactures ready-made garments by a simple process of cutting the clothes in various shapes and sewing the pieces to form the finished dress.

The Sewing Department and the Cutting Department report to the Production Manager who along with Engineering Manager reports to The Director- Manufacturing. The Sales Manager, Publicity Manager and Credit Manager report to the Marketing Director of the company.

The Accounts Department reports the following for the month of March 2006.

Particulars	*Budget* *Rs.*	*Actual* *Rs.*
Cloth utilized	40,000	45,000
Advertising	5,000	5,000
Bad debts losses	7,000	5,000
Audit fee	5,000	5,000
Credit reports	1,500	1,350
Sales representatives:		
Traveling expenses	7,000	8,200
Sales commission	6,000	6,000
Thread	650	600
Sewing labor	19,600	21,000
Cutting labor	7,400	8,000
Credit department salaries	10,000	10,000
Sewing utilities	1,900	1,950
Cutting utilities	1,800	1,700
Marketing manager:		
Salaries and Administrative expenses	25,000	26,400
Production Engineering expenses	15,000	14,200
Publicity Management office expenses	18,000	17,700
Production Management office expenses	19,000	18,000
Directors Manufacturing salaries and Administrative expenses	31,000	30,100

Using the above data, prepare Responsibility Accounting Reports for the Director-Manufacturing, the Director – Marketing and the Production Manager.

Solution

Responsibility Accounting Reports

Particulars	*Budgeted Rs.*	*Actual Rs.*	*Variance Rs.*
For the Production Manager			
Cutting Department			
Cloth	40,000	45,000	5,000 A
Cutting labor	7,400	8,000	600 A
Cutting utilities	1,800	1,700	100 F
Total (A)	49,200	54,700	5,500 A
Sewing Department			
Thread	650	600	50 F
Sewing labor	19,600	21,000	1,400 A
Sewing utilities	1,900	1,950	50 A
Total (B)	22,150	23,550	1,400 A
Total (A + B)	71,350	78,250	6,900 A
Director- Manufacturing			
Production Department	71,350	78,250	6,900 A
Production Engineering expenses	15,000	14,200	800 F
Production Manager – office	19,000	18,000	1,000 F
Total	1,05,350	1,10,450	5,100 A
For the Director – Marketing			
Sales Manager			
Traveling expenses	7,000	8,200	1,200 A
Sales commission	6,000	6,000	—
Total (A)	13,000	14,200	1,200 A
Publicity Manager			
Office expenses	18,000	17,700	300 F
Advertising	5,000	5,000	—
Total (B)	23,000	22,700	300 F
Total (A + B) (C)	36,000	36,900	900 A
Credit Manager			
Salaries	10,000	10,000	—
Credit reports	1,500	1,350	150 F
Bad debt losses	7,000	5,000	2,000 F
Total (D)	18,500	16,350	2,150 F
Grand Total (C + D)	54,500	53,250	1,250 F

Note: Audit fee, salaries and administration expenses of Marketing Manager, Directors– Manufacturing salaries are ignored as Marketing Manager and Director, Manufacturing are not reporting to any one.

Illustration 5

Vishnu Fuels Limited has three production departments Machine Shop, Fabrication and Assembly, which are the responsibility of the Shop Superintendent who along with Material Manager, Planning Superintendent and Maintenance

Engineer, reports to the Works Manager at the factory. The office administration, sales and publicity come under the Sales Manager who, along with the Works Manager, reports to the Managing Director of the company. The following data relating to a month's performance is extracted from the books of the company:

Particulars	*Budgeted* *Rs.*	*Actual* *Rs.*
Raw Material:		
Machine shop	1,900	1,920
Assembly	960	1,000
Fabrication	500	510
Sales commission	1,000	1,050
Publicity expenses	2,100	2,200
Printing and Stationery	4,200	4,000
Travelling expenses	5,000	5,200
Wages:		
Machine shop	700	690
Fabrication	800	820
Assembly	920	930
Utilities:		
Machine shop	540	550
Fabrication	670	610
Assembly	570	540
Maintenance	600	620
Stores	410	370
Planning	280	300
Shop Superintendent Office:		
Salaries and expenses	2,200	2,178
Depreciation: Factory	5,880	6,920
Works Manager's Office:		
General Office:		
Salaries and Administration expenses	4,270	4,300
Managing Directors Office:		
Salaries and Administration expenses	2,800	2,780

(i) Treating the machine shop, fabrication and assembly as Cost Centres, prepare cost sheets for each centre with the help of the following additional information:

The shop-superintendent devotes his time amongst machine shop, fabrication and assembly in the ratio of 4:3:4. Other factory overheads are absorbed on the basis of direct labor in each Cost Centre. Office, administration, selling and distribution overheads are borne equally by the Cost Centres.

*(ii)*Treating the machine shop, fabrication and assembly as responsibility centres, prepare a responsibility accounting report for the shop superintendent.

Solution

(i) Cost Sheets for Machine–shop, Fabrication and Assembly Cost Centres

	Machine-shop		*Fabrication*		*Assembly*	
Particulars	*Budget* *Rs.*	*Actual* *Rs.*	*Budget* *Rs.*	*Actual* *Rs.*	*Budget* *Rs.*	*Actual* *Rs.*
Raw material	1,900	1,920	500	510	960	1,000
Wages	700	690	800	820	920	930
Utilities	540	550	670	610	570	540
Prime Cost (A)	3,140	3,160	1,970	1,940	2,450	2,470

	Machine-shop		*Fabrication*		*Assembly*	
Particulars	*Budget* *Rs.*	*Actual* *Rs.*	*Budget* *Rs.*	*Actual* *Rs.*	*Budget* *Rs.*	*Actual* *Rs.*
Factory Overheads						
Salaries and expenses*	800	792	600	594	800	792
Other factory Overheads**	2,073	2,322	2,370	2,759	2,727	3,129
Factory Cost (Prime Cost + Factory Overheads) (B)	6,013	6,274	4,940	5,293	5,977	6,391
Administrative Overheads						
Administrative expenses***	3,757	3,693	3,757	3,693	3,756	3,694
Cost of Production (Factory Cost + Admn. Overheads) (C)	9,770	9,967	8,697	8,986	9,733	10,085
Selling and Distribution Overheads	2,700	2,816	2,700	2,816	2,700	2,817
Selling and Distribution expenses****	1,2470	12,783	11,397	11,802	12,433	12,902
Total Cost (C + Selling OH)						

Working Notes:

* Shop Superintendent Office Salaries and Expenses

Shop superintendent devotes his time amongst Machine shop, Fabrication and Assembly in the ratio of 4:3:4

	Budget		*Actual*	
Machine shop	2,200 × 4/11	800	2,178 × 4/11	792
Fabrication	2,200 × 3/11	600	2,178 × 3/11	594
Assembly	2,200 × 4/11	800	2,178 × 4/11	792

**** Other Factory Overheads**

Particulars	*Budget* *Rs.*	*Actual* *Rs.*
Stores	410	370
Planning	280	300
Depreciation	5,880	6,920
Maintenance	600	620
Total	7,170	8,210

These are absorbed on the basis of direct labor, i.e., 700: 800: 920 and 690: 820: 930 budgeted and actual respectively.

***** Administration Overheads**

Particulars	*Budget* *Rs.*	*Actual* *Rs.*
Printing and Stationery	4,200	4,000
General Office and Adm. Expenses	4,270	4,300
MD's salary	2,800	2,780
Total	11,270	11,080

Administrative overhead is absorbed by all responsibility centres equally.

******Selling and Administrative Overheads**

Particulars	*Budget* *Rs.*	*Actual* *Rs.*
Sales Commission	1,000	1,050
Publicity expenses	2,100	2,200
Traveling expenses	5,000	5,200
Total	8,100	8,450

Selling and Distribution expenditure is absorbed by all Responsibility Centres equally.

(ii) Responsibility Accounting Report

Particulars	*Budgeted* *Rs.*	*Actual* *Rs.*	*Variance* *Rs.*
For the Shop Superintendent			
Machine shop:			
Material	1,900	1,920	20 A
Labor	700	690	10 F
Utilities	540	550	10 A
Total	3,140	3,160	20 A
Fabrication:			
Material	500	510	10 A
Labor	800	820	20 A
Utilities	670	610	60 F
Total	1,970	1,940	30 F
Assembly:			
Material	960	1,000	40 A
Labor	920	930	10 A
Utilities	570	540	30 F
Total	2,450	2,470	*20 A*
Grand Total	7,560	7,570	10 A

Note: Factory overheads and administrative and selling overheads being common costs which are not influenced by the decision of the Manager of the Responsibility Centre are ignored.

Illustration 6

BHEL manufacturing company has five plants A, B, C, D and E. Each plant has a Forming, Cleaning and Packing Department.

Each level of management has the responsibility over costs incurred at its level.

The budget for the current year has been set up as follows:

Plant:	*Budgeted Cost* *Rs.*
A	1,35,000
B	1,22,500
C	1,08,400
D	1,35,000
E	1,35,000

Budgeted information for plant C is as follows:

	Rs.
Plant Manager's Office	2,350
Forming Department	30,000
Cleaning Department	55,450
Packing Department	20,600
Direct Material	8,167
Direct Labor	15,000
Factory Overheads	6,833
The following additional budgeted data are available	
President Office	16,250
Vice-president, Marketing	20,000
Vice- president, Manufacturing Office	4,168
The following actual costs are incurred during the year:	
Plant A	1,27,650
B	1,24,300
C	1,08,476
D	1,31,100
E	1,36,800
Vice President, Manufacturing Office	4,990
The actual costs for the plant C were as follows:	
Direct Material	8,000
Direct Labor	13,000
Factory Overheads	7,000
Actual costs for plant C (Plant manager) were:	
Plant Manager's Office	2,476
Cleaning Department	57,500
Packing Department	22,500
Forming Department	26,000
Actual costs for the President's level were	
President Office	16,376
Vice-president, Marketing	29,800
Vice-president, Manufacturing	6,33,316

Prepare a Responsibility Report for the year showing the details of the budgeted, actual and variance amounts for the following areas:

Level 1, Forming Department, Plant C
Level 2, Plant Manager, Plant C
Level 3, Vice-President, Manufacturing
Level 4, President

Solution

Responsibility Report

Particulars	*Budgeted* *Rs.*	*Actual* *Rs.*	*Variance* *Rs.*
Forming Department, Plant C (Level 1)			
Direct Material	8,167	8,000	167 F
Direct Labor	15,000	13,000	2,000 F
Factory Overheads	6,833	7,000	167 A
Total Controllable Costs	**30,000**	**28,000**	**2,000 F**
Plant Manager, Plant C **(Level 2)**			
Plant Manager's Office	2,350	2,476	126 A
Forming Department	30,000	26,000	4,000 F
Cleaning Department	55,450	57,500	2,050 A
Packing Department	20,600	22,500	1,900 A
Total Controllable Costs	**1,08,400**	**1,08,476**	**76 A**

Particulars	*Budgeted Rs.*	*Actual Rs.*	*Variance Rs.*
Vice-president, Manufacturing **(Level 3)**			
Vice-president, Manufacturing office	4,168	4,990	822 A
Plant A	1,35,000	1,27,650	7,350 F
Plant B	1,22,500	1,24,300	1,800 A
Plant C	1,08,400	1,08,476	76 A
Plant D	1,35,000	1,31,100	3,900 F
Plant E	1,35,000	1,36,800	1,800 A
Total Controllable Costs	**6,40,068**	**6,33,316**	**6,752 F**
President (Level 4)			
President office	16,250	16,376	126 A
Vice-president, Marketing	20,000	29,800	9,800 A
Vice-president, Manufacturing	6,40,068	6,33,316	6,752 F
Total Controllable Costs	**6,76,318**	**6,79,492**	**3,174 A**

Illustration 7

Shiva Home Needs Limited deals in three products chairs, tables and iron stands and these are sold directly through salesmen in three zones namely Southern, Northern and Western. The responsibility for sales promotion rests with the headquarters and so does the overall control of distribution and sales. Cost of sales as a per cent of sales are: Chairs Rs. 85, Tables Rs. 80 and Iron stands Rs. 75. Details of sales and selling and distribution expenses for the year are as follows:

Zones	*Product*	*Sales Rs.*	*Selling and Distribution expenses allocated direct Rs.*
Southern	Chairs	11,00,000	83,000
	Tables	11,00,000	94,500
	Iron stands	6,50,000	56,000
		28,50,000	**2,33,500**
Northern	Chairs	8,75,000	47,000
	Tables	6,50,000	50,000
	Iron stands	4,25,000	25,000
		19,50,000	**1,22,000**
Western	Chairs	4,25,000	19,000
	Tables	3,80,000	20,000
	Iron stands	6,95,000	80,000
		15,00,000	**1,19,000**

Selling and distribution expenses at headquarters are as follows:

	Rs.
Office expenses	1,50,000
Advertisement	1,76,500
Other expenses	1,83,000

Advertisement costs are allocated to zones and products on the basis of sales. Office expenses and other expenses are apportioned equally to the zones or the products, while computing the profit or loss for the zones or the products as the case may be.

Prepare a Comparative Profit and Loss Statement, presenting Zonal Performance as distinct from Product Performance.

Solution

Comparative Profit and Loss Statement (evaluating Zonal Performance)

Particulars	*Zones*			
	Southern *Rs*	*Northern* *Rs.*	*Western* *Rs.*	*Total* *Rs.*
Sales Revenue (A)	28,50,000	19,50,000	15,00,000	63,00,000
Less: Cost of sales:				
Chairs (85%)	9,35,000	7,43,750	3,61,250	20,40,000
Tables (80%)	8,80,000	5,20,000	3,04,000	17,04,000
Iron Stands (75%)	4,87,500	3,18,750	5,21,250	13,27,500
Total (B)	**23,02,500**	**15,82,500**	**11,86,500**	**50,71,500**
Gross Profit (A-B) (C)	5,47,500	3,67,500	3,13,500	12,28,500
Less: Selling and Distribution Expenses:				
Direct Cost (allocated)	2,33,500	1,22,000	1,19,000	4,74,500
Advertisement (apportioned in Sales Ratio: 285:195:150)	79,845	54,631	42,024	1,76,500
Office Expenses (Equally)	50,000	50,000	50,000	1,50,000
Other Expenses (Equally)	61,000	61,000	61,000	1,83,000
Total Selling and Distribution expenses (D)	**4,24,345**	**2,87,631**	**2,72,024**	**9,84,000**
Net profit (C-D) E	1,23,155	79,869	41,476	2,44,500

Divisional Performance

An Organization consists of many units of parallel authority, which are created into several divisions for the purpose of decentralization and diversification. These units reflect autonomous Responsibility Centres, authorized by the divisional heads to carry out the tasks and achieve the goal confined to the respective division. Generally, divisions refer to Profit Centres in the organization.

The purpose of divisionalisation is to create accountability for generation of profit by those divisions which reflect separate products/services, area, processes, etc. It also enables inter-division comparison relating to profit performance of different divisions and also their impact on the overall profitability of the organization. Divisional performance helps in strategy formulation and operational planning. It poses a challenge to divisional managers by generating an inter-competitive spirit amongst themselves.

For the success of Divisionalisation, it is necessary to verify if the boundary lines between different divisions are specific and clear. Each division has its own link of expenses and revenue authority.

The divisional operations should be carried out in such a way that one division does not affect the profitability of the other. There should be a proper division, i.e., a proper system for the recording and pricing of inter division transfer.

A Divisional Manager has autonomy and is authorized to take production and marketing decisions, which makes him accountable to the top management for the profitability of his division.

The following is the organizational chart that reflects divisionalisation in the Organization.

Division 'A'	**Division 'B'**	**Division 'C'**	**Division 'D'**
Profit Target Personnel	Profit Target Finance	Profit Target Administration	Profit Target Marketing

Evaluation of Divisional Performance

Divisional Performance can be evaluated using the following methods.

(1) The Contribution Margin Approach/Net Profit/Operational Profit Approach

(2) Return on Investment Approach

(3) Residual Income Approach

I. The Net Profit/Operational Profit/Contribution Margin Approach

For the purpose of assessing the profitability of a Division in absolute figures, profit can take the form of net profit either before or after tax. The only disadvantage arising is that, the net profit may be more or less, due to certain non-operating incomes or expenses of higher amounts like profit on sale of capital assets or loss on it.

The other basis can be the figures of Operating Profit. The profit arising from the main business for which a company was incorporated is termed as Operating Profit. Thus, greater the value of absolute net profit/operating profit, better is the performance.

The Contribution Approach Statement can be as follows which includes cost controllability and cost allocation relating to the net profit earned by the Division.

Statement

Sales	***
Less: Variable Costs	***
Less: Controllable Divisional Overheads	***
Controllable Profit	***
Less: Fixed Non Controllable Divisional Overheads	***
Contribution Margin	***
Less: Allocation for Fixed Expenses	***
Net Profit before Tax	***
Less: Tax	**
Net Profit after Tax	****

The following statement explains about the **Analysis of Operational Data** related to Divisions-A, B, C and D.

Particulars	*Div 'A'* *Rs.*	*Div 'B'* *Rs.*	*Div 'C'* *Rs.*	*Div 'D'* *Rs.*
Sales Revenue	1,00,000	1,00,000	1,00,000	1,00,000
Less: Direct Variable Cost	45,000	45,000	45,000	45,000
Contribution Margin	55,000			
Less: Fixed Controllable Expenses		25,000	25,000	25,000
Controllable Profit		30,000		
Less: Fixed Non Controllable Expenses			10,000	10,000
Direct Profit			20,000	
Less: Indirect Costs				15,000
Net Profit				5,000

Given below statement illustrates the **Allocation of Assets and Profit** relating to Divisions-X, Y and Z on an assumption basis.

Statement of Allocation of Assets and Profit

Particulars	*Total* *Rs.*	*Unallocated* *Rs.*	*Division X* *Rs.*	*Division Y* *Rs.*	*Division Z* *Rs.*
Investment					
Cash	1,40,000	30,000	20,000	30,000	60,000
Debtors	2,30,000	—	60,000	80,000	90,000
Inventory	5,20,000	—	1,00,000	1,80,000	2,40,000
Pre-payments	65,000	20,000	10,000	15,000	20,000
Plant and Equipment	10,20,000	60,000	2,00,000	3,20,000	44,000
Investment	1,10,000	1,00,000	10,000	—	—
Total Assets	20,85,000	2,10,000	4,00,000	6,25,000	8,50,000

Particulars	*Total* Rs.	*Unallocated* Rs.	*Division X* Rs.	*Division Y* Rs.	*Division Z* Rs.
Profit					
Revenue	12,00,000		1,00,000	4,00,000	7,00,000
Less: Variable Cost	6,50,000		30,000	2,20,000	4,00,000
Contribution	5,50,000		70,000	1,80,000	3,00,000
Less: Separate Fixed Cost	2,60,000		30,000	90,000	1,40,000
Division Profit	2,90,000		40,000	90,000	1,60,000
Less: Common Fixed Cost	80,000				
Net Profit	2,10,000				

Criteria for Measurement of Divisional Profit

There are three criteria against which Divisional Profit Measurements must be judged before they are considered acceptable.

(1) Divisional Profit should not be increased by any action that reduces the total company's profit.

(2) Each Division's Profit should be as independent as possible of performance efficiency and managerial decisions elsewhere in the company.

(3) Each Division's Profit should reflect all items that are subject to any substantial degree of control by the Division Manager or his subordinates.

II. Return on Investment Method

The most common form of performance evaluation in a divisionalisation company is Return on Investment (ROI) Method. Return on Investment is calculated as a ratio of net divisional profit i.e. before tax, to the net assets employed in the division. This is calculated with the help of the following formula.

ROI = (Profit Margin × 100)/Invested Capital

Or

Sales Revenue / Profit Margin

$$\text{ROI} = \frac{\text{Sale Revenue}}{\text{Investment Capital}} \times \frac{\text{Profit Margin}}{\text{Sale Revenue}}$$

= Return on Capital × Margin on Sales

Note:

(1) Net Divisional Profit means divisional profit before tax

(2) Net Assets should always be taken at book values.

Advantages of ROI

The advantages of this method are:

(1) It relates to level of investment

(2) The ROI can be analyzed into other ratios which are useful for analytical purposes

(3) It can be used for inter firm comparison, provided, the firms whose result are being compared, are of comparable size and of the same industry.

Disadvantages of ROI

The disadvantages of ROI Method are:

(1) Usually, capital employed will be valued at net book value, and the fixed assets are indexed to provide at current cost profit which is usually calculated before deducting tax and after charging controllable allocated head office expenses.

(2) The ROI may influence a divisional manager to select only those investments with high rates of return. But other investments which could increase the value of the business may be rejected.

These types of decisions are sub-optional and result in underinvesting in order to maintain ROI.

III. Residual Income Method

As an alternative to ROI, the performance of a division can be measured by means of Residual Income Method. This Method deducts a charge for the use of assets from divisional profits, and bases this charge on company's cost of capital. It is an operating profit or income of a Division, less the imputed interest on the assets used by the Division.

In other words, interest on the capital invested in the Division is treated as cost and any surplus after deducting this cost, is the residual income.

Residual Income is the excess of net earnings over the cost of capital. This criterion is relevant when managers of Divisions are autonomous and accountable for their performance and makes their own decision on capital investment.

Divisional Residual Income Statement

Particulars	*Rs.*
Revenue	***
Less: Variable Cost	***
Contribution	***
Less: Controllable Fixed Costs	***
Controllable Profit	***
Less: Interest on Controllable Investment	***
Controllable Residual Income	***
Less: Uncontrollable Cost Collected (Head Office Charges)	***
Less: Interest on Uncontrollable Investment	***
Net Residual Income	***

Advantages of Residual Income Method (RI)

(1) Unlike the ROI, the RI approach is not concerned with preserving a relative measure. It strives to maximize the absolute figure, and thus, increase the shareholders wealth.

(2) The cost of capital charge on divisional investments ensures that managers are aware of the opportunity cost of funds.

(3) If each Division is charged with a common group cost of capital, the interest taken at Division level will be compatible with the interest of the Organization as a whole.

Disadvantages of RI

The following are the disadvantages of RI Method.

(1) There may be difficulties in defining the net operating income and the value of the divisional investments

(2) Identifying controllable and uncontrollable factors at divisional level may be difficult. There can be problems in calculating an accurate cost of capital.

It can be understood from the statement below (with the assumed figures) that the Residual Income will be arrived at after charging a notional amount for the target return that should be made on capital investment.

Particulars	*Organization as a whole (Rs.)*	*Division X (Rs.)*	*Division Y (Rs.)*	*Division Z (Rs.)*
Investment	20,85,000	4,00,000	6,25,000	8,50,000
Residual Income:				
Operating Profit	2,10,000	40,000	90,000	1,60,000
Required Return (10% on investment)	2,08,500	40,000	62,500	85,000
Residual Income	1,500	—	27,500	75,000

Summary

Responsibility Accounting means, an accounting process that reports as to how well managers of Responsibility Centres have fulfilled their responsibility. It is closely related to the goal of controllability. Those elements in a certain area of activity which are controllable are identified and a person is given the responsibility for managing such elements. Thus, individuals in an organization are made responsible for only those elements which can be controlled by them.

The process of implementation of Responsibility Accounting involves creation of the Responsibility Centres, setting of the objectives, recording the actual performance, comparison of the actual performance with the standards set, ascertainment of variance and taking remedial action.

The various Responsibility Centres in the organization are Cost Centre, Revenue Centre, Profit Centre and Investment Centre.

The reports can be Responsibility Reporting for Cost Centres and Profit Centres. Responsibility Report contains items and information which are required by the concerned Responsibility Centre Manager and which are within his responsibility area. Responsibility Reporting goes on aggregating information as the reports are prepared for higher level managers in the organizational hierarchy. The amount of details decreases as reports reach higher and higher levels of management. If the information is too detailed and voluminous, the managers cannot make effective use of information as the time at their disposal is very limited. In case, detailed information is required, they can get it and might seek it, if they are concerned about some particular elements of cost.

The main point in reporting is to convey the best information.

The purpose of Divisionalisation is to create accountability for generation of profit by those divisions which reflect separate products/services, areas, processes, etc. It also enables inter-division comparison relating to profit performance of different divisions and also their impact on the overall profitability of the organization. Divisional performance helps in strategy formulation and operational planning. It poses a challenge to divisional managers by generating an inter-competitive spirit amongst themselves.

Glossary

- **Responsibility Accounting:** is that type of Management Accounting that collects and reports both planned and actual accounting information in terms of Responsibility Centres.
- **Cost Centre:** is the Centre where inputs are measured in monetary terms. In Cost Centre Responsibility, the accounting system records only the cost incurred in the centre. Performance of Cost Centre is measured by the monetary terms of input only, where cost of operating the division is directly traceable to it.
- **Revenue Centre:** is a segment of the organization which is primarily responsible for generating sales revenue. This Centre's performance is measured by comparing the actual revenue with the budgeted revenue and the actual marketing expenses with that of the budgeted marketing expenses.
- **Profit Centre:** is a division of the company which produces and markets the products. Managers of Profit Centres have control over both the costs and the revenues because profit is the difference between the revenues and the costs.
- **Investment Centre:** is a division of an organization wherein its performance is assessed by considering not only its costs and revenues but also by establishing the relationship between profit (difference between revenues and costs), capital invested or employed and revenue. It is responsible for both profits and investments.
- **Responsibility Performance Reporting:** is the reporting phase of Responsibility Accounting.
- **Operating Profit:** is the profit arising from the main business for which a company was incorporated.
- **Return on Investment:** is calculated as a ratio of net divisional profit, i.e., profit before tax to the net assets employed in the Division.
- **Residual Income:** is an operating profit or income of a Division less the imputed interest on the assets used by the Division.

Questions

(1) What is Responsibility Accounting? Discuss its significance in measuring the performance of the organization in each Department.

(2) Explain the following concepts: *(i)* Cost Centre *(ii)* Profit Centre *(iii)* Investment Centre

(3) Draw an Organization Structure Chart and explain the Responsibility Centres in an organization.

(4) What is ROI? What are the problems involved in ROI analysis?

(5) Define Residual Profit. Discuss its suitability as a Performance Measure.

(6) "Compare the performance with comparables only" means comparable divisions must follow the same accounting methods. Are you agreeing with this statement?

(7) Distinguish between a Cost Centre, Profit Centre and Investment Centre.

(8) Explain the relationship between Organization Structure and Responsibility Centres.

(9) What are the requirements of an effective Responsibility Accounting System?

(10) What are the advantages of Responsibility Accounting?

(11) What are the major difficulties encountered in introducing Responsibility Accounting?

(12) What are the problems that arise in Performance Evaluation?

(13) What do you understand by Divisional Performance? Explain in brief.

PROBLEMS

(1) 'A' Limited operates a number of Divisions located in different regions. Relevant revenue and cost data pertaining to this Division are as follows:

	Rs.
Sales Revenue	13,00,000
Controllable Variable Cost	7,00,000
Controllable Fixed Costs	4,00,000
Attributable Segment Costs	1,00,000
Common Costs	1,20,000

You are required *(i)* to prepare a Performance Evaluation Report of A Limited in the proper format and *(ii)* advise the management whether its operations should be continued or shut down.

(2) The current year's operating results of the three divisions (X,Y,Z) of Henko Limited are given below:

(Amount in 000 rupees)

Particulars	*Divisions*		
	X	*Y*	*Z*
Sales Revenue	500	500	2,200
Less: Expenses	460	300	2,000
Segment Profit Contribution	40	200	200
Segment Assets	300	900	5,000

Determine the rate of return for the three divisions and rank these divisions assuming that the firm follows Investment Centre Basis of Performance Evaluation.

(3) The sales manager of Mumbai Textiles Limited is judged by the total sales. Exceeding the sales budget is considered good performance. The sales budget and cost data for the current year are shown below:

Products

Particulars	*Ladies' wear* *Rs.*	*Men's wear* *Rs.*	*Children's wear* *Rs.*	*Total* *Rs.*
Budgeted Sales	9,00,000	18,00,000	33,00,000	60,00,000
Less: Variable Cost	4,50,000	9,20,000	12,00,000	25,70,000
Contribution	4,50,000	8,80,000	21,00,000	34,30,000
Actual Sales	27,00,000	22,00,000	12,00,000	61,00,000

There is no change in variable cost per unit.

(i) Did the sales manager perform well? Support your answer with calculations.

(ii) Suggest better performance measurement criterion to be used by the firm.

❑❑❑